CONTENTS

C000194150

THE NATIONWIDE
FOOTBALL ANNUAL
2011–2012

Published by SportsBooks Limited, PO Box 422, Cheltenham, GL50 2YN
First published in 1887

Copyright © Stuart Barnes and SportsBooks 2011
www. sportsbooks.ltd.uk

A CIP catalogue record for this book is available from the British Library.

Editorial compilation by Stuart Barnes

ISBN-13 9781907524042

Front cover photograph of Manchester United celebrating their 19th title win
by PAphotos.

Printed and bound in the UK by CPI UK Reading RG1 8EX

For the first time in eight years we have had to increase the price of this annual. We would
like to take this opportunity to thank all our readers for their continued support.

UNITED FACE THREAT FROM OLD AND NEW

By Stuart Barnes

The old master against the young pretender; the richest club tired of being the poor relations in their own city; a legend determined to restore past glories for his team; a manager who will not rest until some silverware is back on the table. Take your pick from five possible contenders for what promises to be an intriguing race for the 2011–12 Premier League title. For the past seven years it has been the exclusive property of Manchester United and Chelsea, with the odd hint from Arsenal and Liverpool that they might be capable of breaking the mould. Now, Manchester City have put down a marker by winning the FA Cup, qualifying for the Champions League and keeping within striking distance of United throughout the first half of last season. Roberto Mancini believes that along the way his team gathered the level of experience and know-how needed for a sustained challenge – as well as earning the respect of their record-breaking neighbours.

Andre Villas-Boas knows he has to win that respect quickly if Chelsea are to prosper. The league's youngest manager drew plenty of compliments for the way he settled in at Stamford Bridge and shaped up to the job of meeting the demands of the club's owner, Roman Abramovich. The 33-year-old has shown himself to be a winner with domestic and European honours at Porto. The appointment of Roberto di Matteo, who won the hearts of supporters as a player, as his assistant was a shrewd one. How Villas-Boas manages to transmit this confidence and belief to his players will make fascinating watching. At Anfield, the return of Kenny Dalglish put a smile back on the face of a club beset by problems on and off the field. It remained even when United moved ahead of Liverpool in the number of League Championships won. For once, there are no European nights to look forward to. But with the prospect of Steven Gerrard putting his injury problems behind him, £35m Andy Carroll and Luis Suarez forming a productive forward partnership and some talented youngsters breaking through, there is plenty of optimism among supporters. Whether Liverpool are good enough for a first title since 1990 remains to be seen.

Neither can Arsenal's chances of ending their trophy drought be dismissed, despite an unsettled summer at the Emirates. This time, however, Arsene Wenger is aware that his side will have to find something special if unease among fans at this lack of success is not to grow. A summer priority for Wenger has been to strengthen his defence. If Arsenal are to lodge a challenge, they must also stop conceding points to teams lower down the table, having failed several times last season to take advantage of United's slips. Sir Alex Ferguson, aware of the domestic threat from new and old and anxious to bridge the gap Barcelona have opened up in Europe, was quickest off the mark in the transfer window, spending £50m on Edwin van der Sar's replacement, David de Gea, Phil Jones and Ashley Young as a start to reshaping his squad. United's 19th title win was not a vintage one and the manager knows this defence will be a tough one. But Sir Alex continues to relish the challenge and thrive under pressure. It's a measure of their great consistency and character that they remain the side to beat.

The three promoted clubs will offer their own particular qualities to the top flight. Queens Park Rangers return after an absence of 15 years as worthy winners of the Championship, with Neil Warnock describing it as his best moment in 30 years of management. Norwich, relegated in 2005 and later down to League One, won back-to-back promotions under their impressive manager Paul Lambert, who has been busy in the transfer market strengthening his line-up. Swansea make their bow in the Premier League, having earned widespread respect for the quality of their passing game under Brendan Rodgers.

The spotlight will also be on the Football League's two newcomers. AFC Wimbledon's achievement reflects tremendous credit on the supporters who founded their own club after the former FA winners relocated to Milton Keynes and the players and managers involved in the rise through the divisions from the starting point of the Combined Counties League. Wealthy Crawley join them as Conference champions and are already being backed to go straight through to League One, having underlined their pedigree last season when reaching the fifth round of the FA Cup and holding United to 1-0 at Old Trafford.

YOUNG ENGLAND RELFECT ON WHAT MIGHT HAVE BEEN

England were left with a feeling of what might have been after failing to qualify from their group at the European Under-21 Championship Finals in Denmark. Stuart Pearce's team reflected on the way two goals were conceded at the end of the deciding match against the Czech Republic. They looked back at a costly goalless draw with the Ukraine – and at what a difference players like Jack Wilshere and Andy Carroll might have made to their performance. Wilshere, named the PFA's Young Player of the Year after establishing a midfield place with Arsenal and England, was ruled out when his club insisted he was suffering from fatigue. Carroll, Liverpool's £35m signing from Newcastle, had a thigh injury. Both would have been expected to play key roles. Both were missed.

England were solid enough defensively, with Chris Smalling and his new Manchester United team-mate Phil Jones suggesting there is a dominant partnership to come in the future for both club and country. But they lacked rhythm and creativity going forward and were outplayed for much of the opening game against skilful Spain, despite Danny Welbeck's 88th minute equaliser from Kyle Walker's pass. England then failed to break down the more direct Ukrainians prompting Pearce to make changes for the third game, bringing in Swansea's play-off hat-trick hero Scott Sinclair, Fabrice Muamba and Tom Cleverley for Michael Mancienne, Jack Rodwell and Danny Rose. Welbeck headed in a Dean Sturridge cross and it looked to be enough until lapses of concentration led to Jan Chramosta levelling after 89 minutes and fellow-substitute Tomas Pekhart scoring in stoppage-time.

Pearce, who agreed a new two-year contract with the FA before leaving for the tournament, was deflated but determined to learn lessons for the 2013 Championship, for which England's qualifying begins with a match against Azerbaijan on September 1. Their group also features Belgium, Iceland and Norway. Scotland are drawn with Austria, Bulgaria Holland and Luxembourg; Wales play Andorra, Armenia, Czech Republic and Montenegro; Northern Ireland face Denmark, Faroe Islanda, Macedonia and Serbia; Republic of Ireland meet Hungary, Itay Turkey and Liechtenstein.

Spain followed on from their senior's World Cup success by beating Switzerland 2-0 the final in Aarhus with goals from Athletic Bilbao's Anders Herrera and Barcelona's Thiago Alcantara, son of Brazil's 1994 World Cup winner Mazinho.

GROUP A

Match-day 1: Belarus 2 (Voronkov 77 pen, Skavysh 87) Iceland 0. Att: 2,817 (Aarhus). Denmark 0 Switzerland 1 (Shaqiri 48). Att: 10,000 (Aalborg)

Match-day 2: Denmark 2 (Eriksen 22, Jorgensen 71) Belarus 1 (Baga 20). Att: 18,152 (Aarhus). Switzerland 2 (Frei 1, Emeghara 40) Iceland 0. Att: 1,903 (Aalborg)

Match-day 3: Iceland 3 (Sigthorsson 58, Bjarnason 60, Valgardsson 90) Denmark 1 (Kadrii 81). Att: 9,308 (Aalborg). Switzerland 3 (Medmedi 6 pen, 43, Feltsher 90) Belarus 0. Att: 1,604 (Aarhus)

FINAL TABLE

	P	W	D	L	F	A	Pts
Switzerland Q	3	3	0	0	6	0	9
Belarus Q	3	1	0	2	3	5	3
Iceland	3	1	0	2	3	5	3
Denmark	3	1	0	2	3	5	3

GROUP B

Match-day 1: Spain 1 (Ander 14) **England** 1 (Welbeck 88). Att: 8,046 (Herning)
England (4-2-3-1): Fielding (Derby), Walker (Tottenham), Smalling (Manchester Utd), Jones (Blackburn), Bertrand (Chelsea), Henderson (Liverpool), Mancienne (Hamburg) (Rodwell, Everton 67), Cleverley (Manchester Utd) (Sinclair, Swansea 81), Sturridge (Chelsea), Rose (Tottenham) (Lansbury, Arsenal 67), Welbeck (Manchester Utd. Booked: Welbeck
Czech Republic 2 (Dockall 49, 56) Ukraine 1 (Biliy 87). Att: 4,251 (Viborg)

Match-day 2: Ukraine 0 **England** 0. Att: 3,495 (Herning)
England (4-3-3): Fielding (Derby), Walker (Tottenham), Smalling (Manchester Utd), Jones (Blackburn), Bertrand (Chelsea), Rodwell (Everton) (Lansbury, Arsenal 58), Mancienne (Hamburg) (Muamba, Bolton 89), Henderson (Liverpool), Sturridge (Chelsea), Welbeck (Manchester Utd), Rose (Tottenham) (Sinclair, Swansea 58). Booked: Rodwell, Sinclair, Muamba, Jones
Czech Republic 0 Spain 2 (Adrian Lopez 27, 46). Att: 4,556 (Viborg)

Match-day 3: England 1 (Welbeck 76) Czech Republic 2 (Chramosta 89, Pekhart 90). Att: 5,262 (Viborg)
England (4-2-3-1): Fielding (Derby), Walker (Tottenham), Smalling (Manchester Utd), Jones (Blackburn), Bertrand (Chelsea), Muamba (Bolton), Henderson (Liverpool) (Lansburg, Arsenal 64), Cleverley (Manchester Utd) (Albrighton, Aston Villa 76), Sturridge (Chelsea), Sinclair (Swansea) (Rose, Tottenham 87), Welbeck (Manchester Utd)
Ukraine 0 Spain 3 (Mata 10, 72 pen), Adrian Lopez 27). Att: 3,302 (Herning)

FINAL TABLE

	P	W	D	L	F	A	Pts
Spain Q	3	2	1	0	6	1	7
Czech Republic Q	3	2	0	1	4	4	6
England	3	0	2	1	2	3	2
Ukraine	3	0	1	2	1	5	1

SEMI-FINALS

Spain 3 (Adrian Lopez 89, 105, Suarez 113) Belarus 1 (Voronkov 38). Att: 7,521 (aet, Viborg)
Switzerland 1 (Mehmedi 114) Czech Republic 0. Att: 5,038 (aet, Herning)

THIRD/FOURTH PLACE PLAY-OFF

Czech Republic 0 Belarus 1 (Filipenko 88). Att: 300 (Aalborg)

FINAL (June 25, 2011)

Switzerland 0 Spain 2 (Herrera 41, Alcantara 81). Att: 19,444 (Aarhus)

(See page 311 for qualifying results and other Under-21 matches)

AFTER YOU, BROTHER

Gary Neville made his 600th appearance for Manchester United at Stoke last season and a week later brother Phil reached that milestone in Everton's home game against Stoke. It was his 214th match for Everton after playing 386 times for United.

DAY BY DAY DIARY 2010–11

JULY 2010

14 Emile Heskey announces his retirement from internationals after winning 62 England caps.

15 Brendan Rodgers, formerly in charge of Reading, is appointed Swansea's new manager.

16 Howard Webb is given permission to sit out the start of the new Premier League season after refereeing the World Cup Final between Spain and Holland. Sheffield Wednesday's Tommy Miller is fined £2,500 by the FA after admitting 17 breaches of betting regulations.

18 Joe Cole leaves Chelsea for Liverpool, the most high-profile free transfer of the summer.

19 Steven Gerrard ends speculation about his future by pledging it to Liverpool after meeting new manager Roy Hodgson.

20 Nationwide Building Society bring to an end a £5m-a-year sponsorship of the England team after having a £20m offer for another four years turned down by the FA.

21 The International FA Board approve the use of an extra assistant referee behind each goal-line in European Championship qualifiers and Champions League matches, following UEFA's experiment in the Europa League.

22 Martin Jol, Ajax and former Spurs manager, turns down the chance to take charge at Fulham.

23 Manchester City pay £16m for the Lazio full-back Aleksandar Kolarov.

26 Scunthorpe receive a club-record fee of £2.4m from Celtic for striker Gary Hooper.

27 England are beaten 3-1 by Spain in the semi-finals of the European Under-19 Championship.

28 Mark Hughes, former Blackburn and Manchester City manager, takes charge at Fulham.

30 Portsmouth's David James turns down offers to stay in the Premier League and signs for Bristol City.

AUGUST 2010

2 Southend avoid administration by settling a tax bill of £340,000 with the Inland Revenue.

3 Fernando Torres ends speculation about his future by agreeing to stay with Liverpool.

4 Chelsea sign the Brazil midfielder Ramires from Benfica for £18m. Celtic fall at their first Champions League hurdle, losing to Braga in the third qualifying round.

5 Cesc Fabregas, pursued by Barcelona in the summer, agrees to stay at Arsenal. The prospects of survival for debt-ridden Portsmouth are boosted by a High Court victory over the Inland Revenue.

6 Mikel Arteta agrees a new five-year contract with Everton. Cardiff have a transfer embargo lifted by the Football League on the eve of the new season.

7 Fabio Capello names a new-look squad for England's friendly against Hungary following his team's World Cup failure. Football League newcomers Stevenage and Oxford kick off with draws, against Macclesfield and Burton respectively.

8 Paul Robinson, winner of 41 England caps, and Wes Brown, with 21, announce their retirements from international football, despite being included in the squad to face Hungary. Simon Davies, capped 58 times by Wales, also calls it a day. Manchester United beat Chelsea 3-1 in the Community Shield game.

9 Five days before the start of the Premier League season, Martin O'Neill resigns as Aston Villa manager. The FA announce a new fast-track disciplinary procedure to speed up cases.

10 Exeter striker Adam Stansfield, 31, dies of cancer. Stoke pay a club-record fee of £8m for Sunderland's Kenwyne Jones. Republic of Ireland manager Giovanni Trapattoni is taken to hospital on the eve of the friendly international against Argentina and undergoes surgery for an abdominal complaint. Shrewsbury take pride of place in the Carling Cup first round, retrieving a 3-0 deficit to beat Charlton 4-3.

11 Robbie Keane wins his 100th Irish cap in their 1-0 defeat by Argentina at the redeveloped Lansdowne Road, now the Aviva Stadium. Despite England's miserable World Cup, a crowd of 72,000 see Steven Gerrard score twice in a 2-1 win over Hungary. But Fabio Capello comes under more pressure after describing David Beckham as 'too old' to play international football again. David Cotterill, Andy King and Ashley Williams score for Wales for the first time in a 5-1 win over Luxembourg. Brothers Jonny and Corry Evans play together for the first time for Northern Ireland, who lose 2-0 to Montenegro. Cardiff stave off a winding-up order after paying a £1.3m tax bill. Southampton owner Markus Liebherr dies aged 62. Blackpool manager Ian Holloway agrees a new two-year contract.

12 Leicester are bought by a consortium led by Thai businessman Aiyawatt Raksriaksorn. Steve Coppell resigns at Bristol City after less than four months in charge and announces his retirement from management. Coppell's assistant, Keith Millen, takes over.

13 Manchester City take their summer spending beyond £100m by signing the Inter Milan striker Mario Balotelli for £24m. Arsenal manager Arsene Wenger signs a three-year extension to his contract through to June 2014. Celtic's Aiden McGeady joins Spartak Moscow for £9.5m.

14 Mark Halsey referees his first Premier League game since recovering from cancer – Wigan v Blackpool. Kevin Blackwell is sacked as Sheffield United manager after the 3-0 home defeat by Queens Park Rangers.

16 Former Wales captain Gary Speed succeeds Kevin Blackwell at Bramall Lane, his first managerial appointment.

17 Chelsea's Nicolas Anelka is banned for 18 internationals by the French Federation after being sent home from the World Cup and retires from international football. Manchester United's Patrice Evra receives a five-game ban for his part in a players' revolt in South Africa. Giovanni Trapattoni, the Republic of Ireland manager, is released from hospital after surgery for an abdominal complaint.

18 Manchester City's spending reaches nearly £130m when Aston Villa's James Milner moves to Eastlands for £24m. Four days after his club win 4-0 at Wigan in their opening Premier League game, Blackpool chairman Karl Oyston resigns, having previously admitted to being disillusioned with the influence of agents in the game. His decision coincides with figures showing that Championship clubs paid £10m to agents in the 2009–10 season. He later returned to the position.

19 The transfer window's most surprising move takes Manchester City's Craig Bellamy to his home-town club Cardiff on a year's loan. Chris Turner, Hartlepool's director of sport and effectively the club's manager, resigns after differences with chairman Ken Hodcroft.

20 A good day for Crystal Palace, who come out of administration and sign former Holland midfielder Edgar Davids on a pay-as-you-play deal.

21 Michael Oliver, at the age of 25 years and 182 days, becomes the youngest referee to take charge of a Premier League match – Birmingham v Blackburn.

23 A team of FIFA inspectors begin a four-day visit to assess the merits of England's bid for the 2018 World Cup Finals.

24 Rangers captain David Weir returns to Scotland's squad for two European Championship qualifiers at the age of 40. The FA fine Nottingham Forest £12,500 and Leeds £7,500 for a players' confrontation. Forest's Chris Gunter receives a three-match, retrospective ban for a stamping offence caught on camera.

25 A hat-trick by Peter Crouch against Young Boys of Berne puts Tottenham into the group stage of the Champions League for the first time.

26 Aston Villa are knocked out of the Europa League by Rapid Vienna for the second successive season. Liverpool and Manchester City win their play-off matches, but Celtic, Dundee United, Motherwell and the Welsh side TNS are beaten.

27 Former Liverpool manager Rafael Benitez misses out on his first trophy with Inter Milan, who lose 2-0 to Atletico Madrid in the European Super Cup.

28 Liverpool pay £11.5m for Porto's World Cup midfielder player Raul Meireles.

29 Southampton sack Alan Pardew the day after a 4-0 win over Bristol Rovers, claiming he is not the manager to win promotion.

30 Liverpool's Javier Mascherano joins Barcelona for £17.2m in one of the summer's most contentious transfers.

31 Sunderland pay a club-record £13m to Rennes for the Ghana World Cup striker Asamoah Gyan. Other major deals on the final day of the transfer window take Robinho, Manchester City's £32.5m signing, to AC Milan for £16m and Holland midfielder Rafael van der Vaart from Real Madrid to Tottenham for £8m. Total spending by Premier League clubs during the window is around £350m. Elsewhere, the most eye-catching signing is made by Crawley, who pay a record Conference fee of £275,000 for the York striker Richard Brodie.

SEPTEMBER 2010

1 FIFA rule out the possibility of Everton's Mikel Arteta playing for England under residency rules.

3 Jermain Defoe scores a hat-trick and Adam Johnson nets his first international goal as England beat Bulgaria 4-0 in their opening European Championship qualifying match – a record 11th successive victory at Wembley. Two other players are on the mark for the first time on their competitive debuts – Corry Evans with his first touch in Northern Ireland's win in Slovenia and Keith Fahey for the Republic of Ireland, who are also successful 1-0 in Armenia. Scotland share a goalless draw away to Lithuania, while Wales go down 1-0 in Montenegro.

5 John Toshack resigns after nearly six years as Wales manager, declaring he has taken the team as far as he can.

6 England maintain an impressive start to their European Championship qualifying campaign with a 3-1 away win over Switzerland. Wayne Rooney scores his first England goal for a year and Darren Bent nets his first. Scotland need a Stephen McManus goal seven minutes into stoppage-time to beat Liechtenstein 2-1, while the Republic of Ireland defeat Andorra 3-1.

7 Former Liverpool manager Gerard Houllier returns to English football to succeed Martin O'Neill at Aston Villa.

8 Fabio Capello rules out continuing as England manager beyond the 2012 European Championship Finals. Sheffield Wednesday avoid the immediate threat of administration when the club's bank, the Co-operative, agree to settle a £780,000 tax bill.

9 Scott Parker signs a new contract with West Ham, keeping him at the club until 2014.

10 Bobby Zamora agrees a new four-year deal with Fulham, but is then sidelined for six months with a broken leg sustained against Wolves.

11 Wayne Rooney is left out of Manchester United's match against his former club Everton following allegations about his private life.

12 Nigel Adkins, who turned Scunthorpe into a Championship club, resigns to take over at Southampton.

13 Brian Flynn, the Wales youth coach, is appointed caretaker-manager of the senior side for their next two European Championship qualifying games.

15 Manchester United's Antonio Valencia is ruled out for six months with a double-break of his left ankle, sustained in the Champions League game against Rangers.

16 Everton manager David Moyes is fined £8,000 by the FA for confronting referee Martin Atkinson after the game against Manchester United. His assistant, Steve Round, is later fined the same amount. Preston manager Darren Ferguson receives a three-match touchline ban and £4,000 fine for his behaviour towards referee Kevin Friend following the match with Burnley.

17 England beat Switzerland 5-2 on aggregate to reach the 2011 Women's World Cup Finals in Germany.

20 Preston goalkeeper Andy Lonergan is fined £5,000 by the FA for provocative gestures towards Burnley supporters.

21 Arsenal manager Arsene Wenger receives a one-match touchline ban and £8,000 fine from the FA for improper conduct after the game at Sunderland. Brentford beat Everton on penalties in the Carling Cup third round.

22 More Merseyside misery in the Carling Cup as Liverpool lose on penalties to Northampton at Anfield.

23 Coach Ian Baraclough is appointed Scunthorpe's new manager after a brief spell as caretaker.

24 Arsenal announce record annual pre-tax profits of £56m.

27 Manchester United's Dimitar Berbatov turns down a request from Bulgaria's new coach, Lothar Matthaus, to come out of international retirement.

28 Preston, trailing 4-1 at Leeds win 6-4, with Jon Parkin scoring a hat-trick.

29 Chris Sutton resigns after a year as manager of struggling Lincoln, citing 'personal reasons.'

30 West Ham register an interest in moving to the Olympic Stadium after the 2012 Games.

OCTOBER 2010

1 Manchester City announce a record annual loss of £121.3m. Paulo Sousa is sacked after less than three months as Leicester manager with his side bottom of the Championship. Tottenham announce their interest in moving to the Olympic Stadium. Charlton manager Phil Parkinson receives a two-match touchline ban and £1,500 fine from the FA after being sent to the stands during the game against Dagenham & Redbridge.

2 Emile Heskey declines an invitation from Fabio Capello to come out of international retirement and join England's injury-hit squad for the World Cup qualifier against Montenegro.

3 Sven-Goran Eriksson is appointed Leicester's eighth manager since 2004.

4 Manchester City's Nigel de Jong is dropped by Holland following the tackle which left Newcastle's Hatem Ben Arfa with a broken leg. Hibernian, without a win since the opening day of the season, part company with manager John Hughes by mutual agreement. Danny Gabbidon announces his retirement from international football after winning 43 caps with Wales.

5 Liverpool's board accept a takeover bid from New England Sports Ventures, owners of the Boston Red Sox baseball team. After ten league games as Hereford manager, Simon Davey is sacked with his team at the bottom of the table.

6 Liverpool owners Tom Hicks and George Gillett launch a High Court challenge to the sale of the club.

7 The Premier League approve the Liverpool takeover. Manchester United report an annual loss of £80m. Newcastle's Andy Carroll signs a new five-year contract. Former Tottenham captain Graham Roberts is appointed coach of Pakistan.

8 Chris Gunter is sent off in the last minute of a 1-0 defeat for Wales against Bulgaria, Brian Flynn's first match as caretaker-manager. The Republic of Ireland also lose at home in their European Championship qualifier, 3-2 to Russia. Scotland are beaten 1-0 in the Czech Republic, while Northern Ireland share a goalless draw with Italy in the first meeting of the teams at Windsor Park for 52 years.

11 Blackpool manager Ian Holloway is given a one-match touchline ban and £9,500 fine by the FA for his behaviour towards match officials after the game against Blackburn. West Ham's bid to move to the Olympic Stadium receives backing from the governing body of British athletics. Scotland lose 4-2 on aggregate to Iceland in their play-off for a place in the European Under-21 Championship Finals. Brazil beat Ukraine 2-0 in a full international friendly played at Pride Park because of Derby's large Ukrainian population.

12 On a night when none of the home nations manage a win in European Championship qualifying matches, England fail to score for the first time at the new Wembley, sharing a goalless draw with Montenegro. Scotland retrieve a 2-0 deficit against World Cup-winners Spain, but concede the deciding goal and then have Steven Whittaker sent off. Wales's chances of reaching the finals are effectively ended by a third successive defeat, 4-1 in Switzerland, while Northern Ireland suffer an embarrassing 1-1 draw against the Faroe Islands. Robbie Keane has a penalty saved by Everton reserve goalkeeper Jan Mucha as the Republic of Ireland draw 1-1 away to Slovakia. England beat Romania 2-1 on aggregate to reach the European Under-21 Championship Finals.

13 A High Court judge refuses Liverpool owners Tom Hicks and George Gillett permission to delay the £300m sale of the club. Accrington withdraw from the Johnstone's Paint Trophy after fielding a suspended player against Tranmere, who are reinstated after losing the teams' first round tie on penalties. Peterborough and Notts County are fined £15,000 each by the FA for a post-match brawl involving players and coaching staff. County coach Mark Draper receives a three-match touchline ban and £400 fine for violent conduct.

14 Another bid by Tom Hicks and George Gillett, this time in a Texas court, to block the sale of the club also fails.

15 The Liverpool saga ends with New England Sports Ventures taking over at Anfield. Malcolm Allison, one of the game's most flamboyant managers, dies aged 83. Former Southend manager Steve Tilson takes charge at Lincoln.

16 Manager Gordon Chisholm, his assistant Billy Dodds and nine players lose their jobs after

Dundee go into administration for the second time, owing £365,000 in tax.

17 Wayne Rooney is revealed to have told Manchester United he wants to leave Old Trafford. FIFA launch an investigation into World Cup vote-selling allegations in the *Sunday Times* .Former Northampton and Nottingham Forest manager Colin Calderwood takes charge at Hibernian.

18 Gordon Strachan resigns as manager of Middlesbrough with his side fifth from bottom.

19 Sir Alex Ferguson accuses Wayne Rooney of a lack of respect for Manchester United, but says he will try to keep the player.

20 Gareth Bale scores a hat-trick for Tottenham in the San Siro, but it is not enough to prevent a 4-3 Champions League defeat by holders Inter Milan after they concede three goals and have goalkeeper Heurelho Gomes sent off in the first 14 minutes. Wayne Rooney issues a statement claiming not enough money has been spent at Old Trafford on new players. George Best's 1968 European Cup winner's medal is sold at auction for £156,000.

21 Another hat-trick in Europe, this time by Manchester City's Emmanuel Adebayor in the 3-1 Europa League win over Lech Poznan. Gary Speed, Sheffield United manager, is given a one-match touchline ban and fined £2,000 by the FA for improper behaviour at the home game with Watford.

22 With speculation rife about a move to Manchester City or Chelsea, Wayne Rooney does a U-turn, signs a five-year contract worth a reported £200,000 a week and apologises to Sir Alex Ferguson and his team-mates. Portsmouth issue a statement warning they are in danger of going out of business over a £2.5m debt to former owner Sacha Gaydamak.

23 Agreement is reached with Sacha Gaydamak and Portsmouth come out of administration after being sold to a company controlled by Hong Kong businessman Balram Chainrai.

24 Craig Short is sacked after less than five months as manager of Notts County with his team 16th in the table.

25 Chelsea sign a new eight-year sponsorship deal with adidas worth an estimated £160m. Newcastle striker Andy Carroll is fined £1,000 and ordered to pay £2,500 compensation after pleading guilty at Newcastle Crown Court to assaulting a man in a nightclub.

26 Former West Bromwich Albion and Celtic manager Tony Mowbray succeeds Gordon Strachan at Middlesbrough, the club he captained in the 1980s.

27 Nobby Stiles's 1966 World Cup winner's medal is sold at auction to his old club Manchester United for a record £188,200. Paul Ince, formerly in charge of MK Dons and Blackburn, is appointed Notts County's fifth manager in a year.

28 England's 2018 World Cup bid team withdraw a complaint to FIFA following an apology from their Russian rivals for derogatory remarks about London.

29 Referee Dougie McDonald is warned by the Scottish FA for failing to clearly explain why he changed his mind about giving Celtic a penalty against Dundee United.

30 Fifteen players are sent off in League's One and Two, three of them in the Bradford–Oxford match.

31 Jack Wilshere signs a new five-year contract with Arsenal.

NOVEMBER 2010

1 Dundee are deducted 25 points in the Scottish First Division for going into administration for the second time.

2 Gareth Bale wins more widespread acclaim as Tottenham beat holders Inter Milan 3-1 in their Champions League return match.

3 Chelsea reach the knock-out stage of the Champions League with two group matches to spare.

4 Steven Gerrard scores all three of Liverpool's goals against Napoli.

5 West Ham co-owner David Gold is banned from the Birmingham directors' box and boardroom following critical comments about his former club.

6 Celtic score a record Scottish Premier League win – 9-0 against Aberdeen, who suffer the club's worst-ever defeat. The match includes two hat-tricks, three penalties and a red card for each side. Manchester United's Wayne Rooney is sent to an American fitness centre in Portland to continue his recovery from injury.

8 Cristiano Ronaldo accepts substantial, undisclosed libel damages in the High Court over a story in the *Daily Telegraph* in July 2008 that he put his injured ankle at risk by 'living it up' in a Hollywood nightclub.

9 Edgar Davids ends his pay-as-you-play deal at Crystal Palace after three months, having failed to make an impact in the Championship. Ole Gunnar Solskjaer decides to leave Manchester United after 14 years to become manager of the Norwegian club Molde.

10 Bolton record an annual loss of £34.5m. Celtic manager Neil Lennon incurs a two-match touchline ban after being sent to the stands during the defeat at Hearts.

11 Joey Barton is banned for three matches by the FA after being caught on camera punching Morten Gamst Pedersen in Newcastle's game against Blackburn. Chelsea dispense with the services of assistant manager Ray Wilkins.

12 Gabriel Agbonlahor signs a new five-year contract with Aston Villa.

13 Leaders of England's 2018 World Cup bid write to FIFA distancing themselves from corruption allegations made against the world governing body by the British media.

16 Three players score for the first time for Scotland in a 3-0 win over the Faroe Islands – Danny Wilson on his debut, Kris Commons and Jamie Mackie.

17 Substitute Peter Crouch scores with his first touch, but England lose for the first time at Wembley under Fabio Capello – 2-1 to France. Rory Patterson's first international goal, from the penalty spot, gives Northern Ireland a 1-1 draw with Morocco.

18 Two FIFA executive committee members receive unprecedented bans and fines following World Cup vote-selling allegations in the *Sunday Times*. Four other officials are banned and fined. Chelsea promote former Nigeria international Michael Emenalo to replace Ray Wilkins. Former Arsenal winger Robert Pires returns to English football on a six-month contract with Aston Villa.

19 Indian company Venky's take control of Blackburn from the Jack Walker Trust in a £43m deal.

20 Burnley defender Clarke Carlisle succeeds Chris Powell as chairman of the Professional Footballers' Association.

21 Scotland's leading referees, angry about criticisms and concerned for their safety, vote for strike action.

22 Chelsea manager Carlo Ancelotti, worried about three defeats in four Premier League matches and unhappy about the removal of his No 2 Ray Wilkins, insists he will not resign.

23 The Scottish FA look across Europe for replacements for striking referees for the weekend's matches.

24 Wayne Rooney's penalty against Rangers, his first goal since signing a new contract, puts Manchester United into the knock-out stage of the Champions League. Tottenham also reach the last 16. The Premier League uphold Charlie Adam's claim for a £25,000 'survival' bonus from Blackpool.

25 Norwich manager Paul Lambert is given a two-match touchline ban and £2,500 fine by the FA for his behaviour towards match officials after the game at Reading. Newcastle's Mike Williamson receives a three-match ban after being caught on camera head-butting Bolton's Johan Elmander.

26 A fortnight after the controversial departure of Ray Wilkins, director of football Frank Arnesen tells Chelsea he is leaving at the end of the season.

27 Officials from Israel, Malta and Luxembourg take charge of SPL matches as cover for striking Scottish referees. All fixtures in Divisions One, Two and Three are postponed.

29 Three days before the vote for the 2018 World Cup, the BBC's *Panorama* programme makes corruption allegations against four members of FIFA's executive committee.

30 Holders Manchester United lose 4-0 to West Ham in the Carling Cup quarter-finals, their heaviest defeat by the London side for 80 years. Jonathan Spector scores twice, his first goals in English football. Figures released by the Premier League show that Chelsea and Liverpool each paid more than £9m in agents' fees in the year to September 30, with the total for all clubs topping £67m.

DECEMBER 2010

1 Supporters invade the pitch and throw flares at each other after Birmingham's Carling Cup victory over Aston Villa at St Andrew's. Mark McGhee, under pressure since a record 9-0 defeat by Celtic, is sacked as Aberdeen manager. Manchester City reach the knock-out stage of the Europa League. Ray Wilkins agrees a compensation package with Chelsea.

2 England receive only two votes out of 22 – one of them from their own representative Geoff Thompson – and are eliminated in the first round of voting for the 2018 World Cup. Russia are chosen as hosts, with Qatar the successful bidders for the 2022 tournament. Liverpool reach the knock-out stage of the Europa Cup.

3 Anger about England's World Cup embarrassment is followed by acting FA chairman Roger Burden withdrawing his application for the permanent position because he wants nothing more to do with FIFA.

4 The big freeze accounts for 27 matches in England and all but one of the games in Scotland.

6 Newcastle sack manager Chris Hughton with the team just below mid-table, prompting widespread protests from supporters.

7 In a remarkable FA Cup second round replay, Leyton Orient come from 2-0 down to beat Droylsden 8-2 with six goals in extra time. Two players from each side are sent off and two others score hat-tricks.

8 Arsenal reach the knock-out stage of the Champions League for the 11th successive season. Carlos Tevez asks Manchester City for a transfer.

9 Alan Pardew, sacked from his last job at Southampton, is named Newcastle's new manager with a five-year contract.

10 Barcelona sign a world-record, five-year shirt sponsorship deal worth £125m with the Qatar Foundation. It tops the £20m-a-year agreement Manchester United and Liverpool have with Aon and Standard Chartered respectively. Former Scotland manager Craig Brown takes over at Aberdeen, two days after pledging to stay at Motherwell. Queens Park Rangers lose the Football League's only remaining unbeaten record, going down 3-1 at home to Watford.

12 Gary Speed, winner of 85 caps with Wales, agrees to become their manager, four months after taking charge at Sheffield United.

13 Three weeks after being given a vote of confidence by the club's new Indian owners, Blackburn's Sam Allardyce is sacked. Twenty six of the 33 rescued Chilean miners are Manchester United's guests of honour for the game against Arsenal.

14 Former Leicester and Portsmouth owner Milan Mandaric completes a £10m takeover of Sheffield Wednesday.

15 Paul Trollope, League One's second longest-serving manager with five years at Bristol Rovers, is sacked after his team slip into the bottom four.

16 Local father-and-son businessmen Assem and Ehab Allam take over Hull from Russell Bartlett in a £40m deal.

17 Jamie Pitman, a former player and physio with the club, is appointed Hereford manager until the end of the season after a spell as caretaker.

18 The weather again takes its toll, with 30 matches in England and 16 in Scotland postponed.

19 Sir Alex Ferguson becomes Manchester United's longest-serving manager, passing Sir Matt Busby's mark of 24 years, one month and 14 days. United's game at Chelsea is called off, one of a record-equalling seven Premier League postponements over the weekend. David Beckham receives a lifetime achievement award at the BBC Sports Personality of the Year night.

20 Carlos Tevez withdraws his transfer request after a meeting with Manchester City chairman Khaldoon Al Mubarak, chief executive Garry Cook and manager Roberto Mancini.

21 Former coach Steve Kean is given the Blackburn manager's job until the end of the season.

22 David Bernstein, the Wembley and former Manchester City chairman, is named the FA's new chairman.

23 Former Liverpool manager Rafael Benitez is sacked by Inter Milan after six months in charge.

26 The backlog of fixtures continues to pile up, with 29 games in England and 15 in Scotland called off.

27 Steven Taylor signs a new five-and-a-half-year contract with Newcastle.

28 The weather eases somewhat, but there are still 16 games postponed, all in the Football League.

29 Two managers are sacked – Preston's Darren Ferguson with his side bottom of the

Championship and Burnley's Brian Laws following a home defeat by former club Scunthorpe.

30 Micky Adams leaves Port Vale to become Sheffield United's new manager. Former Bradford manager Stuart McCall takes charge at Motherwell.

31 Businessmen Michael Slater and Tony Jimenez take over Charlton from chairman Richard Murray for an undisclosed sum. World Cup Final referee Howard Webb receives an MBE in the New Year Honours List.

JANUARY 2011

1 George Burley (Crystal Palace) and Mark Stimson (Barnet) join the managerial casualty list, sacked with their teams second from bottom of the Championship and League Two respectively.

3 Lee Bowyer is banned for three matches by the FA after being caught on camera stamping on Bacary Sagna in the Birmingham-Arsenal match.

4 Three more managers are dismissed, making seven in a week. Phil Parkinson leaves Charlton, fifth in the table but without a win in five games; Walsall sack Chris Hutchings with his team bottom; Paul Simpson, in charge at Stockport for less than six months, goes with his side fourth from bottom.

5 Jim Gannon, formerly in charge of Stockport, Motherwell and Peterborough, is appointed Port Vale's new manager.

6 Phil Brown, who led Hull into the Premier League, takes charge at Preston.

7 Ipswich sack manager Roy Keane after a run of seven defeats in nine matches. Manchester City sign the Wolfsburg striker Edin Dzeko for £27m.

8 Roy Hodgson is dismissed by Liverpool after six turbulent months as manager and Anfield legend Kenny Dalglish takes over until the end of the season. Newcastle are knocked out of the FA Cup by Stevenage.

9 Barcelona's Lionel Messi wins the inaugural FIFA *Ballon d'Or* – the merged European and World Footballer of the Year awards. Paul Jewell, who took Bradford and Wigan into the Premier League, succeeds Roy Keane at Ipswich.

10 Richard Butcher, 29-year-old Macclesfield midfield player, dies aged 29. Two more managers lose their jobs – Peterborough's Gary Johnson after a difference of opinion with chairman Darragh MacAnthony and Kevin Dillon, sacked by Aldershot following four successive home league defeats. Dave Penney, formerly in charge of Doncaster, Darlington and Oldham, takes over at Bristol Rovers.

11 Vauxhall become England's lead sponsor in a reported £20m deal with the FA through to July 2014. Dougie Freedman is appointed manager of Crystal Palace, where he made 368 appearances and scored 108 goals. Dean Holdsworth, former Wimbledon and Bolton striker, leaves Newport to succeed Kevin Dillon. Celtic manager Neil Lennon appeals against a two-match touchline ban imposed in November and has it trebled by the Scottish FA.

12 Darren Ferguson, dismissed by Preston, returns for a second spell as Peterborough manager.

13 Chris Powell, who had three spells with the club as a player, is appointed Charlton's new manager.

14 David Beckham trains with Tottenham, but a loan move from LA Galaxy is ruled out.

15 Bournemouth's Eddie Howe, one of the country's most highly-rated young managers, takes over at Burnley.

16 West Ham respond to speculation about the future of manager Avram Grant by announcing that he will not be leaving the club.

17 Vauxhall complete a 'clean sweep' of sponsorship for the home nations with deals for Scotland, Wales and Northern Ireland. Liverpool's Ryan Babel is fined £10,000 by the FA for posting a doctored picture on *Twitter* of referee Howard Webb wearing a Manchester United shirt. Plymouth manager Peter Reid is given a one-match touchline ban and £1,000 fine by the FA for criticising referee Paul Tierney.

18 Aston Villa follow up the £6m signing of Jean Makoun from Lyon by paying Sunderland £24m for Darren Bent – a record fee for both clubs.

19 Former Walsall captain Dean Smith is appointed manager until the end of the season after a spell as caretaker.

20 Steve Kean, initially given the manager's job at Blackburn until the end of the season, signs a contract through to the summer of 2013. Burnley defender Clarke Carlisle, chairman of the PFA, becomes the first footballer to appear on the BBC's *Question Time* programme while still playing for a club.

21 Manchester United's Rafael is fined £8,000 by the FA for remonstrating with referee Mike Dean after being sent off at Tottenham. Team-mate Ryan Giggs, 37, signs on for another year at Old Trafford.

23 London Olympics chief Lord Coe calls for the main stadium to be handed over after the 2012 Games to West Ham, not Tottenham, to preserve the athletics track as promised.

24 Presenter Richard Keys and analyst Andy Gray are disciplined by Sky Sports for 'sexist' remarks off-air about assistant referee Sian Massey and West Ham vice-chairman Karren Brady. The Olympic Park Legacy Company postpone a decision about the stadium to seek 'further clarification' from West Ham and Tottenham.

25 Andy Gray is sacked following new evidence of 'offensive behaviour.' Sian Massey is removed from running the line at the Crewe-Bradford match to shield her from the spotlight. Arsenal reach the Carling Cup Final, scoring three second half goals in 16 minutes to beat Ipswich 3-1 on aggregate.

26 Richard Keys resigns, admitting to 'prehistoric banter.' Birmingham come from 3-1 down in the second leg of their Carling Cup semi final to beat West Ham 4-3 on aggregate, Craig Gardner scoring the winner in extra-time.

27 Blackpool are fined £25,000 by the Premier League for fielding a weakened side against Aston Villa. Manchester United goalkeeper Edwin van der Sar, 40, announces he is retiring at the end of the season. Bournemouth striker Lee Bradbury is appointed the club's new manager after a spell as caretaker. England and Wales are unsuccessful with bids to stage the European Under-21 Championship Finals in 2013, UEFA awarding the tournament to Israel. East Stirling are expelled from the Scottish Cup for fielding an ineligible player against Buckie.

28 Liverpool turn down a bid from Chelsea for Fernando Torres, reject a transfer request from the player and agree a club-record £22.7m deal with Ajax for striker Luis Suarez.

30 Crawley, the one remaining non-league side left in the FA Cup, draw Manchester United at Old Trafford in the fifth round.

31 The transfer record between British clubs is broken twice on a remarkable deadline-day for moves. Liverpool pay £35m for Newcastle's Andy Carroll and later accept Chelsea's £50m offer for Fernando Torres. On the day the club report an annual loss of £71m, Chelsea also sign central-defender David Luiz from Benfica for £21.3m. Total Premier League spending is a record £225m.

FEBRUARY 2011

1 Former Foreign Secretary David Miliband becomes a non-executive vice-chairman at Sunderland.

2 Gary Neville, 35, announces his retirement with immediate effect after 602 appearances for Manchester United and a record 85 caps for an England right-back.

3 Two more managers are sacked following poor results – Sheffield Wednesday's Alan Irvine and Brentford's Andy Scott. Barnsley are fined £1,000 by the FA for comments on their website questioning the integrity of referee Peter Quinn following the match against Hull.

4 Gary Megson succeeds Alan Irvine at Hillsborough, the ninth appointment of his managerial career.

5 Newcastle make Premier League history, retrieving a 4-0 deficit to draw 4-4 with Arsenal.

6 West Bromwich Albion manager Roberto di Matteo is sacked after a run of eight defeats in ten matches.

7 Ashley Cole is voted England fans' Player of the Year. Former England manager Steve McClaren is dismissed by the struggling German club Wolfsburg.

8 Gary Speed's first match as Wales manager is a 3-0 defeat by the Republic of Ireland in the new Carling Nations Cup. Former Sky Sports pair Andy Gray and Richard Keys sign up for a daily radio programme on talkSPORT.

9 Ashley Young scores his first England goal and Aston Villa team-mate Darren Bent is also on the mark in a 2-1 away win over Denmark in a friendly international. James McArthur scores his first for Scotland on his full debut in the 3-0 Carling Nations Cup victory over Northern Ireland. A winding-up order from Revenue and Customs against Plymouth is dismissed in the High Court after the club pay off a £760,000 tax bill.

10 Five weeks after being sacked by Liverpool, Roy Hodgson is appointed West Bromwich Albion's new manager.

11 West Ham win the vote over Tottenham to move into the Olympic Stadium after the 2012 Games.

12 Leyton Orient, the club nearest the stadium, challenge the choice of West Ham, fearing for their future.

14 Bolton's Mark Davies signs a contract extension through to the summer of 2015.

15 Tottenham's assistant coach Joe Jordan is butted by AC Milan captain Gennaro Gattuso after the Italian side's 1-0 home defeat in the Champions League.

16 Plymouth's financial problems are underlined by the PFA having to make loans to players who have not been paid.

17 A man who punched Stevenage defender Scott Laird after their FA Cup win over Newcastle is jailed for 12 weeks and banned from grounds for six years.

18 Sir Alex Ferguson, Arsene Wenger and Carlo Ancelotti join fans' groups in protesting at the price of tickets for the Champions League Final at Wembley – costing from £150 to £300, with a £26 administration charge on top, for neutral supporters.

19 Crawley are denied a stoppage-time equaliser by the woodwork in their FA Cup fifth round tie against Manchester United at Old Trafford.

20 Patrice Evra, coveted by Real Madrid and Barcelona, signs a new three-year contract with Manchester United.

21 Plymouth are deducted ten points for entering administration and drop to the bottom of League One. AC Milan captain Gennaro Gattuso is banned for four matches by UEFA for 'assaulting' Tottenham's Joe Jordan.

22 Rangers confirm that assistant manager Ally McCoist will take over at the end of the season when Walter Smith steps down. Reading are fined £40,000 by the FA for a players' fracas at Cardiff.

23 Liverpool, Manchester City and Rangers reach the last 16 of the Europa League.

24 Cheick Tiote, Newcastle's Ivory Coast midfielder, signs a new six-and-a-half-year contract.

25 Steve Bruce, the Sunderland manager, signs a new contract through to 2014.

26 Bradford manager Peter Taylor leaves the club with his side fifth from bottom of League Two.

27 Birmingham beat Arsenal 2-1 in the Carling Cup Final with an 89th minute goal from substitute Obafemi Martins.

28 Wayne Rooney escapes FA disciplinary action after catching James McCarthy with his elbow in Manchester United's win at Wigan.

MARCH 2011

1 Nicky Forster, Brentford striker, is appointed manager until the end of the season following a successful spell as caretaker.

2 Rangers have Steven Whittaker, Madjid Bougherra and El-Hadji Diouf sent off in a Scottish Cup replay at Celtic Park. Eight other players receive yellow cards and Celtic manager Neil Lennon squares up to the Rangers assistant manager Ally McCoist on the touchline. Danny Wilson resigns as Swindon manager after a run of 11 matches without a win. Ian Sampson is sacked by Northampton after seven games without a victory.

3 Manchester City's Kolo Toure is revealed to have failed a drugs test. Paul Hart, football's 'trouble-shooting' manager, takes over at relegation-threatened Swindon until the end of the season.

4 Darren Fletcher signs a new, four-year contract with Manchester United. Gary Johnson, former Bristol City and Peterborough manager, succeeds Ian Sampson at Northampton.

5 The International FA Board, meeting in Newport, pave the way for goal-line technology at the

2014 World Cup by agreeing to extend trials. The game's law-making body also decide to ban players from wearing neck-warming snoods.

7 Dave Penney is sacked after 56 days – two wins in 13 matches – as Bristol Rovers manager. Captain Stuart Campbell takes charge until the end of the season. Macclesfield fine manager Gary Simpson, his assistant Glyn Chamberlain and all the players following a mass brawl during the home match against Wycombe.

8 Arsenal are beaten 4-3 on aggregate by Barcelona after having Robin van Persie sent off in the second leg of their first knock-out round tie. Representatives from Celtic, Rangers, the Scottish FA and Strathclyde Police meet in Edinburgh to discuss ways to combat disorder at Old Firm matches.

9 Tottenham reach the last eight of the Champions League with a 1-0 aggregate victory over AC Milan. Former Wigan and Tranmere manager Ray Mathias takes over at Stockport. Charlton manager Chris Powell receives a one-match touchline ban from the FA for comments to referee David Coote after the game against Tranmere.

10 Ashley Cole escapes police action for accidentally shooting a work placement student with an air rifle at Chelsea's training ground. Celtic manager Neil Lennon is given a four-match touchline ban and Rangers assistant manager Ally McCoist receives a two-game ban from the Scottish FA for their altercation after the teams' Scottish Cup replay. Macclesfield and Wycombe are both fined £9,000 by the FA for a players' brawl.

12 Aston Villa's Richard Dunne and James Collins apologise after clashing with coaching staff during a team break and face club fines.

13 Coventry dismiss manager Aidy Boothroyd after a run of one win in 16 Championship matches.

14 Jens Lehmann comes out of retirement to rejoin Arsenal until the end of the season with the club facing a goalkeeping crisis.

15 Javier Hernandez scores twice to put Manchester United into the last eight of the Champions League for the fifth successive season – 2-1 on aggregate against Marseille.

16 Sir Alex Ferguson is given a five-match touchline ban and £30,000 fine by the FA for criticising referee Martin Atkinson after Manchester United's defeat at Chelsea. Notts County manager Paul Ince receives a one-game ban and £1,000 fine after being sent to the stands during the game at Leyton Orient. Chelsea join United and Tottenham in the quarter-finals of the Champions League by beating Copenhagen 2-0 on aggregate. Ian Baraclough is sacked after six months as manager of relegation-threatened Scunthorpe. Cardiff are fined £5,000 by the FA of Wales for a players' fracas in their match against Reading.

17 Liverpool, Manchester City and Rangers all go out of the European League at the last 16 stage. Manager Arsene Wenger is banned from Arsenal's next match in Europe and fined £8,700 by UEFA for comments to referee Massimo Busacca after the Champions League defeat in Barcelona. Tottenham coach Joe Jordan is banned from the first leg of Tottenham's quarter-final against Real Madrid following his altercation with AC Milan captain Gennaro Gattuso.

18 Gareth Bale signs a new, four-and-a-half-year contract with Tottenham.

19 Fabio Capello restores John Terry to the England captaincy, 13 months after stripping the Chelsea player of the position and giving it to Rio Ferdinand.

20 An extra-time goal by Nikica Jelavic gives Rangers a 2-1 win over Celtic in the Co-operative Insurance Cup Final.

21 The Scottish Government announce a £1m sponsorship of the League Cup, funded by cash seized from criminals. It will be called the Scottish Communities League Cup. Jim Gannon, manager of Port Vale for 74 days, is sacked after his team drop out of the play-off places. Morecambe manager Sammy McIlroy is given a one-match touchline ban and £500 fine by the FA for comments to referee Nigel Miller after the game against Bradford.

22 Ronnie Moore's second spell as Rotherham manager comes to an end after a 5-0 defeat by Chesterfield – even though his side remain in a play-off spot.

23 Martin Allen takes charge of struggling Barnet, where he started his managerial career.

24 Arsenal's Aaron Ramsey, 20, is appointed Wales's youngest-ever captain.

25 Gareth McAuley puts Northern Ireland ahead in a European Championship qualifier played behind closed doors in Belgrade because of previous crowd trouble. But Serbia reply twice in nine minutes to win 2-1.

26 A parcel bomb sent to Celtic manager Neil Lennon is intercepted by the Royal Mail. England score twice in the first 14 minutes through Frank Lampard (pen) and Darren Bent to beat Wales 2-0 at the Millennium Stadium. Aiden McGeady, with his first international goal, and Robbie Keane, with his 46th, give the Republic of Ireland a 2-1 victory over Macedonia in another European Championship qualifier.

27 Scotland are beaten 2-0 by Brazil in a friendly at the Emirates Stadium.

29 Northern Ireland lose further ground in their European Championship qualifying group when held to a goalless draw at home by Slovenia. Andy Carroll scores his first goal for England against Ghana, who equalise in stoppage-time through Sunderland striker Asamoah Gyan. In another absorbing friendly match, the Republic of Ireland lose 3-2 to World Cup semi-finalists Uruguay. Birmingham are fined £20,000 by the FA, with a further £20,000 suspended, after a pitch invasion during their Carling Cup tie against Aston Villa.

30 Manager Alan Knill swops a League Two promotion challenge with Bury for a Championship relegation battle at Scunthorpe.

31 The Premier League announce plans to crack down next season on mass dissent and abuse of referees. Mixu Paatelainen leaves Kilmarnock to become Finland's national coach.

APRIL 2011

1 Dean Smith, appointed Walsall manager until the end of the season, is given the job permanently after improved results.

2 Jose Mourinho suffers his first home league defeat in nine years with Porto, Chelsea and Real Madrid when Sporting Gijon win 1-0 in the Bernabeu.

3 Paul Ince, manager of Notts County for five months, leaves by mutual consent after five successive defeats. Peter Murphy, three times a losing finalist, scores the only goal to give Carlisle victory over Brenford in the Johnstone's Paint Trophy – two days after becoming a father. Fulham owner Mohamed Al Fayed unveils a statue of the late singer Michael Jackson at Craven Cottage.

4 The Football League sign a new TV contract with Sky worth £195m for three seasons from 2012-13 to replace the current £264m deal with Sky and the BBC. Manager Avram Grant is banned from the touchline and fined £6,000 by the FA for comments about referee Mike Jones after West Ham's FA Cup defeat at Stoke.

5 Wayne Rooney is banned for two matches by the FA for swearing into a TV camera after completing a hat-trick for Manchester United at West Ham. Peter Crouch is sent off after 14 minutes as Tottenham lose 4-0 to Real Madrid in their Champions League quarter-final first leg.

6 Wayne Rooney gives Manchester United the edge by scoring the only goal of their Champions League quarter-final first leg against Chelsea at Stamford Bridge. Hereford are docked three points and Torquay one point by the Football League for fielding ineligible players in their League Two match. Both clubs are also fined £10,000.

7 Wayne Rooney's appeal against his two-match ban is turned down and he misses Manchester United's FA Cup semi-final against Manchester City.

8 Accounts show that Roman Abramovich has put nearly £1bn into Chelsea since taking over the club in 2003. Seven players are nominated for the PFA Player of the Year award – Charlie Adam (Blackpool), Gareth Bale (Tottenham), Samir Nasri (Arsenal), Scott Parker (West Ham), Carlos Tevez (Manchester City), Rafael van der Vaart (Tottenham) and Nemanja Vidic (Manchester Utd).

9 Crawley celebrate promotion to the Football League after becoming Conference champions with five matches to spare.

10 American billionaire Stan Kroenke moves towards a takeover of Arsenal after increasing his shareholding in the club to 62%.

11 Martin Allen leaves Barnet after 19 days to become Notts County's sixth manager in 18 months.

12 Manchester United reach the semi-finals of the Champions League for the fourth time in five seasons with a 3-1 aggregate win over Chelsea. Brighton, in League One, become the first side to clinch promotion. Rangers assistant manager Ally McCoist wins his appeal against a two-match touchline ban imposed for a clash with Celtic manager Neil Lennon.

13 Tottenham's Champions League campaign comes to an end with a 5-0 aggregate defeat by Real Madrid. The club apply for a judicial review over West Ham's move to the Olympic Stadium. Former Brentford manager Andy Scott takes charge of Rotherham. The inaugural FA Women's Super League, with eight teams competing, kicks off.

14 The FA announce that top-price FA Cup Final tickets will break through the £100 barrier for the first time. Leyton Orient join Tottenham in applying for a judicial review over West Ham's move.

15 Four players are nominated for the Scottish PFA Player of the Year award – Celtic's Gary Hooper and Emilio Izaguirre, Steven Naismith (Rangers) and Kilmarnock's Alexei Eremenko, on loan from Ukraine club Metalist Kharkiv.

16 Manchester United's bid for the Treble is ended when Yaya Toure scores the only goal of the FA Cup semi-final against Manchester City. United have Paul Scholes sent off. Burnley's Graham Alexander becomes the second outfield player in English football, after Tony Ford, to make 1,000 appearances.

17 Stoke's 5-0 win over Bolton is the biggest in the FA Cup semi-finals for 72 years. Tottenham's Gareth Bale is named PFA Player of the Year.

18 Sunderland's Fraizer Campbell, sidelined since August 2010 with a cruciate knee ligament injury, is ruled out for most of next season.

19 Dundee United have three players sent off and concede three penalties in a 4-0 home defeat by Rangers. Martin Atkinson is named as the FA Cup Final referee.

20 Aston Villa manager Gerard Houllier, 63, who underwent life-saving heart surgery in 2001, is admitted to hospital suffering from chest paints. West Ham's Carlton Cole is fined £20,000 by the FA for improper conduct following comments on *Twitter* during England's friendly with Ghana.

21 Jamie Pitman is given the Hereford manager's job on a permanent basis after steering his side away from the relegation zone.

22 West Ham's Scott Parker is voted Footballer of the Year by the Football Writers' Association.

25 Bury goalkeeper Cameron Belford is attacked by a supporter during the game at Chesterfield.

26 Wayne Rooney scores one goal and makes another for Ryan Giggs as Manchester United beat Schalke 2-0 away from home in the first leg of their Champions League semi-final.

27 Lionel Messi scores twice as Barcelona defeat Real Madrid 2-0 in the Bernabeu. Former Wimbledon and Crystal Palace defender Andy Thorn is appointed Coventry manager after a successful spell as caretaker. UEFA announce a new, three-year deal for Champions League rights with ITV and Sky worth around £400million, similar to the current agreement.

28 Gerard Houllier is released from hospital, but will take no further part in Aston Villa's season.

30 Queens Park Rangers establish an unbeatable lead at the top of the Championship, but FA charges relating to the ownership of midfielder player Alejandro Faurlin cast a shadow over their achievement. Stockport are relegated from the Football League. Hartlepool goalkeeper Scott Flinders heads a stoppage-time equaliser against Bournemouth.

MAY 2011

1 Celtic's Honduran full-back Emilio Izaguirre is named Scotland PFA Player of the Year.

2 Norwich win a second, successive promotion to regain a place in the Premier League.

3 Chairman Ken Bates buys out Swiss-based firm FSF to become Leeds' major shareholder, ending mystery about the club's ownership. Mixu Paatelainen, who left Kilmarnock to become Finland coach, is named Scottish Premier League Manager of the Year. Barcelona complete a 3-1 aggregate win over Real Madrid to go into the Champions League Final.

4 Manchester United reach the Champions League Final for the third time in four years with a 6-1 aggregate win over Schalke.

5 After six months of negotiations, businessman Craig Whyte completes a takeover of Rangers by acquiring Sir David Murray's majority shareholding.

6 Real Madrid coach Jose Mourinho is banned for five European matches – one of them suspended – and fined £44,000 by UEFA for his outbursts during the Champions League semi-final against Barcelona.

7 Queens Park Rangers are fined £875,000 for breaching FA rules over the signing of Alejandro Faurlin, but there is no deduction of points and promotion to the Premier League is confirmed. Lincoln are relegated from the Football League.

8 Whitley Bay win the FA Vase for a record third successive season, beating Coalville 3-2 at Wembley.

9 Sammy McIlroy, the second longest-serving manager in League Two, leaves Morecambe by mutual agreement after five years in the job. Charlton manager Chris Powell, banned from the touchline for one match in March, receives a two-game suspension and £1,000 fine from the FA, this time after being sent to the stands during the match against Bristol Rovers.

10 Speaking to a House of Commons committee, former FA chairman Lord Triesman, claims that four members of the FIFA executive sought bribes to support England's 2018 World Cup bid. Relegated Sheffield United sack Micky Adams. West Ham's Danny Gabbidon is fined £6,000 by the FA for improper conduct over offensive comments on Twitter after the defeat by Aston Villa. The FA fine Leeds £12,500 and Burnley £5,000 for a players' melee. Hamilton are relegated from the Scottish Premier League.

11 Celtic manager Neil Lennon is attacked by a fan on the Tynecastle touchline during the match against Hearts. Birmingham goalkeeper Ben Foster makes himself unavailable for England for the forseeable future

12 Kenny Dalglish is rewarded for transforming Liverpool's fortunes with the manager's job on a permanent basis.

13 Micky Adams returns as Port Vale manager after four months in charge of Sheffield United. Former Wycombe, Fulham and Northern Ireland manager Lawrie Sanchez takes over at Barnet. Morecambe appoint captain Jim Bentley player-manager.

14 A red-letter day for Manchester, as United win a record 19th title and City beat Stoke 1-0 in the FA Cup Final with a goal by Yaya Toure.

15 Manager Avram Grant is sacked after West Ham are relegated from the Premier League. Rangers win the Scottish Premier League title for the third successive year, finishing one point ahead of Celtic. Emileo Izaguirre adds the Scottish Football Writers' Player of the Year award to his Scotland PFA and SPL honours.

16 Mark Robins resigns as Barnsley's manager in a disagreement over the budget for the new season. A tribute match for former Celtic defender John Kennedy, scheduled to take place on May 22, is postponed to a later date because of security fears surrounding manager Neil Lennon.

17 Sir Alex Ferguson and Carlo Ancelotti are warned by the FA for their comments about referee Howard Webb ahead of the crucial Manchester United-Chelsea Premier League game.

18 Andre Villas-Boas, mentored by Sir Bobby Robson and Jose Mourinho, becomes the youngest coach, at 33, to win a UEFA competition when his Porto side beat Braga 1-0 in the Europa League Final in Dublin.

19 Following the controversial World Cup vote, the FA decide not to back either Sepp Blatter or his challenger for the FIFA presidency, Mohamed Bin Hammam.

20 Paolo di Canio, one of the most colourful and controversial players during his time in England and Scotland, is appointed Swindon's new manager. Sir Alex Ferguson is named Manager of the Year and his Manchester United captain Nemanja Vidic Player of the Year by Premier League sponsors Barclays.

21 AFC Wimbledon, founded in 2002 by fans after the former FA Cup-winning club relocated to Milton Keynes, reach the Football League with a fifth promotion. They beat Luton on penalties in the Blue Square Premier League Play-off Final. Celtic defeat Motherwell 3-0 in the Scottish Cup Final. Arsenal are 2-0 winners over Bristol Academy in the Women's FA Cup Final.

22 Birmingham and Blackpool are relegated and Carlo Ancelotti is sacked by Chelsea on the final day of the Premier League season.

23 Sir Alex Ferguson is named Manager of the Year by the League Managers' Association.

Arsenal's Jack Wilshere is omitted from England's squad for the European Under-21 Championship Finals after his club insist he is suffering from fatigue.

24 Stephen Ward and Simon Cox score on their debuts for the Republic of Ireland, who beat Northern Ireland 5-0 in the Carling Nations Cup – Giovanni Trapattoni's biggest win as manager.

25 Martin O'Neill reaches a settlement with Aston Villa over his departure as manager in August 2010. James Morrison, on his 25th birthday, and Christophe Berra score their first international goals as Scotland beat Wales 3-1 in the Carling Nations Cup. Peter Jackson, Bradford's interim manager, is given the job on a permanent basis.

26 Manchester City's Kolo Toure is banned by the FA for six months, backdated to March 2, for failing a drugs test. Fulham win a place in the Europa League through the Fair Play League.

27 Gary Speed gains his first win as Wales manager – 2-0 over Northern Ireland in the Carling Nations Cup. Danny Wilson, a former Sheffield Wednesday manager, takes charge of Sheffield United, three months after resigning at Swindon.

28 Barcelona outclass Manchester United to win the Champions League Final 3-1 at Wembley. Stevenage beat Torquay 1-0 in the League Two Play-off Final to win back-to-back promotions.

29 FIFA's ethics committee suspend vice-presidents Mohamed Bin Hammam and Jack Warner over corruption allegations, but clear president Sepp Blatter. An FA inquiry finds no evidence to back up former chairman Lord Triesman's claims that four members of the FIFA executive sought bribes to support England's 2018 World Cup bid. Robbie Keane's 49th international goal gives the Republic of Ireland victory over Scotland and the inaugural Carling Nations Cup. Peterborough defeat Huddersfield 3-0 in the League One Play-off Final.

30 Scott Sinclair scores a hat-trick as Swansea beat Reading 4-2 in the Championship Play-off Final. Dave Jones, the Championship's longest-serving manager with six years at Cardiff, is sacked for failing to win promotion. Paul Buckle leaves Torquay after losing the League Two Play-off Final to become manager of Bristol Rovers.

31 Paul Scholes announces his retirement after 676 appearances for Manchester United and 66 England caps.

JUNE 2011

1 Aston Villa manager Gerard Houllier, who missed the last month of the season through illness, leaves the club. Sam Allardyce returns to management at West Ham following his sacking by Blackburn. An attempt by the English and Scottish FAs to have the election for the FIFA presidency postponed is unsuccessful and Sepp Blatter is returned unopposed. Keith Hill leaves Rochdale to be Barnsley's new manager. Richie Barker, who sealed promotion for Bury as caretaker after Alan Knill's departure, is given the job on a permanent basis.

2 Manager Mark Hughes activates a break clause in his contract with Fulham and leaves the club.

4 Robbie Keane overtakes Sir Bobby Charlton as the highest international scorer in the British Isles with his 50th and 51st goals for the Republic of Ireland, who beat Macedonia 2-0 in a European Championship qualifier. England draw 2-2 with Switzerland after trailing 2-0.

5 Carlo Ancelotti, sacked by Chelsea and linked with the vacant manager's job at Aston Villa, says he will take a year's sabbatical from the game.

6 Former Tottenham manager Martin Jol succeeds Mark Hughes at Fulham.

7 Two promoted clubs make record signings. Swansea pay £3.5m for Watford's Danny Graham. Brighton sign Watford's Will Buckley for £1m.

8 Liverpool make the first major signing of the summer, paying £16m for Sunderland's Jordan Henderson. Former England captain Bryan Robson resigns as manager of the Thailand national side.

9 Roberto Martinez turns down the chance to become Aston Villa manager to stay at Wigan.

10 Football League chairmen vote to adopt UEFA's financial fair-play system, under which clubs can spend only what they earn. Hearts are hit with a record £100,000 fine from the Scottish FA for a poor disciplinary record – £60,000 immediately and the remainder if it does not improve. Former Manchester City striker Uwe Rosler is appointed Brentford's new manager.

11 Rushden and Diamonds are expelled from the Blue Square Premier League for breaches of rules.

12 Alex McLeish resigns as manager of relegated Birmingham, claiming to have 'issues' with the board. Billy Davies is sacked by Nottingham Forest after failing to win promotion. Former Manchester City youth coach Steve Eyre is appointed Rochdale's new manager. Danny Welbeck scores in the 88th minute to give England a 1-1 draw against Spain in their opening group match of the European Under-21 Championship in Denmark.

13 Former England manager Steve McClaren succeeds Billy Davies at Nottingham Forest. Former Leyton Orient manager Martin Ling takes over at Torquay.

14 Manchester United sign 19-year-old Blackburn defender Phil Jones for £16.5m.

15 England share a goalless draw with Ukraine in the European Under-21 Championship. Caretaker Kenny Shiels is appointed Kilmarnock manager on a permanent basis.

16 UEFA choose Wembley for the 2013 Champions League Final following the success of the Manchester United-Barcelona showpiece. Budwesier replace E.ON as sponsor of the FA Cup in a three-year deal worth a reported £24m.

17 Five days after his controversial departure from Birmingham, Alex McLeish takes over at Aston Villa. Malky Mackay leaves Watford to become Cardiff's new manager.

19 Leading with a minute of normal time remaining, England concede two goals to the Czech Republic and fail to qualify from their group at the European Under-21 Championship.

20 Porto's Andre Villas-Boas, 33, becomes the youngest manager in the Premier League when he takes over at Chelsea. Jack Warner, one of the central figures in bribery allegations within FIFA, resigns all his positions in international football.

21 The FA and British Olympic Association announce that a Great Britain team will compete at the 2012 Games. The football associations from Scotland, Wales and Northern Ireland refuse to support it. Sean Dyche, Malky Mackay's assistant at Watford, is promoted to succeed him – his first managerial appointment.

22 Chris Hughton, sacked from his last job at Newcastle, is appointed Birmingham's new manager.

23 Ashley Young moves from Aston Villa to Manchester United for £16m. Attempts by Tottenham and Leyton Orient for a judicial review blocking West Ham's move to the Olympic Stadium are rejected in the High Court.

24 Arsenal's Alex Song is fined £1,350 by the Cameroon Federation for refusing a conciliatory handshake from Samuel Eto'o following their rift at the 2010 World Cup.

26 A dispute over Tamas Priskin's loan move from Ipswich to Swansea last season is resolved following Ipswich's call for a transfer ban on the Premier League newcomers.

27 England draw 1-1 with Mexico in their opening group match of the Women's World Cup in Germany.

28 Roberto di Matteo, who scored FA Cup Final goals for Chelsea in 1997 and 2000, returns to Stamford Bridge as assistant to new manager Andre Villas-Boas.

29 England move ahead of Brazil and Argentina to fourth in FIFA's latest world rankings, equalling their previous highest position. Ipswich receive a club-record £8.1m from Sunderland for 18-year-old Connor Wickham.

30 David de Gea becomes Britain's most expensive goalkeeper, joining Manchester United from Atletico Madrid for £17.8m.

JULY 2011

1 England beat New Zealand 2-1 in the Women's World Cup.

3 Brighton break their transfer record for the second time, paying £2.5m for Peterborough's Craig Mackail-Smith.

4 Leicester re-name the Walkers Stadium the Kings Power Stadium to tie in with their Thai owners' business group. England lose 3-2 to Germany in the quarter-finals of the Under-17 World Cup in Mexico.

5 For the second time in seven months, Carlos Tevez asks for a move from Manchester City. England reach the quarter-finals of the Women's World Cup with a 2-0 win over Japan.

7 Fulham, the new season's earliest starters, complete a 3-0 aggregate win over the Faroe Islands team Runavik in the Europa League first qualifying round.

8 Manchester United's Wes Brown and John O'Shea become Sunderland's eighth and ninth signings of the summer.

9 England lose 5-4 on penalties to France in the Women's World Cup quarter-finals.

EUROPEAN CHAMPIONSHIP 2012

Robbie Keane's chequered career at club level touched a new low last season when his loan spell at West Ham ended in relegation from the Premier League. But just three weeks later, the striker was on a high with a record-breaking performance which underlined the success he has enjoyed playing international football. Keane scored both goals in a 2-0 win over Macedonia in a European Championship qualifier in Skopje to take his tally for the Republic of Ireland to 51 in 108 matches. They moved him ahead of Sir Bobby Charlton's long-standing total of 49 for England and made him the most prolific marksman in the British Isles. Keane, who returned to Tottenham after the loan at Upton Park, his eighth club, made his Irish debut against the Czech Republic in March 1998 and scored for the first time the following season against Malta. Steve Staunton made him captain after being appointed manager in January 2006. In November that year, he scored his first hat-trick, against San Marino in the last game at the old Lansdowne Road ground in Dublin – now the new Aviva Stadium. Keane won his 100th cap in August 2010 in a friendly against Argentina. Now, having led the side a record 46 times, the 31-year-old will try to fire the Republic towards Euro 2012 in Poland and the Ukraine. They are level on 13 points with Slovakia and Russia and play both these teams in the space of five days in September. The following month, England have a vital qualifier away to Montenegro which is likely to decide top spot in their group. They ended on a disappointing note, held 2-2 by Switzerland at Wembley, although there was something of a let-off when Montenegro dropped two points against Bulgaria on the same day. Scotland will need to beat the Czech Republic to keep alive their slim hopes of finishing runners-up to World Cup winners Spain, who, like beaten finalists Holland and Germany, have still to drop a point. Wales, bottom of England's group, are out of the running and Northern Ireland's chance of qualifying are minimal.

QUALIFYING POSITIONS AFTER 2010-11 SEASON
(group winners through to finals, along with best runners-up, winners of two-leg play-off matches invlving remaining eight second-placed teams and hosts Poland and Ukraine)

GROUP A

	P	W	D	L	F	A	Pts
Germany	7	7	0	0	22	3	21
Belgium	7	3	2	2	15	10	11
Turkey	6	3	1	2	9	7	10
Austria	6	2	1	3	10	10	7
Azerbaijan	6	1	0	5	5	18	3
Kazakhstan	6	1	0	5	2	15	3

Results: Kazakhstan 0 Turkey 3, Belgium 0 Germany 1, Turkey 3 Belgium 2, Austria 2 Kazakhstan 0, Germany 6 Azerbaijan 1, Kazakhstan 0 Belgium 2, Austria 3 Azerbaijan 0, Germany 3 Turkey 0, Azerbaijan 1 Turkey 0, Kazakhstan 0 Germany 3, Belgium 4 Austria 4, Austria 0 Belgium 2, Germany 4 Kazakhstan 0, Turkey 2 Austria 0, Belgium 4 Azerbaijan 1, Austria 1 Germany 2, Belgium 1 Turkey 1, Kazakhstan 2 Azerbaijan 1, Azerbaijan 1 Germany 3

To play: Sept 2: Azerbaijan v Belgium, Turkey v Kazakhstan, Germany v Austria; Sept 6: Azerbaijan v Kazakhstan, Austria v Turkey; Oct 7: Belgium v Kazakhstan, Turkey v Germany, Azerbaijan v Austria; Oct 11: Kazakhstan v Austria, Germany v Belgium, Turkey v Azerbaijan

GROUP B

	P	W	D	L	F	A	Pts
Slovakia	6	4	1	1	6	4	13
Russia	6	4	1	1	9	4	13
Republic of Ireland	6	4	1	1	11	6	13

	P	W	D	L	F	A	Pts
Armenia	6	2	2	2	10	7	8
Macedonia	6	1	1	4	5	8	4
Andorra	6	0	0	6	1	13	0

Results: Armenia 0 Republic of Ireland 1, Andorra 0 Russia 2, Slovakia 1 Macedonia 0, Russia 0 Slovakia 1, Macedonia 2 Armenia 2, Republic of Ireland 3 Andorra 1, Armenia 3 Slovakia 1, Andorra 0 Macedonia 2, Republic of Ireland 2 Russia 3, Armenia 4 Andorra 0, Slovakia 1 Republic of Ireland 1, Macedonia 0 Russia 1, Armenia 0 Russia 0, Andorra 0 Slovakia 1, Republic of Ireland 2 Macedonia 1, Russia 3 Armenia 1, Macedonia 0 Republic of Ireland 2, Slovakia 1 Andorra 0
To play: Sept 2: Andorra v Armenia, Russia v Macedonia, Republic of Ireland v Slovakia; Sept 6: Slovakia v Armenia, Macedonia v Andorra, Russia v Republic of Ireland; Oct 7: Slovakia v Russia, Andorra v Republic of Ireland; Oct 11: Russia v Andorra, Republic of Ireland v Armenia, Macedonia v Slovakia

GROUP C

	P	W	D	L	F	A	Pts
Italy	6	5	1	0	14	1	16
Slovenia	7	3	2	2	9	4	11
Serbia	6	2	2	2	8	9	8
Estonia	7	2	1	4	7	11	7
Northern Ireland	5	1	3	1	3	3	6
Faroe Islands	7	1	1	5	5	18	4

Results: Estonia 2 Faroe Islands 1, Faroe Islands 0 Serbia 3, Estonia 1 Italy 2; Slovenia 0 Northern Ireland 1, Serbia 1 Slovenia 1, Italy 5 Faroe Islands 0, Serbia 1 Estonia 3, Northern Ireland 0 Italy 0, Slovenia 5 Faroe Islands 1, Faroe Islands 1 Northern Ireland 1, Estonia 0 Slovenia 1, Italy 3 Serbia 0 (forfeited: match abandoned at 0-0 after six mins – crowd trouble); Serbia 2 Northern Ireland 1, Slovenia 0 Italy 1, Estonia 1 Serbia 1, Northern Ireland 0 Slovenia 0, Faroe Islands 0 Slovenia 2, Italy 3 Estonia 0, Faroe Islands 2 Estonia 0
To play: Aug 10: Northern Ireland v Faroe Islands; Sept 2: Northern Ireland v Serbia, Slovenia v Estonia, Faroe Islands v Italy; Sept 6: Italy v Slovenia, Serbia v Faroe Islands, Estonia v Northern Ireland; Oct 7: Serbia v Italy, Northern Ireland v Estonia; Oct 11: Slovenia v Serbia, Italy v Northern Ireland

GROUP D

	P	W	D	L	F	A	Pts
France	6	4	1	1	9	2	13
Belarus	7	3	3	1	6	2	12
Bosnia-Herz	6	3	1	2	8	7	10
Romania	6	2	2	2	8	6	8
Albania	6	2	2	2	4	6	8
Luxembourg	7	0	1	6	1	13	1

Results: Romania 1 Albania 1, Luxembourg 0 Bosnia-Herzegovina 3, France 0 Belarus 1, Belarus 0 Romania 0, Albania 1 Luxembourg 0, Bosnia-Herzegovina 0 France 2, Luxembourg 0 Belarus 0, Albania 1 Bosnia-Herzegovina 1, France 2 Romania 0, Belgium 2 Albania 0, France 2 Luxembourg 0, Luxembourg 0 France 2, Bosnia-Herzegovina 2 Romania 1, Albania 1 Belarus 0, Romania 3 Luxembourg 1, Belarus 1 France 1, Romania 3 Bosnia-Herzegovina 0, Belarus 2 Luxembourg 0, Bosnia-Herzegovina 2 Albania 0
To play: Sept 2: Belarus v Bosnia-Herzegovina, Albania v France, Luxembourg v Romania; Sept 6: Luxembourg v Albania, Bosnia-Herzegovina v Belarus, Romania v France; Oct 7: Romania v Belarus, France v Albania, Bosnia-Herzegovina v Luxembourg; Oct 11: France v Bosnia-Herzegovina, Albania v Romania

GROUP E

	P	W	D	L	F	A	Pts
Holland	6	6	0	0	21	5	18
Sweden	6	5	0	1	20	6	15
Hungary	7	4	0	3	18	13	12
Moldova	6	2	0	4	7	9	6
Finland	6	2	0	4	11	11	6
San Marino	7	0	0	7	0	33	0

Results: Moldova 2 Finland 0, Sweden 2 Hungary 0, San Marino 0 Holland 5, Sweden 6 San Marino 0, Holland 2 Finland 1, Hungary 2 Moldova 1, Hungary 8 San Marino 0, Moldova 0 Holland 1, Finland 1 Hungary 2, Holland 4 Sweden 1, San Marino 0 Moldova 2, Finland 8 San Marino 0, Hungary 0 Holland 4, Sweden 2 Moldova 1, Holland 5 Hungary 3, Moldova 1 Sweden 4, San Marino 0 Finland 1, Sweden 5 Finland 0
To play: Sept 2: Hungary v Sweden, Finland v Moldova, Holland v San Marino; Sept 6: Finland v Holland, San Marino v Sweden, Moldova v Hungary; Oct 7: Finland v Sweden, Holland v Moldova; Oct 11: Sweden v Holland, Hungary v Finland, Moldova v San Marino

GROUP F

	P	W	D	L	F	A	Pts
Greece	6	4	2	0	8	3	14
Croatia	6	4	1	1	10	3	13
Israel	7	4	1	2	10	7	13
Georgia	7	2	3	3	5	5	9
Latvia	6	1	1	4	5	9	4
Malta	6	0	0	6	2	13	0

Results: Israel 3 Malta 1, Latvia 0 Croatia 3, Greece 1 Georgia 1, Georgia 0 Israel 0, Malta 0 Latvia 2, Croatia 0 Greece 0, Georgia 1 Malta 0, Greece 1 Latvia 0, Israel 1 Croatia 2, Latvia 1 Georgia 1, Greece 2 Israel 1, Croatia 3 Malta 0, Georgia 1 Croatia 0, Israel 2 Latvia 1, Malta 0 Greece 1, Israel 1 Georgia 0, Croatia 2 Georgia 1, Greece 3 Malta 1, Latvia 1 Israel 2
To play: Sept 2: Israel v Greece, Malta v Croatia, Georgia v Latvia; Sept 6: Malta v Georgia, Latvia v Greece, Croatia v Israel; Oct 7: Greece v Croatia, Latvia v Malta; Oct 11: Georgia v Greece, Malta v Israel, Croatia v Latvia

GROUP G

	P	W	D	L	F	A	Pts
England	5	3	2	0	11	3	11
Montenegro	5	3	2	0	4	1	11
Switzerland	5	1	2	2	7	7	5
Bulgaria	5	1	2	2	2	6	5
Wales	4	0	0	4	1	8	0

Results: Montenegro 1 Wales 0, England 4 Bulgaria 0, Bulgaria 0 Montenegro 1, Switzerland 1 England 3, Wales 0 Bulgaria 1, Montenegro 0 Switzerland 0, Switzerland 4 Wales 1, England 0 Montenego 0, Wales 0 England 2, Bulgaria 0 Switzerland 0, England 2 Switzerland 2, Montenegro 1 Bulgaria 1
To play: Sept 2: Bulgaria v England, Wales v Montenegro; Sept 6: England v Wales, Switzerland v Bulgaria; Oct 7: Montenegro v England, Wales v Switzerland; Oct 11: Bulgaria v Wales, Switzerland v Montenegro

GROUP H

	P	W	D	L	F	A	Pts
Portugal	5	3	1	1	11	7	10
Denmark	5	3	1	1	7	4	10
Norway	5	3	1	1	6	4	10
Cyprus	4	0	2	2	5	8	2
Iceland	5	0	1	4	2	8	1

Results: Iceland 1 Norway 2, Portugal 4 Cyprus 4, Denmark 1 Iceland 0, Norway 1 Portugal 0, Cyprus 1 Norway 2, Portugal 3 Denmark 1, Denmark 2 Cyprus 0, Iceland 1 Portugal 3, Cyprus 0 Iceland 0, Norway 1 Denmark 1, Iceland 0 Denmark 2, Portugal 1 Norway 0
To play: Sept 2: Norway v Iceland, Cyprus v Portugal; Sept 6: Iceland v Cyprus, Denmark v Norway; Oct 7: Cyprus v Denmark, Portugal v Iceland; Oct 11: Denmark v Portugal, Norway v Cyprus

GROUP I

	P	W	D	L	F	A	Pts
Spain	5	5	0	0	15	5	15
Czech Republic	5	3	0	2	6	3	9
Scotland	4	1	1	2	4	5	4
Lithuania	5	1	1	3	3	8	4
Liechtenstein	5	1	0	4	3	10	3

Results: Lithuania 0 Scotland 0, Liechtenstein 0 Spain 4, Czech Republic 0 Lithuania 1, Scotland 2 Liechtenstein 1, Czech Republic 1 Scotland 0, Spain 3 Lithuania 1, Liechtenstein 0 Czech Republic 2, Scotland 2 Spain 3, Spain 2 Czech Republic 1, Czech Republic 2 Liechtenstein 0, Lithuania 1 Spain 3, Liechtenstein 2 Lithuania 0
To play: Sept 2: Lithuania v Liechtenstein; Sept 3: Scotland v Czech Republic; Sept 6: Spain v Liechtenstein, Scotland v Lithuania; Oct 7: Czech Republic v Spain; Oct 8: Liechtenstein v Scotland; Oct 11: Lithuania v Czech Republic, Spain v Scotland

PREVIOUS FINALS

1960	*USSR 2 Yugoslavia 1 (Paris)
1964	Spain 2 USSR 1 (Madrid)
1968	**Italy 2 Yugoslavia 0 (Rome)
1972	West Germany 3 USSR 0 (Brussels)
1976	***Czechoslovakia 2 West Germany 2 (Belgrade)
1980	West Germany 2 Belgium 1 (Rome)
1984	France 2 Spain 0 (Paris)
1988	Holland 2 USSR 0 (Munich)
1992	Denmark 2 Germany 0 (Gothenburg)
1996	+Germany 2 Czech Republic 1 (Wembley)
2000	+France 2 Italy 1 (Rotterdam)
2004	Greece 1 Portugal 0 (Lisbon)
2008	Spain 1 Germany 0 (Vienna)

* After extra-time. ** Replay after 1-1. *** Czechoslovakia won 5-3 on pens.
+ Golden goal winner

ENGLISH TABLES 2010–2011

BARCLAYS PREMIER LEAGUE

			Home					Away						
		P	W	D	L	F	A	W	D	L	F	A	GD	PTS
1	Manchester Urd	38	18	1	0	49	12	5	10	4	29	25	41	80
2	Chelsea	38	14	3	2	39	13	7	5	7	30	20	36	71
3	Manchester City	38	13	4	2	34	12	8	4	7	26	21	27	71
4	Arsenal	38	11	4	4	33	15	8	7	4	39	28	29	68
5	Tottenham	38	9	9	1	30	19	7	5	7	25	27	9	62
6	Liverpool	38	12	4	3	37	14	5	3	11	22	30	15	58
7	Everton	38	9	7	3	31	23	4	8	7	20	22	6	54
8	Fulham	38	8	7	4	30	23	3	9	7	19	20	6	49
9	Aston Villa	38	8	7	4	26	19	4	5	10	22	40	-11	48
10	Sunderland	38	7	5	7	25	27	5	6	8	20	29	-11	47
11	WBA	38	8	6	5	30	30	4	5	10	26	41	-15	47
12	Newcastle	38	6	8	5	41	27	5	5	9	15	30	-1	46
13	Stoke	38	10	4	5	31	18	3	5	13	15	30	-2	46
14	Bolton	38	10	5	4	34	24	2	5	12	18	32	-4	46
15	Blackburn	38	7	7	5	22	16	4	3	12	24	43	-13	43
16	Wigan	38	5	8	6	22	34	4	7	8	18	27	-21	42
17	Wolves	38	8	4	7	30	30	3	3	13	16	36	-20	40
18	Birmingham	38	6	8	5	19	22	2	7	10	18	36	-21	39
19	Blackpool	38	5	5	9	30	37	5	4	10	25	41	-23	39
20	West Ham	38	5	5	9	24	31	2	7	10	19	39	-27	33

Manchester Utd, Chelsea and Manchester City go into Champions League group stage; Arsenal into qualifying two-leg play-off; Tottenham, Fulham, Stoke and Birmingham into Europa League.

TV/merit money: 1 £60.4m, 2 £57.7m, 3 £56.1m, 4 £55.5m, 5 £55.1m, 6 £53.1m, 7 £49.6m, 8 £49.1m, 9 £47.4m, 10 £47.2m, 11 £46.4m, 12 £45.1m, 13 £43.6m, 14 £42.8m, 15 £42.1m, 16 £41.3m, 17 £40.6m, 18 £40.3m, 19 £39.8m, 20 £39.1m

Biggest win: Manchester Utd 7 Blackburn 1, Arsenal 6 Blackpool 0, Chelsea 6 WBA 0, Newcastle 6 Aston Villa 0, Wigan 0 Chelsea 6

Highest aggregate score: Manchester Utd 7 Blackburn 1, Everton 5 Blackpool 3, Newcastle 4 Arsenal 4

Highest attendance: 75,486 (Manchester Utd v Bolton)

Lowest attendance: 14,042 (Wigan v Wolves)

Manager of Year: Sir Alex Ferguson (Manchester Utd)

Player of Year: Nemanja Vidic (Manchester Utd)

Golden Boot: 20 Dimitar Berbatov (Manchester Utd), Carlos Tevez (Manchester City)

Golden Glove: 18 (clean sheets) Joe Hart (Manchester City)

PFA Team of Year: Van der Sar (Manchester Utd), Sagna (Arsenal), Vidic (Manchester Utd), Kompany (Manchester City), Cole (Chelsea), Nani (Manchester Utd), Nasri (Arsenal), Wilshere (Arsenal), Bale (Tottenham), Tevez (Manchester City), Berbatov (Manchester Utd)

Leading scorers (all competitions): 23 Tevez (Manchester City); 22 Van Persie (Arsenal); 21 Berbatov (Manchester Utd); 20 Bent (Aston Villa – 11 for Sunderland), Hernandez (Manchester Utd); 16 Anelka (Chelsea), Rooney (Manchester Utd); 15 Kuyt (Liverpool), Nasri (Arsenal), Odemwingie (WBA), Van der Vaart (Tottenham); 14 Malouda (Chelsea); 13 Adam (Blackpool), Campbell (Blackpool), Carroll (Liverpool – 11 for Newcastle), Dempsey (Fulham), Drogba (Chelsea), Kalou (Chelsea), Lampard (Chelsea), Pavlyuchenko (Tottenham), Walcott (Arsenal).

NPOWER CHAMPIONSHIP

		P		Home					Away					
		P	W	D	L	F	A	W	D	L	F	A	GD	PTS
1	QPR	46	14	7	2	43	15	10	9	4	28	17	39	88
2	Norwich	46	13	6	4	47	30	10	9	4	36	28	25	84
3	Swansea*	46	15	5	3	41	11	9	3	11	28	31	27	80
4	Cardiff	46	12	7	4	41	25	11	4	8	35	29	22	80
5	Reading	46	12	7	4	43	25	8	10	5	34	26	26	77
6	Nottm Forest	46	13	8	2	43	22	7	7	9	26	28	19	75
7	Leeds	46	11	8	4	47	34	8	7	8	34	36	11	72
8	Burnley	46	12	6	5	40	30	6	8	9	25	31	4	68
9	Millwall	46	12	6	5	39	22	6	7	10	23	26	14	67
10	Leicester	46	13	6	4	48	27	6	4	13	28	44	5	67
11	Hull	46	7	8	8	21	19	9	9	5	31	32	1	65
12	Middlesbrough	46	10	7	6	37	32	7	4	12	31	36	0	62
13	Ipswich	46	10	3	10	33	37	8	5	10	29	31	-6	62
14	Watford	46	9	7	7	39	32	7	6	10	38	39	6	61
15	Bristol City	46	10	4	9	30	29	7	5	11	32	36	-3	60
16	Portsmouth	46	8	9	6	31	26	7	4	12	22	34	-7	58
17	Barnsley	46	11	6	6	32	23	3	8	12	23	43	-11	56
18	Coventry	46	9	5	9	27	26	5	8	10	27	32	-4	55
19	Derby	46	8	4	11	35	32	5	2	12	23	39	-13	49
20	Crystal Palace	46	11	6	6	28	24	1	6	16	16	45	-25	48
21	Doncaster	46	7	9	7	26	31	4	6	13	29	50	-26	48
22	Preston	46	7	4	12	27	36	3	8	12	27	43	-25	42
23	Sheffield Utd	46	7	5	11	27	36	4	4	15	17	43	-35	42
24	Scunthorpe	46	5	5	13	21	40	7	1	15	22	47	-44	42

*also promoted

Biggest win: Norwich 6 Scunthorpe 0, Doncaster 0 Ipswich 6
Highest aggregate score: Leeds 4 Preston 6
Highest attendance: 33,622 (Leeds v Sheffield Utd)
Lowest attendance: 4,160 (Scunthorpe v Preston)
Manager of Year: Paul Lambert (Norwich)
Player of the Year: Adel Taarabt (QPR)
Top league scorer: 24 Danny Graham (Watford)
PFA Team of Year: Kenny (QPR), Naughton (Leicester), Williams (Swansea), Morgan (Nottm Forest), Harte (Reading), Sinclair (Swansea), Taarabt (QPR), King (Leicester), Hoolahan (Norwich), Graham (Watford), Holt (Norwich)
Leading scorers (all competitions): 27 Graham (Watford), Sinclair (Swansea); 25 Long (Reading); 23 Holt (Norwich); 20 Becchio (Leeds), Bothroyd (Cardiff); 19 Taarabt (QPR); 18 Gradel (Leeds); 17 Morison (Millwall), 16 King (Leicester), Sharp (Doncaster); 15 Eagles (Burnley), Rodriguez (Burnley), Sordell (Watford); 14 McDonald (Middlesbrough), Nugent (Portsmouth); 13 Commons (Derby), Helguson (QPR), Jackson (Norwich), King (Coventry), McGugan (Nottm Forest). Also: 17 Mclean (Hull – 14 for Peterborough)

NPOWER LEAGUE ONE

			Home					Away						
		P	W	D	L	F	A	W	D	L	F	A	GD	PTS
1	Brighton	46	17	4	2	54	22	11	7	5	31	18	45	95
2	Southampton	46	16	4	3	44	13	12	4	7	42	25	48	92
3	Huddersfield	46	12	8	3	38	21	13	4	6	39	27	29	87
4	Peterborough*	46	15	5	3	69	40	8	5	10	37	35	31	79
5	MK Dons	46	14	5	4	35	23	9	3	11	32	37	7	77
6	Bournemouth	46	13	5	5	47	24	6	9	8	28	30	21	71
7	Leyton Orient	46	12	6	5	37	25	7	7	9	34	37	9	70
8	Exeter	46	12	5	6	40	31	8	5	10	26	42	-7	70
9	Rochdale	46	9	8	6	36	30	9	6	8	27	25	8	68
10	Colchester	46	12	7	4	38	30	4	7	12	19	33	-6	62
11	Brentford	46	9	5	9	24	28	8	5	10	31	34	-7	61
12	Carlisle	46	9	9	7	34	26	7	4	12	26	36	-2	59
13	Charlton	46	10	6	7	29	29	5	8	10	33	37	-4	59
14	Yeovil	46	8	6	9	27	30	8	5	10	29	36	-10	59
15	Sheffield Wed	46	10	5	8	38	29	6	5	12	29	38	0	58
16	Hartlepool	46	9	6	8	32	32	6	6	11	15	33	-18	57
17	Oldham	46	7	9	7	29	31	6	8	9	24	29	-7	56
18	Tranmere	46	9	4	10	28	27	6	7	10	25	33	-7	56
19	Notts Co	46	9	3	11	24	25	5	5	13	22	35	-14	50
20	Walsall	46	9	3	11	33	36	3	9	11	23	39	-19	48
21	Dag and Red	46	8	6	9	28	27	4	5	14	24	43	-18	47
22	Bristol Rovers	46	6	7	10	24	35	5	5	13	24	47	-34	45
23	Plymouth**	46	9	4	10	27	33	6	3	14	24	41	-23	42
24	Swindon	46	5	9	9	20	27	4	5	14	30	45	-22	41

* also promoted, ** 10pts deducted for administration

Biggest win: Peterborough 6 Carlisle 0, Oldham 0 Southampton 6
Highest aggregate score: Peterborough 5 Swindon 4
Highest attendance: 31,653 (Southampton v Walsall)
Lowest attendance: 1,907 (Dagenham v Brentford)
Manager of Year: Gus Poyet (Brighton)
Player of Year: Craig Mackail-Smith (Peterborough)
Top league scorer: 27 Craig Mackail-Smith
PFA Team of Year: Davis (Southampton), Calderon (Brighton), Greer (Brighton), Fonte (Southampton), Harding (Southampton), Pilkington (Huddersfield), Bennett (Brighton), Lallana (Southampton), Oxlade-Chamberlain (Southampton), Mackail-Smith (Peterborough), Wright-Phillips (Charlton).
Leading scorers (all competitions): 35 Mackaill-Smith (Peterborough); 22 Murray (Brighton), Rhodes (Huddersfield); 21 Lambert (Southampton), Wright-Phillips (Charlton – 13 for Plymouth); 20 Barnes (Brighton), Cureton (Exeter), Hoskins (Bristol Rov), Mellor (Sheffield Wed); 19 Jones (Rochdale); 18 Madine (Sheffield Wed – 13 for Carlisle); 17 Austin (Swindon), Boyd (Peterborough), McGleish (Leyton Orient); 16 Hughes (Notts Co), Revell (Leyton Orient); 15 Barnard (Southampton), Bowditch (Yeovil), Harley (Exeter), Jackson (Charlton)

NPOWER LEAGUE TWO

			Home					Away					
		P	W	D	L	F	A	W	D	L	F	A	GD	PTS
1	Chesterfield	46	16	3	4	59	31	8	11	4	26	20	34	86
2	Bury	46	11	6	6	35	23	12	6	5	47	27	32	81
3	Wycombe	46	12	6	5	38	25	10	8	5	31	25	19	80
4	Shrewsbury	46	11	9	3	36	18	11	4	8	36	31	23	79
5	Accrington	46	15	5	3	53	24	3	14	6	20	31	18	73
6	Stevenage*	46	9	11	3	37	24	9	4	10	25	21	17	69
7	Torquay***	46	10	8	5	36	22	7	10	6	38	31	21	68
8	Gillingham	46	10	7	6	29	24	7	10	6	38	33	10	68
9	Rotherham	46	10	8	5	41	26	7	7	9	34	34	15	66
10	Crewe	46	13	6	4	49	18	5	5	13	38	47	22	65
11	Port Vale	46	11	7	5	32	22	6	7	10	22	27	5	65
12	Oxford Utd	46	11	4	8	32	25	6	8	9	26	35	-2	63
13	Southend	46	10	7	6	37	28	6	6	11	25	28	6	61
14	Aldershot	46	8	8	7	26	26	6	11	6	28	28	0	61
15	Macclesfield	46	6	7	10	25	30	8	6	9	34	37	-14	55
16	Northampton	46	8	9	6	40	33	3	10	10	23	38	-8	52
17	Cheltenham	46	6	6	11	24	32	7	7	9	32	45	-21	52
18	Bradford	46	10	3	10	27	30	5	4	14	16	38	-25	52
19	Burton	46	9	8	6	36	31	3	7	13	20	39	-14	51
20	Morecambe	46	6	8	9	26	31	7	4	12	28	42	-19	51
21	Hereford**	46	4	11	8	23	30	8	6	9	27	36	-16	50
22	Barnet	46	8	5	10	30	35	4	7	12	28	42	-19	48
23	Lincoln	46	7	4	12	18	41	6	4	13	27	40	-36	47
24	Stockport	46	4	12	7	31	51	5	2	16	17	45	-48	41

* also promoted, ** 3pts deducted for ineligible player, *** 1pt deducted for ineligible player

Biggest win: Crewe 8 Cheltenham 1, Crewe 7 Barnet 0
Highest aggregate score: Accrington 7 Gillingham 4
Highest attendance: 15,332 (Bradford v Stockport)
Lowest attendance: 1,067 (Macclesfield v Lincoln)
Manager of Year: John Sheridan (Chesterfield)
Player of Year: Ryan Lowe (Bury)
Top league scorer: 28 Clayton Donaldson (Crewe)
PFA Team of Year: Lee (Chesterfield), Batt (Oxford), Sharps (Shrewsbury), Branston (Torquay), Skarz (Bury), Whitaker (Chesterfield), Ainsworth (Wycombe), Ryan (Accrington), Law (Rotherham), Lowe (Bury), Davies (Chesterfield)
Leading scorers (all competitions): 29 Donaldson (Crewe); 28 Lowe (Bury); 25 Davies (Chesterfield), McDonald (Gillingham); 24 Le Fondre (Rotherham); 21 Corr (Southend), 20 M Richards (Port Vale); 19 Harrad (Northampton – 13 for Burton), Miller (Crewe), Rendell (Wycombe), Thomas (Cheltenham); 18 Fleetwood (Hereford); 17 Constable (Oxford), Grimes (Lincoln), Lester (Chesterfield); 16 Robinson (Shrewsbury – 7 for Torquay); 15 Craddock (Oxford), Whitaker (Chesterfield), Zebroski (Torquay)

	Arsenal	Aston Villa	Birmingham	Blackburn	Blackpool	Bolton	Chelsea	Everton	Fulham	Liverpool	Man City	Man Utd	Newcastle	Stoke	Sunderland	Tottenham	WBA	West Ham	Wigan	Wolves
Arsenal		1-2	2-1	0-0	6-0	4-1	3-1	2-1	2-1	1-1	0-0	1-0	0-1	1-0	0-0	2-3	2-3	1-0	3-0	2-0
Aston Villa	2-4		0-0	4-1	3-2	1-1	0-0	1-0	2-2	0-1	1-0	2-2	1-0	1-1	0-1	1-2	2-1	1-0	1-1	0-1
Birmingham	0-3	1-1		2-1	2-0	2-1	1-0	0-2	0-2	0-0	2-2	1-1	0-2	1-0	2-0	1-1	1-3	2-2	0-0	1-1
Blackburn	1-2	2-0	1-1		2-2	1-0	1-2	1-0	0-2	3-1	0-1	1-1	0-0	0-2	0-0	0-1	2-0	1-1	2-1	3-0
Blackpool	1-3	1-1	1-2	1-2		4-3	1-3	2-2	2-2	2-1	2-3	2-3	1-1	0-0	1-2	3-1	2-1	1-3	1-3	2-1
Bolton	2-1	3-2	2-2	2-1	2-2		0-4	2-0	0-0	0-1	0-2	2-2	5-1	2-1	1-2	4-2	2-0	3-0	1-1	1-0
Chelsea	2-0	3-3	3-1	2-0	4-0	1-0		1-1	2-0	0-1	2-1	2-1	2-2	2-0	0-3	2-1	6-0	3-0	1-0	2-0
Everton	1-2	2-2	1-1	2-0	5-3	1-1	1-0		2-1	0-1	2-1	3-3	0-1	2-0	2-0	2-1	1-4	2-2	0-0	2-0
Fulham	2-2	1-1	3-2	1-1	3-0	3-0	0-0	0-0		2-5	1-4	2-2	0-0	2-0	0-0	1-2	3-0	1-3	2-0	2-1
Liverpool	1-1	3-0	5-0	2-1	1-2	2-1	2-0	2-2	1-0		3-0	3-1	3-0	2-0	2-2	1-0	1-0	3-0	1-1	0-3
Man City	0-3	4-0	0-0	1-1	1-0	2-1	1-0	1-2	1-1	3-0		0-0	2-1	3-0	5-0	1-0	2-2	2-1	0-1	4-3
Man Utd	1-0	5-0	5-0	7-1	2-2	1-0	2-1	1-0	2-0	3-2	0-0		3-0	2-1	2-0	1-1	2-2	2-1	4-2	4-1
Newcastle	4-4	6-0	1-1	1-2	0-2	1-1	1-1	1-2	3-1	3-1	1-3	0-0		1-2	5-1	1-1	3-3	5-0	2-2	4-1
Stoke	3-1	2-1	3-2	1-0	0-1	2-0	1-1	2-0	0-2	2-0	1-1	1-2	4-0		3-2	3-2	1-1	1-1	0-1	3-0
Sunderland	1-1	1-0	3-0	3-0	0-2	1-0	2-4	2-2	0-3	0-2	1-0	0-0	1-1	2-0		1-2	2-3	1-0	4-2	1-3
Tottenham	3-3	2-1	4-2	1-3	1-1	2-1	1-1	1-1	1-0	2-1	0-0	0-0	2-0	3-2	1-1		2-2	0-0	0-1	3-1
WBA	2-2	2-1	1-3	3-2	3-2	2-0	1-3	1-0	2-1	1-1	0-2	1-2	3-1	0-3	1-0	1-1		3-3	2-2	1-1
West Ham	0-3	1-2	0-1	0-0	0-0	1-1	1-3	1-1	3-1	3-1	1-3	2-4	1-2	3-0	0-3	0-0	2-2		3-1	2-0
Wigan	2-2	1-2	2-1	4-3	0-4	2-3	0-6	1-1	1-1	1-1	0-2	0-4	0-1	2-2	1-1	3-3	1-0	3-2		1-2
Wolves	0-2	1-2	1-0	2-3	4-0	2-3	1-0	0-3	0-3	0-3	1-1	1-1	1-1	2-1	3-2	3-3	3-1	1-1	1-2	

NPOWER CHAMPIONSHIP RESULTS 2010–2011

	Barnsley	Bristol City	Burnley	Cardiff	Coventry	Crystal Palace	Derby	Doncaster	Hull	Ipswich	Leeds	Leicester	Middlesbrough	Millwall	Norwich	Nottm Forest	Portsmouth	Preston	QPR	Reading	Scunthorpe	Sheffield Utd	Swansea	Watford
Barnsley	–	4-2	3-0	2-2	3-0	2-1	0-2	0-0	2-0	1-1	5-2	0-2	2-0	1-0	0-2	3-1	1-0	2-0	0-1	0-1	2-1	1-0	1-1	0-0
Bristol City	3-3	–	0-0	3-0	1-4	1-1	0-2	1-1	2-4	0-1	0-0	0-2	0-4	1-0	0-2	3-1	3-1	2-0	1-1	1-1	0-2	3-2	0-1	0-2
Burnley	3-0	0-0	–	1-1	2-0	1-0	2-1	1-1	4-0	1-2	2-3	3-0	3-1	0-3	2-1	1-0	1-1	4-3	0-0	0-4	2-0	4-2	2-1	3-2
Cardiff	2-2	3-2	1-1	–	4-1	0-0	4-1	1-0	2-0	0-2	2-3	1-1	0-3	2-1	3-1	1-2	3-0	1-1	2-0	2-2	1-0	1-1	1-0	4-2
Coventry	3-0	1-4	1-1	2-0	–	2-1	2-2	1-0	0-0	1-2	2-1	3-2	1-0	2-1	3-1	1-2	0-2	1-2	2-2	2-2	1-0	1-1	0-1	2-0
Crystal Palace	2-1	0-0	2-0	1-0	2-1	–	5-0	0-0	0-0	1-2	0-0	0-1	1-0	3-3	0-0	0-3	2-1	1-0	0-1	3-3	3-0	0-0	0-3	3-2
Derby	0-0	1-1	2-4	1-0	2-2	2-2	–	1-3	0-1	1-2	1-0	1-0	2-1	2-2	0-2	0-3	4-1	3-0	2-2	1-2	3-2	1-0	4-1	3-2
Doncaster	0-2	1-0	1-0	0-2	5-0	0-0	2-2	–	3-1	0-6	0-0	2-4	0-0	0-0	1-2	0-3	2-0	1-0	2-2	0-3	3-0	0-1	2-1	4-1
Hull	2-0	1-1	1-0	1-3	2-2	2-3	3-1	3-1	–	0-1	2-1	0-2	2-4	2-0	0-1	0-2	0-2	3-0	2-2	1-1	3-2	0-1	2-1	4-1
Ipswich	1-3	2-0	1-2	2-0	1-2	2-1	0-2	3-1	1-1	–	1-0	0-1	2-4	3-1	1-5	0-1	1-2	0-0	1-1	1-0	2-3	1-1	4-1	1-2
Leeds	3-3	0-0	2-3	2-3	2-1	2-1	0-0	2-1	2-1	2-2	–	3-0	3-3	2-0	3-2	1-1	2-1	4-1	1-1	1-3	2-0	3-0	2-0	2-2
Leicester	4-1	1-2	1-0	2-1	1-0	0-1	4-0	1-0	3-0	0-0	2-1	–	1-2	4-2	2-3	4-1	2-2	4-6	0-3	1-3	3-1	2-2	3-4	2-1
Middlesbrough	2-0	0-0	3-1	0-3	2-1	1-0	3-0	0-0	3-1	2-3	1-0	0-0	–	1-0	1-1	0-0	2-0	4-0	2-0	1-1	0-2	1-0	0-2	2-1
Millwall	2-0	1-0	0-3	2-1	1-0	2-1	2-1	0-1	1-0	2-1	4-2	0-1	3-1	–	1-1	0-1	1-1	0-1	1-1	0-0	2-1	1-1	1-1	1-0
Norwich	2-0	0-2	2-1	3-1	3-1	0-0	0-2	1-2	0-1	1-1	2-2	1-5	2-2	2-3	–	0-1	4-1	2-1	1-0	0-1	3-3	1-2	1-0	3-0
Nottm Forest	2-1	3-1	1-0	2-1	2-1	3-0	0-3	3-0	0-2	2-1	2-1	1-1	2-3	1-0	1-1	–	2-1	2-2	1-0	3-4	5-1	4-2	3-1	3-2
Portsmouth	1-0	3-1	1-2	0-3	0-3	1-0	0-2	2-3	2-0	0-0	1-0	0-0	0-0	1-1	0-1	2-1	–	1-0	2-2	1-1	1-0	1-0	0-0	3-1
Preston	1-2	0-4	4-3	1-1	1-2	4-3	0-2	0-2	0-2	2-0	1-2	3-1	1-3	0-0	0-1	1-3	1-0	–	1-1	3-1	2-3	2-0	2-1	3-1
QPR	4-0	0-4	2-1	0-1	4-3	0-0	2-0	0-2	0-2	1-2	1-1	0-0	1-3	0-0	0-1	1-1	1-0	3-1	–	0-0	2-3	3-0	4-0	0-1
Reading	3-0	4-2	0-0	3-0	3-0	3-0	2-1	4-3	1-1	1-0	3-1	3-1	5-2	2-1	3-3	1-1	2-0	0-3	2-0	–	1-2	2-3	0-1	1-3
Scunthorpe	0-0	0-2	2-4	0-2	0-1	3-0	0-0	1-3	1-5	1-1	0-0	0-3	0-2	2-1	1-2	1-0	2-0	0-1	0-3	1-2	–	3-2	0-1	2-2
Sheffield Utd	2-2	0-1	0-2	0-1	2-1	3-2	0-1	2-2	2-3	4-1	2-1	0-1	0-1	1-0	1-2	2-1	1-1	4-0	0-1	0-4	0-4	–	1-0	3-0
Swansea	1-1	0-0	0-1	0-1	2-1	1-1	0-3	2-1	1-1	3-0	3-0	1-2	1-0	3-0	0-1	1-1	1-0	4-0	4-0	1-0	1-0	4-0	–	1-1
Watford	1-0	1-3	1-3	4-1	2-2	1-1	3-0	2-0	2-1	0-1	1-2	3-2	3-1	1-0	2-1	2-1	3-0	2-2	0-2	1-1	2-0	3-0	2-3	–

NPOWER LEAGUE ONE RESULTS 2010–2011

	Bournemouth	Brentford	Brighton	Bristol Rov	Carlisle	Charlton	Colchester	Dag & Red	Exeter	Hartlepool	Huddersfield	Leyton Orient	MK Dons	Notts Co	Oldham	Peterborough	Plymouth	Rochdale	Sheffield Wed	Southampton	Swindon	Tranmere	Walsall	Yeovil
Bournemouth		3-1	1-0	2-1	2-0	3-0	1-2	2-1	3-0	2-2	0-1	1-1	3-2	3-3	3-0	5-1	3-0	1-2	0-0	1-3	3-2	1-2	3-0	2-0
Brentford	1-1		0-1	1-0	2-1	2-1	1-1	1-2	2-4	3-0	4-4	1-0	1-1	1-1	1-3	2-1	2-0	1-3	1-0	0-3	0-1	2-1	1-2	1-2
Brighton	1-1	1-0		2-2	4-3	1-1	2-0	4-3	3-0	4-1	2-3	5-0	1-0	1-0	3-2	3-1	4-0	2-2	2-1	1-2	2-1	2-1	2-1	2-0
Bristol Rov	1-0	0-0	2-4		1-1	3-4	0-1	0-2	2-2	0-0	2-2	1-2	2-1	2-1	1-0	2-2	2-3	1-1	1-1	0-4	3-1	0-1	2-2	0-2
Carlisle	1-0	0-0	0-0	4-0		4-1	4-1	0-2	1-3	0-0	2-2	0-3	2-1	1-0	2-2	0-1	1-1	1-1	0-1	3-2	0-0	2-0	2-2	1-0
Charlton	2-1	0-2	0-4	1-1	1-3		1-0	2-2	1-3	1-0	2-2	3-1	1-0	1-1	1-1	3-2	1-1	3-1	1-0	0-2	2-4	1-1	0-1	3-2
Colchester	1-0	1-1	1-1	0-3	1-1	1-0		2-2	5-1	0-3	0-3	3-2	1-3	3-1	1-0	2-1	1-0	1-0	1-1	0-2	2-1	3-1	2-0	0-0
Dag & Red	1-2	1-1	0-3	0-3	1-1	1-0	1-0		1-1	1-1	0-3	2-0	0-1	3-1	1-0	0-2	1-0	1-0	1-1	1-3	2-1	2-2	1-1	0-0
Exeter	1-2	2-4	1-2	2-2	2-1	1-0	2-2	2-1		1-2	1-4	0-1	1-1	3-1	2-0	0-2	2-0	1-0	5-1	1-2	1-0	1-1	2-1	2-3
Hartlepool	2-0	3-0	3-1	2-2	0-4	2-0	1-0	2-4	2-3		0-1	0-1	3-1	1-1	4-2	2-2	0-2	0-2	5-1	0-0	0-2	1-1	2-1	3-1
Huddersfield	2-2	4-4	2-0	0-1	0-0	3-1	2-1	2-1	0-1	1-0		2-2	4-1	3-0	0-0	1-1	3-2	2-1	4-0	2-0	3-0	0-0	1-0	4-2
Leyton Orient	2-2	1-0	1-0	4-1	0-0	1-3	4-2	1-1	3-0	1-0	1-2		2-2	2-1	0-0	0-3	2-1	4-0	1-4	0-2	3-0	2-0	0-0	1-5
MK Dons	2-0	1-0	1-0	2-0	3-2	1-1	1-2	2-0	1-0	3-0	1-3	2-3		2-1	1-0	2-2	1-3	1-1	1-1	0-2	1-0	2-0	0-0	4-0
Notts Co	0-2	1-1	1-1	0-1	0-1	2-0	0-0	1-1	0-2	3-0	0-3	2-0	2-0		0-2	0-1	3-0	1-2	0-2	1-3	1-0	0-1	1-1	0-0
Oldham	3-3	2-1	0-1	2-2	0-1	0-0	0-0	2-1	3-0	4-0	5-2	2-0	3-0	3-0		1-1	4-2	1-2	2-3	0-6	2-0	2-1	1-1	3-2
Peterborough	1-2	1-2	0-3	3-0	6-0	1-1	1-1	1-1	3-0	4-0	4-2	1-4	2-3	2-1	5-2		2-1	5-3	5-3	4-4	5-4	2-1	4-1	2-2
Plymouth	1-2	1-2	0-2	3-0	2-2	1-2	1-1	0-1	1-1	2-1	2-1	1-0	1-0	1-0	0-2	0-3		2-0	3-2	1-3	1-3	1-3	2-0	0-0
Rochdale	0-0	2-2	2-2	3-1	2-3	3-2	1-2	2-0	0-0	3-0	3-0	1-1	1-4	2-2	0-0	2-2	1-1		2-1	0-2	3-3	3-2	3-2	0-1
Sheffield Wed	1-1	1-3	1-0	6-2	0-1	2-1	0-0	0-0	1-2	4-0	0-1	1-0	2-2	0-0	0-0	1-4	2-4	2-0		0-0	3-1	4-0	3-0	2-2
Southampton	2-0	0-2	0-0	1-0	1-0	0-0	0-0	1-1	4-0	1-1	3-2	1-1	3-2	1-2	4-1	4-1	2-3	2-0	2-0		4-1	2-0	3-0	3-0
Swindon	1-2	0-2	1-1	2-1	1-0	0-3	1-1	0-1	4-2	0-1	1-2	2-2	1-2	0-3	1-2	1-0	2-3	1-1	0-2	1-0		0-0	3-1	2-1
Tranmere	0-3	0-3	1-1	1-1	2-1	1-1	1-0	0-1	4-0	0-1	0-2	4-2	1-1	0-3	1-2	1-0	1-3	1-1	3-0	1-0	0-2		0-0	1-0
Walsall	0-1	3-2	6-1	2-1	0-1	2-0	0-1	1-1	5-2	2-4	2-4	0-2	4-2	0-3	1-1	1-3	1-0	0-0	1-1	1-0	1-2	1-4		3-3
Yeovil	2-2	2-0	0-1	0-1	4-2	1-3	0-1	0-1	2-1	0-1	1-1	1-0	1-1	1-0	1-1	3-3	0-0	1-1	1-1	0-2	3-3	3-1	1-1	

NPOWER LEAGUE TWO RESULTS 2010–2011

Home \ Away	Accrington	Aldershot	Barnet	Bradford	Burton	Bury	Cheltenham	Chesterfield	Crewe	Gillingham	Hereford	Lincoln	Macclesfield	Morecambe	Northampton	Oxford	Port Vale	Rotherham	Shrewsbury	Southend	Stevenage	Stockport	Torquay	Wycombe
Accrington	–	1-1	2-0	3-0	1-1	3-0	1-2	5-2	0-0	3-1	1-1	0-0	2-2	1-2	0-0	0-0	2-0	0-0	1-1	2-2	2-2	0-0	0-0	1-2
Aldershot	1-1	–	1-0	1-0	2-1	1-3	0-2	2-2	3-2	1-2	0-3	2-2	1-0	1-2	1-1	1-2	1-0	2-2	3-0	1-1	1-1	1-0	1-0	0-0
Barnet	2-0	1-2	–	0-2	0-0	1-1	3-1	2-2	2-1	1-0	2-0	4-2	1-1	1-2	4-1	2-2	1-0	1-4	1-1	0-2	0-3	1-3	0-3	0-1
Bradford	3-0	1-4	0-2	–	1-1	1-3	3-1	0-1	1-5	1-1	1-0	3-1	3-2	1-2	2-2	5-0	0-0	2-4	1-2	0-2	0-2	3-2	3-3	3-3
Burton	1-1	2-1	0-0	1-1	–	1-3	2-0	2-2	2-1	1-2	1-0	3-1	3-2	3-2	1-1	0-0	0-1	2-4	0-0	3-1	0-2	2-1	3-3	1-2
Bury	3-0	2-0	0-1	1-0	1-0	–	2-3	1-1	3-1	5-4	1-1	1-0	2-2	1-0	3-0	3-0	0-1	1-1	0-0	3-1	3-0	2-1	1-2	1-3
Cheltenham	1-2	1-2	2-1	4-0	2-1	0-3	–	0-3	3-2	1-2	0-3	1-2	0-1	1-1	1-0	1-1	0-0	1-1	0-1	0-2	1-0	1-0	2-2	1-2
Chesterfield	5-2	1-1	2-2	2-2	0-3	2-3	3-0	–	5-5	2-1	4-0	2-1	2-1	1-1	1-0	1-1	2-1	5-0	4-3	0-2	1-1	4-1	1-0	4-1
Crewe	0-0	3-1	7-0	4-1	2-0	1-3	3-0	5-5	–	1-3	4-0	2-1	1-1	2-0	2-0	2-1	2-1	0-1	1-2	1-0	1-0	4-1	3-3	3-0
Gillingham	3-1	2-1	2-4	2-0	1-0	1-1	8-1	0-2	1-3	–	0-0	2-4	2-1	1-0	1-0	3-0	3-0	3-1	2-0	1-3	0-1	2-0	1-1	0-2
Hereford	1-1	1-2	1-1	1-1	0-0	0-5	3-0	3-0	1-1	0-4	–	0-1	2-4	2-1	0-2	0-2	1-0	0-6	1-5	1-3	1-4	0-0	2-2	0-0
Lincoln	0-0	0-3	1-2	0-0	2-1	0-5	0-2	1-1	1-1	0-4	3-1	–	0-1	0-1	0-2	3-1	1-0	2-2	0-2	0-1	1-1	0-0	0-2	1-2
Macclesfield	2-2	2-0	1-1	1-2	1-1	2-4	0-2	1-1	1-1	2-4	1-1	1-1	–	2-0	1-2	3-2	0-3	0-6	1-0	1-1	0-4	0-3	3-3	0-1
Morecambe	1-2	1-1	2-2	0-1	2-3	1-1	1-1	1-2	6-2	2-1	3-4	2-1	1-2	–	3-1	2-1	2-1	2-1	2-3	2-1	0-0	0-1	0-2	0-3
Northampton	0-0	3-0	3-0	3-0	1-2	1-2	0-1	1-1	2-1	1-1	1-1	2-1	2-1	4-0	–	1-2	2-1	1-0	3-1	1-1	1-1	0-2	0-0	0-0
Oxford	2-0	0-0	3-0	0-0	1-1	6-4	0-1	1-0	2-1	2-2	0-1	2-1	2-1	7-2	3-1	–	5-0	0-1	1-2	1-1	0-0	0-1	1-2	1-3
Port Vale	2-0	2-1	3-1	0-0	0-0	0-3	1-2	2-3	0-1	1-0	4-0	4-0	4-1	1-2	2-1	3-0	–	1-0	0-2	2-2	1-0	1-1	2-1	2-0
Rotherham	0-0	2-1	1-1	0-0	1-1	0-0	1-2	4-1	1-1	3-1	4-0	2-0	4-1	1-3	3-2	1-3	2-2	–	2-2	4-0	3-3	4-0	1-0	3-4
Shrewsbury	1-1	0-0	3-1	4-0	1-1	2-3	1-2	1-1	1-0	2-2	4-0	1-0	1-0	2-3	2-1	3-1	1-3	1-0	–	1-1	3-0	2-0	1-2	1-1
Southend	2-2	2-2	4-2	1-1	0-0	1-1	1-2	1-3	0-2	2-2	0-1	4-0	2-2	0-2	3-2	2-1	1-3	0-5	3-3	–	2-2	1-0	1-1	0-0
Stevenage	2-2	1-1	2-1	1-1	0-0	3-3	1-1	1-1	1-1	3-0	1-1	3-0	1-0	0-2	2-0	0-1	0-5	3-3	1-0	2-2	–	2-2	1-1	2-2
Stockport	0-0	1-1	2-1	0-0	1-1	2-1	1-1	1-3	1-1	0-5	0-5	2-0	1-4	3-1	2-0	3-4	0-5	3-3	0-4	1-1	2-2	–	1-1	0-0
Torquay	0-0	0-1	1-1	1-1	0-0	3-4	2-1	2-2	1-3	1-1	1-3	2-2	1-3	3-1	2-0	3-4	0-1	1-0	5-0	1-1	2-2	2-0	–	0-0
Wycombe	1-2	4-2	1-0	4-1	1-0	2-1	1-1	1-2	2-0	1-0	1-1	2-2	1-2	0-2	2-2	0-0	1-1	1-0	2-2	3-1	0-1	2-0	1-3	–

HIGHLIGHTS OF THE PREMIER LEAGUE
SEASON 2010–11

AUGUST 2010

14 Marlon Harewood scores twice on his debut as Blackpool make a dream start to their first season in the top-flight since 1971, winning 4-0 at Wigan in a fixture switched from Bloomfield Road because of continuing ground improvement work there. The other promoted side in action, West Bromwich Albion, take a 6-0 beating at Chelsea, an unhappy return to the ground he graced as a player for manager Roberto di Matteo. Last season's Golden Boot winner, Didier Drogba, nets a hat-trick for the defending champions. Steven Fletcher is on the mark for his new side Wolves, whose 2-1 victory over Stoke is their first on the opening day of the season since 1999. James Milner wraps up Aston Villa's 3-0 success against West Ham in his final appearance before moving to Manchester City. The first sending-off of the new campaign is Sunderland captain Lee Cattermole in a 2-2 draw with Birmingham.

15 Joe Cole is dismissed on his league debut for Liverpool. So too is Arsenal new boy Laurent Koscielny in a separate incident, but his side earn a point thanks to a last-minute own goal by Jose Reina.

16 The third promoted side, Newcastle, safely negotiate the first half-an-hour at Old Trafford before Dimitar Berbatov's goal paves the way for a 3-0 Manchester United win.

21 Blackpool are brought down to earth by a 6-0 defeat at Arsenal in which Ian Evatt is sent off. Theo Walcott claims a hat-trick and Marouane Chamakh opens his account. Chelsea become the first side to start with two 6-0 victories, destroying Wigan in the second half with five goals, one of them from new-signing Yossi Benayoun. Gareth Bale's brace, the second a volleyed early contender for goal of the season, earns Tottenham a 2-1 win at Stoke. The home side lose Mamady Sidibe for the season with a snapped Achilles tendon and are unlucky when a Jonathan Walters header in stoppage-time looks to have crossed the line. The Hawthorns match programme has no mention of Peter Odemwingie because of his late transfer from Lokomotiv Moscow. But West Bromwich Albion's new striker announces himself in style with the only shout against Sunderland.

22 The high-scoring start to the campaign continues as Andy Carroll fires a hat-trick in Newcastle's 6-0 rout of Aston Villa, this after Villa's John Carew misses a penalty with the scoreline blank. Manchester United's Nani spurns the chance to make it 3-1 against Fulham when his spot-kick is saved by David Stockdale, enabling the home side to take advantage with Brede Hangeland making amends for his earlier own goal by heading the equaliser.

23 Manchester City's owner, Sheik Mansour, pays his first visit to Eastlands and sees the club's biggest win over Liverpool since 1937 – 3-0.

28 Wigan return to White Hart Lane where they crashed 9-1 last season and surprise Tottenham with a late winner from Hugo Rodallega. Fabio Capello watches Wayne Rooney end a run of 13 goalless games for club and country with a penalty in Manchester United's 3-0 victory over West Ham. On a busy day for the England manager, he is also at Blackpool for Luke Varney's scoring debut in a 2-2 draw with Fulham and at Blackburn for Arsenal's 2-1 success. Referee Stuart Attwell shows 12 yellow cards at Molineux, seven of them to Wolves, who face a £25,000 FA fine. The game with Newcastle ends 1-1.

29 Darren Bent's 90th minute penalty, preceded by one of the misses of the season by Carlos Tevez, result in Sunderland beating Manchester City 1-0. Their victory is overshadowed by a knee injury which rules Fraizer Campbell out for the rest of the season. Bolton have goalkeeper Jussi Jaaskelainen sent off and trail Birmingham 2-0, but recover to gain a point with Robbie Blake's equaliser his first for the club. Also dismissed is James Morrison in West Bromwich Albion's 1-0 defeat at Liverpool. At the end of the month, Chelsea are two points ahead of Arsenal and Manchester United.

SEPTEMBER 2010

11 Everton, trailing Manchester United 3-1, pull a point out of the fire with stoppage-time goals by Tim Cahill and Mikel Arteta. Sunderland's record-signing, Asamoah Gyan, scores on his debut at Wigan after captain Lee Cattermole is sent off for the second time in three games. Wigan's equaliser from Antolin Alcaraz is his first for the club. Laurent Koscielny opens his account for Arsenal, 4-1 winners over Bolton who have Gary Cahill dismissed. So does Jelle Van Damme for Wolves, but a 2-1 reversal at Fulham proves even more costly for the club, who incur seven bookings – two of them for Christophe Berra - for the second successive match and this time are fined £50,000. Fulham's match-winner is Moussa Dembele, with his first Premier League match.

18 Arsenal experience a costly afternoon at Sunderland, where they lose Cesc Fabregas to a hamstring injury, have Alex Song sent off and concede an equaliser to Darren Bent in the fifth minute of stoppage-time. In addition, manager Arsene Wenger's argument with match officials costs him a touchline ban and fine from the FA. Rafael van der Vaart, from the penalty spot, and Alan Hutton score their first goals for Tottenham, who master Wolves 3-1. Also on the mark for the first time is Newcastle's Hatem Ben Arfa with the only goal at Everton on his full debut. West Ham gain their first point of the season, 1-1 at Stoke, in the absence of manager Avram Grant, who observes the Jewish holy day of Yom Kippur.

19 Dimitar Berbatov's hat-trick gives Manchester United a 3-2 victory over Liverpool, the third goal coming after two by Steven Gerrard enable his side to retrieve a 2-0 deficit. Yaya Toure gets his first for Manchester City, who win 2-0 at Wigan.

25 A day of surprises and controversy. West Bromwich Albion, without a Premier League away win in 18 matches, beat Arsenal 3-2, despite Chris Brunt having a penalty saved by Manuel Almunia. After five straight victories and 21 goals, Chelsea lose to a Carlos Tevez strike at Manchester City. West Ham take three points for the first time, thanks to Frederic Piquionne's first in the league for the club, against Tottenham. Blackpool's Matt Phillips,19, scores two minutes after coming on for his debut, but Brett Emerton is on the mark in stoppage-time to give Blackburn the verdict 2-1. Despite drawing 2-2 at Liverpool, Sunderland are angry about Dirk Kuyt's goal after Fernando Torres intercepts a ball rolled back by Michael Turner towards his goalkeeper Simon Mignolet for a free-kick to be taken. Birmingham have Craig Gardner sent off in a goalless draw with Wigan

26 Michael Owen's 200th club goal in English football comes during Manchester United's 2-2 draw against Bolton, for whom Martin Petrov scores his first for his new team. Emile Heskey, Owen's former strike partner at Liverpool under Gerard Houllier, gives Houllier a winning start as Aston Villa manager with an 88th minute header for a 2-1 success at Molineux. Wolves midfielder Adlene Guedioura sustains a broken leg. The month ends with Chelsea three points clear of United.

OCTOBER 2010

2 Birmingham's club record-equalling unbeaten run of 18 matches at St Andrew's comes to an end with a 2-0 defeat by Everton, Tim Cahill scoring his 100th English league goal in the season's first success for his team. Rafael van der Vaart, with a goal, a missed penalty and a red card to his name in the Champions League game against FC Twente, rounds off an eventful week with both goals in Tottenham's 2-1 victory over Aston Villa. Clint Dempsey, who embarrassed Robert Green in the England-USA World Cup match, scores against him again in Fulham's 1-1 draw with West Ham. This time the goalkeeper has no chance with the shot. Stoke's Jonathan Walters scores the only one of the game against Blackburn, his first in the league for the club. Karl Henry is dismissed after 11 minutes of a 2-0 defeat for Wolves at Wigan

3 Charlie Adam, with a penalty, and Luke Varney score in front of the Kop to give Blackpool a famous 2-1 win over Liverpool, who languish in the bottom three as a result. Didier Drogba scores his 13th goal in 13 games against Arsenal to set Chelsea on the road to a 2-0 victory. Newcastle's Hatem Ben Arfa suffers a broken leg in the 2-1 defeat at Manchester City.

16 In the space of three minutes of stoppage-time, Ivan Klasnic scores Bolton's winner against Stoke and receives two yellow cards. Arsenal's Jack Wilshere is also dismissed in a 2-1 victory over Birmingham, Arsene Wenger's 800th match as manager of the club. Nikola Zigic is on the mark for Birmingham with his first goal in the Premier League. Fabricio Coloccini celebrates being made captain with his first, seconds from the end, to earn Newcastle a point after Wigan's Charles N'Zogbia scores twice against his old club. A red-letter day, too, for Somen Tchoyi, who opens his account on his first start for West Bromwich Albion, who retrieve a 2-0 half-time deficit against Manchester United at Old Trafford.

17 Liverpool's new owners see their team lose 2-0 to Everton (Tim Cahill and Mikel Arteta) in a Merseyside derby carrying even more significance that usual. David Silva sets up Carlos Tevez for the second of his two goals, then scores for the first time himself in the league for Manchester City, who win 3-2 at Blackpool.

19 Chris Samba is sent off in Blackburn's goalless draw with Sunderland.

23 Chelsea complete a club-record eighth successive Premier League home game without conceding a goal when beating Wolves 2-0. West Bromwich Albion move up to fourth – albeit for 24 hours - with a 2-1 victory over Fulham, Youssouf Mulumbu scoring for the first time in the top-flight. Andy Carroll sets up a goal for Kevin Nolan, with whom he has been ordered to live pending a court appearance, then scores Newcastle's winner at West Ham.

24 Joe Hart saves a penalty from Cesc Fabregas, but Manchester City lose 3-0 at home to Arsenal after Dedryck Boyata is sent off after four minutes. Two goals by Javier Hernandez, his second a remarkable back-header after 86 minutes, bring Manchester United a 2-1 victory at Stoke at the end of a week dominated by Wayne Rooney's change of heart about leaving Old Trafford.

30 The season's most bizarre and controversial goal seals Manchester United's 2-0 victory over Tottenham. Nani handles before putting the ball in the net as goalkeeper Heurelho Gomes prepares to take what he thinks is a free-kick for his team. Nicolas Anelka scores for the 11th time in 15 Premier League matches against Blackburn as Chelsea come from behind to win 2-1 after Benjani scores his first goal for the home team. Chelsea end the month five points clear of United and Arsenal, who need an 88th minute header from Alex Song to beat bottom team West Ham. Wolves also come from behind to master Manchester City 2-1, their first success since the opening day of the season.

31 Kevin Nolan hits a hat-trick as Newcastle record the biggest win in the Tyne-Wear derby for 50 years, 5-1 against Sunderland, who have Titus Bramble sent off and are fined £25,000 for six bookings. Liverpool move out of the bottom three, thanks to the only goal of the game from Maxi Rodriguez after 86 minutes at Bolton.

NOVEMBER 2010

2 Blackpool win for the first time at home in the Premier League, beating West Bromwich Albion 2-1. Albion have Gonzalo Jara and Pablo Ibanez sent off, but the Ibanez red card is later rescinded.

6 Neal Eardley celebrates his 22nd birthday with his first goal for Blackpool, a 25-yard free-kick, in the 2-2 draw with Everton. Seamus Coleman, who helped them reach the top-flight while on loan at Bloomfield Road, scores his first in the Premier League for Everton. Record-signing Asamoah Gyan marks his first league start for Sunderland with both goals in a 2-0 success against Stoke, who are denied a penalty when Lee Cattermole clearly handles on the line and later have Ryan Shawcross sent off. Ji-Sung Park's stoppage-time strike, his second of the game, enables Manchester United to edge past Wolves 2-1. But the win is soured when Owen Hargreaves limps off with a hamstring injury four minutes into his first start for two years following knee surgery. Kevin Davies scores twice and sets up Martin Petrov for another as Tottenham are brought down to earth after their midweek Champions League win over Inter Milan, losing 4-2 at Bolton. Birmingham retrieve a 2-0 deficit for a point against West Ham in a match which has a bizarre start when two sprinklers on the pitch come on.

7 Fernando Torres is on the mark twice as Liverpool overcome Chelsea. Mario Balotelli's double, his first goals in the Premier League, gives Manchester City victory over West Bromwich Albion by the same 2-0 margin. The Italian is later sent off and Albion's Youssouf Mulumbu also sees red in a separate incident. Arsenal fail to take advantage of Chelsea's slip, losing at home to an Andy Carroll header for Newcastle and having Laurent Koscielny dismissed for the second time in his first season at the Emirates.

10 Mixed fortunes for Michael Essien, who heads the only goal of the game for Chelsea against Fulham and is then sent off in the 94th minute. Also dismissed is Marouane Fellaini of Everton, who salvage a point against Bolton in stoppage-time through substitute Jermaine Beckford, his first Premier League goal. Marouane Chamakh scores after 38 seconds for Arsenal at Molineux – the club's fastest goal in the Premier League. The Moroccan adds a second in time added on for a 2-0 victory over Wolves, but Cesc Fabregas courts controversy for lunging at Stephen Ward and apologises afterwards. Ian Holloway makes ten changes for Blackpool's visit to Aston Villa and looks to have earned an unlikely point until a James Collins header in the 89th minute gives the home side the verdict 3-2. An eventful night's football, surprisingly, does not extend to Eastlands, where a defence-dominated Manchester derby ends goalless.

13 Ian Holloway replaces Blackpool's entire midweek starting line-up, reverts to his 'first-choice' side at West Ham and comes away with a goalless draw. Aston Villa look to be on course for their first home league win over Manchester United since 1995 when Ashley Young (pen) and Marc Albrighton establish a two-goal lead with 80 minutes gone. But United rally and draw level through Federico Macheda and Nemanja Vidic. Stoke, fourth from bottom before beating Birmingham 3-2 in midweek, climb further to half-way with a 2-0 victory over Liverpool, who have Lucas sent off. Ricardo Fuller's opener is their first goal from a Rory Delap long throw since March. Gareth Bale scores twice and sets up another for Roman Pavlyuchenko, who also misses a penalty in Tottenham's 4-2 win over Blackburn. An own goal by Richard Stearman after 50 seconds, followed by Stuart Holden's first for the club, point Bolton to a 3-2 success at Wolves.

14 A fortnight after being overwhelmed in the Tyne–Wear derby, Sunderland crush a Chelsea side hit by injuries and suspension 3-0 at Stamford Bridge. Full-back Nedum Onuoha, with a fine solo effort, and fellow-loanee Danny Welbeck score their first goals for the club, while Asamoah Gyan nets his fourth in three matches. Another full-back, Bacary Sagna, makes a big impression, his first goal since March 2008 paving the way for Arsenal's 2-1 win at Everton.

20 Tottenham overturn a two-goal half-time deficit to win 3-2 at the Emirates with goals by Gareth Bale, Rafael van der Vaart from the penalty spot and Younes Kaboul. It is their first away success against Arsenal since 1993 and the first in 69 visits to the traditional 'big four' of Manchester United, Chelsea, Arsenal and Liverpool. Chelsea lose for the third time in four games, Lee Bowyer scoring the only goal for Birmingham and Ben Foster protecting their advantage with outstanding goalkeeping. Manchester United are 2-0 winners over Wigan, who have Antolin Alcaraz and Hugo Rodallega sent off after 59 and 61 minutes respectively. Also dismissed is Newcastle's Fabricio Coloccini in the 5-1 defeat at Bolton, for whom Johan Elmander scores twice and Kevin Davies converts two penalties. Blackpool's 2-1 victory over Wolves is watched from a hospitality box by Prince William and a group of friends.

21 Diego Maradona sees fellow Argentines Carlos Tevez (2) and Pablo Zabaleta lead Manchester City to a 4-1 success over former manager Mark Hughes's Fulham at Craven Cottage. Morten Gamst Pedersen also nets twice as Blackburn defeat Aston Villa 2-0 in front of the club's new owners.

27 Dimitar Berbatov, without a goal for two months, scores five times in the 7-1 rout of Blackburn, leading Manchester United to the top of the table and joining Andy Cole, Alan Shearer and Jermain Defoe in the Premier League record books. Ciaran Clark scores twice for Aston Villa, his first goals for the club, but they are not enough to deny Arsenal, whose 4-2 victory is rounded off by Jack Wilshere's first in the top-flight. Five other players reach personal milestones. Paul Scharner opens his account for West Bromwich Albion, who are 4-1 victors at Goodison Park, where team-mate Youssouf Mulumbu is booked twice in the space of two minutes near the end and Everton have Mikel Arteta dismissed for a straight red. Stephen

Hunt's first for Wolves comes in a 3-2 victory over Sunderland, while on-loan Tom Cleverley's first for Wigan is in a 3-1 reversal at Upton Park. Robert Green saves Mauro Boselli's penalty in that match and Victor Obinna's first league strike of his loan spell further boosts West Ham. Mark Davies also records his first in the league, an 89th minute effort completing Bolton's comeback to a point after they trail Blackpool 2-0.

28 A lean month for Chelsea ends with a 1-1 draw at Newcastle and means they trail Manchester United by two points, with Arsenal third on goal difference. After beating Arsenal then qualifying for the Champions League knock-out stage, Tottenham complete a memorable eight days with Aaron Lennon's stoppage-time winner for 2-1 against Liverpool, who lose Jamie Carragher with a dislocated shoulder.

DECEMBER 2010

4 With Manchester United's match at Blackpool a victim of the weather, Arsenal go top courtesy of two Samir Nasri goals and a 2-1 victory over Fulham. Chelsea's run of poor form continues as Jermaine Beckford's 86th minute header earns Everton a point at Stamford Bridge. Carlos Tevez scores the only goal of the game for Manchester City against Bolton, but the victory is marred by the dismissal of Aleksandar Kolarov and the angry reaction of Tevez to being substituted.

5 Peter Odemwingie scores twice in West Bromwich Albion's 3-1 victory over Newcastle in what proves to be Chris Hughton's last game as manager.

6 Gerard Houllier receives a warm welcome on his return to Anfield as Aston Villa manager, but his side are frozen out by Liverpool, who overcome the absence of the injured Steven Gerrard and father-to-be Jamie Carragher and Fernando Torres to win 3-0.

11 Alan Pardew makes a flying start as the new Newcastle manager, with Andy Carroll netting once and having a hand in goals by Kevin Nolan and Joey Barton for a 3-1 success against Liverpool. Manchester City, helped by Robert Green's own goal, move into the thick of the title race with victory by the same scoreline at West Ham. Blackpool continue to stack up the points, thanks to the only goal of the game by DJ Campbell at Stoke.

12 Didier Drogba has a stoppage-time penalty saved by Heurelho Gomes, so Chelsea have to be satisfied with a 1-1 scoreline at Tottenham. Blackburn go down 2-1 at Bolton, who overcome the dismissal of Mark Davies. Rovers manager Sam Allardyce is sacked the following day.

13 Wayne Rooney fires a penalty over the bar, but Ji-Sung Park is on the mark with a header to give Manchester United a 1-0 victory over Arsenal.

18 Danny Welbeck's fifth goal in six games and Craig Gordon's marvellous save from Zat Knight – which draws comparison with Jim Montgomery's save against Leeds in the 1973 FA Cup Final – enable Sunderland to beat Bolton 1-0 and move above their opponents into sixth place. In the only other match to beat the weather, Junior Stanislas scores his first of the season to earn West Ham a point at Blackburn, who lose 18-year-old defender Phil Jones with a knee injury.

20 Everton, without a win in seven games, overcome Manchester City 2-1 at Eastlands with goals in the first 20 minutes from Tim Cahill and Leighton Baines. They have Victor Anichebe sent off, while City's Kolo Toure receives two yellow cards in the space of 60 seconds near the end.

26 Four players from opposite ends of the table each score two goals, including Rafael van der Vaart as Tottenham are successful 2-1 at Villa Park, despite having Jermain Defoe sent off. Dimitar Berbatov steers Manchester United to a 2-0 victory over Sunderland, Carlos Tevez, is on the mark twice in Manchester City's 3-1 victory over Newcastle and Carlton Cole's double gives struggling West Ham their first away league win in 28 matches – 3-1 against Fulham. Marc Wilson nets his first goal for Stoke, who beat Blackburn 2-0 away.

27 Three goals in the space of nine minutes either side of half-time from Alex Song, Cesc Fabregas and Theo Walcott give Arsenal a 3-1 win over Chelsea.

28 Mario Balotelli converts two penalties in a hat-trick for Manchester City, who outplay Aston Villa 4-0. Manchester United are denied victory at Birmingham by Lee Bowyer's 89th minute equaliser, but go into the New Year leading City on goal difference from two fewer games played. Chris Baird has an afternoon to remember at Stoke with two sweetly-struck goals, his first since joining Fulham in the summer of 2007. A 2-0 scoreline ends his side's run of 27 games without success away from home. Delight turns to despair for Nikola Kalinic, whose brace sets up a first victory for new Blackburn manager Steve Kean – 3-1 at West Bromwich Albion – but who is then sent off. Albion's Gabriel Tamas sees red later on. Another two-goal marksman is DJ Campbell as Blackpool continue to thrive, winning 2-0 at Sunderland. Another dismissal is Tottenham's Younes Kaboul as his team overcome Newcastle 2-0.

29 Pressure mounts on Liverpool manager Roy Hodgson after a home defeat by bottom-of-the-table Wolves, inflicted by the only goal of the game from Stephen Ward, his first in the Premier League. Arsenal miss a golden opportunity for maximum points at Wigan, who trail 2-1 and have Charles N'Zogbia sent off but then force Sebastien Squillaci into conceding an own goal. They finish the month two points behind in third place. Chelsea end a run of six games without a win, thanks to the only goal from Florent Malouda against Bolton.

JANUARY 2011

1 Wayne Rooney scores for the first time in open play for nine months, then supplies the corner for Manchester United's winner from substitute Javier Hernandez against West Bromwich Albion, who rue a penalty miss by Peter Odemwingie for their 2-1 defeat. Manchester City's Carlos Tevez also fails from the spot and is grateful to Adam Johnson for the only goal against Blackpool. Joe Cole comes off the bench to score his first Premier League goal for Liverpool in stoppage-time and give Roy Hodgson a much-needed 2-1 victory over Bolton. Robin van Persie's first of an injury-dogged season launches Arsenal's 3-0 success at Birmingham. West Ham, in the bottom three all season move clear, Freddie Sears sealing the 2-0 defeat of fellow-strugglers Wolves with his first goal for the club since March, 2008.

2 John Terry looks to have given Chelsea the final say against Aston Villa when he makes it 3-2 in the 89th minute, but they are deflated by Ciaran Clark's equaliser in time added on. Villa have seven players booked, resulting in a £25,000 fine.

4 Birmingham, the only side without an away win, erase that statistic by beating Blackpool 2-1, helped by Alex Hleb's first league goal for the club. Dean Whitehead scores Stoke's first goal at Old Trafford since 1980, but it is not enough to prevent Manchester United prevailing 2-1.

5 Chelsea's title defence looks to be over when an own goal by Jose Bosingwa results in a 1-0 reversal at Wolves, leaving his side nine points adrift of Manchester United from an extra game played. With Arsenal and Manchester City goalless, it all goes United's way on the night. Bacary Sagna and Pablo Zabaleta are sent off at the Emirates after clashing, but the City player's red card is later rescinded. Aston Villa's Emile Heskey and Sunderland's Bolo Zenden see red in separate incidents in a match settled by Phil Bardsley's first league goal for Steve Bruce's side. Leon Best has a night to remember, making his first Premier League start and scoring a hat-trick in the 5-0 trouncing of West Ham – his first goals for the club. But another one to forget for Roy Hodgson, who sees Benjani score twice – and Steven Gerrard miss a penalty - in a 3-1 defeat Blackburn and is sacked three days later. Bolton's Rodrigo and Wigan's Ronnie Stam both score for the first time for their respective clubs in a 1-1 scoreline.

11 There is no quick fix for Liverpool with Kenny Dalglish back in charge. They lead through Fernando Torres, but goals by Gary Taylor-Fletcher and DJ Campbell enable Blackpool to repeat their 2-1 win at Anfield and complete a famous double.

15 Manchester City are coasting at 4-1 after two Carlos Tevez goals until Wolves pull two back to ensure a tight finish. Two for Robin van Persie, one from the penalty spot, in Arsenal's 3-0 win at Upton Park increases the pressure on West Ham manager Avram Grant. Peter Odemwingie is also on the mark twice for West Bromwich Albion against Blackpool, his second after 87 minutes settling the match at 3-2. Andy Johnson, dogged by injuries, gets his first in the league since March 2009 to earn Fulham a point at Wigan.

16 All three derbies end all-square, with crowd trouble marring matches at Sunderland and Birmingham. Asamoah Gyan's stoppage-time goal at the Stadium of Light cancels out Kevin Nolan's effort for Newcastle. Roger Johnson puts the home side ahead at St Andrew's, but another central defender, James Collins, earns Aston Villa a point. Sylvain Distin, with his first league goal for the club, and Jermaine Beckford put Everton in charge after Fernando Torres opens the scoring at Anfield. Then, Dirk Kuyt's penalty earns Liverpool a draw. Manchester United have Rafael sent off at Tottenham, but hold on for a goalless draw.

22 Darren Bent delivers an immediate return on his £24m transfer fee with the only goal of the match for Aston Villa against Manchester City. Dimitar Berbatov registers his third hat-trick of the season as Manchester United crush Birmingham 5-0 and Robin van Persie scores all three for Arsenal against Wigan. The Dutchman also misses a penalty, conceded by Gary Caldwell, who is sent off. West Ham's Frederic Piquionne receives a second yellow card for jumping into the crowd to celebrate his goal at Goodison Park. It looks to be enough to win the game, but Marouane Fellaini brings Everton level at 2-2 in stoppage-time. Ryan Shawcross also sees red as Stoke go down 2-0 at Fulham to two Clint Dempsey goals, one from the penalty sport. There is a brace for Sunderland's Kieran Richardson, pushed forward following the departure of Bent, in the 2-1 victory at Blackpool. And two by Fernando Torres enable Kenny Dalglish to celebrate a first victory of his second coming as Liverpool manager - 3-0 at Wolves.

24 Chelsea prolong a remarkable record at Bolton, winning there for the eighth successive season without conceding a goal. Their 4-0 victory is rounded off by Ramires with his first for the club.

25 Manchester United increase their lead at the top over Arsenal to five points when transforming a 2-0 half-time deficit at Blackpool into a 3-2 victory, Dimitar Berbatov scoring the second of his two goals in the 88th minute.

FEBRUARY 2011

1 Wayne Rooney scores twice and provides the pass for Nemanja Vidic's goal as Manchester United beat Aston Villa 3-1 to extend their unbeaten league run to 29 games – equalling the club-record.

2 Roberto Mancini admits Manchester City's championship chances are over after his side twice lose the lead and have to settle for a 2-2 draw at Birmingham. Luis Suarez comes off the bench for his Liverpool debut and claims their second goal in a 2-0 victory over Stoke. Another substitute, Daniel Sturridge, makes his first appearance on loan for Bolton and scores the only goal against Wolves in added time, with his side facing a sixth game without a victory. Victor Obinna follows up his FA Cup hat-trick against Nottingham Forest with a brace as West Ham win 3-1 at Blackpool.

5 Newcastle make Premier League history, Manchester United's undefeated run comes to an end and Louis Saha scores four times as an incident-packed programme of matches produces 41 goals. Arsenal look home and dry at St James' Park when leading 4-0 after 26 minutes through Robin van Persie (2), Theo Walcott and Johan Djourou's first goal for the club. But they fall to pieces after Abou Diaby is sent off. Newcastle, with Andy Carroll sold to Liverpool and Shola Ameobi injured, become the first side to retrieve a four-goal deficit - Joey Barton netting two penalties, Leon Best pulling a third back and Cheik Tiote equalising three minutes from the end of normal time. Nani gives United the lead at Molineux, but bottom-of-the-table Wolves reply through George Elokobi's first Premier League goal and Kevin Doyle. Saha takes the individual honours for Everton, who come back from 3-2 down to defeat Blackpool 5-3. Carlos Tevez, on his 27th birthday, hits all three as Manchester City are 3-0 winners over West Bromwich Albion, whose manager Roberto di Matteo is sacked the following day. Two of them are penalties on a day when a record seven spot-kicks are converted. Wigan edge out Blackburn 4-3 with two goals from James McCarthy, while Robert Huth's second of the game in stoppage-time gives Stoke the verdict by 3-2 against Sunderland after on-loan John Carew gets his first for the club.

6 Fernando Torres, Chelsea's £50m record-signing, has a miserable debut against his former side. He is substituted midway through the second half and watches Raul Meireles volley the only goal of the game for Liverpool at Stamford Bridge. Eleven days after beating West Ham to reach the Carling Cup Final, Birmingham overcome their rivals-in-distress again, this time with a Nikola Zigic header.

12 Wayne Rooney's wonder goal, an acrobatic, airborne volley he describes as the best he has ever scored, settles the Manchester derby 2-1 in United's favour. Robin van Persie's brace in Arsenal's 2-1 win over Wolves, takes his tally to nine in five matches. Graham Dorrans, with his first Premier League goal, puts West Bromwich Albion on the way to a 3-0 lead in 32 minutes against West Ham, who then stage a fine recovery to gain a point, Demba Ba scoring twice on his full debut to leave Albion on a club-record of 24 matches without a clean sheet. Nikola Zigic boosts Birmingham's chances of staying up with the only goal in stoppage-time against Stoke – his third in successive matches. Elliot Grandin's first for Blackpool enables his side to end a run of five successive defeats with a 1-1 draw against Aston Villa, who have Jean Makoun sent off.

14 Fernando Torres is substituted again by Chelsea, who salvage a goalless draw at Fulham thanks to Petr Cech's stoppage-time penalty save from Clint Dempsey.

20 Two on-loan players score for the first time for their respective clubs at the Hawthorns, Jamie O'Hara putting Wolves ahead and substitute Carlos Vela equalising in stoppage-time for West Bromwich Albion in Roy Hodgson's first match in charge.

22 Brett Ormerod becomes the first player to score in all four divisions for Blackpool when rounding off a 3-1 victory over Tottenham.

23 Arsenal move to within a point of Manchester United by beating Stoke 1-0, but pay a price when injuries rule Cesc Fabregas and Theo Walcott out of the Carling Cup Final against Birmingham.

26 With Arsenal preparing for Wembley, Manchester United re-open a four-point lead by winning 4-0 at Wigan, Javier Hernandez scoring twice and Fabio netting his first goal for the club. Wigan protest that Wayne Rooney should have been sent off for catching James McCarthy with his elbow. Three other players are on the mark twice, including Sylvan Ebanks-Blake as Wolves record their biggest victory in top-flight football for 31 years - 4-0 against Blackpool, who have DJ Campbell sent off. Ashley Young's double, one from the penalty spot, comes in a 4-1 success against Blackburn, who have captain Ryan Nelsen dismissed, while Jermaine Beckford's brace gives Everton a 2-0 win over Sunderland. Also shown a red card, on his first league start of the season, is Newcastle's Ryan Taylor in the 1-1 draw with Bolton, for whom Daniel Sturridge gets his fourth goal in four matches.

27 Liverpool's eight-match unbeaten run in domestic and European competition comes to an end with a 3-1 reversal at West Ham. Mark Hughes returns to Manchester City for the first time since his sacking and receives a frosty handshake from Roberto Mancini after his Fulham side earn a 1-1 draw – a legacy of City's 4-1 success at Craven Cottage.

MARCH 2011

1 Wayne Rooney puts Manchester United ahead at Stamford Bridge, but David Luiz, with his first goal for the club, and Frank Lampard (pen) give Chelsea victory.

5 Arsenal miss the chance to close in when held to a goalless draw by Sunderland. At the bottom, Birmingham's Carling Cup celebrations are cut short, despite Jean Beausejour's first Premier League goal for the club. They lose 3-1 at home to West Bromwich Albion, while West Ham continue their improvement when beating Stoke 3-0, Thomas Hitzlsperger scoring his first Premier League goal for the home side. Bobby Zamora, out for six months with a broken leg, comes off the bench and converts a controversial 89th minute penalty to give Fulham a 3-2 success against Blackburn after two earlier goals from Damien Duff. Grant Hanley scores his first for Rovers, who have Gael Givet red-carded for protesting after the final whistle. Jussi Jaskelainen saves Ashley Young's penalty to prevent Bolton going 3-1 down to Aston Villa and his side respond to win 3-2, with former Villa defender Gary Cahill scoring his second of the game and Ivan Klasnic netting the decider after 86th minutes.

6 Ryan Giggs overtakes Sir Bobby Charlton's Manchester United record of 606 league appearances, but Dirk Kuyt steals the show at Anfield with a hat-trick – each goal from inside the six-yard box – as Liverpool win 3-1. United are beaten in back-to-back league matches for the first time in two years. Two-goal Jermain Defoe is denied a hat-trick by the woodwork at Molineux, so Tottenham have to be satisfied with a 3-3 scoreline after Steven Fletcher's 87th minute equaliser for Wolves.

9 John Heitinga scores his first goal for Everton in their 1-1 draw with Birmingham.

19 Manchester United lose Sir Alex Ferguson for the start of a five-match touchline ban and have Jonny Evans sent off. But an 88th minute goal by substitute Dimitar Berbatov breaks the deadlock against Bolton and puts them five points ahead of Arsenal from an extra game played. Arsenal salvage a 2-2 draw after being 2-0 down against West Bromwich Albion, for whom Steven Reid scores his first Premier League goal for nearly five years. Blackburn also come from two down to gain a point after Charlie Adam, back after suspension, puts Blackpool on top with a penalty and a free-kick in a five-minute spell. Stoke move away from a congested relegation area with their biggest Premier League success – 4-0 against Newcastle in which Jermaine Pennant scores his first goal for the club. At the end of the month, the bottom eight teams are separated by only three points. Maynor Figueroa's stoppage-time strike gives Wigan hope with a 2-1 victory over Birmingham, while Matt Jarvis nets the only one of the game for Wolves at Villa Park as a prelude to a surprise England call-up.

20 John Mensah is sent off in Sunderland's 2-0 home defeat by Liverpool, but has the red card rescinded on appeal.

APRIL 2011

2 Wayne Rooney scores a hat-trick as Manchester United win 4-2 at West Ham after trailing to two Mark Noble penalties – then apologises for swearing into a TV camera. United extend their lead over Arsenal, held to a goalless draw at home by ten-man Blackburn, who have Steven Nzonzi sent off. West Bromwich Albion's Chris Brunt is also on the mark twice from the spot to give Roy Hodgson a satisfying 2-1 success against former club Liverpool, who in nine previous Premier League games between the teams had scored 25 goals and conceded none. Veteran Kevin Phillips, making his first league start of the season, puts Birmingham on the way to a 2-1 victory over Bolton with a goal after four minutes, while Darren Bent's brace earns Aston Villa a point at Everton on a good day for three relegation-threatened Midlands sides.

3 Bobby Zamora, starting for the first time since his broken leg, is on the mark twice as Fulham overcome Blackpool 3-0 to go clear of trouble. Sunderland's slide continues with a 5-0 beating at Manchester City.

9 Sir Alex Ferguson's horse pulls up in the Grand National, but his team clear another hurdle in their pursuit of the title by beating Fulham 2-0. West Bromwich Albion look to be safe after their transformation under Roy Hodgson continues. Albion twice come from behind to win 3-2 at Sunderland, with Peter Odemwingie scoring one goal and having a hand in the other two. Wolves, however, remain deep in trouble after a 3-0 home defeat by Everton, for whom Phil Neville scores for the first time for three years. Peter Crouch goes some way to making amends for his red card in Tottenham's 4-0 Champions League defeat by Real Madrid by doubling his league tally for the season with two headed goals in a 3-2 win over Stoke.

10 On his 300th appearance for the club, Cesc Fabregas has a hand in two goals as Arsenal win 3-1 at Blackpool.

11 Andy Carroll opens his account for Liverpool with two goals in a 3-0 victory over Manchester City, who lose Carlos Tevez for the FA Cup semi-final against Manchester United with a hamstring injury.

16 A stoppage-time header by Gabriel Agbonlahor moves Aston Villa away from trouble, thanks to a 2-1 victory at West Ham. Neighbours Birmingham beat Sunderland 2-0, Sebastian Larsson opening the scoring on his 100th Premier League appearance. In another crunch match, Charles N'Zogbia sets up the first goal for Hugo Rodallega and scores the second himself as Wigan climb out of the bottom three by winning 3-1 at Blackpool. Roy Hodgson suffers his first defeat as West Bromwich Albion manager – 3-1 at home to Chelsea, for whom Didier Drogba scores one goal and makes the other two.

17 Arsene Wenger and Kenny Dalglish exchange strong words on the touchline after a goalless 90 minutes is followed by a dramatic period of stoppage-time at the Emirates. Robin van Persie puts Arsenal ahead with a penalty and Dirk Kuyt levels from the spot with the last kick of the game.

19 Missed chances mean Manchester United have to be satisfied with a goalless draw at Newcastle.

20 Arsenal are again unable to take advantage, despite leading Tottenham 3-1. The home side pull back to 3-3, with Rafael van der Vaart scoring twice.

23 Manchester United welcome back Sir Alex Ferguson after his five-match touchline ban with another late winner, this time from Javier Hernandez seven minutes from the end of normal time to end Everton's resistance. A somewhat less familiar sight is Fernando Torres scoring for Chelsea, at the 14th attempt, in a 3-0 victory over West Ham. Best individual performance of the day comes from Maxi Rodriguez with a hat-trick as Liverpool overwhelm Birmingham 5-0. Best team display is by Sunderland. They go behind to Wigan and lose three more players to injury – Phil Bardsley, Danny Welbeck and Asamoah Gyan – but score four times in 19 minutes for a 4-2 victory. Jordan Henderson gets two of them in Steve Bruce's 500th league game as a manager. The statisticians are also on the ball at White Hart Lane, where Tottenham and West Bromwich Albion share four goals. The home side chalk up their 1,000th in the Premier League, Jermain Defoe scores his 100th – as well as his 100th for the club in all competitions – and Simon Cox nets his first for Albion. Manager Mark Hughes, sent to the stands for his reaction to a booking for Brede Hangeland, orders Andy Johnson off the bench and sees the striker score within 20 seconds to earn Fulham a point at Wolves.

24 Wojciech Szczesny saves a penalty from Kevin Davies, but Arsenal's title challenge is ended when they lose 2-1 to Tamir Cohen's 90th minute goal at Bolton.

25 Edin Dzeko scores his first Premier League goal for Manchester City, the only one of the match, at Blackburn.

26 Clint Dempsey becomes Fulham's record Premier League marksman on 33 goals with a brace in the 3-0 win over Bolton.

30 The call for goal-line technology surfaces again as Chelsea record a fifth successive victory to close to within three points of Manchester United from an extra game played. A shot by Frank Lampard, denied a clear goal against Germany in the World Cup, is wrongly ruled to have crossed the line against Tottenham. TV replays also show that Salomon Kalou is offside when scoring an 89th minute winner. Blackburn, without a win in ten matches, boost their prospects of beating the drop from the only goal from Martin Olsson against Bolton. Wigan's chances also receive a lift when Ali Al Habsi saves Mikel Arteta's penalty. But the goalkeeper is beaten by a spot-kick from Leighton Baines, who gives Everton a point against his former club. West Bromwich Albion overcome the dismissal of Paul Scharner to end a run of 17 league and cup matches without a win against Aston Villa dating back to 1985, Youssouf Mulumbu scoring the decider after 84 minutes for a 2-1 scoreline. Simon Davies doubles his tally for the season with a brace as Fulham win 3-0 at Sunderland.

MAY 2011

1 Manchester United's game in hand is cancelled out in a 1-0 defeat by Arsenal, Aaron Ramsey scoring his first goal for the home side since returning from a broken leg. But his side are unable to make the extra man count and have to be satisfied with a 1-1 draw at Birmingham, who have Craig Gardner sent off with an hour of the match still to play. Manchester City, with Nigel de Jong on the mark for the first time, make virtually sure of a Champions League place by beating West Ham 2-1.

7 Blackpool's Charlie Adam has a penalty saved at White Hart Lane by Heurelho Gomes, who concedes another spot-kick from the resulting corner and this time Adam puts it away. But his side are denied what would have been a huge win by Jermain Defoe's 89th minute equaliser for Tottenham. Two other games involving relegation-threatened teams end 1-1. Wigan are pegged back at Villa Park after leading through Charles N'Zogbia, while Thomas Hitzlsperger levels for West Ham against Blackburn. Birmingham's Liam Ridgewell is sent off in the 2-1 defeat at Newcastle.

8 Manchester United close in on the title with a 2-1 victory over Chelsea. Javier Hernandez scores after 36 seconds and Nemanja Vidic heads the second on 23 minutes. Frank Lampard pulls one back. At the bottom, Steven Fletcher continues to boost Wolves' chances of staying up. He follows up goals against Fulham and Birmingham by scoring twice and setting up one for Adlene Guedioura for a 3-1 success against West Bromwich Albion.

9 Maxi Rodriguez scores the fastest goal of the season, after 32 seconds, on the way to his second hat-trick in three games as Liverpool beat Fulham 5-2 at Craven Cottage.

10 Manchester City guarantee Champions League football, thanks to an own goal by Peter Crouch, who in the corresponding fixture the previous season scored the winner to give Tottenham fourth place.

14 Manchester United clinch a record 19th championship, overtaking Liverpool's total, with a 1-1 draw at Blackburn. They fall behind to Brett Emerton's goal, but a disputed penalty, converted by Wayne Rooney after Javier Hernandez tumbles under the challenge of goalkeeper Paul Robinson, secures the point needed. On the day Manchester City win the FA Cup, Blackpool and Bolton evoke memories of one of the finest of all Wembley finals. Blackpool win 4-3 – the same scoreline as the 'Matthews final' of 1953 – to keep alive their chances of beating the drop. Wolves score a vital 3-1 victory at Sunderland, with Steven Fletcher scoring his fifth goal in five matches. It is Mick McCarthy's first success at the Stadium of Light, something he never achieved while manager there. Everton have Diniyar Bilyaletdinov sent off in a 1-0 defeat by West Bromwich Albion.

15 West Ham go down – and manager Avram Grant is sacked – after surrendering a two-goal lead and losing 3-2 at Wigan. Charles N'Zogbia completes the comeback in stoppage-time with his second goal of the game after substitute Conor Sammon gets his first for the club. Birmingham lose at home to two Brede Hangeland goals for Fulham, and along with Wigan, Blackpool, Wolves and Blackburn are covered by a single point going into the final day of the season. Tottenham move above Liverpool into fifth place with their first league win at Anfield for 18 years – 2-0.

17 Manchester City, with two goals from Carlos Tevez, move above Arsenal into third place with a 3-0 victory over Stoke – three days after beating them in the FA Cup Final.

22 Down go Blackpool and Birmingham and out goes Carlo Ancelotti on a dramatic afternoon. Blackpool lead 2-1 at Old Trafford, but an own goal by Ian Evatt puts Manchester United on the way to a 4-2 win – a Premier League record 15th in succession at home and a nine-point advantage at the top to finish with. Three months after winning the Carling Cup, Birmingham are relegated after losing 2-1 at Tottenham. Wigan survive, thanks to the only goal at Stoke scored by Hugo Rodallega. So do Wolves, who lose 3-2 at home to Blackburn but are saved by events at Old Trafford and White Hart Lane. Three first-half goals ensure safety for Rovers. Ancelotti is sacked as Chelsea manager 12 months after winning the Double. His last game is a 1-0 defeat at at Everton, who have Seamus Coleman sent off. Also red-carded are Dean Sturridge in Bolton's 2-0 home defeat by Manchester City and Zoltan Gera, of Fulham, previously the only club without a dismissal. Arsenal's 2-2 draw at Craven Cottage brings Robin van Persie his 18th goal in 17 games – and a Premier League record of scoring in nine successive away matches. Newcastle look certain to finish above Sunderland when leading West Bromwich Albion 3-0. But a hat-trick by Somen Tchoyi leaves them a point behind their rivals, who win 3-0 at West Ham, with Cristian Riveros scoring his first goal for the club and Boudewijn Zenden on the mark in his final appearance. Four days after turning 40, Brad Friedel marks his 400th Premier League appearance with a clean sheet against Liverpool, who are beaten at Villa Park for the first time since 1997– Stewart Downing scoring the only goal.

● Three stoppage-time goals on the final day take the total scored to 1,063, a record for a 38-match season. Manchester United's Dimitar Berbatov and Manchester City's Carlos Tevez share the Golden Boot award with 20 each. City's Joe Hart, with 18 clean sheets, wins the Golden Glove.

HOW MANCHESTER UNITED WON A RECORD TITLE

AUGUST 2010

16   Manchester Utd 3 (Berbatov 33, Fletcher 41, Giggs 85) Newcastle 0. Att: 75,221

22   Fulham 2 (Davies 57, Hangeland 89) Manchester Utd 2 (Scholes 11, Hangeland 84 og). Att: 25,643

28   Manchester Utd 3 (Rooney 33 pen, Nani 50, Berbatov 69) West Ham 0. Att: 75,061

SEPTEMBER 2010

11   Everton 3 (Pienaar 39, Arteta 90, Cahill 90) Manchester Utd 3 (Fletcher 43, Vidic 47, Berbatov 66). Att: 36,556

19   Manchester Utd 3 (Berbatov 42, 59, 84) Liverpool 2 (Gerrard 64 pen, 70). Att: 75,213

26   Bolton 2 (Knight 6, Petrov 67) Manchester Utd 2 (Nani 23, Owen 74). Att: 23,926

OCTOBER 2010

2   Sunderland 0 Manchester Utd 0. Att: 41,709

16   Manchester Utd 2 (Hernandez 5, Nani 25) WBA 2 (Evra 50 og, Tchoyi 55). Att: 75,272

24   Stoke 1 (Tuncay 81) Manchester Utd 2 (Hernandez 27, 86). Att: 27,372

30   Manchester Utd 2 (Vidic 31, Nani 84) Tottenham 0. Att: 75,223

NOVEMBER 2010

6   Manchester Utd 2 (Park 45, 90) Wolves 1 (Ebanks-Blake 66). Att: 75,285

10   Manchester City 0 Manchester Utd 0. Att: 47,679

13   Aston Villa 2 (A Young 72 pen, Albrighton 76) Manchester Utd 2 (Macheda 81, Vidic 85). Att: 40,073

20   Manchester Utd 2 (Evra 45, Hernandez 77) Wigan 0. Att: 74,181

27   Manchester Utd 7 (Berbatov 2, 27, 47, 62, 70, Park 23, Nani 48) Blackburn 1 (Samba 83). Att: 74,850

DECEMBER 2010

13   Manchester Utd 1 (Park 41) Arsenal 0. Att: 75,227

26   Manchester Utd 2 (Berbatov 5, 57) Sunderland 0. Att: 75,269

28   Birmingham 1 (Bowyer 89) Manchester Utd 1 (Berbatov 58). Att: 28,242

JANUARY 2011

1   WBA 1 (Morrison 14) Manchester Utd 2 (Rooney 3, Hernandez 75). Att: 25,499

4   Manchester Utd 2 (Hernandez 27, Nani 62) Stoke 1 (Whitehead 50). Att: 73,401

16   Tottenham 0 Manchester Utd 0. Att: 35,828

22   Manchester Utd 5 (Berbatov 2, 31, 53, Giggs 45, Nani 76) Birmingham 0. Att: 75,326

25   Blackpool 2 (Cathcart 15, Campbell 43) Manchester Utd 3 (Berbatov 72, 88, Hernandez 74). Att: 15,574

FEBRUARY 2011

1   Manchester Utd 3 (Rooney 1, 45, Vidic 63) Aston Villa 1 (Bent 58). Att: 75,256

5   Wolves 2 (Elokobi 10, Doyle 40) Manchester Utd 1 (Nani 3). Att: 28,811

12   Manchester Utd 2 (Nani 41, Rooney 78) Manchester City 1 (Silva 65). Att: 75,322

26   Wigan 0 Manchester Utd 4 (Hernandez 17, 74, Rooney 84, Fabio 87). Att: 18,140

MARCH 2011

1 Chelsea 2 (Luiz 54, Lampard 80 pen) Manchester Utd 1 (Rooney 29). Att: 41,825
6 Liverpool 3 (Kuyt 34, 39, 65) Manchester Utd 1 (Hernandez 90). Att: 44,753
19 Manchester Utd 1 (Berbatov 88) Bolton 0. Att: 75,486

APRIL 2011

2 West Ham 2 (Noble 11, 25 pens) Manchester Utd 4 (Rooney 65, 73, 79 pen, Hernandez 81). Att: 34,546
9 Manchester Utd 2 (Berbatov 12, Valencia 32) Fulham 0. Att: 75,339
19 Newcastle 0 Manchester Utd 0. Att: 49,025
23 Manchester Utd 1 (Hernandez 83) Everton 0. Att: 75,300

MAY 2011

1 Arsenal 1 (Ramsey 56) Manchester Utd 0. Att: 60,107
8 Manchester Utd 2 (Hernandez 1, Vidic 23) Chelsea 1 (Lampard 68). Att: 75,445
14 Blackburn 1 (Emerton 20) Manchester Utd 1 (Rooney 73 pen). Att: 29,867 (clinched title)
22 Manchester Utd 4 (Park 21, Anderson 62, Evatt 74 og, Owen 81) Blackpool 2 (Adam 40, Taylor-Fletcher 57). Att: 75,400

MANCHESTER UNITED'S RECORD 19 TITLE WINS

1907–08

Two players signed from Manchester City assumed key roles in United's first title success, under manager Ernest Mangnall. Welshman Billy Meredith, one of football's first 'superstars' was the provider and Sandy Turnbull the marksman, scoring 27 goals in 25 matches as their team finished well clear of Aston Villa.

	P	W	D	L	F	A	Pts
Manchester Utd	38	23	6	9	81	48	52
Aston Villa	38	17	9	12	77	59	43
Manchester City	38	16	11	11	62	54	43
Newcastle	38	15	12	11	65	54	42
Sheffield Wed	38	19	4	15	73	64	42

1910–11

United were crowned champions at the end of their first full season at Old Trafford. They again finished ahead of Villa, but this time had only a point to spare, clinching the honours with a 5-1 win over Sunderland in the final match while Villa lost to Liverpool.

	P	W	D	L	F	A	Pts
Manchester Utd	38	22	8	8	72	40	52
Aston Villa	38	22	7	9	69	41	51
Sunderland	38	15	15	8	67	48	45
Everton	38	19	7	12	50	36	45
Bradford City	38	20	5	13	51	42	45

1951–52

With Matt Busby now in charge, Roger Byrne establishing himself and Jackie Blanchflower and Mark Jones coming through, United ended a long wait for another First Division success. It was the start of the era of the team that became known as the 'Busby Babes.'

	P	W	D	L	F	A	Pts
Manchester Utd	42	23	11	8	95	52	57
Tottenham	42	22	9	11	76	51	53
Arsenal	42	21	11	10	80	61	53
Portsmouth	42	20	8	14	68	58	48
Bolton	42	19	10	13	65	61	48

1955–56

Roger Byrne lifted the trophy as captain of a great young side with an average age of just 22. It included more Academy products in Eddie Colman, David Pegg and the player recognised as the finest of them all, Duncan Edwards.

	P	W	D	L	F	A	Pts
Manchester Utd	42	25	10	7	83	51	60
Blackpool	42	20	9	13	86	62	49
Wolves	42	20	9	13	89	65	49
Manchester City	42	18	10	14	82	69	46
Arsenal	42	18	10	14	60	61	46

1956–57

Billy Whelan, with 26 goals, and Tommy Taylor, with 22, led the way as United topped 100. The team were in their prime, only to be cut down the following season when the Munich disaster took the lives of eight players – Byrne, Colman, Edwards, Jones, Pegg, Taylor, Whelan and Geoff Bent.

	P	W	D	L	F	A	Pts
Manchester Utd	42	28	8	6	103	54	64
Tottenham	42	22	12	8	104	56	56
Preston	42	23	10	9	84	56	56
Blackpool	42	22	9	11	93	65	53
Arsenal	42	21	8	13	85	69	50

1964–65

Matt Busby harnessed the talents of George Best, Bobby Charlton and European Footballer of the Year Denis Law into a new title-winning team, who beat off the challenge of Don Revie's Leeds to take the crown on goal average.

	P	W	D	L	F	A	Pts
Manchester Utd	42	26	9	7	89	39	61
Leeds	42	26	9	7	83	52	61
Chelsea	42	24	8	10	89	54	56
Everton	42	17	15	10	69	60	49
Nottm Forest	42	17	13	12	67	67	47

1966–67

Matt Busby's last championship success. This time, Bobby Charlton was European Footballer of the Year as United paved the way for more European Cup football the following season when they became the first English side to win the trophy, beating Benfica 4-1 at Wembley.

	P	W	D	L	F	A	Pts
Manchester Utd	42	24	12	6	84	45	60
Nottm Forest	42	23	10	9	64	41	56
Tottenham	42	24	8	10	71	48	56
Leeds	42	22	11	9	62	42	55
Liverpool	42	19	13	10	64	47	51

1992–93

The club's first title for 26 years and the first of many for Sir Alex Ferguson in the inaugural Premier League season. Eric Cantona, signed from Leeds, introduced a a new dimension, while Steve Bruce's two goals against Sheffield Wednesday over Easter tipped the balance in United's favour.

	P	W	D	L	F	A	Pts
Manchester Utd	42	24	12	6	67	31	84
Aston Villa	42	21	11	10	57	40	74
Norwich	42	21	9	12	61	65	72
Blackburn	42	20	11	11	68	46	71
QPR	42	17	12	13	63	55	63

1993–94

Roy Keane was a commanding figure and Peter Schmeichel laid claim to the accolade of the club's finest-ever goalkeeper as United retained the title with another comfortable margin, this time over Blackburn. They went on to complete the Double by beating Chelsea 4-0 in the FA Cup Final.

	P	W	D	L	F	A	Pts
Manchester Utd	42	27	11	4	80	38	92
Blackburn	42	25	9	8	63	36	84
Newcastle	42	23	8	11	82	41	77
Arsenal	42	18	17	7	53	28	71
Leeds	42	18	16	8	65	39	70

1995–96

Experience gave way to youth as Sir Alex Ferguson sold Paul Ince, Mark Hughes and Andrei Kanchelskis and introduced David Beckham, Paul Scholes, Nicky Butt and the Neville brothers. When his side trailed Newcastle by 12 points in mid-January, questions were being asked. But they came good and completed a second Double, beating Liverpool 1-0 at Wembley.

	P	W	D	L	F	A	Pts
Manchester Utd	38	25	7	6	73	35	82
Newcastle	38	24	6	8	66	37	78
Liverpool	38	20	11	7	70	34	71
Aston Villa	38	18	9	11	52	35	63
Arsenal	38	17	12	9	49	32	63

1996–97

David Beckham opened the season by scoring from the half-way line at Wimbledon. Eric Cantona brought it to a close with the shock announcement that he was retiring from football. In between, United made light of drubbings at Newcastle (0-5) and Southampton (3-6) in successive matches to finish ahead of Newcastle again.

	P	W	D	L	F	A	Pts
Manchester Utd	38	21	12	5	76	44	75
Newcastle	38	19	11	8	73	40	68
Arsenal	38	19	11	8	62	32	68
Liverpool	38	19	11	8	62	37	68
Aston Villa	38	17	10	11	47	34	61

1998–99

The season of the historic Treble. United came from behind on the final day at Tottenham to edge out Arsenal, thanks to Andy Cole's winner. Newcastle were beaten 2-0 at Wembley. Then, stoppage-time goals by Teddy Sheringham and Ole Gunnar Solskjaer against Bayern Munich brought the Champions League trophy to Old Trafford.

	P	W	D	L	F	A	Pts
Manchester Utd	38	22	13	3	80	37	79
Arsenal	38	22	12	4	59	17	78
Chelsea	38	20	15	3	57	30	75
Leeds	38	18	13	7	62	34	67
West Ham	38	16	9	13	46	53	57

1999–2000

United returned from the Club World Championship in South America – controversially pulling out of the FA Cup – to race clear of the pack and become champions in April. They won their last 11 matches and scored 37 goals, including a 7-1 victory over West Ham, to finish a record 18 points clear.

	P	W	D	L	F	A	Pts
Manchester Utd	38	28	7	3	97	45	91
Arsenal	38	22	7	9	73	43	73
Leeds	38	21	6	11	58	43	69
Liverpool	38	19	10	9	51	30	67
Chelsea	38	18	11	9	53	34	65

2000–01

A third successive title for Sir Alex Ferguson and his team – and a change of heart about retiring by the manager. They were beaten by Arsenal at Highbury, but won the return fixture 6-1, forcing Arsene Wenger to settle for another runners-up position.

	P	W	D	L	F	A	Pts
Manchester Utd	38	24	8	6	79	31	80
Arsenal	38	20	10	8	63	38	70
Liverpool	38	20	9	9	71	39	69
Leeds	38	20	8	10	64	43	68
Ipswich	38	20	6	12	57	42	66

2002–03

Arsene Wenger talked about a 'shift in power' after Arsenal's success in 2002. When his side established an eight-point lead in this campaign, there was every sign of it. But United, with £30m Rio Ferdinand boosting their defence and David Beckham playing in what proved to be his last season with the club, came storming back to prevail.

	P	W	D	L	F	A	Prs
Manchester Utd	38	25	8	5	74	34	83
Arsenal	38	23	9	6	85	42	78
Newcastle	38	21	6	11	63	48	69
Chelsea	38	19	10	9	68	38	67
Liverpool	38	18	10	10	61	41	64

2006–07

Cristiano Ronaldo made a clean sweep of the domestic individual awards after United re-established supremacy to deny Chelsea a third successive title. The two teams were neck-and-neck for the first half of the season, before United edged clear and went on to pull away when retrieving a 2-0 deficit against Everton to win 4-2

	P	W	D	L	F	A	Prs
Manchester Utd	38	28	5	5	83	27	89
Chelsea	38	24	11	3	64	24	83
Liverpool	38	20	8	10	57	27	68
Arsenal	38	19	11	8	63	35	68
Tottenham	38	17	9	12	57	54	60

2007–08

Cristiano Ronaldo was rewarded with World and European awards for scoring 42 goals in all competitions as United won domestic and European honours. Ronaldo's 31st in the league came on the final day of the season when a 2-0 victory over Wigan proved decisive. Ryan Giggs, equalling Sir Bobby Charlton's record 758 appearances for the club, scored the other and United went on to beat Chelsea on penalties in the Champions League Final.

	P	W	D	L	F	A	Pts
Manchester Utd	38	27	6	5	80	22	87
Chelsea	38	25	10	3	65	26	85
Arsenal	38	24	11	3	74	31	83
Liverpool	38	21	13	4	67	28	76
Everton	38	19	8	11	55	33	65

2008–09

United came from behind to drew level with Liverpool on 18 titles. They trailed their rivals by seven points at one stage, but overtook Chelsea's Premier League record of ten successive clean sheets to close the gap. Then, 17-year-old Federico Macheda scored in stoppage-time on his debut against Aston Villa for a vital victory.

	P	W	D	L	F	A	Pts
Manchester Utd	38	28	6	4	68	24	90
Liverpool	38	25	11	2	77	27	86
Chelsea	38	25	8	5	68	24	83
Arsenal	38	20	12	6	68	37	72
Everton	38	17	12	9	55	37	63

2010–11

A record breaking 19th triumph for the club and a 12th success for both Sir Alex Ferguson and Ryan Giggs. United assumed pole position when Chelsea faltered after a whirlwind start, held off challenges from Manchester City and Arsenal, then resisted a late run by Chelsea, who cut a 15-point deficit to three before losing at Old Trafford.

	P	W	D	L	F	A	Pts
Manchester Utd	38	23	11	4	78	37	80
Chelsea	38	21	8	9	69	33	71
Manchester City	38	21	8	9	60	33	71
Arsenal	38	19	11	8	72	43	68
Tottenham	38	16	14	8	55	46	62

GOALS GALORE IN THE TOP DIVISION

It was the day last season when Newcastle retrieved a 4-0 deficit to earn a point against Arsenal, Louis Saha scored four times for Everton against Blackpool and Carlos Tevez netted all three of Manchester City's goals against West Bromwich Albion. Eight Premier League matches yielded 41 goals. Here, we also look back at two other high-scoring days in top-flight football.

PREMIER LEAGUE – FEBRUARY 5 2011 (Matches – 8, Goals – 41)

Aston Villa 2 (Pantsil og 13, Walker 72) Fulham 2 (Johnson 52, Dempsey 78). Att: 35,899

Everton 5 (Saha 20, 47 76, 84, Beckford 80) Blackpool 3 (Baptiste 37, Puncheon 62, Adam 64). Att: 38,202

Manchester City 3 (Tevez 17 pen, 22, 39 pen,) WBA 0. Att: 46,846

Newcastle 4 (Barton 68 pen, 83 pen, Best 75, Tiote 87) Arsenal 4 (Walcott 1, Djourou 3, Van Persie 10, 26). Att: 51,561

Stoke 3 (Carew 32, Huth 83, 90) Sunderland 2 (Richardson 2, Gyan 48). Att: 26,008

Tottenham 2 (Van der Vaart 6 pen, Kranjcar 90) Bolton 1 (Sturridge 55). Att: 36,197

Wigan 4 (McCarthy 35, 56, Rodallega 50, Watson 65 pen) Blackburn 3 (Roberts 23, Samba 58, Dunn 81 pen). Att: 18,567

Wolves 2 (Elokobi 10, Doyle 40) Manchester Utd 1 (Nani). Att: 28,811

PREMIER LEAGUE – MAY 8, 1993 (Matches – 9, Goals – 47)

Arsenal 3 (Wright 9, Dickov 82, Campbell 89) Crystal Palace 0. Att: 25,225

Blackburn 1 (Sherwood 65) Sheffield Wed 0. Att: 14,956

Coventry 3 (Williams 5, Quinn 40, Ndlovu 73) Leeds 3 (Wallace 6, 89, 90). Att: 19,591

Ipswich 2 (Milton 40, Whitton 52 pen) Nottm Forest 1 (Clough 64 pen). Att: 22,093

Liverpool 6 (Rush 21, 85, Barnes 44, 88, Harkness 47, Walters 82) Tottenham 2 (Sheringham 46, Sedgley 77). Att: 43,385

Manchester City 2 (White 39, Curle 73 pen) Everton 5 (Jackson 6, Beagrie 19, 84, Beardsley 32, Preki 51). Att: 25,180

Middlesbrough 3 (Falconer 34, Wilkinson 65, Hendrie 74) Norwich 3 (Ekoku 14, 66, Johnson 68). Att: 15,155

Oldham 4 (Pointon 29, Olney 44, Ritchie 55, Halle 64) Southampton 3 (Le Tissier 34, 67, 85). Att: 14,597

Sheffield Utd 4 (Scott 7, Rogers 16, Whitehouse 43, 48) Chelsea 2 (Lee 86, Townsend 87). Att: 24,850.

FIRST DIVISION – DECEMBER 26, 1963 (Matches – 10, Goals 66)

Blackpool 1 (Durie) Chelsea 5 (Bridges 2, Murray, Houseman, Venables). Att: 17,163

Burnley 6 (Lochhead 4, Morgan 2) Manchester Utd 1 (Herd). Att: 35,764

Fulham 10 (Leggat 4, Howfield 3, Cook, Robson, Muller) Ipswich 1 (Baker). Att: 19,374

Leicester 2 (Keyworth 2) Everton 0. Att: 30,004

Liverpool 6 (Hunt 4, St John, Arrowsmith) Stoke 1 (Ritchie). Att: 49,942

Nottm Forest 3 (Wignall, Vowden, Storey-Moore) Sheffield Utd 3 (Jones 2, Allchurch). Att: 23,916

Sheffield Wed 3 (Dobson 2, Pearson) Bolton 0. Att: 31,301

WBA 4 (Kaye, Clarke, Fudge, Howe) Tottenham 4 (Greaves 2, Smith, Jones). Att: 37,189

West Ham 2 (Byrne 2) Blackburn 8 (McEvoy 3, Pickering 3, Douglas, Ferguson). Att: 20, 500

Wolves 3 (Crawford 2, Wharton) Aston Villa 3 (Pountney, Crowe, Hateley). Att: 27,569

(ends)

END OF SEASON PLAY-OFFS

Swansea evoked memories of John Toshack, the Vetch Field and Clive Mendonca when reaching the Premier League with a 4-2 win over Reading at Wembley. The victory came 30 years after player-manager Toshack led the club into the old First Division at their old ground, his third promotion in four seasons. Scott Sinclair's hat-trick, the first in a Play-off Final since Mendonca's for Charlton in 1998, completed Swansea's rise this time from League Two to the top-flight in seven seasons. Charlton's victory over Sunderland was eventually secured in a penalty shoot-out - and it was Sinclair's coolness in converting two spot-kicks in normal time that proved decisive. His side led 3-0 at half-time, were pegged back to 3-2, then made sure with Sinclair's second penalty. It was a sweet moment for manager Brendan Rodgers, in his first season at the Liberty Stadium after being sacked by Reading in December 2009 six months into the job. A disappointing afternoon for his old club was compounded when substitute Jay Tabb and assistant manager Nigel Gibbs were sent to the stands for comments made to match officials in the tunnel at half-time.

The day after his father's side had been outplayed by Barcelona in the Champions League Final, Darren Ferguson led high-scoring **Peterborough** back to the Championship at the first attempt. They had scored 106 League One goals and after being denied by Huddersfield until deep into the second half, delivered three more in seven minutes from Tommy Rowe, Craig Mackail-Smith, with his 35th in all competitions, and captain Grant McCann. That 3-0 win was at Old Trafford, where the League Two Final was also staged because of the European showpiece game at Wembley. **Stevenage** followed their Conference title success in 2010 by securing a second, successive promotion, beating Torquay with the only goal of the game four minutes from half-time by John Mousinho. **AFC Wimbledon**, formed by supporters in 2002 when the former FA Cup-winning club relocated to Milton Keynes, completed a notable rise from the Combined Counties League to the Football League with a penalty shoot-out win over Luton after a goalless 120 minutes at the City of Manchester Stadium.

SEMI-FINALS, FIRST LEG

NPOWER CHAMPIONSHIP
Nottm Forest 0 **Swansea** 0. Att: 27,881. **Reading** 0 **Cardiff** 0. Att: 21,485

LEAGUE ONE
Bournemouth 1 (McDermott 60) **Huddersfield** 1 (Kilbane 22). Att: 9,043. **MK Dons** 3 (Powell 47, S Baldock 50, Balanta 56) **Peterborough** 2 (Mackail-Smith 8, McCann 81 pen). Att: 12,662

LEAGUE TWO
Stevenage 2 (Long 24, Byrom 45) **Accrington** 0. Att: 4,424. **Torquay** 2 (Zebroski 29, O'Kane 45) **Shrewsbury** 0. Att: 4,130.

BLUE SQUARE PREMIER LEAGUE
Fleetwood 0 **AFC Wimbledon** 2 (Moore 39, Mohamed 49). Att: 4,112. **Wrexham** 0 **Luton** 3 (Lawless 16, Gnakpa 28, Asafu-Adjaye 35). Att: 7,211

SEMI-FINALS, SECOND LEG

NPOWER CHAMPIONSHIP
Cardiff 0 **Reading** 3 (Long 28, 45 pen, McAnuff 84). Att: 24,081 (**Reading** won 3-0 on agg).
Swansea 3 (Britton 28, Dobbie 33, Pratley 90) **Nottm Forest** 1 (Earnshaw 80). Att: 19,816 (**Swansea** won 3-1 on agg)

LEAGUE ONE
Huddersfield 3 (Peltier 26, Ward 45, Kay 105) **Bournemouth** 3 (Lovell 44 pen, 63, Ings 104).
Att: 16,444 (aet, agg 4-4, **Huddersfield** won 4-2 on pens). **Peterborough** 2 (McCann 11,
Mackail-Smith 54) **MK Dons** 0. Att: 11,920 (**Peterborough** won 4-3 on agg)

LEAGUE TWO
Accrington 0 **Stevenage** 1 (Beardsley 90). Att: 4,185 (**Stevenage** won 3-0 on agg). **Shrewsbury** 0
Torquay 0. Att: 8,452 (**Torquay** won 2-0 on agg)

BLUE SQUARE PREMIER LEAGUE
AFC Wimbledon 6 (Mohamed 1, 35, 63, Kedwell 28, Jolley 67, Mulley 80) **Fleetwood** 1
(Seddon 47). Att: 4,538 (**AFC Wimbledon** won 8-1 on agg). **Luton** 2 (Kroca 29, Walker 81)
Wrexham 1 (Mangan 8). Att: 9,078 (**Luton** won 5-1 on agg).

FINALS

NPOWER CHAMPIONSHIP – MAY 30 2011
Reading 2 (Allen 49 og, Mills 57) **Swansea City** 4 (Sinclair 21 pen, 22, 80 pen, Dobbie 40).
Att: 86,581 (Wembley)
Reading (4-4-2): Federici, Griffin (Robson-Kanu 84), Mills (capt), Khizanishvili, Harte, Kebe,
Leigertwood, Karacan, McAnuff, Long, Hunt (Church 76). **Subs not used:** McCarthy, Tabb,
Howard, Cummings, Pearce. **Booked:** Griffin, Khizanishvili, McAnuff. **Sent off** (half-time): Tabb.
Manager: Brian McDermott
Swansea City (4-3-3): De Vries, Rangel, Monk (capt), Williams, Tate, Dyer, Britton (Gower 77),
Dobbie (Pratley 55), Allen (Moore 89), Sinclair, Borini. **Subs not used:** Ma-Kalambay, Beattie,
Serran, Richards. **Booked:** Borini, Allen, Gower. **Manager:** Brendan Rodgers
Referee: P Dowd (Staffs). **Half-time:** 0-3

LEAGUE ONE – MAY 29 2011
Huddersfield Town 0 **Peterborough United** 3 (Rowe 78, Mackail-Smith 80, McCann 85). Att:
48,410 (Old Trafford)
Huddersfield Town (4-3-3): Bennett, Hunt, Kay, P Clarke (capt), Naysmith, Peltier, Kilbane,
Arfield (Lee 81), Ward (Cadamarteri 79), Roberts, Afobe (Rhodes 81). **Subs not used:** Colgan,
McCombe, Gudjonsson, Novak. **Booked:** Peltier, Hunt, Kay. **Manager:** Lee Clark
Peterborough United (4-3-1-2): Jones, Little, Bennett, Zakuani, Basey (Lee 64), Wesolowski,
McCann (capt), Rowe (Whelpdale 84), Boyd, Tomlin (Ball 90), Mackail-Smith. **Subs not**
used: Richardson, Langmead, Mendez-Laing, Newell. **Booked:** Tomlin, Lee. **Manager:** Darren
Ferguson
Referee: S Tanner (Somerset). **Half-time:** 0-0

LEAGUE TWO – MAY 28 2011
Stevenage 1 (Mousinho 41) **Torquay United** 0. Att: 11,484 (Old Trafford)
Stevenage (4-4-2): Day, Henry, Bostwick, Roberts (capt), Laird, Wilson, Byrom (Murphy 57),
Mousinho, Long, Charles (Beardsley 85), Reid (Harrison 62). **Subs not used:** Welch, Ashton,
May, Winn. **Booked:** Mousinho, Harrison. **Manager:** Graham Westley
Torquay United (4-4-2): Bevan, Mansell, Branston, Robertson, Nicholson (Rowe-Turner 83),
Kee, O'Kane, Lathrope (Oastler 79), Robinson (Stevens 83), Zebroski, Tomlin. **Subs not used:**
Potter, Ellis, Macklin, Halpin. **Booked:** Zebroski, Oastler. **Manager:** Paul Buckle
Referee: D Deadman (Cambs). **Half-time:** 0-0

BLUE SQUARE PREMIER LEAGUE – MAY 21 2011
AFC Wimbledon 0 **Luton Town** 0 (aet, **AFC Wimbledon** won 4-3 on pens). Att: 18,195 (City of
Manchester Stadium)

AFC Wimbledon (4-4-2): Brown, Hatton, Stuart, Johnson, Gwillim (Yakubu 61), Gregory (Minshull 94), Wellard (Mulley 67), Yussuff, Kedwell (capt), Mohamed, Moore. **Subs not used**: Turner, Jolley. **Booked**: Johnson, Moore, Minshull. **Manager**: Terry Brown
Luton Town (4-5-1): Tyler, Gleeson, G Pilkington (capt), Kroca, Asafu-Adjaye, Willmott (Barnes-Homer 61), Keane, Lawless, Howells, Gnakpa (Newton 95), Walker. **Subs not used**: K Pilkington, Graham, Crow. **Booked**: Keane, Lawless. **Manager**: Gary Brabin
Referee: J Adcock (Notts)

PLAY-OFF FINALS – HOME & AWAY

1987: Divs 1/2: Charlton beat Leeds 2-1 in replay (Birmingham) after 1-1 agg (1-0h, 0-1a). Charlton remained in Div 1 Losing semi-finalists: Ipswich and Oldham. **Divs 2/3: Swindon** beat Gillingham 2-0 in replay (Crystal Palace) after 2-2 agg (0-1a, 2-1h). Swindon promoted to Div 2. Losing semi-finalists: Sunderland and Wigan; Sunderland relegated to Div 3. **Divs 3/4: Aldershot** beat Wolves 3-0 on agg (2-0h, 1-0a) and promoted to Div 3. Losing semi-finalists: Bolton and Colchester; Bolton relegated to Div 4

1988: Divs 1/2: Middlesbrough beat Chelsea 2-1 on agg (2-0h, 0-1a) and promoted to Div 1; Chelsea relegated to Div 2. Losing semi-finalists: Blackburn and Bradford City. **Divs 2/3: Walsall** beat Bristol City 4-0 in replay (h) after 3-3 agg (3-1a, 0-2h) and promoted to Div 2. Losing semi-finalists: Sheffield Utd and Notts County; Sheffield Utd relegated to Div 3. **Divs 3/4: Swansea** beat Torquay 5-4 on agg (2-1h, 3-3a) and promoted to Div 3. Losing semi-finalists: Rotherham and Scunthorpe.; Rotherham relegated to Div 4

1989: Div 2: Crystal Palace beat Blackburn 4-3 on agg (1-3a, 3-0h). Losing semi-finalists: Watford and Swindon. **Div 3: Port Vale** beat Bristol Rovers 2-1 on agg (1-1a, 1-0h). Losing semi-finalists: Fulham and Preston **Div.4: Leyton Orient** beat Wrexham 2-1 on agg (0-0a, 2-1h). Losing semi-finalists: Scarborough and Scunthorpe

PLAY-OFF FINALS AT WEMBLEY

1990: Div 2: Swindon 1 Sunderland 0 (att: 72,873). Swindon promoted, then demoted for financial irregularities; Sunderland promoted. Losing semi-finalists: Blackburn and Newcastle Utd **Div 3: Notts County** 2 Tranmere 0 (att: 29,252). Losing semi-finalists: Bolton and Bury. **Div 4: Cambridge Utd** 1 Chesterfield 0 (att: 26,404). Losing semi-finalists: Maidstone and Stockport County

1991: Div 2: Notts County 3 Brighton 1 (att: 59,940). Losing semi-finalists: Middlesbrough and Millwall. **Div 3: Tranmere** 1 Bolton 0 (att: 30,217). Losing semi-finalists: Brentford and Bury. **Div 4: Torquay 2** Blackpool 2 – Torquay won 5-4 on pens (att: 21,615). Losing semi-finalists: Burnley and Scunthorpe

1992: Div 2: Blackburn 1 Leicester 0 (att: 68,147). Losing semi-finalists: Derby and Cambridge Utd. **Div 3: Peterborough** 2 Stockport 1 (att: 35,087). Losing semi-finalists: Huddersfield and Stoke. **Div 4: Blackpool** 1 Scunthorpe 1 aet, Blackpool won 4-3 on pens (att: 22,741). Losing semi-finalists: Barnet and Crewe

1993: Div 1: Swindon 4 Leicester 3 (att: 73,802). Losing semi-finalists: Portsmouth and Tranmere. **Div 2: WBA** 3 Port Vale 0 (att: 53,471). Losing semi-finalists: Stockport and Swansea. **Div 3: York** 1 Crewe 1 aet, York won 5-3 on pens (att: 22,416). Losing semi-finalists: Bury and Walsall

1994: Div 1: Leicester 2 Derby 1 (att: 73,671). Losing semi-finalists: Millwall and Tranmere. **Div 2: Burnley** 2 Stockport 1 (att: 44,806). Losing semi-finalists: Plymouth Argyle and York. **Div 3: Wycombe** 4 Preston 2 (att: 40,109). Losing semi-finalists: Carlisle and Torquay

1995: Div 1: Bolton 4 Reading 3 (att: 64,107). Losing semi-finalists: Tranmere and Wolves. **Div 2: Huddersfield** 2 Bristol Rov 1 (att: 59,175). Losing semi-finalists: Brentford and Crewe. **Div 3: Chesterfield** 2 Bury 0 (att: 22,814). Losing semi-finalists: Mansfield and Preston

1996: Div 1: Leicester 2 Crystal Palace 1 aet (att: 73,573). Losing semi-finalists: Charlton and Stoke. **Div 2: Bradford City** 2 Notts Co 0 (att: 39,972). Losing semi-finalists: Blackpool and Crewe. **Div 3: Plymouth Argyle** 1 Darlington 0 (att: 43,431). Losing semi-finalists: Colchester and Hereford

1997: Div 1: Crystal Palace 1 Sheffield Utd 0 (att: 64,383). Losing semi-finalists: Ipswich and Wolves. **Div 2: Crewe** 1 Brentford 0 (att: 34,149). Losing semi-finalists: Bristol City and Luton. **Div 3: Northampton** 1 Swansea 0 (att: 46,804). Losing semi-finalists: Cardiff and Chester

1998: Div 1: Charlton 4 Sunderland 4 aet, Charlton won 7-6 on pens (att: 77, 739). Losing semi-finalists: Ipswich and Sheffield Utd. **Div 2: Grimsby** 1 Northampton 0 (att: 62,988). Losing semi-finalists: Bristol Rov and Fulham. **Div 3: Colchester** 1 Torquay 0 (att: 19,486). Losing semi-finalists: Barnet and Scarborough

1999: Div 1: Watford 2 Bolton 0 (att: 70,343). Losing semi-finalists: Ipswich and Birmingham. **Div 2: Manchester City** 2 Gillingham 2 aet, Manchester City won 3-1 on pens (att: 76,935). Losing semi-finalists: Preston and Wigan. **Div 3: Scunthorpe** 1 Leyton Orient 0 (att: 36,985). Losing semi-finalists: Rotherham and Swansea

2000: Div 1: Ipswich 4 Barnsley 2 (att: 73,427). Losing semi-finalists: Birmingham and Bolton. **Div 2: Gillingham** 3 Wigan 2 aet (att: 53,764). Losing semi-finalists: Millwall and Stoke. **Div 3: Peterborough** 1 Darlington 0 (att: 33,383). Losing semi-finalists: Barnet and Hartlepool

PLAY-OFF FINALS AT MILLENNIUM STADIUM

2001: Div 1: Bolton 3 Preston 0 (att: 54,328). Losing semi-finalists: Birmingham and WBA. **Div 2: Walsall** 3 Reading 2 aet (att: 50,496). Losing semi-finalists: Stoke and Wigan. **Div 3: Blackpool** 4 Leyton Orient 2 (att: 23,600). Losing semi-finalists: Hartlepool and Hull.

2002: Div 1: Birmingham 1 Norwich 1 aet, Birmingham won 4-2 on pens, (att: 71,597). Losing semi-finalists: Millwall and Wolves. **Div 2: Stoke** 2 Brentford 0 (att: 42,523). Losing semi-finalists: Cardiff and Huddersfield. **Div 3: Cheltenham** 3 Rushden & Diamonds 1 (att: 24,368). Losing semi-finalists: Hartlepool and Rochdale

2003: Div 1: Wolves 3 Sheffield Utd 0 (att: 69,473). Losing semi-finalists: Nott'm Forest and Reading. **Div 2: Cardiff** 1 QPR. 0 aet (att: 66,096). Losing semi-finalists: Bristol City and Oldham. **Div 3: Bournemouth** 5 Lincoln 2 (att: 32,148). Losing semi-finalists: Bury and Scunthorpe

2004: Div 1: Crystal Palace 1 West Ham 0 (att: 72,523). Losing semi-finalists: Ipswich and Sunderland. **Div 2: Brighton** 1 Bristol City 0 (att: 65,167). Losing semi-finalists: Hartlepool and Swindon. **Div 3: Huddersfield** 0 Mansfield 0 aet, Huddersfield won 4-1 on pens (att: 37,298). Losing semi-finalists: Lincoln and Northampton

2005: Championship: West Ham 1 Preston 0 (att: 70,275). Losing semifinalists: Derby Co and Ipswich. **League 1: Sheffield Wed** 4 Hartlepool 2 aet (att: 59,808). Losing semi-finalists: Brentford and Tranmere **League 2: Southend** 2 Lincoln 0 aet (att: 19532). Losing semi-finalists: Macclesfield and Northampton

2006: Championship: Watford 3 Leeds 0 (att: 64,736). Losing semi-finalists: Crystal Palace and Preston. **League 1: Barnsley** 2 Swansea 2 aet (att: 55,419), Barnsley won 4-3 on pens. Losing semi-finalists: Huddersfield and Brentford. **League 2: Cheltenham** 1 Grimsby 0 (att: 29,196). Losing semi-finalists: Wycombe and Lincoln

PLAY-OFF FINALS AT WEMBLEY

2007: Championship: Derby 1 WBA 0 (att: 74,993). Losing semi-finalists: Southampton and Wolves. **League 1: Blackpool** 2 Yeovil 1 (att: 59,313). Losing semi-finalists: Nottm Forest and Oldham. **League 2: Bristol Rov** 3 Shrewsbury 1 (att: 61,589). Losing semi-finalists: Lincoln and MK Dons

2008: Championship: Hull 1 Bristol City 0 (att: 86,703). Losing semi-finalists: Crystal Palace and Watford. **League 1: Doncaster** 1 Leeds 0 (att: 75,132). Losing semi-finalists: Carlisle and Southend. **League 2: Stockport** 3 Rochdale 2 (att: 35,715). Losing semi-finalists: Darlington and Wycombe

2009: Championship: Burnley 1 Sheffield Utd 0 (att: 80,518). Losing semi-finalists: Preston and Reading. **League 1: Scunthorpe** 3 Millwall 2 (att: 59,661). Losing semi-finalists: Leeds and MK Dons. **League 2: Gillingham** 1 Shrewsbury 0 (att: 53,706). Losing semi-finalists: Bury and Rochdale

2010: Championship: Blackpool 3 Cardiff 2 (att: 82,244). Losing semi-finalists: Leicester and Nottm Forest. **League 1: Millwall** 1 Swindon 0 (att:73,108). Losing semi-finalists: Charlton and Huddersfield. **League 2: Dagenham & Redbridge** 3 Rotherham 2 (att: 32,054). Losing semi-finalists: Aldershot and Morecambe

HISTORY OF THE PLAY-OFFS

Play-off matches were introduced by the Football League to decide final promotion and relegation issues at the end of season 1986-87. A similar series styled 'Test Matches' had operated between Divisions One and Two for six seasons from 1893-98, and was abolished when both divisions were increased from 16 to 18 clubs.

Eighty-eight years later, the play-offs were back in vogue. In the first three seasons (1987-88-89), the Finals were played home-and-away, and since they were made one-off matches in 1990, they have featured regularly in Wembley's spring calendar, until the old stadium closed its doors and the action switched to the Millennium Stadium in Cardiff in 2001.

Through the years, these have been the ups and downs of the play-offs:

1987: Initially, the 12 clubs involved comprised the one that finished directly above those relegated in Divisions One, Two and Three and the three who followed the sides automatically promoted in each section. Two of the home-and-away Finals went to neutral-ground replays, in which **Charlton** clung to First Division status by denying Leeds promotion while **Swindon** beat Gillingham to complete their climb from Fourth Division to Second in successive seasons, via the play-offs, Sunderland fell into the Third and Bolton into Division Four, both for the first time. **Aldershot** went up after finishing only sixth in Division Four; in their Final, they beat Wolves, who had finished nine points higher and missed automatic promotion by one point.

1988: Chelsea were relegated from the First Division after losing on aggregate to **Middlesbrough**, who had finished third in Division Two. So Middlesbrough, managed by Bruce Rioch, completed the rise from Third Division to First in successive seasons, only two years after their very existence had been threatened by the bailiffs. Also promoted via the play-offs: **Walsall** from Division Three and **Swansea** from the Fourth. Relegated, besides Chelsea: Sheffield Utd (to Division Three) and Rotherham (to Division Four).

1989: After two seasons of promotion-relegation play-offs, the system was changed to involve the four clubs who had just missed automatic promotion. That format has remained. Steve Coppell's **Crystal Palace**, third in Division Two, returned to the top flight after eight years, beating Blackburn 4-3 on aggregate after extra time. Similarly, **Port Vale** confirmed third place in Division Three with promotion via the play-offs. For **Leyton Orient**, promotion seemed out of the question in Division Four when they stood 15th on March 1. But eight wins and a draw in the last nine home games swept them to sixth in the final table, and two more home victories in the play-offs completed their season in triumph.

1990: The play-off Finals now moved to Wembley over three days of the Spring Holiday weekend. On successive afternoons, **Cambridge Utd** won promotion from Division Four and **Notts Co** from the Third. Then, on Bank Holiday Monday, the biggest crowd for years at a Football

League fixture (72,873) saw Ossie Ardiles' **Swindon** beat Sunderland 1-0 to reach the First Division for the first time. A few weeks later, however, Wembley losers **Sunderland** were promoted instead, by default; Swindon were found guilty of "financial irregularities" and stayed in Division Two.

1991: Again, the season's biggest League crowd (59,940) gathered at Wembley for the First Division Final in which **Notts Co** (having missed promotion by one point) still fulfilled their ambition, beating Brighton 3-1. In successive years, County had climbed from Third Division to First via the play-offs – the first club to achieve double promotion by this route. Bolton were denied automatic promotion in Division Three on goal difference, and lost at Wembley to an extra-time goal by **Tranmere**. The Fourth Division Final made history, with Blackpool beaten 5-4 on penalties by **Torquay** – first instance of promotion being decided by a shoot-out. In the table, Blackpool had finished seven points ahead of Torquay.

1992: Wembley that Spring Bank Holiday was the turning point in the history of **Blackburn.** Bolstered by Kenny Dalglish's return to management and owner Jack Walker's millions, they beat Leicester 1-0 by Mike Newell's 45th-minute penalty to achieve their objective – a place in the new Premier League. Newell, who also missed a second-half penalty, had recovered from a broken leg just in time for the play-offs. In the Fourth Division Final **Blackpool** (denied by penalties the previous year) this time won a shoot-out 4-3 against Scunthorpe., who were unlucky in the play-offs for the fourth time in five years. **Peterborough** climbed out of the Third Division for the first time, beating Stockport County 2-1 at Wembley.

1993: The crowd of 73,802 at Wembley to see **Swindon** beat Leicester 4-3 in the First Division Final was 11,000 bigger than that for the FA Cup Final replay between Arsenal and Sheffield Wed Leicester rallied from three down to 3-3 before Paul Bodin's late penalty wiped away **Swindon**'s bitter memories of three years earlier, when they were denied promotion after winning at Wembley. In the Third Division Final, **York** beat Crewe 5-3 in a shoot-out after a 1-1 draw, and in the Second Division decider, **WBA** beat Port Vale 3-0. That was tough on Vale, who had finished third in the table with 89 points – the highest total never to earn promotion in any division. They had beaten Albion twice in the League, too.

1994: Wembley's record turn-out of 158,586 spectators at the three Finals started with a crowd of 40,109 to see Martin O'Neill's **Wycombe** beat Preston 4-2. They thus climbed from Conference to Second Division with successive promotions. **Burnley**'s 2-1 victory in the Second Division Final was marred by the sending-off of two Stockport players, and in the First Division decider **Leicester** came from behind to beat Derby Co and end the worst Wembley record of any club. They had lost on all six previous appearances there – four times in the FA Cup Final and in the play-offs of 1992 and 1993.

1995: Two months after losing the Coca-Cola Cup Final to Liverpool, Bruce Rioch's **Bolton** were back at Wembley for the First Division play-off Final. From two goals down to Reading in front of a crowd of 64,107, they returned to the top company after 15 years, winning 4-3 with two extra-time goals. **Huddersfield** ended the first season at their new £15m. home with promotion to the First Division via a 2-1 victory against Bristol Rov – manager Neil Warnock's third play-off success (after two with Notts Co). Of the three clubs who missed automatic promotion by one place, only **Chesterfield** achieved it in the play-offs, comfortably beating Bury 2-0.

1996: Under new manager Martin O'Neill (a Wembley play-off winner with Wycombe in 1994), **Leicester** returned to the Premiership a year after leaving it. They had finished fifth in the table, but in the Final came from behind to beat third-placed Crystal Palace by Steve Claridge's shot in the last seconds of extra time. In the Second Division **Bradford City** came sixth, nine points behind Blackpool (3rd), but beat them (from two down in the semi-final first leg) and then clinched promotion by 2-0 v Notts County at Wembley. It was City's greatest day since they won the Cup in 1911. **Plymouth Argyle** beat Darlington in the Third Division Final to earn promotion a year after being relegated. It was manager Neil Warnock's fourth play-off triumph in seven seasons after two with Notts County (1990 and 1991) and a third with Huddersfield in 1995.

1997: High drama at Wembley as **Crystal Palace** left it late against Sheffield Utd in the First Division play-off final. The match was scoreless until the last 10 seconds when David Hopkin lobbed Blades' keeper Simon Tracey from 25 yards to send the Eagles back to the Premiership after two seasons of Nationwide action. In the Second Division play-off final, **Crewe** beat Brentford 1-0 courtesy of a Shaun Smith goal. **Northampton** celebrated their first Wembley appearance with a 1-0 victory over Swansea thanks to John Frain's injury-time free-kick in the Third Division play-off final.

1998: In one of the finest games ever seen at Wembley, **Charlton** eventually triumphed 7-6 on penalties over Sunderland. For Charlton, Wearside-born Clive Mendonca scored a hat-trick and Richard Rufus his first career goal in a match that lurched between joy and despair for both sides as it ended 4-4. Sunderland defender Michael Gray's superb performance ill deserved to end with his weakly struck spot kick being saved by Sasa Ilic. In the Third Division, the penalty spot also had a role to play, as **Colchester's** David Gregory scored the only goal to defeat Torquay, while in the Second Division a Kevin Donovan goal gave **Grimsby** victory over Northampton.

1999: Elton John, watching via a personal satellite link in Seattle, saw his **Watford** side overcome Bolton 2-0 to reach the Premiership. Against technically superior opponents, Watford prevailed with application and teamwork. They also gave Bolton a lesson in finishing through match-winners by Nick Wright and Allan Smart. **Manchester City** staged a remarkable comeback to win the Second Division Final after trailing to goals by Carl Asaba and Robert Taylor for Gillingham. Kevin Horlock and Paul Dickov scored in stoppage time and City went on to win on penalties. A goal by Spaniard Alex Calvo-Garcia earned **Scunthorpe** a 1-0 success against Leyton Orient in the Third Division Final.

2000: After three successive play-off failures, **Ipswich** finally secured a place in the Premiership. They overcame the injury loss of leading scorer David Johnson to beat Barnsley 4-2 with goals by 36-year-old Tony Mowbray, Marcus Stewart and substitutes Richard Naylor and Martijn Reuser. With six minutes left of extra-time in the Second Division Final, **Gillingham** trailed Wigan 2-1. But headers by 38-year-old player-coach Steve Butler and fellow substitute Andy Thomson gave them a 3-2 victory. Andy Clarke, approaching his 33rd birthday, scored the only goal of the Third Division decider for **Peterborough** against Darlington.

2001: Bolton, unsuccessful play-off contenders in the two previous seasons, made no mistake at the third attempt. They flourished in the new surroundings of the Millennium Stadium to beat Preston 3-0 with goals by Gareth Farrelly, Michael Ricketts – his 24th of the season – and Ricardo Gardner to reach the Premiership. **Walsall,** relegated 12 months earlier, scored twice in a three-minute spell of extra time to win 3-2 against Reading in the Second Division Final, while **Blackpool** capped a marked improvement in the second half of the season by overcoming Leyton Orient 4-2 in the Third Division Final.

2002: Holding their nerve to win a penalty shoot-out 4-2, **Birmingham** wiped away the memory of three successive defeats in the semi-finals of the play-offs to return to the top division after an absence of 16 years. Substitute Darren Carter completed a fairy-tale first season as a professional by scoring the fourth spot-kick against Norwich. **Stoke** became the first successful team to come from the south dressing room in 12 finals since football was adopted by the home of Welsh rugby, beating Brentford 2-0 in the Second Division Final with Deon Burton's strike and a Ben Burgess own goal. Julian Alsop's 26th goal of the season helped **Cheltenham** defeat League newcomers Rushden & Diamonds 3-1 in the Third Division decider.

2003: Wolves benefactor Sir Jack Hayward finally saw his £60m investment pay dividends when the club he first supported as a boy returned to the top flight after an absence of 19 years by beating Sheffield Utd 3-0. It was also a moment to savour for manager Dave Jones, who was forced to leave his previous club Southampton because of child abuse allegations, which were later found to be groundless. **Cardiff,** away from the game's second tier for 18 years, returned with an extra-time winner from substitute Andy Campbell against QPR after a goalless 90 minutes in the Division Two final. **Bournemouth,** relegated 12 months earlier, became the first team to score five in the end-of-season deciders, beating Lincoln 5-2 in the Division Three Final.

2004: Three tight, tense Finals produced only two goals, the lowest number since the Play-offs were introduced. One of them, scored by Neil Shipperley, gave **Crystal Palace** victory over West Ham, the much-travelled striker tapping in a rebound after Stephen Bywater parried Andy Johnson's shot. It completed a remarkable transformation for Crystal Palace, who were 19th in the table when Iain Dowie left Oldham to become their manager. **Brighton** made an immediate return to Division One in a poor game against Bristol City which looked set for extra-time until Leon Knight netted his 27th goal of the campaign from the penalty spot after 84 minutes. **Huddersfield** also went back up at the first attempt, winning the Division Three Final in a penalty shoot-out after a goalless 120 minutes against Mansfield.

2005: Goals were few and far between for Bobby Zamora during **West Ham**'s Championship season – but what a difference in the Play-offs. The former Brighton and Tottenham striker scored three times in the 4-2 aggregate win over Ipswich in the semi-finals and was on the mark again with the only goal against Preston at the Millennium Stadium. **Sheffield Wed** were eight minute away from defeat against Hartlepool in the League One decider when Steven MacLean made it 2-2 from the penalty spot and they went on to win 4-2 in extra-time. **Southend**, edged out of an automatic promotion place, won the League Two Final 2-0 against Lincoln, Freddy Eastwood scoring their first in extra-time and making the second for Duncan Jupp. **Carlisle** beat Stevenage 1-0 with a goal by Peter Murphy in the Conference Final to regain their League place 12 months after being relegated.

2006: From the moment Marlon King scored his 22nd goal of the season to set up a 3-0 win over Crystal Palace in the semi-final first leg, **Watford** had the conviction of a team going places. Sure enough, they went on to beat Leeds just as comfortably in the final. Jay DeMerit, who was playing non-league football 18 months earlier, headed his side in front. James Chambers fired in a shot that hit a post and went in off goalkeeper Neil Sullivan. Then Darius Henderson put away a penalty after King was brought down by Shaun Derry, the man whose tackle had ended Boothroyd's playing career at the age of 26. **Barnsley** beat Swansea on penalties in the League One Final, Nick Colgan making the vital save from Alan Tate, while Steve Guinan's goal earned **Cheltenham** a 1-0 win over Grimsby in the League Two Final. **Hereford** returned to the Football League after a nine-year absence with Ryan Green's extra-time winner against Halifax in the Conference Final.

2007: Record crowds, plenty of goals and a return to Wembley for the finals made for some eventful and entertaining matches. Stephen Pearson, signed from Celtic for £650,000 in the January transfer window, took **Derby** back to the Premier League after an absence of five seasons with a 61st minute winner, his first goal for the club, against accounted for West Bromwich Albion. It was third time lucky for manager Billy Davies, who had led Preston into the play-offs, without success, in the two previous seasons. **Blackpool** claimed a place in the game's second tier for the first time for 30 years by beating Yeovil 2-0 – their tenth successive victory in a remarkable end-of-season run. Richard Walker took his tally for the season to 23 with two goals for **Bristol Rov**, who beat Shrewsbury 3-1 in the League Two Final. Sammy McIlroy, who led Macclesfield into the league in 1997, saw his Morecambe side fall behind in the Conference Final against Exeter, but they recovered to win 2-1.

2008: Wembley has produced some unlikely heroes down the years, but rarely one to match 39-year-old Dean Windass. The **Hull** striker took his home-town club into the top-flight for the first time with the only goal of the Championship Final against Bristol City – and it was a goal fit to grace any game. In front of a record crowd for the final of 86,703, Fraizer Campbell, his 20-year-old partner up front, picked out Windass on the edge of the penalty box and a sweetly-struck volley flew into the net. **Doncaster**, who like Hull faced an uncertain future a few years earlier, beat Leeds 1-0 in the League One Final with a header by James Hayter from Brian Stock's corner. Jim Gannon had lost four Wembley finals with **Stockport** as a player, but his first as manager brought a 3-2 win against Rochdale in the League Two Final with goals by Anthony

Pilkington and Liam Dickinson and a Nathan Stanton own goal. Exeter's 1-0 win over Cambridge United in the Conference Final took them back into the Football League after an absence of five years.

2009: Delight for Burnley, back in the big time after 33 years thanks to a fine goal from 20 yards by Wade Elliott, and for their town which became the smallest to host Premier League football. Despair for Sheffield Utd, whose bid to regain a top-flight place ended with two players, Jamie Ward and Lee Hendrie, sent off by referee Mike Dean. Martyn Woolford capped a man-of-the-match performance with an 85th minute winner for Scunthorpe, who beat Millwall 3-2 to make an immediate return to the Championship, Matt Sparrow having scored their first two goals. Gillingham also went back up at the first attempt, beating Shrewsbury with Simeon Jackson's header seconds from the end of normal time in the League Two Final. Torquay returned to the Football League after a two-year absence by beating Cambridge United 2-0 in the Conference Final.

2010: Blackpool, under the eccentric yet shrewd Ian Holloway, claimed the big prize two years almost to the day after the manager was sacked from his previous job at Leicester. On a scorching afternoon, with temperatures reaching 106 degrees, they twice came back from a goal down to draw level against Cardiff through Charlie Adam and Gary Taylor-Fletcher, then scored what proved to be the winner through Brett Ormerod at the end of a pulsating first half. **Millwall**, beaten in five previous play-offs, reached the Championship with the only goal of the game against Swindon from captain Paul Robinson. **Dagenham & Redbridge** defeated Rotherham 3-2 in the League Two Final, Jon Nurse scoring the winner 20 minutes from the end. **Oxford** returned to the Football League after an absence of four years with a 3-1 over York in the Conference Final.

LEAGUE PLAY-OFF CROWDS YEAR BY YEAR

YEAR	MATCHES	AGG. ATT
1987	20	310,000
1988	19	305,817
1989	18	234,393
1990	15	291,428
1991	15	266,442
1992	15	277,684
1993	15	319,907
1994	15	314,817
1995	15	295,317
1996	15	308,515
1997	15	309,085
1998	15	320,795
1999	15	372,969
2000	15	333,999
2001	15	317,745
2002	15	327,894
2003	15	374,461
2004	15	388,675
2005	15	353,330
2006	15	340,804
2007	15	405,278 (record)
2008	15	382,032
2009	15	380,329
2010	15	370,055
2011	15	310,998

NATIONAL REFEREES

Adcock, James (Derbys)
Atkinson, Martin (Yorks)
Attwell, Stuart (Warwicks)
Bates, Tony (Staffs)
Berry, Carl (Surrey)
Booth, Russell (Notts)
Boyeson, Carl (Yorks)
Brown, Mark (Yorks)
Clattenburg, Mark (Co Durham)
Collins, Lee (Surrey)
Coote, David (Notts)
Deadman, Darren (Cambs)
Dean, Mike (Wirral)
Dowd, Phil (Staffs)
Drysdale, Darren (Lincs)
D'Urso, Andy (Essex)
East, Roger (Wilts)
Eltringham, Geoff (Tyne & Wear)
Evans, Karl (Lancs)
Foster, David (Tyne & Wear)
Foy, Chris (Merseyside)
Friend, Kevin (Leics)
Gibbs, Phil (West Mids)
Graham, Fred (Essex)
Haines, Andy (Tyne & Wear)
Hall, Andy (West Mids)
Halsey, Mark (Lancs)
Haywood, Mark (Cheshire)
Hegley, Grant (Herts)
Hill, Keith (Herts)
Hooper, Simon (Wilts)
Horwood, Graham (Beds)
Ilderton, Eddie (Tyne & Wear)
Jones, Mike (Cheshire)
Kettle, Trevor (Rutland)
Langford, Oliver (West Mids)
Lewis, Rob (Shrops)
Linington, James (IOW)
Madley, Andrew (Yorks)
Madley, Bobby (Yorks)
Malone, Brendan (Wilts)

Marriner, Andre (West Mids)
Mason, Lee (Lancs)
Mathieson, Scott (Cheshire)
McDermid, Danny (Hants)
Miller, Nigel (Co Durham)
Miller, Pat (Beds)
Mohareb, Dean (Cheshire)
Moss, Jon (Yorks)
Naylor, Michael (Yorks)
Oliver, Michael (Northumberland)
Pawson, Craig (Yorks)
Penn, Andy (West Mids)
Phillips, David (Sussex)
Probert, Lee (Wilts)
Quinn, Peter (Cleveland)
Rushton, Steve (Staffs)
Russell, Mick (Herts)
Salisbury, Graham (Lancs)
Sarginson, Chris (Staffs)
Scott, Graham (Oxon)
Sheldrake, Darren (Surrey)
Shoebridge, Rob (Derbys)
Stroud, Keith (Hants)
Sutton, Gary (Lincs)
Swarbrick, Neil (Lancs)
Tanner, Steve (Somerset))
Taylor, Anthony (Cheshire)
Tierney, Paul (Lancs)
Walton, Peter (Northants)
Ward, Gavin (Surrey)
Waugh, Jock (Yorks)
Webb, David (Co Durham)
Webb, Howard (Yorks)
Webster, Colin (Tyne & Wear)
Whitestone, Dean (Northants)
Williamson, Iain (Berks)
Woolmer, Andy (Northants)
Wright, Kevin (Cambs)

RECORD 22 NATIONALITIES

A Premier League record 22 different nationalities featured in last season's game between Blackburn and West Bromwich Albion at Ewood Park.

Blackburn: Robinson (England), Salgado (Spain) (Hanley, Scotland 75), Samba (Rep Congo), Givet (France), M Olsson (Sweden), Hoilett (Canada), Jones (USA), Dunn (England) (Nzonzi, France 63), Pedersen (Norway), Kalinic (Croatia) (Roberts, Grenada 63), Santa Cruz (Paraguay)
West Brom: Myhill (Wales), Jara (Chile), J Olsson (Sweden), Tamas (Romania), Cech (Slovakia), Brunt (Northern Ireland), Morrison (Scotland) (Bednar (Czech Republic, 75), Mulumbu (DR Congo) (Tchoyi, Cameroon 56), Scharner (Austria), Thomas (England), Odemwingie (Nigeria).

ENGLISH HONOURS LIST

FA PREMIER LEAGUE

	First	Pts	Second	Pts	Third	Pts
1992–3a	Manchester Utd	84	Aston Villa	74	Norwich	72
1993–4a	Manchester Utd	92	Blackburn	84	Newcastle	77
1994–5a	Blackburn	89	Manchester Utd	88	Nottm Forest	77
1995–6b	Manchester Utd	82	Newcastle	78	Liverpool	71
1996–7b	Manchester Utd	75	Newcastle	68	Arsenal	68
1997–8b	Arsenal	78	Manchester Utd	77	Liverpool	65
1998–9b	Manchester Utd	79	Arsenal	78	Chelsea	75
1999–00b	Manchester Utd	91	Arsenal	73	Leeds	69
2000–01b	Manchester Utd	80	Arsenal	70	Liverpool	69
2001–02b	Arsenal	87	Liverpool	80	Manchester Utd	77
2002–03b	Manchester Utd	83	Arsenal	78	Newcastle	69
2003–04b	Arsenal	90	Chelsea	79	Manchester Utd	75
2004–05b	Chelsea	95	Arsenal	83	Manchester Utd	77
2005–06b	Chelsea	91	Manchester Utd	83	Liverpool	82
2006–07b	Manchester Utd	89	Chelsea	83	Liverpool	68
2007–08b	Manchester Utd	87	Chelsea	85	Arsenal	83
2008–09b	Manchester Utd	90	Liverpool	86	Chelsea	83
2009–10b	Chelsea	86	Manchester Utd	85	Arsenal	75
2010–11b	Manchester Utd	80	Chelsea	71	Manchester City	71

Maximum points: a, 126; b, 114

FOOTBALL LEAGUE

FIRST DIVISION

1992–3	Newcastle	96	West Ham	88	††Portsmouth	88
1993–4	Crystal Palace	90	Nottm Forest	83	††Millwall	74
1994–5	Middlesbrough	82	††Reading	79	Bolton	77
1995–6	Sunderland	83	Derby	79	††Crystal Palace	75
1996–7	Bolton	98	Barnsley	80	††Wolves	76
1997–8	Nottm Forest	94	Middlesbrough	91	††Sunderland	90
1998–9	Sunderland	105	Bradford City	87	††Ipswich	86
1999–00	Charlton	91	Manchester City	89	Ipswich	87
2000–01	Fulham	101	Blackburn	91	Bolton	87
2001–02	Manchester City	99	WBA	89	††Wolves	86
2002–03	Portsmouth	98	Leicester	92	††Sheffield Utd	80
2003–04	Norwich	94	WBA	86	††Sunderland	79

CHAMPIONSHIP

2004–05	Sunderland	94	Wigan	87	††Ipswich	85
2005–06	Reading	106	Sheffield Utd	90	Watford	81
2006–07	Sunderland	88	Birmingham	86	Derby	84
2007–08	WBA	81	Stoke	79	Hull	75
2008–09	Wolves	90	Birmingham	83	††Sheffield Utd	80
2009–10	Newcastle	102	WBA	91	††Nottm Forest	79
2010–11	QPR	88	Norwich	84	Swansea	80

Maximum points: 138 ††Not promoted after play–offs

SECOND DIVISION

1992–3	Stoke	93	Bolton	90	††Port Vale	89
1993–4	Reading	89	Port Vale	88	††Plymouth Argyle	85
1994–5	Birmingham	89	††Brentford	85	††Crewe	83

1995–6	Swindon	92	Oxford Utd	83	††Blackpool	82
1996–7	Bury	84	Stockport	82	††Luton	78
1997–8	Watford	88	Bristol City	85	Grimsby	72
1998–9	Fulham	101	Walsall	87	Manchester City	82
1999–00	Preston	95	Burnley	88	Gillingham	85
2000–01	Millwall	93	Rotherham	91	††Reading	86
2001–02	Brighton	90	Reading	84	††Brentford	83
2002–03	Wigan	100	Crewe	86	††Bristol City	83
2003–04	Plymouth Argyle	90	QPR	83	††Bristol City	82

LEAGUE ONE

2004–05	Luton	98	Hull	86	††Tranmere	79
2005–06	Southend	82	Colchester	79	††Brentford	76
2006–07	Scunthorpe	91	Bristol City	85	Blackpool	83
2007-08	Swansea	92	Nottm Forest	82	Doncaster	80
2008-09	Leicester	96	Peterborough	89	††MK Dons	87
2009-10	Norwich	95	Leeds	86	Millwall	85
2010-11	Brighton	95	Southampton	92	††Huddersfield	87

Maximum points: 138 †† Not promoted after play–offs

THIRD DIVISION

1992–3a	Cardiff	83	Wrexham	80	Barnet	79
1993–4a	Shrewsbury	79	Chester	74	Crewe	73
1994–5a	Carlisle	91	Walsall	83	Chesterfield	81
1995–6b	Preston	86	Gillingham	83	Bury	79
1996–7b	Wigan	87	Fulham	87	Carlisle	84
1997–8b	Notts Co	99	Macclesfield	82	Lincoln	75
1998–9b	Brentford	85	Cambridge Utd	81	Cardiff	80
1999–00b	Swansea	85	Rotherham	84	Northampton	82
2000–01b	Brighton	92	Cardiff	82	*Chesterfield	80
2001–02b	Plymouth Argyle	102	Luton	97	Mansfield	79
2002–03b	Rushden & D	87	Hartlepool Utd	85	Wrexham	84
2003–04b	Doncaster	92	Hull	88	Torquay	81

* Deducted 9 points for financial irregularities

LEAGUE TWO

2004–05b	Yeovil	83	Scunthorpe	80	Swansea	80
2005–06b	Carlisle	86	Northampton	83	Leyton Orient	81
2006–07b	Walsall	89	Hartlepool	88	Swindon	85
2007–08b	MK Dons	97	Peterborough	92	Hereford	88
2008–09b	Brentford	85	Exeter	79	Wycombe	78
2009–10b	Notts Co	93	Bournemouth	83	Rochdale	82
2010–11b	Chesterfield	86	Bury	81	Wycombe 80	

Maximum points: a, 126; b, 138;

FOOTBALL LEAGUE 1888–1992

1888–89a	Preston	40	Aston Villa	29	Wolves	28
1889–90a	Preston	33	Everton	31	Blackburn	27
1890–1a	Everton	29	Preston	27	Notts Co	26
1891–2b	Sunderland	42	Preston	37	Bolton	36

OLD FIRST DIVISION

1892–3c	Sunderland	48	Preston	37	Everton	36
1893–4c	Aston Villa	44	Sunderland	38	Derby	36
1894–5c	Sunderland	47	Everton	42	Aston Villa	39

Season	First		Second		Third	
1895–6c	Aston Villa	45	Derby	41	Everton	39
1896–7c	Aston Villa	47	Sheffield Utd	36	Derby	36
1897–8c	Sheffield Utd	42	Sunderland	39	Wolves	35
1898–9d	Aston Villa	45	Liverpool	43	Burnley	39
1899–1900d	Aston Villa	50	Sheffield Utd	48	Sunderland	41
1900–1d	Liverpool	45	Sunderland	43	Notts Co	40
1901–2d	Sunderland	44	Everton	41	Newcastle	37
1902–3d	The Wednesday	42	Aston Villa	41	Sunderland	41
1903–4d	The Wednesday	47	Manchester City	44	Everton	43
1904–5d	Newcastle	48	Everton	47	Manchester City	46
1905–6e	Liverpool	51	Preston	47	The Wednesday	44
1906–7e	Newcastle	51	Bristol City	48	Everton	45
1907–8e	Manchester Utd	52	Aston Villa	43	Manchester City	43
1908–9e	Newcastle	53	Everton	46	Sunderland	44
1909–10e	Aston Villa	53	Liverpool	48	Blackburn	45
1910–11e	Manchester Utd	52	Aston Villa	51	Sunderland	45
1911–12e	Blackburn	49	Everton	46	Newcastle	44
1912–13e	Sunderland	54	Aston Villa	50	Sheffield Wed	49
1913–14e	Blackburn	51	Aston Villa	44	Middlesbrough	43
1914–15e	Everton	46	Oldham	45	Blackburn	43
1919–20f	WBA	60	Burnley	51	Chelsea	49
1920–1f	Burnley	59	Manchester City	54	Bolton	52
1921–2f	Liverpool	57	Tottenham	51	Burnley	49
1922–3f	Liverpool	60	Sunderland	54	Huddersfield	53
1923–4f	*Huddersfield	57	Cardiff	57	Sunderland	53
1924–5f	Huddersfield	58	WBA	56	Bolton	55
1925–6f	Huddersfield	57	Arsenal	52	Sunderland	48
1926–7f	Newcastle	56	Huddersfield	51	Sunderland	49
1927–8f	Everton	53	Huddersfield	51	Leicester	48
1928–9f	Sheffield Wed	52	Leicester	51	Aston Villa	50
1929–30f	Sheffield Wed	60	Derby	50	Manchester City	47
1930–1f	Arsenal	66	Aston Villa	59	Sheffield Wed	52
1931–2f	Everton	56	Arsenal	54	Sheffield Wed	50
1932–3f	Arsenal	58	Aston Villa	54	Sheffield Wed	51
1933–4f	Arsenal	59	Huddersfield	56	Tottenham	49
1934–5f	Arsenal	58	Sunderland	54	Sheffield Wed	49
1935–6f	Sunderland	56	Derby	48	Huddersfield	48
1936–7f	Manchester City	57	Charlton	54	Arsenal	52
1937–8f	Arsenal	52	Wolves	51	Preston	49
1938–9f	Everton	59	Wolves	55	Charlton	50
1946–7f	Liverpool	57	Manchester Utd	56	Wolves	56
1947–8f	Arsenal	59	Manchester Utd	52	Burnley	52
1948–9f	Portsmouth	58	Manchester Utd	53	Derby	53
1949–50f	*Portsmouth	53	Wolves	53	Sunderland	52
1950–1f	Tottenham	60	Manchester Utd	56	Blackpool	50
1951–2f	Manchester Utd	57	Tottenham	53	Arsenal	53
1952–3f	*Arsenal	54	Preston	54	Wolves	51
1953–4f	Wolves	57	WBA	53	Huddersfield	51
1954–5f	Chelsea	52	Wolves	48	Portsmouth	48
1955–6f	Manchester Utd	60	Blackpool	49	Wolves	49
1956–7f	Manchester Utd	64	Tottenham	56	Preston	56
1957–8f	Wolves	64	Preston	59	Tottenham	51
1958–9f	Wolves	61	Manchester Utd	55	Arsenal	50
1959–60f	Burnley	55	Wolves	54	Tottenham	53

1960–1 f	Tottenham	66	Sheffield Wed	58	Wolves	57
1961–2 f	Ipswich	56	Burnley	53	Tottenham	52
1962–3 f	Everton	61	Tottenham	55	Burnley	54
1963–4 f	Liverpool	57	Manchester Utd	53	Everton	52
1964–5 f	*Manchester Utd	61	Leeds	61	Chelsea	56
1965–6 f	Liverpool	61	Leeds	55	Burnley	55
1966–7 f	Manchester Utd	60	Nottm Forest	56	Tottenham	56
1967–8 f	Manchester City	58	Manchester Utd	56	Liverpool	55
1968–9 f	Leeds	67	Liverpool	61	Everton	57
1969–70 f	Everton	66	Leeds	57	Chelsea	55
1970–1 f	Arsenal	65	Leeds	64	Tottenham	52
1971–2 f	Derby	58	Leeds	57	Liverpool	57
1972–3 f	Liverpool	60	Arsenal	57	Leeds	53
1973–4 f	Leeds	62	Liverpool	57	Derby	48
1974–5 f	Derby	53	Liverpool	51	Ipswich	51
1975–6 f	Liverpool	60	QPR	59	Manchester Utd	56
1976–7 f	Liverpool	57	Manchester City	56	Ipswich	52
1977–8 f	Nottm Forest	64	Liverpool	57	Everton	55
1978–9 f	Liverpool	68	Nottm Forest	60	WBA	59
1979–80 f	Liverpool	60	Manchester Utd	58	Ipswich	53
1980–1 f	Aston Villa	60	Ipswich	56	Arsenal	53
1981–2 g	Liverpool	87	Ipswich	83	Manchester Utd	78
1982–3 g	Liverpool	82	Watford	71	Manchester Utd	70
1983–4 g	Liverpool	80	Southampton	77	Nottm Forest	74
1984–5 g	Everton	90	Liverpool	77	Tottenham	77
1985–6 g	Liverpool	88	Everton	86	West Ham	84
1986–7 g	Everton	86	Liverpool	77	Tottenham	71
1987–8 h	Liverpool	90	Manchester Utd	81	Nottm Forest	73
1988–9 j	††Arsenal	76	Liverpool	76	Nottm Forest	64
1989–90 j	Liverpool	79	Aston Villa	70	Tottenham	63
1990–1 j	Arsenal	83	Liverpool	76	Crystal Palace	69
1991–2 g	Leeds	82	Manchester Utd	78	Sheffield Wed	75

Maximum points: a, 44; b, 52; c, 60; d, 68; e, 76; f, 84; g, 126; h, 120; j, 114
*Won on goal average †Won on goal diff ††Won on goals scored No comp 1915–19 –1939–46

OLD SECOND DIVISION 1892–1992

1892–3 a	Small Heath	36	Sheffield Utd	35	Darwen	30
1893–4 b	Liverpool	50	Small Heath	42	Notts Co	39
1894–5 c	Bury	48	Notts Co	39	Newton Heath	38
1895–6 c	*Liverpool	46	Manchester City	46	Grimsby	42
1896–7 c	Notts Co	42	Newton Heath	39	Grimsby	38
1897–8 c	Burnley	48	Newcastle	45	Manchester City	39
1898–9 d	Manchester City	52	Glossop	46	Leicester Fosse	45
1899–1900 d	The Wednesday	54	Bolton	52	Small Heath	46
1900–1 d	Grimsby	49	Small Heath	48	Burnley	44
1901–2 d	WBA	55	Middlesbrough	51	Preston	42
1902–3 d	Manchester City	54	Small Heath	51	Woolwich Arsenal	48
1903–4 d	Preston	50	Woolwich Arsenal	49	Manchester Utd	48
1904–5 d	Liverpool	58	Bolton	56	Manchester Utd	53
1905–6 e	Bristol City	66	Manchester Utd	62	Chelsea	53
1906–7 e	Nottm Forest	60	Chelsea	57	Leicester Fosse	48
1907–8 e	Bradford City	54	Leicester Fosse	52	Oldham	50
1908–9 e	Bolton	52	Tottenham	51	WBA	51
1909–10 e	Manchester City	54	Oldham	53	Hull	53

Season	Team		Team		Team	
1910–11e	WBA	53	Bolton	51	Chelsea	49
1911–12e	*Derby	54	Chelsea	54	Burnley	52
1912–13e	Preston	53	Burnley	50	Birmingham	46
1913–14e	Notts Co	53	Bradford PA	49	Woolwich Arsenal	49
1914–15e	Derby	53	Preston	50	Barnsley	47
1919–20f	Tottenham	70	Huddersfield	64	Birmingham	56
1920–1f	*Birmingham	58	Cardiff	58	Bristol City	51
1921–2f	Nottm Forest	56	Stoke	52	Barnsley	52
1922–3f	Notts Co	53	West Ham	51	Leicester	51
1923–4f	Leeds	54	Bury	51	Derby	51
1924–5f	Leicester	59	Manchester Utd	57	Derby	55
1925–6f	Sheffield Wed	60	Derby	57	Chelsea	52
1926–7f	Middlesbrough	62	Portsmouth	54	Manchester City	54
1927–8f	Manchester City	59	Leeds	57	Chelsea	54
1928–9f	Middlesbrough	55	Grimsby	53	Bradford City	48
1929–30f	Blackpool	58	Chelsea	55	Oldham	53
1930–1f	Everton	61	WBA	54	Tottenham	51
1931–2f	Wolves	56	Leeds	54	Stoke	52
1932–3f	Stoke	56	Tottenham	55	Fulham	50
1933–4f	Grimsby	59	Preston	52	Bolton	51
1934–5f	Brentford	61	Bolton	56	West Ham	56
1935–6f	Manchester Utd	56	Charlton	55	Sheffield Utd	52
1936–7f	Leicester	5o	Blackpool	55	Bury	52
1937–8f	Aston Villa	57	Manchester Utd	53	Sheffield Utd	53
1938–9f	Blackburn	55	Sheffield Utd	54	Sheffield Wed	53
1946–7f	Manchester City	62	Burnley	58	Birmingham	55
1947–8f	Birmingham	59	Newcastle	56	Southampton	52
1948–9f	Fulham	57	WBA	56	Southampton	55
1949–50f	Tottenham	61	Sheffield Wed	52	Sheffield Utd	52
1950–1f	Preston	57	Manchester City	52	Cardiff	50
1951–2f	Sheffield Wed	53	Cardiff	51	Birmingham	51
1952–3f	Sheffield Utd	60	Huddersfield	58	Luton	52
1953–4f	*Leicester	56	Everton	56	Blackburn	55
1954–5f	*Birmingham	54	Luton	54	Rotherham	54
1955–6f	Sheffield Wed	55	Leeds	52	Liverpool	48
1956–7f	Leicester	61	Nottm Forest	54	Liverpool	53
1957–8f	West Ham	57	Blackburn	56	Charlton	55
1958–9f	Sheffield Wed	62	Fulham	60	Sheffield Utd	53
1959–60f	Aston Villa	59	Cardiff	58	Liverpool	50
1960–1f	Ipswich	59	Sheffield Utd	58	Liverpool	52
1961–2f	Liverpool	62	Leyton Orient	54	Sunderland	53
1962–3f	Stoke	53	Chelsea	52	Sunderland	52
1963–4f	Leeds	63	Sunderland	61	Preston	56
1964–5f	Newcastle	57	Northampton	56	Bolton	50
1965–6f	Manchester City	59	Southampton	54	Coventry	53
1966–7f	Coventry	59	Wolves	58	Carlisle	52
1967–8f	Ipswich	59	QPR	58	Blackpool	58
1968–9f	Derby	63	Crystal Palace	56	Charlton	50
1969–70f	Huddersfield	60	Blackpool	53	Leicester	51
1970–1f	Leicester	59	Sheffield Utd	56	Cardiff	53
1971–2f	Norwich	57	Birmingham	56	Millwall	55
1972–3f	Burnley	62	QPR	61	Aston Villa	50
1973–4f	Middlesbrough	65	Luton	50	Carlisle	49
1974–5f	Manchester Utd	61	Aston Villa	58	Norwich	53

1975–6 *f*	Sunderland	56	Bristol City	53	WBA	53
1976–7 *f*	Wolves	57	Chelsea	55	Nottm Forest	52
1977–8 *f*	Bolton	58	Southampton	57	Tottenham	56
1978–9 *f*	Crystal Palace	57	Brighton	56	Stoke	56
1979–80 *f*	Leicester	55	Sunderland	54	Birmingham	53
1980–1 *f*	West Ham	66	Notts Co	53	Swansea	50
1981–2 *g*	Luton	88	Watford	80	Norwich	71
1982–3 *g*	QPR	85	Wolves	75	Leicester	70
1983–4 *g*	†Chelsea	88	Sheffield Wed	88	Newcastle	80
1984–5 *g*	Oxford Utd	84	Birmingham	82	Manchester City	74
1985–6 *g*	Norwich	84	Charlton	77	Wimbledon	76
1986–7 *g*	Derby	84	Portsmouth	78	††Oldham	75
1987–8 *h*	Millwall	82	Aston Villa	78	Middlesbrough	78
1988–9 *j*	Chelsea	99	Manchester City	82	Crystal Palace	81
1989–90 *j*	†Leeds	85	Sheffield Utd	85	†† Newcastle	80
1990–1 *j*	Oldham	88	West Ham	87	Sheffield Wed	82
1991–2 *j*	Ipswich	84	Middlesbrough	80	†† Derby	78

Maximum points: *a*, 44; *b*, 56; *c*, 60; *d*, 68; *e*, 76; *f*, 84; *g*, 126; *h*, 132; *j*, 138 * Won on goal average † Won on goal difference †† Not promoted after play–offs

THIRD DIVISION 1958–92

1958–9	Plymouth Argyle	62	Hull	61	Brentford	57
1959–60	Southampton	61	Norwich	59	Shrewsbury	52
1960–1	Bury	68	Walsall	62	QPR	60
1961–2	Portsmouth	65	Grimsby	62	Bournemouth	59
1962–3	Northampton	62	Swindon	58	Port Vale	54
1963–4	*Coventry	60	Crystal Palace	60	Watford	58
1964–5	Carlisle	60	Bristol City	59	Mansfield	59
1965–6	Hull	69	Millwall	65	QPR	57
1966–7	QPR	67	Middlesbrough	55	Watford	54
1967–8	Oxford Utd	57	Bury	56	Shrewsbury	55
1968–9	*Watford	64	Swindon	64	Luton	61
1969–70	Orient	62	Luton	60	Bristol Rov	56
1970–1	Preston	61	Fulham	60	Halifax	56
1971–2	Aston Villa	70	Brighton	65	Bournemouth	62
1972–3	Bolton	61	Notts Co	57	Blackburn	55
1973–4	Oldham	62	Bristol Rov	61	York	61
1974–5	Blackburn	60	Plymouth Argyle	59	Charlton	55
1975–6	Hereford	63	Cardiff	57	Millwall	56
1976–7	Mansfield	64	Brighton	61	Crystal Palace	59
1977–8	Wrexham	61	Cambridge Utd	58	Preston	56
1978–9	Shrewsbury	61	Watford	60	Swansea	60
1979–80	Grimsby	62	Blackburn	59	Sheffield Wed	58
1980–1	Rotherham	61	Barnsley	59	Charlton	59
†1981–2	**Burnley	80	Carlisle	80	Fulham	78
†1982–3	Portsmouth	91	Cardiff	86	Huddersfield	82
†1983–4	Oxford Utd	95	Wimbledon	87	Sheffield Utd	83
†1984–5	Bradford City	94	Millwall	90	Hull	87
†1985–6	Reading	94	Plymouth Argyle	87	Derby	84
†1986–7	Bournemouth	97	Middlesbrough	94	Swindon	87
†1987–8	Sunderland	93	Brighton	84	Walsall	82
†1988–9	Wolves	92	Sheffield Utd	84	Port Vale	84
†1989–90	Bristol Rov	93	Bristol City	91	Notts Co	87
†1990–1	Cambridge Utd	86	Southend	85	Grimsby	83
†1991–2	Brentford	82	Birmingham	81	††Huddersfield	78

* Won on goal average ** Won on goal difference † Maximum points 138 (previously 92) †† Not promoted after play–offs

FOURTH DIVISION 1958–92

1958–9	Port Vale 64	Coventry 60	York 60	Shrewsbury 58
1959–60	Walsall 65	Notts Co 60	Torquay 60	Watford 57
1960–1	Peterborough 66	Crystal Palace 64	Northampton 60	Bradford PA 60
1961–2	Millwall 56	Colchester 55	Wrexham 53	Carlisle 52
1962–3	Brentford 62	Oldham 59	Crewe 59	Mansfield 57
1963–4	*Gillingham 60	Carlisle 60	Workington 59	Exeter 58
1964–5	Brighton 63	Millwall 62	York 62	Oxford Utd 61
1965–6	*Doncaster 59	Darlington 59	Torquay 58	Colchester 56
1966–7	Stockport 64	Southport 59	Barrow 59	Tranmere 58
1967–8	Luton 66	Barnsley 61	Hartlepool Utd 60	Crewe 58
1968–9	Doncaster 59	Halifax 57	Rochdale 56	Bradford City 56
1969–70	Chesterfield 64	Wrexham 61	Swansea 60	Port Vale 59
1970–1	Notts Co 69	Bournemouth 60	Oldham 59	York 56
1971–2	Grimsby 63	Southend 60	Brentford 59	Scunthorpe 57
1972–3	Southport 62	Hereford 58	Cambridge Utd 57	Aldershot 56
1973–4	Peterborough 65	Gillingham 62	Colchester 60	Bury 59
1974–5	Mansfield 68	Shrewsbury 62	Rotherham 58	Chester 57
1975–6	Lincoln 74	Northampton 68	Reading 60	Tranmere 58
1976–7	Cambridge Utd 65	Exeter 62	Colchester 59	Bradford City 59
1977–8	Watford 71	Southend 60	Swansea 56	Brentford 59
1978–9	Reading 65	Grimsby 61	Wimbledon 61	Barnsley 61
1979–80	Huddersfield 66	Walsall 64	Newport 61	Portsmouth 60
1980–1	Southend 67	Lincoln 65	Doncaster 56	Wimbledon 56
†1981–2	Sheffield Utd 96	Bradford City 91	Wigan 91	Bournemouth 88
†1982–3	Wimbledon 98	Hull 90	Port Vale 88	Scunthorpe 83
†1983–4	York 101	Doncaster 85	Reading 82	Bristol City 82
†1984–5	Chesterfield 91	Blackpool 86	Darlington 85	Bury 84
†1985–6	Swindon 102	Chester 84	Mansfield 81	Port Vale 79
†1986–7	Northampton 99	Preston 90	Southend 80	††Wolves 79
†1987–8	Wolves 90	Cardiff 85	Bolton 78	††Scunthorpe 77
†1988–9	Rotherham 82	Tranmere 80	Crewe 78	††Scunthorpe 77
†1989–90	Exeter 89	Grimsby 79	Southend 75	††Stockport 74
†1990–1	Darlington 83	Stockport 82	Hartlepool Utd 82	Peterborough 80
1991–2a	Burnley 83	Rotherham 77	Mansfield 77	Blackpool 76

* Won on goal average Maximum points: †, 138; a, 126; previously 92 †† Not promoted after play-offs

THIRD DIVISION – SOUTH 1920–58

1920–1a	Crystal Palace 59	Southampton 54	QPR 53
1921–2a	*Southampton 61	Plymouth Argyle 61	Portsmouth 53
1922–3a	Bristol City 59	Plymouth Argyle 53	Swansea 53
1923–4a	Portsmouth 59	Plymouth Argyle 55	Millwall 54
1924–5a	Swansea 57	Plymouth Argyle 56	Bristol City 53
1925–6a	Reading 57	Plymouth Argyle 56	Millwall 53
1926–7a	Bristol City 62	Plymouth Argyle 60	Millwall 56
1927–8a	Millwall 65	Northampton 55	Plymouth Argyle 53
1928–9a	*Charlton 54	Crystal Palace 54	Northampton 52
1929–30a	Plymouth Argyle 68	Brentford 61	QPR 51
1930–31a	Notts Co 59	Crystal Palace 51	Brentford 50
1931–2a	Fulham 57	Reading 55	Southend 53
1932–3a	Brentford 62	Exeter 58	Norwich 57
1933–4a	Norwich 61	Coventry 54	Reading 54
1934–5a	Charlton 61	Reading 53	Coventry 51
1935–6a	Coventry 57	Luton 56	Reading 54
1936–7a	Luton 58	Notts Co 56	Brighton 53
1937–8a	Millwall 56	Bristol City 55	QPR 53

1938–9a	Newport	55	Crystal Palace	52	Brighton	49
1946–7a	Cardiff	66	QPR	57	Bristol City	51
1947–8a	QPR	61	Bournemouth	57	Walsall	51
1948–9a	Swansea	62	Reading	55	Bournemouth	52
1949–50a	Notts Co	58	Northampton	51	Southend	51
1950–1d	Nottm Forest	70	Norwich	64	Reading	57
1951–2d	Plymouth Argyle	66	Reading	61	Norwich	61
1952–3d	Bristol Rov	64	Millwall	62	Northampton	62
1953–4d	Ipswich	64	Brighton	61	Bristol City	56
1954–5d	Bristol City	70	Leyton Orient	61	Southampton	59
1955–6d	Leyton Orient	66	Brighton	65	Ipswich	64
1956–7d	*Ipswich	59	Torquay	59	Colchester	58
1957–8d	Brighton	60	Brentford	58	Plymouth Argyle	58

THIRD DIVISION – NORTH 1921–58

1921–2b	Stockport	56	Darlington	50	Grimsby	50
1922–3b	Nelson	51	Bradford PA	47	Walsall	46
1923–4a	Wolves	63	Rochdale	62	Chesterfield	54
1924–5a	Darlington	58	Nelson	53	New Brighton	53
1925–6a	Grimsby	61	Bradford PA	60	Rochdale	59
1926–7a	Stoke	63	Rochdale	58	Bradford PA	57
1927–8a	Bradford PA	63	Lincoln	55	Stockport	54
1928–9a	Bradford City	63	Stockport	62	Wrexham	52
1929–30a	Port Vale	67	Stockport	63	Darlington	50
1930–1a	Chesterfield	58	Lincoln	57	Wrexham	54
1931–2c	*Lincoln	57	Gateshead	57	Chester	50
1932–3a	Hull	59	Wrexham	57	Stockport	54
1933–4a	Barnsley	62	Chesterfield	61	Stockport	59
1934–5a	Doncaster	57	Halifax	55	Chester	54
1935–6a	Chesterfield	60	Chester	55	Tranmere	54
1936–7a	Stockport	60	Lincoln	57	Chester	53
1937–8a	Tranmere	56	Doncaster	54	Hull	53
1938–9a	Barnsley	67	Doncaster	56	Bradford City	52
1946–7a	Doncaster	72	Rotherham	64	Chester	56
1947–8a	Lincoln	60	Rotherham	59	Wrexham	50
1948–9a	Hull	65	Rotherham	62	Doncaster	50
1949–50a	Doncaster	55	Gateshead	53	Rochdale	51
1950–1d	Rotherham	71	Mansfield	64	Carlisle	62
1951–2d	Lincoln	69	Grimsby	66	Stockport	59
1952–3d	Oldham	59	Port Vale	58	Wrexham	56
1953–4d	Port Vale	69	Barnsley	58	Scunthorpe	57
1954–5d	Barnsley	65	Accrington	61	Scunthorpe	58
1955–6d	Grimsby	68	Derby	63	Accrington	59
1956–7d	Derby	63	Hartlepool Utd	59	Accrington	58
1957–8d	Scunthorpe	66	Accrington	59	Bradford City	57

Maximum points: a, 84; b, 76; c, 80; d, 92 * Won on goal average

TITLE WINNERS

FA PREMIER LEAGUE

Manchester Utd	12
Arsenal	3
Chelsea	3
Blackburn	1

FOOTBALL LEAGUE CHAMPIONSHIP

Sunderland	2
Newcastle	1
QPR	1
Reading	1
WBA	1
Wolves	1

DIV 1 (NEW)

Sunderland	2
Bolton	1
Brighton	1
Charlton	1
Crystal Palace	1
Fulham	1
Manchester City	1

Middlesbrough 1
Newcastle 1
Norwich 1
Nottm Forest 1
Portsmouth 1

DIV 1 (ORIGINAL)

Liverpool 18
Arsenal 10
Everton 9
Aston Villa 7
Manchester Utd 7
Sunderland 6
Newcastle 4
Sheffield Wed 4
Huddersfield 3
Leeds 3
Wolves 3
Blackburn 2
Burnley 2
Derby 2
Manchester City 2
Portsmouth 2
Preston 2
Tottenham 2
Chelsea 1
Ipswich 1
Nottm Forest 1
Sheffield Utd 1
WBA 1

LEAGUE ONE

Brighton 1
Leicester 1
Luton 1
Norwich 1
Scunthorpe 1

Southend 1
Swansea 1

DIV 2 (NEW)

Birmingham 1
Brighton 1
Bury 1
Chesterfield 1
Fulham 1
Millwall 1
Plymouth Argyle 1
Preston 1
Reading 1
Stoke 1
Swindon 1
Watford 1
Wigan 1
Notts Co 1

DIV 2 (ORIGINAL)

Leicester 6
Manchester City 6
Sheffield Wed 5
Birmingham 4
Derby 4
Liverpool 4
Ipswich 3
Leeds 3
Middlesbrough 3
Notts County 3
Preston 3
Aston Villa 2
Bolton 2
Burnley 2
Chelsea 2
Grimsby 2

Manchester Utd 2
Norwich 2
Nottm Forest 2
Stoke 2
Tottenham 2
WBA 2
West Ham 2
Wolves 2
Blackburn 1
Blackpool 1
Bradford City 1
Brentford 1
Bristol City 1
Bury 1
Coventry 1
Crystal Palace 1
Everton 1
Fulham 1
Huddersfield 1
Luton 1
Millwall 1
Newcastle 1
Oldham 1
Oxford Utd 1
QPR 1
Sheffield Utd 1
Sunderland 1

LEAGUE TWO

Brentford 1
Carlisle 1
Chesterfield 1
MK Dons 1
Notts County 1
Walsall 1
Yeovil 1

APPLICATIONS FOR RE-ELECTION (System discontinued 1987)

14	Hartlepool	4	Norwich	2	Oldham
12	Halifax	3	Aldershot	2	QPR
11	Barrow	3	Bradford City	2	Rotherham
11	Southport	3	Crystal Palace	2	Scunthorpe
10	Crewe	3	Doncaster	2	Southend
10	Newport	3	Hereford	2	Watford
10	Rochdale	3	Merthyr	1	Blackpool
8	Darlington	3	Swindon	1	Brighton
8	Exeter	3	Torquay	1	Bristol Rov
7	Chester	3	Tranmere	1	Cambridge Utd
7	Walsall	2	Aberdare	1	Cardiff
7	Workington	2	Ashington	1	Carlisle
7	York	2	Bournemouth	1	Charlton
6	Stockport	2	Brentford	1	Mansfield
5	Accrington	2	Colchester	1	Port Vale
5	Gillingham	2	Durham	1	Preston
5	Lincoln	2	Gateshead	1	Shrewsbury
5	New Brighton	2	Grimsby	1	Swansea
4	Bradford PA	2	Millwall	1	Thames
4	Northampton	2	Nelson	1	Wrexham

RELEGATED CLUBS (TO 1992)

1892–3	In Test matches, Darwen and Sheffield Utd won promotion in place of Accrington and Notts Co
1893–4	Tests, Liverpool and Small Heath won promotion Darwen and Newton Heath relegated
1894–5	After Tests, Bury promoted, Liverpool relegated
1895–6	After Tests, Liverpool promoted, Small Heath relegated
1896–7	After Tests, Notts Co promoted, Burnley relegated
1897–8	Test system abolished after success of Burnley and Stoke, League extended Blackburn and

Newcastle elected to First Division
Automatic promotion and relegation introduced

FIRST DIVISION TO SECOND DIVISION

1898–9	Bolton, Sheffield Wed
1899–00	Burnley, Glossop
1900–1	Preston, WBA
1901–2	Small Heath, Manchester City
1902–3	Grimsby, Bolton
1903–4	Liverpool, WBA
1904–5	League extended Bury and Notts Co, two bottom clubs in First Division, re–elected
1905–6	Nottm Forest, Wolves
1906–7	Derby, Stoke
1907–8	Bolton, Birmingham
1908–9	Manchester City, Leicester Fosse
1909–10	Bolton, Chelsea
1910–11	Bristol City, Nottm Forest
1911–12	Preston, Bury
1912–13	Notts Co, Woolwich Arsenal
1913–14	Preston, Derby
1914–15	Tottenham, *Chelsea
1919–20	Notts Co, Sheffield Wed
1920–1	Derby, Bradford PA
1921–2	Bradford City, Manchester Utd
1922–3	Stoke, Oldham
1923–4	Chelsea, Middlesbrough
1924–5	Preston, Nottm Forest
1925–6	Manchester City, Notts Co
1926–7	Leeds, WBA
1927–8	Tottenham, Middlesbrough
1928–9	Bury, Cardiff
1929–30	Burnley, Everton
1930–1	Leeds, Manchester Utd
1931–2	Grimsby, West Ham
1932–3	Bolton, Blackpool
1933–4	Newcastle, Sheffield Utd
1934–5	Leicester, Tottenham
1935–6	Aston Villa, Blackburn
1936–7	Manchester Utd, Sheffield Wed
1937–8	Manchester City, WBA
1938–9	Birmingham, Leicester
1946–7	Brentford, Leeds
1947–8	Blackburn, Grimsby
1948–9	Preston, Sheffield Utd
1949–50	Manchester City, Birmingham
1950–1	Sheffield Wed, Everton
1951–2	Huddersfield, Fulham
1952–3	Stoke, Derby
1953–4	Middlesbrough, Liverpool

1954–5	Leicester, Sheffield Wed
1955–6	Huddersfield, Sheffield Utd
1956–7	Charlton, Cardiff
1957–8	Sheffield Wed, Sunderland
1958–9	Portsmouth, Aston Villa
1959–60	Luton, Leeds
1960–61	Preston, Newcastle
1961–2	Chelsea, Cardiff
1962–3	Manchester City, Leyton Orient
1963–4	Bolton, Ipswich
1964–5	Wolves, Birmingham
1965–6	Northampton, Blackburn
1966–7	Aston Villa, Blackpool
1967–8	Fulham, Sheffield Utd
1968–9	Leicester, QPR
1969–70	Sheffield Wed, Sunderland
1970–1	Burnley, Blackpool
1971–2	Nottm Forest, Huddersfield
1972–3	WBA, Crystal Palace
1973–4	Norwich, Manchester Utd, Southampton
1974–5	Chelsea, Luton, Carlisle
1975–6	Sheffield Utd, Burnley, Wolves
1976–7	Tottenham, Stoke, Sunderland
1977–8	Leicester, West Ham, Newcastle
1978–9	QPR, Birmingham, Chelsea
1979–80	Bristol City, Derby, Bolton
1980–1	Norwich, Leicester, Crystal Palace
1981–2	Leeds, Wolves, Middlesbrough
1982–3	Manchester City, Swansea, Brighton
1983–4	Birmingham, Notts Co, Wolves
1984–5	Norwich, Sunderland, Stoke
1985–6	Ipswich, Birmingham, WBA
1986–7	Leicester, Manchester City, Aston Villa
1987–8	Chelsea**, Portsmouth, Watford, Oxford Utd
1988–9	Middlesbrough, West Ham, Newcastle
1989–90	Sheffield Wed, Charlton, Millwall
1990–1	Sunderland, Derby
1991–2	Luton, Notts Co, West Ham

* Subsequently re-elected to First Division when League extended after the war
** Relegated after play-offs

SECOND DIVISION TO THIRD DIVISION

1920–1	Stockport
1921–2	Bradford City, Bristol City
1922–3	Rotherham, Wolves
1923–4	Nelson, Bristol City
1924–5	Crystal Palace, Coventry
1925–6	Stoke, Stockport
1926–7	Darlington, Bradford City
1927–8	Fulham, South Shields
1928–9	Port Vale, Clapton Orient
1929–30	Hull, Notts County
1930–1	Reading, Cardiff
1931–2	Barnsley, Bristol City
1932–3	Chesterfield, Charlton
1933–4	Millwall, Lincoln
1934–5	Oldham, Notts Co
1935–6	Port Vale, Hull

1936–7	Doncaster, Bradford City
1937–8	Barnsley, Stockport
1938–9	Norwich, Tranmere
1946–7	Swansea, Newport
1947–8	Doncaster, Millwall
1948–9	Nottm Forest, Lincoln
1949–50	Plymouth Argyle, Bradford PA
1950–1	Grimsby, Chesterfield
1951–2	Coventry, QPR
1952–3	Southampton, Barnsley
1953–4	Brentford, Oldham
1954–5	Ipswich, Derby
1955–6	Plymouth Argyle, Hull
1956–7	Port Vale, Bury
1957–8	Doncaster, Notts Co
1958–9	Barnsley, Grimsby
1959–60	Bristol City, Hull
1960–1	Lincoln, Portsmouth
1961–2	Brighton, Bristol Rov
1962–3	Walsall, Luton
1963–4	Grimsby, Scunthorpe
1964–5	Swindon, Swansea
1965–6	Middlesbrough, Leyton Orient
1966–7	Northampton, Bury
1967–8	Plymouth Argyle, Rotherham
1968–9	Fulham, Bury
1969–70	Preston, Aston Villa
1970–1	Blackburn, Bolton
1971–2	Charlton, Watford
1972–3	Huddersfield, Brighton
1973–4	Crystal Palace, Preston, Swindon
1974–5	Millwall, Cardiff, Sheffield Wed
1975–6	Portsmouth, Oxford Utd, York
1976–7	Carlisle, Plymouth Argyle, Hereford
1977–8	Hull, Mansfield, Blackpool
1978–9	Sheffield Utd, Millwall, Blackburn
1979–80	Fulham, Burnley, Charlton
1980–1	Preston, Bristol City, Bristol Rov
1981–2	Cardiff, Wrexham, Orient
1982–3	Rotherham, Burnley, Bolton
1983–4	Derby, Swansea, Cambridge Utd
1984–5	Notts Co, Cardiff, Wolves
1985–6	Carlisle, Middlesbrough, Fulham
1986–7	Sunderland**, Grimsby, Brighton
1987–8	Sheffield Utd**, Reading, Huddersfield
1988–9	Shrewsbury, Birmingham, Walsall
1989–90	Bournemouth, Bradford City, Stoke
1990–1	WBA, Hull
1991–2	Plymouth Argyle, Brighton, Port Vale

** Relegated after play–offs

THIRD DIVISION TO FOURTH DIVISION

1958–9	Rochdale, Notts Co, Doncaster, Stockport
1959–60	Accrington, Wrexham, Mansfield, York
1960–1	Chesterfield, Colchester, Bradford City, Tranmere
1961–2	Newport, Brentford, Lincoln, Torquay
1962–3	Bradford PA, Brighton, Carlisle, Halifax
1963–4	Millwall, Crewe, Wrexham, Notts Co

1964–5	Luton, Port Vale, Colchester, Barnsley
1965–6	Southend, Exeter, Brentford, York
1966–7	Doncaster, Workington, Darlington, Swansea
1967–8	Scunthorpe, Colchester, Grimsby, Peterborough (demoted)
1968–9	Oldham, Crewe, Hartlepool Utd, Northampton
1969–70	Bournemouth, Southport, Barrow, Stockport
1970–1	Gillingham, Doncaster, Bury, Reading
1971–2	Mansfield, Barnsley, Torquay, Bradford City
1972–3	Scunthorpe, Swansea, Brentford, Rotherham
1973–4	Cambridge Utd, Shrewsbury, Rochdale, Southport
1974–5	Bournemouth, Watford, Tranmere, Huddersfield
1975–6	Aldershot, Colchester, Southend, Halifax
1976–7	Reading, Northampton, Grimsby, York
1977–8	Port Vale, Bradford City, Hereford, Portsmouth
1978–9	Peterborough, Walsall, Tranmere, Lincoln
1979–80	Bury, Southend, Mansfield, Wimbledon
1980–1	Sheffield Utd, Colchester, Blackpool, Hull
1981–2	Wimbledon, Swindon, Bristol City, Chester
1982–3	Reading, Wrexham, Doncaster, Chesterfield
1983–4	Scunthorpe, Southend, Port Vale, Exeter
1984–5	Burnley, Orient, Preston, Cambridge Utd
1985–6	Lincoln, Cardiff, Wolves, Swansea
1986–7	Bolton**, Carlisle, Darlington, Newport
1987–8	Doncaster, York, Grimsby, Rotherham**
1988–9	Southend, Chesterfield, Gillingham, Aldershot
1989–90	Cardiff, Northampton, Blackpool, Walsall
1990–1	Crewe, Rotherham, Mansfield
1991–2	Bury, Shrewsbury, Torquay, Darlington

** Relegated after plays–offs

DEMOTED FROM FOURTH DIVISION TO CONFERENCE

1987	Lincoln
1988	Newport
1989	Darlington
1990	Colchester
1991	No demotion
1992	No demotion

DEMOTED FROM THIRD DIVISION TO CONFERENCE

1993	Halifax
1994–6	No demotion
1997	Hereford
1998	Doncaster
1999	Scarborough
2000	Chester
2001	Barnet
2002	Halifax
2003	Exeter, Shrewsbury
2004	Carlisle, York

DEMOTED FROM LEAGUE TWO TO BLUE SQUARE PREMIER LEAGUE

2005	Kidderminster, Cambridge Utd
2006	Oxford Utd, Rushden & Diamonds
2007	Boston, Torquay
2008	Mansfield, Wrexham
2009	Chester Luton
2010	Grimsby, Darlington
2011	Lincoln, Stockport

RELEGATED CLUBS (SINCE 1993)

1993
Premier League to Div 1: Crystal Palace, Middlesbrough, Nottm Forest
Div 1 to Div 2: Brentford, Cambridge Utd, Bristol Rov
Div 2 to Div 3: Preston, Mansfield, Wigan, Chester

1994
Premier League to Div 1: Sheffield Utd, Oldham, Swindon
Div 1 to Div 2: Birmingham, Oxford Utd, Peterborough
Div 2 to Div 3: Fulham, Exeter, Hartlepool Utd, Barnet

1995
Premier League to Div 1: Crystal Palace, Norwich, Leicester, Ipswich
Div 1 to Div 2: Swindon, Burnley, Bristol City, Notts Co
Div 2 to Div 3: Cambridge Utd, Plymouth Argyle, Cardiff, Chester, Leyton Orient

1996
Premier League to Div 1: Manchester City, QPR, Bolton
Div 1 to Div 2: Millwall, Watford, Luton
Div 2 to Div 3: Carlisle, Swansea, Brighton, Hull

1997
Premier League to Div 1: Sunderland, Middlesbrough, Nottm Forest
Div 1 to Div 2: Grimsby, Oldham, Southend
Div 2 to Div 3: Peterborough, Shrewsbury, Rotherham, Notts Co

1998
Premier League to Div 1: Bolton, Barnsley, Crystal Palace
Div 1 to Div 2: Manchester City, Stoke, Reading
Div 2 to Div 3: Brentford, Plymouth Argyle, Carlisle, Southend

1999
Premier League to Div 1: Charlton, Blackburn, Nottm Forest
Div 1 to Div 2: Bury, Oxford Utd, Bristol City
Div 2 to Div 3: York, Northampton, Lincoln, Macclesfield

2000
Premier League to Div 1: Wimbledon, Sheffield Wed, Watford
Div 1 to Div 2: Walsall, Port Vale, Swindon
Div 2 to Div 3: Cardiff, Blackpool, Scunthorpe, Chesterfield

2001
Premier League to Div 1: Manchester City, Coventry, Bradford City
Div 1 to Div 2: Huddersfield, QPR, Tranmere
Div 2 to Div 3: Bristol Rov, Luton, Swansea, Oxford Utd

2002
Premier League to Div 1: Ipswich, Derby, Leicester
Div 1 to Div 2: Crewe, Barnsley, Stockport
Div 2 to Div 3: Bournemouth, Bury, Wrexham, Cambridge Utd

2003
Premier League to Div 1: West Ham, WBA, Sunderland
Div 1 to Div 2: Sheffield Wed, Brighton, Grimsby
Div 2 to Div 3: Cheltenham, Huddersfield, Mansfield, Northampton

2004
Premier League to Div 1: Leicester, Leeds, Wolves
Div 1 to Div 2: Walsall, Bradford City, Wimbledon
Div 2 to Div 3: Grimsby, Rushden & Diamonds, Notts Co, Wycombe

2005
Premier League to Championship: Crystal Palace, Norwich, Southampton
Championship to League 1: Gillingham, Nottm Forest, Rotherham
League 1 to League 2: Torquay, Wrexham, Peterborough, Stockport

2006
Premier League to Championship: Birmingham, WBA, Sunderland
Championship to League 1: Crewe, Millwall, Brighton
League 1 to League 2: Hartlepool Utd, MK Dons, Swindon, Walsall

2007
Premier League to Championship: Sheffield Utd, Charlton, Watford
Championship to League 1: Southend, Luton, Leeds
League 1 to League 2: Chesterfield, Bradford City, Rotherham, Brentford

2008
Premier League to Championship: Reading, Birmingham, Derby
Championship to League 1: Leicester, Scunthorpe, Colchester
League 1 to League 2: Bournemouth, Gillingham, Port Vale, Luton

2009
Premier League to Championship: Newcastle, Middlesbrough, WBA
Championship to League 1: Norwich, Southampton, Charlton
League 1 to League 2: Northampton, Crewe, Cheltenham, Hereford

2010
Premier League to Championship: Burnley, Hull, Portsmouth
Championship to League 1: Sheffield Wed, Plymouth, Peterborough
League 1 to League 2: Gillingham, Wycombe, Southend, Stockport

2011
Premier League to Championship: Birmingham, Blackpool, West Ham
Championship to League 1: Preston, Sheffield Utd, Scunthorpe
League 1 to League 2: Dagenham & Redbridge, Bristol Rov, Plymouth, Swindon

QUOTE/UNQUOTE

'It's not the Yorkshire Ripper I'm signing' – **Harry Redknapp**, Tottenham manager, urges fans to forget that new signing William Gallas used to play for arch-rivals Arsenal.

'Well done to Mr Wenger. It was an honour to come here' – **Ian Holloway**, Blackpool manager, after a 6-0 beating at Arsenal.

'I love this club and felt this was the best way to show my commitment' – **Arsene Wenger**, Arsenal manager, after signing a new three-year contract.

ANNUAL AWARDS

FOOTBALL WRITERS' ASSOCIATION

Footballer of the Year: 1948 Stanley Matthews (Blackpool); 1949 Johnny Carey (Manchester Utd); 1950 Joe Mercer (Arsenal); 1951 Harry Johnston (Blackpool); 1952 Billy Wright (Wolves); 1953 Nat Lofthouse (Bolton); 1954 Tom Finney (Preston); 1955 Don Revie (Manchester City); 1956 Bert Trautmann (Manchester City); 1957 Tom Finney (Preston); 1958 Danny Blanchflower (Tottenham); 1959 Syd Owen (Luton); 1960 Bill Slater (Wolves); 1961 Danny Blanchflower (Tottenham); 1962 Jimmy Adamson (Burnley); 1963 Stanley Matthews (Stoke); 1964 Bobby Moore (West Ham); 1965 Bobby Collins (Leeds); 1966 Bobby Charlton (Manchester Utd); 1967 Jack Charlton (Leeds); 1968 George Best (Manchester Utd); 1969 Tony Book (Manchester City) & Dave Mackay (Derby) – shared; 1970 Billy Bremner (Leeds); 1971 Frank McLintock (Arsenal); 1972 Gordon Banks (Stoke); 1973 Pat Jennings (Tottenham); 1974 Ian Callaghan (Liverpool); 1975 Alan Mullery (Fulham); 1976 Kevin Keegan (Liverpool); 1977 Emlyn Hughes (Liverpool); 1978 Kenny Burns (Nott'm Forest); 1979 Kenny Dalglish (Liverpool); 1980 Terry McDermott (Liverpool); 1981 Frans Thijssen (Ipswich); 1982 Steve Perryman (Tottenham); 1983 Kenny Dalglish (Liverpool); 1984 Ian Rush (Liverpool); 1985 Neville Southall (Everton); 1986 Gary Lineker (Everton); 1987 Clive Allen (Tottenham); 1988 John Barnes (Liverpool); 1989 Steve Nicol (Liverpool); Special award to the Liverpool players for the compassion shown to bereaved families after the Hillsborough Disaster; 1990 John Barnes (Liverpool); 1991 Gordon Strachan (Leeds); 1992 Gary Lineker (Tottenham); 1993 Chris Waddle (Sheffield Wed); 1994 Alan Shearer (Blackburn); 1995 Jurgen Klinsmann (Tottenham); 1996 Eric Cantona (Manchester Utd); 1997 Gianfranco Zola (Chelsea); 1998 Dennis Bergkamp (Arsenal); 1999 David Ginola (Tottenham); 2000 Roy Keane (Manchester Utd); 2001 Teddy Sheringham (Manchester Utd); 2002 Robert Pires (Arsenal); 2003 Thierry Henry (Arsenal); 2004 Thierry Henry (Arsenal); 2005 Frank Lampard (Chelsea); 2006 Thierry Henry (Arsenal); 2007 Cristiano Ronaldo (Manchester Utd); 2008 Cristiano Ronaldo (Manchester Utd); 2009 Steven Gerrard (Liverpool), 2010 Wayne Rooney (Manchester Utd), 2011 Scott Parker (West Ham)

PROFESSIONAL FOOTBALLERS' ASSOCIATION

Player of the Year: 1974 Norman Hunter (Leeds); 1975 Colin Todd (Derby); 1976 Pat Jennings (Tottenham); 1977 Andy Gray (Aston Villa); 1978 Peter Shilton (Nott'm Forest); 1979 Liam Brady (Arsenal); 1980 Terry McDermott (Liverpool); 1981 John Wark (Ipswich); 1982 Kevin Keegan (Southampton); 1983 Kenny Dalglish (Liverpool); 1984 Ian Rush (Liverpool); 1985 Peter Reid (Everton); 1986 Gary Lineker (Everton); 1987 Clive Allen (Tottenham); 1988 John Barnes (Liverpool); 1989 Mark Hughes (Manchester Utd); 1990 David Platt (Aston Villa); 1991 Mark Hughes (Manchester Utd); 1992 Gary Pallister (Manchester Utd); 1993 Paul McGrath (Aston Villa); 1994 Eric Cantona (Manchester Utd); 1995 Alan Shearer (Blackburn); 1996 Les Ferdinand (Newcastle); 1997 Alan Shearer (Newcastle); 1998 Dennis Bergkamp (Arsenal); 1999 David Ginola (Tottenham); 2000 Roy Keane (Manchester Utd); 2001 Teddy Sheringham (Manchester Utd); 2002 Ruud van Nistelrooy (Manchester Utd); 2003 Thierry Henry (Arsenal); 2004 Thierry Henry (Arsenal); 2005 John Terry (Chelsea); 2006 Steven Gerrard (Liverpool); 2007 Cristiano Ronaldo (Manchester Utd); 2008 Cristiano Ronaldo (Manchester Utd); 2009 Ryan Giggs (Manchester Utd); 2010 Wayne Rooney (Manchester Utd), 2011 Gareth Bale (Tottenham)

Young Player of the Year: 1974 Kevin Beattie (Ipswich); 1975 Mervyn Day (West Ham); 1976 Peter Barnes (Manchester City); 1977 Andy Gray (Aston Villa); 1978 Tony Woodcock (Nott'm Forest); 1979 Cyrille Regis (WBA); 1980 Glenn Hoddle (Tottenham); 1981 Gary Shaw (Aston Villa); 1982 Steve Moran (Southampton); 1983 Ian Rush (Liverpool); 1984 Paul Walsh (Luton); 1985 Mark Hughes (Manchester Utd); 1986 Tony Cottee (West Ham); 1987

Tony Adams (Arsenal); **1988** Paul Gascoigne (Newcastle); **1989** Paul Merson (Arsenal); **1990** Matthew Le Tissier (Southampton); **1991** Lee Sharpe (Manchester Utd); **1992** Ryan Giggs (Manchester Utd); **1993** Ryan Giggs (Manchester Utd); **1994** Andy Cole (Newcastle); **1995** Robbie Fowler (Liverpool); **1996** Robbie Fowler (Liverpool); **1997** David Beckham (Manchester Utd); **1998** Michael Owen (Liverpool); **1999** Nicolas Anelka (Arsenal); **2000** Harry Kewell (Leeds); **2001** Steven Gerrard (Liverpool); **2002** Craig Bellamy (Newcastle); **2003** Jermaine Jenas (Newcastle); **2004** Scott Parker (Chelsea); **2005** Wayne Rooney (Manchester Utd); **2006** Wayne Rooney (Manchester Utd); **2007** Cristiano Ronaldo (Manchester Utd); **2008** Cesc Fabregas (Arsenal), **2009** Ashley Young (Aston Villa), **2010** James Milner (Aston Villa), **2011** Jack Wilshere (Arsenal)

Merit Awards: 1974 Bobby Charlton & Cliff Lloyd; **1975** Denis Law; **1976** George Eastham; **1977** Jack Taylor; **1978** Bill Shankly; **1979** Tom Finney; **1980** Sir Matt Busby; **1981** John Trollope; **1982** Joe Mercer; **1983** Bob Paisley; **1984** Bill Nicholson; **1985** Ron Greenwood; **1986** England 1966 World Cup-winning team; **1987** Sir Stanley Matthews; **1988** Billy Bonds; **1989** Nat Lofthouse; **1990** Peter Shilton; **1991** Tommy Hutchison; **1992** Brian Clough; **1993** Manchester Utd, 1968 European Champions; Eusebio; **1994** Billy Bingham; **1995** Gordon Strachan; **1996** Pele; **1997** Peter Beardsley; **1998** Steve Ogrizovic; **1999** Tony Ford; **2000** Gary Mabbutt; **2001** Jimmy Hill; **2002** Niall Quinn; **2003** Sir Bobby Robson; **2004** Dario Gradi; **2005** Shaka Hislop; **2006** George Best; **2007** Sir Alex Ferguson; **2008** Jimmy Armfield; **2009** John McDermott, **2010** Lucas Radebe, **2011** Howard Webb

MANAGER OF THE YEAR (1)
(Chosen by a panel from the governing bodies, media and fans)

1966 Jock Stein (Celtic); **1967** Jock Stein (Celtic); **1968** Matt Busby (Manchester Utd); **1969** Don Revie (Leeds); **1970** Don Revie (Leeds); **1971** Bertie Mee (Arsenal); **1972** Don Revie (Leeds); **1973** Bill Shankly (Liverpool); **1974** Jack Charlton (Middlesbrough); **1975** Ron Saunders (Aston Villa); **1976** Bob Paisley (Liverpool); **1977** Bob Paisley (Liverpool); **1978** Brian Clough (Nott'm Forest); **1979** Bob Paisley (Liverpool); **1980** Bob Paisley (Liverpool); **1981** Ron Saunders (Aston Villa); **1982** Bob Paisley (Liverpool); **1983** Bob Paisley (Liverpool); **1984** Joe Fagan (Liverpool); **1985** Howard Kendall (Everton); **1986** Kenny Dalglish (Liverpool); **1987** Howard Kendall (Everton); **1988** Kenny Dalglish (Liverpool); **1989** George Graham (Arsenal); **1990** Kenny Dalglish (Liverpool); **1991** George Graham (Arsenal); **1992** Howard Wilkinson (Leeds); **1993** Alex Ferguson (Manchester Utd); **1994** Alex Ferguson (Manchester Utd); **1995** Kenny Dalglish (Blackburn); **1996** Alex Ferguson (Manchester Utd); **1997** Alex Ferguson (Manchester Utd); **1998** Arsene Wenger (Arsenal); **1999** Alex Ferguson (Manchester Utd); **2000** Sir Alex Ferguson (Manchester Utd); **2001** George Burley (Ipswich); **2002** Arsene Wenger (Arsenal); **2003** Sir Alex Ferguson (Manchester Utd); **2004** Arsene Wenger (Arsenal); **2005** Jose Mourinho (Chelsea); **2006** Jose Mourinho (Chelsea); **2007** Sir Alex Ferguson (Manchester Utd); **2008** Sir Alex Ferguson (Manchester Utd); **2009** Sir Alex Ferguson (Manchester Utd), **2010** Harry Redknapp (Tottenham), **2011** Sir Alex Ferguson (Manchester Utd)

MANAGER OF THE YEAR (2)
(Chosen by the League Managers' Association)

1993 Dave Bassett (Sheffield Utd); **1994** Joe Kinnear (Wimbledon); **1995** Frank Clark (Nott'm Forest); **1996** Peter Reid (Sunderland); **1997** Danny Wilson (Barnsley); **1998** David Jones (Southampton); **1999** Alex Ferguson (Manchester Utd); **2000** Alan Curbishley (Charlton Athletic); **2001** George Burley (Ipswich); **2002** Arsene Wenger (Arsenal); **2003** David Moyes (Everton); **2004** Arsene Wenger (Arsenal); **2005** David Moyes (Everton); **2006** Steve Coppell (Reading); **2007** Steve Coppell (Reading); **2008** Sir Alex Ferguson (Manchester Utd); **2009** David Moyes (Everton); **2010** Roy Hodgson (Fulham), **2011** Sir Alex Ferguson (Manchester Utd)

SCOTTISH FOOTBALL WRITERS' ASSOCIATION

Player of the Year: 1965 Billy McNeill (Celtic); **1966** John Greig (Rangers); **1967** Ronnie Simpson (Celtic); **1968** Gordon Wallace (Raith); **1969** Bobby Murdoch (Celtic); **1970** Pat Stanton (Hibernian); **1971** Martin Buchan (Aberdeen); **1972** David Smith (Rangers); **1973** George Connelly (Celtic); **1974** World Cup Squad; **1975** Sandy Jardine (Rangers); **1976** John Greig (Rangers); **1977** Danny McGrain (Celtic); **1978** Derek Johnstone (Rangers); **1979** Andy Ritchie (Morton); **1980** Gordon Strachan (Aberdeen); **1981** Alan Rough (Partick Thistle); **1982** Paul Sturrock (Dundee Utd); **1983** Charlie Nicholas (Celtic); **1984** Willie Miller (Aberdeen); **1985** Hamish McAlpine (Dundee Utd); **1986** Sandy Jardine (Hearts); **1987** Brian McClair (Celtic); **1988** Paul McStay (Celtic); **1989** Richard Gough (Rangers); **1990** Alex McLeish (Aberdeen); **1991** Maurice Malpas (Dundee Utd); **1992** Ally McCoist (Rangers); **1993** Andy Goram (Rangers); **1994** Mark Hateley (Rangers); **1995** Brian Laudrup (Rangers); **1996** Paul Gascoigne (Rangers); **1997** Brian Laudrup (Rangers); **1998** Craig Burley (Celtic); **1999** Henrik Larsson (Celtic); **2000** Barry Ferguson (Rangers); **2001** Henrik Larsson (Celtic); **2002** Paul Lambert (Celtic); **2003** Barry Ferguson (Rangers); **2004** Jackie McNamara (Celtic); **2005** John Hartson (Celtic); **2006** Craig Gordon (Hearts); **2007** Shunsuke Nakamura (Celtic); **2008** Carlos Cuellar (Rangers); **2009** Gary Caldwell (Celtic), **2010** David Weir (Rangers), **2011** Emilio Izaguirre (Celtic)

SCOTTISH PROFESSIONAL FOOTBALLERS' ASSOCIATION

Player of the Year: 1978 Derek Johnstone (Rangers); **1979** Paul Hegarty (Dundee Utd); **1980** Davie Provan (Celtic); **1981** Mark McGhee (Aberdeen); **1982** Sandy Clarke (Airdrieonians); **1983** Charlie Nicholas (Celtic); **1984** Willie Miller (Aberdeen); **1985** Jim Duffy (Morton); **1986** Richard Gough (Dundee Utd); **1987** Brian McClair (Celtic); **1988** Paul McStay (Celtic); **1989** Theo Snelders (Aberdeen); **1990** Jim Bett (Aberdeen); **1991** Paul Elliott (Celtic); **1992** Ally McCoist (Rangers); **1993** Andy Goram (Rangers); **1994** Mark Hateley (Rangers); **1995** Brian Laudrup (Rangers); **1996** Paul Gascoigne (Rangers); **1997** Paolo Di Canio (Celtic) **1998** Jackie McNamara (Celtic); **1999** Henrik Larsson (Celtic); **2000** Mark Viduka (Celtic); **2001** Henrik Larsson (Celtic); **2002** Lorenzo Amoruso (Rangers); **2003** Barry Ferguson (Rangers); **2004** Chris Sutton (Celtic); **2005** John Hartson (Celtic) and Fernando Ricksen (Rangers); **2006** Shaun Maloney (Celtic); **2007** Shunsuke Nakamura (Celtic); **2008** Aiden McGeady (Celtic); **2009** Scott Brown (Celtic), **2010** Steven Davis (Rangers), **2011** Emilio Izaguirre (Celtic)

Young Player of the Year: 1978 Graeme Payne (Dundee Utd); **1979** Ray Stewart (Dundee Utd); **1980** John McDonald (Rangers); **1981** Charlie Nicholas (Celtic); **1982** Frank McAvennie (St Mirren); **1983** Paul McStay (Celtic); **1984** John Robertson (Hearts); **1985** Craig Levein (Hearts); **1986** Craig Levein (Hearts); **1987** Robert Fleck (Rangers); **1988** John Collins (Hibernian); **1989** Billy McKinlay (Dundee Utd); **1990** Scott Crabbe (Hearts); **1991** Eoin Jess (Aberdeen); **1992** Phil O'Donnell (Motherwell); **1993** Eoin Jess (Aberdeen); **1994** Phil O'Donnell (Motherwell); **1995** Charlie Miller (Rangers); **1996** Jackie McNamara (Celtic); **1997** Robbie Winters (Dundee Utd); **1998** Gary Naysmith (Hearts); **1999** Barry Ferguson (Rangers) ; **2000** Kenny Miller (Hibernian); **2001** Stilian Petrov (Celtic); **2002** Kevin McNaughton (Aberdeen); **2003** James McFadden (Motherwell); **2004** Stephen Pearson (Celtic); **2005** Derek Riordan (Hibernian); **2006** Shaun Maloney (Celtic); **2007** Steven Naismith (Kilmarnock); **2008** Aiden McGeady (Celtic); **2009** James McCarthy (Hamilton), **2010** Danny Wilson (Rangers), **2011:** David Goodwillie (Dundee Utd)

SCOTTISH MANAGER OF THE YEAR

1987 Jim McLean (Dundee Utd); **1988** Billy McNeill (Celtic); **1989** Graeme Souness (Rangers); **1990** Andy Roxburgh (Scotland); **1991** Alex Totten (St Johnstone); **1992** Walter Smith (Rangers); **1993** Walter Smith (Rangers); **1994** Walter Smith (Rangers); **1995** Jimmy Nicholl (Raith); **1996** Walter Smith (Rangers); **1997** Walter Smith (Rangers); **1998** Wim

Jansen (Celtic); **1999** Dick Advocaat (Rangers); **2000** Dick Advocaat (Rangers); **2001** Martin O'Neill (Celtic); **2002** John Lambie (Partick Thistle); **2003** Alex McLeish (Rangers); **2004** Martin O'Neill (Celtic); **2005** Alex McLeish (Rangers); **2006** Gordon Strachan (Celtic); **2007** Gordon Strachan (Celtic); **2008** Billy Reid (Hamilton); **2009** Csaba Laszlo (Hearts), **2010** Walter Smith (Rangers), **2011**: Mixu Paatelainen (Kilmarnock)

EUROPEAN FOOTBALLER OF THE YEAR

1956 Stanley Matthews (Blackpool); **1957** Alfredo di Stefano (Real Madrid); **1958** Raymond Kopa (Real Madrid); **1959** Alfredo di Stefano (Real Madrid); **1960** Luis Suarez (Barcelona); **1961** Omar Sivori (Juventus); **1962** Josef Masopust (Dukla Prague); **1963** Lev Yashin (Moscow Dynamo); **1964** Denis Law (Manchester Utd); **1965** Eusebio (Benfica); **1966** Bobby Charlton (Manchester Utd); **1967** Florian Albert (Ferencvaros); **1968** George Best (Manchester Utd); **1969** Gianni Rivera (AC Milan); **1970** Gerd Muller (Bayern Munich); **1971** Johan Cruyff (Ajax); **1972** Franz Beckenbauer (Bayern Munich); **1973** Johan Cruyff (Barcelona); **1974** Johan Cruyff (Barcelona); **1975** Oleg Blokhin (Dynamo Kiev); **1976** Franz Beckenbauer (Bayern Munich); **1977** Allan Simonsen (Borussia Moenchengladbach); **1978** Kevin Keegan (SV Hamburg); **1979** Kevin Keegan (SV Hamburg); **1980** Karl-Heinz Rummenigge (Bayern Munich); **1981** Karl-Heinz Rummenigge (Bayern Munich); **1982** Paolo Rossi (Juventus); **1983** Michel Platini (Juventus); **1984** Michel Platini (Juventus); **1985** Michel Platini (Juventus); **1986** Igor Belanov (Dynamo Kiev); **1987** Ruud Gullit (AC Milan); **1988** Marco van Basten (AC Milan); **1989** Marco van Basten (AC Milan); **1990** Lothar Matthaus (Inter Milan); **1991** Jean-Pierre Papin (Marseille); **1992** Marco van Basten (AC Milan); **1993** Roberto Baggio (Juventus); **1994** Hristo Stoichkov (Barcelona); **1995** George Weah (AC Milan); **1996** Matthias Sammer (Borussia Dortmund); **1997** Ronaldo (Inter Milan); **1998** Zinedine Zidane (Juventus); **1999** Rivaldo (Barcelona); **2000** Luis Figo (Real Madrid); **2001** Michael Owen (Liverpool); **2002** Ronaldo (Real Madrid); **2003** Pavel Nedved (Juventus); **2004** Andriy Shevchenko (AC Milan); **2005** Ronaldinho (Barcelona); **2006** Fabio Cannavaro (Real Madrid); **2007** Kaka (AC Milan); **2008** Cristiano Ronaldo (Manchester United), **2009** Lionel Messi (Barcelona)

WORLD FOOTBALLER OF YEAR

1991 Lothar Matthaus (Inter Milan and Germany); **1992** Marco van Basten (AC Milan and Holland); **1993** Roberto Baggio (Juventus and Italy); **1994** Romario (Barcelona and Brazil); **1995** George Weah (AC Milan and Liberia); **1996** Ronaldo (Barcelona and Brazil); **1997** Ronaldo (Inter Milan and Brazil); **1998** Zinedine Zidane (Juventus and France); **1999** Rivaldo (Barcelona and Brazil); **2000** Zinedine Zidane (Juventus and France); **2001** Luis Figo (Real Madrid and Portugal); **2002** Ronaldo (Real Madrid and Brazil); **2003** Zinedine Zidane (Real Madrid and France); **2004** Ronaldinho (Barcelona and Brazil); **2005** Ronaldinho (Barcelona and Brazil); **2006** Fabio Cannavaro (Real Madrid and Italy); **2007** Kaka (AC Milan and Brazil); **2008** Cristiano Ronaldo (Manchester United and Portugal), **2009** Lionel Messi (Barcelona and Argentina)

FIFA BALLON D'OR

(replaces European and World Footballer of the Year)
2010: Lionel Messi (Barcelona)

BARCLAYS PREMIER LEAGUE

REVIEWS, APPEARANCES, SCORERS 2010–11

(Figures in brackets denote appearances as substitute)

ARSENAL

A season that seemed likely to end their long wait for a trophy suddenly turned sour for Arsene Wenger and his players. In the space of a fortnight, they lost to rank outsiders Birmingham in the Carling Cup Final, went out of the Champions League to Barcelona after taking a 2-1 lead to the Nou Camp and were beaten by Manchester United in the FA Cup. Then, with confidence shaken particularly by that defeat at Wembley, Arsenal effectively lost the chance of overhauling United in the league by dopping points against West Bromwich Albion and Blackburn and failing to preserve a 3-1 lead at Tottenham. That game at White Hart Lane was their 16th without defeat in the league. But too many of those were drawn for team entertaining title aspirations, including a major slip-up at Newcastle, where a 4-0 lead was surrendered in the second-half. This failure to kill off matches, a tendency to concede late goals, plus goalkeeping and defensive lapses, eventually left them in fourth place and having to qualifying for the Champions League group stage. At least Robin van Persie had something to show at the end – 20 goals in 23 games in all competitions to his name after missing much of the first half of the season through injury.

Almunia M 8	Emmanuel-Thomas J.... - (1)	Sagna B...........................33
Arshavin A 25 (12)	Fabianski L 14	Song A 30 (1)
Bendtner 3 (14)	Fabregas F 22 (3)	Squillaci S 20 (2)
Chamakh M........... 18 (11)	Gibbs K 4 (3)	Szczesny W....................15
Clichy G..........................33	Koscielny T....................30	Vela C........................ - (4)
Denilson 6 (10)	Lehmann J.......................1	Vermaelen T.....................5
Diaby V................... 13 (3)	Nasri S 28 (1)	Walcott T 19 (9)
Djourou J............... 20 (2)	Ramsey A 5 (2)	Wilshere J............... 31 (4)
Eboue E.................... 8 (5)	Rosicky T................. 8 (13)	Van Persie R 19 (6)

League goals (72): Van Persie 18, Nasri 10, Walcott 9, Chamakh 7, Arshavin 6, Song 4, Fabregas 3, Bendtner 2, Diaby 2, Koscielny 2, Djourou 1, Eboue 1, Ramsey 1, Sagna 1, Squillaci 1, Vela 1, Wilshere 1, Opponents 2
FA Cup goals (12): Bendtner 3, Fabregas 2, Chamakh 1, Clichy 1, Nasri 1, Rosicky 1, Sagna 1, Van Persie 1, Oppponents 1. **Carling Cup goals (14):** Bendtner 3, Nasri 2, Walcott 2, Arshavin 1, Fabregas 1, Koscielny 1, Lansbury 1, Van Persie 1, Opponents 2. **Champions League goals (21):** Arshavin 3, Chamakh 3, Fabregas 3, Nasri 2, Vela 2, Van Persie 2, Walcott 2, Koscielny 1, Song 1, Squilaci 1, Wilshere 1
Average home league attendance: 60,025. **Player of Year:** Jack Wilshere

ASTON VILLA

Villa started without a manager when Martin O'Neill resigned five days before the opening match. They finished it without his successor, Gerard Houllier, who was admitted to hospital complaining of chest pains and ordered to rest on his release. In between, there were two record transfers – James Milner to Manchester City and Darren Bent from Sunderland – and a relegation scare. It was a difficult campaign for Houllier, faced with under-performing players, dressing room unrest and dissatisfaction from sections of the crowd. Bent scored goals for him, but the introduction of several youngsters had mixed results and the gamble of bringing in Robert Pires was unsuccessful. In Houllier's last two games, Villa moved clear of trouble with wins over Newcastle and West Ham after slipping to within two points of the bottom three. Gary McAllister, then took over to oversee a final flourish with victories over Arsenal and Liverpool. Houllier did not return and in came Alex McLeish, five days after controversially resigning at Birmingham.

Agbonlahor G 17 (9)	Delfouneso N 2 (9)	Milner J 1
Albrighton M 20 (9)	Delph F 4 (3)	Petrov S 23 (4)
Baker N 4	Downing S 38	Pires R 2 (7)
Bannan B 7 (5)	Dunne N 32	Reo-Coker N 24 (6)
Bent D 16	Friedel B 38	Sidwell S 1 (3)
Beye H 2 (1)	Herd C 1 (5)	Walker K 15
Bradley M .... - (3)	Heskey E 11 (8)	Weimann A .... - (1)
Carew J 6 (4)	Hogg J 5	Warnock S 19
Clark C 16 (3)	Ireland S.................... 6 (4)	Young A 34
Collins J 31 (1)	Lichaj E 3 (2)	Young L 23
Cuellar C 10 (2)	Makoun J 7	

League goals (48): Bent 9, Downing 7, Young A 7, Albrighton 5, Agbonlahor 3, Clark 3, Collins 3, Heskey 3, Delfouneso 1, Milner 1, Petrov 1, Walker 1, Young L 1, Opponents 3
FA Cup goals (6): Albrighton 1, Clark 1, Delfouneso 1, Petrov 1, Pires 1, Walker 1. **Carling Cup goals** (6): Young A 2, Heskey 2, Agbonlahor 1, Downing 1. **Europa League goals** (3): Agbonlahor 1, Bannan 1, Heskey 1
Average home league attendance: 37,180. **Player of Year**: Stewart Downing

BIRMINGHAM CITY

Delight turned to despair at St Andrew's when the club's first trophy for 48 years was followed three months later by relegation. Even the prospect of Europa League football meant little for a side who were caught up in the euphoria of that memorable Carling Cup victory over Arsenal and were never the same afterwards. Birmingham won only two of their final dozen league games and also lost an FA Cup quarter-final to Bolton. Injuries and tiredness took their toll. So did suspensions, with Liam Ridgewell and Craig Gardner both missing the final home game against Fulham when victory would have meant survival. Instead, they laboured to a 2-0 defeat, leaving everything hanging on a visit to White Hart Lane. Gardner's 79th minute equaliser raised hopes, but a second goal which could have made all the difference proved out of reach and Tottenham boke away for a stoppage-time winner. So Birmingham became the first team since Norwich in 1985 to go down from the top division after winning a major trophy. It was a success they worked hard for, coming from behind in three rounds to reach Wembley, then showing great organisation and resilience to overcome the favourites. But all that seemed a long way off when the drop was followed by the controversial resignation of manager Alex McLeish. Chris Hughton, thought by many to have been unfairly sacked by Newcastle, came in.

Beausejour J 9 (8)	Ferguson B 35	McFadden J 3 (1)
Bentley D.................... 9 (4)	Foster B.........................38	Murphy D................... 3 (7)
Bowyer L................. 24 (5)	Gardner C 25 (4)	Mutch J 3
Carr S...........................38	Hleb A 13 (6)	O'Connor G 2 (1)
Dann S 20	Jerome C 30 (4)	Parnaby S 5
Davies C 2 (4)	Jiranek M 10	Phillips K 5 (9)
Derbyshire M 4 (8)	Johnson R......................38	Ridgewell L....................36
Doyle C...................... - (1)	Larsson S 31 (4)	Zigic N 13 (12)
Fahey K 19 (5)	Martins O.................. 3 (1)	

League goals (37): Gardner 8, Zigic 5, Bowyer 4, Larsson 4, Ridgewell 4, Jerome 3, Beausejour 2, Dann 2, Johnson 2, Hleb 1, Fahey 1, Phillips 1
FA Cup goals (12): Jerome 2, Derbyshire 2, Murphy 2, Phillips 2, Beausejour 1, Bentley 1, Martins 1, Parnaby 1. **Carling Cup goals** (15): Zigic 3, Gardner 2, Bowyer 1, Derbyshire 1, Hleb 1, Johnson 1, Larsson 1, Martins 1, McFadden 1, Murphy 1, Phillips 1, Ridgewell 1
Average home league attendance: 25,462. **Player of Year**: Ben Foster

BLACKBURN ROVERS

Rovers saved the best until last to see off the threat of relegation. They went into what was expected to be a tense, tight final match at Wolves in real danger, one of five struggling clubs separated by a single point. But you wouldn't have thought it, watching the free-flowing football which represented their most impressive 45 minutes of an indifferent season. The reward, goals from Jason Roberts, Brett Emerton and Junior Hoilett, lifted all the pressure on manager Steve Kean, whose initial success when taking over from Sam Allardyce had given way to a worrying run of ten matches without a victory. It dragged his side down from seventh to the fringe of the bottom three and led to some supporters questioning the decision of the club's new owners, Indian company Venky's, to sack Allardyce. That followed a defeat by his former club Bolton and with a 7-1 thrashing by Manchester United still fresh in the mind. Former coach Kean, initially given the job until the end of the campaign, was later handed a contract through to the summer of 2013.

Andrews K 2 (3)	Grella V 4 (1)	Nzonzi S................. 13 (8)
Benjani.................. 6 (12)	Hanley G.................. 5 (2)	Olsson M 25 (4)
Biram Diouf M.. 17 (10)	Hoilett D................. 17 (7)	Pedersen M G....... 27 (8)
Bunn M 2 (1)	Jones J.........................15	Roberts J 13 (12)
Chimbonda P 3 (3)	Jones P.................. 24 (2)	Robinson P 36
Diouf E-H 18 (2)	Kalinic I 15 (3)	Rochina R.................. 1 (3)
Dunn D 17 (10)	Linganzi A.............. - (1)	Salgado M....................36
Emerton B 24 (6)	Lowe J................... - (1)	Samba C....................33
Givet G 29	Morris J .... - (4)	Santa Cruz R 7 (2)
Goulon H 1 (3)	Nelsen R....................28	

League goals (46): Hoilett 5, Kalinic 5, Roberts 5, Emerton 4, Pedersen 4, Samba 4, Diouf M B 3, Benjani 3, Nelsen 3, Dunn 2, Olsson 2, Givet 1, Nzonzi 1, Opponents 4
FA Cup goals (2): Hoilett 1, Kalinic 1. **Carling Cup goals** (4): Diouf M B 3, Givet 1
Average home league attendance: 25,000. **Player of Year**: Paul Robinson

BLACKPOOL

Rarely has a team's relegation from the top division been accompanied by such widespread appreciation of their efforts to prevent it. Ian Holloway and his players earned that affection for playing attacking football wherever they went, refusing to compromise when the tide turned against them and succumbing only in the final 20 minutes of the season at Old Trafford. Blackpool, with Charlie Adam an influential presence in midfield, kicked off with a 4-0 victory at Wigan, won at Anfield and St James' Park and after completing the double over Liverpool were looking to cement a mid-table position. Then, the sparkle faded, individual errors were punished and the ability to retrieve them became less evident. When Bolton were beaten 4-3 in the penultimate fixture, it was only their second victory in 17 matches. That, at least, gave them a chance. And, when Gary Taylor-Fletcher made it 2-1 against Manchester United, hope soared. But they self-destructed again with Ian Evatt's own goal, enabling the champions to go on to a 4-2 win. All Blackpool were left with was the knowledge that no side had ever gone down after scoring so many goals – 55.

Adam C 34 (1)	Demontagnac I .... - (1)	Harewood M................. 7 (9)
Baptiste A............. 19 (2)	Eardley N................. 30 (1)	Keinan D 3 (3)
Basham C 1 (1)	Edwards R 1 (1)	Kingson R 19 (1)
Beattie J................. 5 (4)	Euell J..................... 1 (2)	Kornilenko S 3 (3)
Campbell D............ 30 (1)	Evatt I 36 (2)	Ormerod B 6 (13)
Carney D................. 5 (6)	Gilks M.....................18	Phillips M 6 (21)
Cathcart C 28 (2)	Grandin E 21 (2)	Puncheon J............. 6 (5)
Crainey S....................31	Halstead M .... - (1)	Rachubka P 1 (1)

| Reid A | 2 (3) | Sylvestre L | 6 (2) | Varney L | 24 (6) |
| Southern K | 11 (10) | Taylor-Fletcher G | 29 (2) | Vaughan D | 35 |

League goals (55): Campbell 13, Adam 12, Taylor-Fletcher 6, Harewood 5, Varney 5, Puncheon 3, Baptiste 2, Vaughan 2, Cathcart 1, Eardley 1, Evatt 1, Grandin 1, Ormerod 1, Phillips 1, Opponents 1
FA Cup goals: None. **Carling Cup goals (3):** Adam 1, Ormerod 1, Sylvestre 1
Average home league attendance: 15,782. **Player of Year:** David Vaughan

BOLTON WANDERERS

An embarrassing FA Cup semi-final performance put the damper on a season in which Bolton, under Owen Coyle, had shed their direct style of play in favour of a more expansive, entertaining brand of football. They went into the Wembley tie against Stoke full of confidence, but came out it with their tail between their legs after a 5-0 trouncing which Coyle had difficulty explaining. His side seemed to have put the defeat behind them when ending Arsenal's championship chances with a 2-1 victory in which Daniel Sturridge maintained a productive loan spell from Chelsea. It consolidated eighth place in the table, with the incentive to go higher. Instead, Coyle admitted that too many of his players simply ran out of steam as five successive defeats to finish with meant a fall to 14th – the same position as 2010. Particularly disappointing was the away form, with 11 defeats in 12 matches, and the red card shown in the last match against Manchester City to Sturridge, who had scored eight goals in 12 appearances.

Alonso M	4	Elmander J	37	O'Brien A	1 (1)
Blake R	- (8)	Gardner R	3 (2)	Petrov M	18 (10)
Bogdan A	3 (1)	Holden S	26	Ricketts S	14 (3)
Cahill G	36	Jaaskelainen J	35	Robinson P	35
Chung-Yong Lee	25 (6)	Klasnic I	- (22)	Steinsson G	23
Cohen T	3 (5)	Knight Z	34	Sturridge D	11 (1)
Davies K	38	Moreno R	4 (13)	Taylor M	22 (14)
Davies M	9 (15)	Muamba F	32 (4)	Wheater D	5 (2)

League goals (52): Elmander 10, Davies K 8, Sturridge 8, Klasnic 4, Cahill 3, Lee 3, Petrov 3, Holden 2, Taylor 2, Blake 1, Cohen 1, Davies M 1, Knight 1, Moreno 1, Muamba 1, Steinsson 1, Opponents 2
FA Cup goals (7): Davies K 2, Elmander 2, Klasnic 2, Lee 1. **Carling Cup goals (1):** Klasnic 1
Average home league attendance: 22,870. **Player of Year:** Stuart Holden

CHELSEA

When Chelsea repeated their flying start to the previous, title-winning season, this time scoring 21 goals in five successive victories, there was every suggestion of another successful campaign. They stayed on top for three months until a combination of factors brought about a slump – Didier Drogba weakened by a bout of malaria, the influential Florent Malouda's form deserting him, the sudden sacking of popular assistant manager Ray Wilkins. Nine matches yielded a mere seven points, prompting a record £50m fee for Liverpool's Fernando Torres and the £21m purchase of Benfica defender David Luiz. Torres struggled, failing to score in his first 13 appearances, but his new team-mates took on a new lease of life to whittle down Manchester United's lead at the top from 15 to three points. Then came a 2-1 defeat at Old Trafford which put United back in the driving seat and on the way to a nine-point advantage at the end. The surge was enough for the runners-up spot, but not enough to satisfy Roman Abramovich, who also saw his side lose out to United in the Champions League and have their defence of the FA Cup ended by Everton. So, 12 months after presenting him with the 'Double,' Carlo Ancelotti followed Ranieri, Mourinho, Grant and Scolari out of the door. Andre Villas-Boas, fresh from domestic and European success with Porto, replaced him to become the Premier League's youngest manager at 33.

Alex.........................12 (3)	Drogba D 30 (6)	McEachran J................1 (8)
Anelka N...................27 (5)	Essien M..................32 (1)	Mikel J O 28
Benayoun Y...............1 (6)	Ivanovic B................32 (2)	Paulo Ferreira...........12 (9)
Bertrand R ....- (1)	Kakuta G 1 (4)	Ramires 22 (7)
Bosingwa J................13 (7)	Kalou S 16 (15)	Sturridge D ....- (13)
Bruma J.......................1 (1)	Lampard F 23 (1)	Terry J.............................33
Cech P 38	Luiz D 11 (1)	Torres F 8 (6)
Cole A 38	Malouda F................33 (5)	Zhirkov Y 6 (6)

League goals (69): Malouda 13, Drogba 11, Kalou 10, Lampard 10, Anelka 6, Ivanovic 4, Essien 3, Terry 3, Alex 2, Luiz 2, Ramires 2, Benayoun 1, Torres 1, Opponents 1
FA Cup goals (9): Lampard 2, Kalou 2, Sturridge 2, Anelka 1, Opponents 1. **Carling Cup goals** (3): Anelka 2, Van Aanholt 1. **Champions League goals** (17): Anelka 7, Drogba 2, Ivanovic 2, Sturridge 2, Essien 1, Malouda 1, Terry 1, Zhirkov 1. **Community Shield goals** (1): Kalou 1
Average home league attendance: 41,435. **Player of Year:** Petr Cech

EVERTON

David Moyes continues to keep his side on the fringes of the leading group – without the financial muscle to make the breakthrough. This time, he did it after the club's poorest start to the season since 1994-95 – three points from the first six matches. A 2-0 win over Liverpool went some way to restoring the balance and a 2-1 success away to Manchester City helped pave the way for a much more productive second half of the campaign. Everton overcame injuries to Tim Cahill, Mikel Arteta and Marouane Fellaini, and the loss of Steven Pienaar to Tottenham, with Moyes picking out Leon Osman's midfield enterprise as key to the improvement. Osman's eye for goal was also an asset, noticeably a soaring header which set his team on the way to a second victory over City – the only one to do the double. Hopes of making an impact on the FA Cup rose when they knocked out holders Chelsea on penalties at Stamford Bridge, but were ended by a home defeat against Reading in the fifth round.

Anichebe V 8 (8)	Distin S 38	Neville P...........................31
Arteta M 29	Fellaini M 19 (1)	Osman L 20 (6)
Baines L..........................38	Forshaw A ....- (1)	Pienaar S........................18
Baxter J ....- (1)	Gueye M 2 (3)	Rodwell J..................14 (10)
Beckford J 14 (18)	Heitinga J 23 (4)	Saha L 14 (8)
Bilyaletdinov D 10 (16)	Hibbert T 17 (3)	Vaughan J ....- (1)
Cahill T 22 (5)	Howard T........................38	Vellios A ....- (3)
Coleman S 25 (9)	Jagielka P 31 (2)	Yakubu 7 (7)

League goals (51): Cahill 9, Beckford 8, Saha 7, Baines 5, Coleman 4, Osman 4, Arteta 3, Bilyaletdinov 2, Distin 2, Fellaini 1, Heitinga 1, Jagielka 1, Neville 1, Pienaar 1, Yakubu 1, Opponents 1
FA Cup goals (7): Baines 2, Saha 2, Beckford 1, Coleman 1, Fellaini 1. **Carling Cup goals** (6): Beckford 1, Coleman 1, Osman 1, Fellaini 1, Saha 1, Rodwell 1
Average home league attendance: 36,039. **Player of Year:** Leighton Baines

FULHAM

Mark Hughes always believed his side were top-ten material, even when struggling through the first half of the season. They lost Bobby Zamora early on with a broken leg, had only three wins on the board going into the New Year and were languishing in the bottom three. But the manager's faith was justified with victories over West Bromwich Albion, Stoke and Newcastle in a month, along with a 4-0 FA Cup success against Tottenham. Then, with Zamora restored to fitness and looking to make up for lost time, Fulham scored three against Blackburn, Blackpool, Bolton and Sunderland to cement a place in the top half of the table. Although conceding five to

Liverpool at Craven Cottage came as a shock, they responded by inflicting a damaging defeat on Birmingham and went on to finished eighth – the club's second highest placing in ten Premier League campaigns. There was also a place in the Europa League to be had, courtesy of the Fair Play League. Hughes resigned at the end of his contract and was replaced by Martin Jol.

Baird C 25 (4)	Gudjohnsen E 4 (6)	Murphy D 37
Briggs M 3	Halliche R .... - (1)	Pantsil J 15 (1)
Davies S 25 (5)	Hangeland B 37	Riise B H .... - (3)
Dembele M 22 (2)	Hughes A 38	Salcido C 22 (1)
Dempsey C 35 (2)	Johnson A 15 (12)	Schwarzer M 31
Dikgacoi K .... - (1)	Johnson E 1 (10)	Senderos P 3
Duff D 22 (2)	Kakuta G 2 (5)	Sidwell S 10 (2)
Etuhu D 23 (5)	Kamara D 7 (3)	Stockdale D 7
Gera Z 10 (17)	Kelly S 8 (2)	Zamora R 9 (5)
Greening J 6 (4)	Konchesky P 1	

League goals (49): Dempsey 12, Hangeland 6, Zamora 5, Davies 4, Duff 4, Dembele 3, Johnson A 3, Baird 2, Etuhu 2, Kamara 2, Sidwell 2, Gera 1, Hughes 1, Kakuta 1, Opponents 1
FA Cup goals (10): Kamara 3, Murphy 2, Dembele 1, Etuhu 1, Gera 1, Greening 1, Hangeland 1. **Carling Cup goals** (6): Gera 2, Zamora 2, Dembele 1, Dempsey 1
Average home league attendance: 25,043. **Player of Year:** Clint Dempsey

LIVERPOOL

Nearly 20 years after walking out of Anfield, Kenny Dalglish returned as manager to put a smile back on the face of the club and their supporters. He was brought in by the new owners when Roy Hodgson was sacked after a turbulent six months in charge, during which Liverpool made their worst start to a season since relegation 57 years previously, fell into the bottom three after a home defeat by Blackpool and were knocked out of the Carling Cup by Northampton. Dalglish, who ended his first spell as manager because of the pressures of the job and the continuing emotional burden of the Hillsborough disaster, started with an FA Cup loss to Manchester United, followed by another defeat against Blackpool. He sold Fernando Torres, brought in Andy Carroll and Luis Suarez and gave extended runs to young John Flanagan and Jay Spearing. Most of all he restored belief to a side who went on to score 23 goals in a run of eight games producing 19 points and two hat-tricks for Maxi Rodriguez. It included a 3-1 win over United in which Dirk Kuyt also netted three. End of season defeats by Tottenham and Aston Villa pushed them back, but Dalglish had done more than enough to secure the job on a permanent basis.

Agger D 12 (4)	Jovanovic M 5 (5)	Pacheco D .... - (1)
Aurelio F 7 (7)	Kelly M 10 (1)	Poulsen C 9 (3)
Babel R 1 (8)	Konchesky P 15	Reina J 38
Carragher J 28	Kuyt D 32 (1)	Robinson J 1 (1)
Carroll A 5 (2)	Kyrgiakos S 10 (6)	Shelvey J .... - (15)
Cole J 9 (11)	Lucas 32 (1)	Skrtel M 38
Eccleston N .... - (1)	Mascherano J 1	Spearing J 10 (1)
Flanaghan J 7	Maxi Rodriguez........ 24 (4)	Suarez L 12 (1)
Gerrard S 20 (1)	Meireles R 32 (1)	Torres F 22 (1)
Johnson G 28	Ngog D 9 (16)	Wilson D 1 (1)

League goals (59): Kuyt 13, Rodriguez 10, Torres 9, Meireles 5, Gerrard 4, Suarez 4, Carroll 2, Cole 2, Johnson 2, Kyrgiakos 2, Ngog 2, Skrtel 2, Babel 1, Opponents 1
FA Cup goals: None. **Carling Cup goals** (2): Jovanovic 1, Ngog 1. **Europa League goals** (16): Ngog 5, Gerrard 4, Kuyt 2, Babel 1, Cole 1, Jovanovic 1, Lucas 1, Opponents 1
Average home league attendance: 42,820. **Player of Year:** Lucas

MANCHESTER CITY

Is this the start of something big? That's the question being asked, not only among supporters at Eastlands but throughout the game, after City qualified for the Champions League and won the FA Cup in the space of five days. The club's huge outlay on players delivered the first tangible results and many now expect them to go from strength to strength – after another likely summer spending spree. A bid to break the seven-year stranglehold Manchester United and Chelsea have had on the Premier League title is one to relish for the season ahead. This time, they stayed within touching distance until well into the New Year before losing to Aston Villa, being held by Birmingham and falling victim to Wayne Rooney's wonder goal at Old Trafford. It left them eight points adrift of United and not playing well enough to make up the ground. Nevertheless, they never lost their grip on a top-four place and duly sealed it against Tottenham, the team who denied them in 2010. Then came victory over Stoke at Wembley – the club's first major trophy since the League Cup in 1976 – followed by confirmation of a move up to third, their highest finish since 1977.

Adebayor E 2 (6)	Jo 3 (9)	Santa Cruz R .... - (1)
Balotelli M 12 (5)	Johnson A.............. 15 (16)	Silva D 30 (5)
Barry G 31 (2)	Kolarov A 20 (4)	Tevez C 30 (1)
Boateng J 14 (2)	Kompany V 37	Toure K 21 (1)
Boyata D................ 5 (2)	Lescott J 20 (2)	Toure Y 35
Bridge W 1 (2)	McGivern R .... - (1)	Vieira P.............. 4 (11)
De Jong N 30 (2)	Milner J 23 (9)	Wabara R .... - (1)
Dzeko E 8 (7)	Razak A .... - (1)	Wright-Phillips S 2 (5)
Hart J..............38	Richards M 16 (2)	Zabaleta P 21 (5)

League goals (60): Tevez 20, Toure Y 7, Balotelli 6, Johnson A 4, Silva 4, Lescott 3, Barry 2, Dzeko 2, Vieira 2, Zabaleta 2, Adebayor 1, Kolarov 1, Richards 1, Toure K 1, De Jong 1, Opponents 3
FA Cup goals (18): Tevez 3, Toure Y 3, Vieira 3, Dzeko 2, Richards 2, Balotelli 1, Johnson A 1, Kolarov 1, Milner 1, Silva 1. **Carling Cup goals** (1): Jo 1. **Europa League goals** (18): Adebayor 4, Balotelli 3, Dzeko 2, Jo 2, Johnson A 2, Boyata 1, Kolarov ,1, Silva 1, Toure Y 1, Wright-Phillips 1
Average home league attendance: 45,905. **Player of Year:** Vincent Kompany

MANCHESTER UNITED

Two crushing defeats at Wembley cast a shadow over the season, but at the end of it Sir Alex Ferguson and his players could still look back with a sense of great pride. They regained the Premier League title from Chelsea and, more significantly, finished top for a record 19th time, one more than Liverpool. It was a 12th triumph for both Ferguson and Ryan Giggs, the first in 1993 when United trailed their great rivals 18-7 in the championship stakes. They assumed pole position when Chelsea faltered after a whirlwind start, held off challenges from Manchester City and Arsenal, then resisted the defending champions who surged back into contention by cutting a 15-point deficit to just three. Wayne Rooney's penalty clinched the crown at Blackburn in the penultimate game and his team had a nine-point cushion at the end. They were not Ferguson's finest creation, winning only five times away from home. But United were virtually invincible at Old Trafford, where only West Bromwich Albion avoided defeat, displayed a never-say-die spirit to claim 13 points with goals in the last ten minutes and had in Javier Hernandez the find of the season – a player who relegated 20-goal Dimitar Berbatov to the sidelines. The low points were an FA Cup semi-final defeat by City and, most disappointingly, a Champions League Final lesson handed out by Barcelona, which left the manager in no doubt about the need for new blood.

Anderson 14 (4)	Berbatov D......... 24 (8)	Carrick M................. 23 (5)
Bebe .... - (2)	Brown W................... 4 (3)	Evans J................... 11 (2)

Evra P 34 (1)	Kuszczak T 5	Rafael 15 (1)
Fabio..................... 5 (6)	Macheda F 2 (5)	Rooney W 25 (3)
Ferdinand R 19	Nani 31 (2)	Scholes P 16 (6)
Fletcher D............ 24 (2)	Neville G.....................3	Smalling C 11 (5)
Gibson D.............. 6 (6)	O'Shea J 18 (2)	Valencia A............... 8 (2)
Giggs R.................. 19 (6)	Obertan G 3 (4)	Van der Sar E 33
Hargreaves O...............1	Owen M 1 (10)	Vidic N 35
Hernandez J.......... 15 (12)	Ji-Sung Park 13 (2)	

League goals (78): Berbatov 20, Hernandez 13, Rooney 11, Nani 9, Park 5, Vidic 5, Fletcher 2, Giggs 2, Owen 2, Anderson 1, Evra 1, Fabio 1, Macheda 1, Scholes 1, Valencia 1, Opponents 3 **FA Cup goals** (6): Brown 1, Giggs 1, Fabio 1, Hernandez 1, Owen 1, Rooney 1. **Carling Cup goals** (8): Owen 2, Park 2, Bebe 1, Gibson 1, Hernandez 1, Smalling 1. **Champions League goals** (19): Hernandez 4, Rooney 4, Anderson 1, Bebe 1, Fletcher 1, Gibson 1, Giggs 1, Nani 1, Park 1, Obertan 1, Valencia 1. **Community Shield goals** (3): Berbatov 1, Hernandez 1, Valencia 1 **Average home league attendance**: 75,109. **Player of Year**: Javier Hernandez

NEWCASTLE UNITED

Another eventful season at St James' Park embraced highs and lows, controversial comings and goings and one remarkable, record-breaking afternoon. It came when Newcastle retrieved a 4-0 deficit against Arsenal – the first Premier League team to do so – in front of 51,000 disbelieving supporters. Just as satisfying in its own way was the 5-1 beating of neighbours Sunderland, while a 6-0 rout of Aston Villa featuring an Andy Carroll hat-trick was the perfect start to the campaign at home. On the debit side, there were heavy defeats at Bolton and Stoke, along with an FA Cup embarrassment at Stevenage. On the managerial front, Chris Hughton, who led the club back to the top division, was sacked in December after a run of five matches without a win. Almost as surprising was the appointment of Alan Pardew, dismissed by his previous club Southampton, with a five-and-a-half-year contract. Carroll's move to Liverpool also came out of the blue, leaving a big hole. Pardew patched it over with a degree of success, while looking ahead to spending money to fill it permanently and build on a satisfactory 12th place finish.

Amoebi Sam .... - (1)	Guthrie D................ 11 (3)	Perch J 9 (3)
Amoebi Shola........... 21 (7)	Gutierrez J 34 (3)	Ranger N 1 (23)
Barton J.....................32	Harper S.................18	Routledge W 10 (7)
Ben Arfa H 3 (1)	Ireland S................ - (2)	Simpson D 30
Best L 9 (2)	Jose Enrique 36	Smith A 7 (4)
Campbell S 4 (3)	Krul T 20 (1)	Taylor R 3 (3)
Carroll A 18 (1)	Kuqi S .... - (6)	Taylor S 12 (2)
Coloccini F.....................35	Lovenkrands P.......... 18 (7)	Tiote C.....................26
Ferguson S............ 3 (4)	LuaLua K .... - (2)	Williamson M 28 (1)
Gosling D................ - (1)	Nolan K 30	Xisco .... - (2)

League goals (56): Nolan 12, Carroll 11, Ameobi Shola 6, Best 6, Lovenkrands 6, Barton 4, Gutierrez 3, Taylor S 3, Coloccini 2, Ben Arfa 1, Tiote 1, Opponents 1 **FA Cup goals** (1): Barton 1. **Carling Cup goals** (7): Ameobi Shola 3, Taylor R 2, Lovenkrands 1, Ranger 1 **Average home league attendance**: 47,720. **Player of Year**: Joey Barton

STOKE CITY

Their big day proved a big disappointment and cast a shadow over the remainder of the league programme. But Tony Pulis could still look back with considerable satisfaction on a season in which he introduced more subtlety and variety to a team previously characterised by power and aggression. With Jermaine Pennant coming in on the right wing to balance Matthew Etherington's work down the left, Stoke's play had a more pleasing look about it, while maintaining the strengths on which their arrival in the Premier League had been based. This was underlined by a handsome 5-0 FA Cup semi-final win over Bolton which suggested they were up for the challenge of Manchester City in the club's first appearance in the final. It was not to be. Stoke were second best for much of the game and lost out again when the two teams met in a re-arranged league fixture three days later. The final game brought a home defeat by Wigan, resulting in a slide to 13th when a top-half finish had been the target.

Begovic A 28	Higginbotham D 9 (1)	Sorensen T...................10
Carew J...................7 (3)	Huth R 35	Tonge M...................- (2)
Collins D...................23 (2)	Jones K 33 (1)	Walters J...................27 (9)
Delap R 33 (4)	Pennant J 26 (3)	Whelan G...................14 (15)
Diao S 3 (5)	Pugh D 5 (5)	Whitehead D 31 (6)
Etherington M 30 (2)	Tuncay...................5 (9)	Wilkinson A...............21 (1)
Faye A 12 (2)	Shawcross R 36	Wilson M...................21 (7)
Fuller R 9 (19)	Shotton R ....- (2)	
Gudjohnsen E.............- (2)	Sidibe M...................- (2)	

League goals (46): Jones 9, Huth 6, Walters 6, Etherington 5, Fuller 4, Pennant 3, Delap 2, Higginbotham 2, Whitehead 2, Carew 1, Faye 1, Shawcross 1, Tuncay 1, Wilson 1, Opponents 2
FA Cup goals (14): Walters 5, Huth 3, Carew 1, Etherington 1, Higginbotham 1, Jones 1, Shawcross 1, Tuncay 1. **Carling Cup goals** (5): Jones 2, Higginbotham 1, Tuncay 1, Walters 1
Average home league attendance: 26,858. **Player of Year**: Robert Huth

SUNDERLAND

Steve Bruce targeted a place in the top eight for what he regarded as one of the best sides Sunderland have had – and for much of the season the manager looked to be on course. In fact, they climbed as high as sixth, having shaken off a punishing 5-1 defeat at Newcastle with the help of an equally eye-catching 3-0 victory over Chelsea at Stamford Bridge. Then, a transfer request by Darren Bent and the striker's subsequent sale to Aston Villa for a record £24m upset the applecart. Bruce lost other key players through injury and the whole complexion of the season changed. Sunderland took a single point from nine matches and looked to be heading for big trouble. They lost to two teams battling to move clear, West Bromwich Albion and Birmingham, and fell behind to another, Wigan, while at the same time losing three more players, defender Phil Bardsley and strikers Danny Welbeck and Asamoah Gyan. But in an amazing turnaround, four goals in 19 minutes brought a 4-2 victory which ensured survival. Two more wins, over Bolton and West Ham, brought a further climb to tenth.

Angeleri M ....- (2)	Gordon C 15	Onuoha N 31
Bardsley P 32 (2)	Gyan A 20 (11)	Reid A...................- (2)
Bent D...................20	Henderson J...................37	Richardson K 23 (3)
Bramble T...............22 (1)	Laing L...................- (1)	Riveros C 5 (7)
Campbell F...................3	Lynch C...................- (2)	Sessegnon S 12 (1)
Cattermole L 22 (1)	Malbranque S...........24 (11)	Turner M...................15
Colback J...................6 (5)	Mensah J...................15 (3)	Waghorn M...................- (2)
Cook J...................- (3)	Meyler D...................4 (1)	Welbeck D 21 (5)
Da Silva P...................1	Mignolet S...................23	Zenden B...............10 (17)
Elmohamady A 26 (10)	Muntari S...................7 (2)	
Ferdinand A 23 (4)	Noble R...................- (3)	

League goals (45): Gyan 10, Bent 8, Welbeck 6, Richardson 4, Bardsley 3, Henderson 3, Sessegnon 3, Zenden 2, Onuoha 1, Riveros 1, Opponents 4
FA Cup goals (1): Bent 1. **Carling Cup goals** (3): Bent 2, Gyan 1
Average home league attendance: 40,011. **Player of Year**: Phil Bardsley

TOTTENHAM HOTSPUR

Harry Redknapp's side paid a price for an exhilarating run to the Champions League quarter-finals. Premier League form dipped after a famous win over AC Milan and they missed out on qualifying again. A make-or-break match with Manchester City for fourth place looked to be on the cards, just as it was the previous season. But the fixture was rendered meaningless after Tottenham won only once in seven games, then lost controversially to Chelsea to a Frank Lampard shot which TV replays showed had not crossed the line and a goal by Salomon Kalou which should have been ruled offside. Despite the disappointment, there were some special European moments to savour. Spurs scored 18 goals in six group matches, Gareth Bale struck a hat-trick after Inter Milan had established a 4-0 lead and his side won the return 3-1. Then, after Peter Crouch netted the only goal in the San Siro, they held on to the lead at White Hart Lane to reach the last eight. But Crouch received a second yellow card just 14 minutes into the first leg against Real Madrid, who took advantage to establish an unassailable four-goal advantage. Bale's step into world class later earned him the PFA Player of the Year award.

Assou-Ekotto B...............30	Giovani .... - (3)	Modric L..........................32
Bale G 29 (1)	Gomes H.......................30	Palacios W................. 16 (5)
Bassong S................... 7 (5)	Huddlestone T.......... 13 (1)	Pavlyuchenko R...... 18 (11)
Bentley D................... 1 (1)	Hutton A................. 19 (2)	Pienaar S................... 5 (3)
Corluka V................. 13 (2)	Jenas J 14 (5)	Rose D 0
Crouch P.............. 20 (14)	Kaboul Y................. 19 (2)	Sandro....................... 11 (8)
Cudicini C.......................8	Keane R 2 (5)	Van der Vaart R 28
Dawson M.....................24	King L..........................6	Walker K..................... - (1)
Defoe J................. 16 (6)	Kranjcar N 2 (11)	
Gallas W 26 (1)	Lennon A................. 25 (9)	

League goals (55): Van der Vaart 13, Pavlyuchenko 9, Bale 7, Crouch 4, Defoe 4, Lennon 3, Modric 3, Huddlestone 2, Hutton 2, Kranjcar 2, Bassong 1, Dawson 1, Kaboul 1, Sandro 1, Opponents 2
FA Cup goals (3): Defoe 2, Townsend 1. **Carling Cup goals** (1): Keane 1. **Champions League goals** (25): Crouch 7, Bale 4, Pavlyuchenko 4, Defoe 3, Van der Vaart 2, Bassong 1, Kaboul 1, Modric 1, Opponents 2
Average home league attendance: 35,704. **Player of Year**: Luka Modric

WEST BROMWICH ALBION

Albion opened the season strongly under Roberto di Matteo, closed it successfully under Roy Hodgson and shed, at least for the time being, the label of a 'yo-yo' club. They shook off a 6-0 defeat at Chelsea to accumulate 15 points from the first nine matches and climb to sixth in the table. Approaching Christmas, things were still going well, but then came a run of five successive defeats which sent them tumbling. A 3-0 reversal at Manchester City, leaving them out of the bottom three only on goal difference, was followed by the sacking of di Matteo. In came Hodgson, himself dismissed by Liverpool, to transform their fortunes with his customary organisation and attention to detail. With Peter Odemwingie finding his goal touch again, Chris Brunt showing nerves of steel to convert two penalties against Liverpool and the team showing great character to come from behind twice to win at Sunderland, Albion went six games unbeaten under the new manager to move clear of trouble. Then, victory over Everton followed by Somen Tchoyi's hat-trick to retrieve a 3-0 deficit at Newcastle confirmed Albion's highest Premier League placing of 11th.

Barnes G................. 1 (3)	Cox S 8 (11)	Jara G...................... 24 (5)
Bednar R 1 (3)	Dorrans G 16 (5)	Meite A..............................9
Brunt C..........................33	Fortune M-A........... 13 (11)	Miller I .... - (5)
Carson S.......................31	Hurst J 1	Morrison J................. 25 (5)
Cech M................. 14 (1)	Ibanez P 8 (1)	Mulumbu Y.......................33

Myhill B............................6	Scharner P........................32	Thomas J..............32 (1)
Odemwingie P..........29 (3)	Shorey N................24 (3)	Vela C.........................3 (5)
Olsson J.........................23	Tamas G.............22 (4)	Wood C......................- (1)
Reid S................12 (10)	Tchoyi S.................6 (16)	Zuiverloom G..............1 (1)

League goals (56): Odemwingie 15, Mulumbu 7, Tchoyi 6, Brunt 4, Morrison 4, Scharner 4, Thomas 3, Fortune 2, Vela 2, Cox 1, Dorrans 1, Ibanez 1, Jara 1, Olsson 1, Reid 1, Opponents 3
FA Cup goals: None. **Carling Cup goals** (8): Cox 3, Ibanez 1, Reid 1, Tchoyi 1, Wood 1, Zuiverloom 1
Average home league attendance: 24,683. **Player of Year:** Youssouf Mulumbu

WEST HAM UNITED

They had the star of the show in Scott Parker, but not a good enough supporting cast. So West Ham went down and manager Avram Grant was sacked immediately after a 3-2 defeat at Wigan which left them at the foot of the table with no chance of escaping. Two goals by Demba Ba had suggested they might retain a slim chance of survival going into the last day of the season. Instead, the 2-0 advantage was surrendered and, for the 13th time, three or more goals were conceded. Not even the sterling efforts of Parker, voted Footballer of the Year by the Football Writers' Association, could do much about the demise. The writing was on the wall after the club's worst start to a Premier League season, four successive defeats and 12 goals against. There was a hint of a revival when Ba, signed during the winter transfer window, and Thomas Hitzlsperger, finally making his debut after six months out with a thigh injury, began to exert an influence. West Ham climbed out of the bottom three after beating Blackpool, Liverpool and Stoke and led Manchester United with two Mark Noble penalties. But they succumbed to Wayne Rooney's hat-trick, lost Parker with an achilles injury and lost five games on the trot to slip back.

Barrera P....................6 (8)	Faubert J.....................7 (2)	Obinna V..................17 (8)
Behrami V....................6 (1)	Gabbidon D..............24 (2)	O'Neil G......................7 (1)
Ben-Haim T.......................8	Green R...........................37	Parker S...................30 (2)
Boa Morte L...........19 (3)	Hines Z......................4 (5)	Piquionne F...........26 (8)
Boffin R..............................1	Hitzlsperger T................11	Reid W........................3 (4)
Bridge W.......................15	Ilunga H.................10 (1)	Sears F........................9 (2)
Cole C.................21 (14)	Jacobsen L...............22 (2)	Spector J.................10 (4)
Collison J....................2 (1)	Keane R....................5 (4)	Spence J.........................2
Da Costa M.............14 (2)	Kovac R.......................7 (6)	Stanislas J.................4 (2)
Demba Ba.................10 (2)	McCarthy B..............- (6)	Tomkins J................18 (1)
Diamanti A...................- (1)	Noble M...................25 (1)	Upson M.........................30
Dyer K........................8 (3)	Nouble F......................- (2)	

League goals (43): Ba 7, Piquionne 6, Cole 5, Parker 5, Noble 4, Obinna 3, Behrami 2, Hitzlsperger 2, Keane 2, Da Costa 2, Sears 1, Spector 1, Stanislas 1, Tomkins 1, Opponents 2
FA Cup goals (11): Obinna 3, Cole 2, Piquionne 2, Hitzlsperger 1, Reid 1, Sears 1, Spector 1.
Carling Cup goals (13): Cole 4, Obinna 2, Parker 2, Spector 2, Da Costa 1, Noble 1, Piquionne 1
Average home league attendance: 31,668. **Player of Year:** Scott Parker

WIGAN ATHLETIC

A nightmare start, a long, hard slog in the bottom three, then a finish to savour. That was the course Wigan chartered through a tough season, eventually defined by the first back-to-back victories Roberto Martinez had enjoyed in his two years in charge. His side opened up an escape route by beating relegation rivals Birmingham and Blackpool and gaining a point against Everton and Aston Villa. They were back in trouble when trailing West Ham 2-0 at home, before two goals from Charles N'Zogbia and a first for the club by Conor Sammon sent their opponents down instead. Then, in the final match, the outstanding N'Zogbia provided the cross from which Hugo Rodallega headed the only goal at Stoke – one which ensured survival. No wonder chairman Dave Whelan, who brought Martinez over from Spain as a young midfield player, celebrated wildly with his manager and players. It was a far cry from the beginning of the campaign when Wigan lost 4-0 to Blackpool, were trounced 6-0 in another home match by Chelsea and even at that stage looked relegation material.

Al Habsi A 34	Figueroa M............. 32 (1)	Pollitt M .... - (1)
Alcaraz A 34	Gohouri S 26 (1)	Piscu............................1
Boselli M 5 (3)	Gomez J 9 (4)	Rodallega H 34 (2)
Boyce E 20 (2)	Kirkland C.......................4	Sammon C............... 1 (6)
Caldwell G 23	McArthur J 3 (15)	Stam R 17 (8)
Caldwell S............... 8 (2)	McCarthy J...............24	Thomas H 22 (2)
Cleverley T 19 (6)	McManaman C .... - (3)	Watson B 23 (6)
Diame M 30 (6)	Moses V 8 (13)	
Di Santo F 9 (16)	N'Zogbia C............. 32 (2)	

League goals (40): N'Zogbia 9, Rodallega 9, Cleverley 3, McCarthy 3, Watson 3, Alcaraz 1, Diame 1, Di Santo 1, Figueroa 1, Gohouri 1, Gomez 1, Moses 1, Sammon 1, Stam 1, Opponents 4
FA Cup goals (3): Diame 2, McManaman 1. **Carling Cup goals** (7): Gomez 2, Boselli 1, Moses 1, N'Zogbia 1, Watson 1, Opponents 1
Average home league attendance: 16,812. **Player of Year:** Ali Al Habsi

WOLVERHAMPTON WANDERERS

Wolves experienced a rollercoaster ride on the way to beating the drop on the final day of the season. Relegation beckoned when Blackburn led 3-0 at Molineux and results elsewhere looked to be going against them. Jamie O'Hara pulled one back and with three minutes of normal time remaining Stephen Hunt curled in a second which, crucially, boosted their goal difference. Finally, there was confirmation of Birmingham's defeat at Tottenham to lift the pressure on a side who owed much to the way in which the loss of the injured Kevin Doyle for the run-in had been offset by Steven Fletcher's goals. Fletcher scored five in matches against Fulham, Birmingham, West Bromwich Albion and Sunderland which yielded eight precious points. Previously, Wolves had risen to the challenge of the top teams, ending Manchester United's unbeaten record, also beating Manchester City and Chelsea at Molineux and winning at Liverpool. But they struggled too often against lesser opposition and consequently spent most of the time in the bottom three.

Bent M .... - (3)	Hahnemann M................14	Mancienne M 13 (3)
Berra C 32 (1)	Halford G.................. - (2)	Milijas N............... 20 (3)
Craddock J............. 13 (1)	Hammill A 7 (3)	Mouyokolo S 2 (2)
Doyle M 25 (1)	Hennessey W...............24	Mujangi Bia G............. - (1)
Ebanks-Blake S 11 (19)	Henry K 28 (1)	O'Hara J 13 (1)
Edwards D 12 (3)	Hunt S 14 (6)	Stearman R............. 27 (4)
Elokobi G............. 23 (4)	Jarvis M 34 (3)	Van Damme J 4 (2)
Fletcher S 15 (14)	Jones D 11 (1)	Vokes S .... - (2)
Foley K 30 (3)	Keogh A .... - (1)	Ward S 27 (7)
Guedioura A 4 (6)	Kightly M 1 (3)	Zubar R 14 (1)

League goals (46): Fletcher 10, Ebanks-Blake 7, Doyle 5, Jarvis 3, Hunt 3, O'Hara 3, Elokobi 2, Foley 2, Milijas 2, Craddock 1, Edwards 1, Guedioura 1, Jones 1, Van Damme 1, Ward 1, Zubar 1, Opponents 1
FA Cup goals (7): Doyle 1, Fletcher 1, Hunt 1, Jarvis 1, Jones 1, Milijas 1, Bia 1. **Carling Cup goals** (8): Doyle 2, Milijas 2, Elokobi 1, Fletcher 1, Foley 1, Stearman 1
Average home league attendance: 27,696. **Player of Year:** Matt Jarvis

NPOWER CHAMPIONSHIP

BARNSLEY

Mark Robins left Oakwell at the end of a season in which the team achieved their highest position since returning to the game's second tier in 2006. He resigned after 20 months in the job over a disagreement with the board on the budget for the new campaign and the way the club should go forward. Barnsley's improvement to 17th was a modest one, but at least they were free from the relegation worries that dominated some of the recent campaigns. High-spots included home wins over Leeds (5-2) and Nottingham Forest (3-1), with the return matches each yielding a point. In his last match, Robins brought on 17-year-old Reuben Noble-Lazarus and saw the youngster who, in 2008 became the Football League's youngest-ever player, score the winner with a 25-yard drive against Millwall for his first senior goal. Robins was replaced by Rochdale's Keith Hill.

Arismendi, D 24 (7)	Harewood, M 9 (1)	Noble-Lazarus, R 1 (6)
Bennett, S .... - (4)	Hassell, B 34 (3)	Nouble, F....................4
Butterfield, J 18 (22)	Hayes, P 2 (5)	O'Brien, J 20 (13)
Clark, J..................... - (4)	Haynes, D..................20	O'Connor, G 19 (3)
Colace, H.............. 24 (2)	Hill, M......................23	Potter, L 2 (2)
Devaney, M 1 (5)	Hume, I .... - (1)	Rose, D .... - (1)
Dickinson, L............. - (3)	Lovre, G 19 (2)	Shackell, J..................44
Doyle, N 35 (8)	McEveley, J 15 (2)	Steele, L.....................46
Foster, S 32 (1)	McShane, P 10	Taylor, A .... - (2)
Gray, A 24 (10)	Mellis, J 14 (1)	Trippier, K 37 (2)
Hammill, A 25	Morales J .... - (5)	Wood, C 4 (3)

League goals (55): Hammill 8, Gray 7, Haynes 6, Harewood 4, O'Connor 4, Shackell 3, Butterfield 2, Doyle 2, Hill 2, Lovre 2, Mellis 2, Trippier 2, Arismendi 1, Colace 1, Foster 1, Hassell 1, McEveley 1, McShane 1, Noble-Lazarus 1, O'Brien 1, Opponents 3
FA Cup goals: None. **Carling Cup goals:** None
Average home league attendance: 11,855. **Player of Year:** Jason Shackell

BRISTOL CITY

David James hadn't banked on going straight from the World Cup to the bottom of the Championship table after a dozen matches with his new club. Neither did the veteran goalkeeper expect that the man who brought him to Ashton Gate, Steve Coppell, would announce his retirement from management after less than four months as manager. Coppell's assistant, Keith Millen, took over and City eventually began to find some form with three straight wins – along with three clean sheets – against Leicester, Sheffield United and Derby. But further inconsistency meant it was not until well into the second half of the season that they moved clear of the lower reaches of the table on the back of a run of six victories in seven matches. James played in all but one of the 46 matches. Nicky Maynard was restricted to only 11 starts because of a knee injury which ruled him out for six months. But the previous season's leading scorer started to make up for lost time by scoring six goals.

Adomah A................. 45 (1)	Elliott M 46	Keogh A.................... 4 (5)
Akinde J .... - (2)	Fontaine L 30 (1)	Maynard N 11 (2)
Campbell-Ryce J..... 21 (10)	Gerken D 1	McAllister J 33 (1)
Carey L 20 (1)	Haynes D 10 (3)	Nyatanga L 18 (2)
Caulker S..................29	Hunt N 6 (1)	Pitman B 21 (18)
Cisse K 19 (10)	Jackson M.............. - (4)	Reid B .... - (1)
Clarkson D 17 (16)	James D......................45	Ribeiro C 8 (1)
Edwards J 1 (1)	Johnson L 14 (6)	Rose D 13 (4)

93

Skuse C	25 (5)	Stewart D	18 (3)	Wilson J	2
Spence J	11	Vokes S	- (1)	Woolford M	10 (5)
Sproule I	4 (7)	Williams T	- (1)		
Stead J	24 (3)	Williams G	- (3)		

League goals (62): Pitman 13, Stead 9, Elliott 8, Clarkson 7, Maynard 6, Adomah 5, Campbell-Ryce 2, Caulker 2, Haynes 1, Johnson 1, Keogh 1, McAllister 1, Nyatanga 1, Skuse 1, Stewart 1, Opponents 3.
FA Cup goals: None. **Carling Cup goals** (2): McAllister 1, Sproule 1
Average home league attendance: 14,604. **Player of Year:** Albert Adomah

BURNLEY

Eddie Howe left behind one promotion challenge at Bournemouth to take on another at Turf Moor and looked to be leading Burnley towards a crack at an instant return to the Premier League. His new team gathered 16 points from run of six matches to move to within three points off a place in the top six with two fixtures in hand on their rivals. Then they fell away, gaining a single point from the next six matches, before a 2-1 win over Swansea in which 39-year-old Graham Alexander made his 1,000th career appearance. Further victories over Middlesbrough and Derby made up lost ground. But two points dropped at home to Portsmouth and a defeat at Leeds in the penultimate game ended their chances and they finished some way short in eighth position. Howe took over when Brian Laws was sacked following a home defeat by former club Scunthorpe.

Alexander G	15 (17)	Duffy S	1	Jensen B	21
Austin C	2 (2)	Eagles C	37 (6)	Marney D	34 (2)
Bartley M	3 (2)	Easton B	11 (1)	McCann C	4
Bikey A	27 (1)	Edgar D	3 (4)	Mears T	44
Carlisle C	33 (2)	Elliott W	37 (7)	Paterson M	7 (4)
Cork J	36 (4)	Fox D	35	Rodriguez J	37 (5)
Cort L	3 (1)	Grant L	25	Thompson S	2 (27)
Delfouneso N	7 (4)	Guidetti J	2 (3)	Wallace R	24 (16)
Duf M	27 (1)	Iwelumo C	29 (16)l		

League goals (65): Rodriguez 14, Eagles 11, Iwelumo 11, Alexander 3, Cork 3, Marney 3, Wallace 3, Bikey 2, Elliott 2, Paterson 2, Thompson 2, Carlisle 1, Delfouneso 1, Duff 1, Easton 1, Guidetti 1, McCann 1, Mears 1, Opponents 2
FA Cup goals (8): Eagles 3, Alexander 1, Carlisle 1, Mears 1, Paterson 1, Rodriguez 1. **Carling Cup goals** (5): Carlisle 1, Eagles 1, Elliott 1, McDonald 1, Thompson 1
Average home league attendance: 14,930. **Player of Year:** Jay Rodriguez

CARDIFF CITY

Twice at the end of the season, Cardiff fell from grace in front of their own supporters. The result was that a promising-looking promotion bid again fell short, following defeat by Blackpool in the 2010 Play-off Final. This time, they were disputing the runners-up spot with Norwich, and in a rich seam of form, until a 3-0 reversal in the penultimate match against a Middlesbrough team with little apart from pride to play for. It was followed by allegations that some players had been out drinking in the run-up to the game. Things looked brighter when a goalless draw was secured at Reading in the first leg of the play-off semi-final. But Cardiff went into the return without the injured Craig Bellamy, who had been so influential during a season-long loan at his home-town club from Manchester City. Cardiff suffered another 3-0 defeat and Dave Jones, the Championship's longest-serving manager paid the price, sacked after six years at the club. Watford's Malky Mackay took over.

Bellamy, C 34 (1)	Hudson M................. 39 (1)	Olofinjana S 38 (1)
Blake D 13 (13)	Keinan D 18	Parkin J 2 (9)
Bothroyd J 37	Keogh A................. 11 (5)	Quinn P 22 (1)
Burke C 31 (13)	Koumas J............... 5 (18)	Rae G 2 (5)
Bywater S 8	Marshall D....................11	Ramsey A 6
Chopra M................. 25 (7)	Matthews A 2 (6)	Riggott C 2
Drinkwater D 7 (2)	McCormack R............ - (2)	Samuel Jlloyd.............6
Emmanuel-Thomas J... 7 (7)	McNaughton K.............44	Whittingham P 45
Gyepes G 16 (5)	McPhail S............... 23 (5)	Wildig A..................... - (2)
Heaton T.......................27	Naylor L............... 25 (2)	

Play-offs – appearances: Bothroyd 2, Bywater 2, Blake 2, Burke 2, Emmanuel-Thomas 2, Keinan 2, McNaughton 2, Olofinjana 2, Whittingham 2, Chopra 1 (1), Bellamy 1, Quinn 1, Samuel 1, Koumas – (2), Matthews – (1), Naylor – (1), Parkin – (1)

League goals (76): Bothroyd 18, Bellamy 11, Whittingham 11, Chopra 9, Olofinjana 6, Burke 5, Emmanuel-Thomas 2, Keinan 2, Keogh 2, Koumas 2, Naylor 2, Gyepes 1, Parkin 1, Quinn 1, Rae 1, Ramsey 1, Opponents 1. **Play-offs – goals:** None

FA Cup goals (1): Chopra 1. **Carling Cup goals (5):** Bothroyd 2, McCormack 2, Chopra 1

Average home league attendance: 23,193. **Player of Year:** Kevin McNaughton

COVENTRY CITY

Former Wimbledon and Crystal Palace defender Andy Thorn became the latest manager to try to restore Coventry's fortunes. Thorn got the job after eight matches as caretaker, of which he won three, drew three and suffered two stoppage-time defeats. Thorn's attractive football went down well with the fans and he became the club's tenth man in charge since 2001, succeeding Aidy Boothroyd, who was sacked after ten months in the job. Approaching the half-way point of season, Coventry were handily placed, three points off an automatic promotion spot. Then they began to struggle for goals and went ten matches without a victory, before beating Crystal Palace. It was followed by another five games without a win and Boothroyd paid the price with his side sixth from bottom. Thorn was given a boost at the end of the season when the club's transfer embargo was lifted by the Football League.

Baker C 19 (13)	Gunnarsson A 37 (5)	O'Halloran S 10 (1)
Bell D....................... 20 (2)	Hussey C 8 (3)	Platt C................... 22 (12)
Cameron N............. 22 (3)	Ireland D .... - (1)	Quirke M..................... 3 (1)
Carsley L......................25	Jutkiewcz L 34 (8)	Turner B 14
Clarke J 12 (9)	Keogh R 46	Turner I 2
Clingan S 26 (3)	King M 24 (4)	Ward D 4 (1)
Cranie M............... 32 (4)	McIndoe M .... - (6)	Westwood K 41
Deegan G.................... - (1)	McPake J 11 (1)	Wilson C .... - (1)
Doyle M.............. 15 (3)	McSheffrey G 30 (3)	Wood R 35 (5)
Eastwood F 14 (13)	O'Donovan R .... - (2)	

League goals (54): King 12, Jutiewicz 9, McSheffrey 8, Eastwood 5, Gunnarsson 4, Turner 4, Platt 3, Bell 2, Baker 1, Clarke 1, Doyle 1, Keogh 1, Wood 1, Opponents 2

FA Cup goals (4): Baker 1, Eastwood 1, King 1, Wood 1. **Carling Cup goals:** None

Average home league attendance: 16,309. **Player of Year:** Marlon King

CRYSTAL PALACE

Dougie Freedman served Palace with distinction as a player, making 368 appearances and scoring 108 goals in two spells at the club. Now, he will also be remembered as the fledgling manager who led the team away from the threat of relegation. Freedman took over, initially on a caretaker basis, when the experienced George Burley was sacked within an hour of a 3-0 defeat at Millwall on New Year's Day which kept his side in the bottom three. They stayed there for the next month before edging clear, then managed to keep the teams below them at arms length for the rest of the season. It was tough going, with Palace always having to look over their shoulder. A home defeat by Scunthorpe threatened to undo all Freedman's good work, but the job was completed over Easter by a point gained at Doncaster followed by a 1-0 victory over Leeds. That winner came after 80 seconds from Neil Danns, whose red card later did not detract from the influential role he had played in the survival effort.

Agustien K 6 (2)	Dikgacoi K 13	N'Diaye A 4 (8)
Ambrose D 27 (1)	Djilali K 10 (4)	O'Keefe S 1 (3)
Andrew C 1 (12)	Dorman A 14 (6)	Obika J .... - (7)
Barrett A 5 (2)	Easter J 6 (8)	Parsons M 2
Bennett J 10 (3)	Gardner A 26 (2)	Price L ....
Cadogan K 7 (9)	Garvan O..................26	Scannell S 5 (14)
Clyne N 46	Iversen S 11 (6)	Sekajja I .... - (1)
Counago P 17 (13)	Lee A 3	Speroni J.....................45
Danns N 36 (1)	Marrow A 20 (1)	Vaughan J 28 (2)
Davids E 6	McCarthy P 43	Wright D 27 (1)
Davis C 17 (7)	Moxey D 17	Zaha W 26 (15)

League goals (44): Vaughan 9, Danns 8, Ambrose 7, Garvan 3, Counago 2, Iversen 2, Scannell 2, Lee 1, Bennett 1, Cadogan 1, Dikgacoi 1, Dorman 1, Easter 1, Gardner 1, McCarthy 1, Moxey 1, Sekajja 1, Zaha 1
FA Cup goals (1): Danns 1. **Carling Cup goals** (2): Lee 1, Opponents 1
Average home league attendance: 15,351. **Player of Year:** Nathaniel Clyne

DERBY COUNTY

A tough season for Nigel Clough's team, who were expected to make their presence felt in the top half of the table but instead finished deep in the bottom section. Derby were flying after a record six successive victories at Pride Park produced 20 goals and carried them to fourth in the table. Then it all fell apart, with the next nine home matches yielding just two points. A tendency to concede important late goals contributed to an overall run of just two victories in 18 games. There was also a defeat at the hands of non-league Crawley in the FA Cup. Derby had built up a sufficient reserve of points to ward off any prospect of dropping further – and there were brighter performances against promotion-chasing Swansea and Leeds, followed by a committed display to earn a point away to leaders Queens Park Rangers. But four successive defeats to finish with underlined the problems, including one against Bristol City when Robbie Savage made a final home appearance, the 600th start of his career, before retiring.

Addison M 10 (11)	Davies B 10 (3)	Noble R .... - (1)
Anderson R 4 (7)	Davies S 14 (6)	O'Brien M .... - (2)
Atkins R 1	Doyle C 5 (8)	Pearson S 21 (9)
Sanchez Ayala D....... 16 (1)	Fielding F 16	Porter C 6 (12)
Bailey J 32 (4)	Green P 36	Pringle B 3 (12)
Ball C 1 (4)	Hendrick J .... - (4)	Roberts G 24 (2)
Barker S 42 (1)	Hulse R 1	Robinson T 8 (5)
Brayford J 46	Jones B 7	Savage R 37 (3)
Bueno A 25 (4)	Kuqi S 8 (4)	Severn J .... - (1)
Buxton J .... - (1)	Leacock D 22 (3)	Varney L 1
Bywater S 22	Martin D .... - (2)	Ward J 13
Commons K 25 (1)	Moore L 9 (4)	
Cywka T 21 (10)	Moxey D 20 (2)	

League goals (58): Commons 13, Bueno 5, Davies S 5, Ward 5, Cywka 4, Moore 4, Savage 4, Green 2, Kuqi 2, Moxey 2, Porter 2, Robinson 2, Bailey 1, Barker 1, Brayford 1, Davies B 1,

Hulse 1, Leacock 1, Pearson 1, Opponents 1
FA Cup goals (1): Addison. **Carling Cup goals:** None
Average home league attendance: 25,892. **Player of Year:** John Brayford

DONCASTER ROVERS

Doncaster went into the New Year in a healthy mid-table position, within striking distance of the top six and with matches in hand on the teams immediately above them. But the second half of the season was a different story. Goals were hard to come by, wins scarce and a 6-0 home defeat by Ipswich further undermined confidence. There was a worrying slide down the table, interrupted only by a 3-1 success at Derby, where Billy Sharp ended a personal barren spell with two goals. Rovers lost 5-2 at Leeds next time out and although keeping the bottom three at arms length, were grateful for the two goals on-loan Jason Euell scored to earn a point at Barnsley and make them safe. Rovers failed to win any of their final dozen matches and finished one place above the relegation zone.

Brooker S	1 (12)	Hird S	20 (12)	Shiels D	15 (18)
Burge R	- (1)	Keegan P	9 (1)	Souza D	3 (5)
Chambers J	6 (1)	Kilgallon M	7 (5)	Stock B	31 (6)
Coppinger J	38 (2)	Lockwood A	13 (3)	Sullivan N	30 (1)
Dumbuya M	17 (6)	Martis S	24 (2)	Thomas W	17 (4)
Euell J	7 (5)	Mason R	5 (10)	Webster B	1 (6)
Fairhurst W	- (2)	Mills J	17 (1)	Wilson M	15 (12)
Friend G	30 (2)	Moussa F	14	Woods G	16
Gillett S	21 (1)	O'Connor J	34	Woods M	13 (2)
Hayter J	28 (4)	Oster J	41		
Healy D	6 (2)	Sharp B	27 (2)		

League goals (55): Sharp 15, Hayter 9, Coppinger 7, Euell 3, Shiels 3, Healy 2, Mills 2, Moussa 2, O'Connor 2, Stock 2, Brooker 1, Friend 1, Gillett 1, Lockwood 1, Martis 1, Woods M 1, Opponents 2
FA Cup goals (2): Hayter 1, Sharp 1. **Carling Cup goals** (1): Payne 1
Average home league attendance: 10,258. **Player of Year:** Billy Sharp

HULL CITY

A club-record run of unbeaten matches away from home transformed Hull from relegation candidates into challengers for a place in the play-offs. Had their form at the KC Stadium been up to scratch, they would have been in with a chance of an immediate return to the Premier League. Instead, they won only seven matches there and ultimately fell some way short. With his side two points off the top six, manager Nigel Pearson targeted victory in all four remaining matches. But, predictably, they then went down 4-2 at home to Middlesbrough and despite a hard-earned point next time out at Queens Park Rangers, it was not enough to keep hopes alive. That was 17 successive matches without defeat on their travels – and end of the road, with the final game of the season bringing a 3-0 reversal at Bristol City. Even so, a mid-table finish was a marked improvement on their predicament when owner Russell Bartlett agreed to sell his controlling interest in the club to local father-and-son businessmen Assem and Ehab Allam in a deal worth £40m. They were then third from bottom after 16 matches.

Akpan H	1 (1)	Belaid T	3 (5)	Cullen M	4 (13)
Amoo D	1 (6)	Bostock J	8 (3)	Dawson A	45
Ashbee I	19	Bullard J	5 (3)	Devitt J	7 (9)
Atkinson W	3 (1)	Cairney T	16 (6)	Duke M	20 (1)
Sanchez Ayala D	12	Chester J	21	Evans C	17 (1)
Barmby N	8 (23)	Cooper L	2	Fagan C	4 (1)

Folan C	2 (1)	Hobbs J	9 (4)	Simpson J	19 (13)
Fryatt M	21 (1)	Kilbane K	11 (3)	Solano N	6 (5)
Garcia R	16 (9)	Koren R	39 (1)	Stewart C	14
Gardner A	2	Mannone V	10	Vine R	4 (1)
Gerrard A	41	Mclean A	18 (5)	Zayatte K	16
Guzan B	16	McShane P	13 (6)		
Harper J	27 (1)	Rosenior L	26		

League goals (52): Fryatt 9, Koren 7, Simpson 6, Barmby 5, Gerrard 5, Evans 3, Mclean 3, Bostock 2, Bullard 2, Garcia 2, Amoo 1, Ashbee 1, Ayala 1, Cairney 1, Chester 1, Harper 1, Kilbane 1, Opponents 1
FA Cup goals (2): Barmby 2. **Carling Cup goals** (1): Cullen 1
Average home league attendance: 21,168. **Player of Year:** Anthony Gerrard

IPSWICH TOWN

Roy Keane's turbulent 20 months as manager came to an end in mid-season when he was sacked after seven defeats in nine matches sent his team sliding from sixth to 19th in the table. He was replaced by Paul Jewell, who led Bradford and Wigan into the Premier League and who was quickly into his stride with successive wins over Doncaster, Derby and Sheffield United. When 17-yeard-old Connor Wickham underlined his great promise by scoring a hat-trick in an impressive 6-0 victory at Doncaster. Ipswich were well clear of trouble. But they were unable to kick-on and establish a place in the top half. Worst of all, a 5-1 drubbing by Norwich followed a 4-1 beating by their arch-rivals at Carrow Road. Then, limitations were further exposed by a 4-1 defeat away to another promotion-chasing team, Swansea, and a 4-2 reversal at Leicester on the final day of the season.

Ainsley J	- (1)	Fulop M	35	Norris D	35 (1)
Brown T	6 (6)	Healy C	7 (9)	O'Connor S	2 (3)
Bullard J	16	Hyam L	8 (2)	O'Dea D	17 (3)
Carson J	8 (1)	Kennedy M	24 (2)	Peters J	12 (11)
Civelli L	- (9)	Lambe R	- (2)	Priskin T	18 (14)
Colback J	13	Leadbitter G	44	Scotland J	32 (7)
Delaney D	32	Lee-Barrett A	7	Smith T	22
Drury A	4 (8)	Livermore J	8 (4)	Stead J	2 (1)
Dyer K	1 (3)	Martin L	15 (1)	Townsend A	11 (2)
Eastman T	8 (1)	McAuley G	39	Walters J	1
Edwards C	42 (3)	Murphy B	4	Wickham C	24 (13)
Fallon R	4 (2)	Murray R	1 (7)	Zuiverloom G	4

League goals (62): Scotland 10, Wickham 9, Norris 8, Bullard 5, Leadbitter 5, Priskin 4, Edwards 3, Carson 3, Smith 3, Delaney 2, McAuley 2, Healy 2, Fallon 1, Peters 1, Stead 1, Townsend 1, Opponents 2
FA Cup goals: None. **Carling Cup goals** (11): Norris 3, Priskin 3, Edwards 1, Leadbitter 1, Delaney 1, McAuley 1, Murray 1.
Average home league attendance: 19,614. **Player of Year:** Carlos Edwards

LEEDS UNITED

Leeds recovered from the shock of surrendering a 4-1 lead at home to Preston and losing 6-4 to launch a free-scoring run of 12 matches unbeaten to climb to second place behind Queens Park Rangers midway through the season. Jonathan Howson and Luciano Becchio scored hat-tricks against Scunthorpe and Bristol City respectively as a second, succession promotion seemed a real possibility. A notable FA Cup performance at Arsenal, where victory was denied by a 90th minute Cesc Fabregas penalty, seemed to underline their credentials. But despite continuing to contest the runners-up spot until mid-March, they eventually wilted under the pressure of a highly competitive division to finish three points away. A 4-1 success against rivals Nottingham Forest proved the only one of a damaging eight-match run which concluded with defeat at Crystal Palace. At least, Leeds finished on a high, interrupting Queens Park Rangers' championship celebrations with a 2-1 win at Loftus Road.

Bannan B 3 (4)	Grella M .... - (1)	Naylor R 13 (2)
Becchio L 34 (7)	Higgs S 6	Nunez R .... - (2)
Bessone F 6	Howson J 46	O'Brien A..................30
Bromby L 9 (4)	Hughes A 5 (5)	Parker B 1 (1)
Brown J 3 (1)	Johnson B.......... 40 (5)	Paynter B 8 (14)
Bruce A 21	Kilkenny N 29 (8)	Sam L 7 (11)
Clayton A .... - (4)	Kisnorbo P .... - (1)	Schmeichel K............37
Collins N............... 20 (1)	Lichaj E 16	Snodgrass R 34 (3)
Connolly P 30	Livermore J 4 (1)	Somma D 12 (17)
Faye A 6 (2)	McCartney G 32	Watt S 9 (13)
Gradel M 38 (5)	McCormack R.......... 6 (15)	White A 1 (1)

League goals (81): Becchio 19, Gradel 18, Somma 11, Howson 10, Snodgrass 6, Johnson 5, McCormack 2, O'Brien 2, Sam 2, Kilkenny 1, Bruce 1, Naylor 1, Paynter 1, Watt 1, Opponents 1
FA Cup goals (2): Johnson 1, Snodgrass 1. **Carling Cup goals** (5): Becchio 1, Howson 1, Kilkenny 1, Sam 1, Somma 1
Average home league attendance: 27,299. **Player of Year:** Max Gradel

LEICESTER CITY

Sven-Goran Eriksson led Leicester out of early trouble, but they were always playing catch-up and unable to gain a foothold in the scramble for play-off places. The former England coach became their eighth manager since 2004 when Paulo Sousa was sacked, less than three months after taking over, with his side bottom nine matches into the season. The club's worst league start for 16 years – accompanied by a takeover by a consortium led by Thai businessman Aiyawatt Raksriaksorn – gave way to a rapid improvement under Eriksson. Leicester went on to chalk up some handsome victories – 5-1 against Doncaster and four goals scored against Millwall, Barnsley, Burnley, Watford and Ipswich. They also took one of his former clubs, Manchester City, to an FA Cup replay. However, the high level of consistency required to make up the lost ground was never there and they finished eight points adrift of the top six.

Bamba S......................16	Kamara D 5 (2)	Oakley M 22 (12)
Bednar R 4 (1)	Kennedy T 1	Ricardo 8
Berner B 15 (2)	King A 44 (1)	Tunchev A................... - (2)
Bruma J 10 (1)	Kirkland C........................3	Van Aanholt P 12
Campbell D....................3	Lamey M................... 2 (2)	Vassell D 26 (5)
Cunningham G 13	Logan C................. 2 (1)	Vitor M 13 (2)
Davies C 12	Mee B 15	Waghorn M........... 11 (19)
Dyer L 18 (17)	Moreno J....................3	Weale C 28 (1)
Fryatt M 5 (7)	Morrison M 10 (1)	Wellens R 44 (1)
Gallagher P 32 (9)	Moussa C 2 (6)	Yakubu, Aiyegbeni ... 19 (1)
Hobbs J 23 (3)	N'Guessan D 3 (2)	Yuki Abe 25 (11)
Howard S 11 (18)	Naughton K................34	
Ikeme C......................5	Neilson R....................7	

League goals (76): King 15, Yakubu 11, Gallagher 10, Naughton 5, Howard 4, Vassell 4, Waghorn 4, Dyer 3, Vitor 3, Bamba 2, Bruma 2, Fryatt 2, Kamara 2, Oakley 2, Wellens 2, Abe 1, Berner 1, Campbell 1, Moussa 1, Van Aanholt 1
FA Cup goals (4): Bamba 1, Dyer 1, Gallagher 1, King 1. **Carling Cup goals** (9): Fryatt 2,

Wellens 2, Dyer 1, Howard 1, Morrison 1, Neilson 1, Opponents 1
Average home league attendance: 23,709. **Player of Year:** Richie Wellens

MIDDLESBROUGH

For the second successive season, Middlesbrough were among the favourites for a return to the Premier League – and once again failed to justify the odds. This time, they struggled to finish in the top half of the table, a 3-1 home defeat by Ipswich on the opening day proving an accurate indicator of things to come. There was also a worrying slump in support, with lowest-ever league attendances at the Riverside below 14,000. Gordon Strachan resigned in mid-October with his side fifth from bottom, making way for the former West Bromwich Albion and Celtic manager Tony Mowbray. Back at the club he captained in the 1980s, Mowbray was unable to bring about any significant improvement, an FA Cup defeat by Burton adding to his problems. With a dozen games remaining, Middlesbrough were just three points off the relegation zone. Then, after a 5-2 defeat at Reading, results began to pick up, building to a rousing finish which brought successive wins over Hull, Coventry, Cardiff and Doncaster and 12 goals scored.

Arca J 27 (5)	Halliday A 5 (7)	Ripley C .... - (1)
Bailey N 28 (6)	Hines S 14	Robson B 29 (3)
Bates M 31	Hoyte J 14 (3)	Smallwood R 7 (5)
Bennett J 28 (3)	Kilgallon M 2	Smith P 10
Boyd K 18 (9)	Kink T 8 (13)	Steele J 35
Coyne D 1	Lita L 28 (10)	Tavares M 10 (3)
Davies A 5 (1)	McDonald S 34 (4)	Taylor A 20 (1)
Emnes M 18 (5)	McMahon T 28 (6)	Thomson K 18 (1)
Flood W 1 (4)	McManus S 22 (2)	Wheater D 24
Franks J 1 (3)	Miller L .... - (1)	Williams L 5 (1)
Gibson B .... - (1)	O'Neil G 17 (1)	Williams R 10 (2)
Grounds J 5 (1)	Park C .... - (4)	Zemmama M 2 (7)
Haas M 1 (1)	Reach A .... - (1)	

League goals (68): Lita 12, McDonald 12, Boyd 6, Robson 5, Kink 4, Arca 3, Bates 3, Emnes 3, Taylor 3, Wheater 3, McMahon 2, Grounds 2, Halliday 1, Hines 1, McManus 1, Reach 1, Smallwood 1, Williams R 1, Zemmama 1, Opponents 4
FA Cup goals (1): O'Neil 1. **Carling Cup goals** (3): McDonald 2, Arca 1
Average home league attendance: 16,377. **Player of Year:** Julio Arca

MILLWALL

Satisfaction at following promotion with a ninth-place finish was tinged with disappointment that a late charge for the play-offs ran out of steam in the penultimate match. Millwall were in the bottom half of the table, ten points adrift and facing a demanding run of fixtures against five teams above them. They rose to the occasion by beating Queens Park Rangers, Burnley, Hull and Leeds and sharing six goals with Cardiff to close the gap to four points. Then, a goalless draw with Bristol City in which leading scorer Steve Morison was sent off, followed by defeat at Coventry where his strike partner Neil Harris saw red, proved costly. Millwall coped well without the suspended players, overcoming Preston and Scunthorpe with goals from the new front pair of John Marquis and Josh McQuoid. But a home defeat by Swansea ended their hopes.

Abdou N 30 (4)	Dunne A 38 (1)	Hughes-Mason K .... - (1)
Andrew C 3	Eastmond C 4 (2)	Laird M .... - (1)
Barron S 35 (3)	Forde D 46	Lisbie K 10 (10)
Berthel Askou J 1	Grabban L	Marquis J 5 (6)
Bouazza H 3 (9)	Hackett C 7 (9)	McQuoid J 7 (4)
Carter D 5 (5)	Harris N 7 (19)	Mkandawire T 34 (1)
Craig T 21 (3)	Henry J 39 (3)	Morison S 40

100

Puncheon J.....................7	Rowlands M .... - (1)	Townsend A....................11
Purse D 9 (4)	Schofield D............20 (11)	Trotter L..................34 (1)
Robinson P 35 (2)	Shittu D...........................9	Ward D 28 (3)
Robinson T 8 (2)	Smith J..........................9	

League goals (62): Morison 15, Trotter 7, Henry 5, Puncheon 5, Lisbie 4, Marquis 4, Robinson P 3, Robinson T 3, Barron 2, Harris 2, Schofield 2, Townsend 2, Bouazza 1, McQuoid 1, Mkandawire 1, Purse 1, Smith 1, Ward 1, Opponents 2
FA Cup goals (1): Schofield. **Carling Cup goals** (5): Morison 2, Dunne 1, Harris 1, Trotter 1
Average home league attendance: 12,438. **Player of Year:** Tamika Mkandawire

NORWICH CITY

Paul Lambert described it as a 'miracle' after his side won a second successive promotion to bring Premier League football back to Carrow Road. They clinched it on a dramatic day which had seemed likely to send the destination of the runners-up spot behind Queens Park Rangers into the final progamme of matches. Cardiff suffered a surprise 3-0 home defeat by Middlesbrough and two-and-a-half-hours later Norwich took full advantage with a 1-0 victory at Portsmouth. The winner from Canadian international Simeon Jackson was his ninth goal in seven games, including hat-tricks against Scunthorpe and Derby – a remarkable turnaround in fortunes for a player who went five months without scoring earlier in the season. Lambert, who took over at the start of the previous campaign after Norwich were beaten 7-1 by Colchester in their opening match, saw them kick-off this time with a home defeat by Watford. But with Grant Holt playing a captain's role, they soon settled into a successful rhythm – and a never-say-die attitude which would bring 22 points from goals scored in the final 10 minutes. Holt also netted two hat-tricks, in the first of two big wins over arch-rivals Ipswich and against Scunthorpe.

Barnett L 25	Jackson S 20 (18)	Smith K....................19 (9)
Berthel Askou J 2 (3)	Johnson O................ - (4)	Smith S 5 (2)
Crofts A 44	Lansbury H 15 (8)	Surman A 19 (3)
Daley L .... - (1)	Lappin S 20 (7)	Tierney M 14 (2)
Drury A 19 (1)	Martin C 21 (9)	Tudor Jones O 1 (1)
Edwards R .... - (3)	Martin R.......................46	Vokes S 1 (3)
Fox D 30 (2)	McNamee A 5 (12)	Ward E 39
Gill M .... - (4)	Nelson M 7 (1)	Whitbread Z 20 (2)
Holt G 44 (1)	Pacheco D 3 (3)	Wilbraham A 5 (7)
Hoolahan W 36 (5)	Rudd D...........................1	
Hughes S .... - (1)	Ruddy J.......................45	

League goals (83): Holt 21, Jackson 13, Hoolahan 10, Crofts 8, Martin R 5, Lansbury 4, Martin C 4, Surman 3, Nelson 2, Pacheco 2, Barnett 1, Drury 1, Fox 1, Vokes 1, Ward 1, Whitbread 1, Wilbraham 1, Opponents 4
FA Cup goals: None. **Carling Cup goals** (5): Holt 2, Martin C 2, Berthel Askou 1
Average home league attendance: 25,386. **Player of Year:** Grant Holt

NOTTINGHAM FOREST

Former England manager Steve McClaren was handed the task of planning for another push for the Premier League after the club's fourth defeat in the semi-finals of the play-offs in nine years. McClaren replaced Billy Davies, sacked after this latest disappointment. Davies admitted his side did not have the strength in depth for automatic promotion – even when briefly climbing to second behind Queens Park Rangers in mid-February after six successive wins. The manager, however, had no complaints about the efforts of his players in holding on to sixth place and when trying to match Swansea when it came to sudden-death. Forest went into the first leg at the City Ground having scored 14 goals in the final four matches, but were frustrated when their opponents overcame a first minute sending-off to secure a goalless draw. Trailing 2-0 in the return, they were given hope by a goal from Robert Earnshaw, who was then denied an equaliser by the woodwork before Swansea scored a third to make sure of going through. Earlier in the season, Forest extended their unbeaten Championship record at home to 36 matches before losing to Hull.

Adebola D 4 (25)	Earnshaw R 26 (8)	Moloney B 5 (1)
Anderson P 27 (9)	Findley R .... - (2)	Morgan W 46
Bennett J .... - (3)	Gunter C 40 (3)	Moussi S 25 (6)
Bertrand R 19	Konchesky P 14 (1)	Ramsey A 2 (3)
Blackstock D 13 (4)	Lynch J 8 (4)	Rodney N .... - (3)
Boyd K 7 (3)	Majewski R 21 (5)	Tudgay M 19 (3)
Camp L.......................46	McCleary G 7 (11)	Tyson N 11 (19)
Chambers L 43 (1)	McGoldrick D 10 (11)	Wilson K 8 (2)
Cohen C 41 (1)	McGugan L 34 (6)	
Darlow K .... - (1)	McKenna P 30 (2)	

Play-offs – appearances: Camp 2, Chambers 2, Cohen 2, Gunter 2, McGugan 2, Moloney 2, Morgan 2, Boyd 1 (1), Earnshaw 1 (1), Tudgay 1 (1), Tyson 1 (1), Anderson 1, McGoldrick 1, McKenna 1, Moussi 1, Majewski – (1), McCleary – (1).

League goals (69): McGugan 13, Earnshaw 8, Boyd 6, Tudgay 7, Chambers 6, Blackstock 5, McGoldrick 5, Anderson 3, Adebola 2, Cohen 2, Majewski 2, McCleary 2, McKenna 2, Tyson 2, Konchesky 1, Morgan 1, Opponents 2. **Play-offs – goals** (1): Earnshaw 1
FA Cup goals (4): Adebloa 1, Anderson 1, Chambers 1, McGoldrick 1. **Carling Cup goals** (1): Thornhill 1
Average home league attendance: 23,062. **Player of Year:** Luke Chambers

PORTSMOUTH

Another eventful season – on and off the pitch – at Fratton Park. It started in the High Court with prospects of survival for the relegated, debt-ridden club boosted by a 'victory' over the Inland Revenue. A team shredded after relegation kicked off at Coventry with just 15 players, four of them trainees, and were bottom after seven matches yielded just two points. Meanwhile, the club issued a statement warning of the danger of going out of business over a £2.5m debt to Sacha Gaydamak. Agreement was reached with the former owner and Portsmouth came out of administration after being sold to a company controlled by Hong Kong businessman Balram Chainrai. Back on the pitch, things were looking up, a 6-1 win over Leicester opening the way for a climb into the top half of table. The rollercoaster continued – nine matches without a win, six successive victories without conceding a goal and finally another slide. The result, 16th place, was followed by another takeover, this time by a company headed by Russian businessman Vladimir Antonov.

Ashdown J 46	Hreidarsson H 20 (8)	Pack M .... - (1)
Brown M 20 (1)	Hughes R.................. 5 (6)	Ritchie M.................... 2 (3)
Ciftci N................... 4 (15)	Kanu N................. 13 (19)	Rocha R 26 (3)
Cotterill J 12 (3)	Kilbey T .... - (2)	Smith T 3
De Laet R 22	Kitson D 35	Sonko I................... 16 (7)
Dickinson C........... 23 (13)	Lawrence L 28 (3)	Utaka J 23 (2)
Gregory P .... - (1)	Mokoena A 29 (8)	Ward J 33 (9)
Halford G.......................33	Mullins H......................45	Webber D................. 1 (7)
Hogg J 19	Nugent D......................44	Wilson M 4

League goals (53): Nugent 13, Kitson 8, Lawrence 7, Halford 5, Utaka 3, Ward 3, Brown 2, Kanu 2, Mokoena 2, Mullins 2, Ciftci 1, Cotterill 1, Hreidarsson 1, Sonko 1, Opponents 2
FA Cup goals (1): Kilbey 1. **Carling Cup goals** (4): Brown 1, Ciftci 1, Lawrence 1, Nugent 1
Average home league attendance: 15,707. **Player of Year:** Hayden Mullins

PRESTON NORTH END

When a hat-trick from Jon Parkin helped Preston deliver a stunning comeback by turning a 4-1 deficit at Leeds into a 6-4 victory six weeks into the season, the prospect of relegation was the last thing on everyone's mind. For Darren Ferguson and his players, however, it was something they soon had to contend with. The next 13 matches yielded only two victories, which saw them sink to the bottom of the table and Ferguson paid the price after a home defeat by Middlesbrough. Former Hull manager Phil Brown was given the task of rescuing a side seven points from safety – a situation which became increasingly hopeless with the gap extending to 13. Brown achieved his first win in his 12th match in charge – a handsome 3-0 success at Scunthorpe. Then, home victories against Coventry and Swansea restored a bit more pride. But Preston fell away again and finished six points adrift, ending an 11-year stay in the game's second tier. Brown's insistence that they could bounce straight back was the only cause for optimism.

Ashbee I 19	Gray D 12 (10)	Miller G .... - (1)
Barton A 24 (9)	Hayes P 11 (12)	Morgan C 30 (1)
Brown C.............. 12 (4)	Hume I 29 (2)	Nicholson B 18 (4)
Brown W 12 (1)	James M 10	Parkin J 16 (3)
Carter D................ 13 (1)	Johnson E 15 (1)	Parry P 6 (17)
Clarke L 5 (1)	Jones B 43	Proctor J .... - (5)
Cort L..................13	Khumalo B..............6	Pugh D.................5
Coutts P 17 (6)	King J 6 (2)	Russell D 21 (4)
Davidson C......... 17 (1)	Leather S.................2	St Ledger S............31
De Laet R 5	Linganzi A...............1	Tonge M.................5
Devine D.................2	Lonergan A 29	Treacy K 33 (5)
Douglas J............. - (2)	Mayor D............. 5 (16)	Turner I 17
Ellington N 7 (11)	McLaughlin C......... 5 (2)	Wright B .... - (2)
Gardner A..............4	Middleton D........... - (2)	

League goals (54): Hume 12, Treacy 7, Parkin 7, Jones 6, Nicholson 4, Davidson 3, Hayes 2, Ellington 2, Morgan 2, Barton 1, Brown C 1, Clarke 1, Coutts 1, Proctor 1, St Ledger 1, Tonge 1, Opponents 2
FA Cup goals (1): Carter 1. **Carling Cup goals** (8): Hayes 2, Treacy 2, Coutts 1, Davidson 1, James 1, King 1
Average home league attendance: 11,767. **Player of Year**: Billy Jones

QUEENS PARK RANGERS

Manager Neil Warnock and his midfielder Alejando Faurlin experienced a mixture of delight and relief as they held aloft the Championship trophy on a dramatic final day of the season at Loftus Road. Earlier, with kick-off approaching for the final match against Leeds, they were still waiting to hear whether the club would lose points for breaches of rules over the signing of the Argentine player in the summer of 2009. Then, an hour before the start, the FA announced there would be no deduction but a fine of £875,000 – a decision that confirmed Rangers as champions and put them back in the Premier League after a 15-year absence. It was the third team Warnock had led into the top-flight, after Notts County and Sheffield United, and the seventh promotion of his managerial career. They were the dominant force for most of the time, having started with a club-record 19 unbeaten matches and at one stage leading the division by ten points. Their key man was the Moroccan midfielder Adel Taarabt, whose wide-ranging skills influenced so many matches, brought him19 goals and earned the Championship's Player of the Year award. Rangers also had the most dominant defence, which none of their rivals could match.

Agyemang P.......... - (19)	Buzsaky A............ 9 (10)	Clarke L.............. 2 (11)
Andrade B.............. - (1)	Cerny R 2	Connolly M........... 33 (3)
Borrowdale G............... - (1)	Chimbonda P .... - (3)	Derry S 45

Ephraim H 19 (9)	Kenny P.....................44	Rowlands M .... - (4)
Faurlin A.....................40	Leigertwood M............. - (9)	Shittu D..................... 5 (2)
German A .... - (2)	Mackie J.....................25	Smith T 23 (10)
Gorkss K.....................42	Miller I 4 (8)	Taarabt A 43 (1)
Hall F 12 (7)	Orr B 29 (4)	Tofas G .... - (1)
Helguson H 32 (2)	Parker J .... - (1)	Vaagen Moen P.......... 1 (6)
Hill C.....................44	Ramage P .... - (4)	Walker K.....................20
Hulse R 12 (9)	Routledge W 20	

League goals (71): Taarabt 19, Helguson 13, Mackie 9, Smith 6, Routledge 5, Ephraim 3, Faurlin 3, Gorkss 3, Agyemang 2, Hill 2, Hulse 2, Hall 1, Miller 1, Orr 1, Opponents 1
FA Cup goals: None. **Carling Cup goals** (1): German 1
Average home league attendance: 15,635. **Player of Year:** Paddy Kenny

READING

With a month of the season remaining, Reading had built up such a head of steam that there was a real chance of the runners-up spot. Accompanying an FA Cup victory at Everton and a narrow defeat at Manchester City, were eight successive victories and 22 goals scored. Then, after moving to within three points of second place, they lost some of this sparkle, unable to compete with Norwich's surge down the home straight. Goalless draws against Leeds and Coventry sandwiched a home defeat by Sheffield United and left them fifth. Shane Long scored twice to add to his total of 21 in a convincing 3-0 victory at Cardiff in the second leg of the play-offs, but conceding three in the first-half at Wembley proved beyond repair. Matt Mills and an own goal pulled it back to 3-2, but Swansea's fourth ten minutes from the end of normal time settled the issue. This one echoed the late goals Reading conceded earlier in the season, left them trailing the leading group and which, ultimately, had an effect on the outcome of their season.

Antonio M 2 (19)	Hunt N 19 (14)	McCarthy A 12 (1)
Armstrong C 6 (1)	Ingimarsson I 12 (1)	Mills M.....................38
Church S 14 (23)	Karacan J 39 (1)	Pearce A 20 (1)
Cummings S 10	Kebe J 34 (2)	Rasiak G .... - (1)
Federici A.....................34	Khizanishvili Z......... 21 (1)	Robson-Kanu H 12 (15)
Griffin K.....................33	Leigertwood M 21 (1)	Sigurdsson G.....................4
Gunnarsson B.......... 10 (2)	Long S.....................44	Tabb J 15 (6)
Harte I.....................40	Manset M 4 (9)	Williams M.....................3
Howard B................ 19 (5)	McAnuff J.....................40	

Play-offs – appearances: Federici 3, Griffin 3, Hunt 3, Karacan 3, Khizanishvili 3, Mills 3, Harte 3, Leigertwood 3, Long 3, McAnuff 3, Robson-Kanu 1 (1), Cummings 1, Kebe 1, Church – (2), Howard – (1), Manset – (1), Tabb – (1)
League goals (77): Long 21, Harte 11, Hunt 10, Kebe 9, Church 5, Robson-Kanu 5, McAnuff 4, Karacan 4, Mills 2, Manset 2, Sigurdsson 2, Antonio 1, Leigertwood 1, Pearce 1. **Play-offs – goals** (5): Long 2, McAnuff 1, Mills 1, Opponents 1
FA Cup goals (4): Long 2, Leigertwood 1, Mills 1. **Carling Cup goals** (4): Mills 2, Rasiak 1, Robson-Kanu 1
Average home league attendance: 17,681. **Player of Year:** Shane Long

SCUNTHORPE UNITED

The summer departure of prolific strike pair Gary Hooper and Paul Hayes suggested a difficult season ahead at Glanford Park. When Scunthorpe also lost manager Nigel Adkins, who transformed them into a Championship club, to Southampton after five matches, the task of continuing to compete on shoestring gates was made that much more demanding. And when they won only one of the first 13 league matches at home, the writing was on the wall. Coach

Ian Baraclough, who replaced Adkins, signed eight new players – half of them on loan – in the January transfer window and there was a glimmer of hope when his team at last showed some home form to beat promotion-chasing Nottingham Forest and Swansea and come from 2-0 down to overcome Sheffield United. But defensive shortcomings soon resurfaced, Baraclough was sacked and there was precious little room for error for the new man, Bury's Alan Knill, in the eight games remaining. Despite a rousing 4-1 win over champions-elect Queens Park Rangers, Scunthorpe finished bottom.

Byrne C 20 (1)	Jones R 13 (1)	Raynes M 15 (7)
Canavan N 6 (2)	Lillis J 15	Reid P 12
Collins M 19 (13)	McClenahan T .... - (1)	Sears F 9
Cowan-Hall P .... - (1)	McDonald K 3 (2)	Slocombe S................... - (2)
Dagnall C................ 31 (6)	McNulty J 5 (1)	Thompson G................. 4 (8)
Duffy M 19 (3)	Miller L 12 (6)	Togwell S 34 (2)
Forte J 18 (6)	Mirfin D 23	Warner T 2
Garner J 17 (1)	Murphy J 29	Williams M...........................5
Godden M .... - (5)	N'Guessan D 3	Woolford M 18 (6)
Gordon B 13 (1)	Nelson M 20	Wright J 31 (5)
Grant R 7 (20)	Nolan E 32 (3)	Wright A 16 (4)
Hughes A................ 18 (1)	Nunez R 8	
Ibrahim A 4 (7)	O'Connor M.............. 25 (7)	

League goals (43): O'Connor 8, Woolford 6, Garner 6, Dagnall 5, Forte 3, Mirfin 3, Nunez 3, Byrne 2, Collins 1, Duffy 1, Jones 1, McDonald 1, Miller 1, N'Guessan 1, Thompson 1
FA Cup goals (1): Collins 1. **Carling Cup goals (8):** Dagnall 2, Woolford 2, Collins 1, Forte 1, O'Connor 1, Wright J 1
Average home league attendance: 5,547. **Player of Year:** Sam Togwell

SHEFFIELD UNITED

Danny Wilson was installed as the club's fourth manager in nine months at the end of a season which brought relegation to the game's third tier for the first time for 23 years. The turmoil started early, with Kevin Blackwell sacked when a 3-0 home defeat by Queens Park Rangers followed a 2-0 loss to Hartlepool in the Carling Cup. Blackwell was replaced by former Wales captain Gary Speed, whose first job in management had lasted just four months when he agreed to take charge of the national team. Micky Adams left Port Vale to replace Speed with the team six points clear of the relegation zone. That cushion was swallowed up as Adams couldn't buy a win for the next 13 matches. By the time it came against Nottingham Forest, United were six points adrift. There was further encouragement with a 2-0 victory over promotion-chasing Leeds, but successive home defeats by Middlesbrough and Cardiff ended all hope of avoiding the same fate neighbours Wednesday experienced the previous season.

Bartley K 21	Jordan S 14 (1)	Phillskirk D .... - (3)
Batth D....................... - (1)	Kennedy T .... - (1)	Quinn S 33 (4)
Bent M 4 (7)	Kozluk R..................... 2 (6)	Reid A 8 (1)
Bogdanovic D......... 12 (20)	Long G 1	Riise B H 9 (4)
Britton L 22 (2)	Lowry S 17	Simonsen S................ 43 (2)
Calve J 16 (2)	Lowton M 21 (11)	Slew J 5 (2)
Collins N.....................14	Maguire M 4 (1)	Taylor A 7 (2)
Cresswell R 30 (5)	Mattock J 12 (1)	Tonne E .... - (2)
Doyle M 16	McAllister D 1 (1)	Vokes S 4 (2)
Ertl J 25 (3)	Montgomery N.......... 34 (1)	Ward J 13 (6)
Evans C 26 (8)	Morgan C........................8	Williamson L 14 (2)
Harriott M .... - (2)	Nosworthy N 31 (1)	Wright R 2
Henderson D....................8	Parrino E 7 (1)	Yeates M 18 (17)

League goals (44): Evans 9, Bogdanovic 5, Cresswell 5, Yeates 5, Lowton 4, Williamson 3, Henderson 2, Reid 2, Slew 2, Calve 1, Kozluk 1, McAllister 1, Quinn 1, Riise 1, Vokes 1, Opponents 1
FA Cup goals (1): Ward 1. **Carling Cup goals:** None.
Average home league attendance: 20,632. **Player of Year:** Stephen Quinn

SWANSEA CITY

Swansea completed a remarkable rise from the brink of relegation to the Conference to a place in the Premier League by overcoming Reading in the Play-off Final. Scott Sinclair's hat-trick in a 4-2 win came eight years after James Thomas scored three times in a victory over Hull by the same scoreline on the final day of the season to secure the club's survival. After that came promotion from League Two in 2005, then the League One title three years later. Now Brendan Rodgers has led his side into the big time in his first season as manager after being sacked by Reading, reaping the reward for a cultured brand of football that drew widespread approval. Sinclair also joined Swansea in the summer of 2010, following an unsuccessful spell with Chelsea and loan moves to six clubs. The 22-year-old's 19 goals in the regular campaign included seven penalties and he showed that same confidence to score twice from the spot at Wembley. Swansea started the season indifferently, losing three of the first six games, before cementing a top-six spot in October. They held Nottingham Forest to a goalless draw in the semi-finals, after having Neil Taylor sent off inside two minutes, and won the second leg 3-1.

Agustien K 3 (5)	Easter J 2 (4)	Pratley D 28 (6)
Alfei D .... - (1)	Emnes M 3 (1)	Priskin T .... - (4)
Allen J 30 (10)	Gower M 37 (3)	Rangel A 37 (1)
Beattie C 9 (13)	Kuqi S .... - (2)	Richards A 6
Borini F 8 (1)	Lopez J .... - (1)	Serran A 5 (6)
Britton L 10 (7)	Lucas L .... - (1)	Sinclair S 39 (4)
Cotterill D 10 (4)	Monk G 27 (2)	Tate A 39 (1)
De Vries D 46	Moore L 11 (4)	Taylor N 25 (4)
Dobbie S 23 (18)	Nouble F 2 (4)	Williams A 46
Donnelly S .... - (1)	Orlandi A 13 (7)	Van der Gun C 1 (9)
Dyer N 45 (1)	Pintado G .... - (1)	

Play-offs – appearances: Allen 3, Borini 3, Britton 3, De Vries 3, Dobbie 3, Dyer 3, Rangel 3, Sinclair 3, Tate 3, Williams 3, Monk 2 (1), Taylor 1, Moore – (3), Gower – (2), Pratley – (2), Serran – (1)
League goals (69): Sinclair 19, Dobbie 9, Pratley 9, Borini 6, Beattie 4, Moore 3, Williams 3, Allen 2, Dyer 2, Emnes 2, Gower 2, Rangel 2, Britton 1, Cotterill 1, Easter 1, Nouble 1, Priskin 1, Van der Gun 1. **Play-offs – goals** (7): Sinclair 3, Dobbie 2, Britton, Pratley
FA Cup goals (5): Van der Gun 2, Monk 1, Pratley 1, Sinclair 1. **Carling Cup goals** (9): Sinclair 4, Kuqi 2, Van der Gun 2, Pratley 1
Average home league attendance: 15,507. **Player of Year:** Nathan Dyer

WATFORD

A prolific season for Danny Graham was not enough to establish his side in the promotion picture. The former Carlisle striker kicked off with two goals at Norwich on the opening day of the season and went on to become the Championship's leading scorer on 24. With three more in FA Cup and Carling Cup ties, he became the club's most successful marksman since Luther Blissett netted 28 in the 1984-85 season. Defensive weaknesses, however, meant Watford conceded too many to have a chance of reaching the play-offs. They started well, climbing to third after winning 6-1 at Millwall and beating Middlesbrough 3-1. Then, after a lean spell, there were six straight successes, with Graham scoring eight times in the club's best run for more than a decade. Again form dipped and this time eight matches without a victory left them struggling to make up ground. Finally, defeat in the final three matches pushed them into the bottom half of the table.

Malky Mackay resigned to take over at Cardiff and was succeeded by his assistant, Sean Dyche, the former defender's first managerial appointment.

Bennett D 5 (5)	Hoban T .... - (1)	Mutch J 21 (2)
Bryan M 4 (1)	Hodson L 26 (3)	Taylor A 19
Buckley W 27 (6)	Jenkins R 13 (6)	Taylor M 46
Cowie D 37	Loach S 46	Thompson A 7 (3)
Deeney T 17 (19)	Mariappa A 45	Townsend A 2 (1)
Doyley L 36	Massey G .... - (3)	Walker L .... - (5)
Drinkwater D 3 (9)	McGinn S 24 (5)	Weimann A 10 (8)
Eustace J 41	Mingoia P 2 (3)	Whichelow M 4 (15)
Graham D 45	Murray S 1	

League goals (77): Graham 24, Sordell 12, Eustace 6, Taylor 6, Mutch 5, Buckley 4, Cowie 4, Weimann 4, Whichelow 3, Deeney 2, McGinn 2, Hodson 1, Jenkins 1, Mariappa 1, Taylor 1, Thompson 1
FA Cup goals (4): Sordell 2, Graham 1, Mingoia 1. **Carling Cup goals** (4): Graham 2, Deeney 1, Sordell 1
Average home league attendance: 13,108. **Player of Year:** Danny Graham

NPOWER LEAGUE ONE

BOURNEMOUTH

Bournemouth lost their manager and two leading scorers, but won widespread respect for pursuing a second successive promotion to the play-offs. Brett Pitman signed for Bristol City after scoring 26 goals in their successful League Two season. He was followed in November by Josh McQuoid, who moved to Millwall after scoring back-to-back hat-tricks against Tranmere, in the FA Cup, and Walsall. Then, after leading his side to second-in-the-table, Eddie Howe, one of the country's brightest young bosses, left for Burnley. Striker Lee Bradbury replaced him and was unbeaten in his first ten matches in charge. After three straight defeats by Exeter, Southampton and Carlisle pushed them down to fifth, they regrouped to hold on to a place in the leading pack. But there was heartbreak against Huddersfield in the semi-finals, with the teams locked on aggregate at 4-4 at the end of the second leg. Liam Feeney had his spot-kick saved and Anton Robinson struck the crossbar for the home side to go through 4-2.

Arter H 7 (11)	Hollands D 31 (11)	Purches S 6 (3)
Bartley M 24 (2)	Ings D 21 (5)	Robinson A 45
Baudry M 1 (2)	Jalal S 43	Smith A 38
Bignall N 3 (2)	Lovell S 5 (2)	Stewart J 3 (1)
Bradbury L 8 (6)	McDermott D 6 (3)	Stockley J .... - (4)
Cooper S 33 (3)	McQuoid J 15 (2)	Symes M 16 (6)
Cummings W 9 (5)	Molesley M .... - (2)	Taylor L 2 (9)
Dalla Valle L 5 (3)	Partington J 2 (3)	Wiggins R 34 (1)
Feeney L 44 (2)	Pearce J 46	Williamson B .... - (4)
Fletcher S 7 (31)	Pitman B 2	
Garry R 10	Pugh M 40 (1)	

Play-offs – appearances: Cooper 2, Feeney 2, Hollands 2, Ings 2, Jalal 2, Lovell 2, McDermott 2, Pearce 2, Robinson 2, Smith 2, Wiggins 2, Pugh – (2), Baudry – (1), Fletcher – (1), Symes – (1), Williamson – (1)
League goals (75): Pugh 12, McQuoid 9, Symes 8, Hollands 7, Ings 7, Fletcher 6, Robinson 5, Feeney 4, Pearce 2, Pitman 3, Dalla Valle 2, Garry 2, Wiggins 2, Bartley 1, Baudry 1, Lovell 1, McDermott 1, Smith 1. **Play-offs – goals** (4): Lovell 2, Ings, McDermott
FA Cup goals (6): McQuoid 3, Feeney 1, Fletcher 1, Pugh 1. **Carling Cup goals:** None.

BRENTFORD

Andy Scott won the League Two title in 2009 and delivered a season of consolidation to follow it. So there was every indication of more progress at Griffin Park. Instead, Brentford struggled for goals and were bottom after 11 matches. They picked up by winning seven of their next nine to move to within two points of the play-off places, as well as taking Birmingham to penalties in the fourth round of the Carling Cup after knocking out Everton in the previous round. Then the rollercoaster continued, with six defeats in seven – and this time Scott was sacked. Striker Nicky Forster took over as caretaker and was appointed manager until the end of the season after winning four and drawing two of his first six matches. Brentford also reached the Johnstone's Paint Trophy Final, but played poorly and lost 1-0 to Carlisle. Afterwards, six matches brought a single victory for a fall to 11th. Scott's permanent replacement was former Manchester City striker Uwe Rosler.

Adams N.................. 3 (4)	Hudson K .... - (2)	Reed A 8 (3)
Alexander G.............. 37 (1)	Hunt D .... - (3)	Reeves J .... - (1)
Balkestein P.............. 17 (3)	Laird M..................4	Royce S 1 (1)
Bean M.................. 32 (5)	Lee R 22	Saunders S 18 (3)
Bignall N 1 (5)	Legge L 27 (3)	Schlupp J 6 (3)
Byrne N 4 (7)	MacDonald, C......... 28 (2)	Simpson R 11 (16)
Carson T..................1	McCarthy A..................3	Spillane M 18 (6)
Cort C.................. - (3)	McCracken D.............. 1 (1)	Tudur Jones O 4 (2)
Diagouraga T..................32	Moore S 9 (1)	Weston M.............. 33 (9)
Forster N 6 (12)	Neilson R..................15	Wood S 13 (7)
Grabban L 13 (9)	O'Connor K 39 (2)	Woodman C.............. 40 (1)
Hamer B..................10	Osborne K.............. 41 (1)	Wright S 9 (2)

League goals (55): Alexander 9, MacDonald 9, Schlupp 6, Grabban 5, Simpson 4, Bean 3, Legge 3, Weston 3, O'Connor 2, Saunders 2, Balkestein 1, Diagouraga 1, Forster 1, Laird 1, Osborne 1, Spillane 1, Wood 1, Woodman 1, Opponents 1
FA Cup goals (1): MacDonald 1. **Carling Cup goals (6):** Simpson 2, Alexander 1, Bean 1, Wood 1, Woodman 1. **Johnstone's Paint Trophy goals (5):** Alexander 2, Simpson 2, Saunders 1
Average home league attendance: 5,172. **Player of Year:** Richard Lee

BRIGHTON AND HOVE ALBION

Gus Poyet led Brighton to the title in the humble surroundings of the Withdean athletics track. Now the Uruguayan and his players will enjoy it in the lavish surroundings of the American Express Stadium as the club embark on a new era in a ground of their own after being 'homeless' for 14 years. Poyet described it as the proudest achievement of a career which embraced club and country as a player and country and which now looks set to have an impact at managerial level. In his first full season in charge, Brighton adopted a stylish, passing game, went top after eight games and stayed there. They became the first team in the country to win promotion, with five matches to spare, by beating Dagenham & Redbridge 4-3 and clinched the title four days later with a 3-1 victory at Walsall. Poyet then set his team another target, 100 points, but that proved out of reach as some of the season's impetus was lost. There were home defeats against two sides still looking to go up, Southampton and Huddersfield, and by the end a 16-point advantage had been whittled down to just three points by fast-finishing Southampton

Ankergren C 45	Brezovan P................. 1 (1)	El-Abd A 36 (1)
Barnes A................. 31 (11)	Bridcutt L 31 (6)	Elphick T 22 (5)
Battipiedi A................. 3 (5)	Calderon I 44	Greer G.........................32
Baz C .... - (7)	Dicker G 38 (8)	Hart G .... - (3)
Bennett E 45 (1)	Dunk L 2 (3)	Holroyd C................. - (3)

Kasim Y	1	Navarro A	..................2 (2)	Smith J	.....................3 (5)
Kishishev R	......21 (11)	Noone C	..........10 (13)	Sparrow M	........21 (8)
LuaLua K	.........7 (4)	Painter M	46	Taricco M	..................2 (2)
Murray G	........38 (4)	Sandaza F	...........3 (12)	Wood C	.................22 (7)

League goals (85): Murray 22, Barnes 18, Wood 8, Calderon 7, Bennett 6, LuaLua 4, Sparrow 4, Dicker 3, Bridcutt 2, Noone 2, Sandaza 2, El-Abd 1, Elphick 1, Painter 1, Opponents 4
FA Cup goals (11): Sandaza 3, Barnes 2, Bennett 2, Sparrow 2, Calderon 1, Wood 1. **Carling Cup goals:** None. **Johnstone's Paint Trophy goals:** None
Average home league attendance: 7,351. **Player of Year:** Adam El-Abd

BRISTOL ROVERS

A change of fortunes under caretaker-manager Stuart Campbell was not enough to save Rovers from relegation. The team captain took over with a dozen matches remaining and his side five points from safety. Victory by the only goal in four of the next six, against Tranmere, Notts County, Yeovil and Bournemouth took them out of the bottom four. But they were unable to sustain this improvement in a tough run-in and finished three points adrift. The damage had been done with Paul Trollope and then Dave Penney in charge, 18 matches having yielded just one victory. Trollope, League One's second longest-serving manager with five years at the club, was sacked when Rovers slipped into the bottom four after losing 6-2 at Sheffield Wednesday. Penney, formerly in charge of Doncaster, Darlington and Oldham, was dismissed after 56 days in the wake of a home defeat by Dagenham and Redbridge. Campbell's stint in charge was not enough to earn him the job, which went to Torquay's Paul Buckle.

Akinde J	....................9 (5)	Duffy D	.......................- (3)	McCracken D	.............5 (5)
Andersen M	19	Green M	2	Pell H	.....................7 (3)
Anthony B	.............36 (1)	Harrison E	...................- (1)	Powell L	.....................- (1)
Blizzard D	..........3 (2)	Hoskins W	..........41 (2)	Reece C	................6 (8)
Bolger C	...............4 (2)	Howe R	.............8 (4)	Regan C	................19 (2)
Brown W	.......12 (13)	Hughes J	..........40 (2)	Richards E	............2 (11)
Campbell S	37	Ifil J	3	Sawyer G	37
Clarke O	....................- (1)	Kalala J-P	..........10 (1)	Senda D	15
Clough J	............1 (1)	Kuffour J	..........33 (9)	Swallow B	............11 (6)
Coles D	37	Lambe R	.............1 (6)	Tunnicliffe J	.......21 (4)
Daniels L	9	Lines C	............41 (1)	Williams G	...............17 (2)
Davies S	...........4 (3)	Logan C	16		

League goals (48): Hoskins 17, Hughes 10, Kuffour 6, Anthony 3, Brown 3, Lines 3, Williams 2, Howe 1, Richards 1, Opponents 2
FA Cup goals (1): Hoskins 1. **Carling Cup goals** (1): Lines 1. **Johnstone's Paint Trophy goals** (9): Kuffour 3, Hoskins 2, Swallow 2, Hughes 1, Lines 1
Average home league attendance: 6,253. **Player of Year:** Stuart Campbell

CARLISLE UNITED

A red-letter at Wembley for Peter Murphy and his team brought silverware to Brunton Park. They overcame Port Vale, Crewe, Sheffield Wednesday and Huddersfield to reach the final of the Johnstone's Paint Trophy for the fourth time in nine years and Murphy's goal, the only one of the match, finally brought them the trophy. It was a particularly sweet moment for the long-serving central defender, who became a father two days before the match and who conceded the penalty that put Southampton on the way to a 4-1 win in the 2010 final. Carlisle made a bright start to the league season, rising to second behind Brighton with two months gone. But they couldn't maintain that momentum, spent most of the time in the middle reaches of the table and finished 12th for an improvement of two places on the previous year.

Arter H 2 (3)	Grella M 7 (3)	Michalik L.............32
Berrett J 46	Harte I 4	Murphy P 32 (2)
Borrowdale G.............1	Hurst K .... - (2)	Noble L 18 (3)
Bowman R .... - (3)	Kane T .... - (1)	Norwood O 4 (2)
Bridge-Wilkinson M...... - (3)	Kavanagh G............. - (1)	Price J .... - (3)
Chester J 18	Livesey D 5 (5)	Robson M 27 (15)
Collin A 46	Loy R 5 (12)	Simek F 46
Cooper L 6	Madden P 1 (12)	Taiwo T 44 (2)
Cruise T...................3	Madine G...............21	Thirlwell P 21 (2)
Curran C 36 (9)	Marshall B 27 (6)	Wells N .... - (3)
Dudgeon J............. 1 (1)	McDaid S...............12	Zoko F 40 (4)
Evans C 1	Mckenna B .... - (1)	

League goals (60): Berrett 10, Madine 8, Curran 8, Zoko 6, Grella 3, Murphy 3, Marshall 3, Noble 3, Chester 2, Harte 2, Michalik 2, Robson 2, Taiwo 2, Arter 1, Cooper 1, Loy 1, Thirlwell 1, Opponents 2
FA Cup goals (9): Madine 5, Zoko 3, Chester 1. **Carling Cup goals**: None. **Johnstone's Paint Trophy goals** (13): Murphy 4, Marshall 2, Michalik 2, Chester 1, Price 1, Taiwo 1, Zoko 1, Opponents 1
Average home league attendance: 5,207. **Player of Year:** James Berrett

CHARLTON ATHLETIC

Chris Powell made a flying start to his first job in management at the club where he had three spells as a player. Replacing Phil Parkinson midway through the season, Powell gathered 13 points from his first five matches in charge to keep Charlton in the promotion picture. Then it all went wrong – 11 games without another victory and a slide into mid-table. A 3-1 win over Leyton Orient ended the run, but another slump followed, with five of the final seven games of the season goalless and a position in the bottom half of the table the result. Under Parkinson, Charlton climbed to second behind Brighton with five wins on the trot, including the club's first five-goal haul away from home for 11 years – 5-1 at Peterborough. They slipped to fifth, but were still only three points off an automatic promotion place when he was sacked four days after Michael Slater and Tony Jimenez took over at The Valley from chairman Richard Murray.

Abbott P 10 (7)	Fry M 20 (5)	Reid K................... 13 (19)
Anyinsah J 14 (5)	Harriotts C 1 (2)	Semedo J.......................42
Benson P 28 (4)	Jackson J................. 29 (1)	Sodje A................... 1 (14)
Bessone F...............13	Jenkinson C 7 (1)	Solly C 9 (5)
Dailly C........................32	Llera M 14 (1)	Stewart M 6 (3)
Doherty G 35 (3)	Martin L 14 (6)	Sullivan J......................4
Eccleston N 8 (13)	McCormack A.......... 18 (6)	Wagstaff S 35 (5)
Elliot R 35	Nouble F................... 4 (5)	Worner R 7 (2)
Fortune J 12 (3)	Parrett D.....................9	Wright-Phillips B 20 (1)
Francis S 32 (2)	Racon T................... 34 (5)	

League goals (62): Jackson 13, Benson 10, Wagstaff 8, Wright-Phillips 8, Anyinsah 3, Eccleston 3, Racon 3, Llera 2, Martin 2, Abbott 1, Fry 1, McCormack 1, Nouble 1, Parrett 1, Reid 1, Semedo 1, Sodje 1, Solly 1, Opponents 1
FA Cup goals (6): Anyinsah 2, Jackson 2, Reid 1, Wagstaff 1. **Carling Cup goals** (3): Abbott 2, Martin 1. **Johnstone's Paint Trophy goals** (4): Racon 2, Abbott 1, Wagstaff 1
Average home league attendance: 15,582. **Player of Year:** Jose Semedo

COLCHESTER UNITED

Colchester were in third place with a third of the season gone, having lost only once. But in a division boasting some quality sides, it was always going to be difficult staying in touch with the leading group. They gave it a go, collecting seven points from successive matches against four promotion contenders, Bournemouth, Huddersfield, Brighton and Peterborough, early in the New Year. But four successive defeats in March pushed them back, with too much ground to make up. A 5-1 win over Exeter highlighted solid form at home, where three of the four defeats were against top teams. A 2-1 victory over Bristol Rovers enabled two-goal Ian Henderson to finish with five in six games and confirmed relegation for one of manager John Ward's former clubs. It meant a tenth-place finish, following eighth and 12th in the two previous years.

Baldwin P	10 (1)	Henderson L	- (8)	Sanderson J	- (1)
Beevers L	12 (7)	Izzet K	38 (3)	Smith T	6
Bond A	36 (7)	James L	17 (11)	Tierney M	12 (1)
Clarke N	18	Mooney D	37 (2)	Vilhjalmsson M	- (3)
Coker B	20	O'Toole J-J	5 (6)	Vincent A	28 (9)
Cousins M	13 (1)	Odejayi K	18 (26)	White J	15 (7)
Gillespie S	11 (7)	Okuonghae M	14	Williams B	33
Hackney S	- (1)	Perkins D	36	Williams T	7
Heath M	26 (1)	Powell C	2	Wilson B	25 (1)
Henderson I	24 (13)	Reid P	17 (1)	Wordsworth A	26 (9)

League goals (57): Henderson 10, Gillespie 9, Mooney 9, Bond 7, Vincent 5, Wordsworth 5, Odejayi 4, Heath 2, Okuonghae 2, Perkins 1, Williams 1, Wilson 1, Opponents 1.
FA Cup goals (5): Mooney 3, Bond 1, Wilson 1. **Carling Cup goals** (3): Mooney 2, Henderson I 1. **Johnstone's Paint Trophy goals:** None
Average home league attendance: 4,246. **Player of Year:** David Perkins

DAGENHAM AND REDBRIDGE

Disappointed but not downhearted – that was manager John Still's view of an immediate return to League One. Still pointed to the progress the club have made over recent years, the limited resources at his disposal and the fact that a determined bid to beat the drop stretched to the last day. Dagenham were eight points adrift nearing the half-way point of the season, before three wins out of four against Bristol Rovers, Colchester and Charlton offered real hope. With a month remaining, they were out of the bottom four. Then came four damaging defeats, followed by a 3-0 victory over Carlisle in the penultimate game, leaving them a point behind Walsall and two away from Notts County. A visit to Peterborough to face a side with 101 goals to their credit could hardly have proved more demanding. There was only a goal in it with more than an hour gone, but Dagenham had to take chances and conceded three in the final ten minutes to lose 5-0.

Akinde J	8 (1)	Green Danny J	2	Ogogo A	33
Antwi W	9 (2)	Gwillim G	- (2)	Palsson V	2
Arber M	44	Ifil P	13 (1)	Pinney N	- (1)
Benson P	3	Ilesanmi F	24 (1)	Roberts T	43
Bingham B	4 (2)	Lancaster C	- (4)	Savage B	21 (15)
Brown K	3	Lee O	4 (1)	Scannell D	14 (6)
Currie D	12 (10)	Lewington C	3	Scott J	8 (8)
Doe S	38	Lewis S	7 (3)	Taiwo S	16 (2)
Elito M	8 (2)	McCrory D	22 (1)	Tomlin D	16 (3)
Gain P	35 (2)	Morgan M	5 (7)	Vincelot R	46
Green Danny	39	Nurse J	24 (14)	Walsh P	- (3)

League goals (52): Vincelot 12, Green Danny 10, Nurse 10, Savage 3, Akinde 2, Arber 2, Elito 2, Scannell 2, Tomlin 2, Antwi 1, Currie 1, Green Danny J 1, Ogogo 1, Scott 1, Opponents 2

EXETER CITY

Tragedy gave way to a season full of purpose and potential for a side rated among the favourites to go down but keen to make sure there was no repeat of the last-day escape from relegation of a few months earlier. The death of striker Adam Stansfield, 31, cast a long shadow over the club, but the players set about their task commendably, holding their own in mid-table for much of the campaign before a late burst for the play-offs. Ironically, it followed one of their worst days on the pitch – a 5-1 beating at Colchester in which Steve Tully and Scott Golbourne were sent off. Five successive victories followed and, with three matches remaining, they were three points off the top six. There was no margin for error at such a crucial time, however, and a 4-0 defeat at Tranmere ended hopes. Even so, Exeter finished a single point away after two more wins, the final game against Sheffield Wednesday also notable for manager Paul Tisdale making a cameo appearance as a substitute, 11 years after his last appearances for Yeovil.

Archibald-Henville T . 32 (4)	Harley R 40 (2)	O'Flynn J 22 (8)
Bennett S .... - (1)	Jones B 27 (2)	Sercombe L.............. 38 (4)
Cozic B...................... 4 (7)	Jones P...................18	Stewart M 2 (6)
Cureton J.................. 34 (7)	Krysiak A 10	Taylor M 26 (2)
Duffy R.................... 41 (1)	Logan R................ 22 (18)	Thompson J 1 (15)
Dunne J 36 (6)	Nardiello D 15 (15)	Tisdale P..................... - (1)
Edwards R 6 (3)	Nicholls T .... - (1)	Tully S 42 (1)
Goulbourne S 42 (2)	Noble D 29 (7)	
Hamer B........................18	Norwood J....................1	

League goals (66): Cureton 17, Logan 11, Harley 10, Nardiello 10, O'Flynn 6, Sercombe 3, Duffy 2, Golbourne 2, Taylor 2, Archibald-Henville 1, Dunne 1, Tully 1
FA Cup goals: None. **Carling Cup goals** (2): Harley 2. **Johnstone's Paint Trophy goals** (12): Cureton 3, Harley 3, Nardiello 3, Duffy 1, O'Flynn 1, Opponents 1
Average home league attendance: 5,393. **Player of Year:** Jamie Cureton

HARTLEPOOL UNITED

With the previous season's escape from relegation still fresh in the mind, Hartlepool experienced a difficult start to the new campaign, with Chris Turner, the club's director of sport and effectively their manager, resigning after differences with chairman Ken Hodcroft. Coach Mick Wadsworth took over and his team spent most of the campaign in the middle reaches of the table. Their highest position of seventh came after December victories over promotion-contenders Bournemouth and Huddersfield. Those, coupled to a 4-2 FA Cup win against Yeovil after trailing 2-0, brought Wadsworth the club's first Manager of the Month award for four years and skipper Sam Collins the Player of the Month accolade. The final home game against Bournemouth was also one to remember, goalkeeper Scott Flinders heading in a stoppage-time corner from Fabian Yantorno to earn a 2-2 draw.

Austin N 24	Fredriksen J-A............. - (1)	Kean J...........................19
Behan D 1 (12)	Gamble J 25 (5)	Larkin C................ 15 (15)
Bjornsson A............. 3 (15)	Hartley P 38 (2)	Liddle G........................42
Boyd A 9 (10)	Haslam S 22 (7)	Mackay M 1 (2)
Brown J 17 (9)	Holden D 1	McSweeney L........ 24 (22)
Collins S........................42	Horwood E 44 (1)	Monkhouse A 43 (1)
Donaldson R 11 (1)	Humphreys R 14 (1)	Murray P................. 35 (1)
Flinders S 26	Johnson P....................1	Poole J .... - (3)

| Rafferty A ....1 | Sweeney A .... 38 (2) |
| Rowbotham J ....1 | Yantorno F .... 9 (8) |

Hartley 2, Horwood 2, Humphreys 2, McSweeney 2, Brown 1, Flinders 1, Gamble 1, Murray 1, Poole 1, Opponents 2
FA Cup goals (6): Sweeney 4, Brown 1, Humphreys 1. **Carling Cup goals** (2): Boyd 1, Brown 1. **Johnstone's Paint Trophy goals** (6): Behan 1, Horwood 1, McSweeney 1, Monkhouse 1, Sweeney 1, Yantorno 1
Average home league attendance: 2,933. **Player of Year**: Antony Sweeney

HUDDERSFIELD TOWN

There was little consolation to be gained from the fact that in most other years Huddersfield's club-record run would have brought – and merited – promotion. The problem was that they came up against outstanding sides in Brighton and Southampton, who filled the top two places, and a third in play-off opponents Peterborough, who had chalked up 106 League goals. For more than three-quarters of the final, Lee Clark's team had been their equals. Then, they conceded three goals in seven minutes to lose 3-0 – a first defeat in 28 matches and a second successive setback after losing to Millwall in the 2010 semi-finals. Huddersfield had spent a month in the runners-up spot before Southampton caught up using games in hand as the season entered its critical phase. The two were then locked on the same points total until their rivals' victory at Plymouth, together with a superior goal difference, proved decisive with one match remaining.

Afobe B 14 (14)	Garner J.................. 10 (6)	Novak L 12 (19)
Arfield S 33 (7)	Gudjonsson J............ 29 (8)	Peltier L 38
Atkinson C 2	Hunt J 14 (5)	Pilkington A 30 (1)
Bennett I 24	Johnson D 14 (2)	Rhodes J................. 27 (10)
Cadamarteri D 2 (9)	Jordan S 6	Ridehalgh L 15 (5)
Carey G 18 (1)	Kadar T 2	Roberts G 34 (3)
Chippendale A............. - (1)	Kay A 21 (6)	Robinson T .... - (1)
Clarke N 1	Kilbane K 23 (1)	Smithies A 22
Clarke P.......................46	Lee A 17 (11)	Ward D 5 (2)
Clarke T 3 (2)	McCombe J 31 (3)	
Croft L........................ - (3)	Naysmith G.............. 13 (1)	

Play-offs – appearances: Afobe 3, Bennett 3, Clarke P 3, Kay 3, Kilbane 3, Naysmith 3, Peltier 3, Roberts 3, Ward 3, Hunt 2 (1), Arfield 2, Rhodes 1 (1), Gudjonsson 1, Cadamarteri – (2), Lee – (2), Novak – (2), McCombe – (1)
League goals (77): Rhodes 16, Pilkington 10, Roberts 9, McCombe 5, Afobe 5, Novak 5, Arfield 4, Clarke P 4, Cadamarteri 3, Kay 3, Ward 3, Carey 2, Gudjonsson 2, Kilbane 2, Clarke T 1, Hunt 1, Peltier 1, Opponents 1. **Play-offs – goals** (4): Kay 1, Kilbane 1, Peltier 1, Ward 1
FA Cup goals (11): Roberts 3, Afobe 3, Arfield 1, Kay 1, Lee 1, Peltier 1, Pilkington 1, Rhodes 1, McCombe 1. **Carling Cup goals** (2): Rhodes 1, Opponents 1. **Johnstone's Paint Trophy goals** (13): Rhodes 4, Pilkington 3, Afobe 2, Lee 2, Arfield 1, Carey 1
Average home league attendance: 13,728. **Player of Year**: Peter Clarke

LEYTON ORIENT

A successful cup run often has an adverse effect on league form. Not so with Orient, who went from relegation candidates to play-off contenders while reaching the fifth round of the FA Cup and taking Arsenal to a second tie. In doing so, they equalled a 56-year-old club-record by going 14 league games unbeaten, scoring 30 goals and climbing to seventh in the table with games in hand on teams above them. The run came to an end with a 2-1 defeat at Brentford and Orient lost some of their sparkle after that, unable to take advantage of a sequence of home matches. But they still finished a single place away from the play-offs. The cup run took them past Dagenham & Redbridge, Droylsden in an amazing replay won 8-2 after extra-time and leading Championship sides Norwich and Swansea, both away. Then, an 89th minute equaliser by substitute Jonathan Tehoue earned a money-spinning replay at the Emirates, where the run came to a 5-0 end.

Barrett A................14	Dawson S........... 39 (1)	Omozusi E 39 (1)
Brown A.................... 4 (1)	Forbes T 32 (2)	Patulea A.................... - (1)
Brown J 3	Frampton A.....................1	Porter G.................... - (1)
Butcher L 8 (1)	Jarvis R 3 (8)	Revell A 35 (4)
Carroll T 8 (4)	Jones J 35	Smith J................ 25 (6)
Chambers A 23 (6)	Kane H 9 (9)	Spring M.................39
Chorley B 28 (1)	Liddle M.....................1	Tehoue J................ 9 (23)
Cox D 44 (1)	McGleish S 27 (12)	Walker A.................... - (11)
Crowe J................ 5 (7)	Mike C.....................2	Whing A 23 (1)
Daniels C 41 (1)	Mpoku P-J 9 (18)	

League goals (71): Revell 13, Cox 11, McGleish 11, Smith 7, Tehoue 7, Kane 5, Chorley 3, M'Poku 3, Dawson 2, Forbes 2, Jarvis 2, Spring 2, Whing 2, Opponents 1. **FA Cup goals** (16): McGleish 6, Tehoue 4, Revell 2, Smith 2, Chorley 1, M'Poku 1. **Carling Cup goals** (2): Jarvis 1, Revell 1. **Johnstone's Paint Trophy goals** (2): Cox 1, Jarvis 1
Average home league attendance: 4,581. **Player of Year**: Stephen Dawson

MILTON KEYNES DONS

Karl Robinson, the Football League's youngest manager, took his side to the play-offs with a fifth-place finish in his first season in charge. After edging the first leg 3-2 against Peterborough, they were unable to match their high-scoring opponents at London Road and lost 2-0. Although it was the club's third defeat in the semi-finals in five years, there was plenty of optimism at the end of the campaign, with 30-year-old Robinson given a three-year extension to his contract in recognition of progress made. He acknowledged they had sometimes come up short, but in a competitive division Dons were still in contention for an automatic promotion place with eight matches remaining. Then, they paid for missed chances when held 1-1 at home by relegation-threatened Walsall. A week later, a 2-0 lead at Southampton was surrendered and the resulting 3-2 defeat left them too much work to do.

Amoo D .... - (3)	Flanagan T.....................2	Marsh-Brown K......... 12 (5)
Balanta A.............. 12 (6)	Gleeson S 35 (1)	Martin D 43
Baldock G................. 1 (1)	Guy L 20 (14)	McIndoe M 8
Baldock S 20 (10)	Hamann D 12	O'Hanlon S 28 (4)
Carrington M 7 (5)	Howell L .... - (1)	Powell D 23 (6)
Chadwick L 39 (5)	Hughes S 2 (4)	Searle S.....................3
Chicksen A............. 5 (9)	Ibehre J 19 (23)	Stirling J.................... - (4)
Clayton A 1 (5)	Johnson J 2 (5)	Vine R 12 (5)
Collins C .... - (1)	Leven P 40	Wilbraham A 5 (5)
Doumbe M 42 (2)	Lewington D....................42	Woodards D 36 (1)
Easter J 11 (3)	MacKenzie G............ 24 (2)	

Play-offs – appearances: Balanta 2, Baldock S 2, Chadwick 2, Clayton 2, Doumbe 2, Gleeson 2, Lewington 2, MacKenzie 2, Martin 2, O'Hanlon 2, Powell 2, Ibehre – (2), Marsh-Brown – (2), Guy 1
League goals (67): Baldock S 12, Powell 9, Leven 8, Balanta 6, Doumbe 5, O'Hanlon 4, Ibehre 3, Lewington 3, Carrington 2, Gleeson 2, Guy 2, MacKenzie 2, Marsh-Brown 2, Wilbraham 2, Clayton 1, Johnson 1, Vine 1, Woodards 1, Opponents 1. **Play-offs – goals** (3): Balanta 1, Baldock S 1, Powell
FA Cup goals (1): Guy 1. **Carling Cup goals** (7): Easter 2, Ibehre 2, Baldock S 1, Guy 1,

Wilbraham 1. **Johnstone's Paint Trophy goals** (1): Chadwick 1
Average home league attendance: 8,512. **Player of Year:** Luke Chadwick

NOTTS COUNTY

A club-record run of defeats threatened to send County straight back to League Two until Martin Allen, the club's sixth manager in 18 months, steadied the sinking ship. Allen walked out at Barnet three weeks into a salvage operation there to replace Paul Ince, who left Meadow Lane by mutual agreement after his side lost five games in succession. There were four more reversals, two under Allen, before he turned things around. County broke the sequence by winning at Tranmere with a Craig Westcarr penalty. They came from behind to prevail 2-1 at fellow-strugglers Swindon, Alan Judge, with his first for the club, and Lee Hughes scoring late goals. Then, there was a point gained against Brentford to confirm the climb to safety. Ince lasted slightly longer than the man he replaced, Craig Short, sacked after less than five months in charge.

Bishop N 42 (1)	Harley J 39	Pearce K 26 (1)
Brandy F 5 (4)	Hawley K 12 (12)	Ravenhill R 31 (3)
Burch R 14 (1)	Hughes L 24 (7)	Regan C 4
Burgess B 8 (9)	Hunt S 3 (1)	Rodgers L .... - (4)
Chilvers L 17 (4)	Ince T 3 (3)	Smith K 6 (7)
Clifford C 5 (4)	Jervis J 1 (9)	Sodje S 5 (6)
Darby S 23	Judge A 17 (2)	Spicer J 15 (8)
Davies B 22	Lee G 14 (4)	Sproule I 4 (1)
Demba-Nyren N 5 (7)	Martin D 7 (3)	Thompson J 23 (2)
Edwards M 36 (1)	McDonald K 10 (1)	Westcarr C 36 (5)
Fairclough B .... - (1)	Miller L 5 (1)	Wholey J .... - (1)
Gobern L .... - (4)	Nelson S 32 (1)	
Gow A 12 (4)	Nicholas G .... - (1)	

League goals (46): Hughes 13, Westcarr 12, Davies 5, Ince 2, Miller 2, Spicer 2, Bishop 1, Burgess 1, Demba-Nyren 1, Edwards 1, Gow 1, Judge 1, Pearce 1, Smith 1, Opponents 2
FA Cup goals (8): Hughes 2, Bishop 1, Davies 1, Pearce 1, Rodgers 1, Westcarr 1, Opponents 1
Carling Cup goals (5): Smith 2, Davies 1, Hughes 1, Spicer 1. **Johnstone's Paint Trophy goals** (1): Davies 1
Average home league attendance: 6,586. **Player of Year:** Neal Bishop

OLDHAM ATHLETIC

Paul Dickov made a winning start, home and away, to life as a manager as Oldham rubbed shoulders with the early League One leaders. When his team returned to a play-off position with just over half the season gone, the former striker seemed to be on the way to a successful first season in charge. They had put an embarrassing 6-0 home defeat by Southampton behind them to go fifth after a 4-0 victory over Hartlepool. Then, it all changed as confidence drained away and the goals dried up. Dickov could only watch in frustration as Oldham failed to score in ten out of 11 matches – and lost the other one 3-2. A 2-0 success against Notts County proved welcome relief, although by then Oldham had fallen into the bottom half of the table and they finished 17th, one place worse off than in 2010. Dickov came off the bench in the last match against MK Dons to end a playing career which took him to five clubs, another five on loan and brought ten Scotland caps.

Alessandra L 10 (9)	Brill D 30	Dickov P .... - (2)
Amos B 16	Brooke R 2 (11)	Dikaba R 1
Bembo-Leta D 2 (1)	Burns R 1	Evina C 24 (3)
Black P 28 (1)	Christophe J-F .... - (1)	Feeney W 13 (10)

Furman D	42	Lowe J	7	Stephens D	34
Gregan S	.................- (1)	Mantom S	...........3 (1)	Tarkowski J	.... 7 (2)
Hazell R	33	McGrath P	...............- (1)	Taylor C	.... 41 (1)
Jacobson J	...............- (1)	Millar K	.................- (5)	Todd A	.... 5 (1)
Jarrett J	.... 7 (1)	Morais F	.... 20 (3)	Tounkare O	.... 40 (4)
Jones R	.... 21 (10)	Mvoto J-Y	.... 25 (2)	Trotman N	.... 15 (3)
Kelly D	.... 1 (12)	Reid R	.... 11 (8)	White A	.... 19 (5)
Lee K	43	Smalley D	................- (3)	Winchester C	.... 5 (1)

League goals (53): Taylor 11, Stephens 9, Tounkara 7, Furman 5, White 4, Morais 3, Evina 2, Lee 2, Lowe 2, Mvoto 2, Reid 2, Allesandra 1, Jones 1, Kelly 1, Winchester 1
FA Cup goals (2): Feeney 1, Stephens 1. **Carling Cup goals** (1): Bembo-Leta 1. **Johnstone's Paint Trophy goals:** None
Average home league attendance: 4,392. **Player of Year:** Kieran Lee

PETERBOROUGH UNITED

Peterborough didn't just win an immediate return to the Championship. They were unrivalled as the great entertainers, scoring 106 goals in 46 matches, chalking up three or more in 16 of them and barely noticing the departure of Aaron Mclean to Hull in the winter transfer window. But that was only part of the story. A total of 75 were conceded, with relegated Bristol Rovers the only side in the division to have leaked more. So there was never a chance of automatic promotion. It had to be through the play-offs and three late goals in the space of seven minutes from Tommy Rowe, Craig Mackail-Smith and Grant McCann did the trick in the final against Huddersfield at Old Trafford. It capped a successful return to the club after his sacking by Preston for Darren Ferguson, who took over in mid-season when Gary Johnson had a difference of opinion with chairman Darragh MacAnthony. Mackail-Smith, voted League One Player of Year, scored 35 in all competitions, before moving on to bigger things.

Ball D	.... 7 (12)	Langmead K	.... 28 (4)	Ofori-Twumasi N	.... 6 (5)
Basey G	.... 5 (2)	Lee C	.... 26 (8)	Piergianni C	.... - (1)
Bennett R	.... 32 (2)	Lewis J	45	Rowe T	.... 32 (3)
Boyd G	.... 42 (1)	Little M	.... 32 (3)	Taylor P	........................- (1)
Clayton A	.... 6 (1)	Mackail-Smith C	.... 44 (1)	Tomlin L	.... 31 (6)
Davies A	.... 12 (10)	McCann G	.... 34 (3)	Wesolowski J	.... 23 (9)
Frecklington L	.... 3 (6)	Mclean A	19	Whelpdale C	.... 16 (6)
Gill M	4	Mendez-Laing N	...... 8 (25)	Williams M	3
Hibbert D	..................- (7)	Newell J	.... 1 (1)	Zakuani G	.... 29 (1)
Jones P	1	Nyatanga L	3	
Kennedy T	14	Obika J	........................- (1)	

Play-offs – appearances: Bennett 3, Boyd 3, Little 3, Mackail-Smith 3, McCann 3, Rowe 3, Tomlin 3, Zakuani 3, Jones 2 (1), Basey 2, Wesolowski 2, Lee 1 (1), Lewis 1, Mendez-Laing 1, Ball – (2), Whelpdale – (2), Langmead – (1)
League goals (106): Mackail-Smith 27, Boyd 15, Mclean 10, McCann 9, Tomlin 8, Ball 5, Mendez-Laing 5, Rowe 5, Bennett 4, Langmead 3, Wesolowski 2, Zakuani 2, Basey 1, Davies 1, Frecklington 1, Hibbert 1, Lee 1, Obika 1, Whelpdale 1, Opponents 4. **Play-offs – goals** (7): Mackail-Smith 3, McCann 3, Rowe 1
FA Cup goals (9): Tomlin 3, Mackail-Smith 2, Mclean 2, Langmead 1, McCann 1. **Carling Cup goals** (7): Mackail-Smith 3, Boyd 2, Bennett 1, Mclean 1. **Johnstone's Paint Trophy goals** (2): Little 1, Mclean 1
Average home league attendance: 6,449. **Player of Year:** Craig Mackail-Smith

PLYMOUTH ARGYLE

Peter Reid had experienced most things in a playing and managerial career spanning ten clubs, but rarely a season as difficult and demanding as this one. Reid attempted to resurrect a side relegated from the Championship amid mounting financial problems, which eventually forced directors to apply for administration. That resulted in the mandatory deduction of ten points and left Argyle bottom of the table, eight points adrift. There was an immediate response, with successive victories over Colchester, Sheffield Wednesday and Swindon, before another lean spell looked to have ended all hope of surviving. A successful Easter brought wins over Dagenham & Redbridge and MK Dons and cut the deficit to three points with a game in hand on the teams above them. Reid applauded his players for their efforts to beat the odds, but defeats at Exeter and at home to Southampton in the penultimate game sent them down, six points from safety.

Arnason K 39 (1)	Larrieu R 17 (1)	Rickard M .... - (1)
Bhasera O 28 (1)	MacLean S 4 (3)	Seip M 16 (1)
Bolasie Y 25 (10)	Mason J 26 (8)	Stephens J 2 (3)
Button D 29 (1)	Molyneaux L 7 (2)	Summerfield L 4 (3)
Clark C 18 (4)	Nelson C 32 (3)	Timar K 7 (2)
Clifford C 7	Ngala B 23 (3)	Walton S 6 (1)
Duguid K 19 (7)	Noone C 16 (1)	Wright-Phillips B 17
Fallon R 25 (3)	Parrett D 5 (3)	Young L 2 (3)
Fletcher C 37 (1)	Paterson J 21 (7)	Zubar C 29
Harper-Penman J .... - (2)	Patterson R 21 (14)	
Johnson R 15 (2)	Peterlin A 9 (3)	

League goals (51): Wright-Phillips 13, Bolasie 7, Mason 7, Fallon 4, Patterson 4, Noone 3, Fletcher 2, Johnson 2, Zubar 2, Arnason 1, Bhasera 1, Clark 1, N'Gala 1, Parrett 1, Summerfield 1, Walton 1
FA Cup goals: None. **Carling Cup goals:** None. **Johnstone's Paint Trophy goals** (3): Clark 1, Noone 1, MacLean 1
Average home league attendance: 8,613. **Player of Year:** Carl Fletcher

ROCHDALE

A season of consolidation looked to be the target for a side playing in the game's third tier for the first time since 1974. Instead, they exceeded expectations to mount a commendable bid for a second, successive promotion, which tailed off only in the final lap. Keith Hill's team, among the favourites to go down, moved to within a point of a top-six place by beating Sheffield Wednesday 2-1 to extend an unbeaten run to ten matches. They fell back into mid-table, but regained momentum to win six of the next eight matches, overcoming Southampton 2-0 to climb into a play-off position. Then, successive home defeats by Brentford and Carlisle followed by a loss at Charlton, left them too far behind and they finished ninth. After initially stalling on the move, Hill stepped up a division to take charge at Barnsley and was replaced by former Manchester City youth coach Steve Eyre.

Adams N 25 (5)	Elding A 9 (8)	Lillis J 23
Akpa Akpro J-L 8 (24)	Flynn M .... - (1)	O'Grady C 45 (1)
Andre H .... - (1)	Fon Williams O 22	Redshaw J .... - (2)
Atkinson W 15 (6)	Goodall A 3 (2)	Smalley D .... - (3)
Barry-Murphy B 31 (1)	Grant R 5 (1)	Thompson Joe 19 (13)
Daniels L 1	Gray R .... - (2)	Thompson Josh 11 (1)
Dawson C 44 (1)	Holness M 46	Tutte A 5 (2)
Dickinson L 7 (7)	Jones G 45 (1)	Widdowson J 30 (4)
Done M 16 (17)	Kennedy J 44 (1)	Williams R 9
Edwards M .... - (1)	Kennedy T 6	Wiseman S 37

League goals (63): Jones 17, Dawson 10, O'Grady 9, Done 5, Akpa Akpro 4, Kennedy 4, Elding 3, Atkinson 2, Grant 2, Thompson Joe 2, Gray 1, Holness 1, Thompson Josh 1, Opponents 2
FA Cup goals (2): Dawson 1, Elding 1. **Carling Cup goals** (3): Jones 2, Elding 1. **Johnstone's Paint Trophy goals** (1): Done 1
Average home league attendance: 3,486. **Player of Year:** Gary Jones

SHEFFIELD WEDNESDAY

Relegated Wednesday were favourites for an immediate return to the Championship and a flying start to season showed why. They scored twice in first 15 minutes against Dagenham & Redbridge on the opening day of the season and acquired ten points from the first four matches. After that, there was none of the consistency required for a promotion challenge. It was summed up when a 6-2 victory over Bristol Rovers, which took them briefly to second place behind Brighton, was followed immediately by a 5-1 reversal at Exeter. Former Leicester and Portsmouth owner Milan Mandaric, who took over the club in a £10m deal, ran out of patience after a 5-3 defeat at Peterborough, sacked Alan Irvine and brought in Gary Megson for his ninth managerial job. Megson also found it hard going. A home defeat by Brentford left Wednesday only four points off a relegation place, before three wins in the next four games took them away from trouble.

Batth, D...................10	Jones R 8	Otsemobor J 13 (2)
Beevers M.............. 27 (1)	Madine G................ 20 (2)	Palmer L................ 4 (5)
Buxton L................ 29 (1)	Mellor N 24 (9)	Potter D................ 22 (11)
Coke G 22 (5)	Miller T.................. 29 (5)	Purse D........................22
Heffernan P 3 (14)	Morrison C 22 (13)	Reynolds M...................7
Hinds R 4	Morrison M 12	Sedgwick C............. 24 (9)
Jameson A 2	O'Brien J 3 (1)	Spurr T........................26
Johnson J 15 (11)	O'Connor J 25 (11)	Teale G................. 37 (4)
Johnson R 15 (1)	O'Donnell R 8 (1)	Tudgay M............... 15 (2)
Jones D 13 (12)	Osbourne I 9 (1)	Weaver N 36

League goals (67): Mellor 13, Miller 9, Morrison 6, Madine 5, Coke 4, Johnson J 4, Sedgwick 4, Johnson R 3, Heffernan 3, Potter 3, Beevers 2, O'Connor 2, Teale 2, Tudgay 2, Buxton 1, Jones 1, Opponents 3
FA Cup goals (15): Morrison 5, Mellor 2, Miller 2, Teale 2, Beevers 1, Johnson J 1, Potter 1, Spurr 1. **Carling Cup goals** (3): Coke 1, Mellor 1, Tudgay 1. **Johnstone's Paint Trophy goals** (9): Mellor 4, O'Connor 2, Purse 1, Teale 1, Tudgay 1
Average home league attendance: 17,817. **Player of Year:** Neil Mellor

SOUTHAMPTON

Nigel Adkins twice won promotion to the Championship with Scunthorpe and the physio-turned-manager continued to display the midas touch to bring the good times back to St Mary's. Adkins left Glanford Park to replace Alan Pardew, sacked after a 4-0 away win over Bristol Rovers in the third match of the season with the club claiming he was not the one to take them up. The new man soon made his presence felt, with adventurous, attacking football bringing goals from a all areas of the team. Southampton climbed from the lower reaches of the table to join the leading group with 17 scored against Huddersfield, Exeter, Dagenham and Oldham over Christmas and the New Year. Huddersfield, despite the defeat, emerged as their biggest rivals behind runaway leaders Brighton. But they were seen off by a run of 12 wins out of 14, climaxed by a 3-1 win at Plymouth which sealed second place, three points behind Brighton after having trailed the champions at one point by 16. The reward for Adkins was a new, four-and-a-half-year contract.

Barnard L 24 (12)	Butterfield D 32 (2)	Connolly D 8 (7)
Bignall N .... - (3)	Chaplow R 27 (6)	Davis K...........................46

Dickson R 15 (8)	Holmes L .... - (7)	Oxlade-Chamberlain A27 (7)
Do Prado G 23 (11)	Jaidi R 31	Puncheon J 15
Fonte J 43	Lallana A 30 (6)	Richardson F 14 (7)
Forte J 2 (8)	Lambert R.....................45	Schneiderlin M 23 (4)
Gobern O 1 (10)	Martin A 4 (4)	Seaborne D 14 (10)
Hammond D........... 40 (1)	Mills J .... - (2)	Stephens D 5 (1)
Harding D 35 (1)	N'Guessan D 2 (4)	Wotton P .... - (2)

League goals (86): Lambert 21, Barnard 14, Do Prado 9, Oxlade-Chamberlain 9, Lallana 8, Fonte 7, Chaplow 4, Hammond 4, Connolly 3, Jaidi 3, Forte 2, Dickson 1, Gobern 1.
FA Cup goals (8): Do Prado 2, Lallana 2, Barnard 1, Chaplow 1, Connolly 1, Gobern 1. **Carling Cup goals** (2): Lallana 1, Oxlade-Chamberlain 1, **Johnstone's Paint Trophy goals:** None
Average home league attendance: 22,160. **Player of Year:** Jose Fonte

SWINDON TOWN

On the ground where he saw off relegation with Crystal Palace 12 months earlier, 'trouble-shooting' manager Paul Hart experienced the other side of the coin. Swindon went down 3-1 to Sheffield Wednesday at Hillsborough and with the defeat went their last chance of beating the drop. It was the continuation of a run of 22 matches producing only one victory and sending them to the bottom of the table. Hart was brought in when Danny Wilson resigned 11 games into that sequence, but had only a 1-0 victory over Brentford to show for his efforts to stem the tide. It was a far cry from the previous season when Billy Paynter and Charlie Austin fired Swindon to the Play-off Final with 46 goals between them. Paynter, along with key defender Gordon Greer, then moved on, leaving big holes in the side. Austin's goals kept them afloat in the first half of the season, but he went in the January transfer window, leaving no-one to pick up the pieces. Hart left the club once relegation was confirmed and in came Paolo di Canio, the most intriguing of all the managerial arrivals.

Amankwaah K 17 (2)	Ferry S 18 (3)	Obika J 3 (2)
Andrew C 9 (1)	Flint A 2 (1)	Pericard V 11 (7)
Austin C 20 (1)	Frampton A..................23	Prutton D 31 (10)
Ball D 7 (11)	Grella M 6 (1)	Ritchie M.................. 35 (1)
Benyon E 7 (5)	Lescinel J-F 16 (2)	Rose M 27 (8)
Bodin B 2 (3)	Kennedy C 2 (1)	Sheehan A 17 (4)
Caddis P 36 (2)	Lucas D 20 (1)	Smith P 26 (1)
Clark M..................... - (1)	McGovern J-P 30 (8)	Storey M .... - (2)
Cuthbert S 38 (3)	Morrison S 9	Thompson N 2 (1)
Dossevi T 16 (11)	N'Diaye A 2 (4)	Timlin M 18 (4)
Douglas J 38 (1)	O'Brien A................. 8 (13)	

League goals (50): Austin 12, Ritchie 7, Morrison 4, Dossevi 3, McGovern 3, Prutton 3, Rose 3, Ball 2, Cuthbert 2, Pericard 2, Timlin 2, Andrew 1, Benyon 1, Caddis 1, Douglas 1, Grella 1, Jean-Francois 1, Sheehan 1
FA Cup goals (7): Austin 3, McGovern 1, Morrison 1, Pericard 1, Ritchie 1. **Carling Cup goals** (1): McGovern 1. **Johnstone's Paint Trophy goals** (6): Pericard 3, Austin 2, Ball 1
Average home league attendance: 8,457. **Player of Year:** Matt Ritchie

TRANMERE ROVERS

Another season spent looking anxiously over their shoulder suggested another nail-biting finish. Instead, Tranmere turned on some style to ensure safety – with a helping hand from three first-time scorers. They were three points away from the bottom four when a stoppage-time strike by Adam McGurk earned a 2-1 win away to promotion-chasing Bournemouth. Dagenham and Redbridge were seen off 2-0. Then, Lucas Akins (2) and Michael Kay also scored their first goals for the club to set up a 4-0 victory over Exeter and a move well clear of trouble with two matches to spare. Tranmere had previously seemed to be on the right track after successive three-goal performances against Plymouth and Sheffield Wednesday, but slipped back into trouble by failing to win any of the next seven games. At the end of the season, Les Parry was given the go-ahead to continue as manager with a new, one-year contract.

Akins L................ 23 (10)	Gornell T.........................3	Nielsen G.........................2
Bakayogo Z 15 (12)	Grandison J................ 6 (2)	Robinson A 9 (6)
Blanchard M 14 (6)	Gulacsi P.......................12	Showunmi E.....................43
Broomes M 5	Jennings D 25 (4)	Taylor A 23 (3)
Brown K 1 (3)	Kay M...........................22	Thomas-Moore I....... 15 (4)
Cathalina T 6 (1)	Labadie J 29 (5)	Warner T.......................25
Collister J 7	Mantom S.........................2	Weir R 16 (2)
Cresswell A 42 (1)	McChrystal M 21 (2)	Welsh J..........................41
Darville L 8 (1)	McGurk A 3 (18)	Wood N 5 (6)
Elford Alliyu L 13 (3)	McLaren P 6	Wootton S 7
Fraughan R 4 (9)	Mendy A 11 (1)	
Goodison I 40	Morrow S 2 (3)	

League goals (53): Showunmi 11, Thomas-Moore 7, Jennings 6, Ellford-Alliyu 5, Goodison 4, Welsh 4, Cresswell 3, McGurk 3, Atkins 2, Labadie 2, Wootton 2, Bakayogo 1, Kay 1, Mendy 1, Opponents 1
FA Cup goals (3): Cresswell 1, Goodison 1, Thomas-Moore 1. **Carling Cup goals (2):** Goodison 1, Showunmi 1. **Johnstone's Paint Trophy goals (2):** Showunmi 1, Thomas-Moore 1
Average home league attendance: 5,474. **Player of Year:** Enoch Showunmi

WALSALL

Former Walsall captain Dean Smith repaid the club for giving him the manager's job by engineering an improbable escape from relegation. When he was appointed, they were seven points from safety and looking like a side on the way down. Smith instilled a new confidence and belief, which was soon evident as a 6-1 win over Bristol Rovers moved them off the foot of the table. Victory over promotion-chasing Southampton and a 5-2 defeat of Hartlepool helped keep the momentum going. It was still touch and go through to the final day of the season, with a single point lead over fourth-from-bottom Dagenham and Redbridge. But news of Dagenham losing at Peterborough took the pressure off and defeat in their own game was rendered irrelevant. Walsall made a bright enough start to the campaign with two wins in the opening three matches. Then five successive defeats sent them sliding and put the pressure on Chris Hutchings, who was eventually sacked.

Bevan D...........................4	Gray J 42 (1)	Nicholls A 26 (11)
Brain J 16	Grigg W 8 (20)	Paterson J............... 2 (12)
Butler A.........................31	Jones S 9 (4)	Price J...................... 4 (1)
Byfield D................. 8 (11)	Laird M...........................8	Reid R 13 (5)
Cook J 6 (2)	Lancashire O............ 28 (1)	Richards M 46
Davies A 3	Ledesma E 5 (5)	Smith E 23 (2)
Davis D...........................7	Lescott A 34	Taundry R 26 (2)
Devaney M.......................4	Macken J 35 (4)	Walker J.........................26
Dickinson L 2 (2)	Marshall P 12 (6)	Westlake D 26 (2)
Gbarssin M-A 8 (1)	McDonald C 7 (7)	Williams T.......................14
Gill M...........................8	McGivern R....................15	

League goals (56): Gray 10, Macken 9, Richards 8, Nicholls 5, Grigg 4, Butler 3, Reid 3, Byfield 2, Gill 2, Smith 2, Cook 1, Devaney 1, Ledesma 1, Lescott 1, Marshall 1, Price 1, Westlake 1, Williams 1

FA Cup goals (3): Reid 2, Richards 1. **Carling Cup goals**: None. **Johnstone's Paint Trophy goals** (1): Reid
Average home league attendance: 4,033. **Player of Year:** Andy Butler

YEOVIL TOWN

A tendency to give away costly late goals was a major factor in Yeovil struggling through much of the first half of the season. They slipped from second from bottom after tightening up defensively and keeping a clean sheet for five successive matches. With 11 games remaining, they were still in danger, two points off the bottom four. Then, two excellent away performances pointed them in the right direction. Dean Bowditch scored twice as his side twice came from behind to beat Exeter 3-2 and Shaun MacDonald, on his fifth loan from Swansea, netted a hat-trick in the 5-1 win over a Leyton Orient side looking to push on towards the play-offs. When Jon Obika, on loan from Tottenham, scored the only goal of the next game against Carlisle, Yeovil's position had been transformed. They went on to finish with an unbeaten run of six games for a third successive improvement in their league position – this time up to 14th.

Alcock C 19 (7)	Jones N 7 (1)	Stewart C 1 (4)
Ayling L 31 (6)	Kalala J-P 13 (2)	Sullivan J................. 13
Bowditch D 40 (1)	Kiernan R 1 (2)	Tudor Jones O 12 (2)
Calver C.................... - (6)	MacDonald S............ 26	Tutte A 12 (3)
Ehmer M 26 (1)	Obika J.................... 11	Upson E 15 (8)
Freeman L 5 (8)	Parkes T .... - (1)	Virgo A................ 28 (5)
German A .... - (4)	Phillip A .... - (3)	Welsh A 31 (5)
Gibson B................. - (4)	Roberts B .... - (1)	Williams A 27 (10)
Gritton M .... - (2)	Russell A 2 (12)	Williams G 11 (1)
Henderson S 33	Smith N 35 (5)	Williams S 23 (13)
Huntington P............. 40	Sproule I.................... 2	Wotton P................. 23
Johnson O............ 16 (1)	Stam S 3	

League goals (56): Bowditch 15, Williams A 6, Virgo 5, Huntington 4, MacDonald 4, Welsh 4, Johnson 3, Obika 3, Freeman 2, Tutte 2, Williams S 2, Wotton 2, Alcock 1, Tudur Jones 1, Williams G 1, Opponents 1
FA Cup goals (3): Williams A 2, Upson 1. **Carling Cup goals:** None. **Johnstone's Paint Trophy goals** (1): Welsh
Average home league attendance: 4,291. **Player of Year:** Stephen Henderson

NPOWER LEAGUE TWO

ACCRINGTON STANLEY

The club's best season since returning to the Football League in 2006 ended on a sour note in the play-offs against Stevenage. Accrington had two players, Joe Jacobson and Sean McConville, sent off in the space of two minutes midway through the second half of the second leg at the Crown Ground and were beaten 3-0 on aggregate. Manager John Coleman admitted the tie was lost when a below-par performance brought a 2-0 defeat in the first game. But he insisted his players deserved credit for climbing from mid-table to finish fifth with a run of 13 unbeaten matches through to the end of the regular campaign. A 3-1 win over Barnet in the penultimate game made sure of a place in the semi-finals, Jimmy Ryan celebrating his inclusion in the PFA's League Two Team of the Year – the club's first-ever – with a hat-trick. Ryan also contributed to a remarkable 7-4 win over Gillingham in October in which Phil Edwards scored two of his 11 penalties.

Barnett C 31 (8)	Boulding R................ 6 (9)	Burey B .... - (1)
Bateson J................. 12	Brady I 2	Burton A.................... 1

Cisak A.....................21	Joyce L..............24 (3)	Proctor A...............42 (1)
Craney I.....................20	Lindfield C............2 (14)	Putterill R............11 (13)
Dunbavin I.................25	Long K..............11 (4)	Richardson L............3 (8)
Edwards P.................44	McConville S............37 (6)	Ryan J....................45 (1)
Gornell T....................40	Murphy P.............5 (8)	Smyth T................3 (1)
Hessey S.................40 (1)	Owens A...............- (3)	Turner C....................- (13)
Jacobson J.................26	Parkinson A............10 (8)	Winnard D.................45

Play-offs – appearances: Cisak 2, Edwards 2, Gornell 2, Hessey 2, Jacobson 2, Joyce 2, McConville 2, Winnard 2, Murphy 1, Brady 1, Craney 1, Putterill – (1), Turner – (1)
League goals (73): Edwards 13, Gornell 13, McConville 13, Ryan 9, Craney 7, Procter 6, Barnett 2, Boulding 2, Jacobson 2, Parkinson 2, Hessey 1, Joyce 1, Richardson 1, Winnard 1. Play-offs – goals: None.
FA Cup goals (3): Putterill 2, Ryan. **Carling Cup goals** (4): Hessey, Lindfield, Putterill, Turner.
Johnstone's Paint Trophy goals (1): Putterill
Average home league attendance: 1,867. **Player of Year:** Jimmy Ryan

ALDERSHOT TOWN

A shortage of goals undermined Aldershot's bid to repeat the previous season's achievement of reaching the play-offs under Kevin Dillon. They averaged fewer than one a game throughout the first half of the campaign, which ended with four successive home losses and a slide to fifth from bottom. There was also an FA Cup defeat by non-league Dover, leading to Dillon's dismissal after 14 months in the job. His replacement, Newport County's former Wimbledon and Bolton striker Dean Holdsworth, enjoyed immediate success, with seven points from three games. His new team went on to cement a place just below mid-table with a run of ten matches without defeat. It included a best-of-the-season 3-0 win over promotion-chasing Shrewsbury and brought Holdsworth the League Two Manager of the Month award for March. Victory by the same score condemned Lincoln to relegation on the final day.

Bergqvist D................- (1)	Jackson M.................4 (5)	Randall J.................- (1)
Charles A....................41	Jarrett A.................2 (2)	Rodman A.................9 (5)
Connolly R................- (5)	Jones D.................42 (1)	Sills T....................8 (11)
Fortune C.............3 (4)	Little G.................13 (1)	Small W.................18 (11)
Grand S.....................6	McGlashan J.........23 (15)	Spencer D.................9 (9)
Guttridge L.............36 (5)	Medley L.................- (4)	Straker A.................35 (3)
Halls J.................16 (7)	Mekki A.................2 (6)	Vincent J.................24 (1)
Harding B.............29 (6)	Morgan M.................19	Vincenti P.................20 (1)
Henderson L.................1	Morris A.................13 (9)	Young J.................46
Herd B.....................43	Ngo Baheng W...........- (3)	
Hylton D.............24 (9)	Panther E.................20 (3)	

League goals (54): Guttridge 8, Vincenti 6, Charles 5, Hylton 5, Morgan 5, Rodman 5, Small 5, Spencer 4, Harding 2, Sills 2, Straker 2, Halls 1, Herd 1, Jones 1, Little 1, McGlashan 1
FA Cup goals (2): Small 2. **Carling Cup goals:** None. **Johnstone's Paint Trophy goals** (2): Hylton 1, Spencer 1
Average home league attendance: 2,487. **Player of Year:** Ben Herd

BARNET

A second successive cliffhanger at Underhill on the final day of the season – and another great escape. This one was even more dramatic as Barnet faced Port Vale trailing third-from-bottom Lincoln by two points. But a penalty by Izale McLeod secured victory, while their rivals lost at home to Aldershot, giving caretaker-manager Giuliano Grazioli even more satisfaction than he once enjoyed when scoring the goal to give Stevenage an FA Cup draw with Newcastle. Grazioli, helped by former Northern Ireland manager Lawrie Sanchez, was the fourth man in charge, with Mark Stimson sacked on New Year's Day, former manager Paul Fairclough standing in temporarily and chairman Tony Kleanthous then turning to Martin Allen for what he admitted was 'a last throw of the dice.' Allen looked as if he might be the saviour after a point against champions-elect Chesterfield, a 4-1 win at Burton, where Steve Kabba scored all four goals, then victory over Crewe. Instead, Allen walked out after 19 days to take over at Notts County, leaving Grazioli to pick up the pieces, with a big helping hand from McLeod, whose hat-trick in a 4-2 away win over Gillingham had kept hopes alive. Sanchez later took full charge.

Adjeman-PamboekK ...... - (1)	Gallen K 6 (1)	Parsons M 7 (1)
Basey G 11	Holmes R 14 (11)	Poole G 6 (4)
Byrne M 26 (2)	Hughes M 31 (2)	Pulis A 4
Cole J 31	Jarvis R 12 (10)	Southam G 31 (2)
Coulton T 1	Kabba S 23	Stimson C .... - (6)
Cox S 5 (5)	Kamdjo C 28 (4)	Stirling J 5 (1)
Deering S 14 (2)	Kelly D .... - (3)	Taylor C 2 (16)
Dennehy A 4 (1)	Leach D 14	Uddin A 28 (2)
Devera J 43	Marshall M 45 (1)	Vilhete N 6 (14)
Dobson C .... - (1)	McLeod I 25 (4)	Walker S ....
Dunleavy J 1 (2)	Midson J 3 (2)	Walsh P 6 (2)
Francomb G 13	O'Brien L 7 (1)	Wright B .... - (1)
Fraser T 10 (5)	Parkes J 37 (3)	

League goals (58): McLeod 14, Kabba 11, Byrne 6, Marshall 6, Walsh 3, Deering 2, Holmes 2, Hughes 2, Basey 1, Devera 1, Gallen 1, Kamdjo 1, Leach 1, Parkes 1, Poole 1, Southam 1, Taylor 1, Uddin 1, Opponents 2
FA Cup goals: None. **Carling Cup goals**: None. **Johnstone's Paint Trophy goals** (1): Vilhete 1
Average home league attendance: 2,249. **Player of Year**: Joe Devera

BRADFORD CITY

A season to forget for Bradford, who struggled in the lower reaches of the table for much of the time and had a late scare before securing their league status under interim-manager Peter Jackson. The team's one successful run, four wins out of five and 11 goals scored with Peter Taylor in charge, was rewarded with a place in the top half and suggested better times ahead for the second part of the campaign. But a subsequent fall to fifth-from-bottom prompted Taylor to call it a day and brought in former club captain Jackson. There was no significant improvement in results and successive defeats in April against Torquay, Southend and Accrington meant a worrying few days before a 2-1 victory over Aldershot took them clear. Then, a point at Hereford ensured safety and an eventual 18th place. Jackson was later given the job on a permanent basis after the club ended speculation about a move from Valley Parade to Odsal Stadium.

Adeyemi T 30 (4)	Flett A .... - (1)	Pidgeley L 21
Brown R 3	Flynn M 16 (3)	Price J 6 (4)
Bullock L 22 (4)	Gill O 4	Ransden S 2
Chilaka C .... - (4)	Hanson J 31 (5)	Rehman Z 5 (3)
Cullen M 1 (3)	Hendrie L 8 (4)	Rowe D 1 (1)
Daley O 22 (4)	Hunt L 24	Speight J 13 (15)
Dean L .... - (1)	Kiernan N 6 (2)	Stephenson D .... - (1)
Dobie S 8 (5)	McLaughlan J 25	Syers D 30 (7)
Doherty S 17 (1)	Moult L 4 (7)	Threlfall R 16 (4)
Duff S 14	Neilson S 1	Williams S 26 (2)
Eckersley R 12	O'Brien L 37 (5)	Worthington J 16
Ellison K 6 (1)	Oliver L 41 (1)	
Evans G 28 (8)	Osborne L 10 (12)	

League goals (43): Syers 8, Hanson 6, Adeyemi 5, Daley 5, Speight 4, Evans 3, Williams 3, Hendrick 2, Duff 1, Ellison 1, Hunt 1, Moult 1, Oliver 1, Osborne 1, Price 1
FA Cup goals (3): Hanson 2, Syers 1. **Carling Cup goals** (3): Hanson 1, Speight 1, Syers 1.
Johnstone's Paint Trophy goals: None
Average home league attendance: 11,127. **Player of Year:** David Syers

BURTON ALBION

A run to the fourth round of the FA Cup and a number of winter postponements meant Burton had to address a backlog of matches in the league. At one stage, they had seven games in hand on Barnet and three or more to spare on other teams near the basement. So their position did not seem too threatening, particularly after completing the double over leaders Chesterfield. But the workload began to take its toll. With a month of the season remaining, they were separated from second-from-bottom Barnet only on goal difference and had just two fixtures in hand. Salvation came with successive victories over Cheltenham and Aldershot, which removed the threat of a return to Conference football, giving Burton the confidence to end the campaign on six games unbeaten. Two goals in the final ten minutes by leading scorer Shaun Harrad, who later moved to Northampton, earned Burton a notable victory over Middlesbrough, before a fourth round defeat at Burnley.

Austin R	20 (4)	James T	25 (2)	Rodney N	- (3)
Boertien P	15 (1)	Legzdins A	46	Simpson M	1
Bolder A	32 (5)	Maghoma J	39 (2)	Stanton N	22
Collins J	9 (1)	Malone S	18 (4)	Walker R	9 (9)
Corbett A	36 (4)	McGrath J	38 (3)	Webster A	38 (4)
Dyer J	4 (1)	Moore D	32 (2)	Whaley S	1 (2)
Ellison J	- (2)	Parkes T	4 (1)	Winnall S	12 (7)
Gilroy K	- (1)	Pearson G	16 (19)	Young L	9 (10)
Grocott K	- (2)	Penn R	39 (2)	Zola C	14 (4)
Harrad S	16 (4)	Phillips J	10 (13)		
Hughes B	1	Preen G	- (1)		

League goals (56): Webster 11, Harrad 10, Winnall 7, Pearson 5, Collins 4, Maghoma 4, McGrath 3, Penn 3, Zola 3, Bolder 1, Corbett 1, Malone 1, Walker 1, Opponents 2
FA Cup goals (7): Harrad 2, Webster 2, Collins 1, Maghoma 1, Zola 1. **Carling Cup goals** (1): Harrad 1. **Johnstone's Paint Trophy goals** (1): Walker 1
Average home league attendance: 2,947. **Player of Year:** Adam Legzdins

BURY

Any team chasing promotion would be unsettled by the loss of their manager, so Bury deserved great credit for overcoming Alan Knill's departure to Scunthorpe by finishing runners-up to Chesterfield. Knill, who will face his old club this season after his new one went down, left Gigg Lane with the team in fourth place. They proceeded to win the next six matches and went up in style with a 3-2 victory at Chesterfield under caretaker Richie Barker. Key to this success was productive away form. Bury won more times on their travels (12) than anyone in the division, equalling a club-record in the process with six wins in succession and 21 goals scored during the first half of the campaign. Ryan Lowe claimed a record of his own, scoring in nine successive games. The 32-year-old finished with 27 for the season and was voted League Two Player of Year. Barker was later given the job on a permanent basis.

Ajose N	22 (6)	Branagan R	1 (1)	Futcher B	6 (5)
Belford C	39	Carlton D	- (3)	Gunning G	2
Bennett K	13 (19)	Eckersley R	3	Harrop M	- (3)
Bishop A	14 (5)	Fon Williams O	6	Haworth A	20 (20)

Holroyd C	3 (1)	McCarthy L	- (1)	Sodje E	40
John-Lewis L	6 (33)	Mozika D	32 (1)	Sweeney P	18 (7)
Jones M	37 (5)	Picken P	38	Worrall D	27 (13)
Lees T	45	Schumacher S	42 (1)		
Lowe R	46	Skarz J	46		

League goals (82): Lowe 27, Ajose 13, Schumacher 9, Jones 8, Bishop 4, Lees 4, Haworth 4, Sodje 3, Bennett 2, John-Lewis 2, Mozika 2, Worrall 2, Futcher 1, Holroyd 1, Skarz 1
FA Cup goals (3): Lees 1, Lowe 1, Sodje 1. **Carling Cup goals:** None. **Johnstone's Paint Trophy goals:** None
Average home league attendance: 3,313. **Player of Year:** Ryan Lowe

CHELTENHAM TOWN

With new signing Wes Thomas scoring freely, Cheltenham enjoyed a solid first half of the season. They overcame a potentially confidence-sapping 6-4 defeat at Rotherham – after leading 3-1 – to move to within goal difference of a play-off place, helped by four-goal performances against Accrington and Bradford. But a run of eight matches without a victory, starting in the New Year, sent them sliding into mid-table. They struggled to regain momentum, winning only three more matches and suffering an embarrassing 8-1 trouncing at Crewe, described as 'embarrassing' by manager Mark Yates, who apologised to supporters afterwards. Yates had to contend with budget cuts, although there was an improvement of five places in the team's 2010 finish of third-from-bottom, thanks largely to seven victories scored away from home – one more than at Whaddon Road. Thomas had 18 goals to his name.

Andrew D	43	Green M	10 (9)	Riley M	26
Artus F	21 (8)	Haynes K	1	Shroot R	4 (3)
Bird D	27 (12)	Jeffers S	3 (19)	Smikle B	37 (9)
Brown S	46	Lewis T	8 (13)	Thomas W	40 (1)
Eastham A	8 (1)	Low J	28 (2)	Thomson J	3 (2)
Elito M	1 (1)	Lowe K	36	Walsh P	- (4)
Elliott S	39 (2)	Melligan J	14 (13)	Watkins M	- (1)
Gallinagh A	20 (4)	Pack M	32 (6)		
Goulding J	34 (5)	Pook M	25 (4)		

League goals (56): Thomas 18, Goulding 10, Low 7, Andrew 4, Smikle 4, Artus 3, Gallinagh 2, Pack 2, Elliott 1, Jeffers 1, Lowe 1, Pook 1, Shroot 1, Thomson 1
FA Cup goals (1): Thomas 1. **Carling Cup goals** (1): Jeffers 1. **Johnstone's Paint Trophy goals:** None.
Average home league attendance: 2,980. **Player of Year:** Keith Lowe

CHESTERFIELD

John Sheridan's side turned on the style in their new stadium and were crowned worthy champions. They led the table from mid-October, withstood a late charge from Bury and made sure of the title on the final day of the season by beating Gillingham 3-1, watched by another 10,000-plus crowd. There were none of the problems experienced by some teams moving grounds. Early on, Chesterfield came back from 4-1 down to draw 5-5 with Crewe after Danny Whittaker's second penalty in the 89th minute and Craig Clay's equaliser in the third minute of stoppage-time. They also scored three or more goals in other matches. When Jack Lester registered his second hat-trick against Rotherham, the lead was 13 points. When Bury capped a storming run by winning 3-2 at the b2net stadium, that advantage had been whittled down to two points. But Bury couldn't go all the way and there was finally a five-point difference between the two teams. Lester finished with 17 to his credit, Craig Davies led the way with 23, while Sheridan was named League Two's Manager of the Year.

Allott M 33 (3)	Griffiths S 28 (1)	Morris I 13 (6)
Boden S 2 (21)	Holden D 17	Niven D 24 (11)
Bowery J 5 (22)	Hunt J 18 (2)	Page R .... - (1)
Breckin I 19 (6)	Lee T 46	Robertson G 21
Clay C 1 (2)	Lester J 29 (11)	Smalley D 22 (6)
Davies C 41	Lomax K 3 (1)	Talbot D 44
Djilali K 7 (3)	Lowry J .... - (3)	Vidal J 5 (1)
Ford S 31	Mattis D 35 (3)	Whitaker D 43 (3)
Gray D 1 (1)	Morgan D 18 (3)	

League goals (85): Davies 23, Lester 17, Whitaker 15, Smalley 12, Boden 3, Mattis 3, Talbot 3, Holden 2, Bowery 1, Clay 1, Djilali 1, Ford 1, Morgan 1, Morris 1, Niven 1
FA Cup goals (3): Boden 1, Bowery 1, Davies 1. **Carling Cup goals** (1): Mattis 1. **Johnstone's Paint Trophy goals** (4): Morgan 2, Bowery 1, Davies 1
Average home league attendance: 6,972. **Player of Year**: Drew Talbot

CREWE ALEXANDRA

Crewe chartered a modest mid-table course for much of the season – but it was dotted with some far-from-ordinary scorelines. The first was a 7-0 victory over Barnet in their second home match. Then came a 5-5 draw at Chesterfield in which they led 3-0 and 4-1. Next was a 6-2 reversal at Northampton. After that, came the 8-1 rout of Cheltenham in which Clayton Donaldson and Joel Grant both scored hat-tricks. For good measure, Crewe finished off with a 5-1 win against Bradford, ending a run of 11 straight defeats away from home and leaving them with a total of 87 goals – highest in the division. Donaldson, who netted another three against Burton, was top of the individual scoring charts with 28. His team ended up tenth, an improvement of eight places on the previous campaign. Crewe were up to third early in the New Year after a single loss in nine games, but fell back after that result at Northampton.

Ada P 39 (1)	Hughes C .... - (1)	Sarcevic A .... - (6)
Artell D 40	Law B 1	Shelley D 17 (8)
Bell L 45	Leitch-Smith A 5 (11)	Taylor R 44
Blanchett D 38 (1)	Mellor K .... - (1)	Tootle M 36 (3)
Clayton M .... - (2)	Miller S 38 (4)	Turton O .... - (1)
Connerton J .... - (1)	Mitchel-King M 9 (5)	Westwood A M 7 (1)
Davis H .... - (1)	Moore L 27 (10)	Westwood A R 45 (1)
Donaldson C 42 (1)	Murphy L 36 (3)	Zola C 4 (2)
Dugdale A 15 (5)	Phillips S 2 (1)	
Grant J 16 (9)	Powell N .... - (17)	

League goals (87): Donaldson 28, Miller 19, Moore 6, Shelley 6, Grant 5, Leitch-Smith 5, Westwood A R 5, Artell 4, Murphy 3, Ada 1, Bell 1, Sarcevic 1, Zola 1, Opponents 2
FA Cup goals (1): Westwood A R 1, **Carling Cup goals** (1): Opponents 1. **Johnstone's Paint Trophy goals** (5): Artell 1, Donaldson 1, Grant 1, Bell 1, Opponents 1
Average home league attendance: 4,119. **Player of Year**: Clayton Donaldson

GILLINGHAM

Two successive home defeats against lowly opposition at a crucial time of the season put paid to Gillingham's bid for an immediate return to League One. They were one of the favourites to go up and looked a solid bet for a place in the play-offs when a 4-0 win at Lincoln extended their unbeaten run to 15 matches. Instead, sudden defensive frailty was exposed by relegation-threatened Barnet, who came away from Priestfield with a 4-2 victory, and by Macclesfield, who achieved the same scoreline. It left Andy Hessenthaler's side outside the top seven with a goal difference inferior to that of Torquay and Stevenage and facing a visit to leaders Chesterfield in the final match. Cody McDonald's 25th goal of the campaign was not enough to prevent a 3-1 defeat, following which Hessenthaler set about an overhaul of his squad during the summer.

Aborah S.................. - (1)	Kennedy C 3	Palmer C....................18
Akinfenwa A............ 40 (4)	King S 3 (1)	Payne J.................. 25 (6)
Barcham A 18 (6)	Lawrence M 41 (2)	Payne S 1 (15)
Bentley M 15 (10)	Lee C 4	Richards G 15 (2)
Cronin L 7	Maher K 36	Rooney L 2 (21)
Davies C 1	Martin J 12 (5)	Sinclair T 17 (3)
Fuller B 40 (2)	McCammon M .... - (5)	Spiller D 23 (7)
Gowling J............... 21 (1)	McDonald C................41	Weston C 29 (4)
Inkango B 1 (4)	Miller A .... - (1)	Whelpdale C....................4
Jackman D.............. 15 (2)	Nutter J 32 (2)	White A .... - (1)
Julian A....................39	Oli D 3 (18)	

League goals (67): McDonald 25, Akinfenwa 11, Barcham 6, Palmer 4, Weston 4, Whelpdale 3, Bentley 2, Gowling 2, Spiller 2, Jackman 1, Lee 1, Martin 1, Nutter 1, Oli 1, Payne 1, Rooney 1, Opponents 1
FA Cup goals: None. **Carling Cup goals** (1): Palmer 1. **Johnstone's Paint Trophy goals**: None
Average home league attendance: 5,230. **Player of Year**: Cody McDonald

HEREFORD UNITED

Hereford survived an early goal drought and a late points deduction to preserve their league status under physio-turned-manager Jamie Pitman. Former midfielder Pitman took over on a caretaker basis when Simon Davey was sacked with the team bottom, having scored just four goals in ten matches. He enjoyed a major morale-boost when a 3-0 half-time deficit at Northampton was transformed into a 4-3 win by goals from Stuart Fleetwood, James McQuilkin and Mathieu Manset. That was followed by a 5-0 success at Stockport. Hereford, however, did not record a home victory until the return match with Stockport in mid-January, by which time they were back in trouble. The three-point deduction and £10,000 fine for fielding an ineligible player against Torquay added to the pressure. Then, a handsome 3-0 win over leaders Chesterfield gave them breathing space and Pitman was handed the job on a permanent basis, his team finishing three points above the relegation zone.

Bartlett A....................46	Kanoute S.................. - (1)	Purdie R 18 (7)
Bauza G.................. 9 (3)	Kovacs J 21 (4)	Rabihou A.................. 1 (2)
Canham S.............. 7 (9)	Leslie S 10 (1)	Rose R 32 (2)
Colbeck J................ 40 (4)	Lund M 1 (1)	Valentine R 16
Fairhurst W 10 (6)	Lunt K 38 (4)	Stam S....................10
Featherstone N........ 20 (7)	Malsom S 1 (3)	Stratford D................ 2 (5)
Fleetwood S 36 (7)	Manset M 18 (3)	Thompson O.............. 5 (1)
Green R 40 (1)	McQuilkin J 31 (7)	Townsend M 42 (1)
Gwynne S 3 (3)	Ngo Baheng W .... - (2)	Webster B 2
Heath J....................26	Patulea A .... - (6)	Weer T 2 (2)
James T......................6	Pell H 5 (2)	Werling D.................. 4 (2)
Jervis J 3 (1)	Price J...................... 1 (3)	

League goals (50): Fleetwood 14, Manset 7, Colbeck 5, Fairhurst 3, Purdie 3, McQuilkin 3, Bauza 2, Canham 2, Kovacs 2, Leslie 2, Rose 2, Featherstone 1, Green 1, Townsend 1, Opponents 2
FA Cup goals (13): Manset 6, Fleetwood 4, Purdie 2, Rose 1. **Carling Cup goals**: None.
Johnstone's Paint Trophy goals: None
Average home league attendance: 2,516. **Player of Year**: Stuart Fleetwood

LINCOLN CITY

When Lincoln put the big freeze – and five weeks of inactivity – behind them to chalk up five successive victories under Steve Tilson, the possibility of going out of the Football League seemed unthinkable. They were up to mid-table, nine points clear of trouble, and even a 5-1 home defeat by promotion-chasing Shrewsbury, which brought the run to an end, was viewed as not too damaging. A month later, when on-loan Ashley Grimes took his tally to 14 with two goals in the defeat of Tilson's former club Southend, the gap was 11 points. Then, Lincoln crumbled, gathering just two points from the next ten matches and needing to win their final fixture at home to Aldershot to be sure of beating the drop. Instead, with confidence low, they lost it 3-0 and were overhauled by a resurgent Barnet, who won their last match against Port Vale. Tilson, who came in when Chris Sutton resigned after nine games citing 'personal reasons,' faced having to build a new squad under financial restrictions making it a lot tougher to bounce straight back as the club did after going down in 1987.

Anderson J.................... 19 (3)	Hone D.................... 25 (1)	Kerr S....................... 10 (6)
Anyon J 21	Howell L............. 23 (2)	Kilbey T................ 6 (1)
Broughton D............ 9 (14)	Hoyte G 11 (1)	McCallum G 24 (12)
Carayol M 24 (9)	Hughton C 17 (5)	Musselwhite P............. - (1)
Carson T....................16	Hunt S....................14	O'Keefe J................. 33 (4)
Clapham J................ 21 (4)	Hutchinson A .... - (5)	Parish E............................9
Facey D 26 (6)	Hutchinson B........ 26 (10)	Pearce I................... 3 (1)
Fuseini A 15 (3)	Jarrett A 19 (3)	Spencer S................ 2 (8)
Gowling J....................4	Kanyuka P 2 (4)	Swaibu M 12
Green P 14 (3)	Kelly J 21	Turner S................... - (2)
Grimes A................... 24 (3)	Keltie C 16 (2)	Watts A....................40

League goals (45): Grimes 15, Hutchinson B 4, O'Keefe 4, Carayol 3, Facey 3, McCallum 3, Hughton 2, Hunt 2, Swaibu 2, Clapham 1, Green 1, Howell 1, Jarrett 1, Watts 1, Opponents 2
FA Cup goals (6): Grimes 2, Carayol 1, Clapham 1, Facey 1, Jarrett 1. **Carling Cup goals**: None.
Johnstone's Paint Trophy goals: None
Average home league attendance: 3,508. **Player of Year**: Ashley Grimes

MACCLESFIELD TOWN

A modest achievement, perhaps, but still one to savour as Macclesfield finished in their highest position – 15th – since reaching the play-offs in 2005. It came in a season in which tragedy again struck the club when 29-year-old midfielder player Richard Butcher died, ten months after manager Keith Alexander passed away. Butcher's death came with his side going through a difficult spell on the pitch, sliding to within a point of the bottom two after a run of ten matches produced just four points. There was also a 6-0 FA Cup defeat at Huddersfield to contend with. But Macclesfield dug their way out of trouble, passing manager Gary Simpson's target of 50 points and ending on a solid note, with a 4-2 away win over promotion-chasing Gillingham, victory over Cheltenham and a point gained against Southend and Hereford.

Barnett T 45	Diagne T 19 (1)	Nsiala A......................10
Bencherif H 36 (5)	Draper R 34 (6)	Reid I................. 34 (3)
Bolland P................. 31 (1)	Gray D 18 (3)	Roberts A..................... - (2)
Brisley S.................. 12 (2)	Hamshaw M 18 (10)	Sappleton R .... -1 (9)
Brown N 44	Hewitt E.........................1	Sinclair E................. 26 (5)
Butcher R 5 (2)	Lowe M.................... - (1)	Tremarco C............... 20 (5)
Chalmers L 22 (8)	Morgan P................. 27 (1)	Veiga J M......................46
Daniel C 36 (7)	Mukendi V 8 (13)	Wedgbury S............ 13 (10)

League goals (59): Barnett 13, Bencherif 11, Daniel 8, Draper 5, Sinclair 5, Brown 2, Bolland

2, Chalmers 2, Hamshaw 2, Butcher 1, Diagne 1, Gray 1, Mukendi 1, Reid 1, Sappleton 1, Wedgbury 1, Opponents 2

FA Cup goals (4): Brown 1, Daniel 1, Nsiala 1, Sinclair 1. **Carling Cup goals (3):** Brown 1, Daniel 1, Mukendi 1. **Johnstone's Paint Trophy goals (3):** Mukendi 1, Opponents 2

Average home league attendance: 1,807. **Player of Year:** Tyrone Barnett

MORECAMBE

After finishing in the top half of the table in each of their first three seasons in the Football League, Morecambe experienced an indifferent campaign at the new Globe Arena. They were bottom after failing to win any of the first six matches and struggled to build real momentum after that. A 5-0 win over Stockport, in which Phil Jevons scored a hat-trick, put them in better heart, while successive victories over Stockport in the return fixture, Shrewsbury and Torquay hinted at better times in the New Year. Instead, inconsistency continued to be the overriding feature of their play, although there was never any danger of being sucked into a relegation struggle. High spot was a 2-0 away win over leaders Chesterfield. Low point came with a 7-2 defeat in the final away game at Port Vale, which would have been even worse but for overworked goalkeeper Barry Roche. Sammy McIlroy, second longest-serving manager in the division, left by mutual agreement after five years in the job and was replaced by captain Jim Bentley.

Aley Z 1 (1)	Fleming A 23 (7)	Mullin P 15 (11)
Anyon J 4	Haining W 12	Parrish A 41
Bentley J 7 (1)	Hendrie S 1 (6)	Roche B 42
Brown S 19 (13)	Holdsworth A 12 (3)	Rundle A 8 (9)
Capaldi T 17 (1)	Hunter G 27 (6)	Scott P 6 (2)
Carlton D 11 (5)	Hurst K 21	Shuker C 12 (15)
Charnock K 20 (1)	Jevons P 27 (11)	Spencer J 20 (12)
Cowperthwaite N 6 (1)	McCready C 35 (1)	Stanley C 21 (1)
Drummond S 39 (2)	McLachlan F 1	Wainwright N 1 (4)
Duffy M 16 (6)	Moss D 4	Wilson L 37 (1)

League goals (54): Jevons 8, Spencer 8, Drummond 6, McCready 4, Mullin 4, Brown 3, Carlton 3, Wilson 3, Fleming 2, Hurst 2, Shuker 2, Stanley 2, Bentley 1, Charnock 1, Cowperthwaite 1, Haining 1, Holdsworth 1, Hunter 1, Opponents 1

FA Cup goals: None. **Carling Cup goals (3):** Fleming 2, Jevons 1. **Johnstone's Paint Trophy goals:** None.

Average home league attendance: 2,256. **Player of Year:** Barry Roche

NORTHAMPTON TOWN

The relief was palpable as Northampton retained their league status in a tense, final home match. They went into it a single point ahead of second-from-bottom Barnet after a disastrous run which the arrival of new manager Gary Johnson had failed to halt. A third minute goal by Liam Davis calmed nerves and a second after the interval from Michael Uwezu, his first for the club, secured a 2-0 win over promotion-seeking Stevenage, who had two players sent off. It was the team's first win in 19 matches, seven of which had built up by the time Ian Sampson was sacked and replaced by former Bristol City and Peterborough manager Johnson. Sampson had engineered a famous Carling Cup third round win at Liverpool on penalties. It was followed by five successive defeats, but his team worked their way out of trouble and a 6-2 win over Crewe hinted at a play-off challenge, before the rot set in.

Bauza G 9 (1)	Dunn C 39	Harrad S 18
Beckwith D 35 (2)	Gilligan R 20 (2)	Harris S 1 (3)
Collis S 3 (1)	Guinan S 5 (6)	Herbert C 1 (14)
Davis L 32 (1)	Hall M 21 (3)	Holt A 32 (7)

Jacobs M 33 (8)	McKenzie L............ 17 (10)	Tozer B 28 (3)
Jansson O 4	Ofori-Twumasi N.............11	Uwezu M 2 (2)
Jarvis R 3	Osman A................. 37 (1)	Walker J.....................19
Johnson J 38	Parker J 3	Walker P .... - (1)
Kaziboni G .... - (2)	Purcell T 1 (3)	Webster B 8
King C 3 (4)	Reckord J 4 (3)	Wedderburn N 21 (10)
Laurent F 3 (3)	Rodgers P 15 (10)	
McKay B 24 (10)	Thornton K.............. 16 (9)	

League goals (63): McKenzie 10, Holt 7, Harrad 6, Johnson 6, Thornton 6, Jacobs 5, McKay 5, Bauza 4, Beckwith 3, Osman 3, Tozer 3, Davis 2, Gilligan 1, Guinan 1, Uwezu 1
FA Cup goals (5): Guinan 1, Johnson 1, Jacobs 1, McKay 1, Thornton 1. **Carling Cup goals** (8): Jacobs 2, McKay 2, Davis 1, Holt 1, Thornton 1, Opponents 1. **Johnstone's Paint Trophy goals:** None
Average home league attendance: 4,604. **Player of Year:** Michael Jacobs

OXFORD UNITED

Skipper James Constable, whose goals played a big part in promotion the previous season, continued to lead the way as Oxford cemented a top-half finish on their return to the Football League. Constable scored 15, including a hat-trick against Morecambe, plus two in the Carling Cup. To round off a successful campaign, he signed a new, three-year contract. Another hat-trick, from Jack Midson against Torquay, came during a purple patch of seven victories in nine matches which lifted his team from fourth from bottom to within striking distance of a play-off place. They were still in with a chance after victories over Crewe and Burton, but slipped back when tough matches in April against four leading sides, Bury, Wycombe, Accrington and Chesterfield, netted only three points.

Baker R .... - (6)	Doble R 1 (2)	Midson J................ 11 (10)
Batt D 27 (1)	Franks L 4 (1)	Payne J 23 (5)
Bulman D 4 (1)	Futcher B 6	Philliskirk D .... - (1)
Burge R 5	Green M 9 (8)	Potter A 16 (22)
Clarke R 46	Hackney S 2 (11)	Purkiss B 19 (4)
Clist S 16 (7)	Hall A 34 (7)	Sangare D 2 (2)
Cole M .... - (4)	Hanson M .... - (2)	Tonkin A 37 (2)
Constable J 35 (9)	Heslop S 30 (8)	Worley H 41 (2)
Craddock T 36 (3)	Kinniburgh S........... 10 (1)	Wotton P.....................4
Creighton M 5 (2)	MacLean S 26 (5)	Wright J 33 (2)
Deering S .... - (6)	McLaren P 24	

League goals (58): Constable 15, Craddock 15, MacLean 6, Midson 6, Hall 4, Heslop 3, Potter 2, Clist 1, McLaren 1, Payne 1, Worley 1, Opponents 3
FA Cup goals: None. **Carling Cup goals** (6): Constable 2, Heslop 2, Green 1, Midson 1. **Johnstone's Paint Trophy goals:** None.
Average home league attendance: 7,281. **Player of Year:** Ryan Clarke

PORT VALE

Micky Adams spoke of 'unfinished business' on returning as manager after a troubled four months at Sheffield United ended in relegation and the sack. Adams led Vale to the top of table after 18 games with a 5-0 win at Stockport, but they lost their way when he left for Bramall Lane – and the slide continued under Jim Gannon, previously at Stockport, Motherwell and Peterborough. Gannon lasted just 74 days – during which he fell out with assistant manager Geoff Horsfield – before being dismissed when his side dropped out of the play-off places on the back of a 3-0 defeat at Accrington. Mark Grew assumed the role of caretaker for the third time at the club with the decline deep rooted, winning only two of ten matches during a difficult spell in charge. Vale finished three points adrift, but at least rounded off their home programme on a high, Louis Dodds and Justin Richards scoring hat-tricks in a 7-2 win over Morecambe which showed what might have been.

Bell-Baggie A .... - (3)	Johnson J 1 (5)	Richards M 37 (3)
Blizzard D....................1	Lloyd R...................... - (1)	Rigg S 16 (9)
Brown K .... - (4)	Loft D.................... 24 (5)	Roberts G 30 (5)
Collins L 41 (1)	Malbon A .... - (2)	Sawyers R .... - (1)
Cox K .... - (1)	Martin C 12 (2)	Speight J 1 (3)
Davis J .... - (1)	McCombe J..................42	Sutton R 5 (6)
Dodds L................. 14 (19)	Morsy S 12 (4)	Taylor K 15 (5)
Fraser T 7 (5)	O'Shea J 5	Taylor R 21 (15)
Geohaghon E........... 11 (1)	Owen G 35 (1)	Tomlinson S 34 (2)
Griffith A.................. 36 (4)	Pope T.................... 10 (3)	Yates A 45 (1)
Haldane L 14 (9)	Richards J............... 37 (5)	

League goals (54): Richards M 16, Richards J 9, Dodds 7, McCombe 4, Pope 3, Rigg 3, Collins 2, Roberts 2, Griffith 1, Loft 1, Morsy 1, O'Shea 1, Owen 1, Speight 1, Taylor R 1, Opponents 1
FA Cup goals (8): Richards J 2, Richards M 2, Taylor R 2, McCombe 1, Rigg 1. **Carling Cup goals** (3): Richards J 2, Rigg 1. **Johnstone's Paint Trophy goals** (4): Richards M 2, Richards J 1, Opponents 1
Average home league attendance: 5,532. **Player of Year:** John McCombe

ROTHERHAM UNITED

Adam Le Fondre's goals helped keep Rotherham in the promotion picture for the second successive season – but again there was nothing to show for them. This time, his team's challenge faded along with a run of five games without a win, culminating in a 5-0 defeat by leaders Chesterfield. It pushed them down from third – and eventually out of the play-off places – and brought about the end of Ronnie Moore's second spell as manager. Three days after Moore was dismissed, his son, Ian Thomas-Moore, scored a hat-trick in a 6-0 away win over Lincoln to revive hopes. But Rotherham, beaten finalists in 2010, were unable to build on it and Moore's replacement, former Brentford manager Andy Scott had to wait until the final game against Torquay for his first win. They finished two points adrift, with Le Fondre on 23 for the campaign, including four in a 6-4 victory over Cheltenham achieved after trailing 3-1.

Annerson J.................. 8 (1)	Fenton N 31 (1)	Newey T 38
Ashworth L.............. 3 (6)	Geohaghon E..............14	Pope T..................... 9 (9)
Atkinson W 3	Green J 5 (2)	Randall M 3 (7)
Bank O .... - (1)	Harrison D 23 (7)	Taylor J................... 37 (5)
Bradley M 14 (7)	Henderson L 5 (6)	Taylor R 30 (4)
Brogan S......................1	Holden D 4 (2)	Thomas-Moore I.......... 11 (1)
Coid D...........................9	Kennedy C 4 (1)	Tonge D 21 (2)
Cresswell R 21 (1)	Law N.........................44	Warne P................... 3 (8)
Daley O..................... 2 (6)	Le Fondre A 40 (5)	Warrington A..............38
Elliott T 4 (2)	Marshall M............. 26 (10)	
Ellison K................. 20 (3)	Mullins J.......................35	

League goals (75): Le Fondre 23, Taylor R 11, Taylor J 5, Cresswell 4, Harrison 4, Law 4, Ellison 3, Fenton 3, Marshall 3, Thomas-Moore 3, Atkinson 1, Banks 1, Daley 1, Geohaghon 1, Mullins 1, Pope 1, Randall 1, Warne 1, Opponents 4
FA Cup goals: None. **Carling Cup goals** (1): Marshall 1. **Johnstone's Paint Trophy goals** (5): Bradley 1, Cresswell 1, Ellison 1, Le Fondre 1, Taylor, R 1
Average home league attendance: 3,667. **Player of Year:** Adam Le Fondre

SHREWSBURY TOWN

Pre-match celebrations to mark the club's 125th anniversary were cut short by defeat by Torquay in the play-offs. A goalless draw in the second leg against a side who finished 11 points behind them followed a 2-0 defeat at Plainmoor, which Graham Turner admitted proved decisive. It was a double disappointment, with a strong finish to the regular campaign not quite enough to dislodge Wycombe from the third automatic promotion place. Shrewsbury did not concede a goal when accumulating 13 points from the last five fixtures, but were one short at the end. Turner's second spell as manager had got off to a flying start. His side topped the table early on and came from 3-0 down to beat Charlton 4-3 in a memorable Carling Cup tie. They suffered in the depths of winter, with only one win to show from nine matches. Later, there was a 5-0 defeat at Torquay. But they recovered from it well to stay right in contention

Ainsworth L............ 21 (12)	Harrold M 28 (13)	Robinson J............... 20 (2)
Bradshaw T............ 13 (13)	Holden D 11 (2)	Sadler M.......................46
Bright K.................... - (1)	Leslie S 9 (9)	Sharps I.......................43
Canavan N....................3	Lomax K .... - (1)	Smith B........................25
Cansdell-Sherriff S.... 39 (2)	McAllister S 15 (3)	Taylor J 19 (1)
Collins J 22 (2)	McIntyre K 18 (13)	Tutte A........................2
Davis D.........................19	Neal C 21 (1)	Van den Broek B....... - (11)
Disley C 22 (2)	Neal L .... - (2)	Wright M............... 43 (2)
Geohaghon E..................2	O'Donnell D 4 (1)	Wroe N........................18
Goldson C 1 (2)	Obadeyi T 7 (2)	
Grandison J...................13	Raven D 22 (2)	

Play-offs – appearances: Cansdell-Sherriff 2, Davis 2, Grandison 2, Harrold 2, Sadler 2, Sharps 2, Smith 2, Taylor 2, Wright 2, Wroe 2, Ainsworth 1 (1), Collins 1 (1), Bradshaw – (2), Canavan – (1), Leslie – (1)
League goals (72): Wright 14, Ainsworth 9, Collins 8, Harrold 8, Robinson 8, Bradshaw 6, Taylor 6, Wroe 3, Cansdell-Sherriff 2, Davis 2, Disley 2, McIntyre 1, Sharps 1, Opponents 2.
Play-offs – goals: None
FA Cup goals: None. **Carling Cup goals (5):** Harrold 1, Leslie 1, O'Donnell 1, Robinson 1, Opponents 1. **Johnstone's Paint Trophy goals (1):** Leslie 1
Average home league attendance: 5,875. **Player of Year:** Ian Sharps

SOUTHEND UNITED

Barry Corr's goals, coupled to an improvement in results at home, helped ease Southend out of trouble and up to the fringe of a play-off spot. They offered the opportunity of an immediate return to League One after indifferent form had left Paul Sturrock's side just a point off a relegation place with the onset of winter. By the time high-riding Wycombe were beaten at Roots Hall, 11 matches had delivered 22 points. When lowly Barnet had been accounted for, Southend were just a point away, with a game in hand. But they were unable to press home the advantage. Two 4-0 victories, over Hereford and Bradford, were interspersed with too many dropped points, resulting in a finishing position just below mid-table. Corr's tally was 18, plus three in FA Cup and Carling Cup ties.

Asante K.................... 1 (8)	Easton C.......................32	Herd J 6 (3)
Barker C.......................43	Evans R 13	Jarvis N .... - (6)
Bilel M 21 (2)	Fairhurst W 2 (1)	Midson J.........................4
Clohessy S 46	Ferdinand K 19 (3)	Morris G 33
Comminges M 4 (3)	German A 3 (1)	Nesbitt T .... - (2)
Corr B 32 (9)	Gilbert P 26	Paterson M 4 (7)
Coughlan G 28 (5)	Grant A 41 (2)	Phillips M 3 (2)
Crawford H 5 (18)	Hall R 36 (5)	Prosser L 14 (3)

Sawyer L................ 7 (10)	Spencer S................ 1 (4)	Timlin M 8
Simpson J.................17	Stevens J.................1	Woodyard A....................3
Soares L 17 (14)	Sturrock B 34 (9)	Zaaboub S 2 (1)

League goals (62): Corr 18, Hall 9, Grant 8, Sturrock 6, Mohsni 5, Easton 4, Crawford 2, Ferdinand 2, Midson 2, Asante 1, Clohessy 1, Prosser 1, Simpson 1, Timlin 1, Opponents 1
FA Cup goals (4): Corr 2, German 1, Simpson 1. **Carling Cup goals** (4): Paterson 2, Corr 1, Easton 1. **Johnstone's Paint Trophy goals** (3): Paterson 2, Soares 1
Average home league attendance: 5,250. **Player of Year:** Chris Barker

STEVENAGE

When a memorable FA Cup run was followed by stuttering league form, the new boys looked as if they might have to settle for mid-table consolidation. Five matches yielded only three points and resulted in a fall into the bottom half of the table. Instead, Stevenage got back on track with successive wins over Crewe, Port Vale and Cheltenham. Then, after another hiccup, they reeled off six straight victories on the way to a place in the play-offs, confirmed on the final day of the regular season with a point to spare. After a 3-0 aggregate success against Accrington in the semi-finals, a goal four minutes from half-time by John Mousinho against Torquay brought back-to-back promotions for the Blue Square Premier League title winners, who can now look forward to rubbing shoulders with the likes of Charlton, the two Sheffield clubs and Preston in League One. All round, it was a tremendous season. Newcastle were beaten 3-1 in the third round of the Cup and Reading stretched all the way before going through with a goal after 87 minutes.

Play-offs – appearances: Bostwick 3, Byrom 3, Charles 3, Day 3, Henry 3, Laird 3, Long 3, Reid

Ashton J 37 (1)	Foster L 16 (7)	Odubade Y 5 (10)
Atieno T..........................1	Griffin C 13 (2)	Reid C 14 (6)
Beardsley C.............. 14 (9)	Harrison B 11 (9)	Roberts M...................42
Bostwick M..................41	Henry R......................42	Sills T........................1
Boylan L .... - (1)	Holroyd C....................12	Sinclair R 14 (13)
Bridges D............. 8 (11)	Laird S 42 (2)	Vincenti P 1 (4)
Byrom J 5 (2)	Long S 19 (3)	Walker J..........................
Charles D.............. 20 (8)	May B.................. 7 (13)	Williams M.................. - (1)
Daley L .... - (2)	Mousinho J 36 (2)	Wilson L 39 (3)
Day C......................46	Murphy D................. 1 (4)	Winn P 13 (15)
Dixon T..................... - (1)	O'Shea J..........................5	

3, Roberts 3, Wilson 3, Murphy 1 (2), Ashton 1, Mousinho 1, Beardsley – (3), Harrison – (3), Winn – (1)
League goals (62): Harrison 8, Mousinho 7, Holroyd 6, Roberts 6, Wilson 5, Laird 4, Griffin 3, Bostwick 2, Charles 2, Long 2, Reid 2, Sinclair 2, Winn 2, Ashton 1, Beardsley 1, Bridges 1, Foster 1, May 1, Odubade 1, Vincenti 1, Opponents 4. **Play-offs – goals** (4): Beardsley 1, Byrom 1, Long 1, Mousinho 1
FA Cup goals (7): Charles 2, Bostwick 1, Odubade 1, Walker 1, Winn 1, Opponents 1. **Carling Cup goals** (1): Murphy 1. **Johnstone's Paint Trophy goals:** None
Average home league attendance: 2,898. **Player of Year:** Jon Ashton

STOCKPORT COUNTY

A second successive relegation brought to an end 106 years of league football for Stockport. They finished bottom, just as they did in League One in 2010, a continuing legacy of the club's financial predicament and the 14 months spent in administration. Three 5-0 defeats, by Hereford, Morecambe and Port Vale in less than a month, underlined the problems faced by Paul Simpson, who was eventually sacked after less than six months as manager with his side fourth from bottom. Under caretaker Peter Ward, County slipped into the drop zone three weeks later and stayed there. Former Wigan and Tranmere manager Ray Mathias, Ward's technical advisor, replaced him with Stockport four points from safety and having played more matches than the other strugglers. The gap was closed to two with victory over Southend. Port Vale were also beaten. But there was no escape and they finished seven points from safety.

Aldred T 7	Goodall A 13	Pulis A 9 (1)
Assoumani M 34 (2)	Grieve M 3	Rose J 13 (2)
Brown A.........................17	Griffin A 42 (3)	Rowe D 7 (10)
Conlon B................... 5 (4)	Halls A 17 (2)	Salem Y 2 (3)
Darkwah C .... - (6)	Husband S 5	Simpson J.............. 11 (8)
Demontagnac I 7	Lynch M 30 (1)	Swailes D....................13
Doble R 3	Mainwaring M 9 (2)	Tansey G.............. 30 (8)
Donnelly G...................23	McLoughlin I...................5	Turnbull P 39 (2)
Elding A 18 (3)	O'Donnell D 7	Vincent J 13 (7)
Fisher T 6 (21)	Paterson M 9 (1)	Wallace J....................14
Fletcher W 8 (1)	Pilkington D 1 (4)	Williams R 19 (3)
Fon Williams O...............5	Poole D................. 22 (7)	
Glennon M...................36	Procter J.............. 4 (3)	

League goals (48): Tansey 10, Donnelly 8, Turnbull 5, Elding 3, Paterson 3, Demontagnac 2, Husband 2, Poole 2, Assoumani 1, Brown 1, Doble 1, Fisher 1, Fletcher 1, Griffin 1, Pulis 1, Rowe 1, Wallace 1, Williams 1, Opponents 3
FA Cup goals (2): Griffin 1, Tansey 1. **Carling Cup goals**: None. **Johnstone's Paint Trophy goals**: None
Average home league attendance: 4,163. **Player of Year**: Adam Griffin

TORQUAY UNITED

A season that started on a high ended on a low note with defeat in the play-offs and the loss of manager Paul Buckle. Torquay comfortably saw off Shrewsbury and had the edge, on paper, going into the final against Stevenage. They had not lost to the league newcomers in six previous meetings and took four points from the teams' two fixtures in the regular season. But Torquay fell behind four minutes from the interval and despite an improving in the second half, when Jake Robinson's shot hit the crossbar, were unable to come up with an equaliser. Two days later, Buckle left to take charge at Bristol Rovers. He had seen the previous season's club-record run without conceding a goal extended to ten games by a winning start which secured the early leadership of the division. After that, there were mixed fortunes – nine matches without a win, a run of 17 points from seven games and the deduction of a point by Football League for fielding an ineligible player against Hereford. It meant they held on to seventh place with a goal difference superior to that of Gillingham. Buckle was succeeded by former Leyton Orient manager Martin Ling.

Benyon E.................. 22 (1)	Kee B 17 (23)	Robertson C 40 (3)
Bevan S.........................37	Lathrope D.............. 10 (8)	Robinson J.....................22
Branston G...................45	Macklin L 3 (7)	Rose R 2 (3)
Carlisle W 3 (7)	Mansell D....................45	Rowe-Turner L 4 (4)
Charnock K 1 (3)	Murray R.................. 4 (3)	Senda D 2
Ellis M........................ 24 (3)	Nicholson K 42 (2)	Stanley C....................19
Gilligan R .... - (5)	O'Kane E 31 (14)	Stevens D 19 (18)
Gritton M 3 (9)	Oastler J 17 (8)	Tomlin G.....................12
Haldin S .... - (4)	Potter D.........................9	Wroe N......................20
Hemmings A 4 (5)	Pringle B 45	Zebroski C...................44

Play-offs – appearances: Bevan 3, Branston 3, Kee 3, Lathrope 3, Mansell 3, Nicholson 3, O'Kane 3, Robertson 3, Robinson 3, Tomlin 3, Zebroski 3, Oastler – (3), Rowe-Turner – (2), Stevens – (2), Macklin – (1)

League goals (74): Zebroski 14, Benyon 13, Kee 9, Robinson 7, O'Kane 6, Tomlin 4, Nicholson 3, Stevens 3, Wroe 3, Branston 2, Ellis 2, Robertson 2, Murray 1, Rose 1, Rowe-Turner 1, Stanley 1, Opponents 2. **Play-offs – goals** (2): O'Kane 1, Zebroski 1
FA Cup goals (3): Benyon 1, Kee 1, O'Kane 1. **Carling Cup goals:** None. **Johnstone's Paint Trophy goals:** None
Average home league attendance: 2,630. **Player of Year:** Guy Branston

WYCOMBE WANDERERS

Gary Waddock reshaped the struggling side he inherited from Peter Taylor the previous season and won an instant return to League One. They maintained a single point advantage over Shewsbury in the final game by coming from behind to beat Southend with goals from Scott Donnelly, Ben Strevens and leading marksman Scott Rendell. Waddock immediately began ringing the changes again, releasing eight members of his successful squad to make way for new signings aimed at keeping them up this time. Wycombe were again slow starters, the first eight games yielding a single victory, but once into their stride were a force to be reckoned with. They were up to third on New Year's Day and a ten-match unbeaten run through to the end of the campaign kept them there behind Chesterfield and Bury. Rendell scored 19 times in all competitions, while ever-present goalkeeper Nikki Bull rounded off a fine campaign with the club's Player of the Year award.

Ainsworth G	39 (4)	Foster D	37 (1)	Phillips M	1 (2)
Beavon S	30 (7)	Johnson L	22 (1)	Pittman J-P	6 (13)
Bennett A	16 (1)	Kiernan R	2	Rendell S	24 (13)
Betsy K	41 (4)	Lewis S	24 (1)	Sandell A	30 (2)
Bloomfield M	30 (4)	McClure M	- (8)	Scowen J	- (2)
Bull N	46	McCoy M	18 (3)	Straker A	2 (2)
Davies N	5 (3)	Montrose L	27 (9)	Strevens B	36 (4)
Donnelly S	11 (7)	Murtagh K	1 (6)	Westwood C	24 (3)
Federico J	- (1)	Parker J	- (1)	Winfield D	34 (3)

League goals (69): Rendell 14, Ainsworth 10, Strevens 7, Sandell 7, Betsy 6, Montrose 4, Pittman 4, Beavon 3, Bloomfield 3, Donnelly 3, Lewis 2, Winfield 2, Davies 1, Foster 1, Johnson 1, Westwood 1
FA Cup goals (5): Beavon 2, Rendell 2, Ainsworth 1. **Carling Cup goals** (1): Strevens 1. **Johnstone's Paint Trophy goals** (5): Rendell 3, Betsy 1, Davies 1
Average home league attendance: 4,495. **Player of Year:** Nikki Bull

QUOTE/UNQOUTE

'I just saw the ball coming into the box and thought "why not?" Nine times out of ten they end up in the stand' – **Wayne Rooney** on his wonder goal for Manchester United against Manchester City.

'We weren't given a prayer by the bookies and the pundits, but we believed. It was a titanic performance by my players' – **Alex McLeish**, Birmingham manager, after the Carling Cup Final win over Arsenal.

'At the end of the day, football is only a game. There are worse things in life than fighting relegation' – **Demba Ba**, West Ham striker.

LEAGUE CLUB MANAGERS

Figure in brackets = number of managerial changes at club since the War

BARCLAYS PREMIER LEAGUE

Arsenal (11)	Arsene Wenger	October 1996
Aston Villa (21)	Alex McLeish	June 2011
Blackburn (25)	Steve Kean	December 2010
Bolton (20)	Owen Coyle	January 2010
Chelsea (24)	Andre Villas-Boas	June 2011
Everton (16)	David Moyes	March 2002
Fulham (28)	Martin Jol	June 2011
Liverpool (12)	Kenny Dalglish†	January 2011
Manchester City (28)	Roberto Mancini	December 2009
Manchester Utd (8)	Sir Alex Ferguson	November 1986
Newcastle (25)	Alan Pardew	December 2010
Norwich (25)	Paul Lambert	August 2009
QPR (29)	Neil Warnock	March 2010
Stoke (22)	Tony Pulis†	June 2006
Sunderland (23)	Steve Bruce	June 2009
Swansea (30)	Brendan Rodgers	July 2010
Tottenham (20)	Harry Redknapp	October 2008
WBA (28)	Roy Hodgson	February 2011
Wigan (18)	Roberto Martinez	June 2009
Wolves (20)	Mick McCarthy	July 2006

†Second spell at club. Number of changes since elected to Football League: Wigan 1978

NPOWER CHAMPIONSHIP

Barnsley (21)	Keith Hill	June 2011
Birmingham (23)	Chris Hughton	June 2011
Blackpool (25)	Ian Holloway	May 2009
Brighton (30)	Gus Poyet	November 2009
Bristol City (22)	Keith Millen	August 2010
Burnley (23)	Eddie Howe	January 2011
Cardiff (27)	Malky Mackay	June 2011
Coventry (30)	Andy Thorn	March 2011
Crystal Palace (36)	Dougie Freedman	January 2011
Derby (21)	Nigel Clough	December 2008
Doncaster (1)	Sean O'Driscoll	September 2006
Hull (25)	Nigel Pearson	July 2010
Ipswich (12)	Paul Jewell	January 2011
Leeds (22)	Simon Grayson	December 2008
Leicester (26)	Sven-Goran Eriksson	October 2010
Middlesbrough (19)	Tony Mowbray	October 2010
Millwall (28)	Kenny Jackett	November 2007
Nottm Forest (17)	Steve McClaren	June 2011
Peterborough (27)	Darren Ferguson†	January 2011
Portsmouth (28)	Steve Cotterill	June 2010
Reading (18)	Brian McDermott	January 2010
Southampton (23)	Nigel Adkins	September 2010
Watford (27)	Sean Dyche	June 2011
West Ham (13)	Sam Allardyce	June 2011

Number of changes since elected to Football League: Peterborough 1960. Since returning: Doncaster 2003.
†Second spell at club

NPOWER LEAGUE ONE

Bournemouth (22)	Lee Bradbury	January 2011
Brentford (30)	Uwe Rosler	June 2011
Bury (23)	Richie Barker	March 2011
Carlisle (3)	Greg Abbott	November 2008

Club	Manager	Date
Charlton (17)	Chris Powell	January 2011
Chesterfield (18)	John Sheridan	June 2009
Colchester (24)	John Ward	May 2010
Exeter (-)	Paul Tisdale	June 2006
Hartlepool (31)	Mick Wadsworth	August 2010
Huddersfield (24)	Lee Clark	November 2008
Leyton Orient (22)	Russell Slade	April 2010
MK Dons (15)	Karl Robinson	April 2010
Notts Co (35)	Martin Allen	April 2011
Oldham (25)	Paul Dickov	June 2010
Preston (26)	Phil Brown	January 2011
Rochdale (30)	Steve Eyre	June 2011
Scunthorpe (24)	Alan Knill	March 2011
Sheffield Utd (34)	Danny Wilson	May 2011
Sheffield Wed (26)	Gary Megson	February 2011
Stevenage (-)	Graham Westley	May 2008
Tranmere (19)	Les Parry	December 2009
Walsall (33)	Dean Smith	January 2011
Wycombe (9)	Gary Waddock	October 2009
Yeovil (3)	Terry Skiverton	February 2009

Number of changes since elected to Football League: Wycombe 1993, Yeovil 2003, Stevenage 2010. Since returning: Carlisle 2005, Exeter 2008.

NPOWER LEAGUE TWO

Club	Manager	Date
AFC Wimbledon (-)	Terry Brown	May 2007
Accrington (-)	John Coleman	July 1999
Aldershot (2)	Dean Holdsworth	January 2011
Barnet (4)	Lawrie Sanchez	May 2011
Bradford (32)	Peter Jackson	March 2011
Bristol Rov (24)	Paul Buckle	May 2011
Burton (-)	Paul Peschisolido	June 2009
Cheltenham (6)	Mark Yates	December 2009
Crawley (-)	Steve Evans	May 2007
Crewe (20)	Dario Gradi††	October 2009
Dagenham (-)	John Still	April 2004
Gillingham (21)	Andy Hessenthaler†	May 2010
Hereford (3)	Jamie Pitman	October 2010
Macclesfield (9)	Gary Simpson	April 2010
Morecambe (1)	Jim Bentley	May 2011
Northampton (29)	Gary Johnson	March 2011
Oxford Utd (-)	Chris Wilder	December 2008
Plymouth (31)	Peter Reid	June 2010
Port Vale (23)	Micky Adams†	May 2011
Rotherham (23)	Andy Scott	April 2011
Shrewsbury (3)	Graham Turner	June 2010
Southend (27)	Paul Sturrock	July 2010
Swindon (26)	Paolo di Canio	May 2011
Torquay (1)	Martin Ling	June 2011

††Third spell at club. †Second spell at club. Number of changes since elected to Football League: Macclesfield 1997, Cheltenham 1999, Dagenham 2007, Morecambe 2007, Burton 2009, AFC Wimbledon 2011, Crawley 2011. Since returning: Shrewsbury 2004, Barnet 2005, Accrington 2006, Hereford 2006, Aldershot 2008, Torquay 2009, Oxford Utd 2010

MANAGERIAL INS AND OUTS 2010–11

PREMIER LEAGUE

Aston Villa:	Out – Martin O'Neill (August 2010); In – Gerard Houllier – Out (June 2011); In – Alex McLeish
Birmingham:	Out – Alex McLeish (June 2011); In – Chris Hughton
Blackburn:	Out – Sam Allardyce (December 2010); In – Steve Kean

Chelsea:	Out – Carlo Ancelotti (May 2011); In – Andre Villas-Boas
Fulham:	In – Mark Hughes (July 2010) – Out (May 2011); In – Martin Jol
Liverpool:	Out – Roy Hodgson (January 2011); In – Kenny Dalglish
Newcastle:	Out – Chris Hughton (December 2010); In – Alan Pardew
WBA:	Out – Roberto di Matteo (February 2011); In – Roy Hodgson
West Ham:	Out – Avram Grant (May 2011); In – Sam Allardyce

CHAMPIONSHIP

Barnsley:	Out – Mark Robins (May 2011); In – Keith Hill
Bristol City:	Out – Steve Coppell (August 2010); In – Keith Millen
Burnley:	Out – Brian Laws (December 2010); In – Eddie Howe
Cardiff:	Out – Dave Jones (May 2011); In – Malky Mackay
Coventry:	Out – Aidy Boothroyd (March 2011); In – Andy Thorn
Crystal Palace:	Out – George Burley (January 2011); In – Dougie Freedman
Ipswich:	Out – Roy Keane (January 2011); In – Paul Jewell
Leicester:	Out – Paulo Sousa (October 2010); In – Sven-Goran Eriksson
Middlesbrough:	Out – Gordon Strachan (October 2010); In – Tony Mowbray
Nottm Forest:	Out – Billy Davies (June 2011); In Steve McClaren
Preston:	Out – Darren Ferguson (December 2010); In – Phil Brown
Scunthorpe:	Out – Nigel Adkins (September 2010); In – Ian Baraclough – Out (March 2011); In – Alan Knill
Sheffield Utd:	Out – Kevin Blackwell (August 2010); In – Gary Speed – Out (December 2010); In – Micky Adams – Out (May 2011); In – Danny Wilson
Swansea:	In – Brendan Rodgers (July 2010)
Watford:	Out – Malky Mackay (June 2011); In – Sean Dyche

LEAGUE ONE

Bournemouth:	Out – Eddie Howe (January 2011); In – Lee Bradbury
Brentford:	Out – Andy Scott (February 2011); In – Nicky Forster – Out (May 2011); In – Uwe Rosler
Bristol Rov:	Out – Paul Trollope (December 2010); In – Dave Penney – Out – (March 2011); In – Paul Buckle
Charlton:	Out – Phil Parkinson (January 2011); In – Chris Powell
Hartlepool:	Out – Chris Turner (August 2010); In – Mick Wadsworth
Notts Co:	Out – Craig Short (October 2010); In – Paul Ince – Out (April 2011); In – Martin Allen
Peterborough:	Out – Gary Johnson (January 2011); In – Darren Ferguson
Rochdale:	Out – Keith Hill (May 2011); In – Steve Eyre
Sheffield Wed:	Out – Alan Irvine (February 2011); In – Gary Megson
Southampton:	Out – Alan Pardew (August 2010); In – Nigel Adkins
Swindon:	Out – Danny Wilson (March 2011); In – Paolo di Canio
Walsall:	Out – Chris Hutchings (January 2011); In – Dean Smith

LEAGUE TWO

Aldershot:	Out – Kevin Dillon (January 2011); In – Dean Holdsworth
Barnet:	Out – Mark Stimson (January 2011); In – Martin Allen – Out (April 2011); In – Lawrie Sanchez
Bradford:	Out – Peter Taylor (February 2011); In – Peter Jackson
Bury:	Out – Alan Kill (March 2011); In – Richie Barker
Hereford:	Out – Simon Davey (October 2010); In – Jamie Pitman
Lincoln:	Out – Chris Sutton (September 2010); In – Steve Tilson
Morecambe:	Out – Sammy McIlroy (May 2011); In – Jim Bentley
Northampton:	Out – Ian Sampson (March 2011); In – Gary Johnson
Port Vale:	Out – Micky Adams (December 2010); In – Jim Gannon – Out (March 2011); In – Micky Adams
Rotherham:	Out – Ronnie Moore (March 2011); In – Andy Scott
Stockport:	Out – Paul Simpson (January 2011); In Ray Mathias
Torquay:	Out – Paul Buckle (May 2011); In – Martin Ling

FA CUP 2010-11
(sponsored by E.ON)

FIRST ROUND

AFC Wimbledon 0 Ebbsfleet 0
Accrington 3 Oldham 2
Barnet 0 Charlton 0
Bournemouth 5 Tranmere 3
Brentford 1 Aldershot 1
Brighton 0 Woking 0
Burton 1 Oxford Utd 0
Bury 2 Exeter 0
Cambridge Utd 0 Huddersfield 0
Carlisle 6 Tipton 0
Chelmsford 3 Hendon 2
Cheltenham 1 Morecambe 0
Colchester 4 Bradford 3
Corby 1 Luton 1
Dagenham 1 Leyton Orient 1
Darlington 2 Bristol Rov 1
Dartford 1 Port Vale 1
Fleetwood 1 Walsall 1
Forest Green 0 Northampton 3
Gillingham 0 Dover 2
Guiseley 0 Crawley 5
Harrow 0 Chesterfield 2
Hartlepool 0 Vauxhall 0
Havant 0 Droylsden 0
Hayes 1 Wycombe 2
Hereford 5 Hythe 1
Lincoln 1 Nuneaton 0
Macclesfield 2 Southend 2
Mansfield 0 Torquay 1
Notts Co 2 Gateshead 0
Plymouth 0 Swindon Town 4
Rotherham 0 York 0
Rochdale 2 FC United 3
Rushden 0 Yeovil 1
Southampton 2 Shrewsbury 0
Southport 2 Sheffield Wed 5
Stevenage 0 MK Dons 0
Stockport 1 Peterborough 1
Swindon Supermarine 2 Eastwood 1
Tamworth 2 Crewe 1

FIRST ROUND REPLAYS

Aldershot 1 Brentford 0
Charlton 1 Barnet 0
Ebbsfleet 2 AFC Wimbledon 3 (aet)
Huddersfield 2 Cambridge Utd 1
Leyton Orient 3 Dagenham 2
Luton 4 Corby 2

MK Dons 1 Stevenage 1
(aet, Stevenage won 7-6 on pens)
Peterborough 4 Stockport 1
Port Vale 4 Dartford 0
Southend 2 Macclesfield 2
(aet, Macclesfield won 5-3 on pens)
Vauxhall 0 Hartlepool 1
Walsall 2 Fleetwood 0
Woking 2 Brighton 2
(aet, Brighton won 3-0 on pens)
York 3 Rotherham 0

SECOND ROUND

AFC Wimbldeon 0 Stevenage 2
Brighton 1 FC United 1
Burton 3 Chesterfield 1
Bury 1 Peterborough 2
Carlisle 3 Tamworth 2
Charlton 2 Luton 2
Colchester 1 Swindon Supermarine 0
Crawley 1 Swindon Town 1
Darlington 0 York 2
Dover 2 Aldershot 1
Droylsden 1 Leyton Orient 1
Hartlepool 4 Yeovil 2
Hereford 2 Lincoln 2
Huddersfield 6 Macclesfield 0
Notts Co 3 Bournemouth 1
Port Vale 1 Accrington 0
Sheffield Wed 3 Northampton 2
Southampton 3 Cheltenham 0
Torquay 1 Walsall 0
Wycombe 3 Chelmsford 1

SECOND ROUND REPLAYS

FC United 0 Brighton 4
Leyton Orient 8 Droylsden 2 (aet)
Lincoln 3 Hereford 4
Luton 1 Charlton 3
Swindon Town 2 Crawley 3 (aet)

MANCHESTER CITY'S FIRST FA CUP TRIUMPH SINCE 1969

THIRD ROUND	FOURTH ROUND	FIFTH ROUND	SIXTH ROUND	SEMI-FINALS	FINAL
Manchester City....2:4	Manchester City....1:5	*Manchester City....3	*Manchester City....1	Manchester City....1	Manchester City....1
*Leicester....2:2	*Notts Co....1:0	Aston Villa....0	Reading....0		
*Sunderland....1					
Notts Co....2					
*Sheffield Utd....3	*Aston Villa....3	*Everton....0			
Aston Villa....3	Blackburn....1	Reading....1			
*Blackburn....1					
QPR....0					
*Scunthorpe....1	*Everton....1:A1				
Everton....5	Chelsea....1:1				
*Chelsea....7					
Ipswich....0					
*Stevenage....3	*Stevenage....1				
Newcastle....1	Reading....2				
*Reading....1					
WBA....0					
*Southampton....2	*Southampton....1	*Manchester Utd....1	*Manchester Utd....2	Manchester Utd....0	
Blackpool....0	Manchester Utd....2	Crawley....0	Arsenal....0		
*Manchester Utd....2					
Liverpool....0					
*Torquay....1	*Torquay....0				
Carlisle....0	Crawley....1				
*Crawley....1					
Derby....1					
*Swansea....4	*Swansea....1	*Leyton Orient....1:0			
Colchester....0	Leyton Orient....2	Arsenal....1:5			
*Norwich....0					
Leyton Orient....1					
*Arsenal....1:3	*Arsenal....2				
Leeds....1:1	Huddersfield....1				
*Huddersfield....2					
Dover....0					

140

Round 1

*Millwall.............1
Birmingham.........4
*Coventry...........2
Crystal Palace......1
*Bristol City........0
Sheffield Wed.......4
*Wycombe...........0
Hereford.............1
*Fulham..............6
Peterborough.......2
*Tottenham.........3
Charlton.............0
*Bolton.............2
York.................0
*Hull...............2
Wigan...............3
*West Ham.........2
Barnsley............0
*Preston............2
Nottm Forest.......4
*Burnley............4
Port Vale...........2
*Burton.............2
Middlesbrough.....1
*Watford...........4
Hartlepool..........1
*Brighton..........3
Portsmouth.........1
*Doncaster........2:0
Wolves.............2:5
Cardiff..............1:0
*Stoke..............1+:2

Round 2

*Birmingham........3
Coventry............2
*Sheffield Wed......0
Hereford.............1
*Fulham.............0
Tottenham..........0
*Bolton............0:1
Wigan..............0-0
*West Ham..........3
Nottm Forest.......2
*Burnley............3
Burton..............1
*Watford...........0
Brighton............1
*Wolves.............0
*Stoke..............3

Round 3

*Birmingham........2
Sheffield Wed.......0
*Fulham.............0
Bolton..............1
*West Ham..........5
Burnley.............1
Brighton............0
*Stoke..............3

Semi-finals

*Birmingham........2
Bolton..............3
West Ham...........1
*Stoke..............2

Bolton..............0
Stoke...............5

Final

Stoke...............0

*Drawn at home. +After extra-time. A – Everton won 4-3 on pens. Both semi-finals at Wembley.

141

ROUND BY ROUND HIGHLIGHTS

FIRST ROUND

The club formed by disenchanted Manchester United supporters take pride of place. FC United of Manchester win 3-2 at Rochdale with goals by Nicky Platt, Jake Cottrell and a disputed winner four minutes into stoppage-time after Michael Norton seems to kick the ball out of the hands of goalkeeper Josh Lillis. Former Arsenal trainee Adam Birchall sets Dover on the way against their former manager Andy Hessenthaler at Gillingham and Luke I'Anson completes a 2-0 success. Three second-half goals in 13 minutes bring York a 3-0 victory in a replay against Rotherham, with Chris Smith's header followed by two from Michael Rankine, the first from the penalty spot. Tamworth beat Crewe 2-1 thanks to strikes by Alex Rodman and Danny Thomas, while Darlington also overcome league opposition by the same scoreline, accounting for Bristol Rovers with goals by Michael Brough, his first for the club, and Gary Smith. Cambrdge United are in sight of another upset, leading at Huddersfield through Rory McAuley's goal until stoppage-time when Lee Peltier and Gary Roberts turn the replay on its head. Southampton are also grateful for goals in added time from substitute David Connolly and Adam Lallana after Shrewsbury look set for a goalless draw. Gary Madine scores four in Carlisle's 6-0 victory over Tipton and Josh McQuoid gets three as Bournemouth defeat Tranmere 5-3.

SECOND ROUND

No tie in this season's competition can match for incidents the replay at Matchroom Stadium. Leyton Orient, trailing Droylsden 2-0, equalise in the 89th minute and go on to win 8-2 in extra-time with hat-tricks from substitute Jonathan Tehoue and Scott McGleish. Four players are sent off – the home side's Terrell Forbes and Ben Chorley, along with Droylsden's Nathaniel Kerr and Lee Roche. And Droylsden manager Dave Pace is sent to the stands. Dover, managed by former Arsenal stalwart Martin Hayes, continue to flourish by overcoming Aldershot 2-0 with two goals by Adam Birchall, while two for Crawley's Ben Smith, his second two minutes from the end of extra-time, put paid to Swindon 3-2 in a replay at the County Ground. FC United of Manchester take Brighton to a replay before bowing out 4-0 in front of a record crowd for the club of 6,731. Tamworth's run also comes to an end at Carlisle, who need goals from Francois Zoko and James Chester in the final four minutes to scrape through 3-2. A hat-trick by Antony Sweeney points Hartlepool to a 4-2 win over Yeovil.

THIRD ROUND

Thirteen years after taking Kenny Dalglish's Newcastle to a replay, Stevenage go one better, winning 3-1 with an own goal by Mike Williamson and strikes from Michael Bostwick and Peter Winn. But the performance is marred at the end when their full-back Scott Laird is assaulted by a fan. Newcastle have Cheik Tiote sent off and all round it's a dismal day for the north-east. Paul Ince puts one over former Manchester United team-mate Steve Bruce as his Notts County side win 2-1 at Sunderland, with Craig Westcarr and Lee Hughes on the mark. Middlesbrough also go out, beaten 2-1 by two late Shaun Harrad goals at Burton. Beginning a second spell as Liverpool manager, Dalglish suffers as Ryan Giggs scores the only goal of the tie for Manchester United with a debatable penalty after two minutes and his captain Steven Gerrard is later sent off. Ian Holloway makes his priorities clear by fielding a second-string side at Southampton, who go through 2-0 with goals by Lee Barnard and Guly Do Prado, despite their manager Nigel Adkins making eight changes of his own. Crawley achieve another notable success, 2-1 against Derby, thanks to goals by Craig McAllister and then Argentinian Sergio Torres in stoppage-time – and a Michel Kuipers penalty save earlier from Kris Commons. The two other non-league sides bow out with plenty of credit. Bolton need to bring on their big guns, Kevin Davies and Johan Elmander, to shake off York, both scoring in the final ten minutes. Dover go down by the same 2-0 scoreline after conceding twice in the opening eight minutes to Scott Arfield and Gary

Roberts at Huddersfield. Arsenal need a 90th minute penalty by Cesc Fabregas against Leeds at the Emirates to earn a replay, which they win 3-1. No problems, though, for Fulham who beat Peterborough 6-2 with a hat-trick from Diomansy Kamara.

FOURTH ROUND

What a weekend for Crawley, who win 1-0 at Torquay, then draw Manchester United at Old Trafford in round five. Matt Tubbs scores his 25th goal of the season in an eventful tie in which Tubbs and Craig McAllister have penalties saved by Scott Bevan and both sides finish with ten men. Thomas Sorensen saves a stoppage-time spot-kick from Nenad Milijas to enable Stoke to preserve the lead established by Robert Huth's header after 81 minutes at Wolves. But Cesc Fabregas again makes no mistake after keeping Arsenal in the competition with a penalty against Leeds in the previous round. This one, four minutes from the end of normal time, gives ten-man team victory over Huddersfield after Sebastien Squillaci is sent off and Alan Lee threatens an upset by the League One side at the Emirates by cancelling out Peter Clarke's own goal. Holders Chelsea go out on penalties to Everton at Stamford Bridge after Frank Lampard's goal is cancelled out in the last minute of extra-time by Leighton Baines. Three days after overturning a 3-1 aggregate deficit against West Ham to reach the Carling Cup Final, Birmingham retrieve Coventry's 2-0 lead to go through 3-2, Kevin Phillips scoring the winner on his second start of the season. Jimmy Smith follows up his winner at Norwich in round three by putting Leyton Orient ahead at Swansea and his side reach the last 16 for the first time since 1982 by 2-1, courtesy of Alan Tate's 88th minute own goal. Brighton also overcome Championship opposition away from home, Ashley Barnes scoring the only goal at Watford to put them through to round five for the first time since 1986. Notts County threaten another upset when Neal Bishop scores against Manchester City, who need a first goal on his FA Cup debut from Edin Dzeko ten minutes from the end to earn a replay which they win 5-0. West Ham's Victor Obinna nets all three of West Ham's goals in their 3-2 win over Nottingham Forest.

FIFTH ROUND

Crawley go down with flying colours, restricting Manchester United to a Wes Brown goal and coming within inches of earning a replay when Richard Brodie's header hits the crossbar in time added on. Leyton Orient surprise Arsenal with an 89th minute equaliser from substitute Jonathan Tehoue and despite losing the replay 5-0 at the Emirates – Nicklas Bendtner scoring a hat-trick – the players are rewarded by owner Barry Hearn with a holiday in Las Vegas. Reading captain Matt Mills scores the only goal at Goodison Park to knock out Everton and maintain Football League interest in the competition. Thomas Hitzlsperger marks a long-awaited debut after injury with a goal and New Zealand World Cup defender Winston Reid also scores his first for the club as West Ham defeat Burnley 5-1. After Aston Villa's 3-0 defeat by Manchester City, manager Gerard Houllier faces claims of having given up on the tie by fielding a weakened team.

SIXTH ROUND

Sir Alex Ferguson gambles by playing identical twins Rafael and Fabio da Silva in midfield and the two full-backs respond with leading roles in Manchester United's 2-0 win over Arsenal. Rafael features in the build-up to his brother's goal after 28 minutes and a second by Wayne Rooney leaves Arsenal second best again, four days after going out of the Champions League to Barcelona. Kevin Davies, a semi-finalist with Chesterfield 14 years previously, plays a captain's role in the 3-2 success at Birmingham, winning and converting a penalty, then setting up the 90th minute winner for Chung-Yong Lee. Stoke reach the last four for the first time for 39 years, beating West Ham 2-1 despite Matthew Etherington having a disputed penalty saved by Robert Green. Robert Huth, with a header from Rory Delap's long throw, and Danny Higginbotham's free-kick do the trick. Reading, the only surviving Football League side for the second successive season, push Manchester City all the way at Eastlands before falling to a 74th minute Micah Richards header.

143

SEMI-FINALS

Two sharply contrasting ties. Both Manchester sides are without key players – Carlos Tevez (injured) and Wayne Rooney (suspended) - but it is City who prevail, thanks to Yaya Toure's only goal of the game in the 52nd minute. United's bid for the Treble comes to an end and they also have Paul Scholes sent off for a high challenge on Pablo Zabaleta. In the second of the Wembley matches, Stoke overwhelm Bolton 5-0 – the biggest semi-final victory since 1939. Jon Walters (2), Matthew Etherington, Kenwyne Jones and Robert Huth are their marksmen.

FINAL

There may be speculation about whether he really is the Premier League's most highly-paid player on upwards of £200,000 a week, but there can be no argument about the impact Yaya Toure has made on the FA Cup. Toure scored in the 3-0 fifth round win over Aston Villa, and netted the only goal of the semi-final against Manchester United. Then, returning to Wembley, he broke the deadlock – and Stoke's hearts – with the one that gave Manchester City their first triumph in the competition for 42 years. Nor was there any doubt about what the victory meant to Roberto Mancini. Some suggested that securing a place in the Champions League four days earlier was the only thing that mattered to the manager. But when referee Martin Atkinson sounded the final whistle, Mancini raised both arms in celebration to mark what he clearly regarded as a special achievement. Toure's 74th minute strike also continued the Ivory Coast's new-found affinity with the old competition. The powerful midfielder player followed in the Wembley footsteps of compatriot and international team-mate Didier Drogba, who scored the winner for Chelsea against Manchester United in 2007 and Portsmouth in 2010, as well as their first in the 2-1 success against Everton in 2009. The decider came, ironically, at a time when Stoke were beginning to get to grips with the occasion after a first half in which they were second best and owed much to a brilliant save by Thomas Sorensen from Mario Balotelli. Had Kenwyne Jones made full use of Matthew Etherington's long ball over the top, his side could have caused an upset. Instead, Joe Hart produced a smothering save, paving the way for Toure, 28 the day before the final, to dispatch a crisp half-volley, after good work by Balotelli and David Silva, to give City a deserved win and complete a historic day for Manchester after United's record title success two hours earlier.

MANCHESTER CITY 1 STOKE CITY 0
Wembley (88,643); Saturday, May 14 2011

Manchester City (4-2-3-1): Hart, Richards, Kompany, Lescott, Kolarov, De Jong, Barry, (A Johnson 73), Silva (Vieira 90), Y Toure, Balotelli, Tevez (capt) (Zabaleta 87). **Subs not used**: Given, Boyata, Milner, Dzeko. **Scorer**: Y Toure (74). **Manager**: Roberto Mancini

Stoke City (4-4-2): Sorensen, Wilkinson, Shawcross (capt), Huth, Wilson, Pennant, Whelan (Pugh 84), Delap (Carew 80), Etherington (Whitehead 62), Walters, Jones. **Subs not used**: Nash, Collins, Faye, Diao. **Booked**: Huth, Wilkinson. **Manager**: Tony Pulis

Referee: M Atkinson (Yorks). **Half-time**: 0-0

HOW THEY REACHED THE FINAL

MANCHESTER CITY
Round 3: 2-2 away to Leicester (Milner, Tevez); 4-2 home to Leicester (Tevez, Vieira, A Johnson, Kolarov)
Round 4: 1-1 away to Notts Co (Dzeko); 5-0 home to Notts Co (Vieira 2, Tevez, Dzeko, Richards)
Round 5: 3-0 home to Aston Villa (Y Toure, Balotelli, Silva)
Round 6: 1-0 home to Reading (Richards)
Semi-final: 1-0 v Manchester Utd (Y Toure)

STOKE CITY
Round 3: 1-1 home to Cardiff (Tuncay); 2-0 away to Cardiff (Walters 2)
Round 4: 1-0 away to Wolves (Huth)
Round 5: 3-0 home to Brighton (Carew, Walters, Shawcross)
Round 6: 2-1 home to West Ham (Huth, Higginbotham)
Semi-final: 5-0 v Bolton (Walters 2, Etherington, Huth, Jones)

LEADING SCORERS (from first round)
6 Manset (Hereford), McGleish (Leyton Orient); 5 Madine (Carlisle), Morrison (Sheffield Wed), Walters (Stoke); 4 Fleetwood (Hereford), Sweeney (Hartlepool), Tehoue (Leyton Orient)

FINAL FACTS AND FIGURES

- Manchester City won the trophy for the fifth time in nine finals. Their previous successes were in 1904, 1934, 1956 and 1969. The last one was against Leicester 1-0 with Neil Young's goal. Young,66, died in February 2011
- Stoke had never been so far, losing semi-finals in 1899, 1971 and 1972. A 5-0 win over Bolton this time was the biggest in the semi-finals since Wolves defeated Grimsby by the same scoreline in 1939
- Roberto Mancini became the third Italian to manage an FA Cup-winning team, following Chelsea's Carlo Ancelotti (2010) and Gianluca Vialli (2000)
- Stoke's Tony Pulis became the first Welshman to lead a team into the final as a full-time manager. Jimmy Murphy, who took Manchester United there in 1958, was caretaker while Matt Busby was recuperating from injuries suffered in the Munich air crash
- With City qualifying for the Champions League, Stoke secured a place in the Europa League
- War hero Mark Ward, serving with the The Mercian Regiment based in Catterick, presented the trophy. Corporal Ward was awarded the Military Cross for bravery in Afghanistan
- Ticket prices for the final were increased by the FA by up to 22%, with the most expensive breaking through the £100 barrier
- Premier League fixtures were held on the same day as the flagship match, which was brought forward because of UEFA's demand for a clear fortnight before the Champions League Final at Wembley on May 28. The same could happen again in 2012 because of the need for a clear period before the start of the European Championship Finals. A change in the traditional kick-off from 3pm to tea-time is also on the cards to suit television

QUOTE/UNQOUTE

'Can you believe that? A female linesman. Women don't know the offside rule' – **Andy Gray**, Sky Sports analyst, caught off-air talking about assistant referee Sian Massey and later sacked.

'Course they don't.-Somebody better get down there and explain offside to her' – **Richard Keys**, Sky Sports presenter, also lands himself in trouble with his comments and later resigns.

'Those views are inexcusable from anyone at Sky, regardless of their role or seniority, and will rightly offend many of our customers, our people and the wider public' – **Barney Francis**, Sky Sports managing director.

FA CUP FINAL SCORES & TEAMS

1872 **Wanderers** 1 (Betts) Bowen, Alcock, Bonsor, Welch; Betts, Crake, Hooman, Lubbock, Thompson, Vidal, Wollaston. Note: Betts played under the pseudonym 'AH Chequer' on the day of the match **Royal Engineers** 0 Capt Merriman; Capt Marindin; Lieut Addison, Lieut Cresswell, Lieut Mitchell, Lieut Renny-Tailyour, Lieut Rich, Lieut George Goodwyn, Lieut Muirhead, Lieut Cotter, Lieut Bogle

1873 **Wanderers** 2 (Wollaston, Kinnaird) Bowen; Thompson, Welch, Kinnaird, Howell, Wollaston, Sturgis, Rev Stewart, Kenyon-Slaney, Kingsford, Bonsor **Oxford University** 0 Kirke-Smith; Leach, Mackarness, Birley, Longman, Chappell-Maddison Dixon, Paton, Vidal, Sumner, Ottaway. March 29; 3,000; A Stair

1874 **Oxford University** 2 (Mackarness, Patton) Neapean; Mackarness, Birley, Green, Vidal, Ottaway, Benson, Patton, Rawson, Chappell-Maddison, Rev Johnson **Royal Engineers** 0 Capt Merriman; Major Marindin, Lieut W Addison, Gerald Onslow, Lieut Oliver, Lieut Digby, Lieut Renny-Tailyour, Lieut Rawson, Lieut Blackman Lieut Wood, Lieut von Donop. March 14; 2,000; A Stair

1875 **Royal Engineers** 1 (Renny-Tailyour) Capt Merriman; Lieut Sim, Lieut Onslow, Lieut (later Sir) Ruck, Lieut Von Donop, Lieut Wood, Lieut Rawson, Lieut Stafford, Capt Renny-Tailyour, Lieut Mein, Lieut Wingfield-Stratford **Old Etonians** 1 (Bonsor) Thompson; Benson, Lubbock, Wilson, Kinnaird, (Sir) Stronge, Patton, Farmer, Bonsor, Ottaway, Kenyon-Slaney. March 13; 2,000; CW Alcock. aet **Replay – Royal Engineers** 2 (Renny-Tailyour, Stafford) Capt Merriman; Lieut Sim, Lieut Onslow, Lieut (later Sir) Ruck, Lieut Von Donop, Lieut Wood, Lieut Rawson, Lieut Stafford, Capt Renny-Tailyour, Lieut Mein, Lieut Wingfield-Stratford **Old Etonians** 0 Capt Drummond-Moray; Kinnaird, (Sir) Stronge, Hammond, Lubbock, Patton, Farrer, Bonsor, Lubbock, Wilson, Farmer. March 16; 3,000; CW Alcock

1876 **Wanderers** 1 (Edwards) Greig; Stratford, Lindsay, Chappell-Maddison, Birley, Wollaston, C Heron, G Heron, Edwards, Kenrick, Hughes **Old Etonians** 1 (Bonsor) Hogg; Rev Welldon, Lyttleton, Thompson, Kinnaird, Meysey, Kenyon-Slaney, Lyttleton, Sturgis, Bonsor, Allene. March 11; 3,500; WS Rawson aet **Replay – Wanderers** 3 (Wollaston, Hughes 2) Greig, Stratford, Lindsay, Chappel-Maddison, Birley, Wollaston, C Heron, G Heron, Edwards, Kenrick, Hughes **Old Etonians** 0 Hogg, Lubbock, Lyttleton, Farrer, Kinnaird, (Sir) Stronge, Kenyon-Slaney, Lyttleton, Sturgis, Bonsor, Allene. March 18; 1,500; WS Rawson

1877 **Wanderers** 2 (Kenrick, Lindsay) Kinnaird; Birley, Denton, Green, Heron, Hughes, Kenrick, Lindsay, Stratford, Wace, Wollaston **Oxford University** 1 (Kinnaird og) Allington; Bain, Dunnell, Rev Savory, Todd, Waddington, Rev Fernandez, Otter, Parry, Rawson. March 24; 3,000; SH Wright, aet

1878 **Wanderers** 3 (Kinnaird, Kenrick 2) (Sir) Kirkpatrick; Stratford, Lindsay, Kinnaird, Green, Wollaston, Heron, Wylie, Wace, Denton, Kenrick **Royal Engineers** 1 (Morris) Friend; Cowan, (Sir) Morris, Mayne, Heath, Haynes, Lindsay, Hedley, (Sir) Bond, Barnet, Ruck. March 23; 4,500; SR Bastard

1879 **Old Etonians** 1 (Clerke) Hawtrey; Edward, Bury, Kinnaird, Lubbock, Clerke, Pares, Goodhart, Whitfield, Chevalier, Beaufoy **Clapham Rovers** 0 Birkett; Ogilvie, Field, Bailey, Prinsep, Rawson, Stanley, Scott, Bevington, Growse, Keith-Falconer. March 29; 5,000; CW Alcock

1880 **Clapham Rovers** 1 (Lloyd-Jones) Birkett; Ogilvie, Field, Weston, Bailey, Stanley, Brougham, Sparkes, Barry, Ram, Lloyd-Jones **Oxford University** 0 Parr; Wilson, King, Phillips, Rogers, Heygate, Rev Childs, Eyre, (Dr) Crowdy, Hill, Lubbock. April 10; 6,000; Major Marindin

1881 **Old Carthusians** 3 (Page, Wynyard, Parry) Gillett; Norris, (Sir) Colvin, Prinsep, (Sir) Vintcent, Hansell, Richards, Page, Wynyard, Parry, Todd **Old Etonians** 0 Rawlinson; Foley, French, Kinnaird, Farrer, Macauley, Goodhart, Whitfield, Novelli, Anderson, Chevallier. April 9; 4,000; W Pierce-Dix

1882 **Old Etonians** 1 (Macauley) Rawlinson; French, de Paravicini, Kinnaird, Foley, Novelli, Dunn, Macauley, Goodhart, Chevallier, Anderson **Blackburn Rov** 0 Howarth; McIntyre, Suter, Hargreaves, Sharples, Hargreaves, Avery, Brown, Strachan, Douglas, Duckworth. March 25; 6,500; JC Clegg

1883 **Blackburn Olympic** 2 (Matthews, Costley) Hacking; Ward, Warburton, Gibson, Astley, Hunter, Dewhurst, Matthews, Wilson, Costley, Yates **Old Etonians** 1 (Goodhart) Rawlinson; French, de Paravicini, Kinnaird, Foley, Dunn, Bainbridge, Chevallier, Anderson, Goodhart, Macauley. March 31; 8,000; Major Marindin, aet

1884 Blackburn Rov 2 (Sowerbutts, Forrest) Arthur; Suter, Beverley, McIntyre, Forrest, Hargreaves, Brown, Inglis Sowerbutts, Douglas, Lofthouse **Queen's Park 1** (Christie) Gillespie; MacDonald, Arnott, Gow, Campbell, Allan, Harrower, (Dr) Smith, Anderson, Watt, Christie. March 29; 4,000; Major Marindin

1885 Blackburn Rov 2 (Forrest, Brown) Arthur; Turner, Suter, Haworth, McIntyre, Forrest, Sowerbutts, Lofthouse, Douglas, Brown, Fecitt **Queen's Park 0** Gillespie; Arnott, MacLeod, MacDonald, Campbell, Sellar, Anderson, McWhammel, Hamilton, Allan, Gray. April 4; 12,500; Major Marindin

1886 Blackburn Rov 0 Arthur; Turner, Suter, Heyes, Forrest, McIntyre, Douglas, Strachan, Sowerbutts, Fecitt, Brown **WBA 0** Roberts; Green, Bell, Horton, Perry, Timmins, Woodhall, Green, Bayliss, Loach, Bell. April 3; 15,000; Major Marindin **Replay – Blackburn Rov 2** (Sowerbutts, Brown) Arthur; Turner, Suter, Walton, Forrest, McIntyre, Douglas, Strachan, Sowerbutts, Fecitt, Brown **WBA 0** Roberts; Green, Bell, Horton, Perry, Timmins, Woodhall, Green, Bayliss, Loach, Bell. April 10; 12,000; Major Marindin

1887 Aston Villa 2 (Hodgetts, Hunter) Warner; Coulton, Simmonds, Yates, Dawson, Burton, Davis, Albert Brown, Hunter, Vaughton, Hodgetts **WBA 0** Roberts; Green, Aldridge, Horton, Perry, Timmins, Woodhall, Green, Bayliss, Paddock, Pearson. April 2; 15,500; Major Marindin

1888 WBA 2 (Bayliss), Woodhall) Roberts; Aldridge, Green, Horton, Perry, Timmins, Woodhall, Bassett, Bayliss, Wilson, Pearson **Preston 1** (Dewhurst) Mills-Roberts; Howarth, Holmes, Ross, Russell, Gordon, Ross, Goodall, Dewhurst, Drummond, Graham. March 24; 19,000; Major Marindin

1889 Preston 3 (Dewhurst, Ross, Thomson) Mills-Roberts; Howarth, Holmes, Drummond, Russell, Graham, Gordon, Goodall, Dewhurst, Thompson, Ross **Wolves 0** Baynton; Baugh, Mason, Fletcher, Allen, Lowder, Hunter, Wykes, Brodie, Wood, Knight. March 30; 22,000; Major Marindin

1890 Blackburn Rov 6 (Lofthouse, Jack Southworth, Walton, Townley 3) Horne; James Southworth, Forbes, Barton, Dewar, Forrest, Lofthouse, Campbell, Jack Southworth, Walton, Townley **Sheffield Wed 1** (Bennett) Smith; Morley, Brayshaw, Dungworth, Betts, Waller, Ingram, Woolhouse, Bennett, Mumford, Cawley. March 29; 20,000; Major Marindin

1891 Blackburn Rov 3 (Dewar, Jack Southworth, Townley) Pennington; Brandon, Forbes, Barton, Dewar, Forrest, Lofthouse, Walton, Southworth, Hall, Townley **Notts Co 1** (Oswald) Thraves; Ferguson, Hendry, Osborne, Calderhead, Shelton, McGregror, McInnes Oswald, Locker, Daft. March 21; 23,000; CJ Hughes

1892 WBA 3 (Geddes, Nicholls, Reynolds) Reader; Nicholson, McCulloch, Reynolds, Perry, Groves, Bassett, McLeod, Nicholls, Pearson, Geddes **Aston Villa 0** Warner; Evans, Cox, Devey, Cowan, Baird, Athersmith, Devey, Dickson, Hodgetts, Campbell. March 19; 32,810; JC Clegg

1893 Wolves 1 (Allen) Rose; Baugh, Swift, Malpass, Allen, Kinsey, Topham, Wykes, Butcher, Griffin, Wood **Everton 0** Williams; Kelso, Howarth, Boyle, Holt, Stewart, Latta, Gordon, Maxwell, Chadwick, Milward. March 25; 45,000; CJ Hughes

1894 Notts Co 4 (Watson, Logan 3) Toone; Harper, Hendry, Bramley, Calderhead, Shelton, Watson, Donnelly, Logan Bruce, Daft **Bolton 1** (Cassidy) Sutcliffe; Somerville, Jones , Gardiner, Paton, Hughes, Tannahill, Wilson, Cassidy, Bentley, Dickenson. March 31; 37,000; CJ Hughes

1895 Aston Villa 1 (Chatt) Wilkes; Spencer, Welford, Reynolds, Cowan, Russell, Athersmith Chatt, Devey, Hodgetts, Smith **WBA 0** Reader; Williams, Horton, Perry, Higgins, Taggart, Bassett, McLeod, Richards, Hutchinson, Banks. April 20; 42,560; J Lewis

1896 Sheffield Wed 2 (Spikesley 2) Massey; Earp, Langley, Brandon, Crawshaw, Petrie, Brash, Brady, Bell, Davis, Spikesley **Wolves 1** (Black) Tennant; Baugh, Dunn, Owen, Malpass, Griffiths, Tonks, Henderson, Beats, Wood, Black. April 18; 48,836; Lieut Simpson

1897 Aston Villa 3 (Campbell, Wheldon, Crabtree) Whitehouse; Spencer, Reynolds, Evans, Cowan, Crabtree, Athersmith, Devey, Campbell, Wheldon, Cowan **Everton 2** (Bell, Boyle) Menham; Meechan, Storrier, Boyle, Holt, Stewart, Taylor, Bell, Hartley, Chadwick, Milward. April 10; 65,891; J Lewis

1898 Nottm Forest 3 (Capes 2, McPherson) Allsop; Ritchie, Scott, Forman, McPherson, Wragg, McInnes, Richards, Benbow, Capes, Spouncer **Derby 1** (Bloomer) Fryer; Methven, Leiper, Cox, Goodall, Bloomer, Boag, Stevenson, McQueen. April 16; 62,017; J Lewis

1899 Sheffield Utd 4 (Bennett, Beers, Almond, Priest) Foulke; Thickett, Boyle, Johnson, Morren, Needham, Bennett, Beers, Hedley, Almond, Priest **Derby 1** (Boag) Fryer; Methven, Staley, Cox,

147

Paterson, May, Arkesden, Bloomer, Boag, McDonald, Allen. April 15; 73,833; A Scragg

1900 Bury 4 (McLuckie 2, Wood, Plant) Thompson; Darroch, Davidson, Pray, Leeming, Ross, Richards, Wood, McLuckie, Sagar, Plant **Southampton 0** Robinson; Meechan, Durber, Meston, Chadwick, Petrie, Turner, Yates, Farrell, Wood, Milward. April 21; 68,945; A Kingscott

1901 Tottenham 2 (Brown 2) Clawley; Erentz, Tait, Morris, Hughes, Jones, Smith, Cameron, Brown, Copeland, Kirwan **Sheffield Utd 2** (Priest, Bennett) Foulke; Thickett, Boyle, Johnson, Morren, Needham, Bennett, Field, Hedley, Priest, Lipsham. April 20; 110,820; A Kingscott **Replay – Tottenham 3** (Cameron, Smith, Brown) Clawley; Erentz, Tait, Morris, Hughes, Jones, Smith, Cameron, Brown, Copeland, Kirwan. **Sheffield Utd 1** (Priest) Foulke; Thickett, Boyle, Johnson, Morren, Needham, Bennett, Field, Hedley, Priest, Lipsham. April 27; 20,470; A Kingscott

1902 Sheffield Utd 1 (Common) Foulke; Thickett, Boyle, Needham, Wilkinson, Johnson, Bennett, Common, Hedley, Priest, Lipsham **Southampton 1** (Wood) Robinson; Fry, Molyneux, Meston, Bowman, Lee, Turner, Wood Brown, Chadwick, Turner. April 19; 76,914; T Kirkham. **Replay – Sheffield Utd 2** (Hedley, Barnes) Foulke; Thickett, Boyle, Needham, Wilkinson, Johnson, Barnes, Common, Hedley, Priest, Lipsham **Southampton 1** (Brown) Robinson; Fry, Molyneux, Meston, Bowman, Lee, Turner, Wood, Brown, Chadwick, Turner. April 26; 33,068; T Kirkham

1903 Bury 6 (Leeming 2, Ross, Sagar, Wood, Plant) Monteith; Lindsey, McEwen, Johnston, Thorpe, Ross, Richards, Wood, Sagar Leeming, Plant **Derby 0** Fryer; Methven, Morris, Warren, Goodall, May, Warrington, York, Boag, Richards, Davis. April 18; 63,102; J Adams

1904 Manchester City 1 (Meredith) Hillman; McMahon, Burgess, Frost, Hynds, Ashworth, Meredith, Livingstone, Gillespie, Turnbull, Booth **Bolton 0** Davies; Brown, Struthers, Clifford, Greenhalgh, Freebairn, Stokes, Marsh, Yenson, White, Taylor. April 23; 61,374; AJ Barker

1905 Aston Villa 2 (Hampton 2) George; Spencer, Miles, Pearson, Leake, Windmill, Brawn, Garratty, Hampton, Bache, Hall **Newcastle 0** Lawrence; McCombie, Carr, Gardner, Aitken, McWilliam, Rutherford, Howie, Appleyard, Veitch, Gosnell. April 15; 101,117; PR Harrower

1906 Everton 1 (Young) Scott; Crelley, W Balmer, Makepeace, Taylor, Abbott, Sharp, Bolton, Young, Settle, Hardman **Newcastle 0** Lawrence; McCombie, Carr, Gardner, Aitken, McWilliam, Rutherford, Howie, Orr, Veitch, Gosnell. April 21; 75,609; F Kirkham

1907 Sheffield Wed 2 (Stewart, Simpson) Lyall; Layton, Burton, Brittleton, Crawshaw, Bartlett, Chapman, Bradshaw, Wilson, Stewart, Simpson **Everton 1** (Sharp) Scott; W Balmer, B Balmer, Makepeace, Taylor, Abbott, Sharp, Bolton, Young, Settle, Hardman. April 20; 84,594; N Whittaker

1908 Wolves 3 (Hunt, Hedley, Harrison) Lunn; Jones, Collins, Rev Hunt, Wooldridge, Bishop, Harrison, Shelton, Hedley, Radford, Pedley **Newcastle 1** (Howie) Lawrence; McCracken, Pudan, Gardner, Veitch, McWilliam, Rutherford, Howie, Appleyard, Speedie, Wilson. April 25; 74,697; TP Campbell

1909 Manchester Utd 1 (Sandy Turnbull) Moger; Stacey, Hayes, Duckworth, Roberts, Bell, Meredith, Halse, J Turnbull, S Turnbull, Wall **Bristol City 0** Clay; Annan, Cottle, Hanlin, Wedlock, Spear, Staniforth, Hardy, Gilligan, Burton, Hilton. April 24; 71,401; J Mason

1910 Newcastle 1 (Rutherford) Lawrence; McCracken, Whitson, Veitch, Low, McWilliam, Rutherford, Howie, Higgins, Shepherd, Wilson **Barnsley 1** (Tufnell) Mearns; Downs, Ness, Glendinning, Boyle, Utley, Tufnell, Lillycrop, Gadsby, Forman, Bartrop. April 23; 77,747; JT Ibbotson **Replay – Newcastle 2** (Shepherd 2, 1pen) Lawrence; McCracken, Carr, Veitch, Low, McWilliam, Rutherford, Howie, Higgins, Shepherd, Wilson **Barnsley 0** Mearns; Downs, Ness, Glendinning, Boyle, Utley, Tufnell, Lillycrop, Gadsby, Forman, Bartrop. April 28; 69,000; JT Ibbotson.

1911 Bradford City 0 Mellors; Campbell, Taylor, Robinson, Gildea, McDonald, Logan, Speirs, O'Rourke, Devine, Thompson **Newcastle 0** Lawrence; McCracken, Whitson, Veitch, Low, Willis, Rutherford, Jobey, Stewart, Higgins, Wilson. April 22; 69,068; JH Pearson **Replay – Bradford City 1** (Speirs) Mellors; Campbell, Taylor, Robinson, Torrance, McDonald, Logan, Speirs, O'Rourke, Devine, Thompson **Newcastle 0** Lawrence; McCracken, Whitson, Veitch, Low, Willis, Rutherford, Jobey, Stewart, Higgins, Wilson. April 26; 58,000; JH Pearson

1912 Barnsley 0 Cooper; Downs, Taylor, Glendinning, Bratley, Utley, Bartrop, Tufnell, Lillycrop, Travers, Moore **WBA 0** Pearson; Cook, Pennington, Baddeley, Buck, McNeal, Jephcott, Wright, Pailor, Bowser, Shearman. April 20; 54,556; JR Shumacher **Replay – Barnsley 1** (Tufnell) Cooper; Downs, Taylor, Glendinning, Bratley, Utley, Bartrop, Harry, Lillycrop, Travers, Jimmy Moore **WBA 0** Pearson; Cook,

148

Pennington, Baddeley, Buck, McNeal, Jephcott, Wright, Pailor, Bowser, Shearman. April 24; 38,555; JR Schumacher. aet

1913 **Aston Villa 1** (Barber) Hardy; Lyons, Weston, Barber, Harrop, Leach, Wallace, Halse, Hampton, Stephenson, Bache **Sunderland 0** Butler; Gladwin, Ness, Cuggy, Thomson, Low, Mordue, Buchan, Richardson, Holley, Martin. April 19; 120,081; A Adams

1914 **Burnley 1** (Freeman) Sewell; Bamford, Taylor, Halley, Boyle, Watson, Nesbit, Lindley, Freeman, Hodgson, Mosscrop **Liverpool 0** Campbell; Longworth, Pursell, Fairfoul, Ferguson, McKinley, Sheldon, Metcalfe, Miller, Lacey, Nicholl. April 25; 72,778; HS Bamlett

1915 **Sheffield Utd 3** (Simmons, Fazackerly, Kitchen) Gough; Cook, English, Sturgess, Brelsford, Utley, Simmons, Fazackerly, Kitchen, Masterman, Evans **Chelsea 0** Molyneux; Bettridge, Harrow, Taylor, Logan, Walker, Ford, Halse, Thomson, Croal, McNeil. April 24; 49,557; HH Taylor

1920 **Aston Villa 1** (Kirton) Hardy; Smart, Weston, Ducat, Barson, Moss, Wallace, Kirton, Walker, Stephenson, Dorrell **Huddersfield 0** Mutch; Wood, Bullock, Slade, Wilson, Watson, Richardson, Mann, Taylor, Swann, Islip. April 24; 50,018; JT Howcroft. aet

1921 **Tottenham 1** (Dimmock) Hunter; Clay, McDonald, Smith, Walters, Grimsdell, Banks, Seed, Cantrell, Bliss, Dimmock **Wolves 0** George; Woodward, Marshall, Gregory, Hodnett, Riley, Lea, Burrill, Edmonds, Potts, Brooks. April 23; 72,805; S Davies

1922 **Huddersfield 1** (Smith pen) Mutch; Wood, Wadsworth, Slade, Wilson, Watson, Richardson, Mann, Islip, Stephenson, Billy Smith **Preston 0** Mitchell; Hamilton, Doolan, Duxbury, McCall, Williamson, Rawlings, Jefferis, Roberts, Woodhouse, Quinn. April 29; 53,000; JWP Fowler

1923 **Bolton 2** (Jack, JR Smith) Pym; Haworth, Finney, Nuttall, Seddon, Jennings, Butler, Jack, JR Smith, Joe Smith, Vizard **West Ham 0** Hufton; Henderson, Young, Bishop, Kay, Tresadern, Richards, Brown, Watson, Moore, Ruffell. April 28; 126,047; DH Asson

1924 **Newcastle 2** (Harris, Seymour) Bradley; Hampson, Hudspeth, Mooney, Spencer, Gibson, Low, Cowan, Harris, McDonald, Seymour **Aston Villa 0** Jackson; Smart, Mort, Moss, Milne, Blackburn, York, Kirton, Capewell, Walker, Dorrell. April 26; 91,695; WE Russell

1925 **Sheffield Utd 1** (Tunstall) Sutcliffe; Cook, Milton, Pantling, King, Green, Mercer, Boyle, Johnson, Gillespie, Tunstall **Cardiff 0** Farquharson; Nelson, Blair, Wake, Keenor, Hardy, Davies, Gill, Nicholson, Beadles, Evans. April 25; 91,763; GN Watson

1926 **Bolton 1** (Jack) Pym; Haworth, Greenhalgh, Nuttall, Seddon, Jennings, Butler, JR Smith, Jack, Joe Smith, Vizard **Manchester City 0** Goodchild; Cookson, McCloy, Pringle, Cowan, McMullan, Austin, Browell, Roberts, Johnson, Hicks. April 24; 91,447; I Baker

1927 **Cardiff 1** (Ferguson) Farquharson; Nelson, Watson, Keenor, Sloan, Hardy, Curtis, Irving, Ferguson, Davies, McLachlan **Arsenal 0** Lewis; Parker, Kennedy, Baker, Butler, John, Hulme, Buchan, Brain, Blythe, Hoar. April 23; 91,206; WF Bunnell

1928 **Blackburn 3** (Roscamp 2, McLean) Crawford; Hutton, Jones, Healless, Rankin, Campbell, Thornewell, Puddefoot, Roscamp, McLean, Rigby **Huddersfield 1** (Jackson) Mercer; Goodall, Barkas, Redfern, Wilson, Steele, Jackson, Kelly, Brown, Stephenson, Smith. April 21; 92,041; TG Bryan

1929 **Bolton 2** (Butler, Blackmore) Pym; Haworth, Finney, Kean, Seddon, Nuttall, Butler, McClelland, Blackmore, Gibson, Cook **Portsmouth 0** Gilfillan; Mackie, Bell, Nichol, McIlwaine, Thackeray, Forward, Smith, Weddle, Watson, Cook. April 27; 92,576; A Josephs

1930 **Arsenal 2** (James, Lambert) Preedy; Parker, Hapgood, Baker, Seddon, John, Hulme, Jack, Lambert, James, Bastin **Huddersfield 0** Turner; Goodall, Spence, Naylor, Wilson, Campbell, Jackson, Kelly, Davies, Raw, Smith. April 26; 92,488; T Crew

1931 **WBA 2** (WG Richardson 2) Pearson; Shaw, Trentham, Magee, Bill Richardson, Edwards, Glidden, Carter, WG Richardson, Sandford, Wood **Birmingham 1** (Bradford) Hibbs; Liddell, Barkas, Cringan, Morrall, Leslie, Briggs, Crosbie, Bradford, Gregg, Curtis. April 25; 92,406; AH Kingscott

1932 **Newcastle 2** (Allen 2) McInroy; Nelson, Fairhurst, McKenzie, Davidson, Weaver, Boyd, Richardson, Allen, McMenemy, Lang **Arsenal 1** (John) Moss; Parker, Hapgood, Jones, Roberts, Male, Hulme, Jack, Lambert, Bastin, John. April 23; 92,298; WP Harper

1933 **Everton 3** (Stein, Dean, Dunn) Sagar; Cook, Cresswell, Britton, White, Thomson, Geldard, Dunn, Dean, Johnson, Stein **Manchester City 0** Langford; Cann, Dale, Busby, Cowan, Bray, Toseland, Marshall, Herd, McMullan, Eric Brook. April 29; 92,950; E Wood

1934 **Manchester City 2** (Tilson 2) Swift; Barnett, Dale, Busby, Cowan, Bray, Toseland, Marshall, Tilson, Herd, Brook **Portsmouth 1** (Rutherford) Gilfillan; Mackie, Smith, Nichol, Allen, Thackeray, Worrall, Smith, Weddle, Easson, Rutherford. April 28; 93,258; Stanley Rous

1935 **Sheffield Wed 4** (Rimmer 2, Palethorpe, Hooper) Brown; Nibloe, Catlin, Sharp, Millership, Burrows, Hooper, Surtees, Palethorpe, Starling, Rimmer **WBA 2** (Boyes, Sandford) Pearson; Shaw, Trentham, Murphy, Bill Richardson, Edwards, Glidden, Carter, WG Richardson, Sandford, Wally. April 27; 93,204; AE Fogg

1936 **Arsenal 1** (Drake) Wilson; Male, Hapgood, Crayston, Roberts, Copping, Hulme, Bowden, Drake, James, Bastin **Sheffield Utd 0** Smith; Hooper, Wilkinson, Jackson, Johnson, McPherson, Barton, Barclay, Dodds, Pickering, Williams. April 25; 93,384; H Nattrass

1937 **Sunderland 3** (Gurney, Carter, Burbanks) Mapson; Gorman, Hall, Thomson, Johnston, McNab, Duns, Carter, Gurney, Gallacher, Burbanks **Preston 1** (Frank O'Donnell) Burns; Gallimore, Beattie, Shankly, Tremelling, Milne, Dougal, Beresford, O'Donnell, Fagan, O'Donnell. May 1; 93,495; RG Rudd

1938 **Preston 1** (Mutch pen) Holdcroft; Gallimore, Beattie, Shankly, Smith, Batey, Watmough, Mutch, Maxwell, Beattie, O'Donnell **Huddersfield 0** Hesford; Craig, Mountford, Willingham, Young, Boot, Hulme, Issac, MacFadyen, Barclay, Beasley. April 30; 93,497; AJ Jewell. aet

1939 **Portsmouth 4** (Parker 2, Barlow, Anderson) Walker; Morgan, Rochford, Guthrie, Rowe, Wharton, Worrall, McAlinden, Anderson, Barlow, Parker **Wolves 1** (Dorsett) Scott; Morris, Taylor, Galley, Cullis, Gardiner, Burton, McIntosh, Westcott, Dorsett, Maguire. April 29; 99,370; T Thompson

1946 **Derby 4** (Stamps 2. Doherty, B Turner og) Woodley; Nicholas, Howe, Bullions, Leuty, Musson, Harrison, Carter, Stamps, Doherty, Duncan **Charlton Athletic 1** (B Turner) Bartram; Phipps, Shreeve, Turner, Oakes, Johnson, Fell, Brown, Turner, Welsh, Duffy. April 27; 98,000; ED Smith. aet

1947 **Charlton Athletic 1** (Duffy) Bartram; Croker, Shreeve, Johnson, Phipps, Whittaker, Hurst, Dawson, Robinson, Welsh, Duffy **Burnley 0** Strong; Woodruff, Mather, Attwell, Brown, Bray, Chew, Morris, Harrison, Potts, Kippax. April 26; 99,000; JM Wiltshire. aet

1948 **Manchester Utd 4** (Rowley 2, Pearson, Anderson) Crompton; Carey, Aston, Anderson, Chilton, Cockburn, Delaney, Morris, Rowley, Pearson, Mitten **Blackpool 2** (Shimwell pen, Mortensen) Robinson; Shimwell, Crosland, Johnston, Hayward, Kelly, Matthews, Munro, Mortensen, Dick, Rickett. April 24; 99,000; CJ Barrick

1949 **Wolves 3** (Pye 2, Smyth) Williams; Pritchard, Springthorpe Crook, Shorthouse, Wright, Hancocks, Smyth, Pye, Dunn, Mullen **Leicester 1** (Griffiths) Bradley; Jelly, Scott, Harrison, Plummer, King, Griffiths, Lee, Harrison, Chisholm, Adam. April 30; 99,500; RA Mortimer

1950 **Arsenal 2** (Lewis 2) Swindin; Scott, Barnes, Forbes, Compton, Mercer, Cox, Logie, Goring, Lewis, Compton **Liverpool 0** Sidlow; Lambert, Spicer, Taylor, Hughes, Jones, Payne, Baron, Stubbins, Fagan, Liddell. April 29; 100,000; H Pearce

1951 **Newcastle 2** (Milburn 2) Fairbrother; Cowell, Corbett, Harvey, Brennan, Crowe, Walker, Taylor, Milburn, Jorge Robledo, Mitchell **Blackpool 0** Farm; Shimwell, Garrett, Johnston, Hayward, Kelly, Matthews, Mudie, Mortensen, Slater, Perry. April 28; 100,000; W Ling

1952 **Newcastle 1** (G Robledo) Simpson; Cowell, McMichael, Harvey, Brennan, Eduardo Robledo, Walker, Foulkes, Milburn, Jorge Robledo, Mitchell **Arsenal 0** Swindin; Barnes, Smith, Forbes, Daniel Mercer, Cox, Logie, Holton, Lishman, Roper. May 3; 100,000; A Ellis

1953 **Blackpool 4** (Mortensen 3, Perry) Farm; Shimwell, Garrett, Fenton, Johnston, Robinson, Matthews, Taylor, Mortensen, Mudie, Perry **Bolton 3** (Lofthouse, Moir, Bell) Hanson; Ball, Banks, Wheeler, Barass, Bell, Holden, Moir, Lofthouse, Hassall, Langton. May 2; 100,000; M Griffiths

1954 **WBA 3** (Allen 2 [1pen], Griffin) Sanders; Kennedy, Millard, Dudley, Dugdale, Barlow, Griffin, Ryan, Allen, Nicholls, Lee **Preston 2** (Morrison, Wayman) Thompson; Cunningham, Walton, Docherty, Marston, Forbes, Finney, Foster, Wayman, Baxter, Morrison. May 1; 100,000; A Luty

1955 **Newcastle 3** (Milburn, Mitchell, Hannah) Simpson; Cowell, Batty, Scoular, Stokoe, Casey, White,

Milburn, Keeble, Hannah, Mitchell **Manchester City 1** (Johnstone) Trautmann; Meadows, Little, Barnes, Ewing, Paul, Spurdle, Hayes, Revie, Johnstone, Fagan. May 7; 100,000; R Leafe

1956 **Manchester City 3** (Hayes, Dyson, Johnstone) Trautmann; Leivers, Little, Barnes, Ewing, Paul, Johnstone, Hayes, Revie, Dyson, Clarke **Birmingham 1** (Kinsey) Merrick; Hall, Green, Newman, Smith, Boyd, Astall, Kinsey, Brown, Murphy, Govan. May 5; 100,000; A Bond

1957 **Aston Villa 2** (McParland 2) Sims; Lynn, Aldis, Crowther, Dugdale, Saward, Smith, Sewell, Myerscough, Dixon, McParland **Manchester Utd 1** (Taylor) Wood; Foulkes, Byrne, Colman, Blanchflower, Edwards, Berry, Whelan, Taylor, Charlton, Pegg. May 4; 100,000; F Coultas

1958 **Bolton 2** (Lofthouse 2) Hopkinson; Hartle, Banks, Hennin, Higgins, Edwards, Birch, Stevens, Lofthouse, Parry, Holden **Manchester Utd 0** Gregg; Foulkes, Greaves, Goodwin, Cope, Crowther, Dawson, Taylor, Charlton, Viollet, Webster. May 3; 100,000; J Sherlock

1959 **Nottingham Forest 2** (Dwight, Wilson) Thomson; Whare, McDonald, Whitefoot, McKinlay, Burkitt, Dwight, Quigley, Wilson, Gray, Imlach **Luton Town 1** (Pacey) Baynham; McNally, Hawkes, Groves, Owen, Pacey, Bingham, Brown, Morton, Cummins, Gregory. May 2; 100,000; J Clough

1960 **Wolves 3** (McGrath og, Deeley 2) Finlayson; Showell, Harris, Clamp, Slater, Flowers, Deeley, Stobart, Murray, Broadbent, Horne **Blackburn 0** Leyland; Bray, Whelan, Clayton, Woods, McGrath, Bimpson, Dobing, Dougan, Douglas, McLeod. May 7; 100,000; K Howley

1961 **Tottenham 2** (Smith, Dyson) Brown; Baker, Henry, Blanchflower, Norman, Mackay, Jones, White, Smith, Allen, Dyson **Leicester 0** Banks; Chalmers, Norman, McLintock, King, Appleton, Riley, Walsh, McIlmoyle, Keyworth, Cheesebrough. May 6; 100,000; J Kelly

1962 **Tottenham 3** (Greaves, Smith, Blanchflower pen) Brown; Baker, Henry, Blanchflower, Norman, Mackay, Medwin, White, Smith, Greaves, Jones **Burnley 1** (Robson) Blacklaw; Angus, Elder, Adamson, Cummings, Miller, Connelly, McIlroy, Pointer, Robson, Harris. May 5; 100,000; J Finney

1963 **Manchester Utd 3** (Law, Herd 2) Gaskell; Dunne, Cantwell, Crerand, Foulkes, Setters, Giles, Quixall, Herd, Law, Charlton **Leicester 1** (Keyworth) Banks; Sjoberg, Norman, McLintock, King, Appleton, Riley, Cross, Keyworth, Gibson, Stringfellow. May 25; 100,000; K Aston

1964 **West Ham 3** (Sissons, Hurst, Boyce) Standen; Bond, Burkett, Bovington, Brown, Moore, Brabrook, Boyce, Byrne, Hurst, Sissons **Preston 2** (Holden, Dawson) Kelly; Ross, Lawton, Smith, Singleton, Kendall, Wilson, Ashworth, Dawson, Spavin, Holden. May 2; 100,000; A Holland

1965 **Liverpool 2** (Hunt, St John) Lawrence; Lawler, Byrne, Strong, Yeats, Stevenson, Callaghan, Hunt, St John, Smith, Thompson **Leeds 1** (Bremner) Sprake; Reaney, Bell, Bremner, Charlton, Hunter, Giles, Storrie, Peacock, Collins, Johanneson. May 1; 100,000; W Clements. aet

1966 **Everton 3** (Trebilcock 2, Temple) West; Wright, Wilson, Gabriel, Labone, Harris, Scott, Trebilcock, Young, Harvey, Temple **Sheffield Wed 2** (McCalliog, Ford) Springett; Smith, Megson, Eustace, Ellis, Young, Pugh, Fantham, McCalliog, Ford, Quinn. May 14; 100,000; JK Taylor

1967 **Tottenham 2** (Robertson, Saul) Jennings; Kinnear, Knowles, Mullery, England, Mackay, Robertson, Greaves, Gilzean, Venables, Saul. Unused sub: Jones **Chelsea 1** (Tambling) Bonetti; Allan Harris, McCreadie, Hollins, Hinton, Ron Harris, Cooke, Baldwin, Hateley, Tambling, Boyle. Unused sub: Kirkup. May 20; 100,000; K Dagnall

1968 **WBA 1** (Astle) John Osborne; Fraser, Williams, Brown, Talbut, Kaye, Lovett, Collard, Astle Hope, Clark Sub: Clarke rep Kaye 91 **Everton 0** West; Wright, Wilson, Kendall, Labone, Harvey, Husband, Ball, Royle, Hurst, Morrissey. Unused sub: Kenyon. May 18; 100,000; L Callaghan. aet

1969 **Manchester City 1** (Young) Dowd; Book, Pardoe, Doyle, Booth, Oakes, Summerbee, Bell, Lee, Young, Coleman. Unused sub: Connor **Leicester 0** Shilton; Rodrigues, Nish, Roberts, Woollett, Cross, Fern, Gibson, Lochhead, Clarke, Glover. Sub: Manley rep Glover 70. April 26; 100,000; G McCabe

1970 **Chelsea 2** (Houseman, Hutchinson) Bonetti; Webb, McCreadie, Hollins, Dempsey, Ron Harris, Baldwin, Houseman, Osgood, Hutchinson, Cooke. Sub: Hinton rep Harris 91 **Leeds 2** (Charlton, Jones) Sprake; Madeley, Cooper, Bremner, Charlton, Hunter, Lorimer, Clarke, Jones, Giles, Gray Unused sub: Bates. April 11; 100,000; E Jennings. aet **Replay – Chelsea 2** (Osgood, Webb) Bonetti; Webb, McCreadie, Hollins, Dempsey, Ron Harris, Baldwin, Houseman, Osgood, Hutchinson, Cooke. Sub: Hinton rep Osgood 105 **Leeds 1** (Jones) Harvey; Madeley, Cooper, Bremner, Charlton, Hunter, Lorimer, Clarke, Jones, Giles, Gray Unused sub: Bates. April 29; 62,078; E Jennings. aet

1971 **Arsenal 2** (Kelly, George) Wilson; Rice, McNab, Storey, McLintock Simpson, Armstrong, Graham, Radford, Kennedy, George. Sub: Kelly rep Storey 70 **Liverpool 1** (Heighway) Clemence; Lawler, Lindsay, Smith, Lloyd, Hughes, Callaghan, Evans, Heighway, Toshack, Hall. Sub: Thompson rep Evans 70. May 8; 100,000; N Burtenshaw. aet

1972 **Leeds 1** (Clarke) Harvey; Reaney, Madeley, Bremner, Charlton, Hunter, Lorimer, Clarke, Jones, Giles, Gray. Unused sub: Bates **Arsenal 0** Barnett; Rice, McNab, Storey, McLintock, Simpson, Armstrong, Ball, George, Radford, Graham. Sub: Kennedy rep Radford 80. May 6; 100,000; DW Smith

1973 **Sunderland 1** (Porterfield) Montgomery; Malone, Guthrie, Horswill, Watson, Pitt, Kerr, Hughes, Halom, Porterfield, Tueart. Unused sub: Young **Leeds 0** Harvey; Reaney, Cherry, Bremner, Madeley, Hunter, Lorimer, Clarke, Jones, Giles, Gray. Sub: Yorath rep Gray 75. May 5; 100,000; K Burns

1974 **Liverpool 3** (Keegan 2, Heighway) Clemence; Smith, Lindsay, Thompson, Cormack, Hughes, Keegan, Hall, Heighway, Toshack, Callaghan. Unused sub: Lawler **Newcastle 0** McFaul; Clark, Kennedy, McDermott, Howard, Moncur, Smith, Cassidy, Macdonald, Tudor, Hibbitt. Sub: Gibb rep Smith 70. May 4; 100,000; GC Kew

1975 **West Ham 2** (Taylor 2) Day; McDowell, Taylor, Lock, Lampard, Bonds, Paddon, Brooking, Jennings, Taylor, Holland. Unused sub: Gould **Fulham 0** Mellor; Cutbush, Lacy, Moore, Fraser, Mullery, Conway, Slough, Mitchell, Busby, Barrett. Unused sub: Lloyd. May 3; 100,000; P Partridge

1976 **Southampton 1** (Stokes) Turner; Rodrigues, Peach, Holmes, Blyth, Steele, Gilchrist, Channon, Osgood, McCalliog, Stokes. Unused sub: Fisher **Manchester Utd 0** Stepney; Forsyth, Houston, Daly, Greenhoff, Buchan, Coppell, McIlroy, Pearson, Macari, Hill. Sub: McCreery rep Hill 66. May 1; 100,000; C Thomas

1977 **Manchester Utd 2** (Pearson, J Greenhoff) Stepney; Nicholl, Albiston, McIlroy, B Greenhoff, Buchan, Coppell, J Greenhoff, Pearson, Macari, Hill. Sub: McCreery rep Hill 81 **Liverpool 1** (Case) Clemence; Neal, Jones, Smith, Kennedy, Hughes, Keegan, Case, Heighway, Johnson, McDermott. Sub: Callaghan rep Johnson 64. May 21; 100,000; R Matthewson

1978 **Ipswich Town 1** (Osborne) Cooper; Burley, Mills, Talbot, Hunter, Beattie, Osborne, Wark, Mariner, Geddis, Woods. Sub: Lambert rep Osborne 79 **Arsenal 0** Jennings; Rice, Nelson, Price, Young, O'Leary, Brady, Hudson, Macdonald, Stapleton, Sunderland. Sub: Rix rep Brady 65. May 6; 100,000; D Nippard

1979 **Arsenal 3** (Talbot, Stapleton, Sunderland) Jennings; Rice, Nelson, Talbot, O'Leary, Young, Brady, Sunderland, Stapleton, Price, Rix. Sub: Walford rep Rix 83 **Manchester Utd 2** (McQueen, McIlroy) Bailey; Nicholl, Albiston, McIlroy, McQueen, Buchan, Coppell, J Greenhoff, Jordan, Macari, Thomas. Unused sub: Greenhoff. May 12; 100,000; R Challis

1980 **West Ham 1** (Brooking) Parkes; Stewart, Lampard, Bonds, Martin, Devonshire, Allen, Pearson, Cross, Brooking, Pike. Unused sub: Brush **Arsenal 0** Jennings; Rice, Devine, Talbot, O'Leary, Young, Brady, Sunderland, Stapleton, Price, Rix. Sub: Nelson rep Devine 61. May 10; 100,000; G Courtney

1981 **Tottenham 1** (Hutchinson og) Aleksic; Hughton, Miller, Roberts, Perryman, Villa, Ardiles, Archibald, Galvin, Hoddle, Crooks. Sub: Brooke rep Villa 68. **Manchester City 1** (Hutchinson) Corrigan; Ranson, McDonald, Reid, Power, Caton, Bennett, Gow, Mackenzie, Hutchison Reeves. Sub: Henry rep Hutchison 82. May 9; 100,000; K Hackett. aet **Replay – Tottenham 3** (Villa 2, Crooks) Aleksic; Hughton, Miller, Roberts, Perryman, Villa, Ardiles, Archibald, Galvin, Hoddle, Crooks. Unused sub: Brooke **Manchester City 2** (Mackenzie, Reeves pen) Corrigan; Ranson, McDonald, Reid, Power, Caton, Bennett, Gow, Mackenzie, Hutchison Reeves. Sub: Tueart rep McDonald 79. May 14; 92,000; K Hackett

1982 **Tottenham 1** (Hoddle) Clemence; Hughton, Miller, Price, Hazard, Perryman, Roberts, Archibald, Galvin, Hoddle, Crooks. Sub: Brooke rep Hazard 104 **Queens Park Rangers 1** (Fenwick) Hucker; Fenwick, Gillard, Waddock, Hazell, Roeder, Currie, Flanagan, Allen, Stainrod, Gregory. Sub: Micklewhite rep Allen 50. May 22; 100,000; C White. aet **Replay – Tottenham 1** (Hoddle pen) Clemence; Hughton, Miller, Price, Hazard, Perryman, Roberts, Archibald, Galvin, Hoddle, Crooks. Sub: Brooke rep Hazard 67 **Queens Park Rangers 0** Hucker; Fenwick, Gillard, Waddock, Hazell, Neill, Currie, Flanagan, Micklewhite, Stainrod, Gregory. Sub: Burke rep Micklewhite 84. May 27; 90,000; C White

1983 **Manchester Utd 2** (Stapleton, Wilkins) Bailey; Duxbury, Moran, McQueen, Albiston, Davies, Wilkins, Robson, Muhren, Stapleton, Whiteside. Unused sub: Grimes **Brighton 2** (Smith, Stevens) Moseley; Ramsey, Gary A Stevens, Pearce, Gatting, Smillie, Case, Grealish, Howlett, Robinson, Smith. Sub: Ryan rep Ramsey 56. May 21; 100,000; AW Grey, aet **Replay – Manchester Utd 4** (Robson 2, Whiteside, Muhren pen) Bailey; Duxbury, Moran, McQueen, Albiston, Davies, Wilkins, Robson, Muhren, Stapleton, Whiteside. Unused sub: Grimes **Brighton 0** Moseley; Gary A Stevens, Pearce, Foster, Gatting, Smillie, Case, Grealish, Howlett, Robinson, Smith. Sub: Ryan rep Howlett 74. May 26; 100,000; AW Grey

1984 **Everton 2** (Sharp, Gray) Southall; Gary M Stevens, Bailey, Ratcliffe, Mountfield, Reid, Steven, Heath, Sharp, Gray, Richardson. Unused sub: Harper **Watford 0** Sherwood; Bardsley, Price, Taylor, Terry, Sinnott, Callaghan, Johnston, Reilly, Jackett, Barnes. Sub: Atkinson rep Price 58. May 19; 100,000; J Hunting

1985 **Manchester Utd 1** (Whiteside) Bailey; Gidman, Albiston, Whiteside, McGrath, Moran, Robson, Strachan, Hughes, Stapleton, Olsen. Sub: Duxbury rep Albiston 91 Moran sent off 77. **Everton 0** Southall; Gary M Stevens, Van den Hauwe, Ratcliffe, Mountfield, Reid, Steven, Sharp, Gray, Bracewell, Sheedy. Unused sub: Harper. May 18; 100,000; P Willis. aet

1986 **Liverpool 3** (Rush 2, Johnston) Grobbelaar; Lawrenson, Beglin, Nicol, Whelan, Hansen, Dalglish, Johnston, Rush, Molby, MacDonald. Unused sub: McMahon **Everton 1** (Lineker) Mimms; Gary M Stevens, Van den Hauwe, Ratcliffe, Mountfield, Reid, Steven, Lineker, Sharp, Bracewell, Sheedy. Sub: Heath rep Stevens 65. May 10; 98,000; A Robinson

1987 **Coventry City 3** (Bennett, Houchen, Mabbutt og) Ogrizovic; Phillips, Downs, McGrath, Kilcline, Peake, Bennett, Gynn, Regis, Houchen, Pickering. Sub: Rodger rep Kilcline 88. Unused sub: Sedgley **Tottenham 2** (Allen, Mabbutt) Clemence; Hughton Thomas, Hodge, Gough, Mabbutt, C Allen, P Allen, Waddle, Hoddle, Ardiles. Subs: Gary A Stevens rep Ardiles 91; Claesen rep Hughton 97. May 16; 98,000; N Midgley. aet

1988 **Wimbledon 1** (Sanchez) Beasant; Goodyear, Phelan, Jones, Young, Thorn, Gibson Cork, Fashanu, Sanchez, Wise. Subs: Cunningham rep Cork 56; Scales rep Gibson 63 **Liverpool 0** Grobbelaar; Gillespie, Ablett, Nicol, Spackman, Hansen, Beardsley, Aldridge, Houghton, Barnes, McMahon. Subs: Johnston rep Aldridge 63; Molby rep Spackman 72. May 14; 98,203; B Hill

1989 **Liverpool 3** (Aldridge, Rush 2) Grobbelaar; Ablett, Staunton, Nichol, Whelan, Hansen, Beardsley, Aldridge Houghton, Barnes, McMahon. Subs: Rush rep Aldridge 72; Venison rep Staunton 91 **Everton 2** (McCall 2) Southall; McDonald, Van den Hauwe, Ratcliffe, Watson, Bracewell, Nevin, Trevor Steven, Cottee, Sharp, Sheedy. Subs: McCall rep Bracewell 58; Wilson rep Sheedy 77. May 20; 82,500; J Worrall. aet

1990 **Manchester Utd 3** (Robson, Hughes 2) Leighton; Ince, Martin, Bruce, Phelan, Pallister, Robson, Webb, McClair, Hughes, Wallace. Subs: Blackmore rep Martin 88; Robins rep Pallister 93. **Crystal Palace 3** (O'Reilly, Wright 2) Martyn; Pemberton, Shaw, Gray, O'Reilly, Thorn, Barber, Thomas, Bright, Salako, Pardew. Subs: Wright rep Barber 69; Madden rep Gray 117. May 12; 80,000; A Gunn. aet **Replay – Manchester Utd 1** (Martin) Sealey; Ince, Martin, Bruce, Phelan, Pallister, Robson, Webb, McClair, Hughes, Wallace. Unused subs: Robins, Blackmore **Crystal Palace 0** Martyn; Pemberton, Shaw, Gray, O'Reilly, Thorn, Barber, Thomas, Bright, Salako, Pardew. Subs: Wright rep Barber 64; Madden rep Salako 79. May 17; 80,000; A Gunn

1991 **Tottenham 2** (Stewart, Walker og) Thorstvedt; Edinburgh, Van den Hauwe, Sedgley, Howells, Mabbutt, Stewart, Gascoigne, Samways, Lineker, Allen. Subs: Nayim rep Gascoigne 18; Walsh rep Samways 82. **Nottingham Forest 1** (Pearce) Crossley; Charles, Pearce, Walker, Chettle, Keane, Crosby, Parker, Clough, Glover, Woan. Subs: Hodge rep Woan 62; Laws rep Glover 108. May 18; 80,000; R Milford. aet

1992 **Liverpool 2** (Thomas, Rush) Grobbelaar; Jones, Burrows, Nicol, Molby, Wright, Saunders, Houghton, Rush, McManaman, Thomas. Unused subs: Marsh, Walters **Sunderland 0** Norman; Owers, Ball, Bennett, Rogan, Rush, Bracewell, Davenport, Armstrong, Byrne, Atkinson. Subs: Hardyman rep Rush 69; Hawke rep Armstrong 77. May 9; 80,000; P Don

1993 **Arsenal 1** (Wright) Seaman; Dixon, Winterburn, Linighan, Adams, Jensen, Davis, Parlour, Merson, Campbell, Wright. Subs: Smith rep Parlour 66; O'Leary rep Wright 90. **Sheffield Wed 1** (Hirst) Woods; Nilsson Worthington, Palmer, Hirst, Anderson, Waddle, Warhurst, Bright, Sheridan, Harkes. Subs: Hyde rep Anderson 85; Bart-Williams rep Waddle 112. May 15; 79,347; K Barratt. aet **Replay – Arsenal 2** (Wright, Linighan) Seaman; Dixon, Winterburn, Linighan, Adams, Jensen, Davis, Smith, Merson, Campbell, Wright. Sub: O'Leary rep Wright 81. Unused sub: Selley **Sheffield Wed 1** (Waddle) Woods; Nilsson, Worthington, Palmer, Hirst, Wilson, Waddle, Warhurst, Bright, Sheridan, Harkes. Subs: Hyde rep Wilson 62; Bart-Williams rep Nilsson 118. May 20; 62,267; K Barratt. aet

1994   Manchester Utd 4 (Cantona 2 [2pens], Hughes, McClair) Schmeichel; Parker, Bruce, Pallister, Irwin, Kanchelskis, Keane, Ince, Giggs, Cantona, Hughes. Subs: Sharpe rep Irwin 84; McClair rep Kanchelskis 84. Unused sub: Walsh (gk) **Chelsea 0** Kharine; Clarke, Sinclair, Kjeldberg, Johnsen, Burley, Spencer, Newton, Stein, Peacock, Wise Substitutions Hoddle rep Burley 65; Cascarino rep Stein 78. Unused sub: Kevin Hitchcock (gk) May 14; 79,634; D Elleray

1995   Everton 1 (Rideout) Southall; Jackson, Hinchcliffe, Ablett, Watson, Parkinson, Unsworth, Horne, Stuart, Rideout, Limpar. Subs: Ferguson rep Rideout 51; Amokachi rep Limpar 69. Unused sub: Kearton (gk) **Manchester Utd 0** Schmeichel; Neville, Irwin, Bruce, Sharpe, Pallister, Keane, Ince, Brian McClair, Hughes, Butt. Subs: Giggs rep Bruce 46; Scholes rep Sharpe 72. Unused sub: Gary Walsh (gk) May 20; 79,592; G Ashby

1996   Manchester Utd 1 (Cantona) Schmeichel; Irwin, P Neville, May, Keane, Pallister, Cantona, Beckham, Cole, Butt, Giggs. Subs: Scholes rep Cole 65; G Neville rep Beckham 89. Unused sub: Sharpe **Liverpool 0** James; McAteer, Scales, Wright, Babb, Jones, McManaman, Barnes, Redknapp, Collymore, Fowler. Subs: Rush rep Collymore 74; Thomas rep Jones 85. Unused sub: Warner (gk) May 11; 79,007; D Gallagher

1997   Chelsea 2 (Di Matteo, Newton) Grodas; Petrescu, Minto, Sinclair, Lebouef, Clarke, Zola, Di Matteo, Newton, Hughes, Wise. Sub: Vialli rep Zola 89. Unused subs: Hitchcock (gk), Myers **Middlesbrough 0** Roberts; Blackmore, Fleming, Stamp, Pearson, Festa, Emerson, Mustoe, Ravanelli, Juninho, Hignett. Subs: Beck rep Ravanelli 24; Vickers rep Mustoe 29; Kinder, rep Hignett 74. May 17; 79,160; S Lodge

1998   Arsenal 2 (Overmars, Anelka) Seaman; Dixon, Winterburn, Vieira, Keown, Adams, Parlour, Anelka, Petit, Wreh, Overmars. Sub: Platt rep Wreh 63. Unused subs: Manninger (gk); Bould, Wright, Grimandi **Newcastle 0** Given; Pistone, Pearce, Batty, Dabizas, Howey, Lee, Barton, Shearer, Ketsbaia, Speed. Subs: Andersson rep Pearce 72; Watson rep Barton 77; Barnes rep Ketsbaia 85. Unused sub: Hislop (gk); Albert. May 16; 79,183; P Durkin

1999   Manchester Utd 2 (Sheringham, Scholes) Schmeichel; G Neville, Johnsen, May, P Neville, Beckham, Scholes, Keane, Giggs, Cole, Solskjaer. Subs: Sheringham rep Keane 9; Yorke rep Cole 61; Stam rep Scholes 77. Unused subs: Blomqvist, Van Der Gouw **Newcastle 0** Harper; Griffin, Charvet, Dabizas, Domi, Lee, Hamann, Speed, Solano, Ketsbaia, Shearer. Subs: Ferguson rep Hamann 46; Maric rep Solano 68; Glass rep Ketsbaia 79. Unused subs: Given (gk); Barton. May 22; 79,101; P Jones

2000   Chelsea 1 (Di Matteo) de Goey; Melchiot Desailly, Lebouef, Babayaro, Di Matteo, Wise, Deschamps, Poyet, Weah, Zola. Subs: Flo rep Weah 87; Morris rep Zola 90. Unused subs: Cudicini (gk), Terry , Harley **Aston Villa 0** James; Ehiogu, Southgate, Barry, Delaney, Taylor, Boateng, Merson, Wright, Dublin, Carbone. Subs: Stone rep Taylor 79; Joachim rep Carbone 79; Hendrie rep Wright 88. Unused subs: Enckelman (gk); Samuel May 20; 78,217; G Poll

2001   Liverpool 2 (Owen 2) Westerveld; Babbel, Henchoz, Hyypia, Carragher, Murphy, Hamann, Gerrard, Smicer, Heskey, Owen. Subs: McAllister rep Hamann 60; Fowler rep Smicer 77; Berger rep Murphy 77. Unused subs: Arphexad (gk); Vignal **Arsenal 1** (Ljungberg) Seaman; Dixon, Keown, Adams, Cole, Ljungberg, Grimandi, Vieira, Pires, Henry, Wiltord. Subs: Parlour rep Wiltord 76; Kanu rep Ljungberg 85; Bergkamp rep Dixon 90. Unused subs: Manninger (gk); Lauren. May 12; 72,500; S Dunn

2002   Arsenal 2 (Parlour, Ljungberg) Seaman; Lauren, Campbell, Adams, Cole, Parlour, Wiltord, Vieira, Ljungberg, Bergkamp, Henry.Subs: Edu rep Bergkamp 72; Kanu rep Henry 81; Keown rep Wiltord 90. Unused subs: Wright (gk); Dixon **Chelsea 0** Cudicini; Melchiot, Desailly, Gallas, Babayaro, Gronkjaer, Lampard, Petit, Le Saux, Floyd Hasselbaink, Gudjohnsen. Subs: Terry rep Babayaro 46; Zola rep Hasselbaink 68; Zenden rep Melchiot 77. Unused subs: de Goey (gk); Jokanovic. May 4; 73,963; M Riley

2003   Arsenal 1 (Pires) Seaman; Lauren, Luzhny, Keown, Cole, Ljungberg, Parlour, Gilberto, Pires, Bergkamp, Henry. Sub: Wiltord rep Bergkamp 77. Unused subs: Taylor (gk); Kanu, Toure, van Bronckhorst **Southampton 0** Niemi; Baird, Svensson, Lundekvam, Bridge, Telfer, Svensson, Oakley, Marsden, Beattie, Ormerod. Subs: Jones rep Niemi 66; Fernandes rep Baird 87; Tessem rep Svensson 75. Unused subs: Williams, Higginbotham. May 17; 73,726; G Barber

2004 Manchester Utd 3 (Van Nistelrooy [2, 1 pen], Ronaldo) Howard; G Neville, Brown, Silvestre, O'Shea, Fletcher, Keane, Ronaldo, Scholes, Giggs, Van Nistelrooy. Subs: Carroll rep Howard, Butt rep Fletcher, Solskjaer rep Ronaldo 84. Unused subs: P Neville, Djemba-Djemba **Millwall 0** Marshall; Elliott, Lawrence, Ward, Ryan, Wise, Ifill, Cahill, Livermore, Sweeney, Harris. Subs: Cogan rep Ryan, McCammon rep Harris 74 Weston rep Wise 88. Unused subs: Gueret (gk); Dunne. May 22; 71,350; J Winter

2005 Arsenal 0 Lehmann; Lauren, Toure, Senderos, Cole, Fabregas, Gilberto, Vieira, Pires, Reyes, Bergkamp Subs: Ljungberg rep Bergkamp 65, Van Persie rep Fabregas 86, Edu rep Pires 105. Unused subs: Almunia (gk); Campbell **Manchester Utd 0** Carroll; Brown, Ferdinand, Silvestre, O'Shea, Fletcher, Keane, Scholes, Rooney, Van Nistelrooy, Ronaldo. Subs: Fortune rep O'Shea 77, Giggs rep Fletcher 91. Unused subs: Howard (gk); G Neville, Smith. **Arsenal** (Lauren, Ljungberg, van Persie, Cole, Vieira) beat Manchester Utd (van Nistelrooy, Scholes [missed] Ronaldo, Rooney, Keane) 5-4 on penalties

2006 Liverpool 3 (Gerrard 2, Cisse) Reina; Finnan, Carragher, Hyypiä, Riise, Gerrard, Xabi, Sissoko, Kewell, Cisse, Crouch. Subs: Morientes rep Kewell 48, Kromkamp rep Alonso 67, Hamman rep Crouch 71. Unused subs: Dudek (gk); Traoré **West Ham 3** (Ashton, Konchesky, Carragher (og)) Hislop; Scaloni, Ferdinand, Gabbidon, Konchesky, Benayoun, Fletcher, Reo-Coker, Etherington, Ashton, Harewood. Subs: Zamora rep Ashton 71, Dailly rep Fletcher, Sheringham rep Etherington 85. Unused subs: Walker (gk); Collins. **Liverpool** (Hamann, Hyypiä [missed], Gerrard, Riise) beat **West Ham** (Zamora [missed], Sheringham, Konchesky [missed], Ferdinand [missed]) 3-1 on penalties. May 13; 71,140; A Wiley

2007 Chelsea 1 (Drogba) Cech; Ferreira, Essien, Terry, Bridge, Mikel, Makelele, Lampard, Wright-Phillips, Drogba, J Cole Subs: Robben rep J Cole 45, Kalou rep Wright-Phillips 93, A Cole rep Robben 108. Unused subs: Cudicini (gk); Diarra. **Manchester Utd 0** Van der Sar, Brown, Ferdinand, Vidic, Heinze, Fletcher, Scholes, Carrick, Ronaldo, Rooney, Giggs Subs: Smith rep Fletcher 92, O'Shea rep Carrick, Solskjaer rep Giggs 112. Unused subs: Kuszczak (gk); Evra. May 19; 89,826; S Bennett

2008 Portsmouth 1 (Kanu) James; Johnson, Campbell, Distin, Hreidarsson, Utaka, Muntari, Mendes, Diarra, Kranjcar, Kanu. Subs: Nugent rep Utaka 69, Diop rep Mendes 78, Baros rep Kanu 87. Unused subs: Ashdown (gk); Pamarot. **Cardiff 0** Enckelman; McNaughton, Johnson, Loovens, Capaldi, Whittingham, Rae, McPhail, Ledley, Hasselbaink, Parry. Subs: Ramsey rep Whittingham 62, Thompson rep Hasselbaink 70, Sinclair rep Rae 87. Unused subs: Oakes (gk); Purse. May 17; 89,874; M Dean

2009 Chelsea 2 (Drogba, Lampard), Cech; Bosingwa, Alex, Terry, A Cole, Essien, Mikel, Lampard, Drogba, Anelka, Malouda. Subs: Ballack rep Essien 61. Unused subs: Hilario (gk); Ivanovic, Di Santo, Kalou, Belletti, Mancienne. **Everton 1** (Saha) Howard; Hibbert, Yobo, Lescott, Baines, Osman, Neville, Cahill, Pienaar, Fellaini, Saha. Subs: Jacobsen rep Hibbert 46, Vaughan rep Saha 77, Gosling rep Osman 83. Unused subs: Nash, Castillo, Rodwell, Baxter. May 30; 89,391; H Webb

2010 Chelsea 1 (Drogba) Cech; Ivanovic, Alex, Terry, A Cole, Lampard, Ballack, Malouda, Kalou, Drogba, Anelka. Subs: Belletti rep Ballack 44, J Cole rep Kalou 71, Sturridge rep Anelka 90. Unused subs: Hilario (gk); Zhirkov, Paulo Ferreira, Matic. **Portsmouth 0** James; Finnan, Mokoena, Rocha, Mullins, Dindane, Brown, Diop, Boateng, O'Hara, Piquionne. Subs: Utaka rep Boateng 73, Belhadj rep Mullins 81, Kanu rep Diop 81. Unused subs: Ashdown (gk), Vanden Borre, Hughes, Ben Haim. May 15; 88,335; C Foy

VENUES

Kennington Oval 1872; **Lillie Bridge** 1873; **Kennington Oval** 1874 – 1892 (1886 replay at the **Baseball Ground**); **Fallowfield**, Manchester, 1893; **Goodison Park** 1894; **Crystal Palace** 1895 – 1915 (1901 replay at **Burnden Park**; 1910 replay at **Goodison Park**; 1912 replay at **Bramall Lane**); **Old Trafford** 1915; **Stamford Bridge** 1920 – 1922; **Wembley** 1923 – 2000 (1970 replay at **Old Trafford**; all replays after 1981 at **Wembley**); **Millennium Stadium** 2001 – 2006; **Wembley** 2007 – 2011

SUMMARY OF FA CUP WINS

Manchester Utd	11	Wolves	4	Cardiff	1
Arsenal	10	Sheffield Wed		Charlton	1
Tottenham	8	West Ham	3	Clapham Rdv	1
Aston Villa	7	Bury	2	Coventry	1

Liverpool................7	Nottm.Forest......2	Derby................ 1
Blackburn Rov............6	.Old.Etonians......2	Huddersfield
Chelsea................6	Portsmouth.. 2	Ipswich....... 1
Newcastle................6	.Preston............ 2	Leeds................ 1
Everton................5	Sunderland.. 2	Notts.Co........ 1
Manchester City........5	Barnsley........ 1	Old.Carthusians
The Wanderers 5	Blackburn Olympic	Oxford. University
WBA...................5	Blackpool.......1	Royal. Engineers
Bolton 4	Bradford City	.Southampton
Sheffield Utd...............4	Burnley............. 1	Wimbledon.. 1

APPEARANCES IN FINALS

(Figures do not include replays)

Manchester Utd............ 18	The Wanderers* 5	Queen's Park (Glas)........... 2
Arsenal 17	West Ham 5	Blackburn Olympic* 1
Everton...................... 13	Derby............................4	Bradford City* 1
Liverpool...................... 13	Leeds 4	Brighton............................ 1
Newcastle.................... 13	Leicester 4	Bristol City....................... 1
Aston Villa 10	Oxford University 4	Coventry* 1
Chelsea 10	Royal Engineers...............4	Crystal Palace................... 1
West Brom 10	Southampton 4	Fulham.............................. 1
Manchester City............ 9	Sunderland 4	Ipswich* 1
Tottenham 9	Blackpool.........................3	Luton................................ 1
Blackburn Rov............. 8	Burnley............................3	Middlesbrough.................. 1
Wolves........................ 8	Cardiff..............................3	Millwall............................. 1
Bolton 7	Nottm Forest 3	Old Carthusians*.............. 1
Preston 7	Barnsley...........................2	QPR................................. 1
Old Etonians 6	Birmingham 2	Stoke................................ 1
Sheffield Utd................ 6	Bury*................................2	Watford............................. 1
Sheffield Wed.............. 6	Charlton...........................2	Wimbledon* 1
Huddersfield 6	Clapham Rov.....................2	
Portsmouth................. 5	Notts Co 2	

(* Denotes undefeated)

APPEARANCES IN SEMI-FINALS

(Figures do not include replays)

Manchester Utd 27, Arsenal 26, Everton 24, Liverpool 22, Aston Villa 20, WBA 20, Chelsea 19, Blackburn 18, Tottenham 18, Newcastle 17, Sheffield Wed 16, Bolton 14, Wolves 14, Derby 13, Sheffield Utd 13, Nottm Forest 12, Sunderland 12, Manchester City 11, Southampton 11, Preston 10, Birmingham 9, Burnley 8, Leeds 8, Huddersfield 7, Leicester 7, Portsmouth 7, West Ham 7, Fulham 6, Old Etonians 6, Oxford University 6, Notts Co 5, The Wanderers 5, Watford 5, Cardiff 4, Luton 4, Millwall 4, Queen's Park (Glasgow) 4, Royal Engineers 4, Stoke 4, Barnsley 3, Blackpool 3, Clapham Rov 3, *Crystal Palace 3, Ipswich Town 3, Middlesbrough 3, Norwich 3, Old Carthusians 3, Oldham 3, The Swifts 3, Blackburn Olympic 2, Bristol City 2, Bury 2, Charlton 2, Grimsby Town 2, Swansea 2, Swindon 2, Wimbledon 2, Bradford City 1, Brighton 1, Cambridge University 1, Chesterfield 1, Coventry 1, Crewe 1, Darwen 1, Derby Junction 1, Hull 1, Marlow 1, Old Harrovians 1, Orient 1, Plymouth Argyle 1, Port Vale 1, QPR 1, Rangers (Glasgow) 1, Reading 1, Shropshire Wand 1, Wycombe 1, York 1

(*A previous and different Crystal Palace club also reached the semi-final in season 1871–72)

QUOTE/UNQOUTE

'When people look you in the eye and promise you something, you hope they live up to their word' – **Andy Anson**, chief executive of England's unsuccessful World Cup bid team, accuses FIFA executive committee members of double standards.

'We had the best technical bid, the strongest commercial bid, great stadiums and passionate supporters, but it turns out that's not enough' – **David Cameron**, Prime Minister.

'I'm sorry for the fans back home – we did everything we could' – **Prince William**, president of the FA.

'The boys from the 1966 squad had high hopes of walking out at Wembley again. Even if we do get it in 2026, I won't be here to see it and I'm not sure any of the others will be' – **Roger Hunt**, a member of England's winning team under Sir Alf Ramsey.

'You have to think that if we couldn't get it this time, when are we?' – **Alan Shearer**, former England striker.

'The timing of the *Panorama* programme was crucial. I would like the people who said it was in the public interest to come up here and tell the people in Sunderland that' – **Niall Quinn**, Sunderland chairman.

'The role entails liaising closely with FIFA and I want nothing more to do with them. I am not prepared to deal with people I cannot trust. Making promises to the future King of England and the Prime Minister and not keeping their word' – **Roger Burden**, acting chairman of the FA, withdraws his application for the permanent position.

'I was surprised by all the English complaining. Some of them are showing themselves to be bad losers. The outcome came out clearly' – **Sepp Blatter**, FIFA president, defends the voting.

'I was just dumbfounded. Only months before he was saying he was at the greatest club in the world and he wanted to stay for life' – **Sir Alex Ferguson** on Wayne Rooney's intention to leaves Manchester United.

'I did not receive any of the assurances I was seeking about the continued ability of the club to attract the top players in the world' – **Wayne Rooney** on his decision not to sign a new contract.

"If one player does not trust the others, he should not play" – **Patrice Evra**, Manchester United full-back, on Rooney questioning the quality of the team.

'My message is that I care for the club. Some fans may not take to me again very quickly. But I'll give everything to try to build that relationship back' – **Wayne Rooney** says sorry after changing his mind about leaving and signing a five-year contract.

'Sometimes you look in a field and see a cow and you think it's a better cow than you've got in your own field. It never really works that way'- **Sir Alex Ferguson** in Eric Cantona mode on Rooney's U-turn.

'When I arrived in this company, players were on £200,000 a year. Only 15 years later, it is that per week' – **Arsene Wenger**, Arsenal manager, on Rooney's reported new contract.

BIRMINGHAM UPSET THE ODDS FOR WEMBLEY TRIUMPH

THIRD ROUND	FOURTH ROUND	FIFTH ROUND	SEMI-FINALS	FINAL
Arsenal.....+4	Arsenal.....4	*Arsenal.....2	Arsenal.....0:3	Arsenal.....1
*Tottenham.....1	*Newcastle.....0	Wigan.....0		
*Chelsea.....3	*Wigan.....2	*Ipswich.....1	*Ipswich.....1:0	
Newcastle.....4	Swansea.....0	WBA.....0		
*Wigan.....2	*Ipswich.....3	*West Ham.....4	*West Ham.....2:1	
Preston.....1	Northampton.....1	Manchester Utd.....0		
*Peterborough.....1	*Leicester.....1			
Swansea.....3	WBA.....4			
*Millwall.....1	*West Ham.....+3			
Ipswich.....2	Stoke.....1			
*Liverpool.....2	*Manchester Utd.....3			
Northampton.....+A2				
*Portsmouth.....1				
Leicester.....2				
*WBA.....2				
Manchester City.....1				
*Sunderland.....1				
West Ham.....2				
*Stoke.....2				
Fulham.....0				
*Scunthorpe.....2				
Manchester Utd.....5				

Birmingham 2

Wolves 2

*Aston Villa..........+2

Aston Villa 1

Burnley 1

Birmingham ....1+3

Brentford 1

*Birmingham 2

*Birmingham ....+C1

*Wolves ....+4
Notts Co 2

*Aston Villa...........3
Blackburn 1

*Burnley 1
Bolton 0

*Brentford ....+B1
Everton 1

MK Dons...........1
*Birmingham 3

* Drawn at home; in semi-finals, first leg. + After extra-time. A – Northampton won 4-2 on pens; B – Brentford won 4-3 on pens; C – Birmingham won 4-3 on pens

FIRST ROUND

Aldershot 0 Watford 3; Barnsley 0 Rochdale 1; Bradford 2 Nottm Forest 1 (aet); Brentford 2 Cheltenham 1; Cardiff 4 Burton 1 (aet); Carlisle 0 Huddersfield 1; Chesterfield 1 Middlesbrough 2; Crewe 1 Derby 0; Doncaster 1 Accrington 2 (aet); Exeter 2 Ipswich 3 (aet); Hartlepool 2 Sheffield Utd 0; Hereford 0 Colchester 3; Leeds 4 Lincoln 0; Leicester 4 Macclesfield 3; MK Dons 2 Dagenham 1; Morecambe 2 Coventry 0; Northampton 2 Brighton 0; Norwich 4 Gillingham 0; Oxford 6 Bristol Row 1; Peterborough 4 Rotherham 1; Plymouth 0 Notts Co 1; QPR 1 Port Vale 3; Scunthorpe 2 Oldham 1; Sheffield Wed 1 Bury 0; Shrewsbury 4 Charlton 3; Southampton 2 Bournemouth 0; Southend 3 Bristol City 2 (aet); Stevenage 1 Portsmouth 2; Stockport 0 Preston 5; Swansea 3 Barnet 0; Swindon 1 Leyton Orient 2; Torquay 0 Reading 1 (aet); Walsall 0 Tranmere 1; Wycombe 1 Millwall 2 (aet); Yeovil 0 Crystal Palace 1

SECOND ROUND

Accrington 2 Newcastle 3; Birmingham 3 Rochdale 2; Blackburn 3 Norwich 1; Bradford 2 Hull 1; Crewe 0 Ipswich 1 (aet); Everton 5 Huddersfield 1; Hartlepool 1 Wigan 3; Fulham 6 Port Vale 0; Leeds 1 Leicester 2; Leyton Orient 0 WBA 2; Millwall 2 Middlesbrough 1; MK Dons 4 Blackpool 3 (aet); Morecambe 1 Burnley 3; Peterborough 2 Cardiff 1; Portsmouth 1 Crystal Palace 1 (aet, Portsmouth won 4-3 on pens); Reading 3 Northampton 3 (aet, Northampton won 4-2 on pens); Scunthorpe 4 Sheffield Wed 2; Southampton 0 Bolton 1; Stoke 0 Shrewsbury 1; Sunderland 2 Colchester 0; Tranmere 1 Swansea 3; Watford 1 Notts Co 2; West Ham 1 Oxford 0; Wolves 2 Southend 1 (aet)

CARLING CUP FINAL

ARSENAL 1 BIRMINGHAM CITY 2
Wembley (88,851); Sunday, February 27 2011

Arsenal (4-2-3-1): Szczesny, Sagna, Djourou, Koscielny, Clichy, Song, Wilshere, Rosicky, Nasri, Arshavin (Chamakh 77), Van Persie (capt) (Bendtner 69). **Subs not used:** Almunia, Denilson, Squillaci, Eboue, Gibbs. **Scorer:** Van Persie (39). **Booked:** Koscielny, Clichy. **Manager:** Arsene Wenger

Birmingham City (4-5-1): Foster, Carr (capt), Johnson, Jiranek, Ridgewell, Larsson, Gardner (Beausejour 50), Ferguson, Bowyer, Fahey (Martins 83), Zigic (Jerome 90). **Subs not used:** Taylor, Murphy, Phillips, Parnaby. **Scorers:** Zigic (28), Martins (89). **Booked:** Larsson, Ferguson, Jerome. **Manager:** Alex McLeish

Referee: M Dean (Wirral). **Half-time:** 1-1

When Birmingham first lifted the League Cup in 1963, their performance had little impact on English football. The competition was still in its infancy, many of the top teams declined to take part and there was no showpiece conclusion at Wembley. Instead, the final was contested over two legs and this one had a decidedly local feel about it, with Birmingham, under their former goalkeeper Gil Merrick, and Aston Villa, managed by Joe Mercer, separated by just three miles. What a difference to the 2011 victory over Arsenal – achieved against all the odds, delivered in dramatic fashion at the end of an enthralling match and watched by a crowd of nearly 89,000. It was a reflection of the character which had served Alex McLeish's side in good stead throughout the tournament. After coming from behind to overcome Rochdale, they needed a Kevin Phillips equaliser deep into stoppage-time to pave the way for a win over Brentford on penalties. Nikola Zigic came up with an 84th minute strike to see off Villa. Then, in the second leg of the semi-finals, Birmingham trailed West Ham 3-1 on aggregate before Lee Bowyer, Roger Johnson and Craig Gardner came up with the goals that turned the tie on its head.

   McLeish knew his side had to continue this level of resilience, display the organisation and discipline needed to stifle Arsenal's superior passing game and rise above their Premier League relegation struggle. He was not disappointed. Zigic, the 6ft 8in Serb, headed them in front and missed a great chance of establishing a two-goal cushion. Then, after Robin van Persie levelled with a sweetly-struck volley, Keith Fahey hit a post before substitute Obafemi Martins, on loan from the Russian Premier League side Rubin Kazan, took advantage of a horrible mix-up between goalkeeper Wojciech Szczesny and his central defender Laurent Koscielny to prod the winner into an empty net.

   Arsenal argued with some justification that the absence of the injured Cesc Fabregas and Theo Walcott, deprived them of players whose vision and pace could have made all the difference. But there was no disputing that on the day they did not deserve to end the club's six-year wait for a trophy. Birmingham were good value for a result which gave their manager his first success in England after seven trophies with Rangers and the club's owner, Carson Yeung, the perfect 51st birthday present.

HOW THEY REACHED THE FINAL

ARSENAL
Round 3: 4-1 away to Tottenham (Nasri 2 pens, Lansbury, Arshavin) - aet
Round 4: 4-0 away to Newcastle (Walcott 2, Bendtner, Krul og)
Round 5: 2-0 home to Wigan (Bendtner, Alcaraz og)
Semi-finals: v Ipswich – first leg: 0-1 away; second leg: 3-0 home (Bendtner, Koscielny, Fabregas)

BIRMINGHAM
Round 3: 3-1 home to MK Dons (Hleb, Zigic, Gardner)
Round 4: 1-1 home to Brentford (Phillips) – aet, won 4-3 on pens
Round 5: 2-1 home to Aston Villa (Larsson pen, Zigic)
Semi-finals: v West Ham – first leg: 1-2 away (Ridgewell); second leg: 3-1 home (Bowyer, Johnson, Gardner) - aet

LEAGUE CUP – COMPLETE RESULTS

LEAGUE CUP FINALS

1961*	Aston Villa beat Rotherham 3-2 on agg (0-2a, 3-0h)
1962	Norwich beat Rochdale 4-0 on agg (3-0a, 1-0h)
1963	Birmingham beat Aston Villa 3-1 on agg (3-1h, 0-0a)
1964	Leicester beat Stoke 4-3 on agg (1-1a, 3-2h)
1965	Chelsea beat Leicester 3-2 on agg (3-2h, 0-0a)
1966	WBA beat West Ham 5-3 on agg (1-2a, 4-1h)

AT WEMBLEY

1967	QPR beat WBA (3-2)
1968	Leeds beat Arsenal (1-0)
1969*	Swindon beat Arsenal (3-1)
1970*	Manchester City beat WBA (2-1)
1971	Tottenham beat Aston Villa (2-0)
1972	Stoke beat Chelsea (2-1)
1973	Tottenham beat Norwich (1-0)
1974	Wolves beat Manchester City (2-1)
1975	Aston Villa beat Norwich (1-0)
1976	Manchester City beat Newcastle (2-1)
1977†*	Aston Villa beat Everton (3-2 after 0-0 and 1-1 draws)
1978††	Nottm Forest beat Liverpool (1-0 after 0-0 draw)
1979	Nottm Forest beat Southampton (3-2)
1980	Wolves beat Nottm Forest (1-0)
1981†††	Liverpool beat West Ham (2-1 after 1-1 draw)

MILK CUP

1982*	Liverpool beat Tottenham (3-1)
1983*	Liverpool beat Manchester Utd (2-1)
1984**	Liverpool beat Everton (1-0 after *0-0 draw)
1985	Norwich beat Sunderland (1-0)
1986	Oxford Utd beat QPR (3-0)

LITTLEWOODS CUP

1987	Arsenal beat Liverpool (2-1)
1988	Luton beat Arsenal (3-2)
1989	Nottm Forest beat Luton (3-1)
1990	Nottm Forest beat Oldham (1-0)

RUMBELOWS CUP

1991	Sheffield Wed beat Manchester Utd (1-0)
1992	Manchester Utd beat Nottm Forest (1-0)

COCA-COLA CUP

1993	Arsenal beat Sheffield Wed (2-1)
1994	Aston Villa beat Manchester Utd (3-1)
1995	Liverpool beat Bolton (2-1)
1996	Aston Villa beat Leeds (3-0)
1997***	Leicester beat Middlesbrough (*1-0 after *1-1 draw)
1998	Chelsea beat Middlesbrough (2-0)

WORTHINGTON CUP (at Millennium Stadium from 2001)

1999	Tottenham beat Leicester (1-0)
2000	Leicester beat Tranmere (2-1)
2001	Liverpool beat Birmingham (5-4 on pens after *1-1 draw)
2002	Blackburn beat Tottenham (2-1)
2003	Liverpool beat Manchester Utd (2-0)

CARLING CUP (at Wembley from 2008)

2004	Middlesbrough beat Bolton (2-1)
2005*	Chelsea beat Liverpool (3-2)
2006	Manchester Utd beat Wigan (4-0)
2007	Chelsea beat Arsenal (2-1)
2008*	Tottenham beat Chelsea (2-1)
2009	Manchester Utd beat Tottenham (4-1 on pens after ●0-0 draw)
2010	Manchester Utd beat Aston Villa (2-1)
2011	Birmingham beat Arsenal (2-1)

* After extra time. † First replay at Hillsborough, second replay at Old Trafford. †† Replayed at Old Trafford. ††† Replayed at Villa Park. ** Replayed at Maine Road. *** Replayed at Hillsborough

SUMMARY OF LEAGUE CUP WINNERS

Liverpool	7	Birmingham	2	Middlesbrough	1
Aston Villa	5	Manchester City	2	Oxford Utd	1
Chelsea	4	Norwich	2	QPR	1
Nottm Forest	4	Wolves	2	Sheffield Wed	1
Tottenham	4	Blackburn	1	Stoke	1
Manchester Utd	4	Leeds	1	Swindon	1
Leicester	3	Luton	1	WBA	1
Arsenal	2				

LEAGUE CUP FINAL APPEARANCES

10 Liverpool; **8** Aston Villa, Manchester Utd, Tottenham; **7** Arsenal; **6** Chelsea, Nottm Forest; **5** Leicester; **4** Norwich; **3** Birmingham, Manchester City, Middlesbrough, WBA; **2** Bolton, Everton, Leeds, Luton , QPR, Sheffield Wed, Stoke, West Ham, Wolves; **1** Blackburn, Newcastle, Oldham, Oxford Utd, Rochdale, Rotherham, Southampton, Sunderland, Swindon, Tranmere, Wigan (Figures do not include replays).

LEAGUE CUP SEMI-FINAL APPEARANCES

14 Arsenal; **13** Liverpool, Tottenham; **13** Aston Villa,; **12** Manchester Utd **10** Chelsea; **8** West Ham; **6** Nottm Forest; **6** Blackburn, Leeds, Leicester, Manchester City, Middlesbrough, Norwich City; **5** Birmingham; **4** Bolton, Burnley, Everton, Ipswich, Sheffield Wed, WBA; **3**, Crystal Palace, QPR, Sunderland, Swindon , Wolves; **2** Bristol City, Coventry City, Derby, Luton, Oxford Utd, Plymouth Argyle, Southampton, Stoke City, Tranmere, Watford, Wimbledon; **1** Blackpool, Bury, Cardiff, Carlisle, Chester, Huddersfield, Newcastle, Oldham, Peterborough, Rochdale, Rotherham, Sheffield Utd, Shrewsbury, Stockport, Walsall, Wigan, Wycombe
(Figures do not include replays).

JIMMY HILL – THE COMPLETE
FOOTBALL MAN

By Albert Sewell

In the history of professional football, no-one has made such a wide and thorough contribution to the game as Jimmy Hill: player, coach, qualified referee, manager, chairman, director, far-seeing campaigner, TV executive, presenter and pundit. James William Thomas Hill was born at Balham, South London, on July 22, 1928, the son of a milkman-turned-baker. He was busy from boyhood. He played the trumpet with Balham Boys' Brigade, football too. His mother rewarded him with a bar of chocolate if he scored two goals in a match which, in a way, made him a paid professional at the age of ten.

After matriculating at Henry Thornton Grammar School, Clapham, he began work as a stockbroker's clerk. Being called up for National Service at 18 and playing in the Army Cup was the springboard to a career in football. He was spotted by Reading manager Ted Drake, the pre-war Arsenal and England centre-forward, who signed him as an amateur. On demob, he joined Second Division Brentford in 1949 and in March 1952 moved to First Division Fulham in a player-exchange deal. Hill spent the bulk of his playing career at Craven Cottage, making 276 League appearances and scoring 41 goals (five of them in one match, away to Doncaster Rovers). He saw himself as 'just an intelligent, industrious, bread-and-butter inside-forward.' On the field, he never gave less than 100% and he applied himself as fully in all the other directions he took after packing his boots away.

Football's most famous beard was introduced to the jutting jaw in 1957, a year after Hill was voted chairman of the Professional Footballers' Association (formerly the Players' Union). And in that role he made his most indelible mark on the game, successfully campaigning in the High Court in 1961 for the removal of the maximum wage which had restricted players' earnings from the Football League's formation in 1888. The League capitulated four days before the players were due to strike. The immediate effect was that Johnny Haynes, Hill's inside-forward colleague at Fulham, became England's first £100-a-week footballer. Jimmy, himself, had started with Brentford on £7 a week (£6 in the summer). Later, he supplemented the £20 maximum at Fulham with £12 earned by coaching Oxford United and Sutton.

Retiring as a player in 1961, he became an FA staff coach, then moved into management at Coventry City. In six years, he took them from a struggling Third Division club to the First Division, pioneering a new era for football. Hill turned Highfield Road from a decrepit ground into England's first all-seated stadium (to combat hooliganism which threatened the game) and gave supporters special identity via the Sky Blue train taking them to away games. With Hill as figurehead, Coventry were commercially Britain's most successful club. Away from the game, Jimmy was a 12-handicap golfer and rode to hounds in the Cotswolds. Money made from a consultancy with Saudi Arabian football was lost in a venture into America with Detroit Express and Washington Diplomats. Back in England, he campaigned successfully again, advocating three points for a win, instead of two, to make the game more attractive. At first widely opposed, it now operates world-wide.

And so to television, where he made huge impact as presenter and pundit with BBC's *Match of the Day*, ITV's *Big Match* and as Head of Sport with London Weekend. He finished on-screen as a chat-shot host at Sky. There was still one more notable appearance on the pitch, saving LWT's live Arsenal v Liverpool match from threatened abandonment one Sunday afternoon. Play stopped as a linesman pulled a muscle and over Highbury's public address came the appeal: 'Is there a qualified linesman in the house?' Hill responded instantly, stepping down from the directors' box to fill the vacancy on the touchline. He was, in turn, chairman of Coventry, a director of Charlton Athletic and finally back in the chair with his first love, Fulham. Now 83 and living with his wife Bryony in West Sussex, he is, for health reasons, no longer able to drive, but until last year still attended games at Craven Cottage. His honours include the PFA's Special Award, the Football League's Merit Award and an OBE for unrivalled services to the game. Elsewhere in sport, some have been given knighthoods for contributing considerable less.

Football has known no finer communicator. And how he loved an audience, as I recall from when we were with the BBC at the 1998 World Cup in Paris. Leaving a restaurant one evening, Jimmy stopped at a table to talk to a dozen or so England fans and held court for about 20 minutes. When he emerged, I said: 'Are they some people you know from your Fulham days, Jim?' He replied: 'No, I don't know any of them, but they all know me.' Who didn't during his long heyday.

This new season kicks off with a significant milestone. It is 50 years since the maximum wage was lifted, opening the way to contracts upwards of £100,000 a week at top clubs, with Wayne Rooney reputedly paid £200,000 a week by Manchester United. How many of today's millionaire players are aware that the man who made their vast pay-days possible was Jimmy Hill?

(Albert Sewell MBE was football statistician with BBC TV from 1968 until he retired in 2005. He edited this publication from 1983-97 when it was *The News of the World Annual*)

QUOTE/UNQOUTE

'This is not part of the uniform and it can be dangerous' – **Sepp Blatter**, FIFA president, on the decision to ban players from wearing neck-warming snoods.

'When he said sorry he was really disappointed. What do we have to do now – kill him? We have to support him' – **Carlo Ancelotti**, Chelsea manager, after Ashley Cole accidentally shot a work placement student with an air rifle at the club's training ground.

'I'm just looking forward to getting home, having a bacon sandwich and taking my dogs out' – **Harry Redknapp**, Tottenham manager, after the Championship League win over AC Milan.

'How can I hear the whistle in that noise? The referee killed the game' – **Robin van Persie**, Arsenal striker, on his second yellow card against Barcelona for shooting after being given offside.

'I think about it every year when the FA Cup comes around' – **Kevin Davies**, Bolton captain, on reaching the FA Cup-semi-finals, 14 years after doing so with Chesterfield.

'Dare we say "escape for Alcaraz?" – **Gary Lineker**, *Match of the Day* presenter, after Wigan defender Antolin Alcaraz survives a penalty appeal against Birmingham.

'I miss England and my next job will be in England. There is unfinished business' – **Jose Mourinho**, Real Madrid and former Chelsea manager.
'One year's punishment is enough' – **Fabio Capello**, England manager, after restoring John Terry as captain.

'I don't really want to single any players out because that would be unfair' – **Martin Allen**, Barnet manager, is a model of diplomacy after Steve Kabba scores all four goals against Burton.

'If some stupid fans don't understand and appreciate such a gift, they can go to hell' – **Mohamed Al Fayed**, Fulham owner, after unveiling a statue of the late singer Michael Jackson at Craven Cottage.

OTHER COMPETITIONS 2010–11

JOHNSTONE'S PAINT TROPHY

FIRST ROUND
Northern: Hartlepool 4 Northampton 0; Macclesfield 1 Morecambe 0; Oldham 0 Shrewsbury 1; Port Vale 2 Rochdale 1; Rotherham 1 Lincoln 0; Tranmere 1 Accrington 1 (*Accrington won 5-3 on pens); Walsall 1 Chesterfield 2; Sheffield Wed 2 Notts Co 1
Southern: Aldershot 2 Oxford 0; Bournemouth 0 Torquay 0 (Torquay won 3-0 on pens); Brighton 0 Leyton Orient 2; Charlton 1 Dagenham 0; Southampton 0 Swindon 3; Southend 0 Gillingham 0 (Southend won 4-3 on pens); Stevenage 0 Brentford 1; Yeovil 1 Exeter 3
*Accrington withdrew for fielding ineligible player

SECOND ROUND
Northern: Burton 1 Rotherham 2; Bury 0 Shrewsbury 0 (Bury won 6-5 on pens); Carlisle 2 Port Vale 2 (Carlisle won 4-3 on pens); Hartlepool 1 Bradford 0; Huddersfield 3 Peterborough 2; Macclesfield 2 Crewe 4; Sheffield Wed 2 Chesterfield 2 (Sheffield Wed won 8-7 on pens); Tranmere 0 Stockport 0 (Tranmere won 4-3 on pens)
Southern: Barnet 1 Southend 3; Bristol Rov 1 Aldershot 0; Cheltenham 0 Plymouth 2; Colchester 0 Wycombe 2; Hereford 0 Exeter 3; Leyton Orient 0 Brentford 0 (Brentford won 5-4 on pens); MK Dons 1 Charlton 2; Swindon 2 Torquay 0

THIRD ROUND
Northern: Bury 0 Tranmere 1; Carlisle 3 Crewe 1; Rotherham 2 Huddersfield 5; Sheffield Wed 4 Hartlepool 1
Southern: Plymouth 1 Exeter 2; Southend 0 Charlton 1; Swindon 1 Brentford 1 (Brentford won 4-2 on pens); Wycombe 3 Bristol Rov 6

AREA SEMI-FINALS
Northern: Carlisle 3 Sheffield Wed 1; Tranmere 0 Huddersfield 2
Southern: Brentford 0 Charlton 0 (Brentford won 3-1 on pens); Bristol Rov 2 Exeter 2 (Exeter won 5-4 on pens)

AREA FINALS
Northern first leg: Carlisle 4 (Marshall 19, Taiwo 23, Murphy 62, Michalik 65) Huddersfield 0. Att: 3,706. **Second leg:** Huddersfield 3 (Pilkington 30, Lee 70, 81) Carlisle 0. Att: 6,528 (Carlisle won 4-3 on agg)
Southern first leg: Brentford 1 (Alexander 64) Exeter 1 (Cureton 39). Att: 3,093. **Second leg:** Exeter 1 (Nardiello 90) Brentford 2 (Saunders 20, Alexander 26). Att: 5,322 (Brentford won 3-2 on agg)

FINAL
BRENTFORD 0 CARLISLE UNITED 1
Wembley (40,476); Sunday, April 3 2011
Brentford (4-4-2): Moore, Neilson, Legge, Osborne, Woodman (O'Connor 89), Saunders, Diagouraga, Reed (Bean 46), Weston (Grabban 78), Alexander (capt), Schlupp. **Subs not used:** Byrne, Carson. **Booked:** Legge, Diagouraga, Reed. **Sent off:** Diagouraga. **Manager:** Nicky Forster
Carlisle (4-1-3-2): Collin, Simek, Michalik, Murphy, Robson, Thirlwell (capt), Taiwo (Loy 88), Berrett, Marshall (Noble 23), Curran, Zoko (Madden 68). **Subs not used:** Livesey, Craig. **Scorer:** Murphy (12). **Booked:** Michalik, Robson. **Manager:** Greg Abbott
Referee: G Salisbury (Lancs). **Half-time:** 0-1

FA CARLSBERG TROPHY

FIRST ROUND
Alfreton 3 Hyde 0; Ashford 1 Hornchurch 0; Barrow 2 Guiseley 3; Basingstoke 0 Salisbury 2; Blyth 2 Fleetwood 0; Cambridge Utd 2 Forest Green 1; Chasetown 3 Kettering 3; Cirencester 1 Gloucester 1; Crawley 3 Dartford 3; Curzon 0 Altrincham 2; Darlington 3 Tamworth 2; Dorchester 3 St Albans 0; Droylsden 4 Hinckley 3; Eastbourne 3 Boreham Wood 1; Eastleigh 1 Sutton 1; Ebbsfleet 3 Hayes 1; Gateshead 2 Southport 2; Grimsby 3 Redditch 0; Harlow 0 Woking 2; Harrogate 0 Telford 3; Histon 2 Bath 3; Lowestoft 2 Uxbridge 3; Luton 0 Welling 0; Newport 0 Wealdstone 0; Rushden 1 Eastwood 1; Stalybridge 2 Nantwich 1; Sudbury 1 Hampton 4; Wimbledon 3 Braintree 0; Worcester 1 Northwich 0; Worksop 0 Mansfield 5; Wrexham 2 Kidderminster 0; York 0 Boston 1. **Replays:** Dartford 1 Crawley 0; Eastwood 4 Rushden 1 (aet); Gloucester 3 Cirencester 0; Kettering 1 Chasetown 2 (aet); Southport 0 Gateshead 1; Sutton 0 Eastleigh 4; Wealdstone 0 Newport 1 (aet); Welling 1 Luton 2

SECOND ROUND
Alfreton 3 Cambridge Utd 3; Ashford 0 Dartford 1; Blyth 2 Altrincham 1; Boston 0 Gloucester 1; Chasetown 2 Grimsby 1; Darlington 4 Bath 1; Dorchester 3 Eastbourne 3; Droylsden 1 Ebbsfleet 0; Eastleigh 3 Worcester 3; Gateshead 6 Hampton 0; Guiseley 2 Stalybridge 1; Luton 4 Uxbridge 0; Mansfield 4 Newport 2; Salisbury 1 Wrexham 0; Telford 1 Eastwood 0; Wimbledon 2 Woking 3. **Replays:** Cambridge Utd 3 Alfreton 6 (aet); Eastbourne 1 Dorchester 0; Worcester 1 Eastleigh 4

THIRD ROUND
Blyth 2 Droylsden 2; Eastbourne 1 Guiseley 1; Eastleigh 1 Chasetown 3; Gateshead 3 Dartford 0; Luton 1 Gloucester 0; Mansfield 1 Alfreton 1; Telford 0 Darlington 3; Woking 0 Salisbury 2. **Replays:** Alfreton 1 Mansfield 2; Droylsden 0 Blyth 4; Guiseley 2 Eastbourne 1

FOURTH ROUND
Blyth 0 Gateshead 2; Chasetown 2 Mansfield 3; Darlington 2 Salisbury 1; Guiseley 0 Luton 1. **Replay:** Mansfield 3 Chasetown 1

SEMI-FINALS, FIRST LEG
Darlington 3 (Bridge-Wilkinson 55, Hatch 76, 83) Gateshead 2 (Fisher 20, Rundle 44). Att: 4,243. Mansfield 1 (Mitchley 62) Luton 0. Att: 3,208

SEMI-FINALS, SECOND LEG
Gateshead 0 Darlington 0. Att: 5,156 (Darlington won 3-2 on agg). Luton 1 (Owusu 46) Mansfield 1 (Briscoe 118). Att: 6,133 (aet, Mansfield won 2-1 on agg)

FINAL

DARLINGTON 1 MANSFIELD TOWN 0 (aet)
Wembley (24,668): Saturday, May 7 2011
Darlington (4-3-3): Russell, Arnison, Brown, Miller (capt), Hatch, G Smith (Verma 38), Chandler, Bridge-Wilkinson (Terry 100), Moore, Wright, Campbell (Senior 75). **Subs not used:** Gray, St Louis-Hamilton. **Scorer:** Senior (119). **Booked:** Wright, Brown. **Manager:** Mark Cooper **Mansfield Town** (4-4-1-1): Marriott, Silk, Foster, Naylor, Spence, Briscoe, Thompson, Nix, A Smith (Cain 95), Murray (capt), Connor (Mitchley 108). **Subs not used:** Stonehouse, Collett. **Manager:** Duncan Russell **Referee:** S Attwell (Warwicks). **Half-time:** 0-0

FINALS – RESULTS

Associated Members' Cup
1984   (Hull) Bournemouth 2 Hull 1

Freight Rover Trophy
1985   (Wembley) Wigan 3 Brentford 1
1986   (Wembley) Bristol City 3 Bolton 0
1987   (Wembley) Mansfield 1 Bristol City 1 (aet; Mansfield won 5-4 on pens)

Sherpa Van Trophy
1988   (Wembley) Wolves 2 Burnley 0
1989   (Wembley) Bolton 4 Torquay 1

Leyland Daf Cup
1990   (Wembley) Tranmere 2 Bristol Rov 1
1991   (Wembley) Birmingham 3 Tranmere 2

Autoglass Trophy
1992   (Wembley) Stoke 1 Stockport 0
1993   (Wembley) Port Vale 2 Stockport 1
1994   (Wembley) Huddersfield 1 Swansea 1 (aet; Swansea won 3-1 on pens)

Auto Windscreens Shield
1995   (Wembley) Birmingham 1 Carlisle 0 (Birmingham won in sudden-death overtime)
1996   (Wembley) Rotherham 2 Shrewsbury 1
1997   (Wembley) Carlisle 0 Colchester 0 (aet; Carlisle won 4-3 on pens)
1998   (Wembley) Grimsby 2 Bournemouth 1 (Grimsby won with golden goal in extra-time)
1999   (Wembley) Wigan 1 Millwall 0
2000   (Wembley) Stoke 2 Bristol City 1

LDV Vans Trophy
2001   (Millennium Stadium) Port Vale 2 Brentford 1
2002   (Millennium Stadium) Blackpool 4 Cambridge Utd 1
2003   (Millennium Stadium) Bristol City 2 Carlisle 0
2004   (Millennium Stadium) Blackpool 2 Southend 0
2005   (Millennium Stadium) Wrexham 2 Southend 0

Football League Trophy
2006   (Millennium Stadium) Swansea 2 Carlisle 1

Johnstone's Paint Trophy
2007   (Millennium Stadium) Doncaster 3 Bristol Rov 2 (aet)
2008   (Wembley) MK Dons 2 Grimsby 0
2009   (Wembley) Luton 3 Scunthorpe 2 (aet)
2010   (Wembley) Southampton 4 Carlisle 1
2011   (Wembley) Carlisle 1 Brentford 0

OTHER LEAGUE CLUBS' CUP COMPETITIONS

FINALS – AT WEMBLEY

Full Members' Cup (Discontinued after 1992)
1985–86	Chelsea 5 Manchester City 4
1986–87	Blackburn 1 Charlton 0

Simod Cup
1987–88	Reading 4 Luton 1
1988–89	Nottm Forest 4 Everton 3

Zenith Data Systems Cup
1989–90	Chelsea 1 Middlesbrough 0
1990–91	Crystal Palace 4 Everton 1
1991–92	Nottm Forest 3 Southampton 2

ANGLO-ITALIAN CUP (Discontinued after 1996: * Home club)

1970	*Napoli 0 Swindon 3
1971	*Bologna 1 Blackpool 2 (aet)
1972	*AS Roma 3 Blackpool 1
1973	*Fiorentina 1 Newcastle 2
1993	Derby 1 Cremonese 3 (at Wembley)
1994	Notts Co 0 Brescia 1 (at Wembley)
1995	Ascoli 1 Notts Co 2 (at Wembley)
1996	Port Vale 2 Genoa 5 (at Wembley)

FA VASE FINALS

At Wembley (until 2000 and from 2007)
1975	Hoddesdon 2 Epsom & Ewell 1
1976	Billericay 1 Stamford 0*
1977	Billericay 2 Sheffield 1 (replay Nottingham after a 1-1 draw at Wembley)
1978	Blue Star 2 Barton Rov 1
1979	Billericay 4 Almondsbury Greenway 1
1980	Stamford 2 Guisborough Town 0
1981	Whickham 3 Willenhall 2*
1982	Forest Green 3 Rainworth Miners' Welfare 0
1983	VS Rugby 1 Halesowen 0
1984	Stansted 3 Stamford 2
1985	Halesowen 3 Fleetwood 1
1986	Halesowen 3 Southall 0
1987	St Helens 3 Warrington 2
1988	Colne Dynamoes 1 Emley 0*
1989	Tamworth 3 Sudbury 0 (replay Peterborough after a 1-1 draw at Wembley)
1990	Yeading 1 Bridlington 0 (replay Leeds after 0-0 draw at Wembley)
1991	Guiseley 3 Gresley Rov 1 (replay Bramall Lane Sheffield after a 4-4 draw at Wembley)
1992	Wimborne 5 Guiseley 3
1993	Bridlington 1 Tiverton 0
1994	Diss 2 Taunton 1*
1995	Arlesey 2 Oxford City 1
1996	Brigg Town 3 Clitheroe 0
1997	Whitby Town 3 North Ferriby 0
1998	Tiverton 1 Tow Law 0
1999	Tiverton 1 Bedlington 0
2000	Deal 1 Chippenham 0
2001	Taunton 2 Berkhamsted 1 (Villa Park)

2002	Whitley Bay 1 Tiptree 0* (Villa Park)
2003	Brigg 2 AFC Sudbury 1 (Upton Park)
2004	Winchester 2 AFC Sudbury 0 (St Andrews)
2005	Didcot 3 AFC Sudbury 2 (White Hart Lane)
2006	Nantwich 3 Hillingdon 1 (St Andrews)
2007	Truro 3 AFC Totton 1
2008	Kirkham & Wesham (Fylde) 2 Lowestoft 1
2009	Whitley Bay 2 Glossop 0
2010	Whitley Bay 6 Wroxham1
2011	Whitley Bay 3 Coalville 2

* After extra-time

FA TROPHY FINALS

At Wembley

1970	Macclesfield 2 Telford 0
1971	Telford 3 Hillingdon 2
1972	Stafford 3 Barnet 0
1973	Scarborough 2 Wigan 1*
1974	Morecambe 2 Dartford 1
1975	Matlock 4 Scarborough 0
1976	Scarborough 3 Stafford 2*
1977	Scarborough 2 Dagenham 1
1978	Altrincham 3 Leatherhead 1
1979	Stafford 2 Kettering 0
1980	Dagenham 2 Mossley 1
1981	Bishop's Stortford 1 Sutton 0
1982	Enfield 1 Altrincham 0*
1983	Telford 2 Northwich 1
1984	Northwich 2 Bangor 1 (replay Stoke after a 1-1 draw at Wembley)
1985	Wealdstone 2 Boston 1
1986	Altrincham 1 Runcorn 0
1987	Kidderminster 2 Burton 1 (replay WBA after a 0-0 draw at Wembley)
1988	Enfield 3 Telford 2 (replay WBA after a 0-0 draw at Wembley)
1989	Telford 1 Macclesfield 0*
1990	Barrow 3 Leek 0
1991	Wycombe 2 Kidderminster 1
1992	Colchester 3 Witton 1
1993	Wycombe 4 Runcorn 1
1994	Woking 2 Runcorn 1
1995	Woking 2 Kidderminster 1
1996	Macclesfield 3 Northwich 1
1997	Woking 1 Dagenham & Redbridge 0*
1998	Cheltenham 1 Southport 0
1999	Kingstonian 1 Forest Green 0
2000	Kingstonian 3 Kettering 2
2011	Darlington 1 Mansfield 0 *

At Villa Park

2001	Canvey 1 Forest Green 0
2002	Yeovil 2 Stevenage 0
2003	Burscough 2 Tamworth 1
2004	Hednesford Town 3 Canvey 2
2005	Grays 1 Hucknall 1* (Grays won 6-5 on pens)

2006   Grays 2 Woking 0

At Wembley
2007   Stevenage 3 Kidderminster 2
2008   Ebbsfleet 1 Torquay 0
2009   Stevenage 2 York 0
2010   Barrow 2 Stevenage 1*
(*After extra-time)

FA YOUTH CUP WINNERS

Year	Winners	Runners-up	Aggregate
1953	Manchester Utd	Wolves	9-3
1954	Manchester Utd	Wolves	5-4
1955	Manchester Utd	WBA	7-1
1956	Manchester Utd	Chesterfield	4-3
1957	Manchester Utd	West Ham	8-2
1958	Wolves	Chelsea	7-6
1959	Blackburn	West Ham	2-1
1960	Chelsea	Preston	5-2
1961	Chelsea	Everton	5-3
1962	Newcastle	Wolves	2-1
1963	West Ham	Liverpool	6-5
1964	Manchester Utd	Swindon	5-2
1965	Everton	Arsenal	3-2
1966	Arsenal	Sunderland	5-3
1967	Sunderland	Birmingham	2-0
1968	Burnley	Coventry	3-2
1969	Sunderland	WBA	6-3
1970	Tottenham	Coventry	4-3
1971	Arsenal	Cardiff	2-0
1972	Aston Villa	Liverpool	5-2
1973	Ipswich	Bristol City	4-1
1974	Tottenham	Huddersfield	2-1
1975	Ipswich	West Ham	5-1
1976	WBA	Wolves	5-0
1977	Crystal Palace	Everton	1-0
1978	Crystal Palace	Aston Villa	*1-0
1979	Millwall	Manchester City	2-0
1980	Aston Villa	Manchester City	3-2
1981	West Ham	Tottenham	2-1
1982	Watford	Manchester Utd	7-6
1983	Norwich	Everton	6-5
1984	Everton	Stoke	4-2
1985	Newcastle	Watford	4-1
1986	Manchester City	Manchester Utd	3-1
1987	Coventry	Charlton	2-1
1988	Arsenal	Doncaster	6-1
1989	Watford	Manchester City	2-1
1990	Tottenham	Middlesbrough	3-2
1991	Millwall	Sheffield Wed	3-0
1992	Manchester Utd	Crystal Palace	6-3
1993	Leeds	Manchester Utd	4-1
1994	Arsenal	Millwall	5-3
1995	Manchester Utd	Tottenham	†2-2

1996	Liverpool	West Ham	4-1
1997	Leeds	Crystal Palace	3-1
1998	Everton	Blackburn	5-3
1999	West Ham	Coventry	9-0
2000	Arsenal	Coventry	5-1
2001	Arsenal	Blackburn	6-3
2002	Aston Villa	Everton	4-2
2003	Manchester Utd	Middlesbrough	3-1
2004	Middlesbrough	Aston Villa	4-0
2005	Ipswich	Southampton	3-2
2006	Liverpool	Manchester City	3-2
2007	Liverpool	Manchester Utd	††2-2
2008	Manchester City	Chelsea	4-2
2009	Arsenal	Liverpool	6-2
2010	Chelsea	Aston Villa	3-2
2011	Manchester Utd	Sheffield Utd	6-3

(* One match only; † Manchester Utd won 4-3 on pens, †† Liverpool won 4-3 on pens)

WELSH CUP FINAL

Bangor 1 (Bull 51) Llanelli 4 (Griffiths 15, 60, Moses 20, Venables 64) – Llanelli. Att: 1.719

FA VASE FINAL

Coalville 2 (Moore 58, Goodby 80) Whitley Bay 3 (Chow 28, 86, Kerr 61) – Wembley. Att: 8,778

FA WOMEN'S CUP FINAL

Arsenal 2 (Little 19, Fleeting 32) Bristol Academy 0 - Ricoh Arena, Coventry. Att: 13,885

FA WOMEN'S PREMIER LEAGUE CUP FINAL

Barnet 0 Nottingham Forest 0 – Adams Park, Wycombe. Att: 1,281 (aet, Barnet won 4-3 on pens)

FA SUNDAY CUP FINAL

Oyster Martyrs (Liverpool) 1 (McGivern 76) Paddock (Liverpool) 0 – Prenton Park, Tranmere. Att: 1,105

FA COMMUNITY SHIELD

CHELSEA 1 MANCHESTER UNITED 3
Wembley (84,623); Sunday, August 8 2010

Chelsea (4-3-3): Hilario, Paulo Ferreira (Bruma 79) Ivanovic, Terry, Cole (Zhirkov 79), Essien, Mikel (Drogba 60), Lampard, Kalou, Anelka (Sturridge 60), Malouda (Benayoun 73). **Subs not used:** Turnbull, Van Aanholt. **Scorer:** Kalou (83)

Manchester Utd (4-4-2): Van der Sar, O'Shea, Vidic, J Evans, Fabio (Smalling 71), Valencia, Carrick (Fletcher 80), Scholes (Giggs 79), Park (Hernandez 46), Owen (Nani 46), Rooney (Berbatov 46). **Sub not used:** Kuszczak. **Scorers:** Valencia (41), Hernandez 76), Berbatov (90). **Referee:** A Marriner (W Mdlands). **Half-time:** 0-1

CHARITY/COMMUNITY SHIELD RESULTS (POST WAR)

[CHARITY SHIELD]

Year	Winners	Runners-up	Score
1948	Arsenal	Manchester Utd	4-3
1949	Portsmouth	Wolves	*1-1
1950	England World Cup XI	FA Canadian Tour Team	4-2
1951	Tottenham	Newcastle	2-1
1952	Manchester Utd	Newcastle	4-2
1953	Arsenal	Blackpool	3-1
1954	Wolves	WBA	*4-4
1955	Chelsea	Newcastle	3-0
1956	Manchester Utd	Manchester City	1-0
1957	Manchester Utd	Aston Villa	4-0
1958	Bolton	Wolves	4-1
1959	Wolves	Nottm Forest	3-1
1960	Burnley	Wolves	*2-2
1961	Tottenham	FA XI	3-2
1962	Tottenham	Ipswich Town	5-1
1963	Everton	Manchester Utd	4-0
1964	Liverpool	West Ham	*2-2
1965	Manchester Utd	Liverpool	*2-2
1966	Liverpool	Everton	1-0
1967	Manchester Utd	Tottenham	*3-3
1968	Manchester City	WBA	6-1
1969	Leeds	Manchester City	2-1
1970	Everton	Chelsea	2-1
1971	Leicester	Liverpool	1-0
1972	Manchester City	Aston Villa	1-0
1973	Burnley	Manchester City	1-0
1974	Liverpool	Leeds	1-1

(Liverpool won 6-5 on penalties)

Year	Winners	Runners-up	Score
1975	Derby Co	West Ham	2-0
1976	Liverpool	Southampton	1-0
1977	Liverpool	Manchester Utd	*0-0
1978	Nottm Forest	Ipswich	5-0
1979	Liverpool	Arsenal	3-1
1980	Liverpool	West Ham	1-0
1981	Aston Villa	Tottenham	*2-2
1982	Liverpool	Tottenham	1-0
1983	Manchester Utd	Liverpool	2-0
1984	Everton	Liverpool	1-0
1985	Everton	Manchester Utd	2-0
1986	Everton	Liverpool	*1-1
1987	Everton	Coventry	1-0
1988	Liverpool	Wimbledon	2-1
1989	Liverpool	Arsenal	1-0
1990	Liverpool	Manchester Utd	*1-1
1991	Arsenal	Tottenham	*0-0
1992	Leeds	Liverpool	4-3
1993	Manchester Utd	Arsenal	1-1

(Manchester Utd won 5-4 on penalties)

Year	Winners	Runners-up	Score
1994	Manchester Utd	Blackburn	2-0
1995	Everton	Blackburn	1-0

1996	Manchester Utd	Newcastle	4-0
1997	Manchester Utd	Chelsea	1-1

(Manchester Utd won 4-2 on penalties)

1998	Arsenal	Manchester Utd	3-0
1999	Arsenal	Manchester Utd	2-1
2000	Chelsea	Manchester Utd	2-0
2001	Liverpool	Manchester Utd	2-1

COMMUNITY SHIELD

Year	Winners	Runners-up	Score
2002	Arsenal	Liverpool	1-0
2003	Manchester Utd	Arsenal	1-1

(Manchester Utd won 4-3 on penalties)

2004	Arsenal	Manchester Utd	3-1
2005	Chelsea	Arsenal	2-1
2006	Liverpool	Chelsea	2-1
2007	Manchester Utd	Chelsea	1-1

(Manchester Utd won 3-0 on penalties)

2008	Manchester Utd	Portsmouth	0-0

(Manchester Utd won 3-1 on pens)

2009	Chelsea	Manchester Utd	2-2

(Chelsea won 4-1 on pens)

2010	Manchester Utd	Chelsea	3-1

(Fixture played at Wembley 1974–2000 and from 2007). Millennium Stadium 2001–2006)
*Trophy shared

QUOTE/UNQOUTE

'We have PlayStation footballers' – **Carlo Ancelotti**, Chelsea manager, after a second 6-0 win to start the season, this time at Wigan.

'They are probably going to win the Premier League easily' – **Roberto Mancini**, Manchester City manager, gets it wrong when tipping Chelsea to retain the title with five games gone.

'I'm a coach, not Harry Potter' – **Jose Mourinho** warns Real Madrid fans not to expect too much too soon from his new team.

'You create the god and you create the monster' – **Fabio Capello**, England manager, admitting his status was undermined by World Cup failure.

'We've made the decision because he gets terrible abuse here and we don't want to subject him to that' – **Sir Alex Ferguson** after leaving Wayne Rooney out of Manchester United's team at Everton following allegations about the player's private life.

'Perhaps he was just making sure everybody realises that if you play for Manchester United you have to conduct yourself in a manner and our club doesn't really care who you are' – **David Moyes**, the Everton manager, offers a different perspective.

'I have a photo of George Best on the wall of my office and how his life went is one of the saddest things ever. He was the world's first superstar footballer and it cost him. I think we may have a lot more George Bests around if we're not careful' – **Ian Holloway**, Blackpool manager.

SCOTTISH TABLES 2010–2011

CLYDESDALE BANK PREMIER LEAGUE

			Home				Away						
		P	W	D	L	F	A	W	D	L	F	A	GD	PTS
1	Rangers	38	14	2	3	43	14	16	1	2	45	15	59	93
2	Celtic	38	15	3	1	51	11	14	2	3	34	11	63	92
3	Hearts	38	9	5	5	27	21	9	4	6	26	24	8	63
4	Dundee Utd	38	13	1	5	34	22	4	9	6	21	28	5	61
5	Kilmarnock	38	6	4	9	26	31	7	6	6	27	24	-2	49
6	Motherwell	38	8	3	8	24	24	5	4	10	16	36	-20	46
7	Inverness	38	7	4	8	25	24	7	7	5	27	20	8	53
8	St Johnstone	38	6	5	8	10	19	5	6	8	13	24	-20	44
9	Aberdeen	38	6	2	11	22	21	5	3	11	17	38	-20	38
10	Hibernian	38	5	6	8	21	29	5	1	13	18	32	-22	37
11	St Mirren	38	4	6	9	20	27	4	3	12	13	30	-24	33
12	Hamilton	38	1	8	10	12	26	4	3	12	12	33	-35	26

League split after 33 matches with teams staying in top six and bottom six regardless of points won

Rangers go into Champions League third qualifying round; Celtic, Hearts and Dundee Utd into Europa League

Leading scorers (all competitions): 22 Hooper (Celtic), Miller (Rangers); 21 Rooney (Inverness); 20 Stokes (Celtic) – 1 for Hibernian; 19 Goodwillie (Dundee Utd), Jelavic (Rangers); 18 Sammon (Kilmarnock); 17 Sutton (Motherwell); 16 Vernon (Aberdeen); 15 Higdon (St Mirren), Lafferty (Rangers), Naismith (Rangers); 14 Commons (Celtic); 13 Skacel (Hearts); 12 Blackman (Aberden) – 10 for Motherwell, Maguire (Aberdeen), Murphy (Motherwell)

Manager of Year: Mixu Paatelainen (Kilmarnock). **Player of Year**: Emilio Izaguirre (Celtic)

IRN-BRU FIRST DIVISION

			Home				Away						
		P	W	D	L	F	A	W	D	L	F	A	GD	PTS
1	Dunfermline	36	11	6	1	39	14	9	4	5	27	17	35	70
2	Raith	36	9	3	6	25	20	8	6	4	22	15	12	60
3	Falkirk	36	9	3	6	32	22	8	4	6	25	19	16	58
4	Queen of South	36	7	3	8	31	30	7	4	7	23	23	1	49
5	Partick	36	8	6	4	23	11	4	5	9	21	28	5	47
6	Dundee**	36	11	7	0	29	13	8	5	5	25	21	20	44
7	Morton	36	7	5	6	18	17	4	5	9	21	26	-4	43
8	Ross	36	4	7	7	15	17	5	7	6	15	17	-4	41
9	Cowdenbeath*	36	5	4	9	21	31	4	4	10	20	41	-31	35
10	Stirling	36	2	4	12	17	39	2	4	12	15	43	-50	20

*also relegated; ** 25pts deducted for second administration

Leading scorers (all competitions): 20 Kirk (Dunfermline); 18 Doolan (Partick); 17 Stewart (Falkirk); 15 Baird (Raith); 12 Griffiths (Dundee), McMenamin (Queen of South), Smith (Stirling); 11 Tade (Raith)

Play-offs (on agg) – **Semi-finals**: Ayr 7 Forfar 4; Brechin 4 Cowdenbeath 2. **Final**: Ayr 3 Brechin 2

Manager of Year: Jim McIntyre (Dunfermline). **Player of Year**: John Baird (Raith)

IRN-BRU SECOND DIVISION

			Home					Away						
		P	W	D	L	F	A	W	D	L	F	A	GD	PTS
1	Livingston	36	13	5	0	41	14	12	2	4	38	19	46	82
2	Ayr*	36	11	3	4	28	21	7	2	9	34	34	7	59
3	Forfar	36	10	5	3	32	22	7	3	8	18	26	2	59
4	Brechin	36	9	3	6	35	26	6	9	3	28	19	18	57
5	East Fife	36	8	3	7	42	30	6	7	5	35	30	17	52
6	Airdrie	36	5	7	6	24	29	8	2	8	28	31	-8	48
7	Dumbarton	36	7	3	8	33	29	4	4	10	19	41	-18	40
8	Stenhousemuir	36	7	3	8	28	26	3	5	10	18	33	-13	38
9	Alloa **	36	5	6	7	27	31	4	3	11	22	40	-22	36
10	Peterhead	36	5	5	8	27	32	0	6	12	20	44	-29	26

* also promoted, ** also relegated

Leading scorers (all competitions): 29 McAllister (Brechin); 27 Roberts (Ayr); 24 Russell (Livingston); 15 Linn (East Fife); 14 Campbell (Forfar), McKenna (Brechin); 13 McShane (Dumbarton), Templeman (Forfar), Wyness (Peterhead)

Play-offs (on agg) – **Semi-finals**: Albion 3 Queen's Park 1; Annan 2 Alloa 1. **Final**: Albion 4 Annan 3

Manager of Year: Gary Bollan (Livingston). **Player of Year**: Rory McAllister (Brechin)

IRN-BRU THIRD DIVISION

			Home					Away						
		P	W	D	L	F	A	W	D	L	F	A	GD	PTS
1	Arbroath	36	11	4	3	39	24	9	2	7	41	37	19	66
2	Albion*	36	9	4	5	25	16	8	6	4	31	24	16	61
3	Queen's Park	36	10	3	5	31	17	8	2	8	26	26	14	59
4	Annan	36	8	5	5	32	25	8	6	4	26	20	13	59
5	Stranraer	36	10	4	4	39	25	5	8	5	33	32	15	57
6	Berwick	36	7	7	4	38	31	5	6	7	24	25	6	49
7	Elgin	36	8	2	8	30	29	5	4	9	23	34	-10	45
8	Montrose	36	6	4	8	28	27	4	3	11	19	34	-14	37
9	East Stirling	36	6	3	9	18	27	4	1	13	15	35	-29	34
10	Clyde	36	4	5	9	23	31	4	3	11	14	36	-30	32

* also promoted;

Leading scorers (all competitions): 23 Swankie (Arbroath); 22 One (Stranraer); 21 Malcolm (Stranraer); 18 Tosh (Montrose); 17 Gribben (Berwick), Doris (Arbroath), Harty (Annan); 16 Gunn (Elgin)

Manager of Year: Paul Sheerin (Arbroath). **Player of Year**: Gavin Swankie (Arbroath)

SCOTTISH LEAGUE RESULTS 2010–2011

CLYDESDALE BANK PREMIER LEAGUE

	Aberdeen	Celtic	Dundee Utd	Hamilton	Hearts	Hibernian	Inverness	Kilmarnock	Motherwell	Rangers	St Johnstone	St Mirren
Aberdeen		0-3	1-1	4-0	0-1	4-2	1-2	0-1	1-2	2-3	0-1	2-0
				1-0	0-0	0-1	1-0	5-0		0-1	0-2	0-1
Celtic	9-0		1-1	3-1	3-0	2-1	2-2	1-1	1-0	1-3	2-0	4-0
	1-0		4-1	2-0	4-0	3-1			4-0	3-0		1-0
Dundee Utd	3-1	1-2		2-1	2-0	1-0	0-4	1-1	2-0	0-4	1-0	1-2
	3-1	1-3			2-1	3-0	1-0	4-2	4-0		2-0	
Hamilton	0-1	1-1	0-1		0-4	1-2	1-3	2-2	0-0	1-2	1-2	0-0
	1-1		1-1		0-2	1-0	1-2	1-1		0-1	0-0	
Hearts	5-0	2-0	1-1	2-0		1-0	1-1	0-3	0-2	1-2	1-1	3-0
		0-3	2-1					0-2	0-0	1-0	1-0	3-2
									3-3			
Hibernian	1-2	0-3	2-2	1-1	0-2		1-1	2-1	2-1	0-3	0-0	2-0
	1-3			1-2	2-2		2-0	2-1		0-2	1-2	1-1
Inverness	2-0	0-1	0-2	0-1	1-3	4-2		1-3	1-2	1-1	1-1	1-2
	0-2	3-2		1-1	1-1	2-0			3-0		2-0	1-0
Kilmarnock	2-0	1-2	1-2	3-0	1-2	2-1	1-2		0-1	2-3	1-1	2-1
		0-4	1-1		2-2		1-1		3-1	1-5		2-0
		0-2										
Motherwell	1-1	0-1	2-1	0-1	1-2	2-3	0-0	0-1		1-4	4-0	3-1
	2-1	2-0	2-1	1-0		2-0		1-1		0-5		0-1
Rangers	2-0	0-2	4-0	4-0	1-0	0-3	1-1	2-1	4-1		2-1	2-1
		0-0	2-3		4-0		1-0	2-1	6-0		4-0	
			2-0									
St Johnstone	0-1	0-3	0-0	2-0	0-2	2-0	1-0	0-3	0-2	0-2		2-1
	0-0	0-1		1-0		1-1	0-3	0-0	1-0			0-0
St Mirren	2-1	0-1	1-1	2-2	0-2	1-0	1-2	0-2	1-1	1-3	1-2	
	3-2		1-1	3-1		0-1	3-3			0-1	0-0	
				0-1								

IRN-BRU FIRST DIVISION

	Cowdenbeath	Dundee	Dunfermline	Falkirk	Morton	Partick	Queen of South	Raith	Ross	Stirling
Cowdenbeath	–	2-1	0-4	0-0	2-2	2-1	1-3	1-2	0-2	5-1
		1-3	0-1	1-2	0-2	1-1	2-2	0-3	2-1	1-0
Dundee	3-0	–	2-2	2-0	2-1	2-1	1-0	0-0	0-0	2-0
	2-2	–	1-1	1-0	1-1	3-2	2-1	2-1	2-0	1-1
Dunfermline	2-1	3-1	–	1-1	2-0	0-0	1-0	2-2	3-2	3-0
	5-0	0-0	–	3-0	1-3	0-0	6-1	2-1	1-1	4-1
Falkirk	5-1	3-3	0-1	–	2-1	2-3	3-1	0-0	0-1	3-0
	2-0	2-2	1-2	–	1-0	2-0	0-3	2-1	0-1	4-2
Morton	1-2	0-1	2-1	0-0	–	2-0	2-0	0-1	0-0	0-0
	3-0	1-3	0-2	2-2	–	1-0	0-4	0-0	2-1	2-0
Partick	1-0	1-0	0-2	1-0	0-0	–	3-1	0-0	1-1	1-2
	0-1	0-0	2-0	1-2	2-0	–	0-0	3-0	1-1	6-1
Queen of South	3-0	1-2	2-0	1-5	2-0	2-1	–	1-3	3-0	2-2
	2-2	3-0	1-3	0-1	1-4	3-3	–	0-2	0-1	4-1
Raith	2-1	1-2	2-0	2-1	1-0	4-0	0-1	–	1-0	0-2
	2-2	2-1	2-1	1-2	2-2	0-2	0-1	–	1-1	2-1
Ross	1-1	0-3	0-0	0-1	2-2	0-2	1-1	0-0	–	3-1
	3-0	0-1	0-1	2-1	2-0	0-0	1-2	0-1	–	0-0
Stirling	1-3	1-1	1-5	0-5	0-1	4-2	0-0	1-3	0-0	–
	3-4	0-1	1-1	1-2	3-2	0-3	0-2	1-2	0-2	–

IRN-BRU SECOND DIVISION

	Airdrie	Alloa	Ayr	Brechin	Dumbarton	East Fife	Forfar	Livingston	Peterhead	Stenhousemuir
Airdrie	–	0-1	2-2	1-1	1-2	1-1	2-0	0-1	2-2	1-0
	–	0-2	0-5	2-2	2-1	2-2	3-1	2-4	1-0	2-2
Alloa	2-3	–	4-1	2-2	0-0	3-2	3-2	2-2	2-2	1-0
	1-0	–	0-1	2-2	2-3	1-3	0-3	1-3	0-0	1-2
Ayr	1-0	2-1	–	0-2	1-0	0-4	0-1	3-1	1-1	2-0
	3-1	1-0	–	2-0	2-0	1-1	3-1	0-3	2-2	4-3
Brechin	3-1	3-1	0-3	–	3-3	1-3	0-0	1-3	4-2	0-0
	1-2	3-2	1-0	–	6-0	2-3	0-1	1-0	3-1	3-1
Dumbarton	1-3	4-1	3-2	1-3	–	4-1	1-2	1-2	3-0	1-0
	1-1	2-2	1-2	1-2	–	4-2	0-0	0-3	5-2	0-1
East Fife	3-3	4-1	2-3	1-3	6-0	–	1-3	2-4	2-1	6-0
	0-1	3-1	3-2	0-0	1-3	–	3-0	1-3	3-1	1-1
Forfar	1-2	1-1	4-1	1-1	4-1	3-2	–	1-0	1-1	1-1
	1-2	3-1	3-2	2-1	2-1	0-0	–	0-4	2-1	2-0
Livingston	2-1	3-3	0-0	2-0	2-0	1-1	2-0	–	1-0	4-1
	2-0	4-0	3-2	0-0	1-1	4-3	3-0	–	5-1	2-1
Peterhead	5-1	1-0	2-4	0-5	1-0	2-2	1-2	0-0	–	2-2
	2-4	4-1	1-2	1-1	1-2	0-2	1-1	3-0	–	0-3
Stenhousemuir	1-3	0-1	3-1	0-0	4-0	1-1	3-0	1-2	3-1	–
	1-0	2-3	2-1	1-3	2-2	0-2	0-1	0-3	4-2	–

IRN-BRU THIRD DIVISION

	Albion	Annan	Arbroath	Berwick	Clyde	East Stirling	Elgin	Montrose	Queen's Park	Stranraer
Albion	–	0-0	0-2	2-2	3-1	1-0	3-1	3-1	2-1	1-2
	–	0-0	3-0	0-1	1-1	2-0	2-0	0-2	1-2	1-0
Annan	4-1	–	1-2	1-1	0-2	3-1	0-1	2-2	2-1	2-2
	2-2	–	3-0	2-3	1-0	2-1	2-2	2-1	1-2	2-1
Arbroath	1-1	0-2	–	3-2	3-2	2-0	2-0	4-0	1-0	0-0
	3-0	2-1	–	2-1	2-0	3-5	3-5	4-1	2-2	2-2
Berwick	1-6	2-2	4-1	–	2-1	3-0	6-2	1-0	1-1	2-2
	2-2	2-3	0-4	–	1-1	1-1	4-0	0-1	3-1	3-3
Clyde	1-2	0-2	1-1	1-4	–	1-2	1-1	2-0	2-3	2-2
	0-1	0-2	0-3	2-0	–	2-0	3-3	1-1	0-2	4-2
East Stirling	0-0	1-5	1-3	0-0	0-0	–	0-2	2-1	0-1	0-1
	1-2	2-0	2-5	1-0	2-0	–	2-1	1-2	3-2	0-2
Elgin	2-2	2-0	3-5	1-2	0-1	0-2	–	3-2	4-2	1-2
	1-1	2-3	3-2	3-2	0-1	2-0	–	1-0	0-1	2-1
Montrose	0-2	1-1	3-0	1-1	8-1	0-2	0-1	–	1-2	3-3
	0-2	0-1	0-5	1-1	3-1	3-0	1-0	–	0-2	3-2
Queen's Park	0-1	3-0	5-2	0-2	0-1	2-0	1-1	1-0	–	1-3
	2-1	0-1	1-1	1-0	4-0	2-0	1-0	4-1	–	3-3
Stranraer	3-2	2-2	4-1	1-1	3-1	4-1	2-1	1-2	1-0	–
	1-3	1-1	3-4	3-1	3-0	2-0	1-2	2-2	2-1	–

HOW RANGERS WON THIRD SUCCESSIVE TITLE

AUGUST 2010

14   Rangers 2 (Miller 16, Naismith 57) Kilmarnock 1 (Hamill 60 pen). Att: 45,739
22   Hibernian 0 Rangers 3 (Miller 64, 70, 90). Att: 17,145
28   Rangers 2 (Papac 33, Miller 79) St Johnstone 1 (Grainger 25). Att: 46,109

SEPTEMBER 2010

11   Hamilton 1 (Bougherra 56 og) Rangers 2 (Jelavic 6, Miller 90). Att: 5,356
18   Rangers 4 (Dillon 9 og, Miller 69, 82, Naismith 77) Dundee Utd 0. Att: 44,786
26   Aberdeen 2 (Vernon 10, Maguire 30) Rangers 3 (Miller 34 pen, 52, Jelavic 67). Att: 15,307

OCTOBER 2010

2   Hearts 1 (Skacel 12) Rangers 2 (Lafferty 80, Naismith 90). Att: 15,637
16   Rangers 4 (Naismith 47, Davis 62, Miller 65, Weiss 67) Motherwell 1 (Blackman 44). Att: 44,609
24   Celtic 1 (Hooper 45) Rangers 3 (Loovens 49 og, Miller 55, 67 pen). Att: 58,874
30   Rangers 1 (Edu 11) Inverness 1 (Odhiambo 81). Att: 43,697

NOVEMBER 2010

7   St Mirren 1 (Higdon 76 pen) Rangers 3 (McAusland 48 og, Naismith 58, Miller 68). Att: 5,674
10   Rangers 0 Hibernian 3 (Miller 6, Rankin 19, Dickoh 76). Att: 41,514
13   Rangers 2 (Miller 21, Weiss 32) Aberdeen 0. Att: 44,919
20   Kilmarnock 2 (Sammon 21, 59) Rangers 3 (Miller 42 pen, 55, 64). Att: 10,177

DECEMBER 2010

11   Inverness 1 (Hayes 31) Rangers 1 (Miller 57). Att: 6,799
26   Motherwell 1 (Sutton 46) Rangers 4 (Miller 26, 61, Hammell 34 og, Weiss 51). Att: 9,371

JANUARY 2011

2   Rangers 0 Celtic 2 (Samaras 62 pen, 70). Att: 50,222
15   Rangers 4 (Weiss 25, 45, Whittaker 28 pen, Edu 82) Hamilton 0. Att: 44,639
18   Rangers 1 (Davis 45) Inverness 0. Att: 41,623
22   Hearts 1 (Stevenson 77) Rangers 0. Att: 16,737
26   Hibernian 0 Rangers 2 (Bougherra 26, Jelavic 35). Att: 11,696

FEBRUARY 2011

2   Rangers 1 (Lafferty 4) Hearts 0. Att: 44,823
12   Rangers 6 (Naismith 5, Jelavic 34, 37, 79, Hutchinson 76 og, Healy 83) Motherwell 0. Att: 43,789
20   Celtic 3 (Hooper 17, 28, Commons 70) Rangers 0. Att: 58,748
27   Rangers 4 (Jelavic 5, 90, Lafferty 41, Papac 81) St Johnstone 0. Att: 43,125

MARCH 2011

| 6 | St Mirren 0 Rangers 1 (Bartley 24). Att: 5,405 |
| 13 | Rangers 2 (Diouf 38, Clancy 87 og) Kilmarnock 1 (Hamill 61 pen). Att: 42,417 |

APRIL 2011

2	Rangers 2 (Jelavic 10, Naismith 52) Dundee Utd 3 (Robertson 45, Russell 77, Goodwillie 89). Att: 46, 697
5	St Johnstone 0 Rangers 2 (Lafferty 20, Naismith 83). Att: 5,820
10	Hamilton 0 Rangers 1 (Jelavic 44). Att: 4,526
13	Aberdeen 0 Rangers 1 (Jelavic 22). Att: 11,925
16	Rangers 2 (Papac 33, Whittaker 52 pen) St Mirren 1 (McGregor 38). Att: 46,392
19	Dundee Utd 0 Rangers 4 (Whittaker 22 pen, 60 pen, Jelavic 72, Lafferty 83). Att: 11,626
24	Rangers 0 Celtic 0. Att: 50,248
30	Motherwell 0 Rangers 5 (Lafferty 18, Davis 51, Jelavic 64, Naismith 76, 90). Att: 8,968

MAY 2011

7	Rangers 4 (Jelavic 23, Lafferty 40, Davis 44, Stevenson 84 og) Hearts 0. Att: 46,178
10	Rangers 2 (Jelavic 21, Lafferty 25) Dundee Utd 0. Att: 49,267
15	Kilmarnock 1 (Dayton 65) Rangers 5 (Lafferty 1, 7, 53, Naismith 5, Jelavic 49). Att: 16,173 (clinched title)

QUOTE/UNQOUTE

'It's a magical, magical feeling to walk on to this pitch and think that we are the new owners' – **John W Henry** after his company, New England Sports Ventures, complete the takeover of Liverpool.

'The (old) owners are, from beyond the grave, seeking to exercise with their dead hand a continuing grip on this company' – **David Chivers** QC, on the unsuccessful attempts by Tom Hicks and George Gillett to prevent the sale.

'He tore up his contract, so it cost us no compensation. He walked away with no money and that is a measure of the man' – **Steve Gibson**, Middlesbrough chairman, on how the club parted company with manager Gordon Strachan.

'Dearie me, I feel old now' – **Sir Alex Ferguson** reflects on his 2,000th game as a manager with Manchester United, Aberdeen, St Mirren, East Stirling and Scotland.

'There is a culture of drinking in the English game. In my opinion it is better to go out with a woman. This is what I did after matches in Italy It is better' – **Roberto Mancini**, Manchester City manager.

'That's what you call making an impression' – **Owen Coyle**, Bolton manager, after Ivan Klasnic scored the winner against Stoke and received two yellow cards, all in stoppage-time.

SCOTTISH HONOURS LIST

PREMIER DIVISION

	First	Pts	Second	Pts	Third	Pts
1975-6	Rangers	54	Celtic	48	Hibernian	43
1976-7	Celtic	55	Rangers	46	Aberdeen	43
1977-8	Rangers	55	Aberdeen	53	Dundee Utd	40
1978-9	Celtic	48	Rangers	45	Dundee Utd	44
1979-80	Aberdeen	48	Celtic	47	St Mirren	42
1980-81	Celtic	56	Aberdeen	49	Rangers	44
1981-2	Celtic	55	Aberdeen	53	Rangers	43
1982-3	Dundee Utd	56	Celtic	55	Aberdeen	55
1983-4	Aberdeen	57	Celtic	50	Dundee Utd	47
1984-5	Aberdeen	59	Celtic	52	Dundee Utd	47
1985-6	*Celtic	50	Hearts	50	Dundee Utd	47
1986-7	Rangers	69	Celtic	63	Dundee Utd	60
1987-8	Celtic	72	Hearts	62	Rangers	60
1988-9	Rangers	56	Aberdeen	50	Celtic	46
1989-90	Rangers	51	Aberdeen	44	Hearts	44
1990-1	Rangers	55	Aberdeen	53	Celtic	41
1991-2	Rangers	72	Hearts	63	Celtic	62
1992-3	Rangers	73	Aberdeen	64	Celtic	60
1993-4	Rangers	58	Aberdeen	55	Motherwell	54
1994-5	Rangers	69	Motherwell	54	Hibernian	53
1995-6	Rangers	87	Celtic	83	Aberdeen	55
1996-7	Rangers	80	Celtic	75	Dundee Utd	60
1997-8	Celtic	74	Rangers	72	Hearts	67

PREMIER LEAGUE

	First	Pts	Second	Pts	Third	Pts
1998-99	Rangers	77	Celtic	71	St Johnstone	57
1999-2000	Rangers	90	Celtic	69	Hearts	54
2000-01	Celtic	97	Rangers	82	Hibernian	66
2001-02	Celtic	103	Rangers	85	Livingston	58
2002-03	*Rangers	97	Celtic	97	Hearts	63
2003-04	Celtic	98	Rangers	81	Hearts	68
2004-05	Rangers	93	Celtic	92	Hibernian	61
2005-06	Celtic	91	Hearts	74	Rangers	73
2006-07	Celtic	84	Rangers	72	Aberdeen	65
2007-08	Celtic	89	Rangers	86	Motherwell	60
2008-09	Rangers	86	Celtic	82	Hearts	59
2009-10	Rangers	87	Celtic	81	Dundee Utd	63
2010-11	Rangers	93	Celtic	92	Hearts	63

Maximum points: 72 except 1986-8, 1991-4 (88), 1994-2000 (108), 2001-10 (114)
* Won on goal difference

FIRST DIVISION (Scottish Championship until 1975-76)

	First	Pts	Second	Pts	Third	Pts
1890-1a	††Dumbarton	29	Rangers	29	Celtic	24
1891-2b	Dumbarton	37	Celtic	35	Hearts	30
1892-3a	Celtic	29	Rangers	28	St Mirren	23
1893-4a	Celtic	29	Hearts	26	St Bernard's	22
1894-5a	Hearts	31	Celtic	26	Rangers	21
1895-6a	Celtic	30	Rangers	26	Hibernian	24
1896-7a	Hearts	28	Hibernian	26	Rangers	25
1897-8a	Celtic	33	Rangers	29	Hibernian	22
1898-9a	Rangers	36	Hearts	26	Celtic	24
1899-1900a	Rangers	32	Celtic	25	Hibernian	24

Season	First	Second	Third
1900–1c	Rangers 35	Celtic 29	Hibernian 25
1901–2a	Rangers 28	Celtic 26	Hearts 22
1902–3b	Hibernian 37	Dundee 31	Rangers 29
1903–4d	Third Lanark 43	Hearts 39	Rangers 38
1904–5a	†Celtic 41	Rangers 41	Third Lanark 35
1905–6a	Celtic 46	Hearts 39	Rangers 38
1906–7f	Celtic 55	Dundee 48	Rangers 45
1907–8f	Celtic 55	Falkirk 51	Rangers 50
1908–9f	Celtic 51	Dundee 50	Clyde 48
1909–10f	Celtic 54	Falkirk 52	Rangers 49
1910–11f	Rangers 52	Aberdeen 48	Falkirk 44
1911–12f	Rangers 51	Celtic 45	Clyde 42
1912–13f	Rangers 53	Celtic 49	Hearts 41
1913–14g	Celtic 65	Rangers 59	Hearts 54
1914–15g	Celtic 65	Hearts 61	Rangers 50
1915–16g	Celtic 67	Rangers 56	Morton 51
1916–17g	Celtic 64	Morton 54	Rangers 53
1917–18f	Rangers 56	Celtic 55	Kilmarnock 43
1918–19f	Celtic 58	Rangers 57	Morton 47
1919–20h	Rangers 71	Celtic 68	Motherwell 57
1920–1h	Rangers 76	Celtic 66	Hearts 56
1921–2h	Celtic 67	Rangers 66	Raith 56
1922–3g	Rangers 55	Airdrieonians 50	Celtic 40
1923–4g	Rangers 59	Airdrieonians 50	Celtic 41
1924–5g	Rangers 60	Airdrieonians 57	Hibernian 52
1925–6g	Celtic 58	Airdrieonians 50	Hearts 50
1926–7g	Rangers 56	Motherwell 51	Celtic 49
1927–8g	Rangers 60	Celtic 55	Motherwell 55
1928–9g	Rangers 67	Celtic 51	Motherwell 50
1929–30g	Rangers 60	Motherwell 55	Aberdeen 53
1930–1g	Rangers 60	Celtic 58	Motherwell 56
1931–2g	Motherwell 66	Rangers 61	Celtic 48
1932–3g	Rangers 62	Motherwell 59	Hearts 50
1933–4g	Rangers 66	Motherwell 62	Celtic 47
1934–5g	Rangers 55	Celtic 52	Hearts 50
1935–6g	Celtic 68	Rangers 61	Aberdeen 61
1936–7g	Rangers 61	Aberdeen 54	Celtic 52
1937–8g	Celtic 61	Hearts 58	Rangers 49
1938–9f	Rangers 59	Celtic 48	Aberdeen 46
1946–7f	Rangers 46	Hibernian 44	Aberdeen 39
1947–8g	Hibernian 48	Rangers 46	Partick 46
1948–9i	Rangers 46	Dundee 45	Hibernian 39
1949–50i	Rangers 50	Hibernian 49	Hearts 43
1950–1i	Hibernian 48	Rangers 38	Dundee 38
1951–2i	Hibernian 45	Rangers 41	East Fife 37
1952–3i	*Rangers 43	Hibernian 43	East Fife 39
1953–4i	Celtic 43	Hearts 38	Partick 35
1954–5f	Aberdeen 49	Celtic 46	Rangers 41
1955–6f	Rangers 52	Aberdeen 46	Hearts 45
1956–7f	Rangers 55	Hearts 53	Kilmarnock 42
1957–8f	Hearts 62	Rangers 49	Celtic 46
1958–9f	Rangers 50	Hearts 48	Motherwell 44
1959–60f	Hearts 54	Kilmarnock 50	Rangers 42
1960–1f	Rangers 51	Kilmarnock 50	Third Lanark 42
1961–2f	Dundee 54	Rangers 51	Celtic 46
1962–3f	Rangers 57	Kilmarnock 48	Partick 46
1963–4f	Rangers 55	Kilmarnock 49	Celtic 47
1964–5f	*Kilmarnock 50	Hearts 50	Dunfermline 49

1965–6f	Celtic	57	Rangers	55	Kilmarnock	45
1966–7f	Celtic	58	Rangers	55	Clyde	46
1967–8f	Celtic	63	Rangers	61	Hibernian	45
1968–9f	Celtic	54	Rangers	49	Dunfermline	45
1969–70f	Celtic	57	Rangers	45	Hibernian	44
1970–1f	Celtic	56	Aberdeen	54	St Johnstone	44
1971–2f	Celtic	60	Aberdeen	50	Rangers	44
1972–3f	Celtic	57	Rangers	56	Hibernian	45
1973–4f	Celtic	53	Hibernian	49	Rangers	48
1974–5f	Rangers	56	Hibernian	49	Celtic	45

*Won on goal average †Won .... on deciding match ††Title shared
Competition suspended 1940–46 (Second World War)

SCOTTISH CHAMPIONSHIP WINS

Rangers	*54	Hibernian	4	Kilmarnock	1
Celtic	42	Dumbarton	*2	Motherwell	1
Aberdeen	4	Dundee	1	Third Lanark	1
Hearts	4	Dundee Utd	1	(* Incl 1 shared)

FIRST DIVISION (Since formation of Premier Division)

	First	Pts	Second	Pts	Third	Pts
1975–6d	Partick	41	Kilmarnock	35	Montrose	30
1976–7j	St Mirren	62	Clydebank	58	Dundee	51
1977–8j	*Morton	58	Hearts	58	Dundee	57
1978–9j	Dundee	55	Kilmarnock	54	Clydebank	54
1979–80j	Hearts	53	Airdrieonians	51	Ayr	44
1980–1j	Hibernian	57	Dundee	52	St Johnstone	51
1981–2j	Motherwell	61	Kilmarnock	51	Hearts	50
1982–3j	St Johnstone	55	Hearts	54	Clydebank	50
1983–4j	Morton	54	Dumbarton	51	Partick	46
1984–5j	Motherwell	50	Clydebank	48	Falkirk	45
1985–6j	Hamilton	56	Falkirk	45	Kilmarnock	44
1986–7k	Morton	57	Dunfermline	56	Dumbarton	53
1987–8k	Hamilton	56	Meadowbank	52	Clydebank	49
1988–9j	Dunfermline	54	Falkirk	52	Clydebank	48
1989–90j	St Johnstone	58	Airdrieonians	54	Clydebank	44
1990–1j	Falkirk	54	Airdrieonians	53	Dundee	52
1991–2k	Dundee	58	Partick	57	Hamilton	57
1992–3k	Raith	65	Kilmarnock	54	Dunfermline	52
1993–4k	Falkirk	66	Dunfermline	65	Airdrieonians	54
1994–5l	Raith	69	Dunfermline	68	Dundee	68
1995–6l	Dunfermline	71	Dundee Utd	67	Morton	67
1996–7l	St Johnstone	80	Airdrieonians	60	Dundee	58
1997–8l	Dundee	70	Falkirk	65	Raith	60
1998–9l	Hibernian	89	Falkirk	66	Ayr	62
1999–2000l	St Mirren	76	Dunfermline	71	Falkirk	68
2000–01l	Livingston	76	Ayr	69	Falkirk	56
2001–02l	Partick	66	Airdie	56	Ayr	52
2002–03l	Falkirk	81	Clyde	72	St Johnstone	67
2003–04l	Inverness	70	Clyde	69	St Johnstone	57
2004–05l	Falkirk	75	St Mirren	60	Clyde	60
2005–06l	St Mirren	76	St Johnstone	66	Hamilton	59
2006–07l	Gretna	66	St Johnstone	65	Dundee	53
2007–08l	Hamilton	76	Dundee	69	St Johnstone	58
2008–09l	St Johnstone	65	Partick	55	Dunfermline	51
2009–10l	Inverness	73	Dundee	61	Dunfermline	58
2010–11l	Dunfermline	70	Raith	60	Falkirk	58

Maximum points: a, 36; b, 44; c, 40; d, 52; e, 60; f, 68; g, 76; h, 84; i, 60; j, 78;
k, 88; l, 108 *Won on goal difference

SECOND DIVISION

	First	Pts	Second	Pts	Third	Pts
1921–2a	Alloa	60	Cowdenbeath	47	Armadale	45
1922–3a	Queen's Park	57	Clydebank	52	St Johnstone	50
1923–4a	St Johnstone	56	Cowdenbeath	55	Bathgate	44
1924–5a	Dundee Utd	50	Clydebank	48	Clyde	47
1925–6a	Dunfermline	59	Clyde	53	Ayr	52
1926–7a	Bo'ness	56	Raith	49	Clydebank	45
1927–8a	Ayr	54	Third Lanark	45	King's Park	44
1928–9b	Dundee Utd	51	Morton	50	Arbroath	47
1929–30a	*Leith Athletic	57	East Fife	57	Albion	54
1930–1a	Third Lanark	61	Dundee Utd	50	Dunfermline	47
1931–2a	*E Stirling	55	St Johnstone	55	Stenhousemuir	46
1932–3c	Hibernian	55	Queen of South	49	Dunfermline	47
1933–4c	Albion	45	Dunfermline	44	Arbroath	44
1934–5c	Third Lanark	52	Arbroath	50	St Bernard's	47
1935–6c	Falkirk	59	St Mirren	52	Morton	48
1936–7c	Ayr	54	Morton	51	St Bernard's	48
1937–8c	Raith	59	Albion	48	Airdrieonians	47
1938–9c	Cowdenbeath	60	Alloa	48	East Fife	48
1946–7d	Dundee Utd	45	Airdrieonians	42	East Fife	31
1947–8e	East Fife	53	Albion	42	Hamilton	40
1948–9e	*Raith	42	Stirling	42	Airdrieonians	41
1949–50e	Morton	47	Airdrieonians	44	St Johnstone	36
1950–1e	*Queen of South	45	Stirling	45	Ayr	36
1951–2e	Clyde	44	Falkirk	43	Ayr	39
1952–3	E Stirling	44	Hamilton	43	Queen's Park	37
1953–4e	Motherwell	45	Kilmarnock	42	Third Lanark	36
1954–5e	Airdrieonians	46	Dunfermline	42	Hamilton	39
1955–6b	Queen's Park	54	Ayr	51	St Johnstone	49
1956–7b	Clyde	64	Third Lanark	51	Cowdenbeath	45
1957–8b	Stirling	55	Dunfermline	53	Arbroath	47
1958–9b	Ayr	60	Arbroath	51	Stenhousemuir	46
1959–60b	St Johnstone	53	Dundee Utd	50	Queen of South	49
1960–1b	Stirling	55	Falkirk	54	Stenhousemuir	50
1961–2b	Clyde	54	Queen of South	53	Morton	44
1962–3b	St Johnstone	55	E Stirling	49	Morton	48
1963–4b	Morton	67	Clyde	53	Arbroath	46
1964–5b	Stirling	59	Hamilton	50	Queen of South	45
1965–6b	Ayr	53	Airdrieonians	50	Queen of South	47
1966–7b	Morton	69	Raith	58	Arbroath	57
1967–8b	St Mirren	62	Arbroath	53	East Fife	49
1968–9b	Motherwell	64	Ayr	53	East Fife	48
1969–70b	Falkirk	56	Cowdenbeath	55	Queen of South	50
1970–1b	Partick	56	East Fife	51	Arbroath	46
1971–2b	*Dumbarton	52	Arbroath	44	Stirling	50
1972–3b	Clyde	56	Dunfermline	52	Raith	47
1973–4b	Airdrieonians	60	Kilmarnock	58	Hamilton	55
1974–5b	Falkirk	54	Queen of South	53	Montrose	53

SECOND DIVISION (MODERN)

	First	Pts	Second	Pts	Third	Pts
1975–6d	*Clydebank	40	Raith	40	Alloa	35
1976–7f	Stirling	55	Alloa	51	Dunfermline	50
1977–8f	*Clyde	53	Raith	53	Dunfermline	48
1978–9f	Berwick	54	Dunfermline	52	Falkirk	50
1979–80f	Falkirk	50	E Stirling	49	Forfar	46

1980–1f	Queen's Park	50	Queen of South	46	Cowdenbeath	45
1981–2f	Clyde	59	Alloa	50	Arbroath	50
1982–3f	Brechin	55	Meadowbank	54	Arbroath	49
1983–4f	Forfar	63	East Fife	47	Berwick	43
1984–5f	Montrose	53	Alloa	50	Dunfermline	49
1985–6f	Dunfermline	57	Queen of South	55	Meadowbank	49
1986–7f	Meadowbank	55	Raith	52	Stirling	52
1987–8f	Ayr	61	St Johnstone	59	Queen's Park	51
1988–9f	Albion	50	Alloa	45	Brechin	43
1989–90f	Brechin	49	Kilmarnock	48	Stirling	47
1990–1f	Stirling	54	Montrose	46	Cowdenbeath	45
1991–2f	Dumbarton	52	Cowdenbeath	51	Alloa	50
1992–3f	Clyde	54	Brechin	53	Stranraer	53
1993–4f	Stranraer	56	Berwick	48	Stenhousemuir	47
1994–5g	Morton	64	Dumbarton	60	Stirling	58
1995–6g	Stirling	81	East Fife	67	Berwick	60
1996–7g	Ayr	77	Hamilton	74	Livingston	64
1997–8g	Stranraer	61	Clydebank	60	Livingston	59
1998–9g	Livingston	77	Inverness	72	Clyde	53
1999–2000g	Clyde	65	Alloa	64	Ross Co	62
2000–01g	Partick	75	Arbroath	58	Berwick	54
2001–02g	Queen of South	67	Alloa	59	Forfar Athletic	53
2002–03g	Raith	59	Brechin	55	Airdrie	54
2003–04g	Airdrie	70	Hamilton	62	Dumbarton	60
2004–05g	Brechin	72	Stranraer	63	Morton	62
2005–06g	Gretna	88	Morton	70	Peterhead	57
2006–07g	Morton	77	Stirling	69	Raith	62
2007–08g	Ross	73	Airdrie	66	Raith	60
2008–09g	Raith	76	Ayr	74	Brechin	62
2009–10g	*Stirling	65	Alloa	65	Cowdenbeath	59
2010–11g	Livingston	82	*Ayr	59	Forfar	59

Maximum points: a, 76; b, 72; c, 68; d, 52; e, 60; f, 78; g, 108 *Won on goal average/goal difference

THIRD DIVISION (MODERN)

	First	Pts	Second	Pts	Third	Pts
1994–5	Forfar	80	Montrose	67	Ross Co	60
1995–6	Livingston	72	Brechin	63	Caledonian Th	57
1996–7	Inverness	76	Forfar	67	Ross Co	77
1997–8	Alloa	76	Arbroath	68	Ross Co	67
1998–9	Ross Co	77	Stenhousemuir	64	Brechin	59
1999–2000	Queen's Park	69	Berwick	66	Forfar	61
2000–01	*Hamilton	76	Cowdenbeath	76	Brechin	72
2001–02	Brechin	73	Dumbarton	61	Albion	59
2002–03	Morton	72	East Fife	71	Albion	70
2003–04	Stranraer	79	Stirling	77	Gretna	68
2004–05	Gretna	98	Peterhead	78	Cowdenbeath	51
2005–06	*Cowdenbeath	76	Berwick	75	Stenhousemuir	73
2006–07	Berwick	75	Arbroath	70	Queen's Park	68
2007–08	East Fife	88	Stranraer	65	Montrose	59
2008–09	Dumbarton	67	Cowdenbeath	63	East Stirling	61
2009–10	Livingston	78	Forfar	63	East Stirling	61
2010–11	Arbroath	76	Albion	61	Queen's Park	59

Maximum points: 108 * Won on goal difference

RELEGATED FROM PREMIER DIVISION/PREMIER LEAGUE

1975–6	Dundee, St Johnstone	1978–9	Hearts, Motherwell
1976–7	Kilmarnock, Hearts	1979–80	Dundee, Hibernian
1977–8	Ayr, Clydebank	1980–1	Kilmarnock, Hearts

1981–2	Partick, Airdrieonians	1996–7	Raith
1982–3	Morton, Kilmarnock	1997–8	Hibernian
1983–4	St Johnstone, Motherwell	1998–9	Dunfermline
1984–5	Dumbarton, Morton	1999–2000	No relegation
1985–6	No relegation	2000–01	St Mirren
1986–7	Clydebank, Hamilton	2001–02	St Johnstone
1987–8	Falkirk, Dunfermline, Morton	2002–03	No relegation
1988–9	Hamilton	2003–04	Partick
1989–90	Dundee	2004–05	Dundee
1990–1	No relegation	2005–06	Livingston
1991–2	St Mirren, Dunfermline	2006–07	Dunfermline
1992–3	Falkirk, Airdrieonians	2007–08	Gretna
1993–4	St J'stone, Raith, Dundee	2008–09	Inverness
1994–5	Dundee Utd	2009–10	Falkirk
1995–6	Falkirk, Partick	2010–11	Hamilton

RELEGATED FROM FIRST DIVISION

1975–6	Dunfermline, Clyde	1994–5	Ayr, Stranraer
1976–7	Raith, Falkirk	1995–6	Hamilton, Dumbarton
1977–8	Alloa, East Fife	1996–7	Clydebank, East Fife
1978–9	Montrose, Queen of South	1997–8	Partick, Stirling
1979–80	Arbroath, Clyde	1998–9	Hamilton, Stranraer
1980–1	Stirling, Berwick	1999–2000	Clydebank
1981–2	E Stirling, Queen of South	2000–01	Morton, Alloa
1982–3	Dunfermline, Queen's Park	2001–02	Raith
1983–4	Raith, Alloa	2002–03	Alloa Athletic, Arbroath
1984–5	Meadowbank, St Johnstone	2003–04	Ayr, Brechin
1985–6	Ayr, Alloa	2004–05	Partick, Raith
1986–7	Brechin, Montrose	2005–06	Brechin, Stranraer
1987–8	East Fife, Dumbarton	2006–07	Airdrie Utd, Ross Co
1988–9	Kilmarnock, Queen of South	2007–08	Stirling
1989–90	Albion, Alloa	2008–09	*Livingston, Clyde
1990–1	Clyde, Brechin	2009–10	Airdrie, Ayr
1991–2	Montrose, Forfar	2010–11	Cowdenbeath, Stirling
1992–3	Meadowbank, Cowdenbeath	*relegated to Division Three for breaching	
1993–4	Dumbarton, Stirling, Clyde, Morton, Brechin	insolvency rules	

RELEGATED FROM SECOND DIVISION

1993–4	Alloa, Forfar, E Stirling, Montrose, Queen's Park, Arbroath, Albion, Cowdenbeath	2001–02	Morton
		2002–03	Stranraer, Cowdenbeath
		2003–04	East Fife, Stenhousemuir
		2004–05	Arbroath, Berwick
1994–5	Meadowbank, Brechin	2005–06	Dumbarton
1995–6	Forfar, Montrose	2006–07	Stranraer, Forfar
1996–7	Dumbarton, Berwick	2007–08	Cowdenbeath , Berwick
1997–8	Stenhousemuir, Brechin	2008–09	Queen's Park, Stranraer
1998–9	East Fife, Forfar	2009–10	Arbroath, Clyde
1999–2000	Hamilton	2010–11	Alloa, Peterhead
2000–01	Queen's Park, Stirling		

CLYDESDALE BANK PREMIER LEAGUE 2010-2011

ABERDEEN

Aluko S............... 27 (1)	Howard M 8 (1)	Milsom R 18
Anderson M.............. - (1)	Ifil J 13 (4)	Paton M 4 (6)
Blackman N 10 (5)	Jack R 26 (4)	Pawlett P 6 (6)
Considine A............. 26 (1)	Jarvis D .... - (1)	Robertson C 7 (6)
Diamond Z....................32	Langfield J 30 (1)	Shaughnessy J..................1
Folly Y.......................18	Low N...................... - (1)	Smith S 15 (1)
Foster R.................... - (1)	Mackie D 7 (4)	Velicka A 1 (5)
Fraser R.................... - (2)	Magennis J 10 (19)	Vernon S................ 29 (4)
Fyvie F 1 (4)	Maguire C....................35	Vujadinovic N 13 (5)
Grimmer J............... 1 (1)	McArdle R............... 27 (1)	Young D 20 (9)
Hansson H.............. - (1)	McNamee D....................9	
Hartley P 23 (1)	Megginson M 1 (5)	

League goals (39): Vernon 10, Maguire 7, Hartley 4, Magennis 3, Aluko 2, Blackman 2, McArdle 2, Diamond 1, Folly 1, Jack 1, Mackie 1, Milsom 1, Pawlett 1, Velicka 1, Vujadinovic 1, Opponents 1
Scottish Cup goals (10): Maguire 4, Vernon 3, Magennis 1, McArdle 1, Opponents 1. **Co-op Ins Cup goals (9):** Hartley 4, Vernon 3, Maguire 1. McArdle 1
Average home league attendance: 9,129

CELTIC

Brown S............. 26 (2)	Juarez E 5 (8)	McGinn N 6 (5)
Cha Du-Ri............. 14 (2)	Kapo O 1 (1)	Mulgrew C 20 (3)
Commons K 11 (3)	Kayal B 18 (3)	Murphy D................ 9 (9)
Crosas M................... - (1)	Ki Sung-Yeung... 11 (5)	Rogne T 14 (2)
Forrest J 15 (4)	Ledley J 26 (3)	Samaras G 16 (6)
Forster F......................36	Ljungberg F 1 (6)	Stokes A 22 (7)
Fortune M-A..................2	Loovens G...................13	Toshney L .... - (1)
Hooiveld J............. 4 (1)	Majstorovic D.............32	Towell R .... - (1)
Hooper G 26	Maloney S 15 (6)	Wilson M 25
Izaguirre E 33	McCourt P........... 8 (17)	Zaluska L.......................2

League goals (85): Hooper 20, Stokes 14, Commons 11, McCourt 7, Maloney 5, Forrest 3, Murphy 3, Samaras 3, Brown 2, Kayal 2, Ki Sung-Yueng 3, Ledley 2, McGinn 2, Wilson 2, Cha Du-Ri 1, Izaguirre 1, Loovens 1, Majstorovic 1, Rogne 1, Opponents 1.
Scottish Cup goals (14): Ledley 3, Brown 2, Commons 2, Mulgrew 2, Ki Sung-Yueng 1, Majstorovic 1, Maloney 1, Wilson 1, Opponents 1. **Co-op Ins Cup goals (14):** Stokes 5, Samaras 3, Commons 1, Hooper 1, Ledley 1, McGinn 1, Mulgrew 1, Rogne 1. **Champions League goals (2):** Hooper 1, Juarez 1. **Europa League goals (2):** Juarez 1, Samaras 1
Average home league attendance: 48,968

DUNDEE UNITED

Armstrong S............. 2 (10)	Douglas B 19 (4)	Robertson D............. 22 (8)
Buaben P............. 29 (6)	Dow R .... - (1)	Robertson S............ 29 (5)
Cadamarteri D......... 2 (8)	Gomis M 32 (2)	Russell J................ 21 (9)
Conway C 21 (2)	Goodwillie D........... 37 (1)	Severin S 14 (1)
Daly J.................. 18 (11)	Kenneth G 26 (2)	Shala A 1 (9)
Dillon S......................34	Kovacevic M...................2	Swanson D............... 9 (11)
Dixon P............... 28 (1)	Myrie-Williams J .... - (1)	Watson K 27 (2)
Dods D........................3	Pernis D....................38	Van der Meulen T 4 (3)

League goals (55): Goodwillie 17, Daly 9, Russell 9, Robertson D 4, Conway 3, Buaben 2, Douglas 2, Swanson 2, Dillon 1, Gomis 1, Kenneth 1, Severin 1, Shala 1, Watson 1, Opponents 1

HAMILTON ACADEMICAL

Antoine-Curier M 10 (3)	Gordon Z..........................2	Mensing S....................30
Buchanan D............. 27 (1)	Graham A............. 10 (5)	Millar K...................... - (1)
Canning M 23	Hasselbaink N........... 21 (6)	Murdoch S 1
Carrington M 6 (6)	Hopkirk D 2 (3)	Neil A....................... 8 (2)
Casalinuovo D 6 (13)	Imrie D..........................35	Paixao F 26 (4)
Cerny T..........................37	Kilday L 4 (1)	Paixao M.................. 9 (9)
Chambers J................. 6 (3)	Kirkpatrick J 2 (3)	Ross J 2
Crawford A 9 (5)	Lyle D.................. 1 (3)	Routledge J 22 (2)
Devlin M..........................1	McAlister J............. 15 (4)	Skelton G 14 (2)
Elebert D 16 (3)	McDonald G 22 (3)	Thomas J 1 (2)
Elliott T 1 (6)	McLaughlin M 21	Wildig A..................... 2 (1)
Gilliespie G 8 (9)	McQueen B 1	Wilkie K 3 (3)
Goodwin J..................14	Mcglinchey C .... - (1)	

League goals (24): Antoine-Curier 4, Imrie 4, Hasselbaink 3, Mensing 3, Paixao F 3, Buchanan 1, Chambers 1, McLaughlin 1, Paixao M 1, Routledge 1, Opponents 2
Scottish Cup goals (3): Antoine-Curier 1, Hasselbaink 1, Paixao F 1. **Co-op Ins Cup goals:** None
Average home league attendance: 2,898

HEARTS

Barr D 11 (2)	Kyle K 16 (3)	Smith D .... - (1)
Black I 29 (3)	MacDonald J 7	Stevenson R 18 (13)
Bouzid I 31 (1)	McGowan R............ 3 (5)	Templeton D............. 27 (6)
Driver A 4 (10)	Mrowiec A............. 26 (4)	Thomson C............. 20 (7)
Elliot C 11 (8)	Novikovas A 1 (5)	Thomson J 3 (3)
Elliott S 21 (9)	Obua D 7 (6)	Wallace L..........................9
Glen G 2 (9)	Palazuelos R 31 (2)	Webster A..........................9
Holt J .... - (1)	Robinson S 1 (3)	Zaliukas M 28
Jonsson E 29	Santana S................ 16 (3)	
Kello M....................31	Skacel R 27 (2)	

League goals (53): Skacel 13, Elliott 8, Kyle 7, Templeton 7, Stevenson 6, Elliot 4, Black 1, Glen 1, Novikovas 1, Thomson C 1, Zaliukas 1, Opponents 3
Scottish Cup goals: None. **Co-op Ins Cup goals (7):** Kyle 3, Jonsson 1, Novikovas 1, Robinson 1, Santana 1
Average home league attendance: 14,185

HIBERNIAN

Bamba S..........................16	Hogg C 6 (1)	Stephens D 6 (4)
Booth C 17	Horner L .... - (1)	Stevenson L 11 (8)
Brown M....................26	McBride K 10 (1)	Stokes A..........................3
Byrne K .... - (3)	Miller L 30 (3)	Taggart S 2 (1)
De Graaf E 16 (2)	Murray I 14 (6)	Thicot S 4 (3)
Dickoh F 27 (1)	Nish C 11 (9)	Thornhill M 5 (3)
Divis J 3	Palsson V 15 (1)	Towell R................... 15 (1)
Duffy D 2 (5)	Rankin J 14 (3)	Trakys V 4 (5)
Galbraith D 8 (14)	Riordan D 28 (5)	Vaz Te R 7 (3)
Grounds J 13	Scott M 8 (3)	Wotherspoon D 26 (9)
Handling D .... - (1)	Smith G.................. 3 (1)	Zemmama J 3 (1)
Hanlon P 30 (3)	Sodje A................ 13 (2)	
Hart M................. 16 (2)	Stack G..........................6	

League goals (39): Riordan 11, Sodje 6, Miller 5, Bamba 2, Dickoh 2, Hanlon 2, Hogg 2, Wotherspoon 2, Booth 1, Nish 1, Palsson 1, Rankin 1, Stevenson 1, Stokes 1, Vaz Te 1
Scottish Cup goals: None. **Co-op Ins Cup goals** (1): Grounds 1. **Europa League goals** (2): De Graaf 2
Average home league attendance: 11,756

INVERNESS CALEDONIAN THISTLE

Blumenshtein G......... 1 (4)	Hayes J...................... 23 (1)	Polworth L .... - (1)
Cox L........................ 25 (2)	Hogg C..........................10	Proctor D 7 (3)
Doran A 11 (3)	Innes C................... 10 (3)	Rooney A 37 (1)
Duff S 34	MacDonald A............ 2 (8)	Ross N 30 (4)
Duncan R 20 (4)	McBain R .... - (2)	Sanchez D 3 (6)
Esson R 35	McCann K......................8	Shinnie G 19
Foran R 30 (2)	Morrison G 3 (7)	Sutherland S 9 (20)
Gillet K.................... 12 (1)	Munro G 34 (1)	Tokely R................... 34 (1)
Golabeck S .... - (2)	Odhiambo E 18 (13)	Tuffey J 3

League goals (52): Rooney 15, Foran 7, Hayes 6, Munro 4, Odhiambo 4, Doran 3, Duncan 2, Sutherland 2, Cox 1, Duff 1, Innes 1, MacDonald 1, McCann 1, Ross 1, Sanchez 1, Tokely 1, Opponents 1
Scottish Cup goals (8): Rooney 4, Foran 2, Hogg 1, Sanchez 1. **Co-op Ins Cup goals** (6): Rooney 2, Cox 1, Munro 1, Odhiambo 1, Tokely 1
Average home league attendance: 4,526

KILMARNOCK

Agard K 3 (5)	Fowler J..................... 21 (5)	Pascali M.................. 34 (1)
Aubameyang W....... 4 (2)	Gordon B 18	Pursehouse A .... - (1)
Bell C..............................31	Gros W 8 (3)	Rui Miguel 8 (13)
Berntsson B .... - (4)	Hamill J.................... 31 (1)	Sammon C............... 19 (4)
Bryson C 33	Hay G 17 (5)	Silva D 17 (12)
Clancy T 19 (2)	Invincible D 3 (4)	Sissoko M 26 (1)
Dayton J 7 (7)	Jaakkola A 7 (1)	Taouil M 18 (6)
Eremenko A 31	Kelly L 30 (2)	Wright F..........................27
Fisher G...................... - (3)	McKenzie R .... - (1)	
Forrester H................ 3 (4)	O'Leary R 3	

League goals (53): Sammon 15, Hamill 8, Kelly 7, Eremenko 4, Silva 4, Bryson 2, Dayton 2, Pascali 2, Rui Miguel 2, Agard 1, Aubameyang 1, Fowler 1, Gordon 1, Gros 1, Wright 1, Opponents 1
Scottish Cup goals: None. **Co-op Ins Cup goals** (9): Sammon 3, Hamill 2, Kelly 1, Silva 1, Sissoko 1, Wright 1
Average home league attendance: 6,427

MOTHERWELL

Blackman N.............. 15 (3)	Hateley T 36 (2)	Murphy J 31 (4)
Carswell S................. 3 (1)	Hollis L............................1	Page J 3 (6)
Casagolda E 3 (9)	Humphrey C............ 33 (3)	Pollock J.................... - (3)
Charalambous A .... - (1)	Hutchinson S 18 (1)	Randolph D 37
Craigan S................ 32 (3)	Jeffers F 8 (2)	Reynolds M 19
Fitzpatrick M............. 3 (2)	Jennings S 30	Ross M 5 (1)
Forbes R 11 (12)	Jones S 10 (2)	Saunders S 22 (3)
Gow A....................... 9 (6)	Lasley K 26	Smith G .... - (1)
Gunning G 12 (2)	McHugh R .... - (11)	Sutton J 25 (10)
Hammell S.............. 26 (5)	Meechan S .... - (2)	Sutton J 25 (10)

League goals (40): Blackman 10, Sutton 10, Murphy 6, Humphrey 3, Hateley 2, Gow 1, Hutchinson 1, Jeffers 1, Jones 1, Lasley 1, Saunders 1, Opponents 3
Scottish Cup goals (14): Sutton 6, Murphy 3, Craigan 1, Jeffers 1, Jones 1, Jennings 1, Humphrey 1. **Co-op Ins Cup goals** (4): Page 2, Gow 1, Lasley 1. **Europa League goals** (7): Murphy 3, Hateley

1, Jennings 1, Page 1, Sutton 1
Average home league attendance: 5,255

RANGERS

Alexander N 1	Foster R...................11 (4)	Miller K 17 (1)
Bartley K 5	Healy D 2 (6)	Naismith S...............28 (3)
Beattie J 5 (2)	Hutton K...................1 (6)	Ness J 8 (3)
Bougherra M 31	Jelavic N 20 (3)	Papac S...................34
Broadfoot K...................5 (3)	Kerkar S ....- (1)	Webster A 1
Davis S...................37	Lafferty K 23 (8)	Weir D...................37
Diouf E-H 6 (9)	Loy R ....- (1)	Weiss V 17 (6)
Edu M 27 (6)	McCulloch L...............17 (4)	Whittaker S...................36
Fleck J 3 (10)	McGregor A...................37	Wylde G 9 (6)

League goals (88): Miller 21, Jelavic 16, Lafferty 11, Naismith 11, Weiss 5, Davis 4, Whittaker 4, Papac 3, Edu 2, Bartley 1, Bougherra 1, Diouf 1, Healy 1, Opponents 7
Scottish Cup goals (5): Whittaker 2, Lafferty 1, McCulloch 1, Ness 1. **Co-op Ins Cup goals (13):** Jelavic 3, Lafferty 3, Naismith 3, Bougherra 1, Davis 1, Edu 1, Little 1. **Champions League goals (3):** Edu 1, Miller 1, Naismith 1. **Europa League goals (3):** Diouf 1, Edu 1, Whittaker 1
Average home league attendance: 45,305

ST JOHNSTONE

Adams J 9 (2)	Haber M 5 (6)	Morris J 23
Anderson S 24 (1)	Invincible D 8 (2)	Myrie-Williams J 4 (2)
Caddis L 1 (2)	Jackson A 10 (7)	Novikovas A 1 (5)
Craig L 29 (5)	MacDonald P 14 (10)	Parkin S 17 (4)
Davidson M 33 (1)	Mackay D...................32	Reynolds S...................- (5)
Dobie S 1 (3)	May S...................8 (11)	Robertson J...................2 (4)
Duberry M 32 (1)	Maybury A 23 (7)	Rutkiewicz K 4 (6)
Enckelman P...................29	Millar C 29 (1)	Samuel C 20 (8)
Gartland G 4 (3)	Milne S...................1 (1)	Smith G...................9
Grainger D 31 (2)	Moon K...................4 (2)	Taylor C 11 (10)

League goals (23): Craig 5, Parkin 4, Grainger 2, May 2, Samuel 2, Adams 1, Haber 1, Jackson 1, Moon 1, Taylor 1, Opponents 3
Scottish Cup goals (6): Craig 1, Davidson 1, Invincible 1, MacDonald 1, Millar 1, Samuel 1. **Co-op Ins Cup goals (7):** Davidson 2, Dobie 1, Haber 1, Millar 1, Morris 1, Parkin 1
Average home league attendance: 3,841

ST MIRREN

Barron D 4 (5)	Lynch S 8 (6)	Mooy A 7 (6)
Brady G 3 (2)	Mair L 22 (2)	Murray H 21 (3)
Cregg P...................18 (4)	McAusland M 24 (1)	Potter J 32 (2)
Dargo C 14 (8)	McCluskey J ....- (3)	Ramage G ....- (1)
Gallacher P...................27	McGowan P...................33	Robb S 3
Goodwin J 16 (1)	McGregor D...................36	Samson C 11
Hegarty N 2 (1)	McKernon J...................- (1)	Thomson S 25 (2)
Higdon M...................26 (2)	McLean K 10 (9)	Travner J 35 (2)
Lamont M ....- (1)	McLennan M...................- (1)	Wardlaw G 16 (7)
Love A ....- (1)	McQuade P ....- (5)	Van Zanten D 25 (3)

League goals (33): Higdon 14, Thomson 5, Dargo 3, McGregor 3, Wardlaw 3, Lynch 2, McAusland 1, McGowan 1, Travner 1
Scottish Cup goals (10): McGowan 4, Dargo 2, McQuade 2, Mooy 1, Opponents 1. **Co-op Ins Cup goals (3):** Higdon 1, McGowan 1, McGregor 1
Average home league attendance: 4,450

RANGERS RETAIN LEAGUE CUP WITH EXTRA-TIME GOAL

SECOND ROUND	THIRD ROUND	FOURTH ROUND	SEMI-FINALS	FINAL
Bye				
*Inverness 3	*Celtic 6	Celtic 3		Celtic 1
Peterhead 0	Inverness 0		Celtic 4	
*St Johnstone ...2	*St Johnstone ...3	*St Johnstone 2		
Morton 0	Queen of South ..0			
*Queen of South ..4				
Forfar 1				
*Alloa 0	*Aberdeen 3	*Aberdeen 2	Aberdeen 1	
Aberdeen 3	Raith 2			
*Raith 1	*Falkirk 4	Falkirk 1		
Hamilton 0	Hearts 3			
*Partick 0				
Falkirk 1				
*Hearts 4				
Elgin 0				
*Brechin .....+A2	*Brechin 0	*Motherwell 1	Motherwell 1	
Dundee 2	Motherwell 2			
Bye				
*Ross ....+B3	*Ross 1	Dundee Utd 0		
St Mirren 3	Dundee Utd ....+2			
Bye				

192

Rangers .... +2

*Kilmarnock 6
Airdrie 2

Bye

*Kilmarnock 3

Hibernian 1

*Kilmarnock 0

Rangers 2

*Dunfermline 3
Clyde 2

Bye

Dunfermline 2

Rangers 2

*Dunfermline 2

*Rangers 7

CO-OPERATIVE INSURANCE CUP FINAL

CELTIC 1 RANGERS 2 (aet)

Hampden Park (51,181), Sunday, March 20 2011

Celtic (4-4-2): Forster, Wilson, Rogne, Mulgrew, Izaguirre, Brown (capt) (Ki Sung-Yeung 65), Kayal, Ledley, Commons (McCourt 103), Hooper, Samaras. **Subs not used:** Zaluska, Stokes. **Scorer:** Ledley (31). **Booked:** Kayal, Wilson, Mulgrew. **Sent off:** Izaguirre. **Manager:** Neil Lennon
Rangers (4-4-2): Alexander, Whittaker, Bougherra (Hutton 82), Weir (capt), Papac, Lafferty (Weiss 90), Davis, Edu, Wylde, Naismith, Jelavic (Diouf 117). **Subs not used:** McGregor, Healy. **Scorers:** Davis (24), Jelavic (98). **Booked:** Jelavic, Papac, Diouf. **Manager:** Walter Smith
Referee: C Thomson. **Half-time:** 1-1

FIRST ROUND: Albion 0 Airdrie 1; Annan 0 Partick 1; Clyde 2 Cowdenbeath 1; Dundee 3 Montrose 0; Dunfermline 5 Arbroath 2; Elgin 3 Ayr 2 (aet); East Stirling 1 Alloa 2; Inverness 3 Queen's Park 0; Peterhead 1 Berwick 0; Queen of South 5 Dumbarton 1; Raith 4 East Fife 1; Ross 2 Livingston 1; Stenhousemuir 1 Brechin 3; Stirling 1 Forfar 2; Stranraer 1 Morton 7

*Drawn at home. +After extra-time. A - Brechin won 3-1 on pens. B – Ross won 4-3 on pens. Both semi-finals at Hampden Park

193

SCOTTISH LEAGUE CUP FINALS

1946	Aberdeen beat Rangers (3-2)
1947	Rangers beat Aberdeen (4-0)
1948	East Fife beat Falkirk (4-1 after 0-0 draw)
1949	Rangers beat Raith Rov (2-0)
1950	East Fife beat Dunfermline Athletic (3-0)
1951	Motherwell beat Hibernian (3-0)
1952	Dundee beat Rangers (3-2)
1953	Dundee beat Kilmarnock (2-0)
1954	East Fife beat Partick (3-2)
1955	Hearts beat Motherwell (4-2)
1956	Aberdeen beat St Mirren (2-1)
1957	Celtic beat Partick (3-0 after 0-0 draw)
1958	Celtic beat Rangers (7-1)
1959	Hearts beat Partick (5-1)
1960	Hearts beat Third Lanark (2-1)
1961	Rangers beat Kilmarnock (2-0)
1962	Rangers beat Hearts (3-1 after 1-1 draw)
1963	Hearts beat Kilmarnock (1-0)
1964	Rangers beat Morton (5-0)
1965	Rangers beat Celtic (2-1)
1966	Celtic beat Rangers (2-1)
1967	Celtic beat Rangers (1-0)
1968	Celtic beat Dundee (5-3)
1969	Celtic beat Hibernian (6-2)
1970	Celtic beat St Johnstone (1-0)
1971	Rangers beat Celtic (1-0)
1972	Partick beat Celtic (4-1)
1973	Hibernian beat Celtic (2-1)
1974	Dundee beat Celtic (1-0)
1975	Celtic beat Hibernian (6-3)
1976	Rangers beat Celtic (1-0)
1977†	Aberdeen beat Celtic (2-1)
1978†	Rangers beat Celtic (2-1)
1979	Rangers beat Aberdeen (2-1)
1980	Dundee Utd beat Aberdeen (3-0 after 0-0 draw)
1981	Dundee Utd beat Dundee (3-0)
1982	Rangers beat Dundee Utd (2-1)
1983	Celtic beat Rangers (2-1)
1984†	Rangers beat Celtic (3-2)
1985	Rangers beat Dundee Utd (1-0)
1986	Aberdeen beat Hibernian (3-0)
1987	Rangers beat Celtic (2-1)
1988†	Rangers beat Aberdeen (5-3 on pens after 3-3 draw)
1989	Rangers beat Aberdeen (3-2)
1990†	Aberdeen beat Rangers (2-1)
1991†	Rangers beat Celtic (2-1)
1992	Hibernian beat Dunfermline Athletic (2-0)
1993†	Rangers beat Aberdeen (2-1)
1994	Rangers beat Hibernian (2-1)
1995	Raith Rov beat Celtic (6-5 on pens after 2-2 draw)
1996	Aberdeen beat Dundee (2-0)
1997	Rangers beat Hearts (4-3)

1998	Celtic beat Dundee Utd (3-0)
1999	Rangers beat St Johnstone (2-1)
2000	Celtic beat Aberdeen (2-0)
2001	Celtic beat Kilmarnock (3-0)
2002	Rangers beat Ayr (4-0)
2003	Rangers beat Celtic (2-1)
2004	Livingston beat Hibernian (2-0)
2005	Rangers beat Motherwell (5-1)
2006	Celtic beat Dunfermline Athletic (3-0)
2007	Hibernian beat Kilmarnock (5-1)
2008	Rangers beat Dundee Utd (3-2 on pens after 2-2 draw)
2009†	Celtic beat Rangers (2-0)
2010	Rangers beat St Mirren (1-0)
2011+	Rangers beat Celtic (2-1)

(† After extra time; Skol Cup 1985-93, Coca-Cola Cup 1995-97, Co-operative Insurance Cup 1999 onwards)

SUMMARY OF SCOTTISH LEAGUE CUP WINNERS

Rangers	27	Dundee	3	Livingston	1
Celtic	14	East Fife	3	Motherwell	1
Aberdeen	6	Hibernian	3	Partick	1
Hearts	4	Dundee Utd	2	Raith Rov	1

ALBA CHALLENGE CUP 2010–11

First round (north-east): Dundee 2 Alloa 1; Dunfermline 1 Arbroath 0; East Fife 4 Brechin 3 (aet); Elgin 1 Ross 2; Peterhead 5 Montrose 0; Raith 0 Cowdenbeath 1; Stirling 0 Falkirk 0 (aet, Stirling won 3-1 on pens)

First round (south-west): Airdrie 1 Ayr 2; Dumbarton 0 Morton 0 (aet, Morton won 4-3 on pens); Partick 2 Clyde 1; Queen of South 2 Albion 1; Queen's Park 3 Livingston 2 (aet); Stenhousemuir 3 Annan 2; Stranraer 1 East Stirling 2 (aet)

Second round: Ayr 2 Cowdenbeath 0; Dunfermline 1 Queen of South 1 (aet, Queen of South won 6-5 on pens); East Fife 3 Stirling 1; Partick 2 Berwick 1; Peterhead 6 East Stirling 1; Queen's Park 2 Forfar 3 (aet); Ross 3 Morton 1; Stenhousemuir 4 Dundee 1

Third round: Forfar 0 Ross 2; Partick 2 Ayr 1; Peterhead 3 Stenhousemuir 1; Queen of South 5 East Fife 0

Semi-finals: Peterhead 1 (Bavidge 78) Queen of South 2 (Reid 66, Holmes 69). Att: 1,003. Ross 2 (Morrison 54, Barrowman 88) Partick (Kinniburgh 8, Boyle 64). Att: 1,307 (aet, Ross won 4-3 on pens)

FINAL

QUEEN OF THE SOUTH 0 ROSS COUNTY 2
McDiarmid Park, Perth (5,124); Sunday, April 10 2011

Queen of the South: Hutton, Reid, Lilley (capt), McGuffie, Harris, Burns, Johnston, McKenna, McLaren, Holmes, Carmichael (Degnan 72). **Subs not used:** McKenzie, McShane, Black, Smillie. **Booked:** Lilley, McKenna. **Manager:** Kenny Brannigan.

Ross County: McGovern, Miller, Flynn, Boyd, Fitzpatrick, Gardyne (Milne 87), Brittain (capt), Kettlewell, Lawson (Morrison 90), Barrowman (Wood 89), Vigurs. **Subs not used:** Malin, Craig. **Scorers:** Barrowman (9), Vigurs (39). **Booked:** Barrowman, Lawson. **Manager:** Jimmy Calderwood

Referee: E Norris. **Half-time:** 0-2

COMFORTABLE SCOTTISH CUP WIN FOR CELTIC

FOURTH ROUND	FIFTH ROUND	SIXTH ROUND	SEMI-FINALS	FINAL
Motherwell....4				
*Dundee....0	Motherwell....2			
*Stenhousemuir....0:3		Motherwell....2:3		
Stranraer....0:4	*Stranraer....0			
*Hamilton....2			Motherwell....3	
Alloa....0	*Hamilton....1			
*Dundee Utd....0:A0		*Dundee Utd....2:0		
Ross....0:0	Dundee Utd....3			
*East Stirling....B1				Motherwell....0
Buckie....0	*Buckie....0			
*Queen of South....1		*Brechin....2:0		
Brechin....2	Brechin....2			
*Hearts....0			St Johnstone....0	
St Johnstone....1	*St Johnstone....2			
*Falkirk....2:0		St Johnstone....2:1		
Partick....2:1	Partick....0			
*Hibernian....0:0				
Ayr....0:1	*Ayr....1			
*St Mirren....0:6		*St Mirren....1:1		
Peterhead....0:1	St Mirren....2			
*Aberdeen....6			Aberdeen....0	
East Fife....0	*Aberdeen....1			
*Montrose....2:3		Aberdeen....1:2		
Dunfermline....2:5	Dunfermline....0			

Celtic 3

*Drawn at home. +After extra-time. A – Dundee Utd won 4-3 on pens. B – East Stirling expelled for fielding ineligible player. Both semi-finals played at Hampden Park

*Inverness 2
Elgin 0

*Morton 2:5
Airdrie 2:2

*Rangers 3
Kilmarnock 0

*Berwick 0
Celtic 2

*Inverness 5

*Inverness 1
Morton 1

*Rangers 2:0
Celtic 2:1

Celtic 2

Inverness 1
Celtic 4

FIRST ROUND: Beith 2 Linlithgow 0; Civil Service 1 Wigtown 2; Coldstream 1 Forres 3; Deveronvale 0 Inverurie 0; Edinburgh City 1 Clachnacuddin 0; Edinburgh Univ 2 Brora 2; Fraserburgh 3 St Cuthbert 3; Gala 1 Sunnybank 6; Glasgow Univ 1 Burntisland 0; Golspie 2 Fort William 2; Hawick 0 Dalbeattie 3; Huntly 2 Girvan 2; Lossiemouth 0 Whitehill 2; Newton Stewart 1 Preston 1; Rothes 2 Nairn 2; Selkirk 1 Bo'Ness 6; Vale of Leithen 1 Keith 3. **Replays:** Brora 2 Edinburgh Univ 1; Fort William 2 Golspie 3; Girvan 2 Huntly 1; Inverurie 0 Deveronvale 3; Nairn 4 Rothes 1; Preston 3 Newton Stewart 0; St Cuthbert 3 Fraserburgh 1

SECOND ROUND: Albion 0 Sunnybank 1; Beith 8 Glasgow Univ 1; Bo'Ness 2 Queen's Park 1; Clyde 1 Berwick 2; Deveronvale 1 Dalbeattie 0; Edinburgh City 2 Threave 4; Elgin 5 Brora 3; Forres 0 East Stirling 0; Golspie 2 Girvan 2; Keith 0 Spartans 3; Montrose 1 Arbroath 1; Nairn 0 Cove 1; Preston 0 Annan 0; Stranraer 9 St Cuthbert 0; Whitehill 4 Wick 3; Wigtown 1 Buckie 7. **Replays:** Annan 5 Preston 0; Arbroath 2 Montrose 3 (aet); East Stirling 4 Forres 0; Girvan 4 Golspie 0

THIRD ROUND: Airdrie 2 Beith 2; Alloa 4 Raith 2; Ayr 5 Sunnybank 0; Bo'Ness 0 Buckie 2; Brechin 2 Annan 2; Cove 0 Berwick 3; Dumbarton 1 Morton 2; East Fife 3 Forfar 1; Elgin 2 Livingston 1; Montrose 3 Whitehill 1; Peterhead 2 Cowdenbeath 0; Ross 4 Deveronvale 1; Spartans 1 East Stirling 2; Stenhousemuir 2 Threave 2; Stirling 1 Partick 3; Stranraer 4 Girvan 2. **Replays:** Annan 2 Brechin 5; Beith 3 Airdrie 4; Threave 1 Stenhousemuir 5

SCOTTISH CUP FINAL

MOTHERWELL 0 CELTIC 3

Hampden Park (49,618); Saturday, May 21 2011

Motherwell (4-3-3): Randolph, Lasley, Hutchinson, Craigan (capt), Gunning, Hammell (Jeffers 72), Hateley, Jennings, Murphy (Jones 80), Humphrey, Sutton. **Subs not used:** Hollis, Saunders, Forbes. **Booked:** Lasley, Craigan. **Manager:** Stuart McCall

Celtic (4-4-2): Forster, Wilson, Majstorovic, Loovens, Izaguirre, Commons (Forrest 81), Brown (capt), Ki Sung-Yueng, Samaras (Stokes 68), Hooper (McCourt 89). **Subs not used:** Zaluska, Cha Du-Ri. **Scorers:** Ki Sung-Yueng (32), Craigan (76 og), Mulgrew (88). **Booked:** Majstorovic, Brown, Ki Sung-Yueng. **Manager:** Neil Lennon

Referee: C Murray. **Half-time:** 0-1

197

SCOTTISH FA CUP FINALS

1874	Queen's Park beat Clydesdale (2-0)
1875	Queen's Park beat Renton (3-0)
1876	Queen's Park beat Third Lanark (2-0 after 1-1 draw)
1877	Vale of Leven beat Rangers (3-2 after 0-0, 1-1 draws)
1878	Vale of Leven beat Third Lanark (1-0)
1879	Vale of Leven awarded Cup (Rangers withdrew after 1-1 draw)
1880	Queen's Park beat Thornliebank (3-0)
1881	Queen's Park beat Dumbarton (3-1)
1882	Queen's Park beat Dumbarton (4-1 after 2-2 draw)
1883	Dumbarton beat Vale of Leven (2-1 after 2-2 draw)
1884	Queen's Park awarded Cup (Vale of Leven withdrew from Final)
1885	Renton beat Vale of Leven (3-1 after 0-0 draw)
1886	Queen's Park beat Renton (3-1)
1887	Hibernian beat Dumbarton (2-1)
1888	Renton beat Cambuslang (6-1)
1889	Third Lanark beat Celtic (2-1)
1890	Queen's Park beat Vale of Leven (2-1 after 1-1 draw)
1891	Hearts beat Dumbarton (1-0)
1892	Celtic beat Queen's Park (5-1)
1893	Queen's Park beat Celtic (2-1)
1894	Rangers beat Celtic (3-1)
1895	St Bernard's beat Renton (2-1)
1896	Hearts beat Hibernian (3-1)
1897	Rangers beat Dumbarton (5-1)
1898	Rangers beat Kilmarnock (2-0)
1899	Celtic beat Rangers (2-0)
1900	Celtic beat Queen's Park (4-3)
1901	Hearts beat Celtic (4-3)
1902	Hibernian beat Celtic (1-0)
1903	Rangers beat Hearts (2-0 after 0-0, 1-1 draws)
1904	Celtic beat Rangers (3-2)
1905	Third Lanark beat Rangers (3-1 after 0-0 draw)
1906	Hearts beat Third Lanark (1-0)
1907	Celtic beat Hearts (3-0)
1908	Celtic beat St Mirren (5-1)
1909	Cup withheld because of riot after two drawn games in final between Celtic and Rangers (2-2, 1-1)
1910	Dundee beat Clyde (2-1 after 2-2, 0-0 draws)
1911	Celtic beat Hamilton (2-0 after 0-0 draw)
1912	Celtic beat Clyde (2-0)
1913	Falkirk beat Raith (2-0)
1914	Celtic beat Hibernian (4-1 after 0-0 draw)
1915–19	No competition (World War 1)
1920	Kilmarnock beat Albion (3-2)
1921	Partick beat Rangers (1-0)
1922	Morton beat Rangers (1-0)
1923	Celtic beat Hibernian (1-0)
1924	Airdrieonians beat Hibernian (2-0)
1925	Celtic beat Dundee (2-1)
1926	St Mirren beat Celtic (2-0)
1927	Celtic beat East Fife (3-1)

1928	Rangers beat Celtic (4-0)
1929	Kilmarnock beat Rangers (2-0)
1930	Rangers beat Partick (2-1 after 0-0 draw)
1931	Celtic beat Motherwell (4-2 after 2-2 draw)
1932	Rangers beat Kilmarnock (3-0 after 1-1 draw)
1933	Celtic beat Motherwell (1-0)
1934	Rangers beat St Mirren (5-0)
1935	Rangers beat Hamilton (2-1)
1936	Rangers beat Third Lanark (1-0)
1937	Celtic beat Aberdeen (2-1)
1938	East Fife beat Kilmarnock (4-2 after 1-1 draw)
1939	Clyde beat Motherwell (4-0)
1940–6	No competition (World War 2)
1947	Aberdeen beat Hibernian (2-1)
1948†	Rangers beat Morton (1-0 after 1-1 draw)
1949	Rangers beat Clyde (4-1)
1950	Rangers beat East Fife (3-0)
1951	Celtic beat Motherwell (1-0)
1952	Motherwell beat Dundee (4-0)
1953	Rangers beat Aberdeen (1-0 after 1-1 draw)
1954	Celtic beat Aberdeen (2-1)
1955	Clyde beat Celtic (1-0 after 1-1 draw)
1956	Hearts beat Celtic (3-1)
1957†	Falkirk beat Kilmarnock (2-1 after 1-1 draw)
1958	Clyde beat Hibernian (1-0)
1959	St Mirren beat Aberdeen (3-1)
1960	Rangers beat Kilmarnock (2-0)
1961	Dunfermline beat Celtic (2-0 after 0-0 draw)
1962	Rangers beat St Mirren (2-0)
1963	Rangers beat Celtic (3-0 after 1-1 draw)
1964	Rangers beat Dundee (3-1)
1965	Celtic beat Dunfermline (3-2)
1966	Rangers beat Celtic (1-0 after 0-0 draw)
1967	Celtic beat Aberdeen (2-0)
1968	Dunfermline beat Hearts (3-1)
1969	Celtic beat Rangers (4-0)
1970	Aberdeen beat Celtic (3-1)
1971	Celtic beat Rangers (2-1 after 1-1 draw)
1972	Celtic beat Hibernian (6-1)
1973	Rangers beat Celtic (3-2)
1974	Celtic beat Dundee Utd (3-0)
1975	Celtic beat Airdrieonians (3-1)
1976	Rangers beat Hearts (3-1)
1977	Celtic beat Rangers (1-0)
1978	Rangers beat Aberdeen (2-1)
1979†	Rangers beat Hibernian (3-2 after two 0-0 draws)
1980†	Celtic beat Rangers (1-0)
1981	Rangers beat Dundee Utd (4-1 after 0-0 draw)
1982†	Aberdeen beat Rangers (4-1)
1983†	Aberdeen beat Rangers (1-0)
1984†	Aberdeen beat Celtic (2-1)
1985	Celtic beat Dundee Utd (2-1)
1986	Aberdeen beat Hearts (3-0)
1987†	St Mirren beat Dundee Utd (1-0)

1988	Celtic beat Dundee Utd (2-1)
1989	Celtic beat Rangers (1-0)
1990†	Aberdeen beat Celtic (9-8 on pens after 0-0 draw)
1991†	Motherwell beat Dundee Utd (4-3)
1992	Rangers beat Airdrieonians (2-1)
1993	Rangers beat Aberdeen (2-1)
1994	Dundee Utd beat Rangers (1-0)
1995	Celtic beat Airdrieonians (1-0)
1996	Rangers beat Hearts (5-1)
1997	Kilmarnock beat Falkirk (1-0)
1998	Hearts beat Rangers (2-1)
1999	Rangers beat Celtic (1-0)
2000	Rangers beat Aberdeen (4-0)
2001	Celtic beat Hibernian (3-0)
2002	Rangers beat Celtic (3-2)
2003	Rangers beat Dundee (1-0)
2004	Celtic beat Dunfermline (3-1)
2005	Celtic beat Dundee Utd (1-0)
2006†	Hearts beat Gretna (4-2 on pens after 1-1 draw)
2007	Celtic beat Dunfermline (1-0)
2008	Rangers beat Queen of the South (3-2)
2009	Rangers beat Falkirk (1-0)
2010	Dundee Utd bt Ross Co (3-0)
2011	Celtic bt Motherwell (3-0)

† After extra time

SUMMARY OF SCOTTISH CUP WINNERS

Celtic 35, Rangers 33, Queen's Park 10, Aberdeen 7, Hearts 7, Clyde 3, Kilmarnock 3, St Mirren 3, Vale of Leven 3, Dundee Utd 2, Dunfermline 2, Falkirk 2, Hibernian 2, Motherwell 2, Renton 2, Third Lanark 2, Airdrieonians 1, Dumbarton 1, Dundee 1, East Fife 1, Morton 1, Partick 1, St Bernard's 1

FA WOMEN'S PREMIER LEAGUE

	P	W	D	L	F	A	GD	Pts
Sunderland	14	9	3	2	30	16	14	30
Nottm Forest	14	6	5	3	19	16	3	23
Reading	14	6	2	6	24	21	3	20
Leeds	14	5	3	6	17	17	0	18
Barnet	14	4	4	6	20	22	-2	16
Watford	14	3	7	4	21	26	-5	16
Blackburn	14	4	4	6	18	24	-6	16
Millwall	14	3	4	7	22	29	-7	13

BLUE SQUARE PREMIER LEAGUE
2010–2011

				Home					Away					
		P	W	D	L	F	A	W	D	L	F	A	GD	PTS
1	Crawley	46	18	3	2	57	19	13	9	1	36	11	63	105
2	AFC Wimbledon*	46	17	3	3	46	15	10	6	7	37	32	36	90
3	Luton	46	14	7	2	57	17	9	8	6	28	20	48	84
4	Wrexham	46	13	7	3	36	24	9	8	6	30	25	17	81
5	Fleetwood	46	12	8	3	35	19	10	4	9	33	23	26	78
6	K'rminster**	46	13	6	4	40	27	7	11	5	34	33	14	72
7	Darlington	46	13	6	4	37	14	5	11	7	24	28	19	71
8	York	46	14	6	3	31	13	5	8	10	24	37	5	71
9	Newport	46	11	7	5	44	29	7	8	8	34	31	18	69
10	Bath	46	10	10	3	38	27	6	5	12	26	41	-4	63
11	Grimsby	46	7	12	4	37	28	8	5	10	35	34	10	62
12	Mansfield	46	9	6	8	40	37	8	4	11	33	38	-2	61
13	Rushden†	46	10	6	7	37	27	6	8	9	28	35	3	57
14	Gateshead	46	8	9	6	28	28	6	6	11	37	40	-3	57
15	Kettering***	46	8	8	7	33	32	7	5	11	31	43	-11	56
16	Hayes	46	10	2	11	34	38	5	4	14	23	43	-24	51
17	Cambridge	46	7	7	9	32	28	4	10	9	21	33	-8	50
18	Barrow	46	9	6	8	31	22	3	8	12	21	45	-15	49
19	Tamworth	46	6	8	9	28	41	6	5	12	28	42	-21	49
20	Forest Green	46	7	10	6	28	25	3	6	14	25	47	-19	46
21	Southport	46	9	6	8	39	33	2	7	14	17	44	-21	46
22	Altrincham	46	6	8	9	29	38	5	3	15	18	49	-40	44
23	Eastbourne	46	6	5	12	36	46	4	4	15	26	58	-42	39
24	Histon**	46	4	3	16	18	45	4	6	13	23	45	-49	28

*also promoted; † expelled for rule breaches, 5pts deducted for rule breaches; ** 5pts deducted for rule breaches; *** 2 pts deducted for ineligible player

Manager of Year: Steve Evans (Crawley). **Player of Year:** Matt Tubbs (Crawley). **Fair Play award:** Bath

Leading scorers: 37 Tubbs; 25 Connell (Grimsby); 23 Kedwell (AFC Wimbledon); 22 Vieira (Fleetwood); 19 Marna (Kettering); 17 McPhee (Kidderminster), Perry (Tamworth), Shaw (Gateshead)

CHAMPIONS

1979–80	Altrincham	1997–98*	Halifax
1980–81	Altrincham	1998–99*	Cheltenham
1981–82	Runcorn	1999–2000*	Kidderminster
1982–83	Enfield	2000–01*	Rushden
1983–84	Maidstone	2001–02*	Boston
1984–85	Wealdstone	2002–03*	Yeovil
1985–86	Enfield	2003–04*	Chester
1986–87*	Scarborough	2004–05*	Barnet
1987–88*	Lincoln	2005–06*	Accrington
1988–89*	Maidstone	2006–07*	Dagenham
1989–90*	Darlington	2007–08*	Aldershot
1990–91*	Barnet	2008–09*	Burton
1991–92*	Colchester	2009–10*	Stevenage
1992–93*	Wycombe	2010–11*	Crawley
1993–94	Kidderminster	(*Promoted to Football League	
1994–95	Macclesfield	Conference – Record Attendance: 11,065	
1995–96	Stevenage	Oxford v Woking, December 26, 2006	

BLUE SQUARE PREMIER LEAGUE RESULTS 2010–2011

1996–97* Macclesfield

Home \ Away	AFC Wimbledon	Altrincham	Barrow	Bath	Cambridge	Crawley	Darlington	Eastbourne	Fleetwood	Forest Gr	Gateshead	Grimsby	Hayes	Histon	Kettering	Kidderminster	Luton	Mansfield	Newport	Rushden	Southport	Tamworth	Wrexham	York
AFC Wimbledon	-	4-1	2-0	4-0	3-0	2-1	0-2	3-0	1-0	1-1	1-0	2-1	0-0	2-0	1-2	2-0	0-0	2-1	2-2	1-0	5-0	3-0	0-1	1-0
Altrincham	2-0	-	2-0	0-3	2-2	2-2	1-1	3-4	1-0	1-0	1-1	2-2	4-2	0-3	3-2	1-2	0-1	0-4	1-3	1-0	1-1	2-0	0-0	0-0
Barrow	2-0	1-0	-	0-1	4-0	0-1	0-0	4-0	1-1	3-0	1-3	0-2	2-0	2-1	3-2	2-1	0-0	2-0	2-1	2-3	2-0	0-2	0-0	0-0
Bath	2-2	0-1	0-1	-	4-0	1-2	0-1	1-1	1-1	1-1	1-0	2-0	3-1	2-1	1-1	0-1	0-0	2-0	2-2	2-1	2-1	0-1	0-2	2-2
Cambridge	1-2	4-0	2-2	4-0	-	3-0	0-1	2-0	1-1	1-0	5-0	1-1	1-0	0-0	3-0	1-2	0-0	0-0	2-0	0-2	0-0	2-0	1-3	2-1
Crawley	0-0	2-2	0-1	1-2	3-0	-	0-1	3-1	1-1	2-0	1-0	0-1	5-2	5-2	1-1	2-0	0-0	1-5	2-3	4-0	1-0	3-1	3-2	2-1
Darlington	0-0	3-1	0-3	2-1	1-0	1-0	-	1-0	1-0	3-2	2-0	0-0	0-1	3-1	1-1	1-1	0-1	2-0	1-0	1-1	1-0	1-0	1-1	1-1
Eastbourne	2-3	5-0	0-2	2-0	0-2	3-0	2-0	-	0-6	0-1	0-3	2-3	5-0	2-2	1-3	1-1	2-2	1-3	2-0	2-0	4-1	1-4	4-3	2-1
Fleetwood	1-1	3-1	3-2	2-1	1-2	1-1	1-0	6-1	-	1-0	0-0	5-0	1-0	1-1	4-1	1-1	2-4	0-0	0-0	1-1	2-0	1-0	1-0	2-1
Forest Gr	0-0	1-0	0-3	1-1	1-0	2-0	3-2	0-1	1-0	-	2-2	3-0	1-0	2-0	0-0	2-2	0-3	3-0	1-1	2-1	1-0	1-0	0-1	2-1
Gateshead	0-2	3-0	2-3	0-0	5-0	1-0	1-1	3-4	0-2	2-0	-	3-3	3-0	2-0	0-0	3-3	1-1	1-1	1-7	2-2	1-1	4-0	3-0	0-3
Grimsby	2-1	1-1	1-1	1-2	1-1	0-1	0-0	2-2	1-2	1-1	3-1	-	1-0	1-2	3-2	0-4	0-0	7-2	2-0	1-1	1-0	3-1	0-1	2-1
Hayes	0-0	0-1	3-1	0-3	2-2	1-0	3-2	3-0	1-0	3-4	3-1	0-3	-	4-3	0-3	0-1	0-4	4-0	1-2	3-3	2-1	2-2	0-3	0-0
Histon	0-4	3-3	0-1	1-2	2-3	1-0	0-1	2-0	2-5	0-3	1-4	1-2	1-2	-	0-1	1-1	2-3	2-3	0-3	1-1	3-1	1-2	2-1	1-2
Kettering	1-2	2-1	1-1	2-1	1-1	2-1	1-2	4-0	1-3	1-4	2-2	1-2	2-1	5-1	-	1-2	1-3	1-3	0-1	2-2	3-4	1-1	1-0	1-1
Kidderminster	2-0	2-1	1-1	1-0	2-2	2-1	0-0	1-1	1-3	0-1	2-2	3-2	2-1	2-1	1-1	-	3-3	0-2	2-0	1-1	6-0	2-1	0-0	1-1
Luton	3-0	0-0	1-2	2-0	4-0	1-3	1-1	1-3	3-3	4-0	0-4	2-1	2-0	2-2	2-2	1-2	-	2-0	1-3	0-1	2-0	0-1	2-3	0-0
Mansfield	2-5	0-1	0-3	0-1	1-0	4-0	4-1	4-0	3-0	2-1	5-1	0-2	0-0	2-0	1-2	1-2	2-0	-	3-3	3-1	2-2	0-1	1-1	1-0
Newport	3-3	5-0	1-1	3-1	2-1	2-1	2-1	3-3	1-0	2-2	2-7	4-1	4-1	3-1	3-1	3-0	0-0	1-0	-	1-1	0-1	1-1	2-2	1-1
Rushden	1-0	1-0	2-3	2-1	0-2	1-1	1-1	2-0	1-1	2-1	2-2	2-1	2-1	1-1	2-2	1-1	0-1	3-1	1-1	-	1-1	2-1	1-0	2-1
Southport	0-1	2-4	1-1	2-1	1-1	1-4	2-1	1-3	2-0	2-7	1-1	2-0	1-2	2-1	3-1	1-0	0-1	1-0	2-2	1-1	-	0-1	1-1	0-4
Tamworth	2-5	1-1	2-1	1-1	1-0	3-1	1-1	2-0	2-1	2-1	4-0	2-1	2-0	4-0	0-1	2-2	2-1	1-1	2-1	2-1	2-1	-	4-2	0-4
Wrexham	1-2	2-1	1-1	1-1	0-0	2-1	2-1	2-1	2-1	2-1	3-0	1-0	2-0	2-0	0-1	0-0	2-1	1-1	1-0	1-0	2-1	2-1	-	1-3
York	4-1	3-0	3-0	3-0	3-0	2-1	1-1	1-0	1-0	1-1	0-3	1-2	2-0	1-2	1-1	1-1	0-0	1-0	1-1	2-1	2-0	1-2	1-1	-

BLUE SQUARE NORTH

			Home				Away						
		P	W	D	L	F	A	W	D	L	F	A	GD	PTS
1	Alfreton	40	16	3	1	55	11	13	2	5	42	22	64	92
2	Telford*	40	12	6	2	42	17	11	7	2	29	12	42	82
3	Boston	40	13	4	3	34	14	10	6	4	38	19	39	79
4	Eastwood	40	13	2	5	40	23	9	5	6	42	27	32	73
5	Guiseley	40	9	6	5	29	21	11	7	2	27	20	15	73
6	Nuneaton	40	10	5	5	30	21	11	4	5	36	23	22	72
7	Solihull	40	11	4	5	36	24	7	6	7	30	25	17	64
8	Droylsden	40	11	2	7	41	36	6	7	7	28	31	2	60
9	Blyth	40	9	5	6	30	22	7	5	8	31	32	7	58
10	Stalybridge	40	8	6	6	28	23	8	3	9	36	32	9	57
11	Workington	40	10	3	7	32	28	6	3	11	20	32	-8	54
12	Harrogate	40	9	7	4	34	24	4	4	12	19	42	-13	50
13	Corby	40	7	5	8	28	33	6	5	9	30	47	-22	49
14	Gloucester	40	7	3	10	26	31	7	2	11	23	32	-14	47
15	Hinckley	40	9	4	7	47	29	4	3	13	29	47	0	46
16	Worcester	40	7	4	9	29	29	5	6	9	20	26	-6	46
17	Vauxhall	40	7	5	8	28	34	5	4	11	24	37	-19	45
18	Gainsborough	40	4	4	12	20	40	8	1	11	30	34	-24	41
19	Hyde	40	4	3	13	18	38	6	3	11	26	35	-29	36
20	Stafford	40	5	3	12	20	43	3	5	12	19	35	-39	32
21	Redditch**	40	1	6	13	16	52	1	2	17	14	53	-75	9

*also promoted, ** 5pts deducted

BLUE SQUARE SOUTH

			Home				Away						
		P	W	D	L	F	A	W	D	L	F	A	GD	PTS
1	Braintree	42	15	4	2	45	17	12	4	5	33	16	45	89
2	Farnborough	42	12	5	4	37	22	13	2	6	46	25	36	82
3	Ebbsfleet*	42	9	7	5	34	26	13	5	3	41	24	24	78
4	Chelmsford	42	14	3	4	48	16	9	5	7	34	34	32	77
5	Woking	42	13	5	3	35	17	9	5	7	27	25	20	76
6	Welling***	42	14	3	4	44	20	10	5	6	37	27	34	75
7	Dover	42	9	5	7	36	26	13	3	5	44	25	29	74
8	Eastleigh	42	12	1	8	39	30	10	5	6	35	23	21	72
9	Havant	42	8	5	8	31	27	8	5	8	25	24	5	58
10	Dartford	42	9	7	5	37	28	6	5	10	23	32	0	57
11	Bromley	42	7	6	8	24	30	8	6	7	25	31	-12	57
12	Weston-s-Mare	42	12	3	6	34	24	3	5	13	22	43	-11	53
13	Basingstoke	42	8	4	9	34	32	5	6	10	16	31	-13	49
14	Boreham Wood	42	8	5	8	33	4	6	4	11	21	34	-11	47
15	Staines	42	7	5	9	25	30	4	9	8	23	33	-15	47
16	Bishop's Stortford	42	6	3	12	19	38	7	3	11	29	41	-31	45
17	Dorchester	42	5	9	7	23	28	5	5	11	26	31	-10	44
18	Hampton	42	3	8	10	19	30	6	7	8	24	30	-17	42
19	Maidenhead	42	3	6	12	16	34	7	4	10	27	36	-27	40
20	Thurrock	42	5	7	9	28	40	3	6	12	22	37	-27	37
21	Lewes	42	5	5	11	19	38	4	4	13	15	32	-36	36
22	St Albans**	42	3	6	12	15	33	4	7	10	24	42	-36	24

*also promoted, ** 10pts deducted, *** 5pts deducted

OTHER LEAGUES 2010–11

PRINCIPALITY WELSH PREMIER LEAGUE

	P	W	D	L	F	A	GD	Pts
Bangor	32	22	4	6	80	44	36	70
New Saints	32	20	8	4	87	34	53	68
Neath	32	16	10	6	62	41	21	58
Llanelli	32	15	8	9	58	41	17	53
Prestatyn	32	10	10	12	44	46	-2	40
Port Talbot	32	8	12	12	37	48	-11	36
Aberystwyth	32	11	9	12	42	54	-12	42
Airbus	32	11	8	13	53	53	0	41
Newtown	32	8	11	13	40	55	-15	35
Carmarthen	32	10	5	17	39	64	-25	35
Bala	32	10	3	19	41	57	-16	33
Haverfordwest	32	5	4	23	30	77	-47	29

League splits after 22 games, with teams staying in top six and bottom six regardless of points won

RYMAN PREMIER DIVISION

	P	W	D	L	F	A	GD	Pts
Sutton	42	26	9	7	76	33	43	87
Tonbridge*	42	22	10	10	71	45	26	76
Bury	42	22	10	10	67	49	18	76
Lowestoft	42	20	15	7	68	30	38	75
Harrow	42	22	7	13	77	51	26	73
Canvey	42	21	10	11	69	51	18	73
Kingstonian	42	21	9	12	66	50	16	72
Concord	42	21	8	13	72	55	17	71
Cray	42	20	9	13	72	46	26	69
Hornchurch	42	19	12	11	58	46	12	69
Billericay	42	20	9	13	56	45	11	69
Wealdstone	42	16	10	16	58	54	4	58
Carshalton	42	14	10	18	49	57	-8	52
Tooting	42	13	10	19	63	85	-22	49
Hendon	42	12	10	20	61	81	-20	46
Margate	42	11	12	19	52	64	-12	45
Horsham	42	11	11	20	43	77	-34	44
Hastings	42	9	11	22	50	65	-15	38
Aveley	42	10	8	24	35	62	-27	38
Maidstone	42	9	10	23	43	75	-32	37
Croydon**	42	10	4	28	44	95	-51	31
Folkestone	42	5	12	25	34	68	-34	27

* Also promoted, ** 3pts deducted

EVO-STICK PREMIER LEAGUE

	P	W	D	L	F	A	GD	Pts
Halifax	42	30	8	4	108	36	72	98
Colwyn Bay*	42	24	7	11	67	56	11	79
Bradford	42	23	8	11	84	55	29	77
FC United	42	24	4	14	76	53	23	76
North Ferriby	42	22	7	13	78	51	27	73
Buxton	42	20	10	12	71	52	19	70
Kendal	42	21	5	16	80	77	3	68
Marine	42	20	7	15	74	64	10	67
Worksop**	42	21	6	15	72	54	18	66
Chasetown	42	20	6	16	76	59	17	66
Matlock	42	20	6	16	74	59	15	66
Northwich	42	18	9	15	66	55	11	63
Stocksbridge	42	17	6	19	75	75	0	57
Ashton	42	16	5	21	57	62	-5	53
Mickleover	42	15	7	20	70	76	-6	52
Whitby	42	14	9	19	58	77	-19	51
Nantwich	42	13	7	22	68	90	-22	46
Frickley	42	11	11	20	43	68	-25	44
Burscough	42	12	7	23	56	73	-17	43
Hucknall	42	11	10	21	57	80	-23	43
Ossett	42	9	5	28	45	103	-58	32
Retford	42	5	2	35	31	111	-80	17

* Also promoted, ** 3pts deducted

ZAMARETTO PREMIER DIVISION

	P	W	D	L	F	A	GD	Pts
Truro	40	27	6	7	91	35	56	87
Hednesford	40	26	5	9	82	38	44	83
Salisbury*	40	23	10	7	82	45	37	79
Cambridge	40	24	7	9	74	40	34	79
Leamington	40	24	6	10	68	39	29	78
Chesham	40	20	11	9	64	35	29	71
Chippenham	40	18	14	8	54	41	13	68
Stourbridge	40	18	8	14	72	61	11	62
Brackley	40	16	10	14	67	47	20	58
Swindon	40	17	7	16	56	58	-2	58
Bashley	40	14	10	16	55	63	-8	52
Evesham	40	14	9	17	54	49	5	51
Cirencester	40	13	8	19	59	67	-8	47
Oxford	40	11	12	17	48	54	-6	45
Hemel Hempstead	40	13	6	21	50	59	-9	45
Banbury***	40	11	8	21	44	67	-23	40
Bedford	40	10	7	23	41	76	-35	37
Weymouth**	40	12	8	20	55	85	-30	34
Didcot	40	7	11	22	39	69	-30	32
Tiverton	40	7	8	25	33	77	-44	29
Halesowen	40	5	9	26	24	107	-83	24

* Also promoted, ** 10 pts deducted; *** 1pt deducted

SCOT–ADS HIGHLAND LEAGUE

	P	W	D	L	F	A	GD	Pts
Buckie	34	24	5	5	84	42	42	77
Deveronvale	34	23	3	8	100	45	55	72
Cove	34	22	5	7	100	43	57	71
Keith	34	22	4	8	93	54	39	70
Nairn	34	18	9	7	86	49	37	63
Forres	34	19	6	9	72	56	16	63
Inverurie	34	19	5	10	81	50	31	62
Turriff	34	15	8	11	89	60	29	53
Formartine	34	15	3	16	71	68	3	48
Huntly	34	13	6	15	63	72	-9	45
Brora	34	13	6	15	51	64	-13	45
Lossiemouth	34	12	8	14	52	63	-11	44
Fraserburgh	34	11	9	14	69	65	4	42
Wick	34	12	3	19	75	78	-3	39
Clachnacuddin	34	9	7	18	68	89	-21	34
Rothes	34	6	4	24	43	92	-49	22
Strathspey	34	2	4	28	36	131	-95	10
Fort William	34	2	3	29	36	148	-112	9

BARCLAYS PREMIER RESERVE LEAGUE

NORTH
GROUP A

	P	W	D	L	F	A	GD	Pts
Manchester Utd	19	9	8	2	38	24	14	35
Manchester City	19	10	3	6	32	22	10	33
Wigan	19	9	4	6	21	22	-1	31
Newcastle	19	8	4	7	40	40	0	28
Bolton	19	8	3	8	24	32	-8	27

GROUP B

	P	W	D	L	F	A	GD	Pts
Blackburn	19	7	5	7	39	38	1	26
Sunderland	19	6	6	7	29	27	2	24
Liverpool	19	5	8	6	25	26	-1	23
Everton	19	4	3	12	23	34	-11	15
Blackpool	19	4	2	13	23	49	-26	14

North play-off: Manchester Utd 1 Blackburn 2

SOUTH

	P	W	D	L	F	A	GD	Pts
Chelsea	20	11	3	6	42	39	3	36
Arsenal	20	10	5	5	41	34	7	35
Aston Villa	20	8	6	6	37	21	16	30
West Ham	20	8	4	8	31	30	1	28
WBA	20	5	10	5	30	29	1	25
Wolves	20	5	2	13	27	35	-8	17

Play-off final: Chelsea 1 Blackburn 1 (Chelsea won 5-4 on pens)

IRISH FOOTBALL 2010–11

LEAGUE OF IRELAND

PREMIER DIVISION

		P	W	D	L	F	A	Pts
1	Shamrock Rov	36	19	10	7	57	34	67
2	Bohemians	36	19	10	7	50	29	67
3	Sligo Rov	36	17	12	7	62	36	63
4	Sporting Fingal	36	16	14	6	60	38	62
5	St Patrick's Ath	36	16	9	11	55	33	57
6	Dundalk	36	14	6	16	46	50	48
7	UCD	36	11	8	17	47	54	41
8	Galway Utd	36	9	11	16	38	59	38
9	Bray Wand	36	6	9	21	35	72	27
10	Drogheda Utd*	36	4	9	23	30	74	21

* relegated but regained place when Sporting Fingal disbanded
Leading scorer: 20 Gary Twigg (Shamrock Rov). **Player of Year:** Ritchie Ryan (Sligo Rov). **Young Player of Year:** Shaun Williams (Sporting Fingal). **Goalkeeper of Year:** Alan Mannus (Shamrock Rov). **Personality of Year:** Paul Cook (Sligo Rov).

FIRST DIVISION

		P	W	D	L	F	A	Pts
1	Derry City	33	20	9	4	65	24	69
2	Waterford Utd	33	20	6	7	59	27	66
3	Monaghan Utd	33	18	8	7	59	29	62
4	Shelbourne	33	18	7	8	57	31	61
5	Limerick	33	17	6	10	55	35	57
6	Cork City Foras	33	15	7	11	39	31	52
7	Wexford Youth	33	12	6	15	42	54	42
8	Finn Harps	33	10	10	13	37	43	40
9	Longford Town	33	9	8	16	39	53	35
10	Athlone Town	33	6	13	14	35	50	31
11	Mervue Utd	33	5	4	24	34	84	19
12	Salthill Devon	33	3	6	24	26	86	15

Leading scorers: 18 Graham Cummins (Cork City), Willie John Kiely (Waterford). **Player of Year:** Graham Cummins

FAI FORD CUP FINAL
Sligo Rov 0 **Shamrock Rov** 0 (aet, **Sligo** won 2-0 on pens) – Aviva Stadium, Dublin, November 14, 2010
Sligo: Kelly, Keane, Peers, Lauchlan, Davoran, Boco, Ndo, Ventre (O'Grady), McCabe, Russell, Doyle
Shamrock: Mannus, Rice, Sives, Flynn, Steven, Dennehy, Bradley, Turner, Chambers (Baker) (Price), Stewart (Kavanagh), Twigg. Sent off: Bradley

EA SPORTS LEAGUE CUP FINAL
Sligo Rov 1 (Blinkhorn) **Monaghan Utd** 0 – Showgrounds, September 25, 2010

SETANTA SPORTS CUP FINAL
Shamrock Rov 2 (O'Neill, Dennehy) **Dundalk** 0 – Tallaght Stadium, May 14, 2011

CARLING IRISH PREMIER LEAGUE

SECTION A

		P	W	D	L	F	A	Pts
1	Linfield	38	26	7	5	80	29	85
2	Crusaders	38	23	5	10	78	59	74
3	Glentoran	38	20	6	12	63	41	66
4	Cliftonville	38	17	7	14	60	56	58
5	Portadown	38	15	5	18	49	58	50
6	Lisburn Distillery	38	14	6	18	50	66	48

SECTION B

		P	W	D	L	F	A	Pts
7	Coleraine	38	17	5	16	51	50	56
8	Dungannon Swifts	38	14	9	15	50	53	51
9	Ballymena Utd	38	12	13	13	48	56	49
10	Glenavon	38	12	9	17	60	59	45
11	Donegal Celtic	38	8	8	22	55	89	32
12	Newry City	38	6	8	24	37	65	26R

Leading scorer: 23 Peter Thompson (Linfield). **Player of Year:** Stuart Dallas (Crusaders). **Young Player of Year:** Stuart Dallas. **Manager of Year:** David Jeffrey (Linfield)

LADBROKES.COM CHAMPIONSHIP

		P	W	D	L	F	A	Pts
1	Carrick Rgrs	26	18	4	4	57	27	58
2	Limavady Utd	26	15	6	5	53	27	51
3	Dergview	26	15	3	8	51	32	48
4	Bangor	26	11	8	7	45	38	41
5	HW Welders	26	11	6	9	45	38	39
6	Ballinamallard Utd	26	11	6	9	45	38	39
7	Ards	26	9	7	10	37	42	34
8	Institute	26	10	4	12	28	43	34
9	Larne	26	8	6	12	38	41	30
10	Loughall	26	8	6	12	37	48	30
11	Banbridge Town	26	7	7	12	31	39	28
12	Glebe Rgrs	26	7	7	12	36	46	28
13	Ballymoney Utd	26	5	8	13	31	48	23
14	Ballyclare	26	5	6	15	28	55	21

Leading scorer: 19 Ryan Campbell (Dergview). **Player of Year:** Paul Heatley (Carrick Rgrs)

JJB IRISH CUP FINAL

Linfield 2 (Thompson McAllister) **Crusaders** 1 (Caddell) – Windsor Park, May 7, 2011
Linfield: Blayney, Ervin (Tomelty), Douglas, Casement, Curran, Lowry (Mulgrew) Gault, Garrett, Carvill, McAllister, Thompson
Crusaders: Keenan, McKeown, McBride, Magowan, Coates, Dallas, Halliday (Rainey), Morrow (McMaster), Caddell, Owens, Watson
Referee: M Courtney (Cookstown)

CO-OPERATIVE INSURANCE LEAGUE CUP FINAL

Lisburn Distillery 2 (Davidson, Cushley) **Portadown** 1 (Tipton) – Mourneview Park, Lurgan, April 2, 2011

PADDY POWER COUNTY ANTRIM SHIELD FINAL

Glentoran 3 (Waterworth pen, Burrows, Gardiner) **Linfield** 1 (Billie-Joe Burns) – Windsor Park, November 30, 2010

WORLD CUP SUMMARIES 1930–2006

1930 – URUGUAY

WINNERS: Uruguay RUNNERS-UP: Argentina THIRD: USA FOURTH: Yugoslavia
Other countries taking part: Belgium, Bolivia, Brazil, Chile, France, Mexico, Paraguay, Peru, Romania. **Total entries:** 13
Venue: All matches played in Montevideo
Top scorer: Stabile (Argentina) 8 goals
Final (30/7/30): **Uruguay 4** (Dorado 12, Cea 55, Iriarte 64, Castro 89) **Argentina 2** (Peucelle 29, Stabile 35). **Att:** 90,000
Uruguay: Ballesteros; Nasazzi (capt); Mascheroni, Andrade, Fernandez, Gestido, Dorado, Scarone, Castro, Cea, Iriarte
Argentina: Botasso; Della Torre, Paternoster, J Evaristo, Monti, Suarez, Peucelle, Varallo, Stabile, Ferreira (capt), M Evaristo
Referee: Langenus (Belgium). **Half-time:** 1-2

1934 – ITALY

WINNERS: Italy RUNNERS-UP: Czechoslovakia THIRD: Germany FOURTH: Austria
Other countries in finals: Argentina, Belgium, Brazil, Egypt, France, Holland, Hungary, Romania, Spain, Sweden, Switzerland, USA. **Total entries:** 29 (16 qualifiers)
Venues: Bologna, Florence, Genoa, Milan, Naples, Rome, Trieste, Turin
Top scorers: Conen (Germany), Nejedly (Czechoslovakia), Schiavio (Italy), each 4 goals. **Final** (Rome, 10/6/34): **Italy 2** (Orsi 82, Schiavio 97) **Czechoslovakia 1** (Puc 70) after extra-time.
Att: 50,000
Italy: Combi (capt); Monzeglio, Allemandi, Ferraris, Monti, Bertolini, Guaita, Meazza, Schiavio, Ferrari, Orsi
Czechoslovakia: Planicka (capt); Zenisek, Ctyroky, Kostalek, Cambal, Krcil, Junek, Svoboda, Sobotka, Nejedly, Puc
Referee: Eklind (Sweden). **Half-time:** 0-0 (90 mins: 1-1)

1938 – FRANCE

WINNERS: Italy RUNNERS-UP: Hungary THIRD: Brazil FOURTH: Sweden
Other countries in finals: Belgium, Cuba, Czechoslovakia, Dutch East Indies, France, Germany, Holland, Norway, Poland, Romania, Switzerland. **Total entries:** 25 (15 qualifiers)
Venues: Antibes, Bordeaux, Le Havre, Lille, Marseilles, Paris, Reims, Strasbourg, Toulouse
Top scorer: Leonidas (Brazil) 8 goals
Final (Paris, 19/6/38): **Italy 4** (Colaussi 6, 36, Piola 15, 81) **Hungary 2** (Titkos 7, Sarosi 65).
Att: 45,000
Italy: Olivieri; Foni, Rava, Serantoni, Andreolo, Locatelli, Biavati, Meazza (capt), Piola, Ferrari, Colaussi
Hungary: Szabo; Polgar, Biro, Szalay, Szucs, Lazar, Sas, Vincze, Sarosi (capt), Szengeller, Titkos
Referee: Capdeville (France). **Half-time:** 3-1

1950 – BRAZIL

WINNERS: Uruguay RUNNERS-UP: Brazil THIRD: Sweden FOURTH: Spain
Other countries in finals: Bolivia, Chile, England, Italy, Mexico, Paraguay, Switzerland, USA, Yugoslavia. **Total entries:** 29 (13 qualifiers)
Venues: Belo Horizonte, Curitiba, Porto Alegre, Recife, Rio de Janeiro, Sao Paulo
Top scorer: Ademir (Brazil) 9 goals
Deciding Match (Rio de Janeiro, 16/7/50): **Uruguay 2** (Schiaffino 64, Ghiggia 79) **Brazil 1** (Friaca 47). **Att:** 199,850
(For the only time, the World Cup was decided on a final pool system, in which the winners of the four qualifying groups met in a six-match series So, unlike previous and subsequent

tournaments, there was no official final as such, but Uruguay v Brazil was the deciding match in the final pool)

Uruguay: Maspoli; Gonzales, Tejera, Gambetta, Varela (capt), Andrade, Ghiggia, Perez, Miguez, Schiaffino, Moran

Brazil: Barbosa; Augusto (capt), Juvenal, Bauer, Danilo, Bigode, Friaca, Zizinho, Ademir, Jair, Chico

Referee: Reader (England). **Half-time:** 0-0

1954 – SWITZERLAND

WINNERS: West Germany RUNNERS-UP: Hungary THIRD: Austria FOURTH: Uruguay
Other countries in finals: Belgium, Brazil, Czechoslovakia, England, France, Italy, Korea, Mexico, Scotland, Switzerland, Turkey, Yugoslavia. **Total entries:** 35 (16 qualifiers)
Venues: Basle, Berne, Geneva, Lausanne, Lugano, Zurich
Top scorer: Kocsis (Hungary) 11 goals
Final (Berne, 4/7/54): **West Germany 3** (Morlock 12, Rahn 17, 84) **Hungary 2** (Puskas 4, Czibor 9). **Att:** 60,000
West Germany: Turek; Posipal, Kohlmeyer, Eckel, Liebrich, Mai, Rahn, Morlock, O Walter, F Walter (capt), Schaefer
Hungary: Grosics; Buzansky, Lantos, Bozsik, Lorant, Zakarias, Czibor, Kocsis, Hidegkuti, Puskas (capt), J Toth
Referee: Ling (England). **Half-time:** 2-2

1958 – SWEDEN

WINNERS: Brazil RUNNERS-UP: Sweden THIRD: France FOURTH: West Germany
Other countries in finals: Argentina, Austria, Czechoslovakia, England, Hungary, Mexico, Northern Ireland, Paraguay, Scotland, Soviet Union, Wales, Yugoslavia. **Total entries:** 47 (16 qualifiers)
Venues: Boras, Eskilstuna, Gothenburg, Halmstad, Helsingborgs, Malmo, Norrkoping, Orebro, Sandviken, Stockholm, Vasteras
Top scorer: Fontaine (France) 13 goals
Final (Stockholm, 29/6/58): **Brazil 5** (Vava 10, 32, Pele 55, 88, Zagalo 76) **Sweden 2** (Liedholm 4, Simonsson 83). **Att:** 49,737
Brazil: Gilmar; D Santos, N Santos, Zito, Bellini (capt), Orlando, Garrincha, Didi, Vava, Pele, Zagalo
Sweden: Svensson; Bergmark, Axbom, Boerjesson, Gustavsson, Parling, Hamrin, Gren, Simonsson, Liedholm (capt), Skoglund
Referee: Guigue (France). **Half-time:** 2-1

1962 – CHILE

WINNERS: Brazil RUNNERS-UP: Czechoslovakia THIRD: Chile FOURTH: Yugoslavia
Other countries in finals: Argentina, Bulgaria, Colombia, England, Hungary, Italy, Mexico, Soviet Union, Spain, Switzerland, Uruguay, West Germany. **Total entries:** 53 (16 qualifiers)
Venues: Arica, Rancagua, Santiago, Vina del Mar
Top scorer: Jerkovic (Yugoslavia) 5 goals
Final (Santiago, 17/6/62): **Brazil 3** (Amarildo 17, Zito 69, Vava 77) **Czechoslovakia 1** (Masopust 16). **Att:** 68,679
Brazil: Gilmar; D Santos, Mauro (capt), Zozimo, N Santos, Zito, Didi, Garrincha, Vava, Amarildo, Zagalo
Czechoslovakia: Schroiff; Tichy, Novak, Pluskal, Popluhar, Masopust (capt), Pospichal, Scherer, Kvasnak, Kadraba, Jelinek
Referee: Latychev (Soviet Union). **Half-time:** 1-1

1966 – ENGLAND

WINNERS: England RUNNERS-UP: West Germany THIRD: Portugal FOURTH: USSR

Other countries in finals: Argentina, Brazil, Bulgaria, Chile, France, Hungary, Italy, Mexico, North Korea, Spain, Switzerland, Uruguay. **Total entries:** 53 (16 qualifiers)
Venues: Birmingham (Villa Park), Liverpool (Goodison Park), London (Wembley and White City), Manchester (Old Trafford), Middlesbrough, Sheffield (Hillsborough), Sunderland
Top scorer: Eusebio (Portugal) 9 goals
Final (Wembley, 30/7/66): **England 4** (Hurst 19, 100, 120, Peters 78) **West Germany 2** (Haller 13, Weber 89) after extra-time. **Att:** 93,802
England: Banks; Cohen, Wilson, Stiles, J Charlton, Moore (capt), Ball, Hurst, Hunt, R Charlton, Peters
West Germany: Tilkowski; Hottges, Schnellinger, Beckenbauer, Schulz, Weber, Haller, Held, Seeler (capt), Overath, Emmerich
Referee: Dienst (Switzerland). **Half-time:** 1-1 (90 mins: 2-2)

1970 – MEXICO
WINNERS: Brazil RUNNERS-UP: Italy THIRD: West Germany FOURTH: Uruguay
Other countries in finals: Belgium, Bulgaria, Czechoslovakia, El Salvador, England, Israel, Mexico, Morocco, Peru, Romania, Soviet Union, Sweden. **Total entries:** 68 (16 qualifiers)
Venues: Guadalajara, Leon, Mexico City, Puebla, Toluca
Top scorer: Muller (West Germany) 10 goals
Final (Mexico City, 21/6/70): **Brazil 4** (Pele 18, Gerson 66, Jairzinho 71, Carlos Alberto 87) **Italy 1** (Boninsegna 38). **Att:** 107,412
Brazil: Felix; Carlos Alberto (capt), Brito, Piazza, Everaldo, Clodoaldo, Gerson, Jairzinho, Tostao, Pele, Rivelino
Italy: Albertosi; Burgnich, Facchetti (capt), Cera, Rosato, Bertini (Juliano 72), Domenghini, De Sisti, Mazzola, Boninsegna (Rivera 84), Riva
Referee: Glockner (East Germany). **Half-time:** 1-1

1974 – WEST GERMANY
WINNERS: West Germany RUNNERS-UP: Holland THIRD: Poland FOURTH: Brazil
Other countries in finals: Argentina, Australia, Bulgaria, Chile, East Germany, Haiti, Italy, Scotland, Sweden, Uruguay, Yugoslavia, Zaire. **Total entries:** 98 (16 qualifiers)
Venues: Berlin, Dortmund, Dusseldorf, Frankfurt, Gelsenkirchen, Hamburg, Hanover, Munich, Stuttgart
Top scorer: Lato (Poland) 7 goals
Final (Munich, 7/7/74): **West Germany 2** (Breitner 25 pen, Muller 43) **Holland 1** (Neeskens 2 pen). **Att:** 77,833
West Germany: Maier; Vogts, Schwarzenbeck, Beckenbauer (capt), Breitner, Bonhof, Hoeness, Overath, Grabowski, Muller, Holzenbein
Holland: Jongbloed; Suurbier, Rijsbergen (De Jong 69), Haan, Krol, Jansen, Van Hanegem, Neeskens, Rep, Cruyff (capt), Rensenbrink (R Van der Kerkhof 46)
Referee: Taylor (England). **Half-time:** 2-1

1978 – ARGENTINA
WINNERS: Argentina RUNNERS-UP: Holland THIRD: Brazil FOURTH: Italy
Other countries in finals: Austria, France, Hungary, Iran, Mexico, Peru, Poland, Scotland, Spain, Sweden, Tunisia, West Germany. **Total entries:** 102 (16 qualifiers)
Venues: Buenos Aires, Cordoba, Mar del Plata, Mendoza, Rosario
Top scorer: Kempes (Argentina) 6 goals
Final (Buenos Aires, 25678): **Argentina 3** (Kempes 38, 104, Bertoni 115) **Holland 1** (Nanninga 82) after extra-time. **Att:** 77,000
Argentina: Fillol; Passarella (capt), Olguin, Galvan, Tarantini, Ardiles (Larrosa 66), Gallego, Ortiz (Houseman 74), Bertoni, Luque, Kempes
Holland: Jongbloed; Krol (capt), Poortvliet, Brandts, Jansen (Suurbier 73), Haan, Neeskens, W Van der Kerkhof, Rep (Nanninga 58), R Van der Kerkhof, Rensenbrink
Referee: Gonella (Italy). **Half-time:** 1-0 (90 mins: 1-1)

1982 – SPAIN

WINNERS: Italy RUNNERS-UP: West Germany THIRD: Poland FOURTH: France
Other countries in finals: Algeria, Argentina, Austria, Belgium, Brazil, Cameroon, Chile, Czechoslovakia, El Salvador, England, Honduras, Hungary, Kuwait, New Zealand, Northern Ireland, Peru, Scotland, Soviet Union, Spain, Yugoslavia. **Total entries:** 109 (24 qualifiers)
Venues: Alicante, Barcelona, Bilbao, Coruna, Elche, Gijon, Madrid, Malaga, Oviedo, Seville, Valencia, Valladolid, Vigo, Zaragoza
Top scorer: Rossi (Italy) 6 goals
Final (Madrid, 11/7/82): **Italy** 3 (Rossi 57, Tardelli 69, Altobelli 81) **West Germany** 1 (Breitner 84). **Att:** 90,089
Italy: Zoff (capt); Bergomi, Scirea, Collovati, Cabrini, Oriali, Gentile, Tardelli, Conti, Rossi, Graziani (Altobelli 18 – Causio 88)
West Germany: Schumacher; Kaltz, Stielike, K-H Forster, B Forster, Dremmler (Hrubesch 63), Breitner, Briegel, Rummenigge (capt) (Muller 70), Fischer, Littbarski
Referee: Coelho (Brazil). **Half-time:** 0-0

1986 – MEXICO

WINNERS: Argentina RUNNERS-UP: West Germany THIRD: France FOURTH: Belgium
Other countries in finals: Algeria, Brazil, Bulgaria, Canada, Denmark, England, Hungary, Iraq, Italy, Mexico, Morocco, Northern Ireland, Paraguay, Poland, Portugal, Scotland, South Korea, Soviet Union, Spain, Uruguay. **Total entries:** 118 (24 qualifiers)
Venues: Guadalajara, Irapuato, Leon, Mexico City, Monterrey, Nezahualcoyotl, Puebla, Queretaro, Toluca
Top scorer: Lineker (England) 6 goals
Final (Mexico City, 29/6/86): **Argentina** 3 (Brown 23, Valdano 56, Burruchaga 85) **West Germany** 2 (Rummenigge 74, Voller 82). **Att:** 115,026
Argentina: Pumpido; Cuciuffo, Brown, Ruggeri, Olarticoechea, Batista, Giusti, Maradona (capt), Burruchaga (Trobbiani 89), Enrique, Valdano
West Germany: Schumacher; Berthold, K-H Forster, Jakobs, Brehme, Briegel, Eder, Matthaus, Magath (Hoeness 62), Allofs (Voller 45), Rummenigge (capt)
Referee: Filho (Brazil). **Half-time:** 1-0

1990 – ITALY

WINNERS: West Germany RUNNERS-UP: Argentina THIRD: Italy FOURTH: England
Other countries in finals: Austria, Belgium, Brazil, Cameroon, Colombia, Costa Rica, Czechoslovakia, Egypt, Holland, Republic of Ireland, Romania, Scotland, Spain, South Korea, Soviet Union, Sweden, United Arab Emirates, USA, Uruguay, Yugoslavia. **Total entries:** 103 (24 qualifiers)
Venues: Bari, Bologna, Cagliari, Florence, Genoa, Milan, Naples, Palermo, Rome, Turin, Udine, Verona
Top scorer: Schillaci (Italy) 6 goals
Final (Rome, 8/7/90): **Argentina** 0 **West Germany** 1 (Brehme 85 pen). **Att:** 73,603
Argentina: Goycochea; Ruggeri (Monzon 45), Simon, Serrizuela, Lorenzo, Basualdo, Troglio, Burruchaga (Calderon 53), Sensini, Maradona (capt), Dezotti **Sent-off:** Monzon (65), Dezotti (86) – first players ever to be sent off in World Cup Final
West Germany: Illgner; Berthold (Reuter 75), Buchwald, Augenthaler, Kohler, Brehme, Matthaus (capt), Littbarski, Hassler, Klinsmann, Voller
Referee: Codesal (Mexico). **Half-time:** 0-0

1994 – USA

WINNERS: Brazil RUNNERS-UP: Italy THIRD: Sweden FOURTH: Bulgaria
Other countries in finals: Argentina, Belgium, Bolivia, Cameroon, Colombia, Germany, Greece, Holland, Mexico, Morocco, Nigeria, Norway, Republic of Ireland, Romania, Russia, Saudi Arabia, South Korea, Spain, Switzerland, USA. **Total entries:** 144 (24 qualifiers)

Venues: Boston, Chicago, Dallas, Detroit, Los Angeles, New York City, Orlando, San Francisco, Washington
Top scorers: Salenko (Russia), Stoichkov (Bulgaria), each 6 goals
Final (Los Angeles, 17/7/94): **Brazil 0 Italy 0** after extra-time; Brazil won 3-2 on pens
Att: 94,194
Brazil: Taffarel; Jorginho (Cafu 21) Aldair, Marcio Santos, Branco, Mazinho, Mauro Silva, Dunga (capt), Zinho (Viola 105), Romario, Bebeto
Italy: Pagliuca; Mussi (Apolloni 35), Baresi (capt), Maldini, Benarrivo, Berti, Albertini, D Baggio (Evani 95), Donadoni, R Baggio, Massaro
Referee: Puhl (Hungary)
Shoot-out: Baresi missed, Marco Santos saved, Albertini 1-0, Romario 1-1, Evani 2-1, Branco 2-2, Massaro saved, Dunga 2-3, R Baggio over

1998 – FRANCE
WINNERS: France RUNNERS-UP: Brazil THIRD: Croatia FOURTH: Holland
Other countries in finals: Argentina, Austria, Belgium, Bulgaria, Cameroon, Chile, Colombia, Denmark, England, Germany, Iran, Italy, Jamaica, Japan, Mexico, Morocco, Nigeria, Norway, Paraguay, Romania, Saudi Arabia, Scotland, South Africa, South Korea, Spain, Tunisia, USA, Yugoslavia. **Total entries:** 172 (32 qualifiers)
Venues: Bordeaux, Lens, Lyon, Marseille, Montpellier, Nantes, Paris (St Denis, Parc des Princes), Saint-Etienne, Toulouse
Top scorer: Davor Suker (Croatia) 6 goals
Final (Paris St Denis, 12/7/98): **Brazil 0 France 3** (Zidane 27, 45, Petit 90). **Att:** 75,000
Brazil: Taffarel; Cafu, Junior Baiano, Aldair, Roberto Carlos, Dunga (capt), Leonardo (Denilson 46), Cesar Sampaio (Edmundo 74), Rivaldo; Bebeto, Ronaldo
France: Barthez; Thuram, Leboeuf, Desailly, Lizarazu; Karembeu (Boghossian 56), Deschamps (capt), Petit, Zidane, Djorkaeff (Viera 75); Guivarc'h (Dugarry 66) **Sent-off:** Desailly (68)
Referee: Belqola (Morocco). **Half-time:** 0-2

2002 – JAPAN/SOUTH KOREA
WINNERS: Brazil RUNNERS-UP: Germany THIRD: Turkey FOURTH: South Korea
Other countries in finals: Argentina, Belgium, Cameroon, China, Costa Rica, Croatia, Denmark, Ecuador, England, France, Italy, Japan, Mexico, Nigeria, Paraguay, Poland, Portugal, Republic of Ireland, Russia, Saudi Arabia, Senegal, Slovenia, South Africa, Spain, Sweden, Tunisia, USA, Uruguay. **Total entries:** 195 (32 qualifiers)
Venues: Japan – Ibaraki, Kobe, Miyagi, Niigata, Oita, Osaka, Saitama, Sapporo, Shizuoka, Yokohama. **South Korea** – Daegu, Daejeon, Gwangju, Incheon, Jeonju, Busan, Seogwipo, Seoul, Suwon Ulsan
Top scorer: Ronaldo (Brazil) 8 goals
Final (Yokohama, 30/6/02): **Germany 0, Brazil 2** (Ronaldo 67, 79). **Att:** 69,029
Germany: Kahn (capt), Linke, Ramelow, Metzelder, Frings, Jeremies (Asamoah 77), Hamann, Schneider, Bode (Zeige 84), Klose (Bierhoff 74), Neuville
Brazil: Marcos, Lucio, Edmilson, Roque Junior, Cafu (capt) Kleberson, Gilberto Silva, Roberto Carlos, Ronaldinho (Juninho 85), Rivaldo, Ronaldo (Denilson 90)
Referee: Collina (Italy). **Half-time:** 0-0

2006 – GERMANY
WINNERS: Italy RUNNERS-UP: France THIRD: Germany FOURTH: Portugal
Other countries in finals: Angola, Argentina, Australia, Brazil, Costa Rica, Croatia, Czech Republic, Ecuador, England, Ghana, Holland, Iran, Ivory Coast, Japan, Mexico, Paraguay, Poland, Saudi Arabia, Serbia & Montenegro, South Korea, Spain, Sweden, Switzerland, Trinidad & Tobago, Togo, Tunisia, Ukraine, USA. **Total entries:** 198 (32 qualifiers)
Venues: Berlin, Cologne, Dortmund, Frankfurt, Gelsenkirchen, Hamburg, Hanover, Kaiserslautern, Leipzig, Munich, Nuremberg, Stuttgart

Top scorer: Klose (Germany) 5 goals
Final (Berlin, 9/7/06): **Italy** 1 (Materazzi 19) **France** 1 (Zidane 7 pen) after extra-time: Italy
won 5-3 on pens. **Att:** 69,000
Italy: Buffon; Zambrotta, Cannavaro (capt), Materazzi, Grosso, Perrotta (De Rossi 61), Pirlo,
Gattuso, Camoranesi (Del Piero 86), Totti (Iaquinta 61), Toni
France: Barthez; Sagnol, Thuram, Gallas, Abidal, Makelele, Vieira (Diarra 56), Ribery
(Trezeguet 100), Malouda, Zidane (capt), Henry (Wiltord 107) **Sent-off:** Zidane (110)
Referee: Elizondo (Argentina). **Half-time:** 1-1 90 mins: 1-1
Shoot-out: Pirlo 1-0, Wiltord 1-1, Materazzi 2-1, Trezeguet missed, De Rossi 3-1, Abidal 3-2,
Del Piero 4-2, Sagnol 4-3, Grosso 5-3

2010 – SOUTH AFRICA

WINNERS: Spain **RUNNERS-UP:** Holland **THIRD:** Germany **FOURTH:** Uruguay
Other countries in finals: Algeria, Argentina, Australia, Brazil, Cameroon, Chile, Denmark,
England, France, Ghana, Greece, Honduras, Italy, Ivory Coast, Japan, Mexico, New Zealand,
Nigeria, North Korea, Paraguay, Portugal, Serbia, Slovakia, Slovenia, South Africa, South
Korea, Switzerland, USA. **Total entries:** 204 (32 qualifiers)
Venues: Bloemfontein, Cape Town, Durban, Johannesburg (Ellis Park), Johannesburg (Soccer
City), Nelspruit, Polokwane, Port Elizabeth, Pretoria, Rustenburg
Top scorers: Forlan (Uruguay), Muller (Germany), Sneijder (Holland), Villa (Spain) 5 goals
Final (Johannesburg, Soccer City, 11/7/10): **Holland** 0 **Spain** 1 (Iniesta 116) after extra-time;
Att: 84,490
Holland: Stekelenburg, Van der Wiel, Heitinga, Mathijsen, Van Bronckhorst (capt) (Braafheid
105), Van Bommel, De Jong (Van der Vaart 99), Robben, Sneijder, Kuyt (Elia 71), Van Persie.
Sent off: Heitinga (109)
Spain: Casillas (capt), Sergio Ramos, Puyol, Piquet, Capdevila, Busquets, Xabi Alonso
(Fabregas 87), Iniesta, Xavi, Pedro (Jesus Navas 60), Villa (Torres 106)
Referee: H Webb (England). **Half-time:** 0-0

QUOTE/UNQOUTE

'I was cringing with the coverage and some of the stuff that was written – totally embarrassed.
So I stopped reading the papers and turned off the television' – **Phil Neville**, Everton stalwart,
after winning praise for containing Tottenham's in-form Gareth Bale.

'Harry Redknapp and England sounds right to me' – **Owen Coyle**, Bolton manager, on his choice
to succeed Fabio Capello.

'It went horribly wrong' – **Mark McGhee**, Aberdeen manager, after a record 9-0 Scottish Premier
League defeat by Celtic.

'I gave him four days off last week because he'd been working so hard. I told him to go abroad
for a few days. He went to Cardiff to stay at his Mum's' – **Harry Redknapp**, Tottenham manager,
on star winger Gareth Bale.

'We'll have boosted the local licensing trade tonight. I'll probably do it myself as well' –
Brendan Rogers, Swansea manager, after his side's win over Cardiff.

UEFA CHAMPIONS LEAGUE 2010–11

FIRST QUALIFYING ROUND, ON AGGREGATE

Birkirkara 7 Santa Coloma 3; Rudar 7 Tre Fiori 1

SECOND QUALIFYING ROUND, FIRST LEG

Bohemians 1 (Brennan 66) **New Saints** 0. Att: 2,500; **Linfield** 0 Rosenborg 0. Att: 2,800

SECOND QUALIFYING ROUND, SECOND LEG

New Saints 4 (Jones 6, M Williams 14, 73, Sharp 20) **Bohemians** 0. Att: 1,056 (**New Saints** won 4-1 on agg). Rosenborg 2 (Prica 32, Henriksen 86) **Linfield** 0. Att: 4,000 (Rosenborg won 2-0 on agg)

SECOND QUALIFYING ROUND, ON AGGREGATE

AIK Solna 1 Jeunesse Esch 0; Aktobe 3 Olimpi Rustavi 1; Bate Borisov 6 Hafnarfjordur 1; Debrecen 4 Levadia 3; Dinamo Zagreb 5 Koper 4; HJK Helsinki 2 Ekranas 1 (aet); Lech Poznan 1 Inter Baki 1 (aet, Lech Poznan won 9-8 on pens); Litex Lovech 5 Rudar 0; Omonia Nicosia 5 Renova 0; Partizan 4 Pyunik 1; Red Bull Salzburg 5 Torshavn 1; Sheriff Tiraspol 3 Dinamo Tirana 2; Sparta Prague 5 Liepajas Metalurgs 0; Hapoel Tel-Aviv 6 Zeljeznicar 0; Zilina 3 Birkirkara 1

THIRD QUALIFYING ROUND, FIRST LEG

Braga 3 (Alan 26 pen, Echiejile 76, Matheus 89) **Celtic** 0. Att: 12,295. **New Saints** 1 (Jones 52) Anderlecht 3 (Kljestan 7, Legear 18, Suarez 73). Att: 2,486 (played at Wrexham)

THIRD QUALIFYING ROUND, SECOND LEG

Anderlecht 3 (De Sutter 17, Lukaku 69, 74) **New Saints** 0. Att: 21,000 (Anderlecht won 6-1 on agg). **Celtic** 2 (Hooper 51, Juarez 78) Braga 1 (Paulo Cesar 20). Att: 52,000 (Braga won 4-2 on agg)

THIRD QUALIFYING ROUND , ON AGGREGATE

Ajax 4 PAOK Salonika 4 (Ajax won on away goals); Basle 5 Debrecen 1; Copenhagen 3 Bate Borisov 2; Dynamo Kiev 6 Gent 1; Hapoel Tel-Aviv 3 Aktobe 2; Partizan 5 HJK Helsinki 1; Red Bull Salzburg 5 Omonia Nicosia 2; Rosenborg 4 AIK Solna 0; Sheriff Tiraspol 2 Dinamo Zagreb 2 (aet, Sheriff Tiraspol won 6-5 on pens); Sparta Prague 2 Lech Poznan 0; Young Boys 3 Fenerbahce 2; Zenit St Petersburg 1 Unirea Urziceni 0; Zilina 4 Litex Lovech 2

PLAY-OFFS, FIRST LEG

Young Boys 3 (Lulic 4, Bienvenu 13, Hochstrasse 28) **Tottenham** 2 (Bassong 42, Pavlyuchenko 83). Att: 31,275

PLAY-OFFS, SECOND LEG

Tottenham 4 (Crouch 5, 61, 78 pen, Defoe 32) Young Boys 0. Att: 34,709 (**Tottenham** won 6-3 on agg)

PLAY-OFFS, ON AGGREGATE

Ajax 3 Dynamo Kiev 2; Auxerre 2 Zenit St Petersburg 1; Basle 4 Sheriff Tiraspol 0; Braga 5

Sevilla 3; Copenhagen 2 Rosenborg 2 (Copenhagen won on away goal); Hapoel Tel-Aviv 4 Red Bull Salzburg 3; Partizan 4 Anderlecht 4 (aet, Partizan won 3-2 on pens); Werder Bremen 5 Sampdoria 4 (aet); Zilina 3 Sparta Prague 0

GROUP A

September 14, 2010

Twente 2 (Janssen 20, Milito 31 og) **Inter Milan** 2 (Sneijder 13, Eto'o 41). Att: 23,800

Werder Bremen 2 (Hugo Almeida 43, Marin 47) **Tottenham** 2 (Pasanen 12 og, Crouch 18). Att: 30,344

Tottenham (4-4-1-1): Cudicini, Corluka, Kaboul, King, Assou-Ekotto, Lennon (Palacios 75), Huddlestone, Jenas, Bale, Van der Vaart (Keane 49), Crouch. Booked: Huddlestone, Jenas

September 29, 2010

Inter Milan 4 (Eto'o 21, 27, 81, Sneijder 34) **Werder Bremen** 0. Att: 76,392

Tottenham 4 (Van der Vaart 47, Pavlyuchenko 50 pen, 64 pen, Bale 85) **Twente** 1 (Chadli 56). Att: 32,518

Tottenham (4-4-2): Gomes, Hutton, King, Bassong, Assou-Ekotto, Van der Vaart, Huddlestone, Modric (Lennon 81), Bale, Crouch (Jenas 65), Pavlyuchenko (Keane 88). Booked: Van der Vaart. Sent off: Van der Vaart

October 20, 2010

Inter Milan 4 (Zanetti 2, Eto'o 11 pen, 35, Stankovic 14) **Tottenham** 3 (Bale, 52, 90, 90). Att: 70,520

Tottenham (4-4-1-1): Gomes, Hutton, Gallas, Bassong, Assou-Ekotto, Lennon, Jenas, Huddlestone (Palacios 80), Bale, Modric (Cudicini 9), Crouch (Keane 67). Booked: Palacios. Sent off: Gomes

Twente 1 (Janssen 75) **Werder Bremen** 1 (Arnautovic 80). Att: 23,269

November 2, 2010

Tottenham 3 (Van der Vaart 18, Crouch 61, Pavlyuchenko 89) **Inter Milan** 1 (Eto'o 80). Att: 36,310

Tottenham (4-4-1-1): Cudicini, Hutton, Gallas, Kaboul, Assou-Ekotto, Lennon (Palacios 84), Huddlestone, Modric, Bale, Van der Vaart (Jenas 46), Crouch (Pavlyuchenko 75). Booked: Hutton, Jenas, Modric

Werder Bremen 0 **Twente** 2 (Chadli 81, De Jong 84). Att: 30,200

November 24, 2010

Inter Milan 1 (Cambiasso 55) **Twente** 0. Att: 29,466

Tottenham 3 (Kaboul 6, Modric 45, Crouch 79) **Werder Bremen** 0. Att: 33,546

Tottenham (4-4-2): Gomes, Hutton, Gallas, Kaboul, Assou-Ekotto, Lennon, Jenas (Palacios 19), Modric, Bale (Kranjcar 80), Crouch, Pavlyuchenko (Defoe 62)

December 7 2010

Twente 3 (Landzaat 22 pen, Rosales 56, Chadli 64) **Tottenham** 3 (Wisgerhof 12 og, Defoe 47, 60). Att: 24,000

Tottenham (4-4-1-1): Gomes, Corluka, Gallas, Bassong, Assou-Ekotto, Kranjcar (Crouch 86), Palacios, Jenas (Lennon 34), Bale, Pavlyuchenko (Keane 73), Defoe. Booked: Jenas

Werder Bremen 3 (Prodl 39, Arnautovic 49, Pizarro 88) **Inter Milan** 0. Att: 30,400

FINAL TABLE

	P	W	D	L	F	A	Pts
Tottenham Q	6	3	2	1	18	11	11
Inter Milan Q	6	3	1	2	12	11	10
Twente	6	1	3	2	9	11	6
Werder Bremen	6	1	2	3	6	12	5

GROUP B

September 14, 2010
Benfica 2 (Luisao 21, Cardozo 69) **Hapoel Tel-Aviv** 0. Att: 35,125
Lyon 1 (Howedes 21 og) **Schalke** 0. Att: 35,552

September 29, 2010
Hapoel Tel-Aviv 1 (Enyeama 79 pen) **Lyon** 3 (Michel Bastos 7 pen, 36, Pjanic 90). Att: 12,226
Schalke 2 (Farfan 73, Huntelaar 85) **Benfica** 0. Att: 50,436

October 20, 2010
Lyon 2 (Briand 21, Lopez 51) **Benfica** 0. Att: 36,816
Schalke 3 (Raul 3, 58, Jurado 68) **Hapoel Tel-Aviv** 1 (Shechter 90). Att: 51,230

November 2, 2010
Benfica 4 (Kardec 20, Fabio Coentrao 31, 67, Garcia 43) **Lyon** 3 (Gourcuff 75, Gomis 85, Lovren 90). Att: 37,394
Hapoel Tel-Aviv 0 **Schalke** 0. Att: 12,132

November 24, 2010
Hapoel Tel-Aviv 3 (Zahavi 24, 90, Douglas 74) **Benfica** 0. Att: 11,668
Schalke 3 (Farfan 13, Huntelaar 20, 89) **Lyon** 0. Att: 51,132

December 7 2010
Benfica 1 (Luisao 87) **Schalke** 2 (Jurado 19, Howedes 81). Att: 23,348
Lyon 2 (Lopez 61, Lacazette 87) **Hapoel Tel-Aviv** 2 (Sahar 62, Zahavi 68). Att: 32,245

FINAL TABLE

	P	W	D	L	F	A	Pts
Schalke Q	6	4	1	1	10	3	13
Lyon Q	6	3	1	2	11	10	10
Benfica	6	2	0	4	7	12	6
Hapoel Tel-Aviv	6	1	2	3	7	10	5

GROUP C

September 14, 2010
Bursaspor 0 **Valencia** 4 (Costa 16, Aduriz 41, Pablo 68, Soldado 76). Att: 20,300
Manchester Utd 0 **Rangers** 0. Att: 74,408
Manchester Utd (4-4-2): Kuszczak, Brown, Ferdinand, Smalling, Fabio (J Evans 75), Valencia (Giggs 63), Fletcher , Gibson, Park (Owen 75), Hernandez, Rooney. Booked: Giggs
Rangers (5-4-1): McGregor, Broadfoot, Weir, Bougherra, Papac, Whittaker, Davis, McCulloch, Edu, Naismith, Miller (Lafferty 81). Booked: McGregor, McCulloch

September 29, 2010
Rangers 1 (Naismith 18) **Bursaspor** 0. Att: 41,905
Rangers (5-4-1): McGregor, Broadfoot, Weir, Bougherra, Papac,Whittaker, Davis, McCulloch, Edu, Naismith,Miller (Lafferty 87). Booked: Papac
Valencia 0 **Manchester Utd** 1 (Hernandez 85). Att: 34,946
Manchester Utd (4-5-1): Van der Sar, Rafael (O'Shea 90), Ferdinand, Vidic, Evra, Park, Fletcher, Carrick, Anderson (Hernandez 77), Nani, Berbatov (Macheda 85)

October 20, 2010
Manchester Utd 1 (Nani 7) **Bursaspor** 0. Att: 72,610
Manchester Utd (4-3-3): Kuszczak, Rafael, Smalling, Vidic, Evra, Fletcher, Carrick, Anderson (Hernandez 77), Nani, Macheda, Park (Obertan 71). Booked: Nani
Rangers 1 (Edu 34) **Valencia** 1 (Edu 46 og). Att: 45,153
Rangers (5-4-1)): McGregor, Foster, Weir, Bougherra, Papac, Whittaker, Naismith, Davis, Edu, Weiss (Lafferty 88), Miller. Booked: Bougherra, Edu, Weir

November 2, 2010
Bursaspor 0 **Manchester Utd** 3 (Fletcher 48, Obertan 73, Bebe 77). Att: 19,050
Manchester Utd (4-2-3-1): Van der Sar, Rafael, Smalling, Vidic, Evra (Fabio 80), Carrick, Scholes, Nani (Park 29), Fletcher (Bebe 62), Obertan, Berbatov
Valencia 3 (Soldado 34, 71, Costa 90) **Rangers** 0. Att: 26,821
Rangers (5-4-1): McGregor, Broadfoot, Weir, Bougherra, Papac, Whittaker, McCulloch, Davis, Edu (Lafferty 84), Naismith, Miller

November 24, 2010
Rangers 0 **Manchester Utd** 1 (Rooney 87 pen). Att: 49,764
Rangers (5-1-3-1): McGregor, Davis, Whittaker, Broadfoot, Weir, Foster, Naismith, McCulloch, Hutton (Beattie 88), Weiss (Fleck 79), Miller. Booked: Hutton, Naismith, Whittaker
Manchester Utd (4-4-2): Van der Sar, O'Shea, Smalling, J Evans, Fabio, Nani (Obertan 77), Carrick, Scholes (Anderson 67), Giggs, Berbatov (Hernandez 77), Rooney
Valencia 6 (Mata 17 pen, Soldado 21, 55, Aduriz 30, Joaquin 37, Dominguez 78) **Bursaspor** 1 (Batalla 69). Att: 31,225

December 7 2010
Bursaspor 1 (Yildirim 79) **Rangers** 1 (Miller 19). Att: 9,673
Rangers (5-4-1): McGregor, Cole (McMillan 82), Bougherra, Weir, Whittaker, Foster, Davis, McCulloch, Hutton, Naismith (Weiss 71), Miller (Beattie 63). Booked: Beattie.
Manchester Utd 1 (Anderson 62) **Valencia** 1 (Pablo 32). Att: 74,513
Manchester Utd (4-4-2): Amos, Rafael, Ferdinand (Smalling 50), Vidic, Fabio, Nani (Giggs 81), Carrick, Anderson (Fletcher 89), Park, Berbatov, Rooney. Booked: Anderson

FINAL TABLE

	P	W	D	L	F	A	Pts
Manchester Utd Q	6	4	2	0	7	1	14
Valencia Q	6	3	2	1	15	4	11
Rangers	6	1	3	2	3	6	6
Bursaspor	6	0	1	5	2	16	1

GROUP D

September 14, 2010
Barcelona 5 (Messi 22, 45, Villa 33, Pedro 78, Dani Alves 90) **Panathinaikos** 1 (Govou 20). Att: 69,738
Copenhagen 1 (Ndoye 87) **Rubin Kazan** 0. Att: 29,661

September 29, 2010
Panathinaikos 0 **Copenhagen** 2 (Ndoye 28, Vingaard 37). Att: 43,607
Rubin Kazan 1 (Noboa 30 pen) **Barcelona** 1 (Villa 60 pen). Att: 23,950

October 20, 2010
Barcelona 2 (Messi 19, 90) **Copenhagen** 0. Att: 75,852
Panathinaikos 0 **Rubin Kazan** 0. Att: 36,748

November 2, 2010
Copenhagen 1 (Claudemir 33) **Barcelona** 1 (Messi 31). Att: 37,049
Rubin Kazan 0 **Panathinaikos** 0. Att: 16,400

November 24, 2010
Panathinaikos 0 **Barcelona** 3 (Pedro 27, 69, Messi 62). Att: 58,466
Rubin Kazan 1 (Noboa 45 pen) **Copenhagen** 0. Att: 18,517

December 7, 2010
Barcelona 2 (Fontas 51, Vazquez 82) **Rubin Kazan** 0. Att: 50,436
Copenhagen 3 (Vingaard 26, Gronkjaer 50 pen, Cisse 73 og) **Panathinaikos** 1 (Kante 90). Att: 36,797

FINAL TABLE

	P	W	D	L	F	A	Pts
Barcelona Q	6	4	2	0	14	3	14
Copenhagen Q	6	3	1	2	7	5	10
Rubin Kazan	6	1	3	2	2	4	6
Panathinaikos	6	0	2	4	2	13	2

GROUP E

September 15, 2010
Bayern Munich 2 (Muller 78, Klose 83) **Roma** 0. Att: 67,253
Cluj-Napoca 2 (Rada 9, Traore 12) **Basle** 1 (Stocker 45). Att: 9,593

September 28, 2010
Basle 1 (Frei 17) **Bayern Munich** 2 (Schweinsteiger 56 pen, 89). Att: 37,500
Roma 2 (Mexes 69, Borriello 71) **Cluj-Napoca** 1 (Rada 78). Att: 30,252

October 19, 2010
Bayern Munich 3 (Cadu 32 og, Panin 38 og, Gomez 77) **Cluj-Napoca** 2 (Cadu 28, Culio 86). Att: 64,000
Roma 1 (Borriello 21) **Basle** 3 (Frei 12, Inkoom 44, Cabral 90). Att: 22,365

November 3, 2010
Basle 2 (Frei 69, Shaqiri 83) **Roma** 3 (Menez 16, Totti 26 pen, Greco 76). Att: 36,375
Cluj-Napoca 0 **Bayern Munich** 4 (Gomez 12, 24, 70, Muller 90). Att: 14,097

November 23, 2010
Basle 1 (Almerares 15) **Cluj-Napoca** 0. Att: 34,239
Roma 3 (Borriello 49, De Rossi 81, Totti 84 pen) **Bayern Munich** 2 (Gomez 33, 39). Att: 42,789

December 8, 2010
Bayern Munich 3 (Ribery 35, 49, Tymoschuk 37) **Basle** 0. Att: 63,493
Cluj-Napoca 1 (Traore 88) **Roma** 1 (Borriello 21). Att: 20,754

FINAL TABLE

	P	W	D	L	F	A	Pts
Bayern Munich Q	6	5	0	1	16	6	15
Roma Q	6	3	1	2	10	11	10
Basle	6	2	0	4	8	11	6
Cluj-Napoca	6	1	1	4	6	12	4

GROUP F

September 15, 2010
Marseille 0 **Spartak Moscow** 1 (Azpilicueta 81 og). Att:45,729
Zilina 1 (Oravec 55) **Chelsea** 4 (Essien 13, Anelka 24, 28, Sturridge 48). Att: 10,829
Chelsea (4-3-2-1): Cech, Ivanovic, Alex, Terry, Zhirkov, Essien, Mikel, Benayoun (McEachran 79), Sturridge (Kakuta 61), Malouda (Van Aanholt 88), Anelka

September 28, 2010
Chelsea 2 (Terry 7, Anelka 28 pen) **Marseille** 0. Att: 40,675
Chelsea (4-3-3): Cech, Ivanovic, Alex, Terry, Cole, Essien, Mikel (McEachran 88), Zhirkov (Sturridge 73), Kakuta (Ramires 61), Anelka, Malouda. Booked: Mikel
Spartak Moscow 3 (Ari 34, 61, Ibson 89) **Zilina** 0. Att: 33,124

October 19, 2010
Marseille 1 (Diawara 48) **Zilina** 0. Att: 49,250
Spartak Moscow 0 **Chelsea** 2 (Zhirkov 23, Anelka 43). Att: 75,000
Chelsea (4-3-2-1): Cech, Paulo Ferreira, Ivanovic, Terry, Cole (Van Aanholt 87), Essien, Mikel, Zhirkov, Kalou (McEachran 74), Malouda (Kakuta 82), Anelka. Booked: Zhirkov

November 3, 2010
Chelsea 4 (Anelka 49, Drogba 62 pen, Ivanovic 66, 90) **Spartak Moscow** 1 (Bazhenov 86). Att: 40,477
Chelsea (4-3-3): Cech, Paulo Ferreira, Ivanovic, Alex, Cole, Ramires, Mikel (McEachran 68), Zhirkov, Kalou, Drogba (Sturridge 75), Anelka (Kakuta 75). Booked: Mikel
Zilina 0 **Marseille** 7 (Gignac 12, 21, 54, Heinze 24, Remy 36, Gonzalez 51, 63). Att: 9,664

November 23, 2010
Chelsea 2 (Sturridge 51, Malouda 86) **Zilina** 1 (Babatounde 19). Att: 40,266
Chelsea (4-3-3): Turnbull, Paulo Ferreira, Bruma, Ivanovic, Van Aanholt, Ramires, McEachran (Mellis 90), Malouda, Kakuta (Kalou 46), Drogba, Sturridge (Anelka 74). Booked: Ramires
Spartak Moscow 0 **Marseille** 3 (Valbuena 18, Remy 54, Brandao 68). Att: 43,217

December 8, 2010
Marseille 1 (Brandao 81) **Chelsea** 0. Att: 57,650.
Chelsea (4-3-2-1): Cech, Bosingwa (Van Aanholt 79), Ivanovic, Terry (Bruma 72), Paulo Ferreira, Essien, McEachran, Ramires, Kalou, Malouda, Drogba (Sturridge 62)
Zilina 1 (Majtan 48) **Spartak Moscow** 2 (Alex 54, Ibson 61). Att: 7,208

FINAL TABLE

	P	W	D	L	F	A	Pts
Chelsea Q	6	5	0	1	14	4	15
Marseille Q	6	4	0	2	12	3	12
Spartak Moscow	6	3	0	3	7	10	9
Zilina	6	0	0	6	3	19	0

GROUP G

September 15, 2010
AC Milan 2 (Ibrahimovic 66, 69) **Auxerre** 0. Att: 69,317
Real Madrid 2 (Higuain 31, 73) **Ajax** 0. Att: 69,639

September 28, 2010
Ajax 1 (El Hamdaoui 23) **AC Milan** 1 (Ibrahimovic 37). Att: 51,276
Auxerre 0 **Real Madrid** 1 (Di Maria 81). Att: 19,525

October 19, 2010
Ajax 2 (De Zeeuw 7, Suarez 41) **Auxerre** 1 (Birsa 57). Att: 51,383
Real Madrid 2 (Ronaldo 13, Ozil 14) AC Milan O. Att: 71,657

November 3, 2010
AC Milan 2 (Inzaghi 68, 78) **Real Madrid** 2 (Higuain 45, Pedro Leon 90). Att: 76,357
Auxerre 2 (Sammaritano 9, Langil 84) **Ajax** 1 (Alderweireld 80). Att: 18,727

November 23, 2010
Ajax O **Real Madrid** 4 (Benzema 36, Arbeloa 44, Ronaldo 70, 81 pen). Att: 48,491
Auxerre O **AC Milan** 2 (Ibrahimovic 65, Ronaldinho 90). Att: 19,244

December 8, 2010
AC Milan O **Ajax** 2 (De Zeeuw 57, Alderweireld 66). Att: 53,484
Real Madrid 4 (Benzema 11, 72, 88, Ronaldo 49) Auxerre O. Att: 58,932

FINAL TABLE

	P	W	D	L	F	A	Pts
Real Madrid Q	6	5	1	0	15	2	16
AC Milan Q	6	2	2	2	7	7	8
Ajax	6	2	1	3	6	10	7
Auxerre	6	1	0	5	3	12	3

GROUP H

September 15, 2010
Arsenal 6 (Fabregas 9 pen, 53, Arshavin 30, Chamakh 34, Vela 69, 84) Braga O. Att: 59,333
Arsenal (4-2-3-1): Amunia, Sagna, Squillaci, Koscielney, Clichy, Song (Denilson 63), Wilshere, Nasri, Fabregas, Arshavin (Eboue 68), Chamakh (Vela 63). Booked: Sagna
Shakhtar Donetsk 1 (Srna 71) **Partizan** O. Att: 48,512

September 28, 2010
Braga O **Shakhtar Donetsk** 3 (Luiz Adriano 56, 72, Costa 90 pen). Att: 12,083
Partizan 1 (Cleo 33 pen) **Arsenal** 3 (Arshavin 5, Chamakh 71, Squillaci 82). Att: 29,348
Arsenal (4-2-3-1): Fabianski, Sagna, Squillaci, Djourou, Gibbs, Denilson, Song, Rosicky, Wilshere (Nasri 73), Arshavin (Clichy 84), Chamakh (Vela 73)

October 19, 2010
Arsenal 5 (Song 19, Nasri 42, Fabregas 60 pen, Wilshere 66, Chamakh 69) **Shakhtar Donetsk** 1 (Eduardo 82). Att: 60,016
Arsenal (4-2-3-1): Fabianski, Eboue, Squillaci, Djourou, Clichy, Song, Wilshere, Rosicky, Fabregas (Denilson 63), Nasri (Arshavin 72), Chamakh (Walcott 72).
Braga 2 (Lima 35, Matheus 90) **Partizan** O. Att: 11,454

November 3, 2010
Partizan O **Braga** 1 (Moises 35). Att: 28.295
Shakhtar Donetsk 2 (Eastmond 28 og, Eduardo 45) **Arsenal** 1 (Walcott 10). Att: 51,153
Arsenal (4-2-3-1): Fabianski, Eboue, Squillaci, Djourou, Clichy, Eastmond (Vela 59), Wilshere, Walcott (Emmanuel-Thomas 82), Nasri, Rosicky, Bendtner (Chamakh 73). Booked: Eboue

November 23, 2010
Braga 2 (Matheus 83, 90) **Arsenal** O. Att: 14,809
Arsenal (4-2-3-1): Fabianski, Eboue, Squillaci, Djourou, Gibbs, Denilson, Wilshere, Walcott (Vela 76), Fabregas (Nasri 69), Rosicky, Bendtner. Booked: Eboue, Denilson, Djourou, Vela, Rosicky

Partizan 0 **Shakhtar Donetsk** 3 (Stepanenko 52, Jadson 59, Eduardo 68). Att: 17,473

December 8, 2010
Arsenal 3 (Van Persie 30 pen, Walcott 73, Nasri 77) **Partizan** 1 (Cleo 52). Att: 58,845
Arsenal (4-2-3-1): Fabianski, Sagna, Squillaci, Koscielny, Gibbs (Eboue 23), Song, Denilson, Nasri, Van Persie, Arshavin (Walcott 67), Chamakh (Bendtner 76). Sent off: Sagna
Shakhtar Donetsk 2 (Rat 78, Luiz Adriano 83) **Braga** 0. Att: 47,627

FINAL TABLE

		P	W	D	L	F	A	Pts
Shakhtar Donetsk	Q	6	5	0	1	12	6	15
Arsenal	Q	6	4	0	2	18	7	12
Braga		6	3	0	3	5	11	9
Partizan		6	0	0	6	2	13	0

FIRST KNOCK-OUT ROUND, FIRST LEG

February 15, 2011
AC Milan 0 **Tottenham** 1 (Crouch 80). Att: 75,652
Tottenham (4-4-1-1): Gomes, Corluka (Woodgate 59), Gallas, Dawson, Assou-Ekotto, Lennon, Palacios, Sandro, Pienaar (Kranjcar 76), Van der Vaart (Modric 62), Crouch
Valencia 1 (Soldado 17) **Schalke** 1 (Raul 63). Att: 42,703

February 16, 2011
Arsenal 2 (Van Persie 78, Arshavin 83) **Barcelona** 1 (Villa 26). Att: 59,927
Arsenal (4-2-3-1): Szczesny, Eboue, Djourou, Koscielny, Clichy, Song (Arshavin 68), Wilshere, Walcott (Bendtner 77), Fabregas, Nasri, Van Persie. Booked: Nasri, Song, Van Persie
Roma 2 (Perrotta 28, Menez 61) **Shakhtar Donetsk** 3 (Jadson 29, Costa 36, Luiz Adriano 41). Att: 39,876

February 22, 2011
Copenhagen 0 **Chelsea** 2 (Anelka 17, 54). Att: 36,713
Chelsea (4-4-2): Cech, Bosingwa, Ivanovic, Terry, Cole, Ramires, Essien, Lampard, Malouda (Zhirkov 84), Anelka (Drogba 63), Torres (Kalou 90). Booked: Torres, Malouda, Terry
Lyon 1 (Gomis 83) **Real Madrid** 1 (Benzema 65). Att: 40,299

February 23, 2011
Inter Milan 0 **Bayern Munich** 1 (Gomez 90). Att: 71,462
Marseille 0 **Manchester Utd** 0. Att: 57,597
Manchester Utd (4-5-1): Van der Sar, O'Shea, Smalling, Vidic, Evra, Nani, Fletcher, Gibson (Scholes 72), Carrick, Rooney, Berbatov

FIRST KNOCK-OUT ROUND, SECOND LEG

March 8, 2011
Barcelona 3 (Messi 45, 71 pen, Xavi 69) **Arsenal** 1 (Busquets 53 og). Att: 95,486 (**Barcelona** won 4-3 on agg)
Arsenal (4-2-3-1): Szczesny (Almunia 19), Sagna, Djourou, Koscielny, Clichy, Wilshere, Diaby, Rosicky (Arshavin 74), Fabregas (Bendtner 78), Nasri, Van Persie. Booked: Koscielny, Sagna, Wilshere, Van Persie. Sent off: Van Persie
Shakhtar Donetsk 3 (Hubschman 18, Willian 58, Eduardo 87) **Roma** 0. Att: 46,543 (**Shakhtar Donetsk** won 6-2 on agg)

March 9, 2011
Schalke 3 (Farfan 40, 90, Gavranovic 52) **Valencia** 1 (Costa 17). Att: 53,517 (Schalke won 4-2 on agg)

Tottenham 0 **AC Milan** 0. Att: 34,320 (**Tottenham** won 1-0 on agg)
Tottenham (4-4-1-1): Gomes, Corluka, Gallas, Dawson, Assou-Ekotto, Lennon, Sandro, Modric, Pienaar (Jenas 70), Van der Vaart (Bale 66), Crouch (Pavlyuchenko 82)

March 15, 2011
Bayern Munich 2 (Gomez 21, Muller 31) **Inter Milan** 3 (Eto'o 3, Sneijder 63, Pandev 88). Att: 69,000 (Agg 3-3, **Inter Milan** won on away goals).
Manchester Utd 2 (Hernandez 5, 75) **Marseille** 1 (Brown 83 og). Att: 73,996 (**Manchester Utd** won 2-1 on agg)
Manchester Utd (4-4-2): Van der Sar, O'Shea (Rafael 36) (Fabio 70), Smalling, Brown, Evra, Nani (Valencia 62), Carrick, Scholes, Giggs, Rooney, Hernandez. Booked: Hernandez

March 16, 2011
Chelsea 0 **Copenhagen** 0. Att: 36,454 (**Chelsea** won 2-0 on agg)
Chelsea (4-4-2): Cech, Bosingwa, Ivanovic, Terry, Cole, Ramires, Lampard, Mikel (Essien 84), Zhirkov (Malouda 76), Drogba, Anelka (Torres 68). Booked: Drogba
Real Madrid 3 (Marcelo 37, Benzema 66, Di Maria 76) **Lyon** 0. Att: 76,489 (**Real Madrid** won 4-1 on agg)

QUARTER-FINALS, FIRST LEG

April 5, 2011
Inter Milan 2 (Stankovic 1, Milito 33) **Schalke** 5 (Matip 17, Edu 40, 75, Raul 53, Ranocchia 58 og). Att: 72,770
Real Madrid 4 (Adebayor 5, 57, Di Maria 72, Ronaldo 87) **Tottenham** 0. Att: 71,657
Tottenham (4-4-1-1): Gomes, Corluka (Bassong 80), Gallas, Dawson, Assou-Ekotto, Jenas, Sandro, Modric, Bale, Van der Vaart (Defoe 46), Crouch. Booked: Crouch, Van der Vaart, Defoe. Sent off: Crouch

April 6, 2011
Barcelona 5 (Iniesta 2, Dani Alves 34, Pique 53, Keita 60, Xavi 86) **Shakhtar Donetsk** 1 (Rakitskiy 59). Att: 86,847
Chelsea 0 **Manchester Utd** 1 (Rooney 24). Att: 37,915
Chelsea (4-4-2): Cech, Bosingwa (Mikel 78), Ivanovic, Terry, Cole, Ramires, Essien, Lampard, Zhirkov (Malouda 70), Drogba (Anelka 71), Torres. Booked: Zhirkov, Ramires, Essien, Torres
Manchester Utd (4-4-2): Van der Sar, Rafael (Nani 51), Ferdinand, Vidic, Evra, Valencia, Carrick, Park (Smalling 90), Giggs, Rooney, Hernandez (Berbatov 78). Booked: Vidic, Van der Sar

QUARTER-FINALS, SECOND LEG

April 12, 2011
Manchester Utd 2 (Hernandez 43, Park 77) **Chelsea** 1 (Drogba 77). Att: 74,672 (**Manchester Utd** won 3-1 on agg)
Manchester Utd (4-4-2): Van der Sar, O'Shea, Ferdinand, Vidic, Evra, Nani (Valencia 75), Carrick, Giggs, Park, Rooney, Hernandez. Booked: O'Shea, Evra.
Chelsea (4-4-2): Cech, Ivanovic, Alex (Paulo Ferreira 82), Terry, Cole, Essien, Ramires, Lampard, Malouda, Torres (Drogba 45), Anelka (Kalou 60). Booked: Ramires, Malouda, Terry. Sent off: Ramires
Shakhtar Donetsk 0 **Barcelona** 1 (Messi 43). Att: 57,759 (**Barcelona** won 6-1 on agg)

April 13, 2011
Schalke 2 (Raul 45, Howedes 81) **Inter Milan** 1 (Motta 50). Att: 51,759 (Schalke won 7-3 on agg)
Tottenham 0 **Real Madrid** 1 (Ronaldo 50). Att: 34,326 (Real Madrid won 5-0 on agg)

Tottenham (4-4-1-1): Gomes, Corluka, Gallas, Dawson, Assou-Ekotto, Lennon (Defoe 61), Huddlestone (Sandro 71), Modric (Kranjcar 83), Bale, Van der Vaart, Pavlyuchenko

SEMI-FINALS, FIRST LEG

April 26, 2011
Schalke 0 Manchester Utd 2 (Giggs 67, Rooney 69). Att: 54,142
Manchester Utd (4-4-1-1): Van der Sar, Fabio, Ferdinand, Vidic, Evra, Valencia, Carrick, Giggs, Park (Scholes 73), Rooney (Nani 83), Hernandez (Anderson 73). Booked: Fabio

April 27, 2011
Real Madrid 0 Barcelona 2 (Messi 76, 87). Att: 71,567

SEMI-FINALS, SECOND LEG

May 3, 2011
Barcelona 1 (Pedro 54) **Real Madrid** 1 (Marcelo 64). Att: 95,701 (**Barcelona** won 3-1 on agg)

May 4, 2011
Manchester Utd 4 (Valencia 26, Gibson 31, Anderson 72, 76) **Schalke** 1 (Jurado 35). Att: 74,687 (**Manchester Utd** won 6-1 on agg)
Manchester Utd (4-4-1-1): Van der Sar, Rafael (Evra 60), Smalling, J Evans, O'Shea, Valencia, Gibson, Scholes (Fletcher 73), Anderson, Nani, Berbatov (Owen 77). Booked: Gibson, Scholes, Anderson

FINAL

BARCELONA 3 MANCHESTER UNITED 1
Wembley (87,695); Saturday, May 28 2011

Barcelona (4-3-3): Valdes, Dani Alves (Puyol 88), Mascherano, Piquet, Abidal, Busquets, Xavi (capt), Iniesta, Villa (Keita 86), Messi, Pedro (Afellay 90). **Subs not used:** Oier, Bojan, Adriano Correia, Thiago. **Scorers:** Pedro (27), Messi (54), Villa (69). **Booked:** Dani Alves, Valdes. **Coach:** Pep Guardiola
Manchester United (4-4-2): Van der Sar, Fabio (Nani 69), Ferdinand, Vidic (capt), Evra, Valencia, Carrick (Scholes 76), Giggs, Park, Rooney, Hernandez. **Subs not used:** Kuszczak, Smalling, Fletcher, Anderson, Owen. **Scorer:** Rooney (34). **Booked:** Carrick, Valencia. **Manager:** Sir Alex Ferguson
Referee: V Kassai (Hungary). **Half-time:** 1-1

Harry Redknapp spoke of football on a different level, Roy Keane rated it the best he had ever seen and Gareth Southgate said how privileged he felt to be watching. Sir Alex Ferguson echoed those and all the other tributes paid on a memorable night at Wembley by describing Barcelona as the finest team he had faced. It was some accolade from a man approaching 25 years at Old Trafford and not normally given to such lavish praise. But it was spot-on. Two years previously, when the teams met in the final in Rome, Ferguson had also conceded that United were second best, but picked out contributory shortcomings in their own performance. This time, the manager felt his side were better equipped. They also had what he called the 'symbolic' advantage of the stadium and believed there was a real chance of emulating the club's victory over Benfica there in 1968. By the time Ferguson extended a congratulatory touchline handshake to Pep Guardiola, he had been forced to accept they had fallen even further behind. There was a question mark about whether Edwin van der Sar, bringing down the curtain on a distinguished career, should have dealt better with Lionel Messi's shot for the second goal. And certainly substitute Nani was guilty of giving the ball away in the build-up to David Villa's third. Yet these events were overshadowed by the technical, tactical and territorial mastery Barcelona exerted, apart during United's bright opening and a spell after Wayne Rooney's equaliser. There has been no successful defence of Europe's most prestigious trophy by a team since the Champions League replaced the European Cup format in 1993. Who would bet against Barcelona becoming the first in 2012?

FINAL FACTS AND FIGURES

- Barcelona were crowned champions for the third time in six years, having beaten Arsenal in 2006 and Manchester United in 2009

- Their first triumph was at Wembley in 1992 when coach Pep Guardiola was in the side that beat Sampdoria 1-0

- Barcelona and Real Madrid have now won Europe's top completion 13 times, one more than Italian clubs

- Full-back Eric Abidal was chosen to accept the trophy in recognition of a remarkable recovery from illness. He received it from UEFA president Michel Platini 71 days after undergoing a life-saving operation to remove a tumour from his liver

- Lionel Messi's goal was his 53rd of the season in 55 matches. He was top scorer in the tournament – equalling the Champions League record of 12 by Ruud van Nistelrooy in 2002-03 when Nistelrooy was at Manchester United

- It was the third successive year that Messi had been leading marksman, matching the feat of Gerd Muller (Bayern Munich) and Jean-Pierre Papin (Marseille) under the European Cup format

- During Sir Alex Ferguson's near-25 years at Old Trafford, Barcelona have had 11 coaches, among them Terry Venables and Bobby Robson. Guardiola was appointed in June 2008

- Manchester United had been unbeaten leading up to their third final in four seasons, with nine wins and three draws in group and knock-out matches

- Barcelona's one defeat was against Arsenal, 2-1 at the Emirates in the first leg of the first knock-out round

LEADING SCORERS (from group stage)

12 Messi (Barcelona); 8 Eto'o (Inter Milan), Gomez (Bayern Munich); 7 Anelka (Chelsea);
6 Benzema (Real Madrid), Ronaldo (Real Madrid), Soldado (Valencia); 5 Pedro (Barcelona),
Raul (Schalke); 4 Bale (Tottenham), Borriello (Roma), Crouch (Tottenham), Eduardo (Shakhtar Donetsk), Farfan (Schalke), Hernandez (Manchester Utd), Ibrahimovic (AC Milan), Luiz Adriano (Shakhtar Donetsk), Rooney (Manchester Utd), Villa (Barcelona)

EUROPEAN CUP FINALS

1956	Real Madrid 4, Reims 3 (Paris)
1957	Real Madrid 2, Fiorentina 0 (Madrid)
1958†	Real Madrid 3, AC Milan 2 (Brussels)
1959	Real Madrid 2, Reims 0 (Stuttgart)
1960	Real Madrid 7, Eintracht Frankfurt 3 (Glasgow)
1961	Benfica 3, Barcelona 2 (Berne)
1962	Benfica 5, Real Madrid 3 (Amsterdam)
1963	AC Milan 2, Benfica 1 (Wembley)
1964	Inter Milan 3, Real Madrid 1 (Vienna)
1965	Inter Milan 1, Benfica 0 (Milan)
1966	Real Madrid 2, Partizan Belgrade 1 (Brussels)
1967	Celtic 2, Inter Milan 1 (Lisbon)
1968†	Manchester Utd 4, Benfica 1 (Wembley)
1969	AC Milan 4, Ajax 1 (Madrid)
1970†	Feyenoord 2, Celtic 1 (Milan)
1971	Ajax 2, Panathinaikos 0 (Wembley)
1972	Ajax 2, Inter Milan 0 (Rotterdam)
1973	Ajax 1, Juventus 0 (Belgrade)
1974	Bayern Munich 4, Atletico Madrid 0 (replay Brussels, after a 1-1 draw, Brussels)

1975	Bayern Munich 2, Leeds Utd 0 (Paris)
1976	Bayern Munich 1, St. Etienne 0 (Glasgow)
1977	Liverpool 3, Borussia Moenchengladbach 1 (Rome)
1978	Liverpool 1, Brugge 0 (Wembley)
1979	Nott'm. Forest 1, Malmo 0 (Munich)
1980	Nott'm. Forest 1, Hamburg 0 (Madrid)
1981	Liverpool 1, Real Madrid 0 (Paris)
1982	Aston Villa 1, Bayern Munich 0 (Rotterdam)
1983	SV Hamburg 1, Juventus 0 (Athens)
1984†	Liverpool 1, AS Roma 1 (Liverpool won 4-2 on penalties) (Rome)
1985	Juventus 1, Liverpool 0 (Brussels)
1986†	Steaua Bucharest 0, Barcelona 0 (Steaua won 2-0 on penalties) (Seville)
1987	Porto 2, Bayern Munich 1 (Vienna)
1988†	PSV Eindhoven 0, Benfica 0 (PSV won 6-5 on penalties) (Stuttgart)
1989	AC Milan 4, Steaua Bucharest 0 (Barcelona)
1990	AC Milan 1, Benfica 0 (Vienna)
1991†	Red Star Belgrade 0, Marseille 0 (Red Star won 5-3 on penalties) (Bari)
1992	Barcelona 1, Sampdoria 0 (Wembley)
1993	Marseille 1, AC Milan 0 (Munich)
1994	AC Milan 4, Barcelona 0 (Athens)
1995	Ajax 1, AC Milan 0 (Vienna)
1996†	Juventus 1, Ajax 1 (Juventus won 4-2 on penalties) (Rome)
1997	Borussia Dortmund 3, Juventus 1 (Munich)
1998	Real Madrid 1, Juventus 0 (Amsterdam)
1999	Manchester Utd 2, Bayern Munich 1 (Barcelona)
2000	Real Madrid 3, Valencia 0 (Paris)
2001	Bayern Munich 1, Valencia 1 (Bayern Munich won 5-4 on penalties) (Milan)
2002	Real Madrid 2, Bayer Leverkusen 1 (Glasgow)
2003†	AC Milan 0, Juventus 0 (AC Milan won 3-2 on penalties) (Manchester)
2004	FC Porto 3, Monaco 0 (Gelsenkirchen)
2005†	Liverpool 3, AC Milan 3 (Liverpool won 3-2 on penalties) (Istanbul)
2006	Barcelona 2, Arsenal 1 (Paris)
2007	AC Milan 2, Liverpool 1 (Athens)
2008†	Manchester Utd 1, Chelsea 1 (Manchester Utd won 6-5 on penalties) (Moscow)
2009	Barcelona 2 Manchester Utd 0 (Rome)
2010	Inter Milan 2 Bayern Munich 0 (Madrid)
2011	Barcelona 3 Manchester Utd 1 (Wembley)

(† After extra time)

● Champions League since 1993

UEFA EUROPA LEAGUE 2010–11

FIRST QUALIFYING ROUND, FIRST LEG

Grevenmacher 3 (Heinz 63, Pereira 74, Da Silva 76) **Dundalk** 3 (Kudozovic 26, Hatswell 51, Benichou 79 og). **Llanelli** 2 (Thomas 19, Jones 47) Tauras 2 (Kizys 11, 22). **Portadown** 1 (Lecky 37) Skonto 1 (Laizans 90). Reykjavik 3 (Gunnarsson 12, Finnbogason 32, Takefusa 52) **Glentoran** 0. TPS 3 (Riku Riski 24, 35, Babatunde 30) **Port Talbot** 1 (Rose 70)

FIRST QUALIFYING ROUND, SECOND LEG

Dundalk 2 (Fenn 5 pen, Kudozovic 16) Grevenmacher 1 (Muller 90) – **Dundalk** won 5-4 on agg. **Glentoran** 2 (Callacher 22, Hamilton 56 pen) Reykjavik 2 (Finnbogason 45, Black 54 og) – Reykjavik won 5-2 on agg. **Port Talbot** 0 TPS 4 (Babatunde 29, Kolehmainen 31, Riku Riski 66, Roope Riski 90) – TPS won 7-1 on agg. Skonto 0 **Portadown** 1 (Lecky 29) – **Portadown** won 2-1 on agg. Tauras 3 (Irkha 17, 28, Regelskis 104) **Llanelli** 2 (Llewellyn 19, Bowen 36) – aet, Tauras won 5-4 on agg

FIRST QUALIFYING ROUND, ON AGGREGATE

Anorthosis Famagusta 4 Banants 0; Bnei Yehuda 1 Uliss 0; Dacia 1 Zeta 1 (Dacia won on away goal); Dnepr 8 Laci 2; Dinamo Tbilisi 2 Flora 1; Gyor 5 Nitra 3; Kalmar 4 Streymur 0; Mogren 5 Santa Coloma 0; Mypa 7 Trans 0; Olimpia Balti 1 Lankaran 1 (Olimpia Balti won on away goal); Qarabag 5 Metalurg Skopje 2; Rabotnicki 11 Lusitans 0; Randers 7 Dedelange 3; Ruch 3 Karagandy 1; Sibenik 3 Sliema 0; Siroki Brijeg 5 Olimpija Ljubljana 0; Tirana 1 ZTE 0 (aet); Gefle 4 NSI 1; Zestafoni 5 Faetano 0; Zhodino 6 Fylkir 1 Zrinjski 4 Tobol 2

SECOND QUALIFYING ROUND, FIRST LEG

Cliftonville 1 (Caldwell 82) Cibalia 0. Honka 1 (Savage 43) **Bangor City** 1 (Jones 58). Levski Sofia 6 (Yovov 12, Mladenov 14, 46, Dembele 42, Isa 85, 90) **Dundalk** 0. Maritimo 3 (Esteves 79, Cherrad 84, Tcho 90) **Sporting Fingal** 2 (Crowe 32, Fitzgergald 86). **Motherwell** 1 (Forbes 63) Breidablik 0. **Portadown** 1 (Lecky 29) Qarabag 2 (Ismayilov 67, 86). **Shamrock** 1 (Bayly 90) Bnei Yehuda 1 (Afek 26)

SECOND QUALIFYING ROUND, SECOND LEG

Bangor City 2 (Morley 84, Jones 90) Honka 1 (Koskinen 21) – **Bangor City** won 3-2 on agg. Bnei Yehuda 0 **Shamrock** 1 (Stewart 70) – Shamrock won 2-1 on agg. Breidablik 0 **Motherwell** 1 (Murphy 42) – **Motherwell** won 2-0 on agg. Cibalia 0 **Cliftonville** 0 – Cliftonville won 1-0 on agg. **Dundalk** 0 Levski Sofia 2 (Dembele 4, 33) – Levski Sofia won 8-0 on agg. Qarabag 1 (Ismayilov 83) **Portdadown** 1 (Braniff 71) – Qarabag won 3-2 on agg. **Sporting Fingal** 2 (Zayed 81, 90) Maritimo 0 (Alonso 20 pen, Marquinho 67, Kanu 87) – Maritimo won 6-4 on agg

SECOND QUALIFYING ROUND, ON AGGREGATE

Anorthosis Famagusta 3 Sibenik 2 (aet); Apoel Nicosia 6 Tauras 1; Austria Vienna 3 Siroki Brijeg 2; Besiktas 7 Vikingur 0; Banik 6 WIT Georgia 0; Brondby 3 Vaduz 0; Buducnost Podgorica 4 Baki 2; Cercle Bruges 2 TPS 2 (Cercle Bruges won on away goals); Dinamo Bucharest 7 Olimpia Balti 1; Dinamo Minsk 10 Sillamae 1; Dinamo Tbilisi 4 Gefle 2; Dnepr 3 Stabaek 3 (Dnepr won on away goals). Elfsborg 3 Iskra 1; Gyor 5 Atyrau 0; Kalmar 2 Dacia 0; Karpaty Lviv 6 Reykjavik 2; Lausanne 2 Borac 1; Maccabi Tel-Aviv 3 Mogren 2; Maribor 3 Videoton 1; Molde 2 Jelgava 2 (Molde won on away goal); Mypa 8 Sant Julia 5; OFK 3 Zhodino 2; Olimpiacos 11 Besa 1; Rabotnicki 1 Mika 0; Randers 4 Gorica 1; Rapid Vienna 6 Suduva 2; Ruch Chorzow 1 Valletta 1 (Ruch Chorzow won on away goal); Spartak Zlatibor 5 Differdange 3; Teteks 3 Ventspils 1; Utrecht 5 Tirana 1; Wisla Krakow 7 Siauliai 2; Zestafoni 3 Dukla 1; Zrinjski 13 Tre Penne 3

THIRD QUALIFYING ROUND, FIRST LEG

Aalesund 1 (Mathisen 90 pen) **Motherwell** 1 (Murphy 48). Att: 8,450. CSKA Sofia 3 (Vidanov 9, Marquinhos 72, Trifonov 74) **Cliftonville** 0. Att: 2,500. Maribor 3 (Ilicic 32, 52, Tavares 60) **Hibernian** 0. Att: 10,000. Maritimo 8 (Tcho 33, 79, Dias 38, 75, Diawara 50, 78, Kanu 80, Fidelis 90) **Bangor City** 2 (Ward 73, Jebb 90). Att: 2,000. Rabotnicki 0 **Liverpool** 2 (Ngog 17, 59). Att: 23,000. **Shamrock** 0 Juventus 2 (Amauri 3, 75). Att: 5,800

THIRD QUALIFYING ROUND, SECOND LEG

Bangor City 1 (Bull 9) Maritimo 2 (Adilson 48, Marquinho 58). Att: 556 (Maritimo won 10-3 on agg). **Cliftonville** 1 (Boyce 42) CSKA Sofia 2 (Kostadinov 85, Marquinhos 88). Att: 1,200 (CSKA Sofia won 5-1 on agg). **Hibernian** 2 (De Graaf 54, 89) Maribor 3 (Tavares 19, 73, Mezga 67 pen). Att: 12,504 (Maribor won 6-2 on agg). Juventus 1 (Del Piero 74) **Shamrock** 0. Att: 17,000 (Juventus won 3-0 on agg). **Liverpool** 2 (Ngog 22, Gerrard 40 pen) Rabotnicki 0. Att: 31,202 (**Liverpool** won 4-0 on agg). **Motherwell** 3 (Murphy 4, Sutton 13, Page 89) Aalesund 0. Att: 7,721 (**Motherwell** won 4-1 on agg)

THIRD QUALIFYING ROUND ON, AGGREGATE

Anorthosis Famagusta 3 Cercle Bruges 2; AZ 2 Gothenburg 1; Apoel Nicosia 4 Jablonec 1; Aris Salonika 4 Jagiellonia 3; Austria Vienna 6 Ruch Chorzow 1; Besiktas 4 Plzen 1; Brondby 3 Buducnost Podgorica 1; Dinamo Minsk 3 Maccabi Haifa 2; Dnepr 3 Banik 1; Dnipro 3 Spartak Zlatibor 1; Elfsborg 7 Teteks 1; Galatasaray 7 OFK 3; Genk 8 Inter Turku 3; Gyor 1 Montpellier 1 (aet, Gyor won 4-3 on pens); Hajduk Split 4 Dinamo Bucharest 3; Karpaty Lviv 2 Zestafoni 0; Lausanne 4 Randers 3; Levski Sofia 6 Kalmar 3; Maccabi Tel-Aviv 2 Olympiacos 2 (Maccabi Tel-Aviv won on away goals); Odense 5 Zrinjski 3; Qarabag 4 Wisla Krakow 2; Rapid Vienna 4 Beroe 1; Sibir 2 Apollon 2 (Sibir won on away goal); Slovan Bratislava 3 Crvena Zvezda 2; Sporting 3 Nordsjaelland 1; Sturm Graz 3 Dinamo Tbilisi 1; Stuttgart 5 Molde 4; Timisoara 5 Mypa 4; Utrecht 4 Lucerne 1

PLAY-OFFS, FIRST LEG

CSKA Sofia 3 (Aquaro 81, Nelson 82, Delev 90) New Saints 0. Att: 2,950. Celtic 2 (Juarez 19, Samaras 34) Utrecht 0. Att: 35,755. Dundee Utd 0 AEK Athens 1 (Djebbour 11). Att: 12,116. Liverpool 1 (Babel 45) Trabzonspor 0. Att: 40,941. Odense 2 (Sorensen 31, Utaka 78) Motherwell 1 (Hateley 90). Att: 14,911. Rapid Vienna 1 (Nuhiu 32) Aston Villa 1 (Bannan 11). Att: 16,891. Timisoara 0 Manchester City 1 (Balotelli 72). Att: 20,000

PLAY-OFFS, SECOND LEG

AEK Athens 1 (Diop 23) Dundee Utd 1 (Daly 78). Att: 600 (AEK Athens won 2-1 on agg). Aston Villa 2 (Agbonlahor 22, Heskey 77) Rapid Vienna 3 (Nuhiu 52, Sonnleitner 78, Gartler 81). Att: 29,980 (Rapid Vienna won 4-3 on agg). Manchester City 2 (Wright-Phillips 43, Boyata 59) Timisoara 0. Att: 23,542 (Manchester City won 3-0 on agg). Motherwell 0 Odense 1 (Utaka 28). Att: 9,105 (Odense won 3-1 on agg). New Saints 2 (M Williams 14, Evans 62) CSKA Sofia 5 (Aquaro 11, Tiboni 80). Att: 843 (at Wrexham) (CSKA Sofia won 5-2 on agg); Trabzonspor 1 (Gutierrez 4) Liverpool 2 (Kacar 84 og, Kuyt 88). Att: 21,065 (Liverpool won 3-1 on agg). Utrecht 4 (Van Wolfswinkel 12 pen, 20 pen, 47, Maguire 63) Celtic 0. Att: 18,000 (Utrecht won 4-2 on agg)

PLAY-OFFS, ON AGGREGATE

Aris Salonika 2 Austria Vienna 1; AZ 3 Aktobe 2; Bate Borisov 5 Maritimo 1; Bayer Leverkusen 6 Tavriya Symferopol 1; Besiktas 6 HJK Helsinki 0; Borussia Dortmund 5 Qarabag 0; Club Bruges 5 Dinamo Minsk 3; CSKA Moscow 6 Anorthosis Famagusta 1; Debrecen 4 Litex Lovech 1; Dinamo Zagreb 4 Gyor 1; Gent 2 Feyenoord 1; Getafe 2 Apoel Nicosia 1; Hajduk Split 5 Unirea Urziceni 1; Juventus 3 Sturm Graz 1; Karpaty Lviv 1 Galatasaray 1 (Karpaty Lviv won on away goal); Lausanne 1 Lokomotiv Moscow 1 (aet, Lausanne won 4-3 on pens); Lech Poznan 3 Dnipro 0; Levski Sofia 2 AIK Solna 1; Lille 2 Vaslui 0; Metalist Kharkiv 3 Omonia Nicosia 2; Napoli 3 Elfsborg 0; Palermo 5 Maribor 3; PAOK Salonika 2 Fenerbahce 1; Paris Saint-Germain 5 Maccabi Tel-Aviv 4; Porto 7 Genk 2; PSV 5 Sibir Novosibirsk 1; Sporting 3 Brondby 2; Steaua Bucharest 1 Grasshoppers 1 (aet, Steaua Bucharest won 4-3 on pens); Stuttgart 3 Slovan Bratislava 2; Villarreal 7 Dnepr 1

GROUP A

Match-day 1: Juventus 3 (Chiellini 45, 50, Del Piero 68) Lech Poznan 3 (Rudnevs 14 pen, 30, 90). Att: 10,837. Red Bull Salzburg 0 Manchester City 2 (Silva 8, Jo 63). Att: 25,100
Match-day 2: Lech Poznan 2 (Arboleda 47, Peszko 80) Red Bull Salzburg 0. Att: 42,000. Manchester City 1 (A Johnson 37) Juventus 1 (Iaquinta 10). Att: 35,212
Match-day 3: Manchester City 3 (Adebayor 13, 25, 73) Lech Poznan 1 (Tshibamba 50). Att: 33,388. Red Bull Salzburg 1 (Svento 36) Juventus 1 (Krasic 48). Att: 20,000
Match-day 4: Juventus 0 Red Bull Salzburg 0. Att: 15,000. Lech Poznan 3 (Injac 30,

Arboleda 86, Mozdzen 90) **Manchester City** 1 (Adebayor 51). Att: 43,000
Match-day 5: Lech Poznan 1 (Rudnevs 12) Juventus 1 (Iaquinta 84). Att: 28,000.
Manchester City 3 (Balotelli 18, 65, A Johnson 78) Red Bull Salzburg 0. Att: 37,552
Match-day 6: Juventus 1 (Giannetti 43) **Manchester City** 1 (Jo 76). Att: 10,000. Red Bull
Salzburg 0 Lech Poznan 1 (Stilic 30). Att: 5,300

FINAL TABLE

	P	W	D	L	F	A	Pts
Manchester City Q	6	3	2	1	11	6	11
Lech Poznan Q	6	3	2	1	11	8	11
Juventus	6	0	6	0	7	7	6
Red Bull Salzburg	6	0	2	4	1	9	2

GROUP B

Match-day 1: Aris Salonika 1 (Javito 59) Atletico Madrid 0. Att: 22,800. Bayer Leverkusen 4
(Helmes 4, 58, 61, Reinartz 38) Rosenborg 0. Att: 13,065
Match-day 2: Atletico Madrid 1 (Simao 51 pen) Bayer Leverkusen 1 (Derdiyok 39). Att:
35,000. Rosenborg 2 (Moldskred 37, Prica 68) Aris Salonika 1 (Ruiz 43). Att: 12,000
Match-day 3: Aris Salonika 0 Bayer Leverkusen 0. Att: 22,000. Atletico Madrid 3 (Godin 18,
Aguero 66, Costa 78) Rosenborg 0. Att: 25,000
Match-day 4: Bayer Leverkusen 1 (Vidal 90) Aris Salonika 0. Att: 18,265. Rosenborg 1
(Henriksen 52) Atletico Madrid 2 (Aguero 5, Tiago 84). Att: 14,250
Match-day 5: Atletico Madrid 2 (Forlan 11, Aguero 16) Aris Salonika 3 (Koke 2, 51 pen,
Lazaridis 81). Att: 25,000. Rosenborg 0 Bayer Leverkusen 1 (Sam 35). Att: 11,100
Match-day 6: Aris Salonika 2 (Cesarec 45, Faty 90) Rosenborg 0. Att: 22,000. Bayer
Leverkusen 1 (Helmes 69) Atletico Madrid 1 (Merida 72). Att: 18,093

FINAL TABLE

	P	W	D	L	F	A	Pts
Bayer Leverkusen Q	6	3	3	0	8	2	12
Aris Salonika Q	6	3	1	2	7	5	10
Atletico Madrid	6	2	2	2	9	7	8
Rosenborg	6	1	0	5	3	13	3

GROUP C

Match-day 1: Levski Sofia 3 (Santos Joaozinho 43, Dembele 61, Greene 85) Gent 2 (Azofeifa
23, De Smet 49). Att: 29,000. Lille 1 (Frau 57) Sporting 2 (Vukcevic 11, Postiga 34). Att:
25,000
Match-day 2: Gent 1 (De Smet 6) Lille 1 (Frau 20). Att: 8,000. Sporting 5 (Carrico 30,
Maniche 43, Solomao 53, Postiga 61, Fernandez 79) Levski Sofia 0. Att: 15,081
Match-day 3: Lille 1 (Chedjou 49) Levski Sofia 0. Att: 16,000. Sporting 5 (Solomao 7,
Liedson 13, 27, Maniche 38, Postiga 60) Gent 1 (Wils 17). Att: 15,008
Match-day 4: Gent 3 (Smolders 8 pen, Conte 80, Arbeitman 83) Sporting 1 (Saleiro 39). Att:
8,795. Levski Sofia 2 (Dembele 11, Gadzhev 83) Lille 2 (De Melo 35, Ivanov 88 og). Att:
21,000
Match-day 5: Gent 1 (Wallace 77) Levski Sofia 0. Att: 8,662. Sporting 1 (Anderson Polga 28)
Lille 0. Att: 16,569
Match-day 6: Levski Sofia 1 (Mladenov 45) Sporting 0. Att: 1,600. Lille 3 (Obraniak 30, Frau
56, Sow 88) Gent 0. Att: 15,000

FINAL TABLE

	P	W	D	L	F	A	Pts
Sporting Q	6	4	0	2	14	6	12
Lille Q	6	2	2	2	8	6	8
Gent	6	2	1	3	8	13	7
Levski Sofia	6	2	1	3	6	11	7

GROUP D

Match-day 1: Club Bruges 1 (Kouemaha 61) PAOK Salonika 1 (Malezas 78). Att: 15,155. Dinamo Zagreb 2 (Rukavina 18, Sammir 79) Villarreal 0. Att: 22,000

Match-day 2: PAOK Salonika 1 (Ivic 56) Dinamo Zagreb 0. Att: 20,000. Villarreal 2 (Rossi 41, Rodriguez 56) Club Bruges 1 (Donk 45). Att: 23,000

Match-day 3: Dinamo Zagreb 0 Club Bruges 0. Att: 22,000. Villarreal 1 (Ruben 38) PAOK Salonika 0. Att: 20,000

Match-day 4: Club Bruges 0 Dinamo Zagreb 2 (Sammir 55, Biscan 59). Att: 20,000. PAOK Salonika 1 (Vieirinha 70) Villarreal 0. Att: 22,000

Match-day 5: PAOK Salonika 1 (Vieirinha 25) Club Bruges 1 (Scepovic 89). Att: 21,000. Villarreal 3 (Rossi 25 pen, 81, Ruben 62) Dinamo Zagreb 0. Att: 15,000

Match-day 6: Club Bruges 1 (Kouemaha 28) Villarreal 2 (Rossi 30, 34 pen). Att: 19,000. Dinamo Zagreb 0 PAOK Salonika 1 (Salpingidis 59). Att: 34,000

FINAL TABLE

	P	W	D	L	F	A	Pts
Villarreal Q	6	4	0	2	8	5	12
PAOK Salonika Q	6	3	2	1	5	3	11
Dinamo Zagreb	6	2	1	3	4	5	7
Club Bruges	6	0	3	3	4	8	3

GROUP E

Match-day 1: AZ 2 (Gudmundsson 15, Jaliens 83) Sheriff Tiraspol 1 (Nikolic 67). Att: 10,624. Dynamo Kiev 2 (Milevskiy 34, Eremenko 44) Bate Borisov 2 (Rodionov 3, Nekhaychik 54). Att: 11,000

Match-day 2: Bate Borisov 4 (Rodionov 5, Kontsevoy 48, Bressan 77 pen, Olekhnovich 82) AZ 1 (Sigthorsson 89). Att: 13,000. Sheriff Tiraspol 2 (Erokhin 8, Jymmy 37 pen) Dynamo Kiev 0. Att: 14,000

Match-day 3: AZ 1 (Falkenburg 35) Dynamo Kiev 2 (Milevskiy 16, Khacheridi 39). Att: 12,338. Sherriff Tiraspol 0 Bate Borisov 1 (Sosnovskiy 8). Att: 10,000

Match-day 4: Bate Borisov 3 (Rodionov 15, Pavlov 69, Bressan 74) Sheriff Tiraspol 1 (Erokhin 32). Att: 16,500. Dyamo Kiev 2 (Milevskiy 47, 61) AZ 0. Att: 17,500

Match-day 5: Bate Borisov 1 (Nekhaychik 84) Dynamo Kiev 4 (Vukojevic 16, Yarmolenko 43, Gusev 50 pen, Milevskiy 68). Att: 7,000. Sheriff Tiraspol 1 (Rouamba 54) AZ 1 (Holman 17). Att: 3,000

Match-day 6: AZ 3 (Sigthorsson 6, 84, Maher 86) Bate Borisov 0. Att: 14,000. Dynamo Kiev 0 Sheriff Tiraspol 0. Att: 17,000

FINAL TABLE

	P	W	D	L	F	A	Pts
Dynamo Kiev Q	6	3	2	1	10	6	11
Bate Borisov Q	6	3	1	2	11	11	10
AZ	6	2	1	3	8	10	7
Sheriff Tiraspol	6	1	2	3	5	7	5

GROUP F

Match-day 1: Lausanne 0 CSKA Moscow 3 (Vagner Love 22, 82 pen, Ignashevich 68). Att: 11,500. Sparta Prague 3 (Wilfred 17, Kladrubsky 69, Kadlec 75) Palermo 2 (Maccarone 38, Hernandez 83). Att: 13,765
Match-day 2: CSKA Moscow 3 (Doumbia 72, 86, Gonzalez 84 pen) Sparta Prague 0. Att: 15,000. Palermo 1 (Migliaccio 79) Lausanne 0. Att: 10,000
Match-day 3: Palermo 0 CSKA Moscow 3 (Doumbia 34, 59, Necid 82). Att: 10,000. Sparta Prague 3 (Wilfred 10, 23, Kucka 21) Lausanne 3 (Meoli 6, Steuble 75, Silvio 90). Att: 12,430
Match-day 4: CSKA Moscow 3 (Honda 47, Necid 50, 54) Palermo 1 (Maccarone 10). Att: 12,000. Lausanne 1 (Katz 5) Sparta Prague 3 (Wilfred 44, 90, Kweuke 75). Att: 8,000
Match-day 5: CSKA Moscow 5 (Necid 19, 83, Oliseh 22, Tosic 40, Dzagoev 72) Lausanne 1 (Carrupt 90). Att: 15,000. Palermo 2 (Rigoni 24, Pinilla 59 pen) Sparta Prague 2 (Kladrubsky 51 pen, Kucka 63). Att: 7,000
Match-day 6: Lausanne 0 Palermo 1 (Munoz 85). Att: 6,000. Sparta Prague 1 (Kadlec 44) CSKA Moscow 1 (Dzagoev 15). Att: 12,700

FINAL TABLE

	P	W	D	L	F	A	Pts
CSKA Moscow Q	6	5	1	0	18	3	16
Sparta Prague Q	6	2	3	1	12	12	9
Palermo	6	2	1	3	7	11	7
Lausanne	6	0	1	5	5	16	1

GROUP G

Match-day 1: AEK Athens 3 (Djebbour 12, Liberopoulos 65, Scocco 89) Hadjuk Split 1 (Ibricic 29 pen). Att: 20,000. Anderlecht 1 (Juhasz 66) Zenit St Petersburg 3 (Kerzhakov 8, 33, 44). Att: 30,000
Match-day 2: Hajduk Split 1 (Vukusic 90) Anderlecht 0. Att: 32,000. Zenit St Petersburg 4 (Hubocan 2, Bruno Alves 13, Lazovic 43 pen, 57) AEK Athens 2 (Liberopoulos 37, Kafes 83 pen). Att: 21,000
Match-day 3: Anderlecht 3 (Boussoufa 32, Lukaku 71, Juhasz 76) AEK Athens 0. Att: 20,000. Zenit St Petersburg 2 (Bukharov 25, Danny 68) Hajduk Split 0. Att: 20,000
Match-day 4: AEK Athens 1 (Blanco 48 pen) Anderlecht 1 (Polak 54). Att: 17,000. Hajduk Split 2 (Ljubicic 69, Vukusic 83) Zenit St Petersburg 3 (Ionov 31, Huszti 47 pen, Rosina 51). Att: 30,000
Match-day 5: Hajduk Split 1 (Buljat 90) AEK Athens 3 (Scocco 51 pen, Manolas 61, Blanco 84). Att: 10,000. Zenit St Petersburg 3 (Ionov 12, Bukharov 65, Huszti 88) Anderlecht 1 (Kanu 87). Att: 15,000
Match-day 6: AEK Athens 0 Zenit St Petersburg 3 (Bukharov 44, Rosina 67, Denisov 88). Att: 2,200. Anderlecht 2 (De Sutter 11, Suarez 40) Hajduk Split 0. Att: 18,000

FINAL TABLE

	P	W	D	L	F	A	PTS
Zenit St Petersburg Q	6	6	0	0	18	6	18
Anderlecht Q	6	2	1	3	8	8	7
AEK Athens	6	2	1	3	9	13	7
Hajduk Split	6	1	0	5	5	13	3

GROUP H

Match-day 1: Getafe 2 (Arizmendi 51, Rios 82) Odense 1 (Arizmendi 44 og) Att: 4,000. Stuttgart 3 (Cacau 23 pen, Gentner 59, Tasci 90) Young Boys 0. Att: 15,500

Match-day 2: Odense 1 (Johansson 78) Stuttgart 2 (Kuzmanovic 72, Harnik 86). Att: 14,761. Young Boys 2 (Degen 11, 64) Getafe 0. Att: 20,000
Match-day 3: Stuttgart 1 (Marica 28) Getafe 0. Att: 17,400. Young Boys 4 (Bienvenu 26, Sutter 34, Degen 61, Lulic 75) Odense 2 (Utaka 49, Sorensen 85 pen). Att: 12,000
Match-day 4: Getafe 0 Stuttgart 3 (Marica 26, Gebhart 64, Harnik 76). Att: 4,000. Odense 2 (Andreasen 12, 60) Young Boys 0. Att: 5,600
Match-day 5: Odense 1 (Andreasen 90) Getafe 1 (Rios 17). Att: 4,500. Young Boys 4 (Degen 35, Sutter 78, Mayuka 81, 82) Stuttgart 2 (Pogrebniak 48, Schipplock 68). Att: 1,500
Match-day 6: Getafe 1 (Adrian 15) Young Boys 0. Att: 1,500. Stuttgart 5 (Gebhart 20, Hoegh 48 og, Gentner 65, Pogrebniak 71, Marica 90) Odense 1 (Utaka 73). Att: 14,000

FINAL TABLE

	P	W	D	L	F	A	Pts
Stuttgart Q	6	5	0	1	16	6	15
Young Boys Q	6	3	0	3	10	10	9
Getafe	6	2	1	3	4	8	7
Odense	6	1	1	4	8	14	4

GROUP I

Match-day 1: Debrecen 0 Metalist Kharkiv 5 (Edmar 24, 74, Xavier 34, Fininho 77, Valyaev 90). Att: 5,000. PSV 1 (Dzsudzsak 89) Sampdoria 1 (Cacciatore 25). Att: 17,400
Match-day 2: Metalist Kharkiv 0 PSV 2 (Dzsudzsak 28 pen, Berg 30). Att: 25,000. Sampdoria 1 (Pazzini 18 pen) Debrecen 0. Att: 12,159
Match-day 3: Debrecen 1 (Mijadinoski 35) PSV 2 (Engelaar 40, Reiss 66). Att: 5,000. Metalist Kharkiv 2 (Taison 38, Xavier 73) Sampdoria 1 (Koman 32). Att: 25,000
Match-day 4: PSV 3 (Afellay 21, Reis 43, Wuytens 88) Debrecen 0. Att: 17,000. Sampdoria 0 Metalaist Kharkiv 0. Att: 20,000
Match-day 5: Metalist Kharkiv 2 (Bodi 56 og, Oliynyk 88) Debrecen 1 (Czvitkovics 49). Att: 25,000. Sampdoria 1 (Pazzini 40) PSV 2 (Toivonen 51, 90). Att: 25,000
Match-day 6: Debrecen 2 (Kabat 48, 86) Sampdoria 0. Att: 5,000. PSV 0 Metalist Kharkiv 0. Att: 15,000

FINAL TABLE

	P	W	D	L	F	A	Pts
PSV Q	6	4	2	0	10	3	14
Metalist Kharkiv Q	6	3	2	1	9	4	11
Sampdoria	6	1	2	3	4	7	5
Debrecen	6	1	0	5	4	13	3

GROUP J

Match-day 1: Karpaty Lviv 3 (Holodyuk 43, Kopolovets 52, Kozhanov 78) Borussia Dortmund 4 (Sahin 13 pen, Gotze 27, 90, Barrios 87). Att: 25,000. Sevilla 0 Paris St-Germain 0. Att: 29,000
Match-day 2: Borussia Dortmund 0 Sevilla 1 (Cigarini 45). Att: 49,100. Paris St-Germain 2 (Jallet 4, Nene 20) Karpaty Lviv 0. Att: 5,000
Match-day 3: Borussia Dortmund 1 (Sahin 50 pen) Paris St-Germain 1 (Chantome 87). Att: 50,209. Karpaty Lviv 0 Sevilla 1 (Kanoute 34). Att: 20,000
Match-day 4: Paris St-Germain 0 Borussia Dortmund 0. Att: 16,000. Sevilla 4 (Alfaro 9, 43, Cigarini 31, Negredo 51) Karpaty Lviv 0. Att: 25,000
Match-day 5: Borussia Dortmund 3 (Kagawa 5, Hummels 49, Lewandowski 89) Karpaty Lviv 0. Att: 40,100. Paris St-Germain 4 (Bodmer 17, Hoarau 19, 47, Nene 45) Sevilla 2 (Kanoute 32, 36). Att: 5,000

Match-day 6: Karpaty Lviv 1 (Fedetskiy 45) Paris St-Germain 1 (Luyindula 39). Att: 10,000. Sevilla 2 (Romaric 31, Kanoute 35) Borussia Dortmund 2 (Kagawa 4, Subotic 49). Att: 25,000

FINAL TABLE

	P	W	D	L	F	A	Pts
Paris St-Germain Q	6	3	3	0	9	4	12
Sevilla Q	6	3	1	2	10	7	10
Borussia Dortmund	6	2	3	1	10	7	9
Karpaty Lviv	6	0	1	5	4	15	1

GROUP K

Match-day 1: Liverpool 4 (Cole 1, Ngog 56 pen, 90, Lucas 81) Steaua Bucharest 1 (Tanase 13). Att: 25,605. Napoli 0 Utrecht 0. Att: 35,000
Match-day 2: Utrecht 0 **Liverpool** 0. Att: 23,662. Steaua Bucharest 3 (Emilson 2 og, Tanase 11, Kapetanos 17) Napoli 3 (Vitale 44, Hamsik 73, Cavani 90). Att: 20,000
Match-day 3: Napoli 0 **Liverpool** 0. Att: 55,489. Utrecht 1 (Duplan 60) Steaua Bucharest 1 (Schut 75 og). Att: 23,300
Match-day 4: Liverpool 3 (Gerrard 75 pen, 88, 89) Napoli 1 (Lavezzi 28). Att: 33,895. Steaua Bucharest 3 (Gardos 29, Stancu 52, 53) Utrecht 1 (Mertens 33). Att: 9,000
Match-day 5: Utrecht 3 (Van Wolfswinkel 6, 28 pen, Demouge 35) Napoli 3 (Cavani 5, 42, 70 pen). Att: 24,117. Steaua Bucharest 1 (Eder 61) **Liverpool** 1 (Jovanovic 19). Att: 20,000
Match-day 6: Liverpool 0 Utrecht 0. Att: 37,800. Napoli 1 (Cavani 90) Steaua Bucharest 0. Att: 45,000

FINAL TABLE

	P	W	D	L	F	A	Pts
Liverpool Q	6	2	4	0	8	3	10
Napoli Q	6	1	4	1	8	9	7
Steaua Bucharest	6	1	3	2	9	11	6
Utrecht	6	0	5	1	5	7	5

GROUP L

Match-day 1: Besiktas 1 (Ernst 90) CSKA Sofia 0. Att: 28,000. Porto 3 (Rolando 26, Falcao 66, Ruben Micael 79) Rapid Vienna 0. Att: 30,014
Match-day 2: CSKA Sofia 0 Porto 1 (Falcao 16). Att: 17,231. Rapid Vienna 1 (Kavlak 51), Besiktas 2 (Holosko 55, Bobo 64). Att: 47,200
Match-day 3: Besiktas 1 (Bobo 90) Porto 3 (Falcao 27, Hulk 59, 77). Att: 29,000. CSKA Sofia 0 Rapid Vienna 2 (Vennegoor of Hesselink 28, Hoffmann 32). Att: 6,000
Match-day 4: Porto 1 (Falcao 37 pen) Besiktas 1 (Kahveci 61). Att: 24,139. Rapid Vienna 1 (Salihi 57 pen) CSKA Sofia 2 (Yanchev 51, Marquinhos 64). Att: 50,000
Match-day 5: CSKA Sofia 1 (Sheridan 79) Besiktas 2 (Zapotocny 59, Holosko 64). Att: 10,000. Rapid Vienna 1 (Trimmel 39) Porto 3 (Falcao 42, 86, 88). Att: 53,008
Match-day 6: Besiktas 2 (Quaresma 32, Ernst 45) Rapid Vienna 0. Att: 14,000. Porto 3 (Otamendi 22, Ruben Micael 55, Rodriguez 90) CSKA Sofia 1 (Delev 48). Att: 22,930

FINAL TABLE

	P	W	D	L	F	A	Pts
Porto Q	6	5	1	0	14	4	16
Besiktas Q	6	4	1	1	9	6	13
Rapid Vienna	6	1	0	5	5	12	3
CSKA Sofia	6	1	0	5	4	10	3

ROUND OF 32, FIRST LEG

Anderlecht 0 Ajax 3 (Alderweireld 33, Erikson 59, El Hamdaoui 67). Att: 24,000. Aris Salonika 0 **Manchester City** 0. Att: 21,000

Basle 2 (Frei 37, Streller 42) Spartak Moscow 3 (Kombarov 61, Dzjuba 70, Ananidze 90). Att: 13,060. Bate Borisov 2 (Bressan 16, Gordeychuk 81) Paris St-Germain 2 (Erdinc 30, Luyindula 89). Att: 6,000

Benfica 2 (Cardozo 70, Jara 81) Stuttgart 1 (Harnik 21). Att: 40,000. Besiktas 1 (Quaresma 37) Dynamo Kiev 4 (Vukojevic 27, Shevchenko 50, Yussuf 50, Gusev 90 pen). Att: 27,000

Lech Poznan 1 (Rudnevs 72) Braga 0. Att: 29,133. Lille 2 (Gueye 6, De Melo 31) PSV 2 (Bouma 84, Toivonen 85). Att: 16,951

Metalist Kharkiv 0 Bayer Leverkuson 4 (Derdiyok 22, Castro 72, Sam 90, 90). Att: 24,000. Napoli 0 Villarreal 0. Att: 55,000

PAOK Salonika 0 CSKA Moscow 1 (Necid 29). Att: 22,000. **Rangers** 1 (Whittaker 66) Sporting 1 (Fernandez 89). Att: 34,095

Rubin Kazan 0 Twente 2 (De Jong 77, Wisgerhof 88). Att: 500. Seville 1 (Kanoute 67) Porto 2 (Rolando 59, Guarin 85). Att: 30,000

Sparta Prague 0 **Liverpool** 0. Att: 17,564. Young Boys 2 (Lulic 46, Mayuka 90) Zenit St Petersburg 1 (Lombaerts 20). Att: 15,000

ROUND OF 32, SECOND LEG

Ajax 2 (Sulejmani 11, 16) Anderlecht 0. Att: 42,591 (Ajax won 5-0 on agg). Bayer Leverkusen 2 (Rolfes 47, Ballack 70) Metalist Kharkiv 0. Att: 16,212 (Bayer Leverkusen won 6-0 on agg)

Braga 2 (Alan 9, Lima 36) Lech Poznan 0. Att: 10,007 (Braga won 2-1 on agg). CSKA Moscow 1 (Ignashevich 80) PAOK Salonika 1 (Sulimovic 67). Att: 10,000 (CSKA won 2-1 on agg)

Dynamo Kiev 4 (Vukojevic 3, Yarmolenko 55, Gusev 64, Shevchenki 74) Besiktas 0. Att: 15,000 (Dynamo Kiev won 8-1 on agg). **Liverpool** 1 (Kuyt 86) Sparta Prague 0. Att: 42,949 (**Liverpool** won 1-0 on agg)

Manchester City 3 (Dzeko 7, 12, Y Toure 75) Aris Salonika 0. Att: 36,748 (**Manchester City** won 3-0 on agg). Paris St-Germain 0 Bate Borisov 0. Att: 5,000 (Agg 2-2, Paris St-Germain won on away goals)

Porto 0 Sevilla 1 (Luis Fabiano 71). Att: 35,609 (agg 2-2, Porto won on away goals). PSV 3 (Dzsudzsak 55, Lens 67, Marcelo 73) Lille 1 (Frau 22). Att: 28,500 (PSV won 5-3 on agg)

Spartak Moscow 1 (McGeady 90) Basle 1 (Chipperfield 15). Att: 12,000 (Spartak Moscow won 4-3 on agg). Sporting 2 (Mendes 42, Djalo 83) **Rangers** 2 (Diouf 20, Edu 90). Att: 15,375 (agg 3-3, **Rangers** won on away goals)

Stuttgart 0 Benfica 2 (Salvio 31, Cardozo 78). Att: 25,800 (Benfica won 4-1 on agg). Twente 2 (Janssen 45, Franco 47) Rubin Kazan 2 (Ansaldi 22, Noboa 24). Att: 23,000 (Twente won 4-2 on agg)

Villarreal 2 (Nilmar 42, Rossi 45) Napoli 1 (Hamsik 18). Att: 25,000 (Villarreal won 2-1 on agg). Zenit St Petersburg 3 (Lazovic 41, Semak 52, Shirokov 76) Young Boys 1 (Jemal 21). Att: 17,500 (Zenit St Petersburg won 4-3 on agg)

ROUND OF 16, FIRST LEG

Ajax 0 Spartak Moscow 1 (Alex 57). Att: 30,000. Bayer Leverkusen 2 (Kadlec 33, Castro 72) Villarreal 3 (Rossi 42, Nilmar 70, 90). Att: 20,126

Benfica 2 (Maxi Pereira 42, Jara 81) Paris St-Germain 1 (Luyindula 14). Att: 25,000. Braga 1 (Alan 18 pen) **Liverpool** 0. Att: 12,991

CSKA Moscow 0 Porto 1 (Guarin 70). Att: 10,000. Dynamo Kiev 2 (Shevchenko 25, Gusev 77) **Manchester City** 0. Att: 16,000

PSV 0 **Rangers** 0. Att: 30,000. Twente 3 (De Jong 25, 90, Landzaat 56) Zenit St Petersburg 0. Att: 20,750

ROUND OF 16, SECOND LEG

Liverpool 0 Braga 0. Att: 37,494 (Braga won 1-0 on agg). **Manchester City** 1 (Kolarov 39) Dynamo Kiev 0. Att: 27,816 (Dynamo Kiev won 2-1 on agg). **Porto** 2 (Hulk 2, Guarin 24) CSKA Moscow 1 (Tosic 29). Att: 32,712 (Porto won 3-1 on agg). **Paris St-Germain** 1 (Bodmer 35) Benfica 1 (Gaitan 27). Att: 40,000 (Benfica won 3-2 on agg) **Rangers** 0 PSV 1 (Lens 13). Att: 35,373 (PSV won 1-0 on agg). Spartak Moscow 3 (Kombarov 21, Welliton 30, Alex 54) Ajax 0. Att: 45,000 (Spartak Moscow won 4-0 on agg) **Villarreal** 2 (Santi Cazorla 33, Rossi 61) Bayer Leverkusen 1 (Rodriguez 84 og). Att: 23,000 (Villarreal won 5-3 on agg). Zenit St Petersburg 2 (Shirokov 17, Kerzhakov 37) Twente 0. Att: 20,000 (Twente won 3-2 on agg)

QUARTER-FINALS, FIRST LEG

Benfica 4 (Aimar 37, Salvio 45, 51, Saviola 90) PSV 1 (Labyad 80). Att: 60,026. Dynamo Kiev 1 (Yarmolenko 6) Braga 1 (Vukojevic 14 og). Att: 16,000
Porto 5 (Falcao 38, 84, 90, Varela 65, Kombarov 70 og) Spartak Moscow 1 (Kombarov 71). Att: 38,209. Villarreal 5 (Marchena 22, Valero 43, Nilmar 45, 80, Rossi 55). Twente 1 (Janko 90). Att: 24,000

QUARTER-FINALS, SECOND LEG

Braga 0 Dynamo Kiev 0. Att: 18,000 (agg 1-1, Braga won on away goal). PSV 2 (Dzsudzsak 17, Lens 25) Benfica 2 (Luisao 45, Cardozo 63 pen). Att: 30,000 (Benfica won 6-3 on agg) Spartak Moscow 2 (Dzjuba 52, Ari 72) Porto 5 (Hulk 28, Rodriguez 45, Guarin 47, Falcao 54, Ruben Micael 89. Att: 20,000 (Porto won 10-3 on agg). Twente 1 (Bajrami 32) Villarreal 3 (Rossi 59 pen, Ruben 83 pen, Cani 89). Att: 23,000 (Villarreal won 8-2 on agg)

SEMI-FINALS, FIRST LEG

Benfica 2 (Jardel 50, Cardozo 59) Braga 1 (Vandinho 53). Att: 57,788. Porto 5 (Falcao 49 pen, 67, 75, 90, Guarin 61) Villarreal 1 (Cani 45). Att: 44,719

SEMI-FINALS, SECOND LEG

Braga 1 (Custodio 18) Benfica 0. Att: 25,384 (agg 2-2, Braga won on away goal). Villarreal 3 (Cani 17, Capdevila 75, Rossi 80 pen) Porto 2 (Hulk 40, Falcao 48). Att: 18,000 (Porto won 7-4 on agg)

FINAL

PORTO 1 BRAGA 0
Aviva Stadium, Dublin (45,391); Wednesday, May 18 2011

Porto (4-1-2-3): Helton (capt), Sapunaru, Rolando, Otamendi, Pereira, Guarin (Belluschi 73), Fernando, Joao Moutinho, Hulk, Falcao, Varela (J Rodriguez 79). **Subs not used:** Beto, Maicon, Walter, Souza, Ruben Micael. **Scorer:** Falcao (45). **Booked:** Sapunaru, Helton, Rolando. **Coach:** Andre Villas-Boas
Braga (4-2-1-3): Artur, Miguel Garcia, Paulao, A Rodriguez (Kaka 46), Silvio, Custodio, Hugo Viana (Mossoro 46), Vandinho (capt), Alan, Lima (Meyong 66), Paulo Cesar. **Subs not used:** Cristiano, Helder Barbosa, Echiejile, Leandro Salino. **Booked:** Hugo Viana, Silvio, Miguel Garcia, Mossoro, Kaka. **Coach:** Domingos Paciencia
Referee: C Velasco Carballo (Spain). **Half-time:** 1-0

Leading scorers: 17 Falcao (Porto); 11 Rossi (Villarreal); 6 Necid (CSKA Moscow); 5 Cavani (Napoli), Dzsudzsak (Dynamo Kiev), Guarin (Porto), Kanoute (Sevilla), Nilmar (Villarreal), Rudnevs (Lech Poznan), Wilfred (Sparta Prague)

CLUB WORLD CUP FINAL

TP MAZEMBE (DR Congo) 0 INTER MILAN 3
Abu Dhabi (42,120); Saturday, December 18 2010

TP Mazembe (4-4-2): Kidiaba, Kaliyutuka (Ndonga 89) Kimwaki, Kasasula, Nkulukuta, Kabangu, Bedi, Mihayo, Ekanga, Kasongo (Kanda 46), Singuluma. **Booked**: Kaliyutuka, Ekanga, Bedi, Kasusula. **Coach**: Lamine N'Diaye

Inter Milan (4-2-3-1): Julio Cesar, Maicon, Lucio, Cordoba, Chivu (Stankovic 54), Zanetti, Cambiasso, Motta (Mariga 87), Eto'o, Milito (Biabiany 70), Pandev. **Scorers**: Pandev (13), Eto'o (17), Biabiany (85). **Booked**: Pandev. **Coach**: Rafael Benitez

Referee: Y Nishimura (Japan). **Half-time**: 0-2

EUROPEAN SUPER CUP

INTER MILAN 0 ATLETICO MADRID 2
Monaco (18,100); Friday, August 27 2010

Inter Milan (4-2-3-1): Julio Cesar, Maicon, Samuel, Lucio, Chivu, Stankovic (Pandev 68), Zanetti, Cambiasso, Sneijder (Coutinho 78), Eto'o, Milito. **Subs not used**: Castelazzi, Cordoba, Mariga, Biabiany, Materazzi. **Booked**: Samuel. **Coach**: Rafael Benitez

Atletico Madrid (4-4-2): De Gea, Ujfalusi, Perea, Godin, Dominguez, Paulo Assuncao, Reyes (Merida 69), Raul Garcia, Simao (Camacho 90), Aguero, Forlan (Jurado 82). **Subs not used**: Joel, Lopez, Suarez, Costa. **Scorers**: Reyes (62), Aguero (83). **Booked**: Simao, Raul Garcia. **Coach**: Quique Sanchez Flores

Referee: M Busacca (Switzerland. **Half-time**: 0-0

Leading scorers (from group stage): **9** Pizarro (Werder Bremen), Cardozo (Benfica); **6** Forlan (Atletico Madrid), Gera (Fulham), Legear (Standard Liege), Llorente (Athletic Bilbao), Petric (Hamburg), Villa (Valencia), Zamora (Fulham)

UEFA CUP FINALS

1972	**Tottenham** beat Wolves 3-2 on agg (2-1a, 1-1h)
1973	Liverpool beat Borussia Moenchengladbach 3-2 on agg (3-0h, 0-2a)
1974	Feyenoord beat **Tottenham** 4-2 on agg (2-2a, 2-0h)
1975	Borussia Moenchengladbach beat Twente Enschede 5-1 on agg (0-0h, 5-1a)
1976	Liverpool beat Brugge 4-3 on agg (3-2h, 1-1a)
1977	Juventus beat Atletico Bilbao on away goals after 2-2 agg (1-0h, 1-2a)
1978	PSV Eindhoven beat Bastia 3-0 on agg (0-0a, 3-0h)
1979	Borussia Moenchengladbach beat Red Star Belgrade 2-1 on agg (1-1a, 1-0h)
1980	Eintracht Frankfurt beat Borussia Moenchengladbach on away goals after 3-3 agg (2-3a, 1-0h)
1981	Ipswich Town beat AZ 67 Alkmaar 5-4 on agg (3-0h, 2-4a)
1982	IFK Gothenburg beat SV Hamburg 4-0 on agg (1-0h, 3-0a)
1983	Anderlecht beat Benfica 2-1 on agg (1-0h, 1-1a)
1984	**Tottenham** beat Anderlecht 4-3 on penalties after 2-2 agg (1-1a, 1-1h)
1985	Real Madrid beat Videoton 3-1 on agg (3-0a, 0-1h)
1986	Real Madrid beat Cologne 5-3 on agg (5-1h, 0-2a)
1987	IFK Gothenburg beat Dundee Utd 2-1 on agg (1-0h, 1-1a)
1988	Bayer Leverkusen beat Espanol 3-2 on penalties after 3-3 agg (0-3a, 3-0h)
1989	Napoli beat VfB Stuttgart 5-4 on agg (2-1h, 3-3a)
1990	Juventus beat Fiorentina 3-1 on agg (3-1h, 0-0a)
1991	Inter Milan beat AS Roma 2-1 on agg (2-0h, 0-1a)
1992	Ajax beat Torino on away goals after 2-2 agg (2-2a, 0-0h)
1993	Juventus beat Borussia Dortmund 6-1 on agg (3-1a, 3-0h)
1994	Inter Milan beat Salzburg 2-0 on agg (1-0a, 1-0h)

1995	Parma beat Juventus 2-1 on agg (1-0h, 1-1a)
1996	Bayern Munich beat Bordeaux 5-1 on agg (2-0h, 3-1a)
1997	FC Schalke beat Inter Milan 4-1 on penalties after 1-1 agg (1-0h, 0-1a)
1998	Inter Milan beat Lazio 3-0 (one match) – Paris
1999	Parma beat Marseille 3-0 (one match) – Moscow
2000	Galatasaray beat Arsenal 4-1 on penalties after 0-0 (one match) – Copenhagen
2001	Liverpool beat Alaves 5-4 on golden goal (one match) – Dortmund
2002	Feyenoord beat Borussia Dortmund 3-2 (one match) – Rotterdam
2003	FC Porto beat Celtic 3-2 on silver goal (one match) – Seville
2004	Valencia beat Marseille 2-0 (one match) – Gothenburg
2005	CSKA Moscow beat Sporting Lisbon 3-1 (one match) – Lisbon
2006	Sevilla beat Middlesbrough 4-0 (one match) – Eindhoven
2007	Sevilla beat Espanyol 3-1 on penalties after 2-2 (one match) – Hampden Park
2008	Zenit St Petersburg beat Rangers 2-0 (one match) – City of Manchester Stadium
2009†	Shakhtar Donetsk beat Werder Bremen 2-1 (one match) – Istanbul

EUROPA LEAGUE FINALS

2010†	Atletico Madrid beat Fulham 2-1 (one match) – Hamburg
2011	Porto beat Braga 1-0 (one match) – Dublin

(† After extra-time)

FAIRS CUP FINALS

(As UEFA Cup previously known)

1958	Barcelona beat London 8-2 on agg (2-2a, 6-0h)
1960	Barcelona beat Birmingham 4-1 on agg (0-0a, 4-1h)
1961	AS Roma beat Birmingham City 4-2 on agg (2-2a, 2-0h)
1962	Valencia beat Barcelona 7-3 on agg (6-2h, 1-1a)
1963	Valencia beat Dynamo Zagreb 4-1 on agg (2-1a, 2-0h)
1964	Real Zaragoza beat Valencia 2-1 (Barcelona)
1965	Ferencvaros beat Juventus 1-0 (Turin)
1966	Barcelona beat Real Zaragoza 4-3 on agg (0-1h, 4-2a)
1967	Dinamo Zagreb beat Leeds Utd 2-0 on agg (2-0h, 0-0a)
1968	Leeds Utd beat Ferencvaros 1-0 on agg (1-0h, 0-0a)
1969	Newcastle Utd beat Ujpest Dozsa 6-2 on agg (3-0h, 3-2a)
1970	Arsenal beat Anderlecht 4-3 on agg (1-3a, 3-0h)
1971	Leeds Utd beat Juventus on away goals after 3-3 agg (2-2a, 1-1h)

CUP-WINNERS' CUP FINALS

1961	Fiorentina beat Rangers 4-1 on agg (2-0 Glasgow first leg, 2-1 Florence second leg)
1962	Atletico Madrid beat Fiorentina 3-0 (replay Stuttgart, after a 1-1 draw, Glasgow)
1963	Tottenham beat Atletico Madrid 5-1 (Rotterdam)
1964	Sporting Lisbon beat MTK Budapest 1-0 (replay Antwerp, after a 3-3 draw, Brussels)
1965	West Ham Utd beat Munich 1860 2-0 (Wembley)
1966†	Borussia Dortmund beat Liverpool 2-1 (Glasgow)
1967†	Bayern Munich beat Rangers 1-0 (Nuremberg)
1968	AC Milan beat SV Hamburg 2-0 (Rotterdam)
1969	Slovan Bratislava beat Barcelona 3-2 (Basle)
1970	Manchester City beat Gornik Zabrze 2-1 (Vienna)
1971†	Chelsea beat Real Madrid 2-1 (replay Athens, after a 1-1 draw, Athens)
1972	Rangers beat Moscow Dynamo 3-2 (Barcelona)
1973	AC Milan beat Leeds Utd 1-0 (Salonika)
1974	Magdeburg beat AC Milan 2-0 (Rotterdam)
1975	Dynamo Kiev beat Ferencvaros 3-0 (Basle)

1976	Anderlecht beat West Ham Utd 4-2 (Brussels)
1977	SV Hamburg beat Anderlecht 2-0 (Amsterdam)
1978	Anderlecht beat Austria WAC 4-0 (Paris)
1979†	Barcelona beat Fortuna Dusseldorf 4-3 (Basle)
1980†	Valencia beat Arsenal 5-4 on penalties after a 0-0 draw (Brussels)
1981	Dynamo Tbilisi beat Carl Zeiss Jena 2-1 (Dusseldorf)
1982	Barcelona beat Standard Liege 2-1 (Barcelona)
1983†	Aberdeen beat Real Madrid 2-1 (Gothenburg)
1984	Juventus beat Porto 2-1 (Basle)
1985	Everton beat Rapid Vienna 3-1 (Rotterdam)
1986	Dynamo Kiev beat Atletico Madrid 3-0 (Lyon)
1987	Ajax beat Lokomotiv Leipzig 1-0 (Athens)
1988	Mechelen beat Ajax 1-0 (Strasbourg)
1989	Barcelona beat Sampdoria 2-0 (Berne)
1990	Sampdoria beat Anderlecht 2-0 (Gothenburg)
1991	Manchester Utd beat Barcelona 2-1 (Rotterdam)
1992	Werder Bremen beat Monaco 2-0 (Lisbon)
1993	Parma beat Royal Antwerp 3-1 (Wembley)
1994	Arsenal beat Parma 1-0 (Copenhagen)
1995†	Real Zaragoza beat Arsenal 2-1 (Paris)
1996	Paris St Germain beat Rapid Vienna 1-0 (Brussels)
1997	Barcelona beat Paris St Germain 1-0 (Rotterdam)
1998	Chelsea beat VfB Stuttgart 1-0 (Stockholm)
1999	Lazio beat Real Mallorca 2-1 (Villa Park, Birmingham)

(† After extra time)

INTER-CONTINENTAL CUP

Year	Winners	Runners-up	Score
1960	Real Madrid (Spa)	Penarol (Uru)	0-0 5-1
1961	Penarol (Uru)	Benfica (Por)	0-1 2-1 5-0
1962	Santos (Bra)	Benfica (Por)	3-2 5-2
1963	Santos (Bra)	AC Milan (Ita)	2-4 4-2 1-0
1964	Inter Milan (Ita)	Independiente (Arg)	0-1 2-0 1-0
1965	Inter Milan (Ita)	Independiente (Arg)	3-0 0-0
1966	Penarol (Uru)	Real Madrid (Spa)	2-0 2-0
1967	Racing (Arg)	Celtic (Sco)	0-1 2-1 1-0
1968	Estudiantes (Arg)	Manchester Utd (Eng)	1-0 1-1
1969	AC Milan (Ita)	Estudiantes (Arg)	3-0 1-2
1970	Feyenoord (Hol)	Estudiantes (Arg)	2-2 1-0
1971	Nacional (Uru)	Panathanaikos (Gre)	* 1-1 2-1
1972	Ajax (Hol)	Independiente (Arg)	1-1 3-0
1973	Independiente (Arg)*	Juventus* (Ita)	1-0 #
1974	Atletico Madrid (Spa)*	Independiente (Arg)	0-1 2-0
1975	Not played		
1976	Bayern Munich (WGer)	Cruzeiro (Bra)	2-0 0-0
1977	Boca Juniors (Arg)	Borussia Mönchengladbach* (WGer)	2-2 3-0
1978	Not played		
1979	Olimpia Asuncion (Par)	Malmö* (Swe)	1-0 2-1
1980	Nacional (Arg)	Nott'm Forest (Eng)	1-0
1981	Flamengo (Bra)	Liverpool (Eng)	3-0
1982	Penarol (Uru)	Aston Villa (Eng)	2-0
1983	Porto Alegre (Bra)	SV Hamburg (WGer)	2-1
1984	Independiente (Arg)	Liverpool (Eng)	1-0

1985	Juventus (Ita)	Argentinos Juniors (Arg)	2-2 (aet)
		(Juventus won 4-2 on penalties)	
1986	River Plate (Arg)	Steaua Bucharest (Rom)	1-0
1987	Porto (Por)	Penarol (Uru)	2-1 (aet)
1988	Nacional (Uru)	PSV Eindhoven (Hol)	1-1 (aet)
		(Nacional won 7-6 on penalties)	
1989	AC Milan (Ita)	Nacional (Col)	1-0 (aet)
1990	AC Milan (Ita)	Olimpia Asuncion (Par)	3-0
1991	Red Star (Yug)	Colo Colo (Chi)	3-0
1992	Sao Paulo (Bra)	Barcelona (Spa)	2-1
1993	Sao Paulo (Bra)	AC Milan (Ita)	3-2
1994	Velez Sarsfield (Arg)	AC Milan (Ita)	2-0
1995	Ajax (Hol)	Gremio (Bra)	0-0 (aet)
		(Ajax won 4-3 on penalties)	
1996	Juventus (Ita)	River Plate (Arg)	1-0
1997	Borussia Dortmund (Ger)	Cruzeiro (Arg)	2-0
1998	Real Madrid (Spa)	Vasco da Gama (Bra)	2-1
1999	Manchester Utd (Eng)	Palmeiras (Bra)	1-0
2000	Boca Juniors (Arg)	Real Madrid (Spa)	2-1
2001	Bayern Munich (Ger)	Boca Juniors (Arg)	1-0
2002	Real Madrid (Spa)	Olimpia Ascuncion (Par)	2-0
2003	Boca Juniors (Arg)	AC Milan (Ita)	1-1
		(Boca Juniors won 3-1 on penalties)	
2004	FC Porto (Por)	Caldas (Col)	0-0
		(FC Porto won 8-7 on penalties)	

Played as a single match in Japan since 1980
* European Cup runners-up # One match only
Summary: 43 contests; South America 22 wins, Europe 23 wins

CLUB WORLD CHAMPIONSHIP

2005	Sao Paulo beat Liverpool	1-0
2006	Internacional (Bra) beat Barcelona	1-0
2007	AC Milan beat Boca Juniors (Arg)	4-2

CLUB WORLD CUP

2008	Manchester Utd beat Liga de Quito	1-0
2009	Barcelona beat Estudiantes	2-1 (aet)
2010	Inter Milan beat TP Mazembe	3-0

QUOTE/UNQOUTE

'I'm not suited to Bolton or Blackburn. I would be more suited to Inter Milan or Real Madrid. It wouldn't be a problem for me to go and manage those clubs. I would win the double or the league every time. Give me Manchester United or Chelsea, it would be the same, no problem"
Sam Allardyce, Blackburn manager.

EUROPEAN TABLES 2010–2011

FRANCE

	P	W	D	L	F	A	GD	Pts
Lille	38	21	13	4	68	36	32	76
Marseille	38	18	14	6	62	39	23	68
Lyon	38	17	13	8	61	40	21	64
Paris SG	38	15	15	8	56	41	15	60
Sochaux	38	17	7	14	60	43	17	58
Rennes	38	15	11	12	38	35	3	56
Bordeaux	38	12	15	11	43	42	1	51
Toulouse	38	14	8	16	38	36	2	50
Auxerre	38	10	19	9	45	41	4	49
St Etienne	38	12	13	13	46	47	-1	49
Lorient	38	12	13	13	46	48	-2	49
Valenciennes	38	10	18	10	45	41	4	48
Nancy	38	13	9	16	43	48	-5	48
Montpellier	38	12	11	15	32	43	-11	47
Caen	38	11	13	14	46	51	-5	46
Brest	38	11	13	14	36	43	-7	46
Nice	38	11	13	14	33	48	-15	46
Monaco	38	9	17	12	36	40	-4	44
Lens	38	7	14	17	35	58	-23	35
Arles	38	3	11	24	21	70	-49	20

Leading league scorers: 26 Sow (Lille); 22 Gameiro (Lorient); 17 El Arabi (Caen), Lopez (Lyon), Pujol (Valenciennes); 15 Gervinho (Lille), Ideye (Sochaux), Maiga (Sochaux), Remy (Marseille); 14 Nene (Paris SG). **Cup Final:** Lille 1 (Obraniak 89) Paris SG 0

GERMANY

	P	W	D	L	F	A	GD	Pts
Borussia Dortmund	34	23	6	5	67	22	45	75
Bayer Leverkusen	34	20	8	6	64	44	20	68
Bayern Munich	34	19	8	7	81	40	41	65
Hannover	34	19	3	12	49	45	4	60
Mainz	34	18	4	12	52	39	13	58
Nuremberg	34	13	8	13	47	45	2	47
Kaiserslautern	34	13	7	14	48	51	-3	46
Hamburg	34	12	9	13	46	52	-6	45
Freiburg	34	13	5	16	41	50	-9	44
Cologne	34	13	5	16	47	62	-15	44
Hoffenheim	34	11	10	13	50	50	0	43
Stuttgart	34	12	6	16	60	59	1	42
Werder Bremen	34	10	11	13	47	61	-14	41
Schalke	34	11	7	16	38	44	-6	40
Wolfsburg	34	9	11	14	43	48	-5	38
Monchengladbach	34	10	6	18	48	65	-17	36
Eintracht Frankfurt	34	9	7	18	31	49	-18	34
St Pauli	34	8	5	21	35	68	-33	29

Leading league scorers: 28 Gomez (Bayern Munich); 22 Cisse (Freiburg), 17 Novakovic (Cologne); 16 Barrios (Borussia Dortmund), Gekas (Eintracht Frankfurt), Lakic (Kaiserslautern); 15 Schurrie (Mainz); 14 Konan (Hannover); 13 Podolski (Cologne), Raul (Schalke). **Cup Final:** Schalke 5 (Draxler 18, Huntelaar 22, 70, Howedes 42, Jurado 55) Duisburg 0

HOLLAND

	P	W	D	L	F	A	GD	Pts
Ajax	34	22	7	5	72	30	42	73
Twente	34	21	8	5	65	34	31	71
PSV	34	20	9	5	79	34	45	69
Alkmaar	34	17	8	9	55	44	11	59
Groningen	34	17	6	11	65	52	13	57
Roda	34	14	13	7	65	50	15	55
Den Haag	34	16	6	12	63	55	8	54
Heracles	34	14	7	13	65	56	9	49
Utrecht	34	13	8	13	55	51	4	47
Feyenoord	34	12	8	14	53	54	-1	44
Nijmegen	34	10	13	11	57	56	1	43
Heerenveen	34	10	11	13	60	54	6	41
Breda	34	12	5	17	44	60	-16	40
De Graafschap	34	9	11	14	31	56	-25	38
Vitesse Arnhem	34	9	8	17	42	61	-19	35
Excelsior	34	10	5	19	45	66	-21	35
Venlo	34	6	3	25	34	76	-42	21
Willem	34	3	6	25	37	98	-61	15

Leading league scorers: 23 Vleminckx (Nijmegen); 21 Bulykin (Den Haag); Junker (Roda); 16 Matavz (Groningen), Dzsudzsak (PSV); 15 Castaignos (Feyenoord), Everton (Heracles), Overtoom (Heracles), Sigthorsson (Alkmaar), Toivonen (PSV), Van Wolfswinkel (Utrecht). **Cup Final:** Twente 3 (Brama 45, Janssen 56, Janko 118) Ajax 2 (De Zeeuw 20, Ebecilio 40) – aet

ITALY

	P	W	D	L	F	A	GD	Pts
AC Milan	38	24	10	4	65	24	41	82
Inter Milan	38	23	7	8	69	42	27	76
Napoli	38	21	7	10	59	39	20	70
Udinese	38	20	6	12	65	43	22	66
Lazio	38	20	6	12	55	39	16	66
Roma	38	18	9	11	59	52	7	63
Juventus	38	15	13	10	57	47	10	58
Palermo	38	17	5	16	58	63	-5	56
Fiorentina	38	12	15	11	49	44	5	51
Genoa	38	14	9	15	45	47	-2	51
Chievo	38	11	13	14	38	40	-2	46
Parma	38	11	13	14	39	47	-8	46
Catania	38	12	10	16	40	52	-12	46
Cagliari	38	12	9	17	44	51	-7	45
Cesena	38	11	10	17	38	50	-12	43
Bologna*	38	11	12	15	35	52	-17	42
Lecce	38	11	8	19	46	66	-20	41
Sampdoria	38	8	12	18	33	49	-16	36
Brescia	38	7	11	20	34	52	-18	32
Bari	38	5	9	24	27	56	-29	24

* 3pts deducted

Leading league scorers: 28 Di Natale (Udinese); 26 Cavani (Napoli); 21 Eto'o (Inter Milan); 18 Di Vaio (Bologna); 15 Totti (Roma); 14 Ibrahimovic (AC Milan), Pato (AC Milan), Robinho (AC Milan); 12 Caracciolo (Brescia), Gilardino (Fiorentina), Pellissier (Chievo), Sanchez (Udinese). **Cup Final:** Inter Milan 3 (Eto'o 26, 77, Milito 90) Palermo 1 (Munoz 88)

PORTUGAL

	P	W	D	L	F	A	GD	Pts
Porto	30	27	3	0	73	16	57	84
Benfica	30	20	3	7	61	31	30	63
Sporting	30	13	9	8	41	31	10	48
Braga	30	13	7	10	45	33	12	46
Guimaraes	30	12	7	11	36	37	-1	43
Nacional	30	11	9	10	28	31	-3	42
Pacos Ferreira	30	10	11	9	35	42	-7	41
Rio Ave	30	10	8	12	35	33	2	38
Maritimo	30	9	8	13	33	32	1	35
Uniao Leiria	30	9	8	13	25	38	-13	35
Olhanense	30	7	13	10	24	34	-10	34
Setubal	30	8	10	12	29	42	-13	34
Beira Mar	30	7	12	11	32	36	-4	33
Coimbra	30	7	9	14	32	48	-16	30
Portimonense	30	6	7	17	29	49	-20	25
Naval	30	5	8	17	26	51	-25	23

Leading league scorers: 23 Hulk (Porto); 16 Falcao (Porto), Tomas (Rio Ave); 12 Cardozo (Benfica); 11 Baba (Maritimo); 10 Edgar (Guimaraes), Varela (Porto); 9 Carlao (Uniao Leiria), Mejolaro (Setubal), Leandro Tatu (Beira Mar), Saviola (Benfica). **Cup Final**: Porto 6 (Rodriguez) 3, 45, 73, Varela 22, Rolando 36, Hulk 42) Guimaraes 2 (Pereira 21 og, Edgar 34)

SPAIN

	P	W	D	L	F	A	GD	Pts
Barcelona	38	30	6	2	95	21	74	96
Real Madrid	38	29	5	4	102	33	69	92
Valencia	38	21	8	9	64	44	20	71
Villarreal	38	18	8	12	54	44	10	62
Seville	38	17	7	14	62	61	1	58
Athletic Bilbao	38	18	4	16	59	55	4	58
Atletico Madrid	38	17	7	14	62	53	9	58
Espanyol	38	15	4	19	46	55	-9	49
Osasuna	38	13	8	17	45	46	-1	47
Gijon	38	11	14	13	35	42	-7	47
Malaga	38	13	7	18	54	68	-14	46
Santander	38	12	10	16	41	56	-15	46
Zaragoza	38	12	9	17	40	53	-13	45
Sociedad	38	14	3	21	49	66	-17	45
Levante	38	12	9	17	41	52	-11	45
Getafe	38	12	8	18	49	60	-11	44
Mallorca	38	12	8	18	41	56	-15	44
Deportivo	38	10	13	15	31	47	-16	43
Hercules	38	9	8	21	36	60	-24	35
Almeria	38	6	12	20	36	70	-34	30

Leading league scorers: 41 Ronaldo (Real Madrid); 31 Messi (Barcelona); 20 Aguero (Atletico Madrid); 19 Negredo (Sevilla); 18 Llorente (Athletic Bilbao), Rossi (Villarreal), Soldado (Villarreal), Villa (Barcelona); 15 Benzema (Real Madrid); 14 Rondon (Malaga)
Cup Final: Real Madrid 1 (Ronaldo 113) Barcelona 0 – aet

242

FOOTBALL'S CHANGING HOMES

For the best part of 16 years, **Brighton and Hove Albion** were footballing nomads – without a home to call their own. The Goldstone Ground, their base since 1902, was sold, controversially, for development in 1995. The club stayed as tenants for another two years, before spending another two sharing Gillingham's Priestfield Stadium 72 miles away.

Then, they moved in to the cramped surroundings of the Withdean athletics track, where Steve Ovett once trained on his way to becoming Olympic champion and where the capacity was restricted to around 8,500. A total of 16 possible sites were considered for a new ground and one stood out - at Falmer next to the University of Brighton and A27 dual carriageway. A long, drawn-out process followed, with objections from several quarters, before permission to build there was finally granted. Work started towards the end of 2008. Now, Brighton have moved into the £93m, 22,500-seater American Express Community Stadium, named in a sponsorship deal with the financial services company. Fittingly, they kick off in the Championship, having won the League One title last season under manager Gus Poyet, the former Chelsea and Tottenham midfield player. Poyet and his players are guaranteed huge support, starting with a home match against Doncaster on August 6. The club sold out of more than 15,000 season tickets and there is now a waiting list. Some 2,600 corporate packages were also snapped up. One of the game's longest-running sagas has reached a successful conclusion.

Rotherham are also planning a home-coming – to a more modest but equally satisfying new stadium. Work has started at an old foundry on a 12,000-seater project, costing £17m, to be completed for the 2012-13 season. The club have been at Don Valley Stadium in Sheffield since 2008 after agreement with the club's landlords could not be reached on staying at Millmoor. Subject to planning permission, **Bristol Rovers** are another club targeting that season for a move from the Memorial Ground to a £40m arena seating 20,000 on land acquired from the University of the West of England. The aim is to continue sharing with Bristol Rugby Club. **Aberdeen** are closer to moving after receiving permission for a 22,000-seater community stadium at Loirston Loch south of the city and for redeveloping Pittodrie for housing. The £38million project includes an adjacent 3,000-seat ground for Highland League side Cove Rangers. **Hearts** have begun a joint study with Edinburgh Council looking at redeveloping Tynecastle or building a new stadium to the west of the city.

Crystal Palace could move from Selhurst Park to a 40,000-seater ground at the National Sports Centre, the club's original home, under plans unveiled by co-chairman Steve Parish. **Hull** owner Assem Allam wants to transform the KC Stadium into a £100million sports village with an Olympic-size swimming pool, tennis, squash and gymnastics facilities and a hotel. It would involve increasing capacity from 25,000 to 35,000. **West Ham** won the vote to move into the Olympic Stadium after the 2012 Games and say relegation from the Premier League will not affect plans. **Tottenham**, who lost it, and **Leyton Orient**, who are worried about the impact on their club's support, launched legal challenges to the decision. These were rejected in the High Court, prompting Tottenham to resurrect plans for a new 60,000-seater stadium at White Hart Lane. The club have applied to the Government's regional growth fund for help in regenerating the area around the ground. **West Bromwich Albion** are proposing to increase capacity of the Hawthorns to 30,000 within the next three years by installing an extra 3,500 seats. **Yeovil** are planning a new 3,500-capacity stand to raise capacity from 9,665. A retail park is part of development.

BRITISH AND IRISH INTERNATIONALS 2010–11

* Denotes new cap

EUROPEAN CHAMPIONSHIP 2012 QUALIFYING

ENGLAND 4 BULGARIA 0
Group G: Wembley (73,246); Friday, September 3 2010

England (4-4-1-1): Hart (Manchester City), G Johnson (Liverpool), Dawson (Tottenham) (*Cahill, Bolton 57), Jagielka (Everton), Cole (Chelsea), Walcott (Arsenal) (A Johnson, Manchester City 74), Gerrard (Liverpool), Barry (Manchester City), Milner (Manchester City), Rooney (Manchester Utd), Defoe (Tottenham) (A Young, Aston Villa 87). **Scorers:** Defoe (3, 61, 86), A Johnson (83). **Booked:** Milner

Bulgaria (4-2-3-1): Mihailov, Manolev (Minev 65), Ivanov, Stoyanov, Milanov, S Petrov, Angelov, Yankov, Popov (Peev 79), M Petrov, Bojinov (Rangelov 63). **Booked:** Popov

Referee: V Kassai (Hungary). **Half-time:** 1-0

LITHUANIA 0 SCOTLAND 0
Group I: Kaunas (6,539); Friday, September 3 2010

Lithuania (4-5-1): Karcemarskas, Stankevicius, Skerla, Radavicius, Kijanskas, Semberas, Panka, Cesnauskis, Mikoliunas (Poskus 70), Danilevicius (Ivaskevicius 89), Sernas (Luksa 79). **Booked:** Kijanskas, Radavicius, Skerla, Ivaskevicius

Scotland (4-4-2): McGregor (Rangers), Hutton (Tottenham), Weir (Rangers), McManus (Middlesbrough), Whittaker (Rangers) (Berra, Wolves 90), Brown (Celtic) (Morrison, WBA 76), Fletcher (Manchester Utd), Robson (Middlesbrough) (McFadden, Birmingham 69), McCulloch (Rangers), Miller (Rangers), Naismith (Rangers). **Booked:** Brown, McCulloch

Referee: C Cakir (Turkey)

MONTENEGRO 1 WALES 0
Group G: Podgorica (9,862); Friday, September 3 2010

Montenegro (4-4-2): M Bozovic, Zverotic, Djudovic, Pavicevic, Jovanovic, Basa, Vukcevic (Beciraj 87), Boskovic (V Bozovic 73), Pekovic, Vucinic, Djalovic (Novakovic 83). **Scorer:** Vucinic (30). **Booked:** Pavicevic, Djudovic, Pekovic

Wales (4-4-2): Hennessey (Wolves), Gunter (Nottm Forest), Collins (Aston Villa) (Morgan, Preston 75), Williams (Swansea), Ricketts (Bolton), Vaughan (Blackpool), Edwards (Wolves) (Earnshaw, Nottm Forest 68), Ledley (Celtic), Bale (Tottenham), Morison (Millwall) (Church, Reading 78), Bellamy (Manchester City). **Booked:** Morison, Ricketts, Bale

Referee: A Kakos (Greece). **Half-time:** 1-0

John Toshack's last match as Wales manager.

SLOVENIA 0 NORTHERN IRELAND 1
Group C: Maribor (11,582); Friday, September 3 2010

Slovenia (4-4-2): Handanovic, Brecko, Cesar, Jokic, Mavric, Birsa, Radosavljevic, Koren, Kirm (Illicic 74), Novakovic (Dedic 74), Ljubijankic (Matavz 88)

Northern Ireland (4-4-2): Taylor (Birmingham), McAuley (Ipswich), *Cathcart (Blackpool), Craigan (Motherwell), Baird (Fulham), Davis (Rangers) (C Evans (Manchester Utd 67), Hughes (Fulham), McCann (Peterborough), Brunt (WBA) (Gorman, Wolves 89), Healy (Sunderland) (Lafferty, Rangers 67), Feeney (Oldham). **Scorer:** C Evans (70). **Booked:** Healy, Brunt, Lafferty

Referee: P Balaj (Romania). **Half-time:** 0-0

ARMENIA 0 REPUBLIC OF IRELAND 1
Group B: Yerevan (8,682); Friday, September 3 2010

Armenia (4-4-2): Berezovsky, Hovsepyan, Arzumanyan, Mkrtchyan, Arakelyan, Artak Edigaryan (Hambardzumyan 71), Artur Edigaryan (Manoyan 68), Malakyan (Manucharyan 79), Pachajyan, Movsisyanj, Mkhitaryan. **Booked:** Artak Edigaryan

Republic of Ireland (4-4-2): Given (Manchester City), O'Shea (Manchester Utd), Dunne (Aston Villa), St Ledger (Preston), Kilbane (Hull), Lawrence (Stoke), Whelan (Stoke), Green (Derby), McGeady (Spartak Moscow) (Fahey, Birmingham 68), Doyle (Reading), Keane (Tottenham) (Keogh, Wolves 85). **Scorer:** Fahey (76). **Booked:** Whelan
Referee: Z Szabo (Hungary). **Half-time:** 0-0

SWITZERLAND 1 ENGLAND 3
Group G: Basle (39,700); Tuesday, September 7 2010
Switzerland (4-4-2): Benaglio, Lichtsteiner, Grichting, Von Bergen, Ziegler, Margairaz (Shaqiri 46), Inler, Schwegler (Constanzo 83), Degen (Streller 64), Derdiyok, Frei. **Scorer:** Shaqiri (71). **Booked:** Lichtsteiner. **Sent off:** Lichtsteiner
England (4-4-1-1): Hart (Manchester City), G Johnson (Liverpool), Jagielka (Everton), Lescott (Manchester City), Cole (Chelsea), Walcott (Arsenal) (A Johnson, Manchester City 13), Gerrard (Liverpool), Barry (Manchester City), Milner (Manchester City), Rooney (Manchester Utd) (Wright-Phillips, Manchester City 79), Defoe (Tottenham) (Bent, Sunderland 71). **Scorers:** Rooney (10), A Johnson (69), Bent (88). **Booked:** Milner, Cole
Referee: N Rizzoli (Italy). **Half-time:** 0-1

SCOTLAND 2 LIECHTENSTEIN 1
Group I: Hampden Park (37,050); Tuesday, September 7 2010
Scotland (4-4-2): McGregor (Rangers), Hutton (Tottenham), Weir (Rangers), McManus (Middlesbrough), Wallace (Hearts) (Robson, Middlesbrough 54), Brown (Celtic), Fletcher (Manchester Utd), McCulloch (Rangers), McFadden (Birmingham), Miller (Rangers), Boyd (Middlesbrough) (Naismith, Rangers 66). **Scorers:** Miller (63), McManus (90). **Booked:** Robson, McCulloch, McGregor, Hutton
Liechtenstein (4-5-1): Jehle, Oehri, Martin Stocklasa, Michael Stocklasa, Rechsteiner, Polverino, Wieser (Buchel 71), Erne, Frick (D'Elia 79), Burgmeier, D Hasler (N Hasler 90). **Scorer:** Frick (46). **Booked:** Burgmeier, Wieser, Martin Stocklasa, Frick, Rechsteiner, Polverino, D'Elia
Referee: V Shvetsov (Ukraine). **Half-time:** 0-0

REPUBLIC OF IRELAND 3 ANDORRA 1
Group B: Aviva Stadium (40,283); Tuesday, September 7 2010
Republic of Ireland (4-4-2): Given (Manchester City), O'Shea (Manchester Utd) (Kelly, Fulham 75), Dunne (Aston Villa), St Ledger (Preston), Kilbane (Hull), Lawrence (Stoke), Whelan (Stoke) (Gibson, Manchester Utd 61), Green (Derby), McGeady (Spartak Moscow), Doyle (Wolves) (Keogh, Wolves 82), Keane (Tottenham). **Scorers:** Kilbane (15), Doyle (41), Keane (54). **Booked:** Dunne
Andorra (4-5-1): J Gomez, Bernaus, Martinez, Lima, Pujol (Sonejee 86), Escura, S Gomez, Ayala (Andorra 71), Vieira, Moreno, Silva. **Scorer:** Martinez (45). **Booked:** Silva, Lima, Moreno
Referee: L Trattou (Cyprus). **Half-time:** 2-1

CZECH REPUBLIC 1 SCOTLAND 0
Group I: Prague (16,000); Friday, October 8 2010
Czech Republic (4-4-2): Cech, Suchy, Kadlec, Hubnik, Hubschman, Pospech, Plasil (Rajnoch 90), Polak, Rosicky, Magera (Bednar 59), Necid (Holek 84). **Scorer:** Hubnik (69). **Booked:** Necid, Hubschman
Scotland (4-2-4-0): McGregor (Rangers), Hutton (Tottenham), Weir (Rangers), McManus (Middlesbrough), Whittaker (Rangers), G Caldwell (Wigan) (Miller, Rangers 76), Fletcher (Manchester Utd), *Mackie (QPR) (Iwelumo, Burnley 76), Morrison (WBA) (Robson, Middlesbrough 84), Dorrans (WBA), Naismith (Rangers)
Booked: Whittaker, Weir, Robson
Referee: I Bebek (Croatia). **Half-time:** 0-0

WALES 0 BULGARIA 1
Group G: Cardiff City Stadium (14,061); Friday, October 8 2010
Wales (4-2-3-1): Hennessey (Wolves), Gunter (Nottm Forest), J Collins (Aston Villa), Ricketts (Bolton), D Collins (Stoke), Vaughan (Blackpool), Williams (Swansea), Edwards (Wolves) (Church, Reading 69), Ledley (Celtic) (King, Leicester 58), Bale (Tottenham), Morison (Millwall) (Robson-Kanu, Reading 82). **Booked:** Ricketts. **Sent off:** Gunter
Bulgaria (4-4-1-1): Mihaylov, Bodurov, Iliev (Vidanov 36), Ivanov, Zanev, Peev (Rangelov 72), Georgiev, S Petrov, M Petrov, Popov, Makriev. **Scorer:** Popov (48). **Booked:** M Petrov, Bodurov
Referee: J Eriksson (Sweden). **Half-time:** 0-0

NORTHERN IRELAND 0 ITALY 0
Group C: Windsor Park (15,150); Friday, October 8 2010
Northern Ireland (4-4-2): Taylor (Birmingham), McAuley (Ipswich), Hughes (Fulham), Craigan (Motherwell), J Evans (Manchester Utd), Brunt (WBA) (McGinn, Celtic 71), Baird (Fulham), Davis (Rangers), McCann (Peterborough) (C Evans, Manchester Utd 80), Feeney (Oldham), Healy (Sunderland) (Lafferty, Rangers 66)
Italy (4-2-3-1): Viviano, Criscito, Bonucci, Chiellini, Cassani, De Rossi, Pirlo, Mauri (Marchisio 79), Pepe (Rossi 84), Cassano, Borriello (Pazzini 74)
Referee: A Chapron (France)

REPUBLIC OF IRELAND 2 RUSSIA 3
Group B: Aviva Stadium (50,411); Friday, October 8 2010
Republic of Ireland (4-4-2): Given (Manchester City), O'Shea (Manchester Utd), Dunne (Aston Villa), St. Ledger (Preston), Kilbane (Hull), Lawrence (Stoke) (Long, Reading 62), Whelan (Stoke) (Gibson, Manchester Utd 66), Green (Derby), McGeady (Spartak Moscow), Doyle (Wolves) (Fahey, Birmingham 71), Keane (Tottenham). **Scorers:** Keane (72 pen), Long (78). **Booked:** St. Ledger, Doyle
Russia (4-1-2): Akinfeev, Anyukov, Ignashevich, V Berezutsky, Zhirkov, Denisov, Shirokov, Zyryanov (Semshov 68), Dzagoev (A Berezutsky 84), Arshavin, Kerzhakov (Pogrebniak 80). **Scorers:** Kerzhakov (11), Dzagoev (28), Shirokov (50). **Booked:** Denisov, Anyukov, A Berezutsky
Referee: K Blom (Holland). **Half-time:** 0-2

ENGLAND 0 MONTENEGRO 0
Group G: Wembley (73,451); Tuesday, October 12 2010
England (4-4-2): Hart (Manchester City), G Johnson (Liverpool), Ferdinand (Manchester Utd), Lescott (Manchester City), Cole (Chelsea), A Johnson (Manchester Utd), Gerrard (Liverpool), Barry (Manchester City), A Young (Aston Villa) (Wright-Phillips, Manchester City 74), Crouch (Tottenham) (*K Davies, Bolton 68), Rooney (Manchester Utd). **Booked:** Rooney, Young, Barry, K Davies
Montenegro (4-5-1): Bozovic, Savic, Dzudovic (Delibasic 78), Basa, Jovanovic, Vukcevic, Zverotic, Pekovic, Novakovic (Kascelan 62), Djalovic, Boskovic (Beciraj 83). **Booked:** Dzudovic, Savic, Basa, Kascelan, Vukcevic
Referee: M Grafe (Germany)

SCOTLAND 2 SPAIN 3
Group I: Hampden Park (51,322); Tuesday, October 12 2010
Scotland (4-1-4-1): McGregor (Rangers), *Bardsley (Sunderland), Weir (Rangers), McManus (Middlesbrough), Whittaker (Rangers), McCulloch (Rangers) (Adam, Blackpool 46), Fletcher (Manchester Utd), Morrison (WBA) (Maloney, Celtic 87), Dorrans (WBA) (Mackie, QPR 81), Naismith (Rangers), Miller (Rangers). **Scorers:** Naismith (58), Pique (66 og). **Booked:** Whittaker, Miller. **Sent off:** Whittaker
Spain (4-2-3-1): Casillas, Sergio Ramos, Puyol, Pique, Capdevila, Busquets (Marchena 90), Xabi Alonso, Silva (Llorente 76), Iniesta, Cazoria (Xavi 70), Villa. **Scorers:** Villa (44 pen), Iniesta (55), Llorente (79)
Referee: M Busacca (Italy). **Half-time:** 0-1

SWITZERLAND 4 WALES 1
Group G: Basle (26,000); Tuesday, October 12 2010

Switzerland (4-4-2): Benaglio (Wolfli 8), Lichtsteiner, Ziegler, Von Bergen, Grichting, Schwegler (Fernandes 90), Barnetta, Inler, Stocker, Frei (Derdiyok 78), Streller. **Scorers:** Stocker (8, 89), Streller (21), Inler (82 pen). **Booked:** Lichtsteiner, Barnetta.
Wales (4-4-1-1): Hennessey (Wolves), *Blake (Cardiff) (Ribeiro, Bristol City 54), J Collins (Aston Villa), Williams (Swansea), D Collins (Stoke), Crofts (Norwich), Edwards (Wolves) (Morison, Millwall) 77), King (Leicester), Bale (Tottenham),Vaughan (Blackpool) (*MacDonald, Swansea 88), Church (Reading). **Scorer:** Bale (13). **Booked:** King, J Collins
Referee: A Hamer (Luxembourg). **Half-time:** 2-1

FAROE ISLANDS 1 NORTHERN IRELAND 1
Group C: Toftir (1,921); Tuesday, October 12 2010

Faroe Islands (4-5-1): Mikkelsen, Naes, Jacobsen, Davidsen, Gregersen,Udsen (Petersen 67), Benjaminsen, Samuelsen (A Hansen 78), Holst (J Hansen 84), Edmundsson, Elttor. **Scorer:** Holst (60). **Booked:** Naes, Gregersen
Northern Ireland (4-4-2): Taylor (Birmingham), McAuley (Ipswich), Hughes (Fulham), Craigan (Motherwell), J Evans (Manchester Utd), Baird (Fulham), Davis (Rangers), McGinn (Celtic) (C Evans, Manchester Utd, 83), Brunt (WBA), Feeney (Oldham) (Healy, Sunderland) 50), Lafferty (Rangers). **Scorer:** Lafferty (76). **Booked:** Davis.
Referee: C Zimmermann (Switzerland). **Half-time:** 0-0

SLOVAKIA 1 REPUBLIC OF IRELAND 1
Group B: Zilina (10,892); Tuesday, October 12 2010

Slovakia (4-4-2): Mucha, Zabavnik, Salata, Durica, Hubocan, Kucka, Karhan, Hamsik, Weiss (Holosko 69), Jendrisek (Oravec 83), Sestak (Stoch 70). **Scorer:** Durica (36). **Booked:** Hubocan, Sestak, Mucha, Karhan
Republic of Ireland (4-4-2): Given (Manchester City), O'Shea (Manchester Utd), Dunne (Aston Villa), St. Ledger (Preston), Kilbane (Hull), Fahey (Birmingham) (Keogh, Wolves 71), Whelan (Stoke), Green (Derby) (Gibson, Manchester Utd 41), McGeady (Spartak Moscow), Keane (Tottenham), Long (Reading). **Scorer:** St. Ledger (16)
Referee: A Undiano Mallenco (Spain). **Half-time:** 1-1

SERBIA 2 NORTHERN IRELAND 1
Group C: Belgrade (265); Friday, March 25 2011

Serbia (4-4-2): Brkic, Ivanovic, Subotic, Bisevac, Kolarov, Tosic, Ljajic (Jovanovic 46), Krasic (Petrovic 86), Stankovic, Milijas (Ninkovic 46), Pantelic. **Scorers:** Pantelic (65), Tosic (74). **Booked:** Stankovic, Pantelic, Krasic
Northern Ireland (4-4-1-1): *Camp (Nottm Forest), Baird (Fulham), Hughes (Fulham), J Evans (Manchester Utd) (McCourt, Celtic 86), McAuley (Ipswich), Cathcart (Blackpool), C Evans (Manchester Utd), Clingan (Coventry), Gorman (Wolves) (Feeney, Oldham 78), Brunt (WBA), Lafferty (Rangers) (Healy, Rangers 46). **Scorer:** McAuley (40). **Booked:** J Evans, Healy
Referee: S Gumienny (Belgium). **Half-time:** 0-1 (no home fans admitted – previous crowd trouble)

WALES 0 ENGLAND 2
Group G: Millennium Stadium (68,959); Saturday, March 26 2011

Wales (4-2-3-1): Hennessey (Wolves), Gunter (Nottm Forest), J Collins (Aston Villa), Williams (Swansea), D Collins (Stoke), Crofts (Norwich), Ledley (Celtic), Bellamy (Manchester City), Ramsey (Arsenal), King (Leicester) (Vaughan, Blackpool 65), Morison (Millwall) (Evans, Sheffield Utd 65). **Booked:** Crofts, Ledley, Bellamy, J Collins, Vaughan
England (4-3-3): Hart (Manchester City), Johnson (Liverpool), Dawson (Tottenham), Terry (Chelsea), Cole (Chelsea), Lampard (Chelsea), Parker (West Ham) (Jagielka, Everton 89), Wilshere (Arsenal) (Downing, Aston Villa 82), A Young (Aston Villa), Bent (Aston Villa), Rooney (Manchester Utd) (Milner, Manchester City 70). **Scorers:** Lampard (7 pen), Bent (14). **Booked:** Rooney, Johnson
Referee: O Benquerenca (Portugal). **Half-time:** 0-2

REPUBLIC OF IRELAND 2 MACEDONIA 1
Group B: Aviva Stadium (33,200); Saturday, March 26, 2011

Republic of Ireland (4-4-2): Westwood (Coventry), Foley (Wolves), Dunne (Aston Villa), O'Dea (Celtic), Kilbane (Hull), Duff (Fulham), Whelan (Stoke), Gibson (Manchester Utd) (Fahey, Birmingham 77), McGeady (Spartak Moscow), Keane (Tottenham) (*McCarthy, Wigan 87), Doyle (Wolves) (Long, Reading 20). **Scorers:** McGeady (2), Keane (22). **Booked:** Westwood, Dunne, Gibson

Macedonia (4-5-1): Nuredinoski, Shikov, Popov, Noveski, Grncharov, Shumulikosi, Demiri (Georgievski 84), Tasevski (Gjurovski 61), Trichkovski, Pandev, Naumoski (Risticj 68). **Scorer:** Trichovski (45). **Booked:** Grncharov, Popov, Demiri

Referee: I Vad (Hungary). **Half-time:** 2-1

NORTHERN IRELAND 0 SLOVENIA 0
Group C: Windsor Park (11,299); Tuesday, March 29 2011

Northern Ireland (4-4-1-1): Camp (Nottm Forest), Cathcart (Blackpool), McAuley (Ipswich), Craigan (Motherwell), J Evans (Manchester Utd), C Evans (Manchester Utd) (Boyce, Werder Bremen 90), Baird (Fulham), Clingan (Coventry), McCann (Peterborough) (McQuoid, Millwall 71), Brunt (WBA), Feeney (Oldham) (McCourt, Celtic 83). **Booked:** Baird, C Evans, Brunt

Slovenia (4-5-1): Handanovic, Brecko, Suler, Mavric, Jokic, Birsa, Bacinovic (Sukalo 90), Koren, Kirm, Ilicic (Ljubijankic 29), Novakovic (Dedic 84). **Booked:** Koren, Bacinovic

Referee: B Kuipers (Holland)

ENGLAND 2 SWITZERLAND 2
Group G: Wembley (84,459); Saturday, June 4 2011

England (4-3-3): Hart (Manchester City), Johnson (Liverpool), Ferdinand (Manchester Utd), Terry (Chelsea), Cole (Chelsea) (Baines, Everton 63), Wilshere (Arsenal), Parker (West Ham), Lampard (Chelsea) (A Young Aston Villa 46), Walcott (Arsenal) (Downing, Aston Villa 78) Bent (Aston Villa), Milner (Manchester City). **Scorers:** Lampard (37 pen), A Young (51). **Booked:** Wilshere, Ferdinand

Switzerland (4-5-1): Benaglio, Lichtsteiner, Senderos, Djourou, Ziegler, Shaqiri, Behrami (Dzemaili 59), Inler, Barnetta (Emeghara 89), Xhaka, Derdiyok (Mehmedi 75)

Booked: Djourou, Behrami

Referee: D Skomina (Slovenia). **Half-time:** 1-2

MACEDONIA 0 REPUBLIC OF IRELAND 2
Group B: Skopje (30,000); Saturday, June 4 2011

Macedonia (4-5-1): Bogatinov, Grncarov, Noveski, Sikov, Popov, Sumulikoski, Demiri (Savic 71), Despotovski (Gjurovski 56), Pandev, Trickovski, Naumoski (Hasani 10)

Republic of Ireland (4-4-2): Given (Manchester City), Kelly (Fulham), O'Shea (Manchester Utd), O'Dea (Celtic), Kilbane (Hull), McGeady (Spartak Moscow), Whelan (Stoke), Andrews (Blackburn), Hunt (Wolves), Cox (WBA) (Long, Reading 64), Keane (Tottenham). **Scorer:** Keane (7, 36). **Booked:** Cox

Referee: F Meyer (Germany). **Half-time:** 0-2

CARLING NATIONS CUP

REPUBLIC OF IRELAND 3 WALES 0
Aviva Stadium (19,783); Tuesday, February 8 2011

Republic of Ireland (4-4-2): Given (Manchester City), O'Shea (Manchester Utd) (O'Dea, Celtic 85), Dunne (Aston Villa), St Ledger (Preston), *Clark (Aston Villa), *Coleman (Everton) (Fahey, Birmingham 58), Whelan (Stoke) (Green, Derby 76), Gibson (Manchester Utd) (*Wilson, Stoke 81), Duff (Fulham) (Keogh, Wolves 70), Doyle (Wolves) (Long, Reading 46), Walters (Stoke). **Scorers:** Gibson (60), Duff (67), Fahey (80). **Booked:** Gibson

Wales (4-4-2): Hennessy (Wolves), Eardley (Blackpool) (Gunter, Nottm Forest 46), J Collins (Aston Villa), D Collins (Stoke), Ricketts (Bolton) (Nyatanga, Bristol City 83), Crofts (Norwich), Vaughan (Blackpool) (Ledley, Celtic 61), King (Leicester), Robson-Kanu (Reading) (Eastwood,

Coventry 70), Earnshaw (Nottm Forest) (Easter, Crystal Palace 80), Church (Reading)
Referee: M Courtney (Northern Ireland). **Half-time:** 0-0
Gary Speed's first match as Wales manager.

NORTHERN IRELAND 0 SCOTLAND 3
Aviva Stadium (18,742); Wednesday, February 9 2011
Northern Ireland (4-4-2): Tuffey (Inverness), McArdle (Aberdeen) (Hodson, Watford 46), McAuley (Ipswich), Craigan (Motherwell) (*Thompson, Watford 66), Baird (Fulham), McGinn (Celtic) (*Boyce, Werder Bremen 72), C Evans (Manchester Utd), Davis (Rangers) (Norwood, Manchester Utd 58), McCann (Peterborough) (Healy, Rangers 46), McCourt (Celtic), Patterson (Plymouth). **Booked:** Healy
Scotland (4-5-1): McGregor (Rangers), Hutton (Tottenham), S Caldwell (Wigan), Berra (Wolves), Bardsley (Sunderland) (*M Wilson, Celtic 57), Morrison (WBA) (*Maguire, Aberdeen 79), Adam (Blackpool) (Bannan, Aston Villa 57), McArthur (Wigan), Naismith (Rangers) (*Snodgrass, Leeds 57), Commons (Celtic) (Conway, Dundee Utd 72), Miller (Rangers) (D Wilson, Liverpool 90). **Scorers:** Miller (19), McArthur (32), Commons (51). **Booked:** M Wilson
Referee: T Connolly (Republic of Ireland). **Half-time:** 0-2

REPUBLIC OF IRELAND 5 NORTHERN IRELAND 0
Aviva Stadium (12,083); Tuesday, May 24 2011
Republic of Ireland (4-4-2): Given (Manchester City) (Forde, Millwall 72), McShane (Hull), Kelly (Fulham), Delaney (Ipswich), *Ward (Wolves), Coleman (Everton) (Lawrence, Portsmouth 55), Andrews (Blackburn), Foley (Wolves) (Hunt, Wolves 70), Treacy (Preston), Keane (Tottenham) (Keogh, Wolves 62), *Cox (WBA). **Scorers:** Ward (24), Keane (37, 54 pen), Cathcart (45 og), Cox (80)
Northern Ireland (4-4-2): Blayney (Linfield), Thompson (Watford), Cathcart (Blackpool), McAuley (WBA), Hodson (Watford), *Carson (Ipswich) (McGinn, Celtic 73), Davis (Rangers) (Garrett, Linfield 76), Clingan (Coventry), Gorman (Wolves) (Coates, Crusaders 55), McQuoid (Millwall) (Norwood, Manchester Utd 46), Feeney (Oldham) (Boyce, Werder Bremen 72). **Sent off:** Thompson
Referee: C Thomson (Scotland). **Half-time:** 3-0

WALES 1 SCOTLAND 3
Aviva Stadium (6,036); Wednesday, May 25 2011
Wales (4-4-2): Myhill (WBA), Eardley (Blackpool) (*Matthews, Cardiff 61), Morgan (Preston), Blake (Cardiff), Taylor (Swansea) (Gunter, Nottm Forest 46), Tudur Jones (Norwich) (Vaughan, Blackpool 72), Dorman (Crystal Palace) (Cotterill, Swansea 60), King (Leicester) (Ramsey, Arsenal 61), Vokes (Wolves) (Morison, Millwall 72), Earnshaw (Nottm Forest), Easter (Crystal Palace). **Scorer:** Earnshaw (36)
Scotland (4-4-2): McGregor (Rangers), Whittaker (Rangers) (Bardsley, Sunderland 81), G Caldwell (Wigan) (*Hanley, Blackburn 84), Berra (Wolves), Crainey (Blackpool (*R Martin, Norwich 81), Naismith (Rangers), Brown (Celtic), Adam (Blackpool) (McArthur, Wigan 88), Morrison (WBA) (Robson, Middlesbrough 74), McCormack (Leeds) (Bannan, Aston Villa 73), Miller (Bursaspor). **Scorers:** Morrison (55), Miller (64), Berra (70)
Referee: R Crangle (Northern Ireland). **Half-time:** 1-0

WALES 2 NORTHERN IRELAND 0
Aviva Stadium, Dublin (529); Friday, May 27 2011
Wales (4-4-2): Hennessey (Wolves) (Price, Crystal Palace 74 mins), Gunter (Nottm Forest) (Matthews, Cardiff 72), Taylor (Swansea), Gabbidon (West Ham), D Collins (Stoke), Cotterill (Swansea), Collison (West Ham) (Tudur Jones, Norwich 62), Ramsey (Arsenal) (Dorman, Crystal Palace 89), Vaughan (Blackpool), Bellamy (Manchester City) (Earnshaw, Nottm Forest 62), Morison (Millwall) (Vokes, Wolves 80)
Scorers: Ramsey (36), Earnshaw (69). **Booked:** Tudur Jones

Northern Ireland (4-4-2): Tuffey (Inverness), Hodson (Watford), Coates (Crusaders), Cathcart (Blackpool) (*Dallas, Crusaders 63), McAuley (Ipswich), Norwood (Manchester Utd), Carson (Ipswich), Garrett (Linfield) (*Winchester, Oldham 76), McGinn (Celtic) (*Owens, Crusaders 80), Feeney (Oldham) (Boyce, Werder Bremen 73), Gorman (Wolves)
Referee: A Kelly (Republic of Ireland). **Half-time:** 1-0

REPUBLIC OF IRELAND 1 SCOTLAND 0
Aviva Stadium, Dublin (17,694); Sunday, May 29 2011

Republic of Ireland (4-4-2): Given (Manchester City), McShane (Hull), O'Dea (Celtic) (Foley, Wolves 66), Kelly (Fulham), Ward (Wolves), Lawrence (Portsmouth) (Coleman, Everton 62), Andrews (Blackburn), Fahey (Birmingham), Hunt (Wolves), Keane (Tottenham) (Treacy, Preston 83), Cox (WBA). **Scorer:** Keane (23). **Booked:** McShane, Fahey, Foley
Scotland(4-4-2): McGregor (Rangers), Whittaker (Rangers), Hanley (Blackburn), Berra (Wolves), Bardsley (Sunderland) *Forrest (Celtic) (McCormack, Leeds 85), Brown (Celtic), Adam (Blackpool) (Bannan, Aston Villa 63), Robson (Middlesbrough) (Maguire, Aberdeen 75), Naismith (Rangers), Miller (Bursaspor). **Booked:** Adam, Miller
Referee: M Whitby (Wales). **Half-time:** 1-0

FINAL TABLE

	P	W	D	L	F	A	Pts
Republic of Ireland	3	3	0	0	9	0	9
Scotland	3	2	0	1	6	2	6
Wales	3	1	0	2	3	6	3
Northern Ireland	3	0	0	3	0	10	0

FRIENDLY INTERNATIONALS

ENGLAND 2 HUNGARY 1
Wembley (72,024); Wednesday, August 11 2010

England (4-1-4-1): Hart (Manchester City), G Johnson (Liverpool), Jagielka (Everton), Terry (Chelsea) (*Dawson, Tottenham 46), Cole (Chelsea) (*Gibbs, Arsenal 46), Barry (Manchester City), Walcott (Arsenal) (A Young, Aston Villa 46), Lampard (Chelsea) (*Zamora, Fulham 46), Gerrard (Liverpool) (*Wilshere, Arsenal 82), A Johnson (Manchester City), Rooney (Manchester Utd) (Milner, Aston Villa 66). **Scorer:** Gerrard (69, 73)
Hungary (4-4-1-1): Kiraly, Liptak (Komlosi 55), Vanczak (Laczko 46), Juhasz, Szelesi, Vadocz, Dzsudzsak (Koman 46), Rudolf (Priskin 83), Elek (Toth 59), Gera, Huszti (Hajnal 46). **Scorer:** Jagielka 63 og). **Booked:** Rudolf, Laczko, Koman
Referee: S Lannoy (France). **Half-time:** 0-0

SWEDEN 3 SCOTLAND 0
Stockholm (25,249); Wednesday, August 11 2010

Sweden (4-4-2): Isaksson, Lustig (Larsson 45), Mellberg, Majstorovic, Safarin, Svensson (Wendt 73), Wernbloom (Kallstrom 45), Elmander (Berg 78), Toivonen, Bajrami (Wilhelmsson 64), Ibrahimovic (Hysen 59). **Scorers:** Ibrahimovic (4), Bajrami (39), Toivonen (56). **Booked:** Elmander
Scotland (4-4-2): McGregor (Rangers), Broadfoot (Rangers) (Whittaker, Rangers74), *Kenneth (Dundee Utd), Berra (Wolves), Wallace (Hearts), Robson (Middlesbrough) (Iwelumo, Burnley 78), D Fletcher (Manchester Utd), Thomson (Middlesbrough) (Robertson, Dundee Utd 54), Adam (Blackpool) (Morrison, WBA 64), McFadden (Birmingham), S Fletcher (Wolves) (Boyd, Middlesbrough 64). **Booked:** Broadfoot, Robson
Referee: G Rocchi (Italy). **Half-time:** 2-0

WALES 5 LUXEMBOURG 1
Llanelli (4,504); Wednesday, August 11 2010

Wales (4-4-2): Hennessey (Wolves) (Myhill, WBA 46), Ricketts (Bolton), Morgan (Preston), Williams (Swansea) (Eardley, Blackpool 85), Gunter (Nottm Forest), Cotterill (Swansea) (Crofts, Norwich 81), Stock (Doncaster) (King, Leicester 46), Ledley (Celtic), Bellamy (Manchester City), *Morison (Millwall), Earnshaw (Nottm Forest) (Vaughan, Blackpool 46). **Scorers:** Cotterill (35), Ledley (48 pen), King (55), Williams (78), Bellamy (82). **Booked:** Williams, Cotterill

Luxembourg (4-5-1): Joubert, Mutsch, Janisch (Collette 79), Kintziger, Hoffmann, Schnell, Peters. Gerson (Pedro 60), Bettmer (Bernard 86), Da Mota (Laterza 68), Kitenge. **Scorer:** Kitenge (44). **Booked:** Da Mota, Mutsch, Janisch. **Sent off:** Mutsch

Referee: M Gestanius (Finland). Half-time: 1-1

MONTENEGRO 2 NORTHERN IRELAND 0
Podgorica (5,000); Wednesday, August 11 2010

Montenegro (4-4-2): M Bozovic, Pavicevic (D Bozovic 52), Djudjic, Jovanovic (Savic 75), Pekovic (Novakovic 62), Vukcevic, Pejovic (Tomasevic 56), Zverotic (Beciraj 83), V Bozovic, Vucinic, Djalovic (Delabasic 77). **Scorers:** Djalovic (43, 59). **Booked:** Jovanovic

Northern Ireland (4-5-1): Taylor (Birmingham), Little (Rangers), McGivern (Manchester City) (Healy, Sunderland 68), J Evans (Manchester Utd), Craigan (Motherwell), Paterson (Burnley) (C Evans, Manchester Utd 46), Baird (Fulham) (Feeney, Oldham 46), Davis (Rangers), Clingan (Coventry) (*Norwood, Manchester Utd 64), Brunt (WBA) (McCann, Peterborough 46) Lafferty (Rangers) (Gorman, Wolves 58). **Booked:** Paterson, Lafferty, McCann

Referee: B Jovanetic (Serbia). Half-time: 1-0

REPUBLIC OF IRELAND 0 ARGENTINA 1
Aviva Stadium (49,500); Wednesday, August 11 2010

Republic of Ireland (4-4-2): Given (Manchester City), McShane (Hull), Dunne (Aston Villa), O'Shea (Manchester Utd), Kilbane (Hull) (Cunningham, Manchester City 57), Fahey (Birmingham) (*Treacy, Preston 77), Andrews (Blackburn) (Gibson, Manchester Utd 67), Green (Derby), Duff (Fulham), Keane (Tottenham), Sheridan (Celtic) (Keogh, Wolves 56)

Argentina (4-2-3-1): Romero, Demichelis, Burdisso (Zabaleta 46), Samuel (Coloccini 83), Heinze, Mascherano, Gago, Banega, Messi (Lavezzi 58), Di Maria (Gutierrez 75), Higuain (Milito 46). **Scorer:** Di Maria (20). **Booked:** Heinze

Referee: P Rasmussen (Denmark). Half-time: 0-1

SCOTLAND 3 FAROE ISLANDS 0
Pittodrie (10,873); Tuesday, November 16 2010

Scotland (4-1-4-1): Gordon (Sunderland) (*Bell, Kilmarnock 68) Bardsley (Sunderland) (*Saunders, Motherwell 71), S Caldwell (Wigan), *Wilson (Liverpool) (Kenneth, Dundee Utd 60), Crainey (Blackpool), Adam (Blackpool) (*McArthur, Wigan 55), Commons (Derby) (*Goodwillie, Dundee Utd 76), *Bannan (Aston Villa), Fletcher (Manchester Utd) (*Bryson, Kilmarnock 68), Maloney (Celtic), Mackie (QPR). **Scorers:** Wilson (24), Commons (31), Mackie (45)

Faroe Islands (4-5-1): Nielsen, Naes, Davidsen, Gregersen, Jacobsen, Udsen (Juspinusen 86), Petersen (Mouritsen 60), Lokin, Elttor, Holst (Poulsen 56), Edmundsson

Referee: P van Boekel (Holland). Half-time: 3-0

ENGLAND 1 FRANCE 2
Wembley (85,495); Wednesday, November 17 2010

England (4-2-3-1): Foster (Birmingham), Jagielka (Everton), Ferdinand (Manchester Utd) (Richards, Manchester City 46), Lescott (Manchester City), Gibbs (Arsenal) (Warnock, Aston Villa 72), *Henderson (Sunderland), Barry (Manchester City) (A Young, Aston Villa 46), Walcott (Arsenal) (A Johnson, Manchester City 46), Gerrard (Liverpool) (Crouch, Tottenham 85), Milner (Manchester City), *Carroll (Newcastle) (*Bothroyd, Cardiff 72). **Scorer:** Crouch (86). **Booked:** Henderson

France (4-3-2-1): Lloris, Sagna (Reveillere 87), Mexes (Sakho 46), Rami, Abidal, Gourcuff (Hoarau 85), M'Vila, Nasri, Valbuena (Diarra 68), Malouda (Payet 78), Benzema (Remy 68).
Scorers: Benzema (16), Valbeuna (55)
Referee: C Bo Larsen (Denmark). **Half-time:** 0-1

NORTHERN IRELAND 1 MOROCCO 1
Windsor Park (15,000); Wednesday, November 17 2010
Northern Ireland (4-4-2): Tuffey (Inverness) (Blayney, Linfield 46), *Hodson (Watford), McGivern (Manchester City) (Coates, Crusaders 62), Hughes (Fulham) (McArdle, Aberdeen 46), J Evans (Manchester Utd), *Barton (Preston), McGinn (Celtic) (Magennis, Aberdeen, 69), McCourt (Celtic) (O'Connor, Scunthorpe 46), Gorman (Wolves), Patterson (Plymouth), Brunt (WBA) (*McQuoid, Bournemouth 47). **Scorer:** Patterson (86 pen)
Morocco (4-5-1): Lamyaghri, Soulaimani, El Kaddouri, Kantari, Benatia (Berrabeh 78), Hermach (El Ahmadi 89), Belhanda (Benzoukane 75), Kharja, Hadji (El Zhar 80), Chadli, Chamakh (El Arabi 71). **Scorer:** Chamakh (55). **Booked:** Soulaimani, Chamakh
Referee: T Hagen (Norway). **Half-time:** 0-0

REPUBLIC OF IRELAND 1 NORWAY 2
Aviva Stadium, (25,000); Wednesday, November 17 2010
Republic of Ireland (4-4-2): Given (Manchester City), Kelly (Fulham), O'Shea (Manchester Utd), O'Dea (Celtic) (Foley, Wolves 67), Cunningham (Manchester City), Lawrence (Portsmouth) (*Walters, Stoke 46), Whelan (Stoke), Fahey (Birmingham), Duff (Fulham) (Hunt, Wolves 74), Long (Reading), Doyle (Wolves), (McGeady, Spartak Moscow, 46). **Scorer:** Long (5 pen)
Norway (4-4-2): Knudsen (Pettersen 46), Hogli, Waehler, Hangeland, J A Riise, Hauger, Pedersen, Grindheim (Jenssen 55), Moen (Haestad 78), Helstad (B H Riise 46), Huseklepp (Moldskred 90). **Scorers:** Pedersen (34), Huseklepp (86)
Referee: K Jakobsson (Iceland). **Half-time:** 1-1

DENMARK 1 ENGLAND 2
Copenhagen (21,523); Wednesday, February 9 2011
Denmark (4-4-4-1): Sorensen, Jacobsen (Silberbauer 60), Jorgensen (Kjaer 46), Agger, S Poulsen (Wass 46), Rommedahl (Enedvoldsen 82), C Poulsen, Kvist (Vingaard 90), Krohn-Delhi (Pedersen 70), Eriksen, Bendtner. **Scorer:** Agger (7). **Booked:** Kjaer
England (4-4-2): Hart (Manchester City), G Johnson (Liverpool), Dawson (Tottenham) (Cahill, Bolton 60), Terry (Chelsea), Cole (Chelsea) (Baines, Everton 81), Walcott (Arsenal) (Downing, Manchester City 46), Lampard (Chelsea) (Barry, Manchester City 46), Wilshere (Arsenal) (Parker, West Ham 46), Milner (Manchester City), Rooney (Manchester Utd (A Young, Aston Villa 46), Bent (Aston Villa). **Scorers:** Bent (10), A Young (68)
Referee: J Eriksson (Sweden). **Half-time:** 1-1

SCOTLAND 0 BRAZIL 2
Emirates Stadium (53,087); Sunday, March 27 2011
Scotland (4-1-4-1): McGregor (Rangers), Hutton (Tottenham), G Caldwell (Wigan), Berra (Wolves) (Wilson, Liverpool 73), Crainey (Blackpool), Adam (Blackpool) (Snodgrass, Leeds 78), Brown (Celtic), Morrison (WBA) (Cowie, Watford 90), McArthur (Wigan) (Bannan, Aston Villa 56), Whittaker (Rangers) (Commons, Celtic 64), Miller (Bursaspor) (*Mackail-Smith, Peterborough 87)
Brazil (4-3-3): Julio Cesar, Dani Alves, Lucio, Thiago Silva, Andre Santos, Lucas (Sandro 86), Elano (Elias 82), Ramires, Jadson (Lucas Rodriguez 72), Neymar (Renato Augusto 89), Leandro Damiao (Oliveira 78). **Scorers:** Neymar (42, 77 pen).
Referee: H. Webb (England). **Half-time:** 0-1

ENGLAND 1 GHANA 1
Wembley (80,102); Tuesday, March 29 2011

England (4-3-3): Hart (Manchester City), Johnson (Liverpool) (Lescott, Manchester City 46), Cahill (Bolton), Jagielka (Everton), Baines (Everton), Milner (Manchester City), Barry (Manchester City), Wilshere (Arsenal) (*Jarvis Wolves 69), Downing (Aston Villa), Carroll (Liverpool) (Defoe, Tottenham 59), A Young (Aston Villa) (*Welbeck, Manchester Utd 81). **Scorer:** Carroll (43). **Booked:** Milner

Ghana (4-4-2): Kingson, Pantsil, Vorsah (Jonathan Mensah 46), John Mensah, Addy (Opare 46), Adiyah (Tagoe 69), Annan (Boateng 46), Agyemang-Badu, Kwadwo Asamoah (Inkoom 83), Muntari (Ayew 59), Gyan. **Scorer:** Gyan (90). **Booked:** Boateng, Ayew

Referee: C Cakir (Turkey). **Half-time:** 1-0

REPUBLIC OF IRELAND 2 URUGUAY 3
Aviva Stadium (25,611); Tuesday, March 29 2011

Republic of Ireland (4-4-1-1): Westwood (Coventry), Foley (Wolves), O'Dea (Celtic), Kelly (Fulham), Clark (Aston Villa) (Delaney, Ipswich 75), Lawrence (Portsmouth) (McGeady, Spartak Moscow 78), Green (Derby), Fahey (Birmingham) (Gibson, Manchester Utd 66), Keogh (Wolves) (Stokes, Celtic 85), McCarthy (Wigan) (Treacy, Preston 66), Long (Reading). **Scorers:** Long (15), Fahey (48 pen). **Booked:** O'Dea

Uruguay (4-4-2): Muslera, Lugano, Godin, Caceres, M Pereira, Arevalo (Gargano 64), Perez (Scotti 90), A Pereira, Hernandez (Eguren 84), Forlan, Cavani. **Scorers:** Lugano (12), Cavani (22), Hernandez (39). **Booked:** Cavani, Lugano, Eguren

Referee: S Ennjimi (France). **Half-time:** 1-3

REPUBLIC OF IRELAND 2 ITALY 0
Liege (21,516); Tuesday, June 7 2011

Republic of Ireland (4-4-2): Forde (Millwall), McShane (Hull), St Ledger (Preston), O'Dea (Celtic) (Kelly, Fulham 83), Ward (Wolves) (Delaney, Ipswich 90), Coleman (Everton), Andrews (Blackburn), Foley (Wolves) (Whelan, Stoke 60), Hunt (Wolves), Keogh (Wolves) (Treacy, Preston 75), Long (Reading) (Cox 60). **Scorers:** Andrews (36), Cox (90). **Booked:** Hunt, Andrews

Italy (4-3-1-2): Viviano, Cassani, Gamberini, Chiellini, Criscito (Balzaretti 66), Nocerino (Giovinco 59), Pirlo (Palombo 46), Marchisio, Montolivo, Rossi (Matri 46), Pazzini (Gilardino 59)

Referee: S Gumienny (Belgium). **Half-time:** 1-0

HOLDSWORTH TWINS MAKE HISTORY
Dean and David Holdsworth made history in a Blue Square Bet Premier match last season when they became the first twin brothers to face each other in a league game. Dean, in charge of Newport, got the better of Mansfield's David 1-0.

HAT-TRICK OF HEADERS
Neil Mellor scored a hat-trick of headers in Sheffield Wednesday's 4-1 away win over MK Dons in League One last season. They came from crosses by Chris Sedgwick and Gary Teale and a corner by Tommy Spurr.

OTHER BRITISH & IRISH INTERNATIONAL RESULTS

ENGLAND

v ALBANIA

		E	A
1989	Tirana (WC)	2	0
1989	Wembley (WC)	5	0
2001	Tirana (WC)	3	1
2001	Newcastle (WC)	2	0

v ALGERIA

		E	A
2010	Cape Town (WC)	0	0

v ANDORRA

		E	A
2006	Old Trafford (EC)	5	0
2007	Barcelona (EC)	3	0
2008	Barcelona (WC)	2	0
2009	Wembley (WC)	6	0

v ARGENTINA

		E	A
1951	Wembley	2	1
1953*	Buenos Aires	0	0
1962	Rancagua (WC)	3	1
1964	Rio de Janeiro	0	1
1966	Wembley (WC)	1	0
1974	Wembley	2	2
1977	Buenos Aires	1	1
1980	Wembley	3	1
1986	Mexico City (WC)	1	2
1991	Wembley	2	2
1998†	St Etienne (WC)	2	2
2000	Wembley	0	0
2002	Sapporo (WC)	1	0
2005	Geneva	3	2

(*Abandoned after 21 mins – rain)
(† England lost 3-4 on pens)

v AUSTRALIA

		E	A
1980	Sydney	2	1
1983	Sydney	0	0
1983	Brisbane	1	0
1983	Melbourne	1	1
1991	Sydney	1	0
2003	West Ham	1	3

v AUSTRIA

		E	A
1908	Vienna	6	1
1908	Vienna	11	1
1909	Vienna	8	1
1930	Vienna	0	0
1932	Stamford Bridge	4	3
1936	Vienna	1	2
1951	Wembley	2	2
1952	Vienna	3	2
1958	Boras (WC)	2	2
1961	Vienna	1	3
1962	Wembley	3	1

1965	Wembley	2	3
1967	Vienna	1	0
1973	Wembley	7	0
1979	Vienna	3	4
2004	Vienna (WC)	2	2
2005	Old Trafford (WC)	1	0
2007	Vienna	1	0

v AZERBAIJAN

		E	A
2004	Baku (WC)	1	0
2005	Newcastle (WC)	2	0

v BELARUS

		E	B
2008	Minsk (WC)	3	1
2009	Wembley (WC)	3	0

v BELGIUM

		E	B
1921	Brussels	2	0
1923	Highbury	6	1
1923	Antwerp	2	2
1924	West Bromwich	4	0
1926	Antwerp	5	3
1927	Brussels	9	1
1928	Antwerp	3	1
1929	Brussels	5	1
1931	Brussels	4	1
1936	Brussels	2	3
1947	Brussels	5	2
1950	Brussels	4	1
1952	Wembley	5	0
1954	Basle (WC)	4	4
1964	Wembley	2	2
1970	Brussels	3	1
1980	Turin (EC)	1	1
1990	Bologna (WC)	1	0
1998*	Casablanca	0	0
1999	Sunderland	2	1

(*England lost 3-4 on pens)

v BOHEMIA

		E	B
1908	Prague	4	0

v BRAZIL

		E	B
1956	Wembley	4	2
1958	Gothenburg (WC)	0	0
1959	Rio de Janeiro	0	2
1962	Vina del Mar (WC)	1	3
1963	Wembley	1	1
1964	Rio de Janeiro	1	5
1969	Rio de Janeiro	1	2
1970	Guadalajara (WC)	0	1
1976	Los Angeles	0	1
1977	Rio de Janeiro	0	0
1978	Wembley	1	1
1981	Wembley	0	1
1984	Rio de Janeiro	2	0
1987	Wembley	1	1

1990	Wembley	1	0
1992	Wembley	1	1
1993	Washington	1	1
1995	Wembley	1	3
1997	Paris (TF)	0	1
2000	Wembley	1	1
2002	Shizuoka (WC)	1	2
2007	Wembley	1	1
2009	Doha	0	1

v BULGARIA

		E	B
1962	Rancagua (WC)	0	0
1968	Wembley	1	1
1974	Sofia	1	0
1979	Sofia (EC)	3	0
1979	Wembley (EC)	2	0
1996	Wembley	1	0
1998	Wembley (EC)	0	0
1999	Sofia (EC)	1	1
2010	Wembley (EC)	4	0

v CAMEROON

		E	C
1990	Naples (WC)	3	2
1991	Wembley	2	0
1997	Wembley	2	0
2002	Kobe (Japan)	2	2

v CANADA

		E	C
1986	Vancouver	1	0

v CHILE

		E	C
1950	Rio de Janeiro (WC)	2	0
1953	Santiago	2	1
1984	Santiago	0	0
1989	Wembley	0	0
1998	Wembley	0	2

v CHINA

		E	C
1996	Beijing	3	0

v CIS
(formerly Soviet Union)

		E	CIS
1992	Moscow	2	2

v COLOMBIA

		E	C
1970	Bogota	4	0
1988	Wembley	1	1
1995	Wembley	0	0
1998	Lens (WC)	2	0
2005	New York	3	2

v CROATIA

		E	C
1995	Wembley	0	0
2003	Ipswich	3	1
2004	Lisbon (EC)	4	2
2006	Zagreb (EC)	0	2
2007	Wembley (EC)	2	3
2008	Zagreb (WC)	4	1

| 2009 | Wembley (WC) | 5 | 1 |

v CYPRUS

		E	C
1975	Wembley (EC)	5	0
1975	Limassol (EC)	1	0

v CZECH REPUBLIC

		E	C
1998	Wembley	2	0
2008	Wembley	2	2

v CZECHOSLOVAKIA

		E	C
1934	Prague	1	2
1937	White Hart Lane	5	4
1963	Bratislava	4	2
1966	Wembley	0	0
1970	Guadalajara (WC)	1	0
1973	Prague	1	1
1974	Wembley (EC)	3	0
1975*	Bratislava (EC)	1	2
1978	Wembley (EC)	1	0
1982	Bilbao (WC)	2	0
1990	Wembley	4	2
1992	Prague	2	2
(* Aband 0-0, 17 mins prev day – fog)			

v DENMARK

		E	D
1948	Copenhagen	0	0
1955	Copenhagen	5	1
1956	W'hampton (WC)	5	2
1957	Copenhagen (WC)	4	1
1966	Copenhagen	2	0
1978	Copenhagen (EC)	4	3
1979	Wembley (EC)	1	0
1982	Copenhagen (EC)	2	2
1983	Wembley (EC)	0	1
1988	Wembley	1	0
1989	Copenhagen	1	1
1990	Wembley	1	0
1992	Malmo (EC)	0	0
1994	Wembley	1	0
2002	Niigata (WC)	3	0
2003	Old Trafford	2	3
2005	Copenhagen	1	4
2011	Copenhagen	2	1

v EAST GERMANY

		E	EG
1963	Leipzig	2	1
1970	Wembley	3	1
1974	Leipzig	1	1
1984	Wembley	1	0

v ECUADOR

		E	Ec
1970	Quito	2	0
2006	Stuttgart (WC)	1	0

v EGYPT

		E	Eg
1986	Cairo	4	0
1990	Cagliari (WC)	1	0
2010	Wembley	3	1

v ESTONIA

		E	Est
2007	Tallinn (EC)	3	0
2007	Wembley (EC)	3	0

v FIFA

		E	F
1938	Highbury	3	0
1953	Wembley	4	4
1963	Wembley	2	1

v FINLAND

		E	F
1937	Helsinki	8	0
1956	Helsinki	5	1
1966	Helsinki	3	0
1976	Helsinki (WC)	4	1
1976	Wembley (WC)	2	1
1982	Helsinki	4	1
1984	Wembley (WC)	5	0
1985	Helsinki (WC)	1	1
1992	Helsinki	2	1
2000	Helsinki (WC)	0	0
2001	Liverpool (WC)	2	1

v FRANCE

		E	F
1923	Paris	4	1
1924	Paris	3	1
1925	Paris	3	2
1927	Paris	6	0
1928	Paris	5	1
1929	Paris	4	1
1931	Paris	2	5
1933	White Hart Lane	4	1
1938	Paris	4	2
1947	Highbury	3	0
1949	Paris	3	1
1951	Highbury	2	2
1955	Paris	0	1
1957	Wembley	4	0
1962	Hillsborough (EC)	1	1
1963	Paris (EC)	2	5
1966	Wembley (WC)	2	0
1969	Wembley	5	0
1982	Bilbao (WC)	3	1
1984	Paris	0	2
1992	Wembley	2	0
1992	Malmo (EC)	0	0
1997	Montpellier (TF)	1	0
1999	Wembley	0	2
2000	Paris	1	1
2004	Lisbon (EC)	1	2
2008	Paris	0	1
2010	Wembley	1	2

v GEORGIA

		E	G
1996	Tbilisi (WC)	2	0
1997	Wembley (WC)	2	0

v GERMANY/WEST GERMANY

		E	G
1930	Berlin	3	3
1935	White Hart Lane	3	0
1938	Berlin	6	3
1954	Wembley	3	1
1956	Berlin	3	1
1965	Nuremberg	1	0
1966	Wembley	1	0
1966	Wembley (WCF)	4	2
1968	Hanover	0	1
1970	Leon (WC)	2	3
1972	Wembley (EC)	1	3
1972	Berlin (EC)	0	0
1975	Wembley	2	0
1978	Munich	1	2
1982	Madrid (WC)	0	0
1982	Wembley	1	2
1985	Mexico City	3	0
1987	Dusseldorf	1	3
1990*	Turin (WC)	1	1
1991	Wembley	0	1
1993	Detroit	1	2
1996†	Wembley (EC)	1	1
2000	Charleroi (EC)	1	0
2000	Wembley (WC)	0	1
2001	Munich (WC)	5	1
2007	Wembley	1	2
2008	Berlin	2	1
2010	Bloemfontein (WC)	1	4

(*England lost 3-4 on pens)
(† England lost 5-6 on pens)

v GHANA

		E	G
2011	Wembley	1	1

v GREECE

		E	G
1971	Wembley (EC)	3	0
1971	Athens (EC)	2	0
1982	Salonika (EC)	3	0
1983	Wembley (EC)	0	0
1989	Athens	2	1
1994	Wembley	5	0
2001	Athens (WC)	2	0
2001	Old Trafford (WC)	2	2
2006	Old Trafford	4	0

v HOLLAND

		E	H
1935	Amsterdam	1	0
1946	Huddersfield	8	2
1964	Amsterdam	1	1
1969	Amsterdam	1	0
1970	Wembley	0	0
1977	Wembley	0	2
1982	Wembley	2	0
1988	Wembley	2	2
1988	Dusseldorf (EC)	1	3
1990	Cagliari (WC)	0	0
1993	Wembley (WC)	2	2
1993	Rotterdam (WC)	0	2
1996	Wembley (EC)	4	1
2001	White Hart Lane	0	2
2002	Amsterdam	1	1

2005	Villa Park	1	0
2006	Amsterdam	1	1
2009	Amsterdam	2	2

v HUNGARY

		E	H
1908	Budapest	7	0
1909	Budapest	4	2
1909	Budapest	8	2
1934	Budapest	1	2
1936	Highbury	6	2
1953	Wembley	3	6
1954	Budapest	1	7
1960	Budapest	0	2
1962	Rancagua (WC)	1	2
1965	Wembley	1	0
1978	Wembley	4	1
1981	Budapest (WC)	3	1
1981	Wembley (WC)	1	0
1983	Wembley (EC)	2	0
1983	Budapest (EC)	3	0
1988	Budapest	0	0
1990	Wembley	1	0
1992	Budapest	1	0
1996	Wembley	3	0
1999	Budapest	1	1
2006	Old Trafford	3	1
2010	Wembley	2	1

v ICELAND

		E	I
1982	Reykjavik	1	1
2004	City of Manchester	6	1

v ISRAEL

		E	I
1986	Tel Aviv	2	1
1988	Tel Aviv	0	0
2006	Tel Aviv (EC)	0	0
2007	Wembley (EC)	3	0

v ITALY

		E	I
1933	Rome	1	1
1934	Highbury	3	2
1939	Milan	2	2
1948	Turin	4	0
1949	White Hart Lane	2	0
1952	Florence	1	1
1959	Wembley	2	2
1961	Rome	3	2
1973	Turin	0	2
1973	Wembley	0	1
1976	New York	3	2
1976	Rome (WC)	0	2
1977	Wembley (WC)	2	0
1980	Turin (EC)	0	1
1985	Mexico City	1	2
1989	Wembley	0	0
1990	Bari (WC)	1	2
1996	Wembley (WC)	0	1
1997	Nantes (TF)	2	0
1997	Rome (WC)	0	0

| 2000 | Turin | 0 | 1 |
| 2002 | Leeds | 1 | 2 |

v JAMAICA

		E	J
2006	Old Trafford	6	0

v JAPAN

		E	J
1995	Wembley	2	1
2004	City of Manchester	1	1
2010	Graz	2	1

v KAZAKHSTAN

		E	K
2008	Wembley (WC)	5	1
2009	Almaly (WC)	4	0

v KUWAIT

		E	K
1982	Bilbao (WC)	1	0

v LIECHTENSTEIN

		E	L
2003	Vaduz (EC)	2	0
2003	Old Trafford (EC)	2	0

v LUXEMBOURG

		E	L
1927	Luxembourg	5	2
1960	Luxembourg (WC)	9	0
1961	Highbury (WC)	4	1
1977	Wembley (WC)	5	0
1977	Luxembourg (WC)	2	0
1982	Wembley (EC)	9	0
1983	Luxembourg (EC)	4	0
1998	Luxembourg (EC)	3	0
1999	Wembley (EC)	6	0

v MACEDONIA

		E	M
2002	Southampton (EC)	2	2
2003	Skopje (EC)	2	1
2006	Skopje (EC)	1	0
2006	Old Trafford (EC)	0	0

v MALAYSIA

		E	M
1991	Kuala Lumpur	4	2

v MALTA

		E	M
1971	Valletta (EC)	1	0
1971	Wembley (EC)	5	0
2000	Valletta	2	1

v MEXICO

		E	M
1959	Mexico City	1	2
1961	Wembley	8	0
1966	Wembley (WC)	2	0
1969	Mexico City	0	0
1985	Mexico City	0	1
1986	Los Angeles	3	0
1997	Wembley	2	0
2001	Derby	4	0
2010	Wembley	3	1

v MOLDOVA

		E	M
1996	Kishinev	3	0
1997	Wembley (WC)	4	0

v MONTENEGRO

		E	M
2010	Wembley (EC)	0	0

v MOROCCO

		E	M
1986	Monterrey (WC)	0	0
1998	Casablanca	1	0

v NEW ZEALAND

		E	NZ
1991	Auckland	1	0
1991	Wellington	2	0

v NIGERIA

		E	NZ
1994	Wembley	1	0
2002	Osaka (WC)	0	0

v NORWAY

		E	NZ
1937	Oslo	6	0
1938	Newcastle	4	0
1949	Oslo	4	1
1966	Oslo	6	1
1980	Wembley (WC)	4	0
1981	Oslo (WC)	1	2
1992	Wembley (WC)	1	1
1993	Oslo (WC)	0	2
1994	Wembley	0	0
1995	Oslo	0	0

v PARAGUAY

		E	P
1986	Mexico City (WC)	3	0
2002	Anfield	4	0
2006	Frankfurt (WC)	1	0

v PERU

		E	P
1959	Lima	1	4
1961	Lima	4	0

v POLAND

		E	P
1966	Goodison Park	1	1
1966	Chorzow	1	0
1973	Chorzow (WC)	0	2
1973	Wembley (WC)	1	1
1986	Monterrey (WC)	3	0
1989	Wembley (WC)	3	0
1989	Katowice (WC)	0	0
1990	Wembley (EC)	2	0
1991	Poznan (EC)	1	1
1993	Chorzow (WC)	1	1
1993	Wembley (WC)	3	0
1996	Wembley (WC)	2	1
1997	Katowice (WC)	2	0
1999	Wembley (EC)	3	1
1999	Warsaw (EC)	0	0
2004	Katowice (WC)	2	1
2005	Old Trafford (WC)	2	1

v PORTUGAL

		E	P
1947	Lisbon	10	0
1950	Lisbon	5	3
1951	Goodison Park	5	2
1955	Oporto	1	3
1958	Wembley	2	1
1961	Lisbon (WC)	1	1
1961	Wembley (WC)	2	0
1964	Lisbon	4	3
1964	Sao Paulo	1	1
1966	Wembley (WC)	2	1
1969	Wembley	1	0
1974	Lisbon	0	0
1974	Wembley (EC)	0	0
1975	Lisbon (EC)	1	1
1986	Monterrey (WC)	0	1
1995	Wembley	1	1
1998	Wembley	3	0
2000	Eindhoven (EC)	2	3
2002	Villa Park	1	1
2004	Faro	1	1
2004*	Lisbon (EC)	2	2
2006†	Gelsenkirchen (WC)	0	0

(† England lost 1–3 on pens)
(*England lost 5–6 on pens)

v REPUBLIC OF IRELAND

		E	RoI
1946	Dublin	1	0
1950	Goodison Park	0	2
1957	Wembley (WC)	5	1
1957	Dublin (WC)	1	1
1964	Dublin	3	1
1977	Wembley	1	1
1978	Dublin (EC)	1	1
1980	Wembley (EC)	2	0
1985	Wembley	2	1
1988	Stuttgart (EC)	0	1
1990	Cagliari (WC)	1	1
1990	Dublin (EC)	1	1
1991	Dublin (EC)	1	1
1995*	Dublin	0	1

(*Abandoned 27 mins – crowd riot)

v ROMANIA

		E	R
1939	Bucharest	2	0
1968	Bucharest	0	0
1969	Wembley	1	1
1970	Guadalajara (WC)	1	0
1980	Bucharest (WC)	1	2
1981	Wembley (WC)	0	0
1985	Bucharest (WC)	0	0
1985	Wembley (WC)	1	1
1994	Wembley	1	1
1998	Toulouse (WC)	1	2
2000	Charleroi (EC)	2	3

v RUSSIA

		E	R
2007	Wembley (EC)	3	0
2007	Moscow (EC)	1	2

v SAN MARINO

		E	SM
1992	Wembley (WC)	6	0
1993	Bologna (WC)	7	1

v SAUDI ARABIA

		E	SA
1988	Riyadh	1	1
1998	Wembley	0	0

v SERBIA-MONTENEGRO

		E	S-M
2003	Leicester	2	1

v SLOVAKIA

		E	S
2002	Bratislava (EC)	2	1
2003	Middlesbrough (EC)	2	1
2009	Wembley	4	0

v SLOVENIA

		E	S
2009	Wembley	2	1
2010	Port Elizabeth (WC)	1	0

v SOUTH AFRICA

		E	SA
1997	Old Trafford	2	1
2003	Durban	2	1

v SOUTH KOREA

		E	SK
2002	Seoguipo	1	1

v SOVIET UNION (see also CIS)

		E	SU
1958	Moscow	1	1
1958	Gothenburg (WC)	2	2
1958	Gothenburg (WC)	0	1
1958	Wembley	5	0
1967	Wembley	2	2
1968	Rome (EC)	2	0
1973	Moscow	2	1
1984	Wembley	0	2
1986	Tbilisi	1	0
1988	Frankfurt (EC)	1	3
1991	Wembley	3	1

v SPAIN

		E	S
1929	Madrid	3	4
1931	Highbury	7	1
1950	Rio de Janeiro (WC)	0	1
1955	Madrid	1	1
1955	Wembley	4	1
1960	Madrid	0	3
1960	Wembley	4	2
1965	Madrid	2	0
1967	Wembley	2	0
1968	Wembley (EC)	1	0
1968	Madrid (EC)	2	1
1980	Barcelona	2	0
1980	Naples (EC)	2	1
1981	Wembley	1	2
1982	Madrid (WC)	0	0
1987	Madrid	4	2
1992	Santander	0	1
1996*	Wembley (EC)	0	0

		E	S
2001	Villa Park	3	0
2004	Madrid	0	1
2007	Old Trafford	0	1
2009	Seville	0	2

(*England won 4-2 on pens)

v SWEDEN

		E	S
1923	Stockholm	4	2
1923	Stockholm	3	1
1937	Stockholm	4	0
1948	Highbury	4	2
1949	Stockholm	1	3
1956	Stockholm	0	0
1959	Wembley	2	3
1965	Gothenburg	2	1
1968	Wembley	3	1
1979	Stockholm	0	0
1986	Stockholm	0	1
1988	Wembley (WC)	0	0
1989	Stockholm (WC)	0	0
1992	Stockholm (EC)	1	2
1995	Leeds	3	3
1998	Stockholm (EC)	1	2
1999	Wembley (EC)	0	0
2001	Old Trafford	1	1
2002	Saitama (WC)	1	1
2004	Gothenburg	0	1
2006	Cologne (WC)	2	2

v SWITZERLAND

		E	S
1933	Berne	4	0
1938	Zurich	1	2
1947	Zurich	0	1
1949	Highbury	6	0
1952	Zurich	3	0
1954	Berne (WC)	2	0
1962	Wembley	3	1
1963	Basle	8	1
1971	Basle (EC)	3	2
1971	Wembley (EC)	1	1
1975	Basle	2	1
1977	Wembley	0	0
1980	Wembley (WC)	2	1
1981	Basle (WC)	1	2
1988	Lausanne	1	0
1995	Wembley	3	3
1996	Wembley (EC)	1	1
1998	Berne	1	1
2004	Coimbra (EC)	3	0
2008	Wembley	2	1
2010	Basle (EC)	3	1
2011	Wembley (EC)	2	2

v TRINIDAD & TOBAGO

		E	T
2006	Nuremberg (WC)	2	0
2008	Port of Spain	3	0

v TUNISIA

		E	T
1990	Tunis	1	1
1998	Marseille (WC)	2	0

v TURKEY		E	T
1984	Istanbul (WC)	8	0
1985	Wembley (WC)	5	0
1987	Izmir (EC)	0	0
1987	Wembley (EC)	8	0
1991	Izmir (EC)	1	0
1991	Wembley (EC)	1	0
1992	Wembley (WC)	4	0
1993	Izmir (WC)	2	0
2003	Sunderland (EC)	2	0
2003	Istanbul (EC)	0	0

v UKRAINE		E	U
2000	Wembley	2	0
2004	Newcastle	3	0
2009	Wembley (WC)	2	1
2009	Dnipropetrovski (WC)	0	1

v URUGUAY		E	U
1953	Montevideo	1	2
1954	Basle (WC)	2	4
1964	Wembley	2	1
1966	Wembley (WC)	0	0
1969	Montevideo	2	1
1977	Montevideo	0	0
1984	Montevideo	0	2
1990	Wembley	1	2
1995	Wembley	0	0

	2006 Anfield	2	1

v USA		E	USA
1950	Belo Horizonte (WC)	0	1
1953	New York	6	3
1959	Los Angeles	8	1
1964	New York	10	0
1985	Los Angeles	5	0
1993	Boston	0	2
1994	Wembley	2	0
2005	Chicago	2	1
2008	Wembley	2	0
2010	Rustenburg (WC)	1	1

v YUGOSLAVIA		E	Y
1939	Belgrade	1	2
1950	Highbury	2	2
1954	Belgrade	0	1
1956	Wembley	3	0
1958	Belgrade	0	5
1960	Wembley	3	3
1965	Belgrade	1	1
1966	Wembley	2	0
1968	Florence (EC)	0	1
1972	Wembley	1	1
1974	Belgrade	2	2
1986	Wembley (EC)	2	0
1987	Belgrade (EC)	4	1
1989	Wembley	2	1

ENGLAND'S RECORD

England's first international was a 0-0 draw against Scotland in Glasgow, on the West of Scotland cricket ground, Partick, on November 30, 1872 Their complete record at the start of 2009–10 is:

P	W	D	L	F	A
897	508	216	173	1992	90

ENGLAND'S 'B' TEAM RESULTS
England scores first

1937	Stockholm	4	0	1950	Italy (A)	0	5
1948	Highbury	4	2	1950	Holland (H)	1	0
1949	Stockholm	1	3	1950	Holland (A)	0	3
1956	Stockholm	0	0	1950	Luxembourg (A)	2	1
1959	Wembley	2	3	1950	Switzerland (H)	5	0
1965	Gothenburg	2	1	1952	Holland (A)	1	0
1968	Wembley	3	1	1952	France (A)	1	7
1979	Stockholm	0	0	1953	Scotland (A)	2	2
1986	Stockholm	0	1	1954	Scotland (H)	1	1
1988	Wembley (WC)	0	0	1954	Germany (A)	4	0
1989	Stockholm (WC)	0	0	1954	Yugoslavia (A)	1	2
1992	Stockholm (EC)	1	2	1954	Switzerland (A)	0	2
1995	Leeds	3	3	1955	Germany (H)	1	1
1998	Stockholm (EC)	1	2	1955	Yugoslavia (A)	5	1
1999	Wembley (EC)	0	0	1956	Switzerland (H)	4	1
2001	Old Trafford	1	1	1956	Scotland (A)	2	2
2002	Saitama (WC)	1	1	1957	Scotland (H)	4	1
2004	Gothenburg	0	1	1978	W Germany (A)	2	1
2006	Cologne (WC)	2		1978	Czechoslovakia (A)	1	0
21949	Finland (A)	4	0	1978	Singapore (A)	8	0
1949	Holland (A)	4	0	1978	Malaysia (A)	1	1

1978	N Zealand (A)	4	0
1978	N Zealand (A)	3	1
1978	N Zealand (A)	4	0
1979	Austria (A)	1	0
1979	N Zealand (H)	4	1
1980	USA (H)	1	0
1980	Spain (H)	1	0
1980	Australia (H)	1	0
1981	Spain (A)	2	3
1984	N Zealand (H)	2	0
1987	Malta (A)	2	0
1989	Switzerland (A)	2	0
1989	Iceland (A) .	2	0
1989	Norway (A)	1	0
1989	Italy (H)	1	1
1989	Yugoslavia (H)	2	1

1990	Rep of Ireland (A)	1	4
1990	Czechoslovakia (H)	2	0
1990	Algeria (H)	0	0
1991	Wales (A)	1	0
1991	Iceland (H)	1	0
1991	Switzerland (H)	2	1
1991	Spanish XI (A)	1	0
1992	France (H)	3	0
1992	Czechoslovakia (A)	1	0
1992	CIS (A)	1	1
1994	N Ireland (H)	4	2
1995	Rep of Ireland (H)	2	0
1998	Chile (H)	1	2
1998	Russia (H)	4	1
2006	Belarus (H)	1	2
2007	Albania	3	1

GREAT BRITAIN v REST OF EUROPE (FIFA)

		GB	RofE				GB	RofE
1947	Glasgow	6	1		1955	Belfast	1	4

SCOTLAND

v ARGENTINA

		S	A
1977	Buenos Aires	1	1
1979	Glasgow	1	3
1990	Glasgow	1	0
2008	Glasgow	0	1

v AUSTRALIA

		S	A
1985*	Glasgow (WC)	2	0
1985*	Melbourne (WC)	0	0
1996	Glasgow	1	0
2000	Glasgow	0	2

(* World Cup play-off)

v AUSTRIA

		S	A
1931	Vienna	0	5
1933	Glasgow	2	2
1937	Vienna	1	1
1950	Glasgow	0	1
1951	Vienna	0	4
1954	Zurich (WC)	0	1
1955	Vienna	4	1
1956	Glasgow	1	1
1960	Vienna	1	4
1963*	Glasgow	4	1
1968	Glasgow (WC)	2	1
1969	Vienna (WC)	0	2
1978	Vienna (EC)	2	3
1979	Glasgow (EC)	1	1
1994	Vienna	2	1
1996	Vienna (WC)	0	0
1997	Glasgow (WC)	2	0

(* Abandoned after 79 minutes)

2003	Glasgow	0	2
2005	Graz	2	2
2007	Vienna	1	0

v BELARUS

		S	B
1997	Minsk (WC)	1	0
1997	Aberdeen (WC)	4	1
2005	Minsk (WC)	0	0
2005	Glasgow (WC)	0	1

v BELGIUM

		S	B
1947	Brussels	1	2
1948	Glasgow	2	0
1951	Brussels	5	0
1971	Liege (EC)	0	3
1971	Aberdeen (EC)	1	0
1974	Brugge	1	2
1979	Brussels (EC)	0	2
1979	Glasgow (EC)	1	3
1982	Brussels (EC)	2	3
1983	Glasgow (EC)	1	1
1987	Brussels (EC)	1	4
1987	Glasgow (EC)	2	0
2001	Glasgow (WC)	2	2
2001	Brussels (WC)	0	2

v BOSNIA

		S	B
1999	Sarajevo (EC)	2	1
1999	Glasgow (EC)	1	0

v BRAZIL

		S	B
1966	Glasgow	1	1
1972	Rio de Janeiro	0	1
1973	Glasgow	0	1
1974	Frankfurt (WC)	0	0
1977	Rio de Janeiro	0	2
1982	Seville (WC)	1	4
1987	Glasgow	0	2
1990	Turin (WC)	0	1

1998	St Denis (WC)	1	2
2011	Arsenal	0	2

v BULGARIA

		S	B
1978	Glasgow	2	1
1986	Glasgow (EC)	0	0
1987	Sofia (EC)	1	0
1990	Sofia (EC)	1	1
1991	Glasgow (EC)	1	1
2006	Kobe	5	1

v CANADA

		S	C
1983	Vancouver	2	0
1983	Edmonton	3	0
1983	Toronto	2	0
1992	Toronto	3	1
2002	Edinburgh	3	1

v CHILE

		S	C
1977	Santiago	4	2
1989	Glasgow	2	0

v CIS (formerly Soviet Union)

		S	C
1992	Norrkoping (EC)	3	0

v COLOMBIA

		S	C
1988	Glasgow	0	0
1996	Miami	0	1
1998	New York	2	2

v COSTA RICA

		S	C
1990	Genoa (WC)	0	1

v CROATIA

		S	C
2000	Zagreb (WC)	1	1
2001	Glasgow (WC)	0	0
2008	Glasgow	1	1

v CYPRUS

		S	C
1968	Nicosia (WC)	5	0
1969	Glasgow (WC)	8	0
1989	Limassol (WC)	3	2
1989	Glasgow (WC)	2	1

v CZECH REPUBLIC

		S	C
1999	Glasgow (EC)	1	2
1999	Prague (EC)	2	3
2008	Prague	1	3
2010	Glasgow	1	0
2010	Prague (EC)	0	1

v CZECHOSLOVAKIA

		S	C
1937	Prague	3	1
1937	Glasgow	5	0
1961	Bratislava (WC)	0	4
1961	Glasgow (WC)	3	2
1961*	Brussels (WC)	2	4
1972	Porto Alegre	0	0
1973	Glasgow (WC)	2	1

1973	Bratislava (WC)	0	1
1976	Prague (WC)	0	2
1977	Glasgow (WC)	3	1

(*World Cup play-off)

v DENMARK

		S	D
1951	Glasgow	3	1
1952	Copenhagen	2	1
1968	Copenhagen	1	0
1970	Glasgow (EC)	1	0
1971	Copenhagen (EC)	0	1
1972	Copenhagen (WC)	4	1
1972	Glasgow (WC)	2	0
1975	Copenhagen (EC)	1	0
1975	Glasgow (EC)	3	1
1986	Neza (WC)	0	1
1996	Copenhagen	0	2
1998	Glasgow	0	1
2002	Glasgow	0	1
2004	Copenhagen	0	1

v EAST GERMANY

		S	EG
1974	Glasgow	3	0
1977	East Berlin	0	1
1982	Glasgow (EC)	2	0
1983	Halle (EC)	1	2
1986	Glasgow	0	0
1990	Glasgow	0	1

v ECUADOR

		S	E
1995	Toyama, Japan	2	1

v EGYPT

		S	E
1990	Aberdeen	1	3

v ESTONIA

		S	E
1993	Tallinn (WC)	3	0
1993	Aberdeen	3	1
1996	Tallinn (WC)	*No result	
1997	Monaco (WC)	0	0
1997	Kilmarnock (WC)	2	0
1998	Edinburgh (EC)	3	2
1999	Tallinn (EC)	0	0

(* Estonia absent)

2004	Tallinn	1	0

v FAROE ISLANDS

		S	F
1994	Glasgow (EC)	5	1
1995	Toftir (EC)	2	0
1998	Aberdeen (EC)	2	1
1999	Toftir (EC)	1	1
2002	Toftir (EC)	2	2
2003	Glasgow (EC)	3	1
2006	Glasgow (EC)	6	0
2007	Toftir (EC)	2	0
2010	Aberdeen	3	0

v FINLAND

		S	F
1954	Helsinki	2	1

1964	Glasgow (WC)	3	1
1965	Helsinki (WC)	2	1
1976	Glasgow	6	0
1992	Glasgow	1	1
1994	Helsinki (EC)	2	0
1995	Glasgow (EC)	1	0
1998	Edinburgh	1	1

v FRANCE

		S	F
1930	Paris	2	0
1932	Paris	3	1
1948	Paris	0	3
1949	Glasgow	2	0
1950	Paris	1	0
1951	Glasgow	1	0
1958	Orebro (WC)	1	2
1984	Marseilles	0	2
1989	Glasgow (WC)	2	0
1990	Paris (WC)	0	3
1997	St Etienne	1	2
2000	Glasgow	0	2
2002	Paris	0	5
2006	Glasgow (EC)	1	0
2007	Paris (EC)	1	0

v GEORGIA

		S	G
2007	Glasgow (EC)	2	1
2007	Tbilisi (EC)	0	2

v GERMANY/WEST GERMANY

		S	G
1929	Berlin	1	1
1936	Glasgow	2	0
1957	Stuttgart	3	1
1959	Glasgow	3	2
1964	Hanover	2	2
1969	Glasgow (WC)	1	1
1969	Hamburg (WC)	2	3
1973	Glasgow	1	1
1974	Frankfurt	1	2
1986	Queretaro (WC)	1	2
1992	Norrkoping (EC)	0	2
1993	Glasgow	0	1
1999	Bremen	1	0
2003	Glasgow (EC)	1	1
2003	Dortmund (EC)	1	2

v GREECE

		S	G
1994	Athens (EC)	0	1
1995	Glasgow	1	0

v HOLLAND

		S	H
1929	Amsterdam	2	0
1938	Amsterdam	3	1
1959	Amsterdam	2	1
1966	Glasgow	0	3
1968	Amsterdam	0	0
1971	Amsterdam	1	2
1978	Mendoza (WC)	3	2
1982	Glasgow	2	1
1986	Eindhoven	0	0

1992	Gothenburg (EC)	0	1
1994	Glasgow	0	1
1994	Utrecht	1	3
1996	Birmingham (EC)	0	0
2000	Arnhem	0	0
2003*	Glasgow (EC)	1	0
2003*	Amsterdam (EC)	0	6
2009	Amsterdam (WC)	0	3
2009	Glasgow (WC)	0	1

(*Qual Round play-off)

v HUNGARY

		S	H
1938	Glasgow	3	1
1955	Glasgow	2	4
1955	Budapest	1	3
1958	Glasgow	1	1
1960	Budapest	3	3
1980	Budapest	1	3
1987	Glasgow	2	0
2004	Glasgow	0	3

v ICELAND

		S	I
1984	Glasgow (WC)	3	0
1985	Reykjavik (WC)	1	0
2002	Reykjavik (EC)	2	0
2003	Glasgow (EC)	2	1
2008	Reykjavik (WC)	2	1
2009	Glasgow (WC)	2	1

v IRAN

		S	I
1978	Cordoba (WC)	1	1

v ISRAEL

		S	I
1981	Tel Aviv (WC)	1	0
1981	Glasgow (WC)	3	1
1986	Tel Aviv	1	0

v ITALY

		S	I
1931	Rome	0	3
1965	Glasgow (WC)	1	0
1965	Naples (WC)	0	3
1988	Perugia	0	2
1992	Glasgow (WC)	0	0
1993	Rome (WC)	1	3
2005	Milan (WC)	0	2
2005	Glasgow (WC)	1	1
2007	Bari (EC)	0	2
2007	Glasgow (EC)	1	2

v JAPAN

		S	J
1995	Hiroshima	0	0
2006	Saitama	0	0
2009	Yokohama	0	2

v LATVIA

		S	L
1996	Riga (WC)	2	0
1997	Glasgow (WC)	2	0
2000	Riga (WC)	1	0
2001	Glasgow (WC)	2	1

v LIECHTENSTEIN

		S	L
2010	Glasgow (EC)	2	1

v LITHUANIA

		S	L
1998	Vilnius (EC)	0	0
1999	Glasgow (EC)	3	0
2003	Kaunus (EC)	0	1
2003	Glasgow (EC)	1	0
2006	Kaunas (EC)	2	1
2007	Glasgow (EC)	3	1
2010	Kaunas (EC)	0	0

v LUXEMBOURG

		S	L
1947	Luxembourg	6	0
1986	Glasgow (EC)	3	0
1987	Esch (EC)	0	0

v MACEDONIA

		S	M
2008	Skopje (WC)	0	1
2009	Glasgow (WC)	2	0

v MALTA

		S	M
1988	Valletta	1	1
1990	Valletta	2	1
1993	Glasgow (WC)	3	0
1993	Valletta (WC)	2	0
1997	Valletta	3	2

v MOLDOVA

		S	M
2004	Chisinau (WC)	1	1
2005	Glasgow (WC)	2	0

v MOROCCO

		S	M
1998	St Etienne (WC)	0	3

v NEW ZEALAND

		S	NZ
1982	Malaga (WC)	5	2
2003	Edinburgh	1	1

v NIGERIA

		S	N
2002	Aberdeen	1	2

v NORWAY

		S	N
1929	Bergen	7	3
1954	Glasgow	1	0
1954	Oslo	1	1
1963	Bergen	3	4
1963	Glasgow	6	1
1974	Oslo	2	1
1978	Glasgow (EC)	3	2
1979	Oslo (EC)	4	0
1988	Oslo (WC)	2	1
1989	Glasgow (WC)	1	1
1992	Oslo	0	0
1998	Bordeaux (WC)	1	1
2003	Oslo	0	0

v PARAGUAY

		S	P
1958	Norrkoping (WC)	2	3

v PERU

		S	P
1972	Glasgow	2	0
1978	Cordoba (WC)	1	3
1979	Glasgow	1	1

v POLAND

		S	P
1958	Warsaw	2	1
1960	Glasgow	2	3
1965	Chorzow (WC)	1	1
1965	Glasgow (WC)	1	2
1980	Poznan	0	1
1990	Glasgow	1	1
2001	Bydgoszcz	1	1

v PORTUGAL

		S	P
1950	Lisbon	2	2
1955	Glasgow	3	0
1959	Lisbon	0	1
1966	Glasgow	0	1
1971	Lisbon (EC)	0	2
1971	Glasgow (EC)	2	1
1975	Glasgow	1	0
1978	Lisbon (EC)	0	1
1980	Glasgow (EC)	4	1
1980	Glasgow (WC)	0	0
1981	Lisbon (WC)	1	2
1992	Glasgow (WC)	0	0
1993	Lisbon (WC)	0	5
2002	Braga	0	2

v REPUBLIC OF IRELAND

		S	RoI
1961	Glasgow (WC)	4	1
1961	Dublin (WC)	3	0
1963	Dublin	0	1
1969	Dublin	1	1
1986	Dublin (EC)	0	0
1987	Glasgow (EC)	0	1
2000	Dublin	2	1
2003	Glasgow	0	2
2011	Dublin (CC)	0	1

v ROMANIA

		S	R
1975	Bucharest (EC)	1	1
1975	Glasgow (EC)	1	1
1986	Glasgow	3	0
1990	Glasgow (EC)	2	1
1991	Bucharest (EC)	0	1
2004	Glasgow	1	2

v RUSSIA

		S	R
1994	Glasgow (EC)	1	1
1995	Moscow (EC)	0	0

SAN MARINO

		S	SM
91	Serravalle (EC)	2	0
91	Glasgow (EC)	4	0
95	Serravalle (EC)	2	0
95	Glasgow (EC)	5	0
00	Serravalle (WC)	2	0
01	Glasgow (WC)	4	0

SAUDI ARABIA

		S	SA
88	Riyadh	2	2

SLOVENIA

		S	SL
04	Glasgow (WC)	0	0
05	Celje (WC)	3	0

SOUTH AFRICA

		S	SA
02	Hong Kong	0	2
07	Aberdeen	1	0

SOUTH KOREA

		S	SK
02	Busan	1	4

SOVIET UNION (see also CIS and RUSSIA)

		S	SU
7	Glasgow	0	2
1.	Moscow	0	1
2	Malaga (WC)	2	2
1	Glasgow	0	1

SPAIN

		S	Sp
7	Glasgow (WC)	4	2
7	Madrid (WC)	1	4
3	Madrid	6	2
5	Glasgow	0	0
6	Glasgow (EC)	1	2
5	Valencia (EC)	1	1
2	Valencia	0	3
	Glasgow (WC)	3	1
5	Seville (WC)	0	1
8	Madrid	0	0
4*	Valencia	1	1

*abandoned after 59 mins – floodlight failure

		S	Sp
0	Glasgow (EC)	2	3

SWEDEN

		S	Swe
2	Stockholm	1	3
3	Glasgow	1	2
5	Gothenburg	1	1
7	Glasgow	3	1
0	Stockholm (WC)	1	0
1	Glasgow (WC)	2	0
0	Genoa (WC)	2	1
5	Solna	0	2
6	Glasgow (WC)	1	0
7	Gothenburg (WC)	1	2

2004	Edinburgh	1	4
2010	Stockholm	0	3

v SWITZERLAND

		S	Sw
1931	Geneva	3	2
1948	Berne	1	2
1950	Glasgow	3	1
1957	Basle (WC)	2	1
1957	Glasgow (WC)	3	2
1973	Berne	0	1
1976	Glasgow	1	0
1982	Berne (EC)	0	2
1983	Glasgow (EC)	2	2
1990	Glasgow (EC)	2	1
1991	Berne (EC)	2	2
1992	Berne (WC)	1	3
1993	Aberdeen (WC)	1	1
1996	Birmingham (EC)	1	0
2006	Glasgow	1	3

v TRINIDAD & TOBAGO

		S	T
2004	Hibernian	4	1

v TURKEY

		S	T
1960	Ankara	2	4

v UKRAINE

		S	U
2006	Kiev (EC)	0	2
2007	Glasgow (EC)	3	1

v USA

		S	USA
1952	Glasgow	6	0
1992	Denver	1	0
1996	New Britain, Conn	1	2
1998	Washington	0	0
2005	Glasgow	1	1

v URUGUAY

		S	U
1954	Basle (WC)	0	7
1962	Glasgow	2	3
1983	Glasgow	2	0
1986	Neza (WC)	0	0

v YUGOSLAVIA

		S	Y
1955	Belgrade	2	2
1956	Glasgow	2	0
1958	Vaasteras (WC)	1	1
1972	Belo Horizonte	2	2
1974	Frankfurt (WC)	1	1
1984	Glasgow	6	1
1988	Glasgow (WC)	1	1
1989	Zagreb (WC)	1	3

v ZAIRE

		S	Z
1974	Dortmund (WC)	2	0

WALES

v ALBANIA

		W	A
1994	Cardiff (EC)	2	0
1995	Tirana (EC)	1	1

v ARGENTINA

		W	A
1992	Gifu (Japan)	0	1
2002	Cardiff	1	1

v ARMENIA

		W	A
2001	Yerevan (WC)	2	2
2001	Cardiff (WC)	0	0

v AUSTRIA

		W	A
1954	Vienna	0	2
1955	Wrexham	1	2
1975	Vienna (EC)	1	2
1975	Wrexham (EC)	1	0
1992	Vienna	1	1
2005	Cardiff	0	2
2005	Vienna	0	1

v AZERBAIJAN

		W	A
2002	Baku (EC)	2	0
2003	Cardiff (EC)	4	0
2004	Baku (WC)	1	1
2005	Cardiff (WC)	2	0
2008	Cardiff (WC)	1	0
2009	Baku (WC)	1	0

v BELARUS

		W	B
1998	Cardiff (EC)	3	2
1999	Minsk (EC)	2	1
2000	Minsk (WC)	1	2
2001	Cardiff (WC)	1	0

v BELGIUM

		W	B
1949	Liege	1	3
1949	Cardiff	5	1
1990	Cardiff (EC)	3	1
1991	Brussels (EC)	1	1
1992	Brussels (WC)	0	2
1993	Cardiff (WC)	2	0
1997	Cardiff (WC)	1	2
1997	Brussels (WC)	2	3

v BOSNIA-HERZEGOVINA

		W	B-H
2003	Cardiff	2	2

v BRAZIL

		W	B
1958	Gothenburg (WC)	0	1
1962	Rio de Janeiro	1	3
1962	Sao Paulo	1	3
1966	Rio de Janeiro	1	3
1966	Belo Horizonte	0	1
1983	Cardiff	1	1
1991	Cardiff	1	
1997	Brasilia	0	
2000	Cardiff	0	
2006	White Hart Lane	0	

v BULGARIA

		W	
1983	Wrexham (EC)	1	
1983	Sofia (EC)	0	
1994	Cardiff (EC)	0	
1995	Sofia (EC)	1	
2006	Swansea	0	
2007	Bourgas	1	
2010	Cardiff (EC)	0	

v CANADA

		W	
1986	Toronto	0	
1986	Vancouver	3	
2004	Wrexham	1	

v CHILE

		W	
1966	Santiago	0	

v COSTA RICA

		W	
1990	Cardiff	1	

v CROATIA

		W	
2002	Varazdin	1	
2010	Osijek	0	

v CYPRUS

		W	
1992	Limassol (WC)	1	
1993	Cardiff (WC)	2	
2005	Limassol	0	
2006	Cardiff (EC)	3	
2007	Nicosia (EC)	1	

v CZECHOSLOVAKIA (see also RCS)

		W	
1957	Cardiff (WC)	1	
1957	Prague (WC)	0	
1971	Swansea (EC)	1	
1971	Prague (EC)	0	
1977	Wrexham (WC)	3	
1977	Prague (WC)	0	
1980	Cardiff (WC)	1	
1981	Prague (WC)	0	
1987	Wrexham (EC)	1	
1987	Prague (EC)	0	

v CZECH REPUBLIC

		W	
2002	Cardiff	0	
2006	Teplice (EC)	1	
2007	Cardiff (EC)	0	

v DENMARK

		W	
1964	Copenhagen (WC)	0	
1965	Wrexham (WC)	4	

1987	Cardiff (EC)	1	0
1987	Copenhagen (EC)	0	1
1990	Copenhagen	0	1
1998	Copenhagen (EC)	2	1
1999	Anfield (EC)	0	2
2008	Copenhagen	1	0

v EAST GERMANY

		W	EG
1957	Leipzig (WC)	1	1
1957	Cardiff (WC)	4	1
1969	Dresden (WC)	1	2
1969	Cardiff (WC)	1	3

v ESTONIA

		W	E
1994	Tallinn	2	1
2009	Llanelli	1	0

v FAROE ISLANDS

		W	Fl
1992	Cardiff (WC)	6	0
1993	Toftir (WC)	3	0

v FINLAND

		W	F
1971	Helsinki (EC)	1	0
1971	Swansea (EC)	3	0
1986	Helsinki (EC)	1	1
1987	Wrexham (EC)	4	0
1988	Swansea (WC)	2	2
1989	Helsinki (WC)	0	1
2000	Cardiff	1	2
2002	Helsinki (EC)	2	0
2003	Cardiff (EC)	1	1
2009	Cardiff (WC)	0	2
2009	Helsinki (WC)	1	2

v FRANCE

		W	F
1933	Paris	1	1
1939	Paris	1	2
1953	Paris	1	6
1982	Toulouse	1	0

v GEORGIA

		W	G
1994	Tbilisi (EC)	0	5
1995	Cardiff (EC)	0	1
2008	Swansea	1	2

v GERMANY/WEST GERMANY

		W	G
1968	Cardiff	1	1
1969	Frankfurt	1	1
1977	Cardiff	0	2
1977	Dortmund	1	1
1979	Wrexham (EC)	0	2
1979	Cologne (EC)	1	5
1989	Cardiff (WC)	0	0
1989	Cologne (WC)	1	2
1991	Cardiff (EC)	1	0
1991	Nuremberg (EC)	1	4
1995	Dusseldorf (EC)	1	1
1995	Cardiff (EC)	1	2
2002	Cardiff	1	0

2007	Cardiff (EC)	0	2
2007	Frankfurt (EC)	0	0
2008	Moenchengladbach (WC)	0	1
2009	Cardiff (WC)	0	2

v GREECE

		W	G
1964	Athens (WC)	0	2
1965	Cardiff (WC)	4	1

v HOLLAND

		W	H
1988	Amsterdam (WC)	0	1
1989	Wrexham (WC)	1	2
1992	Utrecht	0	4
1996	Cardiff (WC)	1	3
1996	Eindhoven (WC)	1	7
2008	Rotterdam	0	2

v HUNGARY

		W	H
1958	Sanviken (WC)	1	1
1958	Stockholm (WC)	2	1
1961	Budapest	2	3
1963	Budapest (EC)	1	3
1963	Cardiff (EC)	1	1
1974	Cardiff (EC)	2	0
1975	Budapest (EC)	2	1
1986	Cardiff	0	3
2004	Budapest	2	1
2005	Cardiff	2	0

v ICELAND

		W	I
1980	Reykjavik (WC)	4	0
1981	Swansea (WC)	2	2
1984	Reykjavik (WC)	0	1
1984	Cardiff (WC)	2	1
1991	Cardiff	1	0
2008	Reykjavik	1	0

v IRAN

		W	I
1978	Tehran	1	0

v ISRAEL

		W	I
1958	Tel Aviv (WC)	2	0
1958	Cardiff (WC)	2	0
1984	Tel Aviv	0	0
1989	Tel Aviv	3	3

v ITALY

		W	I
1965	Florence	1	4
1968	Cardiff (WC)	0	1
1969	Rome (WC)	1	4
1988	Brescia	1	0
1996	Terni	0	3
1998	Anfield (EC)	0	2
1999	Bologna (EC)	0	4
2002	Cardiff (EC)	2	1
2003	Milan (EC)	0	4

v JAMAICA

		W	J
1998	Cardiff	0	0

v JAPAN

		W	J
1992	Matsuyama	1	0

v KUWAIT

		W	K
1977	Wrexham	0	0
1977	Kuwait City	0	0

v LATVIA

		W	L
2004	Riga	2	0

v LIECHTENSTEIN

		W	L
2006	Wrexham	4	0
2008	Cardiff (WC)	2	0
2009	Vaduz (WC)	2	0

v LUXEMBOURG

		W	L
1974	Swansea (EC)	5	0
1975	Luxembourg (EC)	3	1
1990	Luxembourg (EC)	1	0
1991	Luxembourg (EC)	1	0
2008	Luxembourg	2	0
2010	Llanelli	5	1

v MALTA

		W	M
1978	Wrexham (EC)	7	0
1979	Valletta (EC)	2	0
1988	Valletta	3	2
1998	Valletta	3	0

v MEXICO

		W	M
1958	Stockholm (WC)	1	1
1962	Mexico City	1	2

v MOLDOVA

		W	M
1994	Kishinev (EC)	2	3
1995	Cardiff (EC)	1	0

v MONTENEGRO

		W	M
2009	Podgorica	1	2
2010	Podgorica (EC)	0	1

v NEW ZEALAND

		W	NZ
2007	Wrexham	2	2

v NORWAY

		W	N
1982	Swansea (EC)	1	0
1983	Oslo (EC)	0	0
1984	Trondheim	0	1
1985	Wrexham	1	1
1985	Bergen	2	4
1994	Cardiff	1	3
2000	Cardiff (WC)	1	1
2001	Oslo (WC)	2	3
2004	Oslo	0	0
2008	Wrexham	3	0

v PARAGUAY

		W	P
2006	Cardiff	0	0

v POLAND

		W	P
1973	Cardiff (WC)	2	0
1973	Katowice (WC)	0	3
1991	Radom	0	0
2000	Warsaw (WC)	0	0
2001	Cardiff (WC)	1	2
2004	Cardiff (WC)	2	3
2005	Warsaw (WC)	0	1
2009	Vila-Real (Por)	0	1

v PORTUGAL

		W	P
1949	Lisbon	2	3
1951	Cardiff	2	1
2000	Chaves	0	3

v QATAR

		W	Q
2000	Doha	1	0

v RCS (formerly Czechoslovakia)

		W	RCS
1993	Ostrava (WC)	1	1
1993	Cardiff (WC)	2	2

v REPUBLIC OF IRELAND

		W	RI
1960	Dublin	3	2
1979	Swansea	2	1
1981	Dublin	3	1
1986	Dublin	1	0
1990	Dublin	0	1
1991	Wrexham	0	3
1992	Dublin	1	0
1993	Dublin	1	2
1997	Cardiff	0	0
2007	Dublin (EC)	0	1
2007	Cardiff (EC)	2	2
2011	Dublin (CC)	0	3

v REST OF UNITED KINGDOM

		W	UK
1951	Cardiff	3	2
1969	Cardiff	0	1

v ROMANIA

		W	R
1970	Cardiff (EC)	0	0
1971	Bucharest (EC)	0	2
1983	Wrexham	5	0
1992	Bucharest (WC)	1	5
1993	Cardiff (WC)	1	2

v RUSSIA (See also Soviet Union)

		W	R
2003*	Moscow (EC)	0	0
2003*	Cardiff (EC)	0	1
2008	Moscow (WC)	1	2
2009	Cardiff (WC)	1	3

(*Qual Round play-offs)

v SAN MARINO

		W	SM
1996	Serravalle (WC)	5	0
1996	Cardiff (WC)	6	0
2007	Cardiff (EC)	3	0

2007	Serravalle (EC)	2	1

SAUDI ARABIA

		W	SA
1986	Dahran	2	1

SERBIA & MONTENEGRO

		W	S
2003	Belgrade (EC)	0	1
2003	Cardiff (EC)	2	3

SLOVAKIA

		W	S
2006	Cardiff (EC)	1	5
2007	Trnava (EC)	5	2

SLOVENIA

		W	S
2005	Swansea	0	0

SOVIET UNION (See also Russia)

		W	SU
1965	Moscow (WC)	1	2
1965	Cardiff (WC)	2	1
1981	Wrexham (WC)	0	0
1981	Tbilisi (WC)	0	3
1987	Swansea	0	0

SPAIN

		W	S
1961	Cardiff (WC)	1	2
1961	Madrid (WC)	1	1
1982	Valencia	1	1
1984	Seville (WC)	0	3
1985	Wrexham (WC)	3	0

SWEDEN

		W	S
1958	Stockholm (WC)	0	0
1988	Stockholm	1	4
1989	Wrexham	0	2
1990	Stockholm	2	4
1994	Wrexham	0	2
2010	Swansea	0	1

SWITZERLAND

		W	S
1949	Berne	0	4

1951	Wrexham	3	2
1996	Lugano	0	2
1999	Zurich (EC)	0	2
1999	Wrexham (EC)	0	2
2010	Basle (EC)	1-4	

v TRINIDAD & TOBAGO

		W	T
2006	Graz	2	1

v TUNISIA

		W	T
1998	Tunis	0	4

v TURKEY

		W	T
1978	Wrexham (EC)	1	0
1979	Izmir (EC)	0	1
1980	Cardiff (WC)	4	0
1981	Ankara (WC)	1	0
1996	Cardiff (WC)	0	0
1997	Istanbul (WC)	4	6

v UKRAINE

		W	U
2001	Cardiff (WC)	1	1
2001	Kiev (WC)	1	1

v URUGUAY

		W	U
1986	Wrexham	0	0

v USA

		W	USA
2003	San Jose	0	2

v YUGOSLAVIA

		W	Y
1953	Belgrade	2	5
1954	Cardiff	1	3
1976	Zagreb (EC)	0	2
1976	Cardiff (EC)	1	1
1982	Titograd (EC)	4	4
1983	Cardiff (EC)	1	1
1988	Swansea	1	2

NORTHERN IRELAND

ALBANIA

		NI	A
1965	Belfast (WC)	4	1
1965	Tirana (WC)	1	1
1983	Tirana (EC)	0	0
1983	Belfast (EC)	1	0
1992	Belfast (WC)	3	0
1993	Tirana (WC)	2	1
1996	Belfast (WC)	2	0
1997	Zurich (WC)	0	1
2010	Tirana	0	1

ALGERIA

		NI	A
1986	Guadalajara (WC)	1	1

ARGENTINA

		NI	A
1958	Halmstad (WC)	1	3

v ARMENIA

		NI	A
1996	Belfast (WC)	1	1
1997	Yerevan (WC)	0	0
2003	Yerevan (EC)	0	1
2003	Belfast (EC)	0	1

v AUSTRALIA

		NI	A
1980	Sydney	2	1
1980	Melbourne	1	1
1980	Adelaide	2	1

v AUSTRIA

		NI	A
1982	Madrid (WC)	2	2
1982	Vienna (EC)	0	2
1983	Belfast (EC)	3	1

1990	Vienna (EC)	0	0
1991	Belfast (EC)	2	1
1994	Vienna (EC)	2	1
1995	Belfast (EC)	5	3
2004	Belfast (WC)	3	3
2005	Vienna (WC)	0	2

v AZERBAIJAN

		NI	A
2004	Baku (WC)	0	0
2005	Belfast (WC)	2	0

v BARBADOS

		NI	B
2004	Bridgetown	1	1

v BELGIUM

		NI	B
1976	Liege (WC)	0	2
1977	Belfast (WC)	3	0
1997	Belfast	3	0

v BRAZIL

		NI	B
1986	Guadalajara (WC)	0	3

v BULGARIA

		NI	B
1972	Sofia (WC)	0	3
1973	Sheffield (WC)	0	0
1978	Sofia (EC)	2	0
1979	Belfast (EC)	2	0
2001	Sofia (WC)	3	4
2001	Belfast (WC)	0	1
2008	Belfast	0	1

v CANADA

		NI	C
1995	Edmonton	0	2
1999	Belfast	1	1
2005	Belfast	0	1

v CHILE

		NI	C
1989	Belfast	0	1
1995	Edmonton, Canada	0	2
2010	Chillan	0	1

v COLOMBIA

		NI	C
1994	Boston, USA	0	2

v CYPRUS

		NI	C
1971	Nicosia (EC)	3	0
1971	Belfast (EC)	5	0
1973	Nicosia (WC)	0	1
1973	Fulham (WC)	3	0
2002	Belfast	0	0

v CZECHOSLOVAKIA/CZECH REP

		NI	C
1958	Halmstad (WC)	1	0
1958	Malmo (WC)	2	1
2001	Belfast (WC)	0	1
2001	Teplice (WC)	1	3
2008	Belfast (WC)	0	0

| 2009 | Prague (WC) | 0 | 0 |

v DENMARK

		NI	D
1978	Belfast (EC)	2	1
1979	Copenhagen (EC)	0	4
1986	Belfast	1	1
1990	Belfast (EC)	1	1
1991	Odense (EC)	1	2
1992	Belfast (WC)	0	1
1993	Copenhagen (WC)	0	1
2000	Belfast (WC)	1	1
2001	Copenhagen (WC)	1	1
2006	Copenhagen (EC)	0	0
2007	Belfast (EC)	2	1

v ESTONIA

		NI	E
2004	Tallinn	1	0
2006	Belfast	1	0

v FAROE ISLANDS

		NI	FI
1991	Belfast (EC)	1	1
1991	Landskrona, Sw (EC)	5	0
2010	Toftir (EC)	1	1

v FINLAND

		NI	F
1984	Pori (WC)	0	1
1984	Belfast (WC)	2	1
1998	Belfast (EC)	1	0
1999	Helsinki (EC)	1	4
2003	Belfast	0	1
2006	Helsinki	2	1

v FRANCE

		NI	F
1951	Belfast	2	2
1952	Paris	1	3
1958	Norrkoping (WC)	0	4
1982	Paris	0	4
1982	Madrid (WC)	1	4
1986	Paris	0	0
1988	Belfast	0	0
1999	Belfast	0	1

v GEORGIA

		NI	G
2008	Belfast	4	1

v GERMANY/WEST GERMANY

		NI	G
1958	Malmo (WC)	2	2
1960	Belfast (WC)	3	4
1961	Berlin (WC)	1	2
1966	Belfast	0	2
1977	Cologne	0	5
1982	Belfast (EC)	1	0
1983	Hamburg (EC)	1	0
1992	Bremen	1	1
1996	Belfast	1	1
1997	Nuremberg (WC)	1	1
1997	Belfast (WC)	1	3
1999	Belfast (EC)	0	3

| 1999 | Dortmund (EC) | 0 | 4 |
| 2005 | Belfast | 1 | 4 |

v GREECE

		NI	G
1961	Athens (WC)	1	2
1961	Belfast (WC)	2	0
1988	Athens	2	3
2003	Belfast (EC)	0	2
2003	Athens (EC)	0	1

v HOLLAND

		NI	H
1962	Rotterdam	0	4
1965	Belfast (WC)	2	1
1965	Rotterdam (WC)	0	0
1976	Rotterdam (WC)	2	2
1977	Belfast (WC)	0	1

v HONDURAS

		NI	H
1982	Zaragoza (WC)	1	1

v HUNGARY

		NI	H
1988	Budapest (WC)	0	1
1989	Belfast (WC)	1	2
2000	Belfast	0	1
2008	Belfast	0	2

v ICELAND

		NI	I
1977	Reykjavik (WC)	0	1
1977	Belfast (WC)	2	0
2000	Reykjavik (WC)	0	1
2001	Belfast (WC)	3	0
2006	Belfast (EC)	0	3
2007	Reykjavik (EC)	1	2

v ISRAEL

		NI	I
1968	Jaffa	3	2
1976	Tel Aviv	1	1
1980	Tel Aviv (WC)	0	0
1981	Belfast (WC)	1	0
1984	Belfast	3	0
1987	Tel Aviv	1	1
2009	Belfast	1	1

v ITALY

		NI	I
1957	Rome (WC)	0	1
1957	Belfast	2	2
1958	Belfast (WC)	2	1
1961	Bologna	2	3
1997	Palermo	0	2
2003	Campobasso	0	2
2009	Pisa	0	3
2010	Belfast (EC)	0	0

v LATVIA

		NI	L
1993	Riga (WC)	2	1
1993	Belfast (WC)	2	0
1995	Riga (EC)	1	0
1995	Belfast (EC)	1	2
2006	Belfast (EC)	1	0
2007	Riga (EC)	0	1

v LIECHTENSTEIN

		NI	L
1994	Belfast (EC)	4	1
1995	Eschen (EC)	4	0
2002	Vaduz	0	0
2007	Vaduz (EC)	4	1
2007	Belfast (EC)	3	1

v LITHUANIA

		NI	L
1992	Belfast (WC)	2	2

v LUXEMBOURG

		NI	L
2000	Luxembourg	3	1

v MALTA

		NI	M
1988	Belfast (WC)	3	0
1989	Valletta (WC)	2	0
2000	Ta'Qali	3	0
2000	Belfast (WC)	1	0
2001	Valletta (WC)	1	0
2005	Valletta	1	1

v MEXICO

		NI	M
1966	Belfast	4	1
1994	Miami	0	3

v MOLDOVA

		NI	M
1998	Belfast (EC)	2	2
1999	Kishinev (EC)	0	0

v MONTENEGRO

		W	M
2010	Podgorica	0	2

v MOROCCO

		NI	M
1986	Belfast	2	1
2010	Belfast	1	1

v NORWAY

		NI	N
1974	Oslo (EC)	1	2
1975	Belfast (EC)	3	0
1990	Belfast	2	3
1996	Belfast	0	2
2001	Belfast	0	4
2004	Belfast	1	4

v POLAND

		NI	P
1962	Katowice (EC)	2	0
1962	Belfast (EC)	2	0
1988	Belfast	1	1
1991	Belfast	3	1
2002	Limassol (Cyprus)	1	4
2004	Belfast (WC)	0	3
2005	Warsaw (WC)	0	1
2009	Belfast (WC)	3	2
2009	Chorzow (WC)	1	1

v PORTUGAL

		NI	P
1957	Lisbon (WC)	1	1
1957	Belfast (WC)	3	0
1973	Coventry (WC)	1	1

1973	Lisbon (WC)	1	1
1980	Lisbon (WC)	0	1
1981	Belfast (WC)	1	0
1994	Belfast (EC)	1	2
1995	Oporto (EC)	1	1
1997	Belfast (WC)	0	0
1997	Lisbon (WC)	0	1
2005	Belfast	1	1

v REPUBLIC OF IRELAND

		NI	RI
1978	Dublin (EC)	0	0
1979	Belfast (EC)	1	0
1988	Belfast (WC)	0	0
1989	Dublin (WC)	0	3
1993	Dublin (WC)	0	3
1993	Belfast (WC)	1	1
1994	Belfast (EC)	0	4
1995	Dublin (EC)	1	1
1999	Dublin	1	0
2011	Dublin (CC)	0	5

v ROMANIA

		NI	R
1984	Belfast (WC)	3	2
1985	Bucharest (WC)	1	0
1994	Belfast	2	0
2006	Chicago	0	2

v SAN MARINO

		NI	SM
2008	Belfast (WC)	4	0
2009	Serravalle (WC)	3	0

v SERBIA & MONTENEGRO

		NI	S
2004	Belfast	1	1

v SERBIA

		NI	S
2009	Belfast	0	1
2011	Belgrade (EC)	1	2

v SLOVAKIA

		NI	S
1998	Belfast	1	0
2008	Bratislava (WC)	1	2
2009	Belfast (WC)	0	2

v SLOVENIA

		NI	S
2008	Maribor (WC)	0	2
2009	Belfast (WC)	1	0
2010	Maribor (WC)	1	0
2011	Belfast (EC)	0	0

v SOVIET UNION

		NI	SU
1969	Belfast (WC)	0	0
1969	Moscow (WC)	0	2
1971	Moscow (EC)	0	1
1971	Belfast (EC)	1	1

v SPAIN

		NI	S
1958	Madrid	2	6
1963	Bilbao	1	1
1963	Belfast	0	1
1970	Seville (EC)	0	3
1972	Hull (EC)	1	1
1982	Valencia (WC)	1	0
1985	Palma, Majorca	0	0
1986	Guadalajara (WC)	1	2
1988	Seville (WC)	0	4
1989	Belfast (WC)	0	2
1992	Belfast (WC)	0	0
1993	Seville (WC)	1	3
1998	Santander	1	4
2002	Belfast	0	5
2002	Albacete (EC)	0	3
2003	Belfast (EC)	0	0
2006	Belfast (EC)	3	2
2007	Las Palmas (EC)	0	1

v ST KITTS & NEVIS

		NI	SK
2004	Basseterre	2	0

v SWEDEN

		NI	S
1974	Solna (EC)	2	0
1975	Belfast (EC)	1	2
1980	Belfast (WC)	3	0
1981	Stockholm (WC)	0	1
1996	Belfast	1	2
2007	Belfast (EC)	2	1
2007	Stockholm (EC)	1	1

v SWITZERLAND

		NI	S
1964	Belfast (WC)	1	0
1964	Lausanne (WC)	1	2
1998	Belfast	1	0
2004	Zurich	0	0
2010	Basle (EC)	1	4

v THAILAND

		NI	T
1997	Bangkok	0	0

v TRINIDAD & TOBAGO

		NI	T
2004	Port of Spain	3	0

v TURKEY

		NI	T
1968	Belfast (WC)	4	1
1968	Istanbul (WC)	3	0
1983	Belfast (EC)	2	1
1983	Ankara (EC)	0	1
1985	Belfast (WC)	2	0
1985	Izmir (WC)	0	0
1986	Izmir (EC)	0	0
1987	Belfast (EC)	1	0
1998	Istanbul (EC)	0	3
1999	Belfast (EC)	0	3
2010	Connecticut	0	2

v UKRAINE

		NI	U
1996	Belfast (WC)	0	1
1997	Kiev (WC)	1	2
2002	Belfast	0	0

2003	Donetsk (EC)	0	0

v URUGUAY

		NI	U
1964	Belfast	3	0
1990	Belfast	1	0
2006	New Jersey	0	1

v YUGOSLAVIA

		NI	Y
1975	Belfast (EC)	1	0

1975	Belgrade (EC)	0	1
1982	Zaragoza (WC)	0	0
1987	Belfast (EC)	1	2
1987	Sarajevo (EC)	0	3
1990	Belfast (EC)	0	2
1991	Belgrade (EC)	1	4
2000	Belfast	1	2

REPUBLIC OF IRELAND

v ALBANIA

		RI	A
1992	Dublin (WC)	2	0
1993	Tirana (WC)	2	1
2003	Tirana (EC)	0	0
2003	Dublin (EC)	2	1

v ALGERIA

		RI	A
1982	Algiers	0	2
2010	Dublin	3	0

v ANDORRA

		RI	A
2001	Barcelona (WC)	3	0
2001	Dublin (WC)	3	1
2010	Dublin (EC)	3	1

v ARGENTINA

		RI	A
1951	Dublin	0	1
1979*	Dublin	0	0
1980	Dublin	0	1
1998	Dublin	0	2
2010	Dublin	0	1
(*Not regarded as full int)			

v ARMENIA

		RI	A
2010	Yerevan (EC)	1	0

v AUSTRALIA

		RI	A
2003	Dublin	2	1
2009	Limerick	0	3

v AUSTRIA

		RI	A
1952	Vienna	0	6
1953	Dublin	4	0
1958	Vienna	1	3
1962	Dublin	2	3
1963	Vienna (EC)	0	0
1963	Dublin (EC)	3	2
1966	Vienna	0	1
1968	Dublin	2	2
1971	Dublin (EC)	1	4
1971	Linz (EC)	0	6
1995	Dublin (EC)	1	3
1995	Vienna (EC)	1	3
2009	Limerick	0	3
2009	Limerick	0	3

v BELGIUM

		RI	B
1928	Liege	4	2
1929	Dublin	4	0
1930	Brussels	3	1
1934	Dublin (WC)	4	4
1949	Dublin	0	2
1950	Brussels	1	5
1965	Dublin	0	2
1966	Liege	3	2
1980	Dublin (WC)	1	1
1981	Brussels (WC)	0	1
1986	Brussels (EC)	2	2
1987	Dublin (EC)	0	0
1997*	Dublin (WC)	1	1
1997*	Brussels (WC)	1	2
(*World Cup play-off)			

v BOLIVIA

		RI	B
1994	Dublin	1	0
1996	East Rutherford, NJ	3	0
2007	Boston	1	1

v BRAZIL

		RI	B
1974	Rio de Janeiro	1	2
1982	Uberlandia	0	7
1987	Dublin	1	0
2004	Dublin	0	0
2008	Dublin	0	1
2010	Arsenal	0	2

v BULGARIA

		RI	B
1977	Sofia (WC)	1	2
1977	Dublin (WC)	0	0
1979	Sofia (EC)	0	1
1979	Dublin (EC)	3	0
1987	Sofia (EC)	1	2
1987	Dublin (EC)	2	0
2004	Dublin	1	1
2009	Dublin (WC)	1	1
2009	Sofia (WC)	1	1

v CAMEROON

		RI	C
2002	Niigata (WC)	1	1

v CANADA

		RI	C
2003	Dublin	3	0

v CHILE

		RI	C
1960	Dublin	2	0
1972	Recife	1	2
1974	Santiago	2	1
1982	Santiago	0	1
1991	Dublin	1	1
2006	Dublin	0	1

v CHINA

		RI	C
1984	Sapporo	1	0
2005	Dublin	1	0

v COLOMBIA

		RI	C
2008	Fulham	1	0

v CROATIA

		RI	C
1996	Dublin	2	2
1998	Dublin (EC)	2	0
1999	Zagreb (EC)	0	1
2001	Dublin	2	2
2004	Dublin	1	0

v CYPRUS

		RI	C
1980	Nicosia (WC)	3	2
1980	Dublin (WC)	6	0
2001	Nicosia (WC)	4	0
2001	Dublin (WC)	4	0
2004	Dublin (WC)	3	0
2005	Nicosia (WC)	1	0
2006	Nicosia (EC)	2	5
2007	Dublin (EC)	1	1
2008	Dublin (WC)	1	0
2009	Nicosia (WC)	2	1

v CZECHOSLOVAKIA/CZECH REP

		RI	C
1938	Prague	2	2
1959	Dublin (EC)	2	0
1959	Bratislava (EC)	0	4
1961	Dublin (WC)	1	3
1961	Prague (WC)	1	7
1967	Dublin (EC)	0	2
1967	Prague (EC)	2	1
1969	Dublin (WC)	1	2
1969	Prague (WC)	0	3
1979	Prague	1	4
1981	Dublin	3	1
1986	Reykjavik	1	0
1994	Dublin	1	3
1996	Prague	0	2
1998	Olomouc	1	2
2000	Dublin	3	2
2004	Dublin	2	1
2006	Dublin (EC)	1	1
2007	Prague (EC)	0	1

v DENMARK

		RI	D
1956	Dublin (WC)	2	1
1957	Copenhagen (WC)	2	0
1968*	Dublin (WC)	1	1
1969	Copenhagen (WC)	0	2
1969	Dublin (WC)	1	1
1978	Copenhagen (EC)	3	3
1979	Dublin (EC)	2	0
1984	Copenhagen (WC)	0	3
1985	Dublin (WC)	1	4
1992	Copenhagen (WC)	0	0
1993	Dublin (WC)	1	1
2002	Dublin	3	0

(*Abandoned after 51 mins – fog)

2007	Aarhus	4	0

v ECUADOR

		RI	E
1972	Natal	3	2
2007	New York	1	1

v EGYPT

		RI	E
1990	Palermo (WC)	0	0

v ESTONIA

		RI	E
2000	Dublin (WC)	2	0
2001	Tallinn (WC)	2	0

v FAROE ISLANDS

		RI	F
2004	Dublin (WC)	2	0
2005	Torshavn (WC)	2	0

v FINLAND

		RI	F
1949	Dublin (WC)	3	0
1949	Helsinki (WC)	1	1
1990	Dublin	1	1
2000	Dublin	3	0
2002	Helsinki	3	0

v FRANCE

		RI	F
1937	Paris	2	0
1952	Dublin	1	1
1953	Dublin (WC)	3	5
1953	Paris (WC)	0	1
1972	Dublin (WC)	2	1
1973	Paris (WC)	1	1
1976	Paris (WC)	0	2
1977	Dublin (WC)	1	0
1980	Paris (WC)	0	2
1981	Dublin (WC)	3	2
1989	Dublin	0	0
2004	Paris (WC)	0	0
2005	Dublin (WC)	0	1
2009	Dublin (WC)	0	1
2009	Paris (WC)	1	1

v GEORGIA

		RI	G
2002	Tbilisi (EC)	2	1
2003	Dublin (EC)	2	0
2008	Mainz (WC)	2	1
2009	Dublin (WC)	2	1

v GERMANY/WEST GERMANY

		RI	G
1935	Dortmund	1	3

1936	Dublin	5	2
1939	Bremen	1	1
1951	Dublin	3	2
1952	Cologne	0	3
1955	Hamburg	1	2
1956	Dublin	3	0
1960	Dusseldorf	1	0
1966	Dublin	0	4
1970	Berlin	1	2
1975*	Dublin	1	0
1979	Dublin	1	3
1981	Bremen	0	3
1989	Dublin	1	1
1994	Hanover	2	0
2002	Ibaraki (WC)	1	1
2006	Stuttgart (EC)	0	1
2007	Dublin (EC)	0	0
(*v W Germany 'B')			

v GREECE

		RI	G
2000	Dublin	0	1
2002	Athens	0	0

v HOLLAND

		RI	H
1932	Amsterdam	2	0
1934	Amsterdam	2	5
1935	Dublin	3	5
1955	Dublin	1	0
1956	Rotterdam	4	1
1980	Dublin (WC)	2	1
1981	Rotterdam (WC)	2	2
1982	Rotterdam (EC)	1	2
1983	Dublin (EC)	2	3
1988	Gelsenkirchen (EC)	0	1
1990	Palermo (WC)	1	1
1994	Tilburg	1	0
1994	Orlando (WC)	0	2
1995*	Liverpool (EC)	0	2
1996	Rotterdam	1	3
(*Qual Round play-off)			
2000	Amsterdam (WC)	2	2
2001	Dublin (WC)	1	0
2004	Amsterdam	1	0
2006	Dublin	0	4

v HUNGARY

		RI	H
1934	Dublin	2	4
1936	Budapest	3	3
1936	Dublin	2	3
1939	Cork	2	2
1939	Budapest	2	2
1969	Dublin (WC)	1	2
1969	Budapest (WC)	0	4
1989	Budapest (WC)	0	0
1989	Dublin (WC)	2	0
1992	Gyor	2	1

v ICELAND

		RI	I
1962	Dublin (EC)	4	2
1962	Reykjavik (EC)	1	1

1982	Dublin (EC)	2	0
1983	Reykjavik (EC)	3	0
1986	Reykjavik	2	1
1996	Dublin (WC)	0	0
1997	Reykjavik (WC)	4	2

v IRAN

		RI	I
1972	Recife	2	1
2001*	Dublin (WC)	2	0
2001*	Tehran (WC)	0	1
(*Qual Round play-off)			

v ISRAEL

		RI	I
1984	Tel Aviv	0	3
1985	Tel Aviv	0	0
1987	Dublin	5	0
2005	Tel Aviv (WC)	1	1
2005	Dublin (WC)	2	2

v ITALY

		RI	I
1926	Turin	0	3
1927	Dublin	1	2
1970	Florence (EC)	0	3
1971	Dublin (EC)	1	2
1985	Dublin	1	2
1990	Rome (WC)	0	1
1992	Boston, USA	0	2
1994	New York (WC)	1	0
2005	Dublin	1	2
2009	Bari (WC)	1	1
2009	Dublin (WC)	2	2

v JAMAICA

		RI	J
2004	Charlton	1	0

v LATVIA

		RI	L
1992	Dublin (WC)	4	0
1993	Riga (WC)	2	0
1994	Riga (EC)	3	0
1995	Dublin (EC)	2	1

v LIECHTENSTEIN

		RI	L
1994	Dublin (EC)	4	0
1995	Eschen (EC)	0	0
1996	Eschen (WC)	5	0
1997	Dublin (WC)	5	0

v LITHUANIA

		RI	L
1993	Vilnius (WC)	1	0
1993	Dublin (WC)	2	0
1997	Dublin (WC)	0	0
1997	Zalgiris (WC)	2	1

v LUXEMBOURG

		RI	L
1936	Luxembourg	5	1
1953	Dublin (WC)	4	0
1954	Luxembourg (WC)	1	0
1987	Luxembourg (EC)	2	0
1987	Luxembourg (EC)	2	1

v MACEDONIA

		RI	M
1996	Dublin (WC)	3	0
1997	Skopje (WC)	2	3
1999	Dublin (EC)	1	0
1999	Skopje (EC)	1	1
2011	Dublin (EC)	2	1
2011	Skopje (EC)	2	0

v MALTA

		RI	M
1983	Valletta (EC)	1	0
1983	Dublin (EC)	8	0
1989	Dublin (WC)	2	0
1989	Valletta (WC)	2	0
1990	Valletta	3	0
1998	Dublin (EC)	1	0
1999	Valletta (EC)	3	2

v MEXICO

		RI	M
1984	Dublin	0	0
1994	Orlando (WC)	1	2
1996	New Jersey	2	2
1998	Dublin	0	0
2000	Chicago	2	2

v MONTENEGRO

		RI	M
2008	Podgorica (WC)	0	0
2009	Dublin (WC)	0	0

v MOROCCO

		RI	M
1990	Dublin	1	0

v NIGERIA

		RI	N
2002	Dublin	1	2
2004	Charlton	0	3
2009	Fulham	1	1

v NORWAY

		RI	N
1937	Oslo (WC)	2	3
1937	Dublin (WC)	3	3
1950	Dublin	2	2
1951	Oslo	3	2
1954	Dublin	2	1
1955	Oslo	3	1
1960	Dublin	3	1
1964	Oslo	4	1
1973	Oslo	1	1
1976	Dublin	3	0
1978	Oslo	0	0
1984	Oslo (WC)	0	1
1985	Dublin (WC)	0	0
1988	Oslo	0	0
1994	New York (WC)	0	0
2003	Dublin	1	0
2008	Oslo	1	1
2010	Dublin	1	2

v PARAGUAY

		RI	P
1999	Dublin	2	0
2010	Dublin	2	1

v POLAND

		RI	P
1938	Warsaw	0	6
1938	Dublin	3	2
1958	Katowice	2	2
1958	Dublin	2	2
1964	Cracow	1	3
1964	Dublin	3	2
1968	Dublin	2	2
1968	Katowice	0	1
1970	Dublin	1	2
1970	Poznan	0	2
1973	Wroclaw	0	2
1973	Dublin	1	0
1976	Poznan	2	0
1977	Dublin	0	0
1978	Lodz	0	3
1981	Bydgoszcz	0	3
1984	Dublin	0	0
1986	Warsaw	0	1
1988	Dublin	3	1
1991	Dublin (EC)	0	0
1991	Poznan (EC)	3	3
2004	Bydgoszcz	0	0
2008	Dublin	2	3

v PORTUGAL

		RI	P
1946	Lisbon	1	3
1947	Dublin	0	2
1948	Lisbon	0	2
1949	Dublin	1	0
1972	Recife	1	2
1992	Boston, USA	2	0
1995	Dublin (EC)	1	0
1995	Lisbon (EC)	0	3
1996	Dublin	0	1
2000	Lisbon (WC)	1	1
2001	Dublin (WC)	1	1
2005	Dublin	1	0

v ROMANIA

		RI	R
1988	Dublin	2	0
1990*	Genoa	0	0
1997	Bucharest (WC)	0	1
1997	Dublin (WC)	1	1

(*Rep won 5-4 on pens)

v RUSSIA (See also Soviet Union)

		RI	R
1994	Dublin	0	0
1996	Dublin	0	2
2002	Dublin	2	0
2002	Moscow (EC)	2	4
2003	Dublin (EC)	1	1
2010	Dublin (EC)	2	3

v SAN MARINO

		RI	SM
2006	Dublin (EC)	5	0
2007	Rimini (EC)	2	1

v SAUDI ARABIA

		RI	SA
2002	Yokohama (WC)	3	0

v SERBIA

		RI	S
2008	Dublin	1	1

v SLOVAKIA

		RI	S
2007	Dublin (EC)	1	0
2007	Bratislava (EC)	2	2
2010	Zilina (EC)	1	1

v SOUTH AFRICA

		RI	SA
2000	New Jersey	2	1
2009	Limerick	1	0

v SOVIET UNION
(See also Russia)

		RI	SU
1972	Dublin (WC)	1	2
1973	Moscow (WC)	0	1
1974	Dublin (EC)	3	0
1975	Kiev (EC)	1	2
1984	Dublin (WC)	1	0
1985	Moscow (WC)	0	2
1988	Hanover (EC)	1	1
1990	Dublin	1	0

v SPAIN

		RI	S
1931	Barcelona	1	1
1931	Dublin	0	5
1946	Madrid	1	0
1947	Dublin	3	2
1948	Barcelona	1	2
1949	Dublin	1	4
1952	Madrid	0	6
1955	Dublin	2	2
1964	Seville (EC)	1	5
1964	Dublin (EC)	0	2
1965	Dublin (WC)	1	0
1965	Seville (WC)	1	4
1965	Paris (WC)	0	1
1966	Dublin (EC)	0	0
1966	Valencia (EC)	0	2
1977	Dublin	0	1
1982	Dublin (EC)	3	3
1983	Zaragoza (EC)	0	2
1985	Cork	0	0
1988	Seville (WC)	0	2
1989	Dublin (WC)	1	0
1992	Seville (WC)	0	0
1993	Dublin (WC)	1	3
2002*	Suwon (WC)	1	1
(*Rep lost 3-2 on pens)			

v SWEDEN

		RI	S
1949	Stockholm (WC)	1	3
1949	Dublin (WC)	1	3
1959	Dublin	3	2
1960	Malmo	1	4
1970	Dublin (EC)	1	1
1970	Malmo (EC)	0	1
1999	Dublin	2	0
2006	Dublin	3	0

v SWITZERLAND

		RI	S
1935	Basle	0	1
1936	Dublin	1	0
1937	Berne	1	0
1938	Dublin	4	0
1948	Dublin	0	1
1975	Dublin (EC)	2	1
1975	Berne (EC)	0	1
1980	Dublin	2	0
1985	Dublin (WC)	3	0
1985	Berne (WC)	0	0
1992	Dublin	2	1
2002	Dublin (EC)	1	2
2003	Basle (EC)	0	2
2004	Basle (WC)	1	1
2005	Dublin (WC)	0	0

v TRINIDAD & TOBAGO

		RI	T&T
1982	Port of Spain	1	2

v TUNISIA

		RI	T
1988	Dublin	4	0

v TURKEY

		RI	T
1966	Dublin (EC)	2	1
1967	Ankara (EC)	1	2
1974	Izmir (EC)	1	1
1975	Dublin (EC)	4	0
1976	Ankara	3	3
1978	Dublin	4	2
1990	Izmir	0	0
1990	Dublin (EC)	5	0
1991	Istanbul (EC)	3	1
1999	Dublin (EC)	1	1
1999	Bursa (EC)	0	0
2003	Dublin	2	2

v URUGUAY

		RI	U
1974	Montevideo	0	2
1986	Dublin	1	1
2011	Dublin	2	3

v USA

		RI	USA
1979	Dublin	3	2
1991	Boston	1	1
1992	Dublin	4	1
1992	Washington	1	3
1996	Boston	1	2
2000	Foxboro	1	1
2002	Dublin	2	1

v YUGOSLAVIA

		RI	Y
1955	Dublin	1	4
1988	Dublin	2	0
1998	Belgrade (EC)	0	1
1999	Dublin (EC)	2	1

BRITISH AND IRISH INTERNATIONAL APPEARANCES SINCE THE WAR (1946–2011)

(As at start of season 2011–12 In year shown 2011 = season 2010–11
*Also a pre-war International player. Totals include appearances as substitute)

ENGLAND

Agbonlahor G (Aston Villa, 2009–10)	3	Beattie K (Ipswich, 1975–58)	9
A'Court A (Liverpool, 1958–59)	5	Beckham D (Manchester Utd, Real Madrid,	
Adams T (Arsenal, 1987–2001)	66	LA Galaxy, AC Milan 1997–2010)	115
Allen A (Stoke, 1960)	3	Bell C (Manchester City, 1968–76)	48
Allen C (QPR, Tottenham, 1984–88)	5	Bent D (Charlton, Tottenham	
Allen R (WBA, 1952–55)	5	Sunderland, 2006–11)	10
Anderson S (Sunderland, 1962)	2	Bentley D (Blackburn, 2008–09)	7
Anderson V (Nottm Forest, Arsenal,		Bentley R (Chelsea, 1949–55)	12
Manchester Utd, 1979–88)	30	Berry J (Manchester Utd, 1953–56)	4
Anderton D (Tottenham, 1994–2002)	30	Birtles G (Nottm Forest, 1980–81)	3
Angus J (Burnley, 1961)	1	Blissett L (Watford, AC Milan, 1983–84)	14
Armfield J (Blackpool, 1959–66)	43	Blockley J (Arsenal, 1973)	1
Armstrong D (Middlesbrough,		Blunstone F (Chelsea, 1955–57)	5
Southampton, 1980–4)	3	Bonetti P (Chelsea, 1966–70)	7
Armstrong K (Chelsea, 1955)	1	Bothroyd J (Cardiff, 2011)	1
Ashton D (West Ham, 2008)	1	Bould S (Arsenal, 1994)	2
Astall G (Birmingham, 1956)	2	Bowles S (QPR, 1974–77)	5
Astle J (WBA, 1969–70)	5	Bowyer L (Leeds, 2003)	1
Aston J (Manchester Utd, 1949–51)	17	Boyer P (Norwich, 1976)	1
Atyeo J (Bristol City, 1956–57)	6	Brabrook P (Chelsea, 1958–60)	3
		Bracewell P (Everton, 1985–86)	3
Bailey G (Manchester Utd, 1985)	2	Bradford G (Bristol Rov, 1956)	1
Bailey M (Charlton, 1964–5)	2	Bradley W (Manchester Utd, 1959)	3
Baily E (Tottenham, 1950–3)	9	Bridge W (Southampton, Chelsea,	
Baines L (Everton, 2010–11)	5	Manchester City 2002–10)	36
Baker J (Hibs, Arsenal, 1960–6)	8	Bridges B (Chelsea, 1965–66)	4
Ball A (Blackpool, Everton, Arsenal,		Broadbent P (Wolves, 1958–60)	7
1965–75)	72	Broadis I (Manchester City, Newcastle,	
Ball M (Everton, 2001)	1	1952–54)	14
Banks G (Leicester, Stoke, 1963–72)	73	Brooking T (West Ham, 1974–82)	47
Banks T (Bolton, 1958–59)	6	Brooks J (Tottenham, 1957)	3
Bardsley D (QPR, 1993)	2	Brown A (WBA, 1971)	1
Barham M (Norwich, 1983)	2	Brown K (West Ham, 1960)	1
Barlow R (WBA, 1955)	1	Brown W (Manchester Utd, 1999–2010)	23
Barmby N (Tottenham, Middlesbrough,		Bull S (Wolves, 1989–91)	13
Everton, Liverpool, 1995–2002)	23	Butcher T (Ipswich, Rangers, 1980–90)	77
Barnes J (Watford, Liverpool, 1983–96)	79	Butt N (Manchester Utd, Newcastle,	
Barnes P (Manchester City, WBA,		1997–2005)	39
Leeds, 1978–82)	22	Byrne G (Liverpool, 1963–66)	2
Barrass M (Bolton, 1952–53)	3	Byrne J (Crystal Palace, West Ham,	
Barrett E (Oldham, Aston Villa, 1991–93)	3	1962–65)	11
Barry G (Aston Villa, Manchester City,		Byrne R (Manchester Utd, 1954–58)	33
2000–11)	46		
Barton J (Manchester City, 2007)	1	Cahill G (Bolton, 2011)	3
Barton W (Wimbledon, Newcastle, 1995)	3	Callaghan I (Liverpool, 1966–78)	4
Batty D (Leeds, Blackburn, Newcastle,		Campbell S (Tottenham, Arsenal,	
Leeds, 1991–2000)	42	Portsmouth, 1996–2008)	73
Baynham R (Luton, 1956)	3	Carragher J (Liverpool, 1999–2010)	38
Beardsley P (Newcastle, Liverpool,		Carrick M (West Ham, Tottenham,	
Newcastle, 1986–96)	59	Manchester Utd, 2001–10)	22
Beasant D (Chelsea, 1990)	2	Carroll A (Newcastle, Liverpool, 2011)	2
Beattie J (Southampton, 2003–04)	5	*Carter H (Derby, 1947)	7

Carson S (Liverpool, Aston Villa WBA, 2008–09) 3
Chamberlain M (Stoke, 1983–85) 8
Channon M (Southampton, Manchester City, 1973–78) 46
Charles G (Nottm Forest, 1991) 2
Charlton, J (Leeds, 1965–70) 35
Charlton, R (Manchester Utd, 1958–70) 106
Charnley R (Blackpool, 1963) 1
Cherry T (Leeds, 1976–80) 27
Chilton A (Manchester Utd, 1951–52) 2
Chivers M (Tottenham, 1971–74) 24
Clamp E (Wolves, 1958) 4
Clapton D (Arsenal, 1959) 1
Clarke A (Leeds, 1970–6) 19
Clarke H (Tottenham, 1954) 1
Clayton R (Blackburn, 1956–60) 35
Clemence R (Liverpool, Tottenham, 1973–84) 61
Clement D (QPR, 1976–7) 5
Clough B (Middlesbrough, 1960) 2
Clough N (Nottm Forest, Liverpool, 1989–93) 14
Coates R (Burnley, Tottenham, 1970–71) 4
Cockburn H (Manchester Utd, 1947–52) 13
Cohen G (Fulham, 1964–68) 37
Cole Andy (Manchester Utd, 1995–2002) 15
Cole Ashley (Arsenal, Chelsea, 2001–11) 89
Cole C (West Ham, 2009–10) 7
Cole J (West Ham, Chelsea, 2001–10) 56
Collymore S (Nottm Forest, Aston Villa, 1995–97) 3
Compton L (Arsenal, 1951) 2
Connelly J (Burnley, Manchester Utd, 1960–66) 20
Cooper C (Nottm Forest, 1995) 2
Cooper T (Leeds, 1969–75) 20
Coppell S (Manchester Utd, 1978–83) 42
Corrigan J (Manchester City, 1976–82) 9
Cottee T (West Ham, Everton, 1987–89) 7
Cowans G (Aston Villa, Bari, Aston Villa, 1983–91) 10
Crawford R (Ipswich, 1962) 2
Crouch P (Southampton, Liverpool, Portsmouth, Tottenham, 2005–11) 42
Crowe C (Wolves, 1963) 1
Cunningham L (WBA, Real Madrid, 1979–81) 6
Curle K (Manchester City, 1992) 3
Currie A (Sheffield Utd, Leeds, 1972–79) 17

Daley T (Aston Villa, 1992) 7
Davenport P (Nottm Forest, 1985) 1
Davies K (Bolton, 2011) 1
Dawson M (Tottenham 2011) 4
Deane B (Sheffield Utd, 1991–93) 3

Deeley N (Wolves, 1959) 2
Defoe J (Tottenham, Portsmouth, Tottenham, 2004–11) 46
Devonshire A (West Ham, 1980–84) 8
Dickinson J (Portsmouth, 1949–57) 48
Ditchburn E (Tottenham, 1949–57) 6
Dixon K (Chelsea, 1985–87) 8
Dixon L (Arsenal, 1990–99) 22
Dobson M (Burnley, Everton, 1974–75) 5
Dorigo T (Chelsea, Leeds, 1990–94) 15
Douglas B (Blackburn, 1959–63) 36
Downing S (Middlesbrough, Aston Villa, 2005–11) 27
Doyle M (Manchester City, 1976–77) 5
Dublin D (Coventry, Aston Villa, 1998–99) 4
Dunn D (Blackburn, 2003) 1
Duxbury, M (Manchester Utd, 1984–85) 10
Dyer K (Newcastle, West Ham, 2000–08) 33

Eastham G (Arsenal, 1963–66) 19
Eckersley W (Blackburn, 1950–54) 17
Edwards, D (Manchester Utd, 1955–58) 18
Ehiogu U (Aston Villa, Middlesbrough, 1996–2002) 4
Ellerington W (Southampton, 1949) 2
Elliott W (Burnley, 1952–53) 5

Fantham J (Sheffield Wed, 1962) 1
Fashanu J (Wimbledon, 1989) 2
Fenwick T (QPR, 1984–88) 20
Ferdinand L (QPR, Newcastle, Tottenham, 1993–98) 17
Ferdinand R (West Ham, Leeds, Manchester Utd, 1997–2011) 81
Finney T (Preston, 1947–59) 76
Flowers R (Wolves, 1955–66) 49
Flowers T (Southampton, Blackburn, 1993–98) 11
Foster B (Manchester Utd, Birmingham 2007–11) 5
Foster S (Brighton, 1982) 3
Foulkes W (Manchester Utd, 1955) 1
Fowler R (Liverpool, Leeds, 1996–2002) 26
Francis G (QPR, 1975–76) 12
Francis T (Birmingham, Nottm Forest, Man City, Sampdoria, 1977–86) 52
Franklin N (Stoke, 1947–50) 27
Froggatt J (Portsmouth, 1950–53) 13
Froggatt R (Sheffield Wed, 1953) 4

Gardner A (Tottenham, 2004) 1
Garrett T (Blackpool, 1952–54) 3
Gascoigne P (Tottenham, Lazio, Rangers, Middlesbrough, 1989–98) 57
Gates E (Ipswich, 1981) 2
George C (Derby, 1977) 1
Gerrard S (Liverpool, 2000–11) 89
Gibbs K (Arsenal, 2011) 2
Gidman J (Aston Villa, 1977) 1
Gillard I (QPR, 1975–76) 3
Goddard P (West Ham, 1982) 1

Grainger C (Sheffield Utd, Sunderland, 1956–57) 7
Gray A (Crystal Palace, 1992) 1
Gray M (Sunderland, 1999) 3
Greaves J (Chelsea, Tottenham, 1959–67) 57
Green R (Norwich, West Ham 2005–10) 11
Greenhoff B (Manchester Utd, Leeds, 1976–80) 18
Gregory J (QPR, 1983–84) 6
Guppy S (Leicester, 2000) 1

Hagan J (Sheffield Utd, 1949) 1
Haines J (WBA, 1949) 1
Hall J (Birmingham, 1956–57) 17
Hancocks J (Wolves, 1949–50) 3
Hardwick G (Middlesbrough, 1947–48) 13
Harford M (Luton, 1988–89) 2
Hargreaves O (Bayern Munich, Manchester Utd, 2002–08) 42
Harris G (Burnley, 1966) 1
Harris P (Portsmouth, 1950–54) 2
Hart J (Manchester City, 2010–11) 11
Harvey C (Everton, 1971) 1
Hassall H (Huddersfield, Bolton, 1951–54) 5
Hateley M (Portsmouth, AC Milan, Monaco, Rangers, 1984–92) 32
Haynes J (Fulham, 1955–62) 56
Hector K (Derby, 1974) 2
Hellawell M (Birmingham, 1963) 2
Henderson J (Sunderland, 2011) 1
Hendrie L (Aston Villa, 1999) 1
Henry R (Tottenham, 1963) 1
Heskey E (Leicester, Liverpool, Birmingham, Wigan, Aston Villa 1999–2010) 62
Hill F (Bolton, 1963) 2
Hill G (Manchester Utd, 1976–78) 6
Hilt R (Luton, 1983–86) 3
Hinchcliffe A (Everton, Sheffield Wed, 1997–99) 7
Hinton A (Wolves, Nottm Forest, 1963–65) 3
Hirst D (Sheffield Wed, 1991–92) 3
Hitchens G (Aston Villa, Inter Milan, 1961–62) 7
Hoddle G (Tottenham, Monaco, 1980–88) 53
Hodge S (Aston Villa, Tottenham, Nottm Forest, 1986–91) 24
Hodgkinson A (Sheffield Utd, 1957–61) 5
Holden D (Bolton, 1959) 5
Holliday E (Middlesbrough, 1960) 3
Hollins J (Chelsea, 1967) 1
Hopkinson E (Bolton, 1958–60) 14
Howe D (WBA, 1958–60) 23
Howe J (Derby, 1948–49) 3
Howey S (Newcastle, 1995–96) 4
Huddlestone T (Tottenham, 2010) 3
Hudson A (Stoke, 1975) 2
Hughes E (Liverpool, Wolves, 1970–80) 62
Hughes L (Liverpool, 1950) 3
Hunt R (Liverpool, 1962–69) 34

Hunt S (WBA, 1984) 2
Hunter N (Leeds, 1966–75) 28
Hurst G (West Ham, 1966–72) 49

Ince P (Manchester Utd, Inter Milan, Liverpool, Middlesbrough, 1993–2000) 53

Jagielka P (Everton, 2008–11) 9
James D (Liverpool, Aston Villa, West Ham, Manchester City, Portsmouth, 1997–2010) 53
Jarvis M (Wolves, 2011) 1
Jeffers F (Arsenal, 2003) 1
Jenas J (Newcastle, Tottenham, 2003–10) 21
Jezzard B (Fulham, 1954–56) 2
Johnson A (Crystal Palace, Everton, 2005–08) 8
Johnson A (Manchester City, 2010–11) 6
Johnson D (Ipswich, Liverpool, 1975–80) 8
Johnson G (Chelsea, Portsmouth, Liverpool, 2004–11) 34
Johnson S (Derby, 2001) 1
Johnston H (Blackpool, 1947–54) 10
Jones M (Leeds, Sheffield Utd, 1965–70) 3
Jones R (Liverpool, 1992–95) 8
Jones WH (Liverpool, 1950) 2

Kay A (Everton, 1963) 1
Keegan K (Liverpool, Hamburg, Southampton, 1973–82) 63
Kennedy A (Liverpool, 1984) 2
Kennedy R (Liverpool, 1976–80) 17
Keown M (Everton, Arsenal, 1992–2002) 43
Kevan D (WBA, 1957–61) 14
Kidd B (Manchester Utd, 1970) 2
King L (Tottenham, 2002–10) 21
Kirkland C (Liverpool, 2007) 1
Knight Z (Fulham, 2005) 2
Knowles C (Tottenham, 1968) 4
Konchesky P (Charlton, 2003–06) 2

Labone B (Everton, 1963–70) 26
Lampard F Snr (West Ham, 1973–80) 2
Lampard F Jnr (West Ham, Chelsea, 2000–11) 86
Langley J (Fulham, 1958) 3
Langton R (Blackburn, Preston, Bolton, 1947–51) 11
Latchford R (Everton, 1978–9) 12
Lawler C (Liverpool, 1971–72) 4
*Lawton T (Chelsea, Notts Co, 1947–49) 15
Lee F (Manchester City, 1969–72) 27
Lee J (Derby, 1951) 1
Lee R (Newcastle, 1995–99) 21
Lee S (Liverpool, 1983–84) 14
Lennon A (Tottenham, 2006–10) 19
Le Saux G (Blackburn, Chelsea, 1994–2001) 36
Lescott J (Everton, Manchester City, 2008–11) 13
Le Tissier M (Southampton, 1994–97) 8

Lindsay A (Liverpool, 1974) 4
Lineker G (Leicester, Everton, Barcelona, Tottenham, 1985–92) 80
Little B (Aston Villa, 1975) 1
Lloyd L (Liverpool, Nottm Forest, 1971–80) 4
Lofthouse N (Bolton, 1951–59) 33
Lowe E (Aston Villa, 1947) 3

Mabbutt G (Tottenham, 1983–92) 16
Macdonald M (Newcastle, 1972–76) 14
Madeley P (Leeds, 1971–77) 24
Mannion W (Middlesbrough, 1947–52) 26
Mariner P (Ipswich, Arsenal, 1977–85) 35
Marsh R (QPR, Manchester City, 1972–73) 9
Martin A (West Ham, 1981–87) 17
Martyn N (Crystal Palace, Leeds, 1992–2002) 23
Marwood B (Arsenal, 1989) 1
Matthews R (Coventry, 1956–57) 5
Matthews S (Stoke, Blackpool, 1947–57) 37
McCann G (Sunderland, 2001) 1
McDermott T (Liverpool, 1978–82) 25
McDonald C (Burnley, 1958–59) 8
McFarland R (Derby, 1971–77) 28
McGarry W (Huddersfield, 1954–56) 4
McGuinness W (Manchester Utd, 1959) 2
McMahon S (Liverpool, 1988–91) 17
McManaman S (Liverpool, Real Madrid, 1995–2002) 37
McNab R (Arsenal, 1969) 4
McNeil M (Middlesbrough, 1961–62) 9
Meadows J (Manchester City, 1955) 1
Medley L (Tottenham, 1951–52) 6
Melia J (Liverpool, 1963) 2
Merrick G (Birmingham, 1952–54) 23
Merson P (Arsenal, Middlesbrough, Aston Villa, 1992–99) 21
Metcalfe V (Huddersfield, 1951) 2
Milburn J (Newcastle, 1949–56) 13
Miller B (Burnley, 1961) 1
Mills D (Leeds, 2001–04) 19
Mills M (Ipswich, 1973–82) 42
Milne G (Liverpool, 1963–65) 14
Milner J (Aston Villa, Manchester City, 2010–11) 19
Milton A (Arsenal, 1952) 1
Moore R (West Ham, 1962–74) 108
Morley A (Aston Villa, 1982–83) 6
Morris J (Derby, 1949–50) 3
Mortensen S (Blackpool, 1947–54) 25
Mozley B (Derby, 1950) 3
Mullen J (Wolves, 1947–54) 12
Mullery A (Tottenham, 1965–72) 35
Murphy D (Liverpool, 2002–04) 9

Neal P (Liverpool, 1976–84) 50
Neville G (Manchester Utd, 1995–2009) 85
Neville P (Manchester Utd, Everton, 1996–2008) 59

Newton K (Blackburn, Everton, 1966–70) 27
Nicholls J (WBA, 1954) 2
Nicholson W (Tottenham, 1951) 1
Nish D (Derby, 1973–74) 5
Norman M (Tottenham, 1962–5) 23
Nugent D (Preston, 2007) 1

O'Grady M (Huddersfield, Leeds, 1963–9) 2
Osgood P (Chelsea, 1970–74) 4
Osman R (Ipswich, 1980–84) 11
Owen M (Liverpool, Real Madrid, Newcastle, 1998–2008) 89
Owen S (Luton, 1954) 3

Paine T (Southampton, 1963–66) 19
Pallister G (Middlesbrough, Manchester Utd 1988–97) 22
Palmer C (Sheffield Wed, 1992–94) 18
Parker P (QPR, Manchester Utd, 1989–94) 19
Parker S (Charlton, Chelsea, Newcastle, West Ham, 2004–11) 6
Parkes R (QPR, 1974) 1
Parlour R (Arsenal, 1999–2001) 10
Parry R (Bolton, 1960) 2
Peacock A (Middlesbrough, Leeds, 1962–66) 6
Pearce S (Nottm Forest, West Ham, 1987–2000) 78
Pearson Stan (Manchester Utd, 1948–52) 8
Pearson Stuart (Manchester Utd, 1976–78) 15
Pegg D (Manchester Utd, 1957) 1
Pejic M (Stoke, 1974) 4
Perry W (Blackpool, 1956) 3
Perryman S (Tottenham, 1982) 1
Peters M (West Ham, Tottenham, 1966–74) 67
Phelan M (Manchester Utd, 1990) 1
Phillips K (Sunderland, 1999–2002) 8
Phillips L (Portsmouth, 1952–55) 3
Pickering F (Everton, 1964–65) 3
Pickering N (Sunderland, 1983) 1
Pilkington B (Burnley, 1955) 1
Platt D (Aston Villa, Bari, Juventus, Sampdoria, Arsenal, 1990–96) 62
Pointer R (Burnley, 1962) 3
Powell C (Charlton, 2001–02) 5
Pye J (Wolves, 1950) 1

Quixall A (Sheffield Wed, 1954–55) 5

Radford J (Arsenal, 1969–72) 2
Ramsey A (Southampton, Tottenham, 1949–54) 32
Reaney P (Leeds, 1969–71) 3
Redknapp J (Liverpool, 1996–2000) 17
Reeves K (Norwich, Manchester City, 1980) 2
Regis C (WBA, Coventry, 1982–88) 5

Waiters A (Blackpool, 1964–65) 5
Walcott T (Arsenal, 2006–11) 17
Walker D (Nottm Forest, Sampdoria, Sheffield Wed, 1989–94) 59
Walker I (Tottenham, Leicester, 1996–2004) 4
Wallace D (Southampton, 1986) 1
Walsh P (Luton, 1983–4) 5
Walters M (Rangers, 1991) 1
Ward P (Brighton, 1980) 1
Ward T (Derby, 1948) 2
Warnock S (Blackburn, Aston Villa, 2008–11) 2
Watson D (Sunderland, Manchester City, Werder Bremen, Southampton, Stoke, 1974–82) 65
Watson D (Norwich, Everton, 1984–8) 12
Watson W (Sunderland, 1950–1) 4
Webb N (Nottm Forest, Manchester Utd, 1988–92) 26
Welbeck D (Manchester Utd, 2011) 1
Weller K (Leicester, 1974) 4
West G (Everton, 1969) 3
Wheeler J (Bolton, 1955) 1
White D (Manchester City, 1993) 1
Whitworth S (Leicester, 1975–76) 7
Whymark T (Ipswich, 1978) 1
Wignall F (Nottm Forest, 1965) 2
Wilcox J (Blackburn, Leeds, 1996–2000) 3
Wilkins R (Chelsea, Manchester Utd, AC Milan, 1976–87) 84
Williams B (Wolves, 1949–56) 24
Williams S (Southampton, 1983–85) 6

Willis A (Tottenham, 1952) 1
Wilshaw D (Wolves, 1954–57) 12
Wilshere J (Arsenal, 2011) 5
Wilson R (Huddersfield, Everton, 1960–8) 63
Winterburn N (Arsenal, 1990–93) 2
Wise D (Chelsea, 1991–2001) 21
Withe P (Aston Villa, 1981–85) 11
Wood R (Manchester Utd, 1955–56) 3
Woodcock A (Nottm Forest, Cologne, Arsenal, 1977–86) 42
Woodgate J (Leeds, Newcastle, Middlesbrough, Tottenham, 1999–2008) 8
Woods C (Norwich, Rangers, Sheffield Wed, 1984–93) 43
Worthington F (Leicester, 1974–75) 8
Wright I (Crystal Palace, Arsenal, West Ham, 1991–99) 33
Wright M (Southampton, Derby, Liverpool, 1982–96) 45
Wright R (Ipswich, Arsenal, 2000–02) 2
Wright T (Everton, 1968–70) 11
Wright W (Wolves, 1947–59) 105
Wright–Phillips S (Manchester City, Chelsea, Manchester City, 2005–11) 36

Young A (Aston Villa, 2008–11) 15
Young G (Sheffield Wed, 1965) 1
Young L (Charlton, 2005) 7

Zamora R (Fulham, 2011) 1

SCOTLAND

Adam C (Rangers, Blackpool, 2007–11) 11
Aird J (Burnley, 1954) 4
Aitken G (East Fife, 1949–54) 8
Aitken R (Celtic, Newcastle, St Mirren, 1980–92) 57
Albiston A (Manchester Utd, 1982–6) 14
Alexander G (Preston, Burnley, 2002–10) 40
Alexander N (Cardiff, 2006) 3
Allan T (Dundee, 1974) 2
Anderson J (Leicester, 1954) 1
Anderson R (Aberdeen, Sunderland, 2003–08) 11
Archibald S (Aberdeen, Tottenham, Barcelona, 1980–86) 27
Auld B (Celtic, 1959–60) 3

Baird H (Airdrie, 1956) 1
Baird S (Rangers, 1957–58) 7
Bannan B (Aston Villa, 2011) 5
Bannon E (Dundee Utd, 1980–86) 11
Bardsley P (Sunderland, 2011) 5
Barr D (Falkirk, 2009) 1
Bauld W (Hearts, 1950) 3
Baxter J (Rangers, Sunderland, 1961–68) 34
Beattie C (Celtic, WBA, 2006–08) 7
Bell C (Kilmarnock, 2011) 1
Bell W (Leeds, 1966) 2

Bernard P (Oldham, 1995) 2
Berra C (Hearts, Wolves, 2008–11) 13
Bett J (Rangers, Lokeren, Aberdeen, 1982–90) 26
Black E (Metz, 1988) 2
Black I (Southampton, 1948) 1
Blacklaw A (Burnley, 1963–66) 3
Blackley J (Hibs, 1974–77) 7
Blair J (Blackpool, 1947) 1
Blyth J (Coventry, 1978) 2
Bone J (Norwich, 1972–73) 2
Booth S (Aberdeen, Borussia Dortmund, Twente Enschede 1993–2002) 22
Bowman D (Dundee Utd, 1992–94) 6
Boyd K (Rangers, Middlesbrough, 2006–11) 18
Boyd T (Motherwell, Chelsea, Celtic, 1991–2002) 72
Brand R (Rangers, 1961–62) 8
Brazil A (Ipswich, Tottenham, 1980–83) 13
Bremner D (Hibs, 1976) 1
Bremner W (Leeds, 1965–76) 54
Brennan F (Newcastle, 1947–54) 7
Broadfoot K (Rangers, 2009–11) 4
Brogan J (Celtic, 1971) 4
Brown A (East Fife, Blackpool, 1950–54) 13
Brown H (Partick, 1947) 3
Brown J (Sheffield Utd, 1975) 1

erguson I (Rangers, 1989–97) 9
erguson R (Kilmarnock, 1966–67) 7
ernie W (Celtic, 1954–58) 12
lavell R (Airdrie, 1947) 2
leck R (Norwich, 1990–91) 4
leming C (East Fife, 1954) 1
letcher D (Manchester Utd, 2004–11) 53
letcher S (Hibs, Burnley, Wolves, 2008–11) 8
orbes A (Sheffield Utd, Arsenal, 1947–52) 14
ord D (Hearts, 1974) 3
orrest J (Motherwell, 1958) 1
orrest J (Rangers, Aberdeen, 1966–71) 5
orrest J (Celtic, 2011) 1
orsyth A (Partick, Manchester Utd, 1972–76) 10
orsyth C (Kilmarnock, 1964) 4
orsyth T (Motherwell, Rangers, 1971–78) 22
ox, D (Burnley, 2010) 1
raser D (WBA, 1968–69) 2
raser W (Sunderland, 1955) 2
reedman D (Crystal Palace, 2002) 2

abriel J (Everton, 1961–64) 2
allacher K (Dundee Utd, Coventry, Blackburn, Newcastle, 1988–2001) 53
allacher P (Dundee Utd, 2003–04) 8
allagher P (Blackburn, 2004) 1
alloway M (Celtic, 1992) 1
ardiner I (Motherwell, 1958) 1
emmell T (St Mirren, 1955) 2
emmell T (Celtic, 1966–71) 18
emmill A (Derby, Nottm Forest, Birmingham, 1971–81) 43
emmill S (Nottm Forest, Everton, 1995–2003) 26
ibson D (Leicester, 1963–65) 7
illespie G (Liverpool, 1988–91) 13
ilzean A (Dundee, Tottenham, 1964–71) 22
ass S (Newcastle Utd 1999) 1
avin R (Celtic, 1977) 1
en A (Aberdeen, 1956) 2
oodwillie D (Dundee Utd, 2011) 1
oram A (Oldham, Hibs, Rangers, 1986–98) 43
ordon C (Hearts, Sunderland, 2004–11) 40
ough R (Dundee Utd, Tottenham, Rangers, 1983–93) 61
ould J (Celtic, 2000–01) 2
ovan J (Hibs, 1948–49) 6
raham A (Leeds, 1978–81) 10
raham G (Arsenal, Manchester Utd, 1972–73) 12
ray A (Aston Villa, Wolves, Everton, 1976–85) 20
ay A (Bradford City, 2003) 2
ay E (Leeds, 1969–77) 12
ay F (Leeds, Nottm Forest, 1976–83) 32
ant J (Hibs, 1958) 2

Grant P (Celtic, 1989) 2
Green A (Blackpool, Newcastle, 1971–72) 6
Greig J (Rangers, 1964–76) 44
Gunn B (Norwich, 1990–94) 6

Haddock H (Clyde, 1955–58) 6
Haffey F (Celtic, 1960–61) 2
Hamilton A (Dundee, 1962–66) 24
Hamilton G (Aberdeen, 1947–54) 5
Hamilton W (Hibs, 1965) 1
Hammell S (Motherwell, 2005) 1
Hanley G (Blackburn, 2011) 2
Hansen A (Liverpool, 1979–87) 26
Hansen J (Partick, 1972) 2
Harper J (Aberdeen, Hibs, 1973–78) 4
Hartford A (WBA, Manchester City, Everton, 1972–82) 50
Hartley P (Hearts, Celtic, Bristol City, 2005–10) 25
Harvey D (Leeds, 1973–77) 16
Haughney M (Celtic, 1954) 1
Hay D (Celtic, 1970–74) 27
Hegarty P (Dundee Utd, 1979–83) 8
Henderson J (Portsmouth, Arsenal, 1953–59) 7
Henderson W (Rangers, 1963–71) 29
Hendry C (Blackburn, Rangers, Coventry, Bolton, 1994–2001) 51
Herd D (Arsenal, 1959–61) 5
Herd G (Clyde, 1958–61) 5
Herriot J (Birmingham, 1969–70) 8
Hewie J (Charlton, 1956–60) 19
Holt D (Hearts, 1963–64) 5
Holt G (Kilmarnock, Norwich, 2001–05) 10
Holton J (Manchester Utd, 1973–75) 15
Hope R (WBA, 1968–69) 2
Hopkin D (Crystal Palace, Leeds, 1997–2000) 7
Houliston W (Queen of the South, 1949) 3
Houston S (Manchester Utd, 1976) 1
Howie H (Hibs, 1949) 1
Hughes J (Celtic, 1965–70) 8
Hughes R (Portsmouth, 2004–06) 5
Hughes S (Norwich, 2010) 1
Hughes W (Sunderland, 1975) 1
Humphries W (Motherwell, 1952) 1
Hunter A (Kilmarnock, Celtic, 1972–74) 4
Hunter W (Motherwell, 1960–61) 3
Husband J (Partick, 1947) 1
Hutchison D (Everton, Sunderland, West Ham, 1999–2004) 26
Hutchison T (Coventry, 1974–76) 17
Hutton A (Rangers, Tottenham, 2007–11) 20

Imlach S (Nottm Forest, 1958) 4
Irvine B (Aberdeen, 1991–94) 9
Iwelumo C (Wolves, Burnley, 2009–11) 4

Jackson C (Rangers, 1975–77) 21
Jackson D (Hibs, Celtic, 1995–99) 29

Jardine A (Rangers, 1971–80) 38
Jarvie A (Airdrie, 1971) 3
Jess E (Aberdeen, Coventry, Aberdeen, 1993–99) 17
Johnston A (Sunderland, Rangers, Middlesbrough, 1999–2003) 18
Johnston M (Watford, Celtic, Nantes, Rangers, 1984–92) 38
Johnston W (Rangers, WBA, 1966–78) 21
Johnstone D (Rangers, 1973–80) 14
Johnstone J (Celtic, 1965–75) 23
Johnstone L (Clyde, 1948) 2
Johnstone R (Hibs, Manchester City, 1951–56) 17
Jordan J (Leeds, Manchester Utd, AC Milan, 1973–82) 52

Kelly H (Blackpool, 1952) 1
Kelly J (Barnsley, 1949) 2
Kennedy J (Celtic, 1964–65) 6
Kennedy J (Celtic, 2004) 1
Kennedy S (Rangers, 1975) 5
Kennedy S (Aberdeen, 1978–82) 8
Kenneth G (Dundee Utd, 2011) 2
Kerr A (Partick, 1955) 2
Kerr B (Newcastle, 2003–04) 3
Kyle K (Sunderland, Kilmarnock, 2002–10) 10

Lambert P (Motherwell, Borussia Dortmund, Celtic, 1995–2003) 40
Law D (Huddersfield, Manchester City, Torino, Manchester Utd, 1959–74) 55
Lawrence T (Liverpool, 1963–69) 3
Leggat G (Aberdeen, Fulham, 1956–60) 18
Leighton J (Aberdeen, Manchester Utd, Hibs, Aberdeen, 1983–99) 91
Lennox R (Celtic, 1967–70) 10
Leslie L (Airdrie, 1961) 5
Levein C (Hearts, 1990–95) 16
Liddell W (Liverpool, 1947–55) 28
Linwood A (Clyde, 1950) 1
Little R (Rangers, 1953) 1
Logie J (Arsenal, 1953) 1
Long H (Clyde, 1947) 1
Lorimer P (Leeds, 1970–76) 21

Macari L (Celtic, Manchester Utd, 1972–78) 24
Macaulay A (Brentford, Arsenal, 1947–48) 7
MacDonald A (Rangers, 1976) 1
MacDougall E (Norwich, 1975–76) 7
Mackail-Smith C (Peterborough, 2011) 1
Mackay D (Hearts, Tottenham, 1957–66) 22
Mackay G (Hearts, 1988) 4
Mackay M (Norwich, 2004–05) 5
Mackie J (QPR, 2011) 3
MacLeod J (Hibs, 1961) 4
MacLeod M (Celtic, Borussia Dortmund, Hibs, 1985–91) 20
Maguire C (Aberdeen, 2011) 2

Maloney S (Celtic, Aston Villa, Celtic, 2006–11) 19
Malpas M (Dundee Utd, 1984–93) 55
Marshall D (Celtic, Cardiff, 2005–10)
Marshall G (Celtic, 1992)
Martin B (Motherwell, 1995)
Martin F (Aberdeen, 1954–55)
Martin N (Hibs, Sunderland, 1965–66)
Martin R (Norwich, 2011)
Martis J (Motherwell, 1961)
Mason J (Third Lanark 1949–51)
Masson D (QPR, Derby, 1976–78) 17
Mathers D (Partick, 1954)
Matteo D (Leeds, 2001–02)
McAllister B (Wimbledon, 1997)
McAllister G (Leicester, Leeds, Coventry, 1990–99) 57
McAllister J (Livingston, 2004)
McArthur J (Wigan, 2011)
McAvennie F (West Ham, Celtic, 1986–88)
McBride J (Celtic, 1967)
McCall S (Everton, Rangers, 1990–98) 40
McCalliog J (Sheffield Wed, Wolves, 1967–71)
McCann N (Hearts, Rangers, Southampton, 1999–2006) 26
McCann R (Motherwell, 1959–61)
McClair B (Celtic, Manchester Utd, 1987–93) 30
McCloy P (Rangers, 1973)
McCoist A (Rangers, Kilmarnock, 1986–99) 61
McColl I (Rangers, 1950–58) 14
McCormack R (Motherwell, Cardiff, Leeds, 2008–11)
McCreadie E (Chelsea, 1965–9) 23
McCulloch L (Wigan, Rangers, 2005–11)
McDonald J (Sunderland, 1956)
McEveley, J (Derby, 2008)
McFadden J (Motherwell, Everton, Birmingham, 2002–11) 48
McFarlane W (Hearts, 1947)
McGarr E (Aberdeen, 1970)
McGarvey F (Liverpool, Celtic, 1979–84)
McGhee M (Aberdeen, 1983–84)
McGinlay J (Bolton, 1995–97) 13
McGrain D (Celtic, 1973–82) 62
McGregor A (Rangers, 2007–11)
McGrory J (Kilmarnock, 1965–66)
McInally A (Aston Villa, Bayern Munich, 1989–90)
McInally J (Dundee Utd, 1987–93) 10
McInnes D (WBA, 2003)
McKay D (Celtic, 1959–62) 14
McKean R (Rangers, 1976)
McKenzie J (Partick, 1954–56)
McKimmie S (Aberdeen, 1989–96) 40
McKinlay T (Celtic, 1996–98) 22
McKinlay W (Dundee Utd, Blackburn, 1994–99) 29
McKinnon R (Rangers, 1966–71)

McKinnon R (Motherwell, 1994–95) — 3
McLaren A (Preston, 1947–48) — 4
McLaren A (Hearts, Rangers, 1992–96) — 24
McLaren A (Kilmarnock, 2001) — 1
McLean G (Dundee, 1968) — 1
McLean T (Kilmarnock, Rangers, 1969–71) — 6
McLeish A (Aberdeen, 1980–93) — 77
McLintock F (Leicester, Arsenal, 1963–71) — 9
McManus S (Celtic, Middlesbrough, 2007–11) — 26
McMillan I (Airdrie, 1952–61) — 6
McNamara J (Celtic, Wolves, 1997–2006) — 33
McNamee D (Livingston, 2004–06) — 4
McNaught W (Raith, 1951–55) — 5
McNaughton K (Aberdeen, Cardiff, 2002–08) — 4
McNeill W (Celtic, 1961–72) — 29
McPhail J (Celtic, 1950–54) — 5
McPherson D (Hearts, Rangers, 1989–93) — 27
McQueen G (Leeds, Manchester Utd, 1974–81) — 30
McStay P (Celtic, 1984–97) — 76
McSwegan G (Hearts, 2000) — 2
Millar J (Rangers, 1963) — 2
Miller C (Dundee Utd, 2001) — 1
Miller K (Rangers, Wolves, Celtic, Derby, Rangers, Bursaspor, 2001–11) — 55
Miller L (Dundee Utd, Aberdeen 2006–10) — 3
Miller W (Celtic, 1946–47) — 6
Miller W (Aberdeen, 1975–90) — 65
Mitchell R (Newcastle, 1951) — 2
Mochan N (Celtic, 1954) — 3
Moir W (Bolton, 1950) — 1
Morrison J (WBA, 2008–11) — 13
Moncur R (Newcastle, 1968–72) — 16
Morgan W (Burnley, Manchester Utd, 1968–74) — 21
Morris H (East Fife, 1950) — 1
Mudie J (Blackpool, 1957–58) — 17
Mulhall G (Aberdeen, Sunderland, 1960–64) — 3
Munro F (Wolves, 1971–75) — 9
Munro I (St Mirren, 1979–80) — 7
Murdoch R (Celtic, 1966–70) — 12
Murray I (Hibs, Rangers, 2003–06) — 6
Murray J (Hearts, 1958) — 5
Murray S (Aberdeen, 1972) — 1
Murty G (Reading, 2004–08) — 4

Naismith S (Kilmarnock, Rangers, 2007–11) — 10
Narey D (Dundee Utd, 1977–89) — 35
Naysmith G (Hearts, Everton, Sheffield Utd, 2000–09) — 46
Neilson R (Hearts, 2007) — 1
Nevin P (Chelsea, Everton, Tranmere, 1987–96) — 28

Nicholas C (Celtic, Arsenal, Aberdeen, 1983–89) — 20
Nicholson B (Dunfermline, 2001–05) — 3
Nicol S (Liverpool, 1985–92) — 27

O'Connor G (Hibs, Lokomotiv Moscow, Birmingham, 2002–10) — 16
O'Donnell P (Motherwell, 1994) — 1
O'Hare J (Derby, 1970–72) — 13
O'Neil B (Celtic, VfL Wolfsburg, Derby, Preston, 1996–2006) — 7
O'Neil J (Hibs, 2001) — 1
Ormond W (Hibs, 1954–59) — 6
Orr T (Morton, 1952) — 2

Parker A (Falkirk, Everton, 1955–56) — 15
Parlane D (Rangers, 1973–77) — 12
Paton A (Motherwell, 1952) — 2
Pearson S (Motherwell, Celtic, Derby, 2004–07) — 10
Pearson T (Newcastle, 1947) — 2
Penman A (Dundee, 1966) — 1
Pettigrew W (Motherwell, 1976–77) — 5
Plenderleith J (Manchester City, 1961) — 1
Pressley S (Hearts, 2000–07) — 32
Provan D (Rangers, 1964–66) — 5
Provan D (Celtic, 1980–82) — 10
Quashie N (Portsmouth, Southampton, WBA, 2004–07) — 14
Quinn P (Motherwell, 1961–62) — 9

Rae G (Dundee, Rangers, Cardiff, 2001–09) — 14
Redpath W (Motherwell, 1949–52) — 9
Reilly L (Hibs, 1949–57) — 38
Ring T (Clyde, 1953–58) — 12
Rioch B (Derby, Everton, 1975–78) — 24
Riordan D (Hibs, 2006–10) — 3
Ritchie P (Hearts, Bolton, 1999–2000) — 6
Ritchie W (Rangers, 1962) — 1
Robb D (Aberdeen, 1971) — 5
Robertson A (Clyde, 1955) — 5
Robertson D (Rangers, 1992–94) — 3
Robertson H (Dundee, 1962) — 1
Robertson J (Tottenham, 1964) — 1
Robertson J (Nottm Forest, Derby, 1978–84) — 28
Robertson J (Hearts, 1991–96) — 16
Robertson S (Dundee Utd, 2009–11) — 2
Robinson R (Dundee, 1974–75) — 4
Robson B (Celtic, Middlesbrough, 2008–11) — 14
Ross M (Rangers, 2002–04) — 12
Rough A (Partick, Hibs, 1976–86) — 53
Rougvie D (Aberdeen, 1984) — 1
Rutherford E (Rangers, 1948) — 1

Saunders S (Motherwell, 2011) — 1
Schaedler E (Hibs, 1974) — 1
Scott A (Rangers, Everton, 1957–66) — 16
Scott J (Hibs, 1966) — 1
Scott J (Dundee, 1971) — 2

Scoular J (Portsmouth, 1951–53)	9
Severin S (Hearts, Aberdeen, 2002–07)	15
Sharp G (Everton, 1985–88)	12
Shaw D (Hibs, 1947–49)	8
Shaw J (Rangers, 1947)	4
Shearer D (Aberdeen, 1994–96)	7
Shearer R (Rangers, 1961)	4
Simpson N (Aberdeen, 1983–88)	4
Simpson R (Celtic, 1967–69)	5
Sinclair J (Leicester, 1966)	1
Smith D (Aberdeen, Rangers, 1966–68)	2
Smith G (Hibs, 1947–57)	18
Smith H (Hearts, 1988–92)	3
Smith JE (Celtic, 1959)	2
Smith J (Aberdeen, Newcastle, 1968–74)	4
Smith J (Celtic, 2003)	2
Snodgrass R (Leeds, 2011)	2
Souness G (Middlesbrough, Liverpool, Sampdoria, Rangers, 1975–86)	54
Speedie D (Chelsea, Coventry, 1985–89)	10
Spencer J (Chelsea, QPR, 1995–97)	14
Stanton P (Hibs, 1966–74)	16
Steel W (Morton, Derby, Dundee, 1947–53)	30
Stein C (Rangers, Coventry, 1969–73)	21
Stephen J (Bradford City, 1947–48)	2
Stewart D (Leeds, 1978)	1
Stewart J (Kilmarnock, Middlesbrough, 1977–79)	2
Stewart M (Manchester Utd, Hearts 2002–09)	4
Stewart R (West Ham, 1981–7)	10
St John I (Motherwell, Liverpool, 1959–65)	21
Stockdale R (Middlesbrough, 2002–03)	5
Strachan G (Aberdeen, Manchester Utd, Leeds, 1980–92)	50
Sturrock P (Dundee Utd, 1981–87)	20
Sullivan N (Wimbledon, Tottenham, 1997–2003)	28
Teale G (Wigan, Derby, 2006–09)	13
Telfer P (Coventry, 2000)	1
Telfer W (St Mirren, 1954)	1
Thomson K (Rangers, Middlesbrough, 2009–11)	3
Thompson S (Dundee Utd, Rangers, 2002–05)	16

Thomson W (St Mirren, 1980–84)	7
Thornton W (Rangers, 1947–52)	7
Toner W (Kilmarnock, 1959)	2
Turnbull E (Hibs, 1948–58)	8
Ure I (Dundee, Arsenal, 1962–68)	11
Waddell W (Rangers, 1947–55)	17
Walker A (Celtic, 1988–95)	3
Walker N (Hearts, 1993–96)	2
Wallace I (Coventry, 1978–79)	3
Wallace L (Hearts, 2010–11)	5
Wallace R (Preston, 2010)	1
Wallace W (Hearts, Celtic, 1965–69)	7
Wardhaugh J (Hearts, 1955–57)	2
Wark J (Ipswich, Liverpool, 1979–85)	29
Watson J (Motherwell, Huddersfield, 1948–54)	2
Watson R (Motherwell, 1971)	1
Webster A (Hearts, Rangers, 2003–10)	23
Weir A (Motherwell, 1959–60)	6
Weir D (Hearts, Everton, Rangers, 1997–2011)	69
Weir P (St Mirren, Aberdeen, 1980–84)	6
White J (Falkirk, Tottenham, 1959–64)	22
Whittaker S (Rangers, 2010–11)	12
Whyte D (Celtic, Middlesbrough, Aberdeen, 1988–99)	12
Wilkie L (Dundee, 2002–03)	11
Williams G (Nottm Forest, 2002–03)	5
Wilson A (Portsmouth, 1954)	1
Wilson D (Liverpool, 2011)	3
Wilson D (Rangers, 1961–65)	22
Wilson I (Leicester, Everton, 1987–8)	5
Wilson M (Celtic, 2011)	1
Wilson P (Celtic, 1975)	1
Wilson R (Arsenal, 1972)	2
Wood G (Everton, Arsenal, 1978–82)	4
Woodburn W (Rangers, 1947–52)	24
Wright K (Hibs, 1992)	1
Wright S (Aberdeen, 1993)	2
Wright T (Sunderland, 1953)	3
Yeats R (Liverpool, 1965–66)	2
Yorston H (Aberdeen, 1955)	1
Young A (Hearts, Everton, 19606–6)	8
Young G (Rangers, 1947–57)	53
Younger T (Hibs, Liverpool, 1955–58)	24

WALES

Aizlewood M (Charlton, Leeds, Bradford City, Bristol City, Cardiff, 1986–95)	39
Allchurch I (Swansea City, Newcastle, Cardiff, 1951–66)	68
Allchurch L (Swansea City, Sheffield Utd, 1955–64)	11
Allen B (Coventry, 1951)	2
Allen J (Swansea, 2009–10)	2
Allen M (Watford, Norwich, Millwall, Newcastle, 1986–94)	14
Baker C (Cardiff, 1958–62)	7
Baker W (Cardiff, 1948)	1
Bale G (Southampton, Tottenham, 2006–11)	27

Barnard D (Barnsley, Bradford City, Barnsley, Grimsby, 1998–2004) 22

Barnes W (Arsenal, 1948–55) 22

Bellamy C (Norwich, Coventry, Newcastle, Blackburn, Liverpool, West Ham, Manchester City, 1998–2011) 62

Berry G (Wolves, Stoke, 1979–83) 5

Blackmore C (Manchester Utd, Middlesbrough, 1985–97) 39

Blake D (Cardiff, 2011) 2

Blake N (Sheffield Utd, Bolton, Blackburn, Wolves, 1994–2004) 29

Bodin P (Swindon, Crystal Palace, Swindon, 1990–95) 23

Bowen D (Arsenal, 1955–59) 19

Bowen J (Swansea City, Birmingham, 1994–97) 2

Bowen M (Tottenham, Norwich, West Ham, 1986–97) 41

Boyle T (Crystal Palace, 1981) 2

Bradley M (Walsall, 2010) 1

Brown J (Gillingham, Blackburn, 2006–07) 2

Browning M (Bristol Rov, Huddersfield, 1996–97) 5

Burgess R (Tottenham, 1947–54) 32

Burton A (Norwich, Newcastle, 1963–72) 9

Cartwright L (Coventry, Wrexham, 1974–79) 7

Charles Jeremy (Swansea City, QPR, Oxford Utd, 1981–87) 19

Charles John (Leeds, Juventus, Cardiff, 1950–65) 38

Charles M (Swansea City, Arsenal, Cardiff, 1955–63) 31

Church S (Reading, 2009–11) 12

Clarke R (Manchester City, 1949–56) 22

Coleman C (Crystal Palace, Blackburn, Fulham, 1992–2002) 32

Collins D (Sunderland, Stoke, 2005–11) 12

Collins J (Cardiff, West Ham, Aston Villa, 2004–11) 39

Collison J (West Ham, 2008–11) 8

Cornforth J (Swansea City, 1995) 2

Cotterill D (Bristol City, Wigan, Sheffield Utd, Swansea, 2006–11) 19

Coyne D (Tranmere, Grimsby, Leicester, Burnley, Tranmere, 1996–2008) 16

Crofts A (Gillingham, Brighton, Norwich, 2006–11) 17

Crossley M (Nottm Forest, Middlesbrough, Fulham, 1997–2005) 8

Crowe V (Aston Villa, 1959–63) 16

Curtis A (Swansea City, Leeds, Southampton, Cardiff, 1976–87) 35

Daniel R (Arsenal, Sunderland, 1951–57) 21

Davies A (Manchester Utd, Newcastle, Swansea City, Bradford City, 1983–90) 13

Davies A (Yeovil 2006) 1

Davies C (Charlton, 1972) 1

Davies C (Oxford Utd, Verona, Oldham, 2006–08) 5

Davies D (Everton, Wrexham, Swansea City 1975–83) 52

Davies ER (Newcastle, 1953–58) 6

Davies G (Fulham, Chelsea, Manchester City, 1980–86) 16

Davies RT (Norwich, Southampton, Portsmouth, 1964–74) 29

Davies RW (Bolton, Newcastle, Manr Utd, Man City, Blackpool, 1964–74) 34

Davies S (Manchester Utd, 1996) 1

Davies S (Tottenham, Everton, Fulham, 2001–10) 58

Davis G (Wrexham, 1978) 3

Deacy N (PSV Eindhoven, Beringen, 1977–79) 12

Delaney M (Aston Villa, 2000–07) 36

Derrett S (Cardiff, 1969–71) 4

Dibble A (Luton, Manchester City, 1986–89) 3

Dorman A (St Mirren, Crystal Palace, 2010–11) 3

Duffy R (Portsmouth, 2006–08) 13

Durban A (Derby, 1966–72) 27

Dwyer P (Cardiff, 1978–80) 10

Eardley N (Oldham, Blackpool, 2008–11) 16

Earnshaw R (Cardiff, WBA, Norwich, Derby, Nottm Forest, 2002–11) 54

Easter J (Wycombe, Crystal Palace, 2007–11) 9

Eastwood F (Wolves, Coventry, 2008–11) 11

Edwards C (Swansea City, 1996) 1

Edwards D (Luton, Wolves, 2008–11) 22

Edwards, G (Birmingham, Cardiff, 1947–50) 12

Edwards, I (Chester, Wrexham, 1978–80) 4

Edwards, L (Charlton, 1957) 2

Edwards, R (Bristol City, 1997–98) 4

Edwards, R (Aston Villa, Wolves, 2003–07) 15

Emmanuel W (Bristol City, 1973) 2

England M (Blackburn, Tottenham, 1962–75) 44

Evans B (Swansea City, Hereford, 1972–74) 7

Evans C (Manchester City, Sheffield Utd, 2008–11) 13

Evans I (Crystal Palace, 1976–78) 13

Evans P (Brentford, Bradford City, 2002–03) 2

Evans R (Swansea City, 1964) 1

Evans S (Wrexham, 2007–09) 7

Felgate D (Lincoln, 1984) 1

Fletcher C (Bournemouth, West Ham, Crystal Palace, 2004–09) 36

Flynn B (Burnley, Leeds, 1975–84) 66

Ford T (Swansea City, Sunderland, Aston Villa, Cardiff, 1947–57) 38

Foulkes W (Newcastle, 1952–54) 11

Freestone R (Swansea City, 2000–03) 1

Gabbidon D (Cardiff, West Ham, 2002–11) 44
Garner G (Leyton Orient, 2006) 1
Giggs R (Manchester Utd, 1992–2007) 64
Giles D (Swansea City, Crystal Palace, 1980–83) 12
Godfrey B (Preston, 1964–65) 3
Goss J (Norwich, 1991–96) 9
Green C (Birmingham, 1965–69) 15
Green R (Wolves, 1998) 2
Griffiths A (Wrexham, 1971–77) 17
Griffiths H (Swansea City, 1953) 1
Griffiths M (Leicester, 1947–54) 11
Gunter C (Cardiff, Tottenham, Nottm Forest, 2007–11) 29

Hall G (Chelsea, 1988–92) 9
Harrington A (Cardiff, 1956–62) 11
Harris C (Leeds, 1976–82) 23
Harris W (Middlesbrough, 1954–58) 6
Hartson J (Arsenal, West Ham, Wimbledon, Coventry, Celtic, 1995–2006) 51
Haworth S (Cardiff, Coventry, 1997–8) 5
Hennessey T (Birmingham, Nottm Forest, Derby, 1962–73) 39
Hennessey W (Wolves, 2007–11) 32
Hewitt R (Cardiff, 1958) 5
Hill M (Ipswich, 1972) 2
Hockey T (Sheffield Utd, Norwich, Aston Villa, 1972–74) 9
Hodges G (Wimbledon, Newcastle, Watford, Sheffield Utd, 1984–96) 18
Holden A (Chester, 1984) 1
Hole B (Cardiff, Blackburn, Aston Villa, Swansea City, 1963–71) 30
Hollins D (Newcastle, 1962–66) 11
Hopkins J (Fulham, Crystal Palace, 1983–90) 16
Hopkins M (Tottenham, 1956–63) 34
Horne B (Portsmouth, Southampton, Everton, Birmingham, 1988–97) 59
Howells R (Cardiff, 1954) 2
Hughes C (Luton, Wimbledon, 1992–97) 8
Hughes I (Luton, 1951) 4
Hughes M (Manchester Utd, Barcelona, Bayern Munich, Manchester Utd, Chelsea, Southampton, 1984–99) 72
*Hughes W (Birmingham, 1947) 3
Hughes WA (Blackburn, 1949) 5
Humphreys J (Everton, 1947) 1

Jackett K (Watford, 1983–88) 31
James EG (Blackpool, 1966–71) 9
James L (Burnley, Derby, QPR, Swansea City, Sunderland, 1972–83) 54
James R (Swansea, Stoke, QPR, Leicester, Swansea, 1979–88) 47
Jarvis A (Hull, 1967) 3
Jenkins S (Swansea, Huddersfield, 1996–2002) 16

Johnson A (Nottm Forest, WBA, 1999–2005) 15
Johnson M (Swansea, 1964) 1
Jones A (Port Vale, Charlton, 1987–90) 6
Jones Barrie (Swansea, Plymouth Argyle, Cardiff, 1963–9) 15
*Jones Bryn (Arsenal, 1947–9) 4
Jones C (Swansea, Tottenham, Fulham, 1954–69) 59
Jones D (Norwich, 1976–80) 8
Jones E (Swansea, Tottenham, 1947–9) 4
Jones J (Liverpool, Wrexham, Chelsea, Huddersfield, 1976–86) 72
Jones K (Aston Villa, 1950) 1
Jones L (Liverpool, Tranmere, 1997) 2
Jones M (Leeds, Leicester, 2000–03) 13
Jones M (Wrexham, 2007–08) 2
Jones P (Stockport, Southampton, Wolves, Millwall, QPR, 1997–2007) 50
Jones R (Sheffield Wed, 1994) 1
*Jones TG (Everton, 1946–49) 13
Jones V (Wimbledon, 1995–97) 9
Jones W (Bristol Rov, 1971) 1

Kelsey J (Arsenal, 1954–62) 41
King A (Leicester, 2009–11) 9
King J (Swansea, 1955) 1
Kinsey N (Norwich, Birmingham, 1951–56) 7
Knill A (Swansea, 1989) 1
Koumas J (Tranmere, WBA, Wigan, 2001–09) 34
Krzywicki R (WBA, Huddersfield, 1970–72) 8

Lambert R (Liverpool, 1947–9) 5
Law B (QPR, 1990) 1
Ledley J (Cardiff, Celtic, 2006–11) 37
Lee C (Ipswich, 1965) 2
Leek K (Leicester, Newcastle, Birmingham, Northampton, 1961–65) 13
Legg A (Birmingham, Cardiff, 1996–2001) 6
Lever A (Leicester, 1953) 1
Lewis D (Swansea, 1983) 1
Llewellyn C (Norwich, Wrexham, 1998–2007) 6
Lloyd B (Wrexham, 1976) 3
Lovell S (Crystal Palace, Millwall, 1982–86) 6
Lowndes S (Newport, Millwall, Brighton, Barnsley, 1983–88) 10
Lowrie G (Coventry, Newcastle, 1948–49) 4
Lucas M (Leyton Orient, 1962–63) 4
Lucas W (Swansea, 1949–51) 7

MacDonald, S (Swansea, 2011) 1
Maguire G (Portsmouth, 1990–92) 7
Mahoney J (Stoke, Middlesbrough, Swansea, 1968–83) 51
Mardon P (WBA, 1996) 1

Shortt W (Plymouth Argyle, 1947–53) 12
Showers D (Cardiff, 1975) 2
Sidlow C (Liverpool, 1947–50) 7
Slatter N (Bristol Rov, Oxford Utd, 1983–89) 22
Smallman D (Wrexham, Everton, 1974–6) 7
Southall N (Everton, 1982–97) 92
Speed G (Leeds, Everton, Newcastle, 1990–2004) 85
Sprake G (Leeds, Birmingham, 1964–75) 37
Stansfield F (Cardiff, 1949) 1
Stevenson B (Leeds, Birmingham, 1978–82) 15
Stevenson N (Swansea, 1982–83) 4
Stitfall R (Cardiff, 1953–57) 2
Stock B (Doncaster, 2010–11) 3
Sullivan D (Cardiff, 1953–60) 17
Symons K (Portsmouth, Manchester City, Fulham, Crystal Palace, 1992–2004) 37

Tapscott D (Arsenal, Cardiff, 1954–59) 14
Taylor G (Crystal Palace, Sheffield Utd, Burnley, Nottm Forest, 1996–2005) 15
Taylor N (Wrexham, Swansea, 2010–11) 3
Thatcher B (Leicester, Manchester City, 2004–05) 7
Thomas D (Swansea, 1957–58) 2
Thomas M (Wrexham, Manchester Utd, Everton, Brighton, Stoke, Chelsea, WBA, 1977–86) 51
Thomas M (Newcastle, 1987) 1
Thomas R (Swindon, Derby, Cardiff, 1967–78) 50
Thomas S (Fulham, 1948–49) 4
Toshack J (Cardiff, Liverpool, Swansea, 1969–80) 40
Trollope P (Derby, Fulham, Northampton, 1997–2003) 9

Tudur Jones O (Swansea, Norwich, 2008–11) 6
Van den Hauwe P (Everton, 1985–89) 13
Vaughan D (Crewe, Real Sociedad, Blackpool, 2003–11) 25
Vaughan N (Newport, Cardiff, 1983–85) 10
Vearncombe G (Cardiff, 1958–61) 2
Vernon R (Blackburn, Everton, Stoke, 1957–68) 32
Villars A (Cardiff, 1974) 3
Vokes S (Wolves, 2008–11) 18

Walley T (Watford, 1971) 1
Walsh I (Crystal Palace, 1980–82) 18
Ward D (Bristol Rov, Cardiff, 1959–62) 2
Ward D (Notts Co, Nottm Forest, 2000–04) 5
Webster C (Manchester Utd, 1957–58) 4
Weston R (Arsenal, Cardiff, 2000–05) 7
Williams A (Stockport, Swansea, 2008–11) 25
Williams A (Reading, Wolves, Reading, 1994–2003) 13
Williams A (Southampton, 1997–98) 2
Williams D (Norwich, 1986–87) 5
Williams G (Cardiff, 1951) 1
Williams G (Derby, Ipswich, 1988–96) 13
Williams G (West Ham, 2006) 2
Williams GE (WBA, 1960–69) 26
Williams GG (Swansea, 1961–62) 5
Williams HJ (Swansea, 1965–72) 3
Williams HT (Newport, Leeds, 1949–50) 4
Williams S (WBA, Southampton, 1954–66) 43
Witcomb D (WBA, Sheffield Wed, 1947) 3
Woosnam P (Leyton Orient, West Ham, Aston Villa, 1959–63) 17
Yorath T (Leeds, Coventry, Tottenham, Vancouver Whitecaps 1970–81) 59
Young E (Wimbledon, Crystal Palace, Wolves, 1990–96) 21

NORTHERN IRELAND

Aherne T (Belfast Celtic, Luton, 1947–50) 4
Anderson T (Manchester Utd, Swindon, Peterborough, 1973–79) 22
Armstrong G (Tottenham, Watford, Real Mallorca, WBA, 1977–86) 63

Baird C (Southampton, Fulham, 2003–11) 51
Barr H (Linfield, Coventry, 1962–63) 3
Barton A (Preston, 2011) 1
Best G (Manchester Utd, Fulham, 1964–77) 37
Bingham W (Sunderland, Luton, Everton, Port Vale, 1951–64) 56
Black K (Luton, Nottm Forest, 1988–94) 30
Blair R (Oldham, 1975–76) 5
Blanchflower RD (Barnsley, Aston Villa, Tottenham, 1950–63) 56

Blanchflower J (Manchester Utd, 1954–58) 12
Blayney A (Doncaster, Linfield, 2006–11) 5
Bowler G (Hull, 1950) 3
Boyce L (Werder Bremen, 2011) 4
Braithwaite R (Linfield, Middlesbrough, 1962–65) 10
Braniff K (Portadown, 2010) 2
Brennan R (Luton, Birmingham, Fulham, 1949–51) 5
Briggs W (Manchester Utd, Swansea, 1962–65) 2
Brotherston N (Blackburn, 1980–85) 27
Bruce W (Glentoran, 1961–67) 2
Brunt C (Sheffield Wed, WBA, 2005–11) 33
Bryan, M (Watford, 2010) 2

Camp L (Nottm Forest, 2011) 2

Campbell D (Nottm Forest, Charlton, 1987–88) — 10
Campbell J (Fulham, 1951) — 2
Campbell R (Crusaders, 1963–65) — 2
Campbell R (Bradford City, 1982) — 2
Campbell W (Dundee, 1968–70) — 6
Capaldi A (Plymouth Argyle, Cardiff, 2004–08) — 22
Carey J (Manchester Utd, 1947–49) — 7
Carroll R (Wigan, Manchester Utd, West Ham, 1997–2007) — 19
Carson J (Ipswich, 2011) — 2
Carson S (Coleraine, 2009) — 1
Casey T (Newcastle, Portsmouth, 1955–59) — 12
Casement C (Ipswich, 2009) — 1
Caskey W (Derby, Tulsa, Roughnecks, 1979–82) — 7
Cassidy T (Newcastle, Burnley, 1971–82) — 24
Cathcart C (Blackpool, 2011) — 5
Caughey M (Linfield, 1986) — 2
Clarke C (Bournemouth, Southampton, QPR, Portsmouth, 1986–93) — 38
Cleary J (Glentoran, 1982–85) — 5
Clements D (Coventry, Sheffield Wed, Everton, New York Cosmos, 1965–76) — 48
Clingan S (Nottm Forest, Norwich, Coventry, 2006–11) — 28
Clyde, M (Wolves, 2005) — 3
Coates C (Crusaders, 2009–11) — 6
Cochrane A (Coleraine, Burnley, Middlesbrough, Gillingham, 1976–84) — 26
Cochrane D (Leeds, 1947–50) — 10
Connell T (Coleraine, 1978) — 1
Coote A (Norwich, 1999–2000) — 6
Cowan J (Newcastle, 1970) — 1
Coyle F (Coleraine, Nottm Forest, 1956–58) — 4
Coyle L (Derry City, 1989) — 1
Coyle R (Sheffield Wed, 1973–74) — 5
Craig D (Newcastle, 1967–75) — 25
Craigan S (Partick, Motherwell, 2003–11) — 54
Crossan E (Blackburn, 1950–55) — 3
Crossan J (Sparta Rotterdam, Sunderland, Manchester City, Middlesbrough, 1960–68) — 24
Cunningham W (St Mirren, Leicester, Dunfermline, 1951–62) — 30
Cush W (Glenavon, Leeds, Portadown, 1951–62) — 26

Dallas S (Crusaders, 2011) — 1
D'Arcy S (Chelsea, Brentford, 1952–53) — 5
Davis S (Aston Villa, Fulham, Rangers, 2005–11) — 46
Davison A (Bolton, Bradford City, Grimsby, 1996–97) — 3
Dennison R (Wolves, 1988–97) — 18

Devine J (Glentoran, 1990) — 1
Dickson D (Coleraine, 1970–73) — 4
Dickson T (Linfield, 1957) — 1
Dickson W (Chelsea, Arsenal, 1951–55) — 12
Doherty L (Linfield, 1985–88) — 2
*Doherty P (Derby, Huddersfield, Doncaster, 1946–50) — 6
Doherty T (Bristol City, 2003–05) — 9
Donaghy M (Luton, Manchester Utd, Chelsea, 1980–94) — 91
Donnelly M (Crusaders, 2009) — 1
Dougan D (Portsmouth, Blackburn, Aston Villa, Leicester, Wolves, 1958–73) — 43
Douglas J (Belfast Celtic, 1947) — 1
Dowd H (Glenavon, 1974) — 3
Dowie I (Luton, Southampton, Crystal Palace, West Ham, QPR, 1990–2000) — 59
Duff M (Cheltenham, Burnley, 2002–09) — 22
Dunlop G (Linfield, 1985–90) — 4

Eglington T (Everton, 1947–49) — 6
Elder A (Burnley, Stoke, 1960–70) — 40
Elliott S (Motherwell, Hull, 2001–08) — 38
Evans C (Manchester Utd, 2009–11) — 11
Evans J (Manchester Utd, 2007–11) — 26

Farrell P (Everton, 1947–49) — 7
Feeney J (Linfield, Swansea, 1947–50) — 2
Feeney W (Glentoran, 1976) — 1
Feeney W (Bournemouth, Luton, Cardiff, Oldham, 2002–11) — 42
Ferguson G (Linfield, 1999–2001) — 5
Ferguson S (Newcastle, 2009) — 1
Ferguson W (Linfield, 1966–67) — 2
Ferris R (Birmingham, 1950–52) — 3
Fettis A (Hull, Nottm Forest, Blackburn, 1992–99) — 25
Finney T (Sunderland, Cambridge Utd, 1975–80) — 14
Fleming G (Nottm Forest, Manchester City, Barnsley, 1987–95) — 31
Forde J (Ards, 1959–61) — 4

Gallogly C (Huddersfield, 1951) — 2
Garrett R (Stoke, Linfield, 2009–11) — 5
Gaston R (Coleraine, 1969) — 1
Gault M (Linfield, 2008) — 1
Gillespie K (Manchester Utd, Newcastle, Blackburn, Leicester, Sheffield Utd, 1995–2009) — 86
Gorman J (Wolves, 2010–11) — 8
Gorman W (Brentford, 1947–48) — 4
Graham W (Doncaster, 1951–59) — 14
Gray P (Luton, Sunderland, Nancy, Burnley, Oxford Utd, 1993–2001) — 25
Gregg H (Doncaster, Manchester Utd, 1954–64) — 25
Griffin D (St Johnstone, Dundee Utd, Stockport, 1996–2004) — 29

Hamill R (Glentoran, 1999) 1
Hamilton B (Linfield, Ipswich, Everton, Millwall, Swindon, 1969–80) 50
Hamilton G (Glentoran, Portadown, 2003–08) 5
Hamilton W (QPR, Burnley, Oxford Utd, 1978–86) 41
Harkin J (Southport, Shrewsbury, 1968–70) 5
Harvey M (Sunderland, 1961–71) 34
Hatton S (Linfield, 1963) 2
Healy D (Manchester Utd, Preston, Leeds, Fulham, Sunderland, 2000–11) 86
Healy F (Coleraine, Glentoran, 1982–83) 4
Hegan D (WBA, Wolves, 1970–73) 7
Hill C (Sheffield Utd, Leicester, Trelleborg, Northampton, 1990–99) 27
Hill J (Norwich, Everton, 1959–64) 7
Hinton E (Fulham, Millwall, 1947–51) 7
Hodson L (Watford, 2011) 4
Holmes S (Wrexham, 2002) 1
Horlock K (Swindon, Manchester City, 1995–2003) 32
Hughes A (Newcastle, Aston Villa, Fulham, 1997–2011) 76
Hughes J (Lincoln, 2006) 2
Hughes M (Oldham, 2006) 1
Hughes M (Manchester City, Strasbourg, West Ham, Wimbledon, Crystal Palace, 1992–2005) 71
Hughes P (Bury, 1987) 3
Hughes W (Bolton, 1951) 1
Humphries W (Ards, Coventry, Swansea, 1962–65) 14
Hunter A (Blackburn, Ipswich, 1970–80) 53
Hunter B (Wrexham, Reading, 1995–2000) 15
Hunter V (Coleraine, 1962) 2

Ingham M (Sunderland, Wrexham, 2005–07) 3
Irvine R (Linfield, Stoke, 1962–5) 8
Irvine W (Burnley, Preston, Brighton, 1963–72) 23

Jackson T (Everton, Nottm Forest, Manchester Utd, 1969–77) 35
Jamison J (Glentoran, 1976) 1
Jenkins I (Chester, Dundee Utd, 1997–2000) 6
Jennings P (Watford, Tottenham, Arsenal, Tottenham, 1964–86) 119
Johnson D (Blackburn, Birmingham, 1999–2010) 56
Johnston W (Glenavon, Oldham, 1962–66) 2
Jones J (Glenavon, 1956–57) 3
Jones S (Crewe, Burnley, 2003–08) 29

Keane T (Swansea, 1949) 1
Kee P (Oxford Utd, Ards, 1990–95) 9

Keith R (Newcastle, 1958–62) 23
Kelly H (Fulham, Southampton, 1950–51) 4
Kelly P (Barnsley, 1950) 1
Kennedy P (Watford, Wigan, 1999–2004) 20
Kirk A (Hearts, Boston, Northampton, Dunfermline, 2000–10) 11

Lafferty K (Burnley, Rangers, 2006–11) 29
Lawrie J (Port Vale, 2009–10) 3
Lawther W (Sunderland, Blackburn, 1960–62) 4
Lennon N (Crewe, Leicester, Celtic, 1994–2002) 40
Little A (Rangers, 2009–11) 6
Lockhart N (Linfield, Coventry, Aston Villa, 1947–56) 8
Lomas S (Manchester City, West Ham, 1994–2003) 45
Lutton B (Wolves, West Ham, 1970–4) 6

Magennis J (Cardiff, Aberden, 2010–11) 3
Magill E (Arsenal, Brighton, 1962–66) 26
Magilton J (Oxford Utd, Southampton, Sheffield Wed, Ipswich, 1991–2002) 52
Mannus A (Linfield, 2004–09) 4
Martin C (Glentoran, Leeds, Aston Villa, 1947–50) 6
McAdams W (Manchester City, Bolton, Leeds, 1954–62) 15
*McAlinden J (Portsmouth, Southend, 1947–49) 2
McArdle R (Rochdale, Aberdeen, 2010–11) 4
McAuley G (Lincoln, Leicester, Ipswich, 2005–11) 30
McBride S (Glenavon, 1991–92) 4
McCabe J (Leeds, 1949–54) 6
McCann G (West Ham, Cheltenham, Barnsley, Scunthorpe, Peterborough, 2002–11) 33
McCarthy J (Port Vale, Birmingham, 1996–2001) 18
McCartney G (Sunderland, West Ham, Sunderland 2002–10) 34
McCavana T (Coleraine, 1954–55) 3
McCleary J (Cliftonville, 1955) 1
McClelland J (Arsenal, Fulham, 1961–67) 6
McClelland J (Mansfield, Rangers, Watford, Leeds, 1980–90) 53
McCourt F (Manchester City, 1952–53) 6
McCourt P (Rochdale, Celtic, 2002–11) 7
McCoy R (Coleraine, 1987) 1
McCreery D (Manchester Utd, QPR, Tulsa, Newcastle, 1976–90) 67
McCrory S (Southend, 1958) 1
McCullough W (Arsenal, Millwall, 1961–67) 10
McCurdy C (Linfield, 1980) 1
McDonald A (QPR, 1986–96) 52
McElhinney G (Bolton, 1984–85) 6
McEvilly L (Rochdale, 2002) 1
McFaul W (Linfield, Newcastle, 1967–74) 6

McGarry J (Cliftonville, 1951) 3
McGaughey M (Linfield, 1985) 1
McGibbon P (Manchester Utd, Wigan, 1995–2000) 7
McGinn N (Derry, Celtic, 2009–11) 13
McGivern R (Manchester City, 2009–11) 13
McGovern, M (Ross Co, 2010) 1
McGrath C (Tottenham, Manchester 1974–79) 21
McIlroy J (Burnley, Stoke, 1952–66) 55
McIlroy S (Manchester Utd, Stoke, Manchester City, 1972–87) 88
McKeag W (Glentoran, 1968) 2
McKenna J (Huddersfield, 1950–52) 7
McKenzie R (Airdrie, 1967) 1
McKinney W (Falkirk, 1966) 1
McKnight A (Celtic, West Ham, 1988–89) 10
McLaughlin J (Shrewsbury, Swansea, 1962–66) 12
McLean B (Motherwell, 2006) 1
McMahon G (Tottenham, Stoke, 1995–98) 17
McMichael A (Newcastle, 1950–60) 40
McMillan S (Manchester Utd, 1963) 2
McMordie A (Middlesbrough, 1969–73) 21
McMorran E (Belfast Celtic, Barnsley, Doncaster, 1947–57) 15
McNally B (Shrewsbury, 1987–88) 5
McParland P (Aston Villa, Wolves, 1954–62) 34
McQuoid J (Millwall, 2011) 3
McVeigh P (Tottenham, Norwich, 1999–2005) 20
Montgomery F (Coleraine, 1955) 1
Moore C (Glentoran, 1949) 1
Moreland V (Derby, 1979–80) 6
Morgan S (Port Vale, Aston Villa, Brighton, Sparta Rotterdam, 1972–99) 18
Morrow S (Arsenal, QPR, 1990–2000) 39
Mulgrew J (Linfield, 2010) 2
Mullan G (Glentoran, 1983) 5
Mulryne P (Manchester Utd, Norwich, 1997–2005) 26
Murdock C (Preston, Hibs, Crewe, Rotherham, 2000–06) 34

Napier R (Bolton, 1966) 1
Neill T (Arsenal, Hull, 1961–73) 59
Nelson S (Arsenal, Brighton, 1970–82) 51
Nicholl C (Aston Villa, Southampton, Grimsby, 1975–83) 51
Nicholl J (Manchester Utd, Toronto, Sunderland, Rangers, WBA, 1976–86) 73
Nicholson J (Manchester Utd, Huddersfield, 1961–72) 41
Nolan I (Sheffield Wed, Bradford City, Wigan, 1997–2002) 18
Norwood O (Manchester Utd, 2011) 4

O'Boyle G (Dunfermline, St Johnstone, 1994–99) 13

O'Connor M (Crewe, Scunthorpe, 2008–11) 10
O'Doherty A (Coleraine, 1970) 2
O'Driscoll J (Swansea, 1949) 3
O'Kane W (Nottm Forest, 1970–75) 20
O'Neill C (Motherwell, 1989–91) 3
O'Neill J (Sunderland, 1962) 1
O'Neill J (Leicester, 1980–86) 39
O'Neill M (Distillery, Nottm Forest, Norwich, Manchester City, Notts Co, 1972–85) 64
O'Neill M (Newcastle, Dundee Utd, Hibs, Coventry, 1989–97) 31
Owens J (Crusaders, 2011) 1

Parke J (Linfield, Hibs, Sunderland, 1964–68) 14
Paterson M (Scunthorpe, Burnley 2008–10) 11
Patterson D (Crystal Palace, Luton, Dundee Utd, 1994–99) 17
Patterson R (Coleraine, Plymouth, 2010–11) 5
Peacock R (Celtic, Coleraine, 1952–62) 31
Penney S (Brighton, 1985–89) 17
Platt J (Middlesbrough, Ballymena, Coleraine, 1976–86) 23
Quinn J (Blackburn, Swindon, Leicester, Bradford City, West Ham, Bournemouth, Reading, 1985–96) 46
Quinn SJ (Blackpool, WBA, Willem 11, Sheffield Wed, Peterborough, Northampton, 1996–2007) 50
Rafferty W (Wolves, 1980) 1
Ramsey P (Leicester, 1984–89) 14
Rice P (Arsenal, 1969–80) 49
Robinson S (Bournemouth, Luton, 1997–2008) 7
Rogan A (Celtic, Sunderland, Millwall, 1988–97) 17
Ross W (Newcastle, 1969) 1
Rowland K (West Ham, QPR, 1994–99) 19
Russell A (Linfield, 1947) 1
Ryan R (WBA, 1950) 1
Sanchez L (Wimbledon, 1987–89) 3
Scott J (Grimsby, 1958) 2
Scott P (Everton, York, Aldershot, 1976–79) 10
Sharkey P (Ipswich, 1976) 1
Shields J (Southampton, 1957) 1
Shiels D (Hibs, Doncaster, 2006–10) 9
Simpson W (Rangers, 1951–59) 12
Sloan D (Oxford Utd, 1969–71) 2
Sloan J (Arsenal, 1947) 1
Sloan T (Manchester Utd, 1979) 3
Smith A (Glentoran, Preston, 2003–05) 18
Smyth S (Wolves, Stoke, 1948–52) 9
Smyth W (Distillery, 1949–54) 4

Sonner D (Ipswich, Sheffield Wed, Birmingham, Nottm Forest, Peterborough, 1997–2005) — 13
Spence D (Bury, Blackpool, Southend, 1975–82) — 27
Sproule I (Hibs, 2006–08) — 11
*Stevenson A (Everton, 1947–48) — 3
Stewart A (Glentoran, Derby, 1967–69) — 7
Stewart D (Hull, 1978) —
Stewart I (QPR, Newcastle, 1982–87) — 31
Stewart T (Linfield, 1961) — 1

Taggart G (Barnsley, Bolton, Leicester, 1990–2003) — 51
Taylor M (Fulham, Birmingham, 1999–2011) — 87
Thompson A (Watford, 2011) — 2
Thompson P (Linfield, 2006–08) — 7
Todd S (Burnley, Sheffield Utd, 1966–71) — 11
Toner C (Leyton Orient, 2003) — 2
Trainor D (Crusaders, 1967) — 1
Tuffey J (Partick, Inverness, 2009–11) — 8
Tully C (Celtic, 1949–59) — 10

Uprichard W (Swindon, Portsmouth, 1952–59) — 18

Vernon J (Belfast Celtic, WBA, 1947–52) — 17

Walker J (Doncaster, 1955) — 1
Walsh D (WBA, 1947–50) — 9
Walsh W (Manchester City, 1948–49) — 5
Watson P (Distillery, 1971) — 1
Webb S (Ross Co, 2006–07) — 4
Welsh E (Carlisle, 1966–67) — 4
Whiteside N (Manchester Utd, Everton, 1982–90) — 38
Whitley Jeff (Manchester City, Sunderland, Cardiff, 1997–2006) — 20
Whitley Jim (Manchester City, 1998–2000) — 3
Williams M (Chesterfield, Watford, Wimbledon, Stoke, Wimbledon, MK Dons, 1999–2005) — 36
Williams P (WBA, 1991) — 1
Wilson D (Brighton, Luton, Sheffield Wed, 1987–92) — 24
Wilson K (Ipswich, Chelsea, Notts Co, Walsall, 1987–95) — 42
Wilson S (Glenavon, Falkirk, Dundee, 1962–68) — 12
Winchester C (Oldham, 2011) — 1
Wood T (Walsall, 1996) — 1
Worthington N (Sheffield Wed, Leeds, Stoke, 1984–97) — 66
Wright T (Newcastle, Nottm Forest, Reading, Manchester City, 1989–2000) — 31

REPUBLIC OF IRELAND

Aherne T (Belfast Celtic, Luton, 1946–54) — 16
Aldridge J (Oxford Utd, Liverpool, Real Sociedad, Tranmere, 1986–97) — 69
Ambrose P (Shamrock R, 1955–64) — 5
Anderson J (Preston, Newcastle, 1980–89) — 16
Andrews K (Blackburn, 2009–11) — 20

Babb P (Coventry, Liverpool, Sunderland, 1994–2003) — 35
Bailham E (Shamrock R, 1964) — 1
Barber E (Bohemians, Birmingham, 1966) — 2
Barrett G (Arsenal, Coventry, 2003–05) — 6
Beglin J (Liverpool, 1984–87) — 15
Bennett A (Reading, 2007) — 2
Best L (Coventry, 2009–10) — 7
Braddish S (Dundalk, 1978) — 2
Branagan K (Bolton, 1997) — 1
Bonner P (Celtic, 1981–96) — 80
Brady L (Arsenal, Juventus, Sampdoria, Inter-Milan, Ascoli, West Ham, 1975–90) — 72
Brady R (QPR, 1964) — 6
Breen G (Birmingham, Coventry, West Ham, Sunderland, 1996–2006) — 63
*Breen T (Shamrock R, 1947) — 3
Brennan F (Drumcondra, 1965) — 1
Brennan S (Manchester Utd, Waterford, 1965–71) — 19
Browne W (Bohemians, 1964) — 3
Bruce A (Ipswich, 2007–09) — 2
Buckley L (Shamrock R, Waregem, 1984–85) — 2
Burke F (Cork Ath, 1952) — 1
Butler P (Sunderland, 2000) — 1
Butler T (Sunderland, 2003) — 2
Byrne A (Southampton, 1970–74) — 14
Byrne J (Shelbourne, 2004–06) — 2
Byrne J (QPR, Le Havre, Brighton, Sunderland, Millwall, 1985–93) — 23
Byrne P (Shamrock R, 1984–86) — 8

Campbell A (Santander, 1985) — 3
Campbell N (St Patrick's Ath, Fortuna Cologne, 1971–77) — 11
Cantwell N (West Ham, Manchester Utd, 1954–67) — 36
Carey B (Manchester Utd, Leicester, 1992–94) — 3
*Carey J (Manchester Utd, 1946–53) — 21
Carolan J (Manchester Utd, 1960) — 2
Carr S (Tottenham, Newcastle, 1999–2008) — 44
Carroll B (Shelbourne, 1949–50) — 2
Carroll T (Ipswich, 1968–73) — 17
Carsley L (Derby, Blackburn, Coventry, Everton, 1997–2008) — 39

Cascarino A (Gillingham, Millwall, Aston Villa, Chelsea, Marseille, Nancy, 1986–2000) — 88

Chandler J (Leeds, 1980) — 2

Clark C (Aston Villa, 2011) — 2

Clarke C (Stoke, 2004) — 2

Clarke J (Drogheda, 1978) — 1

Clarke K (Drumcondra, 1948) — 2

Clarke M (Shamrock R, 1950) — 1

Clinton T (Everton, 1951–54) — 3

Coad P (Shamrock R, 1947–52) — 11

Coffey T (Drumcondra, 1950) — 1

Colfer M (Shelbourne, 1950–51) — 2

Coleman S (Everton, 2011) — 4

Colgan N (Hibs, 2002–07) — 9

Conmy O (Peterborough, 1965–70) — 5

Connolly D (Watford, Feyenoord, Excelsior Feyenoord, Wimbledon, West Ham, Wigan, 1996–2006) — 41

Conroy G (Stoke, 1970–77) — 27

Conway J (Fulham, Manchester City, 1967–77) — 20

Corr P (Everton, 1949–50) — 4

Courtney E (Cork Utd, 1946) — 1

Cox S (WBA, 2011) — 4

Coyle O (Bolton, 1994) — 1

Coyne T (Celtic, Tranmere, Motherwell, 1992–98) — 22

Crowe G (Bohemians, 2003) — 2

Cummins G (Luton, 1954–61) — 19

Cuneen T (Limerick, 1951) — 1

Cunningham G (Manchester City, 2010–11) — 3

Cunningham K (Wimbledon, Birmingham, 1996–2006) — 72

Curtis D (Shelbourne, Bristol City, Ipswich, Exeter, 1956–63) — 17

Cusack S (Limerick, 1953) — 1

Daish L (Cambridge Utd, Coventry, 1992–96) — 5

Daly G (Manchester Utd, Derby, Coventry, Birmingham, Shrewsbury, 1973–87) — 48

Daly M (Wolves, 1978) — 2

Daly P (Shamrock R, 1950) — 1

Deacy E (Aston Villa, 1982) — 4

Delaney D (QPR, Ipswich 2008–11) — 5

Delap R (Derby, Southampton, 1998–2004) — 11

De Mange K (Liverpool, Hull, 1987–89) — 2

Dempsey J (Fulham, Chelsea, 1967–72) — 19

Dennehy J (Cork Hibs, Nottm Forest, Walsall, 1972–77) — 11

Desmond P (Middlesbrough, 1950) — 4

Devine J (Arsenal, 1980–85) — 13

Doherty G (Tottenham, Norwich, 2000–06) — 34

Donovan D (Everton, 1955–57) — 5

Donovan T (Aston Villa, 1980) — 2

Douglas J (Blackburn, Leeds, 2004–08) — 8

Doyle C (Shelbourne, 1959) — 1

Doyle C (Birmingham, 2007) — 1

Doyle K (Reading, Wolves, 2006–11) — 41

Doyle M (Coventry, 2004) — 1

Duff D (Blackburn, Chelsea, Newcastle, Fulham, 1998–2011) — 87

Duffy B (Shamrock R, 1950) — 1

Dunne A (Manchester Utd, Bolton, 1962–76) — 33

Dunne J (Fulham, 1971) — 1

Dunne P (Manchester Utd, 1965–67) — 5

Dunne R (Everton, Manchester City, Aston Villa, 2000–11) — 65

Dunne S (Luton, 1953–60) — 15

Dunne T (Bolton, 1975) — 1

Dunning P (Shelbourne, 1971) — 2

Dunphy E (York, Millwall, 1966–71) — 23

Dwyer N (West Ham, Swansea, 1960–65) — 14

Eccles P (Shamrock R, 1986) — 1

Eglington T (Shamrock R, Everton, 1946–56) — 24

Elliott S (Sunderland, 2005–07) — 9

Evans M (Southampton, 1997) — 1

Fagan E (Shamrock R, 1973) — 1

Fagan F (Manchester City, Derby, 1955–61) — 8

Fahey K (Birmingham, 2010–11) — 11

Fairclough M (Dundalk, 1982) — 2

Fallon S (Celtic, 1951–55) — 8

Farrell P (Shamrock R, Everton, 1946–57) — 28

Farrelly G (Aston Villa, Everton, Bolton, 1996–2000) — 6

Finnan S (Fulham, Liverpool, Espanyol 2000–09) — 53

Finucane A (Limerick, 1967–72) — 11

Fitzgerald F (Waterford, 1955–6) — 2

Fitzgerald P (Leeds, 1961–2) — 5

Fitzpatrick K (Limerick, 1970) — 1

Fitzsimons A (Middlesbrough, Lincoln, 1950–59) — 26

Fleming C (Middlesbrough, 1996–8) — 10

Fogarty A (Sunderland, Hartlepool Utd, 1960–64) — 11

Folan C (Hull, 2009–10) — 7

Foley D (Watford, 2000–01) — 6

Foley K (Wolves, 2009–11) — 8

Foley T (Northampton, 1964–67) — 9

Fullam J (Preston, Shamrock R, 1961–70) — 11

Forde D (Millwall, 2011) — 2

Gallagher C (Celtic, 1967) — 2

Gallagher M (Hibs, 1954) — 1

Galvin A (Tottenham, Sheffield Wed, Swindon, 1983–90) — 29

Gamble J (Cork City, 2007) — 2

Gannon E (Notts Co, Sheffield Wed, Shelbourne, 1949–55) — 14

Lawrenson M (Preston, Brighton, Liverpool, 1977–88) 39

Lee A (Rotherham, Cardiff, Ipswich, 2003–07) 9

Leech M (Shamrock R, 1969–73) 8

Long S (Reading, 2007–11) 21

Lowry D (St Patrick's Ath, 1962) 1

McAlinden J (Portsmouth, 1946) 2

McCarthy J (Wigan, 2011) 3

McAteer J (Bolton, Liverpool, Blackburn, Sunderland, 1994–2004) 52

McCann J (Shamrock R, 1957) 1

McCarthy M (Manchester City, Celtic, Lyon, Millwall, 1984–92) 57

McConville T (Dundalk, Waterford, 1972–73) 6

McDonagh J (Everton, Bolton, Sunderland, Notts Co, 1981–86) 25

McDonagh J (Shamrock R, 1984–85) 3

McEvoy A (Blackburn, 1961–67) 17

McGeady A (Celtic, Spartak Moscow, 2004–11) 40

McGee P (QPR, Preston, 1978–81) 15

McGoldrick E (Crystal Palace, Arsenal, 1992–95) 15

McGowan D (West Ham, 1949) 3

McGowan J (Cork Utd, 1947) 1

McGrath M (Blackburn, Bradford City, 1958–66) 22

McGrath P (Manchester Utd, Aston Villa, Derby, 1985–97) 83

Macken J (Manchester City, 2005) 1

Mackey G (Shamrock R, 1957) 3

McLoughlin A (Swindon, Southampton, Portsmouth, 1990–2000) 42

McMillan W (Belfast Celtic, 1946) 2

McNally B (Luton, 1959–63) 3

McPhail S (Leeds, 2000–04) 10

McShane P (WBA, Sunderland, Hull, 2008–11) 26

Macken A (Derby, 1977) 1

Mahon A (Tranmere, 2000) 3

Malone G (Shelbourne, 1949) 1

Mancini T (QPR, Arsenal, 1974–75) 5

Martin C (Glentoran, Leeds, Aston Villa, 1946–56) 30

Martin M (Bohemians, Manchester Utd, 1972–83) 52

Maybury, A (Leeds, Hearts, Leicester, 1998–2005) 10

Meagan M (Everton, Huddersfield, Drogheda, 1961–70) 17

Miller L (Celtic, Manchester Utd, Sunderland, QPR 2004–10) 21

Milligan M (Oldham, 1992) 1

Mooney J (Shamrock R, 1965) 2

Moore A (Middlesbrough, 1996–97) 8

Moran K (Manchester Utd, Sporting Gijon, Blackburn, 1980–94) 71

Moroney T (West Ham, 1948–54) 12

Morris C (Celtic, Middlesbrough, 1988–93) 35

Morrison C (Crystal Palace, Birmingham, Crystal Palace, 2002–07) 36

Moulson G (Lincoln, 1948–49) 3

Mucklan C (Drogheda, 1978) 1

Mulligan P (Shamrock R, Chelsea, Crystal Palace, WBA, Shamrock R, 1969–80) 50

Munroe L (Shamrock R, 1954) 1

Murphy A (Clyde, 1956) 1

Murphy B (Bohemians, 1986) 1

Murphy D (Sunderland, 2007–09) 9

Murphy J (Crystal Palace, 1980) 3

Murphy J (Scunthorpe, 2009–10) 2

Murphy J (WBA, 2004) 1

Murphy P (Carlisle, 2007) 1

Murray T (Dundalk, 1950) 1

Newman W (Shelbourne, 1969) 1

Nolan E (Preston, 2009–10) 3

Nolan R (Shamrock R, 1957–63) 10

O'Brien Alan (Newcastle, 2007) 5

O'Brien Andy (Newcastle, Portsmouth, 2001–07) 26

O'Brien F (Philadelphia Forest, 1980) 3

O'Brien J (Bolton, 2006–08) 3

O'Brien L (Shamrock R, Manchester Utd, Newcastle, Tranmere, 1986–97) 16

O'Brien R (Notts Co, 1976–77) 5

O'Byrne L (Shamrock R, 1949) 1

O'Callaghan B (Stoke, 1979–82) 6

O'Callaghan K (Ipswich, Portsmouth, 1981–87) 21

O'Cearuill J (Arsenal, 2007) 2

O'Connell A (Dundalk, Bohemians, 1967–71) 2

O'Connor T (Shamrock R, 1950) 4

O'Connor T (Fulham, Dundalk, Bohemians, 1968–73) 8

O'Dea D (Celtic, 2010–11) 9

O'Driscoll J (Swansea, 1949) 3

O'Driscoll S (Fulham, 1982) 3

O'Farrell F (West Ham, Preston, 1952–59) 9

*O'Flanagan Dr K (Arsenal, 1947) 3

O'Flanagan M (Bohemians, 1947) 1

O'Halloran S (Aston Villa, 2007) 2

O'Hanlon K (Rotherham, 1988) 1

O'Keefe E (Everton, Port Vale, 1981–85) 5

O'Leary D (Arsenal, 1977–93) 68

O'Leary P (Shamrock R, 1980–1) 7

O'Neill F (Shamrock R, 1962–72) 20

O'Neill J (Everton, 1952–59) 17

O'Neill J (Preston, 1961) 1

O'Neill K (Norwich, Middlesbrough, 1996–2000) 13

O'Regan K (Brighton, 1984–85) 4

O'Reilly J (Cork Utd, 1946) 3

O'Shea J (Manchester Utd, 2002–11) 70

INTERNATIONAL GOALSCORERS 1946–2011

(start of season 2011-12.)

ENGLAND

Charlton R	49
Lineker	48
Greaves	44
Owen	40
Finney	30
Lofthouse	30
Shearer	30
Platt	27
Robson B	26
Rooney	26
Hurst	24
Mortensen	23
Crouch	22
Lampard Frank jnr	22
Channon	21
Keegan	21
Peters	20
Gerrard	19
Haynes	18
Hunt R	18
Beckham	17
Lawton	16
Taylor T	16
Woodcock	16
Defoe	15
Scholes	14
Chivers	13
Mariner	13
Smith R	13
Francis T	12
Barnes J	11
Douglas	11
Mannion	11
Sheringham	11
Clarke A	10
Cole J	10
Flowers R	10
Gascoigne	10
Lee F	10
Milburn	10
Wilshaw	10
Beardsley	9
Bell	9
Bentley	9
Hateley	9
Wright I	9
Ball	8
Broadis	8
Byrne J	8
Hoddle	8

Kevan	8
Anderton	7
Connelly	7
Coppell	7
Fowler	7
Heskey	7
Paine	7
Charlton J	6
Johnson D	6
Macdonald	6
Mullen	6
Rowley	6
Terry	6
Vassell	6
Waddle	6
Wright-Phillips S	6
Adams	5
Atyeo	5
Baily	5
Brooking	5
Carter	5
Edwards	5
Ferdinand L	5
Hitchens	5
Latchford	5
Neal	5
Pearce	5
Pearson Stan	5
Pearson Stuart	5
Pickering F	5
Barmby	4
Barnes P	4
Bull	4
Dixon K	4
Hassall	4
Revie	4
Robson R	4
Steven	4
Watson Dave (Sunderland)	4
Webb	4
Baker	3
Bent	3
Blissett	3
Butcher	3
Currie	3
Elliott	3
Ferdinand R	3
Francis G	3
Grainger	3
Kennedy R	3

McDermott	3
McManaman	3
Matthews S	3
Merson	3
Morris	3
O'Grady	3
Peacock	3
Ramsey	3
Sewell	3
Walcott	3
Wilkins	3
Wright W	3
Allen R	2
Anderson	2
Barry	2
Bradley	2
Broadbent	2
Brooks	2
Cowans	2
Eastham	2
Froggatt J	2
Froggatt R	2
Haines	2
Hancocks	2
Hunter	2
Ince	2
Johnson A	2
Keown	2
King	2
Lee R	2
Lee S	2
Moore	2
Perry	2
Pointer	2
Richardson	2
Royle	2
Smith A (1989–92)	2
Southgate	2
Stone	2
Taylor P	2
Tueart	2
Upson	2
Wignall	2
Worthington	2
Young A	2
A'Court	1
Astall	1
Beattie K	1
Bowles	1
Bradford	1
Bridge	1

Bridges 1
Brown 1
Campbell 1
Carroll 1
Chamberlain 1
Cole Andy 1
Crawford 1
Dixon L 1
Ehiogu 1
Goddard 1
Hirst 1
Hughes E 1
Jeffers 1
Jenas 1
Johnson G................. 1
Kay 1
Kidd 1
Langton 1
Lawler 1
Lee J 1
Le Saux 1
Mabbutt 1
Marsh 1
Medley 1
Melia 1
Mullery 1
Murphy 1
Nicholls 1
Nicholson 1
Nugent 1
Palmer 1
Parry 1
Redknapp 1
Richards 1
Sansom 1
Shackleton 1
Smith A (2001–5) 1
Stiles 1
Summerbee 1
Tambling 1
Thompson Phil 1
Viollet 1
Wallace..................... 1
Walsh 1
Weller 1
Wise 1
Withe 1
Wright M 1

SCOTLAND

Dalglish 30
Law 30
Reilly 22
McCoist 19

McFadden 15
Johnston M 14
Miller K 14
Collins J 12
Gilzean 12
Steel 12
Jordan 11
Collins R 10
Johnstone R 10
Stein 10
Gallacher 9
McStay 9
Mudie 9
St John 9
Brand 8
Gemmill A 8
Leggat 8
Robertson J (1978-84) .. 8
Wilson Davie 8
Boyd K 7
Dodds 7
Durie 7
Gray A 7
Wark 7
Booth 6
Brown A 6
Cooper 6
Dailly 6
Gough 6
Liddell 6
Murdoch 6
Rioch 6
Waddell 6
Henderson W 5
Hutchison 5
Macari 5
Masson 5
McAllister G 5
McQueen 5
Nevin 5
Nicholas 5
O'Hare 5
Scott A 5
Strachan................... 5
Young A 5
Archibald 4
Caldow 4
Crawford................... 4
Fletcher D 4
Hamilton 4
Hartford 4
Herd D 4
Jackson D 4
Johnstone J 4

Lorimer..................... 4
Mackay D 4
Mason 4
McGinlay 4
McKinlay W 4
McLaren 4
O'Connor 4
Smith G 4
Souness 4
Baxter 3
Bremner W 3
Burley C 3
Chalmers 3
Ferguson B 3
Gibson 3
Graham G 3
Gray E 3
Greig 3
Hendry 3
Lennox 3
MacDougall 3
McCann 3
McInally A 3
McNeill 3
McPhail 3
Morris 3
Robertson J (1991-5) ... 3
Sturrock.................... 3
Thompson 3
White 3
Baird S 2
Bauld 2
Brown S.................... 2
Burke 2
Caldwell G 2
Cameron 2
Commons................... 2
Flavell 2
Fleming 2
Graham A 2
Harper 2
Hewie 2
Holton 2
Hopkin 2
Houliston 2
Jess 2
Johnstone A 2
Johnstone D 2
McClair..................... 2
McGhee 2
McMillan 2
McManus 2
Pettigrew 2
Ring 2

Robertson A 2
Shearer D 2
Aitken R 1
Bannon...................... 1
Beattie........................ 1
Berra........................... 1
Bett 1
Bone 1
Boyd T 1
Brazil.......................... 1
Broadfoot................... 1
Buckley....................... 1
Burns 1
Calderwood 1
Campbell R 1
Clarkson 1
Combe 1
Conn 1
Craig 1
Curran 1
Davidson 1
Dickov 1
Dobie 1
Docherty..................... 1
Duncan M 1
Elliott 1
Fernie 1
Fletcher S................... 1
Freedman 1
Gray F 1
Gemmell T 1
Hartley........................ 1
Henderson J 1
Holt 1
Howie 1
Hughes J 1
Hunter W 1
Hutchison T 1
Jackson C 1
Jardine 1
Johnstone L 1
Kyle 1
Lambert....................... 1
Linwood...................... 1
Mackay G 1
Mackie 1
MacLeod...................... 1
Maloney...................... 1
McAvennie.................. 1
McCall 1
McCalliog 1
McArthur..................... 1
McCormack 1
McCulloch 1

McKenzie 1
McKimmie 1
McKinnon 1
McLean........................ 1
McLintock.................... 1
McSwegan 1
Miller W 1
Mitchell....................... 1
Morgan........................ 1
Morrison...................... 1
Mulhall........................ 1
Murray J 1
Narey 1
Naismith...................... 1
Naysmith 1
Ormond....................... 1
Orr 1
Parlane 1
Provan D 1
Quashie....................... 1
Quinn.......................... 1
Ritchie P 1
Sharp 1
Stewart R 1
Thornton..................... 1
Wallace I 1
Webster 1
Weir A 1
Weir D 1
Wilkie 1
Wilson Danny 1

WALES

Rush 28
Allchurch I 23
Ford 23
Saunders 22
Bellamy..................... 18
Earnshaw................... 16
Hughes M 16
Charles John 15
Jones C 15
Hartson...................... 14
Toshack 13
Giggs 12
James L 10
Koumas 10
Davies RT 8
James R 8
Vernon 8
Davies RW 7
Flynn 7
Speed 7
Walsh I......................... 7

Charles M 6
Curtis A....................... 6
Davies S...................... 6
Griffiths A 6
Medwin 6
Pembridge 6
Clarke R 5
Leek 5
Blake 4
Coleman 4
Deacy 4
Eastwood.................... 4
Edwards I 4
Tapscott...................... 4
Thomas M 4
Woosnam.................... 4
Allen M........................ 3
Bale............................. 3
Bodin 3
Bowen M 3
Edwards D 3
England 3
Ledley 3
Melville 3
Palmer D 3
Ramsey 3
Rees R 3
Robinson J 3
Collins J 2
Davies G 2
Durban A 2
Dwyer 2
Edwards G 2
Evans C 2
Giles D 2
Godfrey....................... 2
Griffiths M 2
Hodges 2
Horne 2
Jones Barrie 2
Jones Bryn 2
Lowrie......................... 2
Nicholas 2
Phillips D 2
Reece G 2
Savage........................ 2
Slatter 2
Symons 2
Vokes.......................... 2
Yorath......................... 2
Barnes 1
Blackmore................... 1
Bowen D...................... 1
Boyle T........................ 1

Burgess R 1
Charles Jeremy 1
Church 1
Cotterill 1
Evans I 1
Fletcher 1
Foulkes 1
Harris C 1
Hewitt R 1
Hockey 1
Jones A 1
Jones D 1
Jones J 1
King 1
Krzywicki 1
Llewellyn 1
Lovell 1
Mahoney 1
Moore G 1
O'Sullivan 1
Parry 1
Paul 1
Powell A 1
Powell D 1
Price P 1
Roberts P 1
Robinson C 1
Smallman 1
Taylor 1
Vaughan 1
Williams Adrian 1
Williams Ashley 1
Williams GE 1
Williams GG 1
Young 1

N IRELAND

Healy 35
Clarke 13
Armstrong 12
Quinn JM 12
Dowie 11
Bingham 10
Crossan J 10
McIlroy J 10
McParland 10
Best 9
Whiteside 9
Dougan 8
Irvine W 8
Lafferty 8
O'Neill M (1972–85) ... 8
McAdams 7
Taggart G 7

Wilson S 7
Gray 6
McLaughlin 6
Nicholson J 6
Wilson K 6
Cush 5
Feeney ((2002-9)) 5
Hamilton W 5
Hughes M 5
Magilton 5
McIlroy S 5
Simpson 5
Smyth S 5
Walsh D 5
Anderson T 4
Elliott 4
Hamilton B 4
McCann 4
McGrath 4
McMorran 4
O'Neill M (1989-96) 4
Quinn SJ 4
Brotherston 3
Harvey M 3
Lockhart 3
Lomas 3
McDonald 3
McMordie 3
Morgan S 3
Mulryne 3
Nicholl C 3
Spence D 3
Tully 3
Blanchflower D 2
Casey 2
Clements 2
Davis 2
Doherty P 2
Finney 2
Gillespie 2
Harkin 2
Lennon 2
McAuley 2
McMahon 2
Neill W 2
O'Neill J 2
Peacock 2
Penney 2
Stewart I 2
Whitley 2
Barr 1
Black 1
Blanchflower J 1
Brennan 1
Brunt 1

Campbell W 1
Caskey 1
Cassidy 1
Cochrane T 1
Crossan E 1
D'Arcy 1
Doherty L 1
Elder 1
Evans C 1
Evans J 1
Ferguson 1
Ferris 1
Griffin 1
Hill C 1
Humphries 1
Hunter A 1
Hunter B 1
Johnston 1
Jones J 1
Jones, S. 1
McCartney 1
McClelland (1961) 1
McCrory 1
McCurdy 1
McGarry 1
McVeigh 1
Moreland 1
Morrow 1
Murdock 1
Nelson 1
Nicholl J 1
O'Boyle 1
O'Kane 1
Patterson D 1
Patterson R 1
Rowland 1
Sproule 1
Stevenson 1
Thompson 1
Walker 1
Welsh 1
Williams 1
Wilson D 1

REP OF IRELAND

Keane Robbie 51
Quinn N 21
Stapleton 20
Aldridge 19
Cascarino 19
Givens 19
Cantwell 14
Daly 13
Harte 11

Brady	9	Robinson	4	Ambrose	1
Connolly	9	Tuohy	4	Anderson	1
Doyle	9	Carey J	3	Carroll	1
Duff	9	Coad	3	Dempsey	1
Keane Roy	9	Conway	3	Duffy	1
Kelly D	9	Fahey	3	Elliott	1
Morrison	9	Farrell	3	Fitzgerald J	1
Sheedy	9	Fogarty	3	Fullam J	1
Curtis	8	Haverty	3	Galvin	1
Grealish	8	Kennedy Mark	3	Gibson	1
Kilbane	8	Kinsella	3	Glynn	1
McGrath P	8	McAteer	3	Green	1
Staunton	8	Ryan R	3	Grimes	1
Breen G	7	Waddock	3	Healy	1
Dunne R	7	Walsh M	3	Holmes	1
Fitzsimons	7	Whelan R	3	Hughton	1
Ringstead	7	Andrews	2	Hunt	1
Townsend	7	Barrett	2	Gibson	1
Coyne	6	Conroy	2	Kavanagh	1
Houghton	6	Cox	2	Keogh	1
Long	6	Dennehy	2	Kernaghan	1
McEvoy	6	Eglington	2	Mancini	1
Martin C	6	Fallon	2	McCann	1
Moran	6	Finnan	2	McGeady	1
Cummins	5	Fitzgerald P	2	McPhail	1
Fagan F	5	Foley	2	Miller	1
Giles	5	Gavin	2	Mooney	1
Holland	5	Hale	2	Moroney	1
Lawrenson	5	Hand	2	Mulligan	1
Rogers	5	Hurley	2	O'Brien A	1
Sheridan	5	Kelly G	2	O'Callaghan K	1
Treacy	5	Lawrence	2	O'Keefe	1
Walsh D	5	Leech	2	O'Leary	1
Byrne J	4	McCarthy	2	O'Neill F	1
Doherty	4	McLoughlin	2	O'Shea	1
Ireland	4	O'Connor	2	Ryan G	1
Irwin	4	O'Farrell	2	Slaven	1
McGee	4	O'Reilly J	2	Sloan	1
Martin M	4	St Ledger S	2	Strahan	1
O'Neill K	4	Whelan G	2	Ward	1
Reid A	4	Reid S	2	Waters	1

HOME INTERNATIONAL RESULTS

Note: In the results that follow, WC = World Cup, EC = European Championship, CC = Carling Cup
TF = Tournoi de France For Northern Ireland read Ireland before 1921

ENGLAND V SCOTLAND
Played 110; England 45; Scotland 41; drawn 24 Goals: England 192, Scotland 169

		E	S					E	S
1872	Glasgow	0	0		1879	The Oval		5	4
1873	The Oval	4	2		1880	Glasgow		4	5
1874	Glasgow	1	2		1881	The Oval		1	6
1875	The Oval	2	2		1882	Glasgow		1	5
1876	Glasgow	0	3		1883	Sheffield		2	3
1877	The Oval	1	3		1884	Glasgow		0	1
1878	Glasgow	2	7		1885	The Oval		1	1
					1886	Glasgow		1	1

Year	Venue	E	S		Year	Venue	E	S
1887	Blackburn	2	3		1947	Wembley	1	1
1888	Glasgow	5	0		1948	Glasgow	2	0
1889	The Oval	2	3		1949	Wembley	1	3
1890	Glasgow	1	1		1950	Glasgow (WC)	1	0
1891	Blackburn	2	1		1951	Wembley	2	3
1892	Glasgow	4	1		1952	Glasgow	2	1
1893	Richmond	5	2		1953	Wembley	2	2
1894	Glasgow	2	2		1954	Glasgow (WC)	4	2
1895	Goodison Park	3	0		1955	Wembley	7	2
1896	Glasgow	1	2		1956	Glasgow	1	1
1897	Crystal Palace	1	2		1957	Wembley	2	1
1898	Glasgow	3	1		1958	Glasgow	4	0
1899	Birmingham	2	1		1959	Wembley	1	0
1900	Glasgow	1	4		1960	Glasgow	1	1
1901	Crystal Palace	2	2		1961	Wembley	9	3
1902	Birmingham	2	2		1962	Glasgow	0	2
1903	Sheffield	1	2		1963	Wembley	1	2
1904	Glasgow	1	0		1964	Glasgow	0	1
1905	Crystal Palace	1	0		1965	Wembley	2	2
1906	Glasgow	1	2		1966	Glasgow	4	3
1907	Newcastle	1	1		1967	Wembley (EC)	2	3
1908	Glasgow	1	1		1968	Glasgow (EC)	1	1
1909	Crystal Palace	2	0		1969	Wembley	4	1
1910	Glasgow	0	2		1970	Glasgow	0	0
1911	Goodison Park	1	1		1971	Wembley	3	1
1912	Glasgow	1	1		1972	Glasgow	1	0
1913	Stamford Bridge	1	0		1973	Glasgow	5	0
1914	Glasgow	1	3		1973	Wembley	1	0
1920	Sheffield	5	4		1974	Glasgow	0	2
1921	Glasgow	0	3		1975	Wembley	5	1
1922	Birmingham	0	1		1976	Glasgow	1	2
1923	Glasgow	2	2		1977	Wembley	1	2
1924	Wembley	1	1		1978	Glasgow	1	0
1925	Glasgow	0	2		1979	Wembley	3	1
1926	Manchester	0	1		1980	Glasgow	2	0
1927	Glasgow	2	1		1981	Wembley	0	1
1928	Wembley	1	5		1982	Glasgow	1	0
1929	Glasgow	0	1		1983	Wembley	2	0
1930	Wembley	5	2		1984	Glasgow	1	1
1931	Glasgow	0	2		1985	Glasgow	0	1
1932	Wembley	3	0		1986	Wembley	2	1
1933	Glasgow	1	2		1987	Glasgow	0	0
1934	Wembley	3	0		1988	Wembley	1	0
1935	Glasgow	0	2		1989	Glasgow	2	0
1936	Wembley	1	1		1996	Wembley (EC)	2	0
1937	Glasgow	1	3		1999	Glasgow (EC)	2	0
1938	Wembley	0	1		1999	Wembley (EC)	0	1
1939	Glasgow	2	1					

ENGLAND v WALES

Played 100; England won 65; Wales 14; drawn 21 Goals: England 244, Wales 90

Year	Venue	E	W		Year	Venue	E	W
1879	The Oval	2	1		1889	Stoke	4	1
1880	Wrexham	3	2		1890	Wrexham	3	1
1881	Blackburn	0	1		1891	Sunderland	4	1
1882	Wrexham	3	5		1892	Wrexham	2	0
1883	The Oval	5	0		1893	Stoke	6	0
1884	Wrexham	4	0		1894	Wrexham	5	1
1885	Blackburn	1	1		1895	Queens Club, London	1	1
1886	Wrexham	3	1		1896	Cardiff	9	1
1887	The Oval	4	0		1897	Bramall Lane	4	0
1888	Crewe	5	1		1898	Wrexham	3	0
					1899	Bristol	4	0

Year	Venue	E	I		Year	Venue	E	I
1900	Cardiff	1	1		1951	Cardiff	1	1
1901	Newcastle	6	0		1952	Wembley	5	2
1902	Wrexham	0	0		1953	Cardiff (WC)	4	1
1903	Portsmouth	2	1		1954	Wembley	3	2
1904	Wrexham	2	2		1955	Cardiff	1	2
1905	Anfield	3	1		1956	Wembley	3	1
1906	Cardiff	1	0		1957	Cardiff	4	0
1907	Fulham	1	1		1958	Villa Park	2	2
1908	Wrexham	7	1		1959	Cardiff	1	1
1909	Nottingham	2	0		1960	Wembley	5	1
1910	Cardiff	1	0		1961	Cardiff	1	1
1911	Millwall	3	0		1962	Wembley	4	0
1912	Wrexham	2	0		1963	Cardiff	4	0
1913	Bristol	4	3		1964	Wembley	2	1
1914	Cardiff	2	0		1965	Cardiff	0	0
1920	Highbury	1	2		1966	Wembley (EC)	5	1
1921	Cardiff	0	0		1967	Cardiff (EC)	3	0
1922	Anfield	1	0		1969	Wembley	2	1
1923	Cardiff	2	2		1970	Cardiff	1	1
1924	Blackburn	1	2		1971	Wembley	0	0
1925	Swansea	2	1		1972	Cardiff	3	0
1926	Selhurst Park	1	3		1972	Cardiff (WC)	1	0
1927	Wrexham	3	3		1973	Wembley (WC)	1	1
1927	Burnley	1	2		1973	Wembley	3	0
1928	Swansea	3	2		1974	Cardiff	2	0
1929	Stamford Bridge	6	0		1975	Wembley	2	2
1930	Wrexham	4	0		1976	Wrexham	2	1
1931	Anfield	3	1		1976	Cardiff	1	0
1932	Wrexham	0	0		1977	Wembley	0	1
1933	Newcastle	1	2		1978	Wembley	3	1
1934	Cardiff	4	0		1979	Wembley	0	0
1935	Wolverhampton	1	2		1980	Wrexham	1	4
1936	Cardiff	1	2		1981	Wembley	0	0
1937	Middlesbrough	2	1		1982	Cardiff	1	0
1938	Cardiff	2	4		1983	Wembley	2	1
1946	Maine Road	3	0		1984	Wrexham	0	1
1947	Cardiff	3	0		2004	Old Trafford (WC)	2	0
1948	Villa Park	1	0		2005	Cardiff (WC)	1	0
1949	Cardiff (WC)	4	1		2011	Cardiff (EC)	2	0
1950	Sunderland	4	2					

ENGLAND v N IRELAND
Played 98; England won 75; Ireland 7; drawn 16 Goals: England 323, Ireland 81

Year	Venue	E	I		Year	Venue	E	I
1882	Belfast	13	0		1901	Southampton	3	0
1883	Aigburth, Liverpool	7	0		1902	Belfast	1	0
1884	Belfast	8	1		1903	Wolverhampton	4	0
1885	Whalley Range	4	0		1904	Belfast	3	1
1886	Belfast	6	1		1905	Middlesbrough	1	1
1887	Bramall Lane	7	0		1906	Belfast	5	0
1888	Belfast	5	1		1907	Goodison Park	1	0
1889	Goodison Park	6	1		1908	Belfast	3	1
1890	Belfast	9	1		1909	Bradford PA	4	0
1891	Wolverhampton	6	1		1910	Belfast	1	1
1892	Belfast	2	0		1911	Derby	2	1
1893	Perry Barr	6	1		1912	Dublin	6	1
1894	Belfast	2	2		1913	Belfast	1	2
1895	Derby	9	0		1914	Middlesbrough	0	3
1896	Belfast	2	0		1919	Belfast	1	1
1897	Nottingham	6	0		1920	Sunderland	2	0
1898	Belfast	3	2		1921	Belfast	1	1
1899	Sunderland	13	2		1922	West Bromwich	2	0
1900	Dublin	2	0		1923	Belfast	1	2
					1924	Goodison Park	3	1

Year	Venue			Year	Venue		
1925	Belfast	0	0	1962	Belfast	3	1
1926	Anfield	3	3	1963	Wembley	8	3
1927	Belfast	0	2	1964	Belfast	4	3
1928	Goodison Park	2	1	1965	Wembley	2	1
1929	Belfast	3	0	1966	Belfast (EC)	2	0
1930	Bramall Lane	5	1	1967	Wembley (EC)	2	0
1931	Belfast	6	2	1969	Belfast	3	1
1932	Blackpool	1	0	1970	Wembley	3	1
1933	Belfast	3	0	1971	Belfast	1	0
1935	Goodison Park	2	1	1972	Wembley	0	1
1935	Belfast	3	1	1973	*Goodison Park	2	1
1936	Stoke	3	1	1974	Wembley	1	0
1937	Belfast	5	1	1975	Belfast	0	0
1938	Old Trafford	7	0	1976	Wembley	4	0
1946	Belfast	7	2	1977	Belfast	2	1
1947	Goodison Park	2	2	1978	Wembley	1	0
1948	Belfast	6	2	1979	Wembley (EC)	4	0
1949	Maine Road (WC)	9	2	1979	Belfast	2	0
1950	Belfast	4	1	1979	Belfast (EC)	5	1
1951	Villa Park	2	0	1980	Wembley	1	1
1952	Belfast	2	2	1982	Wembley	4	0
1953	Goodison Park (WC)	3	1	1983	Belfast	0	0
1954	Belfast	2	0	1984	Wembley	1	0
1955	Wembley	3	0	1985	Belfast (WC)	1	0
1956	Belfast	1	1	1985	Wembley (WC)	0	0
1957	Wembley	2	3	1986	Wembley (EC)	3	0
1958	Belfast	3	3	1987	Belfast (EC)	2	0
1959	Wembley	2	1	2005	Old Trafford (WC)	4	0
1960	Belfast	5	2	2005	Belfast (WC)	0	1
1961	Wembley	1	1				

(*Switched from Belfast because of political situation)

SCOTLAND v WALES
Played 105; Scotland won 61; Wales 21; drawn 23 Goals: Scotland 241, Wales 120

Year	Venue	S	W	Year	Venue	S	W
1876	Glasgow	4	0	1905	Wrexham	1	3
1877	Wrexham	2	0	1906	Edinburgh	0	2
1878	Glasgow	9	0	1907	Wrexham	0	1
1879	Wrexham	3	0	1908	Dundee	2	1
1880	Glasgow	5	1	1909	Wrexham	2	3
1881	Wrexham	5	1	1910	Kilmarnock	1	0
1882	Glasgow	5	0	1911	Cardiff	2	2
1883	Wrexham	3	0	1912	Tynecastle	1	0
1884	Glasgow	4	1	1913	Wrexham	0	0
1885	Wrexham	8	1	1914	Glasgow	0	0
1886	Glasgow	4	1	1920	Cardiff	1	1
1887	Wrexham	2	0	1921	Aberdeen	2	1
1888	Edinburgh	5	1	1922	Wrexham	1	2
1889	Wrexham	0	0	1923	Paisley	2	0
1890	Paisley	5	0	1924	Cardiff	0	2
1891	Wrexham	4	3	1925	Tynecastle	3	1
1892	Edinburgh	6	1	1926	Cardiff	3	0
1893	Wrexham	8	0	1927	Glasgow	3	0
1894	Kilmarnock	5	2	1928	Wrexham	2	2
1895	Wrexham	5	2	1929	Glasgow	4	2
1896	Dundee	4	0	1930	Cardiff	4	2
1897	Wrexham	2	2	1931	Glasgow	1	1
1898	Motherwell	5	2	1932	Wrexham	3	2
1899	Wrexham	6	0	1933	Edinburgh	2	5
1900	Aberdeen	5	2	1934	Cardiff	2	3
1901	Wrexham	1	1	1935	Aberdeen	3	2
1902	Greenock	5	1	1936	Cardiff	1	1
1903	Cardiff	1	0	1937	Dundee	1	2
1904	Dundee	1	1	1938	Cardiff	1	2
				1939	Edinburgh	3	2

Year	Venue	S	l
1946	Wrexham	1	3
1947	Glasgow	1	2
1948	Cardiff (WC)	3	1
1949	Glasgow	2	0
1950	Cardiff	3	1
1951	Glasgow	0	1
1952	Cardiff (WC)	2	1
1953	Glasgow	3	3
1954	Cardiff	1	0
1955	Glasgow	2	0
1956	Cardiff	2	2
1957	Glasgow	1	1
1958	Cardiff	3	0
1959	Glasgow	1	1
1960	Cardiff	0	2
1961	Glasgow	2	0
1962	Cardiff	3	2
1963	Glasgow	2	1
1964	Cardiff	2	3
1965	Glasgow (EC)	4	1
1966	Cardiff (EC)	1	1
1967	Glasgow	3	2
1969	Wrexham	5	3
1970	Glasgow	0	0
1971	Cardiff	0	0
1972	Glasgow	1	0
1973	Wrexham	2	0
1974	Glasgow	2	0
1975	Cardiff	2	2
1976	Glasgow	3	1
1977	Glasgow (WC)	1	0
1977	Wrexham	0	0
1977	Anfield (WC)	2	0
1978	Glasgow	1	1
1979	Cardiff	0	3
1980	Glasgow	1	0
1981	Swansea	0	2
1982	Glasgow	1	0
1983	Cardiff	2	0
1984	Glasgow	2	1
1985	Glasgow (WC)	0	1
1985	Cardiff (WC)	1	1
1997	Kilmarnock	0	1
2004	Cardiff	0	4
2009	Cardiff	0	3
2011	Dublin (CC)	3	1

		S	l
1884	Belfast	5	0

SCOTLAND v NORTHERN IRELAND

Played 95; Scotland won 63; Northern Ireland 15; drawn 17; Goals: Scotland 257, Northern Ireland 80

Year	Venue			Year	Venue		
1885	Glasgow	8	2	1924	Glasgow	2	0
1886	Belfast	7	2	1925	Belfast	3	0
1887	Belfast	4	1	1926	Glasgow	4	0
1888	Belfast	10	2	1927	Belfast	2	0
1889	Glasgow	7	0	1928	Glasgow	0	1
1890	Belfast	4	1	1929	Belfast	7	3
1891	Glasgow	2	1	1930	Glasgow	3	1
1892	Belfast	3	2	1931	Belfast	0	0
1893	Glasgow	6	1	1932	Glasgow	3	1
1894	Belfast	2	1	1933	Belfast	4	0
1895	Glasgow	3	1	1934	Glasgow	1	2
1896	Belfast	3	3	1935	Belfast	1	2
1897	Glasgow	5	1	1936	Edinburgh	2	1
1898	Belfast	3	0	1937	Belfast	3	1
1899	Glasgow	9	1	1938	Aberdeen	1	1
1900	Belfast	3	0	1939	Belfast	2	0
1901	Glasgow	11	0	1946	Glasgow	0	0
1902	Belfast	5	1	1947	Belfast	0	2
1902	Belfast	3	0	1948	Glasgow	3	2
1903	Glasgow	0	2	1949	Belfast	8	2
1904	Dublin	1	1	1950	Glasgow	6	1
1905	Glasgow	4	0	1951	Belfast	3	0
1906	Dublin	1	0	1952	Glasgow	1	1
1907	Glasgow	3	0	1953	Belfast	3	1
1908	Dublin	5	0	1954	Glasgow	2	2
1909	Glasgow	5	0	1955	Belfast	1	2
1910	Belfast	0	1	1956	Glasgow	1	0
1911	Glasgow	2	0	1957	Belfast	1	1
1912	Belfast	4	1	1958	Glasgow	2	2
1913	Dublin	2	1	1959	Belfast	4	0
1914	Belfast	1	1	1960	Glasgow	5	1
1920	Glasgow	3	0	1961	Belfast	6	1
1921	Belfast	2	0	1962	Glasgow	5	1
1922	Glasgow	2	1	1963	Belfast	1	2
1923	Belfast	1	0	1964	Glasgow	3	2

		W	I				
1965	Belfast	2	3	1978	Glasgow	1	1
1966	Glasgow	2	1	1979	Glasgow	1	0
1967	Belfast	0	1	1980	Belfast	0	1
1969	Glasgow	1	1	1981	Glasgow (WC)	1	1
1970	Belfast	1	0	1981	Glasgow	2	0
1971	Glasgow	0	1	1981	Belfast (WC)	0	0
1972	Glasgow	2	0	1982	Belfast	1	1
1973	Glasgow	1	2	1983	Glasgow	0	0
1974	Glasgow	0	1	1984	Belfast	0	2
1975	Glasgow	3	0	1992	Glasgow	1	0
1976	Glasgow	3	0	2008	Glasgow	0	0
1977	Glasgow	3	0	2011	Dublin (CC)	3	0

WALES v NORTHERN IRELAND
Played 95; Wales won 44; Northern Ireland won 27; drawn 24; Goals: Wales 189, Northern Ireland 131

		W	I				
				1935	Wrexham	3	1
1882	Wrexham	7	1	1936	Belfast	2	3
1883	Belfast	1	1	1937	Wrexham	4	1
1884	Wrexham	6	0	1938	Belfast	0	1
1885	Belfast	8	2	1939	Wrexham	3	1
1886	Wrexham	5	0	1947	Belfast	1	2
1887	Belfast	1	4	1948	Wrexham	2	0
1888	Wrexham	11	0	1949	Belfast	2	0
1889	Belfast	3	1	1950	Wrexham (WC)	0	0
1890	Shrewsbury	5	2	1951	Belfast	2	1
1891	Belfast	2	7	1952	Swansea	3	0
1892	Bangor	1	1	1953	Belfast	3	2
1893	Belfast	3	4	1954	Wrexham (WC)	1	2
1894	Swansea	4	1	1955	Belfast	3	2
1895	Belfast	2	2	1956	Cardiff	1	1
1896	Wrexham	6	1	1957	Belfast	0	0
1897	Belfast	3	4	1958	Cardiff	1	1
1898	Llandudno	0	1	1959	Belfast	1	4
1899	Belfast	0	1	1960	Wrexham	3	2
1900	Llandudno	2	0	1961	Belfast	5	1
1901	Belfast	1	0	1962	Cardiff	4	0
1902	Cardiff	0	3	1963	Belfast	4	1
1903	Belfast	0	2	1964	Swansea	2	3
1904	Bangor	0	1	1965	Belfast	5	0
1905	Belfast	2	2	1966	Cardiff	1	4
1906	Wrexham	4	4	1967	Belfast (EC)	0	0
1907	Belfast	3	2	1968	Wrexham (EC)	2	0
1908	Aberdare	0	1	1969	Belfast	0	0
1909	Belfast	3	2	1970	Swansea	1	0
1910	Wrexham	4	1	1971	Belfast	0	1
1911	Belfast	2	1	1972	Wrexham	0	0
1912	Cardiff	2	3	1973	*Goodison Park	0	1
1913	Belfast	1	0	1974	Wrexham	1	0
1914	Wrexham	1	2	1975	Belfast	0	1
1920	Belfast	2	2	1976	Swansea	1	0
1921	Swansea	2	1	1977	Belfast	1	1
1922	Belfast	1	1	1978	Wrexham	1	0
1923	Wrexham	0	3	1979	Belfast	1	1
1924	Belfast	1	0	1980	Cardiff	0	1
1925	Wrexham	0	0	1982	Wrexham	3	0
1926	Belfast	0	3	1983	Belfast	1	0
1927	Cardiff	2	2	1984	Swansea	1	1
1928	Belfast	2	1	2004	Cardiff (WC)	2	2
1929	Wrexham	2	2	2005	Belfast (WC)	3	2
1930	Belfast	0	7	2007	Belfast	0	0
1931	Wrexham	3	2	2008	Glasgow	0	0
1932	Belfast	0	4	2011	Dublin (CC)	0	0
1933	Wrexham	4	1	(*Switched from Belfast because of political situation in N Ireland)			
1934	Belfast	1	1				

BRITISH AND IRISH UNDER-21
INTERNATIONALS 2010–11

EUROPEAN CHAMPIONSIP 2011 – QUALIFYING

REPUBLIC OF IRELAND 5 ESTONIA 0
Group 2: Tallaght (3,010); Tuesday, August 10 2010
Republic of Ireland: Henderson (Bristol City), Coleman (Everton) (Oyebanjo, Histon 88), Gunning (Blackburn), Kiernan (Yeovil), Nolan (Preston), McCarthy (Wigan) (Hourihane, Ipswich 81), Gleeson (MK Dons), Garvan (Crystal Palace), Clifford (Chelsea), Sheridan (Celtic) (Judge, Blackburn 77), Stokes (Hibernian). **Booked:** Stokes, Nolan.
Scorers – Republic of Ireland: Stokes (15, 30 pen), McCarthy (62), Coleman (86), Garvan (90). **Half-time:** 2-0

PORTUGAL 0 ENGLAND 1
Group 9: Barcelos (6,821); Friday, September 3 2010
England: Fielding (Blackburn), Walker (Tottenham), Smalling (Manchester Utd), Jones (Blackburn), Bertrand (Chelsea), Cleverley (Manchester Utd), Henderson (Sunderland), Mancienne (Chelsea), Rose (Tottenham), Welbeck (Manchester Utd) (Cork, Chelsea 84), Sturridge (Chelsea) (Delfouneso, Aston Villa 90). **Booked:** Fielding, Bertrand
Scorer – England: Sturridge (32). **Half-time:** 0-1

BELARUS 1 SCOTLAND 1
Group 10: Borisov (4,500); Friday, September 3 2010
Scotland: Martin (Leeds), Caddis (Celtic), Scobbie (Falkirk), Wilson (Liverpool), Hanlon (Hibernian), Arfield (Huddersfield), Wotherspoon (Hibernian), Coutts (Preston) (McGinn, Watford 84), Maguire (Aberdeen), Murphy (Motherwell) (Goodwillie, Dundee Utd 62), Bannan (Aston Villa) (Forrest, Celtic 62). **Booked:** Bannan, Wotherspoon
Scorers – Belarus: Nekhaychik (36). **Scotland:** Maguire (64 pen). **Half-time:** 1-0

NORTHERN IRELAND 4 SAN MARINO 0
Group 5: Coleraine (3,813); Friday, September 3 2010
Northern Ireland: Drummond (Rangers), Hodson (Watford), Thompson (Watford), McGivern (Manchester City), McLaughlin (Newcastle) (Blake, Brentford 86), Ferguson (Newcastle), Weir (Sunderland), Norwood (Manchester Utd), Boyce (Werder Bremen) (Millar, Oldham 55), Little (Rangers), Magennis (Aberdeen) (Grigg, Walsall 71). **Booked:** McGivern
Scorers – Northern Ireland: Little (4, 84 pen), McGivern (15 pen), Grigg (90). **Half-time:** 2-0

SWITZERLAND 1 REPUBLIC OF IRELAND 0
Group 2: Lugano (6,583); Friday, September 3 2010
Republic of Ireland: Henderson (Bristol City), Coleman (Everton), Gunning (Blackburn), Kiernan (Watford), Nolan (Preston), Judge (Blackburn), Towell (Celtic), Hourihane (Ipswich), Clifford (Chelsea) (Mason, Plymouth), Stokes (Hibernian) (Rooney, Inverness 76), Brady (Manchester Utd). **Booked:** Stokes, Nolan, Gunning, **Scorer – Switzerland:** Frei (48). **Half-time:** 0-0

HUNGARY 0 WALES 1
Group 3: Szekesfehervar (5,500); Saturday, September 4 2010
Wales: Maxwell (Wrexham), Matthews (Cardiff) (Richards, Swansea 16), Taylor (Swansea), Doble (Southampton), Stephens (Hibernian), Morris (Aldershot), Allen (Swansea), Bradley (Rotherham), Robson-Kanu (Reading), Williams (Wrexham) (Partington, Bournemouth 60), MacDonald (Swansea). **Booked:** Williams, Robson-Kanu
Scorer – Wales: Robson-Kanu (67). **Half-time:** 0-0

ENGLAND 3 LITHUANIA 0
Group 9: Colchester (7,240); Tuesday, September 7 2010
England: Fielding (Blackburn), Walker (Tottenham) (Wilshere, Arsenal 46), Smalling (Manchester Utd), Jones (Blackburn), Bertrand (Chelsea), Cleverley (Manchester Utd) (Albrighton, Aston Villa 64), Henderson (Sunderland), Mancienne (Chelsea), Rose (Tottenham), Welbeck (Manchester Utd), Sturridge (Chelsea) (Cork, Chelsea 78).
Booked: Jones
Scorers – England: Welbeck (62, 90), Albrighton (79). **Half-time:** 0-0

SCOTLAND 2 AUSTRIA 1
Group 10: Aberdeen (2,064); Tuesday, September 7 2010
Scotland: Martin (Leeds), Caddis (Swindon), Hanlon (Hibernian), Wilson (Liverpool), Scobbie (Falkirk), Arfield (Huddersfield), Coutts (Preston), Wotherspoon (Hibernian) (Forrest, Celtic 71), Bannan (Aston Villa) (McGinn, Watford 90), Maguire (Aberdeen), Goodwillie (Dundee Utd) (Murphy, Motherwell 77). **Booked:** Coutts
Scorers – Scotland: Bannan (29), Maguire (89). **Austria:** Arnautovic (10). **Half-time:** 1-1

ITALY 1 WALES 0
Group 3: Pescara (6,891); Tuesday, September 7 2010
Wales: Maxwell (Wrexham), Matthews (Cardiff) (Richards, Swansea 34), Taylor (Swansea), King (Leicester), Eardley (Blackpool), Morris (Aldershot), Allen (Swansea) (Williams, Wrexham 80), Bradley (Rotherham) (Doble, Southampton 56), Robson-Kanu (Reading), Church (Reading), MacDonald (Swansea). **Booked:** Bradley, MacDonald
Scorer – Italy: Mustacchio (14). **Half-time:** 1-0

GERMANY 3 NORTHERN IRELAND 0
Group 5: Ingolstadt (2,021); Tuesday, September 7, 2010
Northern Ireland: Devlin (Manchester Utd), Thompson (Watford), (Grigg, Walsall 72), Hodson (Watford), Weir (Sunderland), Flynn (Ross), McGivern (Manchester City), Little (Rangers), Norwood (Manchester Utd) (McLaughlin, Newcastle 44), Boyce (Werder Bremen), McKay (Northampton), (Magennis, Aberdeen 64), Ferguson (Newcastle)
Scorers – Germany: Holtby (42, 60), Hermann (67). **Half-time:** 1-0

TURKEY 1 REPUBLIC OF IRELAND 0
Group 2: Izmir (354); Tuesday, September 7 2010
Republic of Ireland: Henderson (Bristol City), Coleman (Everton), Moloney (Nottm Forest), Kiernan (Watford) (McEleney, Derry 58), Conneely (Galway), Towell (Celtic), Hourihane (Ipswich), Clifford (Chelsea) (Mason, Plymouth 79), Rooney (Inverness), Brady (Manchester Utd) (Kearns, Dundalk 35), Carey (Huddersfield). **Booked:** Coleman, Kearns
Scorer – Turkey: Kose (81). **Half-time:** 0-0

QUALIFYING TABLES
(Group winners and four best runners-up to play-offs to determine seven finalists. Denmark qualify as hosts)

GROUP 1

	P	W	D	L	F	A	Pts
Romania	10	8	1	1	23	6	25
Russia	10	7	1	2	22	6	22
Moldova	10	4	2	4	9	13	14
Latvia	10	4	1	5	16	15	13
Faroe Islands	10	3	2	5	8	16	11
Andorra	10	0	1	9	3	25	1

GROUP 2

	P	W	D	L	F	A	Pts
Switzerland	10	6	2	2	15	8	20
Turkey	10	5	1	4	13	11	16
Georgia	10	4	3	3	12	9	15
Armenia	10	4	1	5	18	19	13
Estonia	10	3	3	4	9	16	12
Republic of Ireland	10	1	4	5	11	15	7

GROUP 3

	P	W	D	L	F	A	Pts
Italy	8	5	1	2	12	5	16
Wales	8	5	1	2	15	6	16
Hungary	8	4	1	3	9	7	13
Bosnia-Herzegovina	8	2	2	4	4	8	8
Luxembourg	8	1	1	6	2	16	4

GROUP 4

	P	W	D	L	F	A	Pts
Holland	8	7	0	1	19	5	21
Spain	8	6	1	1	15	5	19
Finland	8	3	1	4	11	11	10
Poland	8	3	0	5	11	13	9
Liechtenstein	8	0	0	8	1	27	0

GROUP 5

	P	W	D	L	F	A	Pts
Czech Republic	8	7	1	0	25	4	22
Iceland	8	5	1	2	29	11	16
Germany	8	3	3	2	26	10	12
Northern Ireland	8	2	1	5	12	16	7
San Marino	8	0	0	8	0	51	0

GROUP 6

	P	W	D	L	F	A	Pts
Sweden	8	6	1	1	15	5	19
Israel	8	5	1	2	18	8	16
Montenegro	8	4	1	3	9	11	13
Kazakhstan	8	1	2	5	7	17	5
Bulgaria	8	1	1	6	8	16	4

GROUP 7

	P	W	D	L	F	A	Pts
Croatia	8	5	2	1	17	10	17
Slovakia	8	4	2	2	11	11	14
Serbia	8	4	1	3	14	12	13
Norway	8	2	1	5	14	18	7
Cyprus	8	2	0	6	8	13	6

GROUP 8

	P	W	D	L	F	A	Pts
Ukraine	8	4	4	0	13	5	16
Belgium	8	4	3	1	8	5	15
France	8	4	3	1	12	6	15
Slovenia	8	2	2	4	6	10	8
Malta	8	0	0	8	0	13	0

GROUP 9

	P	W	D	L	F	A	Pts
Greece	8	6	1	1	13	7	19
England	8	5	2	1	15	7	17
Portugal	8	4	1	3	12	8	13
Lithuania	8	1	2	5	3	11	5
Macedonia	8	0	2	6	9	19	2

GROUP 10

	P	W	D	L	F	A	Pts
Scotland	8	5	2	1	16	7	17
Belarus	8	5	2	1	16	11	17
Austria	8	4	2	2	17	11	14
Albania	8	1	1	6	11	20	4
Azerbaijan	8	1	1	6	8	19	4

PLAY-OFFS

ICELAND 2 SCOTLAND 1
First leg: Reyjkavik (7,255); Thursday, October 7 2010
Scotland: Martin (Leeds), Caddis (Swindon), Scobbie (Falkirk), Wilson (Liverpool), Hanlon (Hibernian), Arfield (Huddersfield), Wotherspoon (Hibernian) (Goodwillie, Dundee Utd 55), McGinn (Watford) Maguire (Aberdeen) Murphy (Motherwell) (Templeton, Hearts 85), Bannan (Aston Villa). **Booked:** Arfield, Goodwillie
Scorers – Iceland: Gudmundsson (34), Ormarsson (78). **Scotland:** Murphy (19)

ENGLAND 2 ROMANIA 1
First leg: Norwich (25,749); Friday, October 8 2010
England: Fielding (Blackburn), Mancienne (Chelsea), Smalling (Manchester Utd), Jones (Blackburn), Bertrand (Chelsea) Cleverley (Manchester Utd), (Albrighton, Aston Villa 75), Henderson (Sunderland), Muamba (Bolton), Wilshere (Arsenal) (Cork, Chelsea 90), Rose (Tottenham), Welbeck (Manchester Utd) Sturridge (Chelsea 80)
Scorers – England: Henderson (63), Smalling (83). **Romania:** Bertrand (71 og). **Half-time:** 0-0

SCOTLAND 1 ICELAND 2 (Iceland won 4-2 on agg)
Second leg: Hibernian (12,320); Monday, October 11 2010
Scotland: Martin (Leeds), Caddis (Swindon), Scobbie (Falkirk) (Griffiths, Dundee 83), Wilson (Liverpool), Hanlon (Hibernian), Wotherspoon (Hibernian), Coutts (Preston), McGinn (Watford) (Goodwillie, Dundee Utd) 81), Bannan (Aston Villa), Murphy (Motherwell) (Templeton, Hearts 86), Maguire (Aberdeen). **Booked:** Maguire, Templeton
Scorers – Scotland: Maguire (75). **Iceland:** Sigurdsson (74, 80). **Half-time:** 0-0

ROMANIA 0 ENGLAND 0 (England won 2-1 on agg)
Second leg: Botosani (6,347); Tuesday, October 12 2010
England: Fielding (Blackburn), Mancienne (Chelsea), Smalling (Manchester Utd), Jones (Blackburn), Bertrand (Chelsea); Cleverley (Manchester Utd), Henderson (Sunderland), Muamba (Bolton), Rose (Tottenham) (Cork, Chelsea 82), Welbeck (Manchester Utd) (Delfouneso, Aston Villa 89), Sturridge (Chelsea) (Lansbury, Arsenal 61). **Booked:** Rose, Mancienne, Sturridge, Cleverley

ON AGGREGATE
Belarus 3 Italy 2 (aet); Czech Republic 5 Greece 0; Spain 5 Croatia 1; Switzerland 5 Sweden 2; Ukraine 3 Holland 3 (Ukraine won on away goals)

EUROPEAN CHAMPIONSHIP 2013
– QUALIFYING

ANDORRA 0 WALES 1
Group 3 : La Vella (350); Tuesday, March 29 2011
Wales: R Taylor (Chelsea), Matthews (Cardiff), Richards (Swansea), Lucas (Swansea) (Bodin, Swindon 60), Alfei (Swansea), Brown (Ipswich), J Taylor (Reading), Partington (Bournemouth), Doble (Southampton), Williams (Crystal Palace) (Ogleby, Hearts 83), Chamberlain (Leicester) (Cassidy, Wolves 69). **Booked:** Brown, Lucas, Ogleby
Scorer – Wales: Fajardo (21 og). **Half-time:** 0-1

FAROE ISLANDS 0 NORTHERN IRELAND 0
Group 4: Gundadalur (500); Tuesday, May 31 2011
Northern Ireland: Devlin (Manchester Utd), Clucas (Preston) (Winchester, Oldham 82), Hanley (Linfield), Norwood (Manchester Utd), Ramsey (Portadown), Hegarty (Rangers), Grigg (Walsall) (Ball, Norwich 71), Lund (Stoke), Boyce (Werder Bremen), Magennis (Aberdeen) (Bryan, Watford 46), Carson (Ipswich). **Booked:** Lund, Grigg, Hegarty

INTERNATIONAL FRIENDLIES

ENGLAND 2 UZBEKISTAN 0
Bristol City (9,821); Tuesday, August 10 2010
England: Fielding (Blackburn) (McCarthy, Reading 77), Walker (Tottenham), Smalling (Manchester Utd), Jones (Blackburn) (Kelly, Liverpool 46), Mancienne (Chelsea), Henderson (Sunderland) (Cork, Chelsea 46), Rodwell (Everton) (Lansbury, Arsenal 61), Cleverley (Manchester Utd), Rose (Tottenham), Sturridge (Chelsea) (Albrighton, Aston Villa, 71), Moses (Wigan) (Welbeck, Manchester Utd 46)
Scorers – England: Rose (64), Kelly (78). **Half-time:** 0-0

MALTA 1 WALES 1
Ta-Qali (750); Tuesday, August 10 2010
Wales: Bond (Watford) (Cornell, Swansea 46), Richards (Swansea) (Alfei, Swansea 46), N Taylor (Swansea), Bradley (Rotherham) (Lucas, Swansea 46), Stephens (Hibernian) (Bender, Colchester 54), Morris (Aldershot), Bodin (Swindon), Partington (Bournemouth) (Williams, Crystal Palace 62), Robson-Kanu (Reading), J Taylor (Reading) (Chamberlain, Leicester 46), MacDonald (Swansea). **Booked:** Bender
Scorers – Malta: Vella (30). **Wales:** Robson-Kanu (82). **Half-time:** 1-0

SCOTLAND 1 SWEDEN 1
St Mirren (2,726); Wednesday, August 11 2010
Scotland: Martin (Leeds) (Gallacher, Rangers 46), Marr (Celtic), Perry (Rangers), Wilson (Liverpool), Hanlon (Hibernian) (Scobbie, Falkirk 46), Bannan (Aston Villa) (Easton, Burnley 72), Shinnie (Rangers) (Saunders, Motherwell 64), Davidson (St Johnstone), Wotherspoon (Hibernian), Maguire (Aberdeen), Murphy (Motherwell) (Inman, Newcastle 46).
Scorers – Scotland: Wotherspoon (90). **Sweden:** Avdic (16). **Half-time:** 0-1

GERMANY 2 ENGLAND 0
Wiesbaden (5,600); Tuesday, November 16 2010
England: Loach (Watford) (Steele, Middlesbrough 46), Trippier (Manchester City), Kelly (Liverpool) (Caulker, Tottenham 78), Mancienne (Chelsea), Bertrand (Chelsea), Rodwell (Everton) (Mee, Manchester City 69), Cork (Chelsea), Lansbury (Arsenal), Rose (Tottenham),

Sinclair (Swansea) (Wickham, Ipswich 69), Delfouneso (Aston Villa) (McEachran, Chelsea 87).
Sent off: Steele
Scorers – Germany: Rausch (36), Tosun (59 pen). **Half-time:** 1-0

SCOTLAND 3 NORTHERN IRELAND 1
Partick (1,764); Wednesday, November 17 2010
Scotland: Barclay (Falkirk), Thomson (Hearts), Hanley (Blackburn), Perry (Rangers), Hanlon (Hibernian) (Booth, Hibernian 67), Armstrong (Dundee Utd) (Duffie, Falkirk 86), Inman (Newcastle) (MacDonald, Burnley 46), Hutton (Rangers) (Ross, Inverness 75), Fleck (Rangers) (Ness, Rangers 75), Russell (Dundee Utd) (Wylde, Rangers 66), Griffiths (Dundee) (Palmer, Sheffield Wed 46)
Northern Ireland: Drummond (Rangers), C McLaughlin (Preston), Breeze (Wigan) (Clucas, Preston 84), McCashin (Jerez), Ferguson (Newcastle), Bryan (Watford) (Lavery, Ipswich 75), P McLaughlin (Newcastle), Devine (Preston) (Bagnall, Sunderland 46), O'Kane (Torquay) (Carson, Ipswich 54), Grigg (Walsall) (Kee, Torquay), Boyce, (Werder Bremen 56)
Scorers – Scotland: Griffiths (12), Hanlon (65), Ross (89). **Northern Ireland:** O'Kane (89).
Half-time: 1-0

WALES 1 AUSTRIA 0
Newport (1,041); Wednesday, November 17 2010
Wales: Taylor (Chelsea) (Cornell, Swansea 46), Richards (Swansea), Bloom (Falkirk) (Dummett, Newcastle 46), Lucas (Swansea) (Brown, Ipswich 56), Stephens (Hibernian) (Bender, Colchester 79), Alfei (Swansea), Partington (Bournemouth), Bodin (Swindon) (Thomas, Swansea 73), Ogleby (Hearts) (Chamberlain, Leicester 70), Doble (Southampton), Craig (Everton) (Williams, Crystal Palace 46).
Scorer – Wales: Chamberlain (74). **Half-time:** 0-0

ITALY 1 ENGLAND 0
Empoli (3,700); Tuesday, February 8 2011
England: Fielding (Blackburn), Naughton (Tottenham), Bennett (Middlesborough), Rodwell (Everton) (Cork, Chelsea 12), Mee (Manchester City), Muamba (Bolton), Albrighton (Aston Villa) (Sinclair (Swansea 73), Lansbury (Arsenal) (Oxlade-Chamberlain, Southampton 60), McEachran (Chelsea) (Trippier, Manchester City 83), Vaughan (Everton) (Rodriguez, Burnley 60), Delfouneso (Aston Villa) (Howson, Leeds 60). **Sent off:** Mee
Scorer – Italy: Macheda (88 pen). **Half-time:** 0-0

WALES 2 NORTHERN IRELAND 0
Wrexham (700); Wednesday, February 9 2011
Wales: R Taylor (Chelsea), Richards (Swansea), Dummett (Newcastle) (Bender, Colchester 55), Lucas (Swansea), Alfei (Swansea), Brown (Ipswich), J Taylor (Reading) (Matthews, Cardiff 81), Jones (Wimbledon) (Partington, Bournemouth 46), Doble (Southampton), Chamberlain (Leicester) (Ogleby, Hearts 74), Williams (Crystal Palace) (Bodin, Swindon 55)
Northern Ireland: Devlin (Manchester Utd), Clucas (Preston), Blake (Brentford) (Millar, Oldham 61), McLaughlin (Newcastle), Hegarty (Rangers) (Devine, Preston 46), McGivern (Manchester City), Lawrie (Telford) (Mitchell, Rangers 74), Lund (Stoke) (Winchester, Oldham 74), Grigg (Walsall) (Gray, unatt 84), Carson (Ipswich) (Magennis, Aberdeen 46), Ferguson (Newcastle)
Scorers – Wales: Alfei (42 pen), Ogleby (75). **Half-time:** 1-0

CYPRUS 0 REPUBLIC OF IRELAND 0
Larnaca (200); Wednesday, February 9, 2011
Republic of Ireland: Branagan (Bury) (McLoughlin, Ipswich 46), Towell (Celtic) (Stevens, Shamrock 72), Duffy (Everton), Kiernan (Watford), Dunleavy (Wolves), Connolly (Bolton), Clifford (Chelsea), Hourihane (Ipswich) (Devitt, Hull 46), Doran (Blackburn) (Doyle, Derby 46), Scannell (Crystal Palace) (Gibbons, Larnaca 80), J Collins (Aston Villa) (M Collins, APEP 75)

DENMARK 0 ENGLAND 4
Viborg (5,126); Thursday, March 24 2011
England: McCarthy (Reading), Naughton (Tottenham), Smalling (Manchester Utd), Richards (Manchester City) (Tomkins, West Ham 4), Bertrand (Chelsea), Cleverley (Manchester Utd) (Cork, Chelsea 79), Muamba (Bolton) (Albrighton, Aston Villa 87), Henderson (Sunderland) (Delfouneso, Aston Villa 79), Sinclair (Swansea) (McEachran, Chelsea 67), Sturridge (Chelsea) (Wickham, Ipswich 87), Welbeck (Manchester Utd) (Rose, Tottenham 67). **Booked:** Cleverley, Bertrand
Scorers – England: Welbeck (23), Sinclair (58), Sturridge (62), Henderson (72). **Half-time:** 0-1

BELGIUM 1 SCOTLAND 0
Deinze (650); Thursday, March 24 2011
Scotland: Adam (Rangers) (Andrews, Falkirk 85), Thomson (Hearts), Booth (Hibernian) (Cole, Rangers 78), Palmer (Sheffield Wed), Hanlon (Hibernian), Perry (Rangers), Wotherspoon (Hibernian) (Armstrong, Dundee Utd 69), Cairney (Hull), Forrest (Celtic), Griffiths (Wolves) (MacDonald, Burnley 58), Rhodes (Huddersfield) (Russell, Dundee Utd 58). **Booked:** Thomson
Scorer – Belgium: Ghanassy (43). **Half-time:** 1-0

PORTUGAL 2 REPUBLIC OF IRELAND 0
Agueda (3,000); Friday, March 25 2011
Republic of Ireland: McLoughlin (Ipswich) (Quirke, Coventry 46), Connolly (Bolton) (Oyebanjo, Histon 46), Gunning (Blackburn) (Dunleavy, Wolves 67), Kiernan (Watford), Canavan (Scunthorpe) (Duffy, Burnley 46), Towell (Celtic), Barton (Preston), Clifford (Chelsea), Henderson (Arsenal) (Madden, Carlisle 55), O'Connor (Ipswich) (Hourihane, Ipswich 46), Doran (Inverness) (Murray, Torquay 76). **Booked:** Quirke
Scorers – Portugal: Josue (90), Abel Camara (90). **Half-time:** 0-0

ENGLAND 1 ICELAND 2
Preston (14,622); Monday, March 28 2011
England: McCarthy (Reading) (Loach, Watford 46), Naughton (Tottenham) (Spence, West Ham 73), Tomkins (West Ham), Baker (Aston Villa), Bertrand (Chelsea) (Bennett, Middlesbrough 74), Albrighton (Aston Villa) (Sinclair, Swansea 82), McEachran (Chelsea) (Mutch, Birmingham 83), Cork (Chelsea) (Cleverley, Manchester Utd 46), Rose (Tottenham), Wickham (Ipswich), Delfouneso (Aston Villa) (Hammill, Wolves 74). **Booked:** Tomkins, Baker
Scorers – England: Delfouneso (13). **Iceland:** Smarason (42), Eyjolfsson (67). **Half-time:** 1-1

ENGLAND 2 NORWAY 0
Southampton (17,996); Sunday, June 5 2011
England: Fielding (Derby). Mancienne (Chelsea), Jones (Blackburn) (Tomkins, West Ham 83), Smalling (Manchester Utd), Bertrand (Chelsea) (Gibbs, Arsenal 46), Henderson (Sunderland) (Lansbury, Arsenal 46), Rodwell (Everton), Muamba (Bolton) (Cork, Chesea 46), Rose (Tottenham) (Albrighton, Aston Villa 46), Sturridge (Chelsea) (Delfouneso, Aston Villa 65), Welbeck (Manchester Utd) (Cleverley, Manchester Utd 46).
Scorers – England: Sturridge (9). Rose (40). **Half-time:** 2-0

TRANSFER TRAIL

I	=	World record fee	D	=	Record fee paid by Scottish club
A	=	Record all-British deal	E	=	Record fee to Scottish club
B	=	British record for goalkeeper	F	=	Record for teenager
C	=	Record deal between English and Scottish clubs	G	=	Most expensive foreign import

	Player	From	To	Date	£
I	Cristiano Ronaldo	Manchester Utd	Real Madrid	7/09	80,000,000
A	Fernando Torres	Liverpool	Chelsea	1/11	50,000,000
	Andy Carroll	Newcastle	Liverpool	1/11	35,000,000
G	Robinho	Real Madrid	Manchester City	9/08	32,500,000
	Dimitar Berbatov	Tottenham	Manchester Utd	9/08	30,750,000
	Andriy Shevchenko	AC Milan	Chelsea	5/06	30,800,000
	Xabi Alonso	Liverpool	Real Madrid	8/09	30,000,000
	Rio Ferdinand	Leeds	Manchester Utd	7/02	29,100,000
	Juan Sebastian Veron	Lazio	Manchester Utd	7/01	28,100,000
	Yaya Toure	Barcelona	Manchester City	7/10	28,000,000
F	Wayne Rooney	Everton	Manchester Utd	8/04	27,000,000
	Edin Dzeko	Wolfsburg	Manchester City	1/11	27,000,000
	Marc Overmars	Arsenal	Barcelona	7/00	25,000,000
	Carlos Tevez	Manchester Utd	Manchester City	7/09	25,000,000
	Emmanuel Adebayor	Arsenal	Manchester City	7/09	25,000,000
	Arjen Robben	Chelsea	Real Madrid	8/07	24,500,000
	Michael Essien	Lyon	Chelsea	8/05	24,400,000
	David Silva	Valencia	Manchester City	7/10	24,000,000
	James Milner	Aston Villa	Manchester City	8/10	24,000,000
	Mario Balotelli	Inter Milan	Manchester City	8/10	24,000,000
	Darren Bent	Sunderland	Aston Villa	1/11	24,000,000
	David Beckham	Manchester Utd	Real Madrid	7/03	23,300,000
	Didier Drogba	Marseille	Chelsea	7/04	23,200,000
	Luis Suarez	Ajax	Liverpool	1/11	22,700,000
	Nicolas Anelka	Arsenal	Real Madrid	8/99	22,300,000
	Fernando Torres	Atletico Madrid	Liverpool	7/07	22,000,000
	Joloen Lescott	Everton	Manchester City	8/09	22,000,000
	David Luiz	Benfica	Chelsea	1/11	21,300,000
	Shaun Wright-Phillips	Manchester City	Chelsea	7/05	21,000,000
	Lassana Diarra	Portsmouth	Real Madrid	12/08	20,000,000
	Alberto Aquilani	Roma	Liverpool	8/09	20,000,000
	Ricardo Carvalho	Porto	Chelsea	7/04	19,850,000
	Ruud van Nistelrooy	PSV Eindhoven	Manchester Utd	4/01	19,000,000
	Robbie Keane	Tottenham	Liverpool	7/08	19,000,000
	Michael Carrick	Tottenham	Manchester Utd	8/06	18,600,000
	Javier Mascherano	Media Sports	Liverpool	2/08	18,600,000
	Rio Ferdinand	West Ham	Leeds	11/00	18,000,000
	Anderson	Porto	Manchester Utd	7/07	18,000,000
	Jo	CSKA Moscow	Manchester City	6/08	18,000,000
	Yuri Zhirkov	CSKA Moscow	Chelsea	7/09	18,000,000
	Ramires	Benfica	Chelsea	8/10	18,000,000
B	David de Gea	Atletico Madrid	Manchester Utd	6/11	17,800,000
	Roque Santa Cruz	Blackburn	Manchester City	6/09	17,500,000
	Jose Reyes	Sevilla	Arsenal	1/04	17,400,000
	Javier Mascherano	Liverpool	Barcelona	8/10	17,250,000

Damien Duff	Blackburn	Chelsea	7/03	17,000,000
Owen Hargreaves	Bayern Munich	Manchester Utd	6/07	17,000,000
Glen Johnson	Portsmouth	Liverpool	6/09	17,000,000
Andrey Arshavin	Zenit St Petersburg	Arsenal	2/09	16,900,000
Hernan Crespo	Inter Milan	Chelsea	8/03	16,800,000
Claude Makelele	Real Madrid	Chelsea	9/03	16,600,000
Luka Modric	Dinamo Zagreb	Tottenham	6/08	16,600,000
Darren Bent	Charlton	Tottenham	6/07	16,500,000
Phil Jones	Blackburn	Manchester Utd	6/11	16,500,000
Jose Bosingwa	Porto	Chelsea	6/08	16,200,000
Michael Owen	Real Madrid	Newcastle	8/05	16,000,000
Thierry Henry	Arsenal	Barcelona	6/07	16,000,000
Aleksander Kolarov	Lazio	Chelsea	7/10	16,000,000
Robinho	Manchester City	AC Milan	8/10	16,000,000
Jordan Henderson	Sunderland	Liverpool	6/11	16,000,000
Ashley Young	Aston Villa	Manchester Utd	6/11	16,000,000
Adrian Mutu	Parma	Chelsea	8/03	15,800,000
Samir Nasri	Marseille	Arsenal	7/08	15,800,000
Jermain Defoe	Portsmouth	Tottenham	1/09	15,750,000
Antonio Valencia	Wigan	Manchester Utd	6/09	15,250,000
Alan Shearer	Blackburn	Newcastle	7/96	15,000,000
Jimmy F Hasselbaink	Atletico Madrid	Chelsea	6/00	15,000,000
Juan Sebastian Veron	Manchester Utd	Chelsea	8/03	15,000,000
Nicolas Anelka	Bolton	Chelsea	1/08	15,000,000
David Bentley	Blackburn	Tottenham	7/08	15,000,000
Marouane Fellaini	Standard Liege	Everton	9/08	15,000,000
Nigel de Jong	Hamburg	Manchester City	1/09	15,000,000
Kolo Toure	Arsenal	Manchester City	7/09	15,000,000
Djibril Cisse	Auxerre	Liverpool	7/04	14,000,000
Wilson Palacios	Wigan	Tottenham	1/09	14,000,000
Roman Pavlyuchenko	Spartak Moscow	Tottenham	8/08	14,000,000
Patrick Vieira	Arsenal	Juventus	7/05	13,700,000
Paulo Ferreira	Porto	Chelsea	7/04	13,500,000
Florent Malouda	Lyon	Chelsea	7/07	13,500,000
Jonathan Woodgate	Newcastle	Real Madrid	8/04	13,400,000
Jaap Stam	Manchester Utd	Lazio	8/01	13,300,000
Robbie Keane	Coventry	Inter Milan	7/00	13,000,000
Sylvain Wiltord	Bordeaux	Arsenal	8/00	13,000,000
Asamoah Gyan	Rennes	Sunderland	8/10	13,000,000
Louis Saha	Fulham	Manchester Utd	1/04	12,825,000
Sulley Muntari	Portsmouth	Inter Milan	7/08	12,700,000
Dwight Yorke	Aston Villa	Manchester Utd	8/98	12,600,000
Afonso Alves	Heerenveen	Middlesbrough	1/08	12,500,000
Cristiano Ronaldo	Sporting Lisbon	Manchester Utd	8/03	12,240,000
Juninho	Middlesbrough	Atletico Madrid	7/97	12,000,000
Jimmy F Hasselbaink	Leeds	Atletico Madrid	8/99	12,000,000
D Tore Andre Flo	Chelsea	Rangers	11/00	12,000,000
Robbie Keane	Inter Milan	Leeds	12/00	12,000,000
Gareth Barry	Aston Villa	Manchester City	6/09	12,000,000
Nicolas Anelka	Paris St Germain	Manchester City	5/02	12,000,000
Arjen Robben	PSV Eindhoven	Chelsea	4/04	12,000,000
Theo Walcott	Southampton	Arsenal	1/06	12,000,000
John Obi Mikel	Manchester Utd	Chelsea	6/06	12,000,000
Nani	Sporting Lisbon	Manchester Utd	7/07	12,000,000

Johan Elmander	Toulouse	Bolton	6/08	12,000,000
James Milner	Newcastle	Aston Villa	8/08	12,000,000
Craig Bellamy	West Ham	Manchester City	1/09	12,000,000
Wayne Bridge	Chelsea	Manchester City	1/09	12,000,000
Robbie Keane	Liverpool	Tottenham	2/09	12,000,000
Stewart Downing	Middlesbrough	Aston Villa	7/09	12,000,000
Alexander Hleb	Arsenal	Barcelona	7/08	11,800,000
Steve Marlet	Lyon	Fulham	8/01	11,500,000
Raul Meireles	Porto	Liverpool	8/10	11,500,000
Aiyegbeni Yakubu	Middlesbrough	Everton	8/07	11,250,000
Sergei Rebrov	Dynamo Kiev	Tottenham	5/00	11,000,000
Frank Lampard	West Ham	Chelsea	6/01	11,000,000
Robbie Fowler	Liverpool	Leeds	11/01	11,000,000
Ryan Babbel	Ajax	Liverpool	7/07	11,000,000
Dimitar Berbatov	Bayer Leverkusen	Tottenham	5/06	10,900,000
Jaap Stam	PSV Eindhoven	Manchester Utd	5/98	10,750,000
Xabi Alonso	Real Sociedad	Liverpool	8/04	10,700,000
Thierry Henry	Juventus	Arsenal	8/99	10,500,000
Laurent Robert	Paris St Germain	Newcastle	8/01	10,500,000
Andrew Johnson	Everton	Fulham	8/08	10,500,000
Ruud van Nistelrooy	Manchester Utd	Real Madrid	7/06	10,200,000
Dirk Kuyt	Feyenoord	Liverpool	8/06	10,200,000
Chris Sutton	Blackburn	Chelsea	7/99	10,000,000
Emile Heskey	Leicester	Liverpool	2/00	10,000,000
El Hadji Diouf	Lens	Liverpool	6/02	10,000,000
Scott Parker	Charlton	Chelsea	1/04	10,000,000
Alexander Hleb	Stuttgart	Arsenal	6/05	10,000,000
Obafemi Martins	Inter Milan	Newcastle	8/06	10,000,000
Shaun Wright-Phillips	Chelsea	Manchester City	8/08	10,000,000
Fabricio Coloccini	Dep La Coruna	Newcastle	8/08	10,000,000
Thomas Vermaelen	Ajax	Arsenal	6/09	10,000,000
Darren Bent	Tottenham	Sunderland	8/09	10,000,000
Diniyar Bilyaletdinov	Lokomotiv Moscow	Tottenham	7/09	10,000,000
Jerome Boateng	Hamburg	Manchester City	7/10	10,000,000

BRITISH RECORD TRANSFERS FROM FIRST £1,000 DEAL

Player	From	To	Date	£
Alf Common	Sunderland	Middlesbrough	2/1905	1,000
Syd Puddefoot	West Ham	Falkirk	2/22	5,000
Warney Cresswell	South Shields	Sunderland	3/22	5,500
Bob Kelly	Burnley	Sunderland	12/25	6,500
David Jack	Bolton	Arsenal	10/28	10,890
Bryn Jones	Wolves	Arsenal	8/38	14,500
Billy Steel	Morton	Derby	9/47	15,000
Tommy Lawton	Chelsea	Notts Co	11/47	20,000
Len Shackleton	Newcastle	Sunderland	2/48	20,500
Johnny Morris	Manchester Utd	Derby	2/49	24,000
Eddie Quigley	Sheffield Wed	Preston	12/49	26,500
Trevor Ford	Aston Villa	Sunderland	10/50	30,000
Jackie Sewell	Notts Co	Sheffield Wed	3/51	34,500
Eddie Firmani	Charlton	Sampdoria	7/55	35,000
John Charles	Leeds	Juventus	4/57	65,000
Denis Law	Manchester City	Torino	6/61	100,000
Denis Law	Torino	Manchester Utd	7/62	115,000

Allan Clarke	Fulham	Leicester	6/68	150,000
Allan Clarke	Leicester	Leeds	6/69	165,000
Martin Peters	West Ham	Tottenham	3/70	200,000
Alan Ball	Everton	Arsenal	12/71	220,000
David Nish	Leicester	Derby	8/72	250,000
Bob Latchford	Birmingham	Everton	2/74	350,000
Graeme Souness	Middlesbrough	Liverpool	1/78	352,000
Kevin Keegan	Liverpool	Hamburg	6/77	500,000
David Mills	Middlesbrough	WBA	1/79	516,000
Trevor Francis	Birmingham	Nottm Forest	2/79	1,180,000
Steve Daley	Wolves	Manchester City	9/79	1,450,000
Andy Gray	Aston Villa	Wolves	9/79	1,469,000
Bryan Robson	WBA	Manchester Utd	10/81	1,500,000
Ray Wilkins	Manchester Utd	AC Milan	5/84	1,500,000
Mark Hughes	Manchester Utd	Barcelona	5/86	2,300,000
Ian Rush	Liverpool	Juventus	6/87	3,200,000
Chris Waddle	Tottenham	Marseille	7/89	4,250,000
David Platt	Aston Villa	Bari	7/91	5,500,000
Paul Gascoigne	Tottenham	Lazio	6/92	5,500,000
Andy Cole	Newcastle	Manchester Utd	1/95	7,000,000
Dennis Bergkamp	Inter Milan	Arsenal	6/95	7,500,000
Stan Collymore	Nottm Forest	Liverpool	6/95	8,500,000
Alan Shearer	Blackburn	Newcastle	7/96	15,000,000
Nicolas Anelka	Arsenal	Real Madrid	8/99	22,500,000
Juan Sebastian Veron	Lazio	Manchester Utd	7/01	28,100,000
Rio Ferdinand	Leeds	Manchester Utd	7/02	29,100,000
Andriy Shevchenko	AC Milan	Chelsea	5/06	30,800,000
Robinho	Real Madrid	Manchester City	9/08	32,500,000
Cristiano Ronaldo	Manchester Utd	Real Madrid	7/09	80,000,000

• World's first £1m transfer: Guiseppe Savoldi, Bologna to Napoli, July 1975

TOP FOREIGN SIGNINGS

Player	From	To	Date	£
Kaka	AC Milan	Real Madrid	06/08	56,000,000
Zinedine Zidane	Juventus	Real Madrid	7/01	47,200,000
Zlatan Ibrahimovic	Inter Milan	Barcelona	7/09	40,000,000
Luis Figo	Barcelona	Real Madrid	7/00	37,200,000
Karim Benzema	Lyon	Real Madrid	7/09	35,800,000
Hernan Crespo	Parma	Lazio	7/00	35,000,000
David Villa	Valencia	Barcelona	5/10	34,000,000
Ronaldo	Inter Milan	Real Madrid	8/02	33,000,000
Gianluigi Buffon	Parma	Juventus	7/01	32,600,000
Christian Vieri	Lazio	Inter Milan	6/99	31,000,000
Alessandro Nesta	Lazio	AC Milan	8/02	30,200,000
Karim Benzema	Lyon	Real Madrid	7/08	30,000,000
Hernan Crespo	Lazio	Inter Milan	8/02	29,000,000
Gaizka Mendieta	Valencia	Lazio	7/01	28,500,000
Mario Gomez	Stuttgart	Bayern Munich	5/09	27,000,000
Pavel Nedved	Lazio	Juventus	7/01	25,000,000
Danny	Dynamo Moscow	Zenit St Petersburg	8/08	25,000,000
Rui Costa	Fiorentina	AC Milan	7/01	24,500,000
Daniel Alves	Sevilla	Barcelona	7/08	23,500,000
Gabriel Batistuta	Fiorentina	Roma	5/00	22,000,000
Lilian Thuram	Parma	Juventus	6/01	22,000,000

Dmytro Chygrynskiy	Shakhtar Donetsk	Barcelona	8/09	22,000,000
Diego	Werder Bremen	Juventus	5/09	22,000,000
Filippo Inzaghi	Juventus	AC Milan	7/01	21,700,000
Denilson	Sao Paulo	Real Betis	7/97	21,400,000
Claudio Lopez	Valencia	Lazio	7/00	21,200,000
Marcio Amoroso	Udinese	Parma	6/99	21,000,000
Ronaldinho	Paris St Germain	Barcelona	7/03	21,000,000
Lisandro Lopez	Porto	Lyon	7/09	20,600,000

WORLD RECORD FEE FOR TEENAGER
£27m for Wayne Rooney, aged 18, Everton to Manchester Utd, Aug 2004

WORLD RECORD FOR 16-YEAR-OLD
£12m for Theo Walcott, Southampton to Arsenal, Jan 2006

RECORD FEE BETWEEN SCOTTISH CLUBS
£4.4m for Scott Brown, Hibernian to Celtic, May 2007

RECORD CONFERENCE FEE
£260,000: George Boyd, Stevenage to Peterborough, Jan 2007

RECORD FEE BETWEEN NON-LEAGUE CLUBS
£275,000: Richard Brodie, York to Crawley, Aug 2010

MILESTONES OF SOCCER

1848: First code of rules compiled at Cambridge University.
1857: Sheffield FC, world's oldest football club, formed.
1862: Notts Co (oldest League club) formed.
1863: Football Association founded – their first rules of game agreed.
1871: FA Cup introduced.
1872: First official International: Scotland 0 England 0. Corner-kick introduced.
1873: Scottish FA formed; Scottish Cup introduced.
1874: Shinguards introduced.
1875: Crossbar introduced (replacing tape).
1876: FA of Wales formed.
1877: Welsh Cup introduced.
1878: Referee's whistle first used.
1880: Irish FA founded; Irish Cup introduced.
1883: Two-handed throw-in introduced.
1885: Record first-class score (Arbroath 36 Bon Accord 0 – Scottish Cup). Professionalism legalised.
1886: International Board formed.
1887: Record FA Cup score (Preston 26 Hyde 0).
1888: Football League founded by William McGregor. First matches on Sept 8.
1889: Preston win Cup and League (first club to complete Double).
1890: Scottish League and Irish League formed.
1891: Goal-nets introduced. Penalty-kick introduced.
1892: Inter-League games began. Football League Second Division formed.
1893: FA Amateur Cup launched.

1894: Southern League formed.

1895: FA Cup stolen from Birmingham shop window – never recovered.

1897: First Players' Union formed. Aston Villa win Cup and League.

1898: Promotion and relegation introduced.

1901: Maximum wage rule in force (£4 a week). Tottenham first professional club to take FA Cup south. First six-figure attendance (110,802) at FA Cup Final.

1902: Ibrox Park disaster (25 killed). Welsh League formed.

1904: FIFA founded (7 member countries).

1905: First £1,000 transfer (Alf Common, Sunderland to Middlesbrough).

1907: Players' Union revived.

1908: Transfer fee limit (£350) fixed in January and withdrawn in April.

1911: New FA Cup trophy – in use to 1991. Transfer deadline introduced.

1914: King George V first reigning monarch to attend FA Cup Final.

1916: Entertainment Tax introduced.

1919: League extended to 44 clubs.

1920: Third Division (South) formed.

1921: Third Division (North) formed.

1922: Scottish League (Div II) introduced.

1923: Beginning of football pools. First Wembley Cup Final.

1924: First International at Wembley (England 1 Scotland 1). Rule change allows goals to be scored direct from corner-kicks.

1925: New offside law.

1926: Huddersfield complete first League Championship hat-trick.

1927: First League match broadcast (radio): Arsenal v Sheffield United. First radio broadcast of Cup Final (winners Cardiff City). Charles Clegg, president of FA, becomes first knight of football.

1928: First £10,000 transfer – David Jack (Bolton to Arsenal). WR ('Dixie') Dean (Everton) creates League record – 60 goals in season. Britain withdraws from FIFA

1930: Uruguay first winners of World Cup.

1931: WBA win Cup and promotion.

1933: Players numbered for first time in Cup Final (1-22).

1934: Sir Frederick Wall retires as FA secretary; successor Stanley Rous. Death of Herbert Chapman (Arsenal manager).

1935: Arsenal equal Huddersfield's Championship hat-trick record. Official two-referee trials.

1936: Joe Payne's 10-goal League record (Luton 12 Bristol Rov 0).

1937: British record attendance: 149,547 at Scotland v England match.

1938: First live TV transmission of FA Cup Final. Football League 50th Jubilee. New pitch marking – arc on edge of penalty-area. Laws of Game re-drafted by Stanley Rous. Arsenal pay record £14,500 fee for Bryn Jones (Wolves).

1939: Compulsory numbering of players in Football League. First six-figure attendance for League match (Rangers v Celtic 118,567). All normal competitions suspended for duration of Second World War.

1945: Scottish League Cup introduced.

1946: British associations rejoin FIFA. Bolton disaster (33 killed) during FA Cup tie with Stoke. Walter Winterbottom appointed England's first director of coaching.

1947: Great Britain beat Rest of Europe 6-1 at Hampden Park, Glasgow. First £20,000 transfer – Tommy Lawton, Chelsea to Notts Co

1949: Stanley Rous, secretary FA, knighted. England's first home defeat outside British Champ. (0-2 v Eire).

1950: Football League extended from 88 to 92 clubs. World record crowd (203,500) at World Cup Final, Brazil v Uruguay, in Rio. Scotland's first home defeat by foreign team (0-1 v Austria).

1951: White ball comes into official use.

1952: Newcastle first club to win FA Cup at Wembley in successive seasons.

1953: England's first Wembley defeat by foreign opponents (3-6 v Hungary).

1954: Hungary beat England 7-1 in Budapest.

1955: First FA Cup match under floodlights (prelim round replay): Kidderminster v Brierley Hill Alliance.

1956: First FA Cup ties under floodlights in competition proper. First League match by floodlight (Portsmouth v Newcastle). Real Madrid win the first European Cup.

1957: Last full Football League programme on Christmas Day. Entertainment Tax withdrawn.

1958: Manchester United air crash at Munich. League re-structured into four divisions.

1960: Record transfer fee: £55,000 for Denis Law (Huddersfield to Manchester City). Wolves win Cup, miss Double and Championship hat-trick by one goal. For fifth time in ten years FA Cup Final team reduced to ten men by injury. FA recognise Sunday football. Football League Cup launched.

1961: Tottenham complete the first Championship–FA Cup double this century. Maximum wage (£20 a week) abolished in High Court challenge by George Eastham. First British £100-a-week wage paid (by Fulham to Johnny Haynes). First £100,000 British transfer – Denis Law, Manchester City to Torino. Sir Stanley Rous elected president of FIFA

1962: Manchester United raise record British transfer fee to £115,000 for Denis Law.

1963: FA Centenary. Season extended to end of May due to severe winter. First pools panel. English "retain and transfer" system ruled illegal in High Court test case.

1964: Rangers' second great hat-trick – Scottish Cup, League Cup and League. Football League and Scottish League guaranteed £500,000 a year in new fixtures copyright agreement with Pools. First televised 'Match of the Day' (BBC2): Liverpool 3 Arsenal 2.

1965: Bribes scandal – ten players jailed (and banned for life by FA) for match-fixing 1960-63. Stanley Matthews knighted in farewell season. Arthur Rowley (Shrewsbury) retires with record of 434 League goals. Substitutes allowed for injured players in Football League matches (one per team).

1966: England win World Cup (Wembley).

1967: Alf Ramsey, England manager, knighted; OBE for captain Bobby Moore. Celtic become first British team to win European Cup. First substitutes allowed in FA Cup Final (Tottenham v Chelsea) but not used. Football League permit loan transfers (two per club).

1968: First FA Cup Final televised live in colour (BBC2 – WBA v Everton). Manchester United first English club to win European Cup.

1970: FIFA/UEFA approve penalty shoot-out in deadlocked ties.

1971: Arsenal win League Championship and FA Cup.

1973: Football League introduce 3-up, 3-down promotion/relegation between Divisions 1, 2 and 3 and 4-up, 4-down between Divisions 3 and 4.

1974: First FA Cup ties played on Sunday. League football played on Sunday for first time. Last FA Amateur Cup Final. Joao Havelange (Brazil) succeeds Sir Stanley Rous as FIFA president.

1975: Scottish Premier Division introduced.

1976: Football League introduce goal difference (replacing goal average) and red/yellow cards.

1977: Liverpool achieve the double of League Championship and European Cup. Don Revie defects to United Arab Emirates when England manager – successor Ron Greenwood.

1978: Freedom of contract for players accepted by Football League. PFA lifts ban on foreign players in English football. Football League introduce Transfer Tribunal. Viv Anderson (Nottm Forest) first black player to win a full England cap. Willie Johnston (Scotland) sent home from World Cup Finals in Argentina after failing dope test.

1979: First all-British £500,000 transfer – David Mills, Middlesbrough to WBA. First British million pound transfer (Trevor Francis – Birmingham to Nottm Forest). Andy Gray moves from Aston Villa to Wolves for a record £1,469,000 fee.

1981: Tottenham win 100th FA Cup Final. Liverpool first British side to win European Cup three times. Three points for a win introduced by Football League. QPR install Football League's first artificial pitch. Death of Bill Shankly, manager–legend of Liverpool 1959–

74. Record British transfer – Bryan Robson (WBA to Manchester United), £1,500,000.

1982: Aston Villa become sixth consecutive English winners of European Cup. Tottenham retain FA Cup – first club to do so since Tottenham 1961 and 1962. Football League Cup becomes the (sponsored) Milk Cup.

1983: Liverpool complete League Championship–Milk Cup double for second year running. Manager Bob Paisley retires. Aberdeen first club to do Cup-Winners' Cup and domestic Cup double. Football League clubs vote to keep own match receipts. Football League sponsored by Canon, Japanese camera and business equipment manufacturers – 3-year agreement starting 1983–4. Football League agree two-year contract for live TV coverage of ten matches per season (5 Friday night, BBC, 5 Sunday afternoon, ITV).

1984: One FA Cup tie in rounds 3, 4, 5 and 6 shown live on TV (Friday or Sunday). Aberdeen take Scottish Cup for third successive season, win Scottish Championship, too. Tottenham win UEFA Cup on penalty shoot-out. Liverpool win European Cup on penalty shoot-out to complete unique treble with Milk Cup and League title (as well as Championship hat-trick). N Ireland win the final British Championship. France win European Championship – their first honour. FA National Soccer School opens at Lilleshall. Britain's biggest score this century: Stirling Alb 20 Selkirk 0 (Scottish Cup).

1985: Bradford City fire disaster – 56 killed. First £1m receipts from match in Britain (FA Cup Final). Kevin Moran (Manchester United) first player to be sent off in FA Cup Final. Celtic win 100th Scottish FA Cup Final. European Cup Final horror (Liverpool v Juventus, riot in Brussels) 39 die. UEFA ban all English clubs indefinitely from European competitions. No TV coverage at start of League season – first time since 1963 (resumption delayed until January 1986). Sept: first ground-sharing in League history – Charlton Athletic move from The Valley to Selhurst Park (Crystal Palace).

1986: Liverpool complete League and Cup double in player-manager Kenny Dalglish's first season in charge. Swindon (4th Div Champions) set League points record (102). League approve reduction of First Division to 20 clubs by 1988. Everton chairman Philip Carter elected president of Football League. Death of Sir Stanley Rous (91). 100th edition of News of the World Football Annual. League Cup sponsored for next three years by Littlewoods (£2m). Football League voting majority (for rule changes) reduced from three-quarters to two-thirds. Wales move HQ from Wrexham to Cardiff after 110 years. Two substitutes in FA Cup and League (Littlewoods) Cup. Two-season League/TV deal (£6.2m):- BBC and ITV each show seven live League matches per season, League Cup semi-finals and Final. Football League sponsored by Today newspaper. Luton first club to ban all visiting supporters; as sequel are themselves banned from League Cup. Oldham and Preston install artificial pitches, making four in Football League (following QPR and Luton).

1987: League introduce play-off matches to decide final promotion/relegation places in all divisions. Re-election abolished – bottom club in Div 4 replaced by winners of GM Vauxhall Conference. Two substitutes approved for Football League 1987–8. Red and yellow disciplinary cards (scrapped 1981) re-introduced by League and FA Football League sponsored by Barclays. First Div reduced to 21 clubs.

1988: Football League Centenary. First Division reduced to 20 clubs.

1989: Soccer gets £74m TV deal: £44m over 4 years, ITV; £30m over 5 years, BBC/ BSB. But it costs Philip Carter the League Presidency. Ted Croker retires as FA chief executive; successor Graham Kelly, from Football League. Hillsborough disaster: 95 die at FA Cup semi-final (Liverpool v Nottm Forest). Arsenal win closest-ever Championship with last kick. Peter Shilton sets England record with 109 caps.

1990: Nottm Forest win last Littlewoods Cup Final. Both FA Cup semi-finals played on Sunday and televised live. Play-off finals move to Wembley; Swindon win place in Div 1, then relegated back to Div 2 (breach of financial regulations) – Sunderland promoted instead. England reach World Cup semi-final in Italy and win FIFA Fair Play Award. Peter Shilton retires as England goalkeeper with 125 caps (world record). Graham Taylor (Aston Villa) succeeds Bobby Robson as England manager. International Board amend offside law (player 'level' no longer offside). FIFA make "professional foul!" a sending-off offence.

English clubs back in Europe (Manchester United and Aston Villa) after 5-year exile.

1991: First FA Cup semi-final at Wembley (Tottenham 3 Arsenal 1). Bert Millichip (FA chairman) and Philip Carter (Everton chairman) knighted. End of artificial pitches in Div 1 (Luton, Oldham). Scottish League reverts to 12-12-14 format (as in 1987–8). Penalty shoot-out introduced to decide FA Cup ties level after one replay.

1992: Introduction of fourth FA Cup (previous trophy withdrawn). FA launch Premier League (22 clubs). Football League reduced to three divisions (71 clubs). Record TV-sport deal: BSkyB/BBC to pay £304m for 5-year coverage of Premier League. ITV do £40m, 4-year deal with Football League. Channel 4 show Italian football live (Sundays). FIFA approve new back-pass rule (goalkeeper must not handle ball kicked to him by team-mate). New League of Wales formed. Record all-British transfer: £3.3m: Alan Shearer (Southampton to Blackburn). Charlton return to The Valley after 7-year absence.

1993: Barclays end 6-year sponsorship of Football League. For first time both FA Cup semi-finals at Wembley (Sat, Sun). Arsenal first club to complete League Cup/FA Cup double. Rangers pull off Scotland's domestic treble for fifth time. FA in record British sports sponsorship deal (£12m over 4 years) with brewers Bass for FA Carling Premiership, from Aug. Brian Clough retires after 18 years as Nottm Forest manager; as does Jim McLean (21 years manager of Dundee Utd). Football League agree 3-year, £3m sponsorship with Endsleigh Insurance. Premier League introduce squad numbers with players' names on shirts. Record British transfer: Duncan Ferguson, Dundee Utd to Rangers (£4m). Record English-club signing: Roy Keane, Nottm Forest to Manchester United (£3.75m). Graham Taylor resigns as England manager after World Cup exit (Nov). Death of Bobby Moore (51), England World Cup winning captain 1966.

1994: Death of Sir Matt Busby. Terry Venables appointed England coach. Manchester United complete the Double. Last artificial pitch in English football goes – Preston revert to grass, summer 1994. Bobby Charlton knighted. Scottish League format changes to four divisions of ten clubs. Record British transfer: Chris Sutton, Norwich to Blackburn (£5m). FA announce first sponsorship of FA Cup – Littlewoods Pools (4-year, £14m deal, plus £6m for Charity Shield). Death of Billy Wright.

1995: New record British transfer: Andy Cole, Newcastle to Manchester United (£7m). First England match abandoned through crowd trouble (v Republic of Ireland, Dublin). Blackburn Champions for first time since 1914. Premiership reduced to 20 clubs. British transfer record broken again: Stan Collymore, Nottm Forest to Liverpool (£8.5m). Starting season 1995–6, teams allowed to use 3 substitutes per match, not necessarily including a goalkeeper. European Court of Justice upholds Bosman ruling, barring transfer fees for players out of contract and removing limit on number of foreign players clubs can field.

1996: Death of Bob Paisley (77), ex-Liverpool, most successful manager in English Football. FA appoint Chelsea manager Glenn Hoddle to succeed Terry Venables as England coach after Euro 96. Manchester United first English club to achieve Double twice (and in 3 seasons). Football League completes £125m, 5-year TV deal with BSkyB starting 1996–7. England stage European Championship, reach semi-finals, lose on pens to tournament winners Germany. Keith Wiseman succeeds Sir Bert Millichip as FA Chairman. Linesmen become known as "referees' assistants". Coca-Cola Cup experiment with own disciplinary system (red, yellow cards). Alan Shearer football's first £15m player (Blackburn to Newcastle). Nigeria first African country to win Olympic soccer. Nationwide Building Society sponsor Football League in initial 3-year deal worth £5.25m Peter Shilton first player to make 1000 League appearances.

1997: Howard Wilkinson appointed English football's first technical director. England's first home defeat in World Cup (0-1 v Italy). Ruud Gullit (Chelsea) first foreign coach to win FA Cup. Rangers equal Celtic's record of 9 successive League titles. Manchester United win Premier League for fourth time in 5 seasons. New record World Cup score: Iran 17, Maldives 0 (qualifying round). Season 1997–8 starts Premiership's record £36m,

4-year sponsorship extension with brewers Bass (Carling).

1998: In French manager Arsene Wenger's second season at Highbury, Arsenal become second English club to complete the Double twice. Chelsea also win two trophies under new player-manager Gianluca Vialli (Coca-Cola Cup, Cup Winners' Cup). France win 16th World Cup competition. In breakaway from Scottish League, top ten clubs form new Premiership under SFA, starting season 1998–9. Football League celebrates its 100th season, 1998–9. New FA Cup sponsors – French insurance giants AXA (25m, 4-year deal). League Cup becomes Worthington Cup in £23m, 5-year contract with brewers Bass. Nationwide Building Society's sponsorship of Football League extended to season 2000–1.

1999: FA buy Wembley Stadium (£103m) for £320m, plan rebuilding (Aug 2000–March 2003) as new national stadium (Lottery Sports fund contributes £110m) Scotland's new Premier League takes 3-week mid-season break in January. Sky screen Oxford Utd v Sunderland (Div 1) as first pay-per-view match on TV. FA sack England coach Glenn Hoddle; Fulham's Kevin Keegan replaces him at £1m a year until 2003. Sir Alf Ramsey, England's World-Cup-winning manager, dies aged 79. With effect 1999, FA Cup Final to be decided on day (via penalties, if necessary). Hampden Park re-opens for Scottish Cup Final after £63m refit. Alex Ferguson knighted after Manchester United complete Premiership, FA Cup, European Cup treble. Starting season 1999–2000, UEFA increase Champions League from 24 to 32 clubs. End of Cup-Winners' Cup (merged into 121-club UEFA Cup). FA allow holders Manchester United to withdraw from FA Cup to participate in FIFA's inaugural World Club Championship in Brazil in January. Chelsea first British club to field an all-foreign line-up at Southampton (Prem). FA vote in favour of streamlined 14-man board of directors to replace its 92-member council.

2000: Scot Adam Crozier takes over as FA chief executive. Wales move to Cardiff's £125m Millennium Stadium (v Finland). Brent Council approve plans for new £475m Wembley Stadium (completion target spring 2003); demolition of old stadium to begin after England v Germany (World Cup qual.). Fulham Ladies become Britain's first female professional team. FA Premiership and Nationwide League to introduce (season 2000–01) rule whereby referees advance free-kick by 10 yards and caution player who shows dissent, delays kick or fails to retreat 10 yards. Scottish football increased to 42 League clubs in 2000–01 (12 in Premier League and 3 divisions of ten; Peterhead and Elgin elected from Highland League). France win European Championship – first time a major international tournament has been jointly hosted (Holland/ Belgium). England's £10m bid to stage 2006 World Cup fails; vote goes to Germany. England manager Kevin Keegan resigns after 1-0 World Cup defeat by Germany in Wembley's last International. Lazio's Swedish coach Sven-Goran Eriksson agrees to become England head coach.

2001: Scottish Premier League experiment with split into 5-game mini leagues (6 clubs in each) after 33 matches completed. New transfer system agreed by FIFA/UEFA is ratified. Barclaycard begin £48m, 3-year sponsorship of the Premiership, and Nationwide's contract with the Football League is extended by a further 3 years (£12m). ITV, after winning auction against BBC's Match of the Day, begin £183m, 3-season contract for highlights of Premiership matches; BSkyB's live coverage (66 matches per season) for next 3 years will cost £1.1bn. BBC and BSkyB pay £400m (3-year contract) for live coverage of FA Cup and England home matches. ITV and Ondigital pay £315m to screen Nationwide League and Worthington Cup matches. In new charter for referees, top men can earn up to £60,000 a season in Premiership. Real Madrid break world transfer record, buying Zinedine Zidane from Juventus for £47.2m. FA introduce prize money, round by round, in FA Cup.

2002: Scotland appoint their first foreign manager, Germany's former national coach Bertie Vogts replacing Craig Brown. Collapse of ITV Digital deal, with Football League owed £178m, threatens lower-division clubs. Arsenal complete Premiership/FA Cup Double for second time in 5 seasons, third time in all. Newcastle manager Bobby Robson knighted in Queen's Jubilee Honours. Brazil win World Cup for fifth time. New record British transfer and world record for defender, £29.1m Rio Ferdinand (Leeds to Manchester United). Transfer window introduced to British football. FA Charity Shield renamed FA Community Shield. After 2-year delay, demolition of Wembley Stadium begins. October: Adam Crozier, FA chief executive, resigns.

2003: FA Cup draw (from 4th Round) reverts to Monday lunchtime. Scottish Premier League decide to end mid-winter shut-down. Mark Palios appointed FA chief executive. For first time, two Football League clubs demoted (replaced by two from Conference). Ban lifted on loan transfers between Premiership clubs. July: David Beckham becomes record British export (Manchester United to Real Madrid, £23.3m). Biggest takeover in British football history – Russian oil magnate Roman Abramovich buys control of Chelsea for £150m Wimbledon leave rented home at Selhurst Park, become England's first franchised club in 68-mile move to Milton Keynes.

2004: Arsenal first club to win Premiership with unbeaten record and only the third in English football history to stay undefeated through League season. Trevor Brooking knighted in Queen's Birthday Honours. Wimbledon change name to Milton Keynes Dons. Greece beat hosts Portugal to win European Championship as biggest outsiders (80-1 at start) ever to succeed in major international tournament. New contracts – Premiership in £57m deal with Barclays, seasons 2004–07. Coca-Cola replace Nationwide as Football League sponsors (£15m over 3 years), rebranding Div 1 as Football League Championship, with 2nd and 3rd Divisions, becoming Leagues 1 and 2. After 3 years, BBC Match of the Day wins back Premiership highlights from ITV with 3-year, £105m contract (2004–07). All-time League record of 49 unbeaten Premiership matches set by Arsenal. Under new League rule, Wrexham forfeit 10 points for going into administration.

2005: Brian Barwick, controller of ITV Sport, becomes FA chief executive. Foreign managers take all major trophies for English clubs: Chelsea, in Centenary year, win Premiership (record 95 points) and League Cup in Jose Mourinho's first season; Arsene Wenger's Arsenal win FA Cup in Final's first penalty shoot-out; under new manager Rafael Benitez, Liverpool lift European Cup on penalties after trailing 0-3 in Champions League Final. Wigan, a League club only since 1978, promoted to Premiership. In new record British-club take-over, American tycoon Malcolm Glazer buys Manchester United for £790m Bury become the first club to score 1,000 goals in each of the four divisions. Tributes are paid world-wide to George Best, who dies aged 59.

2006: Steve Staunton succeeds Brian Kerr as Republic of Ireland manager. Chelsea post record losses of £140m Sven-Goran Eriksson agrees a settlement to step down as England coach. Steve McClaren replaces him. The Premier League announce a new 3-year TV deal worth £1.7 billion under which Sky lose their monopoly of coverage. Chelsea smash the British transfer record, paying £30.8m for Andriy Shevchenko. Italy win the World Cup on penalties. Aston Villa are taken over by American billionaire Randy Lerner. Clydesdale Bank replace Bank of Scotland as sponsor of the SPL. An Icelandic consortium buy West Ham.

2007: Michel Platini becomes the new president of UEFA. Walter Smith resigns as Scotland manager to return to Rangers and is replaced by Alex McLeish. American tycoons George Gillett and Tom Hicks finalise a £450m takeover of Liverpool. The new £800m Wembley Stadium is finally completed. The BBC and Sky lose TV rights for England's home matches and FA Cup ties to ITV and Setanta. World Cup-winner Alan Ball dies aged 61. Lawrie Sanchez resigns as Northern Ireland manager to take over at Fulham. Nigel Worthington succeeds him. Lord Stevens names five clubs in his final report into alleged transfer irregularities. Former Thai Prime Minister Thaksin Shinawatra becomes Manchester City's new owner. Steve McClaren is sacked after England fail to qualify for the European Championship Finals and is replaced by Fabio Capello. The Republic of Ireland's Steve Staunton also goes. Scotland's Alex McLeish resigns to become Birmingham manager.

2008: The Republic of Ireland follow England's lead in appointing an Italian coach – Giovanni

Trapattoni. George Burley leaves Southampton to become Scotland manager. Derby are taken over by an American sports and entertainment group in a deal worth around £50m. David Beckham wins his 100th England cap. Manchester United beat Chelsea in the first all-English Champions League Final. Spain beat Germany 1-0 in the European Championship Final. **Thaksin Shinawatra, who bought Manchester City for £81m in July 2007, agrees to sell the club to the Abu Dhabi United Group for a reported £200m. With their new-found wealth, City smash the British transfer record when signing Robinho from Real Madrid for £32.5m.** Cristiano Ronaldo is named European Footballer of the Year.

2009: Sky secure the rights to five of the six Premier League packages from 2010–13 with a bid of £1.6bn. Setanta keep the Saturday evening slot. Cristiano Ronaldo wins the World Footballer of the Year accolade. Reading's Steve Coppell reaches 1,000 games as a manager. David Beckham breaks Bobby Moore's record number of caps for an England outfield player with his 109th appearance. A British league record for not conceding a goal ends on 1,311 minutes for Manchester United's Edwin van der Sar. AC Milan's Kaka moves to Real Madrid for a world record fee of £56m. Nine days later, Manchester United agree to sell Cristiano Ronaldo to Real for £80m. Setanta goes into administration and ESPN takes over its live games.

Sir Bobby Robson dies aged 76 after a long battle with cancer. Shay Given and Kevin Kilbane win their 100th caps for the Republic of Ireland. The Premier League vote for clubs to have eight home-grown players in their squads. George Burley is sacked as Scotland manager and replaced by Craig Levein.

2010: Former Birmingham owners David Gold and David Sullivan take control of West Ham. John Terry is stripped of the England captaincy after revelations about his private life and replaced by Rio Ferdinand. nPower succeed Coca-Cola as sponsors of the Football League. Portsmouth become the first Premier League club to go into administration. Chelsea achieve the club's first League and FA Cup double. Lord Triesman resigns as chairman of the FA and of England's 2018 World Cup bid after making embarrassing remarks about bribes. Fabio Capello agrees to stay on as England manager for another two years. Robbie Keane wins his 100th Republic of Ireland cap. John Toshack resigns as Wales manager and is replaced by former captain Gary Speed. Liverpool are taken over by New England Sports Ventures. England are humiliated in the vote for the 2018 World Cup which goes to Russia, with the 2022 tournament awarded to Qatar. Sir Alex Ferguson, appointed in 1986, becomes Manchester United's longest-serving manager.

2011: Seven club managers are sacked in a week. The transfer record between Britsh clubs is broken twice in a day, with Liverpool buying Newcastle's Andy Carroll for £35m and selling Fernando Torres to Chelsea for £50m. Vauxhall replace Nationwide as sponsors of England and the other home nations. Businessman Craig Whyte takes over Rangers from Sir David Murray. West Ham beat Tottenham in the vote to move into the Olympic Stadium after the 2012 Games. John Terry is restored as England captain. Burnley's Graham Alexander makes his 1,000th career appearance. FIFA are rocked by bribery and corruption allegations.

FAMILY AFFAIR AT STOCKPORT

The Simpsons got the better of the Stimsons in a League Two match last season. Stockport, managed by Paul Simpson and with his son Jake in midfield, were 2-1 winners over Barnet, managed by Mark Stimson, who brought on his son Charlie as an attacking substitute in the second half.

FINAL WHISTLE – OBITUARIES 2010–11

JULY 2010

KEN BARNES, 81 served Manchester City in various roles for 46 years. He joined the club in 1950, played 283 games and was described by Denis Law as the country's best uncapped wing-half. The father of former City and England winger Peter Barnes, he played in two FA Cup Finals – the 3-1 defeat by Newcastle in 1955 followed a year later by victory over Birmingham by the same scoreline when goalkeeper Bert Trautmann carried on with a broken bone in his neck. He succeeded Roy Paul as captain and also had the distinction of scoring a hat-trick of penalties in a 6-2 victory over Everton. After a spell as player-manager of Wrexham in which they won promotion from Division Four, he returned to Maine Road to work as a coach, assistant manager, chief scout for two decades and finally part-time scout.

STAN MILBURN, 83, was part of one of the most famous football families – the youngest of four brothers who all played professionally. Cousin Jackie was Newcastle's legendary centre-forward and nephews Bobby and Jack Charlton won the World Cup with England. Stan, himself a full-back, made more than 600 appearances for Chesterfield, Leicester and Rochdale between 1947–64. He had a testimonial at each club and played for Rochdale in the 1962 League Cup Final which his side lost 4-0 on aggregate to Norwich. In addition to winning England B honours, he has a unique place in the game after 'sharing' an own goal with Leicester's Jack Froggatt against Chelsea in 1954 when the two players simultaneously booted the ball into their own net.

ALEX WILSON, 76, joined Portsmouth on leaving school in 1949, turned professional the following year and spent 18 years at the club, making 381 appearances. The full-back, won a Third Division Championship medal in 1962 and three years later scored an 86th minute equaliser on the last day of the season at Northampton to prevent the club being relegated. He finished his career at Chelmsford. Wilson won one Scotland cap, against Finland in a warm-up match for the 1954 Word Cup in Switzerland, but did not make their final squad.

DAVE KING, 69, scored twice on his debut for Hull against Sunderland and went on to net 25 goals in 67 appearances between 1959–62. The inside-forward then played non-league football and managed North Ferriby. He later returned to Hull to work with the club's youth players.

SHAUN MAWER, 50, worked his way through the youth team ranks at Grimsby and made his senior debut in September, 1977. The winger-turned-full-back was named the club's Young Player of the Year for that season, but a serious knee injury sustained against Gillingham in 1980 forced him to retire.

AUGUST 2010

ADAM STANSFIELD, 31, was diagnosed with cancer towards the end of the 2009–10 season in which he had continued to play a leading role in the revival of Exeter's Football League fortunes. An operation seemed to be successful and the striker joined his team-mates when they reported back for training for the new campaign. But his condition deteriorated and he died days after it got under way. The club announced that his No 9 shirt would be 'retired' for nine seasons and the team's match against Dagenham and Redbridge was postponed as a mark of respect. Stansfield helped Exeter win successive promotions from the Conference to League One and made 27 appearances, scoring seven goals, in the game's third tier in 2009–10 before the illness took hold. Previously, he shared Hereford's return to league football and scored for Yeovil in their FA Trophy Final win over Stevenage at Villa Park. He made more than 300 appearances for the three clubs.

BRIAN CLARK, 67, was a prolific marksman for Cardiff and Bristol City whose most famous goal gave the Welsh side victory over Real Madrid in a 1971 Cup-Winners' Cup quarter-final first leg at Ninian Park. Playing alongside John Toshack, he was top scorer for three successive seasons before moving to Bournemouth for £100,000. Clark returned for a second spell in 1975, sharing promotion to the Second Division, and scored a total of 91 goals in 240 appearances for the club. He began his career at Ashton Gate, playing alongside City legend John Atyeo for much of the time and scoring 83 goals in 195 league matches. One of them, in 1965, helped clinch promotion to Division Two. Clark also played for Huddersfield, Millwall and Newport.

GORDON BROWN, 81, was right-half in the York team that reached the semi-finals of the FA Cup in 1955, beating Tottenham 3-1 on the way and taking eventual winners Newcastle to a replay before losing 2-0 in front of a 58,000 crowd at Sunderland's Roker Park. Signed from Nottingham Forest, he made 351 appearances in eight years with the club.

KEN BOYES, 75, joined York in 1957 from Scarborough and spent nine years at the club, largely as understudy to centre-half Barry Jackson. He finished his playing career back at Scarborough, was coach to the FA Trophy-winning team of 1973 and was briefly caretaker-manager in 1974.

MARKUS LIEBHERR, 62, bought struggling Southampton in July 2009, took the club out of administration and targeted a return to the Premier League. They won the Johnstone's Paint Trophy at Wembley and finished one place away from the League One play-offs after a ten-point deduction. Hundreds of fans attended his funeral and the club's match against MK Dons was postponed as a mark of respect.

FRANCISCO VARALLO, 100, was the last surviving player from the first World Cup Final. He played for Argentina who lost 4-2 to the hosts Uruguay in 1930. His 194 goals for Boca Juniors remained a club record until it was broken in 2010 by Martin Palermo.

BOBBY MOSS, 58, scored within five minutes of his league debut for Leyton Orient against Watford in 1970. He moved to Colchester, but it was in non-league football that the inside-forward made his mark, notably with Wealdstone and Chelmsford. He also played for Barnet and Wimbledon.

LEN HARRIS, 73, made a club-record 691 appearances for Yeovil in their non-league days. The centre-half spent 14 years there from 1958 and played under six managers.

SEPTEMBER 2010

BOBBY SMITH, 77, scored 33 goals during Tottenham's Double-winning season of 1960–61 when they finished eight points clear of Sheffield Wednesday and beat Leicester 2-0 at Wembley. The barnstorming centre-forward was also on the mark during the 3-1 win over Burnley in the 1962 final and gained another medal when his side overcame holders Atletico Madrid in the 1963 European Cup-Winners' Cup after reaching that final by beating Rangers, Slovan Bratislava and OFK Belgrade. Smith, signed from Chelsea for £16,000, totalled 208 goals in 317 appearances for Tottenham, second only to team-mate Jimmy Greaves in the club's all-time list. He scored 13 times in 15 games for England and was considered by many unlucky not to have played in the 1962 World Cup Finals in Chile. After leaving White Hart Lane, he scored 20 goals in 33 games in Brighton's Division Four Championship-winning season of 1964–65.

JACKIE SINCLAIR, 67, was an influential figure in Newcastle's European Fairs Cup triumph of 1969, the club's last major trophy. He set up important goals for Wyn Davies and Pop Robson and scored himself in the semi-final against Rangers. Newcastle went on to beat Ujpest Dozsa 6-2 on aggregate in the two-leg final, having previously knocked out Feyenoord, Sporting Lisbon, Real Zaragoza and Setubal. Manager Joe Harvey paid £67,500 to take the winger from Leicester, where he scored 53 goals in 113 appearances. He started out under Jock Stein at Dunfermline in 1960, later returned for a second spell there and also played for Sheffield Wednesday, Chesterfield and Stenhousemuir. He won one Scottish cap, against Portugal in 1966.

JIM TOWERS, 76, scored a club-record 163 goals in 282 appearances during a decade with Brentford. He formed a successful partnership with George Francis, who netted 124, and they were known in the game as 'The Terrible Twins.' Both were sold to Queens Park Rangers in 1961 because of the club's precarious financial position. Towers later played for Millwall, Gillingham and Aldershot.

MALCOLM ALLISON, 83, was a flamboyant, larger-than-life coach and manager, who most notably inspired Manchester City to great success at home and abroad. Under Allison's shrewd coaching and the guiding hand of manager Joe Mercer, City won the Second Division Championship in 1966, the Division One title two years later, the FA Cup in 1969 and both the European Cup-Winners' Cup and League Cup in 1970. This success came to an end when Allison took over as manager and tried to rebuild the team around the maverick centre-forward Rodney Marsh. He left to take charge of Crystal Palace in 1973, returning to Maine Road for one further season in 1979–80. Allison, who developed a love of champagne, cigars and his 'lucky' fedora, had a second spell at Selhurst Park, managed Plymouth twice and was also in charge of Middlesbrough, Bristol Rovers, Bath and Yeovil. In Portugal, he led Sporting Lisbon to league and cup success; in Turkey, he spent time at Galatasaray. As a centre-half, Allison made more than 250 appearances for West Ham after playing for Charlton. His career was cut short by tuberculosis.

RONNIE CLAYTON, 76, was the type of footballer rarely seen in the modern game. He spent his entire career at one club and will be remembered as one of Blackburn's finest players, making 665 appearances between 1951–1969. The right-half was a key figure in the Second Division promotion-winning side of 1958 and captained Rovers in the FA Cup Final of 1960 when they lost 3-0 to Wolves. Clayton made 35 appearances for England, five of them as captain, and played in the 1958 World Cup Finals in Sweden. Another memorable occasion for him was marking Pele in front of a crowd of 159,000 at Brazil's Maracana Stadium a year later. After leaving Blackburn, he had a spell as player-manager of Morecambe in the Northern Premier League.

EDDIE BAILY, 85, proved to be one of the most influential figures in Tottenham's post-war history. The skilful, free-scoring inside-forward helped Arthur Rowe's push-and-run side win the Second Division Championship in 1949 and the First Division title a year later. He was rewarded with an England call-up against Spain in the 1950 World Cup Finals and went on to win nine caps. After 325 appearances and 69 goals for the club, Baily joined Port Vale, then helped Nottingham Forest back to top-flight football in 1956. He was a coach at Leyton Orient when they reached the First Division in 1962, before returning to White Hart Lane and spending 11 years as assistant manager to his former team-mate Bill Nicholson. During that time, Tottenham won the FA Cup, the League Cup twice and the UEFA Cup. After that he scouted for West Ham.

MEL HOPKINS, 75, made his debut for Tottenham in 1952 and went on to become one of the best full-backs in the country. He made 240 appearances for the club and won 34 caps for Wales, playing in the 1958 World Cup Finals in Sweden when they reached the quarter-finals before losing to a goal by the young Pele for Brazil. Hopkins, however, missed out on Tottenham's League and FA Cup Double in the 1960–61 season – the first in modern times – after breaking his jaw in an aerial challenge with Scotland's Ian St John at Hampden Park. Hopkins helped Brighton win the Fourth Division in 1965, later played for Bradford Park Avenue and scouted for Derby, managed by former White Hart Lane team-mate Dave Mackay. In 2003, he was given a merit award by the FA of Wales.

JOHN BENSON, 67, began a career spanning more than 40 years as player and manager by signing professional forms at Manchester City in 1958. The full-back went on to captain Torquay and also won promotion from the Fourth Division with Bournemouth, where he had two spells. He served Exeter, followed by Norwich under John Bond, turning down the manager's job at Carrow Road to become Bond's assistant at Manchester City. Benson took charge following Bond's departure in 1983, but inherited a team on the way to relegation and was replaced after four months at the helm by Billy McNeill. He later managed Burnley and Wigan and returned to Norwich to assist John Deehan and then Gary Megson.

IAN BUXTON, 72, was the last all-round sportsman to play football for Derby County and cricket for Derbyshire. He made notable debuts for both in 1959, scoring twice against Ipswich at the Baseball Ground and taking three Yorkshire wickets for five runs in six overs at Queen's Park.

The two clubs had an amicable and flexible agreement about Buxton's services when the seasons overlapped, until the arrival of Brian Clough and Peter Taylor. The inside-forward was sold to Luton after 145 league appearances and 41 goals, moved on to Notts County, then helped Port Vale to promotion from Division Four in 1970. Buxton, who captained Derbyshire from 1970–72, scored 11,803 runs and took 483 wickets in his first-class cricket career.

BOBBY CRAIG, 75, experienced the highs and lows of Scottish football. He made his debut for Celtic in their first home European tie, against Valencia in the Inter-Cities Fairs Cup in 1962. Five years later, he returned to his first club, Third Lanark, and played in their last game, against Dumbarton, before Lanark went out of business. In between, the inside-forward had spells with Sheffield Wednesday, Blackburn, St Johnstone and Oldham and played in Toronto and Johannesburg.

FREDERIC DARRAS, 44, joined Swindon from the Corsican club Bastia in the summer of 1996 and made 55 appearances before returning to his native France in January 1998 to play for Red Star. The full-back was also with Auxerre and Sochaux.

LES FELL, 89, was in the Charlton side beaten 4-1 by Derby in the 1946 FA Cup Final, having scored against Fulham, Wolves and Preston on the way to Wembley. The right-winger was not involved a year later when Charlton won the trophy by beating Burnley 1-0. Fell spent eight years at the club, mainly as a part-time professional, before joining Crystal Palace.

HARRY BALDWIN, 90, saved seven out of the nine penalties he faced for Brighton during the 1947–48 Third Division South season. The goalkeeper joined the club from West Bromwich Albion in 1939 and made 215 appearances during a 13-year stay. He guested for Northampton and Nottingham Forest during the War and later had a spell with Walsall.

COLIN LIPPIATT, 68, joined Yeovil as coach in November, 1997 after helping Woking win the FA Trophy three times. He took over from manager Graham Roberts when the former Tottenham defender left the following February and spent 18 months in charge. Then, he opted to keep his day job as a sales manager rather than be part of the club's move towards full-time status.

NORMAN CHRISTIE, 85, was a centre-half with Third Lanark, Stirling, Ayr, Brechin and Montrose. He spent ten seasons as Montrose manager, had a spell on the coaching staff at Dundee United and trained referees.

JOHNNY MATTHEWS, was a prominent player in the 1940s and 1950s in both the League of Ireland and the Irish League. The left-half turned centre-back also captained their representative teams. He started his career with Brideville and went on to serve St James's Gate, Dundalk, Ards, Glenavon and Transport.

NOVEMBER 2010
RON COCKERILL, 75, made 323 appearances during a decade with Grimsby and helped win promotion from Division Three in the 1961–62 season. The wing-half, who scored 33 goals and was nicknamed 'Cannonball' because of his powerful shooting, was previously at Huddersfield. His sons also played league football. Glenn made more than 700 appearances for seven clubs, including Southampton, Fulham and Sheffield United. John played for Grimsby and had three spells as caretaker-manager of the club.

JIM CRUICKSHANK, 69, made 528 appearances during 17 years with Hearts and is regarded by many as the club's finest-ever goalkeeper. Yet he was never able to win a major honour. His side lost to Kilmarnock in a League Championship decider in 1965, were beaten by Dunfermline and Rangers respectively in the Scottish Cup Finals of 1968 and 1976 and by Rangers in the 1961 League Cup Final replay. Cruickshank left Tynecastle under a cloud in 1977, released following relegation and a testimonial failing to materialise. He had a short spell with Dumbarton before retiring. After winning his first Scotland cap in 1964, he had to wait another six years for the second. There were six in all, including a goalless draw with England, watched by a crowd of more than 137,000 at Hampden in 1970.

JIM FARRY, 56, was one of the most influential figures in Scottish football for 20 years. He became the youngest-ever secretary of the SFL at the age of 24 and spent more than a decade in the post. In 1990, he succeeded Ernie Walker as secretary of the Scottish FA, became chief executive and oversaw the rebuilding of Hampden Park. Farry lost his job in 1999 after an independent commission found that he deliberately delayed the registration of the Portuguese player Jorge Cadete with Celtic.

RON SIMPSON, 76, made his debut on the left-wing for Huddersfield at 17 and played 118 times for the club, including the 7-6 defeat at Charlton in 1957 when Bill Shankly was manager. He went on to make 239 appearances, scoring 47 goals, for Sheffield United, including their Second Division promotion-winning season of 1960–61. Simpson helped home-town club Carlisle to the 1965 Third Division Championship, before ending his career with Queen of the South.

GEORGE NORTHCOTT, 75, was one of the last surviving members of Torquay's first-ever promotion season, achieved in 1959-60 with third place in Division Four. He was at the heart of the defence, with elder brother Tommy leading the attack, George made 172 appearances for the club between 1954-61 and later played for Cheltenham and Exeter.

KEN MONTGOMERY, 69, was chief football writer at the *Sunday Mirror* for 30 years and executive secretary of the Football Writers' Association from 1996 to the summer of 2010.

BILL 'BUSTER' COLLINS, 90, devoted nearly of half his life to Gillingham, first as a wing-half after joining the club from Luton in 1949 and later as reserve-team manager, in charge of the club's youth scheme and as first-team trainer. The Ulsterman was awarded two testimonial matches, against Arsenal and then against Manchester United to mark his retirement at 73

JOHNNY LOVE, 73, was a speedy left-winger who played more than 300 matches for Oxford United between 1955–63, most of them before the club's election to the Football League. The England youth international scored 45 goals, including one on his league debut against Darlington in 1962.

NORMAN SMITH, 90, was Coventry's oldest surviving player. He joined the club in 1938, but lost the best part of his career to the War. The centre-forward made only 15 appearances before moving to Millwall in 1947, then finishing his career with Bedworth, Rugby and Nuneaton.

FELIX MCGROGAN, 68, was one of four Dumbarton brothers who played senior football in Scotland in the 1960s. A winger with Raith and St Johnstone, he had his career ended after breaking his neck while playing for Durban in South Africa.

DECEMBER 2010

RALPH COATES, 64, enjoyed immediate success after Bill Nicholson paid Burnley £190,000 to bring him to Tottenham in 1971. In his first season, the left-winger helped them win the inaugural UEFA Cup with a 3-2 aggregate victory over Wolves in the two-leg final. A year later, he came off the bench to score the only goal in the League Cup Final against Norwich at Wembley. Then, he was in the side beaten 4-2 on aggregate by Feyenoord in the 1974 UEFA Cup Final. Coates finished his career with Leyton Orient, having made a total of 593 appearances and scored 68 goals. He won four England caps and made Alf Ramsey's initial squad for the 1970 World Cup.

AVI COHEN, 54, was the first Israeli to play in English football, joining Liverpool from Maccabi Tel-Aviv for £200,000 in 1979. He made only 24 appearances in two years at Anfield, but won the hearts of supporters when his goal against Aston Villa helped Bob Paisley's side clinch the First Division Championship. Earlier, the left-back had sliced an attempted clearance into his own net. Cohen had a spell at Rangers under former Liverpool team-mate Graeme Souness, coming off the bench in their 1987 League Cup Final win on penalties against Aberdeen. He also played briefly for Sheffield United, Huddersfield and Port Elizabeth in South Africa, before returning to Israel to finish his playing career and go into management. Cohen, who captained his country and played in 51 internationals, died after a motorcycle accident. His death was announced by son Tamir, a midfielder with Bolton.

BILL JONES, 89, won the First Division Championship with Liverpool in 1947 when a 2-1 victory at Molineux on the final day of the season enabled them to finish a point ahead of Manchester United and Wolves. He also played in the club's first Wembley FA Cup Final – a 2-0 defeat by Arsenal in 1950. The centre-half, who won two England caps, made 277 appearances in seven years at Anfield. His grandson, Rob, played for Liverpool in the 1990s. Supporters marked the death of Jones and Avi Cohen at Liverpool's match against Wolves.

ENZO BEARZOT, 83, was Italy's World Cup-winning coach in Spain in 1982. His team squeezed through the first group stage with three draws, then showed a marked improvement to beat Argentina and Brazil in the second phase, Poland in the semi-finals and West Germany 3-1 in the final. Bearzot was also in charge for the 1978 and 1986 World Cups. He was a centre-back with Inter Milan, Catania and Torino and played once for his country.

TERRY BRANSTON, 72, was an uncompromising centre-half in Northampton's fairytale rise from Division Four to Division One, with three promotions gained in five seasons, starting from 1960–61. He left for Luton in 1967 after two successive relegations, leading his new team to the Fourth Division Championship. Branston later played alongside Graham Taylor at Lincoln and narrowly lost out to Taylor for the manager's job there. He was two short of 500 appearances at the end of his career.

JEFF TAYLOR, 80, scored on his debut at centre-forward for Huddersfield against Chelsea in 1949, played alongside Johnny Haynes, Jimmy Hill and Bobby Robson at Fulham, then served Brentford before a serious injury ended his career. But although he spent a decade in the game, his main love was for music. The elder brother of Ken Taylor, who also played for Huddersfield and for Yorkshire and England at cricket, funded his studies with money earned from football. Later, he became one of the finest baritones of his generation, as well as an accomplished pianist, composer and teacher.

DALE ROBERTS, 24, was a goalkeeper who spent time in the academies of Sunderland and Middlesbrough, then came through the youth system at Nottingham Forest. He had loan spells with Eastwood, Alfreton and Rushden and Diamonds, before leaving Forest for Rushden in January 2009. He was voted Player of the Year for 2009–10 for England C, the national non-league team.

TED POLE, 88, made his debut for Ipswich on New Year's Day, 1947 and went on to play 40 first-team matches, scoring 13 goals. After four years at Portman Road, much of the time in the reserves, he had a season with Leyton Orient.

JEFF IRELAND, 76, was a right-winger who made three appearances for Tottenham in 1957–58. He joined Shrewsbury and later played and managed in non-league football.

JANUARY 2011
NAT LOFTHOUSE, 85, was a giant of the post-War game, a prodigious scorer for club and country whose nickname 'Lion of Vienna' reflected the way he played. He was given it after scoring against Austria in1952, despite being elbowed in the face, tackled from behind and brought down by the goalkeeper. The centre-forward netted 30 times in 33 internationals – a strike rate unrivalled by any England player – playing alongside the likes of Stanley Matthews and Tom Finney. He was a one-club man, making more than 500 appearances for home-town side Bolton and scoring 285 goals. In 1953, he led them in the legendary 1953 FA Cup Final, when Matthews inspired Blackpool to a 4-3 victory, and was named Footballer of the Year after scoring 30 goals in the First Division. Five years later, he scored both in Bolton's 2-0 Wembley win over Manchester United, the second when controversially bundling goalkeeper Harry Gregg and the ball into the net. Lofthouse retired with a knee injury in 1960 and went on to serve the club as manager, chief coach and chief scout. He was awarded an OBE, voted Bolton's greatest player and remained club president up to the time of his death.

RICHARD BUTCHER, 29, was a midfield player whose death from natural causes left his club, Macclesfield, in mourning for the second time in ten months. Their manager, Keith Alexander, died in March 2010. Butcher started his career as a trainee at Northampton and went on to serve Rushden & Diamonds, Kettering, Oldham, Peterborough, Notts County and Lincoln. While at Lincoln, he played in two losing Play-off Finals – against Bournemouth in 2003 and Southend two years later. He joined Macclesfield in the summer of 2010 and would have made more than nine appearances but for knee injuries. His last goal was against Bury on New Year's Day and his last appearance two days later against Rotherham. Butcher made 337 appearances and scored 45 goals in his career. Macclesfield retired the player's No 21 shirt as a mark of respect and their match against Burton was postponed.

NORMAN UPRICHARD, 82, won 18 caps for Northern Ireland and featured in their memorable 1958 World Cup campaign. He was No 2 goalkeeper to Harry Gregg, but when the Manchester United player was fog-bound for a crucial qualifier against Italy in Belfast, Uprichard came in for the 2-1 win which booked a place in the finals in Sweden. Then, when Gregg sustained an ankle injury, he came in for a play-off match against Czechoslovakia which the Irish won by the same scoreline to reach the quarter-finals. At club level, Uprichard served Glenavon and Distillery before signing for Arsenal, where he did not figure in the first team. He moved to Swindon, spent seven seasons with Portsmouth and later played for Southend.

BILL HOLDEN, 82, played 431 league games and scored 162 goals in a career which took him to five clubs. The centre-forward spent five years at Burnley from 1950 and made one appearance for England B against Scotland. He served Sunderland and Stockport, then helped Bury to the Third Division title in 1961 before finishing at Halifax.

WALLY HUGHES, 76, started on the ground staff at Liverpool and went on to play for Stockport, Sheffield United, Bradford Park Avenue and Southport. But it was as a coach with New Zealand that he made his mark, taking charge for 12 matches in 1977 and 1978 and helping lay the foundations for the team reaching the World Cup Finals in Spain in 1982. He also had a spell as coach of the Fiji national team.

ALEC BODEN, 85, played 158 games for Celtic and was their centre-half in the Scottish Cup Final win over Motherwell in 1951. He made another major contribution to the club as a scout after his playing career ended, spotting the potential in 1967 of the young Kenny Dalglish. Boden also served as coach and trainer.

FEBRUARY 2011

NEIL YOUNG, 66, was an elegant, free-scoring forward who played an integral role in Manchester City's success under Joe Mercer and Malcolm Allison. He formed a formidable attacking force with Francis Lee, Colin Bell and Mike Summerbee and was leading scorer with 19 goals in their First Division Championship-winning season of 1967–68. Two of those goals came on the final day of the season when City won 4-3 at Newcastle to finish two points ahead of Manchester United. In 1969, Young scored the only goal of the FA Cup Final against Leicester. The following season, he was on the mark twice in the Cup-Winners' Cup semi-final against Schalke, then opened the scoring and won the penalty, converted by Lee, as his team lifted the trophy by beating Gornik Zabrze 2-1 in Vienna. Young netted 107 times in 412 appearances for the club he joined as an apprentice in 1959, but unlike his team-mates never won England recognition. He spent two years with Preston before ending his career at Rochdale in 1974.

DEAN RICHARDS, 36, joined Tottenham from Southampton for £8.1m in 2001, a record fee for a player with no senior international caps. He was restricted to 81 appearances in four years at White Hart Lane, suffering dizzy spells and headaches and having to retire in 2005. The central-defender rejoined home-town club Bradford in 2007 as a part-time coach. He had started his playing career at Valley Parade, moving to Wolves for £1.85m in 1995 and then on to Southampton. Richards, who died after a long illness, was renowned for his skilful breaks out of defence and strength in the air. He had played for the England Under-21 team.

LES STUBBS, 81, was an important part of Chelsea's first League Championship-winning team in 1954–55. The inside-forward spent six seasons at Stamford Bridge, making 122 appearances and scoring 35 goals. He joined the club from Southend for £10,000 in 1952 and returned there to finish his career.

ERIC PARSONS, 87, was another member of Chelsea's successful team of 1954–55. The right-winger played in all 42 matches that season and scored 11 goals, two of them in the 3-0 home win over Sheffield Wednesday which clinched top spot. Nicknamed 'Rabbit' because of his speed, he joined the club from West Ham for a then record £23,000 and was there for six years before moving to Brentford. Parsons played nearly 500 senior games between 1946–60 and appeared twice for England B.

TONY KELLOW, 58, scored twice on his debut for Exeter in 1976, won promotion from Division Four in his first season and went on to become their all-time leading marksman with 150 goals in 377 appearances spread over three spells at the club. Blackpool paid £105,000 for his services in November, 1978 and received £65,000, another record, when he returned in March, 1980 after being unable to settle in Lancashire. Kellow scored a career-best 33 goals in the 1980–81 season, including an FA Cup hat-trick against Leicester. He went on to play for Plymouth, Swansea and Newport, but was back in 1985 to finish his career at St James Park.

TREVOR BAILEY, 87, made his name as an England cricket all-rounder, but he was also an accomplished amateur footballer who won two soccer Blues at Cambridge. He played for Leytonstone in the Isthmian League, then helped Walthamstow Avenue win the Amateur Cup in 1952. A year later Bailey, who could play centre-half or inside-forward, was in their side that drew 1-1 with Manchester United in a fourth round FA Cup tie at Old Trafford. United won the replay 5-2 at Highbury.

JIMMY FELL, 75, was once described as 'an up and coming Stanley Matthews' by commentator Kenneth Wolstenholme. It came after the left-winger's performance in a 7-0 win for his home-town team Grimsby over Bristol Rovers. He made 174 appearances and scored 35 goals between 1957–1961, before a then club-record £20,000 transfer to Everton. Fell moved on to Newcastle, where he was leading scorer with 16 goals in the 1962–63 season, and also played for Walsall, Lincoln and Boston.

NORMAN CORNER, 68, scored a hat-trick of headers for Lincoln in a 5-1 away win over Bradford Park Avenue in 1968. He helped Bradford City win promotion from the Fourth Division the following season and later played for Bradford PA, by then a non-league club. The centre-forward or centre-half had started his career with Hull.

GEORGE CLARKE, 89, was a half-back who spent seven seasons with Ipswich from 1946. He made 37 appearances for the first-team, spending most of his time in the reserves.

BILLY GALLIER, 78, was a youth team player at West Bromwich Albion, had a season at left-half with Walsall in 1955, then played for Tamworth and Hednesford.

MARCH 2011

TREVOR STORTON, 61, made 468 appearances for Chester between 1974–84. One of the highlights was scoring in a 3-0 win over Don Revie's Leeds on the way to the semi-finals of the League Cup, where his side lost to the eventual 1975 winners, Aston Villa. The centre-back, who helped Chester win promotion from Division Four that season, began his career at Tranmere, playing alongside brother Stan. Then, he had a spell under Bill Shankly at Liverpool, collecting, as a squad member, a UEFA Cup-winner's medal from the 3-2 aggregate victory over Borussia Moenchengladbach in the 1973 final. Storton was briefly Chester's assistant manager, served as manager of Bradford Park Avenue and at the time of his death was assistant manager of Halifax.

DANNY PATON, 75, enjoyed two big moments with Hearts in the 1962–63 season. He was in the side that won the Scottish League Cup by beating Kilmarnock 1-0 in the final. Later, he scored a hat-trick in a 4-0 victory over local rivals Hibernian at Easter Road. Paton, a right-winger or inside-forward, spent seven years at the club, before a knee injury forced him into non-league football with Oxford United, Bedford and Cambridge City. He also played for two American teams, Washington and Atlanta.

LES DAGGER, 77, played every match for Carlisle in the 1961–62 season when the club achieved a first-ever promotion, finishing fourth in Division Four. Dagger, a right-winger, had previously spent five years with Preston and went on to serve Southport, before finishing his career in non-league football.

LADISLAV NOVAK, 79, captained Czechoslovakia in the 1962 World Cup Final in Chile which Brazil won 3-1. The left-back also played in the 1954 and 1958 tournaments. He won 75 caps and led the team 71 times.

RAY MATTS, 70, spent 25 years as a *Daily Mail* sportswriter. He was the paper's Midlands football reporter and later its motor racing correspondent.

APRIL 2011

ALLAN BROWN, 84, was a Scottish international who played for Blackpool and twice managed the club. He signed in 1950, after winning the Scottish League Cup with East Fife, for £26,000, then the biggest fee received by a Scottish club. The inside-forward spent six years there, but missed two FA Cup Finals – against Newcastle in 1951 and Bolton in 1953 – through injury, the latter with a broken leg sustained when scoring against Arsenal in the quarter-finals. Brown made it to Wembley in 1959 with Luton, although there was more disappointment when his team lost 2-1 to Nottingham Forest. He also played for Portsmouth and, in their non-league days, Wigan. His 13 caps included games against Austria and Uruguay at the 1954 World Cup Finals in Switzerland. Brown managed Luton to the Division Four title in 1968 and also took charge of Torquay, Bury and Nottingham Forest, before two spells back at Blackpool (1976–78 and 1981–82), with a coaching stint in Kuwait in between.

BILLY GRAY, 83, was a key figure in Nottingham Forest's FA Cup success in 1959 when they beat Luton 2-1 in the final. He scored five goals on the way to Wembley, including one against non-league Tooting & Mitcham when his side looked to be going out in the third round. At the end of his playing and managerial career, he returned to the City Ground as groundsman during the Brian Clough era. The winger-turned-inside-forward, an England B international, started at Leyton Orient in 1947, moving on to Chelsea and Burnley before joining Forest and then completing 500 league appearances as Millwall's player-manager. Gray won successive promotions up to Division Two at The Den (1965 and 1966) and supervised a 59-match unbeaten home record. He went on to manage Brentford and Notts County.

EDDIE TURNBULL, 88, was an accomplished player for club and country, who went on to become an innovative manager. He spent 13 years with Hibernian, lining up in the greatest forward line in the history of Scottish football and winning titles in 1948, 1951 and 1952. Turnbull also played in two losing Scottish Cup Finals, 2-1 to Aberdeen in 1947 and 1-0 to Clyde in 1958. He scored 152 goals in 350 appearances, including the first one by a British player in the European Cup – against the German champions Rot-Weiss Essen in 1955. His eight appearances for Scotland included all three matches at the 1958 World Cup Finals, against Yugoslavia, Paraguay and France, at the age of 35. After retiring and coaching Queen's Park, he led Aberdeen to a 3-1 victory over Celtic in the 1970 Scottish Cup Final and to the league runners-up spot behind Celtic the following season. Then, he spent nearly a decade in charge back at Easter Road, where Hibs were twice runners-up and twice finished third. They beat Celtic 2-1 in the 1972 League Cup Final, took Rangers to a second Scottish Cup Final replay before losing 3-2 in 1979 – and in between scored a memorable 7-0 victory over neighbours Hearts at Tynecastle.

WILLIE O'NEILL, 70, made his debut for Celtic in a losing Scottish Cup Final replay against Dunfermline in 1961 and spent ten years at the club. Although largely a squad player, he made 32 appearances in the 1966–67 season in which they won the domestic Treble and beat Inter Milan 2-1 in the European Cup Final. The full-back was not among the 'Lisbon Lions,' but did play in the League Cup Final against Rangers. He moved to Carlisle for a £10,000 fee, but was forced to retire prematurely with an ankle injury in 1971.

JOHNNY MORRIS, 87, was part of Matt Busby's first great Manchester United team. They won the FA Cup in 1948, beating Blackpool 4-2 in the final, and were Championship runners-up in the first three post-War years. A rift with his manager led to a move to Derby in 1949 for a British transfer record fee of £24,000, followed by three England caps. The inside-forward scored on his debut against Norway (4-1) and netted twice against France (3-1), but never quite reached the heights expected of him. He helped Leicester to two Second Division title wins (1954 and 1957), then became player-manager at Corby and Kettering.

JIM BLAIR, 64, made only 11 appearances for Norwich, but two of them were in cup finals. He was a surprise inclusion in the team beaten 1-0 by Tottenham in the 1973 League Cup at Wembley. The inside-right also played in the second leg of the Texaco Cup Final which his side lost 4-2 on aggregate to Ipswich at the end of that season. Previously, Blair scored 72 goals in 169 games for St Mirren and had a brief spell with Hibernian. He ended his career with the Belgium club Mechelen.

RONNIE COYLE, 46, won Scottish First Division title medals with Raith in 1993 and 1995 and made over 300 appearances for the club. But the central-defender missed through injury, their biggest success – victory over Celtic in the 1994 League Cup Final. He died a fortnight after the club hosted a benefit match for him between the two teams from that final. Coyle began his career with Celtic and also played for Middlesbrough and Rochdale, before spending eight years at Raith. He also served Ayr, Albion, East Fife and Queen's Park, retiring in 1999.

JIMMY 'GUNBOAT' BRIGGS, 74, made 401 appearances for Dundee United between 1955–70 and was captain for their first European match – a 2-1 win over Barcelona in a Fairs Cup tie in the Nou Camp in 1966. Dundee won the return 2-0, before losing to Juventus in the next round. The full-back helped win promotion to the Scottish First Division in 1960 and was inducted into the club's Hall of Fame in 2008. He also played for Montrose and Keith.

DANNY FISZMAN, 66, shortly after selling his stake in Arsenal to American billionaire Stan Kroenke. The Swiss-based diamond dealer joined the board in 1992 and played a key role in the move from Highbury to the Emirates Stadium in 2006.

ALEC WEEKS, 84, set the standard for the way football is covered on television and was executive producer of BBC's *Match of the Day* from 1964–80. His earliest acclaim was for the presentation of England's World Cup triumph in 1966. Weeks, who also supervised the *Grandstand* programme, produced and usually directed eight World Cup tournaments, 16 European finals, and nine summer and winter Olympics. He retired on his 60th birthday in 1987.

MAY 2011

EDDIE LEWIS, 76, was one of Manchester United's original 'Busby Babes. He made 24 appearances in the early 1950s, but because of fierce competition for places was never a regular in the team. Lewis, who started as a centre-forward then switched to full-back, moved on to Preston, helped West Ham win the Second Division title in 1958 and Leyton Orient finish runners-up in 1962. He later coached teams in South Africa after emigrating.

FRANK UPTON, 76, joined Chelsea in 1961 from Derby for £15,000 and helped a young side back to the First Division two years later under Tommy Docherty. He was a strong-tackling wing-half, who moved up to centre-forward at the end of that season when a 7-0 win over Portsmouth clinched the runners-up spot with a goal average 0.4 better than that of Sunderland. Upton was also a League Cup winner, playing in the second leg of the 1965 final when Chelsea beat Leicester 3-2 on aggregate. He returned Derby and also served Northampton, Notts County and Workington. There was a second spell at Stamford Bridge in the late 1970s, before numerous other coaching roles in England and abroad.

SAMMY MCCRORY, 86, was a member of the Northern Ireland squad that reached the quarter-finals of the 1958 World Cup in Sweden. In his one international appearance the previous year, he scored their second goal in a 3-2 win over England at Wembley. The centre-forward started his career with Linfield, scoring in two successive Irish Cup-winning teams, then spent 17 years with Swansea, Ipswich, Plymouth, Southend and Cambridge. At Southend in 1957-58, he was top scorer in the last season of the old Third Division South with 31 goals.

EDDIE MORRISON, 63, scored on his debut for Kilmarnock against Hibernian in 1967 and was a prolific marksman for the next decade. The centre-forward chalked up 154 goals in 352 appearances, helping the club win promotion back to the top division in the 1973-74 season when he and Ian Fleming scored 58 between them. Morrison, who also played for home-town club Morton, returned to Rugby Park in 1984 and was manager for four years.

FRANKIE LANE, 62, was signed by Liverpool manager Bill Shankly in 1971 as understudy to goalkeeper Ray Clemence. He was restricted to reserve-team football during four years at Anfield, making only two appearances for the senior side. Lane eventually moved to Notts County and later played non-league football.

DOUGIE MCCRACKEN, 46, played for Ayr between 1985-1990 and was Ally MacLeod's first signing in his final spell as manager of the club. He also had spells with Dumbarton and East Fife. He was the stepfather of Scottish Formula One driver Paul di Resta.

ERNIE WALKER, 83, was a leading administrator in Scottish football at a time when the national team qualified for five successive World Cup Finals. After a lengthy 'apprenticeship' he served as SFA secretary for 13 years from 1977, receiving an OBE for services to the game. A strict disciplinarian, he cracked down on errant players and managers alike and was given the nickname 'Ayatollah.'

PHILIP GREENE, 90, was a leading Irish broadcaster and head of sport at the RTE station. He was best known for his football commentaries – the first in 1951 when the Republic played Argentina at Dalymount Park. He retired in 1985.

JUNE 2011

MIKE DOYLE, 64, was the most decorated player in Manchester City's history. An imposing defender, he won the League title, FA Cup, European Cup Winners' Cup and League Cup in the golden years under Joe Mercer and Malcolm Allison between 1968-70. He was later made captain and lifted the League Cup again in 1976. Doyle made 550 appearances for the club and won five England caps. He was named in Sir Alf Ramsey's provisional squad for the 1970 World Cup in Mexico, but chose to stay at home with his sick wife Cheryl. He later played for Stoke, Bolton and Rochdale.

GEORGE STEWART, 84, broke Accrington's scoring record in the 1955–56 season with 35 goals, including three hat-tricks. The centre-forward netted 136 in 182 matches before spells with Coventry and Carlisle.

BILL NAYLOR, 86, was a full-back-turned-centre-half who made 224 league appearances for Oldham between 1948–59. He joined from Huddersfield and later played for Stalybridge.

IDWAL ROBLING, 84, was a commentator who won a competition to be part of the BBC team for the 1970 World Cup in Mexico, beating Ian St John in the final round. He had been the Wales amateur captain and was part of Britain's squad at the 1952 Olympics in Helsinki.

JULY 2011

WILLIE FERNIE, 82, was hailed as Scotland's Stanley Matthews in a career which brought him honours for club and country. The inside-forward-cum-winger won the League and Cup double with Celtic in the 1953–54 season and shared one of the club's most celebrated triumphs – a 7-1 victory over Rangers in the League Cup Final four years later. After playing alongside Brian Clough at Middlesbrough, he returned for a second spell at the club, also served St Mirren and Alloa and gained two promotions as Kilmarnock manager. Fernie won 12 Scotland caps and played in the 1954 and 1958 World Cup Finals.

RECORDS SECTION

INDEX

GOALSCORING

(†Football League pre-1992–93)

Highest: Arbroath 36 Bon Accord (Aberdeen) 0 in Scottish Cup 1, Sep 12, 1885. On same day, also in Scottish Cup 1, Dundee Harp beat Aberdeen Rov 35-0.

Internationals: France 0 England 15 in Paris, 1906 (Amateur); Ireland 0 England 13 in Belfast Feb 18, 1882 (record in UK); England 9 Scotland 3 at Wembley, Apr 15, 1961; Biggest England win at Wembley: 9-0 v Luxembourg (Euro Champ), Dec 15, 1982.

Other record wins: Scotland: 11-0 v Ireland (Glasgow, Feb 23, 1901); **Northern Ireland:** 7-0 v Wales (Belfast, Feb 1, 1930); **Wales:** 11-0 v Ireland (Wrexham, Mar 3, 1888); **Rep of Ireland:** 8-0 v Malta (Euro Champ, Dublin, Nov 16, 1983).

Record international defeats: England: 1-7 v Hungary (Budapest, May 23, 1954); **Scotland:** 3-9 v England (Wembley, Apr 15, 1961); **Ireland:** 0-13 v England (Belfast, Feb 18, 1882); **Wales:** 0-9 v Scotland (Glasgow, Mar 23, 1878); **Rep of Ireland:** 0-7 v Brazil (Uberlandia, May 27, 1982).

World Cup: Qualifying round – Australia 31 American Samoa 0, world record international score (Apr 11, 2001); Australia 22 Tonga 0 (Apr 9, 2001); Iran 19 Guam 0 (Nov 25, 2000); Maldives 0 Iran 17 (Jun 2, 1997). **Finals – highest scores:** Hungary 10 El Salvador 1 (Spain, Jun 15, 1982); Hungary 9 S Korea 0 (Switzerland, Jun 17, 1954); Yugoslavia 9 Zaire 0 (W Germany, Jun 18, 1974).

European Championship: Qualifying round – highest scorers: San Marino 0 Germany 13 (Serravalle, Sep 6, 2006). **Finals – highest score:** Holland 6 Yugoslavia 1 (quarter-final, Rotterdam, Jun 25, 2000).

FA Cup: Preston 26 Hyde 0 1st round, Oct 15, 1887.

League Cup: West Ham 10 Bury 0 (2nd round, 2nd leg, Oct 25, 1983); Liverpool 10 Fulham 0 (2nd round, 1st leg, Sep 23, 1986). **Record aggregates:** Liverpool 13 Fulham 2 (10-0h, 3-2a), Sep 23, Oct 7, 1986; West Ham 12 Bury 1 (2-1a, 10-0h), Oct 4, 25, 1983; Liverpool 11 Exeter 0 (5-0h, 6-0a), Oct 7, 28, 1981.

Premier League (beginning 1992–93): Manchester Utd 9 Ipswich 0, Mar 4, 1995. Tottenham 9 Wigan 1, Nov 22, 2009. **Record away win:** Nottm Forest 1 Manchester Utd 8 Feb 6, 1999.

Highest aggregate scores in Premier League –11: Portsmouth 7 Reading 4, Sep 29, 2007; **10:** Tottenham 6 Reading 4, Dec 29, 2007; Tottenham 9 Wigan 1, Nov 22, 2009; **9:** Norwich 4 Southampton 5, Apr 9, 1994; Manchester Utd 9 Ipswich 0, Mar 4, 1995; Southampton 6 Manchester Utd 3, Oct 26, 1996; Blackburn 7 Sheffield Wed 2, Aug 25, 1997; Nottm Forest 1 Manchester Utd 8 Feb 6, 1999; Tottenham 7 Southampton 2, Mar 11, 2000; Tottenham 4 Arsenal 5, Nov 13, 2004; Middlesbrough 8 Manchester City 1, May 11, 2008; Chelsea 7 Sunderland 2, Jan 16, 2010.

†Football League (First Division): Aston Villa 12 Accrington 2, Mar 12, 1892; Tottenham 10 Everton 4, Oct 11, 1958 (highest Div 1 aggregate that century); WBA 12 Darwen 0, Apr 4, 1892; Nottm Forest 12 Leicester Fosse 0, Apr 21, 1909. **Record away win:** Newcastle 1 Sunderland 9, Dec 5, 1908; Cardiff 1 Wolves 9, Sep 3, 1955; Wolves 0 WBA 8, Dec 27, 1893.

New First Division (beginning 1992–93): Bolton 7 Swindon 0, Mar 8, 1997; Sunderland 7 Oxford Utd 0, Sep 19, 1998. **Record away win:** Stoke 0 Birmingham 7, Jan 10, 1998; Oxford Utd 0 Birmingham 7, Dec 12, 1998.

Record aggregate: Grimsby 6 Burnley 5, Oct 29, 2002; Burnley 4 Watford 7, Apr 5, 2003.

Championship (beginning 2004–05): WBA 7 Barnsley 0, May 6, 2007.

Record agregate: Leeds 4 Preston 6, Sep 29, 2010.

†**Second Division:** Manchester City 11 Lincoln 3, Mar 23, 1895; Newcastle 13 Newport Co 0, Oct 5, 1946; Small Heath 12 Walsall Town Swifts 0, Dec 17, 1892; Darwen 12 Walsall 0, Dec 26, 1896; Small Heath 12 Doncaster 0, Apr 11, 1903. **Record away win:** *Burslem Port Vale 0 Sheffield Utd 10, Dec 10, 1892.

New Second Division (beginning 1992–93): Hartlepool 1 Plymouth Argyle 8, May 7, 1994; Hartlepool 8 Grimsby 1, Sep 12, 2003.

New League 1 (beginning 2004–05): Norwich 1 Colchester 7, Aug 8, 2009; Huddersfield 7 Brighton 1, Aug 18, 2009; Nottm Forest 7 Swindon 1, Feb 25, 2006; Swansea 7 Bristol City 1, Sep 10, 2005.

Record aggregate: Peterborough 5 Swindon 4, Oct 16, 2010.

†**Third Division:** Gillingham 10 Chesterfield 0, Sep 5, 1987; Tranmere 9 Accrington 0, Apr 18, 1959; Brighton 9 Southend 1, Nov 22, 1965; Brentford 9 Wrexham 0, Oct 15, 1963. **Record away win:** Halifax 0 Fulham 8, Sep 16, 1969.

New Third Division (beginning 1992–93): Barnet 1 Peterborough 9, Sep 5, 1998.

New League 2 (beginning 2004–05): Crewe 8 Cheltenham 1, Apr 2, 2011.

Record aggregate: Accrington 2 Gillingham 4, Oct 2, 2010.

†**Third Division (North):** Stockport 13 Halifax 0 (still joint biggest win in Football League – see Div 2) Jan 6, 1934; Tranmere 13 Oldham 4, Dec 26, 1935. (17 is highest Football League aggregate score). **Record away win:** Accrington 0 Barnsley 9, Feb 3, 1934.

†**Third Division (South):** Luton 12 Bristol Rov 0, Apr 13, 1936; Bristol City 9 Gillingham 4, Jan 15, 1927; Gillingham 9 Exeter 4, Jan 7, 1951. **Record away win:** Northampton 0 Walsall 8, Apr 8, 1947.

†**Fourth Division:** Oldham 11 Southport 0, Dec 26, 1962; Hartlepool 10 Barrow 1, Apr 4, 1959; Wrexham 10 Hartlepool 1, Mar 3, 1962. **Record away win:** Crewe 1 Rotherham 8 *Crewe 1, 1973.

Scottish Premier – Highest aggregate: 12: Motherwell 6 Hibernian 6, May 5, 2010; **11:** Celtic 8 Hamilton 3, Jan 3, 1987; Motherwell 5 Aberdeen 6, Oct 20, 1999. **Other highest team scores:** Aberdeen 8 Motherwell 0 (Mar 26, 1979); Hamilton 0 Celtic 8 (Nov 5, 1988); Celtic 9 Aberdeen 0 (Nov 6, 2010).

Scottish League Div 1: Celtic 11 Dundee 0, Oct 26, 1895. **Record away win:** Hibs 11 *Airdrie 1, Oct 24, 1959.

Scottish League Div 2: Airdrieonians 15 Dundee Wanderers 1, Dec 1, 1894 (biggest win in history of League football in Britain).

Record modern Scottish League aggregate: 12 – Brechin 5 Cowdenbeath 7, Div 2, Jan 18, 2003.

Record British score since 1900: Stirling 20 Selkirk 0 (Scottish Cup 1, Dec 8, 1984). Winger Davie Thompson (7 goals) was one of 9 Stirling players to score.

LEAGUE GOALS – BEST IN SEASON (Before restructure in 1992)

Div		Goals	Games
1	WR (Dixie) Dean, Everton, 1927–28	60	39
2	George Camsell, Middlesbrough, 1926–27	59	37
3(S)	Joe Payne, Luton, 1936–37	55	39
3(N)	Ted Harston, Mansfield, 1936–37	55	41
3	Derek Reeves, Southampton, 1959–60	39	46
4	Terry Bly, Peterborough, 1960–61	52	46

(Since restructure in 1992)

Div		Goals	Games
1	Guy Whittingham, Portsmouth, 1992–93	42	46

| 2 | Jimmy Quinn, Reading, 1993–94 | 35 | 46 |
| 3 | Andy Morrell, Wrexham, 2002–03 | 34 | 45 |

Premier League – BEST IN SEASON
Andy Cole **34 goals** (Newcastle – 40 games, 1993–94); Alan Shearer **34 goals** (Blackburn – 42 games, 1994–95).

FOOTBALL LEAGUE – BEST MATCH HAULS
(Before restructure in 1992)

Div	Goals	
1	Ted Drake (Arsenal), away to Aston Villa, Dec 14, 1935	7
	James Ross (Preston) v Stoke, Oct 6, 1888	7
2	*Neville (Tim) Coleman (Stoke) v Lincoln, Feb 23, 1957	7
	Tommy Briggs (Blackburn) v Bristol Rov, Feb 5, 1955	7
3(S)	Joe Payne (Luton) v Bristol Rov, Apr 13, 1936	10
3(N)	Robert ('Bunny') Bell (Tranmere) v Oldham, Dec 26, 1935	
	he also missed a penalty	9
3	Barrie Thomas (Scunthorpe) v Luton, Apr 24, 1965	5
	Keith East (Swindon) v Mansfield, Nov 20, 1965	5
	Steve Earle (Fulham) v Halifax, Sep 16, 1969	5
	Alf Wood (Shrewsbury) v Blackburn, Oct 2, 1971	5
	Tony Caldwell (Bolton) v Walsall, Sep 10, 1983	5
	Andy Jones (Port Vale) v Newport Co., May 4, 1987	5
4	Bert Lister (Oldham) v Southport, Dec 26, 1962	6
	*Scored from the wing	

(Since restructure in 1992)

Div	Goals
1	**4 in match** – John Durnin (Oxford Utd v Luton, 1992–93); Guy Whittingham (Portsmouth v Bristol Rov 1992–3); Craig Russell (Sunderland v Millwall, 1995–6); David Connolly (Wolves at Bristol City 1998–99); Darren Byfield (Rotherham at Millwall, 2002–03); David Connolly (Wimbledon at Bradford City, 2002–03); Marlon Harewood (Nottm Forest v Stoke, 2002–03); Michael Chopra (Watford at Burnley, 2002–03); Robert Earnshaw (Cardiff v Gillingham, 2003–04).
2	**5 in match** – Paul Barnes (Burnley v Stockport, 1996–97); Robert Taylor (all 5, Gillingham at Burnley, 1998–99); Lee Jones (all 5, Wrexham v Cambridge Utd, 2001–02).
3	**5 in match** – Tony Naylor (Crewe v Colchester, 1992–93); Steve Butler (Cambridge Utd v Exeter, 1993–4); Guiliano Grazioli (Peterborough at Barnet, 1998–99).
Lge 1	**5 in match** – Juan Ugarte (Wrexham at Hartlepool, 2004–05).

PREMIER LEAGUE – BEST MATCH HAULS
5 goals in match: Andy Cole (Manchester Utd v Ipswich, Mar 4, 1995); Alan Shearer (Newcastle v Sheffield Wed, Sep 19, 1999); Jermain Defoe (Tottenham v Wigan, Nov 22, 2009); Dimitar Berbatov (Manchester Utd v Blackburn, Nov 27, 2010).

SCOTTISH LEAGUE

Div		Goals
Prem	Kris Boyd (Rangers) v Dundee Utd, Dec 30, 2009	5
	Kris Boyd (Kilmarnock) v Dundee Utd, Sep 25, 2004	5
	Kenny Miller (Rangers) v St Mirren, Nov 4, 2000	5
	Marco Negri (Rangers) v Dundee Utd, Aug. 23, 1997	5
	Paul Sturrock (Dundee Utd) v Morton, Nov 17, 1984	5
1	Jimmy McGrory (Celtic) v Dunfermline, Jan 14, 1928	8

1	Owen McNally (Arthurlie) v Armadale, Oct 1, 1927	8
2	Jim Dyet (King's Park) v Forfar, Jan 2, 1930,...	
	on his debut for the club	8
2	John Calder (Morton) v Raith, Apr 18, 1936	8
2	Norman Haywood (Raith) v Brechin, Aug. 20, 1937	8

SCOTTISH LEAGUE – BEST IN SEASON

Prem	Brian McClair (Celtic, 1986–87) 35	
	Henrik Larsson (Celtic, 2000–01)..	35
1	William McFadyen (Motherwell, 1931–32)	53
2	*Jimmy Smith (Ayr, 1927–28 – 38 appearances).....................................	66
	(*British record)	

CUP FOOTBALL

Scottish Cup: John Petrie (Arbroath) v Bon Accord, at Arbroath, 1st round,
Sep 12, 1885 — 13

FA Cup: Ted MacDougall (Bournemouth) v Margate, 1st round, Nov 20,1971 — 9

FA Cup Final: Billy Townley (Blackburn) v Sheffield Wed, at Kennington
Oval, 1890; Jimmy Logan (Notts Co) v Bolton, at Everton, 1894;
Stan Mortensen (Blackpool) v Bolton, at Wembley, 1953 — 3

League Cup: Frank Bunn (Oldham) v Scarborough (3rd round), Oct 25, 1989 — 6

Scottish League Cup: Jim Fraser (Ayr) v Dumbarton, Aug. 13, 1952;
Jim Forrest (Rangers) v Stirling Albion, Aug. 17, 1966 — 5

Scottish Cup: Most goals in match since war: 10 by **Gerry Baker** (St Mirren) in 15-0 win (1st
round) v Glasgow Univ, Jan 30, 1960; 9 by his brother **Joe Baker** (Hibernian) in 15-1 win
(2nd round) v Peebles, Feb 11, 1961.

AGGREGATE LEAGUE SCORING RECORDS

	Goals
*Arthur Rowley (1947–65, WBA, Fulham, Leicester, Shrewsbury)	434
†Jimmy McGrory (1922–38, Celtic, Clydebank)	410
Hughie Gallacher (1921–39, Airdrieonians, Newcastle, Chelsea, Derby,	
Notts Co, Grimsby, Gateshead)	387
William ('Dixie') Dean (1923–37, Tranmere, Everton, Notts Co)	379
Hugh Ferguson (1916–30, Motherwell, Cardiff, Dundee)	362
● Jimmy Greaves (1957–71, Chelsea, Tottenham, West Ham)	357
Steve Bloomer (1892–1914, Derby, Middlesbrough, Derby)	352
George Camsell (1923–39, Durham City, Middlesbrough)	348
Dave Halliday (1920–35, St Mirren, Dundee, Sunderland, Arsenal,	
Manchester City, Clapton Orient)	338
John Aldridge (1979–98, Newport, Oxford Utd, Liverpool, Tranmere)	329
John Atyeo (1951–66, Bristol City)	315
Joe Smith (1908–29, Bolton, Stockport)	315
Victor Watson (1920–36, West Ham, Southampton)	312
Harry Johnson (1919–36, Sheffield Utd, Mansfield)	309
Bob McPhail (1923–1939, Airdrie, Rangers)	306

(*Rowley scored 4 for WBA, 27 for Fulham, 251 for Leicester, 152 for Shrewsbury.
●Greaves's 357 is record top-division total (he also scored 9 League goals for AC Milan).
Aldridge also scored 33 League goals for Real Sociedad. †**McGrory** scored 397 for Celtic, 13
for Clydebank.)

Most League goals for one club: 349 – Dixie Dean (Everton 1925–37); **326–George Camsell**
(Middlesbrough 1925–39); **315 –John Atyeo** (Bristol City 1951–66); **306 – Vic Watson**
(West Ham 1920–35); **291 – Steve Bloomer** (Derby 1892–1906, 1910–14); **259 – Arthur
Chandler** (Leicester 1923–35); **255 – Nat Lofthouse** (Bolton 1946–61); **251 – Arthur Rowley**
(Leicester 1950–58).

More than 500 Goals: Jimmy McGrory (Celtic, Clydebank and Scotland) scored a total of **550** goals in his first-class career (1922–38).

More than 1,000 goals: Brazil's **Pele** is reputedly the game's all-time highest scorer with **1,282** goals in 1,365 matches (1956–77), but many of them were scored in friendlies for his club, Santos. He scored his 1,000th goal, a penalty, against Vasco da Gama in the Maracana Stadium, Rio, on Nov 19, 1969. ● Pele (born Oct 23, 1940) played regularly for Santos from the age of 16. During his career, he was sent off only once. He played 95 'A' internationals for Brazil and in their World Cup-winning teams in 1958 and 1970. † Pele (Edson Arantes do Nascimento) was subsequently Brazil's Minister for Sport. He never played at Wembley, apart from being filmed there scoring a goal for a commercial. Aged 57, Pele received an 'honorary knighthood' (Knight Commander of the British Empire) from the Queen at Buckingham Palace on Dec 3, 1997.

Romario (retired Apr, 2008, aged 42) scored more than 1,000 goals for Vasco da Gama, Barcelona, PSV Eindhoven, Valencia and Brazil (56 in 73 internationals).

MOST LEAGUE GOALS IN SEASON: DEAN'S 60

WR ('Dixie') Dean, Everton centre-forward, created a League scoring record in 1927–28 with 60 in 39 First Division matches. He also scored three in FA Cup ties, and 19 in representative games, totalling 82 for the season.

George Camsell, of Middlesbrough, previously held the record with 59 goals in 37 Second Division matches in 1926–27, his total for the season being 75.

SHEARER'S RECORD 'FIRST'

Alan Shearer (Blackburn) is the only player to score more than 30 top-division goals in 3 successive seasons since the War: 31 in 1993–94, 34 in 1994–95, 31 in 1995–96.

Thierry Henry (Arsenal) is the first player to score more than 20 Premiership goals in five consecutive seasons (2002–06). **David Halliday** (Sunderland) topped 30 First Division goals in 4 consecutive seasons with totals of 38, 36, 36 and 49 from 1925–26 to 1928–29.

MOST GOALS IN A MATCH

Sep 12, 1885: John Petrie set the all-time British individual record for a first-class match when, in Arbroath's 36-0 win against Bon Accord (Scottish Cup 1), he scored **13**

Apr 13, 1936: Joe Payne set the still- existing individual record on his debut as a centre-forward, for Luton v Bristol Rov (Div 3 South). In a 12-0 win he scored **10**

ROWLEY'S ALL-TIME RECORD

Arthur Rowley is English football's top club scorer with a total of 464 goals for WBA, Fulham, Leicester and Shrewsbury (1947–65). There were 434 in the League, 26 FA Cup, 4 League Cup.

Jimmy Greaves is second with a total of 420 goals for Chelsea, AC Milan, Tottenham and West Ham, made up of 366 League, 35 FA Cup, 10 League Cup and 9 in Europe. He also scored nine goals for AC Milan.

John Aldridge retired as a player at the end of season 1997–98 with a career total of 329 League goals for Newport, Oxford Utd, Liverpool and Tranmere (1979–98). In all competitions for those clubs he scored 410 in 737 appearances. He also scored 45 in 63 games for Real Sociedad.

MOST GOALS IN INTERNATIONAL MATCHES

13 by **Archie Thompson** for Australia v American Samoa in World Cup (Oceania Group qualifier) at Coff's Harbour, New South Wales, Apr 11, 2001. Result: 31-0.

7 by **Stanley Harris** for England v France in Amateur International in Paris, Nov 1, 1906. Result: 15-0.

6 by **Nat Lofthouse** for Football League v Irish League, at Wolverhampton, Sep 24, 1952. Result: 7-1.

Joe Bambrick for Ireland against Wales, in Belfast, Feb 1, 1930. Result: 7-0.

WC Jordan in Amateur International for England v France, at Park Royal, Mar 23, 1908. Result: 12-0.
Vivian Woodward for England v Holland in Amateur International, at Chelsea, Dec 11,1909. Result: 9-1.
5 by **Howard Vaughton** for England v Ireland (Belfast) Feb 18, 1882. Result: 13-0.
Steve Bloomer for England v Wales (Cardiff) Mar 16, 1896. Result: 9-1.
Hughie Gallacher for Scotland against Ireland (Belfast), Feb 23, 1929. Result: 7-3.
Willie Hall for England v Northern Ireland, at Old Trafford, Nov 16, 1938. Five in succession (first three in 3'5 mins – fastest international hat-trick). Result: 7-0.
Malcolm Macdonald for England v Cyprus (Wembley) Apr 16, 1975. Result: 5-0.
Hughie Gallacher for Scottish League against Irish League (Belfast) Nov 11, 1925. Result: 7-3.
Barney Battles for Scottish League against Irish League (Firhill Park, Glasgow) Oct 31, 1928. Result: 8-2.
Bobby Flavell for Scottish League against Irish League (Belfast) Apr 30, 1947. Result: 7-4.
Joe Bradford for Football League v Irish League (Everton) Sep 25, 1929. Result: 7-2.
Albert Stubbins for Football League v Irish League (Blackpool) Oct 18, 1950. Result: 6-3.
Brian Clough for Football League v Irish League (Belfast) Sep 23, 1959. Result: 5-0.

LAST ENGLAND PLAYER TO SCORE ...

3 goals: Jermain Defoe v Bulgaria (4-0), Euro Champ qual, Wembley, Sep 3, 2010
4 goals: Ian Wright v San Marino (7-1), World Cup qual, Bologna, Nov 17, 1993.
5 goals: Malcolm Macdonald v Cyprus (5-0), Euro Champ qual, Wembley, Apr 16, 1975.

INTERNATIONAL TOP SHOTS

		Goals	Games
England	Bobby Charlton (1958–70)	49	106
N Ireland	David Healy (2000–11)	35	86
Scotland	Denis Law (1958–74)	30	55
	Kenny Dalglish (1971–86)	30	102
Wales	Ian Rush (1980–96)	28	73
Rep of Ire	Robbie Keane (1998–2011)	51	108

ENGLAND'S TOP MARKSMEN

(As at start of season 2011–12)

	Goals	Games
Bobby Charlton (1958–70)	49	106
Gary Lineker (1984–92)	48	80
Jimmy Greaves (1959–67)	44	57
Michael Owen (1998–2008)	40	89
Tom Finney (1946–58)	30	76
Nat Lofthouse (1950–58)	30	33
Alan Shearer (1992–2000)	30	63
Vivian Woodward (1903–11)	29	23
Steve Bloomer (1895–1907)	28	23
David Platt (1989–96)	27	62
Bryan Robson (1979–91)	26	90
Wayne Rooney (2003-11)	26	70
Geoff Hurst (1966–72)	24	49
Stan Mortensen (1947–53)	23	25
Tommy Lawton (1938–48)	22	23
Peter Crouch (2005–11)	22	42
Mike Channon (1972–77)	21	46
Kevin Keegan (1972–82)	21	63

CONSECUTIVE GOALS FOR ENGLAND

Steve Bloomer scored in **TEN** consecutive appearances (19 goals) for **England** between Mar 1895 and Mar 1899.
Jimmy Greaves scored 11 goals in five consecutive England matches from the start of season 1960–61.
Paul Mariner scored in five consecutive England appearances (7 goals) between Nov 1981 and Jun 1982.

ENGLAND'S TOP FINAL SERIES MARKSMAN

Gary Lineker with 6 goals at 1986 World Cup in Mexico.

ENGLAND TOP SCORERS IN COMPETITIVE INTERNATIONALS

Michael Owen 26 goals in 53 matches; **Gary Lineker** 22 in 39; **Alan Shearer** 20 in 31.

MOST ENGLAND GOALS IN SEASON

13 – **Jimmy Greaves** (1960–61 in 9 matches); 12 – **Dixie Dean** (1926–27 in 6 matches); 10 – **Gary Lineker** (1990–91 in 10 matches); 10 – **Wayne Rooney** – (2008–09 in 9 matches).

MOST ENGLAND HAT-TRICKS

Jimmy Greaves 6; **Gary Lineker** 5, **Bobby Charlton** 4, **Vivian Woodward** 4, **Stan Mortensen** 3.

MOST GOALS FOR ENGLAND U-21s

13 – **Alan Shearer** (11 apps) Francis Jeffers (13 apps)

GOLDEN GOAL DECIDERS

The Football League, in an experiment to avoid penalty shoot-outs, introduced a new golden goal system in the 1994–95 **Auto Windscreens Shield** to decide matches in the knock-out stages of the competition in which scores were level after 90 minutes. The first goal scored in overtime ended play.
Iain Dunn (Huddersfield) became the first player in British football to settle a match by this sudden-death method. His 107th-minute goal beat Lincoln 3-2 on Nov 30, 1994, and to mark his 'moment in history' he was presented with a golden football trophy.
The AWS Final of 1995 was decided when Paul Tait headed the only goal for Birmingham against Carlisle 13 minutes into overtime – the first time a match at Wembley had been decided by the 'golden goal' formula.
First major international tournament match to be decided by sudden death was the Final of the **1996 European Championship** at Wembley in which Germany beat Czech Rep 2-1 by **Oliver Bierhoff**'s goal in the 95th minute.
In the **1998 World Cup Finals** (2nd round), host country France beat Paraguay 1-0 with **Laurent Blanc**'s goal (114).
France won the **2000 European Championship** with golden goals in the semi-final, 2-1 v Portugal (Zinedine Zidane pen, 117), and in the Final, 2-1 v Italy (David Trezeguet, 103).
Galatasaray (Turkey) won the **European Super Cup** 2-1 against Real Madrid (Monaco, Aug 25, 2000) with a 103rd minute golden goal, a penalty.
Liverpool won the **UEFACup** 5-4 against Alaves with a 117th min golden goal, an own goal, in the Final in Dortmund (May 19, 2001).
In the **2002 World Cup Finals**, 3 matches were decided by Golden Goals: in the 2nd round Senegal beat Sweden 2-1 (Henri Camara, 104) and South Korea beat Italy 2-1 (Ahn Jung – hwan, 117); in the quarter-final, Turkey beat Senegal 1-0 (Ilhan Mansiz, 94).
France won the 2003 **FIFA Confederations Cup** Final against Cameroon (Paris, Jun 29) with a 97th-minute golden goal by Thierry Henry.
Doncaster won promotion to Football League with a 110th-minute golden goal winner (3-2) in the Conference Play-off Final against Dagenham at Stoke (May 10, 2003).
Germany won the **Women's World Cup Final** 2-1 v Sweden (Los Angeles, Oct 12, 2003) with a 98th-minute golden goal.

GOLD TURNS TO SILVER

Starting with the 2003 Finals of the UEFA Cup and Champions League/European Cup, UEFA introduced a new rule by which a silver goal could decide the winners if the scores were level after 90 minutes.

Team leading after 15 minutes' extra time win match. If sides level, a second period of 15 minutes to be played. If still no winner, result to be decided by penalty shoot-out.

UEFA said the change was made because the golden goal put too much pressure on referees and prompted teams to play negative football.

Although both 2003 European Finals went to extra-time, neither was decided by a silver goal. The new rule applied in the 2004 European Championship Finals, and Greece won their semi-final against the Czech Republic in the 105th minute.

The **International Board** decided (Feb 28 2004) that the golden/silver goal rule was 'unfair' and that from July 1 competitive international matches level after extra-time would, when necessary, be settled on penalties.

PREMIER LEAGUE TOP SHOTS (1992–2010)

Alan Shearer	260	Robbie Keane	123
Andy Cole	187	Nicolas Anelka	122
Thierry Henry	174	Wayne Rooney	117
Robbie Fowler	163	Ian Wright	113
Les Ferdinand	149	Dion Dublin	111
Michael Owen	149	Emile Heskey	109
Teddy Sheringham	147	Ryan Giggs	105
Frank Lampard	139	Paul Scholes	102
Jimmy Floyd Hasselbaink	127	Matthew Le Tissier	101
Dwight Yorke	123	Jermain Defoe	101

LEAGUE GOAL RECORDS

The highest goal-scoring aggregates in the Football League, Premier and Scottish League are as follows:

For

	Goals	Games	Club	Season
Prem	103	38	Chelsea	2009-10
Div 1	128	42	Aston Villa	1930–31
New Div 1	108	46	Manchester City	2001–02
New Champ	99	46	Reading	2005–06
Div 2	122	42	Middlesbrough	1926–27
New Div 2	89	46	Millwall	2000–01
New Lge 1	106	46	Peterborough	2010–11
Div 3(S)	127	42	Millwall	1927–28
Div 3(N)	128	42	Bradford City	1928–29
Div 3	111	46	QPR	1961–62
New Div 3	96	46	Luton	2001–02
New Lge 2	90	46	Yeovil	2004–05
Div 4	134	46	Peterborough	1960–61
Scot Prem	105	38	Celtic	2003–04
Scot L 1	132	34	Hearts	1957–58
Scot L 2	142	34	Raith Rov	1937–38
Scot L 3 (Modern)	130	36	Gretna	2004–05

Against

	Goals	Games	Club	Season
Prem	100	42	Swindon	1993–94
Div 1	125	42	Blackpool	1930–31

New Div 1	102	46	Stockport	2001–02
New Champ	86	46	Crewe	2004–05
Div 2	141	34	Darwen	1898–99
New Div 2	102	46	Chester	1992–93
New Lge 1	98	46	Stockport	2004–05
Div 3(S)	135	42	Merthyr T	1929–30
Div 3(N)	136	42	Nelson	1927–28
Div 3	123	46	Accrington Stanley	1959–60
New Div 3	113	46	Doncaster	1997–98
New Lge 2	96	46	Stockport	2010-11
Div 4	109	46	Hartlepool Utd	1959–60
Scot Prem	100	36	Morton	1984–85
Scot Prem	100	44	Morton	1987–88
Scot L 1	137	38	Leith A	1931–32
Scot L 2	146	38	Edinburgh City	1931–32
Scot L 3 (Modern)	118	36	East Stirling	2003–04

BEST DEFENSIVE RECORDS – *Denotes under old offside law

Div	Goals Agst	Games	Club	Season
Prem	15	38	Chelsea	2004–05
1	16	42	Liverpool	1978–79
1	*15	22	Preston	1888–89
New Div 1	28	46	Sunderland	1998–99
New Champ	30	46	Preston	2005–06
2	18	28	Liverpool	1893–94
2	*22	34	Sheffield Wed	1899–1900
2	24	42	Birmingham	1947–48
2	24	42	Crystal Palace	1978–79
New Div 2	25	46	Wigan	2002–03
New Lge 1	35	46	Scunthorpe	2006–07
3(S)	*21	42	Southampton	1921–22
3(S)	30	42	Cardiff	1946–47
3(N)	*21	38	Stockport	1921–22
3(N)	21	46	Port Vale	1953–54
3	30	46	Middlesbrough	1986–87
New Div 3	20	46	Gillingham	1995–96
New Lge 2	34	46	Walsall	2006–07
4	25	46	Lincoln	1980–81

SCOTTISH LEAGUE

Div	Goals Agst	Games	Club	Season
Prem	18	38	Celtic	2001–02
1	*12	22	Dundee	1902–03
1	*14	38	Celtic	1913–14
2	20	38	Morton	1966–67
2	*29	38	Clydebank	1922–23
2	29	36	East Fife	1995–96
New Div 3	21	36	Brechin	1995–96

TOP SCORERS (LEAGUE ONLY)

		Goals	Div
2010-11	Clayton Donaldson (Crewe)	28	Lge 2
2009-10	Rickie Lambert (Southampton)	31	Lge 1
2008– 09	Simon Cox (Swindon), Rickie Lambert (Bristol Rov)	29	Lge 1

2007–08	Cristiano Ronaldo (Manchester Utd)	31	Prem
2006–07	Billy Sharp (Scunthorpe)	30	Lge 1
2005–06	Thierry Henry (Arsenal)	27	Prem
2004–05	Stuart Elliott (Hull)	27	1
	Phil Jevons (Yeovil)	27	2
	Dean Windass (Bradford City)	27	1
2003–04	Thierry Henry (Arsenal)	30	Prem
2002–03	Andy Morrell (Wrexham)	34	3
2001–02	Shaun Goater (Manchester City)	28	1
	Bobby Zamora (Brighton)	28	2
2000–01	Bobby Zamora (Brighton)	28	3
1999–00	Kevin Phillips (Sunderland)	30	Prem
1998–99	Lee Hughes (WBA)	31	1
1997–98	Pierre van Hooijdonk (Nottm Forest)	29	1
	Kevin Phillips (Sunderland)	29	1
1996–97	Graeme Jones (Wigan)	31	3
1995–96	Alan Shearer (Blackburn)	31	Prem
1994–95	Alan Shearer (Blackburn)	34	Prem
1993–94	Jimmy Quinn (Reading)	35	2
1992–93	Guy Whittingham (Portsmouth)	42	1
1991–92	Ian Wright (Crystal Palace 5, Arsenal 24)	29	1
1990–91	Teddy Sheringham (Millwall)	33	2
1989–90	Mick Quinn (Newcastle)	32	2
1988–89	Steve Bull (Wolves)	37	3
1987–88	Steve Bull (Wolves)	34	4
1986–87	Clive Allen (Tottenham)	33	1
1985–86	Gary Lineker (Everton)	30	1
1984–85	Tommy Tynan (Plymouth Argyle)	31	3
	John Clayton (Tranmere)	31	4
1983–84	Trevor Senior (Reading)	36	4
1982–83	Luther Blissett (Watford)	27	1
1981–82	Keith Edwards (Hull 1, Sheffield Utd 35)	36	4
1980–81	Tony Kellow (Exeter)	25	3
1979–80	Clive Allen (Queens Park Rangers)	28	2
1978–79	Ross Jenkins (Watford)	29	3
1977–78	Steve Phillips (Brentford)	32	4
	Alan Curtis (Swansea City)	32	4
1976–77	Peter Ward (Brighton)	32	3
1975–76	Dixie McNeil (Hereford)	35	3
1974–75	Dixie McNeil (Hereford)	31	3
1973–74	Brian Yeo (Gillingham)	31	4
1972–73	Bryan (Pop) Robson (West Ham)	28	1
1971–72	Ted MacDougall (Bournemouth)	35	3
1970–71	Ted MacDougall (Bournemouth)	42	4
1969–70	Albert Kinsey (Wrexham)	27	4
1968–69	Jimmy Greaves (Tottenham)	27	1
1967–68	George Best (Manchester Utd)	28	1
	Ron Davies (Southampton)	28	1
1966–67	Ron Davies (Southampton)	37	1
1965–66	Kevin Hector (Bradford PA)	44	4
1964–65	Alick Jeffrey (Doncaster)	36	4
1963–64	Hugh McIlmoyle (Carlisle)	39	4
1962–63	Jimmy Greaves (Tottenham)	37	1
1961–62	Roger Hunt (Liverpool)	41	2
1960–61	Terry Bly (Peterborough)	52	4

100 LEAGUE GOALS IN SEASON

Manchester City, First Div Champions in 2001–02, scored 108 goals.

Bolton, First Div Champions in 1996–97, reached 100 goals, the first side to complete a century in League football since 103 by **Northampton** (Div 4 Champions) in 1986–87.

Last League Champions to reach 100 League goals: **Tottenham** (115 in 1960–61). Last century of goals in the top division: 111 by runners-up **Tottenham** in 1962–63.

Only club to score a century of Premier League goals in season: **Chelsea** (103 in 2009-10, including home scores of 7, 7, 7, 8

Wolves topped 100 goals in four successive First Division seasons (1957–58, 1958–59, 1959–60, 1960–61).

In **1930–31,** the top three all scored a century of League goals: 1 Arsenal (127), 2 Aston Villa (128), 3 Sheffield Wed (102).

Latest team to score a century of League goals: **Peterborough** with 106 in 2010-11 (Lge 1).

100 GOALS AGAINST

Swindon, relegated with 100 goals against in 1993–94, were the first top-division club to concede a century of League goals since **Ipswich** (121) went down in 1964. Most goals conceded in the top division: 125 by **Blackpool** in 1930–31, but they avoided relegation.

MOST LEAGUE GOALS ON ONE DAY

A record of 209 goals in the four divisions of the Football League (43 matches) was set on **Jan 2, 1932:** 56 in Div 1, 53 in Div 2, 57 in Div 3 South and 43 in Div 3 North.

There were two 10-goal aggregates: Bradford City 9, Barnsley 1 in Div 2 and Coventry City 5, Fulham 5 in Div 3 South.

That total of 209 League goals on one day was equalled on **Feb 1, 1936** (44 matches): 46 in Div 1, 46 in Div 2, 49 in Div 3 South and 69 in Div 3 North. Two matches in the Northern Section produced 23 of the goals: Chester 12, York 0 and Crewe 5, Chesterfield 6.

MOST GOALS IN TOP DIV ON ONE DAY

This record has stood since **Dec 26, 1963,** when 66 goals were scored in the ten First Division matches played.

MOST PREMIER LEAGUE GOALS ON ONE DAY

47, in nine matches on **May 8, 1993** (last day of season). For the first time, all 20 clubs scored in the Premier League programme over the weekend of Nov 27-28, 2010

FEWEST PREMIER LEAGUE GOALS IN ONE WEEK-END

10, in 10 matches on **Nov 24/25, 2001**

FEWEST FIRST DIV GOALS ON ONE DAY

For full/near full programme: **Ten goals,** all by home clubs, in ten matches on Apr 28, 1923 (day of Wembley's first FA Cup Final).

SCORERS IN CONSECUTIVE TOP-DIVISION MATCHES

Stan Mortensen scored in 11 consecutive Division One games for Blackpool in season 1950–51. **Ruud van Nistelrooy** (Manchester Utd) scored 13 goals in last 8 games of season 2002–03 and in first 2 of 2003–04. Since the last war, 3 other players scored in 10 successive matches in the old First Division: **Billy McAdams** (Man City, 1957–58), **Ron Davies** (Southampton, 1966–67) and **John Aldridge** (Liverpool, May–Oct 1987).

SCORERS FOR 6 PREMIER LEAGUE CLUBS

Les Ferdinand (QPR, Newcastle, Tottenham, West Ham, Leicester, Bolton); **Andy Cole** (Newcastle, Manchester Utd, Blackburn, Fulham, Manchester City, Portsmouth), **Marcus Bent** (Crystal Palace, Ipswich, Leicester, Everton, Charlton, Wigan), **Nick Barmby** (Tottenham,

Middlesbrough, Everton, Liverpool, Leeds, Hull); **Craig Bellamy** (Coventry, Newcastle, Blackburn, Liverpool, West Ham, Manchester City).

SCORERS FOR 5 PREMIER LEAGUE CLUBS

Stan Collymore (Nottm Forest, Liverpool, Aston Villa, Leicester, Bradford); **Mark Hughes** (Manchester Utd, Chelsea, Southampton, Everton, Blackburn); **Benito Carbone** (Sheffield Wed, Aston Villa, Bradford, Derby, Middlesbrough); **Ashley Ward** (Norwich, Derby, Barnsley, Blackburn Bradford); **Teddy Sheringham** (Nottm Forest, Tottenham, Manchester Utd, Portsmouth, West Ham); **Chris Sutton** (Norwich, Blackburn, Chelsea, Birmingham, Aston Villa); **Nicolas Anelka** (Arsenal, Liverpool, Manchester City, Bolton, Chelsea).

SCORERS IN MOST CONSECUTIVE LEAGUE MATCHES

Arsenal broke the record by scoring in 55 successive Premiership fixtures: the last match in season 2000–01, then all 38 games in winning the title in 2001–02, and the first 16 in season 2002–03. The sequence ended with a 2–0 defeat away to Manchester Utd on December 7, 2002.
Chesterfield previously held the record, having scored in 46 consecutive matches in Div 3 (North), starting on Christmas Day, 1929 and ending on December 27, 1930.

SIX-OUT-OF-SIX HEADERS

When **Oxford Utd** beat Shrewsbury 6–0 (Div 2) on Apr 23, 1996, all six goals were headers.

ALL–ROUND MARKSMEN

Alan Cork scored in four divisions of the Football League and in the Premier League in his 18-season career with Wimbledon, Sheffield Utd and Fulham (1977–95).
Brett Ormerod scored in all four divisions (2, 1, Champ and Prem Lge) for Blackpool in two spells (1997-2002, 2008-11)

MOST CUP GOALS

FA Cup – most goals in one season:20 by **Jimmy Ross** (Preston, runners-up 1887–88); 15 by **Alex (Sandy) Brown** (Tottenham, winners 1900–01).
Most FA Cup goals in individual careers:49 by **Harry Cursham** (Notts Co 1877–89); this century: **44** by **Ian Rush** (39 for Liverpool, 4 for Chester, 1 for Newcastle 1979–98). **Denis Law** was the previous highest FA Cup scorer in the 20th century with 41 goals for Huddersfield Town, Manchester City and Manchester Utd (1957–74).
Most FA Cup Final goals by individual: 5 by **Ian Rush** for Liverpool (2 in 1986, 2 in 1989, 1 in 1992).

HOTTEST CUP HOT-SHOT

Geoff Hurst scored 21 cup goals in season 1965–66: 11 League Cup, 4 FA Cup and 2 Cup-Winners' Cup for West Ham, and 4 in the World Cup for England.

SCORERS IN EVERY ROUND

Twelve players have scored in every round of the FA Cup in one season, from opening to Final inclusive: **Archie Hunter** (Aston Villa, winners 1887); **Sandy Brown** (Tottenham, winners 1901); **Harry Hampton** (Aston Villa, winners 1905); **Harold Blackmore** (Bolton, winners 1929); **Ellis Rimmer** (Sheffield Wed, winners 1935); **Frank O'Donnell** (Preston, beaten 1937); **Stan Mortensen** (Blackpool, beaten 1948); **Jackie Milburn** (Newcastle, winners 1951); **Nat Lofthouse** (Bolton, beaten 1953); **Charlie Wayman** (Preston, winners 1954); **Jeff Astle** (WBA, winners 1968); **Peter Osgood** (Chelsea, winners 1970).
Blackmore and the next seven completed their 'set' in the Final at Wembley; Osgood did so in the Final replay at Old Trafford.
Only player to score in every **Football League Cup** round possible in one season: **Tony Brown** for WBA, winners 1965–66, with 9 goals in 10 games (after bye in Round 1).

TEN IN A ROW

Dixie McNeill scored for Wrexham in ten successive FA Cup rounds (18 goals): 11 in Rounds 1-6, 1977–78; 3 in Rounds 3-4, 1978–79; 4 in Rounds 3-4, 1979–80.

Stan Mortensen (Blackpool) scored 25 goals in 16 FA Cup rounds out of 17 (1946–51).

TOP MATCH HAULS IN FA CUP

Ted MacDougall scored nine goals, a record for the competition proper, in the FA Cup first round on Nov 20, 1971, when Bournemouth beat Margate 11-0. On Nov 23, 1970 he had scored six in an 8-1 first round replay against Oxford City.

Other six-goal FA Cup scorers include **George Hilsdon** (Chelsea v Worksop, 9-1, 1907– 08), **Ronnie Rooke** (Fulham v Bury, 6-0, 1938–39), **Harold Atkinson** (Tranmere v Ashington, 8-1, 1952–53), **George Best** (Manchester Utd v Northampton 1969–70, 8-2 away), **Duane Darby** (Hull v Whitby, 8-4, 1996–97).

Denis Law scored all six for Manchester City at Luton (6-2) in an FA Cup 4th round tie on Jan 28, 1961, but none of them counted – the match was abandoned (69 mins) because of a waterlogged pitch. He also scored City's goal when the match was played again, but they lost 3-1.

Tony Philliskirk scored **five** when Peterborough beat Kingstonian 9-1 in an FA Cup 1st round replay on Nov 25, 1992, but had them wiped from the records.

With the score at 3-0, the Kingstonian goalkeeper was concussed by a coin thrown from the crowd and unable to play on. The FA ordered the match to be replayed at Peterborough behind closed doors, and Kingstonian lost 1-0.

I Two players have scored **ten goals** in FA Cup preliminary round matches: **Chris Marron** for South Shields against Radcliffe in Sep 1947; **Paul Jackson** when Sheffield-based club Stocksbridge Park Steels beat Oldham Town 17-1 on Aug 31, 2002. He scored 5 in each half and all ten with his feet – goal times 6, 10, 22, 30, 34, 68, 73, 75, 79, 84 mins

QUICKEST GOALS AND RAPID SCORING

A goal in **4 sec** was claimed by **Jim Fryatt**, for Bradford PA v Tranmere (Div 4, Apr 25, 1965), and by **Gerry Allen** for Whitstable v Danson (Kent League, Mar 3,1989). **Damian Mori** scored in **4 sec** for Adelaide v Sydney (Australian National League, December 6, 1995).

Goals after **6 sec** – **Albert Mundy** for Aldershot v Hartlepool, Oct 25, 1958; **Barrie Jones** for Notts Co v Torquay, Mar 31, 1962; **Keith Smith** for Crystal Palace v Derby, Dec 12, 1964.

9.6 sec by **John Hewitt** for Aberdeen at Motherwell, 3rd round, Jan 23, 1982 (fastest goal in Scottish Cup history).

Colin Cowperthwaite reputedly scored in **3.5 sec** for Barrow v Kettering (Alliance Premier League) on Dec 8, 1979, but the timing was unofficial.

Phil Starbuck for Huddersfield **3 sec** after entering the field as 54th min substitute at home to Wigan (Div 2) on Easter Monday, Apr 12, 1993. Corner was delayed, awaiting his arrival and he scored with a header.

Malcolm Macdonald after **5 sec** (officially timed) in Newcastle's 7-3 win in a pre-season friendly at St Johnstone on Jul 29, 1972.

World's fastest goal: 2.8 sec, direct from kick-off, Argentinian **Ricardo Olivera** for Rio Negro v Soriano (Uruguayan League), December 26, 1998.

Fastest international goal: 8.3 sec, Davide Gualtieri for San Marino v England (World Cup qual, Bologna, Nov 17, 1993).

Fastest England goal: 17 sec, Tommy Lawton v Portugal in Lisbon, May 25, 1947. **27 sec, Bryan Robson** v France in World Cup at Bilbao, Spain on Jun 16, 1982; **37 sec, Gareth Southgate** v South Africa in Durban, May 22, 2003; **30 sec, Jack Cock** v Ireland, Belfast, Oct 25, 1919; **30 sec, Bill Nicholson** v Portugal at Goodison Park, May 19, 1951. **38 sec, Bryan Robson** v Yugoslavia at Wembley, Dec 13, 1989; **42 sec, Gary Lineker** v Malaysia in Kuala Lumpur, Jun 12, 1991.

Fastest international goal by substitute: 5 sec, John Jensen for Denmark v Belgium (Euro Champ), Oct 12, 1994.

Fastest goal by England substitute: 10 sec, Teddy Sheringham v Greece (World Cup qualifier) at Old Trafford, Oct 6, 2001.

Fastest FA Cup goal: 4 sec, **Gareth Morris** (Ashton Utd) v Skelmersdale, 1st qual round, Sept 15, 2001.

Fastest FA Cup goal (comp proper): 9.7 sec, **Jimmy Kebe** for Reading v WBA, 5th Round, Feb 13, 2010.

Fastest FA Cup Final goal: 25 sec, **Louis Saha** for Everton v Chelsea at Wembley, May 30, 2009.

Fastest goal by substitute in FA Cup Final: 96 sec, **Teddy Sheringham** for Manchester Utd v Newcastle at Wembley, May 22, 1999.

Fastest League Cup Final goal: 45 sec, **John Arne Riise** for Liverpool v Chelsea, 2005.

Fastest goal on full League debut: 7.7 sec, **Freddy Eastwood** for Southend v Swansea (Lge 2), Oct 16, 2004. He went on to score hat-trick in 4-2 win.

Fastest goal in cup final: 4.07 sec, 14-year-old **Owen Price** for Ernest Bevin College, Tooting, beaten 3-1 by Barking Abbey in Heinz Ketchup Cup Final at Arsenal on May 18, 2000. Owen, on Tottenham's books, scored from inside his own half when the ball was played back to him from kick-off.

Fastest Premier League goals: 10 sec, **Ledley King** for Tottenham away to Bradford, Dec 9, 2000; **10.4 sec, Alan Shearer** for Newcastle v Manchester City, Jan 18, 2003: **11 sec, Mark Viduka** for Leeds v Charlton, Mar 17, 2001; **12.5 sec, James Beattie** for Southampton at Chelsea, Aug 28, 2004; **13 sec, Chris Sutton** for Blackburn at Everton, Apr 1, 1995; **13 sec, Dwight Yorke** for Aston Villa at Coventry, Sep 30, 1995.

Fastest top-division goal: 7 sec, **Bobby Langton** for Preston v Manchester City (Div 1), Aug 25, 1948.

Fastest goal in Champions League: 10 sec, **Roy Makaay** for Bayern Munich v Real Madrid (1st ko rd), Mar 7, 2007.

Fastest Premier League goal by substitute: 9 sec, **Shaun Goater**, Manchester City's equaliser away to Manchester Utd (1-1), Feb 9, 2003.

Fastest goal in women's football: 7 sec, **Angie Harriott** for Launton v Thame (Southern League, Prem Div), season 1998–99.

Fastest hat-trick in League history: 2 min 20 sec, Bournemouth's 84th-minute substitute **James Hayter** in 6-0 home win v Wrexham (Div 2) on Feb 24, 2004 (goal times 86, 87, 88 mins).

Fastest First Division hat-tricks since war: Graham Leggat, 3 goals in 3 minutes (first half) when Fulham beat Ipswich 10-1 on Boxing Day, 1963; **Nigel Clough**, 3 goals in **4 minutes** (81, 82, 85 pen) when Nottm Forest beat QPR 4-0 on Dec 13, 1987.

Premier League – fastest hat-trick: 4 min30 sec (26, 29, 31) by **Robbie Fowler** in Liverpool 3, Arsenal 0 on Aug 28, 1994.

Fastest international hat-trick: 3 min 15 sec, **Masashi Nakayami** for Japan in 9-0 win v Brunei in Macao (Asian Cup), Feb 16, 2000.

Fastest international hat-trick in British matches: 3.5 min, **Willie Hall** for England v N Ireland at Old Trafford, Manchester, Nov 16, 1938. (Hall scored 5 in 7-0 win); **4.5 min, Arif Erdem** for Turkey v N Ireland, European Championship, at Windsor Park, Belfast, on Sep 4, 1999.

Fastest FA Cup hat-tricks: In 3 min, **Billy Best** for Southend v Brentford (2nd round, Dec 7, 1968); **2 min 20 sec, Andy Locke** for Nantwich v Droylsden (1st Qual round, Sep 9, 1995).

Fastest Scottish hat-trick: 2 min 30 sec, **Ian St John** for Motherwell away to Hibernian (Scottish League Cup), Aug 15, 1959.

Fastest hat-trick of headers: Dixie Dean's 5 goals in Everton's 7-2 win at home to Chelsea (Div 1) on Nov 14, 1931 included 3 headers between **5th** and **15th-min**.

Fastest all-time hat-trick: Reported at 1 min 50 sec, **Eduardo Magloni** for Independiente against Gimnasia de la Plata in Argentina Div , Mar 18, 1973.

Scored first kick: Billy Foulkes (Newcastle) for Wales v England at Cardiff, Oct 20, 1951, in his first international match.

Preston scored six goals in **7 min** in record 26-0 FA Cup 1st round win v Hyde, Oct 15, 1887.

Notts Co scored six second-half goals in **12 min** (Tommy Lawton 3, Jackie Sewell 3) when beating Exeter 9-0 (Div 3 South) at Meadow Lane on Oct 16, 1948.

Arsenal scored six in **18 min** (71-89 mins) in 7-1 home win (Div 1) v Sheffield Wed, Feb 15, 1992.

Tranmere scored six in first **19 min** when beating Oldham 13-4 (Div 3 North), December 26, 1935.

Sunderland scored eight in **28 min** at Newcastle (9-1 Div 1), December 5, 1908. Newcastle went on to win the title.

Southend scored all seven goals in **29 min** in 7-0 win at home to Torquay (Leyland Daf Cup, Southern quarter-final), Feb 26, 1991. Score was 0-0 until 55th minute.

Plymouth Argyle scored five in first **18 min** in 7-0 home win v Chesterfield (Div 2), Jan 3, 2004.

Five in 20 min: Frank Keetley in Lincoln's 9-1 win over Halifax in Div 3 (North), Jan 16, 1932; **Brian Dear** for West Ham v WBA (6-1, Div 1) Apr 16, 1965. **Kevin Hector** for Bradford PA v Barnsley (7-2, Div 4), Nov 20, 1965.

Four in 5 min: John McIntyre for Blackburn v Everton (Div 1), Sep 16, 1922; **WG (Billy) Richardson** for WBA v West Ham (Div 1), Nov 7, 1931.

Three in 2'5 min: Jimmy Scarth for Gillingham v Leyton Orient (Div 3S), Nov 1, 1952.

Three in three minutes: Billy Lane for Watford v Clapton Orient (Div 3S), December 20, 1933; **Johnny Hartburn** for Leyton Orient v Shrewsbury (Div 3S), Jan 22, 1955; **Gary Roberts** for Brentford v Newport, (Freight Rover Trophy, South Final), May 17, 1985; **Gary Shaw** for Shrewsbury v Bradford City (Div 3), December 22, 1990.

Two in 9 sec: Jamie Bates with last kick of first half, **Jermaine McSporran** 9 sec into second half when Wycombe beat Peterborough 2-0 at home (Div 2) on Sep 23, 2000.

Premier League – fastest scoring: Four goals in 4 min 44 sec, Tottenham home to Southampton on Sunday, Feb 7, 1993.

Premiership – fast scoring away: When **Aston Villa** won 5-0 at Leicester (Jan 31, 2004), all goals scored in **18 second-half min** (50-68).

Four in 13 min by Premier League sub:**Ole Gunnar Solskjaer** for Manchester Utd away to Nottm Forest, Feb 6, 1999.

FASTEST GOALS IN WORLD CUP FINAL SERIES

10.8 sec, Hakan Sukur for Turkey against South Korea in 3rd/4th-place match at Taegu, Jun 29, 2002; **15 sec, Vaclav Masek** for Czechoslovakia v Mexico (in Vina, Chile, 1962); **27 sec, Bryan Robson** for England v France (in Bilbao, Spain, 1982).

TOP MATCH SCORES SINCE WAR

By English clubs: 13-0 by Newcastle v Newport (Div 2, Oct 1946); 13-2 by Tottenham v Crewe (FA Cup 4th. Rd. replay, Feb 1960); 13-0 by Chelsea v Jeunesse Hautcharage, Lux. (Cup-Winners' Cup 1st round, 2nd leg, Sep 1971).

By Scottish club: 20-0 by Stirling v Selkirk (E. of Scotland League) in Scottish Cup 1st round. (Dec 1984). That is the highest score in British first-class football since Preston beat Hyde 26-0 in FA Cup, Oct 1887.

GOALS BY GOALKEEPERS

(Long clearances unless stated)

Pat Jennings for Tottenham v Manchester Utd (goalkeeper Alex Stepney), Aug 12, 1967 (FA Charity Shield).

Peter Shilton for Leicester v Southampton (Campbell Forsyth), Oct 14, 1967 (Div 1).

Ray Cashley for Bristol City v Hull (Jeff Wealands), Sep 18, 1973 (Div 2).

Steve Sherwood for Watford v Coventry (Raddy Avramovic), Jan 14, 1984 (Div 1).

Steve Ogrizovic for Coventry v Sheffield Wed (Martin Hodge), Oct 25, 1986 (Div 1).

Andy Goram for Hibernian v Morton (David Wylie), May 7, 1988 (Scot Prem Div).

Andy McLean, on Irish League debut, for Cliftonville v Linfield (George Dunlop), Aug 20, 1988.

Alan Paterson for Glentoran v Linfield (George Dunlop), Nov 30, 1988 (Irish League Cup Final - only instance of goalkeeper scoring winner in a senior cup final in UK).

Ray Charles for East Fife v Stranraer (Bernard Duffy), Feb 28, 1990 (Scot Div 2).

Iain Hesford for Maidstone v Hereford (Tony Elliott), Nov 2, 1991 (Div 4).

Chris Mackenzie for Hereford v Barnet (Mark Taylor), Aug 12, 1995 (Div 3).

Peter Schmeichel for Manchester Utd v Rotor Volgograd, Sep 26, 1995 (header, UEFA Cup 1).

Mark Bosnich (Aston Villa) for Australia v Solomon Islands, Jun 11, 1997 (penalty in World Cup qual – 13-0)).

Peter Keen for Carlisle away to Blackpool (goalkeeper John Kennedy), Oct 24, 2000 (Div 3).

Steve Mildenhall for Notts Co v Mansfield (Kevin Pilkington), Aug 21, 2001 (free-kick inside own half, League Cup 1).

Peter Schmeichel for Aston Villa v Everton (Paul Gerrard), Oct 20, 2001 (volley, first goalkeeper to score in Premiership)

Mart Poom for Sunderland v Derby (Andy Oakes), Sep 20, 2003 (header, Div 1).

Brad Friedel for Blackburn v Charlton (Dean Kiely), Feb 21, 2004 (shot, Prem).

Paul Robinson for Leeds v Swindon (Rhys Evans), Sep 24, 2003 (header, League Cup 2).

Andy Lonergan for Preston v Leicester (Kevin Pressman), Oct 2, 2004 (Champ).

Gavin Ward for Tranmere v Leyton Orient (Glenn Morris), Sep 2, 2006 (free-kick Lge 1).

Mark Crossley for Sheffield Wed v Southampton (Kelvin Davis), Dec 23, 2006 (header, Champ)

Paul Robinson for Tottenham v Watford (Ben Foster); Mar 17, 2007 (Prem).

Adam Federici for Reading v Cardiff (Peter Enckelman), Dec 28, 2008 (shot, Champ).

Chris Weale for Yeovil v Hereford (Peter Gulacsi), Apr 21, 2009 (header, Lge 1)

Scot Flinders for Hartlepool v Bournemouth (Shwan Jalal), Apr 30, 2011 (header, Lge 1)

MORE GOALKEEPING HEADLINES

Arthur Wilkie, sustained a hand injury in Reading's Div 3 match against Halifax on Aug 31, 1962, then played as a forward and scored twice in a 4-2 win.

Alex Stepney was Manchester Utd's joint top scorer for two months in season 1973–74 with two penalties.

Alan Fettis scored twice for Hull in 1994-95 Div 2 season, as a substitute in 3-1 home win over Oxford Utd (Dec 17) and, when selected outfield, with last-minute winner (2-1) against Blackpool on May 6.

Roger Freestone scored for Swansea with a penalty at Oxford Utd (Div 2, Apr 30, 1995) and twice from the spot the following season against Shrewsbury (Aug 12) and Chesterfield (Aug 26).

Jimmy Glass, on loan from Swindon, kept Carlisle in the Football League on May 8, 1999. With ten seconds of stoppage-time left, he went upfield for a corner and scored the winner against Plymouth that sent Scarborough down to the Conference instead.

Paul Smith, Nottm Forest goalkeeper, was allowed to run through Leicester's defence unchallenged and score direct from the kick-off of a Carling Cup second round second match on Sept 18, 2007. It replicated the 1-0 score by which Forest had led at half-time when the original match was abandoned after Leicester defender Clive Clarke suffered a heart attack. Leicester won the tie 3-2.

Tony Roberts (Dagenham), is the only known goalkeeper to score from open play in the FA Cup, his last-minute goal at Basingstoke in the fourth qualifying round on Oct 27, 2001 earning a 2-2 draw. Dagenham won the replay 3-0 and went on to reach the third round proper.

The only known instance in first-class football in Britain of a goalkeeper scoring direct from a goal-kick was in a First Division match at Roker Park on Apr 14, 1900. The kick by Manchester City's **Charlie Williams** was caught in a strong wind and Sunderland keeper J. E Doig fumbled the ball over his line.

Jose Luis Chilavert, Paraguay's international goalkeeper, scored a hat-trick of penalties when his club Velez Sarsfield beat Ferro Carril Oeste 6-1 in the Argentine League on Nov 28, 1999. In all, he scored 8 goals in 72 internationals. He also scored with a free-kick from just inside his own half for Velez Sarsfield against River Plate on Sep 20, 2000.

Most goals by a goalkeeper in a League season: 5 (all penalties) by **Arthur Birch** for Chesterfield (Div 3 North), 1923–24.

When Brazilian goalkeeper **Rogerio Ceni** (37) converted a free-kick for Sao Paulo's winner (2-1) v Corinthians in a championship match on Mar 27, 2011, it was his 100th goal (56 free-kicks, 44 ;pens) in a 20-season career.

OWN GOALS

Most by player in one season: 5 by **Robert Stuart** (Middlesbrough) in 1934–35.

Three in match by one team: Sheffield Wed's **Vince Kenny**, **Norman Curtis** and **Eddie Gannon** in 5-4 defeat at home to WBA (Div 1) on Dec 26, 1952; Rochdale's **George Underwood**, **Kenny Boyle** and **Danny Murphy** in 7-2 defeat at Carlisle (Div 3 North), Dec 25, 1954; Sunderland's **Stephen Wright** and **Michael Proctor (2)** in 24, 29, 32 minutes at home to Charlton (1-3, Premiership), Feb 1, 2003.

Two in match by one player: Chris Nicholl (Aston Villa) scored all 4 goals in 2-2 draw away to Leicester (Div 1), Mar 20, 1976; **Jamie Carragher** (Liverpool) in first half at home to Manchester Utd (2-3) in Premiership, Sep 11, 1999; **Jim Goodwin** (Stockport) in 1-4 defeat away to Plymouth (Div 2), Sep 23, 2002; **Michael Proctor** (Sunderland) in 1-3 defeat at home to Charlton (Premiership), Feb 1, 2003.

Fastest own goals: 8 sec by **Pat Kruse** of Torquay, for Cambridge Utd (Div 4), Jan 3, 1977; in First Division, 16 sec by **Steve Bould** (Arsenal) away to Sheffield Wed, Feb 17, 1990.

Late own-goal man: Frank Sinclair (Leicester) put through his own goal in the 90th minute of Premiership matches away to Arsenal (L1-2) and at home to Chelsea (2-2) in Aug 1999.

Half an own goal each: Chelsea's second goal in a 3-1 home win against Leicester on December 18, 1954 was uniquely recorded as 'shared own goal'. Leicester defenders **Stan Milburn** and **Jack Froggatt**, both lunging at the ball in an attempt to clear, connected simultaneously and sent it rocketing into the net.

Match of 149 own goals: When Adama, Champions of Malagasy (formerly Madagascar) won a League match 149-0 on Oct 31, 2002, all 149 were own goals scored by opponents Stade Olympique De L'Emryne. They repeatedly put the ball in their own net in protest at a refereeing decision.

MOST SCORERS IN MATCH

Liverpool set a Football League record with **eight** scorers when beating Crystal Palace 9-0 (Div 1) on Sep 12, 1989. Marksmen were: Steve Nicol (7 and 88 mins), Steve McMahon (16), Ian Rush (45), Gary Gillespie (56), Peter Beardsley (61), John Aldridge (67 pen), John Barnes (79), Glenn Hysen (82).

Fifteen years earlier, **Liverpool** had gone one better with **nine** different scorers when they achieved their record win, 11-0 at home to Stromsgodset (Norway) in the Cup-Winners' Cup 1st round, 1st leg on Sep 17, 1974.

Eight players scored for **Swansea** when they beat Sliema, Malta, 12-0 in the Cup-Winners' Cup 1st round, 1st leg on Sep 15, 1982.

Nine Stirling players scored in the 20-0 win against Selkirk in the Scottish Cup 1st Round on December 8, 1984.

LONG SCORING RUNS

Tom Phillipson scored in 13 consecutive matches for Wolves (Div 2) in season 1926–27, which is still an English League record. **Bill Prendergast** scored in 13 successive League and Cup appearances for Chester (Div 3 North) in season 1938–39.

Dixie Dean scored in 12 consecutive games (23 goals) for Everton in Div 2 in 1930–31.

Danish striker **Finn Dossing** scored in 15 consecutive matches (Scottish record) for Dundee Utd (Div 1) in 1964–65.

50-GOAL PLAYERS

With **52** goals for **Wolves** in 1987–78 (34 League, 12 Sherpa Van Trophy, 3 Littlewoods Cup, 3 FA Cup), **Steve Bull** became the first player to score 50 in a season for a League club since **Terry Bly** for Div 4 newcomers Peterborough in 1960–61. Bly's 54 comprised 52 League goals and 2 in the FA Cup, and included 7 hat-tricks, still a post-war League record. Bull was again the country's top scorer with 50 goals in season 1988–89: 37 League, 2 Littlewoods Cup and 11 Sherpa Van Trophy. Between Bly and Bull, the highest individual scoring total for a season was 49 by two players: **Ted MacDougall** (Bournemouth 1970–71, 42 League, 7 FA Cup) and **Clive Allen** (Tottenham 1986–87, 33 League, 12 Littlewoods Cup, 4 FA Cup).

Jimmy Greaves was top Div 1 scorer (League goals) six times in 11 seasons: 32 for Chelsea (1958–59), 41 for Chelsea (1960–61) and, for Tottenham, 37 in 1962–63, 35 in 1963–64, 29 in 1964–65 (joint top) and 27 in 1968–69.

Brian Clough (Middlesbrough) was leading scorer in Div 2 in three successive seasons: 40 goals in 1957–58, 42 in 1958–59 and 39 in 1959–60.

John Hickton (Middlesbrough) was top Div 2 scorer three times in four seasons: 24 goals in 1967–68, 24 in 1969–70 and 25 in 1970–71.

MOST HAT-TRICKS

Nine by **George Camsell** (Middlesbrough) in Div 2, 1926–27, is the record for one season. Most League hat-tricks in career: 37 by **Dixie Dean** for Tranmere and Everton (1924–38).

Most **top division** hat-tricks in a season since last War: six by **Jimmy Greaves** for Chelsea (1960–61). **Alan Shearer** scored five hat-tricks for Blackburn in the Premier League, season 1995–96.

Frank Osborne (Tottenham) scored three consecutive hat-tricks in Div 1 in Oct–Nov 1925, against Liverpool, Leicester (away) and West Ham

Tom Jennings (Leeds) scored hat-tricks in three successive Div 1 matches (Sep–Oct, 1926): 3 goals v Arsenal, 4 at Liverpool, 4 v Blackburn. Leeds were relegated that season.

Jack Balmer (Liverpool) scored his three hat-tricks in a 17-year career in successive Div 1 matches (Nov 1946): 3 v Portsmouth, 4 at Derby, 3 v Arsenal. No other Liverpool player scored during that 10-goal sequence by Balmer.

Gilbert Alsop scored hat-tricks in three successive matches for Walsall in Div 3 South in Apr 1939: 3 at Swindon, 3 v Bristol City and 4 v Swindon.

Alf Lythgoe scored hat-tricks in three successive games for Stockport (Div 3 North) in Mar 1934: 3 v Darlington, 3 at Southport and 4 v Wrexham.

TRIPLE HAT-TRICKS

There have been at least three instances of **3 hat-tricks** being scored for one team in a Football League match:

Apr 21, 1909: Enoch West, Billy Hooper and Alfred Spouncer for Nottm Forest (12-0 v Leicester Fosse, Div 1).

Mar 3, 1962: Ron Barnes, Wyn Davies and Roy Ambler in Wrexham's 10-1 win against Hartlepool (Div 4).

Nov 7, 1987: Tony Adcock, Paul Stewart and David White for Manchester City in 10-1 win at home to Huddersfield (Div 2).

For the first time in the Premiership, **three hat-tricks** were completed on one day (Sep 23, 1995): **Tony Yeboah** for Leeds at Wimbledon; **Alan Shearer** for Blackburn v Coventry; **Robbie Fowler** with 4 goals for Liverpool v Bolton.

In the FA Cup, **Jack Carr**, **George Elliott** and **Walter Tinsley** each scored 3 in Middlesbrough's 9-3 first round win against Goole in Jan, 1915. **Les Allen** scored 5, **Bobby Smith** 4 and **Cliff Jones** 3 when Tottenham beat Crewe 13-2 in a fourth-round replay in Feb 1960.

HAT-TRICKS v THREE KEEPERS

When West Ham beat Newcastle 8-1 (Div 1) on Apr 21, 1986 **Alvin Martin** scored 3 goals against different goalkeepers: Martin Thomas injured a shoulder and was replaced, in turn, by outfield players Chris Hedworth and Peter Beardsley.

Jock Dodds of Lincoln had done the same against West Ham on Dec 18, 1948, scoring past Ernie Gregory, Tommy Moroney and George Dick in 4-3 win.

David Herd (Manchester Utd) scored against Sunderland's Jim Montgomery, Charlie Hurley and Johnny Parke in 5-0 First Division home win on Nov 26, 1966.

Brian Clark, of Bournemouth, scored against Rotherham's Jim McDonagh, Conal Gilbert and Michael Leng twice in 7-2 win (Div 3) on Oct 10, 1972.

On Oct 16, 1993 (Div 3) **Chris Pike** (Hereford) scored a hat-trick in 5-0 win over Colchester, who became the first team in league history to have two keepers sent off in the same game.

On Dec 18, 2004 (Lge 1), in 6-1 defeat at Hull, Tranmere used **John Achterberg** and **Russell Howarth**, both retired injured, and defender **Theo Whitmore**.

On Mar 9, 2008, Manchester Utd had three keepers in their 0-1 FA Cup quarter-final defeat by Portsmouth. **Tomasz Kuszczak** came on at half-time for **Edwin van der Sar** but was sent off when conceding a penalty. **Rio Ferdinand** went in goal and was beaten by Sulley Muntari's spot-kick

Derby used three keepers in a 4-1 defeat at Reading (Mar 10, 2010, Champ). **Saul Deeney**, who took over when **Stephen Bywater** was injured, was sent off for a foul and **Robbie Savage** replaced him.

EIGHT-DAY HAT-TRICK TREBLE

Joe Bradford, of Birmingham, scored three hat-tricks in eight days in Sep 1929–30 v Newcastle (won 5-1) on the 21st, 5 for the Football League v Irish League (7-2) on the 25th, and 3 in his club's 5-7 defeat away to Blackburn on the 28th.

PREMIERSHIP DOUBLE HAT-TRICK

Robert Pires and **Jermaine Pennant** each scored 3 goals in Arsenal's 6-1 win at home to Southampton (May 7, 2003).

TON UP – BOTH ENDS

Manchester City are the only club to score and concede a century of League goals in the same season. When finishing fifth in the 1957–58 season, they scored 104 and gave away 100.

TOURNAMENT TOP SHOTS

Most individual goals in a World Cup Final series: 13 by **Just Fontaine** for France, in Sweden 1958. Most in European Championship Finals: 9 by **Michel Platini** for France, in France 1984.

MOST GOALS ON CLUB DEBUT

Jim Dyet scored eight in King's Park's 12-2 win against Forfar (Scottish Div 2, Jan 2, 1930). **Len Shackleton** scored six times in Newcastle's 13-0 win v Newport (Div 2, Oct 5, 1946) in the week he joined them from Bradford Park Avenue

MOST GOALS ON LEAGUE DEBUT

Five by **George Hilsdon**, for Chelsea (9-2) v Glossop, Div 2, Sep 1, 1906. **Alan Shearer**, with three goals for Southampton (4-2) v Arsenal, Apr 9, 1988, became, at 17, the youngest player to score a First Division hat-trick on his full debut.

CLEAN-SHEET RECORDS

On the way to promotion from Div 3 in season 1995–96, Gillingham's ever-present goalkeeper **Jim Stannard** set a clean-sheet record. In 46 matches. He achieved 29 shut-outs (17 at home, 12 away), beating the 28 by **Ray Clemence** for Liverpool (42 matches in Div 1, 1978–79) and the previous best in a 46-match programme of 28 by Port Vale (Div 3 North, 1953–54). In conceding only 20 League goals in 1995–96, Gillingham created a defensive record for the lower divisions.

Chris Woods, Rangers' England goalkeeper, set a British record in season 1986–87 by going 1,196 minutes without conceding a goal. The sequence began in the UEFA Cup match against Borussia Moenchengladbach on Nov 26, 1986, and ended when Rangers were sensationally beaten 1-0 at home by Hamilton in the Scottish Cup 3rd round on Jan 31, 1987 with a 70th-minute goal by **Adrian Sprott**. The previous British record of 1,156 minutes without a goal conceded was held by Aberdeen goalkeeper **Bobby Clark** (season 1970–01).

Manchester Utd set a new Premier League clean-sheet record of 1,333 minutes (including 14 successive match shut-outs) in season 2008–9 (Nov 15-Feb 21). **Edwin van der Sar's** personal British league record of 1,311 minutes without conceding ended when United won 2-1 at Newcastle on Mar 4, 2009

Most clean sheets in season in top English division: **28** by Liverpool (42 matches) in 1978–79; **25** by Chelsea (38 matches) in 2004–05.

There have been three instances of clubs keeping 11 consecutive clean sheets in the Football League: **Millwall** (Div 3 South, 1925–26), **York** (Div 3, 1973–74) and **Reading** (Div 4, 1978–79). In his sequence, Reading goalkeeper **Steve Death** set the existing League shut-out record of 1,103 minutes.

Sasa Ilic remained unbeaten for over 14 hours with 9 successive shut-outs (7 in Div 1, 2 in play-offs) to equal a Charlton club record in Apr/May 1998. He had 12 clean sheets in 17 first team games after winning promotion from the reserves with 6 successive clean sheets.

Sebastiano Rossi kept a clean sheet in 8 successive away matches for AC Milan (Nov 1993–Apr 1994).

A world record of 1,275 minutes without conceding a goal was set in 1990–01 by **Abel Resino**, the Atletico Madrid goalkeeper. He was finally beaten by Sporting Gijon's Enrique in Atletico's 3-1 win on Mar 19, 1991.

In international football, the record is held by **Dino Zoff** with a shut-out for Italy (Sep 1972 to Jun 1974) lasting 1,142 minutes.

LOW SCORING

Fewest goals by any club in season in Football League: 24 by **Stoke** (Div 1, 42 matches, 1984–85); 24 by **Watford** (Div 2, 42 matches, 1971–72). In 46-match programme, 27 by **Stockport** (Div 3, 1969–70).

Arsenal were the lowest Premier League scorers in its opening season (1992–93) with 40 goals in 42 matches, but won both domestic cup competitions. In subsequent seasons the lowest Premier League scorers were **Ipswich** (35) in 1993–94, **Crystal Palace** (34) in 1994–95, **Manchester City** (33) in 1995–96 and Leeds (28) in 1996–97 until **Sunderland** set the Premiership's new fewest-goals record with only 21 in 2002–03. Then, in 2007–08, **Derby** scored just 20.

LONG TIME NO SCORE

The world international non-scoring record was set by **Northern Ireland** when they played 13 matches and 1,298 minutes without a goal. The sequence began against Poland on Feb 13, 2002 and ended 2 years and 5 days later when David Healy scored against Norway (1-4) in Belfast on Feb 18, 2004.

Longest non-scoring sequences in Football League: 11 matches by **Coventry City** in 1919–20 (Div 2); 11 matches in 1992–93 (Div 2) by **Hartlepool**, who after beating Crystal Palace 1-0 in the FA Cup 3rd round on Jan 2, went 13 games and 2 months without scoring (11 League, 1 FA Cup, 1 Autoglass Trophy). The sequence ended after 1,227 blank minutes with a 1-1 draw at Blackpool (League) on Mar 6.

In the Premier League (Oct–Jan season 1994–95) **Crystal Palace** failed to score in nine consecutive matches.

The British non-scoring club record is held by **Stirling**: 14 consecutive matches (13 League, 1 Scottish Cup) and 1,292 minutes play, from Jan 31 1981 until Aug 8, 1981 (when they lost 4-1 to Falkirk in the League Cup).

In season 1971–72, **Mansfield** did not score in any of their first nine home games in Div 3. They were relegated on goal difference of minus two.

FA CUP CLEAN SHEETS

Most consecutive FA Cup matches without conceding a goal: 11 by **Bradford City**. The sequence spanned 8 rounds, from 3rd in 1910–11 to 4th. Round replay in 1911–12, and included winning the Cup in 1911.

GOALS THAT WERE WRONGLY GIVEN

Tottenham's last-minute winner at home to Huddersfield (Div 1) on Apr 2, 1952: Eddie Baily's corner-kick struck referee W.R Barnes in the back, and the ball rebounded to Baily, who crossed for Len Duquemin to head into the net. Baily had infringed the Laws by playing the ball twice, but the result (1-0) stood. Those two points helped Spurs to finish Championship runners-up; Huddersfield were relegated.

The second goal (66 mins) in **Chelsea's** 2-1 home win v Ipswich (Div 1) on Sep 26, 1970: Alan Hudson's shot hit the stanchion on the outside of goal and the ball rebounded on to the pitch. But instead of the goal-kick, referee Roy Capey gave a goal, on a linesman's confirmation. TV pictures proved otherwise. The Football League quoted from the Laws of the Game: 'The referee's decision on all matters is final.'

When **Watford's** John Eustace and **Reading's** Noel Hunt challenged for a 13th minute corner at Vicarage Road on Sep 20, 2008, the ball was clearly diverted wide. But referee Stuart Attwell signalled for a goal on the instruction on his assistant and it went down officially as a Eustace own goal. The Championship match ended 2-2.

Sunderland's 1-0 Premier League win over **Liverpool** on Oct 17, 2009 was decided by one of the most bizarre goals in football history when Darren Bent's shot struck a red beach ball thrown from the crowd and wrong-footed goalkeeper Jose Reina. Referee Mike Jones wrongly allowed it to stand. The Laws of the Game state: 'An outside agent interfering with play should result in play being stopped and restarted with a drop ball.'

The Republic of Ireland were deprived of the chance of a World Cup place in the second leg of their play-off with France on Nov 18, 2009. They were leading 1-0 in Paris when Thierry Henry blatantly handled before setting up William Gallas to equalise in extra-time time and give his side a 2-1 aggregate victory. The FA of Ireland's call for a replay was rejected by FIFA.

• The most notorious goal in World Cup history was fisted in by Diego Maradona in **Argentina's** 2-1 quarter-final win over England in Mexico City on Jun 22, 1986.

ATTENDANCES

GREATEST WORLD CROWDS

World Cup, Maracana Stadium, Rio de Janeiro, Jul 16, 1950. Final match (Brazil v Uruguay) attendance 199,850; receipts £125,000.

Total attendance in three matches (including play-off) between Santos (Brazil) and AC Milan for the Inter-Continental Cup (World Club Championship) 1963, exceeded 375,000.

BRITISH RECORD CROWDS

Most to pay: 149,547, Scotland v England, at Hampden Park, Glasgow, Apr 17, 1937. This was the first all-ticket match in Scotland (receipts £24,000).

At Scottish FA Cup Final: 146,433, Celtic v Aberdeen, at Hampden Park, Apr 24, 1937. Estimated another 20,000 shut out.

For British club match (apart from a Cup Final): 143,470, Rangers v Hibernian, at Hampden Park, Mar 27, 1948 (Scottish Cup semi-final).

FA Cup Final: 126,047, Bolton v West Ham, Apr 28, 1923. Estimated 150,000 in ground at opening of Wembley Stadium.

New Wembley: 89,874, FA Cup Final, Cardiff v Portsmouth, May 17, 2008.

World Cup Qualifying ties: 120,000, Cameroon v Morocco, Yaounde, Nov 29, 1981; 107,580, Scotland v Poland, Hampden Park, Oct 13, 1965.

European Cup: 135,826, Celtic v Leeds (semi-final, 2nd leg) at Hampden Park, Apr 15, 1970.

European Cup Final: 127,621, Real Madrid v Eintracht Frankfurt, at Hampden Park, May 18, 1960.

European Cup-Winners' Cup Final: 100,000, West Ham v TSV Munich, at Wembley, May 19, 1965.

Scottish League: 118,567, Rangers v Celtic, Jan 2, 1939.

Scottish League Cup Final: 107,609, Celtic v Rangers, at Hampden Park, Oct 23, 1965.

Football League old format: First Div: 83,260, Manchester Utd v Arsenal, Jan 17, 1948 (at

Maine Road); **Div 2** 70,302 Tottenham v Southampton, Feb 25, 1950; **Div 3S:** 51,621, Cardiff v Bristol City, Apr 7, 1947; **Div 3N:** 49,655, Hull v Rotherham, Dec 25, 1948; **Div 3:** 49,309, Sheffield Wed v Sheffield Utd, Dec 26, 1979; **Div 4:** 37,774, Crystal Palace v Millwall, Mar 31, 1961.

Premier League: 76,098, Manchester Utd v Blackburn, Mar 31, 2007.

Football League – New Div 1: 41,214, Sunderland v Stoke, Apr 25, 1998; **New Div2:** 32,471, Manchester City v York, May 8, 1999; **New Div 3:** 22,319, Hull v Hartlepool Utd, Dec 26, 2002. **New Champs:** 52,181, Newcastle v Ipswich, Apr 24, 2010; **New Lge 1:** 38,256, Leeds v Gillingham, May 3, 2008; **New Lge 2:** 17,250, MK Dons v Morecambe, May 3, 2008.

In English Provinces: 84,569, Manchester City v Stoke (FA Cup 6), Mar 3, 1934.

Record for Under-21 International: 55,700, England v Italy, first match at New Wembley, Mar 24, 2007.

Record for friendly match: 104,679, Rangers v Eintracht Frankfurt, at Hampden Park, Glasgow, Oct 17, 1961.

FA Youth Cup: 38,187, Arsenal v Manchester Utd, at Emirates Stadium, Mar 14, 2007.

Record Football League aggregate (season): 41,271,414 (1948–49) – 88 clubs.

Record Football League aggregate (single day): 1,269,934, December 27, 1949, previous day, 1,226,098.

Record average home League attendance for season: 75,691 by Manchester Utd in 2007–08.

Long-ago League attendance aggregates: 10,929,000 in 1906–07 (40 clubs); 28,132,933 in 1937–38 (88 clubs).

Last 1m crowd aggregate, League (single day): 1,007,200, December 27, 1971.

Record Amateur match attendance: 100,000 for FA Amateur Cup Final, Pegasus v Harwich & Parkeston at Wembley, Apr 11, 1953.

Record Cup-tie aggregate: 265,199, at two matches between Rangers and Morton, in Scottish Cup Final, 1947–48.

Abandoned match attendance records: In England – 63,480 at Newcastle v Swansea City FA Cup 3rd round, Jan 10, 1953, abandoned 8 mins (0-0), fog.

In Scotland: 94,596 at Scotland v Austria (4-1), Hampden Park, May 8, 1963. Referee Jim Finney ended play (79 minutes) after Austria had two players sent off and one carried off.

Colchester's record crowd (19,072) was for the FA Cup 1st round tie v Reading on Nov 27, 1948, abandoned 35 minutes (0-0), fog.

SMALLEST CROWDS

Smallest League attendances: 13, Stockport v Leicester (Div 2, May 7, 1921; played at Old Trafford – Stockport ground closed); 469, Thames v Luton (Div 3 South, December 6, 1930).

Lowest post-war League attendance: 450 Rochdale v Cambridge Utd (Div 3, Feb 5, 1974).

Lowest Premier League crowd: 3,039 for Wimbledon v Everton, Jan 26, 1993 (smallest top-division attendance since War).

Lowest Saturday post-war top-division crowd: 3,231 for Wimbledon v Luton, Sep 7, 1991 (Div 1).

Lowest Football League crowds, new format – Div 1: 849 for Wimbledon v Rotherham, (Div 1) Oct 29, 2002 (smallest attendance in top two divisions since War); 1,054 Wimbledon v Wigan (Div 1), Sep 13, 2003 in club's last home match when sharing Selhurst park; **Div 2:** 1,077, Hartlepool Utd v Cardiff, Mar 22, 1994; **Div 3:** 739, Doncaster v Barnet, Mar 3, 1998.

Lowest top-division crowd at a major ground since the war: 4,554 for Arsenal v Leeds (May 5, 1966) – fixture clashed with live TV coverage of Cup-Winners' Cup Final (Liverpool v Borussia Dortmund).

Smallest League Cup attendances: 612, Halifax v Tranmere (1st round, 2nd leg) Sep 6, 2000; 664, Wimbledon v Rotherham (3rd round), Nov 5, 2002.

Smallest League Cup attendance at top-division ground: 1,987 for Wimbledon v Bolton (2nd Round, 2nd Leg) Oct 6, 1992.

Smallest Wembley crowds for England matches: 15,628 v Chile (Rous Cup, May 23, 1989 – affected by Tube strike); 20,038 v Colombia (Friendly, Sep 6, 1995); 21,432 v Czech.

(Friendly, Apr 25, 1990); 21,142 v Japan (Umbro Cup, Jun 3, 1995); 23,600 v Wales (British Championship, Feb 23, 1983); 23,659 v Greece (Friendly, May 17, 1994); 23,951 v East Germany (Friendly, Sep 12, 1984); 24,000 v N Ireland (British Championship, Apr 4, 1984); 25,756 v Colombia (Rous Cup, May 24, 1988); 25,837 v Denmark (Friendly, Sep 14, 1988).

Smallest international modern crowds: 221 for Poland v N Ireland (4-1, friendly) at Limassol, Cyprus, on Feb 13, 2002. Played at neutral venue at Poland's World Cup training base. 265 (all from N Ireland) at their Euro Champ qual against Serbia in Belgrade on Mar 25, 2011. Serbia ordered by UEFA to play behind closed doors because of previous crowd trouble.

Smallest international modern crowds at home: N Ireland: 2,500 v Chile (Belfast, May 26, 1989 – clashed with ITV live screening of Liverpool v Arsenal Championship decider); Scotland: 7,843 v N Ireland (Hampden Park, May 6, 1969); Wales: 2,315 v N Ireland (Wrexham, May 27, 1982).

Smallest attendance for post-war England match: 2,378 v San Marino (World Cup) at Bologna (Nov 17, 1993). Tie clashed with Italy v Portugal (World Cup) shown live on Italian TV.

Smallest paid attendance for British first-class match: 29 for Clydebank v East Stirling, CIS Scottish League Cup 1st round, Jul 31, 1999. Played at Morton's Cappielow Park ground, shared by Clydebank. Match clashed with the Tall Ships Race which attracted 200,000 to the area.

FA CUP CROWD RECORD (OUTSIDE FINAL)

The first FA Cup-tie shown on closed-circuit TV (5th round, Saturday, Mar 11, 1967, kick-off 7pm) drew a total of 105,000 spectators to Goodison Park and Anfield. At Goodison, 64,851 watched the match 'for real', while 40,149 saw the TV version on eight giant screens at Anfield. Everton beat Liverpool 1-0.

LOWEST SEMI-FINAL CROWD

The smallest FA Cup semi-final attendance since the War was 17,987 for the Manchester Utd–Crystal Palace replay at Villa Park on Apr 12, 1995. Palace supporters largely boycotted tie after a fan died in car-park clash outside pub in Walsall before first match.

Previous lowest: 25,963 for Wimbledon v Luton, at Tottenham on Apr 9, 1988.

Lowest quarter-final crowd since the war: 8,735 for Chesterfield v Wrexham on Mar 9, 1997.

Smallest FA Cup 3rd round attendances for matches between League clubs: 1,833 for Chester v Bournemouth (at Macclesfield) Jan 5, 1991; 1,966 for Aldershot v Oxford Utd, Jan 10, 1987.

PRE-WEMBLEY CUP FINAL CROWDS

AT CRYSTAL PALACE

1895 42,560	1902 48,036	1908 74,967
1896 48,036	Replay 33,050	1909 67,651
1897 65,891	1903 64,000	1910 76,980
1898 62,017	1904 61,734	1911 69,098
1899 73,833	1905 101,117	1912 54,434
1900 68,945	1906 75,609	1913 120,028
1901 110,802	1907 84,584	1914 72,778

AT OLD TRAFFORD

1915 50,000

AT STAMFORD BRIDGE

1920 50,018	1921 72,805	1922 53,000

INTERNATIONAL RECORDS

MOST APPEARANCES

Peter Shilton, England goalkeeper, then aged 40, retired from international football after the 1990 World Cup Finals with the European record number of caps – 125. Previous record (119) was set by **Pat Jennings**, Northern Ireland's goalkeeper from 1964–86, who retired on his 41st birthday during the 1986 World Cup in Mexico. Shilton's England career spanned 20 seasons from his debut against East Germany at Wembley on Nov 25, 1970.

Six players have completed a century of appearances in full international matches for England. **Billy Wright** of Wolves, was the first, retiring in 1959 with a total of 105 caps. **Bobby Charlton**, of Manchester Utd, beat Wright's record in the World Cup match against West Germany in Leon, Mexico, in Jun 1970 and **Bobby Moore**, of West Ham, overtook Charlton's 106 caps against Italy in Turin, in Jun, 1973. Moore played 108 times for England, a record that stood until **Shilton** reached 109 against Denmark in Copenhagen (Jun 7, 1989). In season 2008–09, **David Beckham** (LA Galaxy/AC Milan) overtook Moore as England's most-capped outfield player. In the vastly different selection processes of their eras, Moore played 108 full games for his country, whereas Beckham's total of 115 to the end of season 2009-10, included 58 part matches, 14 as substitute and 44 times substituted.

Kenny Dalglish became Scotland's first 100-cap international v Romania (Hampden Park, Mar 26, 1986).

Shay Given earned a record 109th cap for the Republic of Ireland against Norway on Nov 17, 2010.

World's most-capped player: Mohamed Al-Deayea (Saudi Arabia goalkeeper) 173 (1990–2004).

Most-capped European player: Lothar Matthaus 150 Internationals for Germany (1980– 2000).

Most-capped European goalkeeper: Thomas Ravelli, 143 Internationals for Sweden (1981–97).

Gillian Coultard, (Doncaster Belles), England Women's captain, received a special presentation from Geoff Hurst to mark 100 caps when England beat Holland 1-0 at Upton Park on Oct 30, 1997. She made her international debut at 18 in May 1981, and retired at the end of season 1999–2000 with a record 119 caps (30 goals).

BRITAIN'S MOST-CAPPED PLAYERS

(As at start of season 2011-12)

England		Northern Ireland	
Peter Shilton	125	Pat Jennings	119
David Beckham	115	Mal Donaghy	91
Bobby Moore	108	Sammy McIlroy	88
Bobby Charlton	106	Maik Taylor	87
Billy Wright	105	Keith Gillespie	86
		David Healy	86
Scotland			
Kenny Dalglish	102	**Republic of Ireland**	
Keith Gillespie	86	Shay Given	113
Jim Leighton	91	Kevin Kilbane	110
Alex McLeish	77	Robbie Keane	108
Paul McStay	76	Steve Staunton	102
Tommy Boyd	72	Niall Quinn	91
Wales			
Steve Staunton	102		
Neville Southall	92		
Gary Speed	85		
Dean Saunders	75		
Peter Nicholas	73		
Ian Rush	73		

MOST ENGLAND CAPS IN ROW

Most consecutive international appearances: 70 by **Billy Wright,** for England from Oct 1951 to May 1959. He played 105 of England's first 108 post-war matches.

England captains most times: Billy Wright and Bobby Moore, 90 each.

England captains – 4 in match (v Serbia & Montenegro at Leicester Jun 3, 2003): **Michael Owen** was captain for the first half and after the interval the armband passed to **Emile Heskey** (for 15 minutes), **Philip Neville** (26 minutes) and substitute **Jamie Carragher** (9 minutes, including time added).

MOST SUCCESSIVE ENGLAND WINS

10 (Jun 1908–Jun 1909. Modern: 8 (Oct 2005–Jun 2006).

ENGLAND'S LONGEST UNBEATEN RUN

19 matches (16 wins, 3 draws), Nov 1965–Nov 1966.

ENGLAND'S TALLEST

At 6ft 7in, **Peter Crouch** became England's tallest-ever international when he made his debut against Colombia in New Jersey, USA on May 31, 2005.

MOST PLAYERS FROM ONE CLUB IN ENGLAND SIDES

Arsenal supplied seven men (a record) to the England team v Italy at Highbury on Nov 14, 1934. They were: Frank Moss, George Male, Eddie Hapgood, Wilf Copping, Ray Bowden, Ted Drake and Cliff Bastin. In addition, Arsenal's Tom Whittaker was England's trainer.

Since then until 2001, the most players from one club in an England team was six from **Liverpool** against Switzerland at Wembley in Sep 1977. The side also included a Liverpool old boy, Kevin Keegan (Hamburg).

Seven **Arsenal** men took part in the England – France (0-2) match at Wembley on Feb 10, 1999. Goalkeeper David Seaman and defenders Lee Dixon, Tony Adams and Martin Keown lined up for England. Nicolas Anelka (2 goals) and Emmanuel Petit started the match for France and Patrick Vieira replaced Anelka.

Manchester Utd equalled Arsenal's 1934 record by providing England with seven players in the World Cup qualifier away to Albania on Mar 28, 2001. Five started the match – David Beckham (captain), Gary Neville, Paul Scholes, Nicky Butt and Andy Cole – and two went on as substitutes: Wes Brown and Teddy Sheringham.

INTERNATIONAL SUBS RECORDS

Malta substituted all 11 players in their 1-2 home defeat against England on Jun 3, 2000. Six substitutes by England took the total replacements in the match to 17, then an international record.

Most substitutions in match by **England**: 11 in second half by Sven-Goran Eriksson against Holland at Tottenham on Aug 15, 2001; 11 against Italy at Leeds on Mar 27, 2002; Italy sent on 8 players from the bench – the total of 19 substitutions was then a record for an England match; 11 against Australia at Upton Park on Feb 12, 2003 (entire England team changed at half-time); 11 against Iceland at City of Manchester Stadium on Jun 5, 2004.

Forty three players, a record for an England match, were used in the international against Serbia & Montenegro at Leicester on Jun 3, 2003. England sent on 10 substitutes in the second half and their opponents changed all 11 players.

The Republic of Ireland sent on 12 second-half substitutes, using 23 players in all, when they beat Russia 2-0 in a friendly international in Dublin on Feb 13, 2002.

First England substitute: Wolves winger **Jimmy Mullen** replaced injured Jackie Milburn (15 mins) away to Belgium on May 18, 1950. He scored in a 4-1 win.

ENGLAND'S WORLD CUP-WINNERS

At Wembley, Jul 30, 1966, 4-2 v West Germany (2-2 after 90 mins), scorers Hurst 3, Peters.

Team: Banks; Cohen, Wilson, Stiles, J Charlton, Moore (capt), Ball, Hurst, R Charlton, Hunt, Peters. Manager **Alf Ramsey** fielded that same eleven in six successive matches (an England record): the World Cup quarter-final, semi-final and Final, and the first three games of the following season. England wore red shirts in the Final and The Queen presented the Cup to Bobby Moore. The players each received a £1,000 bonus, plus £60 World Cup Final appearance money, all less tax, and Ramsey a £6,000 bonus from the FA The match was shown live on TV (in black and white).

England's non-playing reserves – there were no substitutes – also received the £1,000 bonus, but no medals. That remained the case until FIFA finally decided that non-playing members and staff of World Cup-winning squads should be given replica medals. England's 'forgotten heroes' received theirs at a reception in Downing Street on June 10, 2009 and were later guests of honour at the World Cup qualifier against Andorra at Wembley. The 11 reserves were: Springett, Bonetti, Armfield, Byrne, Flowers, Hunter, Paine, Connelly, Callaghan, Greaves, Eastham.

BRAZIL'S RECORD RUN

Brazil hold the record for the longest unbeaten sequence in international football: 45 matches from 1993–97. The previous record of 31 was held by Hungary between Jun 1950 and Jul 1954.

ENGLAND MATCHES ABANDONED

May 17, 1953 v **Argentina** (Friendly, Buenos Aires) after 23 mins (0-0) – rain.
Oct 29, 1975 v **Czechoslovakia** (Euro Champ qual, Bratislava) after 17 mins (0-0) – fog. Played next day.
Feb 15, 1995 v **Rep of Ireland** (Friendly, Dublin) after 27 mins (1-0) – crowd disturbance.

ENGLAND POSTPONEMENT

Nov 21, 1979 v **Bulgaria** (Euro Champ qual, Wembley postponed for 24 hours – fog.

ENGLAND UNDER COVER

England played indoors for the first time when they beat Argentina 1-0 in the World Cup at the Sapporo Dome, Japan, on Jun 7, 2002.

ALL-SEATED INTERNATIONALS

The first **all-seated crowd** (30,000) for a full international in Britain saw **Wales** and **WestGermany** draw 0-0 at Cardiff Arms Park on May 31, 1989. The terraces were closed.

England's first all-seated international at Wembley was against Yugoslavia (2-1) on December 13, 1989 (attendance 34,796). The terracing behind the goals was closed for conversion to seating.

The first **full-house all-seated** international at Wembley was for England v Brazil (1-0) on Mar 28, 1990, when a capacity 80,000 crowd paid record British receipts of £1,200,000.

FIRST BLACK CAPS

First black player for **England** in a senior international was Nottm Forest full-back **Viv Anderson** against Czechoslovakia at Wembley on Nov 29, 1978.

Aston Villa's **Ugo Ehiogu** was **England's** first black captain (U-21 v Holland at Portsmouth, Apr 27, 1993).

Paul Ince (Manchester Utd) became the first black player to captain **England** in a **full international** (v USA, Boston, Jun 9, 1993).

First black British international was **Eddie Parris** (Bradford Park Avenue) for Wales against N Ireland in Belfast on December 5, 1931.

MOST NEW CAPS IN ENGLAND TEAM

6, by Sir Alf Ramsey (v Portugal, Apr 3, 1974) and **by Sven-Goran Eriksson** (v Australia, Feb 12, 2003; 5 at half-time when 11 changes made).

PLAYED FOR MORE THAN ONE COUNTRY

Multi-nationals in senior international football include: **Johnny Carey** (1938–53) – caps Rep of Ireland 29, N Ireland 7; **Ferenc Puskas** (1945–62) – caps Hungary 84, Spain 4; **Alfredo di Stefano** (1950–56) – caps Argentina 7, Spain 31; **Ladislav Kubala** (1948–58) – caps, Hungary 3, Czechoslovakia 11, Spain 19, only player to win full international honours with 3 countries. Kubala also played in a fourth international team, scoring twice for FIFA v England at Wembley in 1953. Eleven players, including **Carey**, appeared for both N Ireland and the Republic of Ireland in seasons directly after the last war.

Cecil Moore, capped by N Ireland in 1949 when with Glentoran, played for USA v England in 1953.
Hawley Edwards played for England v Scotland in 1874 and for Wales v Scotland in 1876.
Jack Reynolds (Distillery and WBA) played for both Ireland (5 times) and England (8) in the 1890s.
Bobby Evans (Sheffield Utd) had played 10 times for Wales when capped for England, in 1910–11. He was born in Chester of Welsh parents.
In recent years, several players have represented USSR and one or other of the breakaway republics. The same applies to Yugoslavia and its component states. **Josip Weber** played for Croatia in 1992 and made a 5-goal debut for Belgium in 1994.

THREE-GENERATION INTERNATIONAL FAMILY

When Bournemouth striker **Warren Feeney** was capped away to Liechtenstein on Mar 27, 2002, he became the third generation of his family to play for Northern Ireland. He followed in the footsteps of his grandfather James (capped twice in 1950) and father Warren Snr. (1 in 1976).

FATHERS & SONS CAPPED BY ENGLAND

George Eastham senior (pre-war) and **George Eastham** junior; **Brian Clough** and **Nigel Clough**; **Frank Lampard** snr and **Frank Lampard** jnr.

FATHER & SON SAME-DAY CAPS

Iceland made father-and-son international history when they beat Estonia 3-0 in Tallin on Apr 24, 1996. **Arnor Gudjohnsen** (35) started the match and was replaced (62 mins) by his 17-year-old son **Eidur**.

LONGEST UNBEATEN START TO ENGLAND CAREER

Steven Gerrard, 21 matches (W16, D5) 2000–03.

SUCCESSIVE ENGLAND HAT-TRICKS

The last player to score a hat-trick in consecutive England matches was **Dixie Dean** on the summer tour in May 1927, against Belgium (9-1) and Luxembourg (5-2).

POST-WAR HAT-TRICKS v ENGLAND

Nov 25, 1953, **Nandor Hidegkuti** (England 3, Hungary 6, Wembley); May 11, 1958, **Aleksandar Petakovic** (Yugoslavia 5, England 0, Belgrade); May 17, 1959, **Juan Seminario** (Peru 4, England 1, Lima); Jun 15, 1988, **Marco van Basten** (Holland 3, England 1, European Championship, Dusseldorf).

NO-SAVE GOALKEEPERS

Chris Woods did not have one save to make when England beat San Marino 6-0 (World Cup) at Wembley on Feb 17, 1993. He touched the ball only six times.
Gordon Banks had a similar no-save experience when England beat Malta 5-0 (European Championship) at Wembley on May 12, 1971. Malta did not force a goal-kick or corner, and the four times Banks touched the ball were all from back passes.
Robert Green was also idle in the 6-0 World Cup qualifying win over Andorra at Wembley on Jun 10, 2009.

FIFA WORLD YOUTH CHAMPIONSHIP (UNDER-20)

Finals: 1977 (Tunis) Soviet Union 2 Mexico 2 (Soviet won 9-8 on pens.); 1979 (Tokyo) Argentina 3 Soviet Union 1; 1981 (Sydney) W Germany 4 Qatar 0; 1983 (Mexico City) Brazil 1 Argentina 0; 1985 (Moscow) Brazil 1 Spain 0; 1987 (Santiago) Yugoslavia 1 W Germany 1 (Yugoslavia won 5-4 on pens.); 1989 (Riyadh) Portugal 2 Nigeria 0; 1991 (Lisbon) Portugal 0 Brazil 0 (Portugal won 4-2 on pens.); 1993 (Sydney) Brazil 2 Ghana 1; 1995 (Qatar) Argentina 2 Brazil 0; 1997 (Kuala Lumpur) Argentina 2 Uruguay 1; 1999 (Lagos) Spain 4 Japan 0; 2001 (Buenos Aires) Argentina 3 Ghana 0; 2003 (Dubai) Brazil 1 Spain 0; 2005 (Utrecht) Argentina 2 Nigeria 1; 2007 (Toronto) Argentina 2 Czech Republic 1; 2009 (Cairo) Ghana 0 Brazil 0 (aet, Ghana won 4-3 on pens).

FAMOUS CLUB FEATS

Chelsea were Premiership winners in 2004–05, their centenary season with the highest points total (95) ever recorded by England Champions. They set these other records: Most Premiership wins in season (29); most clean sheets (25) and fewest goals conceded (15) in top-division history. They also won the League Cup in 2005.

Arsenal created an all-time English League record sequence of 49 unbeaten Premiership matches (W36, D13), spanning 3 seasons, from May 7, 2003 until losing 2-0 away to Manchester Utd on Oct 24, 2004. It included all 38 games in season 2003–04.

The Double: There have been 11 instances of a club winning the Football League/Premier League title and the FA Cup in the same season. **Manchester Utd** and **Arsenal** have each done so three times: **Preston** 1888–89; **Aston Villa** 1896–97; **Tottenham** 1960–61; **Arsenal** 1970–71, 1997–98, 2001–02; **Liverpool** 1985–86; **Manchester Utd** 1993–94, 1995–96, 1998–99; **Chelsea** 2009-10.

The Treble: **Liverpool** were the first English club to win three major competitions in one season when in 1983–84, Joe Fagan's first season as manager, they were League Champions, League Cup winners and European Cup winners.

Sir Alex Ferguson's **Manchester Utd** achieved an even more prestigious treble in 1998–99, completing the domestic double of Premiership and FA Cup and then winning the European Cup. In season 2008– 09, they completed another major triple success – Premier League, Carling Cup and World Club Cup.

Liverpool completed a unique treble by an English club with three cup successes under Gerard Houllier in season 2000–01: the League Cup, FA Cup and UEFA Cup.

Liverpool the first English club to win five major trophies in one calendar year (Feb– Aug 2001): League Cup, FA Cup, UEFA Cup, Charity Shield, UEFA Super Cup.

As Champions in season 2001–02, **Arsenal** set a Premiership record by winning the last 13 matches. They were the first top-division club since Preston in the League's inaugural season (1888–89) to maintain an unbeaten away record.

(See Scottish section for treble feats by Rangers and Celtic.)

Record Home Runs: Liverpool went 85 competitive first-team games unbeaten at home between losing 2-3 to Birmingham on Jan 21, 1978 and 1-2 to Leicester on Jan 31, 1981. They comprised 63 in the League, 9 League Cup, 7 in European competition and 6 FA Cup.

Chelsea hold the record unbeaten home League sequence of 82 matches (W60, D22), including four full seasons to the end of 2007–08. Last visiting team to take three points at Stamford Bridge were Arsenal (2-1 winners on Feb 21, 2004)

Third to First: Charlton, in 1936, became the first club to advance from the Third to First Division in successive seasons. **Queens Park Rangers** were the second club to achieve the feat in 1968, and **Oxford Utd** did it in 1984 and 1985 as Champions of each division. Subsequently, **Derby** (1987), **Middlesbrough** (1988), **Sheffield Utd** (1990) and **Notts Co** (1991) climbed from Third Division to First in consecutive seasons.

Watford won successive promotions from the modern Second Division to the Premier League in 1997–98, 1998–99. **Manchester City** equalled the feat in 1998–99, 1999–2000.

Fourth to First: Northampton , in 1965 became the first club to rise from the Fourth to the First Division. **Swansea** climbed from the Fourth Division to the First (three promotions in four seasons), 1977–78 to 1980–81. **Wimbledon** repeated the feat, 1982–83 to 1985–86 **Watford** did it in five seasons, 1977–8 to 1981–82. **Carlisle** climbed from Fourth Division to First, 1964–74.

Non-League to First: When **Wimbledon** finished third in the Second Division in 1986, they completed the phenomenal rise from non-League football (Southern League) to the First Division in nine years. Two years later they won the FA Cup.

Tottenham, in 1960–61, not only carried off the First Division Championship and the FA Cup for the first time that century but set up other records by opening with 11 successive wins, registering most First Division wins (31), most away wins in the League's history (16), and equalling Arsenal's First Division records of 66 points and 33 away points. They already held the Second Division record of 70 points (1919–20).

Arsenal, in 1993, became the first club to win both English domestic cup competitions (FA Cup and League Cup) in the same season. Liverpool repeated the feat in 2000–01.

Preston, in season 1888–89, won the first League Championship without losing a match and the FA Cup without having a goal scored against them. Only other English clubs to remain unbeaten through a League season were **Liverpool** (Div 2 Champions in 1893–94) and **Arsenal** (Premiership Champions 2003–04).

Bury, in 1903, also won the FA Cup without conceding a goal.

Everton won Div 2, Div 1 and the FA Cup in successive seasons, 1930–31, 1931–32, 1932–33.

Wolves won the League Championship in 1958 and 1959 and the FA Cup in 1960.

Liverpool won the title in 1964, the FA Cup in 1965 and the title again in 1966. In 1978 they became the first British club to win the European Cup in successive seasons. Nottm Forest repeated the feat in 1979 and 1980.

Liverpool won the League Championship six times in eight seasons (1976–83) under **Bob Paisley's** management.

Sir Alex Ferguson's **Manchester Utd** have won the Premier League in 12 of its 19 seasons (1993–2011). They were runners-up four times and third three times.

Most Premiership wins in season: 29 by Chelsea in 2004–05, 2005–06.

Biggest points-winning margin by League Champions: 18 by Manchester Utd (1999–2000).

COVENTRY UNIQUE

Coventry City are the only club to have played in the Premier League, all four previous divisions of the Football League, in both sections (North and South) of the old Third Division and in the Coca-Cola Championship.

FAMOUS UPS & DOWNS

Sunderland: Relegated in 1958 after maintaining First Division status since their election to the Football League in 1890. They dropped into Division 3 for the first time in 1987.

Aston Villa: Relegated with Preston to the Third Division in 1970.

Arsenal up: When the League was extended in 1919, Woolwich Arsenal (sixth in Division Two in 1914–15, last season before the war) were elected to Division One. Arsenal have been in the top division ever since.

Tottenham down: At that same meeting in 1919 Chelsea (due for relegation) retained their place in Division One but the bottom club (Tottenham) had to go down to Division Two.

Preston and Burnley down: Preston, the first League Champions in season 1888–89, dropped into the Fourth Division in 1985. So did Burnley, also among the League's original members in 1888. In 1986, Preston had to apply for re-election.

Wolves' fall: Wolves, another of the Football League's original members, completed the fall from First Division to Fourth in successive seasons (1984–5–6).

Lincoln out: Lincoln became the first club to suffer automatic demotion from the Football League when they finished bottom of Div 4, on goal difference, in season 1986–87. They were replaced by Scarborough, champions of the GM Vauxhall Conference. Lincoln regained their place a year later.

Swindon up and down: In the 1990 play-offs, Swindon won promotion to the First Division for the first time, but remained in the Second Division because of financial irregularities.

MOST CHAMPIONSHIP WINS

Manchester Utd became champions of England for a record 19th time (7 Football League, 12 Premier League) by winning the title in season 2010–11. They overtook **Liverpool** (18), with **Arsenal** third on 13 wins.

LONGEST CURRENT MEMBERS OF TOP DIVISION

Arsenal (since 1919), **Everton** (1954), **Liverpool** (1962), **Manchester Utd** (1975).

CHAMPIONS: FEWEST PLAYERS

Liverpool used only **14** players (five ever-present) when they won the League Championship in season 1965–66. **Aston Villa** also called on no more than 14 players to win the title in 1980–81, with seven ever-present.

UNBEATEN CHAMPIONS

Only two clubs have become Champions of England with an unbeaten record: **Preston** as the Football League's first winners in 1888–89 (22 matches) and **Arsenal**, Premiership winners in 2003–04 (38 matches).

LEAGUE HAT-TRICKS

Huddersfield created a record in 1924–5–6 by winning the League Championship three years in succession.

Arsenal equalled this hat-trick in 1933–4–5, **Liverpool** in 1982–3–4 and **Manchester Utd** in 1999–2000–01. Sir Alex Ferguson's side became the first to complete two successive hat-tricks (2007– 8– 9).

'SUPER DOUBLE' WINNERS

Since the War, there have been three instances of players appearing in and then managing FA Cup and Championship-winning teams:

Joe Mercer: Player in Arsenal Championship teams 1948, 1953 and in their 1950 FA Cup side; manager of Manchester City when they won Championship 1968, FA Cup 1969.

Kenny Dalglish: Player in Liverpool Championship-winning teams 1979, 1980, 1982, 1983, 1984, player-manager 1986, 1988, 1990: player-manager when Liverpool won FA Cup (to complete Double) 1986; manager of Blackburn, Champions 1995.

George Graham: Played in Arsenal's Double-winning team in 1971, and as manager took them to Championship success in 1989 and 1991 and the FA Cup – League Cup double in 1993.

ORIGINAL TWELVE

The original 12 members of the Football League (formed in 1888) were: **Accrington, Aston Villa, Blackburn, Bolton, Burnley, Derby, Everton, Notts Co, Preston, Stoke, WBA** and **Wolves**.

Results on the opening day (Sep 8, 1888): Bolton 3, Derby 6; Everton 2, Accrington 1; Preston 5, Burnley 2; Stoke 0, WBA 2; Wolves 1, Aston Villa 1. Preston had the biggest first-day crowd: 6,000. Blackburn and Notts Co did not play that day. They kicked off a week later (Sep 15) – Blackburn 5, Accrington 5; Everton 2, Notts Co 1.

Accrington FC resigned from the league in 1893 and later folded. A new club, Accrington Stanley, were members of the league from 1921 until 1962 when financial problems forced their demise. The current Accrington Stanley were formed in 1968 and gained league status in 2007.

FASTEST CLIMBS

Three promotions in four seasons by two clubs – **Swansea City**: 1978 third in Div 4; 1979 third in Div 3; 1981 third in Div 2; **Wimbledon**: 1983 Champions of Div 4; 1984 second in Div 3; 1986 third in Div 2.

MERSEYSIDE RECORD

Liverpool is the only city to have staged top-division football – through Everton and/or Liverpool – in **every season** since League football began in 1888.

EARLIEST PROMOTIONS TO TOP DIVISION POST-WAR

Mar 23, 1974, Middlesbrough; Mar 25, 2006, Reading.

EARLIEST RELEGATIONS POST-WAR

From top division: **QPR** went down from the old First Division on Mar 29, 1969. From modern First Division: **Stockport** on Mar 16, 2002, with 7 matches still to play; **Wimbledon** on Apr 6, 2004, with 7 matches to play.

LEAGUE RECORDS

DOUBLE CHAMPIONS

Nine men have played in and managed League Championship-winning teams:

Ted Drake Player – Arsenal 1934, 1935, 1938. Manager – Chelsea 1955.
Bill Nicholson Player – Tottenham 1951. Manager – Tottenham 1961.
Alf Ramsey Player – Tottenham 1951. Manager – Ipswich 1962.
Joe Mercer Player – Everton 1939, Arsenal 1948, 1953. Manager – Manchester City 1968.
Dave Mackay Player – Tottenham 1961. Manager – Derby 1975.
Bob Paisley Player – Liverpool 1947. Manager – Liverpool 1976, 1977, 1979, 1980, 1982, 1983.
Howard Kendall Player – Everton 1970. Manager – Everton 1985, 1987.
Kenny Dalglish Player – Liverpool 1979, 1980, 1982, 1983, 1984. Player-manager – Liverpool 1986, 1988, 1990. Manager – Blackburn 1995.
George Graham Player – Arsenal 1971. Manager – Arsenal 1989, 1991.

GIGGS RECORD COLLECTION

Ryan Giggs (Manchester Utd) has collected the most individual honours in English football with a total of 32 prizes to the end of season 2010–11. They comprise: 12 Premier League titles, 4 FA Cups, 3 League Cups, 2 European Cups, 1 UEFA Super Cup, 1 Inter-Continental Cup, 1 World Club Cup, 8 Charity Shields/Community Shields.

CANTONA'S FOUR-TIMER

Eric Cantona played in four successive Championship-winning teams: Marseille 1990–01, Leeds 1991–92, Manchester Utd 1992–93 and 1993–94.

ARRIVALS AND DEPARTURES

The following are the Football League arrivals and departures since 1923:

Year	In	Out
1923	Doncaster	Stalybridge Celtic
	New Brighton	
1927	Torquay	Aberdare Athletic
1928	Carlisle	Durham
1929	York Ashington	
1930	Thames	Merthyr Tydfil
1931	Mansfield	Newport Co
	Chester	Nelson
1932	Aldershot	Thames

	Newport Co	Wigan Borough
1938	Ipswich	Gillingham
1950	Colchester, Gillingham	
	Scunthorpe, Shrewsbury	
1951	Workington	New Brighton
1960	Peterborough	Gateshead
1962	Oxford Utd	Accrington (resigned)
1970	Cambridge Utd	Bradford PA
1972	Hereford	Barrow
1977	Wimbledon	Workington
1978	Wigan	Southport
1987	Scarborough	Lincoln
1988	Lincoln	Newport Co
1989	Maidstone	Darlington
1990	Darlington	Colchester
1991	Barnet	
1992	Colchester	Aldershot, Maidstone (resigned)
1993	Wycombe	Halifax
1997	Macclesfield	Hereford
1998	Halifax	Doncaster
1999	Cheltenham	Scarborough
2000	Kidderminster	Chester
2001	Rushden	Barnet
2002	Boston	Halifax
2003	Yeovil, Doncaster	Exeter, Shrewsbury
2004	Chester, Shrewsbury	Carlisle, York
2005	Barnet, Carlisle	Kidderminster, Cambridge Utd
2006	Accrington, Hereford	Oxford Utd, Rushden & Diamonds
2007	Dagenham, Morecambe	Torquay, Boston
2008	Aldershot, Exeter	Wrexham, Mansfield
2009	Burton, Torquay	Chester, Luton
2010	Stevenage, Oxford Utd	Grimsby, Darlington
2011	Crawley, AFC Wimbledon	Lincoln, Stockport

Leeds City were expelled from Div 2 in Oct, 1919; Port Vale took over their fixtures.

EXTENSIONS TO FOOTBALL LEAGUE

Clubs	Season	Clubs	Season
12 to 14	1891–92	44 to 66†	1920–21
14 to 28*	1892–93	66 to 86†	1921–22
28 to 31	1893–94	86 to 88	1923–24
31 to 32	1894–95	88 to 92	1950–51
32 to 36	1898–99	92 to 93	1991–92
36 to 40	1905–06	(Reverted to 92 when Aldershot closed, Mar 1992)	

*Second Division formed. † Third Division (South) formed from Southern League clubs.
†Third Division (North) formed.
Football League reduced to 70 clubs and three divisions on the formation of the FA Premier League in 1992; increased to 72 season 1994–95, when Premier League reduced to 20 clubs.

RECORD RUNS

Arsenal hold the record unbeaten sequence in the English League – 49 Premiership matches (36 wins, 13 draws) from May 7, 2003 until Oct 24, 2004 when beaten 2-0 away to Manchester Utd

The record previously belonged to **Nottm Forest** – 42 First Division matches (21 wins, 21 draws) from Nov 19, 1977 until beaten 2-0 at Liverpool on December 9, 1978.

Best debuts: Ipswich won the First Division at their first attempt in 1961–62.

Peterborough in their first season in the Football League (1960–1) not only won the Fourth Division but set the all-time scoring record for the League of 134 goals. **Hereford** were promoted from the Fourth Division in their first League season, 1972–73.

Wycombe were promoted from the Third Division (via the play-offs) in their first League season, 1993–94.

Record winning sequence in a season: 14 consecutive League victories (all in Second Division): **Manchester Utd** 1904–05, **Bristol City** 1905–06 and **Preston** 1950–51.

Best winning start to League season: 13 successive victories in Div 3 by **Reading**, season 1985–86.

Best starts in 'old' First Division: 11 consecutive victories by **Tottenham** in 1960–61; 10 by **Manchester Utd** in 1985–86. **Newcastle** won their first 11 matches in the 'new' First Division in 1992–93.

Longest unbeaten sequence (all competitions): 40 by **Nottm Forest**, Mar–December 1978. It comprised 21 wins, 19 draws (in 29 League matches, 6 League Cup, 4 European Cup, 1 Charity Shield).

Longest unbeaten starts to League season: 38 matches (26 wins, 12 draws) in **Arsenal's** undefeated Premiership season, 2003–04; 29 matches – **Leeds**, Div 1 1973–74 (19 wins, 10 draws); **Liverpool**, Div 1 1987–88 (22 wins, 7 draws).

Most consecutive League matches unbeaten in a season: 38 **Arsenal** Premiership season 2003–04 (see above); 33 **Reading** (25 wins, 8 draws) 2005–06.

Longest winning sequence in Div 1: 13 matches by **Tottenham** – last two of season 1959–60, first 11 of 1960–61.

Longest winning one-season sequences in League Championship: 13 matches by **Preston** in 1891–92; 13 by **Sunderland**, also in 1891–92.

Longest unbeaten home League sequence in top division: 86 matches (62 wins, 24 draws) by **Chelsea** (Mar 2004– Oct 2008).

League's longest winning sequence with clean sheets: 9 matches by **Stockport** (Lge 2, 2006–07 season).

Premier League – best starts to season: (before **Arsenal** unbeaten through season 2003–04): 12 games unbeaten – **Nottm Forest** in 1995–96, **Arsenal** in 1997–98, **Aston Villa** in 1998–99, **Liverpool** 2002–03.

Best winning start to Premiership season: 9 consecutive victories by **Chelsea** in 2005–06.

Premier League – most consecutive wins (two seasons): 14 by **Arsenal**, Feb–Aug, 2002. Single season:11 by **Manchester Utd** (Dec 2008– Mar 2009)

Most consecutive away League wins in top flight: 11 by **Chelsea** (3 at end 2007– 08 season, 8 in 2008– 9)

Premier League – longest unbeaten away run: 23 matches (W16, D7) by **Arsenal** (Aug 18, 2001–Sep 28, 2002); and by **Arsenal** again (W13, D10), Apr 5, 2003–May 15, 2004.

Record home-win sequences:Bradford Park Avenue won 25 successive home games in Div 3 North – the last 18 in 1926–7 and the first 7 the following season. Longest run of home wins in the top division is 21 by **Liverpool** – the last 9 of 1971–72 and the first 12 of 1972–73.

British record for successive League wins: 25 by **Celtic** (Scottish Premier League), 2003–04.

WORST SEQUENCES

Derby experienced the longest run without a win in League history in season 2007–08 – 32 games from Sep 22 to the end of the campaign (25 lost, 7 drawn). They finished bottom by a 24-point margin. The sequence increased to 36 matches (28 lost, 8 drawn) at the start of the following season.

Cambridge Utd had the previous worst of 31 in 1983–84 (21 lost, 10 drawn). They were bottom of Div 2.

Worst losing start to a League season : 12 consecutive defeats by **Manchester Utd** (Div 1), 1930–31.

Worst Premier League start:Swindon 15 matches without win (6 draws, 9 defeats), 1993–94.

Premier League – most consecutive defeats: 20 **Sunderland** last 15 matches, 2002–03, first five matches 2005–06.

Longest non-winning start to League season: 25 matches (4 draws, 21 defeats) by **Newport**, Div 4. Worst no-win League starts since then: 16 matches by **Burnley** (9 draws, 7 defeats in Div 2, 1979–80); 16 by **Hull** (10 draws, 6 defeats in Div 2, 1989–90); 16 by **Sheffield Utd** (4 draws, 12 defeats in Div 1, 1990–91).

Most League defeats in season: 34 by **Doncaster** (Div 3) 1997–98.

Fewest League wins in season: 1 by **Loughborough** (Div 2, season 1899–1900). They lost 27, drew 6, goals 18-100 and dropped out of the League. (See also Scottish section). 1 by **Derby** (Prem Lge, 2007–08). They lost 29, drew 8, goals 20-89.

Most consecutive League defeats in season: 18 by Darwen (Div 1, 1898–99); 17 by Rochdale (Div 3 North, 1931–32).

Fewest home League wins in season: 1 by **Loughborough** (Div 2, 1899–1900), **Notts Co** (Div 1, 1904–05), **Woolwich Arsenal** (Div 1, 1912–13), **Blackpool** (Div 1, 1966–67), **Rochdale** (Div 3, 1973–74), **Sunderland** (Prem Lge, 2005–06); **Derby** (Prem Lge, 2007–08).

Most home League defeats in season: 18 by **Cambridge Utd** (Div 3, 1984–85).

Away League defeats record: 24 in row by **Nelson** (Div 3 North) – 3 in Apr 1930 followed by all 21 in season 1930–31. They then dropped out of the League.

Biggest defeat in Champions' season: During **Newcastle's** title-winning season in 1908–09, they were beaten 9-1 at home by Sunderland on December 5.

WORST START BY EVENTUAL CHAMPIONS

Sunderland took only 2 points from their first 7 matches in season 1912–13 (2 draws, 5 defeats). They won 25 of the remaining 31 games to clinch their fifth League title.

DISMAL DERBY

Derby were relegated in season 2007–08 as the worst-ever team in the Premier League: fewest wins (1), fewest points (11); fewest goals (20), first club to go down in March (29th).

UNBEATEN LEAGUE SEASON

Only three clubs have completed an English League season unbeaten: **Preston** (22 matches in 1888–89, the League's first season), **Liverpool** (28 matches in Div 2, 1893–94) and **Arsenal** (38 matches in Premiership, 2003–04).

100 PER CENT HOME RECORDS

Five clubs have won every home League match in a season, four of them in the old Second Division: **Liverpool** (14) in 1893–94, **Bury** (15) in 1894–5, **Sheffield Wed** (17) in 1899–1900 and **Small Heath**, subsequently **Birmingham** (17) in 1902–03. The last club to do it, **Brentford**, won all 21 home games in Div 3 South in 1929–30.

Rotherham just failed to equal that record in 1946–47. They won their first 20 home matches in Div 3 North, then drew the last 3-3 v Rochdale.

BEST HOME LEAGUE RECORDS IN TOP FLIGHT

Newcastle, 1906–07 (P19, W18, D1); **Chelsea** 2005–06 (P19, W18, D1).

MOST CONSECUTIVE CLEAN SHEETS

Premier League – 14: **Manchester Utd** (2008– 09); **Football League** – 11: **Millwall** (Div 3 South 1925–26); **York** (Div 3 1973–74); **Reading** (Div 4, 1978–79).

WORST HOME RUNS

Most consecutive home League defeats: 8 by **Rochdale** (Div 3 North) in season 1931–32; 8 by **Stockport** (Div1) in season 2001–02; 8 by **Sunderland** (Premiership), season 2002–03. Between Nov 1958 and Oct 1959 **Portsmouth** drew 2 and lost 14 out of 16 consecutive home games.

West Ham did not win in the Premiership at Upton Park in season 2002–03 until the 13th home match on Jan 29.

MOST AWAY WINS IN SEASON
Doncaster won 18 of their 21 away League fixtures when winning Div 3 North in 1946–47.

AWAY WINS RECORD
Most consecutive away League wins: 10 by **Tottenham** (Div 1) – 8 at start of 1960–61 after ending previous season with 2.

100 PER CENT HOME WINS ON ONE DAY
Div 1 – All 11 home teams won on Feb 13, 1926 and on Dec 10, 1955. **Div 2** – All 12 home teams won on Nov 26, 1988. **Div 3**, all 12 home teams won in the week-end programme of Oct 18–19, 1968.

NO HOME WINS IN DIV ON ONE DAY
Div 1 – 8 away wins, 3 draws in 11 matches on Sep 6, 1986. **Div 2** – 7 away wins, 4 draws in 11 matches on Dec 26, 1987. **Premier League** – 6 away wins, 5 draws in 11 matches on Dec 26, 1994.
The week-end **Premiership** programme on Dec 7–8–9, 1996 produced no home win in the ten games (4 aways, 6 draws). There was again no home victory (3 away wins, 7 draws) in the week-end **Premiership** fixtures on Sep 23–24, 2000.

MOST DRAWS IN A SEASON (FOOTBALL LEAGUE)
23 by **Norwich** (Div 1, 1978–79), **Exeter** (Div 4, 1986–87). **Cardiff** and **Hartlepool** (both Div 3, 1997–98). **Norwich** played 42 matches, the others 46.

MOST DRAWS IN ONE DIV ON ONE DAY
On Sep 18, 1948 **nine** out of 11 First Division matches were drawn.

MOST DRAWS IN PREMIER DIV PROGRAMME
Over the week-ends of December 2–3–4, 1995, and Sep 23–24, 2000, **seven** out of the ten matches finished level.

FEWEST DRAWS IN SEASON (46 MATCHES)
3 by **Reading** (Div 3 South, 1951–52); **Bradford Park Avenue** (Div 3 North, 1956–57); **Tranmere** (Div 4, 1984–85); **Southend** (Div 3, 2002–03).

HIGHEST-SCORING DRAWS IN LEAGUE
Leicester 6, **Arsenal** 6 (Div 1 Apr 21, 1930); **Charlton** 6, **Middlesbrough** 6 (Div 2. Oct 22, 1960)
Latest **6-6** draw in first-class football was between **Tranmere** and **Newcastle** in the Zenith Data Systems Cup 1st round on Oct 1, 1991. The score went from 3-3 at 90 minutes to 6-6 after extra time, and Tranmere won 3-2 on penalties. In Scotland: **Queen of the South** 6, **Falkirk** 6 (Div 1, Sep 20, 1947).
Most recent **5-5** draws in top division: **Southampton** v **Coventry** (Div 1, May 4, 1982); **QPR** v **Newcastle** (Div 1, Sep 22, 1984).

DRAWS RECORDS
Most consecutive drawn matches in Football League: 8 by **Torquay** (Div 3), Oct 25 – Dec 13, 1969; **Chesterfield** (Lge 1), Nov 26 – Jan 2 (2005–06).
Longest sequence of draws by the same score: six 1-1 results by QPR in season 1957–58.
Tranmere became the first club to play **five consecutive 0-0 League draws**, in season 1997–98.

IDENTICAL RECORDS

There is only **one instance** of two clubs in one division finishing a season with identical records. In 1907–08, **Blackburn** and **Woolwich Arsenal** were bracketed equal 14th in the First Division with these figures: P38, W12, D12, L14, Goals 51-63, Pts. 36.

The total of **1195 goals** scored in the Premier League in season 1993–94 was repeated in 1994–95.

DEAD LEVEL

Millwall's record in Division Two in season 1973–74 was P42, W14, D14, L14, F51, A51, Pts 42.

CHAMPIONS OF ALL DIVISIONS

Wolves, **Burnley** and **Preston** are the only clubs to have won titles in the old Divisions1, 2, 3and4. Wolves also won the Third Division North and the new Championship.

POINTS DEDUCTIONS

2000–01: Chesterfield 9 for breach of transfer regulations and falsifying gate receipts.

2002–03: Boston 4 for contractual irregularities.

2004–05: Wrexham, Cambridge Utd 10 for administration.

2005–06: Rotherham 10 for administration.

2006–07: Leeds, Boston 10 for administration; **Bury** 1 for unregistered player.

2007–08: Leeds 15 over insolvency rules; **Bournemouth, Luton, Rotherham** 10 for administration.

2008–09: Luton 20 for failing Insolvency rules, 10 over payments to agents; **Bournemouth, Rotherham** 17 for breaking administration rules; **Southampton, Stockport** 10 for administration - **Southampton** with effect from season 2009–10 **Crystal Palace** 1 for ineligible player.

2009-10: Portsmouth 9, **Crystal Palace** 10 for administration; **Hartlepool** 3 for ineligible player.

2010-11: Plymouth 10 for administration; **Hereford** 3, **Torquay** 1, each for ineligible player

Among previous points penalties imposed:

Nov 1990: **Arsenal** 2, **Manchester Utd** 1 following mass players' brawl at Old Trafford.

Dec 1996: **Brighton** 2 for pitch invasions by fans.

Jan 1997: **Middlesbrough** 3 for refusing to play Premiership match at Blackburn because of injuries and illness.

Jun 1994: **Tottenham** 12 (reduced to 6) and banned from following season's FA Cup for making illegal payments to players. On appeal, points deduction annulled and club re-instated in Cup.

NIGHTMARE STARTS

Most goals conceded by a goalkeeper on League debut: 13 by **Steve Milton** when Halifax lost 13-0 at Stockport (Div 3 North) on Jan 6, 1934.

Post-war: 11 by Crewe's new goalkeeper **Dennis Murray** (Div 3 North) on Sep 29, 1951, when Lincoln won 11-1.

RELEGATION ODD SPOTS

None of the Barclays Premiership relegation places in season 2004–05 were decided until the last day (Sunday, May 15). **WBA** (bottom at kick-off) survived with a 2-0 home win against Portsmouth, and the three relegated clubs were **Southampton** (1-2 v Manchester Utd), **Norwich** (0-6 at Fulham) and **Crystal Palace** (2-2 at Charlton).

In season 1937–38, **Manchester City** were the highest-scoring team in the First Division with 80 goals (3 more than Champions Arsenal), but they finished in 21st place and were relegated – a year after winning the title. They scored more goals than they conceded (77).

That season produced the **closest relegation battle** in top-division history, with only 4 points spanning the bottom 11 clubs in Div 1. WBA went down with **Manchester City**.

Twelve years earlier, in 1925–26, City went down to Division 2 despite totalling 89 goals – still the most scored in any division by a relegated team. Manchester City also scored 31 FA Cup goals that season, but lost the Final 1-0 to Bolton Wanderers.

Cardiff were relegated from Div 1 in season 1928–29, despite conceding fewest goals in the division (59). They also scored fewest (43).

On their way to relegation from the First Division in season 1984–85, **Stoke** twice lost ten matches in a row.

RELEGATION TREBLES

Two Football League clubs have been relegated three seasons in succession. **Bristol City** fell from First Division to Fourth in 1980–1–2 and **Wolves** did the same in 1984–5–6.

OLDEST CLUBS

Oldest Association Football Club is **Sheffield FC** (formed in 1857). The oldest Football League clubs are **Notts Co**, 1862; **Nottm Forest**, 1865; and **Sheffield Wed**, 1866.

FOUR DIVISIONS

In **May, 1957**, the Football League decided to re-group the two sections of the Third Division into Third and Fourth Divisions in **season 1958–59**.

The Football League was reduced to three divisions on the formation of the Premier League in **1992**.

In season 2004–05, under new sponsors Coca-Cola, the titles of First, Second and Third Divisions were changed to League Championship, League One and League Two.

THREE UP – THREE DOWN

The Football League annual general meeting of Jun 1973 agreed to adopt the promotion and relegation system of three up and three down.

The **new system** came into effect in **season 1973–74** and applied only to the first three divisions; four clubs were still relegated from the Third and four promoted from the Fourth.

It was the first change in the promotion and relegation system for the top two divisions in 81 years.

MOST LEAGUE APPEARANCES

Players with more than 700 English League apps (as at end of season 2010-11).

1005	Peter Shilton 1966–97 (286 Leicester, 110 Stoke, 202 Nottm Forest, 188 Southampton, 175 Derby, 34 Plymouth Argyle, 1 Bolton, 9 Leyton Orient).
931	Tony Ford 1975–2002 (423 Grimsby, 9 Sunderland, 112 Stoke, 114 WBA, 5 Bradford City, 76 Scunthorpe, 103 Mansfield, 89 Rochdale).
824	Terry Paine 1956–77 (713 Southampton, 111 Hereford).
822	Graham Alexander 1991–2011 (159 Scunthorpe, 152 Luton, 354 Preston, 157 Burnley).
795	Tommy Hutchison 1968–91 (165 Blackpool, 314 Coventry City, 46 Manchester City, 92 Burnley, 178 Swansea). In addition, 68 Scottish League apps for Alloa 1965–68, giving career League app total of 863.
790	Neil Redfearn 1982–2004 (35 Bolton, 100 Lincoln, 46 Doncaster, 57 Crystal Palace, 24 Watford, 62 Oldham, 292 Barnsley, 30 Charlton, 17 Bradford City, 22 Wigan, 42 Halifax, 54 Boston, 9 Rochdale).
782	Robbie James 1973–94 (484 Swansea, 48 Stoke, 87 QPR, 23 Leicester, 89 Bradford City, 51 Cardiff).
777	Alan Oakes 1959–84 (565 Manchester City, 211 Chester, 1 Port Vale).
773	Dave Beasant 1980–2003 (340 Wimbledon, 20 Newcastle, 4 Grimsby, 4 Wolves, 133 Chelsea, 88 Southampton, 139 Nottm F, 27 Portsmouth, 16 Brighton).
770	John Trollope 1960–80 (all for Swindon, record total for one club).
764	Jimmy Dickinson 1946–65 (all for Portsmouth).
761	Roy Sproson 1950–72 (all for Port Vale).
760	Mick Tait 1974–97 (64 Oxford Utd, 106 Carlisle, 33 Hull, 240 Portsmouth, 99

Reading, 79 Darlington, 139 Hartlepool Utd).

758   Billy Bonds 1964–88 (95 Charlton, 663 West Ham).
758   Ray Clemence 1966–88 (48 Scunthorpe, 470 Liverpool, 240 Tottenham).
757   Pat Jennings 1963–86 (48 Watford, 472 Tottenham, 237 Arsenal).
757   Frank Worthington 1966–88 (171 Huddersfield Town, 210 Leicester, 84 Bolton, 75 Birmingham, 32 Leeds, 19 Sunderland, 34 Southampton, 31 Brighton, 59 Tranmere, 23 Preston, 19 Stockport).
755   Wayne Allison 1986–2008 228 (84 Halifax, 7 Watford, 195 Bristol City, 103 Swindon, 76 Huddersfield, 102 Tranmere, 73 Sheffield Utd, 115 Chesterfield).
749   Ernie Moss 1968–88 (469 Chesterfield, 35 Peterborough, 57 Mansfield, 74 Port Vale, 11 Lincoln, 44 Doncaster, 26 Stockport, 23 Scarborough, 10 Rochdale).
746   Les Chapman 1966–88 (263 Oldham, 133 Huddersfield Town, 70 Stockport, 139 Bradford City, 88 Rochdale, 53 Preston).
744   Asa Hartford 1967–90 (214 WBA, 260 Manchester City, 3 Nottm Forest, 81 Everton, 28 Norwich, 81 Bolton, 45 Stockport, 7 Oldham, 25 Shrewsbury).
743   Alan Ball 1963–84 (146 Blackpool, 208 Everton, 177 Arsenal, 195 Southampton, 17 Bristol Rov).
743   John Hollins 1963–84 (465 Chelsea, 151 QPR, 127 Arsenal).
743   Phil Parkes 1968–91 (52 Walsall, 344 QPR, 344 West Ham, 3 Ipswich).
737   Steve Bruce 1979–99 (205 Gillingham, 141 Norwich, 309 Manchester Utd 72 Birmingham, 10 Sheffield Utd).
734   Teddy Sheringham 1983–2007 (220 Millwall, 5 Aldershot, 42 Nottm Forest, 104 Manchester Utd, 236 Tottenham, 32 Portsmouth, 76 West Ham, 19 Colchester)
732   Mick Mills 1966–88 (591 Ipswich, 103 Southampton, 38 Stoke).
731   Ian Callaghan 1959–81 (640 Liverpool, 76 Swansea, 15 Crewe).
731   David Seaman 1982–2003 (91 Peterborough, 75 Birmingham, 141 QPR, 405 Arsenal, 19 Manchester City).
725   Steve Perryman 1969–90 (655 Tottenham, 17 Oxford Utd, 53 Brentford).
722   Martin Peters 1961–81 (302 West Ham, 189 Tottenham, 207 Norwich, 24 Sheffield Utd).
718   Mike Channon 1966–86 (511 Southampton, 72 Manchester City, 4 Newcastle, 9 Bristol Rov, 88 Norwich, 34 Portsmouth).
716   Ron Harris 1961–83 (655 Chelsea, 61 Brentford).
716   Mike Summerbee 1959–79 (218 Swindon, 357 Manchester City, 51 Burnley, 3 Blackpool, 87 Stockport).
714   Glenn Cockerill 1976–98 (186 Lincoln, 26 Swindon, 62 Sheffield Utd, 287 Southampton, 90 Leyton Orient, 40 Fulham, 23 Brentford).
705   Keith Curle 1981–2003 (32 Bristol Rov, 16 Torquay, 121 Bristol City, 40 Reading, 93 Wimbledon, 171 Manchester City, 150 Wolves, 57 Sheffield Utd, 11 Barnsley, 14 Mansfield).
705   Phil Neal 1968–89 (186 Northampton, 455 Liverpool, 64 Bolton).
705   John Wile 1968–86 (205 Peterborough, 500 WBA).
701   Neville Southall 1980–2000 (39 Bury, 578 Everton, 9 Port Vale, 9 Southend, 12 Stoke, 53 Torquay, 1 Bradford City).

● **Stanley Matthews** made 701 League apps 1932–65 (322 Stoke, 379 Blackpool), incl. 3 for Stoke at start of 1939–40 before season abandoned (war).
● Goalkeeper **John Burridge** made a total of 771 League appearances in a 28-season career in English and Scottish football (1968–96). He played 691 games for 15 English clubs (Workington, Blackpool, Aston Villa, Southend, Crystal Palace, QPR, Wolves, Derby, Sheffield Utd, Southampton, Newcastle, Scarborough, Lincoln, Manchester City and Darlington) and 80 for 5 Scottish clubs (Hibernian, Aberdeen, Dumbarton, Falkirk and Queen of the South).

LONGEST LEAGUE APPEARANCE SEQUENCE

Harold Bell, centre-half of Tranmere, was ever-present for the first nine post-war seasons (1946–55), achieving a League record of 401 consecutive matches. Counting FA Cup and other games, his run of successive appearances totalled 459.

The longest League sequence since Bell's was 394 appearances by goalkeeper **Dave Beasant** for Wimbledon, Newcastle and Chelsea. His nine-year run began on Aug 29, 1981 and was ended by a broken finger sustained in Chelsea's League Cup-tie against Portsmouth on Oct 31, 1990. Beasant's 394 consecutive League games comprised 304 for Wimbledon (1981–88), 20 for Newcastle (1988–89) and 70 for Chelsea (1989–90).

Phil Neal made 366 consecutive First Division appearances for Liverpool between December 1974 and Sep 1983, a remarkable sequence for an outfield player in top-division football.

MOST CONSECUTIVE PREMIER LEAGUE APPEARANCES

266 by goalkeeper **Brad Friedel** (152 Blackburn, 114 Aston Villa in seven ever-present seasons 2004–11)

EVER-PRESENT DEFENCE

The **entire defence** of Huddersfield played in all 42 Second Division matches in season 1952–53, namely, Bill Wheeler (goal), Ron Staniforth and Laurie Kelly (full-backs), Bill McGarry, Don McEvoy and Len Quested (half-backs). In addition, Vic Metcalfe played in all 42 League matches at outside-left.

FIRST SUBSTITUTE USED IN LEAGUE

Keith Peacock (Charlton), away to Bolton (Div 2) on Aug 21, 1965.

FROM PROMOTION TO CHAMPIONS

Clubs who have become Champions of England a year after winning promotion: **Liverpool** 1905, 1906; **Everton** 1931, 1932; **Tottenham** 1950, 1951; **Ipswich** 1961, 1962; **Nottm Forest** 1977, 1978. The first four were placed top in both seasons: Forest finished third and first.

PREMIERSHIP'S FIRST MULTI-NATIONAL LINE-UP

Chelsea made history on December 26, 1999 when starting their Premiership match at Southampton without a single British player in the side.

Fulham's Unique XI: In the Worthington Cup 3rd round at home to Bury on Nov 6, 2002, Fulham fielded 11 players of 11 different nationalities. Ten were full Internationals, with Lee Clark an England U–21 cap.

On Feb 14, 2005 **Arsenal** became the first English club to select an all-foreign match squad when Arsene Wenger named 16 non-British players at home to Crystal Palace (Premiership).

Fifteen nations were represented at Fratton Park on Dec 30, 2009 (Portsmouth 1 Arsenal 4) when, for the first time in Premier League history, not one Englishman started the match. The line-up comprised seven Frenchmen, two Algerians and one from each of 13 other countries.

Players from **22 nationalities** (subs included) were involved in the Blackburn-WBA match at Ewood Park on Jan 23, 2011.

PREMIER LEAGUE'S FIRST ALL-ENGLISH LINE-UP

On Feb 27, 1999 **Aston Villa** (at home to Coventry) fielded the first all-English line up seen in the Premier League (starting 11 plus 3 subs).

THREE-NATION CHAMPION

Trevor Steven earned eight Championship medals in three countries: two with Everton (1985, 1987); five with Rangers (1990, 1991, 1993, 1994, 1995) and one with Marseille in 1992.

LEEDS NO WIN AWAY

Leeds, in 1992–93, provided the first instance of a club failing to win an away League match as reigning Champions.

PIONEERS IN 1888 AND 1992

Three clubs among the twelve who formed the Football League in 1888 were also founder members of the Premier League: **Aston Villa**, **Blackburn** and **Everton**.

CHAMPIONS (MODERN) WITH TWO CLUBS – PLAYERS

Francis Lee (Manchester City 1968, Derby 1975); **Ray Kennedy** (Arsenal 1971, Liverpool 1979, 1980, 1982); **Archie Gemmill** (Derby 1972, 1975, Nottm Forest 1978); **John McGovern** (Derby 1972, Nottm Forest 1978) **Larry Lloyd** (Liverpool 1973, Nottm Forest 1978); **Peter Withe** (Nottm Forest 1978, Aston Villa 1981); **John Lukic** (Arsenal 1989, Leeds 1992); **Kevin Richardson** (Everton 1985, Arsenal 1989); **Eric Cantona** (Leeds 1992, Manchester Utd 1993, 1994, 1996, 1997); **David Batty** (Leeds 1992, Blackburn 1995), **Bobby Mimms** (Everton 1987, Blackburn 1995), **Henning Berg** (Blackburn 1995, Manchester Utd 1999, 2001).

TITLE TURNABOUTS

In Jan 1996, **Newcastle** led the Premier League by 13 points. They finished runners-up to Manchester Utd

At Christmas 1997, **Arsenal** were 13 points behind leaders Manchester Utd and still 11 points behind at the beginning of Mar 1998. But a run of 10 wins took the title to Highbury.

On Mar 2, 2003, **Arsenal**, with 9 games left, went 8 points clear of Manchester Utd, who had a match in hand. United won the Championship by 5 points.

I In Mar 2002, **Wolves** were in second (automatic promotion) place in Nationwide Div 1, 11 points ahead of WBA, who had 2 games in hand. They were overtaken by Albion on the run-in, finished third, then failed in the play-offs. A year later they won promotion to the Premiership via the play-offs.

CLUB CLOSURES

Four clubs have left the Football League in mid-season: **Leeds City** (expelled Oct 1919); **Wigan Borough** (Oct 1931, debts of £20,000); **Accrington Stanley** (Mar 1962, debts £62,000); **Aldershot** (Mar 1992, debts £1.2m). **Maidstone**, with debts of £650,000, closed Aug 1992, on the eve of the season.

FOUR-DIVISION MEN

In season 1986–87, goalkeeper **Eric Nixon**, became the first player to appear in **all four divisions** of the Football League **in one season**. He served two clubs in Div 1: Manchester City (5 League games) and Southampton (4); in Div 2 Bradford City (3); in Div 3 Carlisle (16); and in Div 4 Wolves (16). Total appearances: 44.

Harvey McCreadie, a teenage forward, played in four divisions over two seasons inside a calendar year – from Accrington (Div 3) to Luton (Div 1) in Jan 1960, to Div 2 with Luton later that season and to Wrexham (Div 4) in Nov.

Tony Cottee played in all four divisions in season 2000–01, for Leicester (Premiership), Norwich (Div 1), Barnet (Div 3, player-manager) and Millwall (Div 2).

FATHERS AND SONS

When player-manager **Ian** (39) and **Gary** (18) **Bowyer** appeared together in the **Hereford** side at Scunthorpe (Div 4, Apr 21, 1990), they provided the first instance of father and son playing in the same team in a Football League match for 39 years. Ian played as substitute, and Gary scored Hereford's injury-time equaliser in a 3-3 draw.

Alec (39) and **David** (17) **Herd** were the previous father-and-son duo in League football – for Stockport, 2-0 winners at Hartlepool (Div 3 North) on May 5, 1951.

When Preston won 2-1 at Bury in Div 3 on Jan 13, 1990, the opposing goalkeepers were brothers: **Alan Kelly** (21) for Preston and **Gary** (23) for Bury. Their father, **Alan** (who kept goal for Preston in the 1964 FA Cup Final and won 47 Rep of Ireland caps) flew from America to watch the sons he taught to keep goal line up on opposite sides.

George Eastham Snr (manager) and son George Eastham Jnr were inside-forward partners for Ards in the Irish League in season 1954–55.

FATHER AND SON REFEREE PLAY-OFF FINALS

Father and son refereed two of the 2009 Play-off Finals. Clive Oliver, 46, took charge of Shrewsbury v Gillingham (Lge 2) and Michael Oliver, 26, refereed Millwall v Scunthorpe (Lge 1) the following day.

FATHER & SON BOTH CHAMPIONS

John Aston Snr won a Championship medal with Manchester Utd in 1952 and John Aston Jnr did so with the club in 1967.

FATHER & SON RIVAL MANAGERS

When Bill Dodgin Snr took Bristol Rov to Fulham for an FA Cup 1st Round tie in Nov 1970, the opposing manager was his son, Bill Jnr.

FATHER & SON ON OPPOSITE SIDES

It happened for the first time in FA Cup history (1st Qual Round on Sep 14, 1996) when 21-year-old Nick Scaife (Bishop Auckland) faced his father Bobby (41), who played for Pickering. Both were in midfield. Home side Bishops won 3-1.

THREE BROTHERS IN SAME SIDE

Southampton provided the first instance for 65 years of three brothers appearing together in a Div 1 side when Danny Wallace (24) and his 19-year-old twin brothers Rodney and Ray played against Sheffield Wed on Oct 22, 1988. In all, they made 25 appearances together for Southampton until Sep 1989.

A previous instance in Div 1 was provided by the Middlesbrough trio, William, John and George Carr with 24 League appearances together from Jan 1920 to Oct 1923.

The Tonner brothers, Sam, James and Jack, played together in 13 Second Division matches for Clapton Orient in season 1919–20.

Brothers David, Donald and Robert Jack played together in Plymouth's League side in 1920.

TWIN TEAM-MATES (see also Wallace twins above)

Twin brothers David and Peter Jackson played together for three League clubs (Wrexham, Bradford City and Tranmere) from 1954–62.

The Morgan twins, Ian and Roger, played regularly in the QPR forward line from 1964–68.

WBA's Adam and James Chambers, 18, were the first twins to represent England (v Cameroon in World Youth Championship, Apr 1999). They first played together in Albion's senior team, aged 19, in the League Cup 2nd. Round against Derby in Sep 2000. Brazilian identical twins Rafael and Fabio da Silva (18) made first team debuts at full-back for Manchester Utd in season 2008– 09.

SIR TOM DOES THE HONOURS

Sir Tom Finney, England and Preston legend, opened the Football League's new headquarters on their return to Preston on Feb 23, 1999. Preston had been the League's original base for 70 years before the move to Lytham St Annes in 1959.

SHORTENED MATCHES

The 0-0 score in the Bradford City v Lincoln Third Division fixture on May 11, 1985, abandoned through fire after 40 minutes, was subsequently confirmed as a result. It is the shortest officially- completed League match on record, and was the fourth of only five instances in Football League history of the score of an unfinished match being allowed to stand.

The other occasions: Middlesbrough 4, Oldham 1 (Div 1, Apr 3, 1915), abandoned after 55 minutes when Oldham defender Billy Cook refused to leave the field after being sent off;

Barrow 7, Gillingham 0 (Div 4, Oct 9, 1961), abandoned after 75 minutes because of ba
light, the match having started late because of Gillingham's delayed arrival.

A crucial **Manchester** derby (Div 1) was abandoned after 85 minutes, and the result stood, o
Apr 27, 1974, when a pitch invasion at Old Trafford followed the only goal, scored for City b
Denis Law, which relegated United, Law's former club.

The only instance of a first-class match in England being abandoned **'through shortage of players**
occurred in the First Division at Bramall Lane on Mar 16, 2002. Referee Eddie Wolstenholm
halted play after 82 minutes because **Sheffield Utd** were reduced to 6 players against **WBA**
They had had 3 men sent off (goalkeeper and 2 substitutes), and with all 3 substitutes use
and 2 players injured, were left with fewer than the required minimum of 7 on the field
Promotion contenders WBA were leading 3-0, and the League ordered the result to stand.

The last 60 seconds of **Birmingham v Stoke** (Div 3, 1-1, on Feb 29, 1992) were played behin
locked doors. The ground had been cleared after a pitch invasion.

A First Division fixture, **Sheffield Wed v Aston Villa** (Nov 26, 1898), was abandoned through ba
light after 79 mins with Wednesday leading 3-1. The Football League ruled that the matc
should be completed, and the remaining 10.5 minutes were played four months later (Ma
13, 1899), when Wednesday added another goal to make the result 4-1.

FA CUP RECORDS

(See also Goalscoring section)

CHIEF WINNERS

11 Manchester Utd.
10 Arsenal.
8 Tottenham.
7 Aston Villa, Liverpool.
6 Blackburn, Chelsea, Newcastle
Three Times in Succession: The Wanderers (1876-7-8) and Blackburn (1884-5-6).
Trophy Handed Back: The FA Cup became the Wanderers' absolute property in 1878, but the
handed it back to the Association on condition that it was not to be won outright by any clu
In Successive Years by Professional Clubs: Blackburn (in 1890 and 1891); Newcastle (in 195
and 1952); Tottenham (in 1961 and 1962); Tottenham again (in 1981 and 1982) ar
Arsenal (in 2002 and 2003).
Record Final-tie score: Bury 6, Derby 0 (1903).
Most FA Cup Final wins at Wembley: Manchester Utd 9, Arsenal 7, Tottenham 6, Chelsea
Liverpool 5, Newcastle 5.

SECOND DIVISION WINNERS

Notts Co (1894), **Wolves** (1908), **Barnsley** (1912), **WBA** (1931), **Sunderland** (1973
Southampton (1976), **West Ham** (1980). When **Tottenham** won the Cup in 1901 they we
a Southern League club.

'OUTSIDE' SEMI-FINALISTS

Wycombe, in 2001, became the eighth team from outside the top two divisions to reach th
semi-finals, following **Millwall** (1937), **Port Vale** (1954), **York** (1955), **Norwich** (1959
Crystal Palace (1976), **Plymouth** (1984) and **Chesterfield** (1997). None reached the Final.

FOURTH DIVISION QUARTER-FINALISTS

Oxford Utd (1964), **Colchester** (1971), **Bradford City** (1976), **Cambridge Utd** (1990).

FOURTH ROUND – NO REPLAYS

No replays were necessary in the 16 fourth round ties in January 2008 (7 home wins, 9 away
This had not happened for 51 years, since 8 home and 8 away wins in season 1956-57.

FOUR TROPHIES

The latest FA Cup, first presented at Wembley in 1992, is a replica of the one it replaced, which had been in existence since 1911. 'It was falling apart and was not going to last much longer,' said the FA.

The new trophy is the fourth FA Cup. These were its predecessors:

1895: First stolen from shop in Birmingham while held by Aston Villa. Never seen again.

1910: Second presented to Lord Kinnaird on completing 21 years as FA president. This trophy was bought by Birmingham chairman David Gold at Christie's (London) for £420,000 in May 2005 and presented to the National Football Museum at Preston.

1992: Third 'gracefully retired' after 80 years' service (1911–91).

There are three FA Cups currently in existence. The retired model is still used for promotional work. The present trophy stays with the winners until the following March. A third, identical Cup is secreted in the FA vaults as cover against loss of the existing trophy.

FINALISTS RELEGATED

Five clubs have reached the FA Cup Final in a season of relegation and all lost at Wembley: **Manchester City** 1926, **Leicester** 1969, **Brighton** 1983, **Middlesbrough** 1997; **Portsmouth** 2010.

FA CUP SHOCKS DOWN THE YEARS

(2011 = season 2010-11; rounds shown in brackets; R=replay)

1922 (1)	Everton	0	Crystal Palace	6	1985 (3)	Orient	2	WBA	1
1933 (3)	Walsall	2	Arsenal	0	1985 (4)	York	1	Arsenal	0
1939 (F)	Portsmouth	4	Wolves	1	1985 (4)	Wimbledon	1	Nottm Forest	0R
1948 (3)	Arsenal	0	Bradford PA	1	1986 (3)	Peterborough	1	Leeds	0
1948 (3)	Colchester	1	Huddersfield	0	1986 (3)	Birmingham	1	Altrincham	2
1949 (4)	Yeovil	2	Sunderland	1	1987 (1)	Chorley	3	Wolves0 (at Bolton)
1954 (4)	Arsenal	1	Norwich	2	1988 (F)	Wimbledon	1	Liverpool	0
1955 (5)	York	3	Tottenham	1	1989 (3)	Sutton	2	Coventry	1
1956 (2)	Derby	1	Boston	6	1990 (2)	Whitley Bay	2	Preston	0
1957 (4)	Wolves	0	Bournemouth	1	1991 (3)	WBA	2	Woking	4
1957 (5)	Bournemouth	3	Tottenham	1	1992 (1)	Fulham	0	Hayes	2
1958 (4)	Newcastle	1	Scunthorpe	3	1992 (1)	Telford	2	Stoke	1R
1959 (3)	Norwich	3	Man Utd	0	1992 (3)	Wrexham	2	Arsenal	1
1959 (3)	Worcester	2	Liverpool	1	1993 (1)	Cardiff	2	Bath	3
1961 (3)	Chelsea	2	Crewe	2	1993 (3)	Liverpool	0	Bolton	2R
1964 (3)	Aldershot	2	Aston Villa	1R	1994 (3)	Birmingham	1	Kidderminster	2
1964 (3)	Newcastle	1	Bedford	2	1994 (3)	Liverpool	0	Bristol City	1R
1965 (4)	Peterborough	2	Arsenal	1	1994 (4)	Arsenal	1	Bolton	3R
1967 (3)	Swindon	3	West Ham	0R	2001 (1)	Port Vale	1	Canvey Is	2R
1967 (4)	Man Utd	1	Norwich	2	2001 (1)	Chelsea	0	Stoke	0R
1971 (5)	Colchester	3	Leeds	2	2001 (1)	Wycombe	2	Wolves	1
1972 (3)	Hereford	2	Newcastle	1R	2001 (4)	Everton	0	Tranmere	3
1973 (F)	Sunderland	1	Leeds	0	2002 (1)	Wigan	0	Canvey Island	1
1975 (3)	Burnley	0	Wimbledon	1	2002 (2)	Canvey Is	1	Northampton	0
1978 (4)	Wrexham	4	Newcastle	1R	2002 (3)	Cardiff	2	Leeds	1
1978 (4)	Stoke	2	Blyth	3	2003 (1)	QPR	1	Vauxhall Mot	1R
1980 (3)	Chelsea	0	Wigan	1	(Vauxhall won 4-3 on pens)
1980 (3)	Harlow	1	Leicester	0R	2003 (3)	Shrewsbury	2	Everton	1
1980 (3)	Halifax	1	Man City	0	2005 (3)	Oldham	1	Man City	0
1981 (4)	Exeter	3	Leicester	1R	2006 (3)	Fulham	1	Leyton Orient	2
1981 (5)	Exeter	4	Newcastle	0R	2008 (2)	Chasetown	1	Port Vale	0R
1984 (3)	Bournemouth	2	Man Utd	0	2008 (2)	Notts Co	0	Havant	1

2008 (3)	Havant	4	Swansea	2R		2010 (4)	Liverpool	1	Reading	2R
2008 (5)	Liverpool	1	Barnsley	2		2010 (4)	Wigan	0	Notts Co	2R
2008 (6)	Barnsley	1	Chelsea	0		2011 (1)	Rochdale	2	FC United	3
2009 (1)	Histon	1	Swindon	0		2011 (3)	Stevenage	3	Newcastle	1
2009 (2)	Histon	1	Leeds	0		2011 (3)	Sunderland	1	Notts Co	2
2010 (3)	Man Utd	0	Leeds	1		2011 (3)	Crawley	2	Derby	1

YEOVIL TOP GIANT-KILLERS

Yeovil's victories over Colchester and Blackpool in season 2000–01 gave them a total of 20 FA Cup wins against League opponents. They set another non-League record by reaching the third round 13 times.

This was Yeovil's triumphant (non-League) Cup record against League clubs: 1924–25 Bournemouth 3-2; 1934–35 Crystal Palace 3-0, Exeter 4-1; 1938–39 Brighton 2-1; 1948–49 Bury 3-1, Sunderland 2-1; 1958–59 Southend 1-0; 1960–61 Walsall 1-0; 1963–64 Southend 1-0, Crystal Palace 3-1; 1970–71 Bournemouth 1-0; 1972–73 Brentford 2-1 1987–88 Cambridge Utd 1-0; 1991–92 Walsall 1-0; 1992–93 Torquay 5-2, Hereford 2-1 1993–94 Fulham 1-0; 1998–9 Northampton 2-0; 2000–01 Colchester 5-1, Blackpool 3-1

NON-LEAGUE BEST

Since League football began in 1888, three non-League clubs have reached the FA Cup Final. **Sheffield Wed** (Football Alliance) were runners-up in 1890, as were **Southampton** (Southern League) in 1900 and 1902. **Tottenham** won the Cup as a Southern League team in 1901.

Otherwise, the furthest progress by non-League clubs has been to the 5th round on 6 occasions: **Colchester** 1948, **Yeovil** 1949, **Blyth Spartans** 1978, **Telford** 1985, **Kidderminster** 1994, **Crawley** 2011.

Greatest number of non-League sides to reach the **3rd round** is **8** in 2009: **Barrow, Blyth Eastwood, Forest Green, Histon, Kettering, Kidderminster and Torquay.**

Most to reach **Round 4**: **3** in 1957 (**Rhyl, New Brighton, Peterborough**) and 1975 (**Leatherhead Stafford and Wimbledon**).

Five non-League clubs reaching **round 3** in 2001 was a Conference record. They were **Chester Yeovil, Dagenham, Morecambe and Kingstonian.**

In season 2002–3, Team Bath became the first University-based side to reach the FA Cup 1st Round since **Oxford University** (Finalists in 1880).

NON-LEAGUE 'LAST TIMES'

Last time no non-League club reached round 3: 1951. Last time only one did so: 1969 (**Kettering**).

TOP-DIVISION SCALPS

Victories in FA Cup by non-League clubs over top-division teams since 1900 include: 1900– (Final, replay); Tottenham 3, Sheffield Utd 1 (Tottenham then in Southern League); 1919–20 Cardiff 2, Oldham 0, and Sheffield Wed 0, **Darlington** 2; 1923–24 **Corinthians** 1, Blackburn 0; 1947–48 Colchester 1, Huddersfield 0; 1948–9 **Yeovil** 2, Sunderland 1; 1971–2 **Hereford** 2, Newcastle 1; 1974–75 Burnley 0, **Wimbledon** 1; 1985–86 Birmingham 1, **Altrincham** 2 1988–89 **Sutton** 2, Coventry 1.

MOST WINNING MEDALS

Ashley Cole has won the trophy six times, with (Arsenal 2002–3–5) and Chelsea (2007–9 10). The Hon Arthur Kinnaird (The Wanderers and Old Etonians), **Charles Wollaston** (The Wanderers) and **Jimmy Forrest** (Blackburn) each earned five winners' medals. Kinnaird, late president of the FA, played in nine of the first 12 FA Cup Finals, and was on the winning side three times for The Wanderers, in 1873 (captain), 1877, 1878 (captain), and twice as captain of Old Etonians (1879, 1882).

MANAGERS' MEDALS BACKDATED

In 2010, the FA agreed to award **Cup Final medals** to all living managers who took their teams to the Final before 1996 (when medals were first given to Wembley team bosses). **Lawrie McMenemy** had campaigned for the award since Southampton's victory in 1976

MOST WINNERS' MEDALS AT WEMBLEY

4 – **Mark Hughes** (3 for Manchester Utd, 1 for Chelsea).

3 – **Dick Pym** (3 clean sheets in Finals), **Bob Haworth, Jimmy Seddon, Harry Nuttall, Billy Butler** (all Bolton); **David Jack** (2 Bolton, 1 Arsenal); **Bob Cowell, Jack Milburn, Bobby Mitchell** (all Newcastle); **Dave Mackay** (Tottenham); **Frank Stapleton** (1 Arsenal, 2 Manchester Utd); **Bryan Robson** (3 times winning captain); **Arthur Albiston, Gary Pallister** (all Manchester Utd); **Bruce Grobbelaar, Steve Nicol, Ian Rush** (all Liverpool); **Roy Keane, Peter Schmeichel, Ryan Giggs** (all Manchester Utd); **Dennis Wise** (1 Wimbledon, 2 Chelsea), **Ashley Cole** (all Chelsea)

Arsenal's **David Seaman** and **Ray Parlour** have each earned 4 winners' medals (2 at Wembley, 2 at Cardiff) as have Manchester Utd's **Roy Keane** and **Ryan Giggs** (3 at Wembley, 1 at Cardiff).

MOST WEMBLEY FINALS

Nine players appeared in five FA Cup Finals at Wembley, replays excluded:
- Joe Hulme (Arsenal: 1927 lost, 1930 won, 1932 lost, 1936 won; Huddersfield: 1938 lost).
- Johnny Giles (Manchester Utd: 1963 won; Leeds: 1965 lost, 1970 drew at Wembley, lost replay at Old Trafford, 1972 won, 1973 lost).
- Pat Rice (all for Arsenal: 1971 won, 1972 lost, 1978 lost, 1979 won, 1980 lost).
- Frank Stapleton (Arsenal: 1978 lost, 1979 won, 1980 lost; Manchester Utd: 1983 won, 1985 won).
- Ray Clemence (Liverpool: 1971 lost, 1974 won, 1977 lost; Tottenham: 1982 won, 1987 lost).
- Mark Hughes (Manchester Utd: 1985 won, 1990 won, 1994 won, 1995 lost; Chelsea: 1997 won).
- John Barnes (Watford: 1984 lost; Liverpool: 1988 lost, 1989 won, 1996 lost; Newcastle: 1998 sub, lost): - first player to lose Wembley FA Cup Finals with three different clubs.
- Roy Keane (Nottm Forest: 1991 lost; Manchester Utd: 1994 won, 1995 lost, 1996 won, 1999 won).
- Ryan Giggs (Manchester Utd: 1994 won, 1995 lost, 1996 won, 1999 won, 2007 lost). Stapleton,
- Clemence and Hughes also played in a replay, making six actual FA Cup Final appearances for each of them.
- Glenn Hoddle also made six appearances at Wembley: 5 for Tottenham (incl. 2 replays), in 1981 won, 1982 won and 1987 lost, and 1 for Chelsea as sub in 1994 lost.
- Paul Bracewell played in four FA Cup Finals without being on the winning side - for Everton 1985, 1986, 1989, Sunderland 1992.

MOST WEMBLEY/CARDIFF FINAL APPEARANCES

7 by **Roy Keane** (Nottm Forest: 1991 lost; Manchester Utd: 1994 won; 1995 lost; 1996 won; 1999 won; 2004 won; 2005 lost).

7 by **Ryan Giggs** (Manchester Utd): 1994 won; 1995 lost; 1996 won; 1999 won; 2004 won; 2005 lost; 2007 lost.

7 by **Ashley Cole** (Arsenal: 2001 lost; 2002 won; 2003 won; 2005 won; Chelsea 2007 won; 2009 won; 2010 won

6 by **Paul Scholes** (Manchester Utd): 1995 lost; 1996 won; 1999 won; 2004 won; 2005 lost; 2007 lost.

5 by **David Seaman** and **Ray Parlour** (Arsenal): 1993 won; 1998 won; 2001 lost; 2002 won; 2003 won; **Dennis Wise** (Wimbledon 1988 won; Chelsea 1994 lost; 1997 won; 2000 won; Millwall 2004 lost); **Patrick Vieira** (Arsenal): 1998 won; 2001 lost; 2002 won; 2005 won; (Manchester City) 2011 won

BIGGEST FA CUP SCORE AT WEMBLEY
5-0 by Stoke v Bolton (semi-final, Apr 17, 2011).

WINNING GOALKEEPER-CAPTAINS
1988 **Dave Beasant** (Wimbledon); 2003 **David Seaman** (Arsenal).

MOST-WINNING MANAGER
Sir Alex Ferguson (Manchester Utd) 5 times (1990, 1994, 1996, 1999, 2004).

PLAYER-MANAGERS IN FINAL
Kenny Dalglish (Liverpool, 1986); **Glenn Hoddle** (Chelsea, 1994); **Dennis Wise** (Millwall, 2004).

DEBUTS IN FINAL
Alan Davies (Manchester Utd v Brighton, 1983); **Chris Baird** (Southampton v Arsenal, 2003); **Curtis Weston** (Millwall sub v Manchester Utd, 2004).

SEMI-FINALS AT WEMBLEY
1991 Tottenham 3 Arsenal 1; **1993** Sheffield Wed 2 Sheffield Utd 1, Arsenal 1 Tottenham 0; **1994** Chelsea 2 Luton 0, Manchester Utd 1 Oldham 1; **2000** Aston Villa beat Bolton 4-1 on pens (after 0-0), Chelsea 2 Newcastle 1; **2008** Portsmouth 1 WBA 0, Cardiff 1 Barnsley 0; **2009** Chelsea 2 Arsenal 1, Everton beat Manchester Utd 4-2 on pens (after 0-0); **2010** Chelsea 3 Aston Villa 0, Portsmouth 2 Tottenham 0; **2011** Manchester City 1 Manchester Utd 0, Stoke 5 Bolton 0.

FIRST ENTRANTS (1871–72)
Barnes, Civil Service, Crystal Palace, Clapham Rov, Donnington School (Spalding), Hampstead Heathens, Harrow Chequers, Hitchin, Maidenhead, Marlow, Queen's Park (Glasgow), Reigate Priory, Royal Engineers, Upton Park and Wanderers. Total 15.

FA CUP FIRSTS
Out of country: Cardiff, by defeating Arsenal 1-0 in the 1927 Final at Wembley, became the first and only club to take the FA Cup out of England.
All-English Winning XI: First club to win the FA Cup with all-English XI: Blackburn Olympic in 1883. Others since: WBA in 1888 and 1931, Bolton (1958), Manchester City (1969), West Ham (1964 and 1975).
Non-English Winning XI: Liverpool in 1986 (Mark Lawrenson, born Preston, was a Rep of Ireland player).
Won both Cups: Old Carthusians won the FA Cup in 1881 and the FA Amateur Cup in 1894 and 1897. **Wimbledon** won Amateur Cup in 1963, FA Cup in 1988.

MOST GAMES NEEDED TO WIN
Barnsley played a record 12 matches (20 hours' football) to win the FA Cup in season 1911–12. All six replays (one in round 1, three in round 4 and one in each of semi-final and Final) were brought about by goalless draws.
Arsenal played 11 FA Cup games when winning the trophy in 1979. Five of them were in the 3rd round against Sheffield Wed.

LONGEST TIES
6 matches: (11 hours): Alvechurch v Oxford City (4th qual round, 1971–72). Alvechurch won 1-0.
5 matches: (9 hours, 22 mins – record for competition proper): Stoke v Bury (3rd round, 1954–55). Stoke won 3-2.
5 matches: Chelsea v Burnley (4th round, 1955–56). Chelsea won 2-0.
5 matches: Hull v Darlington (2nd round, 1960–61). Hull won 3-0.

5 matches: Arsenal v Sheffield Wed (3rd round, 1978–79). Arsenal won 2-0.

Other marathons (qualifying comp, all 5 matches, 9 hours): Barrow v Gillingham (last qual round, 1924–25) – winners Barrow; Leyton v Ilford (3rd qual round, 1924–25) – winners Leyton; Falmouth v Bideford (3rd qual round, 1973–74) – winners Bideford.

End of Cup Final replays: The FA decided that, with effect from 1999, there would be no Cup Final replays. In the event of a draw after extra-time, the match would be decided on penalties. This happened for the first time in 2005, when Arsenal beat Manchester Utd 5-4 on penalties after a 0-0 draw. A year later, Liverpool beat West Ham 3-1 on penalties after a 3-3 draw.

FA Cup marathons ended in season 1991–92, when the penalty shoot-out was introduced to decide ties still level after one replay and extra-time.

I In 1932–23 **Brighton** (Div 3 South) played 11 FA Cup games, including replays, and scored 43 goals, without getting past round 5. They forgot to claim exemption and had to play from 1st qual round.

LONGEST ROUND

The longest round in FA Cup history was the **3rd round** in **1962–63**. It took 66 days to complete, lasting from Jan 5 to Mar 11, and included 261 postponements because of bad weather.

LONGEST UNBEATEN RUN

23 matches by **Blackburn** In winning the Cup in three consecutive years (1884–5–6), they won 21 ties (one in a replay), and their first Cup defeat in four seasons was in a first round replay of the next competition.

RE-STAGED TIES

Sixth round, Mar 9, 1974: Newcastle 4, Nottm Forest 3. Match declared void by FA and ordered to be replayed following a pitch invasion after Newcastle had a player sent off. Forest claimed the hold-up caused the game to change its pattern. The tie went to two further matches at Goodison Park (0-0, then 1-0 to Newcastle).

Third round, Jan 5, 1985: Burton 1, Leicester 6 (at Derby). Burton goalkeeper Paul Evans was hit on the head by a missile thrown from the crowd and continued in a daze. The FA ordered the tie to be played again, behind closed doors at Coventry (Leicester won 1-0).

First round replay, Nov 25, 1992: Peterborough 9 (Tony Philliskirk 5), Kingstonian 1. Match expunged from records because, at 3-0 after 57 mins, Kingstonian were reduced to ten men when goalkeeper Adrian Blake was concussed by a 50 pence coin thrown from the crowd. The tie was re-staged on the same ground behind closed doors (Peterborough won 1-0).

Fifth round: Within an hour of holders Arsenal beating Sheffield Utd 2-1 at Highbury on Feb 13, 1999, the FA took the unprecedented step of declaring the match void because an unwritten rule of sportsmanship had been broken. With United's Lee Morris lying injured, their goalkeeper Alan Kelly kicked the ball into touch. Play resumed with Arsenal's Ray Parlour throwing it in the direction of Kelly, but Nwankwo Kanu took possession and centred for Marc Overmars to score the 'winning' goal. After four minutes of protests by manager Steve Bruce and his players, referee Peter Jones confirmed the goal. Both managers absolved Kanu of cheating but Arsenal's Arsene Wenger offered to replay the match. With the FA immediately approving, it was re-staged at Highbury ten days later (ticket prices halved) and Arsenal again won 2-1.

PRIZE FUND

The makeover of the FA Cup competition took off in 2001–02 with the introduction of round-by-round prize-money.

FA CUP FOLLIES

1999–2000 The FA broke with tradition by deciding the 3rd round be moved from its regular Jan date and staged before Christmas. Criticism was strong, gates poor and the 3rd round in

2000–01 reverted to the New Year. By allowing the holders Manchester Utd to withdraw from the 1999–2000 competition in order to play in FIFA's inaugural World Club Championship in Brazil in Jan, the FA were left with an odd number of clubs in the 3rd round. Their solution was a 'lucky losers' draw among clubs knocked out in round 2. Darlington, beaten at Gillingham, won it to re-enter the competition, then lost 2-1 away to Aston Villa.

HAT-TRICKS IN FINAL

There have been three in the history of the competition: **Billy Townley** (Blackburn, 1890), **Jimmy Logan** (Notts Co, 1894) and **Stan Mortensen** (Blackpool, 1953).

MOST APPEARANCES

88 by **Ian Callaghan** (79 for Liverpool, 7 for Swansea City, 2 for Crewe); **87** by **John Barnes** (31 for Watford, 51 for Liverpool, 5 for Newcastle); **86** by **Stanley Matthews** (37 for Stoke, 49 for Blackpool); **84** by **Bobby Charlton** (80 for Manchester Utd, 4 for Preston); **84** by **Pat Jennings** (3 for Watford, 43 for Tottenham, 38 for Arsenal); **84** by **Peter Shilton** for seven clubs (30 for Leicester, 7 for Stoke, 18 for Nottm Forest, 17 for Southampton, 10 for Derby, 1 for Plymouth Argyle, 1 for Leyton Orient); **82** by **David Seaman** (5 for Peterborough, 5 for Birmingham, 17 for QPR, 54 for Arsenal, 1 for Manchester City).

THREE-CLUB FINALISTS

Five players have appeared in the FA Cup Final for three clubs: **Harold Halse** for Manchester Utd (1909), Aston Villa (1913) and Chelsea (1915); **Ernie Taylor** for Newcastle (1951), Blackpool (1953) and Manchester Utd (1958); **John Barnes** for Watford (1984), Liverpool (1988, 1989, 1996) and Newcastle (1998); **Dennis Wise** for Wimbledon (1988), Chelsea (1994, 1997, 2000), Millwall (2004); **David James** for Liverpool (1996), Aston Villa (2000) and Portsmouth (2008, 2010).

CUP MAN WITH TWO CLUBS IN SAME SEASON

Stan Crowther, who played for Aston Villa against Manchester Utd in the 1957 FA Cup Final, appeared for both Villa and United in the 1957–58 competition. United signed him directly after the Munich air crash and, in the circumstances, he was given dispensation to play for them in the Cup, including the Final.

CAPTAIN'S CUP DOUBLE

Martin Buchan is the only player to have captained Scottish and English FA Cup-winning teams – Aberdeen in 1970 and Manchester Utd in 1977.

MEDALS BEFORE AND AFTER

Two players appeared in FA Cup Final teams before and after the War: **Raich Carter** was twice a winner (Sunderland 1937, Derby 1946) and **Willie Fagan** twice on the losing side (Preston 1937, Liverpool 1950).

DELANEY'S COLLECTION

Scotland winger **Jimmy Delaney** uniquely earned Scottish, English, Northern Ireland and Republic of Ireland Cup medals. He was a winner with Celtic (1937), Manchester Utd (1948) and Derry City (1954) and a runner-up with Cork City (1956).

STARS WHO MISSED OUT

Internationals who never won an FA Cup winner's medal include: Tommy Lawton, Tom Finney, Johnny Haynes, Gordon Banks, George Best, Terry Butcher, Peter Shilton, Martin Peters, Nobby Stiles, Alan Ball, Malcolm Macdonald, Alan Shearer.

CUP WINNERS AT NO COST

Not one member of **Bolton**'s 1958 FA Cup-winning team cost the club a transfer fee. Each joined the club for a £10 signing-on fee.

11-NATIONS LINE-UP

Liverpool fielded a team of 11 different nationalities in the FA Cup 3rd round at Yeovil on Jan 4, 2004.

HIGH-SCORING SEMI-FINALS

The **record team score** in FA Cup semi-finals is **6**: 1891–92 WBA 6, Nottm Forest 2; 1907–08 Newcastle 6, Fulham 0; 1933–34 Manchester City 6, Aston Villa 1.

Most goals in semi-finals (aggregate): 17 in 1892 (4 matches) and 1899 (5 matches). In modern times: 15 in 1958 (3 matches, including Manchester Utd 5, Fulham 3 – highest-scoring semi-final since last war); 16 in 1989–90 (Crystal Palace 4, Liverpool 3; Manchester Utd v Oldham 3-3, 2-1. **All 16 goals** in those three matches were scored by **different players**.

Stoke's win against Bolton at Wembley in 2011 was the first 5-0 semi-final result since Wolves beat Grimsby at Old Trafford in 1939.

Last hat-trick in an FA Cup semi-final was scored by **Alex Dawson** for Manchester Utd in 5-3 replay win against Fulham at Highbury in 1958.

SEMI-FINAL VENUES

Villa Park has staged more such matches (55 including replays) than any other ground. Next is Hillsborough (33).

ONE IN A HUNDRED

The 2008 semi-finals included only one top-division club, Portsmouth, for the first time in 100 years – since Newcastle in 1908.

FOUR SPECIAL AWAYS

For the only time in FA Cup history, **all four quarter-finals** in season 1986–87 were won by the away team.

DRAWS RECORD

In season 1985–86, **seven** of the eight 5th round ties went to replays – a record for that stage of the competition.

LUCK OF THE DRAW

In the FA Cup on Jan 11, 1947, eight of **London**'s ten Football League clubs involved in the 3rd round were drawn at home (including Chelsea v Arsenal). Only Crystal Palace played outside the capital (at Newcastle).

In the 3rd round in Jan 1992, Charlton were the only London club drawn at home (against Barnet), but the venue of the Farnborough v West Ham tie was reversed on police instruction. So Upton Park staged Cup ties on successive days, with West Ham at home on the Saturday and Charlton (who shared the ground) on Sunday.

Arsenal were drawn away in every round on the way to reaching the Finals of 1971 and 1972. **Manchester Utd** won the Cup in 1990 without playing once at home.

The 1999 finalists, **Manchester Utd** and **Newcastle**, were both drawn at home every time in Rounds 3–6.

On their way to the semi-finals of both domestic Cup competitions in season 2002–03, **Sheffield Utd** were drawn at home ten times out of ten and won all ten matches – six in the League's Worthington Cup and four in the FA Cup.

ALL TOP-DIVISION VICTIMS

The only instance of an FA Cup-winning club meeting top-division opponents in every round was provided by Manchester Utd in 1947–48. They beat Aston Villa, Liverpool, Charlton, Preston, then Derby in the semi-final and Blackpool in the Final.

In contrast, these clubs have reached the Final without playing top-division opponents on the way: West Ham (1923), Bolton (1926), Blackpool (1948), Bolton (1953), Millwall (2004).

WON CUP WITHOUT CONCEDING GOAL

1873 **The Wanderers** (1 match; as holders, exempt until Final); 1889 **Preston** (5 matches); 1903 **Bury** (5 matches). In 1966 **Everton** reached Final without conceding a goal (7 matches), then beat Sheffield Wed 3-2 at Wembley.

HOME ADVANTAGE

For the first time in FA Cup history, all eight ties in the 1992–93 5th round were won (no replays) by the **clubs drawn at home**. Only other instance of eight home wins at the last 16 stage was in 1889–90, in what was then the 2nd round.

NORTH-EAST WIPE-OUT

For the first time in 54 years, since the 4th round in Jan, 1957, the North-East's 'big three' were knocked out on the same date, Jan 8, 2011 (3rd round). All lost to lower-division opponents – **Newcastle** 3-1 at Stevenage, **Sunderland** 2-1 at home to Notts County and **Middlesbrough** 2-1 at Burton.

FEWEST TOP-DIVISION CLUBS IN LAST 16 (5th ROUND)

5 in 1958; **6** in 1927, 1970, 1982; **7** in 1994, 2003; **8** in 2002, 2004.

SIXTH-ROUND ELITE

For the first time in FA Cup 6th round history, dating from 1926 when the format of the competition changed, all **eight quarter-finalists** in 1995–96 were from the top division.

SEMI-FINAL – DOUBLE DERBIES

There have been only two instances of both FA Cup semi-finals in the same year being local derbies: **1950** Liverpool beat Everton 2-0 (Maine Road), Arsenal beat Chelsea 1-0 after 2-2 draw (both at Tottenham); **1993** Arsenal beat Tottenham 1-0 (Wembley), Sheffield Wed beat Sheffield Utd 2-1 (Wembley).

TOP CLUB DISTINCTION

Since the Football League began in 1888, there has never been an FA Cup Final in which **neither club** represented the top division.

CLUBS THROWN OUT

Bury expelled (Dec 2006) for fielding an ineligible player in 3-1 2nd rd replay win at Chester. **Droylsden** expelled for fielding a suspended player in 2-1 2nd rd replay win at home to Chesterfield (Dec 2008).

SPURS OUT – AND IN

Tottenham were banned, pre-season, from the 1994–95 competition because of financial irregularities, but were re-admitted on appeal and reached the semi-finals.

FATHER & SON FA CUP WINNERS

Peter Boyle (Sheffield Utd 1899, 1902) and **Tommy Boyle** (Sheffield Utd 1925); **Harry Johnson Snr** (Sheffield Utd 1899, 1902) and **Harry Johnson Jnr** (Sheffield Utd 1925); **Jimmy Dunn Snr** (Everton 1933) and **Jimmy Dunn Jnr** (Wolves 1949); **Alec Herd** (Manchester City 1934) and **David Herd** (Manchester Utd 1963); **Frank Lampard Snr** (West Ham 1975, 1980) and **Frank Lampard Jnr** (Chelsea 2007, 2009)

BROTHERS IN FA CUP FINAL TEAMS (Modern Times)

1950 **Denis** and **Leslie Compton** (Arsenal); 1952 **George** and **Ted Robledo** (Newcastle); 1967 **Ron** and **Allan Harris** (Chelsea); 1977 **Jimmy** and **Brian Greenhoff** (Manchester Utd); 1996 and 1999 **Gary** and **Phil Neville** (Manchester Utd).

FIRST SPONSORS

Littlewoods Pools became the first sponsors of the FA Cup in season 1994–95 in a £14m, 4-year deal. French insurance giants **AXA** took over (season 1998–99) in a sponsorship worth £25m over 4 years. German energy company **E.ON** agreed a 4-year sponsorship (worth £32m) from season 2006–07.

FIRST GOALKEEPER-SUBSTITUTE IN FINAL

Paul Jones (Southampton), who replaced injured Antti Niemi against Arsenal in 2003.

LEAGUE CUP RECORDS

(See also Goalscoring section)

Highest scores: West Ham 10-0 v Bury (2nd round, 2nd leg 1983–84; agg 12-1); Liverpool 10-0 v Fulham (2nd round, 1st leg 1986–87; agg 13-2).

Most League Cup goals (career): 49 Geoff Hurst (43 West Ham, 6 Stoke, 1960–75); 49 Ian Rush (48 Liverpool, 1 Newcastle, 1981–98).

Highest scorer (season): 12 Clive Allen (Tottenham 1986–87) in 9 apps.

Most goals in match: 6 Frank Bunn (Oldham v Scarborough, 3rd round, 1989–90).

Most winners' medals: 5 Ian Rush (Liverpool).

Most appearances in Final: 6 Kenny Dalglish (Liverpool 1978–87), Ian Rush (Liverpool 1981–95).

League Cup sponsors: Milk Cup 1981–86, Littlewoods Cup 1987–90, Rumbelows Cup 1991–92, Coca-Cola Cup 1993–98. Worthington Cup 1999–2003, Carling Cup from season 2003–04.

Up for the cup, then down: In 2011, Birmingham became only the second club to win a major trophy (the Carling Cup) and be relegated from the top division. It previously happened to Norwich in 1985 when they went down from the old First Division after winning the Milk Cup.

Liverpool's League Cup records: Winners a record 7 times. **Ian Rush** only player to win 5 times. Rush also first to play in 8 winning teams in Cup Finals **at Wembley**, all with Liverpool (FA Cup 1986–89–92; League Cup 1981–82–83–84–95).

Britain's first under-cover Cup Final: Worthington Cup Final between Blackburn and Tottenham at Cardiff's Millennium Stadium on Sunday, Feb 24, 2002. With rain forecast, the retractable roof was closed on the morning of the match.

DISCIPLINE

SENDINGS-OFF

Season 2003–4 set an **all-time record** of 504 players sent off in English domestic football competitions. There were 58 in the Premiership, 390 Nationwide League, 28 FA Cup (excluding non-League dismissals), 22 League Cup, 2 in Nationwide play-offs, 4 in LDV Vans Trophy.

Most sendings-off in Premier League programme (10 matches): 9 (8 Sat, 1 Sun, Oct 31-Nov 1, 2009)

The 58 Premiership red cards was 13 fewer than the record English **top-division** total of 71 in 2002–03. **Bolton** were the only club in the English divisions without a player sent off in any first-team competition that season.

Worst day for dismissals in English football was Boxing Day, 2007, with **20 red cards** (5 Premier League and 15 Coca-Cola League). Three players, Chelsea's Ashley Cole and Ricardo Carvalho and Aston Villa's Zat Knight were sent off in a 4-4 draw at Stamford Bridge. Luton had three men dismissed in their game at Bristol Rov, but still managed a 1-1 draw.

Previous worst day was Dec 13, 2003, with **19 red cards** (2 Premiership and the 17 Nationwide League).

In the entire first season of post-war League football (1946–47) only 12 players were sent off, followed by 14 in 1949–50, and the total League dismissals for the first nine seasons after the War was 104.

The worst pre-War total was 28 in each of seasons 1921–22 and 1922–23.

ENGLAND SENDINGS-OFF

Robert Green became the 12th England player to be sent off – and the first goalkeeper – when red-carded for a foul after 15 minutes of the World Cup qualifier away to Ukraine on Oct 10, 2009. David Beckham is the only England captain to be sent off.

Jun 5, 1968	**Alan Mullery**	v Yugoslavia (Florence, Eur Champ)
Jun 6, 1973	**Alan Ball**	v Poland (Chorzow, World Cup qual)
Jun 15, 1977	**Trevor Cherry**	v Argentina (Buenos Aires, friendly)
Jun 6, 1986	**Ray Wilkins**	v Morocco (Monterrey, World Cup Finals)
Jun 30, 1998	**David Beckham**	v Argentina (St. Etienne, World Cup Finals)
Sep 5, 1998	**Paul Ince**	v Sweden (Stockholm, Eur Champ qual)
Jun 5, 1999	**Paul Scholes**	v Sweden (Wembley, Eur Champ qual)
Sep 8, 1999	**David Batty**	v Poland (Warsaw, Eur Champ qual)
Oct 16, 2002	**Alan Smith**	v Macedonia (Southampton, Eur Champ qual)
Oct 8, 2005	**David Beckham**	v Austria (Old Trafford, World Cup qual)
Jul 1, 2006	**Wayne Rooney**	v Portugal (Gelsenkirchen, World Cup Finals)
Oct 10, 2009	**Robert Green**	v Ukraine (Dnipropetrovsk, World Cup qual)

Other countries: Most recent sendings-off of players representing other Home Countries:

N Ireland – Adam Thompson (Carling Cup v Rep of Ireland, Dublin, May 24, 2011).

Scotland – Steven Whittaker (European Champ qual v Spain, Hampden Park, Oct 12, 2010).

Wales – Chris Gunter (European Champ qual v Bulgaria, Cardiff, Oct 8, 2010).

Rep of Ireland– Stephen Hunt (European Champ qual v Czech Republic, Prague, Sep 12, 2007).

England dismissals at other levels:

U-23: Stan Anderson (v Bulgaria, Sofia, May 19, 1957); **Alan Ball** (v Austria, Vienna, Jun 2, 1965); **Kevin Keegan** (v E Germany, Magdeburg, Jun 1, 1972); **Steve Perryman** (v Portugal, Lisbon, Nov 19, 1974).

U-21: Sammy Lee (v Hungary, Keszthely, Jun 5, 1981); **Mark Hateley** (v Scotland, Hampden Park, Apr 19, 1982); **Paul Elliott** (v Denmark, Maine Road, Manchester, Mar 26, 1986); **Tony Cottee** (v W Germany, Ludenscheid, Sep 8, 1987); **Julian Dicks** (v Mexico, Toulon, France, Jun. 12, 1988); **Jason Dodd** (v Mexico, Toulon, May 29, 1991; 3 Mexico players also sent off in that match); **Matthew Jackson** (v France, Toulon, May 28, 1992); **Robbie Fowler** (v Austria, Kafkenberg, Oct 11, 1994); **Alan Thompson** (v Portugal, Oporto, Sep 2, 1995); **Terry Cooke** (v Portugal, Toulon, May 30, 1996); **Ben Thatcher** (v Italy, Rieti, Oct 10, 1997); **John Curtis** (v Greece, Heraklion, Nov 13, 1997); **Jody Morris** (v Luxembourg, Grevenmacher, Oct 13, 1998); **Stephen Wright** (v Germany, Derby, Oct 6, 2000); **Alan Smith** (v Finland, Valkeakoski, Oct 10, 2000); **Luke Young** and **John Terry** (v Greece, Athens, Jun. 5, 2001); **Shola Ameobi** (v Portugal, Rio Maior, Mar 28, 2003); **Jermaine Pennant** (v Croatia, Upton Park, Aug 19, 2003); **Glen Johnson** (v Turkey, Istanbul, Oct 10, 2003); **Nigel Reo-Coker** (v Azerbaijan, Baku, Oct 12, 2004); **Glen Johnson** (v Spain, Henares, Nov 15, 2004); **Steven Taylor** (v Germany, Leverkusen, Oct 10, 2006); **Tom Huddlestone** (v Serbia & Montenegro, Nijmegen, Jun 17, 2007); **Tom Huddlestone** (v Wales, Villa Park, Oct 14, 2008); **Michael Mancienne** (v Finland, Halmstad, Jun 15, 2009); **Fraizer Campbell** (v Sweden, Gothenburg, Jun 26, 2009);**Jason Steele** (v Germany, Wiesbaden, Nov 16, 2010); **Ben Mee** (v Italy, Empoli, Feb 8, 2011).

England 'B' (1): Neil Webb (v Algeria, Algiers, Dec 11, 1990).

MOST DISMISSALS IN INTERNATIONAL MATCHES

19 (10 Chile, 9 Uruguay), Jun 25, 1975; **6** (2 Mexico, 4 Argentina), 1956; **6** (5 Ecuador, 1 Uruguay), Jan 4, 1977 (4 Ecuadorians sent off in 78th min, match abandoned, 1-1); **5** (Holland 3, Brazil 2), Jun 6, 1999 in Goiania, Brazil.

INTERNATIONAL STOPPED THROUGH DEPLETED SIDE

Portugal v Angola (5-1), friendly international in Lisbon on Nov 14, 2001, abandoned (68 mins) because Angola were down to 6 players (4 sent off, 1 carried off, no substitutes left).

MOST 'CARDS' IN WORLD CUP FINALS MATCH

20 in Portugal v Holland quarter-final, Nuremberg, Jun 25, 2006 (9 yellow, 2 red, Portugal; 7 yellow, 2 red, Holland).

FIVE OFF IN ONE MATCH

For the first time since League football began in 1888, five players were sent off in one match (two Chesterfield, three Plymouth) in Div 2 at Saltergate on **Feb 22, 1997.** Four were dismissed (two from each side) in a goalmouth brawl in the last minute.

Second instance of **five** sent off in a League match was on Dec 2, 1997: 4 Bristol Rov players, 1 Wigan in Div 2 match at Wigan. Four of those dismissals came in the 45th minute.

Third instance occurred on **Nov 23, 2002:** Exeter 4, Cambridge Utd 3 (Div 3) – all in the last minute.

Matches with **four** Football League club players being sent off in one match:

Jan 8, 1955: Crewe v Bradford City (Div 3 North), two players from each side.

Dec 13, 1986: Sheffield Utd (1 player) v Portsmouth (3) in Div 2.

Aug 18, 1987: Port Vale v Northampton (Littlewoods Cup 1st Round, 1st Leg), two players from each side.

Dec 12, 1987: Brentford v Mansfield (Div 3), two players from each side.

Sep 6, 1992: First instance in British first-class football of **four players from one side** being sent off in one match. Hereford's seven survivors, away to Northampton (Div 3), held out for a 1-1 draw.

Mar 1, 1977: Norwich v Huddersfield (Div 1), two from each side.

Oct 4, 1977: Shrewsbury (1 player), Rotherham (3) in Div 3.

Aug 22, 1998: Gillingham v Bristol Rov (Div 2), two from each side, all after injury-time brawl.

Mar 16, 2001: Bristol City v Millwall (Div 2), two from each side.

Aug 17, 2002: Lincoln (1 player), Carlisle (3) in Div 3.

Aug 26, 2002: Wycombe v QPR (Div 2), two from each side.

Nov 1, 2005: Burnley (1 player) v Millwall (3) in Championship.

Nov 24, 2007: Swindon v Bristol Rov (Lge 1), two from each side.

Mar 4, 2008: Hull v Burnley (Champ) two from each side.

Four Stranraer players were sent off away to Airdrie (Scottish Div 1) on Dec 3, 1994, and that Scottish record was equalled when **four Hearts men** were ordered off away to Rangers (Prem Div) on **Sep 14, 1996. Albion** had four players sent off (3 in last 8 mins) away to Queen's Park (Scottish Div 3) on **Aug 23, 1997.**

In the **Island Games** in Guernsey (Jul 2003), five players (all from Rhodes) were sent off against Guernsey for violent conduct and the match was abandoned by referee Wendy Toms.

Most dismissals one team, one match: Five players of America Tres Rios in first ten minutes after disputed goal by opponents Itaperuna in Brazilian cup match in Rio de Janeiro on Nov 23, 1991. Tie then abandoned and awarded to Itaperuna.

Eight dismissals in one match: Four on each side in South American Super Cup quarter-final (Gremio, Brazil v Penarol, Uruguay) in Oct 1993.

Five dismissals in one season – Dave Caldwell (2 with Chesterfield, 3 with Torquay) in 1987-88.

First instance of four dismissals in Scottish match: three **Rangers** players (all English – Terry Hurlock, Mark Walters, Mark Hateley) and **Celtic's** Peter Grant in Scottish Cup quarter-final at Parkhead on Mar 17, 1991 (Celtic won 2-0).

Four players (3 Hamilton, 1 Airdrie) were sent off in Scottish Div 1 match on Oct 30, 1993.

Four players (3 Ayr, 1 Stranraer) were sent off in Scottish Div 1 match on Aug 27, 1994.

In Scottish Cup first round replays on Dec 16, 1996, there were two instances of three players of one side sent off: Albion Rov (away to Forfar) and Huntly (away to Clyde).

FASTEST SENDINGS-OFF

World record – 10 sec: Giuseppe Lorenzo (Bologna) for striking opponent in Italian League match v Parma, Dec 9, 1990.

World record (non-professional) – 3 sec: David Pratt (Chippenham) at Bashley (British Gas

Southern Premier League, Dec 27, 2008).

Domestic – 13 sec: Kevin Pressman (Sheffield Wed goalkeeper at Wolves, Div 1, Sunday, Aug 14, 2000); **15 sec: Simon Rea** (Peterborough at Cardiff, Div 2, Nov 2, 2002). **19 secs: Mark Smith** (Crewe goalkeeper at Darlington, Div 3, Mar 12, 1994). **Premier League – 72 sec: Tim Flowers** (Blackburn goalkeeper v Leeds Utd, Feb 1, 1995).

In World Cup – 55 sec: Jose Batista (Uruguay v Scotland at Neza, Mexico, Jun 13, 1986).

In European competition – 90 sec: Sergei Dirkach (Dynamo Moscow v Ghent UEFA Cup 3rd round, 2nd leg, Dec 11, 1991).

Fastest FA Cup dismissal – 52 sec: Ian Culverhouse (Swindon defender, deliberate hand-ball on goal-line, away to Everton, 3rd Round, Sunday Jan 5, 1997).

Fastest League Cup dismissal – 33 sec: Jason Crowe (Arsenal substitute v Birmingham, 3rd Round, Oct 14, 1997). Also fastest sending off on debut.

Fastest Sending-off of substitute – 0 sec: Walter Boyd (Swansea City) for striking opponent before ball in play after he went on (83 mins) at home to Darlington, Div 3, Nov 23, 1999. **15 secs: Keith Gillespie** (Sheffield Utd) for striking an opponent at Reading (Premiership), Jan 20, 2007. **90 sec: Andreas Johansson** (Wigan), without kicking a ball, for shirt-pulling (penalty) away to Arsenal (Premiership), May 7, 2006.

MOST SENDINGS-OFF IN CAREER

21 **Willie Johnston** , 1964–82 (Rangers 7, WBA 6, Vancouver Whitecaps 4, Hearts 3, Scotland 1)
21 **Roy McDonough**, 1980–95 (13 in Football League – Birmingham, Walsall, Chelsea, Colchester, Southend, Exeter, Cambridge Utd plus 8 non-league).
13 **Steve Walsh** (Wigan, Leicester, Norwich, Coventry).
13 **Martin Keown** (Arsenal, Aston Villa, Everton).
13 **Alan Smith** (Leeds, Manchester Utd, Newcastle, England U–21, England).
12 **Dennis Wise** (Wimbledon, Chelsea, Leicester, Millwall).
12 **Vinnie Jones** (Wimbledon, Leeds, Sheffield Utd, Chelsea, QPR).
12 **Mark Dennis** (Birmingham, Southampton, QPR).
12 **Roy Keane** (Manchester Utd, Rep of Ireland).
10 **Patrick Vieira** (Arsenal).
10 **Paul Scholes (Manchester Utd, England).**
Most Premier League sendings-off: Patrick Vieira 9, Duncan Ferguson 8, Richard Dunne 8, Vinnie Jones 7, Roy Keane 7.
● **Carlton Palmer** holds the unique record of having been sent off with each of his five Premiership clubs: Sheffield Wed, Leeds, Southampton, Nottm Forest and Coventry.

FA CUP FINAL SENDINGS-OFF

Kevin Moran (Manchester Utd) v Everton, Wembley, 1985; **Jose Antonio Reyes** (Arsenal) v Manchester Utd, Cardiff, 2005.

WEMBLEY SENDINGS-OFF

Aug 1948	**Branko Stankovic** (Yugoslavia) v Sweden, Olympic Games.
Jul 1966	**Antonio Rattin** (Argentina captain) v England, World cup quarter-final.
Aug 1974	**Billy Bremner** (Leeds) and **Kevin Keegan** (Liverpool), Charity Shield.
Mar 1977	**Gilbert Dresch** (Luxembourg) v England, World Cup.
May 1985	**Kevin Moran** (Manchester Utd) v Everton, FA Cup Final.
Apr 1993	**Lee Dixon** (Arsenal) v Tottenham, FA Cup semi-final.
May 1993	**Peter Swan** (Port Vale) v WBA, Div 2 Play-off Final.
Mar 1994	**Andrei Kanchelskis** (Manchester Utd) v Aston Villa, League Cup Final.
May 1994	**Mike Wallace, Chris Beaumont** (Stockport) v Burnley, Div 2 Play-off Final.
Jun 1995	**Tetsuji Hashiratani** (Japan) v England, Umbro Cup.
May 1997	**Brian Statham** (Brentford) v Crewe, Div 2 Play-off Final.
Apr 1998	**Capucho** (Portugal) v England, friendly.
Nov 1998	**Ray Parlour** (Arsenal) and **Tony Vareilles** (Lens), Champions League.

Mar 1999	**Justin Edinburgh** (Tottenham) v Leicester, League Cup Final.
Jun 1999	**Paul Scholes** (England) v Sweden, European Championship qual.
Feb 2000	**Clint Hill** (Tranmere) v Leicester, League Cup Final.
Apr 2000	**Mark Delaney** (Aston Villa) v Bolton, FA Cup semi-final.
May 2000	**Kevin Sharp** (Wigan) v Gillingham, Div 2 Play-off Final.
Aug 2000	**Roy Keane** (Manchester Utd captain) v Chelsea, Charity Shield.
May 2007	**Marc Tierney** (Shrewsbury) v Bristol Rov, Lge 2 Play-off Final.
May 2007	**Matt Gill** (Exeter) v Morecambe, Conf Play-off Final.
May 2009	**Jamie Ward** (Sheffield Utd) and **Lee Hendrie** (Sheffield Utd) v Burnley, Champ Play-off Final (Hendrie after final whistle).
May 2009	**Phil Bolland** (Cambridge Utd) v Torquay, Blue Square Prem Lge Play-off Final.
May 2010	**Robin Hulbert** (Barrow) and **David Bridges** (Stevenage), FA Trophy Final.
Apr 2011	**Paul Scholes** (Manchester Utd) v Manchester City, FA Cup semi-final.
Apr 2011	**Toumani Diagouraga** (Brentford) v Carlisle, Johnstone's Paint Trophy Final.

WEMBLEY'S SUSPENDED CAPTAINS

Suspension prevented four **club captains** playing at Wembley in modern finals, in successive years.

Three were in FA Cup Finals – **Glenn Roeder** (QPR, 1982), **Steve Foster** (Brighton, 1983), **Wilf Rostron** (Watford, 1984). Sunderland's **Shaun Elliott** was banned from the 1985 Milk Cup Final. Roeder was banned from QPR's 1982 Cup Final replay against Tottenham, and Foster was ruled out of the first match in Brighton's 1983 Final against Manchester Utd.

BOOKINGS RECORDS

Most players of one Football League club booked in one match is **TEN** – members of the Mansfield team away to Crystal Palace in FA Cup third round, Jan 1963.

Fastest bookings – 3 seconds after kick-off, **Vinnie Jones** (Chelsea, home to Sheffield Utd, FA Cup fifth round, Feb 15, 1992); 5 seconds after kick-off: **Vinnie Jones** (Sheffield Utd, away to Manchester City, Div 1, Jan 19, 1991). He was sent-off (54 mins) for second bookable offence.

FIGHTING TEAM-MATES

Charlton's **Mike Flanagan** and **Derek Hales** were sent off for fighting each other five minutes from end of FA Cup 3rd round tie at home to Southern League Maidstone on Jan 9, 1979.

Bradford City's **Andy Myers** and **Stuart McCall** had a fight during the 1-6 Premiership defeat at Leeds on Sunday, May 13, 2001.

On Sep 28, 1994 the Scottish FA suspended Hearts players **Graeme Hogg** and **Craig Levein** for ten matches for fighting each other in a pre-season 'friendly' v Raith.

Blackburn's England players **Graeme Le Saux** and **David Batty** clashed away to Spartak Moscow (Champions League) on Nov 22, 1995. Neither was sent off.

Newcastle United's England Internationals **Lee Bowyer** and **Kieron Dyer** were sent off for fighting each other at home to Aston Villa (Premiership on Apr 2, 2005).

Arsenal's **Emmanuel Adebayor** and **Nicklas Bendtner** clashed during the 5-1 Carling Cup semi-final 2nd leg defeat at Tottenham on Jan 22, 2008. Neither was sent off; each fined by their club.

Stoke's **Ricardo Fuller** was sent off for slapping his captain, Andy Griffin, at West Ham in the Premier League on Dec 28, 2008

FOOTBALL'S FIRST BETTING SCANDAL

A Football League investigation into the First Division match which ended Manchester Utd 2, Liverpool 0 at Old Trafford on Good Friday, Apr 2, 1915 proved that the result had been 'squared' by certain players betting on the outcome. Four members of each team were suspended for life, but some of the bans were lifted when League football resumed in 1919 in recognition of the players' war service.

PLAYERS JAILED

Ten professional footballers found guilty of conspiracy to fraud by 'fixing' matches for betting purposes were given prison sentences at Nottingham Assizes on Jan 26, 1965.
Jimmy Gauld (Mansfield), described as the central figure, was given four years. Among the others sentenced, **Tony Kay** (Sheffield Wed, Everton & England), **Peter Swan** (Sheffield Wed & England) and **David 'Bronco' Layne** (Sheffield Wed) were suspended from football for life by the FA.

DRUGS BANS

Abel Xavier (Middlesbrough) was the first Premiership player found to have taken a performance-enchancing drug. He was banned by UEFA for 18 months in Nov 2005 after testing positive for an anabolic steroid. The ban was reduced to a year in Jul 2006 by the Court of Arbitration for Sport. **Paddy Kenny** (Sheffield Utd goalkeeper) was suspended by an FA commission for 9 months from July, 2009 for failing a drugs test the previous May. **Kolo Toure** (Manchester City) received a 6-month ban in May 2011 for a doping offence. It was backdated to Mar 2.

LONG SUSPENSIONS

The longest suspension (8 months) in modern times for a player in British football was imposed on two Manchester Utd players. First was **Eric Cantona** following his attack on a spectator as he left the pitch after being sent off at Crystal Palace (Prem League) on Jan 25, 1995. The club immediately suspended him to the end of the season and fined him 2 weeks' wages (est £20,000). Then, on a separate charge, the FA fined him £10,000 (Feb 1995) and extended the ban to Sep 30 (which FIFA confirmed as world-wide). A subsequent 2-weeks' jail sentence on Cantona for assault was altered, on appeal, to 120 hours' community service, which took the form of coaching schoolboys in the Manchester area.

On Dec 19, 2003 an FA Commission, held at Bolton, suspended **Rio Ferdinand** from football for 8 months (plus £50,000 fine) for failing to take a random drug test at the club's training ground on Sep 23. The ban operated from Jan 12, 2004.

Oct 1998: Paolo Di Canio (Sheff Wed) banned for 11 matches and fined £10,000 for pushing referee Paul Alcock after being sent off at home to Arsenal (Prem), Sep 26.

Mar 2005: David Prutton (Southampton) banned for 10 matches (plus 1 for red card) and fined £6,000 by FA for shoving referee Alan Wiley when sent off at home to Arsenal (Prem), Feb 26.

Sep 2008: Joey Barton (Newcastle) banned for 12 matches (6 suspended) and fined £25,000 by FA for training ground assault on former Manchester City team-mate **Ousmane Dabo.**

Seven-month ban: Frank Barson, 37-year-old Watford centre-half, sent off at home to Fulham (Div 3 South) on Sep 29, 1928, was suspended by the FA for the remainder of the season.

Twelve-month ban: Oldham full-back **Billy Cook** was given a 12-month suspension for refusing to leave the field when sent off at Middlesbrough (Div 1), on Apr 3, 1915. The referee abandoned the match with 35 minutes still to play, and the score (4-1 to Middlesbrough) was ordered to stand.

Long Scottish bans: Sep 1954: Willie Woodburn, Rangers and Scotland centre-half, suspended for rest of career after fifth sending-off in 6 years.

Billy McLafferty, Stenhousemuir striker, was banned (Apr 14) for 8 and a half months, to Jan 1, 1993, and fined £250 for failing to appear at a disciplinary hearing after being sent off against Arbroath on Feb 1.

Twelve-match ban: On May 12, 1994 Scottish FA suspended Rangers forward **Duncan Ferguson** for 12 matches for violent conduct v Raith on Apr 16. On Oct 11, 1995, Ferguson (then with Everton) sent to jail for 3 months for the assault (served 44 days); Feb 1, 1996 Scottish judge quashed 7 matches that remained of SFA ban on Ferguson.

On Sep 29, 2001 the SFA imposed a **17-match suspension** on Forfar's former Scottish international **Dave Bowman** for persistent foul and abusive language when sent off against Stranraer on Sep 22. As his misconduct continued, he was shown **5 red cards** by the referee.

On Apr 3, 2009, captain **Barry Ferguson** and goalkeeper **Allan McGregor** were banned for life from playing for Scotland for gestures towards photographers while on the bench for a World Cup qualifier against Iceland.

TOP FINES

Clubs: £5,500,000 West Ham: Apr 2007, for breaches of regulations involving 'dishonesty and deceit' over Argentine signings Carlos Tevez and Javier Mascherano; **£1,500,000** (increased from original £600,000) Tottenham: Dec 1994, financial irregularities; **£875,000** QPR: May 2011 for breaching rules when signing Argentine Alejandro Faurlin; **£300,000** (reduced to £75,000 on appeal) Chelsea: Jun 2005, illegal approach to Arsenal's Ashley Cole; **£175,000** Arsenal: Oct 2003, players' brawl v Manchester Utd; **£150,000** Leeds: Mar 2000, players' brawl v Tottenham; **£150,000** Tottenham: Mar 2000, players brawl v Leeds; **£115,000** West Ham: Aug 25, 2009, crowd misconduct at Carling Cup; v Millwall; **£105,000** Chelsea: Jan 1991, irregular payments; **£100,000** Boston Utd: Jul 2002, contract irregularities; **£100,000** Arsenal and Chelsea: Mar 2007 for mass brawl after Carling Cup Final; **£100,000** (including suspended fine)Blackburn: Aug 2007, poor disciplinary record; **£62,000** Macclesfield: Dec 2005, funding of a stand at club's ground.

Players: £150,000 Roy Keane (Manchester Utd): Oct 2002, disrepute offence over autobiography; **£100,000** (reduced to £75,000 on appeal) Ashley Cole (Arsenal): Jun 2005, illegal approach by Chelsea; **£45,000** Patrick Vieira (Arsenal): Oct 1999, tunnel incidents v West Ham; **£40,000** Lauren (Arsenal): Oct 2003, players' fracas v Manchester Utd; **£32,000** Robbie Fowler (Liverpool): Apr 1999, simulating drug-taking and incident with Graeme Le Saux v Chelsea; **£30,000** Lee Bowyer (Newcastle): Apr 2005, fighting with team-mate Kieron Dyer v Aston Villa.

*In eight seasons with Arsenal (1996–2004) **Patrick Vieira** was fined a total of £122,000 by the FA for disciplinary offences.

Managers: £200,000 (reduced to £75,000 on appeal) Jose Mourinho (Chelsea): Jun 2005, illegal approach to Arsenal's Ashley Cole; **£30,000** Sir Alex Ferguson (Manchester Utd): Mar 2011 criticising referee Martin Atkinson v Chelsea; **£20,000** Graeme Souness (Newcastle): Jun 2005, criticising referee v Everton; **£20,000** Sir Alex Ferguson (Manchester Utd): Oct 2009, questioning referee's fitness; **£15,000** Graeme Souness (Blackburn): Oct 2002, sent off v Liverpool; **£15,000** Arsene Wenger (Arsenal): Dec 2004, comments about Manchester Utd's Ruud van Nistelrooy;

• Jonathan Barnett, Ashley Cole's agent was fined **£100,000** in Sep 2006 for his role in the 'tapping up' affair involving the player and Chelsea.

*£68,000 FA: May 2003, pitch invasions and racist chanting by fans during England v Turkey, Sunderland.

MANAGERS

INTERNATIONAL RECORDS

(As at start of season 2011–12)

	P	W	D	L	F	A
Fabio Capello (England – appointed Dec 2007)	37	24	7	6	81	33
Craig Levein (Scotland – appointed Dec 2009)	11	5	1	5	14	12
Gary Speed (Wales – appointed Dec 2010)	4	1	0	3	3	8
Nigel Worthington (Northern Ireland – appointed May 2007)	36	8	10	18	29	45
Giovanni Trapattoni (Republic of Ireland – appointed May 2008)	34	16	9	9	50	34

PREVIOUS ENGLAND'S MANAGERS

		P	W	D	L
1946–62	**Walter Winterbottom**	139	78	33	28
1963–74	**Sir Alf Ramsey**	113	69	27	17

1974	**Joe Mercer**, caretaker	7	3	3	1
1974–77	**Don Revie**	29	14	8	7
1977–82	**Ron Greenwood**	55	33	12	10
1982–90	**Bobby Robson**	95	47	30	18
1990–93	**Graham Taylor**	38	18	13	7
1994–96	**Terry Venables**	23	11	11	1
1996–99	**Glenn Hoddle**	28	17	6	5
1999	**Howard Wilkinson**, caretaker	1	0	0	1
1999–2000	**Kevin Keegan**	18	7	7	4
2000	**Howard Wilkinson**, caretaker	1	0	1	0
2000	**Peter Taylor**, caretaker	1	0	0	1
2001–2006	**Sven–Goran Eriksson**	67	40	17	10
2006–2007	**Steve McClaren**	18	9	4	5

INTERNATIONAL MANAGER CHANGES

England: **Walter Winterbottom** 1946–62 (initially coach); **Alf Ramsey** (Feb 1963–May 1974); **Joe Mercer** (caretaker May 1974); **Don Revie** (Jul 1974–Jul 1977); **Ron Greenwood** (Jul 1977–Jul 1982); **Bobby Robson** (Jul 1982–Jul 1990); **Graham Taylor** (Jul 1990–Nov 1993); **Terry Venables**, coach (Jan 1994–Jun 1996); **Glenn Hoddle**, coach (Jun 1996–Feb 1999); **Howard Wilkinson** (caretaker Feb 1999); **Kevin Keegan** coach (Feb 1999–Oct 2000); **Howard Wilkinson** (caretaker Oct 2000); **Peter Taylor** (caretaker Nov 2000); **Sven–Goran Eriksson** (Jan 2001–Aug 2006); **Steve McClaren** (Aug 2006–Nov 2007); **Fabio Capello** (since Dec 2007).

Scotland (modern): **Bobby Brown** (Feb 1967–Jul 1971); **Tommy Docherty** (Sep 1971–Dec 1972); **Willie Ormond** (Jan 1973–May 1977); **Ally MacLeod** (May 1977–Sep 1978); **Jock Stein** (Oct 1978–Sep 1985); **Alex Ferguson** (caretaker Oct 1985–Jun 1986); **Andy Roxburgh**, coach (Jul 1986–Sep 1993); **Craig Brown** (Sep 1993–Oct 2001); **Berti Vogts** (Feb 2002–Oct 2004); **Walter Smith** (Dec 2004–Jan 2007); **Alex McLeish** (Jan 2007–Nov 2007); **George Burley** (Jan 2008-Nov 2009); **Craig Levein** (since Dec 2009).

Northern Ireland (modern): **Peter Doherty** (1951–62); **Bertie Peacock** (1962–67); **Billy Bingham** (1967–Aug 1971); **Terry Neill** (Aug 1971–Mar 1975); **Dave Clements** (player-manager Mar 1975–1976); **Danny Blanchflower** (Jun 1976–Nov 1979); **Billy Bingham** (Feb 1980–Nov 1993); **Bryan Hamilton** Feb 1994–Feb 1998); **Lawrie McMenemy** (Feb 1998–Nov 1999); **Sammy McIlroy** (Jan 2000–Oct 2003); **Lawrie Sanchez** (Jan 2004–May 2007); **Nigel Worthington** (since May 2007).

Wales (modern):**Mike Smith** (Jul 1974–Dec 1979); **Mike England** (Mar 1980–Feb 1988); **David Williams** (caretaker Mar 1988); **Terry Yorath** (Apr 1988–Nov 1993); **John Toshack** (Mar 1994, one match); **Mike Smith** (Mar 1994–Jun 1995); **Bobby Gould** (Aug 1995–Jun 1999); **Mark Hughes** (Aug 1999 – Oct 2004); **John Toshack** (Nov 2004-Sep 2010); **Brian Flynn** (caretaker Sep-Dec 2010); **Gary Speed** (since Dec 2010).

Republic of Ireland (modern): **Liam Tuohy** (Sep 1971–Nov 1972); **Johnny Giles** (Oct 1973–Apr 1980, initially player–manager); **Eoin Hand** (Jun 1980–Nov 1985); **Jack Charlton** (Feb 1986–Dec 1995); **Mick McCarthy** (Feb 1996–Oct 2002); **Brian Kerr** (Jan 2003–Oct 2005); **Steve Staunton** (Jan 2006–Oct 2007); **Giovanni Trapattoni** (since May 2008).

WORLD CUP-WINNING MANAGERS

1930 Uruguay (Alberto Suppici); **1934** and **1938** Italy (Vittorio Pozzo); **1950** Uruguay (Juan Lopez Fontana); **1954** West Germany (Sepp Herberger); **1958** Brazil (Vicente Feola); **1962** Brazil (Aymore Moreira); **1966** England (Sir Alf Ramsey); **1970** Brazil (Mario Zagallo); **1974** West Germany (Helmut Schon); **1978** Argentina (Cesar Luis Menotti); **1982** Italy (Enzo Bearzot); **1986** Argentina (Carlos Bilardo); **1990** West Germany (Franz Beckenbauer); **1994** Brazil (Carlos Alberto Parreira); **1998** France (Aimee Etienne Jacquet); **2002** Brazil (Luiz Felipe Scolari); **2006** Italy (Marcello Lippi); **2010** Spain (Vicente Del Bosque).

Each of the 19 winning teams had a manager/coach of the country's nationality.

FIRST BLACK ENGLAND MANAGER

Chris Ramsey, 36, in charge of England's U-20 squad for World Youth Championship in Nigeria, Apr 1999. He was Brighton's right-back in the 1983 FA Cup Final v Manchester Utd.

FIRST BLACK MANAGER IN FOOTBALL LEAGUE

Tony Collins (Rochdale 1960-68).

YOUNGEST LEAGUE MANAGERS

Ivor Broadis, 23, appointed player-manager of Carlisle, Aug 1946; **Chris Brass**, 27, appointed player-manager of York, Jun 2003; **Terry Neill**, 28, appointed player manager of Hull, Jun 1970; **Graham Taylor**, 28, appointed manager of Lincoln, Dec 1972.

LONGEST-SERVING LEAGUE MANAGERS – ONE CLUB

Fred Everiss, secretary–manager of WBA for 46 years (1902–48); **George Ramsay**, secretary–manager of Aston Villa for 42 years (1884–1926); **John Addenbrooke**, Wolves, for 37 years (1885–1922). Since last war, **Sir Matt Busby**, in charge of Manchester Utd for 25 seasons (1945–69, 1970–71); **Dario Gradi** at Crewe for 26 years (1983–2007, 2009-11); **Jimmy Seed** at Charlton for 23 years (1933–56); **Sir Alex Ferguson** at Manchester Utd for 25 seasons (1986–2011); **Brian Clough** at Nottm Forest for 18 years (1975-93).

LAST ENGLISH MANAGER TO WIN CHAMPIONSHIP

Howard Wilkinson (Leeds), season 1991–92.

1,000-TIME MANAGERS

Only five have managed in more than **1,000 English League games**: Alec Stock, Brian Clough, Jim Smith, Graham Taylor and Dario Gradi.
Sir Matt Busby, Dave Bassett, Lennie Lawrence, Alan Buckley, Denis Smith, Joe Royle, Sir Alex Ferguson, Ron Atkinson, Brian Horton, Neil Warnock, Harry Redknapp and Steve Coppell have each managed more than **1,000 matches in all first class competitions**.

SHORT-TERM MANAGERS

Departed

3 days	Bill Lambton (Scunthorpe)	Apr 1959
7 days	Tim Ward (Exeter)	Mar 1953
7 days	Kevin Cullis (Swansea City)	Feb 1996
10 days	Dave Cowling (Doncaster)	Oct 1997
10 days	Peter Cormack (Cowdenbeath)	Dec 2000
13 days	Johnny Cochrane (Reading)	Apr 1939
13 days	Micky Adams (Swansea City)	Oct 1997
16 days	Jimmy McIlroy (Bolton)	Nov 1970
19 days	Martin Allen (Barnet)	Apr 2011
20 days	Paul Went (Leyton Orient)	Oct 1981
27 days	Malcolm Crosby (Oxford Utd)	Jan 1998
28 days	Tommy Docherty (QPR)	Dec 1968
28 days	Paul Hart (QPR)	Jan 2010
32 days	Steve Coppell (Manchester City)	Nov 1996
34 days	Niall Quinn (Sunderland)	Aug 2006
36 days	Steve Claridge (Millwall)	Jul 2005
39 days	Paul Gascoigne (Kettering)	Dec 2005
41 days	Steve Wicks (Lincoln)	Oct 1995
41 days	Les Reed (Charlton)	Dec 2006
44 days	Brian Clough (Leeds)	Sep 1974
44 days	Jock Stein (Leeds)	Oct 1978
48 days	John Toshack (Wales)	Mar 1994

48 days	David Platt (Sampdoria coach)	Feb 1999
49 days	Brian Little (Wolves)	Oct 1986
49 days	Terry Fenwick (Northampton)	Feb 2003
56 days	Dave Penney (Bristol Rov)	Mar 2011
61 days	Bill McGarry (Wolves)	Nov 1985

- In May 1984, Crystal Palace named **Dave Bassett** as manager, but he changed his mind four days later, without signing the contract, and returned to Wimbledon.
- In May 2007, **Leroy Rosenior** was reportedly appointed manager of Torquay after relegation and sacked ten minutes later when the club came under new ownership.
- **Brian Laws** lost his job at Scunthorpe on Mar 25, 2004 and was reinstated three weeks later.
- In an angry outburst after a play-off defeat in May 1992, Barnet chairman Stan Flashman sacked manager **Barry Fry** and re-instated him a day later.

EARLY-SEASON MANAGER SACKINGS

2010: Kevin Blackwell Sheffield Utd) 8 days; **2009** Bryan Gunn (Norwich) 6 days; **2007:** Neil McDonald (Carlisle) 2 days; Martin Allen (Leicester) 18 days; **2004:** Paul Sturrock (Southampton) 9 days; **2004:** Sir Bobby Robson (Newcastle) 16 days; **2003:** Glenn Roeder (West Ham) 15 days; **2000:** Alan Buckley (Grimsby) 10 days; **1997:** Kerry Dixon (Doncaster) 12 days; **1996:** Sammy Chung (Doncaster) on morning of season's opening League match; **1996:** Alan Ball (Manchester City) 12 days; **1994:** Kenny Hibbitt (Walsall) and Kenny Swain (Wigan) 20 days; **1993:** Peter Reid (Manchester City) 12 days; **1991:** Don Mackay (Blackburn) 14 days; **1989:** Mick Jones (Peterborough) 12 days; **1980:** Bill McGarry (Newcastle) 13 days; **1979:** Dennis Butler (Port Vale) 12 days; **1977:** George Petchey (Leyton O.) 13 days; **1977:** Willie Bell (Birmingham) 16 days; **1971:** Len Richley (Darlington) 12 days.

RECORD START FOR MANAGER

Arsenal were unbeaten in 17 League matches from the start of season 1947–48 under new manager Tom Whittaker.

MANAGER CHOSEN BY POLL

A month after being sacked by Third Division promotion winners Hartlepool, **Mike Newell** became manager of Luton in Jun 2003. He was appointed via a telephone poll which the club, under a new board, conducted among fans, players, shareholders and season-ticket holders.

MANAGER DOUBLES

Four managers have won the League Championship with different clubs: **Tom Watson**, secretary–manager with Sunderland (1892–3–5) and **Liverpool** (1901); **Herbert Chapman** with Huddersfield (1923–24, 1924–25) and Arsenal (1930–31, 1932–33); **Brian Clough** with Derby (1971–72) and Nottm Forest (1977–78); **Kenny Dalglish** with Liverpool (1985–86, 1987–88, 1989–90) and Blackburn (1994–95).

Managers to win the FA Cup with different clubs: **Billy Walker** (Sheffield Wed 1935, Nottm Forest 1959); **Herbert Chapman** (Huddersfield 1922, Arsenal 1930).

Kenny Dalglish (Liverpool) and **George Graham** (Arsenal) completed the Championship/FA Cup double as both player and manager with a single club. **Joe Mercer** won the title as a player with Everton, the title twice and FA Cup as a player with Arsenal and both competitions as manager of Manchester City.

CHAIRMAN–MANAGER

On Dec 20, 1988, after two years on the board, Dundee Utd manager **Jim McLean** was elected chairman, too. McLean, Scotland's longest–serving manager (appointed on Nov 24, 1971), resigned at end of season 1992–93 (remained chairman).

Ron Noades was chairman-manager of Brentford from Jul 1998–Mar 2001. John Reames did both jobs at Lincoln from Nov 1998–Apr 2000)

Niall Quinn did both jobs for five weeks in 2006 before appointing Roy Keane as manager of Sunderland.

TOP DIVISION PLAYER–MANAGERS

Les Allen (QPR 1968–69); **Johnny Giles** (WBA 1976–77); **Howard Kendall** (Everton 1981–82); **Kenny Dalglish** (Liverpool, 1985–90); **Trevor Francis** (QPR, 1988–89); **Terry Butcher** (Coventry, 1990–91); **Peter Reid** (Manchester City, 1990–93); **Trevor Francis** (Sheffield Wed, 1991–94); **Glenn Hoddle**, (Chelsea, 1993–95); **Bryan Robson** (Middlesbrough, 1994–97); **Ray Wilkins** (QPR, 1994–96); **Ruud Gullit** (Chelsea, 1996–98); **Gianluca Vialli** (Chelsea, 1998–2000).

FIRST FOREIGN MANAGER IN ENGLISH LEAGUE

Uruguayan **Danny Bergara** (Rochdale 1988–89).

COACHING KINGS OF EUROPE

When **Jose Mourinho** lifted the Champions League trophy with Inter Milan in 2010, he became only the third coach in European Cup history to win the world's greatest club prize with two different clubs. He had previously done it with Porto in 2004. The others to achieve this double were **Ernst Happel** with Feyenoord (1970) and Hamburg (1983) and **Ottmar Hitzfeld** with Borussia Dortmund (1997) and Bayern Munich (2001).

FOREIGN TRIUMPH

Former Dutch star **Ruud Gullit** became the first foreign manager to win a major English competition when Chelsea took the FA Cup in 1997.

Arsene Wenger and **Gerard Houllier** became the first foreign managers to receive recognition when they were awarded honorary OBEs in the Queen's Birthday Honours in Jun 2003 'for their contribution to English football and Franco–British relations'.

MANAGERS OF POST-WAR CHAMPIONS (*Double winners)

1947 George Kay (Liverpool); **1948** Tom Whittaker (Arsenal); **1949** Bob Jackson (Portsmouth). **1950** Bob Jackson (Portsmouth); **1951** Arthur Rowe (Tottenham); **1952** Matt Busby (Manchester Utd); **1953** Tom Whittaker (Arsenal); **1954** Stan Cullis (Wolves); **1955** Ted Drake (Chelsea); **1956** Matt Busby (Manchester Utd); **1957** Matt Busby (Manchester Utd); **1958** Stan Cullis (Wolves); **1959** Stan Cullis (Wolves).
1960 Harry Potts (Burnley); **1961** *Bill Nicholson (Tottenham); **1962** Alf Ramsey (Ipswich); **1963** Harry Catterick (Everton); **1964** Bill Shankly (Liverpool); **1965** Matt Busby (Manchester Utd); **1966** Bill Shankly (Liverpool); **1967** Matt Busby (Manchester Utd); **1968** Joe Mercer (Manchester City); **1969** Don Revie (Leeds).
1970 Harry Catterick (Everton); **1971** *Bertie Mee (Arsenal); **1972** Brian Clough (*Derby); **1973** Bill Shankly (Liverpool); **1974** Don Revie (Leeds); **1975** Dave Mackay (Derby); **1976** Bob Paisley (Liverpool); **1977** Bob Paisley (Liverpool); **1978** Brian Clough (Nottm Forest); **1979** Bob Paisley (Liverpool).
1980 Bob Paisley (Liverpool); **1981** Ron Saunders (Aston Villa); **1982** Bob Paisley (Liverpool); **1983** Bob Paisley (Liverpool); **1984** Joe Fagan (Liverpool); **1985** Howard Kendall (Everton); **1986** *Kenny Dalglish (Liverpool – player/manager); **1987** Howard Kendall (Everton); **1988** Kenny Dalglish (Liverpool – player/manager); **1989** George Graham (Arsenal).
1990 Kenny Dalglish (Liverpool); **1991** George Graham (Arsenal); **1992** Howard Wilkinson (Leeds); **1993** Alex Ferguson (Manchester Utd); **1994** *Alex Ferguson (Manchester Utd); **1995** Kenny Dalglish (Blackburn); **1996** *Alex Ferguson (Manchester Utd); **1997** Alex Ferguson (Manchester Utd); **1998** *Arsene Wenger (Arsenal); **1999** *Alex Ferguson (Manchester Utd).
2000 Sir Alex Ferguson (Manchester Utd); **2001** Sir Alex Ferguson (Manchester Utd); **2002** *Arsene Wenger (Arsenal); **2003** Sir Alex Ferguson (Manchester Utd); **2004** Arsene Wenger (Arsenal); **2005** Jose Mourinho (Chelsea); **2006** Jose Mourinho (Chelsea); **2007** Sir Alex Ferguson (Manchester Utd); **2008** Sir Alex Ferguson (Manchester Utd); **2009** Sir Alex Ferguson (Manchester Utd); **2010** *Carlo Ancelotti (Chelsea).

SIR ALEX IS TOPS

With 46 major prizes, **Sir Alexander Chapman Ferguson** is the most successful manager in the history of British football. At **Aberdeen** (1978–86) he won 3 Scottish Championships, 4 Scottish Cups, 1 Scottish League Cup, 1 Cup-Winners' Cup, 1 European Super Cup. His triumphs for **Manchester Utd** since taking over in November, 1986 total 36. They comprise: 12 Premier League titles, 5 FA Cups, 4 League Cups, 2 European Cups, 1 Cup-Winners' Cup, 1 UEFA Super Cup, 1 Inter-Continental Cup, 1 FIFA Club World Cup, 9 Charity/Community Shields. Under him, United have set a record of 19 League titles.

BOB PAISLEY'S HONOURS

Bob Paisley won 13 major competitions for Liverpool (1974–83): 6 League Championships, 3 European Cups, 3 League Cups, 1 UEFA Cup.

MOURINHO'S RECORD

Jose Mourinho, who left Chelsea on September 19, 2007, was the most successful manager in the club's history. Appointed in June 2004 after taking Porto to successive Portuguese League titles, he won six trophies in three seasons at Stamford Bridge: Premiership in 2005 and 2006, League Cup in 2005 and 2007, FA Cup in 2007 and Community Shield in 2005. Under Mourinho, Chelsea were unbeaten at home in the Premier League with his record: P60 W46 D14 F123 A28. He won the Italian title with Inter Milan in 2009 and completed the treble of League, Cup and Champions League the following season before taking over at Real Madrid.

FATHER AND SON MANAGERS WITH SAME CLUB

Fulham: Bill Dodgin Snr 1949–53; Bill Dodgin Jnr 1968–72. **Brentford:** Bill Dodgin Snr 1953–57; Bill Dodgin Jnr 1976–80. **Bournemouth:** John Bond 1970–73; Kevin Bond 2006–08. **Derby:** Brian Clough 1967–73; Nigel Clough 2009.

SIR BOBBY'S HAT-TRICK

Sir Bobby Robson, born and brought up in County Durham, achieved a unique hat-trick when he received the Freedom of Durham in Dec 2008. He had already been awarded the Freedom of Ipswich and Newcastle. He died in July 2009 and had an express loco named after him on the East Coast to London line.

MANAGERS WITH MOST FA CUP SUCCESSES

5 Sir Alex Ferguson (Manchester Utd); **4** Arsene Wenger (Arsenal); **3** Charles Foweraker (Bolton), John Nicholson (Sheffield Utd), Bill Nicholson (Tottenham).

HOLE-IN-ONE MANAGER

Three days after appointing **Bobby Williamson** manager, from Hibernian, Plymouth Argyle clinched promotion and the Second Division Championship by beating QPR 2-1 on Apr 24, 2004.

RELEGATION 'DOUBLES'

Managers associated with two clubs relegated in same season: **John Bond** in 1985–86 (Swansea City and Birmingham); **Ron Saunders** in 1985–86 (WBA – and their reserve team – and Birmingham); **Bob Stokoe** in 1986–87 (Carlisle and Sunderland); **Billy McNeill** in 1986–87 (Manchester City and Aston Villa); **Dave Bassett** in 1987–88 (Watford and Sheffield Utd); **Mick Mills** in 1989–90 (Stoke and Colchester).

WEMBLEY STADIUM

NEW WEMBLEY

A new era for English football began in March 2007 with the completion of the new national stadium. The 90,000-seater arena was hailed as one of the finest in the world – but came at a price. Costs soared, the project fell well behind schedule and disputes involving the FA, builders Multiplex and the Government were rife. The old stadium, opened in 1923, was built for £750,000. The new one, originally priced at £326m in 2000, ended up costing around £800m. The first international after completion was an Under-21 match between England and Italy. The FA Cup Final returned to its spiritual home after being staged at the Millennium Stadium in Cardiff for six seasons. Then, England's senior team were back for a friendly against Brazil.

GOAL KING DROGBA

Didier Drogba's FA Cup winner against Portsmouth in May 2010 meant that he had scored in all his 7 appearances for the club at Wembley (6 wins, 1 defeat). They came in: **2007:** FA Cup Final v Manchester Utd (1-0); 2008: League Cup Final v Tottenham (1-2); **2009:** FA Cup semi-final v Arsenal (2-1), Final v Everton (2-1), Community Shield v Manchester Utd (in 4-1 pen shoot-out after 2-2); **2010** FA Cup semi-final v Aston Villa (3-0), Final v Portsmouth (1-0).

INVASION DAY

Memorable scenes were witnessed at the first **FA Cup Final at Wembley,** Apr 28, 1923, between **Bolton** and **West Ham.** An accurate return of the attendance could not be made owing to thousands breaking in, but there were probably more than 200,000 spectators present. The match was delayed for 40 minutes by the crowd invading the pitch. Official attendance was 126,047.

Gate receipts totalled £27,776. The two clubs and the FA each received £6,365 and the FA refunded £2,797 to ticket-holders who were unable to get to their seats. Cup Final admission has since been by ticket only.

REDUCED CAPACITY

Capacity of the all-seated Wembley Stadium was 78,000. The last 100,000 attendance was for the 1985 FA Cup Final between Manchester Utd and Everton. Crowd record for New Wembley: 89,874 for 2008 FA Cup Final (Portsmouth v Cardiff).

WEMBLEY'S FIRST UNDER LIGHTS

Nov 30; 1955 (England 4, Spain 1), when the floodlights were switched on after 73 minutes (afternoon match played in damp, foggy conditions).
First Wembley international played throughout under lights: England 8, N Ireland 3 on evening of Nov 20, 1963 (att: 55,000).

MOST WEMBLEY APPEARANCES BY PLAYER

59 by **Tony Adams** (24 Arsenal, 35 England).

WEMBLEY HAT-TRICKS

Three players have scored hat-tricks in major finals at Wembley: **Stan Mortensen** for Blackpool v Bolton (FA Cup Final, 1953), **Geoff Hurst** for England v West Germany (World Cup Final, 1966) and **David Speedie** for Chelsea v Manchester City (Full Members Cup, 1985).

ENGLAND'S WEMBLEY DEFEATS

England have lost 21 matches to foreign opponents at Wembley:

Nov 1953	3-6 v Hungary	May 1990	1-2 v Uruguay
Oct 1959	2-3 v Sweden	Sep 1991	0-1 v Germany
Oct 1965	2-3 v Austria	Jun 1995	1-3 v Brazil
Apr 1972	1-3 v W Germany	Feb 1997	0-1 v Italy
Nov 1973	0-1 v Italy	Feb 1998	0-2 v Chile
Feb 1977	0-2 v Holland	Feb 1999	0-2 v France
Mar 1981	1-2 v Spain	Oct 2000	0-1 v Germany
May 1981	0-1 v Brazil	Aug 2007	1-2 v Germany

Oct 1982	1-2 v W Germany	Nov 2007	2-3 v Croatia
Sep 1983	0-1 v Denmark	Nov 2010	1-2 v France
Jun 1984	0-2 v Russia		

A further defeat came in **Euro 96**. After drawing the semi-final with Germany 1-1, England went out 6-5 on penalties.

FASTEST GOALS AT WEMBLEY

In first-class matches: **25 sec** by **Louis Saha** for Everton in 2009 FA Cup Final against Chelsea; **38 sec** by **Bryan Robson** for England's against Yugoslavia in 1989; **42 sec** by **Roberto di Matteo** for Chelsea in 1997 FA Cup Final v Middlesbrough; **44 sec** by **Bryan Robson** for England v Northern Ireland in 1982;

Fastest goal in **any** match at Wembley: **20 sec** by **Maurice Cox** for Cambridge University against Oxford in 1979.

FOUR WEMBLEY HEADERS

When Wimbledon beat Sutton 4-2 in the FA Amateur Cup Final at Wembley on May 4, 1963, Irish centre-forward **Eddie Reynolds** headed all four goals.

WEMBLEY ONE-SEASON DOUBLES

In 1989, **Nottm Forest** became the first club to win two Wembley Finals in the same season (Littlewoods Cup and Simod Cup).

In 1993, **Arsenal** made history there as the first club to win the League (Coca-Cola) Cup and the FA Cup in the same season. They beat Sheffield Wed 2-1 in both finals.

SUDDEN-DEATH DECIDERS

First Wembley Final decided on sudden death (first goal scored in overtime): Apr 23, 1995 – **Birmingham** beat Carlisle (1-0, Paul Tait 103 mins) to win Auto Windscreens Shield.

First instance of a golden goal deciding a major international tournament was at Wembley on Jun 30, 1996, when **Germany** beat the Czech Republic 2-1 in the European Championship Final with Oliver Bierhoff's goal in the 95th minute.

SHADOWS OVER SOCCER

DAYS OF TRAGEDY – CLUBS

Season 1988–89 brought the worst disaster in the history of British sport, with the death of 96 Liverpool supporters (200 injured) at the **FA Cup semi-final** against Nottm Forest at **Hillsborough, Sheffield**, on Saturday, Apr 15. The tragedy built up in the minutes preceding kick-off, when thousands surged into the ground at the Leppings Lane end. Many were crushed in the tunnel between entrance and terracing, but most of the victims were trapped inside the perimeter fencing behind the goal. The match was abandoned without score after six minutes' play. The dead included seven women and girls, two teenage sisters and two teenage brothers. The youngest victim was a boy of ten, the oldest 67-year-old Gerard Baron, whose brother Kevin played for Liverpool in the 1950 Cup Final. (*Total became 96 in Mar 1993, when Tony Bland died after being in a coma for nearly four years.)

The two worst disasters in one season in British soccer history occurred at the end of 1984–85. On May 11, the last Saturday of the League season, 56 people (two of them visiting supporters) were burned to death – and more than 200 taken to hospital – when fire destroyed the main stand at the **Bradford City–Lincoln** match at Valley Parade.

The wooden, 77-year-old stand was full for City's last fixture before which, amid scenes of celebration, the club had been presented with the Third Division Championship trophy. The fire broke out just before half-time and, within five minutes, the entire stand was engulfed.

Heysel Tragedy

Eighteen days later, on May 29, at the European Cup Final between **Liverpool** and **Juventus** at the

Heysel Stadium, Brussels, 39 spectators (31 of them Italian) were crushed or trampled to death and 437 injured. The disaster occurred an hour before the scheduled kick-off when Liverpool supporters charged a Juventus section of the crowd at one end of the stadium, and a retaining wall collapsed. The sequel was a 5-year ban by UEFA on English clubs generally in European competition, with a 6-year ban on Liverpool.

On May 26 1985 ten people were trampled to death and 29 seriously injured in a crowd panic on the way into the **Olympic Stadium, Mexico City** for the Mexican Cup Final between local clubs National University and America.

More than 100 people died and 300 were injured in a football disaster at **Nepal's national stadium** in Katmandu in Mar 1988. There was a stampede when a violent hailstorm broke over the capital. Spectators rushed for cover, but the stadium exits were locked, and hundreds were trampled in the crush.

In South Africa, on Jan 13 1991 40 black fans were trampled to death (50 injured) as they tried to escape from fighting that broke out at a match in the gold-mining town of Orkney, 80 miles from Johannesburg. The friendly, between top teams **Kaiser Chiefs** and **Orlando Pirates**, attracted a packed crowd of 20,000. Violence erupted after the referee allowed Kaiser Chiefs a disputed second-half goal to lead 1-0.

Disaster struck at the French Cup semi-final (May 5, 1992), with the death of 15 spectators and 1,300 injured when a temporary metal stand collapsed in the Corsican town of Bastia. The tie between Second Division **Bastia** and French Champions **Marseille** was cancelled. Monaco, who won the other semi-final, were allowed to compete in the next season's Cup-Winners' Cup.

A total of 318 died and 500 were seriously injured when the crowd rioted over a disallowed goal at the National Stadium in Lima, Peru, on May 24, 1964. **Peru** and **Argentina** were competing to play in the Olympic Games in Tokyo.

That remained **sport's heaviest death** toll until Oct 20, 1982, when (it was revealed only in Jul 1989) 340 Soviet fans were killed in Moscow's Lenin Stadium at the UEFA Cup second round first leg match between **Moscow Spartak** and **Haarlem** (Holland). They were crushed on an open stairway when a last-minute Spartak goal sent departing spectators surging back into the ground.

Among other crowd disasters abroad: Jun, 1968 – 74 died in Argentina. Panic broke out at the end of a goalless match between River Plate and Boca Juniors at Nunez, Buenos Aires, when Boca supporters threw lighted newspaper torches on to fans in the tiers below.

Feb 1974 – 49 killed in **Egypt** in crush of fans clamouring to see Zamalek play Dukla Prague.

Sep 1971 – 44 died in **Turkey**, when fighting among spectators over a disallowed goal (Kayseri v Siwas) led to a platform collapsing.

The then worst disaster in the history of British football, in terms of loss of life, occurred at Glasgow Rangers' ground at **Ibrox Park**, Jan 2 1971. Sixty-six people were trampled to death (100 injured) as they tumbled down Stairway 13 just before the end of the **Rangers v Celtic** New Year's match. That disaster led to the 1975 Safety of Sports Grounds legislation.

The Ibrox tragedy eclipsed even the Bolton disaster in which 33 were killed and about 500 injured when a wall and crowd barriers collapsed near a corner-flag at the **Bolton v Stoke** FA Cup sixth round tie on Mar 9 1946. The match was completed after half an hour's stoppage.

In a previous crowd disaster at **Ibrox** on Apr 5, 1902, part of the terracing collapsed during the Scotland v England international and 25 people were killed. The match, held up for 20 minutes, ended 1-1, but was never counted as an official international.

Eight leading players and three officials of **Manchester Utd** and eight newspaper representatives were among the 23 who perished in the air crash at **Munich** on Feb 6, 1958, during take-off following a European Cup-tie in Belgrade. The players were Roger Byrne, Geoffrey Bent, Eddie Colman, Duncan Edwards, Mark Jones, David Pegg, Tommy Taylor, and Liam Whelan, and the officials were Walter Crickmer (secretary), Tom Curry (trainer) and Herbert Whalley (coach). The newspaper representatives were Alf Clarke, Don Davies, George Follows, Tom Jackson, Archie Ledbrooke, Henry Rose, Eric Thompson and Frank Swift (former England goalkeeper of Manchester City).

On May 14, 1949, the entire team of Italian Champions **Torino**, 8 of them Internationals, were killed when the aircraft taking them home from a match against Benfica in Lisbon crashed at Superga, near Turin. The total death toll of 28 included all the club's reserve players, the manager, trainer and coach.

On Feb 8, 1981, 24 spectators died and more than 100 were injured at a match in **Greece**. They were trampled as thousands of the 40,000 crowd tried to rush out of the stadium at Piraeus after Olympiacos beat AEK Athens 6-0.

On Nov 17, 1982, 24 people (12 of them children) were killed and 250 injured when fans stampeded at the end of a match at the Pascual Guerrero stadium in **Cali, Colombia**. Drunken spectators hurled fire crackers and broken bottles from the higher stands on to people below and started a rush to the exits.

On Dec 9, 1987, the 18-strong team squad of **Alianza Lima**, one of Peru's top clubs, were wiped out, together with 8 officials and several youth players, when a military aircraft taking them home from Puccalpa crashed into the sea off Ventillana, ten miles from Lima. The only survivor among 43 on board was a member of the crew.

On Apr 28, 1993, 18 members of **Zambia's international squad** and 5 ZFA officials died when the aircraft carrying them to a World Cup qualifying tie against Senegal crashed into the Atlantic soon after take-off from Libreville, Gabon.

On Oct 16 1996, 81 fans were crushed to death and 147 seriously injured in the '**Guatemala Disaster**' at the World Cup qualifier against Costa Rica in Mateo Flores stadium. The tragedy happened an hour before kick-off, allegedly caused by ticket forgery and overcrowding – 60,000 were reported in the 45,000-capacity ground – and safety problems related to perimeter fencing.

On Jul 9, 1996, 8 people died, 39 injured in riot after derby match between **Libya's two top clubs** in Tripoli. Al-Ahli had beaten Al-Ittihad 1-0 by a controversial goal.

On Apr 6, 1997, 5 spectators were crushed to death at **Nigeria's national stadium** in Lagos after the 2-1 World Cup qualifying victory over Guinea. Only two of five gates were reported open as the 40,000 crowd tried to leave the ground.

It was reported from the **Congo** (Oct 29, 1998) that a bolt of lightning struck a village match, killing all 11 members of the home team Benatshadi, but leaving the opposing players from Basangana unscathed. It was believed the surviving team wore better-insulated boots.

On Jan 10, 1999, eight fans died and 13 were injured in a stampede at **Egypt's Alexandria Stadium**. Some 25,000 spectators had pushed into the ground. Despite the tragedy, the cup-tie between Al-Ittihad and Al-Koroum was completed.

Three people suffocated and several were seriously injured when thousands of fans forced their way into **Liberia's national stadium** in Monrovia at a goalless World Cup qualifying match against Chad on Apr 23, 2000. The stadium (capacity 33,000) was reported 'heavily overcrowded'.

On Jul 9, 2000, 12 spectators died from crush injuries when police fired tear gas into the 50,000 crowd after South Africa scored their second goal in a World Cup group qualifier against Zimbabwe in **Harare**. A stampede broke out as fans scrambled to leave the national stadium. Players of both teams lay face down on the pitch as fumes swept over them. FIFA launched an investigation and decided that the result would stand, with South Africa leading 2-0 at the time of the 84th-minute abandonment.

On Apr 11, 2001, at one of the biggest matches of the South African season, 43 died and 155 were injured in a crush at **Ellis Park, Johannesburg**. After tearing down a fence, thousands of fans surged into a stadium already packed to its 60,000 capacity for the Premiership derby between top Soweto teams Kaizer Chiefs and Orlando Pirates.

The match was abandoned at 1-1 after 33 minutes. In Jan 1991, 40 died in a crowd crush at a friendly between the same clubs at Orkney, 80 miles from Johannesburg.

On Apr 29, 2001, seven people were trampled to death and 51 injured when a riot broke out at a match between two of Congo's biggest clubs, Lupopo and Mazembe at **Lubumbashi**, southern Congo.

On May 6, 2001, two spectators were killed in Iran and hundreds were injured when a glass fibre roof collapsed at the over-crowded Mottaqi Stadium at Sari for the match between Pirouzi and Shemshak Noshahr.

On May 9, 2001, in Africa's worst football disaster, 123 died and 93 were injured in a stampede at the national stadium in **Accra, Ghana**. Home team Hearts of Oak were leading 2-1 against Asante Kotoko five minutes from time, when Asanti fans started hurling bottles on to the pitch. Police fired tear gas into the stands, and the crowd panicked in a rush for the exits, which were locked. It took the death toll at three big matches in Africa in Apr/May to 173.

On Aug 12, 2001, two players were killed by lightning and ten severely burned at a **Guatemala** Third Division match between Deportivo Culquimulilla and Pueblo Nuevo Vinas.

On Nov 1, 2002, two players died from injuries after lightning struck Deportivo Cali's training ground in **Colombia**.

On Mar 12 2004, five people were killed and more than 100 injured when spectators stampeded shortly before the Syrian Championship fixture between Al-Jihad and Al-Fatwa in **Qameshli**, Northern Syria. The match was cancelled.

On Oct 10, 2004, three spectators died in a crush at the African Zone World Cup qualifier between **Guinea** and **Morocco** (1-1) at Conakry, Guinea.

On Mar 25, 2005, five were killed as 100,000 left the Azadi Stadium, **Tehran**, after Iran's World Cup qualifying win (2-1) against Japan.

On Jun 2, 2007, 12 spectators were killed and 46 injured in a crush at the Chillabombwe Stadium, **Zambia**, after an African Nations Cup qualifier against Congo.

On Mar 29, 2009, 19 people died and 139 were injured after a wall collapsed at the Ivory Coast stadium in **Abidjan** before a World Cup qualifier against Malawi. The match went ahead, Ivory Coast winning 5-0 with two goals from Chelsea's Didier Drogba. The tragedy meant that, in 13 years, crowd disasters at club and internationals at ten different grounds across Africa had claimed the lives of 283 people.

On Jan 8, 2010, terrorists at **Cabinda**, Angola machine-gunned the Togo team buses travelling to the Africa Cup of Nations. They killed a driver, an assistant coach and a media officer and injured several players. The team were ordered by their Government to withdraw from the tournament.

On Oct 23, 2010, seven fans were trampled to death when thousands tried to force their way into the Nyayo National Stadium in Nairobi at a Kenya Premier League match between the Gor Mahia and AFC Leopards clubs.

DAYS OF TRAGEDY – PERSONAL

Sam Wynne, Bury right-back, collapsed five minutes before half-time in the First Division match away to Sheffield Utd on Apr 30, 1927, and died in the dressing-room.

John Thomson, Celtic and Scotland goalkeeper, sustained a fractured skull when diving at an opponent's feet in the Rangers v Celtic League match on Sep 5, 1931, and died the same evening.

Sim Raleigh (Gillingham), injured in a clash of heads at home to Brighton (Div 3 South) on Dec 1, 1934, continued to play but collapsed in second half and died in hospital the same night.

James Thorpe, Sunderland goalkeeper, was injured during the First Division match at home to Chelsea on Feb 1, 1936 and died in a diabetic coma three days later.

Derek Dooley, Sheffield Wed centre-forward and top scorer in 1951–52 in the Football League with 46 goals in 30 matches, broke a leg in the League match at Preston on Feb 14, 1953, and, after complications set in, had to lose the limb by amputation.

John White, Tottenham's Scottish international forward, was killed by lightning on a golf course at Enfield, North London in Jul, 1964.

Tony Allden, Highgate centre-half, was struck by lightning during an Amateur Cup quarter-final with Enfield on Feb 25, 1967. He died the following day. Four other players were also struck but recovered.

Roy Harper died while refereeing the York–Halifax (Div 4) match on May 5, 1969.

Jim Finn collapsed and died from a heart attack while refereeing Exeter v Stockport (Div 4) on Sep 16, 1972.

Scotland manager **Jock Stein**, 62, collapsed and died at the end of the Wales-Scotland World Cup qualifying match (1-1) at Ninian Park, Cardiff on Sep 10, 1985.

David Longhurst, York forward, died after being carried off two minutes before half-time in the Fourth Division fixture at home to Lincoln on Sep 8, 1990. The match was abandoned (0-0). The inquest revealed that Longhurst suffered from a rare heart condition.

Mike North collapsed while refereeing Southend v Mansfield (Div 3) on Apr 16, 2001 and died shortly afterwards. The match was abandoned and re-staged on May 8, with the receipts donated to his family.

Marc-Vivien Foe, on his 63rd appearance in Cameroon's midfield, collapsed unchallenged in the centre circle after 72 minutes of the FIFA Confederations Cup semi-final against Colombia in Lyon, France, on Jun 26, 2003, and despite the efforts of the stadium medical staff he could not be revived. He had been on loan to Manchester City from Olympique Lyonnais in season 2002–03, and poignantly scored the club's last goal at Maine Road.

Paul Sykes, Folkestone Invicta (Ryman League) striker, died on the pitch during the Kent Senior Cup semi-final against Margate on Apr 12, 2005. He collapsed after an innocuous off-the-ball incident.

Craig Gowans, Falkirk apprentice, was killed at the club's training ground on Jul 8, 2005 when he came into contact with power lines.

Peter Wilson, Mansfield goalkeeping coach, died of a heart attack after collapsing during the warm-up of the League Two game away to Shrewsbury on Nov 19, 2005.

Matt Gadsby, Hinckley defender, collapsed and died while playing in a Conference North match at Harrogate on Sep 9, 2006.

Phil O'Donnell, 35-year-old Motherwell captain and Scotland midfield player, collapsed when about to be substituted near the end of the SPL home game against Dundee Utd on Dec 29, 2007 and died shortly afterwards in hospital.

GREAT SERVICE

'For services to Association Football', **Stanley Matthews** (Stoke, Blackpool and England), already a CBE, became the first professional footballer to receive a knighthood. This was bestowed in 1965, his last season. Before he retired and five days after his 50th birthday, he played for Stoke to set a record as the oldest First Division footballer (v Fulham, Feb 6, 1965).

Over a brilliant span of 33 years, he played in 886 first-class matches, including 54 full Internationals (plus 31 in war time), 701 League games (including 3 at start of season 1939–40, which was abandoned on the outbreak of war) and 86 FA Cup-ties, and scored 95 goals. He was never booked in his career.

Sir Stanley died on Feb 23, 2000, three weeks after his 85th birthday. His ashes were buried under the centre circle of Stoke's Britannia Stadium. After spending a number of years in Toronto, he made his home back in the Potteries in 1989, having previously returned to his home town, Hanley in Oct, 1987 to unveil a life-size bronze statue of himself. The inscription reads: 'Sir Stanley Matthews, CBE. Born Hanley, 1 Feb 1915.

His name is symbolic of the beauty of the game, his fame timeless and international, his sportsmanship and modesty universally acclaimed. A magical player, of the people, for the people.' On his home-coming in 1989, Sir Stanley was made President of Stoke, the club he joined as a boy of 15 and served as a player for 20 years between 1931 and 1965, on either side of his spell with Blackpool.

In Jul 1992 FIFA honoured him with their 'Gold merit award' for outstanding services to the game.

Former England goalkeeper **Peter Shilton** has made more first-class appearances (1,387) than any other footballer in British history. He played his 1,000th. League game in Leyton Orient's 2-0 home win against Brighton on Dec 22, 1996 and made 9 appearances for Orient in his final season. He retired from international football after the 1990 World Cup in Italy with 125 caps, then a world record. Shilton kept a record 60 clean sheets for England.

Shilton's career spanned 32 seasons, 20 of them on the international stage. He made his League debut for Leicester in May 1966, two months before England won the World Cup.

His 1,387 first-class appearances comprise a record 1,005 in the Football League, 125 Internationals, 102 League Cup, 86 FA Cup, 13 for England U-23s, 4 for the Football League and 52 other matches (European Cup, UEFA Cup, World Club Championship, Charity Shield,

European Super Cup, Full Members' Cup, Play-offs, Screen Sports Super Cup, Anglo-Italian Cup, Texaco Cup, Simod Cup, Zenith Data Systems Cup and Autoglass Trophy).

Shilton appeared more times at Wembley (57) than any other player: 52 for England, 2 League Cup Finals, 1 FA Cup Final, 1 Charity Shield match, and 1 for the Football League. He passed a century of League appearances with each of his first five clubs: Leicester (286), Stoke (110), Nottm Forest (202), Southampton (188) and Derby (175) and subsequently played for Plymouth, Bolton and Leyton Orient.

His club honours, all gained with Nottm Forest: League Championship 1978, League Cup 1979, European Cup 1979 and 1980, PFA Player of Year 1978.

Six other British footballers have made more than 1,000 first-class appearances:

Ray Clemence , formerly with Tottenham, Liverpool and England, retired through injury in season 1987–88 after a goalkeeping career of 1,119 matches starting in 1965–66.

Clemence played 50 times for his first club, Scunthorpe; 665 for Liverpool; 337 for Tottenham; his 67 representative games included 61 England caps.

A third great British goalkeeper, **Pat Jennings**, ended his career (1963–86) with a total of 1,098 first-class matches for Watford, Tottenham, Arsenal and N Ireland. They were made up of 757 in the Football League, 119 full Internationals, 84 FA Cup appearances, 72 League/Milk Cup, 55 European Cup matches, 2 Charity Shield, 3 Other Internationals, 1 Under-23 cap, 2 Texaco Cup, 2 Anglo-Italian Cup and 1 Super Cup. Jennings played his 119th and final international on his 41st birthday, Jun 12, 1986, against Brazil in Guadalajara in the Mexico World Cup.

Yet another outstanding 'keeper, **David Seaman**, passed the 1,000 appearances milestone for clubs and country in season 2002–03, reaching 1,004 when aged 39, he captained Arsenal to FA Cup triumph against Southampton.

With Arsenal, Seaman won 3 Championship medals, the FA Cup 4 times, the Double twice, the League Cup and Cup-Winners' Cup once each. After 13 seasons at Highbury, he joined Manchester City (Jun 2003) on a free transfer. He played 26 matches for City before a shoulder injury forced his retirement in Jan 2004, aged 40.

Seaman's 22-season career composed 1,046 first-class matches: 955 club apps (Peterborough 106, Birmingham 84, QPR 175, Arsenal 564, Manchester City 26); 75 senior caps for England, 6 'B' caps and 10 at U-21 level.

Defender **Graeme Armstrong**, 42-year-old commercial manager for an Edinburgh whisky company and part-time assistant-manager and captain of Scottish Third Division club Stenhousemuir, made the 1000th first team appearance of his career in the Scottish Cup 3rd Round against Rangers at Ibrox on Jan 23, 1999. He was presented with the Man of the Match award before kick-off.

Against East Stirling on Boxing Day, he had played his 864th League game, breaking the British record for an outfield player set by another Scot, Tommy Hutchison, with Alloa, Blackpool, Coventry, Manchester City, Burnley and Swansea City.

Armstrong's 24-year career, spent in the lower divisions of the Scottish League, began as a 1-match trialist with Meadowbank Thistle in 1975 and continued via Stirling Albion, Berwick Rangers, Meadowbank and, from 1992, Stenhousemuir.

Tony Ford became the first English outfield player to reach 1000 senior appearances in Rochdale's 1-0 win at Carlisle (Auto Windscreens Shield) on Mar 7, 2000. Grimsby-born, he began his 26-season midfield career with Grimsby and played for 7 other League clubs: Sunderland (loan), Stoke, WBA, Bradford City (loan), Scunthorpe, Mansfield and Rochdale. He retired, aged 42, in 2001 with a career record of 1072 appearances (121 goals) and his total of 931 League games is exceeded only by Peter Shilton's 1005.

On Apr 16, 2011, **Graham Alexander** (39) reached 1,000 appearances when he came on as a sub for Burnley at home to Swansea. By the end of that season, his total had reached 1,003. He was previously with Preston, Luton and Scunthorpe.

KNIGHTS OF SOCCER

Players, managers and administrators who have been honoured for their services to football: **Charles Clegg** (1927), **Stanley Rous** (1949), **Stanley Matthews** (1965), **Alf Ramsey** (1967),

Matt Busby (1968), Walter Winterbottom (1978) Bert Millichip (1991), Bobby Charlton (1994), Tom Finney (1998), Geoff Hurst (1998), Alex Ferguson (1999), Bobby Robson (2002), Trevor Brooking (2004), Dave Richards (2006).

FOOTBALL IN STATUE

In recognition of **Brian Clough's** outstanding achievements as manager, a 9ft bronze statue was unveiled by his widow Barbara in Market Square, Nottingham on Nov 6, 2008. The bulk of the £60,000 cost was met by supporters of Forest, the club he led to back-to-back European Cup triumphs. There is also a statue of Clough in his home town, Middlesbrough, and at Derby's Pride Park stands a combined statue of the famous management team of Clough and **Peter Taylor**. Other leading managers and players have been honoured over the years. They include **Sir Matt Busby** (Manchester Utd), **Bill Shankly** (Liverpool), **Sir Alf Ramsey** and **Sir Bobby Robson** (Ipswich), **Stan Cullis** (Wolves), **Jackie Milburn** (Newcastle), **Bob Stokoe** (Sunderland) and **Ted Bates** (Southampton).

Bobby Moore, England's World Cup-winning captain, is immortalised by a statue at the new Wembley, where there is a bust of Sir Alf in the tunnel corridor. There are statues of **Sir Stanley Matthews** and **Sir Tom Finney** recognising their playing achievements with Stoke and Preston, and one honouring Manchester Utd's **Sir Bobby Charlton**, **George Best** and **Denis Law** outside Old Trafford. At Upton Park, there is a combined statue of West Ham's World Cup-winning trio, **Bobby Moore**, **Sir Geoff Hurst** and **Martin Peters**. Similarly, Fulham legend **Johnny Haynes** and Charlton's greatest goalkeeper **Sam Bartram** are honoured. The original bust of **Herbert Chapman** remains on its plinth at Arsenal's former home at Highbury (now converted into apartments). A replica is in place at the Emirates Stadium, which also has a bust of the club's most successful manager, **Arsene Wenger**. A bust of **Derby's** record scorer, **Steve Bloomer**, is at Pride Park and there is one of Blackburn's former owner, **Jack Walker**, at Ewood Park. Chelsea honouerd **Peter Osgood** in 2010 and Blackpool did the same for **Jimmy Armfield** the following year.

PENALTIES

The **penalty-kick** was introduced to the game, following a proposal to the Irish FA in 1890 by William McCrum, son of the High Sheriff for Co Omagh, and approved by the International Football Board on Jun 2, 1891.

First penalty scored in a first-class match in England was by John Heath, for Wolves v Accrington Stanley (5-0 in Div 1, Sep 14, 1891).

The greatest influence of the penalty has come since the 1970s, with the introduction of the shoot-out to settle deadlocked ties in various competitions.

Manchester Utd were the first club to win a competitive match in British football via a shoot-out (4-3 away to Hull, Watney Cup semi-final, Aug 5, 1970); in that penalty contest, George Best was the first player to score, Denis Law the first to miss.

The shoot-out was adopted by FIFA and UEFA the same year (1970).

In season 1991–92, penalty shoot-outs were introduced to decide FA Cup ties still level after one replay and extra time.

Wembley saw its first penalty contest in the 1974 Charity Shield. Since then many major matches across the world have been settled in this way, including:

1974	**FA Charity Shield (Wembley):**	Liverpool beat Leeds 6-5 (after 1-1).
1976	**Eur Champ Final (Belgrade):**	Czech beat West Germany 5-3 (after 2-2).
1980	**Cup-Winners' Cup Final (Brussels):**	Valencia beat Arsenal 5-4 (after 0-0).
1980	**Eur Champ 3rd/4th place play-off (Naples):**	Czech beat Italy 9-8 (after 1-1).
1982	**World Cup semi-final (Seville):**	West Germany beat France 5-4 (after 3-3).
1984	**European Cup Final (Rome):**	Liverpool beat Roma 4-2 (after 1-1).
1984	**UEFA Cup Final:**	Tottenham (home) beat Anderlecht 4-3 (2-2 agg).
1984	**Eur Champ semi-final (Lyon):**	Spain beat Denmark 5-4 (after 1-1).
1986	**European Cup Final (Seville):**	Steaua Bucharest beat Barcelona 2-0 (after 0-0). Barcelona's four penalties were all saved.

1987	**Freight Rover Trophy Final (Wembley):** Mansfield beat Bristol City 5-4 (after 1-1).
1987	**Scottish League (Skol) Cup Final (Hampden Park):** Rangers beat Aberdeen 5-3 (after 3-3).
1988	**European Cup Final (Stuttgart):** PSV Eindhoven beat Benfica 6-5 (after 0-0).
1988	**UEFA Cup Final:** Bayer Leverkusen (home) beat Espanyol 3-2 after 3-3 (0-3a, 3-0h).
1990	**Scottish FA Cup Final (Hampden Park):** Aberdeen beat Celtic 9-8 (after 0-0).
1990	**World Cup 2nd Round (Genoa):** Rep of Ireland beat Romania 5-4 (after 0-0); **quarter-final (Florence):** Argentina beat Yugoslavia 3-2 (after 0-0); **semi-final (Naples):** Argentina beat Italy 4-3 (after 1-1); **semi-final (Turin):** West Germany beat England 4-3 (1-1).
1991	**European Cup Final (Bari):** Red Star Belgrade beat Marseille 5-3 (after 0-0).
1991	**Barclays League Div 4 Play-off Final (Wembley):** Torquay beat Blackpool 5-4 (after 2-2).
1992	**FA Cup semi-final replay (Villa Park):** Liverpool beat Portsmouth 3-1 (after 0-0).
1992	**Barclays League Div 4 Play-off Final (Wembley):** Blackpool beat Scunthorpe 4-3 (after 1-1).
1992	**Euro Champ semi-final (Gothenburg):** Denmark beat Holland 5-4 (after 2-2).
1993	**Barclays League Div 3 Play-off Final(Wembley):** York beat Crewe 5-3 (after 1-1).
1993	**FA Charity Shield (Wembley):** Manchester Utd beat Arsenal 5-4 (after 1-1).
1994	**Autoglass Trophy Final (Wembley):** Swansea City beat Huddersfield 3-1 (after 1-1).
1994	**World Cup Final (Los Angeles):** Brazil beat Italy 3-2 (after 0-0).
1994	**Scottish League (Coca-Cola) Cup Final (Ibrox Park):** Raith beat Celtic 6-5 (after 2-2).
1995	**Cup-Winners' Cup semi-final:** Arsenal beat Sampdoria away 3-2 (5-5 agg)
1995	**Copa America Final (Montevideo):** Uruguay beat Brazil 5-3 (after 1-1).
1996	**European Cup Final (Rome):** Juventus beat Ajax 4-2 (after 1-1).
1996	**European U-21 Champ Final (Barcelona):** Italy beat Spain 4-2 (after 0-0).
1996	**Euro Champ quarter-final (Wembley):** England beat Spain 4-2 after 0-0; **semi-final (Wembley):** Germany beat England 6-5 (after 1-1); **semi-final (Old Trafford):** Czech Republic beat France 6-5 (after 0-0).
1997	**Auto Windscreens Shield Final (Wembley):** Carlisle beat Colchester 4-3 (after 0-0)
1997	**UEFA Cup Final:** FC Schalke beat Inter Milan 4-1 (after 1-1 agg).
1998	**Nationwide League Div 1 Play-off Final (Wembley):** Charlton beat Sunderland 7-6 (after 4-4).
1998	**World Cup 2nd round (St Etienne):** Argentina beat England 4-3 (after 2-2).
1999	**Nationwide League Div 2 Play-off Final (Wembley):** Manchester City beat Gillingham 3-1 (after 2-2).
1999	**Women's World Cup Final (Pasedena):** USA beat China 5-4 (after 0-0).
2000	**African Nations Cup Final (Lagos):** Cameroon beat Nigeria 4-3 (after 0-0).
2000	**FA Cup semi-final (Wembley):** Aston Villa beat Bolton 4-1 (after 0-0).
2000	**UEFA Cup Final (Copenhagen):** Galatasaray beat Arsenal 4-1 (after 0-0).
2000	**Euro Champ semi-final (Amsterdam):** Italy beat Holland 3-1 (after 0-0). Holland missed 5 penalties in match – 2 in normal play, 3 in shoot-out.
2000	**Olympic Final (Sydney):** Cameroon beat Spain 5-3 (after 2-2).
2001	**League (Worthington) Cup Final (Millennium Stadium):** Liverpool beat Birmingham 5-4 (after 1-1).
2001	**Champions League Final (Milan):** Bayern Munich beat Valencia 5-4 (after 1-1).
2002	**Euro U-21 Champ Final (Basle):** Czech Republic beat France 3-1 (after 0-0).
2002	**Nationwide League Div 1 Play-off Millennium Stadium):** Birmingham beat Norwich 4-2 (after 1-1).
2002	**World Cup 2nd round: (Suwon):** Spain beat Rep of Ireland 3-2 (after 1-1).
2003	**Champions League Final (Old Trafford):** AC Milan beat Juventus 3–2 (after 0–0).
2003	**FA Community Shield (Millennium Stadium):** Manchester Utd beat Arsenal 4-3 (after 1-1).

2004	**Nationwide League Div 3 Play-off Final (Millennium Stadium):** Huddersfield beat Mansfield 4-1 (after 0-0).
2004	**Euro Champ quarter-final (Lisbon):** Portugal beat England 6-5 (after 2-2).
2004	**Copa America Final (Lima):** Brazil beat Argentina 4-2 (after 2-2).
2005	**FA Cup Final (Millennium Stadium):** Arsenal beat Manchester Utd 5-4 (after 0-0).
2005	**Champions League Final (Istanbul):** Liverpool beat AC Milan 3-2 (after 3-3).
2006	**African Cup of Nations Final (Cairo):** Egypt beat Ivory Coast 4-2 (after 0-0).
2006	**FA Cup Final (Millennium Stadium):** Liverpool beat West Ham 3-1 (after 3-3).
2006	**Scottish Cup Final (Hampden Park):** Hearts beat Gretna 4-2 (after 1-1).
2006	**Coca-Cola League Lge 1 Play-off Final (Millennium Stadium):** Barnsley beat Swansea City 4-3 (after 2-2).
2006	**World Cup 2nd round (Cologne):** Ukraine beat Switzerland 3-0 (after 0-0); **quarter-final (Berlin):** Germany beat Argentina 4-2 (after 1-1); **quarter-final (Gelsenkirchen):** Portugal beat England 3-1 (after 0-0); **Final (Berlin):** Italy beat France 5-3 (after 1-1).
2007	**UEFA Cup Final (Hampden Park):** Sevilla beat Espanyol 3-1 (after 2-2).
2007	**Euro Under-21 Champ semi-final (Heerenveen):** Holland beat England 13-12. (after 1-1).
2007	**FA Community Shield (Wembley):** Manchester Utd beat Chelsea 3-0 (after 1-1).
2008	**Champions League Final (Moscow):** Manchester Utd beat Chelsea 6-5 (after 1-1).
2008	**Euro Champ quarter-final (Vienna):** Turkey beat Croatia 3-1 (after 1-1).
	Euro Champ quarter-final (Vienna): Spain beat Italy 4-2 (after 0-0).
2008	**Scottish League Cup Final (Hampden Park):** Rangers beat Dundee Utd 3-2 (after 2-2).
2008	**FA Community Shield (Wembley):** Manchester Utd beat Portsmouth 3-1 (after 0-0).
2009	**League Cup Final (Wembley):** Manchester Utd beat Tottenham 4-1 (after 0-0).
2009	**Community Shield (Wembley):** Chelsea beat Manchester Utd 4-1 (after 2-2).
2010	**World Cup round of 16 (Pretoria):** Paraguay beat Japan 5-3 (after 0-0); quarter-finals (Johannesburg, Soccer City): Uruguay beat Ghana 4-2 (after 1-1)

In South America in 1992, in a 26-shot competition, **Newell's Old Boys** beat America 11-10 in the Copa Libertadores.

Longest-recorded penalty contest in first-class matches was in Argentina in 1988 – from 44 shots, **Argentinos Juniors** beat Racing Club 20-19. Genclerbirligi beat Galatasaray 17-16 in a Turkish Cup-tie in 1996. Only one penalty was missed.

Highest-scoring shoot-outs in international football: **North Korea** beat Hong Kong 11-10 (after 3-3 draw) in an Asian Cup match in 1975; and **Ivory Coast** beat Ghana 11-10 (after 0-0 draw) in African Nations Cup Final, 1992.

Most penalties needed to settle an adult game in Britain: **44** in Norfolk Primary Cup 4th round replay, Dec 2000. Aston Village side **Freethorpe** beat Foulsham 20-19 (5 kicks missed). All 22 players took 2 penalties each, watched by a crowd of 20. The sides had drawn 2-2, 4-4 in a tie of 51 goals.

Penalty that took 24 days: That was how long elapsed between the award and the taking of a penalty in an Argentine Second Division match between **Atalanta** and Defensores in 2003. A riot ended the original match with 5 minutes left. The game resumed behind closed doors with the penalty that caused the abandonment. Lucas Ferreiro scored it to give Atalanta a 1–0 win.

INTERNATIONAL PENALTIES, MISSED

Four penalties out of five were missed when **Colombia** beat Argentina 3-0 in a Copa America group tie in Paraguay in Jul, 1999. Martin Palmeiro missed three for Argentina and Colombia's Hamilton Ricard had one spot-kick saved.

In the European Championship semi-final against Italy in Amsterdam on Jun 29, 2000, **Holland** missed five penalties – two in normal time, three in the penalty contest which Italy won 3-1 (after 0-0). Dutch captain Frank de Boer missed twice from the spot.

ENGLAND'S SHOOT-OUT RECORD

England have been beaten in six out of eight penalty shoot-outs in major tournaments:
1990 (World Cup semi-final, Turin) 3-4 v West Germany after 1-1.
1996 (Euro Champ quarter-final, Wembley) 4-2 v Spain after 0-0.
1996 (Euro Champ semi-final, Wembley) 5-6 v Germany after 1-1.
1998 (World Cup 2nd round., St Etienne) 3-4 v Argentina after 2-2.
2004 (Euro Champ quarter-final, Lisbon) 5-6 v Portugal after 2-2.
2006 (World Cup quarter-final, Gelsenkirchen) 1-3 v Portugal after 0-0.
2007 (Euro U-21 Champ semi-final, Heerenveen) 12-13 v Holland after 1-1.
2009 (Euro U-21 Champ semi-final, Gothenburg) 5-4 v Sweden after 3-3.

FA CUP SHOOT-OUTS

First penalty contest in the FA Cup took place in 1972. In the days of the play-off for third place, the match was delayed until the eve of the following season when losing semi-finalists Birmingham and Stoke met at St Andrew's on Aug 5. The score was 0-0 and Birmingham won 4-3 on penalties.
Highest-scoring: Preliminary round replay (Aug 30, 2005): Tunbridge Wells beat Littlehampton 16-15 after 40 spot-kicks (9 missed).
Competition proper: Macclesfield beat Forest Green 11-10 in 1st round replay (Nov 28, 2001) – 24 kicks.
Highest-recorded score in shoot-out between Football League clubs: **Aldershot's** 11-10 victory at home to Fulham in Freight Rover Trophy Southern quarter-final (Feb 10, 1987) – 9 missed.
Shoot-out abandoned: The FA Cup 1st round replay between Oxford City and Wycombe at Wycombe on Nov 9, 1999 was abandoned (1-1) after extra-time. As the penalty shoot-out was about to begin, a fire broke out under a stand. Wycombe won the second replay 1-0 at Oxford Utd's ground.
First FA Cup Final to be decided by shoot-out was in 2005 (May 21), when Arsenal beat Manchester Utd 5-4 on penalties at Cardiff's Millennium Stadium (0-0 after extra time). A year later (May 13) Liverpool beat West Ham 3-1 (3-3 after extra-time).

MISSED CUP FINAL PENALTIES

John Aldridge (Liverpool) became the first player to miss a penalty in an FA Cup Final at Wembley when Dave Beasant saved his shot in 1988 to help Wimbledon to a shock 1-0 win. Seven penalties before had been scored in the Final at Wembley.
Previously, **Charlie Wallace**, of Aston Villa, had failed from the spot in the 1913 Final against Sunderland at Crystal Palace, which his team won 1-0
Gary Lineker (Tottenham) had his penalty saved by Nottm Forest's Mark Crossley in the 1991 FA Cup Final.
For the first time, two spot-kicks were missed in an FA Cup Final. In 2010, Petr Cech saved from Portsmouth's **Kevin-Prince Boateng** while Chelsea's **Frank Lampard** put his kick wide.
Another miss at Wembley was by Arsenal's **Nigel Winterburn**, Luton's Andy Dibble saving his spot-kick in the 1988 Littlewoods Cup Final, when a goal would have put Arsenal 3-1 ahead. Instead, they lost 3-2.
Winterburn was the third player to fail with a League Cup Final penalty at Wembley, following **Ray Graydon** (Aston Villa) against Norwich in 1975 and **Clive Walker** (Sunderland), who shot wide in the 1985 Milk Cup Final, also against Norwich who won 1-0. Graydon had his penalty saved by Kevin Keelan, but scored from the rebound and won the cup for Aston Villa (1-0).
Derby's Martin Taylor saved a penalty from **Eligio Nicolini** in the Anglo-Italian Cup Final at Wembley on Mar 27, 1993, but Cremonese won 3-1.

LEAGUE PENALTIES RECORD

Most penalties in Football League match: Five – 4 to Crystal Palace (3 missed), 1 to Brighton (scored) in Div 2 match at Selhurst Park on Mar 27 (Easter Monday), 1989. Crystal Palace won 2-1. Three of the penalties were awarded in a 5-minute spell. The match also produced 5 bookings and a sending-off. Other teams missing 3 penalties in a match: Burnley v Grimsby (Div 2), Feb 13, 1909; Manchester City v Newcastle (Div 1), Jan 17, 1912.

HOTTEST MODERN SPOT-SHOTS

Matthew Le Tissier ended his career in season 2001–02 with the distinction of having netted 48 out of 49 first-team penalties for Southampton. He scored the last 27 after his only miss when Nottm Forest keeper Mark Crossley saved in a Premier League match at The Dell on Mar 24, 1993.

Graham Alexander, at the end of 2010-11, had scored 77 out of 82 penalties in his 23-season career with Scunthorpe, Luton, Preston and Burnley.

SPOT-KICK HAT-TRICKS

Right–back **Joe Willetts** scored three penalties when Hartlepool beat Darlington 6-1 (Div 3N) on Good Friday 1951.

Danish international **Jan Molby**'s only hat-trick in English football, for Liverpool in a 3-1 win at home to Coventry (Littlewoods Cup, 4th round replay, Nov 26, 1986) comprised three goals from the penalty spot.

It was the first such hat-trick in a major match for two years – since **Andy Blair** scored three penalties for Sheffield Wed against Luton (Milk Cup 4th round, Nov 20 1984).

Portsmouth's **Kevin Dillon** scored a penalty hat-trick in the Full Members Cup (2nd round) at home to Millwall (3-2) on Nov 4, 1986.

Alan Slough scored a hat-trick of penalties in an away game, but was on the losing side, when Peterborough were beaten 4-3 at Chester (Div 3, Apr 29, 1978).

Penalty hat-tricks in **international football: Dimitris Saravakos** (in 9 mins) for Greece v Egypt in 1990. He scored 5 goals in match. **Henrik Larsson**, among his 4 goals in Sweden's 6-0 home win v Moldova in World Cup qualifying match, Jun 6, 2001.

MOST PENALTY GOALS (LEAGUE) IN SEASON

13 out of 13 by **Francis Lee** for Manchester City (Div 1) in 1971–72. His goal total for the season was 33. In season 1988–89, **Graham Roberts** scored 12 League penalties for Second Division Champions Chelsea. In season 2004–05, **Andrew Johnson** scored 11 Premiership penalties for Crystal Palace, who were relegated.

PENALTY–SAVE SEQUENCES

Ipswich goalkeeper **Paul Cooper** saved eight of the ten penalties he faced in 1979–80. **Roy Brown** (Notts Co) saved six in a row in season 1972–73.

Andy Lomas, goalkeeper for Chesham (Diadora League) claimed a record eighth **consecutive** penalty saves – three at the end of season 1991–92 and five in 1992–93.

Mark Bosnich (Aston Villa) saved five in two consecutive matches in 1993–94: three in Coca–Cola Cup semi-final penalty shoot–out v Tranmere (Feb 26), then two in Premiership at Tottenham (Mar 2).

MISSED PENALTIES SEQUENCE

Against Wolves in Div 2 on Sep 28, 1991, **Southend** missed their seventh successive penalty (five of them the previous season).

SCOTTISH RECORDS

(See also under 'Goals' & 'Discipline')

RANGERS' MANY RECORDS

Rangers' record-breaking feats include:

League Champions: 54 times (once joint holders) – world record.

Winning every match in Scottish League (18 games, 1898–99 season).

Major hat-tricks: Rangers have completed the domestic treble (League Championship, League Cup and Scottish FA Cup) a record seven times (1948–49, 1963–64, 1975–76, 1977–78, 1992–93, 1998–99, 2002–03).

League & Cup double: 17 times.

Nine successive Championships (1989–97). Four men played in all nine sides: Richard Gough, Ally McCoist, Ian Ferguson and Ian Durrant.

115 major trophies: Championships 54, Scottish Cup 33, League Cup 27, Cup-Winners' Cup 1.

CELTIC'S GRAND SLAM

Celtic's record in 1966–67 was the most successful by a British club in one season. They won the **Scottish League,** the **Scottish Cup,** the **Scottish League Cup** and became the first British club to win the **European Cup.** They also won the **Glasgow Cup.**

Celtic have 3 times achieved the Scottish treble (League Championship, League Cup and FA Cup), in 1966–67, 1968–69 and 2000–01 (in Martin O'Neill's first season as their manager). They became Scottish Champions for 2000–01 with a 1-0 home win against St. Mirren on Apr 7 – the earliest the title had been clinched for 26 years, since Rangers' triumph on Mar 29, 1975. They have won the Scottish Cup 35 times, and have completed the League and Cup double 14 times.

Celtic won nine consecutive Scottish League titles (1966–74) under Jock Stein.

They set a **British record** of 25 consecutive League wins in season 2003–04 (Aug 15 to Mar 14). They were unbeaten for 77 matches (all competitions) at Celtic Park from Aug 22, 2001, to Apr 21, 2004.

UNBEATEN SCOTTISH CHAMPIONS

Celtic and **Rangers** have each won the Scottish Championship with an unbeaten record: Celtic in 1897–98 (P18, W15, D3), Rangers in 1898–99 (P18, W18).

LARSSON SUPREME

After missing most of the previous campaign with a broken leg, Swedish international **Henrik Larsson,** with 53 goals in season 2000–01, set a post-war record for Celtic and equalled the Scottish Premier League record of 35 by Brian McClair (Celtic) in 1986–87. Larsson's 35 earned him Europe's **Golden Shoe** award.

His 7 seasons as a Celtic player ended, when his contract expired in May 2004, with a personal total of 242 goals in 315 apps (third-highest scorer in the club's history). He helped Celtic win 4 League titles, and at 32 he moved to Barcelona (free) on a 2-year contract.

SCOTTISH CUP HAT-TRICKS

Aberdeen's feat of winning the Scottish FA Cup in 1982–3–4 made them only the third club to achieve that particular hat-trick. **Queen's Park** did it twice (1874–5–6 and 1880–1–2), and **Rangers** have won the Scottish Cup three years in succession on three occasions: 1934–5–6, 1948–9–50 and 1962–3–4.

SCOTTISH CUP FINAL DISMISSALS

Four players have been sent off in the Scottish FA Cup Final: **Jock Buchanan** (Rangers v Kilmarnock, 1929), **Roy Aitken** (Celtic v Aberdeen, 1984), **Walter Kidd** (Hearts captain v Aberdeen, 1986), **Paul Hartley** (Hearts v Gretna, 2006).

RECORD SEQUENCES

Celtic hold Britain's League record of 62 matches undefeated, from Nov 13, 1915 to Apr 21, 1917, when Kilmarnock won 2-0 at Parkhead. They won 49, drew 13 (111 points) and scored 126 goals to 26.

Greenock Morton in 1963–64 accumulated 67 points out of 72 and scored 135 goals.

Queen's Park did not have a goal scored against them during the first seven seasons of their existence (1867–74, before the Scottish League was formed).

EARLIEST PROMOTIONS IN SCOTLAND

Dundee promoted from Div 2, Feb 1, 1947; **Greenock Morton** promoted from Div 2, Mar 2, 1964; **Gretna** promoted from Div 3, Mar 5, 2005.

WORST HOME SEQUENCE

After gaining promotion to Div 1 in 1992, **Cowdenbeath** went a record 38 consecutive home League matches without a win. They ended the sequence (drew 8, lost 30) when beating Arbroath 1-0 on Apr 2, 1994, watched by a crowd of 225.

ALLY'S RECORDS

Ally McCoist became the first player to complete 200 goals in the Premier Division when he scored Rangers' winner (2-1) at Falkirk on Dec 12, 1992. His first was against Celtic in Sep 1983, and he reached 100 against Dundee on Boxing Day 1987.

When McCoist scored twice at home to Hibernian (4-3) on Dec 7, 1996, he became Scotland's record post-war League marksman, beating Gordon Wallace's 264.

Originally with St Johnstone (1978–81), he spent two seasons with Sunderland (1981–83), then joined Rangers for £200,000 in Jun 1983.

In 15 seasons at Ibrox, he scored 355 goals for Rangers (250 League), and helped them win 10 Championships (9 in succession), 3 Scottish Cups and earned a record 9 League Cup winner's medals. He won the European Golden Boot in consecutive seasons (1991–92, 1992–93).

His 9 Premier League goals in three seasons for Kilmarnock gave him a career total of 281 Scottish League goals when he retired at the end of 2000–01. McCoist succeeded Walter Smith as manager of Rangers in May 2011.

SMITH'S IBROX HONOURS

Walter Smith, who retired in May, 2011, won a total of 21 trophies in two spells as Rangers manager (10 League titles, 5 Scottish Cups and 6 League Cups).

FIVE IN A MATCH

Paul Sturrock set an individual scoring record for the Scottish Premier Division with 5 goals in Dundee Utd's 7-0 win at home to Morton on Nov 17, 1984. **Marco Negri** equalled the feat with all 5 when Rangers beat Dundee Utd 5-1 at Ibrox (Premier Division) on Aug 23, 1997, and **Kenny Miller** scored 5 in Rangers' 7-1 win at home to St. Mirren on Nov 4, 2000. **Kris Boyd** scored all Kilmarnock's goals in a 5-2 SPL win at home to Dundee Utd on Sep 25, 2004. **Boyd** scored another 5 when Rangers beat Dundee Utd 7-1 on Dec 30, 2009. That took his total of SPL goals to a record 160.

NEGRI'S TEN-TIMER

Marco Negri scored in Rangers' first ten League matches (23 goals) in season 1997–98, a Premier Division record. The previous best sequence was 8 by Ally MacLeod for Hibernian in 1978.

DOUBLE SCOTTISH FINAL

Rangers v Celtic drew **129,643** and **120,073** people to the Scottish Cup Final and replay at Hampden Park, Glasgow, in 1963. Receipts for the two matches totalled £50,500.

MOST SCOTTISH CHAMPIONSHIP MEDALS

13 by Sandy Archibald (Rangers, 1918–34). Post-war record: 10 by **Bobby Lennox** (Celtic, 1966–79).

Alan Morton won **nine** Scottish Championship medals with Rangers in 1921–23–24–25–27–28–29–30–31. **Ally McCoist** played in the Rangers side that won nine successive League titles (1989–97).

Between 1927 and 1939 **Bob McPhail** helped Rangers win nine Championships, finish second twice and third once. He scored 236 League goals but was never top scorer in a single season.

TOP SCOTTISH LEAGUE SCORERS IN SEASON

Raith Rovers (Div 2) 142 goals in 1937–38; **Morton** (Div 2) 135 goals in 1963–64; **Hearts** (Div 1) 132 goals in 1957–58; **Falkirk** (Div 2) 132 goals in 1935–36; **Gretna** (Div 3) 130 goals in 2004–05.

SCOTTISH CUP – NO DECISION

The **Scottish FA** withheld their Cup and medals in 1908–09 after Rangers and Celtic played two drawn games in the Final. Spectators rioted.

FEWEST LEAGUE WINS IN SEASON

Clydebank won only one of 36 matches in Div 1, season 1999–2000. It came on Mar 7 (2-1 at home to Raith).

HAMPDEN'S £63M REDEVELOPMENT

On completion of redevelopment costing £63m **Hampden Park**, home of Scottish football and the oldest first-class stadium in the world, was re-opened full scale for the Rangers-Celtic Cup Final on May 29, 1999.

Work on the 'new Hampden' (capacity 52,000) began in 1992. The North and East stands were restructured (£12m); a new South stand and improved West stand cost £51m. The Millennium Commission contributed £23m and the Lottery Sports Fund provided a grant of £3.75m.

GRETNA'S RISE AND FALL

Gretna, who joined the Scottish League in 2002, won the Bell's Third, Second and First Division titles in successive seasons (2005–6–7). They also become the first team from the third tier to reach the Scottish Cup Final, taking Hearts to penalties (2006). But then it all turned sour. Businessman Brooks Mileson, who had financed their rise to the Premier League, withdrew his backing, causing the club to collapse. They went into administration, finished bottom of the SPL, were demoted to Division Three, then resigned from the League.

DEMISE OF AIRDRIE AND CLYDEBANK

In May 2002, First Division **Airdrieonians**, formed in 1878, went out of business. They had debts of £3m. Their place in the Scottish League was taken by **Gretna**, from the English Unibond League, who were voted into Div 3. Second Division **Clydebank** folded in Jul 2002 and were taken over by the new **Airdrie United** club.

FASTEST GOAL IN SPL

12.4 sec by **Anthony Stokes** for Hibernian in 4-1 home defeat by Rangers, Dec 27, 2009.

YOUNGEST SCORER IN SPL

Fraser Fyvie, aged 16years and 306 days, for Aberdeen v Hearts (3-0) on Jan 27, 2010.

12 GOALS SHARED

There was a record aggregate score for the SPL on May 5, 2010, when **Motherwell** came from 6-2 down to draw 6-6 with **Hibernian**.

25-POINT DEDUCTION

Dundee were deducted 25 points by the Scottish Football League in November 2010 for going into administration for the second time. It left the club on minus 11 points, but they still managed to finish in mid-table in Division One.

GREAT SCOTS

In Feb 1988, the Scottish FA launched a national **Hall of Fame**, initially comprising the first 11 Scots to make 50 international appearances, to be joined by all future players to reach that number of caps. Each member receives a gold medal, invitation for life at all Scotland's home matches, and has his portrait hung at Scottish FA headquarters in Glasgow.

MORE CLUBS IN 2000

The **Scottish Premier League** increased from 10 to 12 clubs in season 2000–01. The **Scottish Football League** admitted two new clubs – Peterhead and Elgin City from the Highland League – to provide three divisions of 10 in 2000–01.

NOTABLE SCOTTISH 'FIRSTS'

I The father of League football was a Scot, **William McGregor**, a draper in Birmingham. The 12–club Football League kicked off in Sep 1888, and McGregor was its first president.

IHibernian were the first British club to play in the European Cup, by invitation. They reached the semi–final when it began in 1955–56.

ICeltic were Britain's first winners of the European Cup, in 1967.

I Scotland's First Division became the **Premier Division** in season 1975–76.

I Football's **first international** was staged at the West of Scotland cricket ground, Partick, on Nov 30, 1872: Scotland 0, England 0.

I Scotland introduced its **League Cup** in 1945–46, the first season after the war. It was another 15 years before the Football League Cup was launched.

I Scotland pioneered the use in British football of **two subs** per team in League and Cup matches.

I The world's **record football score** belongs to Scotland: Arbroath 36, Bon Accord 0 (Scottish Cup 1st rd) on Sep 12, 1885.

I The Scottish FA introduced the penalty **shoot-out** to their Cup Final in 1990.

I On Jan 22, 1994 all six matches in the **Scottish Premier Division** ended as draws.

I Scotland's new Premier League introduced a **3-week shut-down** in Jan 1999 – first instance of British football adopting the winter break system that operates in a number of European countries. The SPL ended its New Year closure after 2003.

IRangers made history at home to St. Johnstone (Premier League, 0-0, Mar 4, 2000) when fielding a team entirely without Scottish players.

John Fleck, aged 16 years, 274 days, became the youngest player in a Scottish FA Cup Final when he came on as a substitute for Rangers in their 3-2 win over Queen of the South at Hampden Park on May 24, 2008

SCOTTISH CUP SHOCK RESULTS

1885–86	(1)	Arbroath 36 Bon Accord 0
1921–22	(F)	Morton 1 Rangers 0
1937–38	(F)	East Fife 4 Kilmarnock 2 (replay, after 1-1)
1960–61	(F)	Dunfermline 2 Celtic 0 (replay, after 0-0)
1966–67	(1)	Berwick 1 Rangers 0
1979–80	(3)	Hamilton 2 Keith 3
1984–85	(1)	Stirling 20 Selkirk 0
1984–85	(3)	Inverness 3 Kilmarnock 0
1986–87	(3)	Rangers 0 Hamilton 1
1994–95	(4)	Stenhousemuir 2 Aberdeen 0
1998–99	(3)	Aberdeen 0 Livingston 1
1999–2000	(3)	Celtic 1 Inverness 3
2003–04	(5)	Inverness 1 Celtic 0
2005–06	(3)	Clyde 2 Celtic 1
2008–09	(6)	St Mirren 1 Celtic 0
2009-10	(SF)	Ross Co 2 Celtic 0

Scottish League (Coca-Cola) Cup Final

1994–95	Raith 2, Celtic 2 (Raith won 6-5 on pens)

MISCELLANEOUS

NATIONAL ASSOCIATIONS FORMED

FA **1863**

FA of Wales	**1876**
Scottish FA	**1873**
Irish FA	**1904**
Federation of International Football Associations (FIFA)	**1904**

NATIONAL & INTERNATIONAL COMPETITIONS LAUNCHED

FA Cup	**1871**
Welsh Cup	**1877**
Scottish Cup	**1873**
Irish Cup	**1880**
Football League	**1888**
Premier League	**1992**
Scottish League	**1890**
Scottish Premier League	**1998**
Scottish League Cup	**1945**
Football League Cup	**1960**
Home International Championship	**1883–4**
World Cup	**1930**
European Championship	**1958**
European Cup	**1955**
Fairs/UEFA Cup	**1955**
Cup-Winners' Cup	**1960**
European Champions League	**1992**
Olympic Games Tournament, at Shepherd's Bush	**1908**

INNOVATIONS

Size of Ball: Fixed in **1872**.

Shinguards: Introduced and registered by Sam Weller Widdowson (Nottm Forest & England) in **1874**.

Referee's whistle: First used on Nottm Forest's ground in **1878**.

Professionalism: Legalised in England in the summer of **1885** as a result of agitation by Lancashire clubs.

Goal-nets: Invented and patented in **1890** by Mr JA Brodie of Liverpool. They were first used in the North v South match in Jan, **1891**.

Referees and linesmen: Replaced umpires and referees in Jan, **1891**.

Penalty-kick: Introduced at Irish FA's request in the season **1891–92**. The penalty law ordering the goalkeeper to remain on the goal-line came into force in Sep, **1905**, and the order to stand on his goal-line until the ball is kicked arrived in **1929–30**.

White ball: First came into official use in **1951**.

Floodlighting: First FA Cup-tie (replay), Kidderminster Harriers v Brierley Hill Alliance, **1955**. First Football League match: Portsmouth v Newcastle (Div 1), **1956**.

Heated pitch to beat frost tried by Everton at Goodison Park in **1958**.

First soccer closed-circuit TV: At Coventry ground in Oct **1965** (10,000 fans saw their team win at Cardiff, 120 miles away).

Substitutes (one per team) were first allowed in Football League matches at the start of season **1965–66**. Three substitutes (one a goalkeeper) allowed, two of which could be used, in Premier League matches, **1992–93**. The Football League introduced three substitutes for **1993–94**.

Three points for a win: Introduced by the Football League in **1981–82**, by FIFA in World Cup games in **1994**, and by the Scottish League in the same year.

Offside law amended, player 'level' no longer offside, and 'professional foul' made sending-off offence, **1990.**
Penalty shoot-outs introduced to decide FA Cup ties level after one replay and extra time, **1991–92.**
New back-pass rule: goalkeeper must not handle ball kicked to him by team-mate, **1992.**
Linesmen became 'referees' assistants', **1998.**
Goalkeepers not to hold ball longer than 6 seconds, **2000.**
Free-kicks advanced by ten yards against opponents failing to retreat, **2000.**

YOUNGEST AND OLDEST

Youngest Caps

	Age
Gareth Bale (Wales v Trinidad & Tobago, May 27, 2006)	**16 years 315 days**
Norman Whiteside (N Ireland v Yugoslavia, Jun 17, 1982)	**17 years 41 days**
Theo Walcott (England v Hungary, May 30, 2006)	**17 years 75 days**
Johnny Lambie (Scotland v Ireland, Mar 20, 1886)	**17 years 92 days**
Jimmy Holmes (Rep of Ireland v Austria, May 30, 1971)	**17 years 200 days**

Youngest England scorer: Wayne Rooney (17 years, 317 days) v Macedonia, Skopje, Sep 6, 2003.
Youngest England hat-trick scorer: Theo Walcott (19 years, 178 days) v Croatia, Zagreb, Sep 10, 2008.
Youngest England captains: Bobby Moore (v Czech., Bratislava, May 29, 1963), 22 years, 47 days; Michael Owen (v Paraguay, Anfield, Apr 17, 2002), 22 years, 117 days.
Youngest England players to reach 50 caps: Michael Owen (23 years, 6 months) v Slovakia at Middlesbrough, Jun 11, 2003; Bobby Moore (25 years, 7 months) v Wales at Wembley, Nov 16, 1966.
Youngest player in World Cup Final: Pele (Brazil) aged 17 years, 237 days v Sweden in Stockholm, Jun 12, 1958.
Youngest player to appear in World Cup Finals: Norman Whiteside (N Ireland v Yugoslavia in Spain – Jun 17, 1982, age 17 years and 42 days.
Youngest First Division player: Derek Forster (Sunderland goalkeeper v Leicester, Aug 22, 1964) aged 15 years, 185 days.
Youngest First Division scorer: At 16 years and 57 days, schoolboy Jason Dozzell (substitute after 30 minutes for Ipswich at home to Coventry on Feb 4, 1984). Ipswich won 3-1 and Dozzell scored their third goal.
Youngest Premier League player: Matthew Briggs (Fulham sub at Middlesbrough, May 13, 2007) aged 16 years and 65 days.
Youngest Premier League scorer: James Vaughan (Everton, home to Crystal Palace, Apr 10, 2005), 16 years, 271 days.
Youngest Premier League captain: Lee Cattermole (Middlesbrough away to Fulham, May 7, 2006) aged 18 years, 47 days.
Youngest player sent off in Premier League: Wayne Rooney (Everton, away to Birmingham, Dec 26, 2002) aged 17 years, 59 days.
Youngest First Division hat-trick scorer: Alan Shearer, aged 17 years, 240 days, in Southampton's 4-2 home win v Arsenal (Apr 9, 1988) on his full debut. Previously, Jimmy Greaves (17 years, 309 days) with 4 goals for Chelsea at home to Portsmouth (7-4), Christmas Day, 1957.
Youngest to complete 100 Football League goals: Jimmy Greaves (20 years, 261 days) when he did so for Chelsea v Manchester City, Nov 19, 1960.
Youngest players in Football League: Reuben Noble-Lazarus (Barnsley 84th minute sub at Ipswich, Sep 30, 2008, Champ) aged 15 years, 45 days; Albert Geldard (Bradford PA v Millwall, Div 2, Sep 16, 1929) aged 15 years, 158 days; Ken Roberts (Wrexham v Bradford Park Avenue, Div 3 North, Sep 1, 1951) also 15 years, 158 days.
Youngest Football League scorer: Ronnie Dix (for Bristol Rov v Norwich, Div 3 South, Mar 3, 1928) aged 15 years, 180 days.
Youngest player in Scottish League: Goalkeeper Ronnie Simpson (Queens Park) aged 15 in 1946.

Youngest player in FA Cup: Andy Awford, Worcester City's England Schoolboy defender, aged 15 years, 88 days when he substituted in second half away to Boreham Wood (3rd qual round) on Oct 10, 1987.

Youngest player in FA Cup proper: Luke Freeman, Gillingham substitute striker (15 years, 233 days) away to Barnet in 1st round, Nov 10, 2007.

Youngest Wembley Cup Final captain: Barry Venison (Sunderland v Norwich, Milk Cup Final, Mar 24, 1985 – replacing suspended captain Shaun Elliott) – aged 20 years, 220 days.

Youngest FA Cup-winning captain: Bobby Moore (West Ham, 1964, v Preston), aged 23 years, 20 days.

Youngest FA Cup Final captain: David Nish aged 21 years and 212 days old when he captained Leicester against Manchester City at Wembley on Apr 26, 1969.

Youngest FA Cup Final player: Curtis Weston (Millwall sub last 3 mins v Manchester Utd, 2004) aged 17 years, 119 days.

Youngest FA Cup Final scorer: Norman Whiteside (Manchester Utd v Brighton in 1983 replay at Wembley), aged 18 years, 19 days.

Youngest FA Cup Final managers: Stan Cullis, Wolves (33) v Leicester, 1949; Steve Coppell, Crystal Palace (34) v Manchester Utd, 1990; Ruud Gullit, Chelsea (34) v Middlesbrough, 1997.

Youngest player in Football League Cup: Chris Coward (Stockport) sub v Sheffield Wed, 2nd Round, Aug 23, 2005, aged 16 years and 31 days.

Youngest Wembley scorer: Norman Whiteside (Manchester Utd v Liverpool, Milk Cup Final, Mar 26, 1983) aged 17 years, 324 days.

Youngest Wembley Cup Final goalkeeper: Chris Woods (18 years, 125 days) for Nottm Forest v Liverpool, League Cup Final on Mar 18, 1978.

Youngest Wembley FA Cup Final goalkeeper: Peter Shilton (19 years, 219 days) for Leicester v Manchester City, Apr 26, 1969.

Youngest senior international at Wembley: Salomon Olembe (sub for Cameroon v England, Nov 15, 1997), aged 16 years, 342 days.

Youngest winning manager at Wembley: Roy McDonough, aged 33 years. 6 months, 24 days as player-manager of Colchester, FA Trophy winners on May 10, 1992.

Youngest scorer in full international: Mohamed Kallon (Sierra Leone v Congo, African Nations Cup, Apr 22, 1995), reported as aged 15 years, 192 days.

Youngest player sent off in World Cup Final series: Rigobert Song (Cameroon v Brazil, in USA, Jun 1994) aged 17 years, 358 days.

Youngest FA Cup Final referee: Kevin Howley, of Middlesbrough, aged 35 when in charge of Wolves v Blackburn, 1960.

Youngest player in England U-23 team: Duncan Edwards (v Italy, Bologna, Jan 20, 1954), aged 17 years, 112 days.

Youngest player in England U-21 team: Theo Walcott (v Moldova, Ipswich, Aug 15, 2006), aged 17 years, 152 days.

Youngest player in Scotland U-21 team: Christian Dailly (v Romania, Hampden Park, Sep 11, 1990), aged 16 years, 330 days.

Youngest player in senior football: Cameron Campbell Buchanan, Scottish-born outside right, aged 14 years, 57 days when he played for Wolves v WBA in War-time League match, Sep 26, 1942.

Youngest player in peace-time senior match: Eamon Collins (Blackpool v Kilmarnock, Anglo-Scottish Cup quarter-final 1st leg, Sep 9, 1980) aged 14 years, 323 days.

World's youngest player in top division match: Centre-forward Fernando Rafael Garcia, aged 13, played for 23 minutes for Peruvian club Juan Aurich in 3-1 win against Estudiantes on May 19, 2001.

Oldest player to appear in Football League: New Brighton manager Neil McBain (51 years, 120 days) as emergency goalkeeper away to Hartlepool (Div 3 North, Mar 15, 1947).

Other oldest post-war League players: Sir Stanley Matthews (Stoke, 1965, 50 years, 5 days); Peter Shilton (Leyton Orient 1997, 47 years, 126 days); Dave Beasant (Brighton 2003, 44 years, 46 days); Alf Wood (Coventry, 1958, 43 years, 199 days); Tommy Hutchison (Swansea

City, 1991, 43 years, 172 days).

Oldest Football League debutant: Andy Cunningham, for Newcastle at Leicester (Div 1) on Feb 2, 1929, aged 38 years, 2 days.

Oldest post-war debut in English League: Defender David Donaldson (35 years, 7 months, 23 days) for Wimbledon on entry to Football League (Div 4) away to Halifax, Aug 20, 1977.

Oldest player to appear in First Division: Sir Stanley Matthews (Stoke v Fulham, Feb 6, 1965), aged 50 years, 5 days – on that his last League appearance, the only 50-year-old ever to play in the top division.

Oldest players in Premier League: Goalkeepers John Burridge (Manchester City v QPR, May 14, 1995), aged 43 years, 5 months, 11 days; Alec Chamberlain (Watford v Newcastle, May 13, 2007) aged 42 years, 11 months, 23 days; Steve Ogrizovic (Coventry v Sheffield Wed, May 6, 2000), aged 42 years, 7 months, 24 days; Neville Southall (Bradford City v Leeds, Mar 12, 2000), aged 41 years, 5 months, 26 days. Outfield: Teddy Sheringham (West Ham v Manchester City, Dec 30, 2006), aged 40 years, 8 months, 28 days. Gordon Strachan (Coventry City v Derby, May 3, 1997), aged 40 years, 2 months, 24 days.

Oldest player for British professional club: John Ryan (owner-chairman of Conference club Doncaster), played as substitute for last minute in 4-2 win at Hereford on Apr 26, 2003), aged 52 years, 11 months, 3 weeks.

Oldest FA Cup Final player: Walter (Billy) Hampson (Newcastle v Aston Villa on Apr 26, 1924), aged 41 years, 257 days.

Oldest captain and goalkeeper in FA Cup Final: David James (Portsmouth v Chelsea, May 15, 2010) aged 39 years, 287 days.

Oldest FA Cup Final scorers: Bert Turner (Charlton v Derby, Apr 27, 1946) aged 36 years, 312 days. Scored for both sides. Teddy Sheringham (West Ham v Liverpool, May 13, 2006) aged 40 years, 41 days. Scored in penalty shoot-out.

Oldest FA Cup-winning team: Arsenal 1950 (average age 31 years, 2 months). Eight of the players were over 30, with the three oldest centre-half Leslie Compton 37, and skipper Joe Mercer and goalkeeper George Swindin, both 35.

Oldest World Cup-winning captain: Dino Zoff, Italy's goalkeeper v W Germany in 1982 Final, aged 40 years, 92 days.

Oldest player capped by England: Stanley Matthews (v Denmark, Copenhagen, May 15, 1957), aged 42 years, 103 days.

Oldest England scorer: Stanley Matthews (v N Ireland, Belfast, Oct 6, 1956), aged 41 years, 248 days.

Oldest British international player: Billy Meredith (Wales v England at Highbury, Mar 15, 1920), aged 45 years, 229 days.

Oldest 'new caps': Goalkeeper Alexander Morten, aged 41 years, 113 days when earning his only England Cap against Scotland on Mar 8, 1873; Arsenal centre-half Leslie Compton, at 38 years, 64 days when he made his England debut in 4-2 win against Wales at Sunderland on Nov 15, 1950. **For Scotland:** Goalkeeper Ronnie Simpson (Celtic) at 36 years, 186 days v England at Wembley, Apr 15, 1967.

Longest Football League career: This spanned 32 years and 10 months, by Stanley Matthews (Stoke, Blackpool, Stoke) from Mar 19, 1932 until Feb 6, 1965.

Shortest FA Cup-winning captain: 5ft 4in – Bobby Kerr (Sunderland v Leeds, 1973).

SHIRT NUMBERING

Numbering players in Football League matches was made compulsory in 1939. Players wore numbered shirts (1-22) in the FA Cup Final as an experiment in 1933 (Everton 1-11 v Manchester City 12-22).

Squad numbers for players were introduced by the Premier League at the start of season 1993–94. They were optional in the Football League until made compulsory in 1999–2000.

Names on shirts: For first time, players wore names as well as numbers on shirts in League Cup and FA Cup Finals, 1993.

SUBSTITUTES

In **1965**, the Football League, by 39 votes to 10, agreed that **one substitute** be allowed for an injured player at any time during a League match. First substitute used in Football League: Keith Peacock (Charlton), away to Bolton in Div 2, Aug 21, 1965.

Two substitutes per team were approved for the League (Littlewoods) Cup and FA Cup in season 1986–87 and two were permitted in the Football League for the first time in 1987–88.

Three substitutes (one a goalkeeper), two of which could be used, introduced by the Premier League for 1992–93. The Football League followed suit for 1993–94.

Three substitutes (one a goalkeeper) were allowed at the World Cup Finals for the first time at US '94.

Three substitutes (any position) introduced by Premier League and Football League in 1995–96.

Seven named substitutes (an increase of two) for Premier League in 2008–09. But still only three to be used.

First substitute to score in FA Cup Final: Eddie Kelly (Arsenal v Liverpool, 1971). The **first recorded use** of a substitute was in 1889 (Wales v Scotland at Wrexham on Apr 15) when Sam Gillam arrived late – although he was a Wrexham player – and Allen Pugh (Rhostellyn) was allowed to keep goal until he turned up. The match ended 0-0.

When **Dickie Roose**, the Welsh goalkeeper, was injured against England at Wrexham, Mar 16, 1908, **Dai Davies** (Bolton) was allowed to take his place as substitute. Thus Wales used 12 players. England won 7-1.

END OF WAGE LIMIT

Freedom from the maximum wage system – in force since the formation of the Football League in 1888 – was secured by the Professional Footballers' Association in 1961. About this time Italian clubs renewed overtures for the transfer of British stars and Fulham's **Johnny Haynes** became the first British player to earn £100 a week.

THE BOSMAN RULING

On Dec 15, 1995 the **European Court of Justice** ruled that clubs had no right to transfer fees for out-of-contract players, and the outcome of the 'Bosman case' irrevocably changed football's player-club relationship. It began in 1990, when the contract of 26-year-old **Jean-Marc Bosman**, a midfield player with FC Liege, Belgium, expired. French club Dunkirk wanted him but were unwilling to pay the £500,000 transfer fee, so Bosman was compelled to remain with Liege. He responded with a lawsuit against his club and UEFA on the grounds of 'restriction of trade', and after five years at various court levels the European Court of Justice ruled not only in favour of Bosman but of all professional footballers.

The end of restrictive labour practices revolutionised the system. It led to a proliferation of transfers, rocketed the salaries of elite players who, backed by an increasing army of agents, found themselves in a vastly improved bargaining position as they moved from team to team, league to league, nation to nation. Removing the limit on the number of foreigners clubs could field brought an increasing ratio of such signings, not least in England and Scotland.

Bosman's one-man stand opened the way for footballers to become millionaires, but ended his own career. All he received for his legal conflict was 16 million Belgian francs (£312,000) in compensation, a testimonial of poor reward and martyrdom as the man who did most to change the face of football.

By 2011, he was living on Belgian state benefits, saying: 'I have made the world of football rich and shifted the power from clubs to players. Now I find myself with nothing.'

INTERNATIONAL SHOCK RESULTS

1950	USA 1 England 0 (World Cup).
1953	England 3 Hungary 6 (friendly).
1954	Hungary 7 England 1 (friendly)
1966	North Korea 1 Italy 0 (World Cup).
1982	Spain 0, Northern Ireland 1; Algeria 2, West Germany 1 (World Cup).

1990	Cameroon 1 Argentina 0; Scotland 0 Costa Rica 1; Sweden 1 Costa Rica 2 (World Cup).
1990	Faroe Islands 1 Austria 0 (European Champ qual).
1992	Denmark 2 Germany 0 (European Champ Final).
1993	USA 2 England 0 (US Cup tournament).
1993	Argentina 0 Colombia 5 (World Cup qual).
1993	France 2 Israel 3 (World Cup qual).
1994	Bulgaria 2 Germany 1 (World Cup).
1994	Moldova 3 Wales 2; Georgia 5 Wales 0 (European Champ qual).
1995	Belarus 1 Holland 0 (European Champ qual).
1996	Nigeria 4 Brazil 3 (Olympics).
1998	USA 1 Brazil 0 (Concacaf Gold Cup).
1998	Croatia 3 Germany 0 (World Cup).
2000	Scotland 0 Australia 2 (friendly).
2001	Australia 1 France 0; Australia 1, Brazil 0 (Confederations Cup).
2001	Honduras 2 Brazil 0 (Copa America).
2001	Germany 1 England 5 (World Cup qual).
2002	France 0 Senegal 1; South Korea 2 Italy 1 (World Cup).
2003:	England 1 Australia 3 (friendly)
2004:	Portugal 0 Greece 1 (European Champ Final).
2005:	Northern Ireland 1 England 0 (World Cup qual).

GREAT RECOVERIES – DOMESTIC FOOTBALL

On Dec 21, 1957, **Charlton** were losing 5-1 against Huddersfield (Div 2) at The Valley with only 28 minutes left, and from the 15th minute, had been reduced to ten men by injury, but they won 7-6, with left-winger Johnny Summers scoring five goals. **Huddersfield** (managed by Bill Shankly) remain the only team to score six times in a League match and lose.

Among other notable comebacks: on Nov 12, 1904 (Div 1), **Sheffield Wed** were losing 0-5 at home to Everton, but drew 5-5. At Anfield on Dec 4, 1909 (Div 1), **Liverpool** trailed 2-5 to Newcastle at half-time, then won 6-5. On Boxing Day, 1927, in Div 3 South, **Northampton** won 6-5 at home to Luton after being 1-5 down at half-time. On Apr 12, 1993 (Div 1) **Swindon** were 1-4 down at Birmingham with 30 minutes left, but won 6-4.

Other turnabouts in Div 1 include: **Grimsby** (3-5 down) won 6-5 at WBA on Apr 30, 1932; and Derby beat Manchester Utd 5-4 (from 1-4) on Sep 5, 1936. With 5 minutes to play, **Ipswich** were losing 3-0 at Barnsley (Div 1, Mar 9, 1996), but drew 3-3. On Sunday, Jan 19, 1997 (Div 1), **QPR** were 0-4 down away to Port Vale at half-time and still trailing 1-4 with 5 minutes left. They drew 4-4. On Nov 19, 2005, **Leeds** retrieved a 3-0 deficit against Southampton in the final 20 minutes to win their **Championship** game 4-3. **Cardiff** were four goals down at the break in their Championship match at Peterborough (Dec 28, 2009) and recovered to gain a point.

Tranmere retrieved a 3-0 half-time deficit to beat Southampton 4-3 in an FA Cup fifth round replay at home on Feb 20, 2001.

Premier League comebacks: Jan 4, 1994 – Liverpool were 3 down after 24 mins at home to Manchester Utd, drew 3-3; Nov 8, 1997 – Derby led 3-0 after 33 mins at Elland Road, but Leeds won 4-3 with last-minute goal; Sep 29, 2001 – Manchester Utd won 5-3 at Tottenham after trailing 3-0 at half-time; Apr 18, 2010 – Wigan beat Arsenal 3-2 after trailing 2-0 with 80 minutes played.

Season 2003–04 produced some astonishing turn-rounds. **Premiership** (Oct 25): In bottom-two clash at Molineux, **Wolves** were 3 down at half-time v Leicester, but won 4-3. Feb 22: **Leicester**, down to 10 men, rallied from 3-1 down at Tottenham to lead 4-3. Result 4-4.

First Division (Nov 8): **West Ham** led 3-0 after 18 mins at home to WBA, but lost 4-3.

FA Cup 4th Round replay (Feb 4): At half-time, Tottenham led 3-0 at home to **Manchester City**, but City, reduced to 10 men, won 4-3.

Season 2010–11 saw a Premier League record on Feb 5 for **Newcastle**, 4-0 down at home to Arsenal but drawing 4-4. Previous instance of a team retrieving that deficit in the top division to draw was on Sep 22 1984 when **Newcastle** trailed at QPR in a game which ended 5-5. **Preston** came back from trailing 4-1 at Leeds to win 6-4 in the Championship on Sep 28 in 2010.

MATCHES OFF

Worst day for postponements: Feb 9, 1963, when 57 League fixtures in England and Scotland were frozen off. Only 7 Football League matches took place, and the entire Scottish programme was wiped out.

Other weather-hit days:

Jan 12, 1963 and Feb 2, 1963 – on both those Saturdays, only 4 out of 44 Football League matches were played.

Jan 1, 1979 – 43 out of 46 Football League fixtures postponed.

Jan 17, 1987 – 37 of 45 scheduled Football League fixtures postponed; only 2 Scottish matches survived.

Feb 8–9, 1991 – only 4 of the week-end's 44 Barclays League matches survived the freeze-up (4 of the postponements were on Friday night). In addition, 11 Scottish League matches were off.

Jan 27, 1996 – 44 Cup and League matches in England and Scotland were frozen off.

On the weekend of Jan 9, 10, 11, 2010, 46 League and Cup matches in England and Scotland were victims of the weather. On the weekend of Dec 18-21, 2010, 49 matches were frozen off in England and Scotland.

Fewest matches left on one day by postponements was during the Second World War – Feb 3, 1940 when, because of snow, ice and fog only one out of 56 regional league fixtures took place. It resulted Plymouth Argyle 10, Bristol City 3.

The Scottish Cup second round tie between Inverness Thistle and Falkirk in season 1978–79 was **postponed 29 times** because of snow and ice. First put off on Jan 6, it was eventually played on Feb 22. Falkirk won 4-0.

Pools Panel's busiest days: Jan 17, 1987 and Feb 9, 1991 – on both dates they gave their verdict on 48 postponed coupon matches.

FEWEST 'GAMES OFF'

Season 1947–48 was the best since the war for English League fixtures being played to schedule. Only six were postponed.

LONGEST SEASON

The latest that League football has been played in a season was **Jun 7, 1947** (six weeks after the FA Cup Final). The season was extended because of mass postponements caused by bad weather in mid-winter.

The latest the FA Cup competition has ever been completed was in season 1981–82, when Tottenham beat QPR 1-0 in a Final replay at Wembley on May 27.

Worst winter hold-up was in season 1962–63. The Big Freeze began on Boxing Day and lasted until Mar, with nearly 500 first-class matches postponed. The FA Cup 3rd round was the longest on record - it began with only three out of 32 ties playable on Jan 5 and ended 66 days and 261 postponements later on Mar 11. The Lincoln–Coventry tie was put off 15 times. The Pools Panel was launched that winter, on Jan 26, 1963.

HOTTEST DAYS

The Nationwide League kicked off season 2003–04 on Aug 9 with pitch temperatures of 102 degrees recorded at Luton v Rushden and Bradford v Norwich. On the following day, there was a pitch temperature of 100 degrees for the Community Shield match between Manchester Utd and Arsenal at Cardiff's Millennium Stadium. Wembley's pitch-side thermometer registered 107 degrees for the 2009 Chelsea–Everton FA Cup Final.

FOOTBALL ASSOCIATION SECRETARIES/CHIEF EXECUTIVES

1863– 66 Ebenezer Morley; 1866– 68 Robert Willis; 1868– 70 RG Graham; 1870– 95 **Charles Alcock** (paid from 1887); 1895–1934 **Sir Frederick Wall**; 1934–62 **Sir Stanley Rous**; 1962–73 Denis Follows; 1973–89 **Ted Croker** (latterly chief executive); 1989–99 **Graham Kelly** (chief executive); 2000–02 **Adam Crozier** (chief executive); 2003–04 **Mark Palios** (chief executive); 2005– 08: **Brian Barwick** (chief executive); 2009-10 **Ian Watmore** (chief executive); 2010 **Alex Horne** (general secretary).

FOOTBALL'S SPONSORS

Football League: Canon 1983–86; Today Newspaper 1986–87; Barclays 1987–93; Endsleigh Insurance 1993–96; Nationwide Building Society 1996–2004; Coca-Cola 2004-10; Npower from 2010.
League Cup: Milk Cup 1982–86; Littlewoods 1987–90; Rumbelows 1991–92; Coca-Cola 1993–98; Worthington 1998–2003; Carling from 2003.
Premier League: Carling 1993–2001; Barclaycard 2001–04; Barclays from 2004.
FA Cup: Littlewoods 1994–98; AXA 1998–2002; E.ON 2006–2011; Budweiser from 2011

SOCCER HEADQUARTERS

Football Association: Wembley Stadium, Wembley, Middx.
Premier League: 30 Gloucester Place, London W1U 8PL.
Football League: Edward VII Quay, Navigation Way, Preston PR2 2YF. London Office: 30 Gloucester Place, London W1U 8FL.
Professional Footballers' Association: 2 Oxford Court, Bishopsgate, Manchester M2 3WQ.
Scottish Football Association: Hampden Park, Glasgow G42 9AY.
Scottish Premier League: Hampden Park, Glasgow G42 9DE.
Scottish Football League: Hampden Park, Glasgow G42 9EB.
Irish Football Association: 20 Windsor Avenue, Belfast BT9 6EG.
Irish Football League: Benmore House, 343-353 Lisburn Road, Belfast BT9 7EN.
League of Ireland: Sports Campus, Abbotstown, Dublin 15.
Football Association of Ireland: Sports Campus, Abbotstown, Dublin 15
Welsh Football Association: 11/12 Neptune Court, Vanguard Way, Cardiff CF24 5PJ.
FIFA: P.O. Box 85, 8030 Zurich, Switzerland.
UEFA: Route de Geneve, CH-1260, Nyon, Geneva, Switzerland.

NEW HOMES OF SOCCER

Newly-constructed League grounds in England since the war: 1946 Hull (Boothferry Park); 1950 Port Vale (Vale Park); 1955 Southend (Roots Hall); 1988 Scunthorpe (Glanford Park); 1990 Walsall (Bescot Stadium); 1990 Wycombe (Adams Park); 1992 Chester (Deva Stadium); 1993 Millwall (New Den); 1994 Huddersfield (Alfred McAlpine Stadium, Kirklees); 1994 Northampton (Sixfields Stadium); 1995 Middlesbrough (Riverside Stadium); 1997 Bolton (Reebok Stadium); 1997 Derby (Pride Park); 1997 Stoke (Britannia Stadium); 1997 Sunderland (Stadium of Light); 1998 Reading (Madejski Stadium); 1999 Wigan (JJB Stadium); 2001 Southampton (St. Mary's Stadium); 2001 Oxford Utd (Kassam Stadium); 2002 Leicester (Walkers Stadium); 2002 Hull (Kingston Communications Stadium); 2003 Manchester City (City of Manchester Stadium); 2003 Darlington (New Stadium); 2005 Coventry (Ricoh Arena); Swansea (Stadium of Swansea, Morfa); 2006 Arsenal (Emirates Stadium); 2007 Milton Keynes Dons (Stadium: MK); Shrewsbury (New Meadow); 2008 Colchester (Community Stadium); Rotherham (Don Valley Stadium, Sheffield); 2009 Cardiff Stadium; 2010 Chesterfield (b2net Stadium), Morecambe (Globe Arena); 2011 Brighton (American Express Stadium).
Huddersfield now Galpharm Stadium; Shrewsbury now Greenhous Meadow Stadium; Swansea now Liberty Stadium; Walsall now Banks's Stadium; Wigan now DW Stadium; Leicester now King Power Stadium

NATIONAL FOOTBALL CENTRE

Ten years after the FA bought the site, building work began in Jan 2011 on the National Football Centre at Burton upon Trent. England's new £105m home, to be known as St George's Park, is scheduled to open in the summer of 2012.

GROUND-SHARING

Crystal Palace and **Charlton** (Selhurst Park, 1985–91; **Bristol Rov** and **Bath City** (Twerton Park, Bath, 1986–96); **Partick Thistle** and **Clyde** (Firhill Park, Glasgow, 1986–91; in seasons 1990–01, 1991–92 **Chester** shared **Macclesfield**'s ground (Moss Rose).
Crystal Palace and **Wimbledon** shared Selhurst Park, from season 1991–92, when **Charlton**

(tenants) moved to rent Upton Park from **West Ham**. **Clyde** moved to Douglas Park, **Hamilton Academical's** home, in 1991–92. **Stirling Albion** shared **Stenhousemuir's** ground, Ochilview Park, in 1992–93. In 1993–94, **Clyde** shared **Partick's** home until moving to Cumbernauld. In 1994–95, **Celtic** shared Hampden Park with **Queen's Park** (while Celtic Park was redeveloped); **Hamilton** shared **Partick's** ground. **Airdrie** shared **Clyde's** Broadwood Stadium. **Bristol Rov** left **Bath City's** ground at the start of season 1996–97, sharing Bristol Rugby Club's Memorial Ground. **Clydebank** shared **Dumbarton's** Boghead Park from 1996–97 until renting **Greenock Morton's** Cappielow Park in season 1999–2000. **Brighton** shared **Gillingham's** ground in seasons 1997–98, 1998–99. **Fulham** shared **QPR's** home at Loftus Road in seasons 2002–03, 2003–04, returning to Craven Cottage in Aug 2004.
Inverness Caledonian Thistle moved to share **Aberdeen's** Pittodrie Stadium in 2004–05 after being promoted to the SPL; **Gretna's** home matches on arrival in the SPL in 2007–08 were held at Motherwell and Livingston.

ARTIFICIAL TURF

QPR were the first British club to install an artificial pitch, in 1981. They were followed by **Luton** in 1985, and **Oldham** and **Preston** in **1986**. QPR reverted to grass in 1988, as did Luton and promoted Oldham in season 1991–92 (when artificial pitches were banned in Div 1). **Preston** were the last Football League club playing 'on plastic' in 1993–94, and their Deepdale ground was restored to grass for the start of 1994–95.
Stirling were the **first Scottish club** to play on plastic, in season 1987–88.

DOUBLE RUNNERS-UP

There have been nine instances of clubs finishing runner-up in **both the League Championship** and **FA Cup** in the same season: 1928 Huddersfield; 1932 Arsenal; 1939 Wolves; 1962 Burnley; 1965 and 1970 Leeds; 1986 Everton; 1995 Manchester Utd; 2001 Arsenal.

CORNER-KICK RECORDS

Not a single corner-kick was recorded when **Newcastle** drew 0-0 at home to **Portsmouth** (Div 1) on Dec 5, 1931. That did not happen again until Chelsea's 6-0 win at Wigan (Prem Lge) on Aug 21, 2010.
The record for **most corners** in a match for one side is believed to be **Sheffield Utd's 28** to West Ham's 1 in Div 2 at Bramall Lane on Oct 14, 1989. For all their pressure, Sheffield Utd lost 2-0.
Nottm Forest led **Southampton** 22-2 on corners (Premier League, Nov 28, 1992) but lost the match 1-2.
Tommy Higginson (Brentford, 1960s) once passed back to his own goalkeeper from a corner kick. When **Wigan** won 4-0 at home to Cardiff (Div 2) on Feb 16, 2002, all four goals were headed in from corners taken by N Ireland international **Peter Kennedy**.
Steve Staunton (Rep of Ireland) is believed to be the only player to score direct from a corner in **two** Internationals.

SACKED AT HALF-TIME

Leyton Orient sacked **Terry Howard** on his 397th appearance for the club – at half-time in a Second Division home defeat against Blackpool (Feb 7, 1995) for 'an unacceptable performance'. He was fined two weeks' wages, given a free transfer and moved to Wycombe.
Bobby Gould resigned as **Peterborough's** head coach at half-time in their 1-0 defeat in the LDV Vans Trophy 1st round at Bristol City on Sep 29, 2004.
Harald Schumacher, former Germany goalkeeper, was sacked as Fortuna Koln coach when they were two down at half-time against Waldhof Mannheim (Dec 15, 1999). They lost 5-1.

MOST GAMES BY 'KEEPER FOR ONE CLUB

Alan Knight made 683 League appearances for Portsmouth, over 23 seasons (1978–2000), a record for a goalkeeper at one club. The previous holder was Peter Bonetti with 600 League games for Chelsea (20 seasons, 1960–79).

PLAYED TWO GAMES ON SAME DAY

Jack Kelsey played full-length matches for both club and country on Wednesday Nov 26, 1958. In the afternoon he kept goal for Wales in a 2-2 draw against England at Villa Park, and he then drove to Highbury to help Arsenal win 3-1 in a prestigious floodlit friendly against Juventus.

On the same day, winger **Danny Clapton** played for England (against Wales and Kelsey) and then in part of Arsenal's match against Juventus.

On Nov 11, 1987, **Mark Hughes** played for Wales against Czechoslovakia (European Championship) in Prague, then flew to Munich and went on as substitute that night in a winning Bayern Munich team, to whom he was on loan from Barcelona.

On Feb 16, 1993 goalkeeper **Scott Howie** played in Scotland's 3-0 U-21 win v Malta at Tannadice Park, Dundee (ko 1.30pm) and the same evening played in Clyde's 2-1 home win v Queen of South (Div 2).

Ryman League **Hornchurch**, faced by end-of-season fixture congestion, played **two matches** on the same night (May 1, 2001). They lost 2-1 at home to Ware and drew 2-2 at Clapton.

CLUB LOSSES

Chelsea made losses of £87.8m in seasons 2003–04 (their first under the ownership of Roman Abramovich) and £140m in 2004–05.

FIRST 'MATCH OF THE DAY'

BBC TV (recorded highlights): Liverpool 3, Arsenal 2 on Aug 22, 1964. **First complete match to be televised:** Arsenal 3, Everton 2 on Aug 29, 1936. **First League match televised in colour:** Liverpool 2, West Ham 0 on Nov 15, 1969.

'MATCH OF THE DAY' – BIGGEST SCORES

Football League: Tottenham 9, Bristol Rov 0 (Div 2, 1977–78). **Premier League:** Nottm Forest 1, Manchester Utd 8 (1998–99); Portsmouth 7 Reading 4 (2007–08).

FIRST COMMENTARY ON RADIO

Arsenal 1 Sheffield Utd 1 (Div 1) broadcast on BBC, Jan 22, 1927.

OLYMPIC SOCCER WINNERS

1908 Great Britain (in London); **1912** Great Britain (Stockholm); **1920** Belgium (Antwerp); **1924** Uruguay (Paris); **1928** Uruguay (Amsterdam); **1932** No soccer in Los Angeles Olympics; **1936** Italy (Berlin); **1948** Sweden (London); **1952** Hungary (Helsinki); **1956** USSR (Melbourne); **1960** Yugoslavia (Rome); **1964** Hungary (Tokyo); **1968** Hungary (Mexico City); **1972** Poland (Munich); **1976** E Germany (Montreal); **1980** Czechoslovakia (Moscow); **1984** France (Los Angeles); **1988** USSR (Seoul); **1992** Spain (Barcelona); **1996** Nigeria (Atlanta); **2000** Cameroon (Sydney); **2004** Argentina (Athens); **2008** Argentina (Beijing).

Highest scorer in Final tournament: Ferenc Bene (Hungary) 12 goals, 1964.
Record crowd for Olympic Soccer Final: 108,800 (France v Brazil, Los Angeles 1984).

MOST AMATEUR CUP WINS

Bishop Auckland set the FA Amateur Cup record with 10 wins, and in 1957 became the only club to carry off the trophy in three successive seasons. The competition was discontinued after the Final on Apr 20, 1974. (Bishop's Stortford 4, Ilford 1, at Wembley).

FOOTBALL FOUNDATION

This was formed (May 2000) to replace the **Football Trust**, which had been in existence since 1975 as an initiative of the Pools companies to provide financial support at all levels, from schools football to safety and ground improvement work throughout the game.

SEVEN-FIGURE TESTIMONIALS

The first was **Sir Alex Ferguson**'s at Old Trafford on Oct 11, 1999, when a full-house of 54,842 saw a Rest of the World team beat Manchester Utd 4-2. United's manager pledged that a large percentage of the estimated £1m receipts would go to charity.

Estimated receipts of £1m and over came from testimonials for **Denis Irwin** (Manchester Utd) against Manchester City at Old Trafford on Aug 16, 2000 (45,158); **Tom Boyd** (Celtic) against Manchester Utd at Celtic Park on May 15, 2001 (57,000) and **Ryan Giggs** (Manchester Utd) against Celtic on Aug 1, 2001 (66,967).

Tony Adams' second testimonial (1-1 v Celtic on May 13, 2002) two nights after Arsenal completed the Double, was watched by 38,021 spectators at Highbury. Of £1m receipts, he donated £500,000 to Sporting Chance, the charity that helps sportsmen/women with drink, drug, gambling problems.

Sunderland and a Republic of Ireland XI drew 0-0 in front of 35,702 at the Stadium of Light on May 14, 2002. The beneficiary, **Niall Quinn**, donated his testimonial proceeds, estimated at £1m, to children's hospitals in Sunderland and Dublin, and to homeless children in Africa and Asia.

A record testimonial crowd of 69,591 for **Roy Keane** at Old Trafford on May 9, 2006 netted more than £2m for charities in Dublin, Cork and Manchester. Manchester Utd beat Celtic 1-0, with Keane playing for both teams.

Alan Shearer's testimonial on May 11, 2006, watched by a crowd of 52,275 at St James' Park, raised more than £1m. The club's record scorer, in his farewell match, came off the bench in stoppage time to score the penalty that gave Newcastle a 3-2 win over Celtic. Total proceeds from his testimonial events, £1.64m, were donated to 14 charities in the north-east.

Ole Gunnar Solskjaer, who retired after 12 years as a Manchester Utd player, had a crowd of 68,868, for his testimonial on Aug 2, 2008 (United 1 Espanyol 0). He donated the estimated receipts of £2m to charity, including the opening of a dozen schools in Africa.

Liverpool's **Jamie Carragher** had his testimonial against Everton (4-1) on Sep 4, 2010. It was watched by a crowd of 35,631 and raised an estimated £1m for his foundation, which supports community projects on Merseyside.

Gary Neville donated receipts of around £1m from his testimonial against Juventus (1-2) in front of 42,000 on May 24, 2011, to charities and building a supporters' centre near Old Trafford.

WHAT IT USED TO COST

Minimum admission to League football was one shilling in 1939 After the war, it was increased to 1s 3d in 1946; 1s 6d in 1951; 1s 9d in 1952; 2s in 1955; 2s 6d.

in 1960; 4s in 1965; 5s in 1968; 6s in 1970; and 8s (40p) in 1972 After that, the fixed minimum charge was dropped.

Wembley's first Cup Final programme in 1923 cost three pence (1½p in today's money). The programme for the 'farewell' FA Cup Final in May, 2000 was priced £10.

FA Cup Final ticket prices in 2011 reached record levels - £115, £85, £65 and £45.

WHAT THEY USED TO EARN

In the 1930s, First Division players were on £8 a week (£6 in close season) plus bonuses of £2 win, £1 draw. The maximum wage went up to £12 when football resumed post-war in 1946 and had reached £20 by the time the limit was abolished in 1961.

EUROPEAN TROPHY WINNERS

European Cup:9 Real Madrid; **7** AC Milan; **5** Liverpool; **4** Ajax, Barcelona, Bayern Munich; **3** Inter Milan, Manchester Utd; **2** Benfica, Juventus, Nottm Forest, Porto; **1** Aston Villa, Borussia Dortmund, Celtic, Feyenoord, Hamburg, Marseille, PSV Eindhoven, Red Star Belgrade, Steaua Bucharest.

Cup-Winners' Cup: 4 Barcelona; **2** Anderlecht, Chelsea, Dynamo Kiev, AC Milan; **1** Aberdeen, Ajax, Arsenal, Atletico Madrid, Bayern Munich, Borussia Dortmund, Dynamo Tbilisi, Everton, Fiorentina, Hamburg, Juventus, Lazio, Magdeburg, Manchester City, Manchester Utd, Mechelen, Paris St. Germain, Parma, Rangers, Real Zaragoza, Sampdoria, Slovan Bratislava, Sporting Lisbon, Tottenham, Valencia, Werder Bremen, West Ham.

UEFA Cup: 3 Barcelona, Inter Milan, Juventus, Liverpool, Valencia; **2** Borussia Moenchengladbach, Feyenoord, Gothenburg, Leeds, Parma, Real Madrid, Sevilla, Tottenham; **1** Anderlecht, Ajax,

Arsenal, Bayer Leverkusen, Bayern Munich, CSKA Moscow, Dynamo Zagreb, Eintracht Frankfurt, Ferencvaros, Galatasaray, Ipswich, Napoli, Newcastle, Porto, PSV Eindhoven, Real Zaragoza, Roma, Schalke, Shakhtar Donetsk, Zenit St Petersburg.

Europa League: 1 Atletico Madrid, Porto

● The Champions League was introduced into the European Cup in 1992–93 to counter the threat of a European Super League. The UEFA Cup became the Europa League, with a new format, in season 2009–10.

BRITAIN'S 32 TROPHIES IN EUROPE

Manchester Utd's success in the 2007–08 Champions League/European Cup took the number of **British** club triumphs in European football to 32:

European Cup (12)	Cup-Winners' Cup (10)	Fairs/UEFA Cup (10)
1967 Celtic	1963 Tottenham	1968 Leeds
1968 Manchester Utd	1965 West Ham	1969 Newcastle
1977 Liverpool	1970 Manchester City	1970 Arsenal
1978 Liverpool	1971 Chelsea	1971 Leeds
1979 Nottm Forest	1972 Rangers	1972 Tottenham
1980 Nottm Forest	1983 Aberdeen	1973 Liverpool
1981 Liverpool	1985 Everton	1976 Liverpool
1982 Aston Villa	1991 Manchester Utd	1981 Ipswich
1984 Liverpool	1994 Arsenal	1984 Tottenham
1999 Manchester Utd	1998 Chelsea	2001 Liverpool
2005 Liverpool		
2008 Manchester Utd		

END OF CUP-WINNERS' CUP

The **European Cup-Winners' Cup**, inaugurated in 1960–61, terminated with the 1999 Final. The competition merged into a revamped **UEFA Cup**.
From its inception in 1955, the **European Cup** comprised only championship-winning clubs until 1998–99, when selected runners-up were introduced. Further expansion came in 1999–2000 with the inclusion of clubs finishing third in certain leagues and fourth in 2002.

EUROPEAN CLUB COMPETITIONS – SCORING RECORDS

European Cup – record aggregate: 18-0 by Benfica v Dudelange (Lux) (8-0a, 10-0h), prelim rd, 1965–66.
Record single-match score: 12-0 by Feyenoord v KR Reykjavik (Ice), 1st rd, 1st leg, 1969–70 (aggregate was 16-0).
Champions League – record single-match score: Liverpool 8-0 v Besiktas, Group A qual (Nov 6, 2007).
Highest match aggregate: 13 – Bayern Munich 12 Sporting Lisbon 1 (5-0 away, 7-1 at home, 1st ko rd, 2008–09)
Cup-Winners' Cup – *record aggregate: 21-0 by Chelsea v Jeunesse Hautcharage (Lux) (8-0a, 13-0h), 1st rd, 1971–72.
Record single-match score: 16-1 by Sporting Lisbon v Apoel Nicosia, 2nd round, 1st leg, 1963–64 (aggregate was 18-1).
UEFA Cup (prev Fairs Cup) – *Record aggregate: 21-0 by Feyenoord v US Rumelange (Lux) (9-0h, 12-0a), 1st round, 1972–73.
Record single-match score: 14-0 by Ajax Amsterdam v Red Boys (Lux) 1st rd, 2nd leg, 1984–85 (aggregate also 14-0).
Record British score in Europe: 13-0 by **Chelsea** at home to Jeunesse Hautcharage (Lux) in Cup-Winners' Cup 1st round, 2nd leg, 1971–72. Chelsea's overall 21-0 win in that tie is highest aggregate by British club in Europe.
Individual scoring record for European tie (over two legs):10 goals (6 home, 4 away) by Kiril Milanov for Levski Spartak in 19-3 agg win Cup-Winners' Cup 1st round v Lahden Reipas,

1976–77. Next highest: **8 goals** by **Jose Altafini** for AC Milan v US Luxembourg (European Cup, prelim round, 1962–63, agg 14-0) and by **Peter Osgood** for Chelsea v Jeunesse Hautcharage (Cup-Winners' Cup, 1st round 1971–72, agg 21-0). Altafini and Osgood each scored 5 goals at home, 3 away.

Individual single-match scoring record in European competition: **6** by **Mascarenhas** for Sporting Lisbon in 16-1 Cup-Winner's Cup 2nd round, 1st leg win v Apoel, 1963–64; and by **Lothar Emmerich** for Borussia Dortmund in 8-0 CWC 1st round, 2nd leg win v Floriana 1965–66; and by **Kiril Milanov** for Levski Spartak in 12-2 CWC 1st round, 1st leg win v Lahden Reipas, 1976–77.

Most goals in single European campaign: 15 by **Jurgen Klinsmann** for Bayern Munich (UEFA Cup 1995–96).

Most goals by British player in European competition: 30 by **Peter Lorimer** (Leeds, in 9 campaigns).

Most European Cup goals by individual player: 49 by **Alfredo di Stefano** in 58 apps for Real Madrid (1955–64).

(*Joint record European aggregate)

First European treble: **Clarence Seedorf** became the first player to win the European Cup with three clubs: Ajax in 1995, Real Madrid in 1998 and AC Milan in 2003.

EUROPEAN FOOTBALL – BIG RECOVERIES

In the most astonishing Final in the history of the European Cup/Champions League, **Liverpool** became the first club to win it from a 3-0 deficit when they beat AC Milan 3-2 on penalties after a 3-3 draw in Istanbul on May 25, 2005. Liverpool's fifth triumph in the competition meant that they would keep the trophy.

The following season, **Middlesbrough** twice recovered from three-goal aggregate deficits in the **UEFA Cup**, beating Basle 4-3 in the quarter finals and Steaua Bucharest by the same scoreline in the semi-finals.

In 2010, **Fulham** beat Juventus 5-4 after trailing 1-4 on aggregate in the second leg of their Europa League, Round of 16 match at Craven Cottage.

Only four clubs have survived a **4-goal** deficit in any of the European club competitions after the first leg had been completed:

1961–62 (Cup-Winners' Cup 1st round): Leixoes (Portugal) beat Chaux de Fonds (Luxembourg) 7-6 on agg (lost 2-6a, won 5-0i).

1962–63 (Fairs Cup 2nd round): Valencia (Spain) beat Dunfermline 1-0 in play-off in Lisbon after 6-6 agg (Valencia won 4-0h, lost 2-6a).

1984–85 (UEFA Cup 2nd round): Partizan Belgrade beat QPR on away goals (lost 2-6 away, at Highbury, won 4-0 home).

1985–86 (UEFA Cup 3rd round): Real Madrid beat Borussia Moenchengladbach on away goals (lost 1-5a, won 4-0h) and went on to win competition.

Two Scottish clubs have won a European tie from a 3-goal, first leg deficit: **Kilmarnock** 0-3, 5-1 v Eintracht Frankfurt (Fairs Cup 1st round, 1964–65); **Hibernian** 1-4, 5-0 v Napoli (Fairs Cup 2nd Round, 1967–68).

English clubs have three times gone out of the **UEFA Cup** after leading 3-0 from the first leg: 1975–76 (2nd Rd) **Ipswich** lost 3-4 on agg to Bruges; 1976–77 (quarter-final) **QPR** lost on penalties to AEK Athens after 3-3 agg; 1977–78 (3rd round) **Ipswich** lost on penalties to Barcelona after 3-3 agg.

● In the **1966 World Cup** quarter-final (Jul 23) at Goodison Park, North Korea led Portugal 3-0, but Eusebio scored 4 times to give **Portugal** a 5-3 win.

HEAVIEST ENGLISH-CLUB DEFEATS IN EUROPE

(Single-leg scores)

European Cup: Artmedia Bratislava 5, **Celtic** 0 (2nd qual round), Jul 2005 (agg 5-4); Ajax 5, **Liverpool** 1 (2nd round), Dec 1966 (agg 7-3); Real Madrid 5, **Derby** 1 (2nd round), Nov 1975 (agg 6-5).

Cup-Winners' Cup: Sporting Lisbon 5, **Manchester Utd** 0 (quarter-final), Mar 1964 (agg 6-4).

Fairs/UEFA Cup: Bayern Munich 6, **Coventry** 1 (2nd round), Oct 1970 (agg 7-3). **Combined**

London team lost 6-0 (agg 8-2) in first Fairs Cup Final in 1958. Barcelona 5, **Chelsea** 0 in Fairs Cup semi-final play-off, 1966, in Barcelona (after 2-2 agg).

SHOCK ENGLISH CLUB DEFEATS

1968–69 (Eur Cup, 1st round): **Manchester City** beaten by Fenerbahce, 1-2 agg.
1971–72 (CWC, 2nd round): **Chelsea** beaten by Atvidaberg on away goals.
1993–94 (Eur Cup, 2nd round): **Manchester Utd** beaten by Galatasaray on away goals.
1994–95 (UEFA Cup, 1st round): **Blackburn** beaten by Trelleborgs, 2-3 agg.
2000–01 (UEFA Cup, 1st round): **Chelsea** beaten by St. Gallen, Switz 1-2 agg.

PFA FAIR PLAY AWARD (Bobby Moore Trophy from 1993)

1988	Liverpool	2000	Crewe
1989	Liverpool	2001	Hull
1990	Liverpool	2002	Crewe
1991	Nottm Forest	2003	Crewe
1992	Portsmouth	2004	Crewe
1993	Norwich	2005	Crewe
1994	Crewe	2006	Crewe
1995	Crewe	2007	Crewe
1996	Crewe	2008	Crewe
1997	Crewe	2009	Stockport
1998	Cambridge Utd	2010	Rochdale
1999	Grimsby		

RECORD MEDAL SALES

West Ham bought (Jun 2000) the late **Bobby Moore**'s collection of medals and trophies for £1.8m at Christie's auction. It was put up for sale by his first wife Tina and included his World Cup-winner's medal.

A No. 6 duplicate red shirt made for England captain **Bobby Moore** for the 1966 World Cup Final fetched £44,000 at an auction at Wolves' ground in Sep, 1999. Moore kept the shirt he wore in that Final and gave the replica to England physio Harold Shepherdson.

Sir Geoff Hurst's 1966 World Cup-winning shirt fetched a record £91,750 at Christie's in Sep, 2000. His World Cup Final cap fetched £37,600 and his Man of the Match trophy £18,800. Proceeds totalling £274,410 from the 129 lots went to Hurst's three daughters and charities of his choice, including the Bobby Moore Imperial Cancer Research Fund.

In Aug, 2001, Sir Geoff sold his World Cup-winner's medal to his former club West Ham Utd (for their museum) at a reported £150,000.

'The **Billy Wright** Collection' – caps, medals and other memorabilia from his illustrious career – fetched over £100,000 at Christie's in Nov, 1996.

At the sale in Oct 1993, trophies, caps and medals earned by **Ray Kennedy**, former England, Arsenal and Liverpool player, fetched a then record total of £88,407. Kennedy, suffering from Parkinson's Disease, received £73,000 after commission. The PFA paid £31,080 for a total of 60 lots – including a record £16,000 for his 1977 European Cup winner's medal – to be exhibited at their Manchester museum. An anonymous English collector paid £17,000 for the medal and plaque commemorating Kennedy's part in the Arsenal Double in 1971.

Previous record for one player's medals, shirts etc collection: £30,000 (**Bill Foulkes**, Manchester Utd in 1992). The sale of **Dixie Dean**'s medals etc in 1991 realised £28,000.

In Mar, 2001, **Gordon Banks**' 1966 World Cup-winner's medal fetched a new record £124,750. TV's Nick Hancock, a Stoke fan, paid £23,500 for **Sir Stanley Matthews**' 1953 FA Cup-winner's medal. He also bought one of Matthews's England caps for £3,525 and paid £2,350 for a Stoke Div 2 Championship medal (1963).

Dave Mackay's 1961 League Championship and FA Cup winner's medals sold for £18,000 at Sotherby's. Tottenham bought them for their museum.

A selection of England World Cup-winning manager **Sir Alf Ramsey**'s memorabilia – England caps, championship medals with Ipswich etc. – fetched more than £80,000 at Christie's. They were offered for sale by his family, and his former clubs Tottenham and Ipswich were among the buyers. **Ray Wilson**'s 1966 England World Cup-winning shirt fetched £80,750. Also in Mar, 2002, the No. 10 shirt worn by **Pele** in Brazil's World Cup triumph in 1970 was sold for a record £157,750 at Christies. It went to an anonymous telephone bidder.

In Oct, 2003, **George Best**'s European Footballer of the Year (1968) trophy was sold to an anonymous British bidder for £167,250 at Bonham's. It was the then most expensive item of sporting memorabilia ever auctioned in Britain.

England captain **Bobby Moore**'s 1970 World Cup shirt, which he swapped with Pele after Brazil's 1-0 win in Mexico, was sold for £60,000 at Christie's in Mar, 2004.

Sep, 2004: England shirt worn by tearful **Paul Gascoigne** in 1990 World Cup semi-final v Germany sold at Christie's for £28,680. At same auction, shirt worn by Brazil's **Pele** in 1958 World Cup Final in Sweden sold for £70,505.

May, 2005: The **second FA Cup** (which was presented to winning teams from 1896 to 1909) was bought for £420,000 at Christie's by Birmingham chairman David Gold, a world record for an item of football memorabilia. It was presented to the National Football Museum, Preston. At the same auction, the World Cup-winner's medal earned by England's **Alan Ball** in 1966 was sold for £164,800.

Oct, 2005: At auction at Bonham's, the medals and other memorabilia of Hungary and Real Madrid legend **Ferenc Puskas** were sold for £85,000 to help pay for hospital treatment.

Nov, 2006: A ball used in the 2006 World Cup Final and signed by the winning Italy team was sold for £1.2m (a world record for football memorabilia) at a charity auction in Qatar. It was bought by the Qatar Sports Academy.

Feb, 2010: A pair of boots worn by **Sir Stanley Matthews** in the 1953 FA Cup Final was sold at Bonham's for £38,400.

Oct, 2010: Trophies and memorabilia belonging to **George Best** were sold at Bonham's for £193,440. His 1968 European Cup winner's medal fetched £156,000.

Oct-Nov 2010: **Nobby Stiles** sold his 1966 World Cup winner's medal at an Edinburgh auction for a record £188,200. His old club, Manchester Utd, also paid £48,300 for his 1968 European Cup medal to go to the club's museum at Old Trafford. In London, the shirt worn by Stiles in the 1966 World Cup Final went for £75,000. A total of 45 items netted £424,438. **George Cohen** and **Martin Peters** had previously sold their medals from 1966.

LONGEST UNBEATEN CUP RUN

Liverpool established the longest unbeaten cup sequence by a Football League club: 25 successive rounds in the League/Milk Cup between semi-final defeat by Nottm Forest (1-2 agg) in 1980 and defeat at Tottenham (0-1) in the third round on Oct 31, 1984. During this period Liverpool won the tournament in four successive seasons, a feat no other Football League club has achieved in any competition.

NEAR £1M RECORD DAMAGES

A High Court judge in Newcastle (May 7, 1999) awarded Bradford City's 28-year-old striker **Gordon Watson** record damages for a football injury: £909,143. He had had his right leg fractured in two places by Huddersfield's Kevin Gray on Feb 1, 1997.

Huddersfield were 'proven negligent for allowing their player to make a rushed tackle'. The award was calculated at £202,643 for loss of earnings, £730,500 for 'potential career earnings' if he had joined a Premiership club, plus £26,000 to cover medical treatment and care.

Watson, awarded £50,000 in an earlier legal action, had a 6-inch plate inserted in the leg. He resumed playing for City in season 1998–99.

BIG HALF-TIME SCORES

Tottenham 10, Crewe 1 (FA Cup 4th round replay, Feb 3, 1960; result 13-2); Tranmere 8, Oldham 1 (Div 3N., Dec 26, 1935; result 13-4); **Chester City 8, York 0** (Div 3N., Feb 1, 1936; result 12-0; believed to be record half-time scores in League football).

Nine goals were scored in the first half – **Burnley 4, Watford 5** in Div 1 on Apr 5, 2003. Result: 4-7.

Stirling Albion led Selkirk 15-0 at half-time (result 20-0) in the Scottish Cup 1st round, Dec 8, 1984.

World record half-time score: **16-0** when **Australia** beat **American Samoa** 31-0 (another world record) in the World Cup Oceania qualifying group at Coff's Harbour, New South Wales, on Apr 11 2001.

• On Mar 4 1933 **Coventry** beat QPR (Div 3 South) 7-0, having led by that score at half-time. This repeated the half-time situation in Bristol City's 7-0 win over Grimsby on Dec 26, 1914.

TOP SECOND-HALF TEAM

Most goals scored by a team in one half of a League match is **11. Stockport** led Halifax 2-0 at half-time in Div 3 North on Jan 6 1934 and won 13-0.

FIVE NOT ENOUGH

Last team to score **5** in League match and lose: **Burton**, beaten 6-5 by Cheltenham (Lge 2, Mar 13, 2010).

LONG SERVICE WITH ONE CLUB

Bill Nicholson, OBE, was associated with Tottenham for 67 years – as a wing-half (1938–55), then the club's most successful manager (1958–74) with 8 major prizes, subsequently chief advisor and scout. He became club president, and an honorary freeman of the borough, had an executive suite named after him at the club, and the stretch of roadway from Tottenham High Road to the main gates has the nameplate Bill Nicholson Way. He died, aged 85, in Oct 2004.

Ted Bates, the Grand Old Man of Southampton with 66 years of unbroken service to the club, was awarded the Freedom of the City in Apr, 2001. He joined Saints as an inside-forward from Norwich in 1937, made 260 peace-time appearances, became reserve-team trainer in 1953 and manager at The Dell for 18 years (1955–73), taking Southampton into the top division in 1966. He was subsequently chief executive, director and club president. He died in Oct 2003, aged 85.

Dario Gradi, MBE, stepped down after completing 24 seasons and more than 1,000 matches as manager of Crewe (appointed Jun 1983). Never a League player, he previously managed Wimbledon and Crystal Palace. At Crewe, his policy of finding and grooming young talent has earned the club more than £20m in transfer fees. He stayed with Crewe as technical director, and twice took charge of team affairs again following the departure of the managers who succeeded him, Steve Holland and Gudjon Thordarson.

Bob Paisley was associated with Liverpool for 57 years from 1939, when he joined them from Bishop Auckland, until he died in Feb 1996. He served as player, trainer, coach, assistant-manager, manager, director and vice-president. He was Liverpool's most successful manager, winning 13 major trophies for the club (1974–83).

Ronnie Moran, who joined Liverpool in as a player 1952, retired from the Anfield coaching staff in season 1998–99.

Ernie Gregory served West Ham for 52 years as goalkeeper and coach. He joined them as boy of 14 from school in 1935, retired in May 1987.

Ted Sagar, Everton goalkeeper, 23 years at Goodison Park (1929–52, but only 16 League seasons because of War).

Alan Knight, goalkeeper, played 23 seasons (1977–2000) for his only club, Portsmouth.

Roy Sproson, defender, played 21 League seasons for his only club, Port Vale (1950–71).

Allan Ball, goalkeeper, 20 seasons with Queen of the South (1963–83).

Pat Bonner, goalkeeper, 19 seasons with Celtic (1978–97).

Danny McGrain, defender, 17 years with Celtic (1970–87).

TIGHT AT HOME

Fewest home goals conceded in League season (modern times): 4 by Liverpool (Div 1, 1978–9); 4 by **Manchester Utd** (Premier League, 1994–95) – both in 21 matches.

FOOTBALL POOLS

Littlewoods launched them in 1923 with a capital of £100. Coupons were first issued (4,000 of them) outside Manchester Utd's ground, the original 35 investors staking a total of £4 7s 6d (pay-out £2 12s).

Vernons joined Littlewoods as the leading promoters. The Treble Chance, leading to bonanza dividends, was introduced in 1946 and the Pools Panel began in Jan 1963, to counter mass fixture postponements caused by the Big Freeze winter.

But business was hard hit by the launch of the National Lottery in 1994. Dividends slumped, the work-force was drastically cut and in Jun 2000 the Liverpool-based Moores family sold Littlewoods Pools in a £161m deal. After 85 years, the name Littlewoods disappeared from Pools betting in Aug 2008. The New Football Pools was formed. Vernons and

Zetters continued to operate under their own name in the ownership of Sportech.

The record prize remains the £2,924,622 paid to a Worsley, Manchester, syndicate in Nov 1994.

Fixed odds football – record pay-out: £654,375 by Ladbrokes (May 1993) to Jim Wright, of Teignmouth, Devon. He placed a £1,000 each-way pre-season bet on the champions of the three Football League divisions – Newcastle (8–1), Stoke (6–1) and Cardiff (9–1).

Record match accumulators: £164,776 to £4 stake on 18 correct results, Oct 5, 6, 7, 2002. The bet, with Ladbrokes in Colchester, was made by Army chef Mark Simmons; £272,629 for £2.50 stake on 9 correct scores (6 English Prem Lge, 3 Spanish Cup) on Jan 5, 2011, by an anonymous punter at Ladbrokes in Berkshire.

TRANSFER WINDOW

This was introduced to Britain in Sep 2002 via FIFA regulations to bring uniformity across Europe (the rule previously applied in a number of other countries). The transfer of contracted players is restricted to two periods: Jun 1–Aug 31 and Jan 1–31). On appeal, Football League clubs continued to sign/sell players (excluding deals with Premiership clubs).

PROGRAMME PIONEERS

Chelsea pioneered football's magazine-style programme when they introduced a 16-page issue for their First Division match against Portsmouth on Christmas Day 1948. It cost sixpence (2.5p).

LONG THROW EXPERTS

Andy Legg's throws for Notts Co were measured at 41m in season 1994–95) and claimed as the longest by any footballer in the world. Then, in 1997–98, **Dave Challinor** (Tranmere) reached 46.3 metres. A range of throws not previously encountered by Premier League defences was provided by Stoke's **Rory Delap** in season 2008–09. Reaching an estimated 37mph, they averaged 38m and were delivered in a combination of high, looping throws and those with a flatter trajectory. Stoke scored nine goals from them.

In 2010, Denmark's **Thomas Gronnemark** was reported to have thrown 51.3m.

BALL JUGGLING: WORLD RECORD CLAIMS

Sam Ik (South Korea) juggled a ball non-stop for 18 hours, 11 minutes, 4 seconds in Mar 1995. Thai footballer **Sam-Ang Sowanski** juggled a ball for 15 hours without letting it touch the ground in Bangkok in Apr 2000.

Milene Domingues, wife of Brazilian star Ronaldo and a player for Italian women's team Fiammonza, Milan, became the 'Queen of Keepy Uppy' when for 9 hours, 6 minutes she juggled a ball 55,187 times.

SUBS' SCORING RECORD

Barnet's 5-4 home win v Torquay (Div 3, Dec 28, 1993) provided the first instance of all **four substitutes** scoring in a major League match in England.

WORLD'S OLDEST FOOTBALL ANNUAL

Now in its 125th edition, this publication began as the 16-page *Athletic News Football Supplement & Club Directory* in 1887. From the long-established *Athletic News*, it became the *Sunday Chronicle Annual* in 1946, the *Empire News* in 1956, the *News of the World & Empire News* in 1961 and the *News of the World Annual* from 1965 until becoming the *Nationwide Annual* in 2008.

BARCLAYS PREMIER LEAGUE CLUB DETAILS AND SQUADS 2011–12

(At time of going to press)

ARSENAL

Ground: Emirates Stadium, Highbury, London, N5 1BU
Telephone: 0207 704 4000. **Club nickname:** Gunners
First-choice colours: Red and white shirts; white shorts; white socks
Record transfer fee: £17,400,000 to Seville for Jose Antonio Reyes, Jan 2004
Record fee received: £25,000,000 from Barcelona for Marc Overmars, Jul 2000 and from Manchester City for Emmanuel Adebayor, Jul 2009
Record attendance: At Highbury: 73,295 v Sunderland (Div 1) 9 Mar, 1935. At Wembley: 73,707 v Lens (Champ Lge) Nov 1998. At Emirates Stadium: 60,161 v Manchester Utd (Prem Lge) 3 Oct, 2007
Capacity for 20011–12: 60,361. **Main sponsor:** Emirates
League Championship: Winners 1930–31, 1932–33, 1933–34, 1934–35, 1937–38, 1947–48, 1952–53, 1970–71, 1988–89, 1990–91, 1997–98, 2001–02, 2003–04
FA Cup: Winners 1930, 1936, 1950, 1971, 1979, 1993, 1998, 2002, 2003, 2005
League Cup: Winners 1987, 1993
European competitions: Winners Fairs Cup 1969–70, Cup-Winners' Cup 1993–94
Finishing positions in Premier League: 1992–93 10th, 1993–94 4th, 1994–95 12th, 1995–96 5th, 1996–97 3rd, 1997–98 1st, 1998–99 2nd, 1999–2000 2nd, 2000–01 2nd, 2001–02 1st, 2002–03 2nd, 2003–04 1st, 2004–05 2nd, 2005–06 4th, 2006–07 4th, 2007–08 3rd, 2008–09 4th, 2009–10 3rd, 2010–11 4th
Biggest win: 12-0 v Loughborough (Div 2) 12 Mar, 1900
Biggest defeat: 0-8 v Loughborough (Div 2) 12 Dec, 1896
Highest League scorer in a season: Ted Drake 42 (1934–35)
Most League goals in aggregate: Thierry Henry 174 (1999–2007)
Longest unbeaten League sequence: 49 matches (2003–04)
Longest sequence without a League win: 23 matches (1912–13)
Most capped player: Thierry Henry (France) 81

Name	Height ft in	Previous club	Birthplace	Birthdate
Goalkeepers				
Almunia, Manuel	6.3	Celta Vigo	Pamplona, Sp	19.05.77
Fabianski, Lukasz	6.3	Legia Warsaw	Kostrzyn, Pol	18.04.85
Mannone, Vito	6.3	Atalanta	Desio, It	02.03.88
Szczesny, Wojciech	6.5	–	Warsaw, Pol	18.04.90
Defenders				
Djourou, Johan	6.3	Etoile Carouge	Abidjan, Iv C	18.01.87
Gibbs, Kieran	5.10	–	Lambeth	26.09.89
Jenkinson, Carl	5.11	Charlton	Harlow	08.02.92
Koscielny, Laurent	6.1	Lorient	Tulle, Fr	10.09.85
Sagny, Bacari	5.9	Auxerre	Sens, Fr	14.02.83
Squillaci, Sebastien	6.1	Sevilla	Toulon, Fr	11.08.80
Traore, Armand	6.1	Monaco	Paris, Fr	08.10.89
Vermaelen, Thomas	6.0	Ajax	Kapellen, Bel	14.11.85
Midfielders				
Arshavin, Andrey	5.8	Zenit St Petersburg	St Petersburg, Rus	29.05.81
Denilson	5.10	Sao Paulo	Sao Paulo, Br	16.02.88

Diaby, Abou	6.2	Auxerre	Paris, Fr	11.05.86
Eastmond, Craig	6.0	–	Wandsworth	09.12.90
Eboue, Emmanuel	5.10	Beveren	Abidjan, Iv C	04.06.83
Emmanuel-Thomas, Jay	6.3	–	Forest Gate	27.12.90
Fabregas, Cesc	5.10	Barcelona	Arenys de Mar, Sp	04.05.87
Frimpong, Emmanuel	6.0		Accra, Gh	10.01.92
Lansbury, Henri	6.0	–	Enfield	12.10.90
Nasri, Samir	5.10	Marseille	Marseille, Fr	26.06.87
Rosicky, Tomas	5.10	Borussia Dortmund	Prague, Cze	04.10.80
Ramsey, Aaron	5.11	Cardiff	Caerphilly	26.12.90
Song, Alex	6.1	Bastia	Douala, Cam	09.09.87
Wilshere, Jack	5.8		Stevenage	01.01.92
Forwards				
Bendtner, Nicklas	6.3	–	Copenhagen, Den	16.01.88
Chamakh, Marouane	6.2	Bordeaux	Tonneins, Fr	10.01.84
Gervinho	5.11	Lille	Anyama, Iv C	27.05.87
Van Persie, Robin	6.0	Feyenoord	Rotterdam, Hol	06.08.83
Vela, Carlos	5.7	Guadalajara	Cancun, Mex	01.03.89
Walcott, Theo	5.8	Southampton	Newbury	16.03.89

ASTON VILLA

Ground: Villa Park, Trinity Road, Birmingham, B6 6HE
Telephone: 0871 423 8101. **Club nickname:** Villans
First-choice colours: Claret and blue shirts; white shorts; blue socks
Record transfer fee: £24,000,000 to Sunderland for Darren Bent, Jan 2011
Record fee received: £24,000,000 for James Milner from Manchester City, Aug 2010
Record attendance: 76,588 v Derby Co (FA Cup 6) 2 Mar, 1946
Capacity for 2011–12: 42,786. **Club sponsor:**
League Championship: Winners 1893–94, 1895–96, 1896–97, 1898–99, 1899–1900, 1909–10, 1980–81
FA Cup: Winners 1887, 1895, 1897, 1905, 1913, 1920, 1957
League Cup: Winners 1961, 1975, 1977, 1994, 1996
European competitions: Winners European Cup 1981–82, European Super Cup 1982–83
Finishing positions in Premier League: 1992–93 2nd, 1993–94 10th, 1994–95 18th, 1995–96 4th, 1996–97 5th, 1997–98 7th, 1998–99 6th, 1999–2000 6th, 2000–01 8th, 2001–02 8th, 2002–03 16th, 2003–04 6th, 2004–05 10th, 2005–06 16th, 2006–07 11th, 2007–08 6th, 2008–09 6th, 2009–10 6th, 2010–11 9th
Biggest win: 12-2 v Accrington (Div 1) 12 Mar, 1892; 11-1 v Charlton (Div 2) 24 Nov, 1959; 10-0 v Sheffield Wed (Div 1) 5 Oct, 1912, v Burnley (Div 1) 29 Aug, 1925. Also: 13-0 v Wednesbury (FA Cup 1) 30 Oct, 1886
Biggest defeat: 0-7 in five League matches from Blackburn (Div 1) 19 Oct, 1889 to Manchester Utd (Div 1) 24 Oct, 1964
Highest League scorer in a season: 'Pongo' Waring 49 (1930–31)
Most League goals in aggregate: Harry Hampton 215 (1904–1915)
Longest unbeaten League sequence: 15 matches (1897, 1909–10 and 1949)
Longest sequence without a League win: 12 matches (1973–74 and 1986–87)
Most capped player: Steve Staunton (Republic of Ireland) 64

Goalkeepers

Guzan, Bradley	6.4	Chivas	Evergreen Park, US	09.09.84
Marshall, Andy	6.2	Coventry	Bury St Edmunds	14.04.75
Defenders				
Baker, Nathan	6.3	–	Worcester	23.04.91

Beye, Habib	5.11	Newcastle	Paris, Fr	19.10.77
Clark, Ciaran	6.2	–	Harrow	26.09.89
Collins, James	6.2	West Ham	Newport	23.08.83
Cuellar, Carlos	6.3	Rangers	Madrid, Sp	23.08.81
Dunne, Richard	6.2	Manchester City	Dublin, Ire	21.09.79
Lichaj, Eric	5.10	Chicago	Downers Grove, US	17.11.88
Warnock, Stephen	5.10	Blackburn	Ormskirk	12.12.81
Young, Luke	6.0	Middlesbrough	Harlow	19.07.79
Midfielders				
Albrighton, Mark	6.1	–	Tamworth	18.11.89
Bannan, Barry	5.11	Derby	Airdrie	01.12.89
Delph, Fabian	5.9	Leeds	Bradford	05.05.91
Downing, Stewart	6.0	Middlesbrough	Middlesbrough	02.07.84
Herd, Chris	5.8	–	Perth, Aus	04.04.89
Ireland, Stephen	5.8	Manchester City	Cork, Ire	22.08.86
Johnson, Daniel	5.9	–	Kingston, Jam	08.10.92
Makoun, Jean	5.8	Lyon	Yaounde, Cam	29.05.83
Petrov, Stiliyan	5.10	Celtic	Montana, Bul	05.07.79
Forwards				
Agbonlahor, Gabriel	5.11	–	Birmingham	13.10.86
Bent, Darren	5.11	Sunderland	Wandsworth	06.02.84
Delfouneso, Nathan	6.1	–	Birmingham	02.02.91
Heskey, Emile	6.2	Wigan	Leicester	11.01.78
Weimann, Andreas	6.2	–	Vienna, Aut	05.08.91

BLACKBURN ROVERS

Ground: Ewood Park, Blackburn BB2 4JF
Telephone: 0871 702 1875. **Club nickname:** Rovers
First-choice colours: Blue and white shirts; white shorts; white socks
Record transfer fee: £8,000,000 to Manchester Utd for Andy Cole, Dec 2001
Record fee received: £17,500,000 from Manchester City for Roque Santa Cruz, Jun 2009
Record attendance: 62,522 v Bolton (FA Cup 6) 2 Mar, 1929
Capacity for 20011–12: 31,154. **Main sponsor:** Crown
League Championship: Winners 1911–12, 1913–14, 1994–95
FA Cup: Winners 1884, 1885, 1886, 1890, 1891, 1928
League Cup: Winners 2002
European competitions: Champions League 1st group stage, 1995–96
Finishing positions in Premier League: 1992–93 4th, 1993–94 2nd, 1994–95 1st, 1995–96 7th, 1996–97 13th, 1997–98 6th, 1998–99 19th, 2001–02 10th, 2002–03 6th, 2003–04 15th, 2004–05 15th, 2005–06 6th, 2006–07 10th, 2007–08 7th, 2008–09 15th, 2009–10 10th, 2010–11 15th
Biggest win: 9-0 v Middlesbrough (Div 2) 6 Nov, 1954. Also: 11-0 v Rossendale (FA Cup 1) 13 Oct, 1884
Biggest defeat: 0-8 v Arsenal (Div 1) 25 Feb, 1933
Highest League scorer in a season: Ted Harper 43 (1925–26)
Most League goals in aggregate: Simon Garner 168 (1978–92)
Longest unbeaten League sequence: 23 matches (1987–88)
Longest sequence without a League win: 16 matches (1978–79)
Most capped player: Henning Berg (Norway) 61

Goalkeepers				
Bunn, Mark	6.0	Northampton	London	16.11.84
Robinson, Paul	6.2	Tottenham	Beverley	15.10.79

Defenders

Givet, Gael	6.0	Marseille	Arles, Fr	09.10.81
Gunning, Gavin	6.1	Crumlin	Dublin, Ire	26.01.91
Hanley, Grant	6.2	–	Dumfries	20.11.91
Nelsen, Ryan	6.0	DC United	Christchurch, NZ	18.10.77
Olsson, Martin	5.7	Hogaborgs	Gavle, Swe	17.05.88
Salgado, Michel	5.9	Real Madrid	Neves, Sp	22.10.75
Samba, Chris	6.5	Hertha Berlin	Creteil, Fr	28.03.84

Midfielders

Aley, Zac	5.11	Southport	Fazakerley	17.08.91
Andrews, Keith	5.11	MK Dons	Dublin, Ire	13.09.80
Dunn, David	5.10	Birmingham	Blackburn	27.12.79
Emerton, Brett	6.1	Feyenoord	Bankstown, Aus	22.02.79
Formica, Mauro	5.10	Newell's OB	Rosario, Arg	04.04.88
Grella, Vince	6.0	Torino	Melbourne, Aus	05.10.79
Linganz, Amine	6.1	St Etienne	Algiers	16.11.89
N'Zonzi, Steven	6.3	Amiens	La Garenne, Fr	15.12.88
Pedersen, Morten Gamst	5.11	Tromso	Vadso, Nor	08.09.81

Forwards

Diouf, El-Hadji	5.11	Sunderland	Dakar, Sen	15.01.81
Doran, Aaron	5.7	–	Dublin, Ire	13.05.91
Hoillett, David	5.8	–	Ottawa, Can	05.06.90
Kalinic, Nikola	6.2	Hajduk Split	Solin, Cro	05.01.88
Roberts, Jason	5.11	Wigan	Park Royal	25.01.78
Rosina, Ruben	5.11	Barcelona	Sagunto, Sp	23.03.91

BOLTON WANDERERS

Ground: Reebok Stadium, Burnden Way, Lostock, Bolton BL6 6JW
Telephone: 0844 871 2932. **Club nickname:** Trotters
First-choice colours: White shirts; white shorts; white socks
Record transfer fee: £12,000,000 to Toulouse for Johan Elmander, Jun 2008
Record fee received: £15,000,000 from Chelsea for Nicolas Anelka, Jan 2008
Record attendance: At Burnden Park: 69,912 v Manchester City (FA Cup 5) 18 Feb, 1933. At Reebok Stadium: 28,101 v Leicester (Prem Lge) Dec 2003
Capacity for 2011–12: 28,101. **Main sponsor:** 188Bet
League Championship: 3rd 1891–92, 1920–21, 1924–25
FA Cup: Winners 1923, 1926, 1929, 1958
League Cup: Runners–up 1995, 2004
European competitions: UEFA Cup rd of 16 2007–08
Finishing positions in Premier League: 1995–96 20th, 1997–98 18th, 2001–02 16th, 2002–03 17th, 2003–04 8th, 2004–05 6th, 2005–06 8th, 2006–07 7th, 2007–08 16th, 2008–09 13th, 2009–10 14th, 2010–11 14th
Biggest win: 8-0 v Barnsley (Div 2) 6 Oct, 1934. Also: 13-0 v Sheffield Utd (FA Cup 2) 1 Feb, 1890
Biggest defeat: 1-9 v Preston (FA Cup 2) 10 Dec, 1887
Highest League scorer in a season: Joe Smith 38 (1920–21)
Most League goals in aggregate: Nat Lofthouse 255 (1946–61)
Longest unbeaten League sequence: 23 matches (1990–91)
Longest sequence without a League win: 26 matches (1902–03)
Most capped player: Jussi Jaaskelainen (Finland) 56

Goalkeepers

Bogdan, Adam	6.4	Vasas	Budapest, Hun	27.09.87

Jaaskelainen, Jussi	6.4	VPS	Mikkeli, Fin	17.04.75
Lainton, Rob	6.1	–	Ashton-under-Lyne	12.10.89
Defenders				
Alonso, Marcos	6.2	Real Madrid	Madrid, Sp	28.12.90
Cahill, Gary	6.2	Aston Villa	Sheffield	19.12.85
Gardner, Ricardo	5.0	Harbour View	St Andrews, Jam	25.09.78
Knight, Zat	6.6	Aston Villa	Solihull	02.05.80
Ricketts, Sam	6.1	Hull	Aylesbury	11.10.81
Robinson, Paul	5.9	WBA	Watford	14.12.78
Steinsson, Greta	6.2	Alkmaar	Siglufjordur, Ice	09.01.82
Wheater, David	6.4	Middlesbrough	Redcar	14.02.87
Midfielders				
Chung–Yong Lee	5.11	Seoul	Seoul, S Kor	02.07.88
Davies, Mark	5.11	Wolves	Wolverhampton	18.02.88
Davis, Sean	5.11	Portsmouth	Clapham	20.09.79
Holden, Stuart	5.10	Houston	Aberdeen	01.08.85
Muamba, Fabrice	5.11	Birmingham	Kinshasa, DR Con	06.04.88
Petrov, Martin	5.11	Manchester City	Vzatza, Bul	15.01.79
Pratley, Darren	6.0	Swansea	Barking	22.04.85
Taylor, Matthew	5.10	Portsmouth	Oxford	27.11.81
Forwards				
Blake, Robbie	5.9	Burnley	Middlesbrough	04.03.76
Davies, Kevin	6.0	Southampton	Sheffield	26.03.77
Eaves, Tom	6.4	Oldham	Liverpool	14.01.92
Klasnic, Ivan	6.1	Nantes	Hamburg, Ger	29.01.80
Obadeyi, Temitope	6.3	–	Birmingham	29.12.89
O'Halloran, Michael	6.2	–	Glasgow	06.01.91

CHELSEA

Ground: Stamford Bridge Stadium, London SW6 1HS
Telephone: 0871 984 1955. **Club nickname:** Blues
First-choice colours: Blue shirts; blue shorts; white socks
Record transfer fee: £50,000,000 to Liverpool for Fernando Torres, Jan 2011
Record fee received: £24,500,000 from Real Madrid for Arjen Robben, Aug 2007
Record attendance: 82,905 v Arsenal (Div 1) 12 Oct, 1935
Capacity for 2011–12: 42,449. **Main sponsor:** Samsung
League Championship: Winners 1954–55, 2004–05, 2005–06, 2009-10
FA Cup: Winners 1970, 1997, 2000, 2007, 2009, 2010
League Cup: Winners 1965, 1998, 2005, 2007
European competitions: Winners Cup-Winners' Cup 1970–71, 1997–98
Finishing positions in Premier League: 1992–93 11th, 1993–94 14th, 1994–95 11th, 1995–96 11th, 1996–97 6th, 1997–98 4th, 1998–99 3rd, 1999–2000 5th, 2000–01 6th, 2001–02 6th, 2002–03 4th, 2003–04 2nd, 2004–05 1st, 2005–06 1st, 2006–07 2nd, 2007–08 2nd, 2008–09 3rd, 2009–10 1st, 2010–11 2nd
Biggest win: 9-2 v Glossop (Div 2) 1 Sep, 1906 and 7-0 in four League matches. Also: 13-0 v Jeunesse Hautcharage, (Cup-Winners' Cup) 29 Sep, 1971
Biggest defeat: 1-8 v Wolves (Div 1) 26 Sep, 1923; 0-7 v Leeds (Div 1) 7 Oct, 1967, v Nottm Forest (Div 1) 20 Apr, 1991
Highest League scorer in a season: Jimmy Greaves 41 (1960–61)
Most League goals in aggregate: Bobby Tambling 164 (1958–70)
Most capped player: Frank Lampard (England) 84
Longest unbeaten League sequence: 40 matches (2004–05)
Longest sequence without a League win: 21 matches (1987–88)

Goalkeepers

Cech, Petr	6.5	Rennes	Plzen, Cze	20.05.82
Hilario, Henrique	6.3	Nacional	Sao Pedro, Por	21.10.75
Turnbull, Ross	6.1	–	Bishop Auckland	04.01.85

Defenders

Alex	6.2	PSV Eindhoven	Niteroi, Br	17.06.82
Bosingwa, Jose	6.0	Porto	Kinshasa, DR Con	24.08.82
Bruma, Jeffrey	6.1	Feyenoord	Rotterdam, Hol	13.11.91
Cole, Ashley	5.8	Arsenal	Stepney	20.12.80
Ferreira, Paulo	6.0	Porto	Lisbon, Por	18.01.79
Ivanovic, Branislav	6.2	Lok Moscow	Mitrovica, Serb	22.02.84
Luiz, David	6.2	Benfica	Didema, Br	22.04.87
Terry, John	6.1	–	Barking	07.12.80
Van Aanholt, Patrick	5.9	PSV	Hertogenbosch, Hol	29.08.90

Midfielders

Benayoun, Yossi	5.10	Liverpool	Dimona, Isr	05.05.80
Essien, Michael	6.0	Lyon	Accra, Gh	03.12.82
Kakuta, Gael	5.8	Lens	Lille, Fr	21.06.91
Lampard, Frank	6.0	West Ham	Romford	20.06.78
Malouda, Florent	5.11	Lyon	Cayenne, Gui	13.06.80
McEachran, Josh	5.10	–	Oxford	01.03.93
Mikel, John Obi	6.2	Lyn Oslo	Jos, Nig	22.04.87
Ramires	5.11	Benfica	Rio de Janeiro, Br	24.03.87
Zhirkov, Yuri	5.10	CSKA Moscow	Tambov, Rus	20.08.83

Forwards

Anelka, Nicolas	6.1	Bolton	Versailles, Fr	14.03.79
Borini, Fabio	5.11	Bologna	Bentivoglio, It	23.03.91
Drogba, Didier	6.2	Marseille	Abidjan, Iv C	11.03.78
Kalou, Salomon	5.10	Feyenoord	Oume, Iv C	05.08.85
Sturridge, Daniel	6.2	Manchester City	Birmingham	01.09.89
Torres, Fernando	6.1	Liverpool	Madrid, Sp	20.03.84

EVERTON

Ground: Goodison Park, Liverpool L4 4EL
Telephone: 0870 442 1878. **Club nickname:** Toffees
First-choice colours: Blue shirts; white shorts; white socks
Record transfer fee: £15,000,000 to Standard Liege for Marouane Fellaini, Aug 2008
Record fee received: £27,000,000 from Manchester Utd for Wayne Rooney, Aug 2004
Record attendance: 78,299 v Liverpool (Div 1) 18 Sep, 1948
Capacity for 2011–12: 40,157. **Main sponsor:** Chang
League Championship: Winners 1890–91, 1914–15, 1927–28, 1931–31, 1938–39, 1962–63, 1969–70, 1984–85, 1986–87
FA Cup: Winners 1906, 1933, 1966, 1984, 1995
League Cup: Runners up 1977, 1984
European competitions: Winners Cup-Winners' Cup 1984–85
Finishing positions in Premier League: 1992–93 13th, 1993–94 17th, 1994–95 15th, 1995–96 6th 1996–97 15th 1997–98 17th 1998–99 14th, 1999–2000 13th, 2000–01 16th, 2001–02 15th, 2002–03 7th, 2003–04 17th, 2004–05 4th, 2005–06 11th, 2006–07 6th, 2007–08 5th, 2008–09 5th, 2009–10 8th, 20010-11 7th
Biggest win: 9-1 v Manchester City (Div 1) 3 Sep, 1906, v Plymouth (Div 2) 27 Dec, 1930. Also: 11-2 v Derby (FA Cup 1) 18 Jan, 1890
Biggest defeat: 0-7 v Portsmouth (Div 1) 10 Sep, 1949 and v Arsenal (Prem Lge) 11 May, 2005

Highest League scorer in a season: Ralph 'Dixie' Dean 60 (1927–28)
Most League goals in aggregate: Ralph 'Dixie' Dean 349 (1925–37)
Longest unbeaten League sequence: 20 matches (1978)
Longest sequence without a League win: 14 matches (1937)
Most capped player: Neville Southall (Wales) 92

Goalkeepers

Howard, Tim	6.3	Manchester Utd	New Jersey, US	03.06.79
Mucha, Jan	6.3	Legia Warsaw	Cirochou, Cze	05.12.82

Defenders

Baines, Leighton	5.7	Wigan	Liverpool	11.12.84
Coleman, Seamus	5.10	Sligo	Donegal, Ire	11.10.88
Dier, Eric	6.2	Sporting	Cheltenham	15.01.94
Distin, Sylvain	6.4	Portsmouth	Paris, Fr	16.12.77
Duffy, Shane	6.4	–	Derry	01.01.92
Heitinga, Johnny	5.11	Atletico Madrid	Alphen, Hol	15.11.83
Hibbert, Tony	5.10	–	Liverpool	20.02.81
Jagielka, Phil	5.11	Sheffield Utd	Manchester	17.08.82
Mustafi, Shkodran	–	Hamburg	Bad Hersfeld, Ger	17.04.92
Neville, Phil	5.11	Manchester Utd	Bury	21.01.77

Midfielders

Arteta, Mikel	5.9	Real Sociedad	San Sebastian, Sp	28.03.82
Barkley, Ross	6.2	–	Liverpool	05.12.93
Bilyaletdinov, Diniyar	6.1	Lokomotiv Moscow	Moscow, Rus	27.02.85
Cahill, Tim	5.10	Millwall	Sydney, Aus	06.12.79
Fellaini, Marouane	6.4	Standard Liege	Etterbeek, Bel	22.11.87
Osman, Leon	5.8	–	Billinge	17.05.81
Rodwell, Jack	6.1	–	Birkdale	17.09.89
Wallace, James	6.0	–	Fazackerly	19.12.91

Forwards

Anichebe, Victor	6.1	–	Lagos, Nig	23.04.88
Baxter, Jose	5.10	–	Bootle	07.02.92
Beckford, Jermaine	6.2	Leeds	Ealing	09.12.83
Gueye, Magaye	5.10	Strasbourg	Nogent, Fr	06.07.90
McAleny, Conor	–	–	Liverpool	12.08.92
Saha, Louis	5.11	Manchester Utd	Paris, Fr	08.08.78
Silva, Joao	6.2	Desportivo	Vila das Aves, Por	21.05.90
Vellios, Apostolos	6.3	Iraklis	Thessalonika, Gre	08.01.92
Yakubu, Aiyegbeni	6.0	Middlesbrough	Benin, Nig	22.11.82

FULHAM

Ground: Craven Cottage, Stevenage Road, London SW6 6HH
Telephone: 0870 442 1222. **Club nickname:** Cottagers
First-choice colours: All white
Record transfer fee: £11,500,000 to Lyon for Steve Marlet, Aug 2001
Record fee received: £12,825,000 from Manchester Utd for Louis Saha, Jan 2004.
Record attendance: 49,335 v Millwall (Div 2) 8 Oct, 1938
Capacity for 2011–12: 25,478. **Main sponsor:** LG
League Championship: 7th 2008–09
FA Cup: Runners-up 1975
League Cup: 5th rd 1968, 1971, 2000
European positions: Europa League final, 2009–10
Finishing positions in Premier League: 2001–02 13th, 2002–03 14th, 2003–04 9th,

2004–05 13th, 2005–06 12th, 2006–07 16th 2007–08 17th, 2008–09 7th; 2009–10 12th, 2010–11 8th
Biggest win: 10-1 v Ipswich (Div 1) 26 Dec, 1963
Biggest defeat: 0-10 v Liverpool (League Cup 2) 23 Sep, 1986
Highest League scorer in a season: Frank Newton 43 (1931–32)
Most League goals in aggregate: Gordon Davies 159 (1978–84 and 1986–91)
Longest unbeaten League sequence: 15 matches (1999)
Longest sequence without a League win: 15 matches (1950)
Most capped player: Johnny Haynes (England) 56

Goalkeepers

Schwarzer, Mark	6.4	Middlesbrough	Sydney, Aus	06.10.72
Somogyi, Csaba	6.3	Rakospalotai	Dunaujvaros, Hun	07.04.85
Stockdale, David	6.3	Darlington	Leeds	28.09.85
Defenders				
Baird, Chris	5.10	Southampton	Ballymoney	25.02.82
Briggs, Matthew	6.2	–	Wandsworth	09.03.91
Halliche, Rafik	6.2	Benfica	Toulon, Fr	02.09.86
Hangeland, Brede	6.5	Copenhagen	Houston, US	20.06.81
Hughes, Aaron	6.1	Aston Villa	Cookstown	08.11.79
Kelly, Stephen	5.11	Birmingham	Dublin, Ire	06.09.83
Salcido, Carlos	5.9	PSV	Ocotian, Mex	02.01.80
Senderos, Philippe	6.3	Arsenal	Geneva, Swi	14.02.85
Midfielders				
Davies, Simon	5.11	Everton	Haverfordwest	23.10.79
Dempsey, Clint	6.1	New England	Nacogdoches, US	09.03.83
Duff, Damien	5.10	Newcastle	Ballyboden, Ire	02.03.79
Etuhu, Dickson	6.2	Sunderland	Kano, Nig	08.06.82
Greening, Jonathan	5.11	WBA	Scarborough	02.01.79
Murphy, Danny	5.9	Tottenham	Chester	18.03.77
Riise, Bjorn Helge	5.9	Lillestrom	Alesund, Nor	21.06.83
Sidwell, Steve	5.10	Aston Villa	Wandsworth	14.12.82
Forwards				
Dalla Valle, Lauri	5.11	Liverpool	Kontiolahti, Fin	14.09.91
Dembele, Moussa	6.1	AZ	Wilrijk, Bel	16.07.87
Johnson, Andy	5.9	Crystal Palace	Bedford	10.02.81
Zamora, Bobby	6.0	West Ham	Barking	16.01.81

LIVERPOOL

Ground: Anfield, Liverpool L4 OTH
Telephone: 0151 263 2361. **Club nickname:** Reds or Pool
First-choice colours: Red shirts; red shorts; red socks
Record transfer fee: £35,000,000 to Newcastle for Andy Carroll, Jan 2011
Record fee received: £50,000,000 from Chelsea for Fernando Torres, Jan 2011
Record attendance: 61,905 v Wolves, (FA Cup 4), 2 Feb, 1952
Capacity for 2011–12: 45,522. **Main sponsor:** Standard Chartered
League Championship: Winners 1900–01, 1905–06, 1921–22, 1922–23, 1946–47, 1963–64, 1965–66, 1972–73, 1975–76, 1976–77, 1978–79, 1979–80, 1981–82, 1982–83, 1983–84, 1985–86, 1987–88, 1989–90
FA Cup: Winners 1965, 1974, 1986, 1989, 1992, 2001, 2006
League Cup: Winners 1981, 1982, 1983, 1984, 1995, 2001, 2003
European competitions: Winners European Cup 1976–77, 1977–78, 1980–81, 1983–84, 2004–05; UEFA Cup 1972–73, 1975–76, 2000–01; European Super Cup 1977, 2005

Finishing positions in Premier League: 1992–93 6th, 1993–94 8th, 1994–95 4th, 1995–96 3rd, 1996–97 4th, 1997–98 3rd, 1998–99 7th, 1999–2000 4th, 2000–01 3rd, 2001–02 2nd, 2002–03 5th, 2003–04 4th, 2004–05 5th, 2005–06 3rd, 2006–07 3rd, 2007–08 4th, 2008–09 2nd, 2009–10 7th, 2010–11 6th
Biggest win: 10-1 v Rotherham (Div 2) 18 Feb, 1896. Also: 11-0 v Stromsgodset (Cup-Winners' Cup 1) 17 Sep, 1974
Biggest defeat: 1-9 v Birmingham (Div 2) 11 Dec, 1954
Highest League scorer in a season: Roger Hunt 41 (1961–62)
Most League goals in aggregate: Roger Hunt 245 (1959–69)
Longest unbeaten League sequence: 31 matches (1987–88)
Longest sequence without a League win: 14 matches (1953–54)
Most capped player: Steven Gerrard (England) 89

Goalkeepers				
Gulacsi, Peter	6.3	Hungaria	Budapest, Hun	06.05.90
Hansen, Martin	6.2	Brondby	Glostrup, Den	15.06.90
Jones, Brad	6.3	Middlesbrough	Armadale, Aus	19.03.82
Reina, Jose	6.2	Villarreal	Madrid, Sp	31.08.82
Defenders				
Agger, Daniel	6.3	Brondby	Hvidovre, Den	12.12.84
Aurelio, Fabio	5.8	Valencia	Sao Carlos, Br	24.09.79
Ayala, Daniel	6.3	Sevilla	El Saucejo, Sp	07.11.90
Carragher, Jamie	6.1	–	Liverpool	28.01.78
Degen, Philipp	6.1	Borussia Dortmund	Holstein, Swi	15.02.83
Flanagan, John			Liverpool	01.01.93
Johnson, Glen	5.11	Portsmouth	Greenwich	23.08.84
Kelly, Martin	6.3	–	Whiston	27.04.90
Konchesky, Paul	5.10	Fulham	Barking	15.05.81
Kyrgiakos, Sotirios	6.4	AEK Athens	Trikala, Gre	23.07.79
Robinson, Jack	5.7	–	Warrington	01.09.93
Skrtel, Martin	6.3	Zenit St Petersburg	Handlova, Slovak	15.12.84
Wilson, Danny	6.2	Rangers	Livingston	27.12.91
Midfielders				
Adam, Charlie	6.1	Blackpool	Dundee	10.12.85
Bruna, Gerardo	5.8	Real Madrid	Mendoza, Arg	29.01.91
Cole, Joe	5.9	Chelsea	Islington	08.11.81
Gerrard, Steven	6.1	–	Whiston	30.05.80
Henderson, Jordan	5.10	Sunderland	Sunderland	17.06.90
Lucas	5.10	Gremio	Dourados, Br	09.01.87
Maxi Rodriguez	5.11	Atletico Madrid	Rosario, Arg	02.01.81
Meireles, Raul	5.11	Porto	Porto, Por	17.03.83
Poulsen, Christian	6.0	Juventus	Asnaes, Den	28.02.80
Shelvey, Jonjo	6.0	Charlton	Romford	27.02.92
Spearing, Jay	5.6		Wirral	25.11.88
Forwards				
Carroll, Andy	6.3	Newcastle	Gateshead	06.01.89
Kuyt, Dirk	6.0	Feyenoord	Katwijk, Hol	22.07.80
Ngog, David	6.3	Paris SG	Gennevilliers, Fr	01.04.89
Pacheco, Daniel	5.6	Barcelona	Malaga, Sp	05.01.91
Suarez, Luis	5.11	Ajax	Salto, Urug	24.01.87

MANCHESTER CITY

Ground: City of Manchester Stadium, Sportcity, Manchester M11 3FF
Telephone: 0870 062 1894. **Club nickname:** City

First-choice-colours: Sky blue shirts; white shorts; sky blue socks
Record transfer fee: £32,500,000 to Real Madrid for Robinho, Aug 2008
Record fee received: £21,000,000 from Chelsea for Shaun Wright-Phillips, Jul 2005
Record attendance: At Maine Road: 84,569 v Stoke (FA Cup 6) 3 Mar, 1934 (British record for any game outside London or Glasgow). At City of Manchester Stadium: 47,370 v Tottenham (Prem Lge) 5 May, 2010
Capacity for 2011–12: 47,715. **Main sponsor:** Etihad
League Championship: Winners 1936–37, 1967–68
FA Cup: Winners 1904, 1934, 1956, 1969, 2011
League Cup: Winners 1970, 1976
European competitions: Winners Cup-Winners' Cup 1969–70
Finishing positions in Premier League: 1992–93 9th, 1993–94 16th, 1994–95 17th, 1995–96 18th, 2000–01: 18th, 2002–03 9th, 2003–04 16th, 2004–05 8th, 2005–06 15th, 2006–07 14th, 2007–08 9th, 2008–09 10th, 2009–10 5th, 2010–11 3rd
Biggest win: 10-1 Huddersfield (Div 2) 7 Nov, 1987. Also: 10-1 v Swindon (FA Cup 4) 29 Jan, 1930
Biggest defeat: 1-9 v Everton (Div 1) 3 Sep, 1906
Highest League scorer in a season: Tommy Johnson 38 (1928–29)
Most League goals in aggregate: Tommy Johnson, 158 (1919–30)
Longest unbeaten League sequence: 22 matches (1946–47)
Longest sequence without a League win: 17 matches (1979–80)
Most capped player: Colin Bell (England) 48

Goalkeepers

Given, Shay	6.1	Newcastle	Lifford, Ire	20.04.76
Hart, Joe	6.3	Shrewsbury	Shrewsbury	19.04.87
Gonzalez, David	6.4	Huracan	Medellin, Col	20.07.82
Nielsen, Gunnar	6.3	Blackburn	Torshavn, Far	07.10.86

Defenders

Boateng, Jerome	6.4	Hamburg	Berlin, Ger	03.09.88
Boyata, Dedryck	6.2	Brussels	Uccle, Bel	28.11.90
Bridge, Wayne	5.10	Chelsea	Southampton	05.08.80
Clichy, Gael	5.11	Arsenal	Toulouse, Fr	26.07.85
Cunningham, Greg	6.0	–	Carnmore, Ire	31.01.91
Kolarov, Aleksandar	6.2	Lazio	Belgrade, Ser	10.11.85
Kompany, Vincent	6.4	Hamburg	Uccle, Bel	10.04.86
Lescott, Joleon	6.2	Everton	Birmingham	16.08.82
Onuoha, Nedum	6.2	–	Warri, Nig	12.11.86
Richards, Micah	5.11	–	Birmingham	24.06.88
Savic, Stefan	6.1	Partizan	Mojkovac, Mont	08.01.91
Toure, Kolo	6.0	Arsenal	Bouake, Iv C	19.03.81
Zabaleta, Pablo	5.10	Espanyol	Buenos Aires, Arg	16.01.85

Midfielders

Barry, Gareth	6.0	Aston Villa	Hastings	23.02.81
De Jong, Nigel	5.8	Hamburg	Amsterdam, Hol	30.11.84
Ibrahim, Abdisalam	6.2	Fjellhamar	Mogadishu, Som	01.05.91
Johnson, Adam	5.9	Middlesbrough	Sunderland	14.07.87
Johnson, Michael	6.0	–	Urmston	03.03.88
Milner, James	5.11	Aston Villa	Leeds	04.01.86
Silva, David	5.7	Valencia	Arguineguin, Sp	08.01.86
Toure, Yaya	6.3	Barcelona	Bouake, Iv C	13.05.83
Weiss, Vladimir	5.8	Inter Bratislava	Bratislava, Slov	30.11.89
Wright-Phillips, Shaun	5.6	Chelsea	Greenwich	25.10.81

Forwards

Adebayor, Emmanuel	6.3	Arsenal	Lome, Tog	24.12.84

Balotelli, Mario	6.3	Inter Milan	Palermo, It	12.08.90
Bellamy, Craig	5.9	West Ham	Cardiff	13.07.79
Caicedo, Felipe	6.1	Basle	Guayaquil, Ec	05.09.88
Dzeko, Edin	6.4	Wolfsburg	Sarajevo, Bos	17.03.86
Jo	6.3	CSKA Moscow	Sao Paulo, Br	20.03.87
Santa Cruz, Roque	6.2	Blackburn	Asuncion, Par	16.08.81
Tchuimeni–Nimely, Alex	5.11	Cotonsport	Monrovia, Lib	11.05.91
Tevez, Carlos	5.8	Manchester Utd	Ciudadela, Arg	05.02.84

MANCHESTER UNITED

Ground: Old Trafford Stadium, Sir Matt Busby Way, Manchester, M16 0RA
Telephone: 0161 868 8000. **Club nickname:** Red Devils
First-choice colours: Red shirts; white shorts; black socks
Record transfer fee: £30,750,000 to Tottenham for Dimitar Berbatov, Aug 2009
Record fee received: £80,000,000 from Real Madrid for Cristiano Ronaldo, Jun 2009
Record attendance: 76,098 v Blackburn (Prem Lge), 31 Mar, 2007. Also: 76,962 Wolves v Grimsby Town (FA Cup semi-final) 25 Mar, 1939. Crowd of 83,260 saw Manchester Utd v Arsenal (Div 1) 17 Jan, 1948 at Maine Road – Old Trafford out of action through bomb damage
Capacity for 2011–12: 75,797. **Main sponsor:** AON
League Championship: Winners 1907–08, 1910–11, 1951–52, 1955–56, 1956–7, 1964–65, 1966–67, 1992–93, 1993–94, 1995–96, 1996–97, 1998–99, 1999–2000, 2000–01, 2002–03, 2006–07, 2007–08, 2008–09, 2010–11
FA Cup: Winners 1909, 1948, 1963, 1977, 1983, 1985, 1990, 1994, 1996, 1999, 2004
League Cup: Winners 1992, 2006, 2009
European competitions: Winners European Cup 1967–68, 1998–99, 2007–08; Cup-Winners' Cup 1990–91; European Super Cup 1991
World Club Cup: Winners 2008
Finishing positions in Premier League : 1992–93 1st, 1993–94 1st, 1994–95 2nd, 1995–96 1st, 1996–97 1st, 1997–98 2nd, 1998–99 1st, 1999–2000 1st, 2000–01 1st, 2001–02 3rd, 2002–03 1st, 2003–04 3rd, 2004–05 3rd, 2005–06 2nd, 2006–07 1st, 2007–08 1st, 2000–09: 1st, 2009–10 2nd, 2010–11 1st
Biggest win: As Newton Heath: 10-1 v Wolves (Div 1) 15 Oct, 1892. As Manchester Utd: 9-0 v Ipswich (Prem Lge), 4 Mar, 1995. Also: 10-0 v Anderlecht (European Cup prelim rd) 26 Sep, 1956
Biggest defeat: 0-7 v Blackburn (Div 1) 10 Apr, 1926, v Aston Villa (Div 1) 27 Dec 1930, v Wolves (Div 2) 26 Dec, 1931
Highest League scorer in a season: Dennis Viollet 32 (1959–60)
Most League goals in aggregate: Bobby Charlton 199 (1956–73)
Longest unbeaten League sequence: 29 matches (1998–99)
Longest sequence without a League win: 16 matches (1930)
Most capped player: Bobby Charlton (England) 106

Goalkeepers
Amos, Ben	6.1	–	Macclesfield	10.04.90
De Gea, David	6.4	Atletico Madrid	Madrid, Sp	07.11.90
Kuszczak, Tomasz	6.3	WBA	Krosno, Pol	20.03.82
Lindegaard, Anders	6.4	Aalesund	Odense, Den	13.04.84

Defenders
Da Silva, Fabio	5.6	Fluminense	Petropolis, Br	09.07.90
Da Silva Rafael	5.6	Fluminense	Petropolis, Br	09.07.90
Evans, Jonny	6.2	–	Belfast	03.01.88
Evra, Patrice	5.8	Monaco	Dakar, Sen	15.05.81
Ferdinand, Rio	6.2	Leeds	Peckham	08.11.78

Jones, Phil	5.11	Blackburn	Blackburn	21.02.92
Smalling, Chris	6.1	Fulham	Greenwich	22.11.89
Vidic, Nemanja	6.3	Spartak Moscow	Uzice, Serb	21.10.81
Midfielders				
Anderson	5.0	Porto	Alegre, Br	13.04.88
Carrick, Michael	6.0	Tottenham	Wallsend	28.07.81
Cleverley, Tom	5.10	–	Basingstoke	12.08.89
Fletcher, Darren	6.0	–	Edinburgh	01.02.84
Gibson, Darron	5.9	–	Derry	25.10.87
Giggs, Ryan	5.11	–	Cardiff	29.11.73
Ji-Sung Park	5.9	PSV Eindhoven	Suwon, S Kor	25.02.81
Nani	5.10	Sporting Lisbon	Praia, Por	17.11.86
Norwood, Oliver	5.11	–	Burnley	12.04.91
Obertan, Gabriel	6.1	Bordeaux	Pantin, Fr	26.02.89
Valencia, Antonio	5.10	Wigan	Lago Agrio, Ec	04.08.85
Young, Ashley	5.10	Aston Villa	Stevenage	09.07.85
Forwards				
Berbatov, Dimitar	6.2	Tottenham	Blagoevgrad, Bul	30.01.81
Diouf, Mame Biram	6.1	Molde	Dakar, Sen	16.12.87
Hernandez, Javier	5.8	Chivas	Guadalajara, Mex	01.06.88
Macheda, Federico	6.0	Lazio	Rome, It	22.08.91
Owen, Michael	5.8	Newcastle	Chester	14.12.79
Rooney, Wayne	5.10	Everton	Liverpool	24.10.85
Welbeck, Danny	5.10	–	Manchester	26.11.90

NEWCASTLE UNITED

Ground: St James' Park, Newcastle-upon-Tyne, NE1 4ST
Telephone: 0844 372 1892. **Club nickname:** Magpies
First-choice colours: Black and white shirts; black shorts; black socks
Record transfer fee: £16,500,000 to Real Madrid for Michael Owen, Aug 2005
Record fee received: £35,000,000 from Liverpool for Andy Carroll, Jan 2011
Record attendance: 68,386 v Chelsea (Div 1) 3 September, 1930
Capacity for 2011–12: 52,339. **Main sponsor:** Northern Rock
League Championship: Winners 1904-05, 1906-07, 1908-09, 1926-27
FA Cup: Winners 1910, 1924, 1932, 1951, 1952, 1955
League Cup: Runners-up 1976
European competitions: Winners Fairs Cup 1968-69, Anglo-Italian Cup 1972-73
Finishing positions in Premier League: 1993-94 3rd 1994-95 6th 1995-96 2nd 1996-97 2nd 1997-98 13th 1998-99 13th, 1999-2000 11th, 2000-01 11th, 2001-02 4th, 2002-03 3rd, 2003-04 5th, 2004-05 14th, 2005-06 7th, 2006-07 13th, 2007-08 12th; 2008-09 18th, 2010-11 12th
Biggest win: 13-0 v Newport (Div 2) 5 Oct, 1946
Biggest defeat: 0-9 v Burton (Div 2) 15 Apr, 1895
Highest League scorer in a season: Hughie Gallacher 36 (1926-27)
Most League goals in aggregate: Jackie Milburn 177 (1946-57)
Longest unbeaten League sequence: 14 matches (1950)
Longest sequence without a League win: 21 matches (1978)
Most capped player: Shay Given (Republic of Ireland) 83

Goalkeepers

Forster, Fraser	6.0	–	Hexham	17.03.88
Harper, Steve	6.2	–	Easington	14.03.75
Krul, Tim	6.3	Den Haag	Den Haag, Hol	03.04.88

Soderberg, Ole	6.3	–		Norrkoping, Swe	20.07.90

Defenders

Coloccini, Fabricio	6.0	Dep La Coruna		Cordoba, Arg	22.01.82
Jose Enrique	6.0	Villarreal		Valencia, Sp	23.01.86
Simpson, Danny	6.0	Manchester Utd		Salford	04.01.87
Perch, James	6.0	Nottm Forest		Mansfield	28.09.85
Taverner, James	5.9	–		Bradford	31.10.91
Taylor, Ryan	5.8	Wigan		Liverpool	19.08.84
Taylor, Steven	6.2	–		Greenwich	23.01.86
Williamson, Mike	6.4	Portsmouth		Stoke	08.11.83

Midfielders

Barton, Joey	5.9	Manchester City		Huyton	02.09.82
Ben Arfa, Hatem	5.10	Marseille		Clamart, Fr	07.03.87
Cabaye, Yohan	5.9	Lille		Tourcoing, Fr	14.01.86
Donaldson, Ryan	5.10	–		Newcastle	01.05.91
Ferguson, Shane	5.11	–		Derry	12.07.91
Gosling, Dan	5.10	Everton		Brixham	02.02.90
Guthrie, Danny	5.9	Liverpool		Shrewsbury	18.04.87
Gutierrez, Jonas	6.0	Real Mallorca		Saenz Pena, Arg	05.07.82
Inman, Bradden	6.1	–		Adelaide, Aus	10.12.91
LuaLua, Kazenga	5.11	–		Kinshasa, DR Con	10.12.90
Marveaux, Sylvain	5.8	Rennes		Vannes, Fr	15.04.86
Abeid, Mehdi	5.10	Lens		Montreuil, Fr	06.08.92
Richardson, Michael	–	–		Newcastle	17.03.92
Routledge, Wayne	5.7	QPR		Eltham	07.01.85
Smith, Alan	5.9	Manchester Utd		Leeds	28.10.80
Tiote, Cheik	5.11	Twente		Yamoussoukro, Iv C	21.06.86
Vuckic, Haris	6.2	Domzale		Ljubljana, Sloven	21.08.92

Forwards

Ameobi, Shola	6.3	–		Zaria, Nig	12.10.81
Best, Leon	6.1	Coventry		Nottingham	19.09.86
Demba Ba	6.3	Hoffenhaim		Sevres, Fr	25.05.85
Lovenkrands, Peter	6.0	Schalke		Horsholm, Den	29.01.80
Ranger, Nile	6.2	–		Highgate	11.04.91

NORWICH CITY

Ground: Carrow Road, Norwich NR1 1JE
Telephone: 01603 760760. **Club nickname:** Canaries
First-choice colours: Yellow shirts; green and yellow shorts; yellow socks
Record transfer fee: £3.5m to WBA for Robert Earnshaw, Jan 2006
Record fee received: £7.25m from West Ham for Dean Ashton, Jan 2006
Record attendance: 43,984 v Leicester City (FA Cup 6), 30 Mar, 1963
Capacity for 2011–12: 27,033. **Main sponsor:** Aviva
League Championship: 3rd 1993
FA Cup: semi-finals 1959, 1989, 1992
League Cup: Winners 1962, 1985
European competitions: UEFA Cup rd 3, 1993-94
Finishing positions in Premier League: 1992-93: 3rd, 1993-94 12th, 1994-95 20th, 2004-05 19th
Biggest win: 10-2 v Coventry (Div 3S) 15 Mar, 1930. Also: 8-0 v Sutton (FA Cup 4) 28 Jan, 1989
Biggest defeat: 2-10 v Swindon (Southern Lge) Sep 5, 1908
Highest League scorer in a season: Ralph Hunt 31 (1955-56)

Most League goals in aggregate: Johnny Gavin 122 (1945-54, 55-58)
Longest unbeaten League sequence: 20 matches (1950)
Longest sequence without a League win: 25 matches (1956-7)
Most capped player: Mark Bowen (Wales) 35

Goalkeepers

Rudd, Declan	6.1	–	Diss	16.01.91
Ruddy, John	6.4	Everton	St Ives, Cam	24.10.86
Steer, Jed	6.0	–	Norwich	23.09.92

Defenders

Barnett, Leon	6.1	WBA	Stevenage	30.11.85
De Laet, Ritchie	6.1	Manchester Utd	Antwerp, Bel	28.11.88
Drury, Adam	5.10	Peterborough	Cambridge	29.08.78
Francomb, George	6.0	–	London	08.09.91
Martin, Russell	6.0	Peterborough	Brighton	04.01.86
Smith, Steven	5.10	Rangers	Bellshill	30.08.85
Tierney, Marc	6.0	Colchester	Prestwich	23.08.85
Ward, Elliott	6.1	Coventry	Harrow	19.01.85
Whitbread, Zak	6.2	Norwich	Houston, US	04.03.84

Midfielders

Adeyemi, Tom	6.0	–	Norwich	24.10.91
Bennett, Elliott	5.9	Brighton	Telford	18.12.88
Crofts, Andrew	5.11	Brighton	Chatham	29.05.84
Dawkin, Josh	5.9	–	Huntingdon	16.01.92
Fox, David	5.9	Norwich	Leek	13.12.83
Hoolahan, Wes	5.7	Blackpool	Dublin, Ire	10.08.83
Hughes, Stephen	5.11	Motherwell	Motherwell	14.11.82
Johnson, Bradley	6.0	Leeds	Hackney	28.04.87
Lappin, Simon	5.11	St Mirren	Glasgow	25.01.83
McNamee, Anthony	5.6	Swindon	Lambeth	13.07.83
Pilkington, Anthony	6.0	Huddersfield	Blackburn	06.06.88
Smith, Korey	6.0	–	Hatfield	31.01.91
Surman, Andrew	5.11	Wolves	Johannesburg, SA	20.08.86
Tudur Jones, Owain	6.2	Swansea	Bangor	15.10.84

Forwards

Daley, Luke	5.10	–	Northampton	10.11.89
Holt, Grant	6.0	Shrewsbury	Carlisle	12.04.81
Jackson, Simeon	5.8	Gillingham	Kingston	28.03.87
Johnson, Oli	5.11	Stockport	Wakefield	06.11.87
Martin, Chris	5.10	–	Beccles	04.11.88
McDonald, Cody	6.0	Dartford	Witham	30.05.86
Morison, Steve	6.2	Millwall	Enfield	29.08.83
Vaughan, James	5.11	Everton	Birmingham	14.07.88
Wilbraham, Aaron	6.3	MK Dons	Knutsford	21.10.79

QUEENS PARK RANGERS

Ground: Loftus Road Stadium, South Africa Road, London W12 7PA
Telephone: 0208 743 0262. **Club nickname:** Hoops
First-choice colours: Blue and white shirts; blue shorts; blue and white socks
Record transfer fee: £3,500,000 to Instituto for Alejandro Faurlin, Jul 2009
Record fee received: £6,000,000 from Newcastle for Les Ferdinand, Jun 1995
Record attendance: 35,353 v Leeds (Div 1) 27 Apr, 1974
Capacity for 2011–12: 18,360. **Main sponsor:** Gulf Air

League Championship: Runners-up: 1975-76
FA Cup: Runners-up 1982
League Cup: Winners 1967
European competitions: UEFA Cup quarter-finals 1976-77
Finishing positions in Premier League: 1992-93 5th, 1993-94 9th, 1994-95 8th, 1995-96 19th
Biggest win: 9-2 v Tranmere (Div 3) 3 Dec, 1960. Also: 8-1 v Bristol Rov (FA Cup 1) 27 Nov, 1937; 8-1 v Crewe (Lge Cup 1) 3 October 1983
Biggest defeat: 1-8 v Mansfield (Div 3) 15 Mar 1965; 1-8 v Manchester Utd (Div 1) 19 Mar 1969
Highest League scorer in a season: George Goddard 37 (1929-30)
Most League goals in aggregate: George Goddard 172 (1926-34)
Longest unbeaten League sequence: 20 matches (1972)
Longest sequence without a League win: 20 matches (1968-69)
Most capped player: Alan McDonald (Northern Ireland) 52

Goalkeepers

Cerny, Radek	6.4	Slavia Prague	Prague, Cze	18.02.74
Kenny, Paddy	6.1	Sheffield Utd	Halifax	17.05.78

Defenders

Borrowdale, Gary	6.0	Coventry	Sutton	16.07.85
Connolly, Matthew	6.1	Arsenal	Barnet	24.09.87
Gorkss, Kaspars	6.3	Blackpool	Riga, Lat	06.11.81
Hall, Fitz	6.4	Wigan	Walthamstow	20.12.80
Hill, Clint	6.0	Crystal Palace	Liverpool	22.02.80
Orr, Bradley	6.0	Bristol City	Liverpool	01.11.82
Ramage, Peter	6.1	Newcastle	Ashington	22.11.83
Shittu, Danny	6.3	Millwall	Lagos, Nig	02.09.80

Midfielders

Buzsaky, Akos	5.11	Plymouth Argyle	Budapest, Hun	07.05.82
Cook, Lee	5.9	Fulham	Hammersmith	03.08.82
Derry, Shaun	5.10	Crystal Palace	Nottingham	06.12.77
Doughty, Michael	6.1	–	Westminster	20.11.92
Ehmer, Max	6.2	–	Frankfurt, Ger	03.02.92
Ephraim, Hogan	5.9	West Ham	Islington	31.03.88
Faurlin, Alejandro	6.1	Instituto	Rosario, Arg	09.08.86
Rowlands, Martin	5.9	Brentford	Hammersmith	08.02.79
Taarabt, Adel	5.11	Tottenham	Taza, Mor	24.05.89
Moen, Petter Vaagan	5.10	Brann	Hamar, Nor	05.02.84

Forwards

Agyemang, Patrick	6.1	Preston	Walthamstow	29.09.81
Clarke, Leon	6.2	Sheffield Wed	Birmingham	10.02.85
German, Antonio	5.10	–	Wembley	26.12.91
Helguson, Heidar	5.10	Bolton	Akureyri, Ice	22.08.77
Hulse, Rob	6.1	Derby	Crewe	25.10.79
Mackie, Jamie	5.08	Plymouth	Dorking	22.09.85
Smith, Tommy	5.10	Portsmouth	Hemel Hempstead	22.05.80

STOKE CITY

Ground: Britannia Stadium, Stanley Matthews Way, Stoke-on-Trent ST4 7EG
Telephone: 0871 663 2008. **Club nickname:** Potters
First-choice colours: Red and white shirts; white shorts; white socks
Record transfer fee: £8,000,000 to Sunderland for Kenwyne Jones, Aug 2010

Record fee received: £4,500,000 from Wolfsburg for Tuncay, Jan 2011
Record attendance: Victoria Ground: 51,380 v Arsenal (Div 1) 29 Mar, 1937
Britannia Stadium: 28,376 v Everton (FA Cup 3) 5 Jan, 2002
Capacity for 2011–12: 27,500. **Main sponsor:** Britannia
League Championship: 4th 1935–36, 1946–47
FA Cup: Final 2011
League Cup: Winners 1972
Finishing position in Premier League: 2008–09 12th, 2009–10 11th, 2010–11 13th
European competitions: UEFA Cup 1972–73, 1974–75
Biggest win: 10-3 v WBA (Div 1) 4 Feb, 1937
Biggest defeat: 0-10 v Preston (Div 1) 14 Sep, 1889
Highest League scorer in a season: Freddie Steele 33 (1936–37)
Most League goals in aggregate: Freddie Steele 142 (1934–49)
Longest unbeaten League sequence: 25 matches (1992–93)
Longest sequence without a League win: 17 matches (1989)
Most capped player: Gordon Banks (England) 37

Goalkeepers

Begovic, Asmir	6.5	Portsmouth	Trebinje, Bos	20.06.87
Nash, Carlo	6.5	Everton	Bolton	13.09.73
Sorensen, Thomas	6.5	Aston Villa	Federica, Den	12.06.76

Defenders

Collins, Danny	5.11	Sunderland	Chester	06.08.80
Davies, Andrew	6.3	Southampton	Stockton	17.12.84
Diao, Salif	5.11	Liverpool	Kedougou, Sen	10.02.77
Higginbotham, Danny	6.1	Sunderland	Manchester	29.12.78
Huth, Robert	6.2	Middlesbrough	Berlin, Ger	18.08.84
Pugh, Danny	6.0	Preston	Manchester	19.10.82
Shawcross, Ryan	6.3	Manchester Utd	Chester	04.10.87
Shotton, Ryan	6.3	–	Stoke	30.09.88
Wilkinson, Andy	5.11	–	Stone	06.08.84
Woodgate, Jonathan	6.2	Tottenham	Middlesbrough	22.01.80

Midfielders

Arismendi, Diego	6.2	Nacional	Montevideo, Uru	25.01.88
Delap, Rory	6.0	Sunderland	Sutton Coldfield	06.07.76
Etherington, Matthew	5.10	West Ham	Truro	14.08.81
Pennant, Jermaine	5.8	Real Zaragoza	Nottingham	15.01.83
Soares, Tom	6.0	Crystal Palace	Reading	10.07.86
Tonge, Michael	5.11	Sheffield Utd	Manchester	07.04.83
Whitehead, Dean	5.11	Sunderland	Abingdon	12.01.82
Whelan, Glenn	5.10	Sheffield Wed	Dublin, Ire	13.01.84
Wilson, Marc	6.2	Portsmouth	Belfast	17.08.87

Forwards

Fuller, Ricardo	6.3	Southampton	Kingston, Jam	31.10.79
Jones, Kenwyne	6.2	Sunderland	Point Fortin, Trin	05.01.84
Marshall, Ben	6.0	Crewe	Salford	29.09.91
Moult, Louis	6.0	–	Stoke	14.05.92
Sidibe, Mamady	6.4	Gillingham	Bamako, Mali	18.12.79
Walters, Jon	6.0	Ipswich	Birkenhead	20.09.83

SUNDERLAND

Ground: Stadium of Light, Sunderland SR5 1SU
Telephone: 0191 551 5000. **Club nickname:** Black Cats

First-choice colours: Red and white shirts; black shorts; black socks
Record transfer fee: £10,000,000 to Tottenham for Darren Bent, Aug 2009
Record fee received: £24,000,000 from Aston Villa for Darren Bent, Jan 2011
Record attendance: At Roker Park: 75,118 v Derby (FA Cup 6 replay) 8 Mar, 1933. At Stadium of Light: 48,707 v Liverpool (Prem Lge) 13 Apr, 2002
Capacity for 2011–12: 49,000. **Main sponsor:** Tombola
League Championship: Winners 1891–92, 1892–93, 1894–95, 1901–02, 1912–13, 1935–36
FA Cup: Winners 1937, 1973
League Cup: Runners-up 1985
European competitions: Cup-Winners' Cup rd 2 1973–74
Finishing positions in Premier League: 1996–97 18th, 1999–2000 7th, 2000–01 7th, 2001–02 17th, 2002–03 20th, 2005–06 20th, 2007–08 15th, 2008–09 16th, 2009–10 13th, 2010–11 10th
Biggest win: 9-1 v Newcastle (Div 1) 5 Dec, 1908. Also: 11-1 v Fairfield (FA Cup 1) 2 Feb, 1895
Biggest defeat: 0-8 v Sheffield Wed (Div 1) 26 Dec, 1911, v West Ham (Div 1) 19 Oct 1968, v Watford (Div 1) 25 Sep, 1982
Highest League scorer in a season: Dave Halliday 43 (1928–29)
Most League goals in aggregate: Charlie Buchan 209 (1911–25)
Longest unbeaten League sequence: 19 matches (1998–99)
Longest sequence without a League win: 22 matches (2003–04)
Most capped player: Charlie Hurley (Republic of Ireland) 38

Goalkeepers

Gordon, Craig	6.4	Hearts	Edinburgh	31.12.82
Mignolet, Simon	6.4	Sint-Truidense	Sint-Truiden, Bel	06.08.88
Westwood, Keiren	6.1	Coventry	Manchester	23.10.84

Defenders

Adams, Blair	5.11	–	South Shields	08.09.91
Angeleri, Marcos	6.0	Estudiantes	La Plata, Arg	07.04.83
Bardsley, Phil	5.11	Manchester Utd	Salford	28.06.85
Bramble, Titus	6.1	Wigan	Ipswich	21.07.81
Brown, Wes	6.1	Manchester Utd	Manchester	13.10.79
Ferdinand, Anton	6.0	West Ham	Peckham	18.02.85
Larsson, Sebastian	5.10	Birmingham	Eskiltuna, Swe	06.06.85
O'Shea, John	6.3	Manchester Utd	Waterford, Ire	30.04.81
Richardson, Kieran	5.10	Manchester Utd	Greenwich	21.10.84
Turner, Michael	6.4	Hull	Lewisham	09.11.83

Midfielders

Cattermole, Lee	5.10	Wigan	Stockton	21.03.88
Colback, Jack	5.9	–	Newcastle	24.10.89
Elmohamady, Ahmed	5.11	ENPPI	El-Mahalla, Egy	09.09.87
Gardner, Craig	5.10	Birmingham	Solihull	25.11.86
Knott, Billy	5.8	Chelsea	Canvey Island	28.11.92
Malbranque, Steed	5.8	Tottenham	Mouscron, Bel	06.01.80
Meyler, David	6.2	Cork	Cork, Ire	29.05.89
Riveros, Cristian	6.0	Cruz Azul	Saldivar, Par	16.10.82
Sessegnon, Stephane	5.8	Paris SG	Allahe, Benin	01.06.84
Vaughan, David	5.7	Blackpool	Rhuddlan	18.02.83

Forwards

Campbell, Fraizer	5.11	Manchester Utd	Huddersfield	13.09.87
Gyan, Asamoah	6.0	Rennes	Accra, Gh	22.11.85
Ji Dong-won	6.2	Chunnam	Jeju-do, S Kor	28.05.91

Lynch, Craig	5.9	–	Durham	25.03.92
Noble, Ryan	6.0	–	Sunderland	06.11.91
Wickham, Connor	6.3	Ipswich	Colchester	31.03.93

SWANSEA CITY

Ground: Liberty Stadium, Morfa, Swansea SA1 2FA
Telephone: 01792 616600. **Club nickname:** Swans
First-choice colours: White and black shirts; white and black shorts; white and black socks
Record transfer fee: £3,500,000 to Watford for Danny Graham, Jun 2011
Record fee received: £2,000,000 from Wigan for Jason Scotland, Jun 2009
Record attendance: Vetch Field: 32,786 v Arsenal (FA Cup 4) 17 Feb,
1968; Liberty Stadium: 19,816 v Nottm Forest (Champ play-off semi-final, 2nd leg) 16 May,
2011
Capacity for 2011–12: 20,532. **Main sponsor:** 32Red
League Championship: 6th 1981-82
FA Cup: Semi-finals 1926, 1964
League Cup: 4th rd 1965, 1977, 2009
European competitions: Cup-winners' Cup rd 2 1982-83
Biggest win: 8-0 v Hartlepool (Div 4) 1 Apr, 1978. Also: 12-0 v Sliema (Cup-winners' Cup 1st
rd 1st leg), 15 Sep, 1982
Biggest defeat: 0-8 v Liverpool (FA Cup 3) 9 Jan, 1990; 0-8 v Monaco (Cup-winners' Cup 1st
rd 2nd leg) 1 October, 1991
Highest League scorer in a season: Cyril Pearce 35 (1931-32)
Most League goals in aggregate: Ivor Allchuch 166 (1949-58, 1965-68)
Longest unbeaten League sequence: 19 matches (1970-71)
Longest sequence without a League win: 15 matches (1989)
Most capped player: Ivor Allchurch (Wales) 42

Goalkeepers

Cornell, David	6.0	–	Swansea	28.03.91
Ma-Kalambay, Yves	6.6	Hibernian	Brussels, Bel	31.01.86
Moreira, Jose	6.1	Benfica	Massarelos, Por	20.03.82

Defenders

Alfei, Daniel	5.11	–	Swansea	23.02.92
Caulker, Steven	6.3	Tottenham	Feltham	29.12.91
Monk, Garry	6.0	Barnsley	Bedford	06.03.79
Rangel, Angel	5.11	Terrassa	Tortosa, Sp	28.10.82
Tate, Alan	6.1	Manchester Utd	Easington	02.09.82
Taylor, Neil	5.9	Wrexham	St Asaph	07.02.89
Walsh, Joe	5.11	–	Cardiff	13.05.92
Williams, Ashley	6.0	Stockport	Wolverhampton	23.08.84

Midfielders

Agustien, Kenny	5.10	AZ	Willemstad, Cur	20.08.86
Allen, Joe	5.7	–	Carmarthen	14.03.90
Britton, Leon	5.5	Sheffield Utd	Merton	16.09.82
Bodde, Ferrie	5.10	Den Haag	Delft, Hol	05.05.82
Cotterill, David	5.9	Sheffield Utd	Cardiff	04.12.87
Dyer, Nathan	5.10	Southampton	Trowbridge	29.11.87
Gower, Mark	5.11	Southend	Edmonton	05.10.78
Harley, Ryan	5.9	Exeter	Bristol	22.01.85
Lucas, Lee	5.10	–	Aberdare	10.06.92
MacDonald, Shaun	6.1	–	Swansea	17.06.88
Orlandi, Andrea	6.0	Alaves	Barcelona	03.08.84

Richards, Ashley	6.1	–	Swansea	12.04.91
Sinclair, Scott	5.10	Chelsea	Bath	25.03.89
Forwards				
Beattie, Craig	6.0	Swansea	Glasgow	16.01.84
Dobbie, Stephen	5.10	Queen of South	Glasgow	05.12.82
Moore, Luke	5.10	WBA	Birmingham	13.02.86
Pintado, Gorka	5.11	Granada	San Sebastian, Sp	24.03.78
Thomas, Casey	5.9	–	Port Talbot	14.11.90

TOTTENHAM HOTSPUR

Ground: White Hart Lane, Tottenham, London N17 OAP
Telephone: 0844 499 5000. **Club nickname:** Spurs
First-choice colours: White shirts; blue shorts; blue and white socks
Record transfer fee: £16,600,000 to Dinamo Zagreb for Luka Modric, Jun 2008
Record fee received: £30,750,000 from Manchester United for Dimitar Berbatov, Aug 2008
Record attendance: 75,038 v Sunderland (FA Cup 6) 5 Mar, 1938
Capacity for 2011–12: 36,230. **Main sponsor:** Autonomy
League Championship: Winners 1950–51, 1960–61
FA Cup: Winners 1901, 1921, 1961, 1962, 1967, 1981, 1982, 1991
League Cup: Winners 1971, 1973, 1999, 2008
European competitions: Winners Cup-Winners' Cup 1962–63, UEFA Cup 1971–72, 1983–84
Finishing positions in Premier League: 1992–93 8th, 1993–94 15th, 1994–95 7th, 1995–96 8th, 1996–97 10th, 1997–98 14th, 1998–99 11th, 1999–2000 10th, 2000–01 12th, 2001–02 9th, 2002–03 10th, 2003–04 14th, 2004–05 9th, 2005–06 5th, 2006–07 5th, 2007–08 11th, 2008–09 8th, 2009–10 4th, 2010–11 5th
Biggest win: 9-0 v Bristol Rov (Div 2) 22 Oct, 1977. Also: 13-2 v Crewe (FA Cup 4 replay) 3 Feb, 1960
Biggest defeat: 0-7 v Liverpool (Div 1) 2 Sep, 1979. Also: 0-8 v Cologne (Inter Toto Cup) 22 Jul, 1995
Highest League scorer in a season: Jimmy Greaves 37 (1962–63)
Most League goals in aggregate: Jimmy Greaves 220 (1961–70)
Longest unbeaten League sequence: 22 matches (1949)
Longest sequence without a League win: 16 matches (1934–35)
Most capped player: Pat Jennings (Northern Ireland) 74

Goalkeepers				
Alnwick, Ben	6.0	Sunderland	Gateshead	01.01.87
Cudicini, Carlo	6.1	Chelsea	Milan, It	06.09.73
Friedel, Brad	6.3	Aston Villa	Lakewood, US	18.05.71
Gomes, Heurelho	6.2	PSV Eindhoven	Joao Pinheiro, Br	15.12.81
Defenders				
Assou-Ekotto, Benoit	5.10	Lens	Arras, Fr	24.03.84
Bale, Gareth	6.0	Southampton	Cardiff	16.07.89
Bassong, Sebastien	6.1	Newcastle	Paris	09.07.86
Corluka, Vedran	6.3	Manchester City	Derventa, Bos	05.02.86
Dawson, Michael	6.2	Nottm Forest	Northallerton	18.11.83
Gallas, William	6.1	Arsenal	Asnieres, Fr	17.08.77
Hutton, Alan	6.1	Rangers	Glasgow	30.11.84
Kaboul, Younes	6.3	Portsmouth	St Julien, Fr	04.01.86
Khumalo, Bongani	6.2	Supersport	Manzini, Swaz	06.01.87
King, Ledley	6.2	–	Bow	12.10.80
Naughton, Kyle	5.10	Sheffield Utd	Sheffield	11.11.88
Walker, Kyle	5.10	Sheffield Utd	Sheffield	28.05.90

Midfielders

Bentley, David	5.10	Arsenal	Peterborough	27.08.84
Huddlestone, Tom	6.1	Derby	Nottingham	28.12.86
Jenas, Jermaine	6.0	Newcastle	Nottingham	18.02.83
Kranjcar, Niko	6.1	Portsmouth	Zagreb, Cro	13.08.84
Lennon, Aaron	5.5	Leeds	Leeds	16.04.87
Livermore, Jake	6.2	–	Enfield	14.11.89
Modric, Luka	5.7	Dinamo Zagreb	Zadar, Cro	09.09.85
Palacios, Wilson	6.0	Wigan	La Ceiba, Hon	29.07.84
Pienaar, Steven	5.9	Tottenham	Johannesburg, SA	17.03.82
Rose, Danny	5.8	Leeds	Doncaster	02.07.90
Sandro	6.2	Internacional	Riachinho, Br	15.03.89
Van der Vaart, Rafael	5.10	Real Madrid	Heemskerk, Hol	11.02.83

Forwards

Crouch, Peter	6.7	Portsmouth	Macclesfield	30.01.81
Defoe, Jermain	5.7	Portsmouth	Beckton	07.10.82
Dos Santos, Giovanni	5.9	Barcelona	Monterrey, Mex	11.05.89
Keane, Robbie	5.9	Liverpool	Dublin, Ire	08.07.80
Pavlyuchenko, Roman	6.1	Spartak Moscow	Mostovskoy, Rus	15.12.81

WEST BROMWICH ALBION

Ground: The Hawthorns, Halfords Lane, West Bromwich B71 4LF
Telephone: 0871 271 1100. **Club nickname**: Baggies
First-choice colours: Blue and white shirts; white shorts; blue socks
Record transfer fee: £4,700,000 to Real Mallora for Borja Valero, Aug 2008
Record fee received: £8,500,000 from Aston Villa for Curtis Davies, July 2008
Record attendance: 64,815 v Arsenal (FA Cup 6) 6 Mar, 1937.
Capacity for 2011–12: 26,500. **Main sponsor**: T-Mobile
League Championship: Winners 1919-20
FA Cup: Winners 1888, 1892, 1931, 1954, 1968
League Cup: Winners 1966
European competitions: Cup-Winners' Cup quarter-finals 1968-69. UEFA Cup quarter-finals 1978-79
Finishing positions in Premier League: 2002-03 19th, 2004-5 17th, 2005-6 19th; 2008-09 20th, 2010–11 11th
Biggest win: 12-0 v Darwen (Div 1) 4 Apr, 1892
Biggest defeat: 3-10 v Stoke (Div 1) 4 Feb, 1937
Highest League scorer in a season: William Richardson 39 (1935-36)
Most League goals in aggregate: Tony Brown 218 (1963-79)
Longest unbeaten League sequence: 17 matches (1957)
Longest sequence without a League win: 14 matches (1995)
Most capped player: Stuart Williams (Wales) 33

Goalkeepers

Daniels, Luke	6.4	Manchester Utd	Bolton	05.01.88
Myhill, Boaz	6.3	Hull	Modesto, US	09.11.82

Defenders

Cech, Marek	6.1	Porto	Trebisov, Slovak	26.01.83
Dawson, Craig	6.2	Rochdale	Rochdale	06.05.90
Downing, Paul	6.1	–	Taunton	26.10.91
Hurst, James		Portsmouth	Sutton Coldfield	31.01.92
Ibanez, Pablo	6.4	Atletico Madrid	Madrigueras, Sp	03.08.81
Jones, Billy	5.11	Preston	Shrewsbury	24.03.87
Mattock, Joe	6.0	Leicester	Leicester	15.05.90

McAuley, Gareth	6.3	Ipswich	Larne	05.12.79
Olsson, Jonas	6.4	Nijmegen	Landskrona, Swe	10.03.83
Shorey, Nicky	5.9	Aston Villa	Romford	19.02.81
Tamas, Gabriel	6.2	Auxerre	Brasov, Rom	09.11.83
Midfielders				
Brown, Kayleden	–	–	Birmingham	15.04.92
Brunt, Chris	6.1	Sheffield Wed	Belfast	14.12.84
Dorrans, Graham	5.9	Livingston	Glasgow	05.05.87
Jara, Gonzalo	5.10	Colo Colo	Santiago, Ch	29.08.85
Mantom, Sam	–	–	Stourbridge	20.02.92
Morrison, James	5.10	Middlesbrough	Darlington	25.05.86
Mulumbu, Youssuf	5.10	Paris SG	Kinshasa, DR Con	25.01.87
Reid, Steven	6.1	Blackburn	Kingston	10.03.81
Sawyers, Romaine	5.9	–	Birmingham	02.11.91
Scharner, Paul	6.3	Wigan	Schiebbs, Aut	11.03.80
Tchoyi, Somen	6.3	Salzburg	Douala, Cam	29.01.83
Thomas, Jerome	6.1	Portsmouth	Wembley	23.03.83
Thorne, George	6.2	–	Chatham	04.01.93
Forwards				
Bednar, Roman	6.4	Hearts	Prague, Cze	26.03.83
Cox, Simon	5.10	Swindon	Reading	28.04.87
Elford-Alliyu, Lateef	5.8	–	Ibadan, Nig	01.06.92
Fortune, Marc-Antoine	6.0	Celtic	Cayenne, Fr Gui	02.07.81
Miller, Ishmael	6.3	Manchester City	Manchester	05.03.87
Odemwingie, Peter	6.0	Lok Moscow	Tashkent, Uzbek	15.07.81
Wood, Chris	6.3	–	Auckland, NZ	07.12.91

WIGAN ATHLETIC

Ground: DW Stadium, Robin Park, Wigan WN5 0UZ
Telephone: 01942 774000. **Club nickname:** Latics
First-choice colours: Blue and white shirts; blue shorts; white socks
Record transfer fee: £7,000,000 to Newcastle for Charles N'Zogbia, Feb 2009
Record fee received: £15,250,000 from Manchester Utd for Antonio Valencia, Jun 2009
Record attendance: At Springfield Park: 27,526 v Hereford (FA Cup 2)
12 Dec, 1953. At DW Stadium: 25,113 v Manchester Utd (Prem Lge) 11 May, 2008
Capacity for 2011–12: 25,133. **Main sponsor:** 12Bet
League Championship: 10th 2005-06
FA Cup: 6th rd 1987
League Cup: Final 2006
Finishing positions in Premier League : 2005–06 10th, 2006–07 17th, 2007–08 14th, 2008–09 11th, 2009–10 16th, 2010–11 16th
Biggest win: 7-1 v Scarborough (Div 3) 11 Mar, 1997). Also: 6-0 v Carlisle (FA Cup 1) 24 Nov, 1934
Biggest defeat: 1-9 v Tottenham (Prem Lge) 22 Nov, 2009
Highest League scorer in a season: Graeme Jones 31 (1996–97)
Most League goals in aggregate: Andy Liddell 70 (1998–2004)
Longest unbeaten League sequence: 25 matches (1999–2000)
Longest sequence without a League win: 14 (1989)
Most capped player: Henri Camara (Senegal) 22

Goalkeepers

| Al Habsi, Ali | 6.5 | Bolton | Muscat, Om | 30.12.81 |
| Kirkland, Chris | 6.3 | Liverpool | Leicester | 02.05.81 |

Pollitt, Mike	6.4	Rotherham	Farnworth	29.02.72
Defenders				
Alcaraz, Antolin	6.2	Bruges	San Roque, Par	30.07.82
Amaya, Antonio	6.3	Rayo Vallecano	Madrid, Sp	31.05.83
Boyce, Emmerson	5.11	Crystal Palace	Aylesbury	24.09.79
Caldwell, Gary	5.11	Celtic	Stirling	12.04.82
Figueroa, Maynor	5.11	Olimpia	Juticalpa, Hond	02.05.83
Gohouri, Steve	6.2	Borussia M'gladbach	Treichville, Iv C	08.02.81
Golobart, Roman	6.4	Espanyol	Barcelona, Sp	21.03.92
Lopez, Adrian	6.0	Dep La Coruna	As Pontes, Sp	25.02.87
Mustoe, Jordan	–	–	Wirral	28.01.91
Robinson, Jordan	5.10	Middlesbrough	Yarm	28.04.91
Stam, Ronnie	5.9	Twente	Breda, Hol	18.06.84
Midfielders				
Diame, Mohamed	6.1	Rayo Vallecano	Creteil, Fr	14.06.87
Gomez, Jordi	5.10	Espanyol	Barcelona, Sp	24.05.85
McArthur, James	5.7	Hamilton	Glasgow	07.10.87
McCarthy, James	5.11	Hamilton	Glasgow	12.11.90
N'Zogbia, Charles	5.8	Newcastle	Harfleur, Fr	28.05.86
Thomas, Hendry	5.11	Olimpia	La Ceiba, Hon	23.02.85
Watson, Ben	5.10	Crystal Palace	Camberwell	09.07.85
Forwards				
Boselli, Mauro	6.0	Estudiantes	Buenos Aires, Arg	22.05.85
Di Santo, Franco	6.4	Chelsea	Mendoza, Arg	07.04.89
McManaman, Callum	5.11	Everton	Knowsley	25.04.91
Moses, Victor	5.10	Crystal Palace	Kaduna, Nig	12.12.90
Rodallega, Hugo	6.0	Necaxa	El Carmelo, Col	25.07.85
Sammon, Conor	6.1	Kilmarnock	Dublin, Ire	06.11.86

WOLVERHAMPTON WANDERERS

Ground: Molineux Stadium, Waterloo Road, Wolverhampton WV1 4QR
Telephone: 0871 222 2220. **Club nickname:** Wolves
First-choice colours: Gold shirts; black shorts; black socks
Record transfer fee: £6,500,000 to Reading for Kevin Doyle, Jun 2009 and to Burnley for Steven Fletcher, Jun 2010
Record fee received: £6,000,000 from Coventry for Robbie Keane, Aug 1999
Record attendance: 61,315 v Liverpool (FA Cup 5) 11 Feb, 1939
Capacity for 2011–12: 29,303. **Main sponsor:** Sportingbet
League Championship: Winners 1953–54, 1957–58, 1958–59
FA Cup: Winners 1893, 1908, 1949, 1960
League Cup: Winners 1974, 1980
European competitions: Runners-up UEFA Cup 1971–72
Finishing positions in Premier League: 2003-04 20th; 2009–10 15th
Biggest win: 10-1 v Leicester (Div 2) 15 Apr, 1938. Also: 14-0 v Crosswell's Brewery (FA Cup 2) 13 Nov, 1886
Biggest defeat: 1-10 v Newton Heath (Div 1) 15 Oct, 1892
Highest League scorer in a season: Dennis Westcott, 38, 1946–47
Most League goals in aggregate: Steve Bull, 250, 1986–98
Longest unbeaten League sequence: 20 matches (1923–24)
Longest sequence without a League win: 19 matches (1984–85)
Most capped player: Billy Wright (England) 105

Goalkeepers				
De Vries, Dorus	5.11	Swansea	Beverwijk, Hol	29.12.80
Hennessey, Wayne	6.0	–	Anglesey	24.01.87
Ikeme Carl	6.2	–	Sutton Coldfield	08.06.86
Defenders				
Batth, Danny	6.3	–	Brierley Hill	21.09.90
Berra, Christophe	6.1	Hearts	Edinburgh	31.01.85
Craddock, Jody	6.2	Sunderland	Redditch	25.07.75
Elokobi, George	6.0	Colchester	Mamfe, Cam	31.01.86
Foley, Kevin	5.9	Luton	Luton	01.11.84
Guedioura, Adlene	6.0	Charleroi	La Roche, Fr	12.11.85
Stearman, Richard	6.2	Leicester	Wolverhampton	19.08.87
Ward, Stephen	5.11	Bohemians	Dublin, Ire	20.08.85
Zubar, Ronald	6.1	Marseille	Les Abymes, Guad	20.09.85
Midfielders				
Davis, David	5.8	–	Smethwick	20.02.91
Edwards, David	5.11	Luton	Pontesbury	03.02.85
Hammill, Adam	5.10	Barnsley	Liverpool	25.01.88
Henry, Karl	6.1	Stoke	Wolverhampton	26.11.82
Hunt, Stephen	5.8	Hull	Port Laoise, Ire	01.08.80
Jarvis, Matt	5.8	Gillingham	Middlesbrough	22.05.86
Kightly, Michael	5.11	Grays	Basildon	24.01.86
Milijas, Nenad	6.2	Red Star Belgrade	Belgrade, Ser	30.04.83
O'Hara, Jamie	5.11	Tottenham	London	25.09.86
Forwards				
Doyle, Kevin	5.11	Reading	Wexford	18.09.83
Ebanks–Blake, Sylvan	5.10	Plymouth	Cambridge	29.03.86
Fletcher, Steven	6.1	Burnley	Shrewsbury	26.03.87
Gorman, Johnny	5.10	Manchester Utd	Sheffield	26.10.92
Griffiths, Leigh	5.9	Dundee	Edinburgh	20.08.90
Keogh, Andy	6.0	Scunthorpe	Dublin, Ire	16.05.86
Spray, James	6.0	–	Birmingham	02.12.92
Vokes, Sam	5.11	Bournemouth	Lymington	21.10.89
Winnall, Sam	5.9	–	Wolverhampton	19.01.91

NPOWER LEAGUE PLAYING STAFFS 2011–12

(At time of going to press)

CHAMPIONSHIP

BARNSLEY

Ground: Oakwell Stadium Barnsley S71 1ET
Telephone: 01226 211211. **Club nickname:** Tykes
First-choice colours: Red shirts; white shorts; red socks
Capacity for 2011–12: 23,287
Record attendance: 40,255 v Stoke (FA Cup 5) 15 Feb, 1936

Name	Height ft in	Previous club	Birthplace	Birthdate
Goalkeepers				
Preece, David	6.2	Odense	Sunderland	28.08.76

Steele, Luke	6.2	WBA	Peterborough	24.09.84
Defenders				
Butterfield, Jacob	5.11	Manchester Utd	Bradford	10.06.90
Edwards, Rob	6.1	Blackpool	Telford	25.12.82
Foster, Stephen	5.11	Burnley	Warrington	10.09.80
Hassell, Bobby	5.9	Mansfield	Derby	04.06.80
McEveley, Jay	6.1	Derby	Liverpool	11.02.85
McNulty, Jim	6.0	Brighton	Liverpool	13.02.85
Miller, Kern	5.10	–	Boston	09.02.91
Perkins, David	5.6	Colchester	Heysham	21.06.82
Potter, Luke	6.4	–	Barnsley	17.07.89
Wiseman, Scott	6.0	Rochdale	Hull	13.12.85
Midfielders				
Done, Matt	5.10	Rochdale	Oswestry	22.07.88
Doyle, Nathan	5.11	Hull	Derby	12.01.87
Haynes, Danny	5.11	Bristol City	Peckham	19.01.88
Lovre, Goran	6.3	Groningen	Zagreb, Cro	23.03.82
O'Brien, Jim	6.0	Motherwell	Vale of Leven	28.09.87
Taylor, Alastair	6.1	–	–	13.09.91
Forwards				
Davies, Craig	6.2	Chesterfield	Burton	09.01.86
Gray, Andy	6.0	Charlton	Harrogate	15.11.77
Noble-Lazarus, Reuben	5.11	–	Huddersfield	16.08.93
Rose, Danny	5.10	–	Barnsley	10.12.93

BIRMINGHAM CITY

Ground: St Andrew's, Birmingham B9 4NH
Telephone: 0844 557 1875. **Club nickname:** Blues
First-choice colours: Blue shirts; white shorts, blue socks
Capacity for 2011–12: 30,079
Record attendance: 66,844 v Everton (FA Cup 5) 11 Feb, 1939

Goalkeepers				
Butland, Jack	6.4	–	Bristol	10.03.93
Doyle, Colin	6.5	–	Cork, Ire	12.08.85
Foster, Ben	6.2	Manchester Utd	Leamington	03.04.83
Defenders				
Caldwell, Steven	5.11	Wigan	Stirling	12.09.80
Carr, Stephen	5.9	Newcastle	Dublin, Ire	29.08.76
Dann, Scott	6.2	Coventry	Liverpool	14.02.87
Davies, Curtis	6.2	Aston Villa	Waltham Forest	15.03.85
Johnson, Roger	6.3	Cardiff	Ashford	28.04.83
Kerr, Fraser	6.3	Motherwell	–	17.01.93
Murphy, David	6.1	Hibernian	Hartlepool	01.06.84
Ozturk, Alpashan	6.0	Beerschot	Antwerp, Bel	16.07.93
Ridgewell, Liam	5.10	Aston Villa	Bexley	21.07.84
Midfielders				
Beausejour, Jean	5.11	Club America	Santiago, Chi	01.06.84
Burke, Chris	5.9	Cardiff	Glasgow	02.12.83
Fahey, Keith	5.10	St Patrick's	Dublin, Ire	15.01.83
Ferguson, Barry	5.10	Rangers	Glasgow	02.02.78
Gomis, Morgaro	5.7	Dundee Utd	Paris, Fr	14.07.85
Michel	6.0	Gijon	Lena, Sp	08.11.85
Mutch, Jordon	5.9	Derby	Birmingham	02.12.91

| Redmond, Nathan | 5.8 | – | Birmingham | 06.03.94 |
| Valles, Enric | 6.3 | Breda | Barcelona, Sp | 01.03.90 |

Forwards

Asante, Akwasi	6.0	–	Amsterdam, Hol	06.09.92
Jerome, Cameron	6.1	Cardiff	Huddersfield	14.08.86
King, Marlon	6.1	Coventry	Dulwich	26.04.80
Rooney, Adam	6.2	Inverness	Dublin, Ire	21.04.88
Zigic, Nikola	6.8	Valencia	Backa Topola, Serb	25.09.80

BLACKPOOL

Ground: Bloomfield Road, Blackpool FY1 6JJ
Telephone: 0871 622 1953. **Club nickname:** Seasiders
First-choice colours: Tangerine shirts; white shorts; tangerine socks
Capacity for 20011–12: 16,220
Record attendance: 38,098 v Wolves (Div 1) 17 Sep, 1955

Goalkeepers

| Gilks, Matthew | 6.1 | Norwich | Rochdale | 04.06.82 |
| Halstead, Mark | 6.3 | – | Blackpool | 01.01.90 |

Defenders

Baptiste, Alex	5.11	Mansfield	Sutton–in–Ashfield	31.01.86
Cathcart, Craig	6.2	Manchester Utd	Belfast	06.02.89
Crainey, Stephen	5.9	Leeds	Glasgow	22.06.81
Eardley, Neal	5.11	Oldham	Llandudno	06.11.88
Eastham, Ashley	6.3	–	Preston	22.03.91
Evatt, Ian	6.3	QPR	Coventry	19.11.81
Hill, Matt	5.8	Barnsley	Bristol	26.03.81
Llera, Miguel	6.4	Charlton	Castillega, Sp	07.08.79

Midfielders

Basham, Chris	5.11	Bolton	Hebburn	18.02.88
Djordic, Bojan	6.0	Videoton	Belgrade, Serb	06.02.82
Grandin, Elliot	5.10	CSKA Mosow	Caen, Fr	17.10.87
Phillips, Matt	6.0	Wycombe	Aylesbury	13.03.91
Southern, Keith	5.10	Everton	Gateshead	21.04.84
Sylvestre, Ludovic	6.0	Mlada Boleslav	Paris, Fr	05.02.84

Forwards

Almond, Louis	5.11	–	Blackburn	05.01.92
Barkhuizen, Thomas	5.9	–	Blackpool	04.07.93
Campbell, Dudley	5.11	Leicester	London	12.11.81
Clarke, Billy	5.8	Ipswich	Cork, Ire	13.12.87
Ormerod, Brett	5.10	Preston	Blackburn	18.10.76
Phillips, Kevin	5.7	Birmingham	Hitchin	25.07.73
Taylor–Fletcher, Gary	6.0	Huddersfield	Liverpool	04.06.81

BRIGHTON AND HOVE ALBION

Ground: American Express Stadium, Village Way, Falmer, Brighton BN1 9BL
Telephone: TBC. **Club nickname:** Seagulls
First-choice colours: Blue and white shirts; white shorts; white socks
Capacity for 2011–12: 22,500
Record attendance: Goldstone Ground: 36,747 v Fulham (Div 2) 27 Dec, 1958;
Withdean Stadium: 8,729 v Manchester City (Carling Cup 2) 23 Sep, 2008

Goalkeepers

| Ankergren, Casper | 6.3 | Leeds | Koge, Den | 09.11.79 |

| Brezonan, Peter | 6.6 | Swindon | Bratislava, Slov | 09.12.79 |
| Walker, Mitch | 6.2 | – | St Albans | 24.09.91 |

Defenders

Calderon, Inigo	5.11	Alaves	Vitoria, Sp	04.01.82
Cook, Steve	6.1	–	Hastings	19.04.91
Dunk, Lewis	6.4	–	Brighton	21.11.91
El-Abd, Adam	6.0	–	Brighton	11.09.84
Elphick, Tommy	5.11	–	Brighton	07.09.87
Greer, Gordon	6.2	Swindon	Glasgow	14.12.80
Painter, Marcos	6.0	Swansea	Birmingham	17.08.86

Midfielders

Bridcutt, Liam	5.9	Chelsea	Reading	08.05.89
Dicker, Gary	6.0	Stockport	Dublin, Ire	31.07.86
Forster-Caskey, Jake	5.10	–	Southend	25.04.94
Kasim, Yaser	–	Tottenham	Baghdad, Iraq	10.05.91
Navarro, Alan	5.10	MK Dons	Liverpool	31.05.81
Noone, Craig	6.3	Plymouth	Fazackerly	17.11.87
Smith, Jamie	5.6	–	Leytonstone	16.09.89
Sparrow, Matt	5.10	Scunthorpe	Wembley	03.10.81

Forwards

Barnes, Ashley	6.0	Plymouth	Bath	31.10.89
Bergkamp, Roland	6.3	Excelsior	Amstelveen, Hol	03.04.91
Buckley, Will	6.0	Watford	Oldham	12.08.88
Hoskins, Will	5.10	Bristol Rov	Nottingham	06.05.86
Mackail-Smith, Craig	6.3	Peterborough	Watford	25.02.84

BRISTOL CITY

Ground: Ashton Gate, Bristol BS3 2EJ
Telephone: 0871 222 6666. **Club nickname:** Robins
First-choice colours: Red shirts; white shorts; red socks
Capacity for 2011–12: 21,497
Record attendance: 43,335 v Preston (FA Cup 5) 16 Feb, 1935

Goalkeepers

| Gerken, Dean | 6.2 | Colchester | Southend | 04.08.85 |
| James, David | 6.5 | Portsmouth | Welwyn Garden City | 01.08.70 |

Defenders

Carey, Louis	5.10	Coventry	Bristol	22.01.77
Edwards, Joe	5.8	–	Gloucester	31.10.90
Fontaine, Liam	6.3	Fulham	Beckenham	07.01.83
Hunt, Nicky	6.1	Bolton	Westhoughton	03.09.83
McAllister, Jamie	5.11	Hearts	Glasgow	26.04.78
Nyatanga, Lewin	6.2	Derby	Burton	18.08.88
Ribeiro, Christian	5.11	–	Neath	14.12.89
Stewart, Damion	6.3	Bradford	Jamaica	08.08.80
Wilson, James	6.2	–	Chepstow	26.02.89

Midfielders

Bolasie, Yannick	6.2	Plymouth	Kinshasa, DR Con	24.05.89
Campbell-Ryce, Jamal	5.7	Barnsley	Lambeth	06.04.83
Cisse, Kalifa	6.1	Reading	Dreux, Fr	09.01.84
Elliott, Marvin	6.0	Millwall	Wandsworth	15.09.84
Johnson, Lee	5.6	Yeovil	Newmarket	07.06.81
Kilkenny, Neil	5.8	Leeds	Enfield	19.12.85
Skuse, Cole	5.9	–	Bristol	29.03.86

Woolford, Martyn	6.0	Scunthorpe	Pontefract	13.10.85
Forwards				
Adomah, Albert	6.1	Barnet	London	13.12.87
Clarkson, David	5.10	Motherwell	Bellshill	10.09.85
Jackson, Marlon	6.2	–	Bristol	06.12.90
Maynard, Nicky	5.11	Crewe	Winsford	11.12.86
Pitman, Brett	6.0	Bournemouth	Jersey	03.01.88
Stead, Jon	6.3	Ipswich	Huddersfield	07.04.83
Taylor, Ryan	6.2	Rotherham	Rotherham	04.05.88

BURNLEY

Ground: Turf Moor, Harry Potts Way, Burnley BB10 4BX
Telephone: 0871 221 1882. **Club nickname:** Clarets
First-choice colours: Claret and blue shirts; white shorts; white socks
Capacity for 2011–12: 22,546.
Record attendance: 54,775 v Huddersfield (FA Cup 4) 23 Feb, 1924

Goalkeepers				
Grant, Lee	6.2	Sheffield Wed	Hemel Hempstead	27.01.83
Jensen, Brian	6.1	WBA	Copenhagen, Den	08.06.75
Defenders				
Bartley, Marvin	5.11	Bournemouth	Reading	01.07.89
Bikey, Andre	6.0	Reading	Douala, Cam	08.01.85
Carlisle, Clarke	6.1	Watford	Preston	14.10.79
Cort, Leon	6.2	Stoke	Southwark	11.07.79
Duff, Mike	6.1	Cheltenham	Belfast	11.01.78
Easton, Brian	6.0	Hamilton	Glasgow	05.03.88
Edgar, David	6.2	Newcastle	Kitchener, Can	19.05.87
Fox, Danny	6.0	Celtic	Winsford	29.05.86
Long, Kevin	6.2	Cork	Cork	18.08.90
Mears, Tyrone	5.11	Derby	Stockport	18.02.83
Midfielders				
Eagles, Chris	6.0	Manchester Utd	Hemel Hempstead	19.11.85
Elliott, Wade	5.10	Bournemouth	Eastleigh	14.12.78
McCann, Chris	6.1	–	Dublin, Ire	21.07.87
MacDonald, Alex	5.7	–	Chester	14.04.90
Marney, Dean	5.11	Hull	Barking	31.01.84
Wallace, Ross	5.6	Preston	Dundee	23.05.85
Forwards				
Austin, Charlie	6.2	Swindon	Hungerford	05.07.89
Iwelumo, Chris	6.3	Wolves	Coatbridge	01.08.78
Fletcher, Wes	5.10	–	Ormskirk	28.02.90
Paterson, Martin	5.9	Scunthorpe	Tunstall	13.05.87
Rodriguez, Jay	6.1	–	Burnley	29.07.89

CARDIFF CITY

Ground: Cardiff City Stadium, Leckwith Road, Cardiff CF11 8AZ
Telephone: 0845 365 1115. **Club nickname:** Bluebirds
First-choice colours: Blue shirts; white shorts; blue socks
Capacity for 2011–12: 26,828
Record attendance: Ninian Park: 61,566 Wales v England, 14 Oct, 1961. Club: 57,800 v Arsenal (Div 1) 22 Apr, 1953. Cardiff City Stadium: 26,058 v QPR (Champ) 23 Apr, 2011

Goalkeepers				
Heaton, Tom	6.1	Manchester Utd	Chester	15.04.86

Marshall, David	6.3	Norwich	Glasgow	05.03.85
Santiago, Jordan	–	Calgary	Calgary, Can	03.04.91
Defenders				
Gerrard, Anthony	6.2	Walsall	Liverpool	06.02.86
Gyepes, Gabor	6.3	Northampton	Budapest, Hun	26.06.81
Hudson, Mark	6.3	Charlton	Guildford	30.03.82
Keinan, Dekel	6.1	Blackpool	Rosh HaNikra, Isr	15.09.84
McNaughton, Kevin	5.10	Aberdeen	Dundee	28.08.82
Naylor, Lee	5.9	Celtic	Bloxwich	19.03.80
Quinn, Paul	6.0	Motherwell	Wishaw	21.07.85
Taylor, Andrew	5.10	Middlesbrough	Hartlepool	01.08.86
Midfielders				
Blake, Darcy	5.10	–	Caerphilly	13.12.88
Conway, Craig	5.8	Dundee Utd	Irvine	02.05.85
Cowie, Don	5.11	Watford	Inverness	15.02.83
Gunnarsson, Aron	5.11	Coventry	Akureyri, Ice	22.04.89
McPhail, Stephen	5.10	Barnsley	Westminster	09.12.79
Meades, Jonathan	6.1	–	Cardiff	02.03.92
Taiwo, Solomon	6.2	Dagenham	London	29.04.85
Whittingham, Peter	5.10	Aston Villa	Nuneaton	08.09.84
Wildig, Adam	5.9	–	Hereford	15.04.92
Forwards				
Earnshaw, Robert	5.8	Nottm Forest	Mufulira, Zam	06.04.81
Jarvis, Nathaniel	6.0	–	Cardiff	20.10.91
Mason, Joe	5.10	Plymouth	Plymouth	13.05.91
Parkin, Jon	6.4	Preston	Barnsley	30.12.81

COVENTRY CITY

Ground: Ricoh Arena, Foleshill, Coventry CV6 6GE
Telephone: 0844 873 1883. **Club nickname:** Sky Blues
First-choice colours: Sky blue shirts; white shorts; sky blue socks
Capacity for 2011–12: 32,400
Record attendance: Highfield Road: 51,455 v Wolves (Div 2) 29 Apr, 1967. Ricoh Arena:
Ricoh Arena: 31,407 v Chelsea (FA Cup 6), 7 Mar 2009

Goalkeepers				
Dunn, Chris	6.4	Northampton	Brentwood	23.10.87
Ireland, Danny	6.0	–	Sydney, Aus	30.09.90
Murphy, Joe	6.2	Scunthorpe	Dublin	21.08.81
Defenders				
Cameron, Nathan	6.2	–	Birmingham	21.11.91
Clarke, Jordan	6.0	–	Coventry	19.11.91
Cranie, Martin	6.0	Portsmouth	Yeovil	26.09.83
Hussey, Chris	5.10	Wimbledon	Hammersmith	02.01.89
Keogh, Richard	6.2	Carlisle	Harlow	11.08.86
McPake, James	6.2	Livingston	Bellshill	24.06.84
Turner, Ben	6.4	–	Birmingham	21.08.88
Wood, Richard	6.3	Sheffield Wed	Ossett	05.07.85
Midfielders				
Baker, Carl	6.2	Stockport	Whiston	26.12.82
Bell, David	5.10	Norwich	Kettering	21.01.84
Clingan, Sammy	5.11	Norwich	Belfast	13.01.84
Deegan, Gary	5.9	Bohemians	Dublin, Ire	28.09.87
McSheffrey, Gary	5.8	Birmingham	Coventry	13.08.72

Forwards

Eastwood, Freddy	5.11	Wolves	Epsom	29.10.83
Jeffers, Sean	6.1	–	Bedford	14.04.92
Jutkiewicz, Lukas	6.1	Everton	Southampton	20.03.89
Platt, Clive	6.4	Colchester	Wolverhampton	27.10.77
Wilson, Callum	5.11	–	Coventry	27.02.92

CRYSTAL PALACE

Ground: Selhurst Park, Whitehorse Lane, London SE25, 6PU
Telephone: 0208 768 6000. **Club nickname:** Eagles
First-choice colours: Red and blue shirts; red shorts; red socks
Capacity for 2011–12: 26,225
Record attendance: 51,482 v Burnley (Div 2), 11 May, 1979

Goalkeepers

Price, Lewis	6.3	Derby	Bournemouth	19.07.84
Speroni, Julian	6.1	Dundee	Buenos Aires, Arg	18.05.79

Defenders

Clyne, Nathaniel	5.9	–	London	05.04.91
Hills, Lee	5.10	Arsenal	Croydon	13.04.90
McCarthy, Patrick	6.1	Charlton	Dublin, Ire	31.05.83
Moxey, Dean	5.11	Derby	Exeter	14.01.86
Parsons, Matthew	5.10	–	London	25.12.91
Wright, David	5.11	Ipswich	Warrington	01.05.80
Wynter, Alex	6.0	–	Beckenham	15.09.93

Midfielders

Ambrose, Darren	5.11	Charlton	Harlow	29.02.84
Cadogan, Kieron	6.4	–	Wandsworth	16.08.90
Dikgacoi, Kagisho	5.11	Fulham	Brandford, SA	24.11.84
Dorman, Andy	6.1	St Mirren	Chester	01.05.82
Garvan, Owen	6.0	Ipswich	Dublin, Ire	29.01.88
Jedinak, Mile	6.3	Genclebirligi	Sydney, Aus	03.08.84
Marrow, Alex	6.1	Blackburn	Salford	12.01.90
O'Keefe, Stuart	5.8	Southend	Norwich	04.03.91
Pinney, Nathaniel	6.0	–	South Norwood	16.11.90

Forwards

Andrew, Calvin	6.0	Luton	Luton	19.12.86
Easter, Jermaine	5.10	MK Dons	Cardiff	15.01.82
Iversen, Steffen	6.1	Rosenborg	Oslo, Nor	10.11.7
Murray, Glenn	6.2	Brighton	Maryport	25.09.83
Scannell, Sean	5.9	–	Croydon	21.03.89
Zaha, Wilf	5.10	–	Abidjan, Iv Coast	10.11.92

DERBY COUNTY

Ground: Pride Park Stadium, Pride Park, Derby DE24 8XL
Telephone: 0871 472 1884. **Club nickname:** Rams
First-choice colours: White shirts; black shorts; white socks
Capacity for 2011–12: 33,100
Record attendance: Baseball Ground: 41,826 v Tottenham (Div 1) 20 Sep, 1969.
Pride Park: 33,475 v Rangers (Ted McMinn testimonial) 1 May, 2006

Goalkeepers

Atkins, Ross	6.0	–	Derby	03.11.89
Bywater, Stephen	6.2	West Ham	Manchester	07.06.81

Deeney, Saul	6.1	Burton	Derry	23.03.83
Fielding, Frank	6.0	Blackburn	Blackburn	04.04.88
Legzdins, Adam	6.0	Burton	Stafford	23.11.86
Severn, James	6.2	–	Nottingham	10.10.91
Defenders				
Anderson, Russell	6.0	Sunderland	Aberdeen	25.10.78
Barker, Shaun	6.2	Blackpool	Nottingham	19.09.82
Brayford, John	5.8	Crewe	Stoke	29.12.87
Buxton, Jake	5.11	Burton	Sutton-in-Ashfield	04.03.85
Leacock, Dean	6.2	Fulham	Croydon	10.06.84
O'Brien, Mark	5.11	Cherry Orchard	Dublin, Ire	20.11.92
Roberts, Gareth	5.8	Doncaster	Wrexham	06.02.78
Shackell, Jason	6.4	Barnsley	Stevenage	27.09.83
Midfielders				
Bailey, James	6.0	Crewe	Macclesfield	18.09.88
Bryson, Craig	5.8	Kilmarnock	Rutherglen	06.11.86
Connolly, Ryan	5.10	–	Castlebar	13.01.92
Croft, Lee	5.9	Norwich	Billinge	21.06.85
Cywka, Tomasz	5.11	Wigan	Gliwce, Pol	27.06.88
Davies, Ben	5.6	Notts Co	Birmingham	27.05.81
Green, Paul	5.10	Doncaster	Sheffield	10.04.83
Martin, David	5.9	Millwall	Erith	03.06.85
Pearson, Stephen	6.0	Celtic	Lanark	02.10.82
Forwards				
Ball, Callum	6.1		Leicester	08.10.92
Davies, Steve	6.1	Tranmere	Liverpool	29.12.87
Doyle, Conor	6.2	Creighton	McKinney, US	13.10.91
Maguire, Chris	5.8	Aberdeen	Bellshill	16.01.89
Robinson, Theo	5.9	Millwall	Birmingham	22.01.89
Tyson, Nathan	6.0	Nottm Forest	Reading	04.05.82
Ward, Jamie	5.5	Sheffield Utd	Birmingham	12.05.86

DONCASTER ROVERS

Ground: Keepmoat Stadium, Stadium Way, Doncaster DN4 5JW
Telephone: 01302 764664. **Club nickname:** Rovers
First-choice colours: Red and white shirts; black shorts; black socks
Capacity for 2011–12: 15,123
Record attendance: Belle Vue: 37,149 v Hull (Div 3 N) 2 Oct, 1948.
Keepmoat Stadium: 14,470 v Huddersfield (Lge 1) 1 Jan, 2007

Goalkeepers				
Sullivan, Neil	6.0	Leeds	Sutton	24.02.70
Woods, Gary	6.0	Manchester Utd	Kettering	01.10.90
Defenders				
Hird, Sam	5.8	Leeds	Doncaster	07.09.87
Chambers, James	5.10	Leicester	Sandwell	20.11.80
Lockwood, Adam	6.0	Yeovil	Wakefield	26.10.81
Martis, Shelton	6.2	WBA	Willemstad, Cur	29.11.82
Naylor, Richard	6.1	Leeds	Leeds	28.02.77
O'Connor, James	5.10	Bournemouth	Birmingham	20.11.84
Spurr, Tommy	6.1	Sheffield Wed	Leeds	13.09.87
Midfielders				
Bennett, Kyle	5.5	Bury	Telford	09.09.90
Dumbuya, Mustapha	5.8	Potters Bar	London	07.08.87

Friend, George	6.0	Wolves	Barnstaple	19.10.87
Gillett, Simon	5.6	Southampton	Oxford	06.11.85
Keegan, Paul		Bohemians	Dublin, Ire	05.07.84
Oster, John	5.9	Crystal Palace	Boston	08.12.78
Shiels, Dean	5.11	Hibernian	Magherafelt	01.02.85
Stock, Brian	5.10	Preston	Winchester	24.12.81
Wilson, Mark	6.0	Dallas	Scunthorpe	09.02.79
Woods, Martin	5.11	Rotherham	Airdrie	01.01.86
Forwards				
Coppinger, James	5.7	Exeter	Middlesbrough	10.01.81
Fairhurst, Waide	5.11	Sheffield Utd	Sheffield	07.05.89
Hayter, James	5.9	Bournemouth	Newport, IOW	09.04.79
Sharp, Billy	5.8	Sheffield Utd	Sheffield	05.02.86

HULL CITY

Ground: Kingston Communications Stadium, Anlaby Road, Hull, HU3 6HU
Telephone: 0870 837 0003. **Club nickname:** Tigers
First-choice colours: Amber shirts; black shorts; black socks
Capacity for 2011–12: 25,417.
Record attendance: At Boothferry Park: 55,019 v Manchester Utd. (FA Cup 6)
26 Feb, 1949. At Kingston Communications Stadium: 25,030 v Liverpool (Prem Lge) 9 May,
2010. Also: 25,280 for England U21 v Holland, 17 Feb, 2004

Goalkeepers				
Oxley, Mark	6.3	Rotherham	Sheffield	02.06.90
Defenders				
Chester, James	5.10	Manchester Utd	Warrington	23.01.89
Dawson, Andy	5.9	Scunthorpe	Northallerton	20.10.78
Dudgeon, Joe		Manchester Utd	Leeds	26.11.90
Hobbs, Jack	6.3	Leicester	Portsmouth	18.08.88
McShane, Paul	6.0	Sunderland	Kilpeddar, Ire	06.01.86
Rosenior, Liam	5.10	Reading	Wandsworth	15.12.84
Midfielders				
Atkinson, Will	5.10	–	Beverley	14.10.88
Barmby, Nick	5.7	Leeds	Hull	11.02.74
Bullard, Jimmy	5.10	Fulham	Newham	23.10.78
Cairney, Tom	6.0	–	Nottingham	20.01.91
Devitt, James	5.10	–	Dublin, Ire	06.07.90
Evans, Corry	5.11	Manchester Utd	Belfast	30.07.90
Harper, James	5.11	Sheffield Utd	Chelmsford	09.11.80
Kilbane, Kevin	6.0	Wigan	Preston	01.02.77
Koren, Robert	5.10	WBA	Radlje, Sloven	20.09.80
McKenna, Paul	5.8	Nottm Forest	Chorley	20.10.77
Olofinjana, Seyi	6.4	Stoke	Lagos, Nig	30.06.80
Stewart, Cameron	5.8	Manchester Utd	Manchester	08.04.91
Forwards				
Adebola, Dele	6.3	Nottm Forest	Lagos, Nig	23.06.75
Cullen, Mark	5.10	–	Ashington	21.04.92
Fryatt, Matty	5.10	Leicester	Nuneaton	05.03.86
Mclean, Aaron	5.6	Peterborough	Hammersmith	25.05.83
Simpson, Jay	5.11	Arsenal	Enfield	01.12.88

IPSWICH TOWN

Ground: Portman Road, Ipswich IP1 2DA

Telephone: 01473 400500. **Club nickname:** Blues/Town
First-choice colours: Blue shirts; white shorts; blue socks
Capacity for 2011–12: 30,311
Record attendance: 38,010 v Leeds (FA Cup 6) 8 Mar, 1975

Goalkeepers

Fulop, Marton	6.6	Sunderland	Budapest, Hun	03.05.83
Lee-Barrett, Arran	6.2	Hartlepool	Ipswich	28.02.84

Defenders

Ainsley, Jack	5.11	–	Ipswich	17.09.91
Cresswell, Aaron	5.7	Tranmere	Liverpool	15.12.89
Delaney, Damien	6.2	Hull	Cork, Ire	29.07.81
Ingimarsson, Ivar	6.0	Reading	Reykjavik, Ice	20.08.77
O'Connor, Shane	5.10	Liverpool	Cork, Ire	14.04.90
Peters, Jaime	5.7	–	Ontario, Can	04.05.87
Smith, Tommy	6.1	–	Macclesfield	31.03.90

Midfielders

Bowyer, Lee	5.9	Birmingham	Canning Town	03.01.77
Carson, Josh	5.9	–	Antrim	03.06.93
Civelli, Luciano	6.1	Banfield	Buenos Aires, Arg	06.10.86
Drury, Andy	5.11	Luton	Chatham	28.11.83
Edwards, Carlos	5.11	Sunderland	Port of Spain, Trin	24.10.78
Griffiths, Jamie	5.11	–	Bury St Edmunds	04.01.92
Healy, Colin	5.11	Cork	Cork, Ire	14.03.80
Hyam, Luke	5.10	–	Ipswich	24.10.91
Hourihane, Conor	5.11	Sunderland	Cork, Ire	02.02.91
Kennedy, Mark	5.11	Cardiff	Dublin, Ire	15.05.76
Leadbitter, Grant	5.9	Sunderland	Sunderland	07.01.86
Martin, Lee	5.10	Manchester Utd	Taunton	09.02.87
Peters, Jaime	5.7	–	Pickering, Can	04.05.87

Forwards

Chopra, Michael	5.9	Cardifff	Gosforth	23.12.83
Ellington, Nathan	5.11	Watford	Bradford	02.07.81
Murray, Ronan	5.8	–	Mayo, Ire	12.09.91
Priskin, Tamas	6.2	Watford	Komarno, Slovak	27.09.87
Scotland, Jason	5.9	Wigan	Morvant, Trin	18.02.79

LEEDS UNITED

Ground: Elland Road, Leeds LS11 0ES
Telephone: 0871 334 1919. **Club nickname:** Whites
First-choice colours: All white
Capacity for 2011–12: 39,457
Record attendance: 57,892 v Sunderland (FA Cup 5 replay) 15 Mar, 1967

Goalkeepers

Rachubka, Paul	6.1	Blackpool	San Luis, US	21.05.81

Defenders

Bessone, Federico	5.11	Swansea	Cordoba, Arg	23.01.84
Bromby, Leigh	5.11	Sheffield Utd	Dewsbury	02.06.80
Bruce, Alex	5.11	Leeds	Norwich	28.09.84
Connolly, Paul	6.0	Derby	Liverpool	29.09.83
Kisnorbo, Patrick	6.2	Leicester	Melbourne, Aus	24.03.81
Lees, Tom	6.0	–	Warwick	18.11.90
O'Brien, Andy	5.10	Bolton	Harrogate	29.06.79
Parker, Ben	5.11	–	Pontefract	08.11.87

White, Aidan	5.7	–	Leeds	10.10.91

Midfielders

Clayton, Adam	5.9	Manchester City	Manchester	14.01.89
Gradel, Max	5.11	Leicester	Abidjan, Iv C	30.11.87
Howson, Jonathan	5.11	–	Leeds	21.05.88
Nunez, Ramon	5.7	Olimpia	Tegucigalpa, Hond	14.11.85
Sam, Lloyd	5.8	Charlton	Leeds	27.09.84

Forwards

Becchio, Luciano	6.2	Merida	Cordoba, Arg	28.12.83
McCormack, Ross	5.10	Cardiff	Glasgow	18.08.86
Paynter, Billy	6.0	Swindon	Liverpool	13.07.84
Snodgrass, Robert	6.0	Livingston	Glasgow	07.09.87
Somma, Davide	6.1	San Jose	Johannesburg, SA	26.03.85

LEICESTER CITY

Ground: King Power Stadium, Filbert Way, Leicester, LE2 7FL
Telephone: 0844 815 6000. **Club nickname:** Foxes
First choice colours: Blue shirts; blue shorts; blue socks
Capacity for 2011–12: 32,312
Record attendance: Filbert Street: 47,298 v. Tottenham (FA Cup 5) 18 Feb, 1928;
Walkers Stadium: 32,148 v Newcastle (Premier League) 26 Dec, 2003

Goalkeepers

Logan, Conrad	6.2	–	Letterkenny, Ire	18.04.86
Schmeichel, Kasper	6.0	Leeds	Copenhagen, Den	05.11.86
Weale, Chris	6.2	Bristol City	Chard	09.02.82

Defenders

Bamba, Sol	6.3	Hibernian	Ivry, Fr	13.01.85
Berner, Bruno	6.1	Blackburn	Zurich, Swi	21.11.77
Kennedy, Tom	5.11	Rochdale	Bury	24.06.85
Mills, Matt	6.3	Reading	Swindon	14.07.86
Neilson, Robbie	5.9	Hearts	Paisley	19.06.80
Parkes, Tom	6.3	–	Mansfield	15.01.92
Peltier, Lee	5.10	Huddersfield	Liverpool	11.12.86
St Ledger, Sean	6.0	Preston	Birmingham	28.12.84
Tunchev, Aleksandar	6.2	CSKA Sofia	Pazardzhik, Bul	10.07.81

Midfielders

Abe, Yuki	5.10	Urawa	Ichikawa, Jap	06.09.81
Danns, Neil	5.9	Crystal Palace	Liverpool	23.11.82
Dyer, Lloyd	5.9	MK Dons	Birmingham	13.09.82
King, Andy	6.0	–	Maidenhead	29.10.88
Moussa, Franck	5.8	Southend	Brussels, Bel	24.09.87
Oakley, Matt	5.10	Derby	Peterborough	17.08.77
Schlupp, Jeffrey	5.8	–	Hamburg, Ger	23.12.92
Teixeira, Joao	5.11	Guimaraes	Urgezes, Por	19.08.81
Wellens, Richie	5.9	Doncaster	Manchester	26.03.80

Forwards

Crncic, Leon	6.1	Aluminij	Slovenia	02.03.90
Gallagher, Paul	6.0	Blackburn	Glasgow	09.08.84
Howard, Steve	6.2	Derby	Durham	10.05.76
N'Guessan, Dany	6.1	Lincoln	Ivry, Fr	11.08.87
Nugent, David	5.11	Portsmouth	Liverpool	02.05.85
Vassell, Darius	5.7	Ankaragucu	Sutton Coldfield	13.06.80
Waghorn, Martyn	5.10	Sunderland	South Shields	23.01.90

MIDDLESBROUGH

Ground: Cellnet Riverside Stadium, Middlesbrough, TS3 6RS
Telephone: 0844 499 6789. **Club nickname:** Boro
First-choice colours: Red shirts; white shorts; red socks
Capacity for 2011–12: 34,998
Record attendance: At Ayresome Park: 53,596 v Newcastle (Div 1) 27 Dec, 1949. At Riverside Stadium: 34,836 v Norwich (Prem Lge) 28 Dec, 2004. Also: 35,000 England v Slovakia 11 Jun, 2003

Goalkeepers

Coyne, Danny	5.11	Tranmere	Prestatyn	27.08.73
Steele, Jason	6.2	–	Bishop Auckland	18.08.90

Defenders

Bates, Matthew	5.8	–	Stockton	10.12.86
Bennett, Joe	5.8	–	Rochdale	28.03.90
Grounds, Jonathan	6.1	–	Thornaby	02.02.88
Hines, Seb	6.2	–	Wetherby	29.05.88
Hoyte, Justin	5.11	Arsenal	Waltham Forest	20.11.84
McMahon, Tony	5.10	–	Bishop Auckland	24.03.86
McManus, Stephen	6.2	Celtic	Lanark	10.09.82
Williams, Rhys	6.1	Joondalup	Perth, Aus	07.07.88

Midfielders

Bailey, Nicky	5.10	Charlton	Hammersmith	10.06.84
Halliday, Andy	5.11	Livingston	Glasgow	11.10.91
Robson, Barry	6.0	Celtic	Inverurie	07.11.78
Thomson, Kevin	6.2	Rangers	Edinburgh	14.10.84
Zemmama, Merouane	5.7	Hibernian	Sale, Mor	07.10.83

Forwards

Emnes, Marvin	5.11	Sparta Rotterdam	Rotterdam, Hol	27.05.88
Franks, Jonathan	5.7	–	Stockton	08.04.90
Kink, Tarmo	6.0	Gyor	Tallinn, Est	06.10.85
Lita, Leroy	5.9	Reading	Kinshasa, DR Con	28.12.84
McDonald, Scott	5.8	Celtic	Melbourne, Aus	21.08.83
Miller, Lee	6.2	Aberdeen	Lanark	18.05.83

MILLWALL

Ground: The Den, Zampa Road, London SE16 3LN
Telephone: 0207 232 1222. **Club nickname:** Lions
First-choice colours: Blue shirts; white shorts; blue socks
Capacity for 2011–12: 19,734
Record attendance: The Den: 48,672 v Derby (FA Cup 5) 20 Feb, 1937;
New Den: 20,093 v Arsenal (FA Cup 3) 10 January, 1994

Goalkeepers

Allsopp, Ryan	6.0	WBA	Birmingham	17.06.92
Forde, David	6.2	Cardiff	Galway, Ire	20.12.79
Mildenhall, Steve	6.4	Southend	Swindon	13.05.78

Defenders

Craig, Tony	6.0	Crystal Palace	Greenwich	20.04.85
Dunne, Alan	5.10	–	Dublin, Ire	23.08.82
Mkandawire, Tamika	6.1	Leyton Orient	Mzuzu, Malaw	28.05.83
Purse, Darren	6.2	Sheffield Wed	Stepney	14.02.77
Robinson, Paul	6.1	–	Barnet	07.01.82
Smith, Jack	5.11	Swindon	Hemel Hempstead	14.11.83

Stewart, Jordan	6.0	Xanthi	Birmingham	03.03.82
Ward, Darren	6.3	Wolves	Kenton	13.09.78
Midfielders				
Abdou, Nadjim	5.10	Plymouth Argyle	Martigues, Fr	13.07.84
Barron, Scott	5.10	Ipswich	Preston	02.09.85
Hackett, Chris	6.0	Hearts	Oxford	01.03.83
Henry, James	6.1	Reading	Reading	10.06.89
Racon, Therry	5.10	Charlton	Villeneuve, Fr	01.05.84
Trotter, Liam	6.2	Ipswich	Ipswich	24.08.88
Forwards				
Batt, Shaun	6.2	Peterborough	Luton	22.02.87
Bouazza, Hameur	5.11	Arles	Evry, Fr	22.02.85
Henderson, Darius	6.1	Sheffield Utd	Doncaster	07.09.81
Marquis, John	6.1	–	Lewisham	16.05.92
McQuoid, Josh	5.10	Bournemouth	Southampton	15.12.89

NOTTINGHAM FOREST

Ground: City Ground, Pavilion Road, Nottingham NG2 5FJ
Telephone: 0115 982 4444. **Club nickname:** Forest
First-choice colours: Red shirts; white shorts; red socks
Capacity for 2011–12: 30,576
Record attendance: 49,945 v Manchester Utd (Div 1) 28 Oct, 1967

Goalkeepers				
Camp, Lee	6.0	QPR	Derby	22.08.84
Darlow, Karl	61	Aston Villa	Northampton	08.10.90
Smith, Paul	6.3	Southampton	Epsom	17.12.79
Defenders				
Chambers, Luke	5.11	Northampton	Kettering	29.08.85
Cohen, Chris	5.11	Yeovil	Norwich	05.03.87
Gunter, Chris	5.11	Tottenham	Newport	21.07.89
Lynch, Joel	6.1	Brighton	Eastbourne	03.10.87
Moloney, Brendan	5.10	–	Beaufort	18.01.89
Morgan, Wes	5.11	–	Nottingham	21.01.84
Midfielders				
Anderson, Paul	5.9	Liverpool	Leicester	23.07.88
McGugan, Lewis	5.10	–	Long Eaton	25.10.88
Mejewski, Radoslaw	5.7	Polonia Warsaw	Pruszkow, Pol	
Moussi, Guy	6.2	Angers	Bondy, Fr	23.01.85
Reid, Andy	5.7	Blackpool	Dublin	29.07.82
Forwards				
Blackstock, Dexter	6.2	Nottm Forest	Oxford	20.05.86
Findley, Robbie	5.9	Real Salt Lake	Phoenix, US	04.08.85
McCleary, Garath	5.11	–	Bromley	15.05.87
McGoldrick, David	6.1	Southampton	Nottingham	29.11.87
Tudgay, Marcus	5.10	Sheffield Wed	Shoreham	03.02.83

PETERBOROUGH UNITED

Ground: London Road Stadium, Peterborough PE2 8AL
Telephone: 01733 563947. **Club nickname:** Posh
First-choice colours: Blue shirts; white shorts; white socks
Capacity for 2011–12: 15,460
Record attendance: 30,096 v Swansea (FA Cup 5) 20 Feb, 1965

Goalkeepers

Jones, Paul	6.3	Exeter	Maidstone	28.06.86
Lewis, Joe	6.5	Norwich	Broome	06.10.87
Richardson, Barry	6.1	Cheltenham	Wallsend	05.08.69

Defenders

Alcock, Craig	5.8	Yeovil	Truro	08.12.87
Basey, Grant	6.1	Charlton	Bromley	30.11.88
Bennett, Ryan	6.2	Grimsby	Orsett	06.03.90
Geohaghon, Exodus	6.5	Kettering	Birmingham	27.02.85
Griffiths, Scott	5.9	Dagenham	London	27.11.85
Korateng, Nathan	6.0	–	London	26.05.92
Langmead, Kelvin	6.1	Shrewsbury	Coventry	23.03.85
Little, Mark	6.1	Wolves	Worcester	20.08.88
Zakuani, Gabriel	6.1	Fulham	Kinshasa, DR Con	31.05.86

Midfielders

Frecklington, Lee	5.8	Lincoln	Lincoln	08.09.85
McCann, Grant	5.10	Scunthorpe	Belfast	14.04.80
Rowe, Tommy	5.11	Stockport	Manchester	01.05.89
Tomlin, Lee	5.11	Rushden	Leicester	12.01.89
Wesolowski, James	5.10	Leicester	Sydney, Aus	25.08.87

Forwards

Ajose, Nicky	5.8	Manchester Utd	Bury	07.10.91
Ball, David	6.0	Manchester City	Whitefield	14.12.89
Boyd, George	5.10	Stevenage	Medway	02.10.85
Hibbert, Dave	6.2	Shrewsbury	Stafford	28.01.86
Mills, Danny	6.3	Crawley	Peterborough	27.11.91
Taylor, Paul	5.11	Anderlecht	Liverpool	04.10.87

PORTSMOUTH

Ground: Fratton Park, Frogmore Road, Portsmouth, PO4 8RA
Telephone: 0239 273 1204. **Club nickname:** Pompey
First choice colours: Blue shirts; white shorts; red socks
Capacity for 2011–12: 20,338
Record attendance: 51,385 v Derby (FA Cup 6) 26 Feb, 1949

Goalkeepers

Ashdown, Jamie	6.3	Reading	Reading	30.11.80
Henderson, Stephen	6.3	Bristol City	Dublin, Ire	02.05.88

Defenders

Hreidarsson, Hermann	6.1	Charlton	Reykjavik, Ice	11.07.74
Mokoena, Aaron	6.1	Blackburn	Johannesburg, SA	25.11.80
Pearce, Jason	5.11	Bournemouth	Hillingdon	06.12.87
Rocha, Ricardo	6.0	Standard Liege	Braga, Por	03.10.78
Ward, Joel	6.1	–	Emsworth	29.10.89

Midfielders

Lawrence, Liam	5.9	Stoke	Retford	14.12.81
Mullins, Hayden	6.0	West Ham	Reading	27.03.79
Norris, David	5.8	Ipswich	Peterborough	22.02.81

Forwards

Kanu, Nwankwo	6.4	WBA	Owerri, Nig	01.08.76
Kitson, Dave	6.3	Stoke	Hitchin	21.01.80
Varney, Luke	5.11	Derby	Leicester	28.09.82

READING

Ground: Madejski Stadium, Junction 11 M4, Reading RG2 OFL
Telephone: 0118 968 1100. **Club nickname:** Royals
First-choice colours: Blue and white shirts; blue shorts; blue socks
Capacity for 2011–12: 24,169
Record attendance: At Elm Park: 33,042 v Brentford (FA Cup 5) 19 Feb, 1927. At Madejski Stadium: 24,135 v Manchester Utd (Prem Lge) 19 Jan, 2008

Goalkeepers

Andersen, Mikkel	6.5	Copenhagen	Herlev, Den	17.12.88
Federici, Adam	6.2	Sardegna	Nowra, Aus	31.01.85
McCarthy, Alex	6.4	–	Guildford	03.12.89

Defenders

Cummings, Shaun	6.0	Chelsea	Hammersmith	28.02.89
Griffin, Andy	5.9	Stoke	Wigan	17.03.79
Harte, Ian	5.10	Carlisle	Drogheda, Ire	31.08.77
Hector, Michael	6.4	–	London	19.07.92
Morrison, Sean	6.1	Swindon	Plymouth	08.01.91
Pearce, Alex	6.0	–	Oxford	09.11.88
Williams, Marcus	5.8	Scunthorpe	Doncaster	08.04.86

Midfielders

Antonio, Michail	5.11	Tooting	London	28.03.90
D'Ath, Lawson	5.9	–	Oxford	24.12.92
Gunnarsson, Brynjar	6.1	Watford	Reykjavik, Ice	16.10.75
Howard, Brian	5.8	Sheffield Utd	Winchester	23.01.83
Karacan, Jem	5.10	–	London	21.02.89
Kebe, Jimmy	5.9	Lens	Vitry, Fr	19.01.84
Leigertwood, Mikele	6.1	QPR	Enfield	12.11.82
McAnuff, Jobi	5.11	Watford	Edmonton	09.11.81
Tabb, Jay	5.7	Coventry	Tooting	21.02.84
Taylor, Jake	5.10	–	Ascot	01.12.91

Forwards

Bignall, Nicholas	5.10	–	Reading	11.07.90
Church, Simon	6.0	–	High Wycombe	10.12.88
Hunt, Noel	5.8	Dundee Utd	Waterford, Ire	26.12.82
Long, Shane	5.10	Cork	Gortnahoe, Ire	22.01.87
Manset, Mathieu	6.1	Hereford	Metz, Fr	05.08.89
Robson-Kanu, Hal	6.0	–	Acton	21.05.89
Walcott, Jacob	5.11	–	Abingdon	26.06.92
Williams, Brett	6.2	Eastleigh	Southampton	01.12.87

SOUTHAMPTON

Ground: St Mary's Stadium, Britannia Road, Southampton, SO14 5FP
Telephone: 0845 688 9448. **Club nickname:** Saints
First-choice colours: White and red; red shorts; black socks
Capacity for 2011–12: 32,689
Record attendance: The Dell: 31,044 v Manchester Utd (Div 1) 8 Oct, 1969; St Mary's: 32,151 v Arsenal (Prem Lge) 29 December, 2003

Goalkeepers

Bialkowski, Bartosz	6.0	Gornik	Braniewo, Pol	06.07.87
Davis, Kelvin	6.1	Sunderland	Bedford	29.09.76
Forecast, Tommy	6.6	Tottenham	Newham	15.10.86

Defenders

Butterfield, Danny	5.9	Crystal Palace	Boston	21.11.79
Cork, Jack	6.1	Chelsea	Carshalton	25.06.89
Fonte, Jose	6.2	Crystal Palace	Penafiel, Por	22.12.83
Harding, Dan	6.0	Ipswich	Gloucester	23.12.83
Jaidi, Radhi	6.4	Birmingham	Tunis	30.08.75
Martin, Aaron	6.1	Eastleigh	Newport, IOW	29.09.89
Mills, Joseph	5.9	–	Swindon	30.10.89
Richardson, Frazer	5.11	Charlton	Rotherham	29.10.82
Seaborne, Daniel	6.0	Exeter	Barnstaple	15.03.87
Stephens, Jack	6.1	Plymouth	Plymouth	27.01.94

Midfielders

Chaplow, Richard	5.9	Preston	Accrington	02.02.85
Cork, Jack	6.1	Chelsea	Carshalton	25.06.89
Dean, Harlee	5.10	Dagenham	Basingstoke	26.07.91
Dickson, Ryan	5.10	Brentford	Saltash	14.12.86
Hammond, Dean	6.0	Colchester	Hastings	07.03.83
Holmes, Lee	5.8	Derby	Mansfield	02.04.87
Oxlade-Chamberlain, Alex	5.11	–	Portsmouth	15.08.93
Puncheon, Jason	5.8	Plymouth	Croydon	26.06.86
Schneiderlin, Morgan	5.11	Strasbourg	Zellwiller, Fr	08.11.89

Forwards

Barnard, Lee	5.10	Southend	Romford	18.07.84
Connolly, David	5.9	Wigan	Willesden	06.06.77
Do Prado, Guly	6.2	Cesena	Campinas, Br	31.12.81
Doble, Ryan	5.10	–	Abergavenny	01.02.91
Forte, Jonathan	6.0	Scunthorpe	Sheffield	25.07.86
Lallana, Adam	5.10	St Albans	Bournemouth	10.05.88
Lambert, Rickie	5.10	Bristol Rov	Liverpool	16.02.82

WATFORD

Ground: Vicarage Road Stadium, Vicarage Road, Watford WD18 OER
Telephone: 0844 856 1881. **Club nickname:** Hornets
First-choice colours: Yellow shirts, black shorts, yellow socks
Capacity for 2011–12: 17,504
Record attendance: 34,099 v Manchester Utd (FA Cup 4 replay) 3 Feb, 1969

Goalkeepers

Bond, Jonathan	6.3	–	Hemel Hempstead	19.05.93
Gilmartin, Rene	6.5	Walsall	Dublin, Ire	31.05.87
Loach, Scott	6.2	Lincoln	Nottingham	14.10.79

Defenders

Bennett, Dale	5.11	–	Enfield	06.01.90
Doyley, Lloyd	5.10	–	Whitechapel	01.12.82
Hodson, Lee	5.11	–	Borehamwood	02.10.91
Mariappa, Adrian	5.11	–	Harrow	03.10.86
Mirfin, David	6.1	Scunthorpe	Sheffield	18.04.85
Oshodi, Eddie	6.0	–	Brent	14.01.92
Taylor, Martin	6.4	Birmingham	Ashington	09.11.79
Thompson, Adam	6.2	–	Harlow	28.09.92

Midfielders

Bryan, Michael	5.8	–	Wexford, Ire	21.02.90
Eustace, John	5.11	Stoke	Solihull	03.11.79
Forsyth, Craig	6.0	Dundee	Carnoustie	24.02.89

Isaac, Chez	5.10	–	Hatfield	16.11.92
Jenkins, Ross	5.11	–	Watford	09.11.90
McGinn, Stephen	5.10	St Mirren	Glasgow	02.12.88
Mingoia, Piero	5.10	–	Enfield	20.10.91
Murray, Sean	5.9	–	Abbots Langley	11.10.93
Walker, Josh	5.11	Middlesbrough	Newcastle	21.02.89
Whichelow, Matt	6.4	–	Islington	28.09.91
Forwards				
Deeney, Troy	5.11	Walsall	Chelmsley	29.06.88
Massey, Gavin	5.10	–	Watford	14.10.92
Sordell, Marvin	5.10	–	Brent	17.02.91

WEST HAM UNITED

Ground: Boleyn Ground, Upton Park, London E13 9AZ
Telephone: 0208 548 2748. **Club nickname:** Hammers
First-choice colours: Claret and blue shirts; white shorts; white socks
Capacity for 2011–12: 35,303
Record attendance: 43,322 v Tottenham (Div 1) 17 Oct, 1970

Goalkeepers				
Boffin, Ruud	6.5	Maastricht	Sint-Truiden, Bel	05.11.87
Green, Robert	6.2	Norwich	Chertsey	18.01.80
Kurucz, Peter	6.1	Ujpest	Budapest, Hun	30.05.88
Stech, Marek	6.3	Sparta Prague	Prague, Cze	28.01.90
Defenders				
Faubert, Julien	5.10	Bordeaux	Le Havre, Fr	01.08.83
Faye, Abdoulaye	6.2	Stoke	Dakar, Sen	26.02.78
Ilunga, Herita	5.11	Toulouse	Kinshasa, DR Con	25.02.82
Reid, Winston	6.3	Midtjlland	Auckland, NZ	03.07.88
Spence, Jordan	6.0	–	Woodford	24.05.90
Tomkins, James	6.3	–	Basildon	29.03.89
Midfielders				
Barrera, Pablo	5.9	Pumas	Tlalnepantia, Mex	21.06.87
Boa Morte, Luis	5.10	Fulham	Lisbon, Por	04.08.77
Collison, Jack	6.0	–	Watford	02.10.88
Noble, Mark	5.11	–	West Ham	08.05.87
Nolan, Kevin	6.1	Newcastle	Liverpool	24.06.82
O'Neil, Gary	5.10	Middlesbrough	Beckenham	18.05.83
Parker, Scott	5.7	Newcastle	Lambeth	13.10.80
Forwards				
Cole, Carlton	6.3	Chelsea	Croydon	12.10.83
Hines, Zavron	5.10	–	Jamaica	27.12.88
Nouble, Frank	6.3	Chelsea	Lewisham	24.09.91
Piquionne, Frederic	6.2	Lyon	Noumea, New Cal	08.12.78
Sears, Freddie	5.10	–	Hornchurch	27.11.89
Stanislas, Junior	6.0	–	Eltham	26.11.89

LEAGUE ONE

EMOUTH

ward Stadium, Dean Court, Bournemouth BH7 7AF
01202 726300. **Club nickname:** Cherries

First-choice colours: Red shirts; black shorts; red socks
Capacity for 2011–12: 9,783
Record attendance: 28,799 v Manchester Utd (FA Cup 6) 2 Mar, 1957

Name	Height ft in	Previous club	Birthplace	Birthdate
Goalkeepers				
Flahavan, Darryl	5.11	Portsmouth	Southampton	28.11.78
Jalal, Shwan	6.2	Peterborough	Baghdad, Iraq	14.08.83
Thomas, Dan	6.2	–	Poole	01.09.91
Defenders				
Barrett, Adam	5.10	Crystal Palace	Dagenham	29.11.79
Baudry, Mathieu	6.2	Troyes	Le Havre, Fr	24.02.88
Cummings, Warren	5.9	Chelsea	Aberdeen	15.10.80
Garry, Ryan	6.0	Arsenal	Hornchurch	29.09.83
Nelson, Mitchell	6.3	Tooting	Lambeth	31.08.89
Purches, Stephen	5.11	Leyton Orient	Ilford	14.01.80
Midfielders				
Arter, Harry	5.9	Woking	Eltham	28.12.89
Cooper, Shaun	5.10	Portsmouth	Newport, IOW	05.10.83
Feeney, Liam	6.0	Salisbury	Hammersmith	28.04.86
Gregory, Steven	6.1	AFC Wimbledon	Aylesbury	19.03.87
Molesley, Mark	6.1	Grays	Hillingdon	11.03.81
Partington, Joe	5.11	–	Portsmouth	01.04.90
Pugh, Marc	5.11	Hereford	Bacup	02.04.87
Robinson, Anton	6.0	Weymouth	Brent	17.02.86
Forwards				
Fletcher, Steve	6.3	Crawley	Hartlepool	26.07.72
Ings, Danny	5.10	–	Winchester	16.03.92
Lovell, Steve	5.11	Partick	Amersham	06.12.80
Stockley, Jayden	6.2	–	Poole	15.09.93
Symes, Michael	6.3	Accrington	Great Yarmouth	31.10.83
Taylor, Lyle	6.2	Concord	Greenwich	29.03.90

BRENTFORD

Ground: Griffin Park, Braemar Road, Brentford TW8 ONT
Telephone: 0845 345 6442. **Club nickname:** Bees
First-choice colours: Red and white shirts; black shorts; black socks
Capacity for 2011–12: 12,702
Record attendance: 39,626 v Preston (FA Cup 6) 5 Mar, 1938

Name	Height ft in	Previous club	Birthplace	Birthdate
Goalkeepers				
Lee, Richard	5.11	Watford	Oxford	05.10.82
Moore, Simon	6.3	Farnborough	IOW	19.05.90
Royce, Simon	6.2	Gillingham	Forest Gate	09.09.71
Defenders				
Balkestein, Pim	6.3	Ipswich	Gouda, Hol	29.04.87
Bean, Marcus	5.11	QPR	Hammersmith	02.11.84
Blake, Ryan	5.10	–	Kingston	08.12.91
Legge, Leon	6.1	Tonbridge	London	28.04.85
Logan, Shaleum	6.1	Manchester City	Manchester	06.11.88
Osborne, Karleigh	6.2	–	Southall	19.03.88
Spillane, Michael	6.1	Norwich	Cambridge	23.03.89
Woodman, Craig	5.9	Wycombe	Tiverton	22.12.82

Midfielders

Diagouraga, Toumani	6.3	Peterborough	Paris, Fr	09.06.87
Douglas, Jonathan	5.11	Swindon	Monaghan	22.11.81
McGinn, Niall	5.8	Celtic	Donaghmore	20.07.87
O'Connor, Kevin	5.11	–	Blackburn	24.02.82
Saunders, Sam	5.11	Dagenham	London	29.08.83
Weston, Myles	5.11	Notts Co	Lewisham	12.03.88
Wood, Sam	6.0	Bromley	London	06.02.88

Forwards

Alexander, Gary	5.11	Millwall	Lambeth	15.08.79
Donaldson, Clayton	6.1	Crewe	Bradford	07.02.84
Hudson, Kirk	5.8	Aldershot	Rochford	12.12.86
MacDonald, Charlie	5.10	Southend	Southwark	13.02.81

BURY

Ground: Gigg Lane, Bury BL9 9HR
Telephone: 08445 790009. **Club nickname:** Shakers
First-choice colours: White shirts; blue shorts; blue socks
Capacity for 2011–12: 11,671
Record attendance: 35,000 v Bolton (FA Cup 3) 9 Jan, 1960

Goalkeepers

Belford, Cameron	5.11	Coventry	Nuneaton	16.10.88
Branagan, Richie	5.11	Bolton	Gravesend	20.10.91

Defenders

Futcher, Ben	6.6	Sheffield Utd	Bradford	04.06.81
Hughes, Mark	6.2	North Queensland	Liverpool	09.12.86
Picken, Phil	5.9	Chesterfield	Droylsden	12.11.85
Skarz, Joe	6.0	Huddersfield	Huddersfield	13.07.89
Sodje, Efe	6.1	Gillingham	Greenwich	05.10.72

Midfielders

Harrop, Max	5.8	–	Oldham	30.06.93
Haworth, Andy	5.11	Blackburn	Lancaster	28.11.88
Jones, Andrai	5.11	Everton	Liverpool	01.01.92
Jones, Michael	6.0	Tranmere	Birkenhead	15.08.87
Mozika, Damien	6.1	Tarbiat Yazd	Corbeil-Essonnes, Fr	15.04.87
Rothwell, Zach	6.1	–	Bury	16.07.92
Schumacher, Steven	6.0	Crewe	Liverpool	30.04.84
Sweeney, Peter	6.0	Grimsby	Glasgow	25.09.84
Worrall, David	6.0	WBA	Manchester	12.06.90

Forwards

Bishop, Andy	6.0	York	Stone	19.10.82
Hudson, Danny	5.11	–	Manchester	12.09.92
John-Lewis, Lenell	5.11	Lincoln	Hammersmith	17.05.89
Lowe, Ryan	5.11	Chester	Liverpool	18.09.78
McCarthy, Luke	5.10	–	Bolton	07.07.93

CARLISLE UNITED

Ground: Brunton Park, Warwick Road, Carlisle CA1 1LL
Telephone: 01228 526237. **Club nickname:** Cumbrians
First-choice colours: Blue shirts; white shorts; white socks
Capacity for 2011–12: 16,981
Record attendance: 27,500 v Birmingham City (FA Cup 3) 5 Jan, 1957, v Middlesbrough (FA Cup 5) 7 Jan, 1970

Goalkeepers

Caig, Tony	6.0	Workington	Whitehaven	11.04.74
Collin, Adam	6.1	Workington	Carlisle	09.12.84
Gillespie, Mark	6.0	–	Newcastle	27.03.92

Defenders

Livesey, Danny	6.3	Bolton	Salford	31.12.84
Michalik, Lubomir	6.4	Leeds	Cadca, Slovak	13.08.83
Murphy, Peter	5.11	Blackburn	Dublin, Ire	27.10.80
O'Halloran, Stephen	6.0	Coventry	Cork, Ire	29.11.87
Simek, Frankie	6.0	Sheffield Wed	St Louis, US	13.10.84
Swinglehurst, Steven	5.11	–	Carlisle	23.10.92

Midfielders

Berrett, James	5.10	Huddersfield	Halifax	13.01.89
Kavanagh, Graham	5.10	Sunderland	Dublin, Ire	02.12.73
McGovern, Jon-Paul	5.10	Swindon	Glasgow	03.10.80
McKenna, Ben	5.10	–	Burnley	16.01.93
Robson, Matty	5.10	Hartlepool	Durham	23.01.85
Taiwo, Tom	5.9	Chelsea	Leeds	27.02.90
Thirlwell, Paul	5.11	Derby	Springwell	13.02.79
Welsh, Andy	5.8	Yeovil	Manchester	24.11.83

Forwards

Curran, Craig	5.9	Tranmere	Liverpool	23.08.89
Loy, Rory	5.10	Rangers	Dumfries	19.03.88
Madden, Patrick		Bohemians	Dublin, Ire	04.03.90
Zoko, Francois	6.0	Oostende	Daloa, Iv C	13.09.83

CHARLTON ATHLETIC

Ground: The Valley, Floyd Road, London SE7 8BL
Telephone: 0208 333 4000. **Club nickname:** Addicks
First-choice colours: Red shirts; white shorts; white socks
Capacity for 2011–12: 27,111
Record attendance: 75,031 v Aston Villa (FA Cup 5) 12 Feb, 1938

Goalkeepers

Elliot, Rob	6.2	Erith	Chatham	30.04.86
Sullivan, John	6.2	Millwall	Brighton	08.03.88

Defenders

Doherty, Gary	6.1	Norwich	Donegal, Ire	31.01.80
Evina, Cedric	5.9	Oldham	Cameroon	16.11.91
Francis, Simon	6.0	Southend	Nottingham	16.02.85
Mambo, Yado	6.3	–	Kilburn	22.10.91
Morrison, Michael	6.1	Sheffield Wed	Bury St Edmunds	03.03.88
Solly, Chris	5.8	–	Rochester	20.01.90
Taylor, Matt	5.10	Exeter	Ormskirk	30.01.82
Wiggins, Rhoys	5.9	Bournemouth	Hillingdon	04.11.87
Youga, Kelly	6.1	Lyon	Bangui, CAF Rep	22.09.85

Midfielders

Mikel Alonso	6.0	Tenerife	Tolosa, Sp	16.05.80
Pritchard, Bradley	6.1	Hayes	Harare, Zim	19.12.85
Green, Danny	6.0	Dagenham	Harlow	09.07.88
Harriott, Callum	5.5	–	London	04.03.94
Hollands, Danny	5.11	Bournemouth	Ashford, Surrey	06.11.85
Jackson, Johnnie	6.1	Notts Co	Camden	15.08.82
McCormack, Alan	5.8	Southend	Dublin, Ire	10.01.84

Stephens, Dale	5.7	Oldham	Bolton	12.06.89
Wagstaff, Scott	5.11	–	Maidstone	31.03.90
Forwards				
Benson, Paul	6.2	Dagenham	Rochford	12.10.79
Hayes, Paul	6.0	Preston	Dagenham	20.09.83
Wright-Phillips, Bradley	5.8	Plymouth	Lewisham	12.03.85

CHESTERFIELD

Ground: b2net Stadium, Whittington Moor, Chesterfield S41 8NZ
Telephone: 01246 209765. **Club nickname:** Spireites
First-choice colours: Blue shirts; white shorts; blue socks
Capacity for 2011–12: 10,338
Record attendance: Saltergate: 30,698 v Newcastle (Div 2) 7 Apr, 1939

Goalkeepers				
Crossley, Mark	6.4	Oldham	Barnsley	16.06.69
Lee, Tommy	6.2	Macclesfield	Keighley	03.01.86
Defenders				
Darikwa, Tendayi	5.10	–	Nottingham	13.12.91
Downes, Aaron	6.1	Frickley	Mudgee, Aus	15.05.85
Ford, Simon	6.1	Kilmarnock	Newham	17.11.81
Holden, Dean	6.1	Shrewsbury	Salford	15.09.79
Lowry, Jamie	6.0	–	Newquay	18.03.87
Robertson, Gregor	6.0	Rotherham	Edinburgh	19.01.84
Midfielders				
Clay, Craig	5.11	–	Nottingham	05.05.92
Mattis, Dwayne	6.0	Walsall	Huddersfield	31.07.81
Niven, Derek	5.10	Raith	Falkirk	12.12.83
Randall, Mark	6.0	Arsenal	Milton Keynes	28.09.89
Smith, Nathan	6.0	Yeovil	Enfield	11.01.87
Whitaker, Danny	5.10	Oldham	Manchester	14.11.80
Forwards				
Allott, Mark	5.11	Tranmere	Manchester	03.10.77
Boden, Scott	5.11	Sheffield Utd	Sheffield	19.12.89
Bowery, Jordan	6.1	–	Nottingham	02.07.91
Lester, Jack	5.10	Nottm Forest	Sheffield	08.10.75
Morgan, Dean	6.0	MK Dons	Edmonton	03.10.83
Talbot, Drew	5.10	Luton	Barnsley	19.07.86

COLCHESTER UNITED

Ground: Weston Homes Community Stadium, United Way, Colchester CO4 5HE
Telephone: 01206 755100. **Club nickname:** U's
First-choice-colours: Blue and white shirts; blue shorts; blue socks
Capacity for 2011–12: 10,110
Record attendance: At Layer Road: 19,072 v Reading (FA Cup 1) 27 Nov, 1948;
Community Stadium: 10,064 v Norwich (Lge 1) 16 Jan, 2010

Goalkeepers				
Cousins, Mark	6.1	–	Chelmsford	09.01.87
Pentney, Carl	6.0	Leicester	Colchester	29.10.89
Williams, Ben	6.0	Carlisle	Manchester	27.08.82
Defenders				
Baldwin, Pat	6.0	Chelsea	London	12.11.82
Bender, Thomas	6.3	–	Harlow	19.01.93
Eastman, Tom	6.3	Ipswich	Colchester	21.10.91

Heath, Matt	6.4	Leeds	Leicester	01.11.81
Okuonghae, Magnus	6.4	Dagenham	Croydon	16.02.86
Rose, Michael	5.11	Swindon	Salford	28.07.82
White, John	6.0	–	Colchester	25.07.86
Wilson, Brian	5.10	Bristol City	Manchester	09.05.83

Midfielders

Bond, Andy	5.11	Barrow	Wigan	16.03.86
Coker, Ben	5.11	Bury Town	Cambridge	01.07.90
Izzet, Kemal	5.8	Charlton	Whitechapel	29.09.80
James, Lloyd	5.11	Southampton	Bristol	16.02.88
O'Toole, John-Joe	6.2	Watford	Harrow	30.09.88
Sanderson, Jordan	6.0	–	Waltham Forest	07.08.93
Wordsworth, Anthony	6.1	–	London	03.01.89

Forwards

Vincent, Ashley	6.0	Cheltenham	Birmingham	26.05.85
Gillespie, Steven	5.9	Cheltenham	Liverpool	04.06.85
Henderson, Ian	5.9	Ankaraguco	Thetford	24.01.85
Odejayi, Kayode	6.2	Barnsley	Ibadon, Nig	21.02.82

EXETER CITY

Ground: St James Park, Stadium Way, Exeter EX4 6PX
Telephone: 01392 411243. **Club nickname:** Grecians
First-choice colours: Red and white shirts, black shorts, black socks
Capacity for 2011–12: 8,830
Record attendance: 20,894 v Sunderland (FA Cup 6) 4 Mar, 1931

Goalkeepers

| Krysiak, Artur | 6.4 | Birmingham | Lodz, Pol | 11.08.89 |
| Pidgeley, Lenny | 6.4 | Bradford | Twickenham | 07.02.84 |

Defenders

Archibald-Henville, Troy	6.2	Tottenham	Newham	04.11.88
Bennett, Scott	5.10	–	Truro	30.11.90
Coles, Danny	6.1	Bristol Rov	Bristol	31.10.81
Duffy, Richard	5.9	Millwall	Swansea	30.08.85
Golbourne, Scott	5.9	Reading	Bristol	29.02.88
Jones, Billy	6.1	Crewe	Gillingham	26.06.83
Tully, Steve	5.9	Weymouth	Paignton	10.02.80

Midfielders

Dunne, James	5.11	Arsenal	Farnborough	18.09.89
Noble, David	6.0	Bristol City	Hitchin	02.02.82
Sercombe, Liam	5.10	–	Exeter	25.04.90
Shephard, Chris	6.3	–	Exeter	02.06.90

Forwards

Bauza, Guillem	6.0	Northampton	Palma	25.10.84
Logan, Richard	6.1	Weymouth	Bury St Edmunds	04.01.82
Nardiello, Danny	5.11	Blackpool	Coventry	22.10.82
O'Flynn, John	5.11	Barnet	Cobh, Ire	11.07.82

HARTLEPOOL UNITED

Ground: Victoria Park, Clarence Road, Hartlepool TS24 8BZ
Telephone: 01429 272584. **Club nickname:** Pool
First-choice colours: Blue and white shirts; blue shorts; white socks
Capacity for 2011–12: 7,787
Record attendance: 17,426 v Manchester Utd (FA Cup 3) 5 Jan, 1957

Goalkeepers

Flinders, Scott	6.4	Crystal Palace	Rotherham	12.06.86
Rafferty, Andy	5.11	Guisborough	Guisborough	27.05.88

Defenders

Austin, Neil	5.10	Darlington	Barnsley	26.04.83
Collins, Sam	6.2	Hull	Pontefract	05.06.77
Hartley, Peter	6.1	Sunderland	Hartlepool	03.04.88
Haslam, Steve	5.11	Bury	Sheffield	06.09.79
Horwood, Evan	6.0	Carlisle	Hartlepool	10.03.86
Humphreys, Richie	5.11	Cambridge Utd	Sheffield	30.11.77
Johnson, Paul	5.10	–	Sunderland	05.04.92

Midfielders

Liddle, Gary	6.1	Middlesbrough	Middlesbrough	15.06.86
Luscombe, Nathan	5.8	Sunderland	Gateshead	06.11.89
Monkhouse, Andy	6.1	Swindon	Leeds	23.10.80
Murray, Paul	5.7	Shrewsbury	Carlisle	31.08.76
Solano, Nolberto	5.9	Hull	Callao, Per	12.12.74
Sweeney, Anthony	6.0	–	Stockton	05.09.83

Forwards

Boyd, Adam	5.9	Leyton Orient	Hartlepool	25.05.82
Brown, James	5.11	–	Cramlington	03.01.87
Larkin, Colin	5.9	Northampton	Dundalk, Ire	27.04.82
Nish, Colin	6.3	Hibernian	Edinburgh	07.03.81
Poole, James	5.11	Manchester City	Stockport	20.03.90

HUDDERSFIELD TOWN

Ground: Galpharm Stadium, Huddersfield HD1 6PX
Telephone: 0870 444 4677. **Club nickname:** Terriers
First-choice colours: Blue and white shirts; white shorts; blue socks
Capacity for 2011–12: 24,554
Record attendance: Leeds Road: 67,037 v Arsenal (FA Cup 6) 27 Feb, 1932;
Galpharm Stadium: 23,678 v Liverpool (FA Cup 3) 12 Dec, 1999

Goalkeepers

Bennett, Ian	6.0	Sheffield Utd	Worksop	10.10.71
Colgan, Nick	6.2	Grimsby	Drogheda, Ire	19.09.73
Smithies, Alex	6.1	–	Huddersfield	25.03.90

Defenders

Clarke, Nathan	6.2	–	Halifax	30.11.83
Clarke, Peter	6.0	Southend	Southport	03.01.82
Clarke, Tom	5.11	–	Halifax	21.12.87
Hunt, Jack	5.9	–	Leeds	06.12.90
McCombe, Jamie	6.5	Bristol City	Pontefract	01.01.83
Naysmith, Gary	5.11	Sheffield Utd	Edinburgh	16.11.78
Pearson, Greg	6.2	–	Halifax	25.12.92
Ridehalgh, Liam	5.10	–	Halifax	20.04.91
Woods, Calum	5.11	Dunfermline	Liverpool	05.02.87

Midfielders

Arfield, Scott	5.10	Falkirk	Livingston	01.11.88
Atkinson, Chris	6.1	–	Huddersfield	13.02.92
Cadamarteri, Danny	5.9	Dundee Utd	Cleckheaton	12.10.79
Chippendale, Aidan	5.8	Bradford	Bradford	24.05.92
Crooks, Matty	6.0	–	Huddersfield	20.01.94
Gobern, Oscar	5.11	Southampton	Birmingham	26.01.91

Gudjonsson, Joey	5.8	Burnley	Akranes, Ice	25.05.80
Kay, Antony	5.11	Tranmere	Barnsley	21.10.82
McDermott, Donal	5.10	Manchester City	Co Meath, Ire	19.10.89
Miller, Tommy	6.1	Sheffield Wed	Shotton	08.01.79
Roberts, Gary	5.10	Ipswich	Chester	18.03.84
Forwards				
Cham, Hatib	6.1	–	Pontefract	14.02.94
Lee, Alan	6.2	Crystal Palace	Galway, Ire	21.08.78
Novak, Lee	6.0	Gateshead	Newcastle	28.09.88
Rhodes, Jordan	6.1	Ipswich	Oldham	05.02.90
Simpson, Robbie	6.0	Coventry	Cambridge	15.03.85
Spencer, James	6.1	–	Leeds	13.12.91

LEYTON ORIENT

Ground: Matchroom Stadium, Brisbane Road, London E10 5NE
Telephone: 0871 310 1881. **Club nickname:** O's
First-choice colours: All red
Capacity for 2011–12: 9,311
Record attendance: 34,345 v West Ham (FA Cup 4) 25 Jan, 1964

Goalkeepers				
Butcher, Lee	6.0	Tottenham	Waltham Forest	11.10.88
Jones, Jamie	6.0	Everton	Kirkby	18.02.89
Defenders				
Chorley, Ben	6.3	Tranmere	Sidcup	30.09.82
Forbes, Terrell	6.0	Yeovil	Southwark	17.08.81
Omozusi, Elliot	5.11	Fulham	Hackney	15.12.88
Midfielders				
Cox, Dean	5.5	–	Brighton	12.08.87
Cuthbert, Scott	6.2	Swindon	Alexandria, Sco	15.06.87
Daniels, Charlie	5.10	Tottenham	Harlow	07.09.86
Dawson, Stephen	5.6	Bury	Dublin, Ire	04.12.85
McSweeney, Leon	6.1	Hartlepool	Cork, Ire	19.02.83
Smith, Jimmy	6.1	Chelsea	Newham	07.01.87
Spring, Matthew	6.0	Charlton	Harlow	17.11.79
Forwards				
Cureton, Jamie	5.8	Exeter	Bristol	28.08.75
Porter, George	5.10	Cray	London	27.06.92
Revell, Alex	6.3	Southend	Cambridge	07.07.83
Tehoue, Jonathan	5.10	Konyaspor	Paris, Fr	03.05.84

MILTON KEYNES DONS

Ground: stadiummk, Stadium Way West, Milton Keynes MK1 1ST
Telephone: 01908 622922. **Club nickname:** Dons
First-choice colours: All white
Capacity for 2011–12: 21,189
Record attendance: Wimbledon: 8,118 v West Ham (Div 1), 25 Nov, 2003; stadiummk: 17,250 v Morecambe (Lge 2), 3 May, 2008

Goalkeepers				
Martin, David	6.2	Liverpool	Romford	22.01.86
Defenders				
Chicksen, Adam	5.8	–	Milton Keynes	01.11.90

Doumbe, Mathias	6.1	Plymouth	Drancy, Fr	28.10.79
Flanagan, Tom	6.2	–	Hammersmith	30.12.91
Lewington, Dean	5.11	–	Kingston	18.05.84
MacKenzie, Gary	6.3	Dundee	Lanark	15.10.85
Midfielders				
Baldock, George	5.9	–	Buckingham	26.01.93
Chadwick, Luke	5.11	Norwich	Cambridge	18.11.80
Coronado, Igor	5.8	–	Brazil	15.04.92
Gleeson, Stephen	6.2	Wolves	Dublin, Ire	03.08.88
Potter, Darren	5.10	Sheffield Wed	Liverpool	21.12.84
Powell, Daniel	6.2	–	Luton	12.03.91
Williams, Shaun	6.0	Sporting Fingal	Dublin	19.09.86
Forwards				
Baldock, Sam	5.8	–	Bedford	15.03.89
Bowditch, Dean	5.11	Yeovil	Bishop's Stortford	15.06.86
Collins, Charlie	6.0	–	Wandsworth	22.11.91
Guy, Lewis	5.10	Doncaster	Penrith	27.08.85
Ibehre, Jabo	6.2	Walsall	Islington	28.01.83

NOTTS COUNTY

Ground: Meadow Lane, Nottingham NG2 3HJ
Telephone: 0115 952 9000. **Club nickname:** Magpies
First-choice colours: Black and white shirts; black shorts; black socks
Capacity for 2011–12: 19,318
Record attendance: 47,310 v York (FA Cup 6) 12 Mar, 1955

Goalkeepers				
Burch, Rob	6.0	Lincoln	Yeovil	08.02.84
Nelson, Stuart	6.1	Aberdeen	Stroud	17.09.81
Defenders				
Edwards, Mike	6.1	Grimsby	Hessle	25.04.80
Hughes, Jeff	6.1	Bristol Rov	Larne	29.05.85
Hunt, Stephen	6.1	Colchester	Southampton	11.11.84
Judge, Alan	6.0	Blackburn	Dublin, Ire	11.11.88
Kelly, Julian	5.9	Reading	Enfield	06.09.89
Pearce, Krystian	6.1	Huddersfield	Birmingham	05.01.90
Sheehan, Alan	5.11	Swindon	Athlone, Ire	14.09.86
Sodje, Sam	6.0	Charlton	Greenwich	25.05.79
Stirling, Jude	6.2	MK Dons	Enfield	29.06.82
Midfielders				
Bencherif, Hamza	6.0	Macclesfield	Paris, Fr	09.02.88
Bishop, Neal	6.0	Barnet	Stockton	07.08.81
Demontagnac, Ishmel	5.10	Blackpool	London	15.06.88
Ravenhill, Ricky	5.10	Darlington	Doncaster	16.01.81
Spicer, John	5.11	Doncaster	Romford	13.09.83
Forwards				
Burgess, Ben	6.3	Blackpool	Buxton	09.11.81
Hawley, Karl	5.8	Preston	Walsall	06.12.81
Hughes, Lee	5.10	Oldham	Smethwick	22.05.76
Westcarr, Craig	5.11	Kettering	Nottingham	29.01.85

OLDHAM ATHLETIC

Ground: Boundary Park, Oldham OL1 2PA
Telephone: 0161 624 4972. **Club nickname:** Latics

First-choice colours: All blue
Capacity for 2011–12: 10,850
Record attendance: 47,761 v Sheffield Wed (FA Cup 4) 25 Jan, 1930

Goalkeepers

Name	Height	Previous club	Birthplace	Birthdate
Cisak, Alex	6.4	Accrington	Krakow, Pol	19.05.89
Gerrard, Paul	6.2	Stockport	Heywood	22.01.73

Defenders

Name	Height	Previous club	Birthplace	Birthdate
Black, Paul	6.0	–	Middleton	18.05.90
Lee, Kieran	6.1	Manchester Utd	Tameside	22.06.88
Mvoto, Jean-Yves	6.4	Sunderland	Paris, Fr	06.09.88
Tarkowski, James	5.11	–	Manchester	19.11.92
Winchester, Carl	5.11	Linfield	Belfast	12.04.93

Midfielders

Name	Height	Previous club	Birthplace	Birthdate
Burns, Ryan	5.10	Cliftonville	Belfast	08.09.92
Carr, Matthew	5.10	–	Bury	23.12.92
Furman, Dean	5.11	Rangers	Cape Town, SA	22.06.88
Hughes, Connor	5.10	–	Bolton	06.05.93
McGrath, Phil	5.9	Glenavon	Belfast	07.04.92
Morais, Filipe	5.9	St Johnstone	Lisbon, Por	21.11.85
Taylor, Chris	5.11	–	Oldham	20.12.86

Forwards

Name	Height	Previous club	Birthplace	Birthdate
Bembo-Leta, Djeny	6.0	–	Kinshasa, DR Con	09.11.91
Brooke, Ryan	6.1	–	Crewe	04.10.90
Feeney, Warren	5.10	Cardiff	Belfast	17.01.81
Millar, Kirk	5.9	Linfield	Belfast	07.07.92
Reid, Reuben	6.0	WBA	Bristol	26.07.88
Smith, Matt	6.6	Solihull Motors	–	–

PRESTON NORTH END

Ground: Deepdale, Sir Tom Finney Way, Preston PR1 6RU
Telephone: 0844 856 1964. **Club nickname:** Lilywhites
First-choice colours: White shirts; blue shorts; blue and white socks
Capacity for 2011–12: 23,408
Record attendance: 42,684 v Arsenal (Div 1) 23 Apr, 1938

Name	Height ft in	Previous club	Birthplace	Birthdate
Goalkeepers				
Arestidou, Andreas	6.2	Shrewsbury	Morecambe	06.12.89
Lonergan, Andy	6.4	–	Preston	19.10.83
Defenders				
Collins, Dominic	5.11	–	Preston	15.04.91
Devine, Daniel	6.0	Linfield	Belfast	07.09.92
Gray, David	5.11	Manchester Utd	Edinburgh	04.05.88
Leather, Scott	6.1	Crewe	Manchester	30.09.92
McLaughlin, Conor	6.0	Linfield	Belfast	26.07.91
Morgan, Craig	6.0	Peterborough	St Asaph	18.06.85
Wright, Bailey	5.10	VIS	Melbourne, Aus	28.07.92
Midfielders				
Ashbee, Ian	6.1	Cambridge Utd	Birmingham	06.09.76
Barton, Adam	5.10	Blackburn	Blackburn	07.01.91
Carter, Darren	6.2	WBA	Solihull	18.12.83
Clucas, Seanan	5.10	Dungannon	Dungannon	08.11.92

Coutts, Paul	6.1	Peterborough	Aberdeen	22.07.88
Mayor, Danny	6.0	–	Leyland	18.10.90
Miller, George	5.9	–	Eccleston	25.11.91
Nicholson, Barry	5.8	Aberdeen	Dumfries	24.08.78
Parry, Paul	5.10	Cardiff	Chepstow	19.08.80
Russell, Darel	5.11	Norwich	Stepney	22.10.80
Treacy, Keith	6.0	Blackburn	Dublin, Ire	13.09.88
Forwards				
Hume, Iain	5.7	Barnsley	Brampton, Can	31.10.83
Proctor, Jamie	6.2	–	Preston	25.03.92

ROCHDALE

Ground: Spotland, Wilbutts Lane, Rochdale OL11 5DS
Telephone: 01706 644648. **Club nickname:** Dale
First-choice colours: Blue and black shirts; white shorts; white socks
Capacity for 2011–12: 10,034
Record attendance: 24,231 v Notts Co (FA Cup 2) 10 Dec, 1949

Goalkeepers				
Edwards, Matthew	6.3	Leeds	Liverpool	22.08.90
Defenders				
Brown, Chris	6.3	–	Hazel Grove	21.02.92
Darby, Stephen	5.9	Liverpool	Liverpool	06.10.88
Holness, Marcus	6.0	Oldham	Oldham	08.12.88
Twaddle, Marc	6.1	Falkirk	Glasgow	27.08.86
Widdowson, Joe	6.0	Grimsby	Forest Gate	29.03.87
Midfielders				
Adams, Nicky	5.10	Brentford	Bolton	16.10.86
Barry-Murphy, Brian	6.0	Bury	Cork, Ire	27.07.78
Hackney, Simon	5.9	Colchester	Manchester	05.02.84
Jones, Gary	5.10	Barnsley	Birkenhead	03.06.77
Kennedy, Jason	6.1	Darlington	Stockton	11.09.86
Thompson, Joe	6.0	–	Rochdale	05.03.89
Tutte, Andrew	5.9	Manchester City	Liverpool	21.09.90
Forwards				
Akpa Apro, Jean-Louis	6.0	Grimsby	Toulouse, Fr	04.01.85
Elding, Anthony	5.7	Ferencvaros	Boston	16.04.82
Gray, Reece	5.7	–	Oldham	01.09.92
Grimes, Ashley	6.0	Millwall	Swinton	09.12.86
O'Grady, Chris	6.1	Oldham	Nottingham	25.01.86

SCUNTHORPE UNITED

Ground: Glanford Park, Doncaster Road, Scunthorpe DN15 8TD
Telephone: 0871 221 1899. **Club nickname:** Iron
First-choice colours: Claret and blue shirts, white shorts; claret socks
Capacity for 2011–12: 9,088
Record attendance: Old Show Ground: 23,935 v Portsmouth (FA Cup 4) 30 Jan, 1954; Glanford Park: 8,921 v Newcastle (Champ) 20 Oct, 2009

Goalkeepers				
Lillis, Josh	6.0	–	Derby	24.06.87
Slocombe, Sam	6.0	Bottesford	Scunthorpe	05.06.88
Turner, Jake	6.1	–	Retford	19.01.93

Defenders

Byrne, Cliff	6.0	Sunderland	Dublin, Ire	26.04.82
Canavan, Niall	6.3	–	Leeds	11.04.91
Nelson, Michael	5.9	Norwich	Gateshead	15.03.82
Nolan, Eddie	6.1	Preston	Waterford, Ire	05.08.88
Palmer, Ashley	6.1	Barnsley	Pontefract	09.11.92
Raynes, Michael	6.3	Stockport	Manchester	15.10.87
Reid, Paul	6.2	Colchester	Carlisle	18.02.82

Midfielders

Barcham, Andy	5.9	Gillingham	Basildon	16.12.86
Collins, Michael	6.0	Huddersfield	Halifax	30.04.86
Duffy, Mark	5.9	Morecambe	Liverpool	07.10.85
Hughes, Andy	5.11	Leeds	Manchester	02.01.78
O'Connor, Michael	6.1	Crewe	Belfast	06.10.87
Ryan, Jimmy	5.10	Accrington	Maghull	06.09.88
Thompson, Garry	5.11	Morecambe	Kendal	24.11.80
Togwell, Sam	5.11	Barnsley	Maidenhead	14.10.85
Wright, Andrew	6.1	West Virginia Univ	Liverpool	15.01.85

Forwards

Dagnall, Chris	5.8	Rochdale	Liverpool	15.04.86
Godden, Matt	5.10	–	Canterbury	29.07.91
Grant, Bobby	5.11	Accrington	Blackpool	01.07.90
Robertson, Jordan	6.0	St Johnstone	Sheffield	12.02.88

SHEFFIELD UNITED

Ground: Bramall Lane, Sheffield S2 4SU
Telephone: 0871 995 1899. **Club nickname:** Blades
First-choice colours: Red and white shirts; black shorts; black socks
Capacity for 2011–12: 32,609
Record attendance: 68,287 v Leeds (FA Cup 5) 15 Feb, 1936

Goalkeepers

Aksalu, Mihkel	6.5	Flora Tallinn	Kuressaare, Est	07.11.84
Long, George	6.4	–	Sheffield	05.11.93
Simonsen, Steve	6.3	Stoke	Federica, Den	12.06.76

Defenders

Collins, Neil	6.3	Leeds	Troon	02.09.83
Conneely, Seamus		Galway	London	09.07.88
Ertl, Johannes	6.2	Crystal Palace	Graz, Aut	13.11.82
Kozluk, Rob	5.8	Barnsley	Sutton-in-Ashfield	05.08.77
Lescinel, Jean-Francois	6.2	Swindon	Cayenne, F Gui	02.10.86
Lowton, Matthew	5.11	–	Chesterfield	09.06.89
Maguire, Harry	6.2	–	Sheffield	05.03.93
Morgan, Chris	6.1	Barnsley	Barnsley	09.11.77
Taylor, Andy	5.11	Tranmere	Blackburn	14.03.86
Warren, Marc	5.8	Central Coast	Sutherland, Aus	11.02.92

Midfielders

Doyle, Michael	5.10	Coventry	Dublin, Ire	08.07.81
McAllister, David	5.11	St Patrick's	Dublin, Ire	29.12.88
Montgomery, Nick	5.9	–	Leeds	28.10.81
Quinn, Stephen	5.6	–	Dublin, Ire	04.04.86
Williamson, Lee	5.10	Watford	Derby	07.06.82
Yeates, Mark	5.9	Middlesbrough	Dublin, Ire	11.01.85

Forwards

Bogdanovic, Daniel	6.2	Barnsley	Misrata, Libya	26.03.80

Evans Ched	6.0	Manchester City	St Asaph	28.12.88
Cresswell, Richard	6.1	Stoke	Bridlington	20.09.77
Philliskirk, Danny	5.10	Chelsea	Oldham	10.04.91

SHEFFIELD WEDNESDAY

Ground: Hillsborough, Sheffield, S6 1SW
Telephone: 0871 995 1867. **Club nickname:** Owls
First-choice colours: Blue and white shirts; black shorts; blue socks
Capacity for 2011–12: 39,812
Record attendance: 72,841 v Manchester City (FA Cup 5) 17 Feb, 1934

Goalkeepers

Jameson, Arron	6.3	–	Sheffield	07.11.89
O'Donnell, Richard	6.2	–	Sheffield	12.09.88
Weaver, Nicky	6.3	Burnley	Sheffield	02.03.79

Defenders

Beevers, Mark	6.4	–	Barnsley	21.11.89
Bennett, Julian	6.1	Nottm Forest	Nottingham	17.12.84
Buxton, Lewis	6.1	Stoke	Newport, IOW	10.12.83
Johnson, Reda	6.3	Plymouth	Marseille, Fr	21.03.88
Jones, Rob	6.7	Scunthorpe	Stockton	03.11.79
Otsemobor, Jon	5.10	Southampton	Liverpool	23.03.83
Reynolds, Mark	6.1	Motherwell	Motherwell	07.05.87
Semedo, Jose	6.0	Charlton	Setubal, Por	11.01.85

Midfielders

Coke, Giles	6.0	Motherwell	Westminster	03.06.86
Johnson, Jermaine	5.9	Bradford	Kingston, Jam	25.06.80
Jones, Daniel	6.2	Wolves	Wordsley	23.12.86
O'Connor, James	5.8	Burnley	Dublin, Ire	01.09.79
Palmer, Liam	5.10	–	Worksop	19.09.91
Prutton, David	6.1	Swindon	Hull	12.09.81
Sedgwick, Chris	5.11	Preston	Sheffield	28.04.80

Forwards

Madine, Gary	6.4	Carlisle	Gateshead	24.08.90
Morrison, Clinton	6.1	Coventry	Wandsworth	14.05.79
Modest, Nathan	5.9	–	Sheffield	29.09.91

STEVENAGE

Ground: Lamex Stadium, Broadhall Way, Stevenage SG2 8RH
Telephone: 01438 223223. **Club nickname:** Borough
First-choice colours: White shirts; red shorts; red socks
Capacity for 2011–12: 7,100.
Record attendance: 8,040 v Newcastle (FA Cup 4) 25 January, 1998

Goalkeepers

| Julian, Alan | 6.2 | Gillingham | Ashford, Kent | 11.03.83 |
| Day, Chris | 6.2 | Millwall | Walthamstow | 28.07.75 |

Defenders

Albrighton, Mark	6.1	Cambridge Utd	Nuneaton	06.03.76
Ashton, Jon	6.2	Grays	Nuneaton	04.10.82
Bostwick, Michael	–	Ebbsfleet	London	17.05.88
Charles, Darius	6.1	Ebbsfleet	Ealing	10.12.87
Edwards, Phil	5.8	Accrington	Kirkby	08.11.85

Henry, Ronnie	5.11	Dublin City	Hemel Hempstead	02.01.84
Laird, Scott	5.9	Plymouth	Taunton	15.05.88
Roberts, Mark	6.1	Northwich	Northwich	16.10.83
Wilson, Lawrie	5.10	Colchester	Collier Row	11.09.87
Midfielders				
Bridges, David	6.0	Kettering	Huntingdon	22.09.82
Byrom, Joel	6.0	Northwich	Oswaldtwistle	14.09.86
Long, Stacy	5.8	Ebbsfleet	Bromley	11.01.85
Mousinho, John	6.1	Wycombe	Isleworth	30.04.86
Murphy, Darren	6.1	Cork	Cork, Ire	28.07.85
Forwards				
Beardsley, Chris	6.0	Kettering	Derby	28.02.84
Madjo, Guy	6.0	Bylis Ballsh	Douala, Cam	01.06.84
Reid, Craig	5.10	Newport	Coventry	17.12.85
Winn, Peter	6.0	Scunthorpe	Grimsby	19.12.88

TRANMERE ROVERS

Ground: Prenton Park, Prenton Road West, Birkenhead CH42 9PY
Telephone: 0871 221 2001. **Club nickname:** Rovers
First-choice colours: All white
Capacity for 2011–12: 16,151
Record attendance: 24,424 v Stoke (FA Cup 4) 5 Feb, 1972

Goalkeepers				
Fon Williams, Owain	6.4	Rochdale	Caernarfon	17.03.87
Defenders				
Bakayogo, Zoumana	6.0	Alfortville	Paris, Fr	17.08.86
Goodison, Ian	6.3	Hull	Kingston, Jam	21.11.72
Holmes, Danny	6.0	New Saints	Wirral	06.01.89
Kay, Michael	6.1	Sunderland	Shotley Bridge	09.12.89
McChrystal, Mark	6.1	Derry	Derry	26.06.84
Midfielders				
Labadie, Joss	6.3	WBA	Croydon	30.08.90
Mahon, Alan	5.10	Burnley	Dublin, Ire	04.04.78
Robinson, Andy	5.9	Leeds	Birkenhead	03.11.79
Taylor, Ash	6.0	–	Bromborough	02.09.90
Weir, Robbie	5.9	Sunderland	Belfast	09.12.88
Welsh, John	6.0	Hull	Liverpool	10.01.84
Forwards				
Akins, Lucas	6.0	Hamilton	Huddersfield	25.02.89
Jennings, Dale	5.7	–	–	21.12.92
McGurk, Adam	5.10	Hednesford	Larne	24.01.89
Showunmi, Enoch	6.4	Falkirk	Kilburn	21.04.82

WALSALL

Ground: Banks's Stadium, Bescot Crescent, Walsall WS1 4SA
Telephone: 01922 622791. **Club nickname:** Saddlers
First-choice colours: Red shirts; white shorts; red socks
Capacity for 2011–12: 10,989
Record attendance: Fellows Park: 25,433 v Newcastle (Div 2) 29 Aug, 1961; Bescot Stadium: 11,307 v Wolves (Div 1) 11 Jan, 2003

Goalkeepers				
Bevan, David	6.2	Aston Villa	Cork, Ire	24.06.89

Walker, Jimmy	5.11	Tottenham	Sutton-in-Ashfield	09.07.73
Defenders				
Butler, Andy	6.0	Huddersfield	Doncaster	04.11.83
Chambers, Adam	5.10	Leyton Orient	Sandwell	20.11.80
Lancashire, Oliver	6.1	Southampton	Basingstoke	13.12.88
Sadler, Mat	5.11	Watford	Birmingham	26.02.85
Smith, Manny	6.2	–	Birmingham	08.11.88
Taundry, Richard	6.0	–	Walsall	15.02.89
Westlake, Darryl	5.9	–	Sutton Coldfield	01.03.91
Midfielders				
Forde, Aaron	5.10	–	Birmingham	21.05.93
Gnakpa, Claude	6.2	Luton	Marseilles, Fr	09.06.83
Gray, Julian	6.1	Barnsley	Lewisham	21.09.79
Hurst, Kevan	6.0	Carlisle	Chesterfield	27.08.85
Richards, Matt	5.9	Ipswich	Harlow	26.12.84
Forwards				
Bowerman, George	5.10	–	Wordsley	06.11.91
Grigg, Will	5.11	Stratford	Solihull	03.07.91
Jarvis, Ryan	5.11	Leyton Orient	Fakenham	11.07.86
Macken, Jon	5.11	Barnsley	Manchester	07.09.77
Nicholls, Alex	5.10	–	Stourbridge	09.12.87
Paterson, Jamie	5.9	–	Coventry	20.12.91

WYCOMBE WANDERERS

Ground: Adams Park, Hillbottom Road, High Wycombe HP12 4HJ
Telephone: 01494 472100. **Club nickname:** Chairboys
First-choice colours: Light and dark blue shirts; dark blue shorts; light and dark blue socks
Capacity for 2011–12: 10,000
Record attendance: 9,921 v Fulham (FA Cup 3) 8 Jan, 2002

Goalkeepers				
Arnold, Steve	6.4	Eastleigh	Welham Gren	
Bull, Nikki	6.2	Brentford	Hastings	02.10.81
Defenders				
Foster, Danny	6.1	Brentford	Enfield	23.09.84
Johnson, Leon	6.0	Gillingham	London	10.05.81
McCoy, Marvin	5.10	Wealdstone	Waltham Forest	02.10.88
Tunnicliffe, James	6.4	Brighton	Manchester	17.01.89
Winfield, Dave	6.3	Aldershot	Aldershot	24.03.88
Midfielders				
Ainsworth, Gareth	5.9	QPR	Blackburn	10.05.73
Betsy, Kevin	6.1	Southend	Woking	20.03.78
Bloomfield, Matt	5.8	Ipswich	Felixstowe	08.02.84
Donnelly, Scott	5.8	Swansea	Hammersmith	25.12.87
Grant, Joel	6.0	Crewe	Hammersmith	27.08.87
Hails, John	6.0	Aldershot	Islington	14.02.82
Harding, Ben	6.1	Aldershot	Carshalton	06.09.84
Harris, Kadeem	5.9	–	London	08.06.93
Lewis, Stuart	5.11	Dagenham	Welwyn Garden City	15.10.87
Forwards				
Beavon, Stuart	5.10	Weymouth	Reading	05.05.84
Benyon, Elliot	5.9	Swindon	High Wycombe	29.08.87
McClure, Matt	5.10	Crystal Palace	Slough	17.11.91
Rendell, Scott	6.1	Peterborough	Ashford, Surrey	21.10.86

Sandell, Andy	6.0	Aldershot	Swindon	08.09.83
Strevens, Ben	6.1	Brentford	Islington	24.05.80

YEOVIL TOWN

Ground: Huish Park, Lufton Way, Yeovil BA22 8YF
Telephone: 01935 423662. **Club nickname:** Glovers
First-choice colours: Green and white shirts; white shorts; white socks
Capacity for 2011–12: 9,665
Record attendance: 9,348 v Liverpool (FA Cup 3) 4 Jan, 2004

Goalkeepers				
Stewart, Gareth	6.0	Welling	Preston	03.02.80
Defenders				
Ayling, Luke	6.1	Arsenal	London	25.08.91
Huntington, Paul	6.2	Stockport	Carlisle	17.09.87
Jones, Nathan	5.7	Brighton	Rhondda	28.05.73
N'Gala, Bondz	6.2	Plymouth	Forest Gate	13.09.89
Midfielders				
Gibson, Billy	6.1	Watford	Watford	30.09.90
Upson, Ed	5.10	Ipswich	Bury St Edmunds	21.11.89
Williams, Gavin	5.11	Bristol Rov	Merthyr	20.07.80
Wotton, Paul	5.11	Southampton	Plymouth	17.08.77
Forwards				
Agard, Kieran	5.10	Everton	London	10.10.89
Williams, Andy	5.11	Bristol Rov	Hereford	14.08.86

LEAGUE TWO

ACCRINGTON STANLEY

Ground: Crown Ground, Livingstone Road, Accrington BB5 5BX
Telephone: 0871 434 1968. **Club nickname:** Stanley
First-choice colours: All red
Capacity for 2011–12: 5,057
Record attendance: 4,368 v Colchester (FA Cup 3) 3 Jan, 2003

Name	Height ft in	Previous club	Birthplace	Birthdate
Goalkeepers				
Dunbavin, Ian	6.1	Halifax	Knowsley	27.05.80
Defenders				
Coid, Danny	5.11	Blackpool	Liverpool	03.10.81
Hessey, Sean	5.10	Macclesfield	Liverpool	19.09.78
Murphy, Peter	6.0	–	Liverpool	13.02.90
Richardson, Leam	5.7	Blackpool	Leeds	19.11.79
Winnard, Dean	5.9	Blackburn	Wigan	20.08.89
Midfielders				
Barnett, Charlie	5.8	Tranmere	Liverpool	19.09.88
Burton, Alan	6.0	–	Blackpool	22.02.91
Craney, Ian	6.0	Fleetwood	Liverpool	21.07.82
Joyce, Luke	5.11	Carlisle	Bolton	09.07.87
McConville, Sean	5.11	Skelmersdale	Liverpool	06.03.89
Procter, Andrew	5.11	Great Harwood	Blackburn	13.03.83

Forwards

Gornell, Terry	5.11	Tranmere	Liverpool	16.12.89

AFC WIMBLEDON

Ground: Kingsmeadow, Kingston Road, Kingston upon Thames KT1 3PB
Telephone: 0208 547 3528. **Club nickname:** Dons
First-choice colours: All blue
Capacity for 2011–12: 4,722
Record attendance: 4,722 v St Albans (Blue Sq South Lge) 25 April, 2009

		Goalkeepers		
Brown, Seb	6.0	Brentford	Sutton	24.11.89
Turner, Jack	6.2	–	Ashford, Middx	17.09.92
Defenders				
Franks, Fraser	6.0	Brentford	–	22.11.90
Hatton, Sam	5.10	Stevenage	St Albans	07.02.88
Jackson, Ryan	5.11	–	Streatham	31.07.90
Johnson, Brett	6.1	Brentford	Hammersmith	15.08.85
Stuart, Jamie	5.10	Rushden	Southwark	15.10.76
Midfielders				
Jones, Reece	6.1	Fulham	Kingston	22.07.92
Minshull, Lee	6.2	Tonbridge	Chatham	11.11.85
Moore, Sammy	5.8	Dover	Deal	07.09.87
Porter, Max	5.10	Rushden	Orsett	29.06.87
Wellard, Ricky	5.11	Ashford, Middx	Hammersmith	09.05.88
Yussuff, Rashid	6.1	Gillingham	Poplar	23.09.89
Forwards				
Ademeno, Charles	5.10	Grimsby	Milton Keynes	12.12.88
Jolley, Christian	5.11	Kingstonian	Aldershot	12.05.88
Kedwell, Danny	5.11	Grays	Gillingham	22.10.85
Midson, Jack	6.2	Oxford	Stevenage	21.09.83
Moore, Luke	5.11	Ebbsfleet	Gravesend	27.04.88

ALDERSHOT TOWN

Ground: EBB Stadium, High Street, Aldershot GU11 1TW
Telephone: 01252 320221. **Club nickname:** Shots
First-choice colours: All red
Capacity for 2011–12: 7,100
Record attendance: 19,138 v Carlisle (FA Cup 4 replay) 28 Jan, 1970

Goalkeepers				
Clement, Jordan	6.0	–	Chertsey	12.06.93
Worner, Ross	6.1	Charlton	Hindhead	03.10.89
Young, Jamie	5.11	Wycombe	Brisbane, Aus	25.08.85
Defenders				
Bergqvist, Doug	5.11	QPR	Stockholm	29.03.93
Brown, Aaron	6.0	Leyton Orient	Wolverhampton	23.06.83
Charles, Anthony	6.1	Barnet	Isleworth	11.03.81
Herd, Ben	5.10	Shrewsbury	Welwyn Garden City	21.06.85
Jones, Darren	6.1	Hereford	Newport	26.08.83
Morris, Aaron	6.0	Cardiff	Rumney	30.12.89
Straker, Anthony	5.9	Crystal Palace	Ealing	23.09.88
Midfielders				
Breimyr, Henrik	5.11	Reading	Stavanger	20.07.93

Collins, Jamie	6.2	Newport	Barking	28.09.84
Guttridge, Luke	5.8	Northampton	Barnstaple	27.03.82
McGlashan, Jermaine	5.7	Ashford, Middx	Croydon	14.04.88
Mekki, Adam	5.9	Reading	Chester	24.12.91
Panther, Emmanuel	6.0	Exeter	Glasgow	11.05.84
Vincenti, Peter	6.2	Stevenage	Jersey	07.07.86
Worsfold, Max	5.11	–	Chertsey	25.10.92
Forwards				
Bubb, Bradley	5.10	Farnborough	Brent	20.05.87
Connolly, Reece	6.0	–	Frimley	22.01.92
Hylton, Danny	6.0	–	Camden	25.02.89
Rankine, Michael	6.2	York	Doncaster	15.01.85
Rodman, Alex	6.2	Tamworth	Sutton Coldfield	15.12.87

BARNET

Ground: Underhill Stadium, Barnet EN5 2DN
Telephone: 0208 441 6932. **Club nickname:** Bees
First-choice colours: Black and amber shirts; black shorts; black socks
Capacity for 2011–12: 5,583
Record attendance: 11,026 v Wycombe (FA Amateur Cup 4), Jan, 1954

Goalkeepers				
O'Brien, Liam	6.4	Portsmouth	Harrow	03.11.91
Defenders				
Dennehy, Darren	6.5	Cardiff	Tralee, Ire	21.09.88
Kamdjo, Clovis	5.11	Reading	Cameroon	15.12.90
Leach, Daniel	6.3	Portland	Redcliffe, Aus	05.01.86
Parkes, Jordan	6.0	Watford	Hemel Hempstead	26.07.89
Uddin, Anwar	6.2	Dagenham	Whitechapel	01.11.81
Midfielders				
Byrne, Mark	5.9	Nottm Forest	Kilnamanagh, Ire	09.11.88
Cox, Sam	5.5	Tottenham	Edgware	10.10.90
Deering, Sam	5.6	Oxford Utd	Tower Hamlets	26.02.91
Fraser, Tommy	5.11	Port Vale	Brighton	05.12.87
Hughes, Mark	5.10	Chester	Dungannon	16.09.83
Marshall, Mark	6.0	Swindon	Manchester, Jam	05.05.87
Vilhete, Mauro	5.9	–	Lisbon, Por	10.05.93
Forwards				
Adjeman-Pamboe, Kwame	5.8	Tampa Bay	London	24.10.87
Holmes, Ricky	6.2	Chelmsford	Uxbridge	19.06.87
Kabba, Steve	5.10	Brentford	Lambeth	07.03.81
McLeod, Izale	6.1	Charlton	Birmingham	15.10.84
Taylor, Charlie	6.2	Sutton	–	01.12.85

BRADFORD CITY

Ground: Coral Windows Stadium, Valley Parade, Bradford BD8 7DY
Telephone: 01274 773355. **Club nickname:** Bantams
First-choice colours: Yellow shirts; claret shorts; claret socks
Capacity for 2011–12: 25,136
Record attendance: 39,146 v Burnley (FA Cup 4) 11 Mar, 1911

| **Goalkeepers** | | | | |
| McLaughlin, Jon | 6.2 | Harrogate | Edinburgh | 09.09.87 |

Defenders

Branston, Guy	6.1	Torquay	Leicester	09.01.79
Hunt, Lewis	5.11	Wycombe	Birmingham	25.08.82
O'Brien, Luke	5.10	–	Halifax	11.09.88
Oliver, Luke	6.4	Wycombe	Hammersmith	04.09.82
Ramsden, Simon	6.0	Rochdale	Bishop Auckland	17.12.81
Threlfall, Robbie	6.0	Liverpool	Liverpool	28.11.88
Williams, Steve	6.4	Bamber Bridge	Preston	24.04.87

Midfielders

Bullock, Lee	5.11	Hartlepool	Stockton	22.05.81
Dean, Luke	5.10	–	Bradford	14.05.91
Flynn, Michael	5.10	Huddersfield	Newport	17.10.80
Mitchell, Chris	5.9	Falkirk	Stirling	21.07.88
Osborne, Leon	5.10	–	Doncaster	28.10.89
Syers, David	5.10	Guiseley	Leeds	30.11.87

Forwards

Hannah, Ross	5.11	Matlock	Sheffield	14.05.86
Hanson, James	6.4	Guiseley	Bradford	09.11.87
Osborne, Leon	5.10	–	Doncaster	28.11.89
Stewart, Mark	5.9	Falkirk	Glasgow	22.06.88

BRISTOL ROVERS

Ground: Memorial Ground, Filton Avenue, Horfield, Bristol BS7 0BF
Telephone: 0117 909 6648. **Club nickname:** Pirates
First-choice colours: Blue and white shirts; white shorts; white socks
Capacity for 2011–12: 11,626
Record attendance: Eastville: 38,472 v Preston (FA Cup 4) 30 Jan, 1960;
Memorial Ground: 11,530 v Bristol City (Johnstone's Paint Trophy, Southern Final, 2nd leg) 27 Feb, 2007

Goalkeepers

Bevan, Scott	6.6	Torquay	Southampton	19.09.79
Cronin, Lance	6.1	Gillingham	Brighton	11.09.85

Defenders

Brown, Lee	6.0	QPR	Farnborough	10.08.90
Byron, Anthony	6.1	Cardiff	Newport	20.09.84
Sawyer, Gary	6.0	Plymouth	Bideford	05.07.85
Smith, Michael	5.11	Ballymena	Ballyclare	04.09.88
Virgo, Adam	6.2	Yeovil	Brighton	25.01.83

Midfielders

Anyinsah, Joe	5.8	Charlton	Bristol	08.10.84
Brown, Wayne	5.9	Fulham	Kingston	06.08.88
Campbell, Stuart	5.10	Grimsby	Corby	09.12.77
Clough, Charlie	6.2	–	Taunton	04.09.90
Gill, Matt	5.11	Norwich	Cambridge	08.11.80
Lines, Chris	6.2	–	Bristol	30.11.85
Reece, Charles	5.11	–	Birmingham	10.07.89
Stanley, Craig	5.8	Morecambe	Bedworth	03.03.83

Forwards

Carayol, Mustapha	5.10	Lincoln	Banjul, Gam	10.06.89
Harrold, Matt	6.1	Shrewsbury	Leyton	25.07.84
Kuffour, Jo	5.7	Bournemouth	Edmonton	17.11.81
McGleish, Scott	5.10	Leyton Orient	Barnet	10.02.74
Powell, Lamar	5.8	–	Bristol	03.09.93

| Richards, Elliot | 5.10 | – | New Tredegar | 10.09.91 |
| Zebroski, Chris | 6.1 | Torquay | Swindon | 29.10.86 |

BURTON ALBION
Ground: Pirelli Stadium, Princess Way, Burton upon Trent DE13 AR
Telephone: 01283 565938. **Club nickname:** Brewers
First-choice colours: Yellow shirts; black shorts; black socks
Capacity for 2011–12: 6,260
Record attendance: 6,191 v Manchester Utd (FA Cup 3) 8 Jan, 2006

Goalkeepers
| Poole, Kevin | 5.10 | Derby | Bromsgrove | 21.07.63 |

Defenders
Austin, Ryan	6.3	Crewe	Stoke	15.11.84
Boertien, Paul	5.10	Walsall	Haltwhistle	20.01.79
Corbett, Andy	6.0	Nuneaton	Worcester	20.02.80
James, Tony	6.3	Weymouth	Cardiff	09.10.78
Moore, Darren	6.2	Barnsley	Birmingham	22.04.74
Palmer, Chris	5.8	Gillingham	Derby	16.10.83
Stanton, Nathan	5.9	Rochdale	Nottingham	06.05.81
Webster, Aaron	6.2	–	Burton	19.12.80

Midfielders
Bolder, Adam	5.9	Millwall	Hull	25.10.80
Dyer, Jack	5.10	Aston Villa	Sutton Coldfield	11.12.91
Maghoma, Jacques	5.11	Tottenham	Lubumbashi, Dr Con	23.10.87
McGrath, John	5.10	Tamworth	Limerick, Ire	27.03.80
Phillips, Jimmy	5.7	Stoke	Stoke	20.09.89
Taylor, Cleveland	5.9	St Johnstone	Leicester	09.09.83

Forwards
Ellison, James	5.10	Liverpool	Liverpool	25.10.91
Pearson, Greg	6.0	Bishop's Stortford	Birmingham	03.04.85
Zola, Calvin	6.2	Crewe	Kinshasa, DR Con	31.12.84

CHELTENHAM TOWN
Ground: Abbey Business Stadium, Whaddon Road, Cheltenham GL52 5NA
Telephone: 01242 573558. **Club nickname:** Town
First-choice colours: Red and white shirts; red shorts; red socks
Capacity for 2011–12: 7,136
Record attendance: 8,326 v Reading (FA Cup 1) 17 Nov, 1956

Goalkeepers
| Brown, Scott | 6.0 | Bristol City | Wolverhampton | 26.04.85 |

Defenders
Andrew, Danny	5.11	Peterborough	Boston	23.12.90
Bennett, Alan	6.2	Wycombe	Cork	04.10.81
Elliott, Steve	6.2	Bristol Rov	Derby	29.10.78
Gallinagh, Andy	5.10	–	Sutton Coldfield	16.03.85
Haynes, Kyle	5.11	Birmingham	Wolverhampton	29..12.91
Jombati, Sido	6.1	Bath	Lisbon, Por	20.08.87
Lowe, Keith	6.2	Hereford	Wolverhampton	13.09.85

Midfielders
Bird, David	5.8	Cinderford	Gloucester	26.12.84
Low, Josh	6.1	Peterborough	Bristol	15.02.79
Pack, Marlon	6.2	Portsmouth	Portsmouth	25.03.91

Penn, Russ	6.0	Burton	Wordsley	08.11.85
Pook, Michael	5.11	Swindon	Swindon	22.10.85
Smikle, Brian	5.11	Kidderminster	Tipton	03.11.85
Forwards				
Goulding, Jeff	6.2	Bournemouth	Reading	13.05.84
Lewis, Theo	5.10	–	Oxford	10.08.91
Mohamed, Kaid	5.11	AFC Wimbledon	Cardiff	23.07.84
Moore, Ethan	6.0	Aston Villa	–	06.03.93

CRAWLEY TOWN

Ground: Broadfield Stadium, Winfield Way, Crawley RH11 9RX
Telephone: 01293 410000. **Club nickname:** Reds
First-choice colours: All red
Capacity for 2011–12: 4,996
Record attendance: 4,522 v Weymouth (Dr Martens Lge) 6 Mar, 2004

Goalkeepers				
Kuipers, Michael	6.2	Brighton	Amsterdam, Hol	26.06.72
Shearer, Scott	6.2	Wrexham	Glasgow	15.02.81
Defenders				
Dempster, John	6.0	Kettering	Kettering	01.04.83
Howell, Dean	6.1	Aldershot	Burton	29.11.80
McFadzean, Kyle	6.1	Alfreton	Sheffield	28.02.87
Mills, Pablo	5.11	Rotherham	Birmingham	27.05.84
Wilson, Glenn	6.1	Rushden	Lewisham	16.03.86
Midfielders				
Akpan, Hope	6.0	Everton	Liverpool	14.08.91
Bulman, Dannie	5.8	Oxford	Ashford, Surrey	24.01.79
Dance, James	6.0	Kettering	Coleshill	15.03.87
Davies, Scott	6.0	Reading	Aylesbury	10.03.88
Day, Jamie	5.9	Rushden	High Wycombe	07.05.86
Gibson, Willie	5.9	Dumfermline	Dumfries	06.08.84
Hunt, David	5.11	Brentford	Dulwich	10.09.82
Neilson, Scott	5.10	Bradford	Enfield	15.05.87
Simpson, Josh	5.9	Peterborough	Cambridge	06.03.87
Smith, Ben	5.8	Hereford	Chelmsford	23.11.78
Torres, Sergio	5.11	Peterborough	Mar del Plata, Arg	08.11.83
Forwards				
Akinde, John	6.2	Bristol City	Gravesend	08.07.89
Barnett, Tyrone	6.3	Macclesfield	Birmingham	28.10.85
Thomas, Wes	6.0	Cheltenham	Barking	23.01.87
Tubbs, Matt	5.9	Salisbury	Salisbury	15.07.84

CREWE ALEXANDRA

Ground: Alexandra Stadium, Gresty Road, Crewe CW2 6EB
Telephone: 01270 213014. **Club nickname:** Railwaymen
First-choice colours: Red shirts; white shorts; red socks
Capacity for 2011–12: 10,109
Record attendance: 20,000 v Tottenham (FA Cup 4) 30 Jan, 1960

Goalkeepers				
Garratt, Ben	6.1	–	Shrewsbury	25.04.93
Phillips, Steve	6.1	Crewe	Bath	06.05.78

Defenders

Artell, David	6.2	Morecambe	Rotherham	22.11.80
Davis, Harry	6.2	–	Burnley	24.09.91
Dugdale, Adam	6.3	Telford	Liverpool	13.09.87
Martin, Carl	6.1	Wealdstone	London	24.10.86
Mellor, Kelvin	6.2	Nantwich	Copenhagen, Den	25.01.91
Shelley, Danny	6.0	–	Stoke	29.12.90
Tootle, Matt	5.8	–	Knowsley	11.10.90
Westwood, Ashley R	5.9	–	Nantwich	01.04.90

Midfielders

Bell, Lee	5.11	Macclesfield	Crewe	26.01.83
Murphy, Luke	6.2	–	Alsager	21.10.89
Powell, Nick	6.0	–	Crewe	23.03.94
Sarcevic, Anton	5.11	Woodley	Manchester	13.03.92

Forwards

Connerton, Jordan	5.10	Lancaster	Lancaster	02.10.89
Leitch-Smith, Ajay	5.11	–	Crewe	06.03.90
Miller, Shaun	5.10	–	Alsager	25.09.87
Moore, Byron	6.0	–	Stoke	24.08.88

DAGENHAM AND REDBRIDGE

Ground: Dagenham Stadium, Victoria Road, Dagenham RM10 7XL
Telephone: 0208 592 1549. **Club nickname:** Daggers
First-choice colours: Red and blue shirts; blue shorts; blue socks
Capacity 2011–12: 6,077
Record attendance: 5,949 v Ipswich (FA Cup 3), 5 Jan, 2002

Goalkeepers

Hogan, David	6.0	–	Harlow	31.05.89
Lewington, Chris	6.2	Fisher	Sidcup	23.08.88
Roberts, Tony	6.0	St Albans	Holyhead	04.08.69

Defenders

Antwi, Will	6.2	Wycombe	Ashford, Kent	19.10.82
Arber, Mark	6.1	Stevenage	Johannesburg, SA	09.10.77
Bingham, Billy	5.10	Crystal Palace	London	15.07.90
Doe, Scott	6.1	Weymouth	Reading	06.11.88
McCrory, Damien	6.2	Plymouth	Croom, Ire	23.02.90
Ogogo, Abu	5.10	Arsenal	Epsom	03.11.89
Reynolds, Duran				
Vincelot, Romain	5.10	Gueugnon	Poitiers, Fr	29.10.85
Wilkinson, Luke	6.2	Portsmouth	–	02.12.91

Midfielders

Currie, Darren	5.11	Chesterfield	Hampstead	29.11.74
Elito, Medy	5.11	Colchester	Kinshasa, DR Con	20.03.90
Gain, Peter	5.9	Peterborough	Hammersmith	02.11.76
Scannell, Damian	5.10	Southend	Croydon	28.04.85

Forwards

Nurse, Jon	5.9	Stevenage	Bridgetown, Barb	01.03.81
Osborn, Alex	5.11	Grays	Walshamstow	25.07.93
Scott, Josh	6.2	Hayes	London	10.05.85
Walsh, Phil	6.3	Dorchester	Hartlepool	04.02.84

GILLINGHAM

Ground: Priestfield Stadium, Redfern Avenue, Gillingham ME7 4DD
Telephone: 01634 300000. **Club nickname:** Gills
First-choice colours: Blue and white shirts; blue shorts; blue socks
Capacity for 2011–12: 11,440
Record attendance: 23,002 v QPR. (FA Cup 3) 10 Jan, 1948

Goalkeepers				
Flitney, Ross	6.3	Dover	Hitchin	01.06.84
Defenders				
Essam, Connor	6.0	–	Chatham	09.07.92
Frampton, Andy	5.11	Millwall	Wimbledon	03.09.79
Fuller, Barry	5.10	Stevenage	Ashford, Kent	25.08.84
Jackman, Danny	5.5	Northampton	Worcester	03.01.83
King, Simon	6.0	Barnet	Oxford	11.04.83
Lawrence, Matt	6.0	Crystal Palace	Northampton	19.06.74
Richards, Garry	6.3	Southend	Romford	11.06.86
Midfielders				
Lee, Charlie	5.11	Peterborough	Whitechapel	05.01.87
Maher, Kevin	6.0	Oldham	Ilford	17.10.76
Martin, Joe	6.0	Blackpool	Dagenham	29.11.89
Montrose, Lewis	6.2	Wycombe	Manchester	17.11.88
Payne, Jack	5.9	–	Gravesend	05.12.91
Rance, Dean	5.10	–	Maidstone	14.05.91
Rooney, Luke	5.11	–	Bermondsey	28.12.90
Southall, Nicky	5.10	Dover	Middlesbrough	28.01.72
Spiller, Danny	5.10	Dagenham	Maidstone	10.10.81
Weston, Curtis	5.11	Leeds	Greenwich	24.01.87
Whelpdale, Chris	6.0	Peterborough	Harold Wood	27.01.87
Forwards				
Kedwell, Danny	5.11	AFC Wimbledon	Gillingham	03.08.83
Oli, Dennis	6.0	Grays	Newham	28.01.84
Payne, Stefan	5.11	Fulham	Lambeth	10.08.91

HEREFORD UNITED

Ground: Edgar Street Ground, Edgar Street, Hereford HR4 9JU
Telephone: 0844 2761939. **Club nickname:** Bulls
First-choice colours: White and black shirts, black shorts, white socks
Capacity for 2011–12: 7,149
Record attendance: 18,114 v Sheffield Wed (FA Cup 3) 4 Jan, 1958

Goalkeepers				
Bartlett, Adam	6.0	Kidderminster	Newcastle	27.02.86
Connor, Dan	6.2	St Patrick's	Dublin, Ire	31.01.81
Defenders				
Green, Ryan	5.8	Bristol Rov	Cardiff	20.10.80
Heath, Joe	5.11	Exeter	Birkenhead	04.10.88
Kovacs, Janos	6.4	Luton	Budapest, Hun	11.09.85
Stam, Stefan	6.2	Yeovil	Amersfoot, Hol	14.09.79
Townsend, Michael	6.2	Cheltenham	Walsall	17.05.86
Midfielders				
Colbeck, Joe	5.11	Oldham	Bradford	29.11.86
Featherstone, Nicky	5.8	Hull	Goole	22.09.88

Lunt, Kenny	5.10	Sheffield Wed	Runcorn	20.11.79
McQuilkin, James	5.8	Tescoma	West Bromwich	09.01.89
Pell, Harry	6.2	Bristol Rov	Chadwell St Mary	21.10.91
Purdie, Rob	5.9	Oldham	Leicester	28.09.82
Weir, Tyler	5.10	–	Hereford	21.12.90
Forwards				
Canham, Sean	5.10	Notts Co	Exeter	26.09.84
Facey, Delroy	6.0	Lincoln	Huddersfield	22.04.80
Fleetwood, Stuart	5.8	Charlton	Gloucester	23.04.86

MACCLESFIELD TOWN

Ground: Moss Rose, London Road, Macclesfield SK11 7SP
Telephone: 01625 264686. **Club nickname:** Silkmen
First-choice colours: Blue shirts; white shorts; blue socks
Capacity for 2011–12: 6,141
Record attendance: 9,003 v Winsford (Cheshire Senior Cup 2) 14 Feb, 1948

Goalkeepers				
Cudworth, Jack	6.2	Rhyl	Preston	11.09.90
Veiga, Jose	6.2	Hereford	Lisbon	18.12.76
Defenders				
Bateson, Jon	6.1	Accrington	Preston	20.09.89
Brisley, Shaun	5.11	–	Macclesfield	06.05.90
Brown, Nat	6.2	Wrexham	Sheffield	15.06.81
Diagne, Tony	6.0	Aubervilliers	Aubergenville, Fr	17.09.90
Kay, Scott	5.10	Manchester City	Denton	18.09.89
Lane, Jack	5.10	–	Winsford	26.02.93
Morgan, Paul	5.11	Bury	Belfast	23.10.78
Tremarco, Carl	5.11	Wrexham	Liverpool	11.10.85
Midfielders				
Chalmers, Lewis	6.0	Aldershot	Manchester	04.02.86
Daniel, Colin	5.11	Crewe	Nottingham	15.02.88
Draper, Ross	5.10	Hednesford	Wolverhampton	20.10.88
Hamshaw, Matt	5.10	Notts Co	Rotherham	01.01.82
Roberts, Adam	5.9	–	Manchester	30.12.91
Thomas, Michael	6.1	–	Manchester	12.08.92
Wedgbury, Sam	6.1	Sheffield Utd	Oldbury	26.02.89
Forwards				
Daniels, Greg	5.11	–	Manchester	21.01.93
Mukendi, Vinny	6.2	–	Sheffield	12.03.92
Sinclair, Emile	6.0	Nottm Forest	Leeds	29.12.87

MORECAMBE

Ground: Globe Arena, Christie Way, Westgate, Morecambe LA4 4TB
Telephone: 01524 411797. **Club nickname:** Shrimps
First-choice colours: Red shirts, white shorts, red socks
Capacity for 2011–12: 6,476
Record attendance: Christie Park: 9,383 v Weymouth (FA Cup 3) 6 Jan 1962. Globe Arena: 3,521 v Bradford (Lge 2) 12 Mar, 2011

Goalkeepers				
Roche, Barry	6.4	Chesterfield	Dublin, Ire	06.04.82
Defenders				
Bentley, Jim	6.1	Telford	Liverpool	11.06.76

Charnock, Kieran	5.11	Torquay	Preston	03.08.84
Cowperthwaite, Niall	5.11	–	Barrow	28.01.92
Haining, Will	6.0	St Mirren	Glasgow	02.10.82
McCready, Chris	6.1	Northampton	Chester	05.09.81
Parrish, Andy	6.0	Bury	Bolton	22.06.88
Scott, Paul	5.11	Bury	Wakefield	05.11.79
Wilson, Laurence	5.10	Chester	Liverpool	10.10.86
Midfielders				
Drummond, Stewart	6.2	Shrewsbury	Preston	11.12.75
Ellison, Kevin	6.0	Rotherham	Liverpool	23.02.79
Fleming, Andy	5.11	Wrexham	Liverpool	05.10.87
McDonald, Gary	6.1	Hamilton	Irvine	10.04.82
Reid, Izak	5.5	Macclesfield	Sheffield	13.09.89
Forwards				
Alessandra, Lewis	5.10	Oldham	Oldham	08.02.89
Carlton, Danny	6.0	Bury	Leeds	22.12.83
Hunter, Garry	5.10	–	Morecambe	01.01.85
Jevons, Phil	5.11	Huddersfield	Liverpool	01.08.79

NORTHAMPTON TOWN

Ground: Sixfields Stadium, Upton Way, Northampton NN5 5QA
Telephone: 01604 683700. **Club nickname:** Cobblers
First-choice colours: Claret shirts; white shorts; claret socks
Capacity for 2011–12: 7,300
Record attendance: County Ground: 24,523 v Fulham (Div 1) 23 Apr, 1966; Sixfields Stadium: 7,557 v Manchester City (Div 2) 26 Sep, 1998

Goalkeepers				
Hall, Freddy	6.2	Quinnipiac Univ	St George's, Ber	03.03.85
Walker, Paul	5.10	–	–	18.04.92
Defenders				
Holt, Andy	6.1	Wrexham	Manchester	21.05.78
Johnson, John	6.0	Middlesbrough	Middlesbrough	16.09.88
Nana-Ofori, Seth	5.8	Peterborough	Accra, Gh	15.05.90
Tozer, Ben	6.1	Newcastle	Plymouth	01.03.90
Webster, Byron	6.5	Doncaster	Leeds	31.03.87
Midfielders				
Built, Michael	5.10	–	Hamilton, NZ	12.11.92
Davies, Arron	5.9	Peterborough	Cardiff	22.06.84
Gilligan, Ryan	5.10	Watford	Swindon	18.01.87
Jacobs, Michael	5.9	–	Northampton	22.03.92
Kaziboni, Greg	5.9	–	Northampton	16.05.92
McKoy, Nick	6.0	Kettering	Newham	03.09.86
Thornton, Kevin	5.7	Nuneaton	Drogheda, Ire	09.07.86
Turnbull, Paul	6.0	Stockport	Handforth	23.01.89
Wedderburn, Nathaniel	6.1	Stoke	Wolverhampton	30.06.91
Young, Lewis	5.9	Burton	Stevenage	27.09.89
Forwards				
Akinfenwa, Adebayo	6.1	Gillingham	West Ham	10.05.82
Harrad, Shaun	5.10	Burton	Nottingham	11.12.84
McKay, Billy	5.8	Leicester	Corby	22.10.88
Purcell, Tadgh	5.11	Darlington	Dublin, Ire	09.02.85
Robinson, Jake	5.8	Shrewsbury	Brighton	23.10.86
Uwezu, Michael	5.6	Fulham	Irete, Nig	12.12.90

OXFORD UNITED

Ground: Kassam Stadium, Grenoble Road, Oxford OX4 4XP
Telephone: 01865 337500. **Club nickname:** U's
First-choice colours: Yellow and blue shirts; blue shorts; blue socks.
Capacity for 2011–12: 12,500
Record attendance: Manor Ground: 22,730 v Preston (FA Cup 6) 29 February, 1964; Kassam Stadium: 12,177 v Aston Villa (League Cup 3) 7 November, 2002

Goalkeepers

Clarke, Ryan	6.3	Salisbury	Bristol	30.04.82

Defenders

Batt, Damien	5.10	Grays	Hoddesdon	16.09.84
Capaldi, Tony	6.0	Morecambe	Porsgrunn, Nor	12.08.81
Duberry, Michael	6.1	St Johnstone	Enfield	14.10.75
Tonkin, Anthony	5.11	Cambridge Utd	Newlyn	17.01.80
Whing, Andy	6.0	Leyton Orient	Birmingham	20.09.84
Worley, Harry	6.4	Leicester	Warrington	25.11.88
Wright, Jake	5.11	Brighton	Keighley	11.03.86

Midfielders

Leven, Peter	5.11	MK Dons	Glasgow	27.09.83
McLaren, Paul	6.1	Tranmere	High Wycombe	17.11.76
Hall, Asa	6.2	Luton	Sandwell	29.11.86
Heslop, Simon	5.11	Barnsley	York	01.05.87
Payne, Josh	6.0	Doncaster	Basingstoke	25.11.90
Potter, Alfie	5.7	Peterborough	London	09.01.89

Forwards

Constable, James	6.2	Shrewsbury	Malmesbury	04.10.84
Craddock, Tom	5.11	Luton	Darlington	14.10.86
Pittman, Jon-Paul	5.9	Wycombe	Oklahoma City, US	24.10.86
Smalley, Deane	6.0	Oldham	Chadderton	05.09.88
Woodley, Aaron	–	–	Oxford	13.10.92

PLYMOUTH ARGYLE

Ground: Home Park, Plymouth PL2 3DQ
Telephone: 01752 562561. **Club nickname:** Pilgrims
First-choice colours: Green shirts; white shorts; green socks
Capacity for 2011–12: 19,810
Record attendance: 42,684 v Aston Villa (Div 2) 10 Oct, 1936

Goalkeepers

Larrieu, Romain	6.2	Valence	Mont de Marsan, Fr	31.08.76

Defenders

Berry, Durrell	5.11	Aston Villa	–	27.05.92
Bhasera, Onismo	5.8	Kaizer Chiefs	Mutare, Zim	07.01.86
Nelson, Curtis	5.11	Stoke	Newcastle-u-Lyme	21.05.93
Williams, Robbie	5.10	Rochdale	Pontefract	02.10.84
Zubar, Stephane	6.2	Vaslui	Pointe-a-Pitre, Guad	09.10.86

Midfielders

Fletcher, Carl	5.10	Crystal Palace	Camberley	07.04.80
Harper-Penman, Jed	5.10	Barnstaple	Barnstaple	02.02.94
Johnson, Damien	5.10	Birmingham	Lisburn	18.11.78
Walton, Simon	6.1	QPR	Leeds	13.09.87
Young, Luke	5.10	–	Plymouth	22.02.93

Forwards

Dickinson, Liam	6.4	Barnsley	Salford	04.10.85
Patterson, Rory	5.11	Glentoran	Strabane	16.07.84

PORT VALE

Ground: Vale Park, Hamil Road, Burslem, Stoke-on-Trent ST6 1AW
Telephone: 01782 655800. **Club nickname:** Valiants
First-choice colours: White shirts, black shorts, shirt socks
Capacity for 2011–12: 19,148
Record attendance: 50,000 v Aston Villa (FA Cup 5) 20 Feb, 1960

Goalkeepers

Martin, Chris	6.0	–	Mansfield	21.07.90
Tomlinson, Stuart	6.0	Barrow	Chester	17.03.84
Defenders				
Collins, Lee	5.11	Wolves	Telford	28.09.88
Davis, Joe	5.10	–	Burnley	10.11.93
James, Kingsley	6.1	Sheffield Utd	Rotherham	17.02.92
McCombe, John	6.2	Hereford	Pontefract	07.05.85
McDonald, Clayton	6.6	Walsall	Liverpool	06.12.88
Owen, Gareth	6.1	Stockport	Stoke	21.09.82
Taylor, Rob	6.0	Nuneaton	Shrewsbury	16.01.85
Yates, Adam	5.10	Morecambe	Stoke	28.05.83
Midfielders				
Burge, Ryan	5.10	Hyde	Cheltenham	12.10.88
Dodds, Louis	5.10	Leicester	Sheffield	08.10.86
Griffith, Anthony	6.0	Doncaster	Huddersfield	28.10.86
Haldane, Lewis	6.0	Bristol Rov	Trowbridge	13.03.85
Loft, Doug	6.0	Brighton	Maidstone	25.12.86
Lloyd, Ryan	5.10	–	Newcastle-u-Lyme	01.02.94
Morsy, Sam	5.9	–	Wolverhampton	10.09.91
Rigg, Sean	5.9	Bristol Rov	Bristol	01.10.88
Roberts, Gary	5.8	Rotherham	Chester	04.02.87
Taylor, Rob	6.0	Nuneaton	Shrewsbury	16.01.85
Forwards				
Richards, Justin	6.0	Cheltenham	Sandwell	16.10.80
Richards, Marc	5.11	Barnsley	Wolverhampton	08.07.82
Williamson, Ben	5.11	Hyde	London	25.12.88

ROTHERHAM UNITED

Ground: Don Valley Stadium, Sheffield, S9 3TL
Telephone: 0844 414 0733 . **Club nickname:** Millers
First-choice colours: Red shirts; white shorts; red socks
Capacity for 2011–12: 10,000
Record attendance: Millmoor: 25,000 v Sheffield Wed (Div 2) 26 Jan, 1952 and v Sheffield Wed (Div 2) 13 Dec, 1952; Don Valley Stadium: 7,082 v Aldershot (Lge 2 play-off semi-final, 2nd leg) 19 May 2010

Goalkeepers

Annerson, Jamie	6.2	Sheffield Utd	Sheffield	21.06.88
Warrington, Andy	6.3	Bury	Sheffield	10.06
Defenders				
Brown, Troy	5.10	Ipswich	London	17.09.90

Cresswell, Ryan	6.2	Bury	Rotherham	22.12.87
Foster, Luke	6.2	Stevenage	Mexborough	08.09.85
Mullins, John	5.11	Stockport	Hampstead	06.11.85
Newey, Tom	5.10	Bury	Sheffield	31.10.82
Midfielders				
Harrison, Danny	5.11	Tranmere	Liverpool	04.11.82
Pringle, Ben	6.1	Derby	Newcastle	27.05.89
Schofield, Danny	5.10	Millwall	Doncaster	10.04.80
Taylor, Jason	6.2	Stockport	Ashton-under-Lyne	28.01.87
Tonge, Dale	5.10	Barnsley	Doncaster	07.05.85
Warne, Paul	5.8	Yeovil	Norwich	08.05.73
Forwards				
Evans, Gareth	6.0	Bradford	Macclesfield	26.04.88
Grabban, Lewis	6.0	Brenford	Croydon	12.01.88
Holroyd, Chris	5.11	Brighton	Nantwich	24.10.86
Le Fondre, Adam	5.9	Rochdale	Stockport	02.12.86
Marshall, Marcus	5.10	Blackburn		17.10.89

SHREWSBURY TOWN

Ground: Greenhous Meadow Stadium, Oteley Road, Shrewsbury SY2 6ST
Telephone: 01743 289177. **Club nickname:** Shrews
First-choice colours: Blue shirts; white shorts; blue socks
Capacity for 2011–12: 10,000
Record attendance: Gay Meadonw: 18,917 v Walsall (Div 3) 26 Apr, 1961; Greenhous
Meadow: 8,817 v Oxford (Lge 2) 7 May, 2011

Goalkeepers				
Neal, Chris	6.2	–	St Albans	23.10.85
Smith, Ben	6.1	Doncaster	Whitley Bay	05.09.86
Defenders				
Cansdell-Sherriff, Shane	6.0	Tranmere	Sydney, Aus	10.11.82
Grandison, Jermaine	6.4	Coventry	Birmingham	15.12.90
Hazell, Reuben	5.11	Oldham	Birmingham	24.04.79
Jacobson, Joe	5.11	Accrington	Cardiff	17.11.86
Sharps, Ian	6.4	Rotherham	Warrington	23.10.80
Midfielders				
Ainsworth, Lionel	5.9	Huddersfield	Nottingham	01.10.87
Leslie, Steven	5.10	–	Shrewsbury	05.11.87
McAllister, Sean	5.8	Sheffield Wed	Bolton	15.08.87
Taylor, Jon	5.11	–	Liverpool	20.07.92
Wright, Mark	5.11	Bristol Rov	Wolverhampton	24.02.82
Wroe, Nicky	5.11	Torquay	Sheffield	28.09.85
Forwards				
Bradshaw, Tom	5.6	Aberystwyth	Shrewsbury	27.07.92
Collins, James	6.2	Aston Villa	Coventry	28.05.78
Morgan, Marvin	6.4	Aldershot	Manchester	13.04.83

SOUTHEND UNITED

Ground: Roots Hall, Victoria Avenue, Southend SS2 6NQ
Telephone: 01702 304050. **Club nickname:** Shrimpers
First-choice colours: All blue
Capacity for 2011–12: 12,163
Record attendance: 31,033 v Liverpool (FA Cup 3) 10 Jan, 1979

Goalkeepers

Morris, Glenn	6.0	Leyton Orient	Woolwich	20.12.83

Defenders

Barker, Chris	6.0	Plymouth	Sheffield	02.03.80
Bilel, Mohsni	6.3	St Genevieve	Tunisia	21.07.87
Clohessy, Sean	5.10	Bath	Croydon	12.12.86
Coughlan, Graham	6.2	Shrewsbury	Dublin, Ire	18.11.74
Gilbert, Peter	5.9	Northampton	Newcastle	31.07.83
Phillips, Mark	6.2	Brentford	Lambeth	27.01.82
Prosser, Luke	6.3	Port Vale	Enfield	28.05.88

Midfielders

N'Diaye, Alassane	6.4	Crystal Palace	Audincourt, Fr	25.02.90
Ferdinand, Kane	6.1	–	Newham	07.10.92
Grant, Anthony	5.10	Chelsea	Lambeth	04.06.87
Hall, Ryan	5.10	Bromley	Dulwich	04.01.88
Sawyer, Lee	5.11	Woking	London	10.09.89

Forwards

Corr, Barry	6.3	Exeter	Newcastle, NI	02.04.85
Crawford, Harry	6.1	–	Watford	10.12.91
Harris, Neil	5.11	Millwall	Orsett	12.07.77
Johnson, Jemal	6.0	Lokomotiv Sofia	Paterson, US	03.05.85
Paterson, Matt	6.2	Southampton	Dunfermline	18.10.89
Sturrock, Blair	6.0	Mansfield	Dundee	25.08.81

SWINDON TOWN

Ground: County Ground, County Road, Swindon SN1 2ED
Telephone: 0871 423 6433. **Club nickname:** Robins
First-choice colours: All red
Capacity for 2011–12: 14,983
Record attendance: 32,000 v Arsenal (FA Cup 3) 15 Jan, 1972

Goalkeepers

Lanzano, Mattia	6.1	Gavorrano	Grosseto, It	07.04.90
Scott, Mark	6.0	Aldershot	Ash Vale	03.01.91

Defenders

Amankwaah, Kevin	6.1	Swansea	Kenton	19.05.82
Caddis, Paul	5.7	Celtic	Irvine	19.04.88
Clark, Matt	5.10	–	Swindon	16.11.92
Comazzi, Alberto	6.0	Spezia	Novara, It	16.04.79
Devera, Joe	6.2	Barnet	Southgate	06.02.87
Flint, Aden	6.2	Alfreton	Nottingham	11.07.89
Kennedy, Callum	6.1	Reading	Chertsey	09.11.89
Misun, Milan	6.1	Celtic	Pribram, Cze	21.02.90

Midfielders

Bodin, Billy	5.11	–	Swindon	24.03.92
Ferry, Simon	5.8	Celtic	Dundee	11.01.88
Pavett, Jordan	–	Redbridge	Enfield	16.12.91
Ritchie, Matt	5.8	Portsmouth	Gosport	10.09.89
Smith, Jonathan	5.8	York	Preston	17.10.86
Timlin, Michael	5.8	Fulham	Lambeth	19.03.85

Forwards

De Vita, Raffaela	5.11	Livingston	Rome, It	23.09.87

TORQUAY UNITED

Ground: Plainmoor, Torquay TQ1 3PS
Telephone: 01803 328666. **Club nickname:** Gulls
First-choice colours: All yellow
Capacity for 2011–12: 6,000
Record attendance: 21,908 v Huddersfield (FA Cup 4) 29 Jan, 1955

Goalkeepers

Olejnik, Robert	6.0	Falkirk	Vienna, Aut	26.11.86

Defenders

Nicholson, Kevin	5.8	Forest Green	Derby	02.10.80
Leadbitter, Daniel	6.3	–	Newcastle	07.10.90
Oastler, Joe	6.1	QPR	Portsmouth	03.07.90
Robertson, Chris	6.3	Sheffield Utd	Dundee	11.10.86
Rowe-Turner, Lathaniel	6.1	Leicester	Leicester	12.11.89
Saah, Brian	6.1	Cambridge Utd	Rush Green	16.12.86

Midfielders

Ellis, Mark	6.2	Bolton	Plymouth	30.09.88
Halpin, Sean	6.1	–	Truro	31.05.91
Mansell, Lee	5.9	Oxford	Gloucester	23.09.82
O'Kane, Eunan	5.8	Coleraine	Derry	10.07.90
McPhee, Chris	5.11	Kidderminster	Eastbourne	20.03.83
Stevens, Danny	5.10	Luton	Enfield	26.11.86
Lathrope, Damon	5.10	Norwich	Stevenage	28.10.89

Forwards

Kee, Billy	5.9	Leicester	Leicester	01.12.90
Macklin, Lloyd	5.9	Swindon	Camberley	02.08.91

CLYDESDALE SCOTTISH PREMIER LEAGUE SQUADS 2011–12

(at time of going to press)

ABERDEEN

Ground: Pittodrie Stadium, Pittodrie Street, Aberdeen AB24 5QH. **Capacity:** 21,421.
Telephone: 01224 650400. **Colours:** Red and white. **Nickname:** Dons
Goalkeepers: Scott Bain, David Gonzalez, Jamie Langfield
Defenders: Myles Anderson, Andrew Considine, Zander, Diamond, Dean Jarvis, Youl Mawene, Rory McArdle, Clark Robertson, Scott Ross, Joe Shaughnessy, Stirling Smith
Midfielders: Sone Aluko, Jordan Brown, Chris Clark, Yoann Folly, Ryan Fraser, Fraser Fyvie, Ryan Jack, Robert Milsom, Isaac Osbourne, Peter Pawlett
Forwards: Darren Mackie, Josh Magennis, Michael Paton, Scott Vernon

CELTIC

Ground: Celtic Park, Glasgow G40 3RE. **Capacity:** 60, 355. **Telephone:** 0871 226 1888.
Colours: Green and white. **Nickname:** Bhoys
Goalkeepers: Dominic Cervi, Lukasz Zaluska
Defenders: Cha Du-Ri, Emilio Izaguirre, Jos Hooiveld, Daniel Majstorovic, Jason Marr, Charlie Mulgrew, Darren O'Dea, Glenn Loovens, Adam Matthews, Thomas Rogne, Josh Thompson, Kevin Wilson, Victor Wanyama, Mark Wilson
Midfielders: Scott Brown, Kris Commons, James Forrest, Efrain Juarez, Beram Kayal, Ki

Sung-Yueng, Joe Ledley, Shaun Maloney, Pat McCourt, Richard Towell, Filip Twardzik, Patrik Twardzik

Forwards: Gary Hooper, Daryl Murphy, Morten Rasmussen, Georgios Samaras, Anthony Stokes

DUNDEE UNITED

Ground: Tannadice Park, Tannadice Street, Dundee DD3 7JW. **Capacity:** 14,223. **Telephone:** 01382 833166. **Colours:** Tangerine and white. **Nickname:** Terrors

Goalkeepers: Steve Banks, Filip Mentel, Dusan Pernis

Defenders: Sean Dillon, Paul Dixon, Barry Douglas, Gary Kenneth, Scott Robertson, Scott Severin, Ross Smith, Keith Watson

Midfielders: Scott Allan, Stuart Armstrong, Willo Flood, Dale Hilson, John Rankin, Danny Swanson

Forwards: Jon Daly, Ryan Dow, David Goodwillie, Johnny Russell

DUNFERMLINE ATHLETIC

Ground: East End Park, Halbeath Road, Dunfermline KY12 7RB. **Capacity:** 11,984 **Telephone:** 01383 724295. **Colours:** Black and white. **Nickname:** Pars

Goalkeepers: Paul Gallacher, Chris Smith

Defenders: Patrick Boyle, Andy Dowie, Alex Keddie, Austin McCann, John Potter, Kevin Rutkiewicz, Jason Thomson

Midfielders: Steven Bell, Paul Burns, Joe Cardle, Martin Hardie, Gary Mason, Nick Phinn, Ryan Thomson, Paul Willis

Forwards: Liam Buchanan, Andy Barrowman, Pat Clarke, David Graham, Andy Kirk, Steven McDougall

HEARTS

Ground: Tynecastle Stadium, McLeod Street Edinburgh EH11 2NL. **Capacity:** 17,590. **Telephone:** 0871 663 1874. **Colours:** Maroon and white. **Nickname:** Jam Tarts

Goalkeepers: Janos Balogh, Marian Kello, Jamie MacDonald, Mark Ridgers

Defenders: Darren Barr, Danny Grainger, Ryan McGowan, David Obua, Lee Wallace, Andy Webster, Marius Zaliukas

Midfielders: Ian Black, Michael Deland, Andrew Driver, Jamie Hamill, Eggert Jonsson, Dylan McGowan, Adrian Mrowiec, Denis Prychynenko, Suso Santana, Rudi Skacel, Ryan Stevenson, Mehdi Taouil, John Wood

Forwards: Calum Elliot, Stephen Elliott, Gary Glen, Kevin Kyle, Aryvdas Novikovas, Scott Robinson, John Sutton, David Templeton

HIBERNIAN

Ground: Easter Road Stadium, Albion Place, Edinburgh EH7 5QG. **Capacity:** 20,250. **Telephone:** 031 661 2159. **Colours:** Green and white. **Nickname:** Hibees

Goalkeepers: Callum Antell, Mark Brown, Graham Stack

Defenders: Callum Booth, Paul Hanlon, Michael Hart, Ian Murray, Sean O'Hanlon, Scott Smith, David Stephens

Midfielders: David Crawford, Edwin de Graaf, Danny Galbraith, Lewis Horner, Victor Palsson, Martin Scott, Ivan Sproule, Lewis Stevenson, Scott Taggart, Matt Thornhill, Sean Welsh, David Wotherspoon

Forwards: Garry O'Connor, Akpo Sodje

INVERNESS CALEDONIAN THISTLE

Ground: Caledonian Stadium, Stadium Road, Inverness IV1 1FF. **Capacity:** 7,750. **Telephone:** 01463 222880. **Colours:** Blue. **Nickname:** Caley Thistle

Goalkeepers: Ryan Esson, Jonathan Tuffey

Defenders: Tom Aldred, Kenny Gillet, Kevin McCann, Josh Meekings, David Proctor, Graeme Shinnie, Ross Tokely
Midfielders: Lee Cox, Stuart Duff, Jonathan Hayes, Gavin Morrison, Nick Ross, Andrew Shinnie, Greg Tansey
Forwards: Richie Foran, Liam Polworth, Shane Sutherland, Gregory Tade

KILMARNOCK

Ground: Rugby Park, Kilmarnock KA 1 2DP. **Capacity:** 18,128. **Telephone:** 01563 545300.
Colours: White and blue. **Nickname:** Killie
Goalkeepers: Cameron Bell, Anssi Jaakkola, Kyle Letheren
Defenders: Patrick Ada, Billy Berntsson, Tim Clancy, Gary Fisher, James Fowler, Garry Hay, Zdenek Kroca, Ryan O'Leary
Midfielders: Danny Buijs, Ross Davidson, James Dayton, Scott Evans, Gaey Harkins, Liam Kelly, Matthew Kennedy, Callum McCluskey, Daniel McKay, Danny Racchi, Manuel Pascali, David Silva
Forwards: William Gros, Paul, Heffernan, Rory McKenzie

MOTHERWELL

Ground: Fir Park, Firpark Street, Motherwell ML1 2QN. **Capacity:** 13,677. **Telephone:** 01698 333333. **Colours:** Clarent and amber. **Nickname:** Well
Goalkeepers: Tom Hateley, Lee Hollis, Darren Randolph
Defenders: Stephen Craigan, Jordan Halsman, Steve Hammell, Shaun Hutchinson, Nicky Law, Ross McKinnon, Jonathan Page, Dario Quinn, Steven Saunders
Midfielders: Tom Hateley, Chris Humphrey, Peter Innes, Steve Jennings, Ross Forbes, Keith Lasley
Forwards: Michael Higdon, Steve Howarth, Robert McHugh, Steven Lawless, Jamie Murphy, Jamie Pollock, Gary Smith

RANGERS

Ground: Ibrox Park, Edmison Drive, Glasgow G51 2XD. **Capacity:** 51,076. **Telephone:** 0141 580 8500. **Colours:** Blue and white. **Nickname:** Gers
Goalkeepers: Grant Adam, Neil Alexander, Scott Gallacher, Allan McGregor
Defenders: Madjid Bougherra, Kirk Broadfoot, Darren Cole, Jordan McMillan, Sasa Papac, David Weir, Steven Whittaker, Gregg Wylde
Midfielders: Steven Davis, Maurice Edu, Lee McCulloch, Jamie Ness, Juan Manuel Ortiz
Forwards: John Fleck, David Healy, Kyle Hutton, Nikica Jelavic, Salim Kerkar, Kyle Lafferty, Andrew Little, Steven Naismith

ST JOHNSTONE

Ground: McDiarmid Park, Crieff Road, Perth PH1 2SJ. **Capacity:** 10,673. **Telephone:** 01738 459090. **Colours:** Blue and white. **Nickname:** Saints
Goalkeepers: Zander Clark, Peter Enckelman
Defenders: Steven Anderson, Callum Davidson, Graham Gartland, David Mackay, Alan Maybury, David McCracken, Frazer Wright
Midfielders: Jamie Adams, Liam Caddis, Liam Craig, Murray Davidson, Chris Millar, Jody Morris, Kevin Moon, David Robertson
Forwards: Carl Finnigan, Sean Higgins, Peter MacDonald, Sam Parkin

ST MIRREN

Ground: St Mirren Park, Greenhill Road, Paisley PA3, 1RU. **Capacity:** 8,029. **Telephone:** 0141 889 2558. **Colours:** Black and white. **Nickname:** Buddies
Goalkeepers: Adam McHugh, Craig Samson, Graeme Smith

Defenders: David Barron, Dominic Kennedy, Lee Mair, Mark McAusland, Darren McGregor, David van Zanten
Midfielders: Jim Goodwin, Jamie McKernon, Kenny McLean, Aaron Mooy, Hugh Murray, Gary Teale, Steven Thomson
Forwards: Jon McShane, Nigel Hasselbaink, Paul McGowan, Paul McQuade, Steven Thompson

QUOTE/UNQUOTE

'I can't get upset every time the fans chant someone else's name. I can only continue to do the best job I can under the circumstances' – **Roy Hodgson**, Liverpool manager, hears supporters calling for Kenny Dalglish to take over.

'Do you think if you play with four strikers it means you will score four goals? If you think like this, you don't know football' – **Roberto Mancini**, Manchester City manager, after successive goalless draws against Manchester United and Birmingham.

'The minute a footballer becomes more important than the manager, your club is dead' – **Sir Alex Ferguson,** Manchester United manager, on player power and agents.

'The last time I played fit? Maybe five years, maybe more' – **John Terry**, Chelsea captain, on playing through the pain.

'I always seem to be the last resort' – **Peter Crouch** after coming off the bench to score his 22nd goal England goal in 42 internationals.

'It makes no sense. Here is a guy who has done an unbelievable job. He got the club back into the Premier League and any manager would have been rewarded with a new contract' – **Sol Campbell**, Newcastle defender, on the sacking of manager Chris Hughton.

'I've never heard of such a stupid decision in all my life. It's absolutely ridiculous' – **Sir** Alex Ferguson, Manchester United manager, on the sacking of Blackburn's Sam Allardyce.

'Football fans don't care. Saddam Hussein could own their club and if he's putting money into it, they'll be quite happy. They'll all be singing: "There's only one Saddam" – **Harry Redknapp**, Tottenham manager.

'It's not often you beat this lot 3-0 in their own back yard. It won't happen again very often, either' – **Steve Bruce**, Sunderland manager, after his side's victory over Chelsea at Stamford Bridge.

'Footballers are role models, but I'm not even a role model to myself' – **Joey Barton**, Newcastle midfielder, after landing himself in more trouble by punching Blackburn's Morten Gamst Pedersen.

'Supporting Bolton is a bit like having a three-legged dog. You wish it had all four, but you still love it' – **Ray Heaton**, Wanderers supporter.

'I'd go back to the days before we had the Premier League when it was the best team wins. Now, it's just about money' – **Delia Smith**, Norwich owner.

ENGLISH FIXTURES 2011–2012

Friday, 5 August
npower Championship
Hull v Blackpool

Saturday, 6 August
npower Championship
Brighton v Doncaster
Bristol City v Ipswich
Burnley v Watford
Coventry v Leicester
Derby v Birmingham
Middlesbrough v Portsmouth
Nottm Forest v Barnsley
Peterborough v Crystal Palace
Reading v Millwall
Southampton v Leeds

npower League 1
Brentford v Yeovil
Carlisle v Notts Co
Charlton v Bournemouth
Huddersfield v Bury
MK Dons v Hartlepool
Oldham v Sheffield Utd
Preston v Colchester
Sheffield Wed v Rochdale
Stevenage v Exeter
Tranmere v Chesterfield
Walsall v Leyton Orient
Wycombe v Scunthorpe

npower League 2
AFC Wimbledon v Bristol Rov
Bradford v Aldershot
Gillingham v Cheltenham
Macclesfield v Dag & Red
Morecambe v Barnet
Northampton v Accrington
Port Vale v Crawley
Rotherham v Oxford
Shrewsbury v Plymouth
Southend v Hereford
Swindon v Crewe
Torquay v Burton

Sunday, 7 August
npower Championship
West Ham v Cardiff

Saturday, 13 August
Barclays Premier League
Blackburn v Wolves
Fulham v Aston Villa

Liverpool v Sunderland
Newcastle v Arsenal
QPR v Bolton
Tottenham v Everton
Wigan v Norwich

npower Championship
Barnsley v Southampton
Birmingham v Coventry
Crystal Palace v Burnley
Doncaster v West Ham
Ipswich v Hull
Leeds v Middlesbrough
Leicester v Reading
Millwall v Nottm Forest
Portsmouth v Brighton
Watford v Derby

npower League 1
Bournemouth v Sheffield Wed
Bury v Carlisle
Chesterfield v Stevenage
Colchester v Wycombe
Exeter v MK Dons
Hartlepool v Walsall
Leyton Orient v Tranmere
Notts Co v Charlton
Rochdale v Huddersfield
Scunthorpe v Preston
Sheffield Utd v Brentford
Yeovil v Oldham

npower League 2
Accrington v Southend
Aldershot v Northampton
Barnet v Port Vale
Bristol Rov v Torquay
Burton v Shrewsbury
Cheltenham v Swindon
Crawley v Macclesfield
Crewe v Gillingham
Dag & Red v AFC Wimbledon
Hereford v Morecambe
Oxford v Bradford
Plymouth v Rotherham

Sunday, 14 August
Barclays Premier League
Stoke v Chelsea
WBA v Manchester Utd

npower Championship
Blackpool v Peterborough
Cardiff v Bristol City

Monday, 15 August
Barclays Premier League
Manchester City v Swansea

Tuesday, 16 August
npower Championship
Barnsley v Middlesbrough
Crystal Palace v Coventry
Doncaster v Nottm Forest
Ipswich v Southampton
Leeds v Hull
Portsmouth v Reading
Watford v West Ham

npower League 1
Bournemouth v Stevenage
Bury v Sheffield Wed
Chesterfield v Preston
Colchester v Charlton
Exeter v Brentford
Hartlepool v Huddersfield
Leyton Orient v Wycombe
Notts Co v Tranmere
Rochdale v Carlisle
Scunthorpe v Oldham
Sheffield Utd v Walsall
Yeovil v MK Dons

npower League 2
Accrington v Bradford
Aldershot v Torquay
Barnet v Gillingham
Bristol Rov v Northampton
Burton v Port Vale
Cheltenham v Morecambe
Crawley v Southend
Crewe v Rotherham
Dag & Red v Swindon
Hereford v Macclesfield
Oxford v Shrewsbury
Plymouth v AFC Wimbledon

Wednesday, 17 August
npower Championship
Blackpool v Derby
Cardiff v Brighton
Leicester v Bristol City
Millwall v Peterborough

Saturday, 20 August
Barclays Premier League
Arsenal v Liverpool
Aston Villa v Blackburn
Chelsea v WBA
Everton v QPR
Norwich v Stoke
Sunderland v Newcastle

Swansea v Wigan
Wolves v Fulham

npower Championship
Brighton v Blackpool
Bristol City v Portsmouth
Burnley v Cardiff
Coventry v Watford
Derby v Doncaster
Hull v Crystal Palace
Nottm Forest v Leicester
Peterborough v Ipswich
Reading v Barnsley
Southampton v Millwall
West Ham v Leeds

npower League 1
Brentford v Leyton Orient
Carlisle v Bournemouth
Charlton v Scunthorpe
Huddersfield v Colchester
MK Dons v Chesterfield
Oldham v Rochdale
Preston v Exeter
Sheffield Wed v Notts Co
Stevenage v Hartlepool
Tranmere v Sheffield Utd
Walsall v Yeovil
Wycombe v Bury

npower League 2
AFC Wimbledon v Hereford
Bradford v Dag & Red
Gillingham v Plymouth
Macclesfield v Bristol Rov
Morecambe v Aldershot
Northampton v Cheltenham
Port Vale v Accrington
Rotherham v Barnet
Shrewsbury v Crewe
Southend v Burton
Torquay v Crawley

Sunday, 21 August
Barclays Premier League
Bolton v Manchester City

npower Championship
Middlesbrough v Birmingham

npower League 2
Swindon v Oxford

Monday, 22 August
Barclays Premier League
Manchester Utd v Tottenham

Saturday, 27 August

Barclays Premier League
Aston Villa v Wolves
Blackburn v Everton
Chelsea v Norwich
Liverpool v Bolton
Newcastle v Fulham
Swansea v Sunderland
WBA v Stoke
Wigan v QPR

npower Championship
Brighton v Peterborough
Crystal Palace v Blackpool
Derby v Burnley
Doncaster v Bristol City
Hull v Reading
Ipswich v Leeds
Leicester v Southampton
Middlesbrough v Coventry
Millwall v Barnsley
Nottm Forest v West Ham
Portsmouth v Cardiff

npower League 1
Bournemouth v Walsall
Brentford v Tranmere
Bury v Charlton
Colchester v Oldham
Exeter v Chesterfield
Huddersfield v Wycombe
Leyton Orient v Carlisle
MK Dons v Stevenage
Preston v Notts Co
Rochdale v Hartlepool
Sheffield Wed v Scunthorpe
Yeovil v Sheffield Utd

npower League 2
Accrington v Burton
Bradford v Barnet
Bristol Rov v Hereford
Cheltenham v Crawley
Dag & Red v Torquay
Macclesfield v AFC Wimbledon
Northampton v Morecambe
Oxford v Aldershot
Plymouth v Crewe
Port Vale v Southend
Rotherham v Gillingham
Shrewsbury v Swindon

Sunday, 28 August

Barclays Premier League
Manchester Utd v Arsenal
Tottenham v Manchester City

npower Championship
Watford v Birmingham

Saturday, 3 September

npower League 1
Carlisle v MK Dons
Charlton v Sheffield Wed
Chesterfield v Leyton Orient
Hartlepool v Exeter
Notts Co v Bournemouth
Oldham v Huddersfield
Scunthorpe v Colchester
Sheffield Utd v Bury
Stevenage v Rochdale
Tranmere v Yeovil
Walsall v Brentford
Wycombe v Preston

npower League 2
AFC Wimbledon v Port Vale
Aldershot v Cheltenham
Barnet v Accrington
Burton v Plymouth
Crawley v Bristol Rov
Crewe v Oxford
Gillingham v Shrewsbury
Hereford v Dag & Red
Morecambe v Bradford
Southend v Northampton
Swindon v Rotherham
Torquay v Macclesfield

Saturday, 10 September

Barclays Premier League
Arsenal v Swansea
Bolton v Manchester Utd
Everton v Aston Villa
Manchester City v Wigan
Stoke v Liverpool
Sunderland v Chelsea
Wolves v Tottenham

npower Championship
Barnsley v Leicester
Blackpool v Ipswich
Bristol City v Brighton
Burnley v Middlesbrough
Cardiff v Doncaster
Coventry v Derby
Leeds v Crystal Palace
Peterborough v Hull
Reading v Watford
Southampton v Nottm Forest
West Ham v Portsmouth

npower League 1
Bournemouth v Chesterfield
Bury v Rochdale

Carlisle v Hartlepool
Charlton v Exeter
Colchester v Leyton Orient
Huddersfield v Tranmere
Notts Co v Walsall
Oldham v Stevenage
Preston v Yeovil
Scunthorpe v Sheffield Utd
Sheffield Wed v MK Dons
Wycombe v Brentford

npower League 2
Aldershot v AFC Wimbledon
Bradford v Bristol Rov
Cheltenham v Macclesfield
Crewe v Barnet
Gillingham v Accrington
Morecambe v Crawley
Northampton v Torquay
Oxford v Burton
Plymouth v Port Vale
Rotherham v Dag & Red
Shrewsbury v Hereford
Swindon v Southend

Sunday, 11 September
Barclays Premier League
Fulham v Blackburn
Norwich v WBA

npower Championship
Birmingham v Millwall

Monday, 12 September
Barclays Premier League
QPR v Newcastle

Tuesday, 13 September
npower League 1
Brentford v Colchester
Chesterfield v Bury
Exeter v Notts Co
Hartlepool v Preston
Leyton Orient v Bournemouth
MK Dons v Charlton
Rochdale v Scunthorpe
Sheffield Utd v Huddersfield
Stevenage v Sheffield Wed
Tranmere v Carlisle
Walsall v Oldham
Yeovil v Wycombe

npower League 2
AFC Wimbledon v Northampton
Accrington v Rotherham
Barnet v Plymouth
Bristol Rov v Shrewsbury

Burton v Crewe
Crawley v Swindon
Dag & Red v Oxford
Hereford v Aldershot
Macclesfield v Morecambe
Port Vale v Bradford
Southend v Gillingham
Torquay v Cheltenham

Saturday, 17 September
Barclays Premier League
Aston Villa v Newcastle
Blackburn v Arsenal
Bolton v Norwich
Everton v Wigan
Fulham v Manchester City
Sunderland v Stoke
Swansea v WBA
Wolves v QPR

npower Championship
Barnsley v Watford
Blackpool v Cardiff
Crystal Palace v Middlesbrough
Hull v Portsmouth
Ipswich v Coventry
Leeds v Bristol City
Leicester v Brighton
Millwall v West Ham
Nottm Forest v Derby
Peterborough v Burnley
Reading v Doncaster
Southampton v Birmingham

npower League 1
Brentford v Preston
Chesterfield v Carlisle
Exeter v Bournemouth
Hartlepool v Bury
Leyton Orient v Oldham
MK Dons v Huddersfield
Rochdale v Charlton
Sheffield Utd v Colchester
Stevenage v Notts Co
Tranmere v Wycombe
Walsall v Scunthorpe
Yeovil v Sheffield Wed

npower League 2
AFC Wimbledon v Cheltenham
Accrington v Crewe
Barnet v Oxford
Bristol Rov v Aldershot
Burton v Swindon
Crawley v Bradford
Dag & Red v Morecambe
Hereford v Gillingham
Macclesfield v Northampton

Port Vale v Shrewsbury
Southend v Plymouth
Torquay v Rotherham

Sunday, 18 September
Barclays Premier League
Manchester Utd v Chelsea
Tottenham v Liverpool

Friday, 23 September
npower Championship
Brighton v Leeds

Saturday, 24 September
Barclays Premier League
Arsenal v Bolton
Chelsea v Swansea
Liverpool v Wolves
Manchester City v Everton
Newcastle v Blackburn
Stoke v Manchester Utd
WBA v Fulham
Wigan v Tottenham

npower Championship
Birmingham v Barnsley
Bristol City v Hull
Burnley v Southampton
Cardiff v Leicester
Coventry v Reading
Derby v Millwall
Doncaster v Crystal Palace
Middlesbrough v Ipswich
Portsmouth v Blackpool
Watford v Nottm Forest
West Ham v Peterborough

npower League 1
Bournemouth v Hartlepool
Bury v MK Dons
Carlisle v Stevenage
Charlton v Chesterfield
Colchester v Walsall
Huddersfield v Leyton Orient
Notts Co v Rochdale
Oldham v Brentford
Preston v Tranmere
Scunthorpe v Yeovil
Sheffield Wed v Exeter
Wycombe v Sheffield Utd

npower League 2
Aldershot v Crawley
Bradford v AFC Wimbledon
Cheltenham v Hereford
Crewe v Port Vale
Gillingham v Burton

Morecambe v Bristol Rov
Northampton v Dag & Red
Oxford v Accrington
Plymouth v Macclesfield
Rotherham v Southend
Shrewsbury v Torquay
Swindon v Barnet

Sunday, 25 September
Barclays Premier League
QPR v Aston Villa

Monday, 26 September
Barclays Premier League
Norwich v Sunderland

Tuesday, 27 September
npower Championship
Birmingham v Leeds
Brighton v Crystal Palace
Bristol City v Reading
Burnley v Nottm Forest
Cardiff v Southampton
Coventry v Blackpool
Derby v Barnsley
Doncaster v Hull
Middlesbrough v Leicester
Portsmouth v Peterborough
Watford v Millwall
West Ham v Ipswich

Friday, 30 September
npower League 2
Macclesfield v Swindon
Southend v Shrewsbury

Saturday, 1 October
Barclays Premier League
Aston Villa v Wigan
Blackburn v Manchester City
Everton v Liverpool
Fulham v QPR
Manchester Utd v Norwich
Sunderland v WBA
Swansea v Stoke
Wolves v Newcastle

npower Championship
Barnsley v Coventry
Blackpool v Bristol City
Crystal Palace v West Ham
Hull v Cardiff
Ipswich v Brighton
Leeds v Portsmouth
Leicester v Derby
Millwall v Burnley
Nottm Forest v Birmingham

Peterborough v Doncaster
Reading v Middlesbrough
Southampton v Watford

npower League 1
Brentford v Huddersfield
Chesterfield v Colchester
Exeter v Oldham
Hartlepool v Sheffield Wed
Leyton Orient v Preston
MK Dons v Notts Co
Rochdale v Wycombe
Sheffield Utd v Charlton
Stevenage v Scunthorpe
Tranmere v Bournemouth
Walsall v Carlisle
Yeovil v Bury

npower League 2
AFC Wimbledon v Gillingham
Accrington v Aldershot
Barnet v Northampton
Bristol Rov v Cheltenham
Burton v Bradford
Crawley v Plymouth
Dag & Red v Crewe
Hereford v Oxford
Port Vale v Rotherham
Torquay v Morecambe

Sunday, 2 October
Barclays Premier League
Bolton v Chelsea
Tottenham v Arsenal

Saturday, 8 October
npower League 1
Bournemouth v Rochdale
Bury v Exeter
Carlisle v Brentford
Charlton v Tranmere
Colchester v Yeovil
Huddersfield v Stevenage
Notts Co v Hartlepool
Oldham v MK Dons
Preston v Sheffield Utd
Scunthorpe v Leyton Orient
Sheffield Wed v Chesterfield
Wycombe v Walsall

npower League 2
Aldershot v Macclesfield
Bradford v Torquay
Cheltenham v Dag & Red
Crewe v Southend
Gillingham v Port Vale
Morecambe v AFC Wimbledon

Northampton v Crawley
Oxford v Bristol Rov
Plymouth v Accrington
Rotherham v Burton
Shrewsbury v Barnet
Swindon v Hereford

Friday, 14 October
npower League 2
Bristol Rov v Rotherham
Burton v Cheltenham

Saturday, 15 October
Barclays Premier League
Arsenal v Sunderland
Chelsea v Everton
Liverpool v Manchester Utd
Norwich v Swansea
QPR v Blackburn
Stoke v Fulham
WBA v Wolves
Wigan v Bolton

npower Championship
Brighton v Hull
Bristol City v Peterborough
Burnley v Reading
Cardiff v Ipswich
Coventry v Nottm Forest
Derby v Southampton
Doncaster v Leeds
Middlesbrough v Millwall
Portsmouth v Barnsley
Watford v Crystal Palace
West Ham v Blackpool

npower League 1
Brentford v Scunthorpe
Chesterfield v Notts Co
Exeter v Huddersfield
Hartlepool v Wycombe
Leyton Orient v Bury
MK Dons v Bournemouth
Rochdale v Colchester
Stevenage v Charlton
Tranmere v Oldham
Walsall v Preston
Yeovil v Carlisle

npower League 2
AFC Wimbledon v Crewe
Accrington v Swindon
Barnet v Aldershot
Crawley v Shrewsbury
Dag & Red v Plymouth
Hereford v Bradford
Macclesfield v Oxford

Port Vale v Northampton
Southend v Morecambe
Torquay v Gillingham

Sunday, 16 October
Barclays Premier League
Manchester City v Aston Villa
Newcastle v Tottenham

npower Championship
Birmingham v Leicester

npower League 1
Sheffield Utd v Sheffield Wed

Tuesday, 18 October
npower Championship
Barnsley v Burnley
Blackpool v Doncaster
Crystal Palace v Bristol City
Ipswich v Portsmouth
Leeds v Coventry
Millwall v Brighton
Nottm Forest v Middlesbrough
Peterborough v Cardiff
Reading v Derby
Southampton v West Ham

Wednesday, 19 October
npower Championship
Hull v Birmingham
Leicester v Watford

Friday, 21 October
npower League 2
Accrington v Cheltenham

Saturday, 22 October
Barclays Premier League
Arsenal v Stoke
Aston Villa v WBA
Blackburn v Tottenham
Bolton v Sunderland
Fulham v Everton
Liverpool v Norwich
Newcastle v Wigan
Wolves v Swansea

npower Championship
Blackpool v Nottm Forest
Brighton v West Ham
Bristol City v Birmingham
Cardiff v Barnsley
Coventry v Burnley
Hull v Watford
Ipswich v Crystal Palace
Leicester v Millwall

Middlesbrough v Derby
Peterborough v Leeds
Portsmouth v Doncaster
Reading v Southampton

npower League 1
Bournemouth v Bury
Charlton v Carlisle
Chesterfield v Hartlepool
Exeter v Rochdale
Huddersfield v Preston
Leyton Orient v Sheffield Utd
MK Dons v Scunthorpe
Notts Co v Brentford
Oldham v Wycombe
Sheffield Wed v Colchester
Stevenage v Yeovil
Tranmere v Walsall

npower League 2
AFC Wimbledon v Crawley
Bradford v Northampton
Burton v Bristol Rov
Crewe v Macclesfield
Dag & Red v Aldershot
Gillingham v Oxford
Hereford v Barnet
Plymouth v Swindon
Port Vale v Morecambe
Rotherham v Shrewsbury
Southend v Torquay

Sunday, 23 October
Barclays Premier League
Manchester Utd v Manchester City
QPR v Chelsea

Tuesday, 25 October
npower League 1
Brentford v Stevenage
Bury v Notts Co
Carlisle v Sheffield Wed
Colchester v Bournemouth
Hartlepool v Tranmere
Preston v Oldham
Rochdale v Chesterfield
Scunthorpe v Huddersfield
Sheffield Utd v MK Dons
Walsall v Exeter
Wycombe v Charlton
Yeovil v Leyton Orient

npower League 2
Aldershot v Burton
Barnet v Southend
Bristol Rov v Port Vale
Cheltenham v Crewe

Crawley v Dag & Red
Macclesfield v Bradford
Morecambe v Rotherham
Northampton v Hereford
Oxford v Plymouth
Shrewsbury v Accrington
Swindon v Gillingham
Torquay v AFC Wimbledon

Saturday, 29 October
Barclays Premier League
Chelsea v Arsenal
Everton v Manchester Utd
Manchester City v Wolves
Norwich v Blackburn
Sunderland v Aston Villa
Swansea v Bolton
WBA v Liverpool
Wigan v Fulham

npower Championship
Barnsley v Bristol City
Birmingham v Brighton
Burnley v Blackpool
Crystal Palace v Reading
Derby v Portsmouth
Doncaster v Coventry
Leeds v Cardiff
Millwall v Ipswich
Nottm Forest v Hull
Southampton v Middlesbrough
Watford v Peterborough
West Ham v Leicester

npower League 1
Brentford v Chesterfield
Bury v Stevenage
Carlisle v Oldham
Colchester v Notts Co
Hartlepool v Charlton
Preston v Bournemouth
Rochdale v Leyton Orient
Scunthorpe v Tranmere
Sheffield Utd v Exeter
Walsall v MK Dons
Wycombe v Sheffield Wed
Yeovil v Huddersfield

npower League 2
Aldershot v Crewe
Barnet v Burton
Bristol Rov v Dag & Red
Cheltenham v Plymouth
Crawley v Accrington
Macclesfield v Southend
Morecambe v Gillingham
Northampton v Rotherham
Oxford v Port Vale

Shrewsbury v AFC Wimbledon
Swindon v Bradford
Torquay v Hereford

Sunday, 30 October
Barclays Premier League
Tottenham v QPR

Monday, 31 October
Barclays Premier League
Stoke v Newcastle

Tuesday, 1 November
npower Championship
Barnsley v Hull
Birmingham v Ipswich
Burnley v Leicester
Crystal Palace v Portsmouth
Derby v Cardiff
Doncaster v Middlesbrough
Leeds v Blackpool
Millwall v Coventry
Nottm Forest v Reading
Southampton v Peterborough
Watford v Brighton
West Ham v Bristol City

Saturday, 5 November
Barclays Premier League
Arsenal v WBA
Aston Villa v Norwich
Blackburn v Chelsea
Bolton v Stoke
Liverpool v Swansea
Manchester Utd v Sunderland
Newcastle v Everton
QPR v Manchester City

npower Championship
Blackpool v Millwall
Bristol City v Burnley
Cardiff v Crystal Palace
Coventry v Southampton
Hull v West Ham
Ipswich v Doncaster
Leicester v Leeds
Middlesbrough v Watford
Peterborough v Derby
Portsmouth v Nottm Forest
Reading v Birmingham

npower League 1
Bournemouth v Scunthorpe
Charlton v Preston
Chesterfield v Yeovil
Exeter v Carlisle
Huddersfield v Walsall

Leyton Orient v Hartlepool
MK Dons v Rochdale
Notts Co v Wycombe
Oldham v Bury
Sheffield Wed v Brentford
Stevenage v Sheffield Utd
Tranmere v Colchester

npower League 2
AFC Wimbledon v Barnet
Accrington v Bristol Rov
Bradford v Cheltenham
Burton v Macclesfield
Crewe v Torquay
Dag & Red v Shrewsbury
Gillingham v Northampton
Hereford v Crawley
Plymouth v Morecambe
Port Vale v Swindon
Rotherham v Aldershot
Southend v Oxford

Sunday, 6 November
Barclays Premier League
Fulham v Tottenham
Wolves v Wigan

npower Championship
Brighton v Barnsley

Saturday, 19 November
Barclays Premier League
Everton v Wolves
Manchester City v Newcastle
Norwich v Arsenal
Stoke v QPR
Sunderland v Fulham
Swansea v Manchester Utd
WBA v Bolton
Wigan v Blackburn

npower Championship
Barnsley v Doncaster
Birmingham v Peterborough
Burnley v Leeds
Coventry v West Ham
Derby v Hull
Leicester v Crystal Palace
Middlesbrough v Blackpool
Millwall v Bristol City
Nottm Forest v Ipswich
Reading v Cardiff
Southampton v Brighton
Watford v Portsmouth

npower League 1
Brentford v Charlton
Colchester v MK Dons

Huddersfield v Notts Co
Leyton Orient v Stevenage
Oldham v Chesterfield
Preston v Rochdale
Scunthorpe v Hartlepool
Sheffield Utd v Carlisle
Tranmere v Sheffield Wed
Walsall v Bury
Wycombe v Bournemouth
Yeovil v Exeter

npower League 2
AFC Wimbledon v Swindon
Aldershot v Gillingham
Bradford v Rotherham
Bristol Rov v Barnet
Cheltenham v Port Vale
Crawley v Oxford
Dag & Red v Southend
Hereford v Burton
Macclesfield v Accrington
Morecambe v Crewe
Northampton v Shrewsbury
Torquay v Plymouth

Sunday, 20 November
Barclays Premier League
Chelsea v Liverpool

Monday, 21 November
Barclays Premier League
Tottenham v Aston Villa

Saturday, 26 November
Barclays Premier League
Arsenal v Fulham
Bolton v Everton
Chelsea v Wolves
Manchester Utd v Newcastle
Norwich v QPR
Sunderland v Wigan
WBA v Tottenham

npower Championship
Blackpool v Birmingham
Brighton v Coventry
Bristol City v Southampton
Cardiff v Nottm Forest
Crystal Palace v Millwall
Doncaster v Watford
Hull v Burnley
Ipswich v Reading
Leeds v Barnsley
Peterborough v Middlesbrough
Portsmouth v Leicester
West Ham v Derby

npower League 1
Bournemouth v Oldham
Bury v Preston
Carlisle v Colchester
Charlton v Huddersfield
Chesterfield v Sheffield Utd
Exeter v Tranmere
Hartlepool v Yeovil
MK Dons v Wycombe
Notts Co v Scunthorpe
Rochdale v Brentford
Sheffield Wed v Leyton Orient
Stevenage v Walsall

npower League 2
Accrington v Dag & Red
Barnet v Macclesfield
Burton v AFC Wimbledon
Crewe v Hereford
Gillingham v Bradford
Oxford v Cheltenham
Plymouth v Northampton
Port Vale v Torquay
Rotherham v Crawley
Shrewsbury v Morecambe
Southend v Bristol Rov
Swindon v Aldershot

Sunday, 27 November
Barclays Premier League
Liverpool v Manchester City
Swansea v Aston Villa

Monday, 28 November
Barclays Premier League
Stoke v Blackburn

Tuesday, 29 November
npower Championship
Barnsley v Crystal Palace
Birmingham v Portsmouth
Burnley v Ipswich
Coventry v Cardiff
Derby v Brighton
Leicester v Blackpool
Middlesbrough v West Ham
Millwall v Doncaster
Nottm Forest v Leeds
Reading v Peterborough
Southampton v Hull
Watford v Bristol City

Saturday, 3 December
Barclays Premier League
Aston Villa v Manchester Utd
Blackburn v Swansea
Everton v Stoke

Fulham v Liverpool
Manchester City v Norwich
Newcastle v Chelsea
QPR v WBA
Tottenham v Bolton
Wigan v Arsenal
Wolves v Sunderland

npower Championship
Blackpool v Reading
Brighton v Nottm Forest
Bristol City v Middlesbrough
Cardiff v Birmingham
Crystal Palace v Derby
Doncaster v Southampton
Hull v Leicester
Ipswich v Watford
Leeds v Millwall
Peterborough v Barnsley
Portsmouth v Coventry
West Ham v Burnley

Saturday, 10 December
Barclays Premier League
Arsenal v Everton
Bolton v Aston Villa
Chelsea v Manchester City
Liverpool v QPR
Manchester Utd v Wolves
Norwich v Newcastle
Stoke v Tottenham
Sunderland v Blackburn
Swansea v Fulham
WBA v Wigan

npower Championship
Barnsley v Ipswich
Birmingham v Doncaster
Burnley v Portsmouth
Coventry v Hull
Derby v Bristol City
Leicester v Peterborough
Middlesbrough v Brighton
Millwall v Cardiff
Nottm Forest v Crystal Palace
Reading v West Ham
Southampton v Blackpool
Watford v Leeds

npower League 1
Brentford v Hartlepool
Colchester v Bury
Huddersfield v Bournemouth
Leyton Orient v Exeter
Oldham v Sheffield Wed
Preston v Stevenage
Scunthorpe v Carlisle
Sheffield Utd v Rochdale

Tranmere v MK Dons
Walsall v Charlton
Wycombe v Chesterfield
Yeovil v Notts Co

npower League 2
AFC Wimbledon v Accrington
Aldershot v Shrewsbury
Bradford v Plymouth
Bristol Rov v Swindon
Cheltenham v Southend
Crawley v Burton
Dag & Red v Port Vale
Hereford v Rotherham
Macclesfield v Gillingham
Morecambe v Oxford
Northampton v Crewe
Torquay v Barnet

Friday, 16 December
npower League 2
Barnet v Cheltenham
Southend v Bradford

Saturday, 17 December
Barclays Premier League
Aston Villa v Liverpool
Blackburn v WBA
Everton v Norwich
Fulham v Bolton
Manchester City v Arsenal
Newcastle v Swansea
QPR v Manchester Utd
Tottenham v Sunderland
Wigan v Chelsea
Wolves v Stoke

npower Championship
Blackpool v Watford
Brighton v Burnley
Bristol City v Nottm Forest
Cardiff v Middlesbrough
Crystal Palace v Birmingham
Doncaster v Leicester
Hull v Millwall
Ipswich v Derby
Leeds v Reading
Peterborough v Coventry
Portsmouth v Southampton
West Ham v Barnsley

npower League 1
Bournemouth v Sheffield Utd
Bury v Brentford
Carlisle v Wycombe
Charlton v Oldham
Chesterfield v Walsall

Exeter v Scunthorpe
Hartlepool v Colchester
MK Dons v Preston
Notts Co v Leyton Orient
Rochdale v Yeovil
Sheffield Wed v Huddersfield
Stevenage v Tranmere

npower League 2
Accrington v Torquay
Burton v Dag & Red
Crewe v Crawley
Gillingham v Bristol Rov
Oxford v Northampton
Plymouth v Hereford
Port Vale v Aldershot
Rotherham v AFC Wimbledon
Shrewsbury v Macclesfield
Swindon v Morecambe

Tuesday, 20 December
Barclays Premier League
QPR v Sunderland
Tottenham v Chelsea
Wigan v Liverpool
Wolves v Norwich

Wednesday, 21 December
Barclays Premier League
Aston Villa v Arsenal
Blackburn v Bolton
Everton v Swansea
Fulham v Manchester Utd
Manchester City v Stoke
Newcastle v WBA

Monday, 26 December
Barclays Premier League
Arsenal v Wolves
Bolton v Newcastle
Chelsea v Fulham
Liverpool v Blackburn
Manchester Utd v Wigan
Norwich v Tottenham
Stoke v Aston Villa
Sunderland v Everton
Swansea v QPR
WBA v Manchester City

npower Championship
Barnsley v Blackpool
Birmingham v West Ham
Burnley v Doncaster
Coventry v Bristol City
Derby v Leeds
Leicester v Ipswich
Middlesbrough v Hull

Millwall v Portsmouth
Nottm Forest v Peterborough
Reading v Brighton
Southampton v Crystal Palace
Watford v Cardiff

npower League 1
Brentford v Bournemouth
Colchester v Stevenage
Huddersfield v Chesterfield
Leyton Orient v MK Dons
Oldham v Hartlepool
Preston v Carlisle
Scunthorpe v Bury
Sheffield Utd v Notts Co
Tranmere v Rochdale
Walsall v Sheffield Wed
Wycombe v Exeter
Yeovil v Charlton

npower League 2
AFC Wimbledon v Oxford
Aldershot v Southend
Bradford v Crewe
Bristol Rov v Plymouth
Cheltenham v Shrewsbury
Crawley v Gillingham
Dag & Red v Barnet
Hereford v Port Vale
Macclesfield v Rotherham
Morecambe v Accrington
Northampton v Burton
Torquay v Swindon

Friday, 30 December
npower Championship
Southampton v Bristol City

npower League 1
Tranmere v Bury

npower League 2
Cheltenham v Rotherham
Dag & Red v Gillingham

Saturday, 31 December
Barclays Premier League
Arsenal v QPR
Bolton v Wolves
Chelsea v Aston Villa
Liverpool v Newcastle
Manchester Utd v Blackburn
Norwich v Fulham
Stoke v Wigan
Sunderland v Manchester City
Swansea v Tottenham
WBA v Everton

npower Championship
Barnsley v Leeds
Birmingham v Blackpool
Burnley v Hull
Coventry v Brighton
Derby v West Ham
Leicester v Portsmouth
Middlesbrough v Peterborough
Millwall v Crystal Palace
Nottm Forest v Cardiff
Reading v Ipswich
Watford v Doncaster

npower League 1
Brentford v MK Dons
Colchester v Exeter
Huddersfield v Carlisle
Leyton Orient v Charlton
Oldham v Notts Co
Preston v Sheffield Wed
Scunthorpe v Chesterfield
Sheffield Utd v Hartlepool
Walsall v Rochdale
Wycombe v Stevenage
Yeovil v Bournemouth

npower League 2
AFC Wimbledon v Southend
Aldershot v Plymouth
Bradford v Shrewsbury
Bristol Rov v Crewe
Crawley v Barnet
Hereford v Accrington
Macclesfield v Port Vale
Morecambe v Burton
Northampton v Swindon
Torquay v Oxford

Monday, 2 January
Barclays Premier League
Aston Villa v Swansea
Blackburn v Stoke
Everton v Bolton
Fulham v Arsenal
Manchester City v Liverpool
Newcastle v Manchester Utd
QPR v Norwich
Tottenham v WBA
Wigan v Sunderland
Wolves v Chelsea

npower Championship
Blackpool v Middlesbrough
Brighton v Southampton
Bristol City v Millwall
Cardiff v Reading
Crystal Palace v Leicester
Doncaster v Barnsley

Hull v Derby
Ipswich v Nottm Forest
Leeds v Burnley
Peterborough v Birmingham
Portsmouth v Watford
West Ham v Coventry

npower League 1
Bournemouth v Wycombe
Bury v Walsall
Carlisle v Sheffield Utd
Charlton v Brentford
Chesterfield v Oldham
Exeter v Yeovil
Hartlepool v Scunthorpe
MK Dons v Colchester
Notts Co v Huddersfield
Rochdale v Preston
Sheffield Wed v Tranmere
Stevenage v Leyton Orient

npower League 2
Accrington v Macclesfield
Barnet v Bristol Rov
Burton v Hereford
Crewe v Morecambe
Gillingham v Aldershot
Oxford v Crawley
Plymouth v Torquay
Port Vale v Cheltenham
Rotherham v Bradford
Shrewsbury v Northampton
Southend v Dag & Red
Swindon v AFC Wimbledon

Saturday, 7 January
npower League 1
Carlisle v Leyton Orient
Charlton v Bury
Chesterfield v Exeter
Hartlepool v Rochdale
Notts Co v Preston
Oldham v Colchester
Scunthorpe v Sheffield Wed
Sheffield Utd v Yeovil
Stevenage v MK Dons
Tranmere v Brentford
Walsall v Bournemouth
Wycombe v Huddersfield

npower League 2
AFC Wimbledon v Macclesfield
Aldershot v Oxford
Barnet v Bradford
Burton v Accrington
Crawley v Cheltenham
Crewe v Plymouth
Gillingham v Rotherham

Hereford v Bristol Rov
Morecambe v Northampton
Southend v Port Vale
Swindon v Shrewsbury
Torquay v Dag & Red

Saturday, 14 January
Barclays Premier League
Aston Villa v Everton
Blackburn v Fulham
Chelsea v Sunderland
Liverpool v Stoke
Manchester Utd v Bolton
Newcastle v QPR
Swansea v Arsenal
Tottenham v Wolves
WBA v Norwich
Wigan v Manchester City

npower Championship
Brighton v Bristol City
Crystal Palace v Leeds
Derby v Coventry
Doncaster v Cardiff
Hull v Peterborough
Ipswich v Blackpool
Leicester v Barnsley
Middlesbrough v Burnley
Millwall v Birmingham
Nottm Forest v Southampton
Portsmouth v West Ham
Watford v Reading

npower League 1
Bournemouth v Notts Co
Brentford v Walsall
Bury v Sheffield Utd
Colchester v Scunthorpe
Exeter v Hartlepool
Huddersfield v Oldham
Leyton Orient v Chesterfield
MK Dons v Carlisle
Preston v Wycombe
Rochdale v Stevenage
Sheffield Wed v Charlton
Yeovil v Tranmere

npower League 2
Accrington v Barnet
Bradford v Morecambe
Bristol Rov v Crawley
Cheltenham v Aldershot
Dag & Red v Hereford
Macclesfield v Torquay
Northampton v Southend
Oxford v Crewe
Plymouth v Burton
Port Vale v AFC Wimbledon

Rotherham v Swindon
Shrewsbury v Gillingham

Saturday, 21 January
Barclays Premier League
Arsenal v Manchester Utd
Bolton v Liverpool
Everton v Blackburn
Fulham v Newcastle
Manchester City v Tottenham
Norwich v Chelsea
QPR v Wigan
Stoke v WBA
Sunderland v Swansea
Wolves v Aston Villa

npower Championship
Barnsley v Millwall
Birmingham v Watford
Blackpool v Crystal Palace
Bristol City v Doncaster
Burnley v Derby
Cardiff v Portsmouth
Coventry v Middlesbrough
Leeds v Ipswich
Peterborough v Brighton
Reading v Hull
Southampton v Leicester
West Ham v Nottm Forest

npower League 1
Bournemouth v Tranmere
Bury v Yeovil
Carlisle v Walsall
Charlton v Sheffield Utd
Colchester v Chesterfield
Huddersfield v Brentford
Notts Co v MK Dons
Oldham v Exeter
Preston v Leyton Orient
Scunthorpe v Stevenage
Sheffield Wed v Hartlepool
Wycombe v Rochdale

npower League 2
Aldershot v Accrington
Bradford v Burton
Cheltenham v Bristol Rov
Crewe v Dag & Red
Gillingham v AFC Wimbledon
Morecambe v Torquay
Northampton v Barnet
Oxford v Hereford
Plymouth v Crawley
Rotherham v Port Vale
Shrewsbury v Southend
Swindon v Macclesfield

Saturday, 28 January
npower League 1
Brentford v Wycombe
Chesterfield v Bournemouth
Exeter v Charlton
Hartlepool v Carlisle
Leyton Orient v Colchester
MK Dons v Sheffield Wed
Rochdale v Bury
Sheffield Utd v Scunthorpe
Stevenage v Oldham
Tranmere v Huddersfield
Walsall v Notts Co
Yeovil v Preston

npower League 2
AFC Wimbledon v Aldershot
Accrington v Gillingham
Barnet v Crewe
Bristol Rov v Bradford
Burton v Oxford
Crawley v Morecambe
Dag & Red v Rotherham
Hereford v Shrewsbury
Macclesfield v Cheltenham
Port Vale v Plymouth
Southend v Swindon
Torquay v Northampton

Tuesday, 31 January
Barclays Premier League
Bolton v Arsenal
Manchester Utd v Stoke
Sunderland v Norwich
Swansea v Chelsea
Tottenham v Wigan
Wolves v Liverpool

npower Championship
Barnsley v Derby
Blackpool v Coventry
Crystal Palace v Brighton
Hull v Doncaster
Ipswich v West Ham
Leeds v Birmingham
Leicester v Middlesbrough
Millwall v Watford
Nottm Forest v Burnley
Peterborough v Portsmouth
Reading v Bristol City
Southampton v Cardiff

Wednesday, 1 February
Barclays Premier League
Aston Villa v QPR
Blackburn v Newcastle
Everton v Manchester City
Fulham v WBA

Saturday, 4 February
Barclays Premier League
Arsenal v Blackburn
Chelsea v Manchester Utd
Liverpool v Tottenham
Manchester City v Fulham
Newcastle v Aston Villa
Norwich v Bolton
QPR v Wolves
Stoke v Sunderland
WBA v Swansea
Wigan v Everton

npower Championship
Birmingham v Southampton
Brighton v Leicester
Bristol City v Leeds
Burnley v Peterborough
Cardiff v Blackpool
Coventry v Ipswich
Derby v Nottm Forest
Doncaster v Reading
Middlesbrough v Crystal Palace
Portsmouth v Hull
Watford v Barnsley
West Ham v Millwall

npower League 1
Bournemouth v Exeter
Bury v Hartlepool
Carlisle v Chesterfield
Charlton v Rochdale
Colchester v Sheffield Utd
Huddersfield v MK Dons
Notts Co v Stevenage
Oldham v Leyton Orient
Preston v Brentford
Scunthorpe v Walsall
Sheffield Wed v Yeovil
Wycombe v Tranmere

npower League 2
Aldershot v Bristol Rov
Bradford v Crawley
Cheltenham v AFC Wimbledon
Crewe v Accrington
Gillingham v Hereford
Morecambe v Dag & Red
Northampton v Macclesfield
Oxford v Barnet
Plymouth v Southend
Rotherham v Torquay
Shrewsbury v Port Vale
Swindon v Burton

Friday, 10 February
npower League 2
Southend v Rotherham

Saturday, 11 February
Barclays Premier League
Aston Villa v Manchester City
Blackburn v QPR
Bolton v Wigan
Everton v Chelsea
Fulham v Stoke
Manchester Utd v Liverpool
Sunderland v Arsenal
Swansea v Norwich
Tottenham v Newcastle
Wolves v WBA

npower Championship
Barnsley v Birmingham
Blackpool v Portsmouth
Crystal Palace v Doncaster
Hull v Bristol City
Ipswich v Middlesbrough
Leeds v Brighton
Leicester v Cardiff
Millwall v Derby
Nottm Forest v Watford
Peterborough v West Ham
Reading v Coventry
Southampton v Burnley

npower League 1
Brentford v Oldham
Chesterfield v Charlton
Exeter v Sheffield Wed
Hartlepool v Bournemouth
Leyton Orient v Huddersfield
MK Dons v Bury
Rochdale v Notts Co
Sheffield Utd v Wycombe
Stevenage v Carlisle
Tranmere v Preston
Walsall v Colchester
Yeovil v Scunthorpe

npower League 2
AFC Wimbledon v Bradford
Accrington v Oxford
Barnet v Swindon
Bristol Rov v Morecambe
Burton v Gillingham
Crawley v Aldershot
Dag & Red v Northampton
Hereford v Cheltenham
Macclesfield v Plymouth
Port Vale v Crewe
Torquay v Shrewsbury

Tuesday, 14 February
npower Championship
Birmingham v Hull
Brighton v Millwall

Bristol City v Crystal Palace
Burnley v Barnsley
Cardiff v Peterborough
Coventry v Leeds
Derby v Reading
Doncaster v Blackpool
Middlesbrough v Nottm Forest
Portsmouth v Ipswich
Watford v Leicester
West Ham v Southampton

npower League 1
Bournemouth v Leyton Orient
Bury v Chesterfield
Carlisle v Tranmere
Charlton v MK Dons
Colchester v Brentford
Huddersfield v Sheffield Utd
Notts Co v Exeter
Oldham v Walsall
Preston v Hartlepool
Scunthorpe v Rochdale
Sheffield Wed v Stevenage
Wycombe v Yeovil

npower League 2
Aldershot v Hereford
Bradford v Port Vale
Cheltenham v Torquay
Crewe v Burton
Gillingham v Southend
Morecambe v Macclesfield
Northampton v AFC Wimbledon
Oxford v Dag & Red
Plymouth v Barnet
Rotherham v Accrington
Shrewsbury v Bristol Rov
Swindon v Crawley

Saturday, 18 February
npower Championship
Barnsley v Portsmouth
Blackpool v West Ham
Crystal Palace v Watford
Hull v Brighton
Ipswich v Cardiff
Leeds v Doncaster
Leicester v Birmingham
Millwall v Middlesbrough
Nottm Forest v Coventry
Peterborough v Bristol City
Reading v Burnley
Southampton v Derby

npower League 1
Brentford v Carlisle
Chesterfield v Sheffield Wed
Exeter v Bury

Hartlepool v Notts Co
Leyton Orient v Scunthorpe
MK Dons v Oldham
Rochdale v Bournemouth
Sheffield Utd v Preston
Stevenage v Huddersfield
Tranmere v Charlton
Walsall v Wycombe
Yeovil v Colchester

npower League 2
AFC Wimbledon v Morecambe
Accrington v Plymouth
Barnet v Shrewsbury
Bristol Rov v Oxford
Burton v Rotherham
Crawley v Northampton
Dag & Red v Cheltenham
Hereford v Swindon
Macclesfield v Aldershot
Port Vale v Gillingham
Southend v Crewe
Torquay v Bradford

Saturday, 25 February
Barclays Premier League
Arsenal v Tottenham
Chelsea v Bolton
Liverpool v Everton
Manchester City v Blackburn
Newcastle v Wolves
Norwich v Manchester Utd
QPR v Fulham
Stoke v Swansea
WBA v Sunderland
Wigan v Aston Villa

npower Championship
Birmingham v Nottm Forest
Brighton v Ipswich
Bristol City v Blackpool
Burnley v Millwall
Cardiff v Hull
Coventry v Barnsley
Derby v Leicester
Doncaster v Peterborough
Middlesbrough v Reading
Portsmouth v Leeds
Watford v Southampton
West Ham v Crystal Palace

npower League 1
Bournemouth v MK Dons
Bury v Leyton Orient
Carlisle v Yeovil
Charlton v Stevenage
Colchester v Rochdale
Huddersfield v Exeter

Notts Co v Chesterfield
Oldham v Tranmere
Preston v Walsall
Scunthorpe v Brentford
Wycombe v Hartlepool

npower League 2
Aldershot v Barnet
Bradford v Hereford
Cheltenham v Burton
Crewe v AFC Wimbledon
Gillingham v Torquay
Morecambe v Southend
Northampton v Port Vale
Oxford v Macclesfield
Plymouth v Dag & Red
Rotherham v Bristol Rov
Shrewsbury v Crawley
Swindon v Accrington

Sunday, 26 February
npower League 1
Sheffield Wed v Sheffield Utd

Saturday, 3 March
Barclays Premier League
Blackburn v Aston Villa
Fulham v Wolves
Liverpool v Arsenal
Manchester City v Bolton
Newcastle v Sunderland
QPR v Everton
Stoke v Norwich
Tottenham v Manchester Utd
WBA v Chelsea
Wigan v Swansea

npower Championship
Barnsley v Nottm Forest
Birmingham v Derby
Blackpool v Hull
Cardiff v West Ham
Crystal Palace v Peterborough
Doncaster v Brighton
Ipswich v Bristol City
Leeds v Southampton
Leicester v Coventry
Millwall v Reading
Portsmouth v Middlesbrough
Watford v Burnley

npower League 1
Bournemouth v Charlton
Bury v Huddersfield
Chesterfield v Tranmere
Colchester v Preston
Exeter v Stevenage
Hartlepool v MK Dons

Leyton Orient v Walsall
Notts Co v Carlisle
Rochdale v Sheffield Wed
Scunthorpe v Wycombe
Sheffield Utd v Oldham
Yeovil v Brentford

npower League 2
Accrington v Port Vale
Aldershot v Morecambe
Barnet v Rotherham
Bristol Rov v Macclesfield
Burton v Southend
Cheltenham v Northampton
Crawley v Torquay
Crewe v Shrewsbury
Dag & Red v Bradford
Hereford v AFC Wimbledon
Oxford v Swindon
Plymouth v Gillingham

Tuesday, 6 March
npower Championship
Brighton v Cardiff
Bristol City v Leicester
Burnley v Birmingham
Coventry v Crystal Palace
Derby v Blackpool
Hull v Leeds
Middlesbrough v Barnsley
Nottm Forest v Doncaster
Peterborough v Millwall
Reading v Portsmouth
Southampton v Ipswich
West Ham v Watford

npower League 1
Brentford v Exeter
Carlisle v Rochdale
Charlton v Colchester
Huddersfield v Hartlepool
MK Dons v Yeovil
Oldham v Scunthorpe
Preston v Chesterfield
Sheffield Wed v Bury
Stevenage v Bournemouth
Tranmere v Notts Co
Walsall v Sheffield Utd
Wycombe v Leyton Orient

npower League 2
AFC Wimbledon v Plymouth
Bradford v Accrington
Gillingham v Barnet
Macclesfield v Hereford
Morecambe v Cheltenham
Northampton v Bristol Rov
Port Vale v Burton

Rotherham v Crewe
Shrewsbury v Oxford
Southend v Crawley
Swindon v Dag & Red
Torquay v Aldershot

Saturday, 10 March
Barclays Premier League
Arsenal v Newcastle
Aston Villa v Fulham
Bolton v QPR
Chelsea v Stoke
Everton v Tottenham
Manchester Utd v WBA
Norwich v Wigan
Sunderland v Liverpool
Swansea v Manchester City
Wolves v Blackburn

npower Championship
Brighton v Portsmouth
Bristol City v Cardiff
Burnley v Crystal Palace
Coventry v Birmingham
Derby v Watford
Hull v Ipswich
Middlesbrough v Leeds
Nottm Forest v Millwall
Peterborough v Blackpool
Reading v Leicester
Southampton v Barnsley
West Ham v Doncaster

npower League 1
Brentford v Sheffield Utd
Carlisle v Bury
Charlton v Notts Co
Huddersfield v Rochdale
MK Dons v Exeter
Oldham v Yeovil
Preston v Scunthorpe
Sheffield Wed v Bournemouth
Stevenage v Chesterfield
Tranmere v Leyton Orient
Walsall v Hartlepool
Wycombe v Colchester

npower League 2
AFC Wimbledon v Dag & Red
Bradford v Oxford
Gillingham v Crewe
Macclesfield v Crawley
Morecambe v Hereford
Northampton v Aldershot
Port Vale v Barnet
Rotherham v Plymouth
Shrewsbury v Burton
Southend v Accrington

Swindon v Cheltenham
Torquay v Bristol Rov

Saturday, 17 March
Barclays Premier League
Aston Villa v Bolton
Blackburn v Sunderland
Everton v Arsenal
Fulham v Swansea
Manchester City v Chelsea
Newcastle v Norwich
QPR v Liverpool
Tottenham v Stoke
Wigan v WBA
Wolves v Manchester Utd

npower Championship
Barnsley v Reading
Birmingham v Middlesbrough
Blackpool v Brighton
Crystal Palace v Hull
Doncaster v Derby
Ipswich v Peterborough
Leeds v West Ham
Leicester v Nottm Forest
Millwall v Southampton
Portsmouth v Bristol City
Watford v Coventry

npower League 1
Bournemouth v Carlisle
Bury v Wycombe
Chesterfield v MK Dons
Colchester v Huddersfield
Exeter v Preston
Hartlepool v Stevenage
Leyton Orient v Brentford
Notts Co v Sheffield Wed
Rochdale v Oldham
Scunthorpe v Charlton
Sheffield Utd v Tranmere
Yeovil v Walsall

npower League 2
Accrington v Northampton
Aldershot v Bradford
Barnet v Morecambe
Bristol Rov v AFC Wimbledon
Burton v Torquay
Cheltenham v Gillingham
Crawley v Port Vale
Crewe v Swindon
Dag & Red v Macclesfield
Hereford v Southend
Oxford v Rotherham
Plymouth v Shrewsbury

Sunday, 18 March
npower Championship
Cardiff v Burnley

Tuesday, 20 March
npower Championship
Blackpool v Leicester
Brighton v Derby
Bristol City v Watford
Crystal Palace v Barnsley
Doncaster v Millwall
Hull v Southampton
Leeds v Nottm Forest
Peterborough v Reading
Portsmouth v Birmingham
West Ham v Middlesbrough

npower League 1
Bournemouth v Brentford
Bury v Scunthorpe
Carlisle v Preston
Charlton v Yeovil
Chesterfield v Huddersfield
Exeter v Wycombe
Hartlepool v Oldham
MK Dons v Leyton Orient
Notts Co v Sheffield Utd
Rochdale v Tranmere
Sheffield Wed v Walsall
Stevenage v Colchester

npower League 2
Accrington v Morecambe
Barnet v Dag & Red
Burton v Northampton
Crewe v Bradford
Gillingham v Crawley
Oxford v AFC Wimbledon
Plymouth v Bristol Rov
Port Vale v Hereford
Rotherham v Macclesfield
Shrewsbury v Cheltenham
Southend v Aldershot
Swindon v Torquay

Wednesday, 21 March
npower Championship
Cardiff v Coventry
Ipswich v Burnley

Saturday, 24 March
Barclays Premier League
Arsenal v Aston Villa
Bolton v Blackburn
Chelsea v Tottenham
Liverpool v Wigan
Manchester Utd v Fulham

Norwich v Wolves
Stoke v Manchester City
Sunderland v QPR
Swansea v Everton
WBA v Newcastle

npower Championship
Barnsley v Peterborough
Burnley v West Ham
Coventry v Portsmouth
Derby v Crystal Palace
Leicester v Hull
Middlesbrough v Bristol City
Millwall v Leeds
Nottm Forest v Brighton
Reading v Blackpool
Southampton v Doncaster
Watford v Ipswich

npower League 1
Brentford v Rochdale
Colchester v Carlisle
Huddersfield v Charlton
Leyton Orient v Sheffield Wed
Oldham v Bournemouth
Preston v Bury
Scunthorpe v Notts Co
Sheffield Utd v Chesterfield
Tranmere v Exeter
Walsall v Stevenage
Wycombe v MK Dons
Yeovil v Hartlepool

npower League 2
AFC Wimbledon v Burton
Aldershot v Swindon
Bradford v Gillingham
Bristol Rov v Southend
Cheltenham v Oxford
Crawley v Rotherham
Dag & Red v Accrington
Hereford v Crewe
Macclesfield v Barnet
Morecambe v Shrewsbury
Northampton v Plymouth
Torquay v Port Vale

Sunday, 25 March
npower Championship
Birmingham v Cardiff

Friday, 30 March
npower Championship
Doncaster v Birmingham

npower League 2
Southend v Cheltenham

Saturday, 31 March
Barclays Premier League
Aston Villa v Chelsea
Blackburn v Manchester Utd
Everton v WBA
Fulham v Norwich
Manchester City v Sunderland
Newcastle v Liverpool
QPR v Arsenal
Tottenham v Swansea
Wigan v Stoke
Wolves v Bolton

npower Championship
Blackpool v Southampton
Brighton v Middlesbrough
Bristol City v Derby
Cardiff v Millwall
Crystal Palace v Nottm Forest
Hull v Coventry
Ipswich v Barnsley
Leeds v Watford
Peterborough v Leicester
Portsmouth v Burnley
West Ham v Reading

npower League 1
Bournemouth v Yeovil
Bury v Tranmere
Carlisle v Huddersfield
Charlton v Leyton Orient
Chesterfield v Scunthorpe
Exeter v Colchester
Hartlepool v Sheffield Utd
MK Dons v Brentford
Notts Co v Oldham
Rochdale v Walsall
Sheffield Wed v Preston
Stevenage v Wycombe

npower League 2
Accrington v AFC Wimbledon
Barnet v Torquay
Burton v Crawley
Crewe v Northampton
Gillingham v Macclesfield
Oxford v Morecambe
Plymouth v Bradford
Port Vale v Dag & Red
Rotherham v Hereford
Shrewsbury v Aldershot
Swindon v Bristol Rov

Friday, 6 April
npower Championship
Burnley v Brighton
Nottm Forest v Bristol City
Watford v Blackpool

npower League 1
Colchester v Hartlepool
Leyton Orient v Notts Co
Scunthorpe v Exeter
Tranmere v Stevenage
Wycombe v Carlisle

npower League 2
AFC Wimbledon v Rotherham
Bradford v Southend
Cheltenham v Barnet
Dag & Red v Burton
Macclesfield v Shrewsbury
Morecambe v Swindon
Northampton v Oxford

Saturday, 7 April
Barclays Premier League
Arsenal v Manchester City
Bolton v Fulham
Chelsea v Wigan
Liverpool v Aston Villa
Manchester Utd v QPR
Norwich v Everton
Stoke v Wolves
Sunderland v Tottenham
Swansea v Newcastle
WBA v Blackburn

npower Championship
Barnsley v West Ham
Birmingham v Crystal Palace
Coventry v Peterborough
Derby v Ipswich
Leicester v Doncaster
Middlesbrough v Cardiff
Millwall v Hull
Reading v Leeds
Southampton v Portsmouth

npower League 1
Brentford v Bury
Huddersfield v Sheffield Wed
Oldham v Charlton
Preston v MK Dons
Sheffield Utd v Bournemouth
Walsall v Chesterfield
Yeovil v Rochdale

npower League 2
Aldershot v Port Vale
Bristol Rov v Gillingham
Crawley v Crewe
Hereford v Plymouth
Torquay v Accrington

Monday, 9 April
Barclays Premier League
Aston Villa v Stoke
Blackburn v Liverpool
Everton v Sunderland
Fulham v Chelsea
Manchester City v WBA
Newcastle v Bolton
QPR v Swansea
Tottenham v Norwich
Wigan v Manchester Utd
Wolves v Arsenal

npower Championship
Blackpool v Barnsley
Bristol City v Coventry
Cardiff v Watford
Crystal Palace v Southampton
Doncaster v Burnley
Hull v Middlesbrough
Ipswich v Leicester
Leeds v Derby
Peterborough v Nottm Forest
West Ham v Birmingham

npower League 1
Bournemouth v Huddersfield
Bury v Colchester
Carlisle v Scunthorpe
Charlton v Walsall
Chesterfield v Wycombe
Exeter v Leyton Orient
Hartlepool v Brentford
MK Dons v Tranmere
Notts Co v Yeovil
Sheffield Wed v Oldham
Stevenage v Preston

npower League 2
Accrington v Hereford
Barnet v Crawley
Burton v Morecambe
Crewe v Bristol Rov
Gillingham v Dag & Red
Oxford v Torquay
Plymouth v Aldershot
Port Vale v Macclesfield
Rotherham v Cheltenham
Shrewsbury v Bradford
Southend v AFC Wimbledon
Swindon v Northampton

Tuesday, 10 April
npower Championship
Brighton v Reading
Portsmouth v Millwall

Npower League 1
Rochdale v Sheffield

Saturday, 14 April
Barclays Premier League
Arsenal v Wigan
Bolton v Tottenham
Chelsea v Newcastle
Liverpool v Fulham
Manchester Utd v Aston Villa
Norwich v Manchester City
Stoke v Everton
Sunderland v Wolves
Swansea v Blackburn
WBA v QPR

npower Championship
Barnsley v Cardiff
Birmingham v Bristol City
Burnley v Coventry
Crystal Palace v Ipswich
Derby v Middlesbrough
Doncaster v Portsmouth
Leeds v Peterborough
Millwall v Leicester
Nottm Forest v Blackpool
Southampton v Reading
Watford v Hull
West Ham v Brighton

npower League 1
Brentford v Notts Co
Bury v Bournemouth
Carlisle v Charlton
Colchester v Sheffield Wed
Hartlepool v Chesterfield
Preston v Huddersfield
Rochdale v Exeter
Scunthorpe v MK Dons
Sheffield Utd v Leyton Orient
Walsall v Tranmere
Wycombe v Oldham
Yeovil v Stevenage

npower League 2
Aldershot v Dag & Red
Barnet v Hereford
Bristol Rov v Burton
Cheltenham v Accrington
Crawley v AFC Wimbledon
Macclesfield v Crewe
Morecambe v Port Vale
Northampton v Bradford
Oxford v Gillingham
Shrewsbury v Rotherham
Swindon v Plymouth
Torquay v Southend

Tuesday, 17 April

npower Championship
Blackpool v Leeds
Brighton v Watford
Bristol City v West Ham
Cardiff v Derby
Coventry v Millwall
Hull v Barnsley
Ipswich v Birmingham
Leicester v Burnley
Middlesbrough v Doncaster
Peterborough v Southampton
Portsmouth v Crystal Palace
Reading v Nottm Forest

Friday, 20 April

npower League 2
Southend v Barnet

Saturday, 21 April

Barclays Premier League
Arsenal v Chelsea
Aston Villa v Sunderland
Blackburn v Norwich
Bolton v Swansea
Fulham v Wigan
Liverpool v WBA
Manchester Utd v Everton
Newcastle v Stoke
QPR v Tottenham
Wolves v Manchester City

npower Championship
Blackpool v Burnley
Brighton v Birmingham
Bristol City v Barnsley
Cardiff v Leeds
Coventry v Doncaster
Hull v Nottm Forest
Ipswich v Millwall
Leicester v West Ham
Middlesbrough v Southampton
Peterborough v Watford
Portsmouth v Derby
Reading v Crystal Palace

npower League 1
Bournemouth v Colchester
Charlton v Wycombe
Chesterfield v Rochdale
Exeter v Walsall
Huddersfield v Scunthorpe
Leyton Orient v Yeovil
MK Dons v Sheffield Utd
Notts Co v Bury
Oldham v Preston
Sheffield Wed v Carlisle

Stevenage v Brentford
Tranmere v Hartlepool

npower League 2
AFC Wimbledon v Torquay
Accrington v Shrewsbury
Bradford v Macclesfield
Burton v Aldershot
Crewe v Cheltenham
Dag & Red v Crawley
Gillingham v Swindon
Hereford v Northampton
Plymouth v Oxford
Port Vale v Bristol Rov
Rotherham v Morecambe

Saturday, 28 April

Barclays Premier League
Chelsea v QPR
Everton v Fulham
Manchester City v Manchester Utd
Norwich v Liverpool
Stoke v Arsenal
Sunderland v Bolton
Swansea v Wolves
Tottenham v Blackburn
WBA v Aston Villa
Wigan v Newcastle

npower Championship
Barnsley v Brighton
Birmingham v Reading
Burnley v Bristol City
Crystal Palace v Cardiff
Derby v Peterborough
Doncaster v Ipswich
Leeds v Leicester
Millwall v Blackpool
Nottm Forest v Portsmouth
Southampton v Coventry
Watford v Middlesbrough
West Ham v Hull

npower League 1
Brentford v Sheffield Wed
Bury v Oldham
Carlisle v Exeter
Colchester v Tranmere
Hartlepool v Leyton Orient
Preston v Charlton
Rochdale v MK Dons
Scunthorpe v Bournemouth
Sheffield Utd v Stevenage
Walsall v Huddersfield
Wycombe v Notts Co
Yeovil v Chesterfield

npower League 2
Aldershot v Rotherham
Barnet v AFC Wimbledon
Bristol Rov v Accrington
Cheltenham v Bradford
Crawley v Hereford
Macclesfield v Burton
Morecambe v Plymouth
Northampton v Gillingham
Oxford v Southend
Shrewsbury v Dag & Red
Swindon v Port Vale
Torquay v Crewe

Saturday, 5 May
Barclays Premier League
Arsenal v Norwich
Aston Villa v Tottenham
Blackburn v Wigan
Bolton v WBA
Fulham v Sunderland
Liverpool v Chelsea
Manchester Utd v Swansea
Newcastle v Manchester City
QPR v Stoke
Wolves v Everton

npower League 1
Bournemouth v Preston
Charlton v Hartlepool
Chesterfield v Brentford
Exeter v Sheffield Utd
Huddersfield v Yeovil
Leyton Orient v Rochdale

MK Dons v Walsall
Notts Co v Colchester
Oldham v Carlisle
Sheffield Wed v Wycombe
Stevenage v Bury
Tranmere v Scunthorpe

npower League 2
AFC Wimbledon v Shrewsbury
Accrington v Crawley
Bradford v Swindon
Burton v Barnet
Crewe v Aldershot
Dag & Red v Bristol Rov
Gillingham v Morecambe
Hereford v Torquay
Plymouth v Cheltenham
Port Vale v Oxford
Rotherham v Northampton
Southend v Macclesfield

Sunday, 13 May
Barclays Premier League
Chelsea v Blackburn
Everton v Newcastle
Manchester City v QPR
Norwich v Aston Villa
Stoke v Bolton
Sunderland v Manchester Utd
Swansea v Liverpool
Tottenham v Fulham
WBA v Arsenal
Wigan v Wolves

SCOTTISH FIXTURES 2011–2012

Saturday, 23 July
Clydesdale Bank Premier League
Aberdeen v St Johnstone
Motherwell v Inverness
Rangers v Hearts

Sunday, 24 July
Clydesdale Bank Premier League
Dundee Utd v Kilmarnock
Hibernian v Celtic

Monday, 25 July
Clydesdale Bank Premier League
Dunfermline v St Mirren

Saturday, 30 July
Clydesdale Bank Premier League
Celtic v Dunfermline Postponed
Inverness v Hibernian
Kilmarnock v Motherwell

St Johnstone v Rangers
St Mirren v Aberdeen

Sunday, 31 July
Clydesdale Bank Premier League
Hearts v Dundee Utd

Saturday, 6 August
Clydesdale Bank Premier League
Dundee Utd v St Mirren
Dunfermline v Inverness
Hibernian v St Johnstone Postponed
Rangers v Kilmarnock Postponed

Irn-Bru First Division
Ayr v Hamilton
Livingston v Queen of South
Partick v Dundee
Raith v Falkirk
Ross v Morton

Irn-Bru Second Division
Airdrie v Dumbarton
Arbroath v Albion
Brechin v Stenhousemuir
Forfar v Cowdenbeath
Stirling v East Fife

Irn-Bru Third Division
Annan Athletic v Queens Park
Clyde v Peterhead
East Stirling v Montrose
Elgin v Berwick
Stranraer v Alloa

Sunday, 7 August
Clydesdale Bank Premier League
Aberdeen v Celtic
Motherwell v Hearts

Saturday, 13 August
Clydesdale Bank Premier League
Celtic v Dundee Utd
Hearts v Aberdeen
Inverness v Rangers
Kilmarnock v Hibernian
St Johnstone v Dunfermline
St Mirren v Motherwell

Irn-Bru First Division
Dundee v Ayr
Falkirk v Partick
Hamilton v Ross
Morton v Livingston
Queen of South v Raith

Irn-Bru Second Division
Albion v Forfar
Cowdenbeath v Brechin
Dumbarton v Stirling
East Fife v Airdrie
Stenhousemuir v Arbroath

Irn-Bru Third Division
Alloa v Clyde
Berwick v East Stirling
Montrose v Elgin
Peterhead v Annan Athletic
Queens Park v Stranraer

Saturday, 20 August
Clydesdale Bank Premier League
Aberdeen v Inverness
Dundee Utd v Dunfermline
Hibernian v St Mirren
Kilmarnock v Hearts
Motherwell v Rangers

Irn-Bru First Division
Ayr v Falkirk
Livingston v Dundee
Partick v Hamilton
Raith v Morton
Ross v Queen of South

Irn-Bru Second Division
Airdrie v Cowdenbeath
Arbroath v East Fife
Brechin v Dumbarton
Forfar v Stenhousemuir
Stirling v Albion

Irn-Bru Third Division
Annan Athletic v Alloa
Clyde v Montrose
East Stirling v Peterhead
Elgin v Queens Park
Stranraer v Berwick

Sunday, 21 August
Clydesdale Bank Premier League
Celtic v St Johnstone

Saturday, 27 August
Clydesdale Bank Premier League
Dunfermline v Motherwell
Hearts v Hibernian
Inverness v Kilmarnock
Rangers v Aberdeen
St Johnstone v Dundee Utd

Irn-Bru First Division
Ayr v Raith
Dundee v Morton
Falkirk v Ross
Hamilton v Livingston
Partick v Queen of South

Irn-Bru Second Division
Albion v Brechin
Arbroath v Stirling
East Fife v Dumbarton
Forfar v Airdrie
Stenhousemuir v Cowdenbeath

Irn-Bru Third Division
Alloa v Peterhead
Annan Athletic v Clyde
Elgin v East Stirling
Montrose v Stranraer
Queens Park v Berwick

Sunday, 28 August
Clydesdale Bank Premier League
St Mirren v Celtic

Saturday, 10 September
Clydesdale Bank Premier League
Celtic v Motherwell
Dundee Utd v Rangers
Inverness v Hearts
Kilmarnock v Dunfermline
St Mirren v St Johnstone

Irn-Bru First Division
Livingston v Falkirk
Morton v Ayr
Queen of South v Hamilton
Raith v Dundee
Ross v Partick

Irn-Bru Second Division
Airdrie v Albion
Brechin v Forfar
Cowdenbeath v East Fife
Dumbarton v Arbroath
Stirling v Stenhousemuir

Irn-Bru Third Division
Berwick v Montrose
Clyde v Queens Park
East Stirling v Alloa
Peterhead v Elgin
Stranraer v Annan Athletic

Sunday, 11 September
Clydesdale Bank Premier League
Hibernian v Aberdeen

Saturday, 17 September
Clydesdale Bank Premier League
Aberdeen v Kilmarnock
Dundee Utd v Inverness
Dunfermline v Hibernian
Hearts v St Mirren
Motherwell v St Johnstone
Rangers v Celtic

Irn-Bru First Division
Falkirk v Dundee
Hamilton v Raith
Partick v Ayr
Queen of South v Morton
Ross v Livingston

Irn-Bru Second Division
Albion v Stenhousemuir
Arbroath v Airdrie
Dumbarton v Cowdenbeath
East Fife v Brechin
Stirling v Forfar

Irn-Bru Third Division
Berwick v Peterhead
East Stirling v Stranraer
Elgin v Clyde
Montrose v Annan Athletic
Queens Park v Alloa

Saturday, 24 September
Clydesdale Bank Premier League
Celtic v Inverness
Dunfermline v Rangers
Hibernian v Dundee Utd
Motherwell v Aberdeen
St Johnstone v Hearts
St Mirren v Kilmarnock

Irn-Bru First Division
Ayr v Queen of South
Dundee v Hamilton
Livingston v Partick
Morton v Falkirk
Raith v Ross

Irn-Bru Second Division
Airdrie v Stirling
Brechin v Arbroath
Cowdenbeath v Albion
Forfar v Dumbarton
Stenhousemuir v East Fife

Irn-Bru Third Division
Alloa v Montrose
Annan Athletic v East Stirling
Clyde v Berwick
Peterhead v Queens Park
Stranraer v Elgin

Saturday, 1 October
Clydesdale Bank Premier League
Aberdeen v Dunfermline
Dundee Utd v Motherwell
Hearts v Celtic
Inverness v St Mirren
Kilmarnock v St Johnstone
Rangers v Hibernian

Irn-Bru First Division
Hamilton v Falkirk
Livingston v Raith
Partick v Morton
Queen of South v Dundee
Ross v Ayr

Irn-Bru Second Division
Airdrie v Stenhousemuir
Arbroath v Cowdenbeath
Dumbarton v Albion

East Fife v Forfar
Stirling v Brechin

Irn-Bru Third Division
Berwick v Annan Athletic
East Stirling v Queens Park
Elgin v Alloa
Montrose v Peterhead
Stranraer v Clyde

Saturday, 15 October
Clydesdale Bank Premier League
Aberdeen v Dundee Utd
Dunfermline v Hearts
Hibernian v Motherwell
Kilmarnock v Celtic
Rangers v St Mirren
St Johnstone v Inverness

Irn-Bru First Division
Ayr v Livingston
Dundee v Ross
Falkirk v Queen of South
Morton v Hamilton
Raith v Partick

Irn-Bru Second Division
Albion v East Fife
Brechin v Airdrie
Cowdenbeath v Stirling
Forfar v Arbroath
Stenhousemuir v Dumbarton

Irn-Bru Third Division
Alloa v Berwick
Annan Athletic v Elgin
Clyde v East Stirling
Peterhead v Stranraer
Queens Park v Montrose

Saturday, 22 October
Clydesdale Bank Premier League
Celtic v Aberdeen
Dundee Utd v St Johnstone
Hearts v Rangers
Inverness v Dunfermline
Motherwell v Kilmarnock
St Mirren v Hibernian

Irn-Bru First Division
Ayr v Dundee
Livingston v Morton
Partick v Falkirk
Raith v Queen of South
Ross v Hamilton

Irn-Bru Second Division

Albion v Arbroath
Cowdenbeath v Forfar
Dumbarton v Airdrie
East Fife v Stirling
Stenhousemuir v Brechin

Saturday, 29 October
Clydesdale Bank Premier League
Aberdeen v Rangers
Celtic v Hibernian
Dunfermline v Dundee Utd
Hearts v Kilmarnock
Inverness v Motherwell
St Johnstone v St Mirren

Irn-Bru First Division
Dundee v Partick
Falkirk v Raith
Hamilton v Ayr
Morton v Ross
Queen of South v Livingston

Irn-Bru Second Division
Airdrie v East Fife
Arbroath v Stenhousemuir
Brechin v Cowdenbeath
Forfar v Albion
Stirling v Dumbarton

Irn-Bru Third Division
Annan Athletic v Peterhead
Clyde v Alloa
East Stirling v Berwick
Elgin v Montrose
Stranraer v Queens Park

Saturday, 5 November
Clydesdale Bank Premier League
Hibernian v Dunfermline
Kilmarnock v Inverness
Motherwell v Celtic
Rangers v Dundee Utd
St Johnstone v Aberdeen
St Mirren v Hearts

Irn-Bru First Division
Ayr v Morton
Dundee v Raith
Falkirk v Livingston
Hamilton v Queen of South
Partick v Ross

Irn-Bru Second Division
Albion v Airdrie
Arbroath v Dumbarton
East Fife v Cowdenbeath
Forfar v Brechin
Stenhousemuir v Stirling

Irn-Bru Third Division
Alloa v Stranraer
Berwick v Elgin
Montrose v East Stirling
Peterhead v Clyde
Queens Park v Annan Athletic

Saturday, 12 November
Irn-Bru First Division
Livingston v Hamilton
Morton v Dundee
Queen of South v Partick
Raith v Ayr
Ross v Falkirk

Irn-Bru Second Division
Airdrie v Forfar
Brechin v Albion
Cowdenbeath v Stenhousemuir
Dumbarton v East Fife
Stirling v Arbroath

Irn-Bru Third Division
Berwick v Queens Park
Clyde v Annan Athletic
East Stirling v Elgin
Peterhead v Alloa
Stranraer v Montrose

Saturday, 19 November
Clydesdale Bank Premier League
Aberdeen v Motherwell
Dundee Utd v Hearts
Hibernian v Kilmarnock
Inverness v Celtic
Rangers v St Johnstone
St Mirren v Dunfermline

Saturday, 26 November
Clydesdale Bank Premier League
Celtic v St Mirren
Dunfermline v Aberdeen
Hearts v Inverness
Kilmarnock v Rangers
Motherwell v Dundee Utd
St Johnstone v Hibernian

Irn-Bru First Division
Ayr v Partick
Dundee v Falkirk
Livingston v Ross
Morton v Queen of South
Raith v Hamilton

Irn-Bru Second Division
Airdrie v Arbroath
Brechin v East Fife

Cowdenbeath v Dumbarton
Forfar v Stirling
Stenhousemuir v Albion

Irn-Bru Third Division
Alloa v East Stirling
Annan Athletic v Stranraer
Elgin v Peterhead
Montrose v Berwick
Queens Park v Clyde

Saturday, 3 December
Clydesdale Bank Premier League
Dundee Utd v Celtic
Hearts v St Johnstone
Kilmarnock v Aberdeen
Motherwell v Hibernian
Rangers v Dunfermline
St Mirren v Inverness

Irn-Bru First Division
Falkirk v Morton
Hamilton v Dundee
Partick v Livingston
Queen of South v Ayr
Ross v Raith

Irn-Bru Second Division
Albion v Cowdenbeath
Arbroath v Brechin
Dumbarton v Forfar
East Fife v Stenhousemuir
Stirling v Airdrie

Irn-Bru Third Division
Berwick v Clyde
East Stirling v Annan Athletic
Elgin v Stranraer
Montrose v Alloa
Queens Park v Peterhead

Saturday, 10 December
Clydesdale Bank Premier League
Aberdeen v St Mirren
Celtic v Hearts
Dunfermline v Kilmarnock
Hibernian v Rangers
Inverness v Dundee Utd
St Johnstone v Motherwell

Irn-Bru First Division
Ayr v Ross
Dundee v Queen of South
Falkirk v Hamilton
Morton v Partick
Raith v Livingston

Irn-Bru Second Division
Albion v Dumbarton
Brechin v Stirling
Cowdenbeath v Arbroath
Forfar v East Fife
Stenhousemuir v Airdrie

Irn-Bru Third Division
Alloa v Queens Park
Annan Athletic v Montrose
Clyde v Elgin
Peterhead v Berwick
Stranraer v East Stirling

Saturday, 17 December
Clydesdale Bank Premier League
Aberdeen v Hibernian
Hearts v Dunfermline
Kilmarnock v Dundee Utd
Motherwell v St Mirren
Rangers v Inverness
St Johnstone v Celtic

Irn-Bru First Division
Hamilton v Morton
Livingston v Ayr
Partick v Raith
Queen of South v Falkirk
Ross v Dundee

Irn-Bru Second Division
Airdrie v Brechin
Arbroath v Forfar
Dumbarton v Stenhousemuir
East Fife v Albion
Stirling v Cowdenbeath

Irn-Bru Third Division
Berwick v Alloa
East Stirling v Clyde
Elgin v Annan Athletic
Montrose v Queens Park
Stranraer v Peterhead

Saturday, 24 December
Clydesdale Bank Premier League
Celtic v Kilmarnock
Dundee Utd v Hibernian
Dunfermline v St Johnstone
Hearts v Motherwell
Inverness v Aberdeen
St Mirren v Rangers

Monday, 26 December
Irn-Bru First Division
Ayr v Raith
Dundee v Morton

Falkirk v Ross
Hamilton v Livingston
Partick v Queen of South

Irn-Bru Second Division
Albion v Brechin
Arbroath v Stirling
East Fife v Dumbarton
Forfar v Airdrie
Stenhousemuir v Cowdenbeath

Irn-Bru Third Division
Alloa v Elgin
Annan Athletic v Berwick
Clyde v Stranraer
Peterhead v Montrose
Queens Park v East Stirling

Wednesday, 28 December
Clydesdale Bank Premier League
Aberdeen v Hearts
Celtic v Rangers
Hibernian v Inverness
Motherwell v Dunfermline
St Johnstone v Kilmarnock
St Mirren v Dundee Utd

Monday, 2 January
Clydesdale Bank Premier League
Dundee Utd v Aberdeen
Dunfermline v Celtic
Hibernian v Hearts
Inverness v St Johnstone
Kilmarnock v St Mirren
Rangers v Motherwell

Irn-Bru First Division
Livingston v Falkirk
Morton v Ayr
Queen of South v Hamilton
Raith v Dundee
Ross v Partick

Irn-Bru Second Division
Airdrie v Albion
Brechin v Forfar
Cowdenbeath v East Fife
Dumbarton v Arbroath
Stirling v Stenhousemuir

Irn-Bru Third Division
Berwick v Montrose
Clyde v Queens Park
East Stirling v Alloa
Peterhead v Elgin
Stranraer v Annan Athletic

Saturday, 7 January
Irn-Bru Third Division
Alloa v Peterhead
Annan Athletic v Clyde
Elgin v East Stirling
Montrose v Stranraer
Queens Park v Berwick

Saturday, 14 January
Clydesdale Bank Premier League
Aberdeen v Kilmarnock
Celtic v Dundee Utd
Dunfermline v Hibernian
Hearts v St Mirren
Motherwell v Inverness
St Johnstone v Rangers

Irn-Bru First Division
Dundee v Livingston
Falkirk v Ayr
Hamilton v Partick
Morton v Raith
Queen of South v Ross

Irn-Bru Second Division
Albion v Stirling
Cowdenbeath v Airdrie
Dumbarton v Brechin
East Fife v Arbroath
Stenhousemuir v Forfar

Irn-Bru Third Division
Alloa v Annan Athletic
Berwick v Stranraer
Montrose v Clyde
Peterhead v East Stirling
Queens Park v Elgin

Saturday, 21 January
Clydesdale Bank Premier League
Dundee Utd v Motherwell
Hibernian v St Johnstone
Inverness v Hearts
Kilmarnock v Dunfermline
Rangers v Aberdeen
St Mirren v Celtic

Irn-Bru First Division
Ayr v Hamilton
Livingston v Queen of South
Partick v Dundee
Raith v Falkirk
Ross v Morton

Irn-Bru Second Division
Airdrie v Dumbarton
Arbroath v Albion

Brechin v Stenhousemuir
Forfar v Cowdenbeath
Stirling v East Fife

Irn-Bru Third Division
Annan Athletic v Queens Park
Clyde v Peterhead
East Stirling v Montrose
Elgin v Berwick
Stranraer v Alloa

Saturday, 28 January
Clydesdale Bank Premier League
Aberdeen v Dunfermline
Dundee Utd v Kilmarnock
Hearts v Celtic
Inverness v St Mirren
Motherwell v St Johnstone
Rangers v Hibernian

Irn-Bru First Division
Falkirk v Dundee
Hamilton v Raith
Partick v Ayr
Queen of South v Morton
Ross v Livingston

Irn-Bru Second Division
Airdrie v Stirling
Brechin v Arbroath
Cowdenbeath v Albion
Forfar v Dumbarton
Stenhousemuir v East Fife

Irn-Bru Third Division
Alloa v Montrose
Annan Athletic v East Stirling
Clyde v Berwick
Peterhead v Queens Park
Stranraer v Elgin

Saturday, 4 February
Irn-Bru Second Division
Albion v Stenhousemuir
Arbroath v Airdrie
Dumbarton v Cowdenbeath
East Fife v Brechin
Stirling v Forfar

Irn-Bru Third Division
Berwick v Peterhead
East Stirling v Stranraer
Elgin v Clyde
Montrose v Annan Athletic
Queens Park v Alloa

Saturday, 11 February
Clydesdale Bank Premier League
Celtic v Inverness
Dunfermline v Rangers
Hibernian v Aberdeen
Kilmarnock v Hearts
St Johnstone v Dundee Utd
St Mirren v Motherwell

Irn-Bru First Division
Ayr v Queen of South
Dundee v Hamilton
Livingston v Partick
Morton v Falkirk
Raith v Ross

Irn-Bru Second Division
Albion v East Fife
Brechin v Airdrie
Cowdenbeath v Stirling
Forfar v Arbroath
Stenhousemuir v Dumbarton

Irn-Bru Third Division
Alloa v Berwick
Annan Athletic v Elgin
Clyde v East Stirling
Peterhead v Stranraer
Queens Park v Montrose

Saturday, 18 February
Clydesdale Bank Premier League
Aberdeen v St Johnstone
Dundee Utd v St Mirren
Dunfermline v Inverness
Hibernian v Celtic
Motherwell v Hearts
Rangers v Kilmarnock

Irn-Bru First Division
Hamilton v Falkirk
Livingston v Raith
Partick v Morton
Queen of South v Dundee
Ross v Ayr

Irn-Bru Second Division
Airdrie v Stenhousemuir
Arbroath v Cowdenbeath
Dumbarton v Albion
East Fife v Forfar
Stirling v Brechin

Irn-Bru Third Division
Berwick v Annan Athletic
East Stirling v Queens Park
Elgin v Alloa

Montrose v Peterhead
Stranraer v Clyde

Saturday, 25 February
Clydesdale Bank Premier League
Celtic v Motherwell
Hearts v Dundee Utd
Inverness v Rangers
Kilmarnock v Hibernian
St Johnstone v Dunfermline
St Mirren v Aberdeen

Irn-Bru First Division
Ayr v Livingston
Dundee v Ross
Falkirk v Queen of South
Morton v Hamilton
Raith v Partick

Irn-Bru Second Division
Albion v Forfar
Cowdenbeath v Brechin
Dumbarton v Stirling
East Fife v Airdrie
Stenhousemuir v Arbroath

Irn-Bru Third Division
Alloa v Clyde
Berwick v East Stirling
Montrose v Elgin
Peterhead v Annan Athletic
Queens Park v Stranraer

Saturday, 3 March
Clydesdale Bank Premier League
Aberdeen v Celtic
Dundee Utd v Inverness
Dunfermline v Motherwell
Hibernian v St Mirren
Kilmarnock v St Johnstone
Rangers v Hearts

Irn-Bru First Division
Ayr v Falkirk
Livingston v Dundee
Partick v Hamilton
Raith v Morton
Ross v Queen of South

Irn-Bru Second Division
Airdrie v Cowdenbeath
Arbroath v East Fife
Brechin v Dumbarton
Forfar v Stenhousemuir
Stirling v Albion

Irn-Bru Third Division
Annan Athletic v Alloa
Clyde v Montrose
East Stirling v Peterhead
Elgin v Queens Park
Stranraer v Berwick

Saturday, 10 March
Irn-Bru First Division
Dundee v Ayr
Falkirk v Partick
Hamilton v Ross
Morton v Livingston
Queen of South v Raith

Irn-Bru Second Division
Albion v Airdrie
Arbroath v Dumbarton
East Fife v Cowdenbeath
Forfar v Brechin
Stenhousemuir v Stirling

Irn-Bru Third Division
Alloa v East Stirling
Annan Athletic v Stranraer
Elgin v Peterhead
Montrose v Berwick

Saturday, 17 March
Clydesdale Bank Premier League
Celtic v Dunfermline
Dundee Utd v Rangers
Hearts v Hibernian
Inverness v Kilmarnock
Motherwell v Aberdeen
St Mirren v St Johnstone

Irn-Bru First Division
Livingston v Hamilton
Morton v Dundee
Queen of South v Partick
Raith v Ayr
Ross v Falkirk

Irn-Bru Second Division
Airdrie v Forfar
Brechin v Albion
Cowdenbeath v Stenhousemuir
Dumbarton v East Fife
Stirling v Arbroath

Irn-Bru Third Division
Berwick v Queens Park
Clyde v Annan Athletic
East Stirling v Elgin
Peterhead v Alloa
Stranraer v Montrose

Tuesday, 20 March
Irn-Bru Third Division
Queens Park v Clyde

Saturday, 24 March
Clydesdale Bank Premier League
Aberdeen v Inverness
Dunfermline v St Mirren
Hibernian v Dundee Utd
Kilmarnock v Motherwell
Rangers v Celtic
St Johnstone v Hearts

Irn-Bru First Division
Ayr v Morton
Dundee v Raith
Falkirk v Livingston
Hamilton v Queen of South
Partick v Ross

Irn-Bru Second Division
Airdrie v Arbroath
Brechin v East Fife
Cowdenbeath v Dumbarton
Forfar v Stirling
Stenhousemuir v Albion

Irn-Bru Third Division
Alloa v Queens Park
Annan Athletic v Montrose
Clyde v Elgin
Peterhead v Berwick
Stranraer v East Stirling

Saturday, 31 March
Clydesdale Bank Premier League
Celtic v St Johnstone
Dundee Utd v Dunfermline
Hearts v Aberdeen
Inverness v Hibernian
Motherwell v Rangers
St Mirren v Kilmarnock

Irn-Bru First Division
Falkirk v Morton
Hamilton v Dundee
Partick v Livingston
Queen of South v Ayr
Ross v Raith

Irn-Bru Second Division
Albion v Cowdenbeath
Arbroath v Brechin
Dumbarton v Forfar
East Fife v Stenhousemuir
Stirling v Airdrie

Irn-Bru Third Division
Berwick v Clyde
East Stirling v Annan Athletic
Elgin v Stranraer
Montrose v Alloa
Queens Park v Peterhead

Saturday, 7 April
Irn-Bru First Division
Ayr v Partick
Dundee v Falkirk
Livingston v Ross
Morton v Queen of South
Raith v Hamilton

Irn-Bru Second Division
Albion v Dumbarton
Brechin v Stirling
Cowdenbeath v Arbroath
Forfar v East Fife
Stenhousemuir v Airdrie

Irn-Bru Third Division
Alloa v Elgin
Annan Athletic v Berwick
Clyde v Stranraer
Peterhead v Montrose
Queens Park v East Stirling

Tuesday, 10 April
Irn-Bru First Division
Dundee v Queen of South
Falkirk v Hamilton
Morton v Partick
Raith v Livingston

Wednesday, 11 April
Irn-Bru First Division
Ayr v Ross

Saturday, 14 April
Irn-Bru First Division
Hamilton v Morton
Livingston v Ayr
Partick v Raith
Queen of South v Falkirk
Ross v Dundee

Irn-Bru Second Division
Airdrie v Brechin
Arbroath v Forfar
Dumbarton v Stenhousemuir
East Fife v Albion
Stirling v Cowdenbeath

Irn-Bru Third Division
Berwick v Alloa

East Stirling v Clyde
Elgin v Annan Athletic
Montrose v Queens Park
Stranraer v Peterhead

Saturday, 21 April
Irn-Bru First Division
Dundee v Partick
Falkirk v Raith
Hamilton v Ayr
Morton v Ross
Queen of South v Livingston

Irn-Bru Second Division
Albion v Arbroath
Cowdenbeath v Forfar
Dumbarton v Airdrie
East Fife v Stirling
Stenhousemuir v Brechin

Irn-Bru Third Division
Alloa v Stranraer
Berwick v Elgin
Montrose v East Stirling
Peterhead v Clyde
Queens Park v Annan Athletic

Saturday, 28 April
Irn-Bru First Division
Ayr v Dundee
Livingston v Morton
Partick v Falkirk
Raith v Queen of South
Ross v Hamilton

Irn-Bru Second Division
Airdrie v East Fife
Arbroath v Stenhousemuir
Brechin v Cowdenbeath
Forfar v Albion
Stirling v Dumbarton

Irn-Bru Third Division
Annan Athletic v Peterhead
Clyde v Alloa
East Stirling v Berwick
Elgin v Montrose
Stranraer v Queens Park

Saturday, 5 May
Irn-Bru First Division
Dundee v Livingston
Falkirk v Ayr
Hamilton v Partick
Morton v Raith
Queen of South v Ross

Irn-Bru Second Division
Albion v Stirling
Cowdenbeath v Airdrie
Dumbarton v Brechin
East Fife v Arbroath
Stenhousemuir v Forfar

Irn-Bru Third Division
Alloa v Annan Athletic
Berwick v Stranraer
Montrose v Clyde
Peterhead v East Stirling
Queens Park v Elgin

BLUE SQUARE PREMIER LEAGUE
FIXTURES 2011–2012

Saturday, 13 August
AFC Telford v Luton
Barrow v Tamworth
Darlington v Braintree
Ebbsfleet v York
Forest Green v Stockport
Grimsby v Fleetwood
Hayes v Alfreton
Kettering v Newport
Kidderminster v Gateshead
Mansfield v Bath
Southport v Lincoln
Wrexham v Cambridge

Tuesday, 16 August
Alfreton v Southport
Bath v Wrexham
Braintree v Grimsby
Cambridge v AFC Telford
Fleetwood v Darlington
Gateshead v Mansfield
Lincoln v Kidderminster
Luton v Forest Green
Newport v Hayes
Stockport v Kettering
Tamworth v Ebbsfleet
York v Barrow

Saturday, 20 August
Alfreton v Forest Green
Bath v Barrow
Braintree v Mansfield
Cambridge v Kidderminster
Fleetwood v Hayes
Gateshead v Kettering
Lincoln v Wrexham
Luton v Southport
Newport v Grimsby
Stockport v Ebbsfleet
Tamworth v Darlington
York v AFC Telford

Tuesday, 23 August
AFC Telford v Lincoln
Barrow v Fleetwood
Darlington v Alfreton

Ebbsfleet v Newport
Forest Green v Braintree
Grimsby v Cambridge
Hayes v Bath
Kettering v York
Kidderminster v Stockport
Mansfield v Luton
Southport v Gateshead
Wrexham v Tamworth

Saturday, 27 August
AFC Telford v Newport
Alfreton v Wrexham
Barrow v Gateshead
Bath v Tamworth
Cambridge v Hayes
Ebbsfleet v Forest Green
Fleetwood v York
Grimsby v Darlington
Kidderminster v Southport
Lincoln v Stockport
Luton v Braintree
Mansfield v Kettering

Monday, 29 August
Braintree v Ebbsfleet
Darlington v Lincoln
Forest Green v Bath
Gateshead v Grimsby
Hayes v Luton
Kettering v Cambridge
Newport v Kidderminster
Southport v Barrow
Stockport v Mansfield
Tamworth v AFC Telford
Wrexham v Fleetwood
York v Alfreton

Saturday, 3 September
Braintree v Lincoln
Darlington v Mansfield
Ebbsfleet v Barrow
Forest Green v Grimsby
Gateshead v Alfreton
Kettering v Fleetwood
Newport v Cambridge

Southport v AFC Telford
Stockport v Luton
Wrexham v Kidderminster
York v Bath

Sunday 4 September
Hayes v Tamworth

Saturday, 10 September
AFC Telford v Stockport
Alfreton v Braintree
Barrow v Wrexham
Bath v Southport
Cambridge v Forest Green
Fleetwood v Gateshead
Grimsby v Hayes
Kidderminster v Ebbsfleet
Lincoln v Kettering
Luton v Darlington
Mansfield v Newport
Tamworth v York

Saturday, 17 September
AFC Telford v Bath
Barrow v Mansfield
Braintree v Newport
Darlington v Hayes
Ebbsfleet v Fleetwood
Forest Green v Southport
Gateshead v Cambridge
Kettering v Tamworth
Kidderminster v Alfreton
Luton v Lincoln
Stockport v Grimsby
Wrexham v York

Tuesday, 20 September
Alfreton v Barrow
Bath v Luton
Cambridge v Ebbsfleet
Fleetwood v Kidderminster
Grimsby v Kettering
Hayes v Braintree
Lincoln v Gateshead
Mansfield v AFC Telford
Newport v Stockport
Southport v Wrexham
Tamworth v Forest Green
York v Darlington

Saturday, 24 September
Alfreton v Ebbsfleet
Bath v Kettering
Cambridge v Darlington
Fleetwood v AFC Telford
Grimsby v Wrexham
Hayes v Gateshead
Lincoln v Forest Green

Mansfield v Kidderminster
Newport v Barrow
Southport v Braintree
Tamworth v Stockport
York v Luton

Tuesday, 27 September
AFC Telford v Alfreton
Barrow v Lincoln
Braintree v Tamworth
Darlington v Southport
Ebbsfleet v Bath
Forest Green v Newport
Gateshead v York
Kettering v Hayes
Kidderminster v Grimsby
Luton v Cambridge
Stockport v Fleetwood
Wrexham v Mansfield

Saturday, 1 October
AFC Telford v Hayes
Braintree v Fleetwood
Darlington v Newport
Forest Green v Mansfield
Gateshead v Tamworth
Grimsby v Alfreton
Kettering v Kidderminster
Lincoln v Bath
Luton v Barrow
Southport v Cambridge
Stockport v York
Wrexham v Ebbsfleet

Saturday, 8 October
Alfreton v Kettering
Barrow v AFC Telford
Bath v Darlington
Cambridge v Stockport
Ebbsfleet v Gateshead
Fleetwood v Forest Green
Kidderminster v Luton
Mansfield v Grimsby
Newport v Southport
Tamworth v Lincoln
York v Braintree

Sunday 9 October
Hayes v Wrexham

Tuesday, 11 October
Alfreton v Lincoln
Bath v Cambridge
Ebbsfleet v Luton
Fleetwood v Newport
Gateshead v Wrexham
Grimsby v Barrow
Hayes v Forest Green

Kettering v Braintree
Kidderminster v AFC Telford
Southport v York
Stockport v Darlington

Saturday, 15 October
AFC Telford v Ebbsfleet
Barrow v Hayes
Braintree v Bath
Cambridge v Alfreton
Darlington v Kidderminster
Forest Green v Kettering
Lincoln v Fleetwood
Luton v Gateshead
Mansfield v Southport
Newport v Tamworth
Wrexham v Stockport
York v Grimsby

Tuesday, 18 October
Alfreton v Fleetwood
Bath v Stockport
Darlington v Barrow
Ebbsfleet v Grimsby
Forest Green v AFC Telford
Gateshead v Southport
Kidderminster v Braintree
Lincoln v Mansfield
Luton v Wrexham
Newport v Kettering
Tamworth v Hayes
York v Cambridge

Saturday, 22 October
AFC Telford v Gateshead
Barrow v Kidderminster
Braintree v Darlington
Cambridge v Lincoln
Fleetwood v Bath
Grimsby v Luton
Hayes v York
Kettering v Ebbsfleet
Mansfield v Alfreton
Southport v Tamworth
Stockport v Forest Green
Wrexham v Newport

Saturday, 5 November
Bath v Grimsby
Darlington v AFC Telford
Forest Green v Alfreton\
Gateshead v Braintree
Kettering v Southport
Kidderminster v Tamworth
Lincoln v Barrow
Luton v Fleetwood
Mansfield v Cambridge
Newport v Ebbsfleet

Stockport v Hayes
York v Wrexham

Saturday, 19 November
AFC Telford v Mansfield
Alfreton v Gateshead
Barrow v York
Braintree v Forest Green
Cambridge v Luton
Ebbsfleet v Darlington
Fleetwood v Stockport
Grimsby v Newport
Hayes v Kidderminster
Southport v Bath
Tamworth v Kettering
Wrexham v Lincoln

Saturday, 26 November
AFC Telford v Barrow
Alfreton v Hayes
Bath v Mansfield
Braintree v Wrexham
Darlington v Tamworth
Forest Green v York
Gateshead v Fleetwood
Kettering v Grimsby
Kidderminster v Cambridge
Lincoln v Ebbsfleet
Newport v Luton
Stockport v Southport

Tuesday, 29 November
Barrow v Alfreton
Cambridge v Bath
Ebbsfleet v Kidderminster
Fleetwood v Kettering
Grimsby v Stockport
Hayes v Newport
Luton v AFC Telford
Mansfield v Gateshead
Southport v Forest Green
Tamworth v Braintree
Wrexham v Darlington
York v Lincoln

Saturday, 3 December
Barrow v Ebbsfleet
Bath v AFC Telford
Cambridge v Grimsby
Darlington v Forest Green
Gateshead v Kidderminster
Luton v Stockport
Mansfield v Braintree
Newport v Lincoln
Southport v Alfreton
Tamworth v Wrexham
York v Kettering

Sunday 4 December
Hayes v Fleetwood

Tuesday, 6 December
AFC Telford v York
Alfreton v Newport
Braintree v Hayes
Ebbsfleet v Cambridge
Fleetwood v Barrow
Forest Green v Tamworth
Grimsby v Mansfield
Kettering v Darlington
Kidderminster v Bath
Lincoln v Luton
Stockport v Gateshead
Wrexham v Southport

Saturday, 17 December
Braintree v AFC Telford
Darlington v Cambridge
Forest Green v Lincoln
Grimsby v Ebbsfleet
Hayes v Barrow
Kettering v Bath
Newport v Fleetwood
Southport v Mansfield
Stockport v Alfreton
Tamworth v Luton
Wrexham v Gateshead
York v Kidderminster

Monday, 26 December
AFC Telford v Wrexham
Alfreton v Tamworth
Barrow v Stockport
Bath v Newport
Cambridge v Braintree
Ebbsfleet v Hayes
Fleetwood v Southport
Gateshead v Darlington
Kidderminster v Forest Green
Lincoln v Grimsby
Luton v Kettering
Mansfield v York

Sunday 1 January
Braintree v Cambridge
Darlington v Gateshead
Forest Green v Kidderminster
Grimsby v Lincoln
Hayes v Ebbsfleet
Kettering v Luton
Newport v Bath
Southport v Fleetwood
Stockport v Barrow
Tamworth v Alfreton
Wrexham v AFC Telford
York v Mansfield

Saturday, 7 January
AFC Telford v Kettering
Alfreton v Grimsby
Barrow v Darlington
Bath v Braintree
Cambridge v Southport
Ebbsfleet v Wrexham
Fleetwood v Tamworth
Gateshead v Stockport
Kidderminster v Hayes
Lincoln v York
Luton v Newport
Mansfield v Forest Green

Saturday, 21 January
AFC Telford v Cambridge
Alfreton v Kidderminster
Braintree v Stockport
Darlington v Fleetwood
Gateshead v Lincoln
Grimsby v Bath
Mansfield v Hayes
Newport v Forest Green
Southport v Luton
Tamworth v Barrow
Wrexham v Kettering
York v Ebbsfleet

Tuesday, 24 January
Barrow v Grimsby
Bath v Alfreton
Cambridge v Newport
Ebbsfleet v Tamworth
Fleetwood v Braintree
Forest Green v Wrexham
Hayes v Darlington
Kettering v Gateshead
Kidderminster v York
Lincoln v Southport
Luton v Mansfield
Stockport v AFC Telford

Saturday, 28 January
Braintree v Barrow
Cambridge v Tamworth
Darlington v York
Ebbsfleet v Mansfield
Forest Green v Fleetwood
Gateshead v Newport
Grimsby v AFC Telford
Hayes v Southport
Kettering v Lincoln
Luton v Alfreton
Stockport v Kidderminster
Wrexham v Bath

Saturday, 4 February
AFC Telford v Forest Green

Alfreton v Stockport
Barrow v Luton
Bath v Hayes
Fleetwood v Ebbsfleet
Kidderminster v Wrexham
Lincoln v Cambridge
Mansfield v Darlington
Newport v Braintree
Southport v Kettering
Tamworth v Grimsby
York v Gateshead

Tuesday, 7 February
AFC Telford v Kidderminster
Alfreton v Mansfield
Gateshead v Hayes
Kettering v Forest Green

Saturday, 11 February
Braintree v Southport
Cambridge v Barrow
Darlington v Wrexham
Ebbsfleet v Alfreton
Forest Green v Luton
Gateshead v Bath
Grimsby v York
Hayes v Lincoln
Kettering v AFC Telford
Mansfield v Fleetwood
Stockport v Newport
Tamworth v Kidderminster

Tuesday, 14 February
Lincoln v Braintree
Southport v Darlington

Saturday, 18 February
AFC Telford v Braintree
Alfreton v Darlington
Barrow v Kettering
Bath v Ebbsfleet
Fleetwood v Cambridge
Forest Green v Gateshead
Kidderminster v Lincoln
Luton v Tamworth
Newport v Mansfield
Southport v Grimsby
Wrexham v Hayes
York v Stockport

Tuesday, 21 February
Tamworth v Newport

Saturday, 25 February
Barrow v Forest Green
Bath v Kidderminster
Braintree v Kettering
Cambridge v Gateshead

Darlington v Luton
Ebbsfleet v Southport
Fleetwood v Alfreton
Hayes v Grimsby
Lincoln v AFC Telford
Mansfield v Tamworth
Newport v York
Stockport v Wrexham

Saturday, 3 March
Alfreton v AFC Telford
Darlington v Stockport
Forest Green v Cambridge
Gateshead v Ebbsfleet
Grimsby v Braintree
Kettering v Wrexham
Kidderminster v Barrow
Luton v Bath
Mansfield v Lincoln
Southport v Newport
Tamworth v Fleetwood
York v Hayes

Tuesday, 6 March
Barrow v Bath
Cambridge v Mansfield
Ebbsfleet v Stockport
Fleetwood v Grimsby
Wrexham v Luton
York v Tamworth

Saturday, 10 March
AFC Telford v Southport
Bath v York
Braintree v Gateshead
Grimsby v Forest Green
Hayes v Kettering
Kidderminster v Fleetwood
Lincoln v Alfreton
Luton v Ebbsfleet
Newport v Darlington
Stockport v Cambridge
Tamworth v Mansfield
Wrexham v Barrow

Saturday, 17 March
AFC Telford v Fleetwood
Bath v Lincoln
Braintree v Kidderminster
Cambridge v York
Darlington v Ebbsfleet
Forest Green v Hayes
Gateshead v Luton
Grimsby v Tamworth
Kettering v Alfreton
Mansfield v Barrow
Newport v Wrexham
Southport v Stockport

Saturday, 24 March
Alfreton v Cambridge
Barrow v Braintree
Ebbsfleet v Kettering
Fleetwood v Mansfield
Hayes v AFC Telford
Kidderminster v Darlington
Lincoln v Newport
Luton v Grimsby
Stockport v Bath
Tamworth v Gateshead
Wrexham v Forest Green
York v Southport

Saturday, 31 March
AFC Telford v Darlington
Bath v Fleetwood
Braintree v Alfreton
Cambridge v Wrexham
Forest Green v Barrow
Grimsby v Kidderminster
Kettering v Stockport
Lincoln v Tamworth
Luton v York
Mansfield v Ebbsfleet
Newport v Gateshead
Southport v Hayes

Saturday, 7 April
Braintree v Luton
Darlington v Grimsby
Forest Green v Ebbsfleet
Gateshead v Barrow
Hayes v Cambridge
Kettering v Mansfield
Newport v AFC Telford
Southport v Kidderminster
Stockport v Lincoln
Tamworth v Bath
Wrexham v Alfreton
York v Fleetwood

Monday, 9 April
AFC Telford v Tamworth
Alfreton v York
Barrow v Southport
Bath v Forest Green
Cambridge v Kettering

Ebbsfleet v Braintree
Fleetwood v Wrexham
Grimsby v Gateshead
Kidderminster v Newport
Lincoln v Darlington
Luton v Hayes
Mansfield v Stockport

Saturday, 14 April
Alfreton v Luton
Barrow v Cambridge
Darlington v Bath
Ebbsfleet v AFC Telford
Fleetwood v Lincoln
Gateshead v Forest Green
Hayes v Mansfield
Kidderminster v Kettering
Stockport v Braintree
Tamworth v Southport
Wrexham v Grimsby
York v Newport

Saturday, 21 April
AFC Telford v Grimsby
Bath v Gateshead
Braintree v York
Cambridge v Fleetwood
Forest Green v Darlington
Kettering v Barrow
Lincoln v Hayes
Luton v Kidderminster
Mansfield v Wrexham
Newport v Alfreton
Southport v Ebbsfleet
Stockport v Tamworth

Saturday, 28 April
Alfreton v Bath
Barrow v Newport
Darlington v Kettering
Ebbsfleet v Lincoln
Fleetwood v Luton
Gateshead v AFC Telford
Grimsby v Southport
Hayes v Stockport
Kidderminster v Mansfield
Tamworth v Cambridge
Wrexham v Braintree
York v Forest Green